HANDBOOK OF
Child and
Adolescent
Psychiatry

Volume Six

HANDBOOK OF
Child and Adolescent Psychiatry

Joseph D. Noshpitz / Editor-in-Chief

VOLUME SIX

Basic Psychiatric Science and Treatment

NORMAN E. ALESSI, JOSEPH T. COYLE,
SAUL ISAAC HARRISON, AND SPENCER ETH

EDITORS

John Wiley & Sons, Inc.
New York • Chichester • Weinheim • Brisbane • Singapore • Toronto

ISBN 0-471-55079-5 (vol. 1)
      0-471-55075-2 (vol. 2)
      0-471-55076-0 (vol. 3)
      0-471-55078-7 (vol. 4)
      0-471-19330-5 (vol. 5)
      0-471-19331-3 (vol. 6)
      0-471-19332-1 (vol. 7)
      0-471-19329-1 (vols. 5, 6, 7)
      0-471-19328-3 (7-volume set)

Printed in the United States of America

10 9 8 7 6 5 4 3 2 1

In Memoriam

Joseph D. Noshpitz, M.D.
1922–1997

DEDICATION

This set of volumes grows out of an attitude that reflects the field itself. To put it succinctly, the basic theme of child and adolescent psychiatry is hope. Albeit formally a medical discipline, child and adolescent psychiatry is a field of growth, of unfolding, of progressive advance; like childhood itself, it is a realm of building toward a future and finding ways to better the outcome for the young. But within the field, at even greater theme inspires an even more dominant regard. For, beyond treating children, child and adolescent psychiatry is ultimately about rearing children. This is literally the first time in human history that we are on the verge of knowing *how* to rear a child. While people have reared children since we were arboreal, they did it by instinct, or by cultural practice, or in keeping with grandma's injunctions, or by reenacting the memories, conscious and unconscious, of their own childhood experiences. They did what they did for many reasons, but never because they really knew what their actions portended, what caused what, what was a precondition for what, or what meant what.

At this moment in history, however, things are different. The efforts of researchers, neuroscientists, child developmental specialists—in short, of the host of those who seek to understand, treat, and educate children and to work with parents—are beginning to converge and to produce a body of knowledge that tells us what children are, what they need, what hurts them, and what helps them. Hard science has begun to study the fetus, rating scales and in-depth therapeutic techniques have emerged for the mother with the infant in her arms, increasing precision is being achieved in assessing temperament, in measuring mother/infant fit, and in detecting the forerunners of personality organization. Adolescence and the intricacies of pubertal transformation are being explored as never before. Indeed, a quiet revolution is coming into being: the gradual dissemination of knowledge about child rearing that, within a few generations, could well alter the quality of the human beings who fall under its aegis.

If children—all children—could be reared in a fashion that gave them a healthier organization of conscience, that preserved the buds of cognitive growth and helped these to flower (instead of pinching them off as so many current practices do), that could recognize from the outset any special needs a child might have in respect to impulse control or emotional stability—and could step in from the earliest moments in development with the appropriate tactics and strategies, anodynes and remedies, techniques of healing and practices of enabling to allow the youngster to better manage his or her inner life and interpersonal transactions—consider what fruit this would bear.

Today this is far more than a dream, far more than a wistful yearning for a better day to come. The beginnings are already accomplished, much of the initial work has been done, the directions of future research are becoming ever more evident. The heretofore cryptic equations of development are beginning to be found and some of their solutions to be discerned, the once-mystical runes are being read—and are here inscribed in page after page of research report and clinical observation.

Some of the initial changes are already well under way. As with all science first a process of demystification must occur. Bit by bit, we have had to unlearn a host of formulaic mythologies about children and about parenting that have been part of Western civilization for centuries.

We have indeed begun to do so. We have been able to admit to the realities of child abuse, first to the violence directed toward children and then to their sexual exploitation. And we have had to admit to children's sexuality. Simply to allow those things to appear in print, to become part of common parlance, has taken immense cultural energy, the overcoming of tremendous defensiveness; after all, such things had been known but not spoken of for generations. Right now the sanctity, the hallowed quality of family life, is the focus of enormous cultural upheaval. There is much to suggest that the nuclear family set in the bosom of a body of extended kin relationships that had for so long served as the basic site for human child rearing is no longer the most likely context within which future generations of our children will grow. The quest is on for new social arrangements, and it is within this milieu that the impact of scientific knowledge, the huge and ever-increasing array of insights into the nature of childhood, the chemistry of human relationships, the psychodynamics of parent-child interplay—in short, within the area of development that this work so carefully details—that we find the wellsprings of hope. As nursery schools, kindergartens, grade schools, and high schools become more sophisticated, as the psychiatric diagnostic manuals become more specific and more differentiated, as doctors become better trained and better prepared to address human issues with dynamic understanding, as what children need in order to grow well becomes ever more part of everyday cultural practice, the realization of this hope will slowly and quietly steal across the face of our civilization, and we will produce children who will be emotionally sounder, cognitively stronger, and mentally healthier than their parents. These volumes are dedicated to advancing this goal.

Joseph D. Noshpitz, M.D.
Editor-in-Chief

PREFACE

Some 16 years ago the first two volumes of the *Basic Handbook of Child Psychiatry* were published, to be followed shortly by volumes III and IV, and then, in 1985, by the fifth volume. More than a decade has passed since that volume was released, during which time the field of child psychiatry has advanced at a remarkable pace. Indeed, it has even changed its name to be more inclusive of the teenage years. New advances in neuroscience, in genetics, in psychoanalytic theory, in psychopharmacology, in animal studies—new findings in a host of areas have poured out during these years. It is therefore necessary to revise the handbook, to reorganize it, to update many of the clinical accounts, and to bring it to the level where the active practitioner can use its encyclopedic format to explore the enormous variety of clinical possibilities he or she may encounter.

The focus of this work is on development. It is no exaggeration to look on child development as the basic science of child and adolescent psychiatry. Development is so vital a concern that in this revision, we have abandoned the classical way of presenting the material. Rather than following tradition, wherein development, diagnosis and assessment, syndromes, treatment, and so on are discussed for a variety of related topics, in these volumes the bulk of the material is presented developmentally. Thus, volumes I, II, and III focus on development and syndromes of infancy and preschool, of grade school, and of adolescence, respectively. Within each of these larger sections, the material on development comes first, followed by chapters on syndromes, conceptualized as disturbances of development. While syndromes are described in depth, they are discussed only within the framework of the developmental level under study. Volume IV, entitled, "Varieties of Development," explores a host of ecological niches within which children are reared.

Volume V includes an unusually rich banquet of studies on the assessment and evaluation of children, adolescents, and their families. Volume VI reports on the basic science issues of the field and the current status of the various treatment techniques. Volume VII contains sections on consultation/liaison, emergencies in child and adolescent psychiatry, the prehistory of child and adolescent psychiatry, current cultural issues that impinge on young people, forensic issues involving children and youth, and professional challenges facing the child and adolescent psychiatrist.

The intention of the work is to be as comprehensive and as readable as possible. In an encyclopedic work of this sort, concerns always arise as to how much space to allot to each topic and to which topics should be covered. To deal with such questions, a number of readers reviewed each submission. One editor had primary responsibility for each section; a coeditor also reviewed submissions. Then the editor of another section reviewed the submissions, exchanging his or her chapters with the first colleague so that someone outside the section read each chapter. In addition, one editor reviewed all submissions with an eye to contradictions or excessive overlap. Finally, the editor-in-chief reviewed and commented on a large proportion of the materials submitted. In short, while the submission process was not juried, a number of readers reviewed each chapter.

Each author was confronted with the in cumulative critiques and asked to make appropriate changes. Most did so cheerfully, although not always with alacrity.

The writing and review process lasted from about 1990 to 1996. For much of this time, a host of authors were busy writing, revising, and polishing their work. The editors worked unstintingly, suffering all the ups and downs that accompany large projects: many meetings, huge expenses, moments of despair, episodes of elation, professional growth on the part of practically all the participants (a couple of authors who never came through with their material may be presumed to have shrunk), profound disappointments and thrilling breakthroughs, lost causes that were snatched from the jaws of defeat and borne aloft to victory, and, ultimately, the final feeling that we did it!

I speak for all the editors when I say that it was our purpose and it is our earnest wish that these volumes make for better understanding of young people, greater access to knowledge about children and adolescents, a richer sense of what this field of human endeavor entails, and a better outcome for the growth, development, mental health, and happiness of all the young in our land and of those who would help them.

Joseph D. Noshpitz, M.D.
Editor-in-Chief

CONTENTS

Contents

CONTRIBUTORS

NORMAN E. ALESSI, M.D.
Associate Professor, Department of Psychiatry, University of Michigan Hospitals, Ann Arbor, Michigan.

SETH ARONSON, Psy.D.
Assistant Clinical Professor of Psychiatry, Mount Sinai School of Medicine; Assistant Professor, Yeshiva and Long Island Universities, New York, New York.

MARION TAYLOR BAER, Ph.D., R.D.
Associate Director, USC University Affiliated Program, Center for Child Development and Developmental Disabilities; Adjunct Associate Professor, Division of Community Health Services, University of California at Los Angeles School of Public Health, Los Angeles, California.

CHRISTIANE A.M. BALTAXE, M.D., Ph.D.
University of California at Los Angeles (UCLA-NPI), Los Angeles, California.

DENNIS J. BARR, Ed.D.
Staff Psychologist, Menville School of the Judge Baker Children's Center; Instructor of Psychology, Department of Psychiatry, Harvard Medical School; Research Associate, Facing History and Ourselves, a non-profit teacher training organization, Boston, Massachusetts.

MARK D. BEALE, M.D.
Assistant Professor, Department of Psychiatry and Behavioral Sciences, Medical University of South Carolina, Charleston, South Carolina.

HILARY J. BERNSTEIN, M.S.W.
Instructor, Department of Psychiatry and Behavioral Sciences, Medical University of South Carolina, Charleston, South Carolina.

JAMES BLACK
University of Illinios at Urbana-Champaign, Beckman Institute, Urbana, Illinois.

KELLY N. BOTTERON, M.D.
Assistant Professor of Psychiatry (Child) and Radiology, Mallinckrodt Institute of Radiology, Washington University School of Medicine, St. Louis, Missouri.

JAMES M. BRIESMEISTER, Ph.D.
Shelby Township, Michigan.

SAUL L. BROWN, M.D.
Private Practice, Malibu, California.

EDWIN H. COOK, JR., M.D.
Associate Professor of Psychiatry and Pediatrics; Director, Laboratory of Developmental Neuroscience, University of Chicago, Chicago, Illinois.

JOSEPH T. COYLE, M.D.
Eben S. Draper Professor of Psychiatry and of Neuroscience; Chair of the Consolidated Department of Psychiatry, Harvard Medical School, Boston, Massachusetts.

CEETTA MEDLOCK CRAYTON, M.S., R.T.C., C.L.P.
Associate Professor, Coordinator of Therapeutic Recreation, California State University, Long Beach, California.

E. KIRSTEN DAHL, Ph.D.
Associate Clinical Professor, Yale University Child Study Center, New Haven, Connecticut.

STEPHANIE SERGENT DANIEL, M.A.
Doctoral Candidate, Department of Psychology, University of North Carolina at Greensboro, Greensboro, North Carolina.

JANET M. DEMB, Ph.D.
Assistant Professor of Psychiatry, Yeshiva University, Albert Einstein College of Medicine, Bronx, New York; Private Practice, Scarsdale, New York.

Contributors

JAMES DILLON, M.D.
University of Michigan Medical Center, Department of Psychiatry, Ann Arbor, Michigan.

ELIZABETH M. DOONE, PH.D., A.B.D.
Research Assistant, Department of At-Risk Children, Youth, and Their Families at USF; Preschool Teacher, Tampa, Florida.

SPENCER ETH, M.D.
Vice-Chair and Clinical Director, Department of Psychiatry, Saint Vincents Hospital and Medical Center, New York, New York; Professor of Psychiatry, New York Medical College, Valhalla, New York.

GORDON K. FARLEY, M.D.
Professor Emeritus of Psychiatry, University of Colorado School of Medicine, Denver, Colorado.

VINCENT J. FONTANA, M.D., F.A.A.P.
Medical Director, New York Foundling Hospital, New York, New York.

STEWART GABEL, M.D.
Chairman, Department of Psychiatry and Behavioral Sciences, The Children's Hospital; Associate Professor of Psychiatry and Pediatrics, University of Colorado Health Sciences Center, Denver, Colorado.

DAVID B. GOLDSTON, PH.D.
Associate Professor of Psychiatry, Bowman Gray School of Medicine, Wake Forest University, Winston-Salem, North Carolina.

MAYU P. B. GONZALES, M.D.
Director of Mental Health Services, New York Foundling Hospital; Attending Staff, Department of Psychiatry and Preceptor, Department of Pediatrics, St. Vincents Hospital and Medical Center; Private Practice of Child and Adolescent Psychiatry, New York, New York; Clinical Assistant Professor of Psychiatry, New York Medical College, Valhalla, New York.

WILLIAM T. GREENOUGH, PH.D.
University of Illinois at Urbana-Champaign, Beckman Institute, Urbana, Illinois.

SANDRA GREENE, MA, OTR
Private Practice, Occupational Therapy with Children, Santa Monica, California.

ELISABETH B. GUTHRIE, M.D.
Chief, Department of Psychiatry/Psychology, Blythedale Children's Hospital, Valhalla, New York; Assistant Clinical Professor of Pediatrics and Psychiatry, Columbia University College of Physicians and Surgeons, New York, New York.

SUSAN HAIMAN, M.P.S. O.T.R./L., F.A.O.T.A.
Assistant Professor and Academic Fieldwork Coordi-
nator, Philadelphia College of Pharmacy and Science, Division of Health Sciences, Department of Occupational Therapy, Philadelphia, Pennsylvania.

AMY HAMMEL, M.T.-B.C., D.A.
Children's and Family Psychotherapist, The New York Hospital-Corenell Medical Center, White Plains, New York; Faculty of Music Therapy Graduate Program, New York University, New York, New York; Music Therapist, Music Therapy Center of Greenwich, Greenwich, Connecticut.

GORDON HARPER, M.D.
Director of Inpatient Psychiatry, Children's Hospital, Boston, Massachusetts.

SAUL ISAAC HARRISON, M.D.
Professor Emeritus, University of Michigan, Ann Arbor, Michigan; Adjunct Professor of Psychiatry and Biobehavioral Sciences, University of California at Los Angeles, Los Angeles, California.

STEVE HARVEY, PH.D., A.D.T.R., R.D.T., R.T.P./S.
United States Army.

LAWRENCE G. HORNSBY, M.D.
Department of Psychiatry, University of Texas Medical School, Houston, Texas.

MARTIN IRWIN, M.D.
Director, Division of Child Psychiatry; Associate Professor, Psychiatry and Pediatrics, State University of New York, Health Science Center, Syracuse, New York.

STEVEN L. JAFFE, M.D.
Professor of Psychiatry, Emory University School of Medicine; Clinical Professor of Psychiatry, Morehouse School of Medicine; Medical Director of Child and Adolescent Services, Charter Peachford Hospital, Atlanta, Georgia.

JOSEPH J. JANKOWSKI, M.D.
Associate Clinical Professor of Psychiatry and Pediatrics; Director of Child and Adolescent Residency Training and Triple Board Residency Program; Director of Consultation/Liaison Program for Child and Adolescent Psychiatry, New England Medical Center; Academic Appointment at Tufts University School of Medicine, Boston, Massachusetts.

THERESA A. JONES
University of Illinois at Urbana-Champaign, Beckman Institute, Urbana, Illinois.

ALLAN M. JOSEPHSON, M.D.
Professor of Psychiatry; Chief of Child, Adolescent, and Family Psychiatry, Department of Psychiatry and Health Behavior, Medical College of Georgia, Augusta, Georgia.

Contributors

MICHAEL J. KARCHER, ED.D.
Resident in Pediatric Psychology, University of Texas at San Antonio, Health Science Center, San Antonio, Texas; Ph.D. Candidate, The University of Texas at Austin, Austin, Texas.

CHARLES H. KELLNER, M.D.
Professor, Department of Psychiatry and Behavioral Sciences and Department of Neurology, Medical University of South Carolina, Charleston, South Carolina.

NANA KOCH, ED.D., A.D.T.R., C.M.A.
Former Coordinator, Dance/Movement Therapy Master's Program, Hunter College of the City University of New York, New York, New York; Consultant, North Shore University Hospital, Manhasset, New York; Writer/Researcher, Office of Advancement, Manhattanville College, Purchase, New York.

ROBERT A. KOWATCH, M.D.
Associate Professor of Psychiatry, The University of Texas, Southwestern Medical Center at Dallas; Center for Pediatric Psychiatry, Dallas, Texas.

CYNTHIA A. KUROWSKI
Department of Education and Psychology, University of Texas at Austin, Austin, Texas.

HELEN B. LANDGARTEN, M.A., B.-C. A.T.R.
Research Associate, Harbor-UCLA Medical Center; Professor Emeritus, Loyola Marymount University, Los Angeles, California.

ELISSA LANG, M.ED., M.A., C.R.C.
Director of Housing and Clinical Services, YWCA of White Plains and Central Westchester, White Plains, New York.

JAMES F. LECKMAN, M.D.
Director of Research, Neison Harris Professor of Child Psychiatry and Pediatrics, Yale University Child Study Center, New Haven, Connecticut.

BENNETT L. LEVENTHAL, M.D.
Professor of Psychiatry and Pediatrics; Chair (Interim), Department of Psychiatry, University of Chicago, Chicago, Illinois.

PAUL LOMBROSO, M.D.
Associate Professor, Yale University Child Study Center, New Haven, Connecticut.

JUAN LOPEZ, M.D.
University of Michigan, Department of Psychiatry, Mental Health Research Institute, Ann Arbor, Michigan.

F. VINCENT MANNINO, PH.D.
Scientist Director, U.S. Public Health Service; National Institute of Mental Health, NIH, (retired);

Private Practice (p/t), Consulting Family Psychology, Silver Spring, Maryland.

STEVEN MARANS, M.S.W., PH.D.
Harris Assistant Professor of Child Psychoanalysis, Yale University Child Study Center, New Haven, Connecticut.

W. DOUGLAS McCOARD, M.S.W., M. DIV.
Executive Director, Huckleberry House, Columbus, Ohio.

VIRGINIA ANNE McDERMOTT, PH.D.
Candidate, Chicago Center for Psychoanalysis, Chicago, Illinois; Clinical Faculty, Department of Psychiatry, University of Minnesota and Private Practice, Minneapolis, Minnesota.

BARBARA MELSON, M.S., A.T.R.
Dance/Movement Psychotherapist, Private Practice, and Soho Parenting Center, New York, New York.

BARBARA E. MILONE, C.S.W.
Private Practice, Katonah, New York; Consultant to Preschools, White Plains, New York and Residential Treatment Schools, Yonkers, New York; Formerly Program Coordinator Child and Adolescent Psychiatry Division, The New York Hospital-Cornell Medical Center, White Plains, New York.

ROGER J. MINNER, M.S.W., L.I.S.W.
Associate Director, Huckleberry House, Columbus, Ohio.

FRANK MONCHER, PH.D.
Assistant Professor of Psychiatry, Department of Psychiatry and Health Behavior, Medical College of Georgia, Augusta, Georgia.

JOHN MORDOCK
Clinical Director, Astor Mental Health Programs, Poughkeepsie, New York.

CHARLES NELSON
University of Illinois at Urbana-Champaign, Beckman Institute, Urbana, Illinios.

PATRICIA NOVAK, M.P.H., R.D., C.L.E.
Maternal-Child Health, Sierra Vista Regional Medical Center, San Luis Obispo, California.

KAREN BELINGER PETERLIN, M.S.W.
Consultant, Private Practice, Brooklyn, New York.

CHARLES W. POPPER, M.D.
Belmont, Massachusetts.

SCOTT W. POWERS, PH.D.
Assistant Professor of Pediatrics, University of Cincinnati College of Medicine, Children's Hospital Medical Center; Assistant Professor of Psychology

(Adjunct), University of Cincinnati, Cincinnati, Ohio.

PAUL QUINLAN, D.O.
University of Michigan Medical Center, Department of Psychiatry, Ann Arbor, Michigan.

HELEN REID, L.C.S.W.
Coordinator, Early Childhood Center, Cedars Sinai Medical Center, Los Angeles, California.

MARIO RENDON, M.D.
Director, Department of Psychiatry, Lincoln Medical and Mental Health Center, Bronx, New York.

ANNE REYSA
Department of Education and Psychology, University of Texas at Austin, Austin, Texas.

ROBERT L. SELMAN, PH.D.
Professor of Psychology, Department of Psychiatry, Harvard Medical School; Professor of Education, Harvard Graduate School of Education, Boston, Massachusetts.

MILTON F. SHORE, PH.D., A.B.P.P.
Consultant, LAB School of Washington; Adjunct Professor, Catholic University of America; Private Practice, Silver Spring, Maryland.

LINMARIE SIKICH, M.D.
Assistant Professor, Department of Psychiatry, University of North Carolina, Chapel Hill, North Carolina.

RICHARD E. SLOVES, PSY.D.
Assistant Professor of Psychiatry, Health Science Center of Brooklyn, State University of New York; Director of Brief Psychotherapy, Child and Adolescent Psychiatry, Kings County Hospital Center, Brooklyn, New York.

JEFFREY A. SMITH, PH.D.
Assistant Professor of Psychiatry, Bowman Gray School of Medicine, Wake Forest University, Winston-Salem, North Carolina.

WILLIAM A. SONIS, M.D.
Associate Professor, MCP-Hahnemann University; Director of Child and Adolescent Residency Training, Allegheny University Hospitals, Eastern Penn-

sylvania Psychiatric Institute, Philadelphia, Pennsylvania.

EVA SPERLING, M.D.
Assistant Clinical Professor of Psychiatry, Albert Einstein College of Medicine of Yeshiva University, New York, New York; Director, The Therapeutic Nursery, The Guidance Center, New Rochelle, New York.

ANTHONY SPIRITO, M.D.
Associate Professor of Psychiatry and Human Behavior, Brown University School of Medicine, Rhode Island Hospital, Providence, Rhode Island.

KEVIN D. STARK
Department of Education and Psychology, University of Texas at Austin, Austin, Texas.

RONALD J. STEINGARD, M.D.
Director of Child Psychiatry, Cambridge Hospital, Cambridge, Massachusetts; Assistant Professor of Psychiatry, Harvard Medical School, Boston, Massachusetts.

MAX SUGAR, M.D.
Professor of Clinical Psychiatry, Department of Psychiatry, Louisiana State University Medical School and Tulane University Medical School, New Orleans, Louisiana.

SUSAN M. SWEARER
Department of Education and Psychology, University of Texas at Austin, Austin, Texas.

DELIA M. VAZQUEZ, M.D.
University of Michigan, Department of Pediatrics and Communicable Diseases, Department of Psychiatry, Ann Arbor, Michigan.

LINDA MANS WAGENER, PH.D.
Assistant Professor of Psychology; Director of Training, Graduate School of Psychology, Fuller Theological Seminary, Pasadena, California.

GAIL B. WERBACH, M.A., C.E.T., F.A.E.T.
Private Practice, Educational Therapy, Los Angeles, California.

SARA G. ZIMET, ED.D.
Professor Emerita of Psychiatry, University of Colorado Health Sciences Center, Denver, Colorado.

SECTION I
Basic Psychiatric Science

1 / Developmental Neuroendocrinology

Delia M. Vázquez and Juan F. López

In the past decades, it has become clear that the brain is an endocrine organ. In response to internal and external stimuli, the brain is capable of modulating and controlling the secretion of pituitary hormones. The brain is, at the same time, the target of circulating hormones (Krisch, 1989). The classical definition of a hormone is that of a substance (usually a peptide) produced by a group of cells which is transported in the circulation to exert specific metabolic effects on another distant group of cells. On the other hand, neurotransmitters are defined as chemicals that are released by neurons and act on other (usually nearby) neurons to alter their function. However, in the last decades, this distinction has been blurred by the realization that many hormones also can act as neurotransmitters and many of the classic brain neurotransmitters can act as hormones. In addition, hormones can exert trophic as well as metabolic functions. Maintaining an optimal hormonal environment is thus essential for the normal development of the organism and in particular the development of the nervous system.

This chapter reviews some of the basic mechanisms of hormone secretion and action during development and the impact of the dysfunction of these hormones on the developing human. Due to space limitations, we focus on the hormonal systems that are part of the anterior pituitary (or adenohyphophysis) and whose brain control is exerted by the hypothalamus. However, it is important to remember that the posterior pituitary (or neurohypophysis) also plays an essential role in the life of the developing organism. The neurohypophyseal hormones (vasopressin, oxytosin, neurophysin) control such important functions as salt and water balance, blood pressure regulation, parturition, and adaptation to intrauterine stress.

We would like to thank Ramin Eskandari for help with the illustrations in this chapter.

The Developing Hypothalamus and Neuroendocrine Control

The hypothalamus area is the final common pathway and integrator of the multiple brain signals that modulate hormonal response. This brain area is an integral component of most endocrine systems in mammals (Krisch, 1989). In humans as well as in other mammals, the hypothalamus is localized around the third ventricle, below the hypothalamic sulcus (Clark, Beattie, Riddoch, & Dott, 1938). Its intimate nervous and vascular connections to the pituitary makes it possible for the hypothalamus to influence hormonal secretion. The hypothalamus is in turn influenced by several other brain areas that send both direct and indirect projections to several hypothalamic nuclei. Therefore, the convergence of these projections containing different neurotransmitters allows the central nervous system to adjust hormonal secretion to a multitude of both internal and external demands. The hypothalamus sends abundant nerve fibers to the posterior lobe of the hypophysis. There is also a vascular link between the hypothalamus and the anterior lobe of the pituitary, through the hypophysial stalk (the hypophysial portal system) (Clark et al., 1938). It is well established that several hypothalamic neurotransmitter and peptides are released into the portal circulation and control the secretion of anterior pituitary hormones in the adult organism as well as during postnatal development. The hypothalamic releasing factors or hormones that are known to influence anterior pituitary secretion in mammals are discussed later; they include: growth hormone-releasing hormone (GHRH), somatostatin (SRIF), luteinizing-releasing hormone (LHRH), thyrotropin-releasing hormone (TRH), corticotropin-releasing hormone (CRH), and vasopressin (AVP) (Meister, 1993).

The hypothalamus is an intricate region that contains several groups of cells or nuclei. The nu-

3

TABLE 1.1

Effect of Selected Neurotransmitters on Anterior Pituitary Hormone Secretion

Neurotransmitter	Hormone				
	Prolactin	TSH	GH	ACTH	Somatostatin
Dopamine	−	−	+	−	+
Norepinephrine	+	+	+	+	+
Serotonin	+	+,−	+	+	−
Opioid peptides	+	−	+	+,−	−
Acetylcholine	?	?	+	+	?
GABA	+	−	?	−	−

Note: From "Inhibition of Opiate Tolerance by Non-Competitive N-methyl–D–aspartate Receptor Antagonists," by K. Trujillo and H. Aril, 1994, *Brain Research,* 633. Copyright 1994. Adapted with permission.
+ = stimulation; − = inhibition; ? = effective is not known or study findings are contradictory.

clei most closely associated with hormonal control of pituitary function include the supraoptic nucleus (which contains AVP), the paraventricular nucleus (AVP and CRH), the medial preoptic area (LHRH), the arcuate nucleus (GHRH), and the periventricular nucleus (SRIF). A detailed description of the efferent and afferent hypothalamic projections is beyond the scope of this chapter. However, it is clear that some of the major brain nuclei containing classical neurotransmitters systems (e.g., acetylcholine, serotonin, norepinephrine, GABA, histamine, and dopamine) have direct projection to this brain area (Tuomisto & Mannisto, 1985). For example, the hypothalamus contains very high concentrations of noradrenaline, the highest concentrations of which are found in the retrochiasmatic area and in the dorsomedial and paraventricular nuclei. Dopamine, an important inhibitor of prolactin secretion, is also highly concentrated in these nuclei, whereas serotonin is most abundant in the basal and posterior hypothalamic nuclei. Acetylcholine-containing cells are found in several hypothalamic nuclei but are absent in others (Shutte & Lewis, 1966). These neurotransmitters are not only capable of influencing secretion of the hypothalamic peptides or factors that control anterior pituitary secretion but also can act directly at the level of the adenohypophysis. Table 1.1 summarizes the effects of a few selected neurotransmitters on anterior pituitary function. It is important to keep in mind that in many research studies, the effect of some of these neurotransmitters may differ de-

pending on the route of administration, the receptor activated, and the brain pathway stimulated.

Developmentally, the hypothalamus arises from the prosencephalon, the most cephalad part of the neural tube. In humans, specific hypothalamic nuclei are already recognized by the 8th week of gestation (Gilmore, 1992). Around this time, specific neurotransmitters (e.g., norepinephrine, serotonin, and dopamine) as well hypothalamic hormones (e.g., GNRH, SRIF, TRH) can be detected there also. By 14 weeks, hypothalamic nuclei and fiber tracts are fairly well differentiated. Although the full range of neurotransmitters and peptides present in the adult brain is identifiable very early in embryonic life, it is doubtful that these neurotransmitters and peptides can influence anterior pituitary function in early development. This is due to the fact that a full vascular connection between the brain and the pituitary is not established until midgestation. Nevertheless, it has been shown that hypothalamic factors present in human fetuses are functional, since extracts from this region are capable of affecting hormonal secretion from rat anterior pituitaries (McNeilly, Gilmore, Dobbie, & Chard, 1977). Therefore, the possibility exists that, under certain circumstances, hypothalamic peptides could be transported through the cerebrospinal fluid and influence anterior pituitary function early in development.

Catecholaminergic and indolaminergic neurons can be detected in the brains of human fetuses as early as 7 weeks, and monoaminergic immunoreactive fibers have been detected in human hypothalamus of 3-month-old human fetuses. Many other hypothalamic neurotransmitters and peptides have been detected early in human fetal life. Examples include cholecystokinin (9 weeks), substance P (8 weeks), γ-hydroxybutyric acid or GHBA (6 weeks), and many others (Gilmore, 1992). The opioid peptide β-endorphin has been detected in GNRH neurons in the hypothalamic of 17-week-old human fetuses. Although neurotransmitters can be synthesized and stored in the newly formed neurons, they probably cannot act postsynaptically until considerable differentiation of the central nervous system takes place. Studies in brains of nonhuman primates showed that the nuclei of monoaminergic cells develop during the first quarter of gestation, but the cell stomata of the nuclei continue to differentiate through gestation, until the second month after birth.

By midgestation, the hypothalamic-pituitary system already forms a well-differentiated and functional unit, and in most mammals (including humans) the different hypothalamic neurotransmitters and hormones can influence pituitary hormone secretion by the second half of gestation. As the organism matures postnatally, an intact hypothalamic-pituitary unit is essential for the optimal functioning of the different hormonal systems. As will be seen in the sections that follow, alterations or dysfunctions in any of these hormonal systems can have potential catastrophic consequences to the developing organism.

Development and Anatomy of the Anterior Pituitary

Since the anterior pituitary gland produces at least 7 hormones, it has been called the master gland and the conductor of the endocrine symphony orchestra.

The pituitary gland has 2 parts: one portion of neural origin, the neurohypophysis, and a second portion, the adenohypophysis, which is ectodermal in origin, derived from the pharynx. In embryonic development, an evagination from the roof of the pharynx (stomodeum) pushes dorsally to reach and surround a ventrally directed evagination from the base of the diencephalon. The dorsal projecting envagination from the pharynx

is the Rathke's pouch, which is visualized by the 4th week postconception and forms the adenohypophysis. The evagination originating from diencephalon forms the neurohypophysis. The neurohypophysis has 3 parts: the median eminence, the infundibular stem, and the neural lobe itself. The median eminence lies ventral to the floor of the third ventricle and represents the intrahypothalamic portion of the neurohypophysis. The main part of the neural lobe is connected to the median eminence by the infundibular stem. Surrounding this area is adenohypophysis tissue called pars tuberalis. The infundibular stem and surrounding pars tuberalis constitute the pituitary stalk. The adenohypophysis also can be divided into 3 parts: the pars distalis, which is the ventral portion or anterior pituitary lobe (AP); the pars intermedia, which is that portion adjacent to the neural lobe and separated from the AP by a residual lumen from the Rathke's pouch; and the pars tuberalis. In the rodent, the pars intermedia consist exclusively of proopiomelanocortin- (POMC) secreting cells. In humans, it is a rudimentary structure, except during early development and during pregnancy, when POMC-synthesizing cells are functional. By 14 weeks postconception, the pituitary gland is morphologically mature (Moore, 1977).

There is no functional neural innervation of the adenohypophysis and the hypothalamus. Instead, a portal system of capillary loops in the median eminence drains blood in parallel long veins down the pituitary stalk. In the AP the long portal vessels break down into sinusoids that provide the blood supply. In addition to the long portal vessels, there are also short portal venous vascular connections that arise in the neural lobe and pass the pars intermedia to the AP. The presence of fenestrated capillaries within the gland enables uptake and delivery of the hormones from the vascular system. Capillary pressure in the gland is very low and the permeability of these capillaries is high, thus ultrafiltration into the capillary bed to distribute the hormones systemically is achieved at a very low sinusoidal pressure.

The various pituitary cell types can be identified by light microscopy at 10 weeks postconception (Gluckman, 1992; Moore, 1977). These are classified as acidophils, basophils, and chromophobes, depending on the affinity of the cytoplasm to either acidic or basic dyes. The acidophils produce prolactin and growth hormone. All

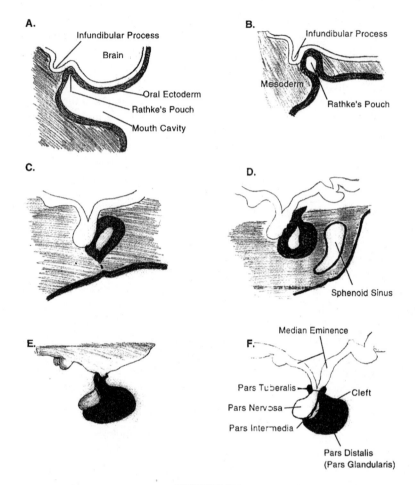

FIGURE 1.1.

Development of the pituitary gland. Sketches A through D illustrate the sequential stages of the developing pituitary gland starting with the appearance of the Rathke's pouch in the 24-day-old embryo. Panel E shows the relationship of the anterior pituitary gland (AP) surrounding the neural lobe. Panel F is a sagittal section of the pituitary illustrating each of its components.

other hormones—thyrotropin (TSH), adrenocorticotropin (ACTH), melanocyte-stimulating hormone (MSH), follicle-stimulating (FSH), and luteinizing hormone (LH)—are from basophilic subtypes. Electron microscopy can further subdivide these cells based on secretion granule size, granule number, and secreting pituitary hormone. For example, lactotrophs secrete prolactin; corticotrophs secrete ACTH. Certain cells may secrete more than one hormone. An example of this is the gonadotroph, which can secrete one or both gonadotropins (FSH and/or LH).

At least 7 distinct hormones are synthesized by cells within the AP. In this review we concentrate on those hormones that have an impact on neuro-

genesis and subsequent development of neuropsychiatric disorders. Studies on the effects of hormones on development can be assessed using at least 3 different approaches (Hamburgh, 1961): the naturalistic approach, where deficiency or excess proves that a hormone is important for the control or differentiation of tissue; the analytical approach, where specific target cells and the critical period in which the hormone acts on these cells is identified; and the cellular approach, where the hormones' action is determined in terms of the cellular mechanisms activated, in particular the repression or expression of genes that code for the synthesis of specific proteins that are needed for the cell to differentiate, disappear

6

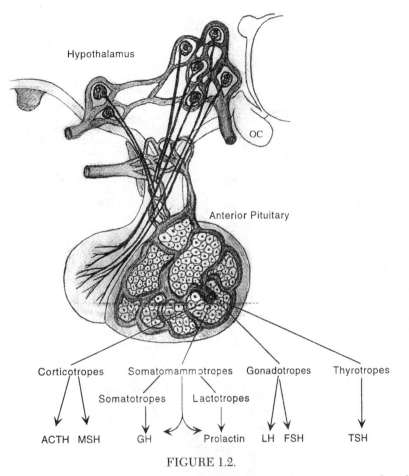

FIGURE 1.2.

The pituitary gland's portal system transports hypothalamic-releasing hormones to stimulate the secretion of the individual anterior pituitary cells. In contrast, the posterior lobe or neurohypophysis receives axonal terminals directly from the magnocellular portion of the paraventricular nucleus (mcPVN) and supraoptic nucleus (SON), which contain vasopressin (AVP) and oxytocin. OC = optic chiasm.

(apoptosis), or to function. We focus on: growth hormone and prolactin, thyroid hormone, gonadotropins, and the stress limbic hypothalamic pituitary adrenal axis. The development of each of these systems and abnormal physiology is described.

Development of the Limbic Hypothalamic Pituitary Adrenal (LHPA) System

The limbic hypothalamic pituitary adrenal (LHPA) axis consists of limbic structures particu-larly the hippocampus, modulating the hypothalamic secretagogues, such as corticotropin-releasing factor (CRF) and AVP, which in turn controls the secretion of corticotropin (ACTH) from the anterior pituitary corticotrophs (Vale, Rivier, & Rivier, 1981). Circulating ACTH interacts with receptors on the adrenal cortex, causing steroidogenesis and elevation of plasma glucocorticoids (GC) (cortisol in the human, corticosterone in the rodent). The rapid increase of GC constitutes one of several mechanisms of negative feedback. This so-called fast negative feedback exerts its action by inhibiting both the releasing factors in the hypothalamus and the release of pituitary hormones, leading to a decrease of circulating ACTH. In addition to this level of regulation, GC act at the transcriptional level by suppressing POMC and CRF gene

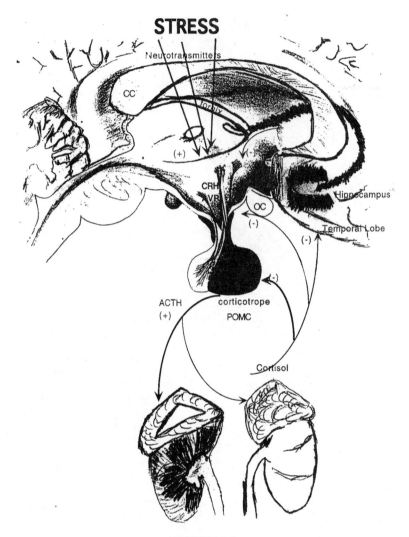

FIGURE 1.3.

The limbic-hypothalamic-pituitary-adrenal axis. Stress signals are received through the various senses and converge at the paraventricular nucleus of the hypothalamus (parvocellular portion—pcPVN) where the two secretagogues, CRH and AVP, are synthesized. CRH and AVP reach the AP through the portal system, where POMC-producing cells secrete ACTH, one of the peptide cleavage products of the POMC molecule. ACTH in turn activates the release of the glucocorticoid cortisol from the adrenal cortex. To close the activation loop, circulating cortisol interacts with glucocorticoid receptors present at the level of the pituitary and the pcPVN and with glucocorticoid and mineralocorticoid receptors present in the hippocampus.

expression, therefore decreasing their stores. Removing circulating GC, such as by adrenalectomy, causes the opposite effects. It promotes the release of CRF and of ACTH and causes an increase in specific POMC gene transcription and mRNA (Fremeau, Lundblad, Pritchett, Wilcox, & Roberts, 1986).

The organization and function of the LHPA axis in the rodent is similar to the human. In fact, much has been learned from this system using the rodent as a model. The development of this system also has been studied in rodents, where the gestational period is a total of 21 days and weaning from the mother is at 21 days postnatal. Although the immediate postnatal period in the rat corresponds to the third trimester in the human, many parallels can be drawn. For example, the adrenocortical response to stress is greatly reduced during the first 2 weeks of the rodent's life. This is termed the stress hyporesponsive period (SHRP). Although less studied, an equivalent SHRP is observed in the premature neonate (Sperling, 1980). Rapid growth characterizes fetal life and the immediate postnatal period. In view of the catabolic influence of corticosteroids on growing and differentiating systems, the SHRP serves an important adaptive function allowing anabolic events to predominate.

Several factors contribute to the SHRP: limited biosynthetic capacity from the hypothalamic CRF and AVP secreting neurons; unique processing of the ACTH precursor molecule coupled with a limited corticotroph biosynthetic capacity; and decreased adrenal sensitivity to circulating ACTH. In addition, stress activation and inhibitory neuronal pathways appear to be immature. The latter is clearly evident in the weanling rodent, which upon stressful stimuli, is able to activate the LHPA axis effectively. However, it fails to swiftly terminate glucocorticoid secretion, exhibiting high and sustained levels of circulating corticosteroids (Goldman, Winget, Holinshead, & Levine, 1978) and ACTH (Vazquez & Akil, 1993). Only at about 4 weeks of age does the rat LHPA axis achieve an adult pattern of responsiveness to stress (De Kloet, Rosenfeld, Van Eekelen, Sutanto, & Levine, 1988). Next we briefly summarize each of these key components of the developing LHPA axis.

CRF AND AVP IN THE DEVELOPING PARAVENTRICULAR NUCLEUS OF THE HYPOTHALAMUS

The hypothalamus is the final common path of the stress response (Lopez, Young, Herman, Akil, & Watson, 1991). In the rat, the appearance of the neurosecretory neurons of the paraventricular nucleus (PVN) begins at a time that coincides with the earliest detection of CRH mRNA in that nucleus (gestational day 17, in the rat and in the 14th to 16th week of human fetal development). Approximately at the time of CRH mRNA detection, axon terminals containing granular vesicles can be seen in the external layer of the median eminence. Maturation of the PVN is mostly completed by postnatal day 28 (Bugnon, Fellmann, Gouget, & Cardot, 1982). Less is known about the exact appearance of arginine vasopressin (AVP) in

the PVN parvocellular neurons. While studies have examined the general developmental pattern of AVP in the whole nucleus (Choy & Watskins, 1979; Rundle & Funder, 1988), there is a critical need to distinguish the parvo- from the magnocellular component of the PVN, as the latter plays a more important role in water balance than stress responsiveness. The relative level of expression of AVP and CRH in the parvocellular PVN is likely to be a critical determinant of stress responsiveness early in life.

It is known that the stress signal involves activation of several neuronal pathways converging on the release of corticotropin-releasing hormone and AVP from hypothalamic neurons. Many of these pathways do not appear to be fully operational during this time. This fact is supported by reports in the literature revealing that serotonergic and catecholaminergic innervation of the hypothalamus and pituitary is a postnatal event reaching an adult pattern on the 4th to 5th week of life (Khachaturian & Sladek, 1980; Loizou 1972). In addition, Grino and associates support the idea that, although the endogenous expression of hypothalamic CRH gene increases steadily after postnatal day 3, peptide release may be impaired due to an incomplete development of the paraventricular nucleus stimulating pathways (Grino, Scott Young, & Burgunder, 1989). The fact that the developing AP is responsive to activation by exogenous CRH during the first 3 weeks of life, both by in vitro and in vivo stimulation, supports this (Guillet, Saffran, & Michaelson, 1980; Walker, Perrin, Vale, & Rivier, 1986). Taken together, these results suggest that the SHRP may occur because the pituitary is not activated appropriately by endogenous secretagogues.

PROOPIOMELANOCORTIN PROCESSING AND REGULATION DURING DEVELOPMENT

Another factor to consider is the availability of pituitary peptides to activate the adrenal. Proopiomelanocortin (POMC) is the precursor molecule that contains the active code of the stress hormone ACTH (ACTH $_{1-39}$). The biosynthesis and processing of the POMC molecule involves an orderly series of proteolytic cleavages, amidations, glycosylations, and amino terminal (N) acetylations that are tissue-specific (Akil, Young, & Watson, 1981; Eipper & Mains, 1980; Herbert

A.
**Anterior Pituitary
Corticotropes**

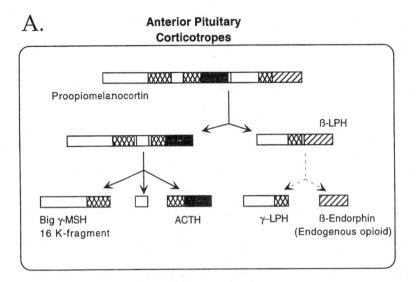

B.
**Neurointermediate Pituitary
Melanotropes**

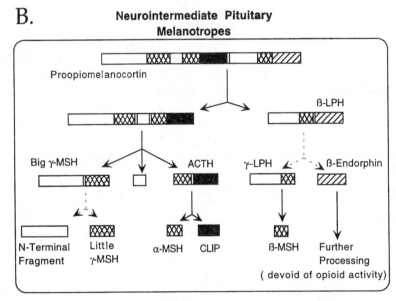

FIGURE 1.4.

Proopiomelanocortin posttranslational processing. Panel A shows the peptide cleavage process leading to ACTH and β-endorphin formation. On Panel B, POMC processing in the neurointermediate lobe cleaves ACTH to αMSH and β-endorphin opioid activity is eliminated with sequential N-acetylations and C-terminal cleavages. The neurointermediate lobe disappears in the mature pituitary but is active during fetal life and may be reactivated during pregnancy.

et al., 1979). In adult corticotrophs, POMC is cleaved to yield equimolar amounts of 16K N fragment, beta-lipotropin (β-LPH) and $ACTH_{1-39}$. One third of the β-LPH is further cleaved to give the active opioid beta-endorphin (βE). By contrast, in the intermediate lobe (IL) or pars intermedia, 16K N fragment, β-LPH and $ACTH_{1-39}$ serve as biosynthetic intermediates to give rise to gamma melanotropin stimulating hormone from the first domain, αMSH (Nac $ACTH_{1-13}NH2$), and corticotropinlike intermediate lobe peptide (CLIP) from the second domain. β-endorphin is produced from the third domain and is further modified to give the opiate inactive forms NAc $βE_{1-27}$ and NAc $βE_{1-26}$. Ninety percent of the stored IL peptides are either MSH or βE forms.

10

Unlike the adult pituitary where the anterior and intermediate lobe POMC products are distinct the developing pituitary lobes have similar POMC products (Allen, Pintar, Stack, & Kendall, 1984; Sato & Mains, 1985; Seizinger, Hollt, & Herz, 1984; Vazquez & Akil, 1992). The immature AP produces more βE than the IL during the first week of life, and some of it may be N-acetylated. Molecular sieving studies coupled with HPLC have revealed that 10% of the ACTH immunoreactivity corresponds to αMSH compared to 1% in the adult AP (Sato & Mains, 1985). It is curious that the AP is producing a large proportion of αMSH during development. However, the hypertrophic and secretagogue effects of ACTH and MSH forms on the adrenal are well known (Challis & Torosis, 1977; Dallman, 1984–85). Likewise, αMSH has been suggested to be an important somatic agent, with effects paralleling those of growth factors during fetal growth and development (Swaab, 1980; Swaab, Visser, & Tilders, 1976). At a time in which anabolic functions predominate in the organism, it is of functional value to have the pituitary POMC systems synthesizing primarily those peptide forms that would promote anabolic effects.

DEVELOPMENT OF THE ADRENAL

The development of the adrenal gland is also tightly linked to the ontogeny of the adrenocortical response. The gland consists of 2 parts, the cortex and the medulla. The cortex is derived from mesoderm and the medulla from ectoderm, which differentiates into neural crest as the neural tube forms. The differentiation of the cortical components begins on the 5th to 6th week of human development. The cortex develops first from the base of the dorsal mesentery near the mesonephros or the primitive kidney. Cells proliferate rapidly and penetrate the retroperitoneum to form the primitive or "fetal cortex." The fetal cortex soon becomes surrounded by a thin layer of more compact cells that become the "permanent cortex." By the 8th week of gestation, the adrenal cortex achieves considerable size and is much larger than the developing kidney. The fetal cortex constitutes the chief bulk of the organ at birth. However, by the 2nd week after birth, the adrenals have lost a third of their weight due to degeneration of the bulky primitive cortex. The outer permanent cortex, which is thin at birth, begins to differentiate as the inner primitive cortex undergoes involution. The zona glomerulosa and fasciculata are present at birth, but full differentiation of the reticularis is not completed until about the third year of life (Moore, 1977).

The fetal and postnatal period is a time when the structure of the adrenal is changing in organization, cell number and in responsiveness to ACTH vs. αMSH (Challis & Torosis, 1977; Glickman, Carson, & Challis, 1979; Silman et al., 1978; Van Dorp & Deane, 1950). Prenatally, the "fetal cortex" is the most active zone for steroidogenesis, producing primarily adrogenic precursors that serve to maintain the fetal placental unit (Martin, Cake, Hartman, & Cook, 1977; Siler-Khodr, 1992). In general, αMSH appears more active at simulating steroidogenesis in the fetal gland while ACTH is more potent in the adult gland (Challis & Torosis, 1977; Glickman et al., 1979). The gradual change in sensitivities appears to involve the specific activation by ACTH of the expression of cytochrome $P-450_{scc}$ and 11β/18 hydroxylase enzyme systems (Ramírez, Bournot, & Maume, 1985; Simpson & Waterman, 1983).

INHIBITION OF THE LHPA AXIS: GLUCOCORTICOID INTERACTIONS IN THE BRAIN

Inhibition of stress responsiveness by glucocorticoids seems to operate through 3 relatively independent types of mechanisms, a rate sensitive fast feedback, an intermediate feedback, and a delayed feedback. Fast feedback is a rapid phenomenon (within minutes) whereby the rate of rise of glucocorticoid (rather than the absolute level) is monitored and inhibition is achieved partly by glucocorticoid binding to specific receptors in the hypothalamus and to limbic structures, including the hippocampus. Intermediate and delayed feedback, on the other hand, work over the course of hours to days, during which time the translocated glucocorticoid-receptor complex acts at the transcriptional level by suppressing CRH and POMC gene expression, therefore decreasing the secretory drive and the peptide stores in the pituitary (Brett, Chong, Coyle, & Levine, 1981). Thus these nested, multiple feedback loops operate in different time domains and through neuronal signaling as well as through gene regulatory controls to maintain the organism in an ideal state of stress responsiveness. To understand the effects of the steroid hormones, we need to summarize what is currently known about the steroid receptors that mediate their actions in the brain.

Glucocorticoid and Mineralocorticoid Receptors: It is well established that the brain is a major target of glucocorticoids. Early demonstrations of the binding of adrenal steroids to brain tissue (McEwen, De Kloet, & Rostene, 1986; McEwen, Weiss, & Schwartz, 1968) revealed a unique anatomical pattern with particularly high levels of expression in the hypothalamus and in the hippocampus. These corticosteroid binding sites were then shown to subsume 2 classes of receptors, a type I, which has a particularly high affinity for corticosterone (subnanomolar) and also recognized aldosterone; and a type II, which has a somewhat lower affinity to corticosterone, does not recognize aldosterone, but does bind the synthetic steroid dexamethasone (Reul & De Kloet, 1986). Following the cloning, expression, and pharmacological characterization of members of the steroid receptor family (Ariza et al., 1987; Hollenberg et al., 1985; Patel, Sherman, Goldman, & Watson, 1989), the type I and type II receptors were recognized to be the mineralocorticoid receptor (MR) and the glucocorticoid receptor (GR), respectively. Not only did these receptors exhibit the appropriate pharmacological signatures, but they also had the appropriate anatomy, which revealed particularly high levels of expression of both MR and GR in the pyramidal cells and in the dentate gyrus (DG) of the HC (Morris, Dausse, Devnick, & Meyer, 1980; Trujillo & Akil, 1994). While MR is primarily expressed in HC, GR is seen throughout the neuroaxis, including the PVN. The unique aspect of these receptors within the brain is that both GR and MR are occupied by circulating glucocorticoids. In the kidney, the main ligand for the MR is aldosterone, because the enzyme 11-β dehydrogenase inactivates corticosterone and cortisol allowing the binding of aldosterone, for which MR has a weaker affinity. In contrast, in the brain MR often is described as a high-affinity, low-capacity glucocorticoid receptor system. Conversely, GR is known as a *low*-affinity, high-capacity receptor system. It binds CS with a lower affinity compared to MR. Its highest affinity is for potent synthetic glucocorticoids, such as dexamethasone. These receptor characteristics *complement* each other and put both the MR and GR in a position to modulate LHPA responses. The MR receptors appear to be operative at low CS concentrations and may offer tonic inhibition to the axis during the nadir of the circadian rhythm (Bodnoff et al., 1995; Bugnon et al., 1982). When high concentrations are present, MR receptors saturate, and the GR receptors appear to "take over" acting coordinately to ensure the return of homeostasis. Therefore, the dual action of these receptors, which are present in the hippocampus, appears to be central to the modulation of the LHPA. There is also evidence of complex interactions, whereby MR may be inactive and GR may be active, raising the possibility the MR may act as an antagonist of GR in certain cases (Funder, 1993; Pearce & Yamamoto, 1993). Such interactions are of interest, as a number of functional studies suggest that GR and MR may not always work in the same direction and that the relative balance of GR and MR may be very important for ultimate physiologic function (De Kloet, 1991; De Kloet & Joels, 1991).

Developmental Pattern of Glucocorticoid and Mineralocorticoid Receptors: The abundance and distribution of GR and MR mRNA follows individually distinct patterns in the developing hippocampal formation and dentate gyrus (DG) (Vazquez, Morano, Lopez, Watson, & Akil, 1993). Postnatal day 10 exhibits the highest signal intensity in virtually all subfields for both GR and MR messages. Beyond this age, GR mRNA expression resembles the adult distribution (Herman et al., 1989). This progression of the GR gene expression agrees well with the ontogenic progression of the protein as revealed by a monoclonal GR antibody (Rosenfeld, Van Eekelen, Levine, & De Kloet, 1988; Van Eekelen, Kiss, Westphal, & De Kloet, 1987). In contrast, MR mRNA continues to be very abundant in the DG and does not acquire an adultlike distribution until after postnatal day 28 (Herman, Patel, Akil, & Watson, 1989; Vazquez et al., 1993). As we mentioned earlier, when the young rat emerges from the SHRP, it fails to terminate its stress response swiftly following certain stressors. While such a pattern is correlated with a loss of hippocampal glucocorticoid receptors in chronically stressed adults or aged animals (Sapolsky, Krey, & McEwen, 1985), this does not appear to be the case during development (Rosenfeld, Sutanto, Levine, & De Kloet, 1988; Vazquez et al., 1993). As we just described, the expression of these receptors increases steadily with age; furthermore, the affinity of GR and MR does not change with age. In fact, the greatest absolute increase for both receptors occurs between days 22 and 45, at a time when failure to terminate the adrenocortical response is described, suggesting that the receptor number and affinity is not the explanation for an impaired "turn-off" of the stress response. Of course, a reasonable possibility is that the connections of the hippocampus to the PVN are not yet fully established at this age.

ABNORMAL PHYSIOLOGY

Glucocorticoids are potent hormones that affect numerous targets, including the brain and the pituitary. Thus it is not surprising that the system is intricately controlled via neuronal and hormonal feedback mechanisms to produce optimal responses allowing the organism to deal with various physiological and environmental events swiftly and adaptively. Dysfunction of the LHPA axis has been studied in various endocrine disorders (e.g., Cushing's disease) and psychiatric disorders (e.g., endogenous depression). In addition, this system is thought to be altered with age; in particular, aged animals and patients with dementia of the Alzheimer's type may demonstrate increased baseline cortisol and abnormalities of negative feedback mechanisms at the hippocampal level (Young & Vazquez, 1996). More important, numerous behavioral endocrine and clinical studies have shown that various stressors, both physical and psychological, that occur early in life can produce profound alterations in the organism's growth, development, and consequent adult life (Pollit, Eichler, & Chan, 1975; Powell, Hopwood, & Barratt, 1973; Smith, Su-Yong, & S., 1995; Stanton, Gutierrez, & Levine, 1988; Weinstock, Matlina, Maor, Rosen, & McEwen, 1992). Most notable is the psychosocial dwarf syndrome seen in children experiencing chronic psychological and social stress (Bowden & Hopwood, 1982). Clearly, the proper development of this axis, both structurally and functionally, is of critical importance to the survival of the organism in early life and for the appropriate control of stress responsiveness in adult life.

Development of the Somatotropic and Lactogenic Systems

Growth hormone (GH) and prolactin (PRL) share several structural and biological features. This is not surprising, as they are derived from a common ancestral gene that encodes GH, PRL, and placental lactogen (and related proteins) (Goffin, Shiverick, Delly, & Martial, 1996). Fetal growth and maturation proceed normally in the absence of PRL or GH, and this endocrine system is autonomous from the maternal system (neither GH nor PRL cross the placenta). Thus the role of GH and PRL in fetal and perinatal physiology have been an enigma.

In adults, GH is believed to be under the dual control of 2 hypothalamic peptides: GH releasing hormone (GHRH) and somatostatin (SRIF). GH secretion occurs in episodic bursts once every 3 hours (Daughaday, 1989). GHRH is secreted into the median eminence into the hypophysial portal circulation to reach the anterior pituitary, where it stimulates the somatotrophs to release GH. A host of neurotransmitters affect GHRH or SRIF release. The effects of GH on peripheral tissues are multiple and complex and include both direct and indirect actions. Although high GH levels are detected during fetal life, the appearance of hepatic GH and somatomedin (IGF-1) receptors during the late infancy period mark the onset of GH effect on somatic growth (Dubois & Hemming, 1987). Thus linear growth in humans becomes GH-*dependent* during late infancy and childhood.

Prolactin is controlled in a complex manner by hypothalamic factors. The major influence is the tonic inhibition exerted by dopamine neurons present in the medial basal hypothalamus. Thyrotropin-releasing hormone (TRH) is a PRL-releasing factor. Thus primary hypothyroidism is associated with hyperprolactenemia. Other hormones also influence PRL release in a complex way. For example, estrogen directly increases synthesis and release of PRL, but it also increases the number of TRH receptors on the lactotrophs and antagonizes dopamine action.

Limited data are available from the human fetus for both these systems, but more is known about the regulation of these hormones from the

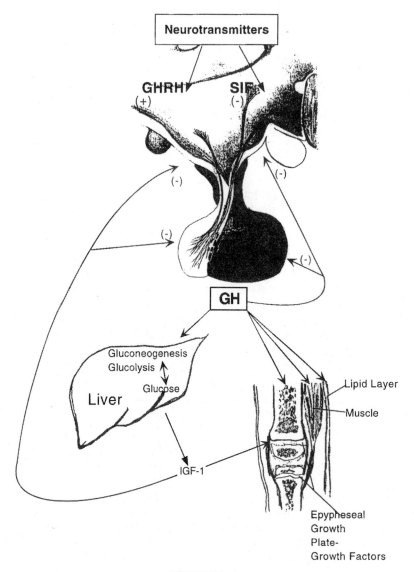

FIGURE 1.5.

The somatotrophic or GH axis. The 2 main modulators of growth hormone (GH) secretion are GH-releasing hormone (GHRH) and somatostatin (SIF). GH release from somatotropes acts directly in tissue and indirectly through growth factors, one of which is insulin growth factor-1 (IGF-1). In addition to the trophic actions, GH has effects on glucose, amino acid, and lipid metabolism.

neonate. We describe briefly the development of somatotrophs and lactotrophs, followed by a description of the regulation of their hormone secretion.

DEVELOPMENT OF SOMATOTROPHS AND LACTOTROPHS

One-third of human pituitary cells secrete both GH and PRL, as observed on fetal tissue obtained at 18 and 20 weeks of gestation (Gluckman, 1992). It has been suggested that there is a common somatomamotrope precursor. Growth hormone is clearly visualized by immunocytochemical techniques at 8 weeks postconception (Gluckman, 1992). The morphology of these cells changes as embryogenesis progresses, which may indicate further differentiation from the somatomamotrope precursor. Large cells with diffuse pale immunoreactivity predominate prior to 20 weeks,

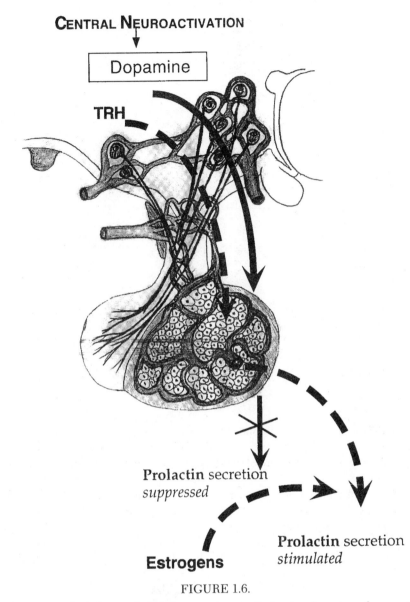

CENTRAL NEUROACTIVATION

Dopamine

TRH

Prolactin secretion
suppressed

Prolactin secretion
stimulated

Estrogens

FIGURE 1.6.

The lactotrope and control of prolactin secretion. Prolactin release is under negative modulation of dopamine. TRH activates prolactin synthesis and release. Several mechanisms are involved in estrogen prolactin stimulating effects, including suppression of dopamine release and down-regulation of pituitary dopamine receptors.

whereas small cells with dense cytoplasmic staining predominate after 20 weeks of gestation. Prolactin-secreting cells are detected at 12 weeks, but their numbers are low until after 26 weeks of gestation. The content of mRNA coding for PRL increases tenfold between 26 and 27 weeks with an even greater increase in pituitary peptide content. The number of GH cells increases progressively through pregnancy.

Tissue-specific nuclear proteins known as transactivators are responsible for the transcriptional activation of GH and PRL genes that ultimately would decide on a differentiated phenotype (Cooke, 1995). The nuclear protein Pit1 has been found to be necessary for the efficient transcriptional activation of both the GH and PRL genes. However, other transacting factors must be involved in the specific cell types since Pit1 in lacto-

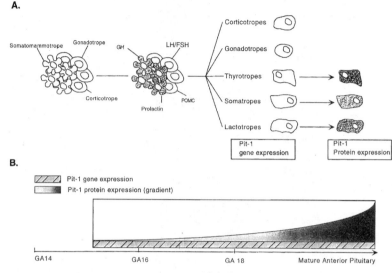

FIGURE 1.7.

Differentiation of anterior pituitary endocrine cells and its relation to Pit-1 protein expression. Panel A shows the sequence of events, where only those cells that translate the Pit-1 gene product differentiate to thyrotrophs, somatotropes, and lactotropes. Panel B illustrates the pit-1 protein increasing levels in the rat, from gestational age 14 (GA14) to birth.

Note: From *Prolactin: Basic Physiology*, by N. E. Cooke, 1995, Philadelphia: W. B. Saunders. Copyright 1995. Adapted with permission.

trophs will activate PRL gene expression but not GH expression. This fact suggests that restrictive mechanisms exist to exclude the GH expression in lactotrophs. The timing of Pit1 expression in pituitary cells is consistent with the morphological and immunological findings presented earlier. The embryonic appearance of Pit1 protein probably represents one of the last steps in the pathway leading to full differentiation of lactotrophs and somatotrophs.

REGULATORY PEPTIDES DURING FETAL DEVELOPMENT

Hypothalamic nuclei are detectable in the human fetus early in gestation. Although the development of the hypothalamus has been described already, a brief discussion here is needed to describe GH and PRL regulation. At 8 weeks postconception the median eminence is distinguishable, and by 15 weeks, all nuclei found in the adult hypothalamus are identifiable. Growth hormone releasing hormone axonal terminals are present by 18 weeks of gestation within the median eminence. An increase in staining is observed later in gestation, and a marked reduction is seen at birth. Somatostatin (SRIF), the negative modulator of GH, is first detected in the human hypothalamus by 11 weeks of gestation. GH effects can be exerted directly or mediated by secondary modulators, insulin growth factor 1 and 2. These proteins, produced primarily by the liver, inhibit GH secretion (Bala, Lopotka, & Leung, 1981). Between 12 and 26 weeks of gestation biologically active forms ($SRIF_{1-14}$, $SRIF_{1-28}$) increase in relation to its larger precursors. SRIF axonal terminal staining is visualized at 16 weeks in the median eminence. Thyroid-releasing hormone, which can activate PRL release from the AP, is detected in the hypothalamus by 8 weeks' gestation and increases in content late in gestation.

The placenta produces neurotransmitters and hormones closely related to GH and PRL. Chorionic somatomamotropin and proliferins are examples of hormones structurally related to GH and PRL that appear to have functions restricted to placental development. However, other hormones and neurotransmitters may act on the fetus. For example, both amniotic fluid and placenta contain dopamine. (TRH and SRIF are also detected in the placenta or amniotic fluid.) In experiments in which pituitary stalk disconnection was performed in sheep fetus, persistent dopaminergic inhibition of PRL secretion was documented. This fact suggests the possibility that placental dopamine and perhaps other hormones or neurotransmitters can influence fetal pituitary function.

Several agents are used clinically to stimulate GH secretion or to induce inhibition. Insulin hypoglycemia, arginine, exercise, levo-dopa and the β-blocker propanolol are potentiators, whereas the a-adrenergic blocker phentolamine inhibits release. As we will see later, opposite effects from those observed in adults are observed in preterm and full-term infants.

REGULATION AND FUNCTION AFTER BIRTH

Growth Hormone: There is evidence to suggest that many components of the hypothalamic control of GH secretion are present at birth. However, the fine control of the system does not appear to be present at this time. High concentrations of GH are present in the neonate, and hyperglycemia stimulates rather than inhibits GH release in the neonate (Reitano, 1977). Similarly, arginine infusion, which is a classical secretagogue for this hormone, is associated with a depression of GH release (Gluckman, 1992; Gluckman, Grumbach, & Kaplan, 1981; Stubbe & Wolf, 1975). Paradoxical effects also are reported about dopamine and pyridoxine on neonatal GH release. However, many aspects of the hypothalamic control are operant at this age. For example, SRIF inhibits GH release in the term infant (Delitala, 1978) and feeding stimulates GH release in both premature and term neonates (Adrian, 1983). However, the activation of the system appears to be more efficient than the inhibitory function during this period. In studies performed in sheep, which follow a similar pattern of GH secretion as in the human neonate, it is evident that while fetal hypothalamic ablation is associated with more than a 90% decrease in plasma GH concentrations, infusion of any inhibitor does not decrease GH secretion by more than 50% (SRIF, β-adrenergic agents, dopaminergic agents, IGF-1-insulinlike growth factor I) (Gluckman et al., 1981). It is possible that these altered responses

are a consequence of an immature hypothalamic inhibitory control, immaturity of the neonatal somatotrope, or both. Interestingly, in the neonate and infant, IGF-1 levels are quite low and pituitary receptors may be fewer in number, factors that also can contribute to this hypersecretory GH state.

The physiological significance of high GH concentrations in fetal and neonatal circulation is uncertain. The action of GH is dependent on binding to somatotropic receptors. In the growing postnatal mammal, the GH actions are mediated directly by GH or by the stimulation of IGF-1 secretion. In addition, GH mediates a number of metabolic effects including: diabetogenic, antilipogenic, and lipolytic. However, GH does not appear to have a major role in fetal growth. Insulin and insulinlike growth factors, on the other hand, are major determinants of fetal growth. Some in utero GH actions cannot be completely excluded since the hypophysectomized fetal lamb retains excess adiposity, and this is reversed by administration of GH (Stevens & Alexander, 1986). In addition, GH is reported to stimulate islet cell proliferation early in gestation and may have actions on preadipocyte differentiation. (See Gluckman, 1992, for review.) However, it is evident from multiple animal studies that the limiting step for GH action with regard to somatic growth is the expression of the GH receptor in tissues, especially in the liver (Gluckman, 1992). In every species studied (monkey, rabbit, sheep, pig, and rat), the number of GH receptors in the liver increases after birth. The induction signal does not appear to be environmental changes but intrinsic genomic events.

Prolactin: Prolactin is present in fetal circulation at very low levels between 12 and 26 weeks postgestation. A sharp increase is noted at birth, when a cord level of 170 nanograms per milliliter is detected in full-term neonates, a level that is 8 times greater than adults. This level declines by more than 60% during the first week of life. This decrease is delayed in premature infants (Gluckman et al., 1981). It is very likely that estrogen levels during late gestation influence the rise of PRL during this part of the gestation period, since estrogen receptors can bind close to one of the enhancer elements in the PRL gene (an ERE)

(Cooke, 1995). While the decline at birth correlates with the withdrawal of placental estrogen, it is difficult to explain why premature infants have a delayed decline. It has been suggested that ongoing maturation within the hypothalamus is also involved in these events. It is clear, however, that dopaminergic tonic inhibition is operational during late gestation.

Prolactin receptors are present in a variety of fetal tissues, including liver and lung. Prolactin appears to be an important factor for fetal lung maturation (Gluckman, 1992; Gluckman et al., 1981). Studies in sheep have shown that PRL acts synergistically with cortisol and thyroid hormones to promote lung maturation. Prolactin also may act as an osmoregulatory hormone, as it does in amphibians. Experimentally induced increases in PRL levels in the newborn rabbit causes water retention; therefore, the loss of total body water after birth could be due in part to the decline in plasma PRL levels observed during the immediate neonatal period (Coulter, 1983).

ABNORMAL PHYSIOLOGY

Disorders of the hypothalamic pituitary unit have made possible our understanding of the role of GH in fetal life. The anancephalic infant has a small pituitary. The proportion of somatotropes within the pituitary are normal, but the GH content is reduced. The responses to pharmacological stimuli are variable, probably due to variable development of the diencephalon, where the hypothalamus resides. Trunk, limb size, birth length, and weight are found to be only slightly reduced in newborn infants with hypopituitarism (Johanson, 1995).

Pituitary agenesis is the only condition associated with PRL deficiency. Although an essential role for PRL is not identified clinically in this condition, the observations are confounded by the presence of lactogens from placental origin.

Theoretically, mutations of Pit-1 should abolish GH and PRL expression. Pit-1 mRNA is detected in corticotrophs, gonadotrophs, thyrotrophs, somatotrophs, and lactotrophs. However, Pit-1 protein expression is only found in thyrotrophs, somatotrophs, and lactotrophs. Thus mutations of the Pit-1 gene would lead to a dwarf phenotype by virtue of GH and/or thyroid hormone deficiency. Three genetically dwarf mouse strains have been identified to contain a mutation in the Pit-1 gene complex: allelic Snell and Jackson strains (dw) and the nonallelic Ames dwarf mouse (df). (For review, see Johanson, 1995.) In the dw mutations, the pituitary is hypoplastic with no evidence of thyrotrophs, somatotrophs, and lactotrophs. The mutations abolish Pit-1 binding to the DNA. (Snell strain has a point mutation in the POU domain, while Jackson contains a 4-kb insertion in the gene, which disrupts the binding domain.) The third strain, Ames dwarf mouse, does not express Pit-1 protein. Pit-1 mutations have been found in human kindreds with dwarfism. The families had different point mutations that lead to reduced binding affinity of Pit-1 to the genome with resulting cretinism and GH and PRL deficiencies. These are the first recognized conditions resulting from mutations in transcription factor genes.

Development of the Hypothalamic-Pituitary-Gonadal Axis (HPG)

Pituitary gonadotropin secretion is regulated precisely by hypothalamic and gonadal factors. The gonadotropins, luteinizing hormone (LH) and follicle-stimulating hormone (FSH), are important for the function of the differentiated gonad in utero and regulate their function in later life. LH and FSH are secreted by the same pituitary cell, the gonadotroph. Both hormones are structurally related and belong to the family of glycoproteins: LH, FSH, TSH (thyroid-stimulating hormone) and hCG (human chorionic gonadotropin). Human chorionic gonadotropin is a placental hormone that behaves like LH. (It binds to LH receptors.) Each of these hormones consists of α and β subunits, with the β subunit conferring biological specificity. The secreted gonadotropins divide the gonad into 2 compartments: the gametogenic compartment controlled by FSH and the steroidogenic compartment, largely dependent on LH. Normal reproductive function is dependent on the collaboration of these 2 gonadal components as well as their feedback via gonadal steroids and other peptides, such as inhibin (which inhibits FSH secretion), acting at the level of both the pi-

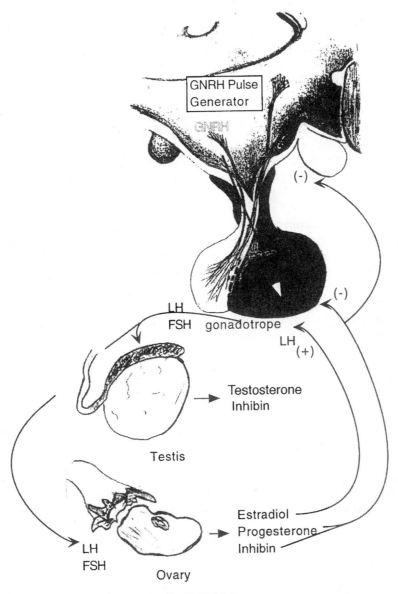

FIGURE 1.8.

*The hypothalamic-pituitary-gonadal axis. Gonadotropin-releasing hormone (GNRH)
neurons secrete GNRH in a pulsatile fashion, which translates to pulsatile LH secretion from the
pituitary. Both LH and FSH are secreted to stimulate the testis and ovary (see text). Inhibition of the
pulses is achieved with inhibin, testosterone, and progestins. Gonadal failure is characterized by high
levels of FSH, while pituitary or hypothalamic failure is identified with low circulating levels of LH
and FSH. GNRH challenge is helpful for the differentiation of hypothalamic hypogonadism (low LH
and FSH) from pituitary failure (high LH and FSH).*

tuitary and the hypothalamus. Recently it has become evident that exposure to gonadal steroid in
utero also influences brain development, which
ultimately would have an impact on mating and
parental behavior.

DEVELOPMENT OF HYPOTHALAMIC AND PITUITARY ELEMENTS

Pituitary secretion of gonadotropins is initiated
by the pulsatile secretion of gonadotropin-

releasing hormone (GnRH or LHRH-luteinizing hormone-releasing hormone) from the hypothalamus. Neurons that contain GnRH are scattered throughout the anterior parts of the hypothalamus, preoptic area, septal complex, medial basal hypothalamus, and arcuate nucleus. Developmentally, GnRH neurons originate outside the developing central nervous system in the olfactory placode and migrate to the median eminence, where they make contact with the hypothalamic-pituitary portal circulation (Schwanzel-Fekuda & Pfaff, 1991). In the human, GnRH is detected in hypothalamic extracts by week 4.5 of gestation. Fetal hypothalamic GnRH neurons have been detected at 9 weeks, and functional connections are established by 16 weeks' gestation (Grambach & Kaplan, 1990). LH and FSH are detected in the AP at 10 weeks and are measurable in blood by 12 weeks gestation (Kaplan & Grumbach, 1976). Some experimental evidence points to a role for GnRH in pituitary gonadotroph development. The first clue came from anancephalic fetuses that have differentiated gonadotrophs but low levels of gonadotropins in the pituitary and serum (Kaplan & Grumbach, 1976). Anancephalics also have persistent secretion of the α subunit of glycoproteins. Studies performed on hypothalamic fetal tissue obtained during the second trimester and on rat fetal pituitary have shown that GnRH stimulates the differentiation of fetal pituitary gonadotrophs (Cuttler, 1992) and GnRH also induces the synthesis of LH β mRNA synthesis (Castillo, Matteri, & Dumesic, 1992; Kaplan & Grumbach, 1976). However, since pituitary gonadotroph differentiation can proceed at a distance from the brain (transplanted under the kidney capsule), it is evident that other unknown factors (paracrine and endocrine) may influence gonadotroph development and function (Cuttler, 1992).

REGULATION AND FUNCTION OF GONADOTROPINS IN THE FETUS AND NEWBORN

The factors involved in the periodic synthesis and release of GnRH are not fully understood. However, there is evidence for influences by gonadal steroids, endogenous opioids, prostaglandins, and central neurotransmitters including norepinephrine, serotonin, dopamine, acetylcholine, and γ-amino-butyric acid (Cuttler, 1992). GnRH neurons are assumed to be electrophysiologically active, and changes in the number of action potentials appear to determine relative synchronization and level of hormonal secretion. The origin and modulation of the "GnRH pulse generator" has been the theme of much investigation and is beyond the scope of this chapter. Suffice it to say that since the GnRH neurons are scattered through out the medial hypothalamus, they are likely to be linked at a central level through interneurons and/or reciprocal connections that orchestrate the synchronization of the GnRH pulses. In addition, most remarkable is the observation that intrinsic pulsatile secretory activity is present in cultures of immortalized GnRH neurons (Wetzel, Valenca, & Merchenthaler, 1992). Thus it is not surprising that so complex a system of communication includes such an array of intrinsic factors and neurotransmitters.

Sexual dimorphism exists as a consequence of the developing of the hypothalamic-pituitary-gonadal axis (HPG). Female fetuses have a preponderance of the FSH over LH when compared to male fetuses. In addition, both LH and FSH peak earlier in the female fetus, with FSH levels remaining elevated throughout gestation and into the neonatal period, infancy, and up to 7 years of age. This is consistent with a late development of gonadal feedback in the female. In effect, both testosterone and inhibin are by the testis as early as 10 weeks gestation. Evidence of gonadal feedback is demonstrated in the male primate fetus by midgestation (Cuttler, 1992). In contrast, FSH receptors are not present in ovaries until the ninth month of pregnancy. In addition, inhibin is minimally expressed in the absence of FSH receptors (Huhtaniemi, Yamomoto, & Ranta, 1987; Robinovici, Goldsmith, & Roberts, 1991). Thus the minimal amounts of steroids and inhibin secreted by the fetal ovary during development may explain the high pituitary and circulating FSH observed in the female. Despite these differences, both the male and female fetus develop in an environment that is rich in estrogen of fetoplacental origin. However, the contribution of androgens in the male fetus and the lack of these in the female results in a differential neuronal organization, operation of motor systems, and processing of sensory stimuli. This conclusion is derived from work in rodents (rats and hamsters) in which organization of neural pathways mediating copulatory behavior and parental behavior (maternal and paternal) have been mapped. In addition, estrogen and progesterone modulation of hypothalamic gene products associated to these behaviors and alterations of these patterns from androgen exposure in utero have been explored. (See Pfaff & Lauber, 1995, for a comprehensive review.) Interestingly, although androgen exposure is important to elicit male behavior, androgen receptors do not always exclusively mediate these behaviors. In fact, the estrogen receptor has been identified as an important player in adults and in the masculinization process of the neonatal brain since a large amount of estradiol is generated from the amortization of testosterone to estradiol (Pfaff, 1980; Pfaff & Lauber, 1995). It appears, then, that androgen, estrogen, and progestin receptors all contribute, with more or less strength, to female reproductive behavior, masculine behavior, and parental behavior.

ONSET OF PUBERTY

The onset of puberty is characterized by a reactivation of the hypothalamic GnRH pulsatile secretion. The mechanism that dictates this event is the subject of much investigation in the endocrine field. The quality of the GnRH pulses and frequency dictate the resultant changes in the quantity of gonadotropins released. The earliest change in the pattern of gonadotropin secretion is an increase in the frequency of LH release associated with sleep (stage 3). As puberty progresses, the LH peaks become more frequent and occur throughout day and night. In contrast to the male, where equivalent LH and FSH levels are seen, in the adolescent female FSH secretion predominates. In addition, FSH glycosylated forms, which confer a longer half-life in circulation, are abundant during puberty. Over time the ovarian feedback is established, with the development of estrogen-induced positive feedback on LH. This represents the final modulation milestone reached in the female and the onset of ovulatory reproductive cycles.

ABNORMAL PHYSIOLOGY

Abnormalities of reproductive function may lie at the level of the hypothalamus, pituitary, the gonad, or the outflow tract (uterus in the female, vas deferens in the male). Because the HPG axis is active during the neonatal period, suspected endocrine disorders can be diagnosed during the first few months of life (0 to 4 months old) with GnRH challenge and up to 4 years based on basal gonadotropin secretion. As in the adult, the level of endocrine abnormality can be localized based on hormonal levels or hormonal levels after a GnRH challenge test (Cuttler, 1992; Hall & Crowley, 1995). In patients with abnormalities at the gonadal level (Klinefelter's-XXY karyotype or Turner's syndrome-X0 karyotype), gonadotropin levels will be elevated in the presence of low levels of gonadal steroids, since gonadal feedback is not present. Patients with either a hypothalamic or pituitary site of pathology will have low or normal levels of gonadotropins. However, after a GnRH challenge test, low levels will prevail in pituitary dysfunction, while an increase of LH and FSH will be detected in the patient with hypothalamic site of disruption.

Microphallus and undescended testes should alert the physician to a pituitary or hypothalamic hormonal deficiency. The full-term AGA (adequate-for-gestational-age) male neonate with panhypopituitarism is identified by hypoglycemia and microphallus. This presentation is consistent with congenital deficiencies of growth hormone and ACTH. Both cortisol and growth hormone treatment are indicated. However, this is the only instance where growth does not dictate growth hormone treatment but rather the hypoglycemia. Kallman's syndrome, a familial condition associated with X-linked, autosomal dominant or autosomal recessive mode of inheritance, should be considered under the category of hypothalamic GnRH deficiency. These patients may present with microphallus and cryptorchidism at birth and have family history of anosmia. In the X-linked form of Kallman's, GnRH neurons fail to migrate from the olfactory placode to their position into the various nuclei that contain GnRH neurons in the hypothalamus due to a gene deletion that has high homology with N-CAM, a neural adhesion molecule involved in cell migration (Cuttler, 1992; Hall & Crowley, 1995). Midfacial defects such as cleft lip and palate, deafness, and color blindness may be present with hypogonadotropic hypogonadism or may be expressed separately in affected families.

Prematurity and phototherapy treatment for

TABLE 1.2

Effect of Thyroid Hormone on the Developing Organism

Thyroid Hormone Action	Age (years)				
	Fetus	0–3	3–12	12–20	>20
Brain Development	±	+4	±	0	0
Somatic Growth[a]	0	+4	+3	+2	0
Bone Maturation	+1	+4	+3	+2	0
Dental Development	0	+4	+2	+1	0
Metabolic	±	+2	+3	+3	+1
Hypothalamic-Pituitary Feedback	0	±	+2	+3	+1

Note: From *Thyroid Disease in the Neonate and in Childhood,* by D. A. Fisher, 1989, Philadelphia: W. B. Saunders. Copyright 1989. Adapted with permission.
[a]synergism with GH action

neonatal hyperbilirubinemia have been reported to transiently increase gonadotropin secretion.

Development of the Hypothalamic-Pituitary-Thyroid Axis

Thyroid hormones affect energy metabolism and the metabolism of a variety of molecules which are important building blocks in cells. For example, important effects are exerted on the metabolism of lipids, carbohydrates, protein, nucleic acids, vitamins and inorganic ions. Thyroid hormones also alter metabolic responses to a variety of humoral stimuli (e.g. cardiovascular tone). While these are functions that are present during childhood, adolescence and adulthood, the effects on cell differentiation and growth are unique to the first twenty years of life. Thus, the importance and effect of thyroid hormone varies with age, as can be seen in Table 1.2. We will summarize in this section the development of the thyroid gland and hypothalamic pituitary thyroid axis followed by a brief description of abnormal thyroid physiology.

DEVELOPMENT OF THE THYROID GLAND

The thyroid gland develops in the third week of gestation from an endodermal invagination present on the floor of the primordial pharynx (Ericson, 1990; Polk & Fisher, 1992). The invagination becomes a diverticulumlike structure that grows downward but remains connected to its origin at the base of the tongue (foramen cecum). The distal end of the diverticulum gradually descends to its normal anatomical position in the neck area, where it becomes bilobed as cell proliferate and fills in the structure into a solid mass. A narrow thyroglossal duct is the structural evidence of the thyroid gland descent from the primitive pharynx. The duct undergoes atrophy and disappears, but its distal end may develop into the pyramidal lobe that connects to the isthmus of the gland. Partial atrophy of the thyroglossal duct leads to cysts, fistulae, and ectopic thyroid tissue in the trajectory of descent. The gland may descend further into the anterior mediastinum, where ectopic thyroid gland tissue may be identified. During the seventh week of gestation, epithelium from the fourth brachial pouch and cells from neural crest origin become part of the thyroid tissue. Each of these respective cell clusters will give rise to the parathyroid glands and the calcitonin-producing parafollicular cells or C cells.

Specific thyroid gland functions develop as the individual components of the gland develop (Ericson, 1990). For example, the ability to synthesize thyroglobin is marked by the development of the rough endoplasmic reticulum (RER) and is observed before follicle organization. Iodination of the thyroglobulin is not evident until follicles are fully developed. Iodinated thyroglobulin has been documented in 75-day-old human fetuses. Shortly after this event, low levels of thyroid hormones

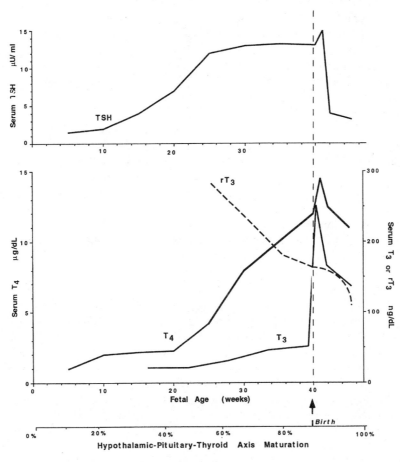

FIGURE 1.9.

Thyroid hormone secretory patterns during human gestation and at birth. The hypothalamic-pituitary-thyroid axis maturation can be followed in the lower panel.

Note: From *Thyroid Disease in the Fetus, Neonate, and Child*, by D. A. Fisher and D. H. Polk, 1995, Philadelphia: W. B. Saunders. Copyright 1995. Adapted with permission.

are present in plasma, indicating a functional secretory mechanism. Larger amounts of thyroid hormone synthesis are apparent at 18 weeks of gestation and steadily increase until final weeks of pregnancy.

DEVELOPMENT OF THYROID HYPOTHALAMIC-PITUITARY AXIS

The fetal thyroid and hypothalamic-pituitary-thyroid axis develop primarily to provide large amounts of thyroid hormones for normal postnatal development. During fetal life, thyroid hormone is present but the pituitary-thyroid axis is independent from the maternal system. The placenta is impermeable to maternal TSH and thy-

roid hormones (Roti, 1983), but the fetal environment provides many extrahypothalamic sources for TRH (e.g., pancreas and gut) (Polk & Fisher, 1992). However, TRH is not required for TSH secretion during early development (Theodoropoulas & Braverman, 1979). Thus, the significance of TRH in the developing fetus is not clear.

After 18 weeks gestation, the fetal total T_4 and free T_4 increases steadily. (See Figure 1.8.) Fetal T_3 concentration is low during this time until 30 weeks of gestation when it slowly increases. The inactive form of the hormone, reverse T_3 (rT_3), predominates during this time. Since the difference between T_3 and rT_3 is the position of iodide (3′ vs. 5′ position), this change from predominant rT_3 to T_3 indicates a progressive maturation of outer ring iodothyronine deiodinase activity and increasing hepatic, brown fat and kidney conversion of T_4 to T_3. These changes in thyroid hormone milieu develop under the influence of moderately high TSH levels during the second trimester. However, the increase in serum T_4 that is seen during the last trimester is associated with a decrease of TSH levels, suggesting the start of a T_4 sensitive pituitary. The free T_4-to-TSH ratio increases during this period of time, a change that is due more to an increase in free T_4 than a TSH decrease. Therefore, it is also apparent that the thyroid gland itself is also more sensitive to TSH stimulation during the later part of gestation.

The production and secretion of thyroid hormones are markedly increased by events surrounding parturition. Four- to sixfold increases on T_4 and T_3 hormone levels are observed which peak at 24 to 36 hours after birth. Thyroid hormone levels, T_4 being the most important, feed back into the hypothalamus and pituitary, inhibiting TRH and TSH release. Circulating thyroid hormone levels ultimately decrease by 72 to 96 hours after birth. However, newborn thyroid levels are normally high when compared to adult standards; they do not approach adult levels until about 1 month of age.

The thyroid gland increases in size during infancy, childhood, and adolescence. The thyroid function also changes with age, with infancy characterized by a relative hyperactive state. Thyroid hormone replacement is thus high during early life (10–15 μg/k per kilogram (kg) per day (d) during the first year) and progressively decreases up to adolescence, when adult replacement doses are adequate (2–4 μg/kg/d). The changes in hormone replacement requirements correlate with age-related decreases in oxygen consumption rate, a decrease in serum thyroglobulin concentration, and a decrease in T_4 degradation rate. Serum thyroxine-binding globulin also decreases with age and in part by androgens during puberty. Circulating hormonal levels, however, remain constant after the initial neonatal period.

DEVELOPMENT OF THYROID HORMONE EFFECTS

Thyroid actions include skin and brain maturation, tissue thermogenesis, body and muscle growth, skeletal maturation, and hormone and growth factor production and action (Fisher & Polk, 1989). In some species, it is apparent that some of these actions require an intact HPT axis during the last part of gestation (Breall & al., 1985; Polk, 1988). In the sheep hypothyroidism induced with thyroidectomy during the final weeks of gestation is associated with impaired thermogenesis and decreased cardiovascular function at birth. However, if the T_4 and T_3 surge is abolished upon parturition, the normal transient neonatal hypothermia and cardiovascular adaptation is observed at birth. Human infants with congenital hypothyroidism have few symptoms at birth even when thyroid agenesis is detected. The most reliable sign of congenital hypothyroidism observed in 10 to 15% of neonates is a large posterior fontanella with widely opened cranial sutures, which results from the delayed skeletal maturation prenatally (Mäenpää, 1972). Growth and weight are typically not affected. Delayed bone maturation is not only diagnostic but also a prognostic feature of congenital hypothyroidism (Mäenpää, 1972). Severe bone maturation delay indicates significant intrauterine hypothyroidism and a worse prognosis for mental development.

Most effects of thyroid hormone occur postnatally. The actions of these hormones are mediated through specific activation of gene products (tissue-specific growth factors) by the thyroid receptor and/or through complex events. Evidently coupling to postreceptor events is also important in this process, since it is known that, in humans, thyroid receptors are expressed in fetal lung, brain, heart, and liver at 13 to 19 weeks of gestation, yet effects are not seen until late gestation and postnatal life. (See Table 1.2.) It is also evident that complex events may be involved in many aspects of thyroid hormone function. For example, the effect on somatic growth and skeletal maturation is at least in part through activation of gene products, since synthesis and release of growth hormone (GH) and growth factors (IGF-1) are noted. Hypothyroid animals have a marked reduction in pituitary GH content (Solomon & Greep, 1959), and cell culture experiments have demonstrated that GH synthesis is dependent on thyroid hormone (Samuels, Stanley, & Shapiro, 1976). Although GH binding to liver receptors stimulates IGF-1 production, which in turn mod-

TABLE 1.3

Clinical Conditions Identified by the Newborn Screening Test

Low T_4 (2–5 days old)	
TSH Normal	TSH Elevated
Transient hypothyroxinemia	Primary hypothyroidism
Normal repeat free T_4 and TSH	Agenesis, dysgenesis, ectopia: 80%
	Dyshormogenesis: 10–15%
	Deficiency or excessive iodine
Prematurity	Transient hypothyroidism
	Maternal Grave's disease
	based on normal thyroid function without change in replacement dose
Hypothalamic or pituitary hypothyroidism	
Congenital TBG deficiency (thyroid binding globulin)	
X-linked dominant	
1:9,000 births	
diagnosis confirmed with TBG levels	
Primary hypothyroidism	
rare, but possible	

ulates bone and muscle growth, T4 also has been shown to increase serum IGF-1 independent of GH action. In contrast, effects on epidermal growth factor (EGF) content of various tissues have been shown to be thyroid hormone responsive, but T_4 also increases EGF receptor binding, an effect that is related to both receptor levels and binding capacity (Fisher, 1989). Yet another level of complexity is the indirect interaction of steroid receptor family, of which thyroid receptor is a member, with transcription initiation factors, which in turn influence the activation or inhibition of gene expression or cross-talk with other signaling pathways. (See Beato and Sánchez-Pacheco, 1986, for a review.)

ABNORMAL PHYSIOLOGY

Newborn: Newborn screening in the United States measures serum T_4. If this level is low (<2 standard deviations below the mean), TSH levels along with a free T_4 are obtained. A free T_4 in term, premature, and sick infants is an accurate indicator of thyroid function and allows the differentiation of hypothyroid state common to prematurity and euthyroid infants. Although a T_4 measurement within the first 24 to 48 hours of birth could potentially be missed compensated hypothyroidism (normal T_4, elevated TSH), a TSH measurement as an initial screening would be confusing since TSH may be physiologically elevated. The clinical conditions associated with an abnormal thyroid screening are presented on Table 1.3.

Childhood: Childhood causes of hypothyroidism are summarized in Table 1.4. Late-onset thyroid dysgenesis and inborn defect of thyroid synthesis represent those infants with residual thyroid function at birth who manifest hypothyroidism after 2 to 4 years of age. Peripheral thyroid hormone resistance is a heterogeneous condition of thyroid hormone action caused by mutations in the thyroid receptor. (See Jameson and DeGroot, 1995, for review.) It has an autosomal dominant inheritance, and the patient may have failure to thrive or florid symptoms consistent with hypothyroidism with or without a goiter.

However, increased levels of thyroid hormone are present with inappropriately elevated or normal TSH. A common mistake is to suppress the thyroid to correct the thyroid hormone levels. These patients require thyroid hormone treatment, not suppression of the thyroid.

Drugs associated with acquired hypothyroidism include: iodides, cobalt containing drugs, lithium salts, p-aminosalicylic acid, aminoglutethimide, phenylbutazone (PTU, perchlorate, thyocyanate). Natural goitrogens have been reported in groundwater, soybeans, and plant members of *Brassica* (e.g., cabbage).

The most common cause of acquired hypothyroidism in childhood (after 6 years old) is chronic autoimmune thyroiditis or Hashimoto's thyroiditis. Prevalence is from 2 to 6% in the general population but as high as 10% in patients with autoimmune disorders, such as insulin-dependent diabetes mellitus (Fisher & Polk, 1995). It is reported with increased frequency in gonadal dysgenesis (Turner's syndrome), Down syndrome, and Kleinfelter's and Noonan's syndrome.

Nonthyroidal Illness: "Low T_3 state" with normal or depressed TSH levels in patients who do not have preexisting thyroid disease is characteristic of nonthyroidal illness. This is also referred to as euthyroid sick syndrome, since there is also a paucity of hypothyroid symptoms. Many disease states give rise to nonthyroidal illness, including acute and chronic systemic illnesses and injuries such as burns and surgery. (See Table 1.4.) Altered metabolic states, such as fasting, diabetes, and ketogenic diets, also trigger the cascade of events that lead to the low T_3 state of nonthyroidal illness. Variants also exist in which the classical pattern of this phenomenon is altered. These conditions include liver and kidney disease, pregnancy, and psychiatric disorders. Thus nonthyroidal illness accounts for the most common alteration of thyroid function.

The mechanism by which the low T_3 state is reached is believed to be a decrease in the conversion of T_4 to T_3 by peripheral tissue 5'-deiodinase enzyme system. (See Table 1.5) (Nicoloff & LoPresti, 1995). Conversely, serum reverse T_3 (rT_3), an inactive iodotyronine, usually is elevated. However, the rT_3 elevation is due to a decrease clearance and not from a change in the thyroid synthetic pathways. Serum total T_4 and free T_4

TABLE 1.4
Hypothyroidism in Childhood: Differential Diagnosis

Late-onset hypothyroidism
   Dysgenesis
   Dyshormogenesis
Peripheral thyroid hormone deficiency
Drugs or goitrogens
Acquired hypothalamic-pituitary hypothyroidism
   craniopharingiomas
   brain tumors or sequela from treatment
Hashimoto's thyroiditis
Cystinosis
Endemic goiter
Chromosomal abnormalities
   Turner's syndrome
   Noonan's syndrome
   Kleinfelter's syndrome
   Down syndrome
Iatrogenic

remain within normal limits, as does the TSH level. Evidently there is a resetting of the pituitary thyrotrophs, which seems to be coordinated with the alteration of T_4 to T_3 conversion, the mechanism of which is not understood. As the severity of the illness progresses, a low T_3–T_4 state is evident. This appears to be due to a decrease T_4 binding to TBG, since free T_4 levels remain normal. However, this state is associated with an increased mortality rate (correlated with the magnitude of T_4 fall). As recovery of the illness is noted, a reversal of these thyroid hormone changes is seen in a reverse sequence. Thus the TBG binding improves, increasing the total T_4 levels, followed by decreasing rT_3 levels, and finally, a normalization of T_3 serum concentrations.

Psychiatric disorders may cause alterations in thyroid hormone levels, the mechanism for which is not clearly understood (Hein & Jackson, 1990). For example, psychotic patients have significant elevations of both total T_4 and free T_4 values in association with normal T_3 levels when admitted

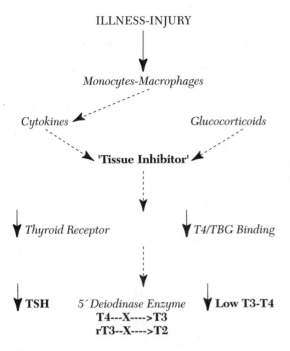

Conclusions

The hormonal axes reviewed here represent an intricate system of checks and balances geared at maintaining homeostasis and at securing an optimal functioning of the developing organism. Although the primary role of hormones in the mature animal is to regulate some aspects of cell metabolism, in the developing animal function and structure are less separated. For example, in the developing nervous system, hormones have effects on cell replication, differentiation, apoptosis, and the organization of brain circuitry. Hormones also have important interactions with neurotransmitters, modulating their function at all ages. The ultimate effect of an hormonal imbalance in the developing organism depends not only on the nature of the dysfunction but also on the stage of development at which the insult occurs. It is also important to keep in mind that, in addition to genetically determined disturbances in neuroendocrine organization, environmental insults (toxins, infectious agents, drugs) can have an impact in this process. Therefore, it is easy to see how alterations in one or more of these neuroendocrine systems, in particular during a vulnerable developmental period, could result in long-lasting negative consequences to the brain, including neuropsychiatric and behavioral disorders.

to psychiatric hospitals. TSH levels are mildly depressed or detectable by third-generation radioimmunoassays. Thyroid hormone levels return to normal after several days of hospitalization and appropriate therapy. Therefore, it is reasonable to hold off further thyroid evaluation in these patients for several days until psychiatric treatment is instituted and psychotic symptoms ameliorate.

REFERENCES

Adrian, T. E. (1983). Growth hormone response to feeding in term and preterm neonates. *Acta Paediatrica Scandinavica, 72,* 251–258.

Akil, H., Young, E., & Watson, S. J. (1981). Opiate binding properties of naturally occurring N and C terminus modified β-endorphin. *Peptides, 2,* 289–292.

Allen, R. G., Pintar, J. E., Stack, J., & Kendall, J. W. (1984). Biosynthesis and processing of proopimelanocortin-derived peptides during the pituitary development. *Developmental Biology, 102,* 43.

Ariza, J. L., Weinberger, C., Cerelli, G., Glaser, T. M., Handelin, B. M., Housman, D. E., & Evans, R. (1987). Cloning of the human mineralocorticoid receptor complementary DNA; Structural and functional kinship with the glucocorticoid receptor. *Science, 237,* 268–275.

Bala, R. M., Lopotka, J., & Leung, A. (1981). Serum immunoreactive somatomedin levels in normal adults, pregnant women at term, children at various ages and children with constitutionally delayed growth. *Journal of Clinical Endocrinology and Metabolism, 52,* 508–512.

Beato, M., & Sánchez-Pacheco, A. (1986). Interaction of steroid hormone receptors with the transcription initiation complex. *Endocrine Review, 17,* 587–609.

Bodnoff, S. R., Humphreys, A. G., Lehman, J. C., Diamond, D. M., Rose, G. M., & Meaney, M. J. (1995). Enduring effects of chronic corticosterone treatment on spatial learning, synaptic plasticity, and hippocampal neuropathology in young and mid-aged rats. *Journal of Neuroscience, 15,* 61–69.

Bowden, M. L., & Hopwood, N. J. (1982). Psychosocial dwarfism: Identification, intervention and planning. *Social Work and Health Care, 7,* 15–36.

Breall, J. A., & al., E. (1985). Role of thyroid hormone in postnatal circulatory and metabolic adjustments. *Journal of Clinical Investigation, 73,* 1418–1425.

Brett, L. P., Chong, G. S., Coyle, S., & Levine, S. (1981). The pituitary-adrenal response to novel stimulation and ether stress in young adult and aged rats. *Neurobiology of Aging, 4,* 133–138.

Bugnon, C., Fellmann, D., Gouget, A., & Cardot, J. (1982). Ontogeny of the corticoliberin neuroglandular system in rat brain. *Nature, 298,* 159.

Castillo, G. H., Matteri, R. L., & Dumesic, A. D. (1992). Luteinizing hormone synthesis in cultured fetal human pituitary cells exposed to gonadotropin-releasing hormone. *Journal of Clinical Endocrinology and Metabolism, 75,* 318–322.

Challis, J., & Torosis, J. (1977). "Is αMSH a trophic hormone to adrenal function in the fetus?" *Nature, 269,* 818–819.

Choy, Y. J., & Watskins, W. B. (1979). Maturation of the hypothalamic-hypophyseal system: I. Localization of neurophysin, oxytocin and vasopressin in the hypothalamus and neural lobe of the developing brain. *Cell Tissue Research, 197,* 325–336.

Clark, W. E. L. G., Beattie, J., Riddoch, J., & Dott, N. M. (1938). *The hypothalamus. Morphological, functional, clinical and surgical aspects.* Edinburgh: Oliver and Boyd.

Cooke, N. E. (1995). *Prolactin: Basic physiology.* Philadelphia: W. B. Saunders.

Coulter, D. M. (1983). Prolactin: A hormonal regulator of the neonatal tissue water reservoir. *Pediatric Research, 17,* 665–674.

Cuttler, L. (1992). *LH and FSH secretion in the fetus and newborn.* Philadelphia: W. B. Saunders.

Dallman, M. F. (1984–85). Control of adrenocortical growth in vivo. *Endocrine Research, 10,* 213–242.

Daughaday, W. H. (1989). *Growth hormone: Normal synthesis, secretion, control and mechanisms of action.*

De Kloet, E. R. (1991). Brain, corticosteroid receptor balance and homeostatic control. *Frontiers in Neuroendocrinology, 12,* 95–164.

De Kloet, E. R., & Joels, M. (1991). Neurosteroids and brain function. *Annals of the New York Academy of Sciences, 8,* 3–9.

De Kloet, E. R., Rosenfeld, P., Van Eekelen, J. A. M., Sutanto, W., & Levine, S. (1988). Stress, glucocorticoids and development. *Progress in Brain Research, 73,* 101–120.

Delitala, G. (1978) Action of somatostatin, levodopa and pyridoxine on growth hormone secretion in newborn infants. *Biomedicine, 29,* 13–15.

Dubois, P. M., & Hemming, F. J. (1987). The ontogeny of hormones of the somatotrophic axis. *Reprod Nutr Dev, 27,* 441–459.

Eipper, A., & Mains, R. E. (1980). Structure and biosynthesis of pro-adrenocorticotropin/endorphin and related peptides. *Endocrine Review, 1,* 1–27.

Ericson, L. E. (1990). *Phylogeny and ontogeny of the thyroid gland.* New York: Raven Press.

Fisher, D. A. (1989). *Thyroid disease in the neonate and in childhood.* Philadelphia: W. B. Saunders.

Fisher, D. A., & Polk, D. H. (1989). *Maturation of thyroid hormone actions.* New York: Plenum Press.

Fisher, D. A., & Polk, D. H. (1995). *Thyroid disease in the fetus, neonate, and child.* Philadelphia: W. B. Saunders.

Fremeau, R. T., Lundblad, J. R., Pritchett, D. B., Wilcox, J. N., & Roberts, J. L. (1986). Regulation of pro-opiomelanocortin gene transcription in individual cell nuclei. *Science, 234,* 1265–1269.

Funder, J. W. (1993). Mineralocorticoids, glucocorticoids, receptors, and response elements. *Science, 259,* 1132–1133.

Gilmore, D. P. (1992). Neurosecretions and neurotransmitters of the fetal hypothalamus. In R. A. Polinn & W. W. Fox (Eds.), *Fetal and neonatal physiology* (Vol. 2, pp. 1779–1785). Philadelphia: W. B. Saunders.

Glickman, J. A., Carson, G. D., & Challis, J. R. G. (1979). Differential effects of synthetic ACTH 1–24 and αMSH on adrenal function in human and sheep fetuses. *Endocrinology, 104,* 34–39.

Gluckman, P. D. (1992). *Growth hormone and prolactin.* Philadelphia: W. B. Saunders.

Gluckman, P. D., Grumbach, M. M., & Kaplan, S. L. (1981). The neuroendocrine regulation and function of growth hormone and prolactin in the mammalian fetus. *Endocrine Review, 2,* 363–395.

Goffin, V., Shiverick, K. T., Delly, P. A., & Martial, J. A. (1996). Sequence-function relationships within the expanding family of prolactin, growth hormone, placental lactogen and related proteins in mammals. *Endocrine Review, 17,* 385–410.

Goldman, L., Winget, C., Holinshead, G., & Levine, S. (1978). Postweaning development of negative feedback in the pituitary adrenal system of the rat. *Neuroendocrinology, 12,* 188–211.

Grambach, M. M., & Kaplan, S. L. (1990). *The neuroendocrinology of human puberty: An ontogenetic perspective.* Baltimore, MD: Williams & Wilkins.

Grino, M., Scott Young, W., & Burgunder, J. M. (1989). Ontogeny of expression of the corticotropin releasing factor gene in the hypothalamic paraventricular nucleus and on the proopiomelanocortin gene in rat pituitary. *Endocrinology, 124,* 60–69.

Guillet, R., Saffran, M., & Michaelson, S. M. (1980). Pituitary-adrenal response in neonatal rats. *Endocrinology, 106,* 991–993.

Hall, J. E., & Crowley, W. F. (1995). *Gonadotropins and the gonad: Normal physiology and their disturbances in clinical endocrine diseases.* Philadelphia: W. B. Saunders.

Hamburgh, M. (1961). The role of thyroid and growth hormones in neurogenesis. *Curr To Dev Biol 4,* 109–112.

Hein, M. D., & Jackson, I. M. (1990). Review: Thyroid function in psychiatric illness. *General Hospital Psychiatry, 12,* 232–244.

Herbert, E., Roberts, J. L., Phillips, M., Rosa, P. A., Budarf, M., Allen, R. G., Policastro, P. F., Paquette, T. L., & Hinman, M. (1979). *Biosynthesis and processing of a common precursor to adrenocorticotropin and β-LPH in mouse pituitary cells.* New York: Macmillan.

Herman, J. P., Patel, P. D., Akil, H., & Watson, S. J. (1989). Localization and regulation of glucocorticoid and mineralocorticoid receptor mRNAs in the hippocampal formation of the rat. *Molecular Endocrinology, 3* (11), 1886–1894.

Herman, J. P., Schafer, M. K.-H., Young, E. A., Thompson, R. C., Douglass, J. O., Akil, H., & Watson, S. J. (1989). Evidence for hippocampal regulation of neuroendocrine neurons of the hypothalamic-pituitary-adrenocortical axis. *Journal of Neuroscience, 9,* 3072–3082.

Hollenberg, S. M., Weinberger, C., Ong, E. S., Cerelli, G., Oro, A., Lebo, R., Thompson, E. B., Rosenfeld, M. G., & Evans, R. M. (1985). Primary structure and expression of a functional human glucocorticoid receptor cDNA. *Nature, 318,* 635–641.

Huhtaniemi, I. T., Yamomoto, M., & Ranta, T. (1987). Follicle-stimulating hormone receptors appear earlier in the primate fetal testis than in the ovary. *Journal of Clinical Endocrinology and Metabolism, 65,* 1210–1214.

Jameson, J. L., & DeGroot, L. J. (1995). *Mechanisms of thyroid action.* Philadelphia: W. B. Saunders.

Johanson, A. J. (1995). *Growth hormone disorders and treatment.* New York: Marcel Dekker.

Kaplan, S. L., & Grumbach, M. M. (1976). The ontogenesis of human foetal hormones. II. Luteinizing hormone (LH) and follicle stimulating hormone (FSH). *Acta Endocrinol 81,* 808–829.

Khachaturian, H., & Sladek, J. J. R. (1980). Simultaneous monoamine histofluorescence and neuropeptide immunocytochemistry: III. Ontogeny of catecholamine varicosities and neurophysin neurons in the rat supraoptic and paraventricular nuclei. *Peptides, 1,* 77–95.

Krisch, B. (1989). The hypothalamo-hypophyseal complex: a paradigm of the paraneuron concept. *Archives of Histology and Cytology, 52* (Suppl.), 365–373.

Loizou, L. A. (1972). The postnatal ontogeny of monoamine-containing neurones in the central nervous system of the albino rat. *Brain Research, 40,* 395–418.

Lopez, J. F., Young, E. A., Herman, J. P., Akil, H., & Watson, S. J. (1991). *Regulatory biology of the HPA axis: An integrative approach.* Washington, DC: American Psychiatric Press.

Mäenpää, J. (1972). Congenital hypothyroidism: Aetiological and clinical aspects. *Archives of Diseases of Children, 47,* 914–923.

Martin, C. E., Cake, M. H., Hartman, P. E., & Cook, I. F. (1977). Relationship between fecat corticosterois, maternal progesterone and parturition. *Acta Endocrinol 84,* 167–176.

McEwen, B. S., De Kloet, E. R., & Rostene, W. H. (1986). Adrenal steroid receptors and actions in the nervous system. *Physiology Review, 66,* 1121–1150.

McEwen, B. S., Weiss, J. M., & Schwartz, L. S. (1968). Selective retention of corticosterone by limbic structures in rat brain. *Nature, 220* (170), 911–912.

McNeilly, A. S., Gilmore, D., Dobbie, G., & Chard, T. (1977). Prolactin releasing activity in the early human foetal hypothalamus. *Journal of Endocrinology, 73,* 533–534.

Meister, B. (1993). Gene expression and chemical diversity in hypothalamic neurosecretory neurons. *Molecular Neurobiology, 7,* 87–110.

Moore, K. L. (1977). *The developing human.* Philadelphia: W. B. Saunders.

Morris, M. J., Dausse, J. P., Devnick, M. A., & Meyer, P. (1980). Onotogeny of alpha 1 and alpha 2 adrenoreceptors in rat brain. *Brain Research, 190,* 268–291.

Nicoloff, J. T., & LoPresti, J. S. (1995). *Nonthyroidal illness.* Philadelphia: W. B. Saunders.

Patel, P. D., Sherman, T. G., Goldman, D. J., & Watson, S. J. (1989). Molecular cloning of a mineralocorticoid (Type I) receptor complementary DNA from rat hippocampus. *Molecular Endocrinology, 3,* 1877–1885.

Pearce, D., & Yamamoto, K. R. (1993). Mineralocorticoid and glucocorticoid receptor activities distinguished by nonreceptor factors at a composite response element. *Science, 259,* 1161–1165.

Pfaff, D. W. (1980). *Estrogens and brain function.* New York: Springer-Verlag.

Pfaff, D. W., & Lauber, A. H. (1995). *Hypothalamus and hormone-regulated behaviors.* Philadelphia: W. B. Saunders.

Polk, D. (1988). Thyroid hormone effects on neonatal thermogenesis. *Seminars in Perinatology, 12,* 151–166.

Polk, D. H., & Fisher, D. A. (1992). *Fetal and neonatal thyroid physiology.* Philadelphia: W. B. Saunders.

Pollit, E., Eichler, A. W., & Chan, C. (1975). Psychosocial development and behavior of mothers of failure-to-thrive children. *American Journal of Orthopsychiatry, 45,* 525–535.

Powell, G. F., Hopwood, N. J., & Barratt, E. S. (1973). Growth hormone studies before and during catch-up growth in a child with emotional deprivation and short stature. *Journal of Clinical Endocrinology and Metabolism, 37,* 674–679.

Ramírez, L. C., Bournot, P., & Maume, B. F. (1985). The role of ACTH in determining the metabolic pathways of deoxycorticosterone by newborn rat adrenal cells in primary culture. *Journal of Steroid Biochemistry, 22,* 249–256.

Reitano, M. (1977). *Regulation of insulin and GH secretion in the human foetus and newborn.* London: Academic Press.

Reul, J. M., & De Kloet, R. (1986). Anatomical resolution of two types of corticosterone receptor sites in rat brain with *in vitro* autoradiography and computerized image analysis. *Journal of Steroid Biochemistry, 24,* 269–272.

Robinovici, J., Goldsmith, P. C., & Roberts, V. J. (1991).

Localization and secretion of inhibin/activin subunits in the human and subhuman primate fetal gonads. *Journal of Clinical Endocrinology and Metabolism, 68,* 1141–1149.

Rosenfeld, P., Sutanto, W., Levine, S., & De Kloet, E. R. (1988). Ontogeny of type I and II corticosteroid receptors in the rat hippocampus. *Developmental Brain Research, 42,* 113–138.

Rosenfeld, P., Van Eekelen, J. A. M., Levine, S., & De Kloet, E. R. (1988). Ontogeny of the type 2 glucocorticoid receptor in discrete rat brain regions: An immunocytochemical study. *Developmental Brain Research, 42,* 119–127.

Roti, E. (1983). The placental transport, synthesis and metabolism of hormones and drugs which affect thyroid function. *Endocrine Review, 4,* 131–143.

Rundle, S. E., & Funder, J. W. (1988). Ontogeny of corticotropin-releasing factor and arginine vasopressin in the rat. *Neuroendocrinology, 47,* 374–378.

Samuels, H. H., Stanley, F., & Shapiro, L. E. (1976). Dose-dependent depletion of nuclear receptors for L-triodothyronine: Evidence for a role in induction of growth hormone synthesis in cultured GH cells. *Proceedings of the National Academy of Science, 73,* 3877–3881.

Sapolsky, R., Krey, L., & McEwen, B. (1985). Prolonged glucocorticoid exposure reduces hippocampal neuron number: Implications for aging. *Journal of Neuroscience, 5,* 1121–1227.

Sato, S. M., & Mains, R. E. (1985). Post-translational processing of pro-adrenocorticotropin endorphin-derived peptides during postnatal development in the rat pituitary. *Endocrinology, 117,* 773–786.

Schwanzel-Fekuda, M., & Pfaff, D. W. (1991). Migration of LHRH-immunoreactive neurons from the olfactory placode rationalizes olfacto-hormonal relationships. *Journal of Steroid Biochemistry and Molecular Biology, 39,* 565–572.

Seizinger, B. R., Hollt, V., & Herz, A. (1984). Postnatal development of β-endorphin-related peptides in rat anterior and intermediate pituitary lobes: Evidence of contrasting development of proopiomelanocortin processing. *Endocrinology, 115,* 136–147.

Shutte, C. C. D., & Lewis, P. R. (1966). Cholinergic and monoaminergic pathways in the hypothalamus. *British Medical Bulletin, 22,* 221–226.

Siler-Khodr, T. M. (1992). *Endocrine and paracrine function of the human placenta.* Philadelphia: W. B. Saunders.

Silman, R. E., Holland, D., Chard, T., Lowry, P. J., Hope, J., Robinson, J. S., & Thorburn, G. D. (1978). The ACTH "family tree" of the rhesus monkey changes in development. *Nature, 276,* 526–528.

Simpson, E. R., & Waterman, M. R. (1983). Regulation by ACTH of steroid hormone biosynthesis in the adrenal cortex. *Canadian Journal of Biochemistry and Cell Biology, 61,* 692–707.

Smith, M. A., Su-Yong, K., & S., L. (1995). Maternal separation alters expression of stress-responsive genes in neonatal rats. *34th Annual Meeting of the American College of Neuropsychopharmacology,* 225.

Solomon, J., & Greep, R. D. (1959). The effect of alterations in thyroid function on the pituitary growth hormone content and acidophil cytology. *Endocrinology, 65,* 158–164.

Sperling, M. A. (1980). *Newborn adaptation: Adrenocortical hormones and ACTH.* Philadelphia: W. B. Saunders.

Stanton, M. E., Gutierrez, Y. R., & Levine, S. (1988). Maternal deprivation potentiates pituitary-adrenal stress responses in infant rats. *Behavioral Neuroscience, 102,* 692–700.

Stevens, D., & Alexander, G. (1986). Lipid deposition after hypophysectomy and growth hormone treatment in the sheep fetus. *Journal of Developmental Physiology, 8,* 139–145.

Stubbe, P., & Wolf, H. (1975). Glucosebelastungen und arginin-infusionen bei neugegorenen. *Lin Wochenschr, 48,* 918–924.

Swaab, D. F. (1980). Neuropeptides and brain development: A working hypothesis. In C. DiBenede, R. Balags, G. Gombos, & P. Pocellati (Eds.), *A multidisciplinary approach to brain development* (p. 181). Amsterdam: North Holland/Elsevier.

Swaab, D. F., Visser, M., & Tilders, F. J. H. (1976). Stimulation of intrauterine growth in rat by α-melanocyte stimulating hormone. *Journal of Endocrinology, 70,* 445–455.

Theodoropoulas, T., & Braverman, L. E. (1979). Thyrotropin releasing hormone is not required for thyrotropin secretion in the perinatal rat. *Journal of Clinical Investigations, 63,* 588–592.

Trujillo, K., & Akil, H. (1994). Inhibition of opiate tolerance by non-competitive N-methyl-D-aspartate receptor antagonists. *Brain Research, 633,* 178–188.

Tuomisto, J., & Mannisto, P. (1985). Neurotransmitter regulation of anterior pituitary hormones. *Pharmacology Review, 37,* 249–332.

Vale, W. W., J., S., Rivier, J., & Rivier, C. (1981). Characterization of 41-residue ovine hypothalamic peptide that stimulates secretions of corticotropin and β-endorphin. *Science, 213,* 1394–1397.

Van Dorp, A. W., & Deane, H. W. (1950). A morphological and cytological study of the postnatal development of the rat's adrenal cortex. *Anat Rec, 107,* 265–281.

Van Eekelen, J. A. M., Kiss, J. Z., Westphal, H. M., & De Kloet, E. R. (1987). Immunocytochemical study on the intracellular localization of the type 2 glucocorticoid receptor in the rat brain. *Brain Research, 436,* 120–128.

Vazquez, D. M., & Akil, H. (1992). Development of pituitary pro-opiomelanocortin gene and peptide expression: Characterization and effect of repeated intermittent maternal isolation. *Neuroendocrinology, 56,* 320–330.

Vazquez, D. M., & Akil, H. (1993). Pituitary-adrenal response to ether vapor in the weanling animal: Characterization of the inhibitory effect of glucocorticoids on adrenocorticotropin secretion. *Pediatric Research, 34*, 646–653.

Vazquez, D. M., Morano, I. M., Lopez, J. F., Watson, S. J., & Akil, H. (1993). Short-term adrenalectomy increases glucocorticoid and mineralocorticoid receptor mRNA in selective areas of the developing hippocampus. *Molecular and Cellular Neurosciences, 4,* 455–471.

Walker, C. D., Perrin, M., Vale, W. W., & Rivier, C. L. (1986). Ontogeny of the stress response in the rat: Role of the pituitary and hypothalamus. *Endocrinology, 118*, 1445–1455.

Weinstock, M., Matlina, E., Maor, G. I., Rosen, H., & McEwen, B. S. (1992). Prenatal stress selectively alters the reactivity of the hypothalamic-pituitary adrenal system in the female rat. *Brain Research, 595*, 195–200.

Wetzel, W. C., Valenca, M. M., & Merchenthaler, I. (1992). Intrinsic pulsatile secretory activity of immortalized luteinizing-hormone-releasing hormone-secreting neurons. *Proceedings of the National Academy of Science, 89*, 4149–4153.

Young, E. A., & Vazquez, D. M. (1996). Hypercortisolemia, hippocampal glucocorticoid receptors, and fast feedback. *Molecular Psychiatry, 1*, 149–159.

2 / **Neuronal Plasticity and the Developing Brain**

James E. Black, Theresa A. Jones, Charles A. Nelson, and William T. Greenough

Over the last decade, researchers from a variety of disciplines have contributed substantially to our understanding of human brain development. Important contributions have come from developmental psychologists and neuroscientists. Borrowing from these sources, we have argued (Black & Greenough, 1986; Greenough & Black, 1992) that brain development can be described as a complex scaffolding of 3 categories of neural processes: gene driven, experience expectant, and experience dependent. Gene-driven processes, which are largely insensitive to experience, serve to guide the migration of neurons, to target many of their synaptic connections, and to determine their differentiated functions. Experience-expectant processes roughly correspond to "sensitive periods," developmentally timed periods of neural plasticity that "expect" certain types of predictable experience to be present for all juvenile members of a species. The third category, experience dependent, roughly corresponds to ordinary learning and memory, that is, encoding information that has adaptive value to an individual but is unpredictable in its timing or nature. In this chapter we review the evidence for these 3 processes, integrate them into a general model of brain development, provide evidence that the human brain is similarly plastic, and then apply this information to issues of child psychiatry.

Gene-Driven Processes

It is sometimes too easy to overemphasize the genetic contribution to behavior, especially in psychiatric disorders, because of the recent explosion of knowledge in this area. We now know much of the molecular biology of cell differentiation, neuron migration, and cell regulation and signaling. These processes are capable of building enormously complex neural structures without any input from the external environment. Indeed, in order to protect brain development, much of the basic organization of most nervous systems is largely impervious to experience. Neural activity that is intrinsically driven, such as that arising from the retina of the cat or monkey in utero, can play a role in these organization processes.

This work was supported by a National Association for Research on Schizophrenia & Affective Disorders Young Investigator award to JEB and Senior Investigator Award to WTG; grants NS32755 and NS32976 to CAN; grants MH10422 and MH56361 to TAJ; grants MH 35321, AG43830, AA0938, the Kiwanis Foundation, and the FRAXA foundation to WTG; and the MacArthur Foundation Network on the Development of Psychopathology (to WTG and CAN). We also thank K. Bates for assistance in preparing the manuscript.

The entrenchment (or resistance to environmental influences) during embryonic development was termed *canalization* by Waddington (1971). Clearly, minor perturbations of pH or temperature should not have drastic effects on embryogenesis if a species is to survive. Extending that concept to the postnatal period, it would seem adaptive for many species that brain development not be too sensitive to minor variations in nutrition or experience. Evidence for the importance of gene-driven processes can be found in the tens of thousands of genes uniquely expressed in rat brain development (Chaudhari & Hahn, 1983; Milner & Sutcliffe, 1983). This canalization can be a two-edged sword, however, in the case of genetic diseases, with brain development being dragged down a maladaptive path while remaining relatively impervious to any corrective experience or therapeutic interventions.

We are not advocating a determinist view of brain development, however. Some species have a survival advantage if they can adapt to the environment or incorporate information from it. Indeed, many mammalian species have evolved specialized structures that can incorporate massive amounts of information. Because they have a long evolutionary history, the specialized systems vary across species and occur in multiple brain regions, such that there is not a single "place" or "process" for learning and memory. We argue that some types of neural plasticity have evolved to be incorporated into the developmental schedule of brain development, whereas others have evolved to serve the individual's needs by incorporating information unique to their environment.

Although we resort to metaphors of "schedules" and "scaffolding," we would like to emphasize a more contemporary model of brain development, that derived from the study of dynamic, nonlinear systems. From the dynamic systems perspective, individuals can use the interaction of genetic constraints and environmental information to self-organize highly complex systems (especially brains; e.g., Quartz & Sejnowski, in press). Each organism follows a potentially unique and partly self-determined developmental path of brain assembly to the extent that it has unique experiences. The genetically determined restrictions (e.g., the initial cortical architecture) serve as constraints to the system, allowing environmental information interacting with existing neural structures to substantially organize and refine neural connections.

We will not go into further detail here, but we wish to emphasize a balanced view of genotype-driven processes providing much of the basic structure of the brain, which is to an extent resistant to experience. Some of these genetically determined structures have evolved to constrain and organize experiential information, facilitating its storage in the brain in massive quantities. Although much of the rest of this chapter focuses on neural plasticity, it is important to remember that all such processes have a complex and genetically determined foundation. Deviations in that foundation (e.g., genetic disease or structural lesions) can have a profound impact on how experience shapes the brain as well as how therapeutic efforts can help restore it.

Experience-Expectant Development

Although numerous examples of neural plasticity have been found in mammalian species, we believe that much of plasticity can be classified into 2 basic categories, experience-expectant and experience-dependent development. *Experience-expectant* development involves a readiness of the brain to receive specific types of information from the environment. This readiness occurs during critical or sensitive stages in development during which there are central adaptations to information that is reliably present for all members of the species. This information includes major sensory experience, such as patterned visual information, as well as information affecting social, emotional, and cognitive development. One aspect of the brain's readiness to receive this expected information is the overproduction of neural connections, of which a subset is selectively retained on the basis of experience.

A general process observed in many mammalian species is that a surplus of connections is produced, a large portion of which are subsequently eliminated. Evidence for overproduction and partial elimination of synapses during development has been found in many brain regions and species including cat (Cragg, 1975), rodent (Greenough & Chang, 1988), monkey (Boothe, Greenough, Lund, & Wrege, 1979; Bourgeois, Goldman-Rakic,

Rakic, 1994), and humans (Conel, 1939–67). The overshoot in the number of synapses produced in cortical areas in many animals, including humans, has been estimated to be roughly double the number found in adults (Huttenlocher & de Courten, 1987; see Huttenlocher, 1994, for review). In humans, synaptic density and estimates of total synapse numbers in the visual cortex reach a peak at approximately 8 months of age, with synapse numbers declining thereafter (Huttenlocher & de Courten, 1987). Another important finding by Huttenlocher (1979) is that frontal cortex has its blooming and pruning of synapse substantially delayed, with its peak occurring during childhood. While synapse density and absolute synapse number may differ, depending on other tissue elements, for purposes of this discussion we will assume that they are equivalent.

The process of overproduction and selective elimination of synapses appears to be a mechanism whereby the brain is made ready to capture critical and highly reliable information from the environment. This possibility is supported by several lines of research, reviewed later, indicating that the pruning into structured patterns of functional neural connections requires appropriate patterns of neural activity, which are obtained through experience. These events occur during known critical or sensitive periods. Furthermore, the pruning appears to be driven by competitive interactions between neural connections such that inactive neural connections are lost and connections that are most actively driven by experience are selectively maintained. In many cases, it appears that regulation of neural plasticity systems has evolved to take advantage of information that could be "expected" for all juvenile members (i.e., it is as if it has an adaptive value for the whole species, not just individuals). Many of the experiments described in this section disturb some aspect of the "expected" experience, often with substantial disruptions of further development. Many of the patients in child psychiatry similarly have had disturbed experience with subsequently disrupted development.

VISUAL DEPRIVATION EXPERIMENTS

Studies of the effects of early visual deprivation have provided some of the strongest examples of experience inducing neural structure during development. Together they indicate a direct link between patterns of experience-expectant visual information and patterns of neural connectivity. Experimental visual deprivation falls into 2 main classes. Binocular deprivation of vision can be complete, depriving animals of all visual stimuli, or partial, depriving animals of patterned visual stimuli. This is achieved, for example, by raising animals in complete darkness or by suturing both eyelids shut, respectively. Partial deprivation reduces or distorts visual experience in some fashion. Complete deprivation of both eyes leads to a loss in complex visuomotor learning and in the precision of neuronal response properties, but it preserves balance in eye dominance and basic perceptual skills (Zablocka & Zernicki, 1990). In contrast, selective deprivation of 1 eye during the critical period leads to a drastic reduction in its control over visual cortex neurons and behavior, while the nondeprived eye correspondingly gains in control. The degree of recovery from deprivation depends on the species and the deprivation period's onset and duration.

BINOCULAR DEPRIVATION

Studies of binocular deprivation have shown that appropriate visual stimulation during certain stages of development is critical for the development of normal neural connectivity in the visual system. Dark rearing or bilateral lid closure in developing animals results in behavioral, physiological, and structural abnormalities in visual pathways (Michalski & Wrobel, 1994; Riesen, 1965; Wiesel & Hubel, 1965). The severity and reversibility of the visual impairments is dependent on the onset and duration of the deprivation, corresponding to defined sensitive periods of a given species (Walk & Gibson, 1961). Even short periods of early visual deprivation can result in impairments in visuomotor skills, such as visually guided placement of the forepaw in cats (Crabtree & Riesen, 1979). The structural effects of dark rearing include smaller neuronal dendritic fields, reduced spine density, and reduced numbers of synapses per neuron within the visual cortex (Coleman & Riesen, 1968; Cragg, 1975; Gabbot & Stewart, 1987; Valverde, 1971). In kittens, for example, developmental binocular deprivation results in a 40% reduction in the number of adult visual cortex synapses (Cragg, 1975).

SELECTIVE DEPRIVATION

Selective deprivation experiments have indicated the importance of specific types of visual experience to normal brain development. For example, kittens reared in a strobe-illuminated environment have plentiful visual pattern but are selectively deprived of any experience of movement (i.e., movement in the visual field would appear "jerky" or disconnected). Specific impairments in motion perception have been found in such kittens (Marchand, Cremieux, & Amblard, 1990). These animals had visual cortical neurons that were insensitive to visual motion (Cynader & Cmerneko, 1976), and they were impaired on visuomotor behavioral tasks that utilize motion (Held, Hein, & Gower, 1970).

Other work has limited visual experience to specific visual patterns, or contours. Hirsch and Spinelli (1970) raised kittens in chambers with 1 eye exposed just to horizontal stripes and the other eye just to vertical stripes. Physiological recordings of visual cortical neurons of these kittens revealed that they were most responsive to stimuli oriented in the direction of the stripes they had experienced. Behaviorally, stripe-reared animals perform best on tests using stimuli in the orientation that they were exposed to during development (Corrigan & Carpenter, 1979; Pettigrew & Freeman, 1973). Unlike dark rearing or bilateral lid closure, stripe rearing does not appear to result in an overall diminishment of neuronal size, but it does alter the orientation of the neuronal dendritic arbors (Coleman, Flood, Whitehead, & Emerson, 1981; Tieman & Hirsch, 1982). Thus neural function appears to be determined by the pattern, in addition to the overall number, of neural connections.

MONOCULAR DEPRIVATION

We have learned a great deal about experience-expectant processes from a particular deprivation model. In species with stereoscopic vision, including cats and monkeys, binocular regions of the cortex receive information from each eye via projections from the lateral geniculate nucleus in adjacent stripes or columns within cortical layer IV, termed ocular dominance columns. With normal experience early in development, the cortical input associated with each eye initially projects in overlapping terminal fields within layer IV. During development in normal animals, these axonal terminal fields are selectively pruned, resulting in sharply defined borders between ocular dominance columns in adult animals. The neurons of this layer send convergent input to other layers, made up in large majority by binocularly driven neurons (LeVay, Wiesel, & Hubel, 1980).

Studies of monocular deprivation in stereoscopic animals have shown that the formation of the ocular dominance columns is dependent on competitive interactions between the visual input from each eye (reviewed in Shatz, 1990). In monocularly deprived monkeys, the axons projecting from the deprived eye regress whereas the axons from the experienced eye do not. This results in the thinning of the columns corresponding to the deprived eye while the columns of the nondeprived eye are enlarged relative to normal animals (Antonini & Stryker, 1993; LeVay et al., 1980). Thus the axonal terminals from the dominant eye appear to be selectively maintained at the expense of the inactive input of the deprived eye, which has its excessive synapses eliminated. Physiologically, the number and responsiveness of cells activated by the deprived eye are severely decreased (Wiesel & Hubel, 1965). Functionally, monocular deprivation for an extended period during development results in near blindness to visual input in the deprived eye. In contrast, binocular deprivation principally results in a loss of visual acuity. Physiologically, it reduces but does not abolish the response of neurons to visual stimuli (Wiesel & Hubel, 1965). It also does not prevent the formation of ocular dominance columns, although the segregation of columns is well below normal (LeVay et al., 1980; Mower, Caplan, Christen, & Duffy, 1985; Swindale, 1988). Thus in binocular deprivation, cortical input from the eyes may be partially maintained in the absence of competing information.

The physiological and anatomical effects of monocular deprivation occur fairly rapidly. Antonini and Stryker (1993) found that the shrinkage of geniculocortical arbors corresponding to the deprived eye was profound in cats with only 6 to 7 days of monocular deprivation, similar to that found after 33 days of deprivation. Like binocular deprivation, the recovery from the deprivation is sensitive to the time of onset and duration of the deprivation. Monocular deprivation corresponding to the sensitive period of a given species results in enduring impairments and physiological nonresponsiveness (e.g., Wiesel & Hubel, 1965), whereas even very extensive deprivation in adult animals has little effect (Blakemore, Garey, & Vital-Durand, 1978). In humans, early monocular deprivation resulting from congenital cataracts can have severe effects on acuity, even after treatment, whereas adults who develop cataracts in 1 eye show little posttreatment impairment (Bowering, Maurer, Lewis, & Brent, 1993). The sensitive period for monocular deprivation effects can be affected by prior experience. For example, the maximum sensitivity to monocular deprivation effects in kittens is normally during the fourth and fifth weeks after birth (Hubel & Wiesel, 1970; Olson & Freeman, 1978). Cynader and Mitchell (1980) found that kittens dark-reared from birth to several months of age maintain a physiological sensitivity to monocular deprivation at ages when normal kittens are insensitive. Dark-reared animals do not, however, simply show normal visual development at this later age. With binocular deprivation early in life, the ocular dominance columns of layer IV do not segregate in a fully normal pattern and do not maintain a structural sensitivity to monocular deprivation effects (Mower et al., 1985).

DEPRIVATION IN OTHER SENSORY SYSTEMS

Although much of the research has utilized the visual system, experience-expectant processes can be observed in other sensory systems. Within layer IV of the somatosensory cortex in rodents, each whisker is represented by a distinctly clustered group of neurons arranged in what have been called "barrels" (Woolsey & van der Loos, 1970). The cell bodies of these neurons form the barrel walls with a cell sparse region forming the barrel hollow. In adult animals, the input from each whisker (via the thalamus) terminates predominantly within the barrel hollows. Positioned to receive this input, most of the dendrites of the neurons lining the barrel wall also are oriented into the barrel hollow. This distinctive pattern of barrel walls surrounding a hollow forms postnatally, prior to which neurons in this region appear homogeneous. Because there is simultaneous regression of dendrites inside the barrel walls and continued growth of dendrites in the barrel hollows, these overlapping processes mask the expected synapse overproduction and pruning back because the overall pattern is one of dendritic expansion (Greenough & Chang, 1988). Were it not for the location of information provided by the structure of the barrel, this dendritic regression would be overlooked.

Many rodents use their vibrissae (highly developed whiskers) to navigate in the dark (along with heightened olfactory perception). Therefore, it might be expected that the whisker barrel region, with its overlapping blooming and pruning of synapses, would be sensitive to experience. Indeed, Glazewski and Fox (1996) were able to demonstrate experience-expectant plasticity in the barrel field cortex of young rats by reducing the complement of vibrissae on one side of the muzzle to a single whisker for a period of 7, 20, or 60 days. The vibrissa dominance distribution was shifted significantly toward the spared vibrissa, which gained control of more neurons in barrel cortex while the deprived whiskers lost control. As the deprived whiskers grew back in, they progressively gained back some control of neurons from the spared whisker. Whisker deprivation had the strongest effects in weanling animals and very little in adult rats.

Humans appear to have something like a critical period for attachment, in that if the "expected" nurturing behavior does not occur in a timely manner then subsequent emotional development will be disrupted. Human and primate studies have revealed substantial effects of disrupted attachment on behavior and endocrine function, but little is known about any underlying neural plasticity. The phenomenon known as imprinting (e.g., by which newly hatched chicks learn to recognize mothers) involves both the formation of new synapses and elimination of preexisting synapses (Horn, 1986; Patel, Rose, & Stewart, 1988). Imprinting fits our definition of experience-expectant neural plasticity, but it is an example of social rather than perceptual development. It is important to note that various primate species are differentially sensitive to maternal deprivation (Sackett et al., 1979), and it would appear that humans are one of the relatively sensitive species. Rhesus monkeys, for example, raised in isolation show an enduring and heightened response to stress, abnormal motor behaviors including stereotyped movements, sexual dysfunction, eating disorders, and various extreme forms of social and emotional dysfunction (Harlow & Harlow, 1973; Sackett, 1972). The effects of total social isolation are more severe than partial isolation, which permits visual and auditory interactions with other animals but without direct contact. Dendritic arbors of neurons within the neocortex (Struble & Riesen, 1978) and the cerebellum (Floeter & Greenough, 1979) have been found to be poorly developed in socially deprived monkeys relative to normal animals. Martin, Spicer, Lewis, Gluck, and Cork (1991) found that socially deprived rhesus monkeys show a marked reduction in the dopaminergic and peptidergic innervation within the caudate-putamen, substantia nigra, and globus pallidus. In addition to evidence of reduced neuronal growth and development, socially deprived monkeys show brain abnormalities more typical of neurological disorders. It is important to note, however, that many of the preceding studies confound social deprivation with experiential deprivation, such that we still know relatively little about structural brain changes related to each social experience.

Another phenomenon that might involve a different type of disruption of the systems involved in attachment and social development leading to pathology is the fragile X mental retardation syndrome. This syndrome is caused by impaired or blocked expression of the fragile X mental retardation protein (FMRP) due to a triplet repeat mutation in the regulatory region of the gene. In addition to cognitive impairment and learning disabilities, fragile X retardation often is accompanied by symptoms of attention deficit hyperactivity disorder and of autism (Baumgardner, Reiss, Freund, & Abrams, 1995). There is also abundant evidence for a link between fragile X and psychiatric symptoms. Even individuals with relatively small expansion of the CGG repeat, who were "unaffected" cognitively, exhibited anxiety disorder (31%), bipolar disorder (23%), panic disorder (17%), and social phobia (11%) (Franke, Maier, Iwers, Hautzinger, & Froster, 1995). Adult fragile X males exhibit elevated schizoid and schizotypal features (Kerby & Dawson, 1994). "Mood lability" that does not reach criterion for bipolar diagnosis is also common in fragile X patients (Sobesky, Hull, & Hagerman, 1994). Of particular note is the frequent report of social problems such as "gaze avoidance" and other disturbances. A plausible etiology of these disturbances might include the failure to develop normal social skills through experience. We recently have presented evidence that FMRP expression at synapses is involved in activity-dependent synapse maturation (Comery, Harris, Willems, Oostra, & Greenough, 1997; Weiler et al., 1997), such that failure of this process could lead to such abnormalities by impeding normal experience-expectant aspects of the social development process.

Experience-Dependent Development

Experience-dependent development involves the brain's adaptation to information that is unique to an individual. This type of adaptation does not occur within strictly defined critical periods, as the timing or nature of such experience cannot be reliably anticipated. Therefore, this type of neural plasticity is likely to be active throughout life. It is important to recognize, however, that such systems cannot be constantly "on" and recording information. They need to have some kind of regulatory process that helps filter important information from the extraneous material. Although this type of process does not have fixed "windows" of plasticity, there may be necessary sequential dependencies on prior development. For example, children learn algebra before they master calculus. Sometimes experience-dependent processes will depend on prior experience-expectant ones, as in language development with a universal sensitive period followed by more idiosyncratic expansion of grammar and vocabulary.

MANIPULATING ENVIRONMENTAL COMPLEXITY

One important central mechanism for experience-dependent development is the formation of new neural connections, in contrast to the overproduction and pruning back of synapses often associated with experience-expectant processes. This idea was supported initially by experiments in which the overall complexity of an animal's environment is manipulated as well as from experiments using specific learning tasks. Modifying the complexity of an animal's environment can have profound effects on behavior and on brain structure both in late development (e.g., after weaning in rats) and in adulthood. In experimental manipulations, animals are typically housed in 1 of 3 conditions: individual cages (IC) in which the animals are housed alone in standard laboratory cages, social cages (SC) in which animals are housed with another rat in the same type of cage, and complex or "enriched" environment (EC) in which animals are housed in large groups in cages filled with changing arrangements of toys and other objects. Raising animals in an enriched environment provides ample opportunity for exploration and permits them to experience complex social interactions, including play behavior, and to gain experience with the manipulation and spatial components of complex multidimensional arrangements of objects.

Following a tradition established by the well-known Berkeley group (e.g., Bennett, Diamond, Krech, & Rosenzweig, 1964), the experimental groups often are referred to as "enriched" and "impoverished." It is important to emphasize that these are more accurately described in terms of varying degrees of *deprivation,* relative to the typical environment of feral rats. Barring considerations of stress or nutrition, we would argue that EC rats experience something close to "normal" brain development and that EC brains would closely resemble those of rats raised in the wild. Although a great deal of useful information can be obtained from laboratory animals, it is important in this chapter to understand that standard animals generally are overfed, understimulated, and physically out of shape.

Animals raised in complex environments are superior on many different types of learning tasks (reviewed in Greenough & Black, 1992). Various studies have suggested that EC animals may use more and different types of cues to solve tasks and may possess enhanced information processing rates and capacities (Greenough, Wood, & Madden, 1972; Juraska, Henderson, & Muller, 1984; Ravizza & Herschberger, 1966; Thinus-Blanc, 1981). Their superiority in complex mazes may rely in part on a greater familiarity with complicated spatial arrangements obtained through their rearing environment. These abilities are generalized across a wide range of other learning tests, however, suggesting that the EC's abilities do not lie simply in specific types of information gathered from the rearing environment. Rather, the brain adaptation to complex environment rearing involves changing how information is processed; in other words, the EC rat appears to have learned to learn better.

Examinations of brain structure in complex environment animals reveals a growth of neurons and synaptic connections in comparison to siblings raised in standard cages. This situation has been most studied in the visual cortex, which in complex-environment rats shows an overall increase in thickness, volume, and weight (Bennett et al., 1964); an increase in dendritic branching complexity and spine density (Holloway, 1966; Greenough & Volkmar, 1973), more synapses per neuron (Turner & Greenough, 1983, 1985); and larger synaptic contacts (Sirevaag & Greenough, 1985). The number of synapses in EC rats is elevated by approximately 20 to 25% within superficial layers of the visual cortex (Turner & Greenough, 1985). The visual cortex also shows physiological alterations that indicate an enhancement of neuronal firing in EC animals in comparison to animals housed in standard cages (Greenough & Wang, 1993). Very comparable anatomical data have been reported in cats given complex experience (Beaulieu & Colonnier, 1987), also with concomitant electrophysiological alterations (Beaulieu & Cynader, 1990).

The effects of environmental complexity have many different dimensions. The EC effects on brain structure cannot be attributed to general metabolic, hormonal, or stress differences across the different rearing conditions (reviewed in Black, Sirevaag, Wallace, Savin, & Greenough, 1989). Thus the structural brain changes may be specifically the result of altered neuronal activity and information storage. Young EC rats will add new capillaries to visual cortex, presumably in support of increased metabolic activity (Black, Sirevaag, & Greenough, 1987). Rats reared in a complex environment tend to have slower growth of skeleton and internal organs (Black et al., 1989) as well as altered immune system responsivity (Kingston & Hoffman-Goetz, 1996). Evidence that male and female rats differ in their responses to the complex environment in both the visual cortex and the hippocampus suggest at least a modulatory role for sex hormones in the EC/IC brain effects, at least in early postnatal development (Juraska, 1984). Multiple brain regions can show evidence of structural change in EC animals, including the temporal cortex (Greenough, Volkmar, & Juraska, 1973), the striatum (Comery, Shaw, & Greenough, 1995), the hippocampus (Juraska, 1984), the superior colliculus (Fuchs, Montemayor, & Greenough, 1990), and cerebellum (Floeter & Greenough, 1979; Pysh & Weiss, 1979). Mice reared in a complex environment will have more neurons in the dentate gyrus (Kempermann, Kuhn, & Gage, 1997). Significant changes in rat cortical thickness and dendritic branching can be detected after just 4 days of enrichment (Wallace, Kilman, Withers, & Greenough, 1992). These effects are not limited to young animals, as changes in neuronal dendrites and synapses in adult rats placed in the complex environment are substantial although smaller than those found in rats reared from weaning in EC (Green, Greenough, & Schlumpf, 1983; Juraska, Greenough, Elliott, Mack, & Berkowitz, 1980).

STRUCTURAL EFFECTS OF LEARNING

Although a variety of activities occur in an EC environment, clearly one of the important activities is learning. If learning in the EC environment results in structural brain changes, then similar changes would be expected in animals in response to a variety of training procedures. Such studies have indeed demonstrated that major brain changes occur during learning. These changes have been found in the specific brain regions apparently involved in the learning. For example, training in complex mazes requiring visuospatial memory has been found to result in increased dendritic arbors of the visual cortex in adult rats (Greenough, Juraska, & Volkmar, 1979). When split brain procedures were performed and unilateral occluders placed in one eye, dendrites of neurons in the monocular cortex mediating vision in the unoccluded eye showed greater growth in comparison to the ipsilateral cortex (Chang & Greenough, 1982).

Training animals on motor learning tasks also has been found to result in site-specific neuronal changes. Rats extensively trained to use 1 forelimb to reach through a tube to receive cookies show dendritic growth within the region of the cortex involved in forelimb function (Greenough, Larson, & Withers, 1985) in comparison to controls. When rats were allowed to use only 1 fore-limb for reaching, dendritic arborizations within the cortex opposite the trained forelimb were significantly increased relative to the cortex opposite the untrained forelimb. Furthermore, reach training selectively alters only certain subpopulations of neurons (e.g., Layer II/III pyramidal neurons showing forked apical shafts; Withers & Greenough, 1989). Reach training may produce similar results in developing animals as well. Rat pups trained to reach with 1 forelimb over 9 days beginning at weaning show increased cortical thickness in the hemisphere opposite the trained limb in comparison to the nontrained limb (Díaz, Pinto-Hamuy, & Fernández, 1994).

A critical question is whether these training-induced brain changes are due to special processes of information storage or simply an effect of increased activity within the affected brain systems. This question has been addressed in a motor learning paradigm in which rats are required to master several new complex motor coordination tasks ("acrobatic" rats). These animals showed increased numbers of synapses per Purkinje neuron within the cerebellum in comparison to inactive controls (Black et al., 1990). Animals exhibiting greater amounts of motor activity in running wheels or treadmills where little information was learned (Black, Isaacs, Anderson, Alcantara, & Greenough, 1990), or yoked-control animals that made an equivalent amount of movement in a simple straight alley (Kleim et al., 1997), did not show significant alterations in synaptic connections in the cerebellum. Thus learning, and not simply the repetitive use of synapses that may occur during dull physical exercise, led to synaptogenesis in the cerebellum.

Interestingly, the exercising animals did show some structural changes: The density of capillaries in the involved region of cerebellum was significantly increased, corresponding to what would be seen if new blood vessels developed to support increased metabolic demand (Black et al., 1990). This fact indicates that the brain can generate independently adaptive changes in different cellular components. When metabolic "stamina" is required, then vasculature is added. When motor skills need to be learned or refined, new synapses modify neural organization.

The cerebellar synaptic changes are accompanied by functional changes in electrophysiological recording. Stimulation of parallel fibers, constituting the primary excitatory input to Purkinje cells and accounting for the bulk of the added synapses, evoked larger postsynaptic changes in acrobatic rats than in motor activity controls (Swain, Bendre, Wheeler, & Greenough, submitted), indicating that the training-induced synapses are functional. This effect probably also reflects increased parallel fiber input to inhibitory neurons, also evident in morphological changes of the acrobatic rats (Kleim et al., submitted).

Experience Effects on Pathological Brains

At this point it is quite clear that abnormal experience (e.g., dark rearing) can cause abnormal neural and behavioral development, but can experience help repair brain damage caused by different factors? This topic is of considerable interest in a number of disciplines, from nutrition, to stroke rehabilitation, to neurotoxicology. In many of these studies the neuropathology occurs as a model for a human syndrome, with the experiential manipulation intended as a corrective or therapeutic treatment. In the following text we have chosen to highlight a few lines of investigation that support the finding that experience can affect and be affected by brain abnormalities. These examples support the view that behavioral experiences can significantly influence the behavioral manifestation and brain changes associated with brain pathology. They also support the idea that the nature of those experiences can be dramatically biased as a result of brain abnormalities and as a result of earlier behavioral experiences.

SENSORY DEPRIVATION

If the organism has been set off on a maladaptive developmental path by aberrant experience during a sensitive period, can other parts of the brain use neural plasticity to make compensatory changes? Many of the experimental paradigms used to describe experience-expectant processes left the animal impaired in some respects, but perhaps other brain regions were strengthened in compensation. Korte and Rauschecker (1993)

found that binocularly deprived kittens had improved spatial tuning of neurons in the auditory cortex (i.e., the neurons became better able to locate sounds in space). Vibrissae removal in rats results in an increase in spine density in the auditory cortex (Ryugo, Ryugo, Globus, & Killackey, 1975). Spine density in auditory cortex increases following visual or somatic deafferentation). Cats with vibrissae clipped from birth show earlier and better performance on visual cliff tests (Turkewitz, Gilbert, & Birch, 1974). Symons and Tees (1990) in an investigation of the effects of vibrissae removal on visual behavior found that these effects are mediated in part by experience. Rats with the vibrissae cauterized at birth showed an increase in the orientation to visual stimulation if they were raised in a complex environment. In each of these examples, deprivation in 1 sensory modality may have created a demand for improved perception in other modalities, thus eliciting compensatory neural changes. Clearly, however, these animals needed adequate and appropriate experience to make such compensatory changes.

EFFECTS OF EARLY STRESS

Animals born to mothers that were severely stressed during pregnancy show a variety of developmental and behavioral abnormalities, including heightened emotionality, altered motor development, abnormal adult sexual behavior (Ward, 1984), and altered patterns of juvenile play and exploration (Deminiére et al., 1992; Poltyrev, Keshet, Kay, & Weinstock, 1996; Takahashi, Haglin, & Kalin, 1992). The stressors used to induce these effects in rat models include exposure to intensely bright light, inescapable foot shock, and restraint during pregnancy. Prenatal stress leads to increased plasma levels of corticosterone, a hormone elevated during stress, in both mothers and fetuses (Ward & Weisz, 1984) as well as elevated levels of corticosterone and adrenocorticotropic hormone (ACTH) in the young offspring after birth (Takahashi, Baker, & Kalin, 1990). At least some of the behavioral and developmental abnormalities associated with prenatal stress can be mitigated by the postnatal environment. Barlow, Knight, and Sullivan (1978) cross-fostered prenatally stressed rats or normal rats immediately after birth with either stressed or nonstressed mothers. The most marked growth and behavioral abnormalities were found in prenatally stressed rats reared with stressed mothers. Relatively mild and approximately equivalent abnormalities were found in stressed pups reared with normal mothers and normal pups reared with stressed mothers.

In terms of the monkey, it is known that maternal exposure to loud sounds presented unpredictably during mid- to late gestation results in offspring with neurobehavioral symptoms, such as jitteriness, and neurochemical abnormalities, such as elevated levels of circulating catecholamines (Schneider, 1992). In addition, monkeys raised from birth in social isolation manifest behavioral symptoms of emotional dysregulation and neuroanatomical abnormalities of brain regions that contribute to emotional and/or cognitive behavior (Ginsberg, Hof, McKinney, & Morrison, 1993).

In addition to a demonstrable sensitivity to postnatal experience, prenatal stress effects exemplify biases in an animal's responses to experience. Prenatally stressed rats show increases in indices of emotionality in response to novelty, an effect that may involve heightened corticosterone secretion in response to environmental stimulation (Henry, Kabbaj, Simon, Le Moal, & Maccari, 1994). Takahashi et al. (1992) examined play behavior in prenatally stressed rats placed with siblings in an unfamiliar environment. These rats eventually did engage in rigorous play behavior, but they were much slower to initiate play. This effect was largely absent upon a repeated exposure to the environment but could be reinstated by subsequent mild stress. These data suggest that prenatal stress induces a long-term wariness in offspring in unfamiliar environments. Such an effect may greatly diminish an animal's ability to benefit from experience by reducing active seeking of new information.

In contrast to the effects of severe prenatal stress, early experience can be associated with brain changes that positively influence an animal's later responses to stress. Glucocorticoid production is controlled by a negative feedback system involving many brain regions, most prominently the hypothalamus, anterior pituitary, and hippocampus. The hippocampus is rich in glucocorticoid receptors, and it appears to be an important mediator of the negative feedback response to stress.

Rat pups that are briefly removed from their mothers and handled daily during the first few days after birth appear to show an enhancement of the negative feedback control over stress responses (reviewed in Francis et al., 1996). Measurements of stress hormones upon later exposure to stressors indicate that rats gently handled as pups show a reduced peak stress response to mild stressors, including a quicker return to normal levels of corticosterone and other stress-associated hormones, than animals that were not handled during development (Levine, 1956; Meaney, Aitken, Viau, Sharma, & Sarrieau, 1989). This effect appears to be mediated at least in part by alterations in the hippocampus in rats handled during development. Animals that are handled shortly after birth show an apparently permanent elevation in a subset of hippocampal glucocorticoid receptors (Meaney et al., 1989). Moreover, there is a sensitive period for the early stress effects. Rats handled during the first week after birth show a maximum elevation in glucocorticoid receptor binding in the hippocampus; handling begun in the second week produces diminished effects; by the third week of life, handling produces no elevation in glucocorticoid receptors (Meaney & Aitken, 1985). This corresponds to the developmental expression of glucocorticoid receptors, which are low in the first week of life and increase to approximately adult levels around 3 weeks.

FETAL ALCOHOL SYNDROME

Several researchers have argued that the outcome of prenatal exposure to alcohol in fetal alcohol syndrome (FAS) and exposure (FAE) is strongly influenced by postnatal environmental factors (Brown et al., 1991). This view is supported by experiments using animals models of fetal alcohol syndrome (Gallo & Weinberg, 1982). For example, Hannigan, Berman, and Zajac (1993) found that the behavioral effects of prenatal exposure to low to moderate levels of alcohol in rats were greatly attenuated by raising the animals in a complex environment. FAS animals that were raised from weaning in isolation showed ataxia and impairments in learning spatial tests. These alcohol-induced effects were largely absent in FAS rats raised in a complex environment. While this group found no indication of rehabilitation effects on hippocampal morphology, we recently demonstrated that a program of forced motor skill training (similar to the "acrobatic" training described earlier) nearly eliminated motor dysfunction in FAE rats, and it substantially increased synapse number in their cerebellar cortexes (Klintsova, Matthews, Goodlett, Napper, & Greenough, in press).

MODELS OF LEARNING DISABILITIES

Special strains of mice have been used as tentative models of developmental learning disorders because they possess cortical ectopias that are structurally similar to those found in humans with developmental dyslexia and show impairments in several types of learning tasks (Denenberg et al., 1991; Sherman, Galaburda, Behan, & Rosen, 1987). Some learning impairments in animals with cortical ectopias have been found to be almost completely abolished by rearing in a complex environment. Schrott et al. (1992) have found that ectopic mice raised in a complex environment perform near control levels on a spatial learning test. Other tests, such as the number of correct choices made on discrimination and avoidance tests, however, were not affected. These data suggest that enriched experience can have a powerful effect on specific types of learning impairments, whereas other types of impairments might remain relatively unaffected.

FOCAL BRAIN TRAUMA

Perhaps the most thorough attention to environment effects on brain dysfunction can be found in investigations of recovery from brain damage. Increasing the complexity of the environment before and/or after brain damage in developing and adult animals enhances recovery from the impairments produced by damage to various neocortical (e.g., Stein, Finger & Hart, 1982; Whishaw, Zaborowski, & Kolb, 1984) and subcortical areas (Donovick, Burright, & Swidler, 1973). A prominently held explanation for the enhanced recovery is that complex environments improve the brain-damaged animal's ability to develop behavioral compensation for the impairments. Performance by rats on tasks that are particularly dependent on the sensory modality most affected by the lesion (Bland & Cooper, 1969) or tasks that

do not require a significant learning component (Rose, Davies, Love, & Dell, 1987) often have not been found to be affected by environmental manipulations. Thus these findings indicate that the exposure to the complex environment typically aids the use of alternative strategies in task solutions and not specifically the recovery of the lost functions (e.g., Rose, al-Khamees, Davey, & Attree, 1993; Stein et al., 1982).

Investigations of the neural basis of this enhanced recovery have yet to show effects that are clearly distinguishable from EC effects in intact animals. Kolb and Gibb (1991) have found that, following bilateral frontal cortex lesions in adult rats, environmental enrichment produced increased dendritic arborization of the occipital cortex that was comparable to enrichment effects in intact animals. Lesioned animals in either complex or isolated environments showed equivalent increases in the arborization of pyramidal neurons in the sensorimotor cortex whereas nonlesioned animals in either condition did not. That is, the environment and the lesion produced independent effects on 2 different cortical areas. It is nevertheless conceivable that EC after brain damage promotes plasticity in sites and forms that are unique to brain-damaged animals.

Localized damage to regions of the motor cortex can produce alterations in remaining tissue in the cortical maps (homunculi) of the periphery, the movements that a particular cortical region is capable of eliciting. In investigations in primates, unilateral ischemic damage to a small portion of the hand territory of the cortex results in a loss of some of the undamaged hand territory adjacent to the lesion (Nudo, Wise, SiFuentes, & Milliken, 1996). When monkeys were trained on a reaching task with the impaired limb, the undamaged hand territory was not lost and in some monkeys it expanded. In a dramatic example of plasticity in the motor system of the monkey, Pons and colleagues (1991) reported on a group of cynomolgus monkeys that 12 years earlier had received deafferentations of an upper limb. Many years after the original intervention, the investigators examined the electrophysiological response of the brain to the loss of limb sensations. Neuronal responses were elicited from the region of somatosensory cortex that normally would correspond to the deafferented portion of the limb, including the fingers, palm, and adjacent areas (area S1). The investigators reported that this region of the brain now responded to stimulation in an area of the face. Not coincidentally, this region of facial sensation normally would border the cortical region innervated by the deafferented limb. Training rats to bar press after more extensive bilateral lesions of the forelimb area was associated with the appearance of a new representation of the forelimb in the cortical tissue near the lesion (Castro-Alamancos & Borrell, 1995). Together these findings indicate that reorganization of cortical regions not directly damaged may be impacted by behavioral manipulations. Manipulations aimed at improving the function of the affected extremities may not always be therapeutic, however. Recent work by Kozlowski, James, and Schallert (1996) indicates that at least some of the degenerative effects of unilateral damage to the forelimb motor cortex of rats may be worsened by overuse of the opposite forelimb. Forced use of the impaired forelimb during the first 2 weeks after the lesion resulted in an increase in the extent of damage in cortical tissue contiguous to the lesion and worsened behavioral function. These authors concluded that "use it but don't overuse it" may apply to the cortex of the lesioned hemisphere, perhaps especially early after the damage.

EFFECTS OF BEHAVIORAL DYSFUNCTION ON NEURAL PLASTICITY

Work such as that just discussed has shown that central processes of neural plasticity and degeneration following brain damage can influence the functional outcome from the damage and that these processes may be sensitive to experience. An important related issue is how behavioral changes that occur as a result of the damage may influence central processes of plasticity. Because manipulations of the behavior of intact animals can lead to central structural changes, it seems reasonable to expect that the behavioral changes produced by the brain damage also can influence brain structure. This possibility is supported by 2 lines of research using adult rats. Although it has yet to be demonstrated, it seems reasonable to expect that a similar type of behavior-dependent plasticity operates after brain damage in developing animals as well.

Work by Huston and his colleagues suggests that the behavior of an animal plays a role in the growth of new connections following injury. Using methods to trace axonal projections, they have found that large unilateral lesions of the telencephalon, unilateral substantia nigra lesions, and peripheral nerve hemitransections each result in the sprouting of new connections from the substantia nigra of the intact hemisphere to the thalamus of the opposite, damaged, hemisphere (e.g., Pritzel, Huston, & Sarter, 1983). Each of these manipulations also results in a propensity for animals to turn in the direction of the damage. This turning behavior was linked to the sprouting because the cessation of lesion-induced turning during behavioral recovery coincided with the appearance of the crossed connections (Pritzel et al., 1983). In addition, preventing the turning behavior by suspending the animals within hammocks results in the absence of the crossed connections (Morgan, Huston, & Pritzel, 1983). These studies provide strong evidence that the behavioral activity of the animal is involved in the neuronal sprouting.

Another line of work has suggested that behavioral changes developed by animals to compensate for brain damage leads to structural changes. When unilateral damage is made to the region of the cortex involved in forelimb movements in rats, the forelimb opposite the damage is impaired in both sensory and motor function (Barth, Jones, & Schallert, 1990). In apparent compensation for these deficits, animals develop a hyperreliance on the nonimpaired forelimb ipsilateral to the lesion. The motor cortex opposite the damage, which "drives" the nonimpaired forelimb, shows an increase in the thickness, dendritic branching, and synapses per neuron (Jones, Kleim, & Greenough, 1996; Jones & Schallert, 1994). These lesions result in impairments in the sensory and motor functions of the forelimb opposite the damage (Barth, Jones, & Schallert, 1990) and, in apparent compensation for these deficits, animals develop a hyperreliance on the forelimb ipsilateral to the lesion. Because this is the forelimb that "drives" the cortex demonstrating growth, it seemed reasonable that this compensatory behavior was involved in the postlesion neuronal growth. To test this possibility, animals with unilateral lesions were placed in 1-holed vests that permitted normal movements of all limbs except the forelimb opposite the intact hemisphere. This situation prevented the lesion-induced growth of dendrites opposite the damage (Jones & Schallert, 1994). In contrast, animals that were allowed to use both forelimbs or only the intact forelimb showed increases in the dendritic arborization opposite the lesion, indicating that the postlesion hyper-reliance on the intact forelimb was responsible for the dendritic growth. Functionally, the rats that were prevented from using the intact limb showed the most extensive impairments of the animals with lesions, suggesting that the compensatory behavior and neuronal growth may have adaptive value for functional outcome. Forcing intact animals to use only 1 forelimb did not lead to dendritic growth in the region affected in lesioned animals. This fact suggests that the brain damage promoted a special sensitivity to behaviorally induced plasticity that goes beyond changes seen in normal adult animals and that an important strategy for enhancing behavioral outcome may be to capitalize on naturally occurring compensatory behaviors.

Evidence for Human Neural Plasticity

Due to ethical and technical limitations, it has been quite difficult to demonstrate that the human brain has neural plasticity processes similar to those for other species. Considering the massive amount of information that humans incorporate (e.g., consider language learning alone) and the fact that this material can be retained for decades without rehearsal, that information seemingly must be stored as lasting structural neural changes. Although present evidence cannot describe any changes in synaptic strength or number directly, human neural plasticity can be described in terms of experience-expectant and experience-dependent processes.

One kind of human experience-expectant process sensitive to selective deprivation involves perceptual mismatch from both eyes—for example, when 1 eye is deviated outward (strabismus) during early development. Similar to the cat and monkey studies described earlier, if the 2 eyes are sending competing and conflicting signals to the visual cortex during the sensitive period, the

brain effectively "shuts down" or becomes insensitive to the nondominant eye. In humans, the resulting perceptual disorder is termed amblyopia (or "lazy eye"), and it results in clear perceptual deficits if surgery does not correct this visual misalignment during the critical period. The strabismus-related perceptual deficit was the first and is still the best-established example of human neural plasticity (Crawford, Harwerth, Smith, & von Noorden, 1993). Recent technology, such as positron emission tomography (PET scans), has demonstrated that patients with uncorrected strabismus use different areas of cortex for visual processing than do normal controls (Demer, 1993). Although the timing, regulation, and structural changes of this sensitive period need further study, the early evidence suggests a clear parallel to the studies described of kittens with selective deprivation of vision.

Another developmental process with innate roots but nonetheless quite dependent on early experience is language acquisition (Locke, 1992). Although the question of whether language has an innate deep structure is still debated, it is clear that children rapidly acquire an enormous amount of vocabulary, grammar, and related information. For middle-class American families, the rate of vocabulary acquisition is related directly to the amount of verbal stimulation the caregiver provides (Huttenlocher, Haight, Bryk, Seltzer, & Lyons, 1991). Apparently there exists a sensitive period for acquiring the ability to discriminate speech contrasts. For example, Kuhl (1994) has reported that prior to 6 or so months of life, infants from English-speaking homes are able to discriminate speech contrasts from a variety of languages, including Thai, Czech, and Swedish, much the way native adult speakers are able to. However, sometime between 6 and 12 months, this ability is gradually lost, such that after this age, infants become more like adults who are most proficient in discriminating the speech contrasts from their native language.

Some preliminary evidence exists that humans can alter brain function with extensive training, corresponding to the experience-dependent processes described earlier. For example, using functional magnetic resonance imaging (fMRI) to measure regional blood flow in the brain, Karni et al. (1995) demonstrated increased cortical involvement after training subjects in a finger-tapping sequence. Elbert, Pantev, Weinbruch, Rockstroh, and Taub (1995) showed substantial expansion of cortical involvement associated with the amount of training to play the violin. Rehabilitation therapy after brain injury produced similar fMRI changes (Frackiowak, 1996). At this time no one can show directly that humans produce new synapses with this type of learning, but the fMRI changes are what we would expect if synaptogenesis were occurring in an experience-dependent process.

Impressive findings of cortical reorganization after peripheral injury in adult humans correspond well to the nonhuman primate work described earlier (reviewed in Weinberger, 1995). For example, Ramachandran, Rogers-Ramachandran, and Stewart (1992) examined adults who had experienced various forms of amputation, such as amputation of the forearm. One such individual (comparable to others in his situation) experienced sensation in the limb that had, in fact, been amputated (i.e., phantom limb phenomenon). Ramachandran then examined sensitivity to tactile stimulation along the regions of the face known to innervate the somatosensory cortex adjacent to the area previously innervated by the missing limb. When this region of the face was lightly stimulated, the patient reported sensation in both the face and the missing limb. Eventually Ramachandran was able to determine the degree to which the cortical surface had been reorganized to subsume the area previously occupied by the missing limb.

Not all experience-related changes in human brain function are positive adaptations. Just as rats can suffer hippocampal damage and memory impairment when exposed to chronic stress, there is emerging evidence that stress can affect humans as well. Initial studies of Vietnam veterans who had experienced combat stress revealed memory impairment in otherwise healthy, middle-age men (Bremner et al., 1993). Just as in the rat studies, early trauma can have lasting effects on stress regulation. For example, Yehuda et al. (1995) demonstrated endocrine dysregulation persisting for decades following exposure to trauma, in this case with survivors of the Holocaust. Bremner et al. (1995) later confirmed that the memory deficits in Vietnam veterans were associated with atrophy of the hippocampus, reflecting possible neuron damage or cell death. Patients, both young and old, often describe an indelibility of the trauma memory with lasting effects on affective regulation (sometimes manifested as posttraumatic stress disorder or personality disorders), suggesting that structural changes may underlie these symptoms.

Putting it all Together to Build a Brain

A number of important principles of brain development can be extracted from the preceding discussion. We would like to emphasize the dynamic systems perspective, such that early brain pathology or distorted experience may set a maladaptive course for development, but the organism often will make efforts to compensate for it. At one level, different parts of the brain may try to compensate, and beyond that the organism may seek out new experience in areas where it has strength. Plasticity is a central feature of mammalian brains, and early brain damage or aberrant experience should not be considered as determining the organism's fate forever.

In describing information storage mechanisms, we have tried to define the similarities and differences between maturation, experience-sensitive development, and learning. Some aspects of experience (e.g., play in juvenile EC/IC rearing) may influence both experience-expectant and experience-dependent processes. In fact, these processes probably cannot be isolated entirely, since they have substantial interactive consequences for how the brain processes information and they share mechanisms at the cellular level.

The evidence that different species have different susceptibility to experience and that brain areas are differentially influenced by experience suggests that information storage mechanisms have not remained stable through evolution. We suggest that, as more complicated sensory, motor, and information processing schemes evolved, experience was utilized in 2 ways: to shape common features of the nervous system through experiences common to members of the species and to provide for storage of information about the unique environment of the individual. The underlying mechanisms may have diverged to meet these separate needs, such that system-wide overproduction at a specific maturational stage, followed by selection, subserves storage of common information, while local activity-dependent synaptogenesis, again followed by selection, subserves later storage of unique information.

Experience-expectant processes have been described here in terms of the species-wide reliability of some types of experience. We suggested that species survival may be facilitated by information storage processes anticipating an experience with identical timing and features for all juvenile members. A structural correlate of "expectation" may be a temporary overproduction of synapses during the sensitive period with a subsequent pruning back of inappropriate synapses. This experience-expectant blooming of new synapses is distributed more or less uniformly across the entire population of homologous cells. The neuromodulatory event that triggers this synapse overproduction may be under maturational control or may be activity dependent (as after eye-opening), but it is diffuse and pervasive. The expected experience produces patterned activity of neurons, effectively targeting which synapses will be selected, as illustrated for monocular deprivation in binocular species.

Experience-dependent mechanisms, on the other hand, may utilize synapse generation and preservation in different balance for a quite different effect. Because these neural plasticity mechanisms cannot anticipate the timing or specific features of such idiosyncratic experience, the "sensitive period" is necessarily left wide open. Here synapses are generated locally, upon demand of some modulatory signal. The specific nature of modulation, which could be elicited locally by neural activity or by hormonal signals, remains an open question for future research. The organism's active participation is important in obtaining and stabilizing experience. For example, juvenile play or adult attention may serve both to extract new information (increase contrast) and help repeat it or stabilize it (increase coherence). This experience-dependent localized shaping of connectivity suggests that very multimodal and diverse experience (as in EC) would produce widespread increases in synaptic frequency but that relatively specific experience (as in training tasks) would produce more localized increases.

Animals raised in EC differ from ICs primarily in the complexity of experience available, so that self-initiation of experience (e.g., exploratory activity) is a key determinant of timing and quality of experience. This feature is consistent with the dynamic systems perspective of development (Thelen & Smith, 1995), in that the connectivity modifications observed in the EC animals appear more related to how neural activity is processed than to how much is processed. For example, both EC and IC animals use approximately the same amount of light (average intensity on the retina) quite differently, 1 with self-initiated activity and its visual consequences, the other with dull routine. Some species (probably including humans) have altered behavior so as to increase the likelihood of obtaining enriched experience. For example, weanling rats generally are quite playful and active in comparison to adults, probably due to the same burst of playful activity we observe in kittens, puppies, and toddlers. The burst of playfulness may be developmentally programmed and generally useful to all members of a species (Ikemoto & Panksepp, 1992; Smith, 1982).

We argued earlier that brain development can be viewed as an elaborate scaffolding of gene-driven, experience-expectant, and experience-dependent processes. While it is oversimplifying to use linear terms such as *scaffolding* or schedule, it is important to see that many components are quite dependent on the completion of earlier steps. Thus the later synaptic blooming and pruning of human frontal cortex compared to visual cortex may reflect a sequential dependency. Neural and cognitive development may require the strictly ordered sequence of the development of sensory modalities (e.g., touch before vision) (Gottlieb, 1973; Turkewitz & Kenny, 1982)—multiple sensitive periods may prevent competition between modalities and help integrate information across modalities (e.g., touch coming before vision may help in the development of visuomotor skills). It is interesting to speculate on the specific roles of the protracted synapses overproduction and loss observed by Huttenlocher (1994) in human prefrontal cortex. In visual cortex, properties such as stereoscopic depth perception and the orientation tuning of receptive fields develop through experience during the early part of postnatal life. If a particular aspect of experience is missing, then subsequent visual function is disturbed. It might be of value for students of cognitive development to consider, for prefrontal cortex, what constitutes the cognitive equivalent of exposure to "expected" visual experience.

The scaffolding of information from 1 domain being used to support a new domain of development can be seen in an older but still elegant series of experiments (Hein & Diamond, 1971; Held & Hein, 1963), in which kittens rode in a gondola that allowed vision but restricted movement, wore large collars that allowed free movement but prevented visualization of their paws, or had surgery that prevented their eyes from tracking their paws in space. These kittens had normal overall amounts of visual and proprioceptive information, but the lack of perceptual integration in these modalities caused profound behavioral pathology. Note that all of the types of deprivation described here either interfere with contrast (less information; e.g., monocular deprivation, strobe rearing, or stripe rearing) or coherence (less consistency of input; e.g., strabismus, wearing prisms, or riding in gondolas).

Although more speculative than we might like, a possible example of behavioral changes that lead to synaptic changes might be in several of the functions known to be subserved by the prefrontal cortex. For example, it has long been known that the ability to use strategies to solve problems and to engage in hypothetico-deductive reasoning is heavily dependent on regions of the prefrontal cortex. Generally it is not until formal schooling begins that these problem-solving skills are fostered, encouraged, and eventually required. Given the long trajectory of synaptic pruning that goes on in this region of the brain (see Huttenlocher, 1994, for review), it would stand to reason that these experiences may cultivate the circuits that eventually will lead to more sophisticated forms of thought, such as the cluster of abilities referred to as "executive functions."

Applications in Child Psychiatry

The general conclusions about mammalian neural plasticity reviewed in this chapter have some important implications for understanding both pathogenesis and potential treatment in child psy-chiatry. Clearly some children have either genetic or acquired brain pathology from early on, and these structural problems will interact differently with subsequent experience and neural plasticity processes. Another large group of children has either deficient or maladaptive experience, such that their subsequent neural development is affected by deprivation or trauma. And last, we have argued that a dynamic systems perspective builds on complex interactions between brain structure and experience during development, such that the culture, the family, and the child all make the contributions in obtaining and organizing experience.

In the early part of this chapter we emphasized the importance of gene-driven processes in constructing a brain that is enormously complex prior to any effects of experience. This structure is the foundation upon which any subsequent modification by experience will be made. Clearly if a child is born with a different brain, his or her experience of the world may be dramatically different. For example, if an infant with cerebral palsy is unable to control eye and hand movements smoothly, then processes using coordinated information from both inputs will be disrupted. Even if the subsequent experience-expectant and dependent processes are themselves unimpaired, the experience distorted by neuropathology will not be utilized appropriately. One implication for this is already widely applied: Children with experience distorted or impoverished by neuropathology can utilize corrective or enabling technology to restore the quality of experience. Although it may be conceptualized somewhat differently, this is why the law mandates that children with hearing or vision impairments be provided with corrective devices as early as possible in order to restore the quality of their experience. Recently developed computer technology has allowed children with motor problems to control their actions better and to improve their communication greatly (Merzenich et al., 1996). In summary, children with different brains need to have their environment adapted to their need; otherwise their experience will be further distorted or impoverished and development will go astray.

We believe that canalization, or the intrinsic resistance to environmental manipulation in some systems, has substantially frustrated some interventions. If the epigenetic landscape for an autistic child is imagined, the neuropathology has resulted in a developmental "groove" that will carry development forward. Therapeutic manipulations may perturb this trajectory initially, but development will fall back into the existing track if the canalization is sufficiently entrenched. However, if the perturbation is large enough, then the trajectory can be shifted out of one equilibrium and into another, and from there brain development will proceed down a different pathway. As development proceeds, canalization generally deepens—developmental trajectories progressively become more difficult to redirect by experience. This perspective supports the common therapeutic strategies that early intervention is better than late and that more intervention may work better than less. Autistic children, for example, often are considered incapable of significant recovery, largely because nearly all efforts at treatment have been largely ineffective. Some preliminary evidence, however, suggests that if Herculean efforts at behavior modification are made early on, a substantial number of autistic children will show a lasting and substantial remission of their language and social deficits (McEachin, Smith, & Lovaas, 1993). Preliminary results of this intensive intervention with children with Rett's syndrome have been disappointing, perhaps because of the degenerative course of that disease (Smith, Klevstrand, & Lovaas, 1995). If the positive findings with autistic children hold up with replication and can be extended to other populations, then it would appear that substantial recovery from some severe neuropsychiatric disorders is possible if there is a wise investment of early and intense clinical efforts.

Some children with relatively normal brains at birth may suffer from the effects of either impoverishment or poor quality of information during development. If uncorrected, the effects of conflicting visual input with early strabismus is functional blindness in 1 eye. Children's vocabularies can be determined significantly by the amount of verbal experience provided by their caregiver. From the animal research described in this chapter, we would expect that human brain development can be influenced substantially by the quality and the amount of experience. (Some preliminary evidence even suggests that education and large brain size offer some protection against Alzheimer's disease; Cobb, Wolf, Au, White, & D'Agostino, 1995). Finally, we also might speculate about the importance of children's early emotional relationship with a caregiver in fostering subsequent healthy emotional development. It is well known that children's attachment to their primary caregiver takes place over the first 2 years of life and, perhaps most critically, between 6 and 18 months of life. Beyond this period of development infants are at risk for not developing healthy attachment relationships, which ultimately may prove maladaptive in both the emotional and cognitive domains (e.g., securely attached children tend to be better at problem solving than insecurely attached children). The fact that this sensitive period exists behaviorally is likely based on the vulnerability to those circuits that are critically involved in emotion, emotion regulation, and memory (e.g., cortico-limbic). Collectively, these observations would support efforts at enrichment of experience for young children (e.g., the Head Start program).

We believe this argument is strongest with regard to cognitive development, but it probably also extends to other important aspects of development, such as social abilities or attachment. Given that early experience can have lasting and profound effects on emotional regulation and social behavior (along with associated neurochemical and neuroendocrine changes), we suspect that neural plasticity underlies these effects as well. It appears that humans have something like a sensitive period for emotional and social development, and it thus becomes important to determine what brain regions may use associated experience-expectant processes to shape the brain. From this knowledge, clinical efforts can be directed in a more timely or focused manner to redirect brain development.

A corollary of early and intensive intervention is that clinicians should not allow children to languish with active symptoms of their disorder. Delayed intervention may "waste" a sensitive period, making subsequent clinical intervention much more difficult and possibly leading to relatively irreversible pathology. In addition, both experience-expectant and experience-dependent mechanisms may continue to operate in various pathological states, and a child who incorporates "pathological" experience in these circumstances may very well add neuropathology in instead of functional connections. Consider what may happen to a child's brain structure after years of experience with auditory hallucinations, drug abuse, depression, or violence. For example, Post (1992) has used findings from epilepsy research to suggest that repeated episodes of mania or depression cumulatively "prime" the brain to suffer more frequent and more severe episodes.

From a dynamic systems perspective, it is apparent that there is another sort of "canalization" active in human development. In some respects, children are resilient and can thrive in a wide variety of environments, and we suggest that children are actively involved in obtaining and structuring experience that is developmentally appropriate

for them. One well-known aspect of this self-structuring of experience is play, a developmental process used by many mammalian species to improve skills and learn socialization. Just as D. W. Winnicott proposed that a "good-enough mother" often can suffice for normal emotional development, we would suggest that many children can extract what they need from a "good-enough environment." Clearly parents play an important role in facilitating a child's experience, and their role should be extensively considered in studies of what might constitute a good-enough environment.

REFERENCES

Antonini, A., & Stryker, M. P. (1993). Rapid remodeling of axonal arbors in the visual cortex. *Science, 260,* 1819–1821.

Barlow, S. M., Knight, A. F., & Sullivan, F. M. (1978). Delay in postnatal growth and development of offspring produced by maternal restraint stress during pregnancy in the rat. *Teratology, 18,* 211–218.

Barth, T. M., Jones, T. A., & Schallert, T. (1990). Functional subdivisions of the rat somatic sensorimotor cortex. *Behavioral Brain Research, 39,* 73–95.

Baumgardner, T., Reiss, A. L., Freund, L. S., & Abrams, M. T. (1995). Specifications of the neurobehavioral associations in males with fragile X syndrome. *Pediatrics, 95,* 744–752.

Beaulieu, C., & Colonnier, M. (1987). Effect of the richness of the environment on the cat visual cortex. *Journal of Comparative Neurology, 266,* 478–494.

Beaulieu, C., & Cynader, M. (1990). Effect of the richness of the environment on neurons in cat visual cortex. I. Receptive field properties. *Brain Research & Development, 53,* 71–81.

Bennett, E. L., Diamond, M. C., Krech, D., & Rosenzweig, M. R. (1964). Chemical and anatomical plasticity of brain. *Science, 146,* 610–619.

Black, J. E., & Greenough, W. T. (1986). Induction of pattern in neural structure by experience: Implications for cognitive development. In M. E. Lamb, A. L. Brown, & B. Rogoff (Eds.), *Advances in developmental psychology* (Vol. 4, pp. 1–50). Hillsdale, NJ: Lawrence Erlbaum.

Black, J. E., Isaacs, K. R., Anderson, B. J., Alcantara, A. A., & Greenough, W. T. (1990). Learning causes synaptogenesis, while motor activity causes angiogenesis, in cerebellar cortex of adult rats. *Proceedings of the National Academy of Sciences, 87,* 5568–5572.

Black, J. E., Sirevaag, A. M., & Greenough, W. T. (1987). Complex experience promotes capillary formation in young rat visual cortex. *Neuroscience Letters, 83,* 351–355.

Black, J. E., Sirevaag, A. M., Wallace, C. S., Savin, M. H., & Greenough, W. T. (1989). Effects of complex experience on somatic growth and organ development in rats. *Developmental Psychobiology, 22,* 727–752.

Blakemore, C., Garey, L. J., & Vital-Durand, F. (1978). The physiological effects of monocular deprivation and their reversal in the monkey's visual cortex. *Journal of Physiology* (London), 283, 223–262.

Bland, B. H., & Cooper, R. M. (1969). Posterior neodecortication in the rat: Age at operation and experience. *Journal of Comparative Physiological Psychology, 69,* 345–354.

Boothe, R. G., Greenough, W. T., Lund, J. S., & Wrege, K. (1979). A quantitative investigation of spine and dendritic development of neurons in visual cortex (area 17) of Macaca nemistrina monkeys. *Journal of Comparative Neurology, 186,* 473–490.

Bourgeois, J. P., Goldman-Rakic, P. S., & Rakic, P. (1994). Synaptogenesis in the prefrontal cortex of rhesus monkeys. *Cerebral Cortex, 4,* 78–96.

Bowering, E. R., Maurer, D., Lewis, T. L., & Brent, H. P. (1993). Sensitivity in the nasal and temporal hemifields in children treated for cataract. *Investigatory Ophthalmology and Vision Science, 34,* 3501–3509.

Bremner, J. D., Innis, R. B., Ng, C. K., Staib, L. H., Salomon, R. M., Bronen, R. A., Duncan, J., Southwick, S. M., Krystal, J. H., Rich, D., Zubal, G., Dey, H., Soufer, R., & Charney, D. S. (1995). MRI-based measurement of hippocampal volume in patients with combat-related posttraumatic stress disorder. *American Journal of Psychiatry, 152,* 973–981.

Bremner, J. D., Scott, T. M., Delaney, R. C., Southwick, S. M., Mason, J. W., Johnson, D. R., Innis, R. B., McCarthy, G., & Charney, D. S. (1993). Deficits in short-term memory in post-traumatic stress disorder. *American Journal of Psychiatry, 150,* 1015–1019.

Brown, R. T., Coles, C. D., Smith, I. E., Platzman, K. A., Silverstein, J., Erickson, S., & Falek, A. (1991). Effects of prenatal alcohol exposure at school age. II. Attention and behavior. *Neurotoxicology and Teratology, 13,* 369–376.

Castro-Alamancos, M. A., & Borrell, J. (1995). Functional recovery of forelimb response capacity after forelimb primary motor cortex damage in the rat is due to the reorganization of adjacent areas of cortex. *Neuroscience, 68,* 793–805.

Chang, F.-L. F., & Greenough, W. T. (1982). Lateralized effects of monocular training on dendritic branching in adult split-brain rats. *Brain Research, 232,* 283–292.

Chaudhari, N., & Hahn, W. E. (1983). Genetic expression in the developing brain. *Science, 220,* 924–928.

Cobb, J. L., Wolf, P. A., Au, R., White, R., & D'Agostino, R. B. (1995). The effect of education on the incidence of dementia and Alzheimer's disease in the Framingham study. *Neurology, 45,* 1707–1712.

Coleman, P. D., Flood, D. G., Whitehead, M. C., & Emerson, R. C. (1981). Spatial sampling by dendritic trees in visual cortex. *Brain Research, 214,* 1–21.

Coleman, P. D., & Riesen, A. H. (1968). Environmental effects on cortical dendritic fields. I. Rearing in the dark. *Journal of Anatomy, 102,* 363–374.

Comery, T. A., Harris, J. B., Willems, P. J., Oostra, B. A. & Greenough, W. T. (in press). Abnormal dendritic spines in fragile-X knockout mice: Maturation and pruning deficits. *Proceedings of the National Academy of Sciences, 94,* 5401–5404.

Comery, T. A., Shah, R., & Greenough, W. T. (1995). Differential rearing alters spine density on medium-sized spiny neurons in the rat corpus striatum: Evidence for association of morphological plasticity with early response gene expression. *Neurobiology of Learning Memory, 63,* 217–219.

Conel, J. L. (1939–67). *The postnatal development of the human cerebral cortex* (Vols. 1–8). Cambridge, MA: Harvard University Press.

Corrigan, J. G., & Carpenter, D. L. (1979). Early selective visual experience and pattern discrimination in hooded rats. *Developmental Psychobiology, 12,* 67–72.

Crabtree, J. W., & Riesen, A. H. (1979). Effects of the duration of dark rearing on visually guided behavior in the kitten. *Developmental Psychobiology, 12,* 291–303.

Cragg, B. G. (1975). The development of synapses in the visual system of the cat. *Journal of Comparative Neurology, 160,* 147–166.

Crawford, M. L., Harwerth, R. S., Smith, E. L., & von Noorden, G. K. (1993). Keeping an eye on the brain: The role of visual experience in monkeys and children. *Journal of General Psychology, 120,* 7–19.

Cynader, M., & Cmerneko, G. (1976). Abolition of direction selectivity in the visual cortex of the cat. *Science, 193,* 504–505.

Cynader, M., & Mitchell, D. E. (1980). Prolonged sensitivity to monocular deprivation in dark-reared cats. *Journal of Neurophysiology, 43,* 1026–1040.

Demer, J. L. (1993). Positron emission tomographic studies of cortical function in human amblyopia. *Neuroscience and Biobehavioral Review, 17,* 469–476.

Deminiére, J. M., Piazza, P. V., Guegan, G., Abrous, N., Maccari, S., Le Moal, M., & Simon, H. (1992). Increased locomotor response to novelty and propensity to intravenous amphetamine self-administration in adult offspring of stressed mothers. *Brain Research, 586,* 135–139.

Denenberg, V. H., Mobraaten, L. E., Sherman, G. F., Morrison, L., Schrott, L. M., Waters, N. S., Rosen, G. D., Behan, P. O., & Galaburda, A. M. (1991). Effects of the autoimmune uterine/maternal environment upon cortical ectopias, behavior and autoimmunity. *Brain Research, 563,* 114–122.

Díaz, E., Pinto-Hamuy, T., & Fernández, V. (1994). Interhemispheric structural asymmetry induced by a lateralized reaching task in the rat motor cortex. *European Journal of Neuroscience, 6,* 1235–1238.

Donovick, P. J., Burright, R. G., & Swidler, M. A. (1973). Presurgical rearing environment alters exploration, fluid consumption, and learning of septal lesioned and control rats. *Physiology and Behavior, 11,* 543–553.

Elbert, T., Pantev, C., Weinbruch, C., Rockstroh, B., & Taub, E. (1995). Increased cortical representation of the fingers of the left hand in string players. *Science, 270,* 305–307.

Floeter, M. K., & Greenough, W. T. (1979). Cerebellar plasticity: Modification of Purkinje cell structure by differential rearing in monkeys. *Science, 206,* 227–229.

Frackiowak, R. S. J. (1996). Plasticity and the human brain: Insights from functional imaging. *The Neuroscientist, 2,* 353–362.

Francis, D., Diorio, J., LaPlante, P., Weaver, S., Seckl, J. R., & Meaney, M. J. (1996). The role of early environmental events in regulating neuroendocrine development. Moms, pups, stress, and glucocorticoid receptors. *Annals of the New York Academy of Sciences, 794,* 136–140.

Franke, P., Maier, W., Iwers, B., Hautzinger, M., & Froster, U. G. (1995, August 2–5). *Fragile X carrier females: Evidence for a distinct psychopathological phenotype?* Paper presented at the 7th International Workshop on the Fragile X and X-Linked Mental Retardation, Tromso, Norway.

Fuchs, J. L., Montemayor, M., & Greenough, W. T. (1990). Effect of environmental complexity on size of the superior colliculus. *Behavioral and Neural Biology, 54,* 198–203.

Gabbott, P. L., & Stewart, M. G. (1987). Quantitative morphological effects of dark-rearing and light exposure on the synaptic connectivity of layer 4 in the rat visual cortex (area 17). *Experimental Brain Research, 68*, 103–114.

Gallo, P. V., & Weinberg, J. (1982). Neuromotor development and response inhibition following prenatal ethanol exposure. *Neurobehavioral Toxicology and Teratology, 4*, 505–513.

Ginsberg, S. D., Hof, P. R., McKinney, W. T., & Morrison, J. H. (1993). The noradrenergic innervation density of the monkey paraventricular nucleus is not altered by early social deprivation. *Neuroscience Letters, 158*, 130–134.

Glazewski, S., & Fox, K. (1996). Time course of experience-dependent synaptic potentiation and depression in barrel cortex of adolescent rats. *Journal of Neurophysiology, 75*, 1714–1729.

Gottlieb, G. (1973). Introduction to behavioral embryology. In G. Gottlieb (Ed.), *Studies on the development of behavior and the nervous system, Vol. 1, Behavioral Embryology* (pp. 3–45). New York: Academic Press.

Green, E. J., Greenough, W. T., & Schlumpf, B. E. (1983). Effects of complex or isolated environments on cortical dendrites of middle-aged rats. *Brain Research, 264*, 233–240.

Greenough, W. T., & Black, J. E. (1992). Induction of brain structure by experience: Substrates for cognitive development. *Minnesota Symposium on Child Development, 24*, 155–200.

Greenough, W. T., & Chang, F.-L. F. (1988). Plasticity of synapse structure and pattern in the cerebral cortex. In A. Peters & E. G. Jones (Eds.), *Cerebral cortex* (Vol. 7, pp. 391–440). New York: Plenum Press.

Greenough, W. T., Juraska, J. M., & Volkmar, F. R. (1979). Maze training effects on dendritic branching in occipital cortex of adult rats. *Behavioral and Neural Biology, 26*, 287–297.

Greenough, W. T., Larson, J. R., & Withers, G. S. (1985). Effects of unilateral and bilateral training in a reaching task on dentritic branching of neurons in the rat motor-sensory forelimb cortex. *Behavioral and Neural Biology, 44*, 301–314.

Greenough, W. T., & Volkmar, F. R. (1973). Pattern of dendritic branching in occipital cortex of rats reared in complex environments. *Experimental Neurology, 40*, 491–504.

Greenough, W. T., Volkmar, F. R., & Juraska, J. M. (1973). Effects of rearing complexity on dendritic branching in frontolateral and temporal cortex of the rat. *Experimental Neurology, 41*, 371–378.

Greenough, W. T., & Wang, X. (1993). Altered postsynaptic response in the visual cortex in vivo of rats reared in complex environments. *Society for Neuroscience Abstracts, 19*, 164.

Greenough, W. T., Wood, W. E., & Madden, T. C. (1972). Possible memory storage differences among mice reared in complex environments. *Behavioral Biology, 7*, 717–722.

Hannigan, J. H., Berman, R. F., & Zajac, C. S. (1993). Environmental enrichment and the behavioral ef-

fects of prenatal exposure to alcohol in rats. *Neurotoxicology and Teratology, 15*, 261–266.

Harlow, H. F., & Harlow, M. K. (1973). The affectonal systems. In A. M. Schrier (Ed.), *Behavior of nonhuman primates* (Vol. 2, pp. 287–334). New York: Academic Press.

Hein, A., & Diamond, R. (1971). Contributions of eye movements to the representation of space. In A. Hein & M. Jeannerod (Eds.), *Spatially oriented behavior* (pp. 119–134). New York: Springer.

Hein, A., Held, R., & Gower, E. C. (1970). Development and segmentation of visually controlled movement by selective exposure during rearing. *Journal of Comparative Physiological Psychology, 73*, 181–187.

Held, R., & Hein, A. (1963). Development and segmentation of visually controlled movement by selective exposure during rearing. *Journal of Comparative and Physiological Psychology, 73*, 181–187.

Henry, C., Kabbaj, M., Simon, H., Le Moal, M., & Maccari, S. (1994). Prenatal stress increases the hypothalamo-pituitary-adrenal axis response in young and adult rats. *Journal of Neuroendocrinology, 6*, 341–345.

Hirsch, H. V. B. & Spinelli, D. N. (1970). Visual experience modifies distribution of horizontally and vertically oriented receptive fields in cats. *Science, 168*, 869–871.

Holloway, R. L. (1966). Dendritic branching: Some preliminary results of training and complexity in rat visual cortex. *Brain Research, 2*, 393–396.

Horn, G. (1986). Imprinting, learning, and memory. *Behavioral Neuroscience, 100*, 825–832.

Hubel, D. H., & Wiesel, T. N. (1970). The period of susceptibility to the physiological effects of unilateral eye closure in kittens. *Journal of Physiology* (London), *206*, 419–436.

Huttenlocher, P. R. (1979). Synaptic density in human frontal cortex—developmental changes and effects of aging. *Brain Research, 163*, 195–205.

Huttenlocher, P. R. (1994). Synaptogenesis, synapse elimination, and neural plasticity in human cerebral cortex. In C. A. Nelson (Ed.), Threats to optimal development: Integrating biological, psychological, and social risk factors. *Minnesota Symposia on Child Psychology* (Vol. 27, pp. 35–54). Hillsdale, NJ: Lawrence Erlbaum.

Huttenlocher, P. R. & de Courten, C. (1987). The development of synapses in striate cortex of man. *Human Neurobiology, 6*, 1–9.

Huttenlocher, J., Haight, W., Bryk, A., Seltzer, M., & Lyons, T. (1991). Early vocabulary growth: Relation to language input and gender. *Developmental Psychology, 27*, 236–248.

Ikemoto, S., & Panksepp, J. (1992). The effects of early social isolation on the motivation for social play in juvenile rats. *Developmental Psychobiology, 25*, 261–274.

Jones, T. A., Kleim, J. A., & Greenough, W. T. (1996). Synaptogenesis and dendritic growth in the cortex opposite unilateral sensorimotor cortex damage in adult rats: A quantitative electron microscopic examination, *Brain Research, 733,* 142–148.

Jones, T. A., & Schallert, T. (1992). Overgrowth and pruning of dendrites in adult rats recovering from neocortical damage, *Brain Research, 581,* 156–160.

Jones, T. A., & Schallert, T. (1994). Use-dependent growth of pyramidal neurons after neocortical damage. *Journal of Neuroscience, 14,* 2140–2152.

Juraska, J. M. (1984). Sex differences in dendritic response to differential experience in the rat visual cortex. *Brain Research, 295,* 27–34.

Juraska, J. M., Greenough, W. T., Elliott, C., Mack, K. J., & Berkowitz, R. (1980). Plasticity in adult rat visual cortex: An examination of several cell populations after differential rearing. *Behavioral and Neural Biology, 29,* 157–167.

Juraska, J. M., Henderson, C., & Muller, J. (1984). Differential rearing experience, gender, and radial maze performance. *Developmental Psychobiology, 17,* 209–215.

Karni, A., Meyer, G., Jezzard, P., Adams, M. M., Turner, R., & Ungerleider, L. G. (1995). Functional MRI evidence for adult motor cortex plasticity during motor skill learning. *Nature, 377,* 155–1588.

Kempermann, G., Kuhn, H. G., & Gage, F. H. (1997). More hippocampal neurons in adult mice living in an enriched environment. *Nature, 386,* 483–485.

Kerby, D. S., & Dawson, B. L. (1994). Autistic features, personality, and adaptive behavior in males with the fragile X syndrome and no autism. *American Journal of Mental Retardation, 9,* 455–462.

Kingston, S. G., & Hoffman-Goetz, L. (1996). Effect of environmental enrichment and housing density on immune system reactivity to acute exercise stress. *Physiology and Behavior, 60,* 145–150.

Kleim, J. A., Swain, R. A., Czerlanis, C. M., Kelly, J. L., Pipitone, M. A., & Greenough, W. T. (1997). Learning-dependent dendritic hypertrophy of cerebellar stellate cells: Plasticity of local circuit neurons. *Neurobiology of Learning and Memory, 67,* 29–33.

Klintsova, A. Y., Matthews, J. T., Goodlett, C. R., Napper, R. M. A., & Greenough, W. T. *Therapeutic motor training increases parallel fiber synapse number per Purkinje neuron in cerebellar cortex of rats given postnatal binge alcohol exposure.* (Manuscript submitted for publication.)

Kolb, B., & Gibb, R. (1991). Environmental enrichment and cortical injury: behavioral and anatomical consequences of frontal cortex lesions. *Cerebral Cortex, 1,* 189–198.

Korte, M., & Rauschecker, J. P. (1993). Auditory spatial tuning of cortical neurons is sharpened in cats with early blindness. *Journal of Neurophysiology, 70,* 1717–1721.

Kozlowski, D. A., James, D. C., & Schallert, T. (1996). Use-dependent exaggeration of neuronal injury after unilateral sensorimotor cortex lesions. *Journal of Neuroscience, 16,* 4776–4786.

Kuhl, P. K. (1994). Innate predispositions and the effects of experience in speech perception, the native language magnet theory. In B. de Boysson-Bardies, S. de Schonen, P. Juscyzyk, P. McNeilage, & J. Morton (Eds.), *Developmental neurocognition: Speech and face processing in the first year of life.* Dordrecht, NL. 132–151. Kluwer Academic.

LeVay, S., Wiesel, T. N., & Hubel, D. H. (1980). The development of ocular dominance columns in normal and visually deprived monkeys. *Journal of Comparative Neurology, 191,* 1–51.

Levine, S. (1956). A further study of infantile handling and adult avoidance conditioning. *Journal of Personality, 25,* 70–80.

Locke, J. L. (1992). Thirty years of research on developmental neurolinguistics. *Pediatric Neurology, 8,* 245–250.

Marchand, A. R., Cremieux, J., & Amblard, B. (1990). Early sensory determinants of locomotor speed in adult cats: II. Effects of strobe rearing on vestibular functions. *Behavioral Brain Research, 37,* 227–235.

Martin, L. J., Spicer, D. M., Lewis, M. H., Gluck, J. P., & Cork, L. C. (1991). Social deprivation of infant rhesus monkeys alters the chemoarchitecture of the brain: I. Subcortical regions. *Journal of Neuroscience, 11,* 3344–3358.

McEachin, J. J., Smith, T., & Lovaas, O. I. (1993). Long-term outcome for children with autism who received early intensive behavioral treatment. *American Journal of Mental Retardation, 97,* 359–372.

Meaney, M. J., & Aitken, D. H. (1985). The effects of early postnatal handling on hippocampal glucocorticoid receptor concentrations: temporal parameters. *Brain Research, 354,* 301–304.

Meaney, M. J., Aitken, D. H., Viau, V., Sharma, S., & Sarrieau, A. (1989). Neonatal handling alters adrenocortical negative feedback sensitivity and hippocampal type II glucocorticoid receptor binding in the rat. *Neuroendocrinology, 50,* 597–604.

Merzenich, M. M., Jenkins, W. M., Johnston, P., Schreiner, C., Miller, S. L., & Tallal, P. (1996). Temporal processing deficits of language-learning impaired children ameliorated by training. *Science, 271,* 77–81.

Michalski, A., & Wrobel, A. (1994). Correlated activity of lateral geniculate neurones in binocularly deprived cats. *Acta Neurobiologica Experimenta, 54,* 3–10.

Milner, R. J., & Sutcliffe, J. G. (1983). Gene expression in the rat brain. *Nucleic Acids Research, 11,* 5497–5520.

Morgan, S., Huston, J. P., & Pritzel, M. (1983). Effects of reducing sensory-motor feedback on the appearance of crossed nigro-thalamic projections and recovery from turning induced by unilateral substantia nigra lesions. *Brain Research Bulletin, 11,* 721–727.

Mower, G. D., Caplan, C. J., Christen, W. G., & Duffy, F. H. (1985). Dark rearing prolongs physiological but not anatomical plasticity of the cat visual cortex. *Journal of Comparative Neurology, 235,* 448–466.

Nudo, R. J., Wise, B. M., SiFuentes, F., & Milliken,

G. W. (1996). Neural substrates for the effects of rehabilitative training on motor recovery after ischemic infarct. *Science, 272,* 1791–1794.

Olson, C. R., & Freeman, R. D. (1978). Monocular deprivation and recovery during sensitive period in kittens. *Journal of Neurophysiology, 41,* 65–74.

Patel, S. N., Rose, S. P., & Stewart, M. G. (1988). Training induced dendritic spine density changes are specifically related to memory formation processes in the chick, Gallus domesticus. *Brain Research, 463,* 168–173.

Pettigrew, J. D., & Freeman, R. D. (1973). Visual experience without lines: effect on developing cortical neurons. *Science, 182,* 599–601.

Poltyrev, T., Keshet, G. I., Kay, G., & Weinstock, M. (1996). Role of experimental conditions in determining differences in exploratory behavior of prenatally stressed rats. *Developmental Psychobiology, 29,* 453–462.

Pons, T. P., Garraghty, P. E., Ommaya, A. K., Kaas, J. H., Taub, E., & Mishkin, M. (1991). Massive cortical reorganization after sensory deafferentation in adult macaques. *Science, 252,* 1857–1860.

Post, R. M. (1992). Transduction of psychosocial stress into the neurobiology of recurrent affective disorder. *American Journal of Psychiatry, 149,* 999–1010.

Pritzel, M., & Huston, J. P. (1981). Neural and behavioral plasticity: crossed nigro-thalamic projections following unilateral substantia nigra lesions. *Behavioral Brain Research, 3,* 393–399.

Pritzel, M., Huston, J. P., & Sarter, M. (1983). Behavioral and neuronal reorganization after unilateral substantia nigra lesions: evidence for increased interhemispheric nigrostriatal projections. *Neuroscience, 9,* 879–888.

Pysh, J. J., & Weiss, M. (1979). Exercise during development induces an increase in Purkinje cell dendritic tree size. *Science, 206,* 230–232.

Quartz, S. R. & Sejnowski, T. J. (in press). The neural basis of cognitive development: a constructivist manifesto. *Behavioral and Brain Sciences.*

Ravizza, R. J. & Herschberger, A. C. (1966). The effects of prolonged motor restriction upon later behavior of the rat. *Psychological Record, 16,* 73–80.

Ramachandran, V. S., Rogers-Ramachandran, D., & Stewart, M. (1992). Perceptual correlates of massive cortical reorganization. *Science, 258,* 1159–1160.

Riesen, A. H. (1965). Effects of visual deprivation on perceptual function and the neural substrate. In J. DeAjuriaguerra (Ed.), *Symposium bel air II, desafferentation experimentale et Clinique* (pp. 47–66). Geneva: George & Cie.

Rose, F. D., al-Khamees, K., Davey, M. J., & Attree, E. A. (1993). Environmental enrichment following brain damage: An aid to recovery or compensation? *Behavioral Brain Research, 56,* 93–100.

Rothblat, L. A., & Schwartz, M. L. (1979). The effect of monocular deprivation on dendritic spines in visual cortex of young and adult albino rats: Evidence for a sensitive period. *Brain Research, 161,* 156–161.

Ryugo, D. K., Ryugo, R., Globus, A., & Killackey, H. P. (1975). Increased spine density in auditory cortex following visual or somatic deafferentation. *Brain Research, 90,* 143–146.

Sackett, G. P. (1972). Prospects for research on schizophrenia. 3. Neurophysiology. Isolation-rearing in primates. *Neuroscience Research Program Bulletin, 10,* 388–392.

Sackett, G. P. (1984). A nonhuman primate model of risk for deviant development. *American Journal of Mental Deficiency, 88,* 469–476.

Schneider, M. L. (1992). The effect of mild stress during pregnancy on birthweight and neuromotor maturation in Rhesus monkey infants (Macaca mulatta). *Infant Behavior and Development, 15,* 389–403.

Schrott, L. M., Denenberg, V. H., Sherman, G. F., Waters, N. S., Rosen, G. D., & Galaburda, A. M. (1992). Environmental enrichment, neocortical ectopias, and behavior in the autoimmune NZB mouse. *Brain Research and Development, 67,* 85–93.

Shatz, C. J. (1990). Impulse activity and the patterning of connections during CNS development. *Neuron, 5,* 745–756.

Sherman, G. F., Galaburda, A. M., Behan, P. O., & Rosen, G. D. (1987). Neuroanatomical anomalies in autoimmune mice. *Acta Neuropathologica* (Berlin), *74,* 239–242.

Sirevaag, A. M., & Greenough, W. T. (1985). Differential rearing effects on rat visual cortex synapses. II. Synaptic morphometry. *Developmental Brain Research, 19,* 215–226.

Smith, P. K. (1982). Does play matter? Functional and evolutionary aspects of animal and human play. *Behavioral and Brain Sciences, 5,* 139–184.

Smith, T., Klevstrand, M., & Lovaas, O. I. (1995). Behavioral treatment of Rett's disorder: Ineffectiveness in three cases. *American Journal of Mental Retardation, 100,* 317–322.

Sobesky, W. E., Hull, C. E., & Hagerman, R. J. (1994). Symptoms of schizotypal personality disorder in fragile X females. *Journal of the American Academy of Child and Adolescent Psychiatry, 33,* 247–255.

Stein, D. G., Finger, S., & Hart, T. (1983). Brain damage and recovery: Problems and perspectives. *Behavioral and Neural Biology, 37,* 185–222.

Struble, R. G., & Riesen, A. H. (1978). Changes in cortical dendritic branching subsequent to partial social isolation in stumptailed monkeys. *Developmental Psychobiology, 11,* 479–486.

Swain, R. A., Bendre, A. A., Wheeler, B. C., & Greenough, W. T. *Augmentation of parallel fibre to Purkinje cell transmission following complex motor learning but not motor activity.* (Manuscript submitted for publication.)

Swindale, N. V. (1988). Role of visual experience in promoting segregation of eye dominance patches in the visual cortex of the cat. *Journal of Comparative Neurology, 267,* 472–488.

Symons, L. A. & Tees, R. C. (1990). An examination of the intramodal and intermodal behavioral consequences of long-term vibrissae removal in rats. *Developmental Psychobiology, 23,* 849–867.

Takahashi, L. K., Baker, E. W., & Kalin, N. H. (1990). Ontogeny of behavioral and hormonal responses to stress in prenatally stressed male rat pups. *Physiology and Behavior, 47,* 357–364.

Takahashi, L. K., Haglin, C., & Kalin, N. H. (1992). Prenatal stress potentiates stress-induced behavior and reduces the propensity to play in juvenile rats. *Physiology and Behavior, 51,* 319–323.

Thelen, E., & Smith, A. (1995). *A dynamic systems approach to the development of cognition and action.* Cambridge, MA: MIT Press.

Thinus-Blanc, C. (1981). Volume discrimination learning in golden hamsters: Effects of the structure of complex rearing cages. *Developmental Psychobiology, 14,* 397–403.

Tieman, S. B., & Hirsch, H. V. B. (1982). Exposure to lines of only one orientation modifies dendritic morphology of cells in the visual cortex of the cat. *Journal of Comparative Neurology, 211,* 353–362.

Turkewitz, G., Gilbert, M., & Birch, H. G. (1974). Early restriction of tactile stimulation and visual functioning in the kitten. *Developmental Psychobiology, 7,* 243–248.

Turkewitz, G., & Kenny, P. A. (1982). Limitations on input as a basis for neural organization and perceptual development: a preliminary theoretical statement. *Developmental Psychobiology, 15,* 357–368.

Turner, A. M. & Greenough, W. T. (1983). Synapses per neuron and synaptic dimensions in occipital cortex of rats reared in complex, social, or isolation housing. *Acta Stereologica, 2* (Suppl. I), 239–244.

Turner, A. M., & Greenough, W. T. (1985). Differential rearing effects on rat visual cortex synapses. I. Synaptic and neuronal density and synapses per neuron. *Brain Research, 329,* 195–203.

Valverde, F. (1971). Rate and extent of recovery from dark rearing in the mouse. *Brain Research, 33,* 1–11.

Waddington, C. H. (1971). Concepts of development. In E. Tobach, L. R. Aronson, E. Shaw (Eds.), *The biopsychology of development* (pp. 17–23). New York: Academic Press.

Walk, R. D., & Gibson, E. J. (1961). A comparative and analytical study of visual depth perception. *Psychological Monographs, 75* (15).

Wallace, C. S., Kilman, V. L., Withers, G. S., & Greenough, W. T. (1992). Increases in dendritic length in occipital cortex after four days of differential housing in weanling rats. *Behavioral and Neural Biology, 58,* 64–68.

Ward, I. L. (1984). The prenatal stress syndrome: current status. *Psychoneuroendocrinology, 9,* 3–11.

Ward, I. L., & Weisz, J. (1984). Differential effects of maternal stress on circulating levels of corticosterone, progesterone, and testosterone in male and female rat fetuses and their mothers. *Endocrinology, 114,* 1635–1644.

Weiler, I. J., Irwin, S. A., Klintsova, A. Y., Spencer, C. M., Brazelton, A. D., Miyashiro, K., Comery, T. A., Patel, B., Eberwine, J. & Greenough, W. T. (in press). Fragile-X mental retardation protein is translated near synapses in response to neurotransmitter activation. *Proceedings of the National Academy of Sciences, 94,* 5395–5400.

Weinberger, N. M. (1995). Dynamic regulation of receptive fields and maps in the adult sensory cortex. *Annual Review of Neuroscience, 18,* 129–158.

Whishaw, I. Q., Zaborowski, J. A., & Kolb, B. (1984). Postsurgical enrichment aids adult hemidecorticate rats on a spatial navigation task. *Behavioral and Neural Biology, 42,* 183–190.

Wiesel, T. N., & Hubel, D. H. (1965). Comparison of the effects of unilateral and bilateral eye closure on cortical unit responses in kittens. *Journal of Neurophysiology, 28,* 1029–1040.

Withers, G. S., & Greenough, W. T. (1989). Reach training selectively alters dendritic branching in subpopulations of layer II–III pyramids in rat motor-somatosensory forelimb cortex. *Neuropsychologia, 27,* 61–69.

Woolsey, T., & van der Loos, H. (1970). The structural organization of Layer IV (SI) of the mouse cerebral cortex: The description of a cortical field composed of discrete cytoarchitectonic units. *Brain Research, 17,* 205–242.

Yehuda, R., Kahana, B., Binder-Brynes, K., Southwick, S. M., Mason, J. W., & Giller, E. L. (1995). Low urinary cortisol excretion in Holocaust survivors with posttraumatic stress disorder. *American Journal of Psychiatry, 152,* 982–986.

Zablocka, T., & Zernicki, B. (1990). Partition between stimuli slows down greatly discrimination learning in binocularly deprived cats. *Behavioral Brain Research, 36,* 13–19.

3 / The Genetics of Childhood Psychiatric Disorders

Linmarie Sikich, Paul J. Lombroso, and James F. Leckman

Understanding how we develop has been a major question throughout history. Much of the more recent work has been built on observational studies of normal and abnormal development. Over the past century researchers have extended their efforts into studies of the development of the brain. There has been an exponential increase in our understanding of many of the fundamental processes involved in neurodevelopment as a consequence of the development of molecular biological techniques. However, directly relating much of this work in developmental neurobiology to human development has been difficult. Knowledge of the underlying genetic mechanisms involved in specific developmental psychiatric disorders has tremendous potential to bridge the gap between more basic studies and our understanding of human development. This chapter reviews the mechanisms by which genes may cause disorders, the research strategies that are utilized in psychiatric genetics, and our current understanding of the genetic contribution to a number of childhood psychiatric disorders.

There are many reasons to be optimistic that our understanding of genetic factors that contribute to childhood psychiatric disorders will improve greatly over the next several years. Many psychiatric disorders affecting children and adolescents have been observed to run in families. Without doubt, these disorders are complex and subject to numerous interacting influences, many of which are not genetic. However, for most of these illnesses, it is also clear that genetic factors play a significant role. Identifying the specific genes involved in the transmission and expression of particular disorders will play a crucial role in our understanding of the normal function of those genes in central nervous system development. The tremendous advances in molecular genetic techniques and in genetic modeling over the past decade have made identification of such genes a real possibility. These techniques already have been used to identify the genes involved in a number of Mendelian disorders, including cystic fi-brosis, muscular dystrophy, Huntington's disease and fragile X syndrome, despite the fact that each of these disorders has considerable phenotypic variability (Online Mendelian Inheritance in Man, 1997). Significant progress has been made in understanding the functional role of these identified genes and has laid the groundwork for a more thorough analysis of relevant gene-environment interactions.

Although many had disparaged the likelihood of identifying genes involved in relatively common disorders with complex, polygenic inheritance patterns, substantial progress has been made recently in one such disorder, diabetes mellitus. Despite the fact that insulin-dependent diabetes mellitus has only modest heritability and is influenced by multiple genetic and environmental factors, a genome-wide screening of affected sibling pairs identified several genes that influence its development (Davies et al., 1994; Hashimoto et al., 1994). Subsequent animal models of diabetes have been used with great advantage to elaborate upon the human genetic studies. In this case the observation that identical mutations of the *NOD1* gene led to diabetes only in select strains of mice despite identical environments led to the search for additional diabetes-associated genes. Backcrosses between sensitive strains and resistant strains provided important information about which additional genes were likely to be involved (Risch, Ghosh, & Todd, 1993). Similar research strategies offer tremendous potential for identifying the genetic factors involved in childhood psychiatric disorders. Thomson (1994) and Lander and Schork (1994) discuss such methods further. Rutter (1997) explicitly discusses the relevance of such methods for child psychiatry.

In addition to increasing our understanding of human development, knowledge of the genetic mechanisms influencing childhood psychiatric disorders will have important consequences for the diagnosis and treatment of such disorders. The identification of specific genes has improved our ability to determine carrier status and to make prenatal diagnoses. In addition, knowledge of the different genetic mechanisms underlying a particular syndrome will facilitate the development of more specific and effective treatments. In such cases, DNA analyses will have the potential to distinguish between phenocopies of a disorder and thereby to help physicians choose the most appropriate treatment for a specific individual. Accurately identifying children at risk for a given disorder will allow more precise evaluation of various interventions and thus improve their efficacy.

Gene Structure and Function

Genetic information resides in each individual's DNA, which is organized into 22 pairs of chromosomes and the 2 sex chromosomes. Normally each parent contributes 1 complete set of chromosomes. It is estimated that the human genome contains 100,000 genes, which are the sequences of DNA that code for proteins. In addition, DNA contains a large number of regions that do not code for proteins. A minority of these regions clearly are involved in regulating the transcription of DNA to RNA and in the posttranscriptional modifications of RNA. However, we do not yet understand the function of most of these noncoding DNA sequences even though many of them have been highly conserved over the course of evolution. A single gene may be made up of several coding regions, termed *exons,* separated by noncoding regions, or *introns.*

There are 2 copies of most genes, 1 from each parent. The exception to this is genes on the sex chromosomes, where there usually is only 1 copy. Often the 2 copies of the gene will differ somewhat in their DNA sequence; different forms of a gene are known as *alleles.* Each allele of the gene is distinguished by its own unique DNA sequence, which arises from changes—*mutations*—in the DNA sequence of the ancestral gene. Often the different alleles of a gene will produce identical proteins because the mutation has not changed the protein's amino acid sequence. Such changes are known as *silent mutations.* They are responsible for many of the genetic polymorphisms observed in normal populations. In other cases, the alleles produce proteins that can-

not be distinguished functionally, as the altered amino acids are very similar in structure. Such changes are called *conservative.* Infrequently, different alleles lead to changes in a critical amino acid within the protein and have significant functional effects. These mutations often result in illness. Similarly, mutations in the noncoding regions of DNA may have no functional significance or may have clinical consequences if the mutation affects the expression of a nearby gene or the way in which different exons within a gene are spliced together.

Changes in the expression and/or function of the protein may occur at several levels. At one extreme are *null mutations,* which completely prevent the intact protein from being made. In the middle are mutations leading to normal amounts of a protein that, however, functions abnormally. At the other extreme are mutations that result in the overproduction of the protein. Furthermore, in some cases the amount of protein expressed is normal, but occurs in the wrong tissues or during inappropriate developmental periods. *Loss-of-function mutations* result in a decrease in the functional activity of the protein; *gain-of-function mutations* lead to an increase in the protein's functional activity.

In certain situations, 1 of the 2 copies of each gene will be inactivated or differentially expressed. Normally this happens with the entire X chromosome in girls. It also has been shown to happen with individual genes in which either the maternally or paternally donated gene is inactivated in a process known as *imprinting.* In diseases involving imprinted genes, mutations (and chromosomal abnormalities) will have an effect only if they occur within the gene that is expressed.

Genetic Influences on Disease

Genes mechanistically influence the development of illnesses in 2 main ways. Rarely, genes code for a protein whose malfunction leads to the disease. Such disorders are referred to as *Mendelian.* More often, genes act indirectly to increase an individual's susceptibility to a disorder. This increased susceptibility is influenced by wide-ranging environmental influences, including interpersonal experiences, exogenous toxins, dietary factors, or even other disease-associated gene products. Genetic disorders caused in this way are referred to as *complex.*

Mendelian disorders involve a functionally significant alteration in a single specific protein. In *autosomal dominant disorders,* a single copy of the disease-associated allele inherited from 1 parent is sufficient to cause the disorder. In such cases, the mutated protein has a *direct negative effect,* or interacts with the other form of the protein to prevent it from functioning normally. Achondroplasia is an example of such a disorder in which mutation of the fibroblast growth factor receptor-3 gene (*FGFR3*) leads to a single amino acid change in the receptor that dramatically interferes with the proliferative ability of long bone growth cartilage despite the fact that half of the FGFR3 protein is normal (Rousseau et al., 1994; Shiang et al., 1994). In *sex-linked disorders,* usually only a single copy of the mutated gene is necessary because there is no corresponding gene on the other chromosome. The mutation in this case may have either a direct negative effect or a loss-of-function effect. In *autosomal recessive disorders,* both alleles must have a disease-associated mutation to produce the disorder. In these disorders, half of the amount of normal protein is sufficient to prevent disease, and the abnormal protein does not have a direct negative effect. For example, in Tay-Sachs disease, homozygous individuals have almost no activity of hexosaminidase A. In contrast, heterozygous individuals have half the normal level of enzymatic activity. The illness becomes apparent only in homozygotes after toxic metabolites build up due to inactivity of hexosaminidase A.

For most disorders, there is a certain degree of heterogeneity. *Genetic heterogeneity* exists when very similar clinical pictures are produced by mutation in different genes. For example, phenylketonuria can be caused by mutations in any of the enzymes or cofactors involved in the metabolism of phenylalanine to phenylpyruvic acid or phenylethylamine (Behrman, 1992; McKusick, 1994). Similarly, Pfeiffer syndrome, which is characterized by premature fusion of specific cranial sutures, widely spaced eyes, and short, broad thumbs and great toes, has been linked both to

mutations in the Fibroblast Growth Factor Receptor 1 (FGFR1) gene and, in different individuals, the Fibroblast Growth Factor Receptor 2 (FGFR2) gene (Muenke et al., 1994; Rutland et al., 1995). *Allelic heterogeneity* occurs when different mutations of the same gene are associated with a single disorder. Five different mutations of the FGFR2 gene have been identified in patients with Pfeiffer syndrome. *Phenotypic heterogeneity* occurs when mutations in a single gene lead to distinct clinical presentations. Often these differences result from mutations within varying regions of the protein that lead to different alterations in the protein's function. For example, mutations of the *CFTR* gene, which prematurely truncate the protein, are associated with severe lung and pancreatic dysfunction whereas those that involve substituting 1 charged amino acid for another often result only in lung dysfunction. A more extreme and intriguing example is provided by the craniofacial syndromes, where identical mutations in the *FGFR2* gene can result either in Pfeiffer syndrome or Crouzon syndrome, which is not associated with limb abnormalities but does lead to abnormalities of the jaw (Mulvihill, 1995). It seems likely that the different symptomatic consequences in such cases result from the differences in both the genetic and nongenetic environment of the different individuals.

As our understanding increases, it has become increasingly clear that disorders directly caused by a mutation in a single gene are extremely rare. Most disorders have complex genetic influences in which specific genes modulate an individual's susceptibility to a particular disorder. In such cases a person with the disease-associated form of the gene is much more likely to develop the disease than someone without it, given the same environmental exposures. However, in the absence of exposure to the appropriate environmental factors, the person with the disease-associated allele would not develop the disorder. The failure of all persons with the disease-associated gene to develop the disease is called *incomplete penetrance.* There are also likely to be cases in which an individual who lacks the disease-associated gene develops the disorder as a result of exposure to particularly potent environmental factors resulting in nongenetic forms of the illness called *phenocopies.* For instance, someone with no genetic vulnerability to Parkinson's disease would likely develop the disorder with exposure to the neurotoxin MPTP (1-methyl-4-phenyl-1,2,3,6-tetrahydopyridine) (Singer, Castagnoli, Ramsay, & Trevor, 1987). Disorders are termed *oligogenic* if only a few genes must interact in order to cause them and *polygenic* if the interaction of many genes is required in addition to environmental factors.

Although the heterogeneity of genetic effects makes identifying the genetic basis of any disorder a considerable challenge, additional complications are present in childhood psychiatric disorders. These complications arise both due to the intricate processes of development and to the problems of accurate diagnosis of these disorders.

Clinical ascertainment provides unique challenges. In most psychiatric disorders, there is usually some continuity between the observed symptoms and normal behavior. All of us have felt sad and discouraged, but we are not all depressed. There also is considerable variability in clinical presentation of different individuals. One person with depression may have difficulty falling asleep while another may wake up frequently through the night. These problems are accentuated in childhood disorders since "normal" behaviors change markedly with time and there is considerable variability in the developmental progress of different individuals. Thus any childhood psychiatric disorder must be defined carefully within the appropriate developmental context. Such normal developmental changes also complicate the assessment of family members. Often individuals will have difficulty accurately recalling behaviors from their past. In addition, manifestations of childhood disorders may be different or lacking altogether in adult relatives as a result of normal developmental processes rather than due to an absence of genetic vulnerability.

Determining the Heritability in a Disorder

In this section, we review the standard research methods used to establish and define the role of genetic factors in particular disorders. Historically, the initial step in this process has been to conduct family studies that can establish whether a given disorder is familial; such studies cannot address questions about the genetic basis of the disorder. Twin and adoption studies are used to determine the relative contribution of genetic factors. Segregation analyses are used to model the mode of genetic transmission.

FAMILY STUDIES

Family studies consist of determining the incidence of a given illness in the biologic relatives of a proband and comparing it to the incidence of the illness in the general population or a control population. They are useful as an initial step in exploring the potential role of genetic factors in a given psychiatric illness, and they are relatively easy to conduct. However, they have 2 major limitations. Most fundamental is their inability to distinguish between familiality, which can arise from genetic, environmental, or combined factors, and heritability. In addition, the results of family studies are always limited by the accuracy with which the illness is diagnosed in individual family members. Accurate ascertainment often is difficult due to problems recalling previous symptoms and illnesses, variabilities in the age of onset, differences in the developmental expression of the disorder, and variability in the phenotypic expression of a given disorder.

Family studies also have been used to determine whether different disorders are etiologically related. Rates of the disorder that is hypothesized to be related are compared in families of probands with only the originally identified disorder and the families of probands with only the second disorder. These studies assume that environmental factors predisposing to the development of the second disorder are greatest in families of probands with that disorder. Consequently, they attribute similarities in rates of the secondary disorder to shared genetic influences. Such family studies have been important in establishing that some forms of obsessive-compulsive disorder are etiologically related to Tourette's disorder (Pauls, Towbin, Leckman, Zahner, & Cohen, 1986). Recent work has also suggested that there may be cotransmission of genetic vulnerability to alcoholism and bipolar affective disorder (Todd, 1997).

A less rigorous variation of such studies involves comparing the rates of the second disorder in families identified through a proband with the first disorder and in families identified through a proband with a disorder that is hypothesized to be unrelated. This method has been employed to argue that depression and social phobia are genetically related to autism (Smalley et al., 1995).

Studies of blended families provide unique and important opportunities for examining the differential influences of environmental and genetic influences. In this case, all children of the blended family are assumed to be subject to similar environmental factors after the families were integrated while genetic influences differ substantially. Stepchildren of an affected parent share no genetic material with the biologic children. Half siblings would be expected to share on average one-quarter of their genes as compared to full siblings, who share, on average, half their genes. Differences in the rates of the illness in full, half, and step siblings are attributed to genetic differences. Such studies may provide special advantages in the study of childhood psychiatric disorders since they minimize problems of recall and differential developmental expression of different disorders. However, they are likely to underestimate the role of nonshared environmental influences, which might be expected to be especially prominent in blended families. Additionally, the different environments experienced before the family blended must be acknowledged. This may be problematic since early experiences are likely to play a significant role in the development of childhood psychiatric disorders.

TWIN STUDIES

The underlying rationale for twin studies is straightforward. Monozygotic (MZ) twins derive from a single fertilized egg and are genetically identical. Dizygotic (DZ) twins derive from 2 separately fertilized eggs and share approximately half their DNA. A second premise is that twins reared together are subject to very similar environmental events (in contrast to siblings of different ages) and that the extent of environmental similarity is equivalent for MZ and DZ twins. Traditional studies consist of comparing the rates of a given disorder in populations of MZ twins and DZ twins. A finding of significantly higher concor-

dance for the presence of the disorder in the MZ twins argues for genetic susceptibility for developing the disorder.

These analyses can be extended in several ways. The most fundamental extension is to determine quantitatively the magnitude of the genetic effect by accounting for the population prevalence of the disorder; this is the *heritability* h^2 of the disorder (reviewed by LaBuda, Gottesman, & Pauls, 1993). Twin studies finding the same concordance rates have very different heritabilities depending on the population prevalence of the disorder. The heritability of a disorder increases as its population prevalence decreases. For example, the difference in concordance between MZ and DZ twins for reading disability and for bipolar affective disorder are both about 50%; however, the heritability of bipolar disorder is about 80% in contrast to the heritability of reading disorder, which is about 60% because bipolar disorder is 5 to 10 times less prevalent than reading disorder in the general population.

Inferences about both environmental influences and genetic mechanisms also can be drawn from twin studies. The rate of concordance in MZ twins provides information about the other, nonshared environmental factors involved in the disorder. Perfect concordance (100%) between MZ twins would suggest that genes were the sole determinant of the disorder, whereas lower levels of concordance would suggest that environmental factors exert a significant influence on the development of the disorder. Ideally, the individual environmental differences between MZ twins could be analyzed to identify particular protective or noxious factors. For example, there is compelling evidence that perinatal factors play an important role in the severity of expression of Tourette's disorder (Hyde, Aaronson, Randolph, Rickler, & Weinberger, 1992; Leckman, Weissman, Pauls, & Kidd, 1987). The magnitude of various environmental factors can be determined using concordance information from both MZ and DZ twins in computer modeling programs such as LISREL (reviewed by Neale, Heath, Hewitt, Eaves, & Fulker, 1989).

The magnitude of difference in concordance between MZ and DZ pairs also gives some indication of the number of genes involved in the disorder. If a single gene is required to develop the disorder, the DZ rate would be expected to be about half (for an autosomal dominant trait) to one-quarter (for an autosomal recessive trait) the rate in the MZ twins. However, if the rate in DZ twins is much less than the rate in MZ twins, it suggests that more than 1 gene is required to develop the disease.

A variant form of twin study involves analyzing the rates of illness in the offspring of nonconcordant MZ twins. In such cases the subjects are presumed to have the same genetic risk for developing the disorder but quite different environments. Similar rates of illness in the discordant twins' children suggests a strong genetic etiology for the disorder.

In all twin studies it is essential that zygotic status be determined accurately. Both parents' perceptions and subject questionnaires have been shown to have a limited accuracy of 90% (Cederlof, Friberg, & Johnson, 1961; Goldsmith, 1991). Instead blood types and/or DNA typing are generally required to definitively establish the twins status. In addition, it is important to use only same-sex DZ twins in the studies, since many developmental neuropsychiatric disorders have markedly different prevalences in boys and girls, probably as a result of differing microenvironments (e.g., different hormonal exposures during brain development). Finally, most researchers feel that population-based studies are more objective than recruited twin studies, which tend to overrepresent both MZ twins and concordant twins (Lykken, McGue, & Tellegen, 1987).

The main criticism of twin studies arises from the underlying assumption of equivalent environments among MZ and DZ twin pairs. Although several studies have shown that MZ twins may in fact experience a more similar environment than DZ twins with respect to dressing and friendships, these differences are quite small (Morris-Yates, Andrews, Howie, & Henderson, 1990). In addition, some have questioned whether results from twin studies can be generalized. The extent to which this is possible clearly depends on the disorder in question. For example, delays in the development of language appear much more frequent in twins than in the general population, whereas the prevalence of major depression is the same in twins and in the general population. Finally, concerns have been raised that twin studies (particularly of psychiatric disorders) may underestimate genetic influences due to assortative mating.

ADOPTION STUDIES

Adoption studies distinguish between genetic and environmental effects by comparing the rates of psychiatric disorders in biologic and adoptive families. These studies can be done in several ways. The most common is the *adoptees' study method,* which begins by identifying parents with a specific illness who have adopted away their children and a control group of parents without known psychiatric illness whose children also have been adopted away. The rates of a particular illness can then be ascertained among both groups of adopted children. Genetic influences are suggested if the rate in the adopted-away children of ill parents is significantly higher than that of adoptees whose biological parents do not have the illness.

The *adoptees' family method* is based on identifying an adopted individual with a psychiatric illness and comparing the rates of that illness in his or her biologic and adoptive family members. An increased rate of illness in the biologic family suggests genetic influences, while an increased rate in adoptive family members implicates shared environmental influences. This method may be particularly useful in childhood psychiatric disorders, since probands can be identified readily and accurately, but its use is greatly limited by difficulties in identifying the child's biologic parents.

The *cross-fostering* paradigm involves identifying adoptive parents with a specific psychiatric illness and examining the rate of the illness in the children in their care whose biologic parents do not have the illness. The rate of illness in these adoptive children can be compared to biologic children of the ill adoptive parent or population rates for the illness. Environmental factors influencing development of the disorder are suggested by an increase in the rate of illness in the adoptive children. These studies are seldom performed because prospective adoptive parents often are excluded if there is evidence of mental illness. Another seldom-used variant of adoption studies is the study of *monozygotic twins separated* early in life. In these cases, differences of rates in illness between the genetically identical twins reflect differences in their environments that are much larger than for twins reared together (Farber, 1982; Pedersen, Friberg, Floderus-Myrhead, McClearn, & Plomin, 1984).

Adoption studies provide a powerful opportunity for distinguishing between genetic and environmental influences on susceptibility to psychiatric disorders. However, they suffer from a number of significant limitations. Foremost among these is the difficulty in fully assessing psychiatric disorders among the biologic families of adoptees. Very often the biologic father cannot be identified, so his disease status is unknown. Even in cases in which both biologic parents are known, it may be difficult to assess accurately the presence of specific illnesses. This is an especially prominent issue in studying childhood psychiatric illnesses since retrospective evaluations of symptoms have proven difficult. Studies also have shown that adoptees (regardless of their biologic risks) have a greater incidence of psychiatric disorders, which may result in underestimates of genetic influences in the adoptees' study method. Similarly, increasing efforts to choose adoptive families with similar characteristics to biologic families may lead to underestimates of both genetic and environmental influences.

SEGREGATION ANALYSES

In instances where genetic factors have been strongly implicated, analyses of the pattern of ill individuals in large families with multiple affected members can provide a great deal of information. The simplest case of this occurs when the observed pattern unequivocally matches a known Mendelian pattern. For example, approximately half of the members of each generation should be affected in an autosomal dominant disorder, while approximately a quarter should be affected in an autosomal recessive disorder. Such a result strongly suggests a single gene etiology. The involvement of multiple genes is suggested when there is a greater than fourfold decrease in the incidence of an illness from the first to the second generation, since on average successive generations share one-half to one-quarter of the relevant genes.

Segregation analyses provide a sensitive and sophisticated mechanism for mathematically assessing patterns of genetic transmission. These analyses statistically compare the observed family pattern with computer-generated patterns of genetic transmission based on hypothesized parameters. This allows researchers to test different models about the prevalence, penetrance, age of onset, dominance state, and/or number of genes involved in the development of the given disease. They are particularly useful in examining complex forms of inheritance, such as those observed in most psychiatric disorders. Most important, they provide a powerful means of rejecting specific forms of genetic transmission. However, they cannot unequivocally establish that disease susceptibility is transmitted in the hypothesized way. Indeed, because it is possible to test so many different models (which may have little empirical basis), there is a substantial risk of false positives.

Gene Mapping: Locating Genes Involved in Particular Disorders

In this section we discuss the techniques available for identifying the specific gene or genes involved in a specific disorder. Over the past 10 years tremendous progress has been made in this arena. Technological advances in genetic modeling, in the identification of genetic polymorphisms throughout the genome, and in recombinant DNA have revolutionized the field. More than 400 illnesses have been genetically mapped. Unfortunately, no psychiatric disorders are unequivocally included. In order to prove that a specific gene is etiologically related to a given disorder, the following conditions must be met. First, transmission of the illness must correlate statistically with transmission of specific genetic alleles in a subset of families with the disorder. Second, the disease-associated allele must be functionally different from the non–disease-associated allele. Finally, manipulation of the disease-associated gene in a model system (e.g., knock-out mice) should lead to physiologic abnormalities typical of the disorder.

Three methods have been developed to correlate the transmission of specific genes and a given disorder: association studies, linkage analysis, and allele-sharing studies. In *association* or *case-control studies,* the frequency of a given genetic allele is examined in a group of individuals with the illness and in an unaffected control group. In *linkage analysis,* familial patterns of the inheritance of specific alleles and of the illness are compared. *Allele-sharing methods* determine whether particular alleles are shared consistently by relatives affected by the illness. (Please see Lander and Schork, 1994, for a comprehensive review of these methods.) Each method requires that an identified gene has at least 2 polymorphic variants. In addition, each method becomes increasingly sensitive with increasing allelic variability. The utility of all of the methods has been enhanced dramatically by the identification of a large number of highly polymorphic areas of DNA known as variable nucleotide tandem repeats (VNTRs). Many of these VNTRs and a large number of genes have been physically mapped to the human genome and can serve as genetic markers. Usually these methods identify a linked genetic region. Single associated genes can then be identified by repeating these studies using increasingly dense markers or by positional cloning of the intervening region. Each of these methods has its own advantages and disadvantages. However, like the family, twin, and adoption methods used to study heritability, they can be particularly powerful when used in concert.

ASSOCIATION STUDIES

Association studies are performed simply by comparing the frequency of different allelic forms of a gene in a defined patient population and a "control" population. A statistical difference in the allelic distribution between the 2 groups ideally suggests that the identified gene is involved in disease susceptibility or expression. However, positive associations may be found in 2 other cases. It is quite possible that the identified gene is simply a marker for the truly relevant gene; because the 2 genes are in close physical proximity, they are cotransmitted. In this case, association yields useful information that can be investigated further. Positive association may be completely spurious if there is a systematic difference between the patient group and the control group that is not etiologically related to the disease. Such differences often are found when the ethnicity of the 2 groups is not precisely matched. For instance, the association between specific *DRD2* alleles and alcoholism initially reported by Blum et al. (1990) appears to have resulted from ethnic differences in the control group (Gelertner, Goldman, & Risch, 1993). Adequate controls for subtle differences in ethnicity are almost impossible unless one studies an extremely isolated population that is completely free of interbreeding with other populations.

Fortunately, the haplotype relative risk strategy initially developed by Falk and Rubenstein (1987) can overcome the problem of adequate controls. In this method, the alleles of each patient's parents serve as the control population and provide precise ethnic matches. Haplotype relative risk strategies are now the accepted standard for association studies. Positive results from association studies can be substantiated fairly easily using the transmission disequilibrium test (TDT) in an independent sample from the same population (Hodge, 1993; Spielman et al., 1993). In the TDT, only patients whose parents are heterozygous for the gene being studied are used, and the question asked is whether the "associated" allele is transmitted more often.

Frequently, association studies are the initial step in trying to characterize the molecular basis of disorders because (1) they generally study candidate genes whose functional relationship to the disorder is fairly clear, (2) it is relatively easy to recruit and identify subjects, and (3) fewer overall subjects are necessary (Risch & Merikangas, 1996; Gelernter & Crowe, 1997). Association studies played a key role in establishing the link between the Apo protein E4 allele and some forms of Alzheimer's disease (Schader et al., 1994; Singer et al., 1992). Often association studies are particularly helpful in identifying genes of relatively small effect. Their chief disadvantage is the high likelihood of spurious results if a heterogeneous population is studied without using appropriate controls for ethnic admixture. This difficulty can best be overcome by using the haplotype relative risk method. In addition, they have less statistical power than linkage studies which correctly specify the model of genetic inheritance do.

LINKAGE STUDIES

Linkage analysis asks whether an illness is transmitted with an identified polymorphic genetic marker whose genomic location is known. Formally, the likelihood that the marker and disease-associated gene are transmitted together according to a specified model of transmission (probability of M_1) and the likelihood that recombination between the genetic marker and the unknown disease-associated gene occurs randomly (probability of M_0) are compared. *Recombination* between homologous portions of each pair of chromosomes during meiosis results in changes in the sequence of specific alleles between a parent's chromosome and the offspring's chromosome. Such recombination usually occurs over a relatively large distance and is unlikely to occur between 2 closely spaced or adjacent genes. Genes that are so physically close together that no recombination occurs are said to be *linked.* Different parts of the chromosomes, such as their ends, are more likely to recombine; this leads to more recombination between closely spaced genes than expected on other parts of the chromosome.

Typically, several models of transmission like those used in segregation analysis (e.g., specifying allele frequencies, penetrance, and extent of disease heterogeneity) are tested. The model that produces the maximal likelihood ratio, LR = (probability of M_1)/(probability of M_0), is reported. The statistical significance of linkage is measured by the *lod score,* $Z = \log_{10}LR$. A lod score of 4 would mean that the probability of linkage is 10,000 times greater than that expected by chance. Linkage studies can yield 3 types of results. Linkage will be supported when the genetic marker studied and the gene that actually confers susceptibility to the illness are so physically close to one another on the chromosome that genetic recombination very rarely occurs. Typically this distance is taken to be ~1 centimorgan, or about 1,000 kilobases. A lod score equal to or greater than 3 generally is accepted as evidence of linkage, although many geneticists have questioned whether this level should be increased (to 3.3–4.0), given the large number of markers and genetic models tested. (Lander & Schork, 1994, provide a fuller discussion of this debate.) Results that clearly exclude linkage also can be very helpful. Linkage generally is excluded when the lod score is minus 2 or more. Studies yielding lod scores between 3 and minus 2 are uninformative. However, the power of linkage studies depends on correctly specifying the mode of genetic transmission which generally is unknown.

Initially, linkage studies were utilized in large extended pedigrees that contained many individuals with the disease. In such families, there is a greater likelihood that the illness will indeed be homogeneous. However, often it is difficult to locate such families and to ascertain disease status correctly in all relevant members. It also has been difficult to account for the possibility that someone marrying into the pedigree is bringing his or her own different gene that confers susceptibility to the disorder. This situation is especially likely with relatively common disorders such as depression. In some cases, performing an affecteds-only analysis in which unaffected individuals are counted as having an unknown phenotype has been useful. Accurate ascertainment is a particular problem in studying childhood psychiatric disorders due to problems with recall and differential presentations throughout development. Multiple small nuclear families also may be studied, but doing so inevitably increases the likelihood of disease heterogeneity. Restricting the phenotype studied to the greatest extent possible has been particularly helpful in heterogeneous disorders. For instance, it was extremely helpful to limit breast cancer linkage studies to families with very early onset. Linkage studies also have had difficulty detecting genes of relatively small effect. Methods have evolved to specify increasingly complex genetic models that partially account for disease heterogeneity, for the interaction of multiple genes in the etiology of the illness, and for bilineality, the transmission of the illness from both maternal and paternal stocks. However, correct specification of complex genetic models remains the major limitation of linkage studies.

ALLELE-SHARING STUDIES

Allele-sharing methods determine whether specific alleles are shared more frequently than expected given random Mendelian segregation in pairs of relatives affected by a given illness. (See reviews by Shah & Green, 1994, and Brown, Gorin, & Weeks, 1994.) If a given allele is shared significantly more often than would occur randomly, the assumption is made that it is related to disease susceptibility. The lod score statistic is used to measure significance but generally is required to be somewhat higher (3.6–4.0) than in traditional linkage studies.

Ideally, the genotypes of the parents of the relative pair are available so that the identity by descent (IBD) of specific alleles can be examined. However, methods are available to evaluate alleles that are identical by state (IBS) if genotype information is not available for the previous generation. The most widely used paradigm for allele-sharing studies is known as the *affected sib-pair* method. It involves studying pairs of siblings who are both affected by the illness and can share either no alleles, 1 allele, or 2 alleles at any given loci with a 25%–50%–25% distribution expected with random segregation. If a particular allele is shared more often than 50% of the time, it is assumed to be related to the illness. Significance is measured with a chi square test. Methods also exist for studying other relative pairs (e.g., grandparent, grandchild; first cousins; etc.) and making the appropriate corrections in the random distributions of shared alleles.

These methods differ from association studies in that the presence of a specific allele is compared between 2 affected individuals who are assumed to have the same genetic basis for the illness rather than between affected and nonaffected individuals. In contrast to linkage studies that require the model of inheritance to be specified, no assumptions are made about the mode of genetic transmission in allele-sharing studies. This nonparametric approach greatly increases the likelihood that any genetic locus involved in a complex disorder will be detected, although the level of significance ascribed to the locus may be falsely reduced. Consequently, many geneticists now advocate using allele-sharing methods to scan the entire genome to identify all genes, including those with small effect, that are involved in complex disorders such as psychiatric illnesses. Brown, Gorin and Weeks (1994) have reported an 84% true positive rate scanning the 305 loci spaced across the entire genome in 20 centimorgan intervals with a 2-cut point strategy. The progress made to date on the Human Genome Project makes such screening highly feasible since more than 5,000 markers with an average distance of 0.7 kilobases have been described so far (McKusick et al., 1997). Allele-sharing methods have resulted in the identification of at least 11 genes associated with insulin-dependent diabetes (Davies et al., 1994) and confirmed the relationship suggested by association studies between the Apoprotein E4 allele and late-onset Alzheimer's disease. (Corder 1993).

QUANTITATIVE TRAIT LOCI

Another strategy for identifying candidate genes involves identifying traits that can be measured and exist along a continuum (e.g., weight or blood pressure). Once this has been done, allele-sharing techniques can be used to compare the genetic makeup of groups of individuals at opposite ends of the spectrum. The genes that consistently differ between the 2 groups become candidates. These studies have been used extensively in animal models of illnesses and are then extended into human studies. This strategy has been used to identify the genes likely to be involved in mouse preferences for substances of abuse (Crabbe, Belknap, & Buck, 1994). A similar strategy was used to identify a gene associated with reading disability on chromosome 6 (Cardon et al., 1994).

PHYSICAL MAPPING STRATEGIES

Once the disease has been correlated with a genetic marker, it is necessary to precisely define the specific disease-associated gene (reviewed by Williamson and Wicking, 1991). This process can be extremely time-consuming; for instance, it took 10 years to identify the Huntington gene once chromosomal linkage was established. Usually researchers begin by systematically studying ever more closely spaced markers until the region of maximal linkage is identified. Then overlapping portions of the identified chromosomal region are cloned so that the DNA can be amplified and sequenced in a process known as *positional cloning*. Increased availability of contiguous yeast artificial chromosomes (YACs) has greatly aided this process. Then the resulting DNA sequences are analyzed to identify start-and-stop codons and map the intron and exon boundaries within the gene; in this way the areas coding for proteins are determined.

This process can be shortcut in 3 ways. It may be possible to narrow the region by examining the sites of recombination in affected individuals. Although a single recombination absolutely excludes areas of the linked chromosomal region in single-gene disorders, it is unlikely to be as helpful in complex disorders where not all affected individuals will necessarily possess a gene of small effect. Candidate genes previously identified in the linked region also can be examined. Additional candidate genes may be identified by hybridizing specific genes from other animals (with functions speculated to be relevant to the disease being studied) to the linked region; this is called zoo blotting.

Next, it is necessary to establish whether that identified gene is mutated in affected individuals as compared to unaffected individuals. Several methods exist for mutational analysis (reviewed by Gejman & Gelernter, 1993). These methods allow researchers to determine whether a mutation is present rapidly. However, DNA sequencing of the disease-associated and "normal" alleles is ultimately necessary to confirm and precisely identify mutations.

Chemical and enzymatic *cleavage methods* are based on the reaction of single-stranded nucleic acids with 1 of several chemicals or enzymes. The most promising of these involves hybridizing subject DNA with a synthetic RNA probe containing the normal sequence and exposing the resulting DNA-RNA dimers to *RNase I cleavage;* the enzyme will cut the RNA probe at the site of mutations in the subject DNA because the RNA will not be able to bind to the altered DNA nucleotide(s) (Murthy, Shen, & Banville, 1995). This method can be used to detect mutations in DNA fragments of up to 1,000 base pairs.

Denaturing gradient gel electrophoresis (DGGE) methods are based on the 2 properties of DNA. First, the denaturation of double-stranded DNA is exquisitely dependent on its sequence such that a single base pair change in a gene will alter its melting point. Second, double-stranded DNA becomes immobile under particular electrophoretic gel conditions as soon as it starts to denature. In DGGE, the electrophoretic mobility of DNA from at least 2 individuals is compared. Any differences reflect mutations in 1 of the DNA sequences. DGGE techniques have been shown to have 100% sensitivity (provided a guanidine-cytosine [G-C] clamp is added) in DNA fragments of 500 base pairs or less.

Single-stranded conformational polymorphism (SSCP) techniques rely on the fact that the mobility of single-stranded nucleic acids in particular electrophoretic gels is dependent on their conformation, which is exquisitely dependent on the sequence of the nucleic acid. Mutations in a gene are expected to result in different conformations, which will lead to changes in electrophoretic mo-

bility. SSCP techniques are extremely simple and very widely used. However, they are less sensitive than the other available techniques particularly when nucleic acid fragments greater than 200 base pairs are studied.

FUNCTIONAL RELEVANCE TO DISEASE PATHOPHYSIOLOGY

Finally, it must be established that the mutated gene is involved in the pathophysiology of the illness. The initial step is to determine whether the DNA change results in an amino acid change in the protein. Deletions or insertions will always result in protein changes because they alter the reading frame of the gene, but single base pair substitutions may be silent, leading to no change in the amino acids of the protein. If the mutation results in a protein change, its effect on the functional activity the protein sometimes can be inferred from examining the location(s) of the mutation(s) with respect to the purported functional domains of the protein. For example, a mutation that changes an amino acid in the transmembrane region of an ion channel might well change the activity of the channel and, thus, the electrical potential and reactivity of the cell. The effects of mutations within noncoding regions of the gene may be less obvious. However, they often influence the expression of the protein or splice sites within introns, which then change the protein's composition. For instance, the fragile X mutation in the promoter region of the *FMR1* gene has profound effects on the expression of the protein. If the function of the mutated gene is not known, often it is helpful to demonstrate that it is expressed in areas related to the illness. For example, the FMR1 gene is abundantly expressed in the brain. Similarly, a gene linked to Tourette's disorder might be expected to be expressed in basal ganglia.

The most definitive ways to link a putative gene to a disorder are to study the effects of the mutated genes in experimental systems. Sometimes this can be done in vitro by expressing the mutated and wild-type genes in separate cell lines and comparing the functional activity (e.g., ligand binding or second messenger activity) of the 2 cell lines. However, particularly in developmental disorders, it may be difficult to correlate in vitro findings with specific disorders. In cases where the disease-associated mutation eliminates production of a protein, knockout mice provide a good system for establishing its pathophysiologic consequences. In less extreme cases, it is likely to be necessary to introduce the mutated gene or its resulting protein into an animal and examine its behavior. Transgenic mice provide the best means for studying the developmental consequences of a mutation. Ultimately the findings in animals must be correlated to the human disorder.

Empirical Findings

In this section we review the empirical findings regarding genetic factors in several selected childhood psychiatric disorders. These findings are summarized in Table 3.1. We have chosen disorders in which genetic factors appear to play a significant role, although certainly not an exclusive one. Research in many of these disorders is progressing rapidly, and likely more molecular information will become available in the near future. Further information also may be found in the chapters focusing directly on each disorder.

AUTISM AND OTHER PERVASIVE DEVELOPMENTAL DISORDERS

Autism is a very rare disorder that appears to be etiologically heterogeneous with a population prevalence of 5 to 10 per 10,000. Infrequently it has been found to be associated with a number of well-known genetic disorders, including phenylketonuria, tuberous sclerosis, and neurofibromatosis and with some congenital infections including cytomegalovirus and rubella. There is also a strong association with mental retardation. Approximately 70% of individuals with autism are mentally retarded, and between 4% and 8% of all individuals with mental retardation have autism (Gillberg, Persson, Grufman, & Themner, 1986). There has been a long-standing view that fragile X and autism are etiologically related, with early reports estimating that as many as half of individuals with the fragile X syndrome had autistic symptoms (Hagerman, Jackson, Levitas, Rimland, & Braden, 1986) and that about a fifth of autistic

males possess the fragile X anomaly (Blomquist et al., 1985; Gillberg & Wahlstrom, 1985). More recently, these estimates have fallen dramatically, with fewer than 7% of fragile X males meeting full criteria for autistic disorder (Dykens, Leckman, Paul, & Watson, 1988; Dykens et al., 1989), and less than 5% of autistic males demonstrating the fragile X anomaly (Bailey & Bolton, 1993). These lower estimates have raised questions about the specificity of the relationship between autism and fragile X.

As recently as 1976, people argued that idiopathic autism is not a genetic disorder. However, subsequent analyses that have considered the very low population prevalence of autism have demonstrated that it is one of the most highly heritable childhood neuropsychiatric disorders (reviewed by Bailey et al., 1995; Folstein & Rutter, 1987; Smalley et al., 1988; Smalley, 1997).

Family studies have shown an incidence of autism in siblings of autistic individuals ranging from 2 to 8.6%, which represents a 50- to 200-fold increase in risk from the general population (August, Stewart, & Tsai, 1981; Baird & August, 1985; Folstein & Rutter, 1977; Gillberg, Gillberg, & Steffenburg, 1992; Macdonald, Rutter, Rios, & Bolton, 1989; Ritvo, Jorde, et al., 1989; Rutter et al., 1990). Ritvo's group (1989a) has suggested that the siblings of female autistic probands are at particularly high risk, with rates of 14.5% in their nonpopulation-based sample of recruited families. The results of the family studies are likely to underestimate the true risk to siblings since parents often curtail their childbearing after the birth of an autistic child.

The 5 twin studies done to date have consistently demonstrated a major genetic effect (Bailey et al., 1995; Folstein & Rutter, 1977; LeCouteur, Bailey, Rutter, & Gottesman, 1989; Ritvo et al., 1985; Steffenburg et al., 1989). These studies have found MZ concordance rates ranging from 36% to 89% and DZ concordance rates of 0% in all but the study by Ritvo and colleagues, which found 24% DZ concordance. Many have suggested that this elevated DZ concordance is likely the result of using recruited twin pairs and of including opposite-sex DZ pairs rather than conducting a population-based study and of using same-sex DZ twins. The latter point may be especially problematic if autistic disorders in females are etiologically distinct from those in males as

TABLE 3.1

Genetic Statistics in Childhood Psychiatric Disorders

Disorder	Population Prevalence	Sex Ratio	Prevalence in Relatives			Concordance Rates		Heritability	Mode of Transmission	?Related Disorder	Adoption
			Offspring	Sibs	Parent	MZ%	DZ%	h²%			
Fragile X	0.0005	M>>F	5–7X ?						Sex-linked dominant	Autism	
Autism	0.0005	M>F		50x		36–89 80(B)	0–24 10(B)		Polygenic? Autosomal?	MR, NF, PKU, TS, MDD, Social	
Reading Disability	.05–.10	4M:1F		↑d		67–88	25–30	50–70	Polygenic single gene?		
Attention Deficit Hyperactivity Disorder	00.08 00.02	4M:1F	5X↑ (31.5 vs. 5.7)			62	26	40	Polygenic	MDD, ODD, CD, ASP	Yes
Conduct Disorder	.04–.055	4M:1F				87	72	40–90			Yes
Anorexia	.00006 all 0.22–0.84 in teens	9F>M	3X↑ Anorexia 5–6X↑ any			23–83	5–27	50	Polygenic	Other eating MDD	
Bulimia	.01			2X↑		29	8.7	55	polygenic	MDD anxiety ETOH	

Tourette's Disorder	.0003–.006	9M:1F	20–400X↑	?53%	8%			Single major additive	CMT OCD	
Obsessive Compulsive Disorder	.02–.03		30%	OCD						
Alcoholism	Use: >.10	M>F	?	4X↑	F 90 M 50	F 10 M 50	40–50 ~80F		?ODD, ASP ?MDE	Yes
Schizophrenia	.01 adults .0003 kids	M=F	40X↑ if both	8X↑	55	12	60–70	Polygenic ?gene of major effect	?Bipolar but prof 2° to misdx	Yes
Major Depression	preteen .005–.025 teen .02–.08 Adult .05–.23	Kids M=F >10 F>M	14.2 X↑	2–4X			Kids 40–23 Adol 80 Adults 30–46	Polygenic additive	Alcoholism ?Anxiety	
Bipolar Affective Disorder	.005–.02	M=F	4–10 X↑	7–15 ↑ 4–16 X↑	79	24	80		MDD Anxiety	

this same group has suggested, based on their family studies. The markedly increased concordance rate in MZ twins as compared with DZ twins or other siblings strongly suggests that autism is an oligogenic disorder. In addition, the absence of 100% concordance rates in MZ pairs suggests that environmental factors influence the expression of the disorder. No adoption studies have been undertaken due both to the difficulty in finding adoptive homes for autistic individuals and the exceptionally low likelihood that an autistic individual will reproduce.

Evidence from family and twin studies also has suggested that less severe social and cognitive disabilities may represent alternative forms of the underlying genetic disorder leading to autism. Cognitive abnormalities have been found in 15% of the siblings of autistic individuals as compared with 3 to 4.5% of the siblings of individuals with Down syndrome (August et al., 1981; Macdonald et al., 1989). These differences do not appear to be limited to autistic individuals with mental retardation (Bartak, Rutter, & Cox, 1975; Piven, Gayle, Landa, Wzorek, & Folstein, 1991). Macdonald and colleagues (1989) also found a significant incidence of social abnormalities (12%) in the siblings of autistic individuals but not of Down syndrome individuals (0%). Abnormalities also have been found in the social use of language by the parents of autistic individuals (Wolff, Narayan, & Moyes, 1988).

Several twin studies from England also have strongly supported the concept of a broader diagnostic continuum. MZ concordance rates for cognitive disorders have been about 80% while DZ concordance rates have been about 10% (Folstein & Rutter, 1977; LeCouteur et al., 1989; Bailey et al., 1995). In contrast, Steffenburg and colleagues (1989) have not found a high MZ concordance for cognitive problems, although their concordance rates for autism, as they broadly define it, are comparable to the British rates for cognitive disorders. Further support for a broader diagnostic continuum is provided by a follow-up study of the MZ twins who were nonconcordant for strict autism from Folstein and Rutter's initial study; nearly all had significant social disabilities in adult life (LeCouteur et al., 1989). Several groups also have suggested that there is an association between autism and affective disorders, particularly depression and social anxiety (Dunger &

DeLong, 1987; Piven et al., 1991; Smalley et al., 1995). These are all family studies and are considerably less rigorous than the previously cited twin studies that demonstrate linkage between cognitive disabilities and autism.

Segregation analyses of autism are limited by the rarity of multiplex and multigenerational families. Ritvo and colleagues tested several segregation models using their sample of recruited multiplex families. They found that both a multifactorial polygenic model and autosomal dominant model could be excluded, leading them to conclude that autosomal recessive inheritance was most likely in this rather unique subset of autistic families (Jorde et al., 1991). However, Pickles et al. (1995a,b) have found that a 3-gene model gives the best fit for their family data.

Several groups have been conducting molecular studies in autism. Herault's group has conducted several association studies using a group of autistic patients in their day treatment program and a group of local schoolchildren as controls. They have found initial associations between autism and the c-Harvey-Ras-1 (HRAS-1) gene (Herault et al., 1993) and a homeobox-containing gene EN2 involved in cerebellar development (Petit et al., 1995). However, these associations must be regarded as tentative until they are replicated in independently ascertained samples. In addition, questions can be raised about the adequacy of the control group, since very little information is provided about the ethnicity of subjects; a haplotype relative risk study would clarify this point. In addition, Comings's group has reported an association between the DRD2 gene and several neuropsychiatric disorders, including autism (Comings et al., 1991).

Several groups have conducted linkage studies. Spence and colleagues (1985) examined 30 markers on multiple chromosomes and found no evidence of linkage using an autosomal recessive model in their study sample of high-density families. Too few and too widely spaced markers were used to make any definitive statements on excluding genetic markers. The Stanford group also has studied multiplex families but analyzed their data using several different models, including a nonparametric model. Thus far they have excluded linkage to the fragile X locus under all models (Hallmayer et al., 1994). Further results are expected during the next several years.

LEARNING DISORDERS: READING DISABILITY

Reading disability is an extremely common problem, affecting about 5 to 10% of children (Berger, Yule, & Rutter, 1975; Stevenson et al., 1982). Four times as many boys as girls are affected (Wadsworth et al., 1992). The consequences of reading problems are significant, affecting children's short- and long-term achievement. In addition, reading problems often are associated with an increased incidence of psychiatric problems (Yule & Rutter, 1985).

Reading disabilities are among the best studied of the learning disabilities and provide a model for their future studies. Despite this, there are significant questions about what defines a reading disability. Most epidemiologic studies have reported a bimodal distribution in reading abilities, with many more children falling into the reading-disabled range than would be predicted by a normal distribution curve (Dobbins & Tafa, 1992; Rutter & Yule, 1975; Stevenson, 1988), although there are notable exceptions (Shaywitz, Escobar, Shaywitz, Fletcher, & Makuch, 1992). This argues that reading disability is a distinct entity rather than the lower extreme of a continuous variable. Numerous studies have attempted to divide reading disability into meaningful subtypes, although as yet none of these categorization schemes has been generally accepted (Boder, 1971; DeFries & Decker, 1981; Mattis, French, & Rapin, 1975). Recently individuals with reading disability have been reported to have a distinct organization of the visual cortex as assessed by functional magnetic resonance imaging (Eden et al., 1996). Support that reading disability is a distinct entity rather than part of a continuum also is provided by recent genetic evidence suggesting that phonological awareness and single-word reading are linked to different chromosomal regions (6p23–21.3 and 15pter-qter respectively) (Grigorenko et al., 1997). This study also suggests ways in which multiple genetic liabilities may interact to produce a clinically recognizable disorder.

Reading disability has long been recognized as familial. Numerous family studies done over the past 90 years have found that relatives of probands are much more likely to have reading disability than relatives of control groups (reviewed by Lombroso et al., 1994; Rutter, MacDonald, Le-Couteur, et al. 1990a).

Results from twin studies have indicated that genetic factors are responsible for a considerable amount of this familiality despite the fact that such studies are likely to underestimate genetic influences because reading difficulties have consistently been shown to be more prevalent in twins than singletons (Hay, O'Brien, Johnston, & Prior, 1984). Monozygotic concordance rates have been found to range between 67 to 88%, while dizygotic rates have been consistently lower, ranging between 30 to 25% (Bakwin, 1973; Ho, Gilger, & Decker, 1988). DeFries, Fulker, and La-Buda (1987) have estimated heritability to be between 50 to 70%. No adoption studies have been reported, to our knowledge. Several different models of inheritance have been proposed, including polygenic with a gender-influenced threshold (DeFries, 1989) and single gene (Finucci, Guthrie, Childs, Abbey, & Childs, 1976; reviewed by Lewitter, DeFries, & Elston, 1980). However, segregation analyses do not support one model better than the others, which leads to the conclusion that reading disability is genetically heterogeneous.

Despite the problems entailed by the presumed genetic and etiologic heterogeneity, the significant influence of environmental factors, the lack of a consistently defined phenotype, and the relatively high population prevalence, several molecular linkage studies have been undertaken with encouraging positive results. Smith and colleagues (1983) initially reported a linkage to the heteromorphic region of chromosome 15 in a sample of multiplex families. Although they were not been able to replicate this finding, Grigorenko and colleagues (1997) found linkage to D15S143 for single word reading with a lod score of 3.15. There also has been linkage reported to chromosome 1p36-p34, which awaits verification (Rabin et al. 1993). Most recently, linkage to the human leukocyte antigen (HLA) region at 6p21.3 of chromosome 6 has been reported (Cardon et al., 1994). This linkage is intriguing as earlier studies suggested an association between autoimmune disorders and reading disability. DeFries and colleagues have independently assessed this linkage in 2 samples using nonparametric allele-sharing methods. The first included 358 siblings in their sample of 19 multiplex families; the second consisted of 50 dizygotic twin pairs. In combination, the 2 samples provided evidence of linkage within a 2-centimorgan region with a significance level of $p < 0.0002$. When the phenotype was limited to those individuals with the most severe forms of reading disability, the significance was even greater, at $p < 0.00001$. Grigorenko and colleagues (1997) also replicated this finding by showing significant linkage ($p < 10^{-6}$) between 5 adjacent markers on 6p23–6p21.3 and phonologic awareness. This is the most convincing linkage finding thus far in a childhood neuropsychiatric disorder. Further work will focus on identifying the specific genes that are linked to aspects of reading disability.

ATTENTION DEFICIT HYPERACTIVITY DISORDER

Attention deficit hyperactivity disorder is one of the most prevalent childhood psychiatric disorders, affecting approximately 8% of all boys and 2% of girls. Symptoms frequently persist and cause considerable distress into adolescence and adulthood. The disorder is clearly heterogeneous, with some cases related to head trauma (Rutter, 1981), toxins (Shaywitz, Cohen, & Shaywitz, 1983), and infectious agents (Shaywitz & Shaywitz, 1982). However, in a considerable number of cases, genetic factors appear to be important (reviewed in Pauls, 1990; Smalley, 1997).

Several studies have examined the incidence of attention deficit hyperactivity disorder in families of affected children (Cantwell, 1972; Farone, Biederman, Keenan, & Tsuangm, 1991; Pauls et al., 1983; Szatmari et al., 1989; Taylor et al., 1986b; Schacher & Wachsmuth, 1990). Their results are consistent with those of Biederman and colleagues (1986, 1987), who found that relatives of children with attention deficit hyperactivity disorder were 5 times as likely to have the disorder as those of control children (31.5 vs. 5.7%). Numerous twin studies have been undertaken and support a major role for genetic factors in the ultimate expression of the disorder (Goodman & Stevenson, 1989a,b; Lopez, 1965; Stevenson, 1992; Vandenberg, 1962). Goodman and Stevenson's study is representative. They found that a covariance of 0.62 in monozygotic twins vs. 0.26 in dizygotic twins, which suggested a heritability of about 40%. Several adoption studies also have provided support for the role of genetic factors in attentional problems (reviewed by McMahon, 1980).

Studies of adoptive siblings who either were or were not biologically related to one another found that genetic factors accounted for about 47% of the variance (VanDeNoord, Boomsma, & Verhulst, 1994). Safer (1973) identified probands with attention deficit hyperactivity disorder and found increased rates of the disorder in their biologic siblings who had been adopted away. Morrison and Stewart (1973) and Cantwell (1975) have reported that adoptive parents raising children with attention deficit hyperactivity disorder have significantly fewer attentional difficulties than biologic parents raising their own children with the disorder. However, these results should be interpreted cautiously, since the biological parents of the adopted children with the disorder were not examined. There also may be some bias for selecting adoptive parents who are free of psychiatric problems, although this may be less of an issue with a disorder not traditionally diagnosed in adult populations.

Numerous questions have been raised about the relationship between attention deficit hyperactivity disorder and other psychiatric disorders. Initial work by Biederman and colleagues found an increased incidence of major depression, oppositional defiant disorder, conduct disorder, and antisocial personality disorder in the families of children with attention deficit hyperactivity disorder. Further analysis revealed that the increased incidence of these disorders, particularly antisocial personality disorder, was limited to the families of probands with both attention deficit hyperactivity disorder and comorbid conduct or oppositional defiant disorder; the risk to families of probands with only attention deficit hyperactivity disorder was 11% compared with 7% for relatives of children with unrelated psychiatric problems or 4% for relatives of normal controls (Faraone et al., 1991). Adoption studies have provided more convincing evidence of a genetic link between attention deficit hyperactivity disorder and antisocial personality disorder. Both Cunningham et al. (1975) and Bohman, Cloninger, Sigvardsson, & von Knorring (1982) have found an increased incidence of attention deficit hyperactivity disorder in adopted children whose biological parents had histories of criminality as compared to those whose biological parents did not. Cadoret and Stewart (1991) have confirmed these results, although they also demonstrate a significant increase in attention deficit hyperactivity disorder and adult antisocial personality disorder if the adoptive parents have psychiatric problems or are financially disadvantaged. They believe that attention deficit hyperactivity disorder predisposes individuals to aggression, which in turn predisposes to the development of antisocial personality disorder. However, these studies are limited by the absence of a clinical diagnoses in the biological parents and the inability to exclude coexisting attention deficit hyperactivity disorder in the biological parents. Finally, it has been suggested that attention deficit hyperactivity disorder may be related to Tourette's disorder due to the high level of comorbidity between the 2 disorders. However, Pauls and colleagues (1993) have specifically tested this hypothesis with segregation analyses of 2 large kindreds and failed to demonstrate a relationship.

It has not been possible to determine a clear model of genetic transmission in attention deficit hyperactivity disorder. Despite the disproportionate number of boys affected, there is no evidence of sex-linked transmission (Omenn, 1973). Morrison and Stewart (1974) have demonstrated that a model of polygenic inheritance best fits the data from their family study. To our knowledge, no linkage studies have been undertaken of attention deficit hyperactivity disorder. However, some associations with genetic markers have been reported. Comings et al. (1991) reported an association between the DRD2 gene and several psychiatric disorders, including attention deficit hyperactivity disorder. Similarly, a highly significant association between a mutation in the thyroid receptor-b gene that results in generalized resistance to thyroid hormone and attention deficit hyperactivity disorder was reported (Hauser et al., 1993), but disappeared when comorbid mental retardation (which results from hypothyroidism) was considered (Weiss et al., 1994). Since that time Hauser and colleagues (1997) have found a correlation between thyroid hormone levels and symptoms of hyperactivity but not inattention reopening the question about a related gene. More recently, Cook and colleagues (1995) have reported an association between the dopamine transporter locus and attention deficit hyperactivity disorder using the haplotype relative risk method. By using this method, this study overcomes many of the methodological concerns of

the other studies. Very importantly, Gill and colleagues (1997) independently found linkage between the dopamine transporter gene and attention deficit hyperactivity disorder. All of these studies remain to be replicated in independently ascertained samples.

CONDUCT DISORDER

Antisocial behavior in adulthood appears to be strongly influenced by both genetic and environmental factors. Relatively few studies have directly addressed the role of genetic factors in conduct disorder and other disruptive behavior disorders of childhood. However, extant studies suggest that genetic factors are relatively less important in childhood disruptive behavior disorders.

Family studies suggest that the relatives of children with either oppositional defiant disorder or conduct disorder and attentional problems are more likely to have antisocial personality disorder; however, it is unclear whether these relatives are at greater risk for conduct disorder symptoms as children (Biederman et al., 1987; Faraone et al., 1991). Twin studies focusing on delinquent behavior during childhood show a much more modest genetic effect than do twin studies of adult antisocial personality disorder (Christiansen, 1977; Dalgaard & Kreinglen, 1976; Graham & Stevenson, 1985; Rowe, 1983, 1986). In a comprehensive review of these studies, McGuffin and Gottesman (1985) reported a combined MZ concordance of 87% and DZ concordance of 72%. They concluded that shared environmental factors play a more significant role on the development of antisocial behaviors during childhood than genetic factors do.

Several other investigators have approached the question of the genetic influence on conduct disorder through twin studies, examining various behavioral scales that are likely to be involved in conduct disorders. The results from these studies have suggested that genetic factors account for 40 to 90% of the variance in the incidence of different externalizing behaviors. In the most recent of these studies, Slutske and colleagues (1997) retrospectively studied more than 2500 twin pairs from the Australian twin registry and found that genetic factors accounted for 71% of the variance observed. Other researchers have felt that it is necessary to break conduct disorder into ~4 latent classes, that are influenced by genetic factors to varying degrees (Silberg et al., 1996; Eaves et al., 1993). Cadoret and colleagues (1995) have explored possible gene-environment interactions in conduct disorder aggression.

Adoption studies also suggest that genetic factors have a limited influence on childhood conduct disorders. Bohman (1971, 1972) and Cadoret (1978) both found no significant differences in the rates of disruptive behavior disorders in adoptees whose biological parents were antisocial and those whose parents were not. In a more recent study, van de Noord et al. (1994) found that externalizing behaviors reported on the Child Behavior Checklist were more similar in biological adoptive siblings than in unrelated adoptive siblings. Using LISREL computer analysis, they estimated that genetic factors account for 70% of aggressive behavior variance and approximately 40% of the variance on the delinquent behavior scale.

Two factors appear to contribute to the significant difference in the magnitude of the genetic effect on childhood and adult antisocial behavior disorders. The first is methodological. In contrast to the adult studies, which focused on the well-defined outcomes of antisocial personality disorder and recurrent criminality, studies of children have failed to utilize consistent and clearly meaningful phenotypes. Clinical diagnostic criteria were employed only in the family studies from Biederman's group. Similarly the relationships among conduct disorders, delinquent behavior, externalizing behaviors, and aggression are not well defined, so it is difficult to correlate findings from different studies.

The second factor is more substantive. Conduct disorders and externalizing behaviors are quite prevalent (as reflected in the high concordance rates observed in the juvenile studies) and very heterogeneous. The course of conduct problems also varies greatly; only a small minority of children with conduct disorders subsequently develop antisocial personality disorder. It may be more feasible to identify environmental factors that seem to influence the expression of conduct disorders. In studies of adults, the following environmental factors have been identified as playing a significant role in the development of antisocial personality disorder: institutional care in infancy

(Cloninger & Gottesman, 1987; Crowe, 1972, 1974; Rutter, Quinton, & Hill, 1990), multiple placements (Cloninger & Gottesman, 1987), and lower socioeconomic status (Cloninger & Gottesman, 1987; Mednick et al., 1983). The influence of these factors on childhood conduct disorders should be examined.

FEEDING AND EATING DISORDERS

Anorexia nervosa and bulimia nervosa have many similarities and appear to be influenced by many of the same environmental factors. However, it remains unclear to what extent they are part of the same disease continuum or are distinct disorders. Anorexia nervosa is a disorder that commonly begins during the transition from childhood to adolescence. About two-thirds of cases resolve by age 40. It is primarily a disorder of girls; about a tenth as many boys are affected (Nielson, 1990). The incidence of anorexia has been estimated at between 6.3 to 8.2 per 100,000 in recent epidemiological studies (Hoek et al., 1991; Lucas et al., 1991); its prevalence among adolescents has been estimated to be between 0.22 and 0.84% (Culberg & Engstrom-Lindberg, 1988; Lucas et al., 1991; Rastam et al., 1989; Whitaker et al., 1990). Anorexia is rarely observed in several ethnic groups, including blacks and Chinese (reviewed in Dolan, 1991).

Bulimia nervosa shares many features of anorexia nervosa but has a quite distinct onset and epidemiology. Bulimia generally begins in late adolescence, during the transition to adulthood. It also affects women much more often than men. It is more common than anorexia and has been estimated to affect about 1% of adolescents and young adults (Fairburn & Beglin, 1990; Stein & Brinza, 1989). The incidence of both anorexia and bulimia have been increasing over the past few decades (Jones et al., 1980; Lucas et al., 1991; Kendell et al., 1973; Kendler, 1991; Szmukler et al., 1986), which is likely to reflect, at least in part, the increasing value placed on slimness and physical attractiveness in most Western societies.

Despite the clear environmental factors involved in anorexia, there is considerable evidence that familiality is involved in the expression of both disorders. Family studies have shown that relatives of probands with anorexia are 3 times as likely as relatives of control groups to have a history of anorexia and 5 to 6 times as likely to have a history of any eating disorder (Strober, 1991). Two studies have found that relatives of bulimic patients are at approximately 2 times greater risk for developing bulimia than controls (Hudson, Pope, Jonas, Yurgelun-Todd, & Frankenburg, 1987; Kassett et al., 1989).

Twin studies have suggested that there is a significant genetic influence on anorexia with an MZ concordance significantly greater than DZ concordance (Garfinkel & Garner, 1982; Holland, Hall, Murray, Russell, & Crisp, 1984; Walters & Kendler, 1995). Holland and colleagues (1984) found a 56% MZ concordance as compared to a 5% DZ concordance in their sample, although this may well represent an overestimate since their study was not population-based. The large MZ/DZ discrepancy suggests that multiple genes are involved in susceptibility. Twin studies also support a significant genetic influence on the development of bulimia. Ficter and Noegel (1990) found an 83% MZ concordance rate and a 27% DZ concordance rate in their recruited sample of 27 twin pairs. Kendler and colleagues (1991) also found a significant MZ/DZ difference, but their overall rates of concordance were much lower: 23% MZ and 9% DZ. They estimated heritability at approximately 50%. It remains unclear to what extent genetic factors specifically increase susceptibility for anorexia as opposed to generally increasing susceptibility for both anorexia and bulimia. Treasure and Holland (1990) have argued for narrow susceptibility, while family studies suggest more continuity in the disorder. To date, no molecular studies have been performed examining either anorexia or bulimia.

It has been postulated that both anorexia and bulimia may be genetically related to major depression. Comorbid depression is extremely common in individuals with eating disorders. Both Strober's group (1982) and Hudson's group (1983) have found that relatives of individuals with eating disorders are more likely than those of control groups to have depression. It is controversial to what extent the increased familial risk for depression is limited to individuals with comorbid affective diagnoses. Strober & Humphrey (1990) and Biederman et al. (1985) find it to be limited, while Gershon et al. (1984) and Hudson et al.

(1987) find it more generally. In Kendler et al.'s sample (1991), 51% of the individuals with bulimia also had major depression, which generally began prior to their bulimic symptoms. However, anxiety disorders and alcoholism were also very frequent. Kendler and colleagues conclude that there is no etiologic relationship between affective disorder and bulimia. Similarly, attempts to demonstrate an increased risk for eating disorders in the relatives of depressed probands have been unsuccessful (Strober et al., 1990).

These studies suggest that multiple genes act to increase the susceptibility for developing anorexia. Some of these same genes also may influence the development of bulimia and, to a much lesser extent, depression. However, environmental factors play a crucial role. Kendler's group has found high neuroticism, dieting status, and various attributes of parents to play an important role in the development of both disorders (Kendler et al., 1991; Walters & Kendler, 1995). In addition, the following environmental factors appear to have a significant impact on bulimia: birth after 1960, slim ideal body image, external locus of control, and low self-esteem. Child psychiatrists should actively seek family history of eating disorders and contributing environmental effects when evaluating patients with possible eating disorders. In addition, they should assess possible comorbid depression.

TOURETTE'S DISORDER

Tourette's disorder is a neuropsychiatric disorder characterized by chronic intermittent vocal and motor tics with onset in childhood. Reported prevalence rates have ranged from 2.9 per 10,000 (Caine et al., 1988) to 59 per 10,000 (Comings et al., 1990) with boys affected 9 times as often as girls (Burd et al., 1986).

Ever since its initial description, Tourette's disorder has been recognized as highly familial. Numerous family studies done during the past several years have confirmed this impression. Studies that relied on the family history method have reported about a 4% incidence of Tourette's disorder and an 11% incidence of chronic motor tics (Comings, Comings, Devor, Cloninger, 1984), while studies using direct interview of first-degree relatives have reported significantly higher rates of approximately 13% incidence of Tourette's and 20% of chronic motor tics (Pauls & Leckman, 1986). Pauls and Leckman (1986) also found an increased incidence of obsessive-compulsive disorder among probands. Furthermore, they found a marked difference in the incidence of various symptoms in male and female relatives, with Tourette's and chronic motor tics being about 3.5 times as likely in male relatives and obsessive-compulsive symptoms being 2.5 times as common in female relatives (Pauls, Raymond, Leckman, & Stevenson, 1991). The only twin study done suggests that the familiality observed has a strong genetic basis. In a recruited twin sample with an excess of MZ pairs, Price, Kidd, Cohen, Pauls, and Leckman (1985) found an MZ concordance rate of 53% for strict Tourette's disorder and 77% for Tourette's or chronic multiple tics; DZ concordance rates were 8 and 23%, respectively. Although the recruitment and assessment methods of this study were not optimal, the findings strongly support a substantial genetic influence on the development of Tourette's. Environmental influences also appear important, since the MZ concordance is significantly less than 1; however, no specific factors have been identified. We are unaware of any adoption studies of Tourette's disorder.

A number of questions have been raised about the extent of the Tourette's phenotype. Although transient tics do not appear to increase the risk to family members for developing Tourette's, chronic motor tics do increase the risk for family members and also are more common among relatives of Tourette probands (Pauls, Kruger, Leckman, Cohen, & Kidd, 1984). Questions also have been raised about the inclusion of both obsessive-compulsive disorder and attention deficit disorder within the Tourette's phenotype since many Tourette patients have comorbid diagnoses (Comings & Comings, 1984; Grad, Pelcovitz, Olson, Matthews, & Grad, 1987; Robertson, Trimble, & Lees, 1988). The incidence of obsessive-compulsive disorder in relatives of patients with Tourette's alone, with Tourette's and obsessive-compulsive disorder, and with obsessive-compulsive disorder alone are all comparable, which argues that obsessive-compulsive disorder is indeed part of the Tourette's spectrum (Pauls et al., 1986). In contrast, the same study reported dissimilar results for attention deficit disorder; attention deficit disorder was increased only in the

relatives of probands with both Tourette's and attention deficit disorder. Finally, Comings & Comings (1984) has suggested that agoraphobia and Tourette's panic disorder are part of the spectrum. However, Pauls, Leckman, & Cohen (1994) did not find any evidence of this in their family study, and it is generally thought that these disorders are distinct from Tourette's.

Numerous molecular studies have been conducted in Tourette's. Several association studies have examined the role of various dopamine receptors in the disorder. Comings and colleagues (1991) reported a highly significant association between a polymorphism of the dopamine D-2 receptor (*DRD-2*) using population-based controls. However, Nothen and colleagues (1994) were unable to replicate this association with the *DRD-2* receptor using the more stringent haplotype relative risk strategy. Similarly, Catalano and colleagues (1994) have been unable to replicate an association between the dopamine D-3 receptor (*DRD-3*) and Tourette's disorder. Finally, a significant association was identified between 1 allele of the dopamine D-4 receptor (*DRD-4*) and Tourette's (Grice et al., 1996). If this association can be replicated in another sample, it will be interesting to determine any functional differences in these alleles.

Linkage studies also have been undertaken. Thus far, no regions that are linked with Tourette's disorder have been identified; however, a large portion of the genome (~80%), including all of chromosome 18, has been putatively excluded from linkage (Heutink, van de Wetering, Breedveld, & Oostra, 1992; reviewed in Leckman (1997); Pakstis et al., 1991; Pauls et al., 1990).

Attempts to model the inheritance of Tourette's disorder have consistently found that a single major locus best explains the family data. However, there is less agreement about the mode of inheritance. Three groups have argued for an autosomal dominant model with sex specific penetrances: Baron, Shapiro, Shapiro, and Rainer (1981); Comings et al. (1984); and Price, Kidd, and Weissman (1987); while others have argued for that an additive model also should be considered (Devor, 1984; Kidd and Pauls, 1982). Inclusion of obsessive-compulsive disorder as part of the Tourette's phenotype in the transmission model significantly improved the fit (Pauls & Leckman, 1986).

OBSESSIVE-COMPULSIVE DISORDER

Obsessive-compulsive disorder is characterized by sudden, recurrent upsetting thoughts or images that intrude into consciousness (obsession) and/or rule-governed acts that the person feels driven to perform (compulsions). Onset is typically during childhood with continued symptoms throughout life. Frequently, obsessive-compulsive disorder is associated with marked impairment and disability. The disorder appears to be quite heterogeneous with idiopathic forms, tic-associated forms, and possibly infection-associated forms. In addition, there is considerable symptomatic overlap with other disorders, including pervasive developmental disorders and eating disorders. Obsessive-compulsive disorder is quite prevalent, affecting 2 to 3.5% of all adults (Robins et al., 1981).

The familial nature of obsessive-compulsive disorder has been observed since the 1930s with family studies reporting as much as a 10-fold increase in incidence among first-degree relatives of affected individuals (Lenane et al., 1990; Leonard et al., 1992; Pauls, Alsbrook, Goodman, Rasmussen, 1995; Riddle et al., 1990). Relatives of early-onset probands appear to be at the highest risk for obsessive-compulsive disorder (Bellodi, Sciuto, Diaferia, Ronchi, & Smeraldi, 1992; Pauls et al., 1995). Studies do exist that have failed to find significant familiality (Black et al., 1992; McKeon & Murray, 1987). They may be studying heterogeneous forms of obsessive-compulsive disorder, some of which do not show a significant familial nature. Recent studies focusing on children with obsessive-compulsive disorder found that 35% of their first-degree relatives were also affected by obsessive-compulsive disorder or significant but subthreshold symptoms of the disorder (Lenane et al., 1990; Riddle et al., 1990). These studies also show a high incidence of tic disorders among relatives even though the obsessive-compulsive disorder probands were specifically selected to not have comorbid Tourette's disorder. However, the risk for tic disorders is markedly increased in families of probands with comorbid tics (10.6%) compared to the families of probands without tics (3.2%) (Pauls et al., 1995).

Twin studies suggest that a significant portion of the observed familiality has a genetic basis. Concordance rates for MZ twins range from 53 to 87% compared to rates in DZ twins, which ranges from 22 to 47% (Carey & Gottesman, 1981; Rasmussen & Tsuang, 1986). Twin studies have emphasized the overlap between obsessive-compulsive disorder and other anxiety disorders (Torgerson, 1983). Adoption studies have not been performed, to our knowledge. Similarly, studies of the molecular genetics of obsessive-compulsive disorder have not yet been undertaken. Such studies will require investigators to identify more homogenous subtypes of the disorder. Both age of onset and association with Tourette's disorder are likely to be important distinguishing criteria.

These results point to the importance of obtaining family history of both obsessive-compulsive disorder and tic disorders in children in whom a clinical diagnosis of obsessive-compulsive disorder is being considered. Likely increased monitoring for tic symptoms in the identified patient and emerging obsessive-compulsive and tic symptoms in other family members will be necessary. It is also prudent to monitor for symptoms of other anxiety disorders.

SUBSTANCE ABUSE DISORDERS: ALCOHOLISM

Despite the fact that alcoholism and the abuse of other substances are growing problems in our society, with nearly 40% of high school seniors admitting to heavy alcohol use, very few studies have specifically addressed the etiology and course of alcohol dependence in adolescents. However, evidence from adults indicates significant continuity between drinking problems that begin early in life and those that persist into adulthood. Given the evidence for strong genetic vulnerabilities to alcoholism in adults (particularly those with early onset), it is quite likely that genetic factors are also important in children and adolescent substance abusers.

Family studies of adult alcoholics have demonstrated that relatives of alcoholic probands are about 4 times as likely to also be alcoholic than relatives of controls (reviewed in Dinwiddie & Reich, 1993). Studies of the offspring of alcoholic parents also report an increased risk for developing alcoholism before adulthood as well as other childhood psychiatric disorders (Bennett, Wolin, & Reiss, 1988; Earls, Reich, Jung, & Cloninger, 1988). Both adoption and twin studies provide strong evidence that such familiality is significantly influenced by genetic factors. Several adoption studies have shown that adoptees with an alcoholic biological parent are significantly more likely to develop alcohol problems than adoptees whose biological parents are not affected, while they are not at greater risk for other psychiatric disorders (Cloninger, Bohman, & Signardsson, 1981; Goodwin et al., 1973). In addition, adoptees without a biologic history of alcoholism raised by adoptive parents with alcoholism have not been shown to be at increased risk for developing alcoholism (Cloninger et al., 1981). This genetic effect has been postulated to be most pronounced in a subgroup of male individuals with onset by the early 20s and particularly severe symptomatology (Cloninger et al., 1981). The only adoption study examining adopted young men with substance abuse problems found an increase in both alcoholism and antisocial personality in their biological relatives but not in their adoptive families (Cadoret, Troughton, O'Gorman, & Heywood, 1986). This suggests that early alcohol misuse may be more genetically heterogeneous than adult alcoholism with a significant number of cases resulting from inherited personality traits rather than a specific susceptibility to alcoholism.

Most twin studies also have supported a significant genetic role in alcoholism with MZ rates of ~55% and DZ rates of ~28% and heritability between 40 and 60% (Heath & Martin, 1988; Kaprio et al., 1987; Kendler, 1994; Pickens et al., 1991). Heath and Martin (1988) demonstrated a significant MZ/DZ split in both teenage drinking as well as adult alcoholism. They also found a difference between men and women in that female twins showed a significant MZ/DZ split with respect to the age of onset of drinking but no MZ/DZ difference was observed among male twins. The primary exception to these findings is a study by Gurling and associates (1981), which is limited by its lack of diagnostic rigor.

In most studies, environmental factors also have been shown to exert a significant influence on the development of alcohol problems. Cadoret and colleagues (1986) found a significant increase in alcoholism in adoptees when there had been divorce or psychiatric illness in the adopting family. Most twin studies also have suggested a significant role for unspecified environmental factors. The study by Kendler, Gruenberg, and

Kinney (1994) of women with alcoholism is unique in that it showed nearly all the variance was genetic. This finding may be further evidence of genetic distinctions between alcoholism in men and women.

Numerous molecular studies have been undertaken in alcoholism. Thus far no chromosomal region has been clearly linked to alcoholism. An association was reported with the *DRD2* gene using a population control group (Blum et al., 1990). However, studies using the haplotype relative risk methodology, which controls for ethnic variation, do not support an association (Gelernter et al., 1993).

These findings suggest that it is especially important for child psychiatrists to address on a regular basis the dangers of substance abuse with the children of alcoholics. It is also clear that children of substance abusers who are in stressful situations, such as divorce or chaotic family situations, may be particularly vulnerable to substance use and that helping such children develop adaptive coping skills will be especially important.

SCHIZOPHRENIA

Although schizophrenia was originally thought of as an adult disorder, very often onset of the disorder occurs during adolescence. Moreover, there is evidence that onset may occur as early as 5 years of age. Schizophrenia is a fairly common disorder with a prevalence in adults of about 1 percent (Robins, 1984) and prevalences in younger children in the range of 3 per 10,000 (Kolvin, 1971). Questions have been raised repeatedly about the diagnostic continuity between schizophrenia occurring during childhood and schizophrenia in adolescents and adults. Longitudinal studies strongly support continuity between the 2 disorders with developmental variations in expression such as the relative absence of well-formed complex delusions in schizophrenia of childhood (Eggers, 1978; reviewed by Werry & Taylor, 1994, and Werry, 1992).

Schizophrenia is regarded as a highly familial disorder that is subject to considerable genetic influence (reviewed by Gottesman, 1994; Prescott & Gottesman, 1993). In general, family studies have demonstrated that first-degree relatives of schizophrenic individuals are about 8 times as likely to develop schizophrenia or a related psychotic disorder as relatives of normal controls (Guze et al., 1983; Kendler et al., 1985). The risk is significantly greater if both parents have schizophrenia (40%) or if an identical twin has schizophrenia (55%). There may be even greater familiality among schizophrenics with early-adolescent onsets (Hanson & Gottesman, 1976; Pulver et al., 1990). In addition, rates of bipolar affective disorder have been found to be elevated in relatives of schizophrenics when compared to relatives of normal controls but decreased compared to relatives of bipolar probands (Kendler et al., 1985; McGuffin, Katz, & Bebbington, 1987). Most have ascribed this result to misdiagnosis of probands since it may be difficult to distinguish between schizophrenia and chronic mania; but others have argued that it reflects a continuum of psychosis (Crow, 1986).

Twin studies have provided strong evidence that the familiality observed has a strong genetic component. Generally MZ concordance rates are about 55% while DZ concordance rates are about 12% (Gottesman & Shields, 1982). This leads to estimates of heritability in the range of 60 to 70% (Fischer, 1973; Kendler, 1988). However, it is clear that environmental factors also exert a significant influence. To date specific environmental factors have not been identified within high-risk contexts.

Adoptive studies also strongly support the importance of genetic factors. Adoptees whose biologic mother had schizophrenia have a higher rate of schizophrenia than those adoptees whose biologic mother did not. In addition, adoptees with no affected biological relatives who were raised by a schizophrenic adoptive parent did not show any increase in risk (Wender et al., 1977, reviewed in Tienari & Wynne, 1994). Tienari and colleagues (1990) have performed careful studies of the environment within the adoptive home in attempts to tease apart gene-environment interactions. They have found that an adverse environment in the adopting home is associated with an increased risk of psychotic illness, which is particularly great among children with biologic risks for developing schizophrenia.

Attempts to model the transmission of schizophrenia have proven very difficult. The familial patterns observed are not consistent with Mendelian inheritance. The addition of corrections for reduced penetrance, strong environmental influ-

ences, and phenocopies have not significantly improved the fit of single-gene models. Better fit has been obtained in multifactorial polygenic models or models in which a single gene of major effect interacts with several other genes of lesser effect. Latent structure analysis is compatible with the transmission of a single latent trait that may be manifest either as schizophrenia or as eye tracking problems in an autosomal dominant fashion (Matthysse, Holzman, & Langer, 1986). However, the evidence that eye tracking problems are a valid latent trait is limited.

There have probably been more molecular studies examining schizophrenia than any other psychiatric disorder which are reviewed by Rao (1997). Associations have been found for several genes, including neurotrophin-3 (Nanko et al., 1994a), the dopamine D2 receptor (DRD2) (Hattori et al., 1994), the dopamine D3 receptor (DRD3) (Catalano et al., 1993) and the dopamine D4 receptor (DRD4). However, none of these associations has been replicated (Daniels et al., 1994; Macciardi et al., 1994). Several linkage studies also are being conducted. Some of these studies have focused on neurotransmitter-related genes while others were based on chromosomal abnormalities found in high-density families. The specific genetic regions that have been "excluded" include the DRD2 gene (Hallmayer et al., 1994; Moises et al., 1991); the DRD4 gene (Nanko, Fukuda et al., 1994b); the tyrosine hydroxylase gene (Maier et al., 1994); the pseudoautosomal region of the X chromosome (Damato et al., 1994); the amyloid beta A4 precursor protein (APP) (Coon et al., 1993; Morris et al., 1984); and the pericentric region of chromosome 9 (Nanko et al., 1994a). Initially, a positive linkage to chromosome 5 was reported (Sherrington et al., 1988). However, this finding has not been replicated despite numerous attempts to do so (Aschauer et al., 1990; Crowe, 1991; Kennedy et al., 1988; St. Clair et al., 1989). Recently linkage has been reported to the nicotinic acetylcholine receptor a-7 subunit on chromosome 15 (15q13-q14) in a group of 9, multiplex families with a maximal lod score of 5.3 (Freedman et al., 1997). This finding awaits replication.

Two collaborative groups are conducting genome-wide screens for genes involved in schizophrenia. Several regions have appeared promising. Both Coon and colleagues (1994) and Pulver and colleagues (1994) have drawn attention to the 22q13.31 region of chromosome 22 and found consistently positive lod scores, although these scores have not reached significance under any of the models tested, including nonparametric allele-sharing paradigms. Interest in this region has been further heightened by the frequent emergence of psychotic symptoms during adolescence in velocardiofacial syndrome, which results from a 22q11 deletion (Pulver et al., 1994) and the presence of 1.5 to 2 Mb interstitial deletions on 22q11 in a sample of schizophrenic patients (Karayiorgou et al., 1995). Velocardiofacial syndrome is the most common genetic etiology of cleft palate and frequently is associated with nasal speech, mental retardation, learning disabilities and congenital heart abnormalities. However, in many individuals the full syndrome is not expressed; for example, individuals with velocardiofacial syndrome may present with nasal speech rather than a dramatic cleft palate or with no significant cardiac abnormalities. Some have felt that the psychotic symptoms observed in velocardiofacial syndrome are more consistent with a bipolar disorder rather than schizophrenia (Golding-Kushner, Weller, & Shprintzen, 1985; Shprintzen, Goldberg, Golding-Kushner, & Marion, 1992).

Even more robust findings of linkage to D65296, a marker on 6pter-22 have emerged from several groups involved in genome screens (Wang et al., 1995; Straub et al., 1995; Antonavakis et al., 1995; Schwab et al., 1995, Gurling et al., 1995). A combined total lod score for the two nonoverlapping samples reported by Wang & Straud is 3.6 to 4.0. It is estimated that this locus could influence vulnerability in 15 to 30% of families affected with schizophrenia.

These findings suggest that child psychiatrists who are evaluating children and adolescents with psychotic illnesses should carefully ascertain family history both for psychotic illnesses and signs of velocardiofacial syndrome in both the patient and family members. Although recognition of velocardiofacial syndrome at this time does not have direct treatment implications, prenatal genetic testing is available.

MAJOR DEPRESSION

Several studies have established that affective disorders occurring in adults have a significant heritable component. However, relatively few studies have directly assessed the familiality of childhood-onset depression. Questions about whether clinically significant childhood-onset depressive symptoms are the same as adult-onset depression have been addressed in several studies, which compared the rates of depression in children of depressed individuals with those in children of other psychiatric patients or the general population. These studies consistently have found increased rates of depression in the offspring of depressed patients (Hammen, Burger, Burney, & Adrian, 1990; Kashani, Burk, & Reid, 1985; Orvaschel et al., 1988; Weissman, Fendrich, Warner, & Wickramaratne, 1992; for reviews, see Beardslee, Bemporad, Keller, & Klerman, 1983; La Roche et al., 1987). The risk appears greatest (14.2 times the baseline incidence) for individuals whose parents had onset of depression before age 20 (Price et al., 1987). In addition, Weissman and colleagues (1987, 1988) have noted a progressively earlier age of onset in patients with heavy familial loading for depression. The average age of onset in children with a positive family history of depression was 12 years rather than 16 years for those without a positive family history. Some of these studies also have shown an increased incidence of other psychiatric conditions in the children, including attention deficit disorder (Biederman et al., 1991; Puig-Antich et al., 1989) and conduct disorder (Harrington, Fudge, Rutter, Pickles, & Hull, 1990; Kovacs, Paulauskas, Gatsonis, & Richards, 1988; Puig-Antich et al., 1989; Radke-Yarrow et al., 1992).

The familiality of depression also has been established in studies comparing the rates of affective illness in relatives of children who have been diagnosed with depression and in relatives of children without depression; rates are generally 2 to 4 times greater in the families of depressed children (Livingston et al., 1985; Mitchell, McCauley, Burke, Calderon, & Schloredt, 1989). The most comprehensive studies have been done by Puig-Antich and colleagues (1989), who examined the families of depressed children, children with other nonaffective psychiatric illnesses, and children with no identified psychiatric problems. They found that the rate of major depression was significantly higher in the depressed children's families (53%) than in the families of either the psychiatric or normal control groups (28%). They also found a significant increase in the number of relatives with alcoholism and other psychiatric problems as compared with relatives of normal controls but not relatives of children with other psychiatric problems. Harrington et al. (1993) have found increases of a similar magnitude, although their absolute rates were decreased; 22% of depressed children's relatives and only 7% of nonpsychiatrically ill children had major depression. These studies clearly establish familial transmission of depression in childhood and adolescence but do not distinguish between genetic and environmental features.

Two twin studies have addressed the genetic basis of depressive disorders in children (Rende et al., 1993; Thapar & McGuffin, 1994). Thapar and McGuffin's study is more comprehensive in that it assessed 313 pairs of twins identified through a population registry, although the conclusions that can be drawn from it are limited by its exclusive reliance on questionnaires and the absence of clinical assessments of major depression. They found that depressive symptoms were best explained by an additive genetic model and that the magnitude of the genetic effect differed significantly between the 114 children (ages 8–11 years) and the 108 adolescents (12–16 years) studied. In children, concordance for depressive symptoms was best explained by a shared environment model (accounting for 60–77% of the variance) whereas in adolescents, genetic effects exerted the major influence with a heritability of 80%. Population-based twin studies of depression in adults have estimated heritability at between 30 and 46% (Jardine, Martin, & Henderson, 1984; Kendler & Eaves, 1986). Taken together, these findings suggest that significant depressive symptoms occurring in young adolescents are greatly influenced by genetic factors while the same depressive symptoms in younger children may have a different etiologic basis. Interestingly, there is no clear evidence of heritability in mild dysthymic states (Cadoret, O'Gorman, Heywood, & Troughton, 1985; McGuffin & Katz, 1986; Slater & Shield, 1969).

Thus far, there have been no reports of molecular studies of major depression associating the illness with any particular chromosomal region or candidate gene. Several groups have examined the role of various environmental factors in children at high genetic risk for developing depression. Chronic distress, disciplinary styles, and lack of consistency appear to have a significant impact (Angst, Merikangas, Scheidegger, & Wicki, 1990; Cohen, Brook, Cohen, Velez, & Garcia, 1990; Downey & Coyne, 1990; Parker, 1979).

BIPOLAR AFFECTIVE DISORDER

In adults, bipolar affective disorder appears to be influenced by genetic factors to an even greater extent than major depression, with heritability estimated as high as 80% (Bertelsen, Harvald, & Hauge, 1977; McGuffin & Katz, 1986; reviewed by Kelsoe, 1997). Recent findings are reviewed by Kelsoe (1997). There is also strong evidence of heritability in adolescents. Several studies have reported an increase of affective illness in the offspring of patients with bipolar affective disorder, ranging from 4 to 10 times that of control populations (Akiskal et al., 1985; Decina et al., 1983; Dwyer & DeLong, 1987; Grigordiu-Serbanescu et al., 1989; Hammen et al., 1987, 1990; Klein & Depue, 1985; Nurngerger et al., 1988). However, other studies have failed to find significant differences (Gershon et al., 1982), and all also found a considerable increase in the incidence of other psychiatric disorders. Todd, Reich, & Reich (1994) have extended these studies by directly examining all of the children in a large multigenerational kindred affected by bipolar affective disorder. They found that children were more likely to have an affective disorder if they were more closely related to an ill individual. They were also significantly more likely to have a disruptive behavior disorder, suggesting that such disorders may represent an early manifestation of bipolar affective disorder.

Strober et al. (1988) compared the rates of affective illness in adolescents with diagnoses of either bipolar affective disorder or schizophrenia. They found that 15% of the bipolar probands' relatives also had bipolar disorder while none of the schizophrenic probands' relatives had bipolar disorder. There was also an increased incidence of other affective illnesses (30% versus 4%) in bipolar families. In addition, the relatives of probands who had presented with any psychiatric illness prior to age 12 were at even greater risk for developing bipolar disorder (44%) than the relatives of adolescents who first developed symptoms in adolescence (24%). To date, there have been no twin or adoption studies looking specifically at the incidence of childhood- or adolescent-onset bipolar affective disorder.

Recently Nylander and colleagues (1994) examined the age of onset in a large kindred and found that the age of onset was earlier for a great proportion of those affected in later generations. They have argued that this reflects "anticipation," a form of inheritance in which each subsequent generation is more severely affected than previous ones. The molecular basis for this inheritance pattern often has been found to be the expansion of a nucleotide triplet repeat, and this mutation was determined as the basis for most cases of fragile X syndrome. However, because Nylander and colleagues did not correct for the onset of cases that may develop in the younger generation subsequent to their analysis, this conclusion may be questioned. McMahon and colleagues (1995) have suggested that bipolar affective disorder is preferentially transmitted through the maternal line with about a twofold greater risk and that mitochondrial transmission or imprinting might account for this. However, another group (Stine et al., 1995) has reported that paternal alleles are shared more frequently in affected individuals. It remains unclear whether disease heterogeneity leads to 2 differently imprinted forms of bipolar disorder or if the findings are spurious.

A large number of molecular studies have been done on bipolar affective disorder. Initially linkage was reported to chromosome 11p15 in an Old Amish kindred (Egeland et al., 1987) and to the X chromosome in European (Factor IX at Xq27) and Israeli pedigrees (glucose-6-phosphate dehydrogenase at Xq28) (Baron et al., 1987; Mendlewicz et al., 1987). However, none of these studies has been replicated and now all are generally thought to be spurious (Gejman et al., 1990; Kelsoe et al., 1989). Interestingly, Baron, Hamburger, Sandkuyl, and colleagues (1990) have reexamined their data and have stated that linkage to the X chromosome may be present if the phenotype is restricted to very early onset, multiplex cases.

Subsequent work has proceeded in 2 ways. Numerous groups have tested specific candidate genes for association and/or linkage with no consistently positive results. Some of these candidates were chosen on the basis of chromosomal abnormalities identified in a subset of individuals with bipolar disorder, specifically 11q21–25, 15q11–13, and Xq28 (Craddock & Owen, 1994). The candidate genes tested thus far include *HRAS 1, INS* (Law et al., 1992), *DRD4* (Lim et al., 1994; Maier et al., 1994; Nanko et al., 1994); *DRD2, DRD3* (Nanko et al., 1994); *TH* (Maier et al., 1994); *GABA A* (Ewald, Mors, Flint, & Kruse, 1994); G_s-*alpha* (Le et al., 1994); chromosome 15q11–13 (Ewald et al., 1994); and chromosome 9q34 (*ABO, AK1, ORM*) (Sherrington et al., 1994). Linkage to several of these sites (*DRD4, DRD2, DRD3, TH*, and chromosome 15q11–13) has been "excluded."

The other approach has been to undertake more systematic genome screening using both standard linkage methods and affected-sib-pair, allele-sharing methods. The most exciting evidence appears to identify a susceptibility gene on chromosome 18p near the D18S21 loci. The association to this locus is significant at the $p < 0.001$ level with sib-pair studies and at the $p < 0.0001$ level in affected pedigree designs (Berrettini et al., 1994, 1997). Stine and colleagues (1995) also have studied chromosome 18 in 28 nuclear families and have found evidence of excess allele sharing both in the region described by Berrettini (maximal at D18S37) and in a subset of families on the long arm of chromosome 18. Freimer (1996) also has some evidence suggestive of a linked region on 18q22–23 in a Costa Rican sample. However, the 18p region was excluded in the full Old Order Amish sample (Pauls et al., 1995). At best, 18p and 18q will account for the transmission of bipolar affective disorder in only a portion of affected individuals.

Similar studies also have yielded positive results at other sites, but each finding must be replicated in an independently ascertained sample before it is fully accepted. Blackwood and colleagues (1996) have found evidence of linkage on chromosome 4p at D4S394 in 12 Scottish families (maximal lod score 4.8) and a larger group including these same 12 families and 11 additional families. Studies of the pericentromeric region of chromosome 11 have found evidence of linkage in a subgroup of families but not the entire sample (Berrettini et al., 1994). Coon and colleagues (1993) have used the affected pedigree member method in 8 families and found evidence of linkage to the distal part of 5q (D5S62). Genome screening has found evidence of linkage to 15 markers on chromosome 21q22.3 (with a maximal lod score of 3.41 for 1 marker) in a sample of 47 families (Straub et al., 1994). Finally, in an expanded sample of the Old Order Amish, genome-wide screening has supported susceptibility loci on chromosomes 6, 13, and 15 (Ginns, Ott, & Egeland, 1996).

At this point, it is clear that children and adolescents whose parents or siblings are affected with bipolar affective disorder are at increased risk for developing the disorder themselves. In such cases, it is prudent to consider whether younger children presenting with subclinical affective disorders or disruptive behavior disorders are in fact showing early signs of bipolar disorder and should be treated accordingly. In addition, parental guidance to reduce environmental stressors may be essential. The molecular studies done to date suggest that bipolar disorder is a heterogeneous disorder with a complex, polygenic basis. Ultimately it may be possible to distinguish subtypes of the disorder that will respond to specific treatments. Identification of specific genes which confer vulnerability will be important in designing more effective treatments.

Gene Environment Interactions

Identification of genetic factors involved in developmental psychiatric disorders is of limited value in and of itself. Only in exceptional cases is the expression and outcome of a neurodevelopmental disorder completely determined by genetic factors. Therefore, it is essential to understand and identify the ways in which environmental factors interact with genetic factors to influence a particular disorder (also discussed by Rutter and Plomin (1997).

Kendler and Eaves (1986) have postulated that gene-environment interactions can occur in 3 ways. In the first case, the effects of the gene and the environmental factor associated with development of the disorder are independent but additive. In this case, an increase in either genetic loading or environmental exposure would lead to an increased incidence of the disorder. The inci-

dence would be greatest in individuals with both genetic and environmental risks. In the second model, genes act to control sensitivity to the environment. Here individuals with genetic sensitivity would be expected to have a markedly increased rate of illness in a predisposing environment. In the third case, the susceptibility genes act by increasing exposure to a predisposing environment. In this case, all individuals have the same likelihood of developing the disorder in a predisposing environment, but those with genetic susceptibility are much more likely to be in a predisposing environment. It is likely that most genes act in multiple ways; for instance, a gene might increase both exposure and sensitivity to a predisposing environment. Frequently a given gene will have different sorts of interactions with different environment factors. For instance, the gene for familial hypercholesterolemia seems to have an additive effect with respect to hypertension and a sensitivity effect with respect to dietary cholesterol.

It is possible to identify specific environmental factors that are likely to interact with genetic factors in a given disorder even before the genes involved are identified. Careful mathematical analyses of twin studies (reviewed in Neale et al., 1989) can be used to estimate the extent to which similarities between twins result from either shared or nonshared environmental influences rather than from genetic influences. Factor analyses of such results may be useful in identifying specific factors that influence expression of the disorder. Studies of adoptive siblings and of blended families (whose numbers are steadily increasing) also allow for the identification of shared environmental factors that have similar neuropsychiatric consequences in the absence of shared genetic factors. In addition, longitudinal studies of children at high genetic risk for developing a given disorder may allow researchers to identify environmental factors associated with either increases or decreases in expression of the disorder. Work with such high-risk populations allows for the examination of the effect of environmental interventions on the expression of the disorder.

Identification of specific genes associated with a given disorder can provide important advantages to the study of environmental mediators. Knowledge of specific genotypes associated with susceptibility allows for phenocopies of the disorder that may be influenced by different environmental factors to be distinguished. Such accurate identification of the at risk population increases the likelihood that important environmental factors will be detected.

In addition, identification of susceptibility genes provides opportunities to examine experimentally the potential neurobiological consequences of specific environmental factors on aspects of the gene's or protein's function. At the most basic level, the ways in which expression of the gene is modified by different growth factors and chemicals (including neurotransmitters and environmental toxins) within culture systems can be examined. Such in vitro systems provide an important means of investigating the differential effects of environmental factors on the functional activities of the mutated and wild-type forms of the gene. In vivo studies provide opportunities to study gene-environment interactions in a much broader context and are likely to be far more relevant to neuropsychiatric disorders. One strategy is to artificially introduce the gene or specific blockers of it (antisense DNA) into experimental animals at various ages and under various conditions. Another is to create transgenic animals in which a particular gene has been functionally deleted—these animals are known as "knockouts" for that gene. Transgenic animals can also be bred that overexpress the resulting protein because additional copies of the gene have been introduced. The development of transgenic animals can be very demanding technically, but currently it provides the most comprehensive way to assess the biologically relevant functions and interactions of a gene. In addition, transgenic animals with double gene knockouts allow gene-gene interactions to be assessed. Finally, transgenic technologies can be used to assess the function and environmental regulation of a given gene throughout the course of development. Such longitudinal assessments are especially important for better understanding childhood psychiatric disorders.

Conclusion

In this chapter we have reviewed the ways in which genes may influence the expression of developmental neuropsychiatric disorders. We have examined the research tools that are available to assess the contribution of genetic influences and to identify specific genes and environmental factors involved in the expression of particular disorders. Finally, we have reviewed the current understanding of the molecular basis for a number of childhood psychiatric disorders. Although tremendous progress has been made, there is a great deal more to learn. It is hoped that the next few decades will bring major advances both in our understanding of which genetic factors are involved and in how they interact with environmental factors. Knowledge of these complex interactions should help us more accurately diagnose neuropsychiatric illnesses and develop more effective and less toxic treatments.

REFERENCES

Akiskal, H. S., Downs, J., Jordan, P., Watson, S., Daugherty, D., & Pruitt, D. B. (1985). Affective disorders in referred children and younger siblings of manic depressives: Mode of onset and prospective course. *Archives of General Psychiatry, 42,* 996–1003.

Angst, J., Merikangas, K. R., Scheidegger, P., & Wicki, W. (1990). Recurrent brief depression: A new subtype of affective disorder. *Journal of Affective Disorders, 19,* 37–38.

Aschauer, H. N., Aschauer-Treiber, G., Isenberg K. E., et al. (1990). No evidence for linkage between chromosome 5 markers and schizophrenia. *Human Heredity, 40,* 109–115.

August, G. J., Stewart, M. A., & Tsai, L. (1981). The incidence of cognitive disabilities in the siblings of autistic children. *British Journal of Psychiatry, 138,* 416–422.

Bailey, A. J., Bolton, P. (1993). Prevalence of the fragile X anomaly amongst autistic twins and singletons. *Journal of Child Psychology and Psychiatry, 34,* 673–688.

Bailey, et al. (1995). *Psychological Medicine 25:* 63–78.

Baird, T. D., & August, G. J. (1985). Familial heterogeneity in infantile autism. *Journal of Autism and Developmental Disorders, 15,* 315–321.

Bakwin, H. (1973). Reading disability in twins. *Development Medicine and Child Neurology, 15,* 184–187.

Barley, A., LeCouteur, A., Gottesman, I. I., Bolton, P.,

Simonoff, E., Rutter, M., & Yuzda, E. (1995). Autism as a strongly genetic disorder: evidence from a British twin study. *Psychol Medicine.*

Baron, M., Hamburger, R., Sandkuyl, L. A., et al. (1990). The impact of phenotypic variation on genetic analysis: application to x-linkage in manic-depressive illness. *Acta Psychiatrica Scandinavica, 83,* 196–203.

Baron, M., Risch, N., Hamburger, R., Mandel, B., Kushner, S., Newman, M., & Belmarker, R. H. (1987). Genetic linkage between X-chromosome marks and bipolar affective illness. *Nature, 326,* 289–292.

Baron, M., Shapiro, E., Shapiro, A., & Rainer, J. D. (1981). Genetic analysis of Tourette syndrome suggesting major gene effects. *American Journal of Human Genetics, 33,* 767–775.

Barr, C. L., Kennedy, J. L., Pakstis, A. J., et al. (1994). Progress in a genome scan for linkage in schizophrenia in a large Swedish kindred. *American Journal of Medical Genetics, 54,* 51–58.

Bartak, L., Rutter, M., & Cox, A. (1975). A comparative study of infantile autism and specific developmental receptive language disorder: The children. *British Journal of Psychiatry, 126,* 127–145.

Beardslee, W. R., Bemporad, J., Keller, M. B., & Klerman, G. L. (1983). Children of parents with major affective disorder: A review. *American Journal of Psychiatry, 140,* 825–832.

Behrman, R. E. (1992). *Nelson textbook of pediatrics* (14th ed.). Philadelphia: W. B. Saunders.

Bellodi, L., Sciuto, G., Diaferia, G., Ronchi, P., & Smeraldi, E. (1992). Psychiatric disorders in the families of patients with obsessive-compulsive disorder. *Psychiatry Research, 42,* 111–120.

Benkelfat, C., Ellenbogen, M. S., Dean, P., et al. (1994). Mood lowering effect of tryptophan depletion—enhanced susceptibility in young men at genetic risk for major affective disorders. *Archives of General Psychiatry, 51,* 687–697.

Bennett, L. A., Wolin, S. J., & Reiss, D. (1988). Cognitive, behavioral and emotional problems among school-age children of alcoholic parents. *American Journal of Psychiatry, 145,* 185–190.

Berger, M., Yule, W., & Rutter, M. (1975). Attainment and adjustment in two geographical areas. II. The prevalence of specific reading retardation. *British Journal of Psychiatry, 126,* 510–519.

Berrettini, W. H., Goldin, L. R., Glernter, J., et al. (1990). X-chromosome markers and manic-depressive illness. Rejection of linkage to Xq28 in nine bipolar pedigrees. *Archives of General Psychiatry 47:* 366–373.

Berrettini, W. H., Ferraro, T. N., Goldin, L. R., et al. (1994). Chromosome 18 DNA markers and manic depressive illness—evidence for a susceptibility gene. *Proceedings of the National Academy of Sciences, 91,* 5918–5921.

Berrettini, W. H., Ferraro, T. N., Goldin, L. R., et al. (1997). A linkage study of bipolar illness. *Archives of General Psychiatry, 54,* 27–35.

Bertelsen, A., Harvald, B., & Hauge, M. (1977). A Danish twin study of manic-depressive disorders. *British Journal of Psychiatry, 130,* 330–351.

Biederman, J., Faraone, S. V., Keenan, K., et al. (1992). Further evidence for family-genetic risk factors in attention deficit hyperactivity disorder: Patterns of comorbidity in probands and relatives in psychiatrically and pediatrically referred samplees. *Archives of General Psychiatry, 49,* 728–738.

Biederman, J., Munir, K., Knee, D., et al. (1986). A family study of parents with attention deficit hyperactivity disorder and normal controls. *J Psychiatric Research, 20:* 263–274.

Biederman, J., Munir, K., & Knee, D. (1987). Conduct and oppositional disorder in clinically referred children with attention deficit disorder: A controlled family study. *Journal of the American Academy of Child and Adolescent Psychiatry, 26,* 724–727.

Biederman, J., Newcorn, J., & Sprich, S. (1991). Comorbidity of attention deficit hyperactivity disorder with conduct, depressive, anxiety, and other disorders. *American Journal of Psychiatry 148:* 564–577.

Biederman, J., Rivinus, T., Kemper, K., Hamilton, D., MacFadyen, J., & Harmatz, J. (1985). Depressive disorders in relatives of anorexia nervosa patients with and without a current episode of nonbipolar major depression. *American Journal of Psychiatry, 142,* 1495–1496.

Blackwood, D. H. R., He, L., Morris, S. W., et al. (1996). A locus for bipolar affective disorder on chromosome 4p. *12,* 427–430.

Blomquist, H. K., Bohman, M., Edvinsson, S. O., Gillberg, C., Gustavson, K. H., Holmgren, G., & Wahlström, J. (1985). Frequency of the Fragile X syndrome in infantile autism: a Swedish multicenter study. *Clinical Genetics 27:* 113–117.

Blum, K., Noble, E. P., Sheridan, P. J., Montgomery, A., Ritchie, T., Jagadeeswaran, P., Nogami, H., Briggs, A. H., & Cohn, J. B. (1990). Allelic association of human dopamine D2 receptor gene in alcoholism. *Journal of the American Medical Association, 263,* 2055–2060.

Boder, E. (1971). Developmental dyslexia: Prevailing diagnostic concepts and a new diagnostic approach. In M. R. Myklebust (Ed.), *Progress in learning disabilities* (Vol. 2). New York: Grune & Stratton.

Bohman, M. (1971). A comparative study of adopted children, foster children and children in their biological environment born after undesired pregnancies. *Acta Paediatrica Scandinavica* (Suppl. 221).

Bohman, M. (1972). The study of adopted children, their background, environment and adjustment. *Acta Paediatrica Scandinavia, 61,* 90–97.

Bohman, M., Cloninger, C. R., Sigvardsson, S., & von Knorring, A.-L. (1982). Predisposition to petty criminality in Swedish adoptees. I. Genetic and environmental heterogeneity. *Archives of General Psychiatry, 39,* 1233–1241.

Braun, D. L., Sunday, S. R., & Halmi, K. A. (1994). Psychiatric comorbidity in patients with eating disorders. *Psychological Medicine, 24,* 859–867.

Brent, D. A., Perper, J. A., Moritz, G., et al. (1994). Suicide in affectively ill adolescents—a case control study. *Journal of Affective Disorders, 31,* 193–202.

Brown, D., Gorin, M. B., & Weeks, D. E. (1994). Efficient strategies for genomic searching using the affected pedigree member method of linkage analysis. *Am J Human Genetics, 54, 544.*

Burd, L., Kerbeshian, L., Wikenhelser, M., & Fisher, W. (1986). A prevalence study of Gilles de la Tourette syndrome in North Dakota school-age children. *Journal of the American Academy of Child Psychiatry, 25:* 552.

Cadoret, R. J. (1978). Evidence for genetic inheritance of primary affective disorder in adoptees. *American Journal of Psychiatry, 133,* 463–466.

Cadoret, R. J., O'Gorman, T. W., Heywood, E., & Troughton, E. (1985). Genetic and environmental factors in major depression. *Journal of Affective Disorders, 9,* 155–164.

Cadoret, R. J., Troughton, E., O'Gorman, T. W., & Heywood, M. A. (1986). An adoption study of genetic and environmental factors in drug abuse. *Archives of General Psychiatry, 43,* 1131–1136.

Cadoret, R. J., & Stewart, M. A. (1991). An adoption study of attention deficit/hyperactivity/aggression and their relationship to adult antisocial personality. *Comprehensive Psychiatry, 32,* 73–82.

Cadoret, R. J., Yates, W. R., Troughton, E., et al. (1995). Genetic-environment interaction in the genesis of aggressivity and conduct disorders. *Archives of General Psychiatry, 52, 916–924.*

Caine, E. D., Mcbride, M. C., Chiverton, P., Bamford, K. A., Rediess, S., & Shiao, S. (1988). Tourette syndrome in Monroe County school children. *Neurology 38:* 472–475.

Cannon, T. D., & Marco, E. (1994). Structural brain abnormalities as indicators of vulnerability to schizophrenia. *Schizophrenia Bulletin, 20,* 89–102.

Cannon, T. D., & Mednick, S. A. (1993). The schizophrenia high-risk project in Copenhagen: Three decades of progress. *Acta Psychiatrica Scandinavica* (Suppl. 370), 33–47.

Cannon, T. D., Mednick, S. A., Parnas, J., et al. (1993). Developmental brain abnormalities in the offspring of schizophrenic mothers. I. Contributions of genetic and perinatal factors. *Archives of General Psychiatry, 50,* 551–564.

Cantwell, D. P. (1972). Psychiatric illness in the families of hyperactive children. *Archives of General Psychiatry 27:* 414–417.

Cantwell, D. P. (1975). Genetic studies of hyperactive children: Psychiatric illness in biological and adopting parents. In R. Fieve, D. Rosenthal, & H. Brill (Eds.), *Genetic research in psychiatry* (pp. 273–280). Baltimore, MD: Johns Hopkins University Press.

Cardon, A. G., & McGuffin, P. (1994). The molecular genetics of schizophrenia. *Neuropathology and Applied neurobiology, 20,* 344–349.

Cardon, L. R., Smith, S. D., Fulker, D. W., et al. (1994). Quantitative trait locus for reading disability on chromosome 6. *Science, 266,* 276–279.

Carey, G., & Gotteman, I. I. (1981). Twin and family studies of anxiety, phobic and obsessive disorders. In D. F. Klein & J. Rankin (Eds.), *Anxiety: New research and changing concepts.* New York: Raven Press.

Catalano, M., Sciuto, G., DiBella, D., et al. (1994). Lack of association between obsessive-compulsive disorder and the dopamine D-3 receptor gene—some preliminary considerations. *American Journal of Medical Genetics, 54,* 253–255.

Cederlof, R., Friberg, L., Johnson, E., & Kau, L. (1961). Studies of similarity diagnosis in twins with the aid of mailed questionnaires. *Acta Genetica* (Basel), *11,* 338–362.

Christiansen, K. O. (1977). A review of studies of criminality among twins. In S. Mednick & K. O. Christiansen (Eds.), *Biosocial bases of criminal behavior* (pp. 45–88). New York: Gardner Press.

Clerget-Darpous, F., Babron, M. C., & Banaiti-Pellie, C. (1990). Assessing the effect of multiple linkage tests in complex diseases. *Genetic Epidemiology, 7,* 245–253.

Cloninger, C. R., Bohman, M., & Signardsson, S. (1981). Inheritance of alcohol abuse: Cross-fostering analysis of adopted men. *Archives of General Psychiatry, 38,* 861–868.

Cloninger, C. R., & Gottesman, I. I. (1987). Genetic and environmental factors in antisocial behavior disorders. In S. A. Mednick, T. E. Moffitt, & S. A. Stack (Eds.), *Cause of crime: New biological approaches* (pp. 92–109). Cambridge: Cambridge University Press.

Cohen, P., Brook, J. S., Cohen, J., Velez, N., & Garcia, M. (1990). Common and uncommon pathways to adolescent psychopathology and problem behavior. In L. Robins & M. Rutter (Eds.), *Straight and devious pathways from childhood to adulthood* (pp. 252–258). London: Cambridge University Press.

Comings, D. E., & Comings, B. G. (1984). Tourette's syndrome and attention deficit disorder with hyperactivity: Are they genetically related? *Journal of the American Academy of Child Psychiatry, 23,* 138–146.

Comings, D. E., Comings, B. G., Devor, E. J., & Cloninger, E. R. (1984). Detection of major gene for Gilles de al Tourette syndrome. *American Journal of Human Genetics, 36,* 586–600.

Comings, D. E., & Comings, B. G. (1987). Hereditary agorophobia and obsessive compulsive behavior in the relatives of patients with Gilles de la Tourette's syndrome. *British J Psychiatry 151:* 195–199.

Comings, D. E., Comings, B. G., Muhleman, D., et al. (1991). The dopamine D_2 receptor locus as a modifying gene in neuropsychiatric disorders. *Journal of the American Medical Association, 266,* 1793–1800.

Comings, D. E., Himes, J. A., & Comings, B. G. (1990). An epidemiological study of Tourette's syndrome in a single school district. *Journal of Clinical Psychiatry 51:* 463–469.

Cook, E. H. Jr, Stein, M. S., Krasowski, M. D., et al. (1995). Association of attention deficit disorder and the dopamine transporter gene. *Am J Human Genetics 56:* 993–996.

Coon, H., Hoff, M., Holik, J., Delisi, L. E., Crowe, T., Freedman, R., Shields, G., Boccio, A. M., Lerman, M., Gershon, E. S., Gejman, P. V., Leppert, M., & Byerley, W. (1993). C toT nucleotide substitution in codon 713 of amyloid precursor protein gene not found in 86 unrelated schizophrenics from multiplex families. *American Journal of Medical Genetics, 48,* 36–39.

Coon, H., Jensen, S., Holik, J., et al. (1994). Genomic scan for genes predisposing to schizophrenia. *American J Human Genetics 54:* 59–71.

Corder, E. H., Saunders, A. M., Stritlmatter, W. J., et al. (1993). Gene dose of apoprotein E type 4 allele and the risk of Alzheimer's Disease in late onset families. *Science 261:* 921–923.

Corder, E. H., Saunders, A. M., Risch, N. J., et al. (1994). Protective effect of apoprotein E type 2 allele for late onset Alzheimer's Disease. *Nature Genetics 7:* 180–184.

Crabbe, J. C., Belknap, J. K., & Buck, K. J. (1994). Genetic animal models of alcohol and drug abuse. *Science, 264,* 1715–1724.

Craddock, N., & Owen, M. (1994). Chromosomal aberrations and bipolar affective disorder. *British Journal of Psychiatry, 164,* 507–512.

Crowe, R. R. (1972). The adopted offspring of women criminal offenders: A study of their arrest records. *Archives of General Psychiatry, 27,* 600–603.

Crowe, R. R. (1974). An adoption study of antisocial personality. *Archives of General Psychiatry, 31,* 785–791.

Crowe, R. R. (1990). The application of genetic methods to the study of disease associations in psychiatry. *Psychiatric Clinics of North America, 13,* 585–596.

Crowe, R. R. (1991). Lack of linkage to chromosome 5q11-q13 markers in six schizophrenia pedigrees. *Archives of General Psychiatry, 58,* 357–361.

Crow, T. J. (1986). The continuum of psychosis and its implication for the structure of the gene. *British Journal of Psychiatry 149:* 419–429.

Crow, T. J. (1994). Chromosomal aberration and bipolar affective disorder. *British Journal of Psychiatry, 165,* 693.

Cunningham, L., Cadoret, R., Loftus, R., & Edwards, J. E. (1975). Studies of adoptees from psychiatrically disturbed biological parents. *British Journal of Psychiatry 126:* 534–539.

Dalgaard, O. C., & Kringlen, E. (1976). A Norwegian twin study of criminality. *British Journal of Criminology, 16,* 213–232.

Damato, T., Waksman, G., Martinez, M., et al. (1994). Pseudoautosomal region in schizophrenia—linkage analysis of seven loci by sib-pair and LOD-score methods. *Psychiatry Research, 52,* 135–137.

Daniels, J., Williams, J., Mant, R., et al. (1994). Repeat length variation in the dopamin D4 receptor gene shows no evidence of association with schizophrenia. *American Journal of Medical Genetics, 54,* 256–258.

Davies, J. L., Kawaguchi, Y., Bennett, S. T., et al. (1994). A genome-wide search for human type 1 diabetes susceptibility genes. *Nature, 371,* 130–136.

De bruyn, A., Mendelbaum, K., Sandkuijl, L. A., et al. (1994). Nonlinkage of bipolar illness to tyrosine hydroxylase, tyrosinase, and D2 and D4 dopamine receptor genes on chromosome 11. *American Journal of Psychiatry, 151,* 102–106.

Decina, P., Kestenbaum, C. J., Farber, S., Kron, L., Gargan, M., Sackeim, H. A., & Fieve, R. R. (1983). Clinical and psychological assessment of children of bipolar probands. *American Journal of Psychiatry, 140,* 548–553.

DeFries, J. C., & Gillis, J. J. (1993). Genetics of reading disability. In R. Plomin & G. E. McClearn (Eds.), *Nature, nurture and psychology* (pp. 121–146). Washington, DC: American Psychological Association.

DeFries, J. C., & Decker, S. N. (1981). Genetic aspects of reading disability: The Colorado Family Reading Study. In P. G. Aaron & M. Malatesha (Eds.), *Neuropsychological and neuropsycholinguistic aspects of reading disability.* New York: Academic Press.

DeFries, J. C., Fulker, D. W., & LaBuda, M. C. (1987). Evidence for a genetic etiology in reading disability of twins. *Nature, 329,* 537–539.

DeFries, J. C. (1989). Gender ratios in reading disabled children and their affected relatives: a commentary. *J of Learning Disability 22:* 544–545.

DeFries, J. C., Singer, S. M., Foch, T. Y., & Lewite, F. I. (1978). Familial nature of reading disability. *British Journal of Psychiatry, 132,* 361–367.

DeGroot, C. M., & Bornstein, R. A. (1994). Obsessive characteristics in subjects with Tourette's syndrome are related to symptoms in their parents. *Comprehensive Psychiatry, 35,* 248–251.

DeLong, G., & Dwyer, J. (1988). Correlation of family history with specific autistic subgroups: Asperger's syndrome and bipolar affective disease. *J of Autism & Devel Disorders 18:* 593–600.

Deterawadleigh, S. D., Hsieh, W. T., Berrettini, E. H., et al. (1994). Genetic linkage mapping for a susceptibility locus to bipolar illness—chromosomes 2, 3, 4, 7, 9, 10P, 11P, 22, and XPTER. *American Journal of Medical Genetics, 54,* 206–218.

Devor, E. J. (1984). Complex segregation analysis of Gilles de la Tourette syndrome: Further evidence for a major locus mode of transmission. *American Journal of Human Genetics, 36,* 704–709.

Dinwiddie, S. H., & Reich, T. (1993). Genetic and family studies in psychiatric illness and alcohol and drug dependence. *Journal of Addictive Diseases, 12,* 17–27.

Dobbins, D. A., & Tafa, E. (1992). The 'stability' of identification of underachieving readers over different measures of intelligence and reading. *British Journal of Educational Psychology 61:* 155–163.

Dolan, B. (1991). Cross cultural aspects of anorexia nervosa and bulimia: a review. *International J of Eating Disorders 10:* 67–80.

Dwyer, J. T., & DeLong, G. R. (1987). A family history study of 20 probands with childhood manic-depressive illness. *Journal of the American Academy of Child and Adolescent Psychiatry, 26,* 176–180.

Dykens, E., Leckman, J. F., Paul, R., & Watson, M. (1988). Cognitive, behavioral and adaptive functioning in fragile X and non–fragile X retarded men. *Journal of Autism and Developmental Disorders, 18,* 41–52.

Dykens, E. M., Hodapp, R. M., Ort, S., Finucane, B., Shapiro, L. R., & Leckman, J. F. (1989). The trajectory of cognitive development in males with fragile X syndrome. *Journal of the American Academy of Child and Adolescent Psychiatry, 28,* 422–426.

Eagles, J. M. (1994). Strength of the genetic effect in schizophrenia. *British Journal of Psychiatry, 165,* 266.

Earls, F., Reich, W., Jung, K., & Cloninger, C. R. (1988). Psychopathology in children of alcoholic and antisocial parents. *Alcoholism: Clinical and Experimental Research, 12,* 481–487.

Eaves, L. J., Silberg, J. L., Hewitt, J. K., Rutter, M., Meyer, J. M., Neale, M. G., Pickles, A., et al. (1993). Analyzing twin resemblance in multisymptom data: Genetic applications of a latent class model for symptoms of conduct disorder in juvenile boys. *Behavior Genetics, 23,* 5–19.

Eden, G. F., Van Meter, J. W., Rumocy, J. M., Maisog, J. M., Woods, R. P., Zeffiro, T. A. (1996). Abnormal processing of visual motion in dyslexia revealed by functional brain imaging. *Nature 382:* 66–69.

Egeland, J. A., Gerhard, D. S., Pauls, D. L., Sussex, J. N., Kidd, K. K., Allen, C. R., Histetter, A. M., & Housman, D. E. (1987). Bipolar affective disorders linked to DNA markers on chromosome 11. *Nature, 325,* 783–786.

Eggers, C. (1978). Course and prognosis in childhood schizophrenia. *Journal of Autism and Childhood Schizophrenia 8:* 21–36.

Ewald, H., Mors, O., Flint, T., & Kruse, T. S. (1994). Manic-depressive illness and the region on chromosome 15Q involved in Prader-Willi syndrome, including two GABA(a) receptor subtype genes. *Human Heredity, 44,* 287–294.

Fairburn, C. G., & Beglin, S. J. (1990). Studies of the epidemiology of bulimia nervosa. *Journal of Psychosomatic Research 32:* 635–646.

Falk, C. T., & Rubinstein, P. (1987). Haplotype relative risks: An easy reliable way to construct a proper control sample for risk calculations. *Annals of Human Genetics, 51,* 227–233.

Faraone, S. V., Biederman, J., Keenan, K., & Tsuangm, M. T. (1991). Separation of DM-II attention deficit disorder and conduct disorder: Evidence from a family-genetic study of American child psychiatric patients. *Psychological Medicine, 21,* 109–121.

Farber, S. L. (1982). *Identical twins reared apart: A re-analysis.* New York: Basic Books.

Finucci, J. M., Guthrie, J. T., Childs, A. L., Abbey, H., & Childs, B. (1976). The genetics of specific reading disability. *Annals of Human Genetics, 40,* 1–23.

Fischer, M. (1971). Psychoses in the offspring of schizophrenic monozygotic twins and their normal co-twins. *British Journal of Psychiatry 118:* 43–52.

Flint, J. (1992). Editorial: Implications of genomic imprinting for psychiatric genetics. *Psychological Medicine, 22,* 5–10.

Folstein, S., & Rutter, M. (1988). Autism familial aggregation & genetic implications. *J Autism & Developmental Disorders 18:* 3–30.

Freedman, R., Coon, H., Myles-Worsley, M., et al. (1997). Linkage of a neurophysiological deficit in schizophrenia to a chromosome 15 locus. *Proceedings National Academy of Sciences, 94,* 587–592.

Freimer, N. B. (1996). An approach to investigating linkage for bipolar disorder using large Costa Rican pedigrees. *American Journal of Medical Genetics, 67,* 254–263.

Garfinkel, P. E., & Garner, D. M. (1982). *Anorexia nervosa: A multidimensional perspective.* New York: Brunner-Mazel.

Gejman, P. V., Detera-Wadleigh, S., Martinez, M. M., et al. (1990). Manic depressive illness not linked to factor IX region in an independent series of pedigrees. *Genomics, 8,* 648–655.

Gejman, P. V., & Gelernter, J. (1993). Mutational analysis of candidate genes in psychiatric disorders. *American Journal of Medical Genetics, 48,* 184–191.

Gelernter, J., & Crowe, R. R. (1997). Candidate genes and psychiatric genetics: tomorrow never knows. *Psychiatric Annals 27:* 262–266.

Gelernter, J., Goldman, D., & Risch, N. (1993). The A1 allele at the D2 dopamine receptor gene and alcoholism. *Journal of the American Medical Association, 269,* 1673–1677.

Gershon, E. S., Hamovit, J., Guroff, J. J., et al. (1982). A family study of schizoaffective, bipolar I, bipolar II, unipolar, and normal control probands. *Archives of General Psychiatry 39:* 1157–1167.

Gershon, E. S., Martinez, M., Goldin, L. R., & Gejman, P. V. (1990). Genetic mapping of common diseases: The challenges of manic-depressive illness and schizophrenia. *Trends in Genetics, 6,* 282–287.

Gershon, E. S., Schreiber, J. L., Hamovit, J. R., Dibble, E. D., Kaye, W. H., Nurnberger, J. I., Andersen, A., & Ebert, M. H. (1984). Clinical findings in patients with anorexia nervosa and affective illness in their relatives. *American Journal of Psychiatry, 141,* 1419–1422.

Gershon, P. E., & Garner, D. M. (1982). *Anorexia nervosa: A multidimensional perspective.* New York: Brunner-Mazel.

Gill, M., Daly, G., Heron, S., Hawi, Z., & Fitzgerald, M. (1997). Conformation of association between hyperactivity attention deficit disorder and adopamine transporter polymorphism. *Molecular Psychiatry 2:* 311–313.

Gillberg, C., Gillberg, I. C., & Steffenburg, S. (1992). Siblings and parents of children with autism: A controlled population-based study. *Developmental Medicine and Child Neurology, 34,* 389–398.

Gillberg, C., Persson, E., Grufman, M., & Themner, U. (1986). Psychiatric disorders in mildly and severely mentally retarded urban children and adolescents: Epidemiological aspects. *British Journal of Psychiatry, 149,* 68–74.

Ginns, E. I., Ott, J., & Egeland, J. A. (1996). A genome-wide search for chromosomal loci linked to bipolar affective disorder in the Old Order Amish. *Nature Genetics 12,* 431–435.

Goldin, L. R., & Gershon, E. S. (1988). Power of the affected-sib-pair method for heterogeneous disorders. *Genetic Epidemiology, 5,* 35–42.

Golding-Kushner, K. J., Weller, G., & Shprintzen, R. J. (1985). Velo-cardio-facial syndrome: Language and psychological profiles. *Journal of Craniofacial Genetics, 51,* 259–266.

Goldsmith, H. H. (1991). A zygosity questionnaire for young twins: a research note. *Behavior Genetics, 21,* 257–270.

Goodfellow, P. N., & Schmitt, K. (1994). From the simple to the complex. *Nature 371:* 104–105.

Goodman, R., & Stevenson, J. (1989a). A twin study of hyperactivity. I. An examination of hyperactivity scores and categories derived from Rutter teacher and parent questionnaires. *Journal of Child Psychology and Psychiatry, 30,* 671–689.

Goodman, R., & Stevenson, J. (1989b). A twin study of hyperactivity. II. The aetiological role of genes, family relationships and perinatal adversity. *Journal of Child Psychology and Psychiatry, 30,* 691–709.

Goodwin, D. W., Schulsinger, F., Hermansen, L., Guze, S. B., & Winokur, G. (1973). Alcohol problems in adoptees raised apart from alcoholic biological parents. *Archives of General Psychiatry 28:* 238–243.

Goodwin, D. W., Schulsinger, F., & Knop, J. (1977). Psychopathology in adopted and non-adopted daughters of alcoholics. *Archives of General Psychiatry, 34,* 1005–1009.

Gottesman, I. I. (1994). Schizophrenia epigenesis—past, present and future. *Acta Psychiatrica Scandinavica, 90,* 26–33.

Gottesman, I. I., & Shields, J. (1982). *Schizophrenia: The epigenetic puzzle.* New York: Cambridge University Press.

Grad, L. R., Pelcovitz, D., Olson, M., Matthews, M., & Grad, G. J. (1987). Obsessive-compulsive symptomatology in children with Tourette's syndrome. *Journal of the American Academy of Child and Adolescent Psychiatry, 26,* 69–73.

Graham and Stevenson, 1985.

Graham, P., & Stevenson, J. (1985). A twin study of genetic influences on behavioral deviance. *Journal of the American Academy of Child Psychiatry, 24,* 33–.

Greenberg, D. A. (1992). There is more than one way to collect data for linkage analysis: What a study of epilepsy can tell us about linkage strategy for psychiatric disease. *Archives of General Psychiatry, 49,* 745–750.

Greenberg, D. A., & Berger, B. (1994). Using LOD-score differences to determine mode of inheritance—a simple, robust method even in the presence of heterogeneity and reduced penetrance. *American Journal of Human Genetics, 55,* 834–840.

Grice, D. E., Leckman, J. F., Pauls, D. L., et al. (1996). Linkage disequilibrium between an allele at the dopamine D4 receptor locus and Tourette syndrome, by the transmission disequilibrium test. *American Journal of Human Genetics, 59,* 644–651.

Grigorenko, E. L., Wood, F. B., Meyer, M. S., Hart, L. A., Speed, W. C., Shuster, A., & Pauls, D. L. (1997). Susceptibility loci for distinct components of developmental dyslexia on chromosomes 6 and 15. *American Journal of Human Genetics, 60,* 27–39.

Grigoroiu-Serbanescu, M., Christodorescu, D., Jipescu, I., Totoescu, A., Marinescu, E., & Ardelean, V. (1989). Psychopathology in children aged 10–17 of bipolar parents: Rates and correlates of the severity of the psychopathology. *Journal of Affective Disorders, 16,* 167–179.

Grof, P., Alda, M., Grof, E., et al. (1994). Lithium Response and genetics of affective disorders. *Journal of Affective Disorders, 32,* 85–95.

Grove, W. M., Eckert, E. D., Heston, L., et al. (1990). Heritability of substance abuse and antisocial behavior: A study of monozygotic twins reared apart. *Biological Psychiatry, 27,* 1293–1304.

Guo, S. W., & Thompson, E. A. (1994). Monte Carlo estimation of mixed models for large complex pedigrees. *Biometrics, 50,* 417–432.

Gurling, H. M. (1990). Genetic linkage and psychiatric disease. *Nature, 344,* 298–299.

Gurling, H. M. (1990). Recent advances in the genetics of psychiatric disorder. *Ciba Foundation Symposium, 149,* 48–62.

Gurling, H. M., Clifford, L. A., & Murray, R. M. (1981). Genetic contribution to alcohol dependence and its effects in brain function. In: Gedda, L., Pinsi, P., & Nance, W. A. (Eds.), *Twin Research* (pp. 77–87). Alan R. Lissi: New York.

Hagerman, R. J., Jackson, A. W., Levitas, A., Rimland, B., & Braden, M. (1986). An analysis of autism in fifty males with the fragile X syndrome. *American Journal of Medical Genetics, 23,* 359–374.

Hallmayer, J., Maier, W., Schwab, S., et al. (1994). No evidence of linkage between the dopamine D-2 receptor gene and schizophrenia. *Psychiatry Research, 53,* 203–215.

Hammen, C., Burge, D., Burney, E., & Adrian, C. (1990). Longitudinal study of diagnoses in children of women with unipolar and bipolar affective disorder. *Archives of General Psychiatry, 47,* 1112–1120.

Hammen, C., Gordon, D., Burge, D., Adrian, C., Jaenick, C., & Hiroto, D. (1987). Maternal affective disorder, illness, and stress: risk for children's psychopathology. *American Journal of Psychiatry, 144,* 736–741.

Hanson, D. R., & Gottesman, I. I. (1976). The genetics, if any, of infantile autism and childhood schizophrenia. *Journal of Autism and Childhood Schizophrenia, 6,* 209–233.

Harrington, R., Fudge, H., Rutter, M., Pickles, A., & Hill, J. (1990). Adult outcomes of childhood and adolescent depression. I. Psychiatric status. *Archives of General Psychiatry, 47,* 465–473.

Harrington, R., Fudge, H., Rutter, M., et al. (1993). Child and adult depression: A test of continuities with data from a family study. *British Journal of Psychiatry, 162,* 627–633.

Hattori, M., Nanko, S., Dai, X. Y., et al. (1994). Mismatch PCR RFLP detection of DRD2 SER311 CYS polymorphism and schizophrenia. *Biochemical and Biophysical Research Communications, 202,* 757–763.

Hauser, P., Zametkin, A. J., Martinez, P., Vitiello, B., Matochik, J. A., Mixson, A. J., & Weintraub, B. D. (1993). Attention deficit hyperactivity disorder in people with generalized resistance to thyroid hormone. *New England J of Medicine 328:* 997–1001.

Hauser, P., Soler, R., Brucker-Davis, F., & Weintraub, P. D. (1997). Thyroid hormones correlate with symptoms of hyperactivity but not inattention in attention deficit hyperactivity disorder. *Psychoneuroendocrinology 22:* 107–114.

Hay, D. A., O'Brien, P. J., Johnston, C. J., & Prior, M. (1984). The high incidence of reading disability in twin boys and its implications for genetic analyses. *Acta Geneticae Medicae et Gemellologiae, 33,* 223–236.

Heath, A. C., & Martin, N. G. (1988). Teenage alcohol use in the Australian Twin Register: Genetic and social determinants of starting to drink. *Alcoholism: Clinical and Experimental Research, 12,* 736–741.

Herault, J., Perrot, A., Barthelemy, C., Buchler, M., Cherpi, C., et al. (1993). Possible association of c-Harvey-Ras-1 (*HRAS-1*) marker with autism. *Psychiatry Research 46:* 261–267.

Heutink, P., van de Wetering, B. J. M., Breedveld, G. J., & Oostra, B. A. (1992). Genetic study on Tourette syndrome in the Netherlands. *Advances in Neurology, 58,* 167–172.

Hill, E. M., Blow, F. C., Young, J. P., & Singer, K. M. (1994). Family history of alcoholism and childhood adversity—joint effects on alcohol consumption and dependence. *Alcoholism—Clinical and Experimental Research, 18,* 1083–1090.

Ho, H. Z., Gillger, J. W., & Decker, S. M. (1988). A twin study of Bannatyne's "genetic dyslexic" sub-type. *Journal of Child Psychology and Psychiatry, 29,* 63–72.

Hodge, S. E. (1992). Do bilineal pedigrees represent a problem for linkage analysis? *Genetic Epidemiology, 9,* 191–206.

Hodge, S. E. (1993). Linkage analysis versus association analysis: Distinguishing between two models that explain disease-marker associations. *American Journal of Human Genetics, 53,* 367–384.

Hodge, S. E., & Elston, R. C. (1994). LODS, WRODS, and MODS—the interpretation of LOD scores calculated under different models. *Genetic Epidemiology, 11,* 329–342.

Holland, A. J., Hall, A., Murray, R., Russell, G. F. M., & Crisp, A. H. (1984). Anorexia nervosa: A study of 34 twin pairs and one set of triplets. *British Journal of Psychiatry, 145,* 414–419.

Holroyd, S., Reiss, A. L., & Bryan, R. N. (1991). Autistic features in Joubert syndrome: a genetic disorder with agenesis of the cerebellar vermis. *Biological Psychiatry, 29,* 287–294.

Hoek, H. W. (1991). The incidence and prevalence of anorexia nervosa and bulimia nervosa in primary care. *Psychological Medicine 21:* 455–460.

Holzman, P. S. (1992). Behavioral markers of schizophrenia useful for genetic studies. *Journal of Psychiatric Research, 26,* 427–445.

Hudson, J. I., Pope, H. G., Jonas, J. M., & Yurgelun-Todd, D. (1983). Family history study of anorexia nervosa and bulimia. *British Journal of Psychiatry, 142,* 133–138.

Hudson, J. I., Pope, H. G., Jonas, J. M., Yurgelun-Todd, D., & Frankenburg, F. R. (1987). A controlled family history study of bulimia. *Psychological Medicine, 17,* 883–890.

Hwang, S. J., Beaty, T. H., Liang, K. Y., et al. (1994). Minimum sample size estimation to detect gene environment interaction in case-control designs. *American Journal of Epidemiology, 140,* 1029–1037.

Hyde, T. M., Aaronson, B. A., Randolph, C., Rickler, K. C., & Weinberger, D. L. (1992). Relationship of birth weight to the phenotypic expression of Gilles de la Tourette's syndrome in monozygotic twins. *Neurology, 42,* 652–658.

Irwin, M., Cox, N., & Kong, A. (1994). Sequential imputation for multilocus linkage analysis. *Proceedings of the National Academy of Science USA, 91,* 11684–11688.

Iversen, L. (1993). The D4 and schizophrenia. *Nature, 365,* 393.

Jardine, R., Martin, N. G., & Henderson, A. S. (1984). Genetic covariation between neuroticism and the symptoms of anxiety and depression. *Genetic Epidemiology, 1,* 89–107.

Jones, D. J., Fox, M. M., Babigian, H. M., & Hutton, H. E. (1980). Epidemiology of anorexia nervosa in Monroe County, New York: 1960–1976. *Psychosomatic Medicine 42:* 551–558.

Jorde, L. B., Hasstedt, S. J., Ritvo, E. R., Mason-Brothers, A., Freeman, B. J., Pingree, C., McMahon, W. M., Peterson, B., Jenson, W. R., & Moll, A. (1991). Complex segregation analysis of autism. *Am J Human Genetics 49:* 932–938.

Kaprio, J., Koskenvuo, M., Langinvainio, H., Romanov, K., Sarna, S., & Rose, R. J. (1987). Genetic influences in use and abuse of alcohol: A study of 5638 adult Finnish twin brothers. *Alcoholism: Clinical and Experimental Research, 11,* 349–356.

Karayiorgan, M., Morris, M. A., Morrow, B., Shprintzen, R. J., Goldberg, R., et al. (1995). Schizophrenia susceptibility associated with interstitial deletions of chromosome 22q11. *Proceedings of the National Academy of Science USA 92:* 7612–7616.

Kashani, J. H., Burk, J. P., & Reid, J. C. (1985). Depressed children of depressed parents. *Canadian Journal of Psychiatry, 30,* 265–269.

Kassett, J. A., Gershon, E. S., Maxwell, M. E., Gurholt, J. J., Kazuba, D. M., Smith, A. L., Brandt, H. A., & Simerson, D. C. (1989). Psychiatric disorders in the first degree relatives of probands with bulimia nervosa. *American Journal of Psychiatry 146:* 1468–1471.

Kelsoe, J. R., Ginns, E. I., Egeland, J. A., Goldstein, A. M., Bale, S. J., Pauls, D. L., Long, R. T., Conte, G., Gerhard, D. S., Housman, D. E., & Paul, S. M. (1989, August 3–5). *Re-evaluation of the linkage relationship between chromosome 11p loci and the gene for bipolar affective disorder in the Old Order Amish.* Paper presented at the First World Congress on Psychiatric Genetics, Churchill College, Cambridge.

Kelsoe, J. R. (1997). The genetics of bipolar disorder. *Psychiatric Annals 27:* 285–292.

Kendell, R. E., Hale, D. J., Hailey, A., & Babigian, H. M. (1973). The epidemiology of anorexia nervosa. *Psychological Medicine 3:* 200–203.

Kendler, K. S. (1988). The genetics of schizophrenia: an overview. In Tsuang, M. T. & Simpson, J. C. (Eds.), *Handbook of Schizophrenia vol. 3,* pp. 437–462. Elsevier, New York.

Kendler, K. S. (1994). Genetic research in psychiatry. *Behavior Genetics, 24,* 191–192.

Kendler, K. S., & Eaves, L. J. (1986). Models for the joint effect of genotype and environment on liability to psychiatric illness. *American Journal of Psychiatry, 143,* 279–289.

Kendler, K. S., Heath, A. C., Neale, M. C., et al. (1992). A population-based twin study of alcoholism in women. *Journal of the American Medical Association, 268,* 1877–1882.

Kendler, K. S., Gruenberg, A. M., & Kinney, D. K. (1994). Independent diagnoses of adoptees and relatives as defined by DSM-III in the provincial and national samples of the Danish adoption study of schizophrenia. *Archives of General Psychiatry, 51,* 456–468.

Kendler, K. S., Gruenberg, A. M., & Tsuang, M. T. (1985). Psychiatric illness in first degree relatives of schizophrenic and surgical control patients. *Archives of General Psychiatry 42:* 770–779.

Kendler, K. S., Heath, A., Martin, N. G., & Eaves, L. J. (1986). Symptoms of anxiety and depression in a volunteer twin population: The etiologic role of genetic and environmental factors. *Archives of General Psychiatry, 43,* 213–221.

Kendler, K. S., MacLean, C., Neale, M., et al. (1991). The genetic epidemiology of bulimia nervosa. *American Journal of Psychiatry, 148,* 1627–1637.

Kendler, K. S., Neale, M. C., Kessler, R. C., et al. (19). Parental treatment and the equal environment assumption in twin studies of psychiatric illness. *Psychological Medicine, 24,* 579–590.

Kendler, K. S., Neale, M. C., Kwaalwe, R. C., et al. (1992). A population-based twin study of major depression in women. The impact of varying definitions of illness. *Archives of General Psychiatry, 49,* 257–266.

Kendler, K. S., Pedersen, N., Johnson, L., et al. (1993). A pilot Swedish twin study of affective illness, including hospital- and population-ascertained subsamples. *Archives of General Psychiatry, 50,* 699–700.

Kennedy, J. L., Giuffra, L. A., Moises, H. W., Cavalli-Sforza, L. L., Pakstis, A. J., Kidd, J. R., Castiglione, C. M., Sjogren, B., Wetterberg, L., & Kidd, K. K. (1988). Evidence against linkage of schizophrenia to markers on chromosome 5 in a northern Swedish pedigree. *Nature, 336,* 167–170.

Kidd, K. K., & Pauls, D. L. (1982). Genetic hypotheses for Tourette syndrome. In A. J. Friedhoff & T. N. Chase (Eds.), *Gilles de la Tourette syndrome.* New York: Raven Press.

Klein, D. N., & Depue, R. A. (1985). Obsessional personality traits and risk for bipolar affective disorder: An offspring study. *Journal of Abnormal Psychology, 94,* 291–297.

Knott, S. A. (1994). Prediction of the power of detection of marker-quantitative trait locus linkages using analysis of variance. *Theoretical and Applied Genetics, 89,* 318–322.

Kolvin, I. (1971). Studies in the childhood psychoses. *British Journal of Psychiatry 118:* 381–419.

Kovacs, M., Paulauskas, S., Gatsonis, C., & Richards, C. (1988). Depressive disorders in childhood. III. A longitudinal study of comorbidity with and risk for conduct disorders. *Journal of Affective Disorders, 15,* 205–217.

Kremen, W. S., Tsuang, M. T., Faraone, S. V., & Lyons, M. J. (1992). Using vulnerability indicators to compare conceptual models of genetic heterogeneity in schizophrenia. *Journal of Nervous and Mental Disease, 180,* 141–152.

Kringlen, E. (1991). Adoption studies in functional psychosis. *European Archives of Psychiatry and Clinical Neuroscience, 240,* 307–313.

Kurlan, R., Eapen, V., Stern, J., et al. (1994). Bilineal transmission in Tourette's syndrome families. *Neurology, 44,* 2336–2342.

LaBuda, M. C., Gottesman, I. I., & Pauls, D. L. (1993). Usefulness of twin studies for exploring the etiology of childhood and adolescent psychiatric disorders. *American Journal of Medical Genetics, 48,* 47–59.

Lander, E. S., & Schork, N. J. (1994). Genetic dissection of complex traits. *Science, 265,* 2037–2048.

LaRoche, C., Sheiner, R., Lester, E., Benierakis, C., Marrache, M., Engelsmann, F., & Chiefetz, P. (1987). Children of parents with manic-depressive illness: A follow-up study. *Canadian Journal of Psychiatry, 32,* 563–569.

Law, A., Richard, C. W., Cottingham, R. W., et al. (1992). Genetic linkage analysis of bipolar affective disorder in an Old Order Amish pedigree. *Human Genetics, 88,* 562–568.

Le, F., Mitchell, P., Vivero, C., et al. (1994). Exclusion of close linkage of bipolar disorder to the G(S)-alpha subunit gene in nine Australian pedigrees. *Journal of Affective Disorders, 32,* 187–195.

Leckman, J. F. (1997). What genes confer vulnerability to Gilles de la Tourette's syndrome? *Psychiatric Annals 27:* 293–296.

Leckman, J. F., Weissman, M. M., Pauls, D. L., & Kidd, K. K. (1987). Family-genetic studies and identification of valid diagnostic categories in adult and child psychiatry. *British Journal of Psychiatry, 151,* 39–44.

LeCouteur, A., Bailey, A. J., Rutter, M., & Gottesman, I. I.(1989, August 3–5). *An epidemiologically based twin study of autism.* Paper presented at the First World Congress on Psychiatric Genetics, Churchill College, Cambridge.

Lenane, M. C., Swedo, S. E., Leonard, H., et al. (1990). Psychiatric disorders in first degree relatives of children and adolescents with obsessive compulsive disorder. *Journal of the American Academy of Child and Adolescent Psychiatry, 29,* 407–412.

Leonard, H. L., Lenane, M. C., Swedo, S. E., Rettew, D. C., Gershon, E. S., & Rapoport, J. L. (1992). Tics and Tourette's disorder: A 2- to 7-year follow-up of 54 obsessive-compulsive children. *American Journal of Psychiatry, 149,* 1244–1251.

Levinson, D. F., & Mowry, B. J. (1991). Defining the schizophrenia spectrum: Issues for genetic linkage studies. *Schizophrenia Bulletin, 17,* 491–514.

Lewitter, F. I., DeFries, J. C., & Elston, R. C. (1980). Genetic models of reading disability. *Behavior Genetics, 10,* 9–30.

Lichterkonecki, U., Rupp, A., Konecki, D. S., et al. (1994). Relation between phenylalanine hydroxylase genotypes and phenotypic parameters of diagnosis and treatment of hyperphenylalaninaemic disorders. *Journal of Inherited Metabolic Disease, 17,* 362–365.

Lidz, T. (1991). Genetic and environmental factors in psychiatric disorders. *American Journal of Psychiatry, 148,* 1617.

Lim, L. C. C., Nothen, M. M., Korner, J., et al. (1994). No evidence of association between dopamine D4 receptor variants and bipolar affective disorder. *American Journal of Medical Genetics, 54,* 259–263.

Livingston, R., Nugent, H., Rader, L., & Smith, G. R. (1985) Family histories of depressed and severely anxious children *American Journal of Psychiatry 142:* 1497–1499.

Lombroso, P. I., Pauls, D. L., & Leckman, J. F. (1994). Genetic mechanisms in childhood psychiatric disorders. *J Amer Academy of Child & Adolescent Psychiatry 33:* 921–938.

Lopez, E. (1965). Hyperactivity in twins. *Canadian Psychiatric Association Journal, 10,* 421–426.

Lucas, A. R., Beard, C. M., O'Fallon, W. M., & Kurlahd, L. T. (1991). Fifty-year trends in the incidence of anorexia nervosa in Rochester, Minnesota: a population based study. *American J of Psychiatry 148:* 917–922.

Lykken, D. T., McGue, M., & Tellegen, A. (1987). Recruitment bias in twin research: The rule of two-thirds reconsidered. *Behavior Genetics, 17,* 343–362.

Macciardi, F., Verga, M., Kennedy, J. L., et al. (1994). An association study between schizophrenia and the dopamine receptor genes DRD3 and DRD4 using haplotype relative risk. *Human Heredity, 44,* 328–336.

Macdonald, H., Rutter, M., Rios, P., & Bolton, P. (1989, August 3–5). *Cognitive and social abnormalities in the siblings of autistic and Down's syndrome probands.*

Paper presented at the First World Congress on Psychiatric Genetics, Churchill College, Cambridge.

Maier, W. (1993). Genetic epidemiology of psychiatric disorders. *European Archives of Psychiatry and Clinical Neuroscience, 243,* 119–120.

Maier, W., Schwab, S., Hallmayer, J., et al. (1994). Absence of linkage between schizophrenia and the dopamine D-4 receptor gene. *Psychiatry Research, 53,* 77–86.

Mangin, B., Goffinet, B., & Rebai, A. (1994). Constructing confidence intervals for QTL location. *Genetics, 138,* 1301–1308.

Mansfield, D. C., Brown, A. F., Green, D. K., et al. (1994). Automation of genetic linkage analysis using fluorescent microsatellite markers. *Genomics, 24,* 225–233.

Matthysse, S., Holzman, P. S., & Lange, K. (1986). The genetic transmission of schizophrenia: Application of Mendelian latent structure analysis to eye tracking dysfunctions in schizophrenia and affective disorders. *Journal of Psychiatric Research, 20,* 57–76.

Matthysse, S., Levy, D. L., Kinney, D., et al. (1992). Gene expression in mental illness: A navigation chart to future progress. *Journal of Psychiatric Research, 26,* 461–473.

Mattis, S., French, J. H., & Rapin, I. (1975). Dyslexia in children and young adults. Three independent neuropsychological syndromes. *Developmental Medicine and Child Neurology, 17,* 281–300.

Maziade, M., Roy, M. A., Fournier, J. P., et al. (1992). Reliability of best-estimate diagnosis in genetic linkage studies of major psychoses: Results from the Quebec pedigree studies. *American Journal of Psychiatry, 149,* 1674–1686.

McGuffin, P., & Gottesman, I. I. (1985). Genetic influences on normal and abnormal development. In M. Rutter & L. Hersov (Eds.), *Child and adolescent psychiatry: Modern approaches* (2nd ed., pp. 17–33). Oxford: Blackwell Scientific.

McGuffin, P., & Katz, R. (1986). Nature, nurture and affective disorder. In J. F. W. Deakin (Ed.), *The biology of depression* (pp. 26–552). London: The Royal College of Psychiatrists/Gaskell Press.

McGuffin, P., Katz, R., & Bebbington, P. (1987). Hazard, heredity and depression: A family study. *Journal of Psychiatric Research, 21,* 365–375.

McKusick, V. A. (1994). *Mendelian Inheritance in Man. Catalogs of Human Genes and Genetic Disorders. 11th ed.* Baltimore: Johns Hopkins University Press.

McInnes, L. A., Escamilla, M. A., Service, S. K., et al. (1996). A complete genome screen for genes predisposing to severe bipolar disorder in two Costa Rican pedigrees. *93,* 13060–13065.

McMahon, F. J., Stine, O. C., Meyers, D. A., Simpson, S. G., & DePaulo, J. R. (1995). Patterns of maternal transmission in bipolar affective disorder. *56,* 1277–1286.

McMahon, R. C. (1980). Genetic etiology in the hyperactive child syndrome: A critical review. *American Journal of Orthopsychiatry, 50,* 145–150.

Mednick, S. A., Moffit, T. E., Pollock, V., Talovic, S.,

Gabrielli, W. F., & Van Dusen, K. T. (1983). The inheritance of human deviance. In D. Magnusson & V. A. Allen (Eds.), *Human development: An interactional perspective* (pp. 221–242). New York: Academic Press.

Mendlewicz, J., Simon, P., Sevy, S., Charon, F., Brocas, H., Legros, S., & Vassart, G. (1987). Polymorphic DNA marker and X-chromosome and manic depression. *Lancet, 1,* 1230–1232.

Merikangas, K. R., & Gelernter, C. S. (1990). Comorbidity for alcoholism and depression. *Psychiatric Clinics of North America, 13,* 613–632.

Merikangas, K. R., Risch, N. J., & Weissman, M. M. (1994). Comorbidity and cotransmission of alcoholism, anxiety and depression. *Psychological Medicine, 24,* 69–80.

Mitchell, J., McCauley, E., Burke, P., Calderon, R., & Schloredt, K. (1989). Psychopathology in parents of depressed children and adolescents. *Journal of the American Academy of Child and Adolescent Psychiatry, 28* (3), 352–357.

Moises, H. W., Gelernter, J., Giuffra, L. A., et al. (1991). No linkage between D2 dopamine receptor gene region and schizophrenia. *Archives of General Psychiatry, 48,* 6443–647. See 49:383.

Morris, S., Leung, J., Sharp, C., Blackwood, D., Muir, W., & St. Clair, D. (1994). Screening schizophrenic patients for mutations in the amyloid precursor gene. *Psychiatric Genetics 4:* 23–27.

Morris-Yates, A., Andrews, G., Howie, P., & Henderson, S. (1990). Twins: A test of the equal environments assumption. *Acta Psychiatrica Scandinavica, 81,* 322–326.

Morrison, J., & Stewart, M. (1973). The psychiatric status of the legal families of adopted hyperactive children. *Archives of General Psychiatry, 28,* 888–891.

Morrison, J. R., & Stewart, M. (1974). Bilateral inheritance as evidence for polygenicity in the hyperactive child syndrome. *Journal of Nervous and Mental Disease, 158,* 226–228.

Motro, U., & Thompson, G. (1985). The affected sib pair method. I. Statistical features of the affected sib pair method. *Genetics, 110,* 525–538.

Muenke, et al. (1994). *Nature Genetics, 8,* 269–274.

Mulvihill, J. J. (1995). Craniofacial syndromes: No such thing as a single gene disorder. *Nature Genetics, 9,* 101–103.

Murthy, K. K., Shen, S. H., & Banville, D. (1995). A sensitive method for detection of mutations. *DNA & Cell Biology 14:* 87–94.

Nanko, S., Fukuda, R., Hattori, M., et al. (1994a). Further evidence of no linkage between schizophrenia and the dopamine D3 receptor gene locus. *American Journal of Medical Genetics, 54,* 264–267.

Nanko, S., Fukuda, R., Hattori, M., et al. (1994). No evidence of linkage or allelic association of schizophrenia with DNA markers at pericentric region of chromosome 9. *Biological Psychiatry, 36,* 589–594.

Nanko, S., Fukuda, R., Hattori, M., et al. (1994b). Linkage studies between affective disorder and dopamine D-2, D-3, and D-4 receptor gene loci in four Japanese pedigrees. *Psychiatry Research, 52,* 149–157.

Nanko, S., Hattori, M., Kuwata, S., et al. (1994). Neurotrophin-3 gene polymorphism associated with schizophrenia. *Acta Psychiatrica Scandinavica, 89,* 390–392.

Nanko, S., Sasaki, T., Fukuda, R., et al. (1993). A study of the association between schizophrenia and the dopamine D3 receptor gene. *Human Genetics, 92,* 336–338.

Neale, M. C., Heath, A. C., Hewitt, J. K., Eaves, L. J., & Fulker, D. W. (1989). Fitting genetic models with LISREL: Hypothesis testing. *Behavior Genetics, 19,* 37–49.

Nielsen, S. (1990). The epidemiology of anorexia nervosa in Denmark from 1973 to 1987: a nationwide register study of psychiatric admission. *Acta Psychiatrica Scandinavica 81:* 507–514.

Nothen, M. M., Hebebrand, J., Knapp, M., et al. (1994). Association analysis of the dopamine D-2 receptor gene in Tourette's syndrome using the haplotype relative risk method. *American Journal of Medical Genetics, 54,* 249–252.

Nurnberg, J. I., Hamovit, J., Hibbs, E., Pellegrini, D., Guroff, J. J., Maxwell, M. E., Smith, A., & Gershon, E. S. (1988). A high risk study of primary affective disorder: Selection of subjects, initial assessment, and 1- to 2-year follow-up. In D. L. Dunner, E. Gershon, & J. E. Barrett (Eds.), *Relatives at risk for mental disorder* (pp. 161–177). New York: Raven Press.

Nylander, P. O., Engstrom, C., Chotai, J., et al. (1994). Anticipation in Swedish families with bipolar affective disorder. *Journal of Medical Genetics, 31,* 686–689.

O'Donovan, M. C., & Owen, M. J. (1992). Advances and retreats in the molecular genetics of major mental illness. *Annals of Medicine, 24,* 171–177.

Online Mendelian Inheritance in Man, OMIM (TM). Center for Medical Genetics, Johns Hopkins University (Baltimore, MD) and National Center for Biotechnology Information, National Library of Medicine (Bethesda, MD), 1997. World Wide Web URL: http://www.ncbi.nlm.nih.gov/omim/.

Omenn, G. S. (1973). Genetic issues in the syndrome of minimal brain dysfunction. *Seminars in Psychiatry, 5,* 5–17.

Orvaschel, H., Walsh-Allis, G., & Ye, W. (1988). Psychopathology in children of parents with recurrent depression. *Journal of Abnormal Child Psychology 16:* 17–28.

Owen, M., Craufurd, D., & St. Clair, D. (1990). Localisation of a susceptibility locus for schizophrenia on chromosome 5. *British Journal of Psychiatry, 157,* 123–127.

Owen, M. J., & McGuffin, P. (1992). The molecular genetics of schizophrenia. *British Medical Journal, 305,* 664–665.

Owen, M. J., & McGuffin, P. (1993). Association and linkage: Complementary strategies for complex disorders. *Journal of Medical Genetics, 30,* 638–639.

Pakstis, A. J., Heutink, P., Pauls, D. L., et al. (1991). Progress in the search for genetic linkage with Tourette syndrome: An exclusion map covering more than 50% of the autosomal genome. *American Journal of Human Genetics, 48,* 281–294.

Pam, A. (1990). A critique of the scientific status of biological psychiatry. *Acta Psychiatrica Scandinavica, 362* [Suppl.], 1–35.

Papoles, D. F., Faedda, G. L., Yeit, S., Goldberg, R., Morrow, B., Kucherlapati, R. & Shprintzen, R. J. (1996). Bipolar spectrum disorders in patients diagnosed with Velo-Cardio-Facial Syndrome. Does a homozygous deletion of 22q11 result in bipolar affective disorder? *American J of Psychiatry 153:* 1541–1547.

Papolos, D. F. (1997). Bipolar disorder: Genes to behavior to symptomatology. *American Academy of Child and Adolescent Psychiatry, Scientific Proceedings of the Annual Meeting, XIII:* 14

Parker, G. (1979). Parental characteristics in relation to depressive disorders. *British Journal of Psychiatry, 134,* 138–147.

Pauls, D. L. (1990). Genetic influences on child psychiatric conditions. In: *Child & Adolescent Psychiatry: A comprehensive textbook,* Lewis, M., ed. Baltimore, Williams & Wilkins, pp. 351–363.

Pauls, D. L. (1993). Behavioral disorders: Lessons in linkage. *Nature Genetics, 3,* 4–5.

Pauls, D. L., Alsbrook, J. P. II, Goodman, W., Rasmussen, S., & Leckman, J. F. (1995). A family study of obsessive compulsive disorder. *American Journal of Psychiatry, 152,* 76–84.

Pauls, D. L., Kruger, S. D., Leckman, J. F., Cohen, D. J., & Kidd, K. K. (1984). The risk of Tourette's syndrome and chronic multiple tics among relatives of Tourette's syndrome patients obtained by direct interview. *Journal of the American Academy of Child Psychiatry, 23,* 134–137.

Pauls, D. L., & Leckman, J. F. (1986). The inheritance of Gilles de la Tourette's syndrome and associated behaviors: Evidence for autosomal dominant transmission. *New England Journal of Medicine, 315,* 993–997.

Pauls, D. L., Leckman, J. F., & Cohen, D. J. (1993). Familial relationship between Gilles de la Tourette's syndrome, attention deficit disorder, learning disabilities, speech disorders, and stuttering. *Journal of the American Academy of Child and Adolescent Psychiatry, 32,* 1044–1050.

Pauls, D. L., Leckman, J. F., & Cohen, D. J. (1994). Evidence against a genetic relationship between Tourette's syndrome and anxiety, depression, panic and phobic disorders. *British Journal of Psychiatry, 164,* 215–221.

Pauls, D. L., Pakstis, A. J., Kurlan, R., et al. (1990). Segregation and linkage analyses of Tourette's syndrome and related disorders. *Journal of the American Academy of Child and Adolescent Psychiatry, 29,* 195–203.

Pauls, D. L., Raymond, C. L., Leckman, J. F., & Stevenson, J. M. (1991). A family study of Tourette's syndrome. *American Journal of Human Genetics, 48,* 154–163.

Pauls, D. L., Shaywitz, S., Kramer, P., et al. (1983). Demonstration of vertical transmission of attention deficit disorder. *Annals of Neurology, 14,* 363.

Pauls, D. L., Towbin, K. E., Leckman, J. F., Zahner, G. E. P., & Cohen, D. J. (1986). Evidence supporting an etiological relationship between Gilles de la Tourette syndrome and obsessive compulsive disorder. *Archives of General Psychiatry, 43,* 1180–1182.

Pedersen, N. L., Friberg, L., Floderus-Myrhead, B., McClearn, G. E., & Plomin, R. (1984). Swedish early separated twins: Identification and characterization. *Acta Geneticae Medicae et Gemelloglogiae, 33,* 243–250.

Petit, E., Herault, J., Martineau, J., Perrot, A., Barthelemy, C., Hameury, L., Sauvage, D., Lelord, G., & Pierre, J. (1995). Association study with two markers of a human homeogene in infantile autism. *American Journal of Medical Genetics (Neuropsychiatric Genetics) 60:.*

Phillips, J. A. (1994). DNA mapping growth and developmental disorders. *Hormone Research, 41,* 157–168.

Pickens, R. W., Svikis, D. S., McGue, M., Lykken, D. T., Heston, L. L., & Clayton, P. J. (1991). Heterogeneity in the inheritance of alcoholism: a study of male and female twins. *Archives of General Psychiatry 48:* 19–28.

Pickles, A., Bolton, P., Macdonald, H., Bailey, A., LeCouteur, A., Sim, C.-H., & Rutter, M. (1995). Latent class analysis of recurrence risks for complex phenotypes with selection and measurement error: a twin and family history study of autism. *American J of Human Genetics 57:* 717–726.

Pickles, A., Crouchley, R., Simonoff, E., et al. (1994). Survival models for developmental genetic data: Age of onset of puberty and antisocial behavior in twins. *Genetic Epidemiology, 11,* 155–170.

Piven, J., Gayle, J., Landa, R., Wzorek, M., & Folstein, S. (1991). The prevalence of the fragile X in a sample of autistic individuals diagnosed using a standardized interview. *Journal of the American Academy of Child and Adolescent Psychiatry, 30,* 825–830.

Plomin, R., & Bergeman, C. S. (1991). The nature of nurture: Genetic influence on "environmental" measures. *Behavioral Brain Sciences, 14,* 373–386.

Prescott, C. A., & Gottesman, I. I. (1993). Genetically mediated vulnerability to schizophrenia. *Psychiatric Clinics of North America, 16,* 245–267.

Price, R. A., Kidd, K. K., Cohen, D. J., Pauls, D. L., & Leckman, J. F. (1985). A twin study of Tourette's syndrome. *Archives of General Psychiatry, 42,* 815–820.

Price, R. A., Kidd, K. K., & Weissman, M. M. (1987). Early onset (under age 30 years) and panic disorder as markers for etiologic homogeneity in major depression. *Archives of General Psychiatry, 44,* 434–440.

Propping, P., Nothen, M. M., Korner, J., et al. (1994). Association tests in psychiatric disorders—concepts and findings. *Nervenarzt, 65,* 725–740.

Puig-Antich, J., Goetz, D., Davies, M., Kaplan, T., Davies, S., Ostrow, L., Asnis, L., Twomey, J., Iyengar, S., & Ryan, N. D. (1989). A controlled family history study of prepubertal major depressive disorder. *Archives of General Psychiatry, 46*, 406–418.

Pulver, A. E., Brown, C. H., Wolyntec, P., McGrath, J., Tam, D., Adler, L., Carpenter, T., & Childs, B. (1990). Schizophrenia: age at onset, gender and familial. risk. *Acta Psychiatrica Scandinavica 82:* 344–357.

Pulver, A. E., Karayiorgou, M., Lasseter, V. K., et al. (1994). Follow-up of a report of a potential linkage for schizophrenia on chromosome 22q12-q13.1: Part 2. *American Journal of Medical Genetics, 54,* 44–50.

Rabin, M., Wen, X. L., Hepburn, M., & Lubs, H. A. (1993). Suggestive linkage of developmental dyslexia to chromosome 1p34-p35. *Lancet 342:* 178.

Radke-Yarrow, M., Nottelmann, E., Martinez, P., Fox, M. B., & Belmont, B. (1992). Young children of affectively ill parents: a longitudinal study of psychosocial development. *Journal of the American Academy of Child Psychiatry 31:* 68–77.

Rao, P. A. (1997). Review of gene mapping and molecular genetic studies of schizophrenia. *Psychiatric Annals 27:* 279–284.

Rasmussen, S. A., & Tsuang, M. T. (1986). Clinical characteristics and family history in DSM-III obsessive compulsive disorder. *American Journal of Psychiatry, 143,* 317–322.

Råstam, M., Gillberg, C., & Garton, M. (1989). Anorexia nervosa in a Swedish urban region. *British J of Psychiatry 155:* 642–646.

Råstam, M., & Gillberg, C. (1991). The family background in anorexia nervosa: A population based study. *Journal of the American Academy of Child & Adolescent Psychiatry 30:* 283–289.

Reiss, D., Plomin, R., & Hetherington, E. M. (1991). Genetics and psychiatry: An unheralded window on the environment. *American Journal of Psychiatry, 148,* 283–291.

Reiss, A. L., & Freund, L. (1990). Fragile X syndrome. *Biological Psychiatry, 27,* 223–240.

Remick, R. A., Sadovnick, A. D., Gimbarzevsky, B., et al. (1993). Obtaining a family psychiatric history: Is it worth the effort? *Canadian Journal of Psychiatry, 38,* 590–594.

Rende, R. D., Plomin, R., Reiss, D., et al. (1993). Genetic and environmental influences on depressive symptomatology in adolescence: Individual differences and extreme scores. *Journal of Child Psychology and Psychiatry, 34,* 1387–1398.

Riddle, M. A., Scahill, L., King, R., Hardin, M. T., Towbin, K. E., Ort, S. I., Leckman, J. F., & Cohen, D. J. (1990). Obsessive compulsive disorder in children and adolescents: phenomenology and family history. *Journal of the American Academy of Child and Adolescent Psychiatry, 29,* 766–772.

Risch, N. (1990a). Genetic linkage and complex diseases, with special reference to psychiatric disorders. *Genetic Epidemiology, 7,* 3–16.

Risch, N. (1990b). Linkage strategies for genetically complex traits. I. Multilocus models. II. The power of affected relative pairs. III. The effect of marker polymorphism on analysis of affected relative pairs. *American Journal of Human Genetics, 46,* 222–253.

Risch, N., Ghosh, S., & Todd, J. A. (1993). Statistical evaluation of multiple-locus linkage data in experimental species and its relevance to human studies: Application of non-obese diabetic (NOD) mouse to human insulin dependent diabetes (IDDM). *Am J Hum Genetics 53:* 702–714.

Risch, N., & Merikangas, K. R. (1993). Linkage studies of psychiatric disorders. *European Archives of Psychiatry and Clinical Neuroscience, 243,* 143–149.

Risch, N., & Merikangas, K. (1996). The future of genetic studies of complex human diseases. *Science 273:* 1516–1517.

Ritvo, E. R., Freeman, B. J., Mason-Brothers, A., Mo, A., & Ritvo, A. M. (1985). Concordance for the syndrome of autism in 40 pairs of afflicted twins. *American Journal of Psychiatry, 142,* 74–77.

Ritvo, E. R., Freeman, B. J., Pingree, C., et al. (1989a). The UCLA–University of Utah epidemiologic survey of autism: Prevalence. *American Journal of Psychiatry, 146,* 194–199.

Ritvo, E. R., Jorde, L., Mason-Brothers, A., et al. (1989). The UCLA–University of Utah epidemiologic survey of autism: Recurrence risk estimates and genetic counseling. *American Journal of Psychiatry, 146,* 1032–1036.

Robertson, M. M. (1991). The Gilles de la Tourette syndrome and obsessional disorder. *International Journal of Clinical Psychopharmacology, 6* [Suppl. 3], 69–82.

Robertson, M. M., Trimble, M. R., & Lees, A. J. (1988). The psychopathology of the Gilles de la Tourette syndrome: A phenomenological analysis. *British Journal of Psychiatry, 152,* 383–390.

Robins, L. N. (1984). Sturdy childhood predictors of adult outcomes replications from longitudinal studies. *Psychological Medicine, 8,* 611–622.

Robins, L., Helzer, J., Crougham, J., & Ratcliffe, K. (1981). The NIMH epidemiologic catchment area study. *Archives of General Psychiatry 38:* 381–389.

Rousseau, F., Bonaventure, J., Legeal-Mallet, L., Pelet, A., Rozet, J.-M., Maroteaux, P., Le Merrer, M., & Munnich, A. (1994). Mutations in the gene encoding fibroblast growth factor receptor-3 in achondroplasia. *Nature 371:* 252–254.

Rowe, D. C. (1983). Biometric models of self-reported delinquent behavior: a twin study. *Behavior Genetics, 13,* 473–489.

Rowe, D. C. (1986). Genetic and environmental components of antisocial pairs: A study of 265 twin pairs. *Criminology, 24,* 513–532.

Roy, M. A., & Kendler, K. S. (1994). The effect of diagnostic hierarchy in genetic epidemiological studies of psychiatric disorders. *Archives of General Psychiatry, 51,* 926–927.

Rutland et al. (1995). *Nature Genetics, 9,* 173–175.

Rutter, M. (1981). Psychological sequelae of brain damage in children. *American Journal of Psychiatry 138:* 1533–1544.

Rutter, M. (1986). The developmental psychopathology of depression: issues and perspectives. In M. Rutter, C. Izard, & P. Read (Eds.), *Depression in young people: Developmental and clinical perspectives* (pp. 3–30). New York: Guilford Press.

Rutter, M. (1994). Psychiatric genetics—research challenges and pathways forward. *American Journal of Medical Genetics, 54,* 185–198.

Rutter, M. (1997). Implications of genetic research for child psychiatry. *Canadian Journal of Psychiatry 42:* 569–575.

Rutter, M., Bailey, A., Bolton, P., & LeCouteur, A. (1993). Autism: Syndrome definition and possible genetic mechanisms. In R. Plomin & G. E. McClearn (Eds.), *Nature, nurture and psychology* (pp. 269–284).

Rutter, M., Bolton, P., Harrington, R., et al. (1990b). Genetic factors in child psychiatric disorder—I. A review of research strategies. *Journal of Child Psychology and Psychiatry and Allied Disciplines, 31,* 3–37.

Rutter, M., Macdonald, H., LeCouteur, A., et al. (1990a). Genetic factors in child psychiatric disorder—II. Empirical Findings. *Journal of Child Psychology and Psychiatry and Allied Disciplines, 31,* 39–83.

Rutter, M., & Plomin, R. (1997). Opportunities for psychiatry from genetic findings. *British Journal of Psychiatry 171:* 209–219.

Rutter, M., Quinton, D., & Hill, J. (1990). Adult outcome of institution reared children. Males and females compared. In L. Robins & M. Rutter (Eds.), Straight & devious pathways from childhood to adulthood. Cambridge: Cambridge Univ. Press.

Sadovnick, A. D., Remick, R. A., Lam, R., et al. (1994). Mood disorder service genetic database: Morbidity risks for mood disorders in 3,942 first-degree relatives of 671 index cases with single depression, recurrent depression, bipolar I, or bipolar II. *American Journal of Medical Genetics, 54,* 132–140.

Schachar, R., & Wachsmuth, R. (1990). Hyperactivity and parental psychopathology. *Journal of Child Psychology & Psychiatry 31:* 381–392.

Schaid, D. J., & Sommer, S. S.(1994). Comparison of statistics for candidate-gene association studies using cases and parents. *American Journal of Human Genetics, 55,* 402–409.

Schork, N. U., Boehnke, M., Terwilliger, J. D., & Ott, J. (1994). Two-locus versus one-locus LODS for complex traits—reply. *American Journal of Human Genetics, 55,* 856–858.

Schrieber, H., Stolz-Born, G., Heinrich, H., et al. (1992). Attention, cognition and motor perseveration in adolescents at genetic risk for schizophrenia and control subjects. *Psychiatry Research, 44,* 125–140.

Schwab, S. G., Albus, M., Hallmayer, J., Honig, S., Borrmann, M., Lichtermann, D., Ebstein, R. P., Ackenheil, M., Lerer, B., Risch, N., Maier, W., & Wildenauer, D. B. (1995). Evaluation of a suscepti-

bility gene for schizophrenia on chromosome 6p by multipoint affected sib-pair linkage analysis. *Nature Genet. 11,* 325–327.

Shah, S., & Green, J. R. (1994). Disease susceptibility genes and the sib-pair method—a review of recent methodology. *Annals of Human Genetics, 58,* 381–395.

Sham, P. C., Gottesman, I. I., MacLean, C. J., & Kendler, K. S. (1994). Schizophrenia—sex and familial morbidity. *Psychiatry Research, 52,* 125–134.

Sham, P. C., Jones, P., Russell, A., et al. (1994). Age at onset, sex and familial psychiatric morbidity in schizophrenia—Camberwell collaborative psychosis study. *British Journal of Psychiatry, 165,* 466–473.

Sham, P. C., MacLean, C. J., & Kendler, K. S. (1994). Two-locus versus one-locus LODS for complex traits. *American Journal of Human Genetics, 55,* 855–856.

Sham, P. C., Morton, N. E., Muir, W. J., et al. (1994). Segregation analysis of complex phenotypes: An application to schizophrenia and auditory P300 latency. *Psychiatric Genetics, 4,* 29–38.

Shaywitz, S. E., & Shaywitz, B. A. (1982). Biologic influences in attention deficit disorders. In M. D. Levine, W. S. Carey, A. C. Crocker, et al. (Eds.), *Developmental-behavioral pediatrics.* Philadelphia: W. B. Saunders.

Shaywitz, S. E., Cohen, D. J., & Shaywitz, B. A. (1983). Pharmacotherapy of attention deficit disorder. In K. Swaiman (Ed.), *Pediatric update.* New York: Elsevier.

Shaywitz, S. E., Escobar, M. D., Shaywitz, B. A., Fletcher, J. M., & Makuch, R. (1992). Evidence that dyslexia may represent the lower tail of a normal distribution of reading ability. *New England Journal of Medicine, 326,* 145–150.

Sherrington, R., Curtis, D., Brynjolfsson, J., et al. (1994). A linkage study of affective disorder with DNA markers for the *ABO-AK1-ORM* linkage group near the dopamine beta hydroxylase gene. *Biological Psychiatry, 36,* 434–442.

Sherrington, R., Brynjolfsson, J., Petursson, H., Potter, M., Dudleston, K., Barraclough, B., Wasmuth, J., Dodds, M., & Gurling, H. (1988). Localization of a susceptibility locus for schizophrenia on chromosome 5. *Nature, 336,* 164–167.

Shiang, R., et al. (1993). *Nature Genetics 5:* 351–358.

Shprintzen, R. J., Goldberg, R., Golding-Kushner, K. J., & Marion, R. (1992). Late-onset psychosis in the velo-cardio-facial syndrome. *American Journal of Medical Genetics, 42,* 141–142.

Silber, J. L., Heath, A. C., Kessler, R., et al. (1990). Genetic and environmental effects on self-reported depressive symptoms in a general population twin sample. *Journal of Psychiatric Research, 24,* 197–212.

Silberg, J., Meyer, J., Pickles, A., Simonoff, E., Eaves, L., Hewitt, J., Maes, H., & Rutter, M. (1996). Heterogeneity among juvenile antisocial behaviors: findings from the Virginia Twin Study of Adolescent

Development. *Ciba Foundation Symposium 194:* 76–92.

Simonoff, E., McGuffin, P., & Gottesman, I. I.(1994). Genetic influences on normal and abnormal development. In M. Rutter, E. Taylor, & L. Ersov (Eds.), *Child and adolescent psychiatry: Modern approaches* (3rd ed., pp. 129–151). Oxford: Blackwell Scientific.

Singer, T. P., Castagnoli, N., Jr., Ramsay, R. R., & Trevor, A. J. (1987). Biochemical events in the development of Parkinsonism induced by 1-methyl-4-phenyl-1,2,3,6-tetrahydropyridine. *Journal of Neurochemistry, 49,* 1–8.

Slater, E., & Shields, J. (1969). Genetical aspects of anxiety. In M. H. Lasider (Ed.), *Studies of anxiety.* British Journal of Psychiatry Special Publication No. 3. Ashford, U.K.: Headley Brothers.

Slutske, W. S., Heath, A. C., Dinwiddie, S. H., Madden, P. A., Bucholz, K. K., Dunne, M. P., Stratham, O. J., & Martin, N. G. (1997). Modeling genetic and environmental influences in the etiology of conduct disorder: a study of 2682 adult twin pairs. *J of Abnormal Psychology 106:* 266–279.

Smalley, S. L., Asarnow, R. F., & Spence, M. A. (1988). Autism & genetics: a decade of research. *Archives of Gen Psychiatry 45:* 953–961.

Smalley, S., McCracken, J., & Tanguay, P. (1995). Autism affective disorders and social phobia. *American Journal of Medical Genetics (Neuropsychiatric Genetics) 60:* 19–26.

Smalley, S. L. (1997). Genetic influences in childhood psychiatric disorders: autism and attention deficit hyperactivity disorder. *American J Human Genetics 60:* 1276–1282.

Smith, S. D., Pennington, B. F., Kimerling, W. J., & Ing, P. S. (1990). Familial dyslexia: use of genetic linkage data to define subtypes. *J American Academy Child & Adolescent Psychiatry 29:* 204–213.

Spence, M. A., Bishop, D. T., Boehnke, M., et al. (1993). Methodological issues in linkage analyses for psychiatric disorders: Secular trends, assortative mating, bilineal pedigrees. Report of the MacArthur Foundation Network I Task Force on Methodological Issues. *Human Heredity, 43,* 166–172.

Spence, M., Ritvo, E., Marazita, M., Funderburk, S., Sparkes, S., & Freeman, B. (1985). Gene mapping studies with the syndrome of autism. *Behavior Genetics 15:* 1–13.

Spielman, R. S., McGinnis, R. E., & Ewens, W. J. (1993). Transmission test for linkage disequilibrium: The insulin gene region and insulin dependent diabetes mellitus. *J Hum Genetics 52:* 506–516.

St. Clair, D., Blackwood, D., Muir, W., Baillie, D., Hubbard, A., Wright, A., & Evans, H. J. (1989). No linkage of chromosome 5q11-q13 markers to schizophrenia in Scottish families. *Nature, 339,* 305–308.

Steffenburg, S., Gillberg, C., Hellgren, L., et al. (1991). A twin study of autism in Denmark, Finland, Iceland, Norway and Sweden. *J Child Psychology & Psychiatry 30:* 405–416.

Stein, D. M., & Brinza, S. R. (1989). Bulimia: prevalence estimates in female junior high and high school students. *Journal of Clinical Child Psychology 18:* 206–213.

Stevenson, H. W., Stigler, J. W., Lucker, G. W., Lees, Y., Hsu, C. C., & Kitmura, S. (1982). Reading disabilities: the case of Chinese, Japanese and English. *Child Devel 33:* 1164–1181.

Stevenson, J. (1992). Evidence for a genetic etiology in hyperactivity in children. *Behavior Genetics 22:* 337–344.

Stine, O. C., Xu, J., Koskela, R., et al. (1995). Evidence for linkage of bipolar disorder to chromosome 18 with a parent of origin effect. *Am Journal of Human Genetics, 57,* 1384–1394.

Straub, R. E., Lehner, T., Luo, Y., et al. (1994). A possible vulnerability locus for bipolar affective disorder on chromosome 21Q22.3. *Nature Genetics, 8,* 291–296.

Straub, R. E., MacLean, C. J., O'Neill, F. A., Burke, J., Murphy, B., Duke, F., Shinkwin, R., Webb, B. T., Zhang, J., Walsh, D., & Kenderler, K. S. (1995). A potential vulnerability locus for schizophrenia chromosome 6p24–22: Evidence for genetic heterogeneity. *Nature Genetics, 11,* 287–293.

Strober, M. (1991). Family genetic studies of eating disorders. *J of Clinical Psychiatry 52 S10:* 9–12.

Strober, M., Lampert, C., Morrell, W., Burroughs, J., & Jacobs, L. (1990). A controlled family study of anorexia nervosa: evidence of familial aggregation and lack of shared transmission with affective disorders. *International Journal of Eating Disorders 9:* 239–253.

Strober, M., Morrell, W., Burroughs, J., Lampert, C., Danforth, H., & Freeman, R. (1988). A family study of bipolar I disorder in adolescence; early onset of symptoms linked to increased familial loading and lithium resistance. *Journal of Affective Disorders 15:* 255–268.

Strober, M., Salkin, B., Burroughs, J., & Morrell, W. (1982). Validity of the bulimia-restricter distinction in anorexia nervosa. Parental personality characteristics and family psychiatric morbidity. *Journal of Nervous and Mental Disease, 170,* 345–351.

Strumwasser, F. (1994). The relations between neuroscience and human behavioral science. *Journal of the Experimental Analysis of Behavior, 61,* 307–317.

Szatmari, P., Offord, D. R., & Boyle, M. H. (1989). Ontario Child Health Study: prevalence of attention deficit disorder with hyperactivity. *Journal of Child Psychology & Psychiatry 30:* 219–230.

Szmukler, G., McCane, C., McCrone, L., & Hunter, D. (1986). Anorexia nervosa: a psychiatric case register study from Aberdeen. Psychological Medicine 16: 49–58.

Taylor, M. A., & Amir, N. (1994). Are schizophrenia and affective disorder related—the problem of schizoaffective disorder and the discrimination of the psychoses by signs and symptoms. *Comprehensive Psychiatry, 35,* 420–429.

Taylor, E., Schachar, R., Thorley, G., & Wieselberg, H. M. (1986). Conduct disorder and hyperactivity. I. Separation of hyperactivity and antisocial conduct in

British child psychiatric patients. *British Journal of Psychiatry, 149,* 760–767.

Terwilliger, J. D., & Ott, J. (1992). A haplotype-based "haplotype relative risk" approach to detecting allelic association. *Human Heredity, 42,* 337–342.

Thapar, A., & McGuffin, P. (1994). A twin study of depressive symptoms in childhood. *British Journal of Psychiatry, 165,* 259–265.

Thapar, A., Gottesman, I. I., Owen, M. J., et al. (1994). The genetics of mental retardation. *British Journal of Psychiatry, 164,* 747–758.

Thomas, A., Skolnick, M. H., & Lewis, C. M. (1994). Genomic mismatch scanning in pedigrees. *IMA Journal of Mathematics Applied in Medicine and Biology, 11,* 1–16.

Thompson, E. A. (1994). Monte Carlo likelihood in the genetic mapping of complex traits. *Philosophical Transactions of the Royal Society of London Series B-Biological Sciences, 344,* 345–351.

Thomson, G., & Motro, U. (1994). Affected sib pair identity by state analyses. *Genetic Epidemiology, 11,* 353–364.

Tienari, P., Lathi, I., Sorri, A., Naarala, M., Moring, J., Kaleva, M., Wahlberg, K.-E., & Wynne, L. C. (1990). Adopted-away offspring of schizophrenics and controls: The Finnish adoptive family study of schizophrenia. In L. N. Robins & M. Rutter (Eds.), *Straight and devious pathways from childhood to adulthood.* Cambridge: Cambridge University Press.

Tienari, P., & Wynne, L. C. (1994). Adoption studies of schizophrenia. *Annals of Medicine, 26,* 233–237.

Tienari, P., Wynne, L. C., Moring, J., et al. (1994). The Finnish adoptive family study of schizophrenia. Implications for family research. *British Journal of Psychiatry* [Suppl. 23], 20–26.

Todd, R. D. (1997). Transmission of early onset affective disorder and alcoholism. *Amer. Acad. Child Add Psych, Scientific Proceedings of the Annual Meeting XIII:* 51.

Todd, R. D., Reich, W., & Reich, T. (1994). Prevalence of affective disorder in the child and adolescent offspring of a single kindred: A pilot study. *Journal of the American Academy of Child and Adolescent Psychiatry, 33,* 198–207.

Torgerson, S. (1983). Genetic factors in anxiety disorders. *Archives of General Psychiatry 40:* 1085–1089.

Treasure, J., & Holland, A. (1990). Genetic vulnerability to eating disorders: evidence from twin and family studies. In H. Remschmidt & M. H. Schmidt (Eds.), *Anorexia Nervosa,* pp. 59–68. Hogrefe & Huber, Toronto.

Tsuang, M. T., Faraone, S. V., & Lyons, M. J. (1993). Identification of the phenotype in psychiatric genetics. *European Archives of Psychiatry and Clinical Neuroscience, 243,* 131–142.

Tsui, L. C. (1992). The spectrum of cystic fibrosis mutations. *Trends in Genetics, 8,* 392–398.

Vandenberg, S. G. (1962). The hereditary abilities study: Hereditary components in a psychological test battery. *American Journal of Human Genetics, 14,* 220–237.

VanDeNoord, E. J. C. G., Boomsma, D. I., & Verhulst, F. C. (1994). A study of problem behaviors in 10- to 15-year-old biologically related and unrelated international adoptees. *Behavior Genetics, 24,* 193–205.

Vieland, V. J., Hodge, S. E., & Greenberg, D. A. (1992). Adequacy of single-locus approximations for linkage analyses of oligogenic traits. *Genetic Epidemiology, 9,* 45–59.

Wadsworth, S. J., DeFries, J. C., Stevenson, J., Gilger, J. W., & Pennington, B. F. (1992). Gender ratios among reading-disabled children and their siblings as a function of parental impairment. *J of Child Psychol & Psychiatry 33:* 1229–1239.

Walker, E., Downey, G., & Caspi, A. (1991). Twin studies of psychopathology: Why do the concordance rates vary? *Schizophrenia Research, 5,* 211–221.

Walters, E. E., & Kendler, K. S. (1995). Anorexia nervosa and anorexic-like syndromes in a population-based female twin sample. *American J of Psychiatry 152:* 64–71.

Wang, S., Sun, C., Walczak, C. A., Ziegle, J. S., Kipps, B. R., Goldin, L. R., & Diehl, S. R. (1995). Evidence for a susceptibility locus for schizophrenia on chromosome 6pter-p22. *Nature Genetics, 10,* 41–46.

Waternaux, C. (1986). A family study of patients with attention deficit disorder and normal controls. *Journal of Psychiatric Research, 20,* 263–274.

Watkins, W. S., Zenger, R., O'Brien, E., et al. (1994). Linkage disequilibrium patterns vary with chromosomal location—a case study from the von Willebrand fractor region. *American Journal of Human Genetics, 55,* 348–355.

Weiss, R. E., Stein, M. A., Duck, S. C., Ohyna, B., Phillips, W., O'Brien, T., Gutermuth, L., & Refetoff, S. (1994). Low intelligence but not attention deficit hyperactivity disorder is associated with resistance to thyroid hormone caused by mutation R316H in the thyroid hormone receptor beta gene. *Journal of Clinical Endocrinology and Metabolism, 78,* 1525–1528.

Weissman, M., Fendrich, M., Warner, V., & Wickramaratne, P. (1992). Incidence of psychiatric disorder in offspring at high and low risk for depression. *Journal of the American Academy of Child and Adolescent Psychiatry, 4,* 460–648.

Weissman, M. M., Gammon, D., John, K., Merikangas, K. R., Warner, V., Prusoff, B. A., & Sholomkas, D. (1987). Children of depressed parents: increased psychopathology and early onset of major depression. *Archives of General Psychiatry 44:* 847–853.

Weissman, M. M., Prusoff, B. A., Gammon, G. D., Merikangas, K., Leckman, J., & Kidd, K. (1984). Psychopathology in children (ages 6–18) of depressed and normal parents. *Journal of the American Academy of Child Psychiatry 23:* 78–84.

Weissman, M. M., Warner, V., Wickramaratne, P., & Prusoff, B. A. (1988). Early-onset major depression in parents and their children. *Journal of Affective Disorders 15:* 269–277.

Wender, P. H., Kety, S. S., Rosenthal, D., Schulsinger, F., Ortmann, J., & Lunde, I. (1986). Psychiatric disorders in the biological and adoptive families of adopted individuals with affective disorders. *Archives of General Psychiatry 43:* 923–929.

Wender, P. H., Rosenthal, D., Kety, S. S., Schulsinger, F., & Welner, J. (1974). Cross fostering: A research strategy for clarifying the role of genetic and experimental factors in the etiology in schizophrenia. *Archives of General Psychiatry, 30,* 121–128.

Wender, P. H., Rosenthal, D., Rainer, J. D., Greenhill, L., & Sarlin, M. B. (1977). Schizophrenic's adopting parents: psychiatric status. *Archives of General Psychiatry 34:* 777–784.

Werry, J. S. (1992). Child and adolescent (early-onset) schizophrenia: a review in light of DSM-III-R. *Journal of Autism and Developmental Disorders 22:* 601–624.

Werry, J. S., & Taylor, E. (1994). Schizophrenic and allied disorders. In: Child and Adolescent Psychiatry: Modern Approaches (3rd edition), Rutter M., Taylor, E., & Hersov, L. (Eds.), pp. 594–615. Oxford: Blackwell Scientific.

Whitaker, A., Johnson, J., Shaffer, D., Rapoport, J. L., Kalikow, K., Walsh, T., Davies, M., Braiman, S., & Dolinsky, A. (1990). Uncommon troubles in young people. Prevalence estimates of selected psychiatric

disorders in a nonreferred population. *Archives of General Psychiatry 47:* 487–496.

Wickramaratne, P., & Weissman, M. M. (1994). The effect of diagnostic hierarchy in genetic epidemiological studies of psychiatric disorders—reply. *Archives of General Psychiatry, 51,* 927.

Williamson, B., & Wicking, C. (1991). From linked marker to gene. *Trends in Genetics 7:* 282–287.

Wilson, A. F., Elston, R. C., Tran, L. D., & Siervogel, R. M. (1992). Use of the robust sib-pair method to screen for single-locus, multiple-locus and pleiotropic effects: Application to traits related to hypertension. *American Journal of Human Genetics, 48,* 862–872.

Wolff, S., Narayan, S., & Moyes, B. (1988). Personality characteristics of parents of autistic children. *Journal of Child Psychology and Psychiatry, 29,* 143–154.

Woodside, D. B. (1993). Anorexia nervosa and bulimia nervosa in children and adolescents. *Current Opinion in Pediatrics, 5,* 415–418.

Yule, W., & Rutter, M. (1985). Reading and other learning difficulties. In M. Rutter & L. Hersov (Eds.), Child and adolescent psychiatry: Modern approaches (2nd ed., pp. 444–464). Oxford: Blackwell Scientific.

4 / Brain Development

Ronald J. Steingard and Joseph T. Coyle

The integration of developmental neuroscience and child and adolescent psychiatry is a challenging task. The rapid and interrelated physical, cognitive, and emotional growth that occurs during development is paralleled by dramatic changes in brain structure and function. Current diagnostic schemata are grounded in classification based on behavioral phenomenology and result in an array of disorders that may not adequately reflect the underlying etiologic complexity. In the future it may be possible to restructure the system of classification to one based on more objective criteria, so that clinicians may be better equipped to discriminate between phenomenologically homogeneous but etiologically heterogeneous disorders. One way of approaching this reclassification is to apply knowledge derived from studies of brain development.

The brain is our most complex organ and is responsible for the regulation of all physical, cognitive, and emotional functions. The nature of its function dictates that it be as changeable as the environment with which it constantly interacts. The brain evolves in a sequential series of highly integrated stages. Normal development at each successive stage is contingent upon the successful completion of all preceding developmental processes. Alterations in this developmental pathway may result in aberrant physical, cognitive, and/or emotional development.

To understand the role of neurodevelopment in the evolution of psychopathology, several areas of interest need to be studied. These include the normal process of brain development and the impact of any deviations in this developmental path on subsequent cognitive and behavioral functioning. This chapter focuses on an overview of these areas of interest and attempts to relate these basic concepts to an in-depth examination of 2 neuro-psychiatric disorders, schizophrenia and autism.

Brain Development

The human brain is comprised of over 100 billion cells. All neurons and glial cells are derived from a shared "ancestor" cell. During the period of cell proliferation, the fetus is producing more than 250,000 neurons per minute (Cowan, 1979; Kolb, 1989). Once these cells are generated, they must migrate to the correct location in the developing brain, differentiate with regards to their ultimate function, and establish up to 15,000 connections per neuron (Kolb, 1989). Brain development occurs in stages and proceeds in a stepwise fashion following a genetically encoded plan that is influenced by environmental events. Each stage of development is dependent on the successful completion of the preceding stages. Alterations in these processes can result in aberrant neural development, connectivity, or function. Typically, early disruption in the developmental process is associated with a greater and more diffuse pathology, while later disruption is associated with less severe pathology and more discrete neurological lesions.

Prenatal Development

Prenatal brain development is focused on cellular events of a progressive nature, including neurogenesis, cell proliferation, cell migration, differentiation, and synaptogenesis. These cellular events trigger structural changes that lead to the initiation of regional specification and encephalization.

NEUROGENESIS

During early embryogenesis, the basic anatomic structures of the central nervous system are formed. This phase of development is characterized by the simultaneous initiation of cellular specialization and gross structural changes. As cells from the primitive streak of the mammalian em-bryo grow anteriorly, they form the dorsal meso-derm. These cells have the capacity to "induce" overlying ectodermal cells to become neural ectoderm. The capacity for cells to be induced to form neural ectoderm depends on cell lineage and cell interactions, which are mediated by diffusible agents provided by the mesodermal cells. It has been suggested that the duration of exposure to these diffusible inducing agents may influence the direction and nature of subsequent regional specialization in the central nervous system.

At 3 weeks, the earliest sign of the nervous system is grossly apparent. The neural ectoderm, which is initially a flat sheet of cells, becomes columnar in shape and forms the neural plate. This columnar plate of neural cells subsequently invaginates and forms the neural groove. The edges of this groove approach each other in the midline, where they fuse to form the neural tube. The neural tube forms initially in the middle of the neural plate, which will correspond to the spinal level of C4. The process of fusion proceeds in both rostral and caudal directions. This is the earliest example of the *spatiotemporal heterogeneity* (Bayer, 1989), the sequential staging of developmental events, that will characterize all of neural development. Presently the neural groove completes the process of fusion, and by the end of the fourth week of gestation, neural tube formation is fully achieved.

The neural tube and the cells that form it are called neuroepithelium. They are the progenitors of all central nervous system cells, including neurons, oligodendroglial cells, ependymal cells, and the spinal cord. (Microglial cells are thought to be of mesodermal origin and "invade" the central nervous system (CNS) at the time of vasculature development.) The center of the neural tube forms the spinal canal and the ventricular system. The caudal portion of the neural tube forms the spinal cord, while the anterior section of the tube will go on to differentiate to form the cerebrum, midbrain, cerebellum, pons, and medulla-oblongata.

CELL PROLIFERATION, MIGRATION, AND DIFFERENTIATION

During the early stages of central nervous system development, neural cells proliferate rapidly. The postmitotic cells migrate out from the germinal zone of the neural tube to their appropriate groupings or nuclei. Development of the neocortex typically proceeds in an "inside out" fashion; cells that form the innermost layer of the cortex are generated first, whereas later-dividing cells migrate from the germinal zone through existing layers of neurons to find their correct locations. As cells proliferate and migrate, the embryonic brain begins to show evidence of regionally specific structures and the initiation of cortical development.

Neuronal Proliferation: Early in the development of the central nervous system, the cells of the neural tube are columnar in shape and extend from the tube's inner ventricular surface to the outer pial surface of the primitive central nervous system. Cell mitosis occurs at the ventricular, innermost, surface. Following mitosis, newly formed cells migrate toward the pial surface of the neural tube, eventually migrating to predetermined positions in the developing central nervous system. As the nervous system continues to develop and the neural tube thickens, actively mitotic cells remain localized in a clump along the ventricular surface, forming the ventricular germinal zone. While it is not fully understood what factors control cell proliferation rates, regional differences in rates probably account for the complex structural foldings that begin to occur.

Neuronal Migration: As noted, in areas of the brain that have a laminar structure (cortex and cerebellar cortices), development proceeds in an inside-out fashion in which neurons located in the deepest laminae arrive first and neurons destined to migrate to more superficial laminae arrive progressively later (Angevine & Sidman, 1961; Brown, Hopkins, & Keynes, 1991). In contrast, nuclear regions of the central nervous system (i.e., thalamus, hypothalamus) appear to develop in an outside-in sequence (Rakic, 1977).

The migration of cells appears to be guided by radially oriented glial cells, which extend from the ventricular surface of the neural tube to the pial surface (Rakic, 1972, 1988a, 1988b). Animal experiments suggest that the distance a cell migrates is determined prior to the initiation of migration (Caviness, 1982; Rakic, 1988a, b).

In mammals, a second proliferative zone can develop above the ventricular germinal zone. Rakic (1972) has speculated that these areas represent discrete proliferative zones. The progeny of these zones appear to migrate as a unit and may provide the developmental basis for the columnar organization seen in the adult cortex (Rakic, 1988a, b).

Once cells have migrated to their correct location, neuronal cells begin to differentiate and develop the biochemical and anatomic characteristics of the neuronal cell type they are destined to become. The factors that influence the direction of neurite extension and the identification of target cells are discussed later.

Neuronal Differentiation: Cell differentiation appears to be influenced by both genetic and environmental influences. Differentiation of the neuronal phenotype depends on either the presence of extrinsic local environmental signals (i.e., neurotransmitters and trophic factors) or convergence of phase-specific cell characteristics and the occurrence of critical periods of brain development. The subdivision of the brain by regional and spatial segmentation also can influence local patterns of cell differentiation. This process is regulated by a family of genes known as homeobox genes, which serve as transcription factors regulating gene expression. The homeobox genes were first identified in fruit fly nervous system development. They are highly conserved in evolution with specific types being expressed during the differentiation of a given segment of the central nervous system.

DEVELOPMENT OF REGIONAL HETEROGENEITY AND INITIAL ENCEPHALIZATION

The pattern of initial differentiation of the anterior section of the neural tube into the primary brain vesicles is the result of the interplay between localized accelerations in mitotic activity of the neuroepithelium (cell proliferation) and the physical spatial constraints of the developing head of the fetus (Bayer, 1989; Richman, Steward, Hutchinsin, & Caviness, 1975). The 3 primary brain vesicles, the prosencephalon, mesencephalon, and rhomboencephalon, are the earliest evidence of regional specialization in the central nervous system.

During subsequent stages of fetal development, these primary brain vesicles differentiate further into the structures that become the adult regions of the brain. The prosencephalon differentiates into the inner diencephalon, from which the thalamus and hypothalamus are derived, and the outer telencephalon, which eventually becomes the cerebral cortex and basal ganglia. Midbrain structures are derived from the neuroepithelium of the mesencephalon; the anterior portion of the rhombencephalon will form the pons and cerebellum, and its posterior region forms the structures of the medulla.

Recent findings that arose from research on the molecular mechanisms regulating the development of the nervous system of the fruit fly have disclosed a family of genes whose sequential expression determine segmentation of the fly's nervous system (Brown et al., 1991; Jacobson, 1991). These highly conserved homeobox genes serve a similar function in the differentiation of the mammalian nervous system. Additional genes in this family have been characterized in the primordial forebrain structures not represented in the fly's nervous system. These homeobox genes represent potential candidate genes in disorders in which disruption of cortical neurogenesis has been implicated, such as schizophrenia.

Postnatal Development

With the exception of a few brain regions, including the hippocampal formation, humans are born with nearly a full complement of neurons. Therefore, the major process of postnatal brain development involves the establishment and maintenance of appropriate connections between neurons. While many of the processes of postnatal development are initiated prenatally, cellular events of a progressive nature (migration, differentiation, axonal/dendritic growth, gliogenesis, synaptogenesis, and myelination) continue postnatally. In addition, during this phase of development, regressive cellular events (programmed cell death, process withdrawal) become critical. Over time, as the nervous system is sculpted by the emergence of functionally effective connectivity in the context of environmental interactions, these processes can continue into adulthood. Finally, a continuing active process of neuronal plasticity persists throughout life and provides the central nervous system with the capacity to be responsive to a constantly changing environment. In this regard,

growth-associated protein (GAP) is expressed by neurons during synaptognesis and synaptic remodeling (Gordon-Weeks, 1988; Jacobson, 1991).

NEURITE ELABORATION: THE DEVELOPMENT OF AXONS AND DENDRITES

Dendrites are specialized extensions of neurons that serve the purpose of integrating synaptic input, whereas axons conduct a wave of depolarization, the action potential, from the cell body to its terminals. The nerve terminal has a specialized structure, the synapse, where it makes contact with a receptive neuron.

The establishment of synaptic connections involves the purposeful elaboration of neurites, which are led by the growth cone (Brown et al., 1991; Jacobson, 1991). The growth cone is structurally and functionally different from the rest of the cell and can be seen as enlargements on the terminal end of the outgrowth. The growth cone carries all the necessary components (mitochondria, vesicles, microfilaments, microtubules) to fuel and provide for neurite extension. The filopodia are fine, mobile extensions that lead the growth cone in order to "sample" the local environment for cell adhesion molecules, trophic factors, and other chemical cues. As the outgrowth matures, their task is to facilitate the location of target sites.

The extent and direction of growth are determined by many signals, including growth factors, extracellular matrix molecules, and local neurotransmitters. The role of the growth factors is to promote neurite extension, help maintain cell viability prior to the establishment of synapse, and maintain the mature neuron. The extracellular matrix molecules provide the physical structure to direct the outgrowth. Neurotransmitters function to identify target sites, promote specialization of neuronal cells, maintain cell viability after the establishment of the synapse, and induce cell death/process withdrawal in normal and disease processes.

SYNAPTOGENESIS

The process of synaptogenesis requires several components. As axons approach their target sites, they must be able to recognize the correct target cells in order to establish viable and long-lasting connections. After recognition, axons make initial contact with their target sites. This contact triggers the process of synaptogenesis. This initial contact between axon and target cell is then stabilized through the development of specialized structures, both pre- and postsynaptically.

Axons are able to recognize target cells by type (type specificity) and position (place specificity). Target cells are identified by type using local signals, such as the neurotransmitters the target cells release. While grossly mismatched axons and targets will not establish long-lasting connections, cells can be made to form less stable connections with matched targets that utilize signals of a similar but not identical nature. Place specificity implies that target cells also can be recognized by their spatial position. Wigston and Sanes (Wigston & Sanes, 1982, 1985) demonstrated that while intercostal muscles taken from different rib spaces in rats could establish connections with axons from mismatched intercostal spaces, the muscles were most intensively innervated by sympathetic axons derived from the same intercostal space.

The process by which axons and their target cells mature into specialized pre- and postsynaptic structures is dependent on active communication between neuron and target. Once the connection is made and target innervation is established, trophic factor is transferred efficiently from target cell to the innervating efferent, which maintains the latter's survival.

REGRESSIVE CELLULAR EVENTS: PROGRAMMED CELL DEATH/PROCESS WITHDRAWAL

Postnatal development heralds the utilization of regressive processes as a developmental agent. The brain overproduces cells by a factor of as much as 2 to 1. This process of neuronal overproduction followed by loss is referred to as programmed cell death, or apoptosis. Supernumerary synaptic connections also are pruned through this mechanism. This process is not random. Rather it reflects the stabilization of appropriate synaptic connections and will continue into late adolescence.

Programmed cell death affects most types of neurons in the human central nervous system. In some areas of the brain, almost half of the neurons are generated in that region. The process of cell death begins shortly after axons have reached and activated their target. Therefore, the number of cells in any given region peaks then, after reaching the final destination, the number of cells begins to diminish. Programmed cell death is a major event and plays an important role in *normal* development of the central nervous system.

The purpose of cell death is complex. Typically, cells are eliminated (1) if their axons have failed to reach their intended target, (2) in order to match the number of connections with the size of the target, and (3) to eliminate target errors. However, in some areas excess neurons may be temporary circuits that are established and required at critical periods of development only to require elimination at a later developmental stage. For example, evidence suggests that prior to 30 weeks of fetal age, the predominant olivocerebellar pathway is a projection from the olivary nucleus to the cerebellar nuclei. However, at some later point in development, this connection is replaced by circuitry that is normal in adults and connects the inferior olivary nucleus directly to the Purkinje cells. Persistence of the more primitive circuit path not only reflects developmental neuropathology but has implications with regard to the nature of the ensuing disease process and its subsequent behavioral and cognitive pathology.

Therefore, programmed cell death typically functions to increase the efficiency and accuracy of the system and to facilitate the strategic unfolding of phase-specific developments within the central nervous system. While this process of overgrowth and pruning appears to be inefficient, the alternative is a significantly more precisely programmed development system that accurately predetermines the number of cells required and guides their outgrowths to the appropriate target precisely and without error. In the event of error, however, when the end product is a system as complex as the human central nervous system, this alternative process may be associated with greater risk. Furthermore, overgrowth and pruning provide opportunities for plastic, use-dependent modification of synaptic connectivity in response to environmental experiences. For example, recent functional brain imaging studies indicate that those with congenital deafness who acquire sign language early in life exhibit a much broader activation of cortex during signing than those who acquire the skill in adulthood. Similarly, in congenitally blind individuals, the sensory experience of "reading" Braille activates the visual cortex. Both examples point to a use-dependent preservation of sensory cortical projection that would otherwise have been pruned.

Developmental Disorders
of Behavior

A growing body of evidence suggests that many psychiatric disorders are associated with abnormal brain development. As noted, the earlier the disruption, the greater the impact and the more obvious the role of developmental aberration. Late-onset developmental disruptions are more subtle in their impact and may only convey a vulnerability for pathology to the affected individual, a vulnerability which may be mitigated by environmental factors. However, even with severe disorders of behavior and cognition, such as autism and schizophrenia, it is evident in both clinical practice and current research that environmental factors have a significant impact on the severity of the disorder and outcome. Next we briefly explore neurodevelopmental issues as they relate to the pathology of autism and schizophrenia.

AUTISM

Autism is a neurodevelopmental disorder that affects 10 per 10,000 children (Bryson, Clark, & Smith, 1988) and disrupts multiple areas of functioning, including language development, social interaction, symbolic play, memory function, impulse control, and affect regulation (Rapin, 1991). Autism has an onset prior to the age of 30 months. Familial and twin studies strongly implicate heritable risk factors in autism, although fetal brain insults such a congenital rubella can produce the syndrome. A growing body of evidence suggests that a prenatal alteration in neurodevelopment underlies the appearance of subsequent behavioral and cognitive neuropathology.

Neuroanatomic Findings: Neuroanatomic observation (Bauman & Kemper, 1994) derived from autopsy data have led to hypotheses regarding the neuropathology associated with autism. These hypotheses provide a way of understanding the cognitive and behavioral symptoms as well as the timing of the onset of both the symptoms and the loss of function seen in some individuals at the time of symptom recognition.

While the gross brain structures and myelination of autistic patients are comparable to those of normal controls, autopsies of autistic individuals reveal multiple cytoarchitectonic abnormalities. The findings in the cortex are widespread and include the hippocampus, subiculum, entorhinal cortex, amygdala, mamillary bodies, anterior cingulate cortex, and septum. These areas comprise a major portion of the limbic system of the central nervous system. For the most part, these areas demonstrate increased cell packing; in addition, the cells in these areas are reduced in size. This pattern of decreased cell size and increased cell packing density is a characteristic of a defect expressed at an early stage of brain development, suggesting a curtailment of normal prenatal brain development. In a single region of the septum, the nucleus of the diagonal band of Broca, this pattern was not seen. In contrast, cells in younger patients were unusually large and adequate in number, while cells in the older patients were small and reduced in number.

In addition to the findings in the cortex, the cerebellum and inferior olive were the only other areas that showed abnormalities at autopsy. While most areas of the cerebellum showed a decrease in the number of Purkinje cells, there was no evidence of significant gliosis, suggesting that these changes occurred early in development. In addition, a pattern similar to that found in the nucleus of the diagonal band of Broca was seen in the fastigeal, emboliform, and globose nuclei. Cells in these regions were enlarged and adequate in number in the younger patients and small and reduced in number in the older patients.

This finding in the inferior olivary nucleus is intriguing. Typically, cells in the inferior olive will demonstrate retrograde loss and atrophy when there is peri- or postnatal Purkinje cell loss. This is not the case in the autopsied autistic individuals. Like the findings in the nucleus of the diagonal band of Broca, the cells of the inferior olivary nucleus were enlarged in the younger individuals and small in the older subjects, but, unlike the findings in the diagonal band of Broca, there were adequate numbers of cells in both samples and no evidence of cell loss or atrophy.

Recent magnetic resonance imaging studies using quantitative morphometry indicate that adult autistics actually exhibit increased brain size, consistent with increased brain weight found at autopsy (Piven et al., 1995). In light of the neuropathologic evidence of the increased neuronal density in the cortex and a disproportionate survival of olivary cells, a defect in programmed cell death exists in autism. Such a defect could disrupt the establishment of appropriate synaptic connections in the distributed systems essential for memory, language, and social relations.

Implications of Neuroanatomic Findings: In attempting to understand these findings, several crucial hypotheses have been generated that may explain both the timing of onset and the nature of symptoms in autistic individuals (Bauman & Kemper, 1994). These hypotheses also highlight ways in which an understanding of brain development can enhance our clinical appreciation of disorders like autism.

The areas affected in the limbic system are reciprocally connected at once to associative cortical structures, which are involved in the integration and interpretation of sensory input in all modalities, and to the reticular core, whose structures are involved in the regulation of affective states, attention, and motivation. In adult animals, lesions in this circuitry produce alterations in emotion, motivation, memory, and learning. However, there are relevant differences in outcome between animals lesioned as adults and animals lesioned as neonates or infants. In 1 experiment, bilateral amygdalectomies in infant monkeys resulted in "normal" development until the age of 8 months, when deficits in social development became apparent. These animals subsequently developed hyperactivity at 3 years of age and severe perturbation in interpersonal relationships. A delay in the expression of symptoms has been demonstrated in a study of neonatal monkeys that underwent bilateral resection of both the amygdala and hippocampus. These findings suggest that developmental events may affect the expression of dysfunction that is related to known underlying neuropathology. Disease expression may require not only the presence of neuropathology but demands placed on the damaged system by age-related acquisition of skills. For example, a discrete prenatal lesion in speech centers in the central nervous system may not become evident until there is a normal expectation of the onset of language development. Even though the neuropathology is present at birth, a subtle speech dysfunction would not be diagnosed in a neonate.

Memory Function and Limbic System Abnormalities: Limbic system structures also are involved in memory and learning (Killiany & Moss, 1994). In humans there are at least 2 short-term memory systems, procedural (habit) memory and representational (declarative) memory. Procedural memory is involved in skill learning and the automatic connection between stimulus and response (Killiany & Moss, 1994; Oakley, 1981; Squire, 1986). This type of memory is not accessible to conscious recollection and is thought to reside in the striatum and the neocortex (both of which are spared in autistic individuals) (Bauman & Kemper, 1994). Representational memory involves all sensory modalities and mediates both the processing of facts and the integration and generalization of information that lead to higher-order cognition and learning. Representational memory is dependent on normal functioning of limbic structures and prefrontal cortex.

The relationship of the limbic system to memory function and learning can lead to salient explanations regarding the nature of the pathology seen in autistic individuals and the timing of the onset of the disorder (Bauman & Kemper, 1994; Killiany & Moss, 1994). Early lesions in the limbic system could lead to disruptions in the acquisition of and, of even greater importance, the assignment of meaning to novel sensory stimuli. This potentially would lead to the type of disordered cognition, social interactions, and language that is characteristic of individuals with autism. In addition, the preservation of the procedural memory system would lead to the type of repetitive behavior and seemingly obsessive need for sameness seen in these individuals; it also could explain the agitation that typically occurs with minor alteration in routine or environment that might render the setting unrecognizable. In addition, the presence of an intact procedural memory system could account for the presence of the outstanding memory for rote information seen in some autistics.

Furthermore, the onset of the disorder also may be explained through this mechanism. Studies from both human and nonhuman primates suggest the presence of a very well-formed procedural memory system early in life (Bachevalier & Mishkin, 1984; Killiany & Moss, 1994). By contrast, these same studies suggest that representational memory is acquired slowly and may not begin to be utilized in humans until approximately 19 months of age, the time when for most affected children the symptomatic features of autism and pervasive developmental disorder appear. Therefore, like all other aspects of motor and cognitive development, memory represents a distributed system comprised of smaller components that mature at different rates (Killiany & Moss, 1994). As a result, the deficit in representational memory may not be as readily apparent at birth as it is at age 19 months, when skill acquisition related to the function of representational memory is expected. It is conceivable that the impact of this developmental shift, from functioning dependent primarily on an intact procedural memory system to functioning dependent on both procedural and representational memory, may be perceived as a loss of function rather than the failure of a new system to come "on-line."

Cerebellar Findings: While the behavioral and cognitive implications of these findings are only beginning to be appreciated, the findings in the cerebellum highlight the developmental aspect of the lesions that are apparent in children with autism. The finding of variations in pathology in individuals of different ages is intriguing. The following hypotheses have been put forth to try to explain these findings (Bauman & Kemper, 1994; Schmahmann, 1994).

The olivocerebellar tracts show evidence of advance myelination at 28 weeks gestation, suggesting the existence of a functional circuit. However, connections between the Purkinje cells and the inferior olive usually occur at about 30 weeks gestation. It has been shown that prior to establishing connections with the Purkinje cells, olivary climbing fibers establish synaptic connections in a transitory zone called the lamina dessicans (Rakic, 1971). This transitory zone is no longer evident after 30 weeks of gestation (Rakic & Sidman, 1970), presumably having been replaced by direct synaptic connections between the inferior olivary nucleus and the Purkinje cells. It is assumed that, given the absence of the retrograde loss of olivary

cells, which would have been an obligatory consequence of the loss of established connections with the Purkinje cells, the lesion seen in the cerebellum of autistic individuals occurs prior to the establishment of these connections (Bauman & Kemper, 1994). Therefore, it is theorized that the abnormalities seen at autopsy were the result of events that occurred prior to the loss of the lamina dessicans at 30 weeks gestation.

Furthermore, it is assumed that the early olivocerebellar pathway involves the cerebellar nuclei. Subsequently, this is replaced by a more mature pathway that involves the Purkinje cells, which is the predominant system postnatally. The absence of adequate numbers of Purkinje cells in autistic individuals may lead to the persistence of the more primitive pathway involving the cerebellar nuclei. In turn, these cells initially could hypertrophy in response to the unusual demand placed on this primitive circuit. However, these cells presumably would be unable to sustain themselves in response to this demand, which could lead to the reduction in cell volume and number with advancing age (Bauman & Kemper, 1994).

Summary of Findings in Autism: These findings support several notions regarding the role of neurodevelopment in disease processes. Autism appears to be the result of a lesion that occurs prenatally, probably prior to 30 weeks gestation. The lesion involves alterations in the normal development of limbic and cerebellar structures, which in turn affects the development of olivocerebellar connections. These areas normally determine functions that include language development, language utilization, affect regulation, motor regulation, motivation, memory, cognitive learning, and motor learning. All of these functions are adversely affected in autistic children. Despite the fact that the lesion occurs prenatally, the effects of the lesion may not be apparent until 20 to 30 months of age. This fact can be accounted for by the intricate interplay between the presumed function of the affected areas and the normal anlagen of development. The deficit becomes apparent only when the function is required. Furthermore, by understanding what brain regions are affected and how these regions function, clinicians may be better able to understand the phenomenology to approach it in different ways and to conceive of more appropriate interventions.

The "obsessive-compulsive" symptoms of the autistic child may be better construed as a cognitive-behavioral response to a deficit in representational memory rather than as a variant of another phenomenologically defined disorder such as obsessive-compulsive disorder. This nuance may lead clinicians to think creatively about intervention based on a bottom-up approach to symptom development. This is better than using top-down approach to understanding neuropathology by just templating an intervention designed for a very different population of patients onto autistic children.

SCHIZOPHRENIA

Schizophrenia is a disorder that affects approximately 1% of adults. It has a typical age of onset between 16 and 30 years of age (Black & Andreasen, 1994). There appears to be a strong correlation between perinatal insult and increased risk for the development of schizophrenia. Evidence from histopathological investigations of brains of schizophrenics suggests that this is a neurodevelopmental disorder. The vulnerability conveyed by the underlying neurological defect requires normal maturational changes to trigger the onset of the illness in late adolescence and early adulthood. The following material reviews the evidence supporting a neurodevelopmental hypothesis.

Neuroanatomic Findings in Support of a Neurodevelopmental Hypothesis: Histopathological studies of schizophrenic patients have been consistent in demonstrating the presence of a reduction in neuronal cell numbers in multiple regions of the brain. However, like autism, on histopathological examination there is no evidence of a concomitant increase in the number of glial cells, which normally would accompany the process of neuronal necrosis (Benes, 1986; Falkai & Bogerts, 1986; Falkai, Bogerts, & Rozumek, 1988).

Detailed histopathological studies reveal that schizophrenic patients have discrete abnormalities within the cortical layer II of the anterior cingulate region, prefrontal cortex, and entorhinal cortex (Benes, 1995; Benes, McSparren, Bird, Vincent, & SanGiovanni, 1991; Jakob & Beckmann, 1986). Cells migrating to this area normally complete migration in the second trimester of fetal life and continue to differentiate through the first postnatal year (Benes, 1995). Therefore, the findings in schizophrenia are consistent with a disruption in normal neuronal migration early in life and may explain the finding of volume loss without accompanying gliosis (Benes, 1995). It has been further suggested that Gamma-aminobutyric acid neurons in this layer may be particularly sensitive to injury in the perinatal period (Benes, 1993, 1995).

Implications of Neuroanatomic Findings with Regard to "Late Onset": At first glance, it appears difficult to reconcile the findings suggesting disruption of central nervous system development in the perinatal period with a disorder that has a typical age of symptomatic onset in young adults. However, 2 lines of investigation provide some clarity (Benes, 1995).

Monkeys lesioned in the dorsolateral prefrontal (DLPF) cortex shortly after birth and tested shortly thereafter do not show the expected deficits in performance on a test (the delayed-response task) that assesses the functioning of this region of the brain (Goldman, 1974). However, repeat testing at age 2 to 3 years of age (the equivalent of adolescence in humans) fails to demonstrate the normal age-appropriate improvement in performance of the same task (Goldman, 1974). This finding suggests that the discrepancy in the acquisition of skills may be the result of late postnatal changes in this region of the brain (Goldman, 1974). Benes (1995) has proposed 2 hypotheses relating postnatal cortical changes to the onset of schizophrenia in late adolescence and early adulthood.

During adolescence, there is a significant increase in myelination in the superior medullary lamina. This area of the brain contains critical afferent fibers connecting the entorhinal and cingulate cortices with the hippocampal formation. Benes (1995) has suggested that alterations in the myelination of these areas during adolescence may act to "trigger" the appearance of schizophrenia at this time. She has proposed that an increased excitatory flow in the corticolimbic circuit accompanies this increased myelination. The activation of the relative excess of glutamatergic cells (due to loss of GABA cells) in layer II cells at this time could cause excitotoxic injury to this lamina in schizophrenic patients.

Alternatively, the role of GABA in mediating the activity of other neurotransmitter systems also may play a role in the onset of the disorder (Benes, 1995). The cortical GABA system interacts with the dopamine system, which plays a central role in the mediation of the effects of antipsychotic medication. There is a marked increase in dopamine release in the prefrontal cortex during periods of acute stress. As this system matures, the dopaminergic response to acute stress presumably increases. Benes (1995) suggests that in late adolescence, a patient with a vulnerability to schizophrenia and the concomitant alterations in GABA functioning in cortical layer II could experience disruption of cortical activity during times of severe stress. This situation would result from the unbridled release of dopamine in the prefrontal cortex in the absence of adequate inhibitory modulation by GABAergic neurons.

In summary, the evidence supports the notion that schizophrenia is a neurodevelopmental disorder (Benes, 1988, 1995; Weinberger, 1987). In this regard, schizophrenia is more similar to autism than it is to disorders associated with central nervous system volume loss, such as Alzheimer's or Huntington's disease. Like autism, schizophrenia is associated with cell loss without significant gliosis, which suggests early disruption in the normal process of development of the central nervous system and the failure of critical circuit pathways to develop. In addition, the disorder becomes symptomatically manifest only at a time in maturation when the missing circuits would be expected to come "on-line." The hypotheses derived from these observations help explain both the cognitive/behavioral pathology and clinical course associated with schizophrenia on the one hand and the role of stress in the etiology of the disorder on the other. Furthermore, the notion of an etiology based on the developmental interplay between functional neurotransmitter systems could

lead to novel pharmacological approaches to the treatment of schizophrenia.

Discussion

The course of normal brain development is a very complex yet highly coordinated process. The overall success of this developmental schema rests on the successful completion of successive interdependent stages. Any aberration in this developmental plan has the capacity to cause not only a "point" lesion in the area that is directly involved but a "cascading" effect on all subsequent developmental processes that rely on this region. The earlier the lesion, the greater the impact.

Understanding the underlying neuropathology in relation to developmental schema aids in translating neuropathology into clinical phenomenology. The "obsession" preoccupation of the autistic child is understood not solely as a variant of another phenomenologically defined disorder, obsessive-compulsive disorder, but as a consequence of the mismatch in the development of procedural memory. In addition, the insight gained through the understanding of developmental neurology allows us to make sense of the timing of onset of complex disorders. Both the intricate interplay between the developmental demands of late adolescence and the inherent deficit in stress modulation incurred by virtue of the underlying neuropathology as one aspect, or the interplay between developmental forces in young autistic children and their relative inability to use representational memory as the other, may allow us to conceive of ways to identify at-risk individuals earlier and to construct a series of interventions designed to reduce their risk of disease expression.

REFERENCES

Angevine, J., & Sidman, B. (1961). Autoradiographic study of cell migration during histogenesis of cerebral cortex in mouse. *Nature, 192,* 766–768.

Bachevalier, J., & Mishkin, M. (1984). An early and late developing system for learning and retention in infant monkeys. *Behavioral Neuroscience, 98,* 770–778.

Bauman, M., & Kemper, T. (1994). Neuroanatomic observations of the brain in autism. In M. Bauman & T. Kemper (Eds.), *The neurobiology of autism* (pp.

119–145). Baltimore, MD: Johns Hopkins University Press.

Bayer, S. (1989). Cellular aspects of brain development. *Neurotoxicology, 10,* 307–320.

Benes, F. (1986). Quantitative cytoarchitectural studies of cerebral cortex of schizophrenics. *Archives of General Psychiatry, 43,* 31–35.

Benes, F. (1988). Post-mortem structural analysis of schizophrenic brain. Study designs and the interpretation of data. *Psychiatric Development, 6:* 213–226.

Benes, F. (1993). Relationship of cingulate cortex to schizophrenia and other psychiatric disorders. In B. Vogt & M. Gabriel (Eds.), *Neurobiology of cingulate cortex and limbic thalamus* (pp. 581–605). Boston: Birkhauser.

Benes, F. (1995). Is there a neuroanatomic basis for schizophrenia? An old question revisited. *The Neuroscientist, 1,* 104–115.

Benes, F., McSparren, J., Bird, E., Vincent, S., & SanGiovanni, J. (1991). Deficits in small interneurons in prefrontal and anterior cingulate cortex of schizophrenic and schizoaffective patients. *Archives of General Psychiatry, 48,* 996–1001.

Black, D., & Andreasen, N. (1994). Schizophrenia, schizophreniform disorder, and delusional (paranoid) disorder. In R. Hales, S. Yudofsky, & J. Talbott (Eds.), *The American Psychiatric Press textbook of psychiatry* (pp. 411–464). Washington, DC: American Psychiatric Press.

Brown, M., Hopkins, W., & Keynes, R. (1991). *Essentials of neural development.* Cambridge: Cambridge University Press.

Bryson, S., Clark, B., & Smith, I. (1988). First Canadian report of a epidemiological study of autistic syndromes. *Journal of Child Psychology and Psychiatry and Allied Disciplines, 29,* 433–445.

Caviness, V. (1982). Neocortical histogenesis in normal and reeler mice: A developmental study based upon 3H-thymidine autoradiography. *Developmental Brain Research, 4,* 293–302.

Cowan, W. (1979). The development of the brain. In W. Cowan (Ed.), *The brain* (pp. 56–69). San Francisco: W. H. Freeman.

Falkai, P., & Bogerts, B. (1986). Cell loss in the hippocampus of schizophrenics. *European Archives of Psychiatry and Clinical Neuroscience, 236,* 154–161.

Falkai, P., Bogerts, B., & Rozumek, M. (1988). Cell loss and volume reduction in the entorhinal cortex of schizophrenics. *Biological Psychiatry, 24,* 515–521.

Goldman, P. (1974). An alternative to developmental plasticity. In D. Stein, J. Rosen, & M. Butters (Eds.), *Plasticity and recovery of function in the CNS* (pp. 149–174). New York: Academic Press.

Gordon-Weeks, P. (1988). RNA transport in dendrites. *Trends in Neuroscience, 11,* 342–342.

Jacobson, M. (1991). *Developmental neurobiology.* New York: Plenum Press.

Jakob, H., & Beckmann, H. (1986). Prenatal developmental disturbances in the limbic allocortex in schizophrenics. *Journal of Neural Transmission, 65,* 303–326.

Killiany, R., & Moss, M. (1994). Memory function and autism. In M. Bauman & T. Kemper (Eds.), *The neurobiology of autism* (pp. 170–194). Baltimore, MD: Johns Hopkins University Press.

Kolb, B. (1989). Brain development, plasticity and behavior. *American Psychologist, 44,* 1203–1212.

Oakley, D. (1981). Brain mechanisms of mammalian memory. *British Medical Bulletin, 37,* 175–180.

Piven, J., Arndt, S., Bailey, J., Havercamp, S., Andreasen, N., & Palmer, P. (1995). An MRI study of brain size in autism. *American Journal of Psychiatry, 152,* 1145–1149.

Rakic, P. (1971). Neuron-glia relationship during granule cell migration in developing cerebellar cortex. *Journal of Comparative Neurology, 141,* 282–312.

Rakic, P. (1972). Mode of cell migration to superficial layers of fetal monkey neocortex. *Journal of Comparative Neurology, 145.*

Rakic, P. (1977). Genesis of the dorsal lateral geniculate nucleus in the rhesus monkey. *Journal of Comparative Neurology, 145,* 23–52.

Rakic, P. (1988a). Defects of neuronal migration and the pathogenesis of cortical malformations. In G. Boer, M. Feenstra, M. Mirmiran, D. Swaab, & F. Van Haaren (Eds.), *Progress in brain research* (pp. 15–37). Elsevier Science Publishers.

Rakic, P. (1988b). Specification of cerebral cortical areas. *Science, 241,* 170–176.

Rakic, P., & Sidman, R. (1970). Histogenesis of cortical layers in human cerebellum particularly the lamina dessicans. *Journal of Comparative Neurology, 139,* 473–500.

Rapin, I. (1991). Autistic children: Diagnosis and clinical features. *Pediatrics, 87,* 751–760.

Richman, D., Steward, R., Hutchinsin, H., & Caviness, V. (1975). Mechanical model of brain convolutional development. *Science, 189,* 18–21.

Schmahmann, J. (1994). The cerebellum in autism: Clinical and anatomic perspectives. In M. Bauman & T. Kemper (Eds.), *The neurobiology of autism* (pp. 195–226). Baltimore, MD: Johns Hopkins University Press.

Squire, L. (1986). Mechanisms of memory. *Science, 232,* 1612–1619.

Weinberger, D. (1987). Implications of normal brain development for the pathogenesis of schizophrenia. *Archives of General Psychiatry, 44,* 660–669.

Wigston, D., & Sanes, J. (1982). Selective reinnervation of adult mammalian muscle by axons from different segmental levels. *Nature, 299,* 464–467.

Wigston, D., & Sanes, J. (1985). Selective reinnervation of intercostal muscle transplanted from different segmental levels to a common site. *Journal of Neuroscience, 5,* 1208–1221.

5 / Molecular Genetics and the Developing Brain

Edwin H. Cook, Jr., and Bennett L. Leventhal

This chapter discusses the mechanisms by which genes are involved in brain development. Molecular genetic mechanisms are involved in brain development even before conception; in fact, the brain development of any given child may be influenced by genetic events occurring many generations before his or her birth. In this chapter we explore the role of genetic function in the developmental process. More precisely, we examine the complex process that transfers information from chromosomes into protein production. This process has many steps, each of which may be involved in abnormal brain development leading to psychopathology. This entire discussion takes place with a bit of caution, because even though there have been many important advances in the field of molecular genetics, at the present time most cases of developmental disorders do not have a specific known etiology. However, it is becoming increasing clear that genetics plays a key role in the development of psychopathology, and knowledge of molecular genetics now can assist parents and patients in understanding at least the genetic risk facing their offspring. Equally important, the informed clinician must recognize that molecular genetics technology is evolving rapidly, thus setting the stage for the study of specific effects of molecular genetic pathology and the development of new treatments in the coming decades. However, contrary to the naive view of some that the understanding of genetics will lead to greater uniformity among humans, in fact, the myriad of genetic mechanisms almost guarantee that there will be a vast diversity in developmental outcomes among individuals both in terms of normal variations and in pathology.

The authors would like to thank the late Roland Ciaranello, who led the field in emphasizing the importance of molecular genetics in the study of normal and pathological brain development.

GAMETOGENESIS (PRODUCTION OF EGG AND SPERM)

Much of this section concerns deoxyribonucleic acid (DNA). In humans, DNA is packaged into chromosomes. The average human has 46 chromosomes, consisting of 22 pairs of autosomes and 2 sex chromosomes (XX or XY). The genetic material from the 2 parents is combined during the process of gametogenesis, or the production of sperm and eggs. It is the combining of sperm and egg that ultimately leads to the production of the cells of the body, each of which has 2 copies of the genetic material, known as the diploid state. However, each normal gamete (a sperm or an egg) has only a single copy of chromosomal material, known as the haploid state. This haploid state is developed in the first step of meiosis, which yields a cell that has 1 copy of each autosome and a single gonosome (either 1 X or 1 Y chromosome). During meiosis, recombination takes place randomly between adjacent stretches of each chromosome. This leads to a mixing of the chromosomes. This random mixing means that no 2 children of 2 parents are genetically identical, except for monozygotic twins—nature's clones; thus enormous individual diversity exists. This diversity is advantageous to the species. Genetic diversity is also advantageous to molecular genetic studies, because mutations near specific markers are not statistically likely to recombine while mutations on different chromosomes or on the opposite ends of a large chromosome are expected to recombine about 50% of the time. These variations and combinations make it possible for geneticists to identify the transmission and sharing of specific sequences of genetic material between family members through linkage and linkage disequilibrium mapping.

Down syndrome is currently the most common genetic form of mental retardation. As it turns out, abnormal meiosis contributes to the development of this disorder by leaving each cell with 3 copies (triploid) of chromosome 21 rather than the usual 2 copies (diploid). Chromosome 21 is particularly vulnerable during the time of maternal gametogenesis. In the first meiotic phase, chromosome 21 fails to segregate into 2 parts to form 2 haploid cells. This process is called nondisjunction. In this instance the precursor cells divide to create 2 ovum, one of which receives both copies of chromosome 21 while the other ovum receives no copies of that chromosome. As a result, when the abnormal diploid ovum is combined with the sperm with 1 copy of chromosome 21, the cell becomes triploid, or has 3 copies of the 21st chromosome. The development of triploid cells usually occurs during the first of the 2 maternal meiotic stages; however, it also may occur during the second division or, even more rarely, during spermatogenesis (Epstein et al., 1991). In any case, it is the presence of this trisomy 21 that leads to the clinical syndrome of Down syndrome.

Tripling or trisomies can occur with other chromosomes. A more complicated result of an initial trisomy can occur after formation of the zygote (early product of sperm and egg fusion). An example of this situation is resolution of trisomy 15. Usually trisomies of chromosomes larger than chromosome 21 are lethal. On occasion, zygotes with trisomy 15 lose the additional chromosome. Thus what started as 3 copies of chromosome 15 ends up with 2; however, most often these 2 copies are copies of the maternal chromosome, with no contribution from the paternal genetic pool. As the resulting child has what seems to be a normal diploid state, previously it was assumed that the situation would not contribute to child and adolescent psychopathology. However, recently molecular genetic tools combined with astute clinical skills have demonstrated that this situation can lead to severe psychopathology in the form of Prader-Willi syndrome when both chromosomes come from the mother (Ledbetter & Engel, 1995) and Angelman syndrome when both chromosomes come from the father. These 2 chromosomal syndromes have demonstrated the importance of the parent of origin of particular pieces of the DNA. Most cases of Prader-Willi and Angelman syndrome have deletions in the same region of the proximal portion of the long arm of chromosome 15. However, the phenotypes (the clinical signs and symptoms that patients actually exhibit) differ considerably. That is, most patients with Prader-Willi syndrome have mild mental retardation and obesity as a result of compulsive overeating. In contrast, patients with Angelman syndrome present with severe mental retardation, ataxic movements, the absence of language, and abnormal electroencephalograms. The factors that appear to account for this difference have to do with which portion of chromosome 15 is deleted. In Prader-Willi syndrome, the deletion in chromosome 15 is in that part that came from the father, in Angelman syndrome, the deletion is in the area of the genetic material that came from the mother. This is quite striking and has led to the understanding that at least on a molecular level, some genes are active only if they come from the father or the mother. Some of the overlap in these 2 syndromes (e.g., ritualistic behavior) may be due to the deletion of active genes from either maternal or paternal chromosomes. This mechanism of relative activation of 1 chromosome as opposed to the other in a diploid pair is termed imprinting.

It remains quite unclear why these variations in gametogenesis take place. Certain risk factors do seem to increase the likelihood that such abnormalities will occur. For example, advanced maternal age appears to be a powerful risk factor for chromosomal abnormalities, particularly trisomy 21. The reasons for this remain elusive now but as understanding of the process of gametogenesis evolves, not only an understanding but also a mechanism for preventing such abnormalities may develop.

FERTILIZED EGG

The net result of fertilization—the combination of the male and female gametes—is the production of a cell line with a single set of genetic material. Once the chromosomes have been added up and the effects of imprinting are in place, the process does not end. Indeed, there are continuing modifications to the genetic material. For example, while both the sperm and the egg each contribute roughly equivalent amounts of DNA to the individual's genetic material, the egg contributes the vast bulk of the cellular material, or cytoplasm. This maternally derived cytoplasm contains messenger ribonucleic acid (mRNA) and proteins that have been derived solely from the mother. In addition, the mother contributes organelles, in particular, the mitochondria, a critical part of the mechanism for energy production. As it turns out, the mitochondria have special DNA that exist outside of the nucleus. Several disorders of mitochondrial metabolism have been demonstrated to be due to mutations of mitochondrial DNA. The fact that mitochondrial DNA is uniquely transmitted from the mother accounts for maternal transmission of mitochondrial disorders, including metabolic crises, diabetes, and seizures (Wallace, 1995). Since these disorders typically involve the most metabolically active cells, it would not be surprising if some cases of developmental disorders ultimately were found to be related to mitochondrial DNA.

Even after cell division of the embryo has begun, DNA still may undergo additional modifications. As the embryo further divides, modifications that occur in the DNA may not be reflected in each and every cell in the body. This event is known as mosaicism. Even though only some cells have an altered number of chromosomes, many chromosomal abnormalities are characterized by mosaicism. For example, many of the higher-functioning patients with Down syndrome exhibit mosaicism: While many of their cells are normal, a sufficient number of other cells have 3 copies of the 21st chromosome for them to have the syndrome. Another example of a somatic mosaicism can occur when translocations (movements of small pieces of DNA from a normal chromosomal location to an atypical location) take place during late stages of cell division. This turn of events can lead to malignant cells occurring in an environment in which most of the remaining cells in the body are chromosomally normal.

Trinucleotide repeat expansions also may begin after embryonic cell division has begun. Trinucleotide repeats are repetitive patterns of 3 nucleotides in DNA. Interestingly enough, if they expand beyond a certain threshold, they become progressively longer in successive generations. As a result, a grandparent may have 40 trinucleotide repeats and no symptoms of a disorder, a parent may have 150 repeats, again with no symptoms of a disorder; the child may have 300 repeats with clear symptoms, such as fragile X syndrome. The exact number of repeats and thresholds varies with the disorder. Trinucleotide repeats have been discovered only recently as mechanisms for specific developmental neurobiological disorders. The best known of these disorders is fragile X syndrome. In fragile X syndrome, DNA instability leads to differing sizes of trinucleotide repeat expansions in different cells. Most interestingly, the full mutation occurs after separation of the germ cell line (the cells which later produce eggs and sperm) from the other cell lines in the body. This means that the developing embryo can create the cells that make sperm and ova without excessive numbers of trinucleotide repeats but the rest of the cells in the body have long expansions, which lead to pathology. An interesting paradox results with fully affected boys with fragile X syndrome having sperm that do not have the full expansion of the DNA.

TRANSCRIPTION

DNA is composed of about 3 billion base pairs. Base pairs are matched combinations of 1 of 4 nucleotides, adenine (A), guanine (G), cytosine (C), and thymine (T). They are linked in a double helix to form the basic genetic code that directs the synthesis of virtually all proteins in cells. Each cell in the body (with some exceptions noted earlier) has the same 3 billion base pairs in spite of the fact that there is a wide variety of cell types and cell function. Thus what differentiates one cell from another is not the totality of the genetic code contained within it but rather which genes are activated or repressed at any particular time within that cell.

The genes consist of patterns of base pairs in a sequence on the DNA that do not themselves make the proteins. Rather, the gene serves as a template for the production of ribonucleic acid, or RNA. The RNA is made from a similar sequence of base pairs, which are derived from the strand of DNA, except the thymine (T) is replaced with uracil (U). The process of making RNA based on a DNA template is known as transcription (see figure 5.1). In order for transcription to be initiated, DNA and the constituents to form RNA have to be present as do specific proteins known as transcription factors that facilitate the process. The specific transcription factors determine the

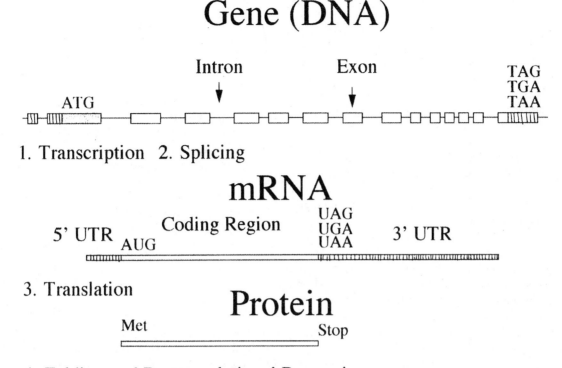

FIGURE 5.1.

Transcription of DNA to mRNA and translation of mRNA to protein. Rectangles designate exons and thin lines designate introns, which are not included in the mRNA. Vertical lines indicate portions of exons and mRNA that are not translated into protein but that may alter processing of mRNA. ATG is an initiation codon (3 nucleotides) that transcribed to AUG and signals the initiation of protein translation with the amino acid methionine. TAG, TGA, and TAA are stop codons present in DNA that are transcribed to UAG, UGA, and UAA respectively. These 3 nucleotides signal the termination of an amino acid chain (protein).

cell type to be produced and contribute to the phenotypic expression of each cell. Most important, transcription factors are themselves regulated, and this regulation often is mediated by the cell's individual environment. This regulation of transcription is considered to be a key mechanism in the translation of effects of experience on protein production and, in particular, the acquisition of knowledge and skills. Although much remains to be learned about regulation of transcription in the central nervous system, the mechanisms by which experiences lead to changes in the central nervous system development are becoming ever better understood. This developing understanding of transcriptional regulatory processes creates the possibility that there will be treatments for

specific pathological conditions arising out of experience. For example, posttraumatic stress disorder appears to be the result of a traumatic environmental event that changes central nervous system functioning through psychological experience. There is some evidence that this change results from a modification in the regulation of cellular mechanisms, including activation of certain genes. More important, it is important to recognize that child abuse, neglect, and malnutrition affect molecular genetic mechanisms, leading to long-term central nervous system changes. These problems are best treated by prevention.

Transcription factors themselves are proteins that recognize specific DNA sequences. Often transcription factors are regulated by phosphorylation through receptor activation, which in turn affects second and third messenger systems. Many hormones, such as glucocorticoids, act by binding to receptors. This process leads to the activation or expression of genes, including transcription factors. Transcription factors interact with specific areas on the DNA, called promoters, leading to the initiation of transcription. Many promoters have DNA sequences, such as the glucocorticoid response element (GRE) to which the activated protein binds. When an activated protein binds to one of these activated elements, a specific gene is transcribed. This complex process allows for the interaction among body functions, environment, and genes.

In addition to transcription factors, chromosomal structure varies from cell to cell. When tightly wound in the nucleus in repeating structures—nucleosomes—DNA is protected from transcription by a covering layer of histone proteins. The process of activating a gene first requires the acetylation of the protected histones by transcriptional regulators. When this occurs, only specific regions of the DNA are likely to be uncovered, thus increasing the likelihood of initiating transcription in that region (Wolffe & Pruss, 1996).

The inactivation of a full chromosome can be another factor that controls genetic response. In addition to containment in the nucleosome, chromosomal activation occurs on the largest scale in females when 1 of the X chromosomes is inactivated in each cell. It has recently been demonstrated that this can be a mechanism for variability in the phenotype or presentation of a child and adolescent mental disorder. Women who have the full fragile X mutation have been shown to have less severe symptoms than males since they have at least 1 normal X chromosome. However, there is considerable variability of cognitive impairment for women with a full fragile X mutation. Reiss and colleagues (Reiss, Freund, Baumgardner, Abrams, & Denckla, 1995) have shown that women with a lower proportion of active normal X chromosomes had more cognitive impairment than women with a higher proportion of active normal X chromosomes. This finding demonstrates that it is not simply the presence of chromosomal abnormality that is necessary for a disorder but the relative availability of the genes on that chromosome for transcription that is important for expression of the disorder.

SPLICING

In genes with multiple exons (exons are the parts of DNA that become part of the messenger RNA [mRNA]), after transcription of DNA to RNA (composed of A,G,C, or U), RNA must be spliced to its mature mRNA form. Introns, on the other hand, are the part of the DNA that are spliced out after transcription; accordingly, they do not become part of mRNA. There are several examples where mutation in introns leads to altered splicing and change of proteins; this, in turn, leads to disease. One recently discovered example is mutation of intronic sequence of UBE 3A, which leads to Angelman syndrome (Kishino, Lalande, & Wagstaff, 1997). Disruption of the nucleotide sequences recognized by the splicing proteins interferes with normal gene splicing.

TRANSLATION

Messenger RNA serves as a template for the production of proteins. With a few exceptions (where the RNA acts as an enzyme [ribozyme]), DNA and mRNA functions to guide the primary structure of proteins. The code for the design of a protein is initiated at a 3-nucleotide sequence called a codon. This beginning codon, composed of adenine-thymine-guanine (ATG), starts the construction of each protein with the amino acid methionine. Subsequently, each 3 nucleotides code for 1 of the 20 amino acids that make up the human body or for 1 of the 3 stop codons. In this way, the DNA nucleotide sequence may be read to determine the primary structure (amino acid sequence) of a protein.

By definition, any change in the structure of DNA is called a mutation. Mutations in DNA may have any one of several outcomes. They may lead to no amino acid change (conservative mutation often useful for genetic mapping), may lead to an amino acid change (missense mutation), or may give rise to shift of the reading frame (frame shift) if base pairs are inserted or deleted in any number that is not a multiple of 3. Frame shifts, in turn, lead to changes in several amino acids with frequent truncation (premature translation termination). Protein changes have many effects, ranging from no effect, to loss of function (common in recessive disorders), to a loss of regulatory sites, to some gain of function (commonly present in dom-

TABLE 5.1

Molecular Genetic Mechanisms and Examples of Disorders with Child and Adolescent Psychiatric Symptoms

Mechanism	Disorder	Symptoms
Meiosis	Down syndrome	Mental retardation
Imprinting	Prader-Willi syndrome	Mental retardation, compulsive eating
Mitochondrial DNA	Mitochondrial myopathy, encephalopathy, lactic acidosis, and strokelike episodes	Diabetes, seizures, metabolic crises
Mosaicism	Down syndrome	Less severe cognitive impairment
Minisatellites (tandem repeats)	Fragile X syndrome	Mental retardation and pervasive developmental disorder symptoms
Transcription	Psychological trauma	Increased arousal
Splicing	Angelman syndrome (rare point mutations)	Mental retardation, seizures, autistic disorder
Point mutation	Phenylketonuria	Mental retardation and frequent autism

inant disorders), to dominant negative effects. (These occur in proteins that organize into tertiary protein structure in which several protein subunits combine into a functional unit. When one of the component subunits undergoes an alteration of structure, the protein function may be disrupted.)

Once proteins are produced by translation outside of the nucleus, in ribosomes, they are then processed in the endoplasmic reticulum. Typically this involves the common addition of oligosaccharides (sugar molecules). Proteins are essential in every phase of central nervous system development. After production, they are commonly regulated by the addition (phosphorylation) or removal of phosphate groups at the amino acids threonine, serine, or tyrosine.

One key function of proteins is to regulate cell-cell contact during development of the central nervous system. Such cell-cell contact is mediated by cell adhesion molecules and cytokines and affects the development of other neurons or glial cells. Usually the adhesion molecules influence other cells by acting at receptors on the cell membrane. These receptors, in turn, lead to changes within the second cell, through second and third messengers. These messengers alter the activity of the proteins (by modulation of phosphorylation) that regulate the transcription of those genes necessary for appropriate response to cell-cell contact. This mediates such vital functions as neu-

ronal migration or neuronal survival through prevention of programmed cell death.

Molecular Genetic Disorders Leading to Abnormal Brain Development

Several molecular genetic disorders have been demonstrated to alter brain development and thus lead to various kinds of psychopathology, particularly to cognitive impairment. Such disorders illustrate the role of the normal molecular genetic process in normal brain development. In addition, it becomes increasingly important to recognize these disorders because of their implications for genetic counseling and for specific intervention (See Table 5.1).

The complexity of gene regulation along with the associated processes leading to protein regulation are clues to understanding the diversity of illness. Although a single developmental neurobiological disorder such as tuberous sclerosis may be caused by 2 different genes (locus heterogeneity), cystic fibrosis provides an excellent example of a single gene with several different mutations. Different mutations of the cystic fibrosis transmembrane regulator (CFTR) gene lead to different organ system involvement as well as differing severity. Different mutations in the CFTR gene, which alter protein production (nonsense, frame shift, and splicing mutations), regulation (missense), conduction (missense), and synthesis (splicing), lead to different clinical expressions of cystic fibrosis, ranging from obstructive azoospermia (infertility) to severe cystic fibrosis with pulmonary complications with or without pancreatic insufficiency. Although this situation seems complex enough, still other genes have been shown to influence the severity of a mouse model of cystic fibrosis (Estivill, 1996).

CODING REGION MUTATIONS

The most direct mutations are those in a coding region that lead to abnormal protein production or function. Phenylketonuria remains an excellent example. Several different mutations reduce the function of the phenylalanine hydroxylase gene on chromosome 12q24.1. When such a mutation is present, it leads to a toxic accumulation of metabolites, which in turn results in mental retardation and, in some cases, comorbid autism. However, it is possible to prevent the occurrence of the retardation through appropriate dietary intervention, in particular, through a phenylalanine diet. This is an important point because all too many assume that mutations affecting protein function inevitably lead to disease. In addition, phenylketonuria provides an example of a disorder with locus genetic heterogeneity (that is to say, the condition can be engendered by genes at different loci), since mutations in dihydropteridine reductase may lead to phenylketonuria through a different point in the pathway, namely, a failure to provide activation of the cofactor biopterin necessary for normal levels of phenylalanine hydroxylase activity.

TRINUCLEOTIDE REPEAT DISORDERS

Trinucleotide repeat disorders are due to expansion of normally occurring repeating units of 3 nucleotides. Trinucleotide repeat disorders illustrate both the complexity of single-gene disorders and the relevance of considering the location of mutations in the coding region, on introns, or on untranslated regions of mRNA (Warren, 1996). Until the 1990s, trinucleotide repeat disorders

were unknown. Now at least 3 have been shown to be associated with child and adolescent psychopathology. It is likely that in the near future, more child and adolescent psychiatric disorders will be demonstrated to be due to other disorders of this character.

5' Untranslated Region (Fragile X Syndrome): There is considerable normal variation in the fragile X mental retardation (FRAXA) gene. In particular, this variation occurs in the number of CGG repeats in the 5' untranslated region (5' UTR). Indeed, these can range up to 50 CGG repeats. The 5' untranslated region is a part of the gene that does become part of the mRNA; however, it is located on the part of the gene that is situated before the start codon and therefore is not translated into the protein. It is difficult to determine the effect of a change in a gene that does not lead to a change in the coding of a protein. The first step in the mutation of fragile X syndrome is a premutation. This extends the CGG repeats from the normal up to 50 to a range of 50 to 200. This premutation leads to subtle, if any, changes in psychopathology. However, in the course of transmitting the gene from one generation to the next, expansion of the repeat from a premutation mother to an affected son leads to expansion of the CGG repeats beyond 200. With this, moderate mental retardation follows along with other psychopathological symptoms, including stereotypic behavior and difficulty in cognitive tasks requiring sequencing (Verkerk et al., 1991). Many patients with fragile X syndrome have pervasive developmental disorders. Physical features include long ears and macroorchidism. Fragile X syndrome may now be diagnosed by chromosomal analysis, but such an examination must be specifically requested, since the fragile Xq27.3 is seen only when the cells are grown in a folate-deficient medium.

Mothers of boys with fragile X syndrome originally were considered to be unaffected carriers. However, a series of studies demonstrated a difference between mothers who were cytogenetically positive (had 1 X chromosome with a fragile site and 1 normal X chromosome) and cytogenetically negative (both X chromosomes normal). Cytogenetically normal mothers have 50 to 200 repeats (premutation) and cytogenetically positive mothers have 50 to 200 repeats but who themselves carry greater than 200 CGG repeats (full mutation). More recently, females with greater than 200 CGG repeats of 1 X chromosome have been demonstrated to have lower IQ if certain conditions are met. In particular, they display this difference if the unaffected chromosome was preferentially inactivated during the process of lyonization where within each female cell, one of each X chromosome is inactivated (Reiss, Freund, et al., 1995).

The mechanism of disease in fragile X syndrome is that the genetic changes lead to reduced fragile X mental retardation (FMR1) protein production. The sequence of events is as follows. The increase in CGG repeats leads to methylation of the CpG island before the FMR1 gene (Oberlé et al., 1991). This, in turn, brings about a reduction in FMR1 transcription. As a result, less protein is produced. Genetic changes lead to reduced FMR1 protein production. Although the specific effects of reduced FMR1 are not yet entirely understood and are being investigated, one possibility is a secondary reduction in adenylyl cyclase activity (Berry-Kravis & Sklena, 1993).

A rarer fragile site at Xq28 has been shown to be due to a CGG expansion in yet another gene called FRAXE. This disorder is rarer, has a more variable clinical expression, and has been shown to both expand and contract in terms of number of CGG repeats (Knight et al., 1993).

Coding Region (Huntington's Disease): In a manner similar to what occurs in fragile X syndrome, in the coding region of the Huntingtin gene, there is diversity in the number of CAG repeats that code for repeating glutamine. Expansion beyond 35 CAG repeats usually leads to Huntington's disease (Huntington's Disease Collaborative Research Group, 1993). It is not surprising that the number of repeats necessary to lead to disease in a coding region trinucleotide repeat disorder is much smaller than that of an untranslated expansion, since coding region expansion leads to an increase in the length of the amino acid repeat and total length of the protein.

Huntington's disease has considerable variability in age of onset and can appear as early as 5 years of age. It leads to dementia as well as to psychosis and mood dysregulation. A correlation has been found between CAG repeat length and age of onset, such that the greater the repeat length, the earlier the age of onset.

One paradox is how a protein such as huntingtin, which is so ubiquitously expressed, can lead to specific neuropathology. A possibility is that it interacts with another protein that has a more limited distribution, such as huntingtin-associated protein (HAP-1) (Li et al., 1995).

Other identified CAG repeat disorders are due to coding region mutations; these include Kennedy's disease, majado Joseph's disease/spinocerebellar ataxia 3 (*SCA 3*), spinocerebellar ataxia 1 (*SCA 1*), and dentatorubral and pallidolluysian atrophy, all of which, like Huntington's disease, lead to motor degeneration.

Intron (Friedrich's Ataxia): In contrast to the previously identified trinucleotide repeat disorders, Friedrich's ataxia is an autosomal recessive disorder. Therefore it was surprising when the condition was found to be due to GGA expansion in the intron of *frataxin*. In this case, it appears that the increase in GGA interferes with the usual sequence necessary for proper recognition of splice sites. It thus leads to abnormal mRNA and protein production (Campuzano et al., 1996).

3′ Untranslated Region (Myotonic Dystrophy (DM): An increase in CTG repeats leads to myotonic dystrophy (Brook et al., 1992). This increase occurs in the 3′ UTR of the DM protein kinase (DMPK) gene beyond $(CTG)_{200}$. The expansion leads to impaired posttranscriptional processing and a reduction in DMPK mRNA and protein (Krahe et al., 1995). This molecular genetic process leads to the clinical phenomenon of anticipation, in which the age of onset is earlier with each generation within the family. Myotonic dystrophy of childhood or congenital onset also may be associated with developmental disorders such as Asperger's disorder (Blondis, Cook, Koza-Taylor, & Finn, 1996).

Chromosomal Abnormalities Leading to Abnormal Brain Development

Abnormalities in chromosomes lead to changes (increases or decreases) in the number of genes or to interruption of genes. Most chromosomal abnormalities lead to abnormal central nervous system development, likely due to the simultaneous involvement of several contiguous genes. It is important to grasp the complexity of central nervous system development; in the development of a single structure such as the hippocampus, more than 6,000 genes are involved. The intricate and interconnected quality of the brain also contributes to developmental vulnerability. If any element is left out, serious consequences can follow. With the smallest typical chromosomal deletions involving at least 3 megabases (1/1000 of the genome), it is likely that in the wake of any such disturbance, 6 to 10 genes would be deleted, 1 of which is likely to be important in at least 1 location for brain development at any point in time. In addition, chromosomal abnormalities usually are associated with distinctive patterns of other organ involvement, including development of facial features, limbs, heart, kidney, and other structures. Chromosomal abnormalities often have distinctive psychiatric presentations (Dykens, 1996).

CHROMOSOMAL DELETION SYNDROMES (MILLER-DIEKER LISSENCEPHALY, WILLIAMS-BEUREN SYNDROME, SMITH-MAGENIS SYNDROME, VELOCARDIOFACIAL SYNDROME, CRI DU CHAT)

In addition to the deletion syndromes already noted (Prader-Willi syndrome and Angelman syndrome), other deletion syndromes are known that also lead to abnormal brain development with subsequent psychopathology.

Miller-Dieker lissencephaly is a deletion syndrome on chromosome 17p13.3. Here the gene lissencephaly-1 (LIS1) is deleted (Reiner et al., 1993). LIS1 is necessary for normal neuronal migration, and the deletion leads to the absence of the normal convolutions of the cerebral cortex (Reiner et al., 1995). Cloning of LIS1 has provided information about normal neuronal migration. Another form of lissencephaly is X-linked.

William-Beuren syndrome is a chromosomal deletion (7q11.2) syndrome leading to gregarious personality, "elfin" facies, characteristic cognitive disability (poor visual-motor integration, poor sustained attention, but relatively stronger language, social, naming, and musical skills) with frequent mental retardation, hyperacusis, supravalvular aortic stenosis, short stature, and infantile hypercalcemia. Although many cases include all of these features, smaller deletions lead to elfin facies with supravalvular aortic stenosis or cognitive

impairment with neither stenosis nor elfin facies. Although many cases of William-Beuren syndrome are detected on routine chromosomal analysis, over 35% of cases will be missed by conventional cytogenetic testing. If clinical suspicion is present of any specific deletion syndrome, fluorescent in situ hybridization (FISH) should be performed. Since 96% of cases will be detected with a probe of the elastin locus, a DNA probe should be employed that hybridizes to sequence in this region. A positive FISH test will reveal the absence of FISH signal for the William's locus on 1 chromosome 7.

Smith-Magenis syndrome results from a deletion on chromosome 17p11.2. The patient presents a phenotype that consists of broad flat midface, a broad nasal bridge, and brachycephaly. Since such midface hypoplasia also is seen in fetal alcohol syndrome, this suggests that both environmental (teratologic) and genetic effects may lead to similar changes in the development of the brain and other tissues. In addition, patients with Smith-Magenis syndrome frequently display brachydactyly, speech delay, a hoarse deep voice, decreased sensitivity to pain, self-destructive behavior (pulling out fingernails and toenails and/or insertion of foreign bodies into body orifices), and sleep disturbance (Greenberg et al., 1991). In view of the sleep and behavioral disturbances, it is noteworthy that the serotonin transporter has been mapped near this region (Gelernter, Pakstis, & Kidd, 1995).

Velocardiofacial syndrome results from a deletion on chromosome 22q11. The phenotype that the patient presents includes cleft palate, cardiac anomalies, typical facies (including bulbous nasal tip), learning disabilities (in the realms of abstraction, reading comprehension, and mathematics), blunt or inappropriate affect in childhood, and ultimately psychosis in adolescence and adulthood (Shprintzen, Goldberg, Golding-Kushner, & Marion, 1992). Although the gene leading to abnormal brain development in velocardiofacial syndrome has not been defined, the presence in this region of catechol-O-methyltransferase (COMT), an enzyme that metabolizes catecholamines, is a suggestive candidate gene. Properly available, this enzyme should regulate brain development, particularly in the limbic system; when reduced in dosage, it may not be present in sufficient quantity to accomplish this mission.

Deletions of the end of the small arm of chromosome 5 often lead to Cri du Chat syndrome. Here the child displays a characteristic "cat's cry" and profound mental retardation. Dissection of deletions with different breakpoints leading to differing missing genes has led to mapping of the cat's cry condition to distal 5p15.2 and proximal 5p15.3. Another group of patients with more distal deletions at 5p15.3 has been reported to have speech delay (Church, Bengtsson, Nielsen, Wasmuth, & Niebuhr, 1995). Although these children were reported not to be hyperactive, behavioral data were not presented. In general, children with language disorder are considered to be at increased risk for comorbid attention deficit hyperactivity disorder (Baker & Cantwell, 1987).

CHROMOSOMAL DUPLICATION SYNDROMES (TRISOMY 21, DUPLICATION OF CHROMOSOME 15)

The most common genetic syndrome identified to date is Down syndrome, where the majority of cases are due to maternal nondisjunction leading to 2 maternally derived chromosome 21s and a third paternally derived chromosome 21. It is important to recognize that Down syndrome is *not* the most common inherited syndrome. Fragile X syndrome (FRAXA) has that dubious distinction. In Down syndrome, a minority of cases display translocations leading to triplication of a portion of chromosome 21. These translocations have led to mapping of the obligate region of chromosome 21 necessary to lead to core Down syndrome clinical features to a 2.5 Mb region at 21q22.1–q22.2 (Lucente et al., 1995).

Duplication of the proximal end of the long arm of chromosome 15 leads to mental retardation and autistic disorder with seizures (Gillberg et al., 1991; Leana-Cox et al., 1994). Almost all of these duplications are maternal, leading to the possibility that maternally imprinted genes are involved in this syndrome (Cook et al., 1997). When one considers an imprinted gene, the gene dosage increase would be 100% (2 active transcripts compared to 1 normally active transcript). This stands in contrast to a gene active from both maternally and paternally derived chromosomes in which the increase would be 50% (3 active transcripts compared to the 2 normally active transcripts). In families with a single autistic child without a specific chromosomal anomaly, the recurrence risk of autistic disorder in siblings is approximately 6% compared to 0.1% for the population as a whole. Intrachromosomal duplications of the proximal long arm of chromosome 15 increase this risk to 50%.

Mitochondrial Genetic Syndromes

The vast majority of DNA is contained within the nucleus. However, the mitochondria contain genes necessary for the production of some mitochondrial proteins. Since mitochondria are energy-producing organelles, it is not surprising that mitochondrial disorders commonly lead to developmental abnormalities of the central nervous system. For example, deafness and seizures commonly result from mitochondrial deletions or mutations. Since mitochondria are transmitted as independent organelles and only the egg contributes mitochondria to the zygote (fertilized egg) (Wallace, 1992), mitochondrial disorders are also unique in that transmission occurs exclusively from mother to child.

Another interesting finding in mitochondrial inheritance is mosaicism. Typically, mitochondrial deletions are found only in a portion of mitochondria. Therefore, in the case of monozygotic (identical) twins, their nuclear DNA may be identical, but they each may have different percentages of mitochondrial deletions. As a result, for each twin, different developing central nervous system cells may have different percentages of mitochondrial deletions. Such mosaicism is also present in disorders such as fragile X syndrome, in which the extent of the repeat expansion may vary among cells.

Online Mendelian Inheritance of Man

As the pace of clinical and research findings in molecular genetics accelerates, tracking all of the genetic syndromes contributing to abnormal brain development becomes challenging. A useful resource with the latest information ranging from diagnostic features and behavioral phenotypes to the sequence of identified mutations is Online Mendelian Inheritance of Man (OMIM). Along with other National Center for Biotechnology Information data bases, this may be accessed at http://www.ncbi.nlm.nih.gov.

Molecular Genetics, Experience, and Brain Development

In order to ascertain their risk for having a next child with a severe developmental neurobiological condition such as autistic disorder, many parents are interested in molecular genetic information. Over and above its clinical utility, identification of a specific molecular genetic mechanism is important because of the potential it offers to clarify its effect on central nervous system development. Neuroimaging studies of specific genetic syndromes (e.g., fragile X syndrome or deletion/duplication syndromes) may permit an understanding of the net effects of the proteins coded for by missing or defective genes in these syndromes (Reiss, Abrams, Greenlaw, Freund, & Denckla, 1995). To study the effects of a specific gene product on the cascade of events underlying brain development, a fragile X mouse has been created in

which the effects of FMR1 CGG expansion may be studied in the developing brain (Godfraind et al., 1996; Kooy et al., 1996). This is likely to lead to a better understanding of normal as well as abnormal central nervous system development. As FMR1 function comes to be better understood through molecular modeling, efforts will be made to develop a replacement for either the FMR1 protein or for targets of FMR1. In this way, it may become possible to develop pharmacological interventions for at least part of the syndrome. Gene therapy is certainly possible, but more traditional pharmacological strategies have the advantage of easier delivery across the blood-brain barrier.

For complex disorders, including all child psychiatric disorders, development of animal models may provide the opportunity to study the interactions between genetic susceptibility and the impact of environmental experience.

Both in health and in disease, molecular genetic modalities and findings are likely to be essential tools in the increased understanding of central nervous system development. Such understanding provides the opportunity to move from a serendipitous development of pharmacotherapy to the rational design of improved therapeutic or preventive interventions. These interventions could relieve the dreadful burdens imposed by many developmental neurobiological syndromes, including mental retardation, obsessive-compulsive disorder, attention deficit hyperactivity disorder, autistic disorder, and Tourette's disorder.

REFERENCES

Baker, L., & Cantwell, D. (1987). A prospective psychiatric follow-up of children with speech/language disorders. *Journal of the American Academy of Child and Adolescent Psychiatry, 26,* 546–553.

Berry-Kravis, E., & Sklena, P. (1993). Demonstration of abnormal cyclic AMP production in platelets from patients with fragile X syndrome. *American Journal of Medical Genetics, 45,* 81–87.

Blondis, T., Cook, E., Koza-Taylor, P., & Finn, T. (1996). Asperger syndrome associated with dystrophia myotonica of Steinert. *Developmental Medicine and Child Neurology, 38,* 840–847.

Brook, J., McCurrach, M., Harley, H., Buckler, A., Church, D., Aburatani, H., Hunter, K., Stanton, V., Thirion, J.-P., Hudson, T., Sohn, R., Zemelman, B., Snell, R., Rundle, S., Crow, S., Davies, J., Shel-

bourne, P., Buxton, J., Jones, C., Juvonen, V., Johnson, K., Harper, P., Shaw, D., & Housman, D. (1992). Molecular basis of myotonic dystrophy: Expansion of a trinucleotide (CTG) repeat at the 3′ end of a transcript encoding a protein kinase family member. *Cell, 68,* 799–808.

Campuzano, V., Montermini, L., Molto, M. D., Pianese, L., Cossee, M., Cavalcanti, F., Monros, E., Rodius, F., Duclos, F., Monticelli, A., Zara, F., Canizares, J., Koutnikova, H., Bidichandani, S. I., Gellera, C., Brice, A., Trouillas, P., De Michele, G., Filla, A., De Frutos, R., Palau, F., Patel, P. I., Di Donato, S., & Mandel, J. L. (1996). Friedreich's ataxia: Autosomal recessive disease caused by an intronic GAA triplet repeat expansion. *Science, 271,* 1423–1427.

Church, D., Bengtsson, U., Nielsen, K., Wasmuth, J., &

Niebuhr, E. (1995). Molecular definition of deletions of different segments of distal 5p that result in distinct phenotypic features. *American Journal of Human Genetics, 56,* 1162–1172.

Cook, E., Lindgren, V., Leventhal, B., Courchesne, R., Lincoln, A., Shulman, C., Lord, C., & Courchesne, E. (1997). Autism or atypical autism in maternally but not paternally derived proximal 15q duplication. *American Journal of Human Genetics, 60,* 928–934.

Dykens, E. (1996). DNA meets DSM: The growing importance of genetic syndromes in dual diagnosis. *Mental Retardation, 34,* 125–127.

Epstein, C. J., Korenberg, J. R., Anneren, G., Antonarakis, S. E., Ayme, S., Courchesne, E., Epstein, L. B., Fowler, A., Groner, Y., Huret, J. L., et al. (1991). Protocols to establish genotype-phenotype correlations in Down syndrome. *American Journal of Human Genetics, 49,* 207–235.

Estivill, X. (1996). Complexity in a monogenic disease. *Nature Genetics, 12,* 348–350.

Gelernter, J., Pakstis, A. J., & Kidd, K. K. (1995). Linkage mapping of serotonin transporter protein gene SLC6A4 on chromosome 17. *Human Genetics, 95,* 677–680.

Gillberg, C., Steffenburg, S., Wahlström, J., Gillberg, I., Sjöstedt, A., Martinsson, T., Liedgren, S., & Eeg-Olofsson, O. (1991). Autism associated with marker chromosome. *Journal of the American Academy of Child and Adolescent Psychiatry, 30,* 489–494.

Godfraind, J. M., Reyniers, E., De Boulle, K., De Deyn, P. P., Bakker, C. E., Oostra, B. A., Kooy, R. F., & Willems, P. J. (1996). Long-term potentiation in the hippocampus of fragile X knockout mice. *American Journal of Medical Genetics, 64,* 246–251.

Greenberg, F., Guzzetta, V., Montes de Oca-Luna, R., Magenis, R. E., Smith, A. C. M., Richter, S. F., Kondo, I., Dobyns, W. B., Patel, P. I., & Lupski, J. R. (1991). Molecular analysis of the Smith-Magenis syndrome: A possible contiguous-gene syndrome associated with del(17)(p11.2). *American Journal of Human Genetics, 49,* 1207–1218.

Huntington's Disease Collaborative Research Group. (1993). A novel gene containing a trinucleotide repeat that is expanded and unstable on Huntington's disease chromosomes. *Cell, 72,* 971–983.

Kishino, T., Lalande, M., & Wagstaff, J. (1997). UBE3A/E6-AP mutations cause Angelman syndrome. *Nature Genetics, 15,* 70–73.

Knight, S., Flannery, A., Hirst, M., Campbell, L., Christodoulou, Z., Phelps, S., Pointon, J., Middleton-Price, H., Barnicoat, A., Pembrey, M., Holland, J., Oostra, B., Bobrow, M., & Davies, K. (1993). Trinucleotide repeat amplification and hypermethylation of a CpG island in *FRAXE* mental retardation. *Cell, 74,* 127–134.

Kooy, R. F., Reyniers, E., Bakker, C. E., Nagels, G., De Boulle, K., Storm, K., Clincke, G., De Deyn, P. P., Oostra, B. A., & Willems, P. J. (1996). Transgenic mouse model for the fragile X syndrome. *American Journal of Medical Genetics, 64,* 241–245.

Krahe, R., Ashizawa, T., Abbruzzese, C., Roeder, E.,

Carango, P., Giacanelli, M., Funanage, V. L., & Siciliano, M. J. (1995). Effect of myotonic dystrophy trinucleotide repeat expansion on DMPK transcription and processing. *Genomics, 28,* 1–14.

Leana-Cox, J., Jenkins, L., Palmer, C., Plattner, R., Sheppard, L., Flejter, W., Zackowski, J., Tsien, F., & Schwartz, S. (1994). Molecular cytogenetic analysis of inv dup(15) chromosomes, using probes specific for the Prader-Willi/Angelman syndrome region: Clinical implications. *American Journal of Human Genetics, 54,* 748–756.

Ledbetter, D. H., & Engel, E. (1995). Uniparental disomy in humans: Development of an imprinting map and its implications for prenatal diagnosis. *Human Molecular Genetics, 4,* 1757–1764.

Li, X. J., Li, S. H., Sharp, A. H., Nucifora, F. C., Jr., Schilling, G., Lanahan, A., Worley, P., Snyder, S. H., & CA, R. O. (1995). A huntingtin-associated protein enriched in brain with implications for pathology. *Nature, 378,* 398–402.

Lucente, D., Chen, H. M., Shea, D., Samec, S. N., Rutter, M., Chrast, R., Rossier, C., Buckler, A., Antonarakis, S. E., & McCormick, M. K. (1995). Localization of 102 exons to a 2.5 Mb region involved in Down syndrome. *Human Molecular Genetics, 4,* 1305–1311.

Oberlé, I., Rousseau, F., Heitz, D., Kretz, C., Devys, D., Hanauer, A., Boué, J., Bertheas, M. F., & Mandel, J. L. (1991). Instability of a 550-base pair DNA segment and abnormal methylation in fragile X syndrome. *Science, 252,* 1097–1102.

Reiner, O., Albrecht, U., Gordon, M., Chianese, K. A., Wong, C., Gal-Gerber, O., Sapir, T., Siracusa, L. D., Buchberg, A. M., Caskey, C. T., & Eichele, G. (1995). Lissencephaly gene (LIS1) expression in the CNS suggests a role in neuronal migration. *Journal of Neuroscience, 15,* 3730–3738.

Reiner, O., Carrozzo, R., Shen, Y., Wehnert, M., Faustinella, F., Dobyns, W., Caskey, C., & Ledbetter, D. (1993). Isolation of a Miller-Dieker lissencephaly gene containing G protein β-subunit-like repeats. *Nature, 364,* 717–721.

Reiss, A., Abrams, M., Greenlaw, R., Freund, L., & Denckla, M. (1995). Neurodevelopmental effects of the FMR-1 full mutation in humans. *Nature Medicine, 1,* 159–167.

Reiss, A. L., Freund, L. S., Baumgardner, T. L., Abrams, M. T., & Denckla, M. B. (1995). Contribution of the FMR1 gene mutation to human intellectual dysfunction. *Nature Genetics, 11,* 331–334.

Shprintzen, R. J., Goldberg, R., Golding-Kushner, K. J., & Marion, R. (1992). Late-onset psychosis in the velo-cardio-facial syndrome. *American Journal of Medical Genetics, 42,* 141–142.

Verkerk, A. J., Pieretti, M., Sutcliffe, J. S., Fu, Y. -H., Kuhl, D. P. A., Pizzuti, A., Reiner, O., Richards, S., Victoria, M. F., Zhang, F., Eussen, B. E., van Ommen, G. -J. B., Blonden, L. A. J., Riggins, G. J., Chastain, J. L., Kunst, C. B., Galjaard, H., Caskey, C. T., Nelson, D. L., Oostra, B. A., & Warren, S. T. (1991). Identification of a gene (FMR-1) containing a CGG repeat coincident with a breakpoint cluster region exhibiting length variation in fragile X syndrome. *Cell, 65,* 905–914.

Wallace, D. (1992). Diseases of the mitochondrial DNA. *Annual Review of Biochemistry, 61,* 1175–1212.

Wallace, D. (1995). 1994 William Allan Award Address. Mitochondrial DNA variation in human evolution, degenerative disease, and aging. *American Journal of Human Genetics, 57,* 201–223.

Warren, S. (1996). The expanding world of trinucleotide repeats. *Science, 271,* 1374–1375.

Wolffe, A., & Pruss, D. (1996). Targeting chromatin disruption: Transcription regulators that acetylate histones. *Cell, 84,* 817–829.

6 / Developmental Psychopharmacology

Paul E. Quinlan and James E. Dillon

In the years since publication of the *Basic Handbook of Child Psychiatry,* the role of psychotropic medication in treating child and adolescent psychiatric disorders has grown dramatically. The year 1980 marked the shift from the theoretically based nosology of the second *Diagnostic and Statistical Manual of Mental Disorders (DSM-II)* to a descriptive, reliable, and empirically based diagnostic system in *DSM-III* and *DSM-IV,* from which the medical model of psychiatric treatment of children and adolescents gained credibility. The very idea of major depressive disorder in children was novel and controversial in the 1970s, despite reports of apparently successful treatments with tricyclic antidepressants (Puig-Antich et al., 1987). Childhood hyperactivity, previously relegated to the exotic obscurity of pediatric neurologic practice precisely because of its responsivity to medication, became the diagnosis *du jour* of *DSM-III.* It soon became apparent that the majority of referrals of severely disturbed children to psychiatric clinics might benefit from judicious application of drugs. The growing role of drugs challenged a cherished belief that years of therapy were needed to bring about meaningful change in emotionally disturbed children.

Progress in child and adolescent psychopharmacology paralleled the biological revolution in general psychiatry. Treatments of psychosis, mania, depression, anxiety, and aggression in children were borrowed, with varying success, from better-established practices in adult psychiatry, while adult psychiatrists learned from their child and adolescent counterparts how to manage autistic and behavior disorders across the life span.

Impressive advances in the disciplines of developmental neuroscience and developmental neuropharmacology, however, had limited direct impact on the clinical practice of child and adolescent psychopharmacology.

The "Decade of the Brain" has brought increasing appreciation of the complexity of neural development. Yet limited information on developmental pharmacodynamics and pharmacokinetics of psychotropic drugs has been accessible to child and adolescent psychiatrists. Although we know much about what drugs do and where they do it, the mystery of how they exert far-reaching effects on behavior and emotion is just beginning to unfold. Enough has been learned about the ontogeny of the human central nervous system, the physiological maturation of metabolic processes, and the variability in the pharmacokinetic and pharmacodynamic properties of psychotropic medications across development that it is time to bring this information into the standard accounts of pediatric psychopharmacology. The growing literature of controlled and uncontrolled clinical drug trials for child and adolescent psychiatric disorders, on the other hand, has been reviewed repeatedly elsewhere, both in this volume and in other publications (Dillon, Tsai, & Alessi, 1996).

This chapter attempts to bring together available information on psychotropic drug mechanisms and pharmacology from a developmental perspective, within the framework of recent advances in neuroscience. We begin with a general discussion of neurotransmitter systems in the maturing mammalian and human central nervous system, then review current knowledge on devel-

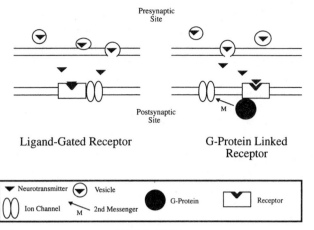

FIGURE 6.1.

The figure above represents synaptic transmission of a neuron. The neurotransmitter in the synaptic vesicle is released into the synaptic cleft. The neurotransmitter reaches the receptor on the postsynaptic site. Depending on the receptor type, the neurotransmitter can have different effects. The two types of receptors are Ligland-Gated and G-Protien Linked. The Ligland-Gated receptor has direct effect on the ion channel while the G-Protien Linked affects the ion channel via a G-Protien and multiple messenger system. In either case, the ion diffusion is altered by the effect of the ion channel promoting signal transmission.

opmental aspects of pharmacokinetics in children and adolescents, and conclude by discussing specific drugs in light of this rapidly changing and growing body of knowledge.

Neurotransmitter Systems

The human brain is rapidly developing at the moment of birth (Dobbing & Sands, 1979). With cellular migration and specialization having taken place during gestation, neuronal networks mature in infancy to subserve behavioral milestones such as gross and fine motor coordination, speech and language, and sphincter control. Extensive myelinization of nervous tissue in the critical years through age 2 or 3 is significantly dependent on social stimulation and becomes the nervous foundation for attachment and social relatedness.

All neuronal networks, whether subserving classical motor and sensory functions or more complex emotional and behavioral states, rely on neurotransmitters for communication across the synapse, as illustrated in Figure 6.1.

While signal mediation is the primary function of mature neurons, immature cells also can produce and release neurotransmitters that function as neurotrophic factors, facilitating growth of the network (Emerit, Riad, & Hamon, 1992). Increasingly complex neural networks underlie mood and behavioral states as well as the motor and sensory functions of classic neurology. The brain is never static, its plasticity in memory, learning, and adaptation continues throughout life.

The major neurotransmitters associated with behavior and emotion fall into 3 categories: the amino acids, the classical neurotransmitters including the biogenic amines and acetylcholine, and the neuropeptides. Each nerve produces 1 principle neurotransmitter, although other neurotransmitters may be present as synthetic intermediates. In some cases, multiple neurotransmitters systems may be present in a single neuron.

Type I neurotransmitters include the simple amino acids gamma-aminobutyric acid, glutamate, aspartate, and glycine. Rapid information transmitters, they compose up to 90% of all synaptic transmissions. They are abundant and are measured in the range of micromoles per gram of the wet brain weight.

Type II neurotransmitters are the "classical" neurotransmitters and include acetylcholine; the catecholamines dopamine, epinephrine, and norepinephrine; and the indoleamines histamine serotonin. They are slow compared to Type I neurotransmitters, functioning as modulators in the central nervous system. Their levels of concentration are approximately 1/1000th that of Type I neurotransmitters.

Type III neurotransmitters are extensive in number but minuscule in individual concentration. They include cholecytokinin; substance P; vasoactive intestinal peptide; somatostatin; vasopressin; oxytocin; thyrotropin-releasing hormone; luteinizing-hormone releasing hormone; alpha-, beta-, and gamma-melanocyte stimulating hormone; corticotropin; beta-endorphin; dynorphin A and B; and met- and leu-enkephalin. These neuropeptides for the most part act as neuromodulators and control the activity of receptors. Their concentrations are one millionth to one billionth that of Type I neurotransmitters.

THE CLASSICAL NEUROTRANSMITTER SYSTEMS

Biogenic Amines: Biogenic amine systems, the most common targets of psychotropic medication, have been studied extensively in animal models, especially the rat, and, to a lesser extent, in uncontrolled case studies of human fetal tissue and postmortem brain specimens of children and adolescents. Although animal models have limitations, including differences from humans in the rate, manner, and final product of brain development, they provide an essential means of comparing the variability of neurotransmitter systems across age groups in a controlled manner. The rat is the model of choice, because it is inexpensive, convenient, and can be extensively inbred to produce genetically homogeneous subjects. Nonhuman primates that are phylogenetically more closely related to *Homo sapiens* and whose social behavior often resembles that of people have been used less extensively, primarily owing to their high cost. Accordingly, our knowledge of the ontogeny of neurotransmitters is based largely on experiments in rats.

Biogenic amines include the catecholamines—norepinephrine (noradrenaline), epinephrine (adrenaline), and dopamine—and the indoleamines, of which serotonin is the most important example. Catecholamines are formed presynaptically through conversion of tyrosine to DOPA via tyrosine hydroxylase, the rate-limiting step in catecholamine synthesis. DOPA is then decarboxylated to dopamine, which serves as the neurotransmitter for nigrostriatal and mesolimbic projections. Noradrenergic cells containing dopamine-beta-hydroxylase, projecting from cell bodies in the locus coeruleus, take the synthesis an additional step to norepinephrine. Epinephrine-producing cells, plentiful peripherally in the adrenal medulla, have not been implicated as critical in the central nervous system actions of psychotropic drugs.

The neurotransmitter serotonin (5-hydroxytryptamine or 5-HT), localized in neurons projecting widely from the brain stem raphe nuclei, is synthesized in a 2-step process beginning with the rate-limiting hydroxylation of trytophan.

The biogenic amines share a brain stem localization and relatively broad fields of projection, suggesting that they may have the function of modulating and, in the sense of sending similar signals to diverse targets, coordinating neural processes occurring at higher levels.

Biogenic Amine Receptors: Biogenic amine neurotransmitter systems are associated with many receptor subtypes, summarized in Table 6.1. These fall into 2 main groups, the G protein-linked receptors and the ligand-gated receptors. The 2 groups are distinguished from one another by the transductive mechanisms leading to changes in the aperture of ion channels that produce changes in polarization of the receptor cell. G protein receptors rely on intermediaries called second messengers to open ion channels, whereas ligand-gated receptors open channels directly. (See Figure 6.1.)

Classical neurotransmitter receptors are predominantly G protein-linked types with the exception of the serotonin 5-HT_3 and the nicotinic acetylcholine receptors. Second messengers via G protein-linked receptors contribute to cell depolarization or hyperpolarization depending on if they are excitatory or inhibitory, respectively. Second messengers can lead to modification of the cell's response to future signals by modulating neurotransmitter synthesis and metabolism, synaptogenesis, and the expression of genes governing synthesis of ion channels, receptors, and messengers. Second messengers include cyclic AMP, cyclic GMP, calcium, and metabolites of phosphatidylinositol. These second messengers then lead biological responses when coupled with 1 or more

TABLE 6.1

Central Nervous System Neurotransmitter Systems Receptor Subtypes

Neurotransmitter	Subtype	Ligand (L) vs. G-protein (G)
Biogenic Amines		
dopamine	D_{1-5}	G
norepinephrine,	alpha-$_1$A,B,C,D	G
epinephrine	alpha-$_2$A,B,C	G
	beta-$_{1-3}$	G
serotonin	5-HT$_{1A}$[a]	G
	5-HT$_{1B}$	G
	5-HT$_{1D}$	G
	5-HT$_{2A}$	G
	5-HT$_{2B}$	G
	5-HT$_{2D}$	G
	5-HT$_3$	L
	5-HT$_4$	G
	5-HT$_6$	G
	5-HT$_7$	G
acetylcholine	M$_{1-5}$[b]	G
	nicotinic	L
Amino acids		
GABA[c]	B	G
GABA	A	L
glutamate	NMDA[d]	L
	AMPA[e]	L
Opioid Neuropeptides		
enkephalins, dynorphins, endorphins	mu, delta, kappa	G (all)

[a]HT-hydroxytryptamine
[b]M-muscarinic
[c]GABA-gamma-aminobutyrate acid
[d]NMDA-N-methyl-D-aspartate
[e]AMPA-alpha-amino-3-hydroxy-5-methyl-4-isoxalone propionic acid

additional messengers. Ligand-gated ion channels, by contrast, can be opened without the second messenger as intermediary. The ligand-gated receptor mechanism can affect these messengers as well, but not as quickly as G protein types (Hyman & Nestler, 1993).

Although genetic control may guide the development of essential pathways, the central nervous system can modify its structure according to experience, making learning, memory, association, rec-

ognition, and higher cortical functions possible. The plasticity of the central nervous system is based on the series of messengers and their effects.

Localization of Biogenic Amine Neurotransmitter Systems: Biogenic amine neurotransmitters in the human brain have been mapped, and their cell bodies and terminals have been localized. Groups of cell bodies comprise the brain nuclei from which neuronal projections originate, carrying signals to termination points elsewhere in the central nervous system. Thus, for example, dopamine cell bodies in the arcuate nucleus project to the pituitary, where they influence hormone levels. Norepinephrine cell bodies found principally in the locus coeruleus have terminals in the brain stem nuclei, cerebellum, cerebral cortex, spinal cord, and thalamus. Other norepinephrine cell bodies are present in the lateral tegmental system, pons, and medulla, with terminals in the basal forebrain, brain stem, hypothalamus, thalamus, and spinal cord. Epinephrine-containing cell bodies lie in the medulla and project to brain stem, thalamus, and spinal cord.

Dopaminergic cell bodies are located in the substantia nigra, ventral tegmentum, arcuate nucleus, olfactory bulb, and retina. Projections from the substantia nigra terminate in the striatum, while ventral tegmental projections terminate in the cerebral cortex and limbic forebrain (mesolimbic system). The arcuate nucleus terminates in the pituitary. Projections from the retina and olfactory bulb terminate locally.

Serotonin cell bodies reside in the raphe nuclei, pons, and medulla and project to the brain stem, cerebellum, cerebral cortex, spinal cord, and thalamus.

The Ontogeny of Biogenic Amines: The ontogeny of neurotransmitter systems has been well characterized in the rat. The typography of monoamine neurotransmitter systems, examined in the fetal central nervous system, is organized much as in humans (Nabin & Bjorklund, 1973). Human and rat development progress at quite different rates, however; rat gestation lasts only 3 weeks and leaves much brain growth for the postnatal period (Dobbing & Sands, 1979). Humans, in contrast, exhibit peak brain growth velocity at about the time of birth and have a better developed sensory system.

Levels of biogenic amines have been described in the postnatal rat as a percentage of adult neurotransmitter levels. Unfortunately, these levels do not provide a full description of the process of development of neurotransmitter systems. The homogenization of brain regions to obtain these levels disregards localized variations in neurotransmitter concentrations. For this reason, histochemical and immunohistochemical visualization of the systems has offered a better description of neurotransmitter systems including their projections and termination sites.

By birth the rat has developed dopamine cell bodies elsewhere in the central nervous system (Specht, Pickel, Joh, & Reis, 1981) but not in the retina (Foster, Schultzberg, Goldstein, & Hokfelt, 1985). Projections from the dopamine cell bodies also have developed prior to birth and continue to develop postnatally. Hypothalamic dopamine content increases gradually into adulthood in the rat (Leret & Freile, 1985; Orosco, Trouvin, Cohen, & Jacquot, 1986), perhaps due to variability in the expression of the tyrosine hydroxylase enzyme (Simerly, 1989). In humans, dopamine has been detected in the hypothalamus and striatum in a fetus with a crown-rump length of 400 millimeters (Ehringer & Hornykiewicz, 1960). Tyrosine hydroxylase–containing cell bodies, however, typically are observed between 14 and 17 weeks of gestation in humans. Thus both human and rat dopaminergic systems arise during gestation and continue to develop pathways in early life. These systems, however, appear to be largely complete by the time children have reached an age at which psychiatric disabilities are likely to receive attention.

The serotonergic system in the rat can be identified at day 12 to 13 of gestation (Aitken & Tork, 1988). Cell bodies of what will become the raphe nuclei are being formed in the week prior to birth in the rat. Projections descending from the caudal raphe nuclei to the spinal cord reach their adult pattern by postnatal day 21. The serotonergic system, like the dopaminergic system, has developed its cell bodies and is sending out projections prior to birth. Thus in rats biogenic amine systems begin developing before birth, reach peak expression early in the postnatal period, and are maintained into adulthood. Developing human brains, for which considerably less data are available, show similar development early in gestation.

THE CHOLINERGIC NEUROTRANSMITTER SYSTEM

Acetylcholine is a small molecule that does not readily fit into a major neurotransmitter classification. Its role in the central nervous system, however, is significant, and psychotropic medications often affect it. Acetylcholine is synthesized in the cell body or terminal from acetyl coenzyme A (acetyl coA) and choline via the enzyme choline acetyl transferase. The acetylcholine is stored in vesicles prior to release into the cleft during synaptic transmission. Glucose and/or citrate is believed to be the source of acetyl coenzyme A while choline comes either from active transport across the blood-brain barrier or from hydrolysis of acetylcholine in the synaptic cleft. Acetylcholinesterase catalyzes hydrolysis of acetylcholine. The cholinergic neurotransmitter system employs 2 types of receptors, muscarinic and nicotinic. Nicotinic receptors are the ligand-gated type while muscarinic receptors are of the G protein type. Although we think of these receptor types as quite distinct, they may coexist in a neuron. Muscarinic synapses may corelease vasoactive intestinal peptide, which modulates acetylcholine response via autoreceptors on the presynaptic terminal.

Localization of the Cholinergic Neurotransmitter System: Like biogenic amines, acetylcholine cell bodies have been localized in the central nervous system. Acetylcholine cell bodies in the basal forebrain project to the cerebral cortex diencephalon and hypothalamus. Cell bodies in the dorsal pons (lateral tegmental area) project to the thalamus and diencephalon. Local termination occurs within the neostriatum.

The Ontogeny of the Cholinergic Neurotransmitter System: Acetylcholine reaches adult levels in the rat cerebral cortex at approximately 40 days postnatally (Johnston & Coyle, 1980) while human cortical levels rise to approximately 80% of adult levels by age 2 (Diebler, Farkus-Bargeton, & Wehrle, 1979).

In the rat, cholinergic cell bodies developing in a caudal-to-rostral sequence begin to send projections prior to birth, reaching full maturation at about 1 month of age. In humans, acetylcholine has been identified in the nucleus basalis as early as 9 weeks' gestation (Candy et al., 1985; Kostovic, 1986). The acetylcholine system in humans, like that of the rat, appears prenatally and begins sending projections out into the central nervous system prior to birth.

AMINO ACID NEUROTRANSMITTER SYSTEMS

While the classical neurotransmitters are formed from cells comprising discrete brainstem nuclei, the amino acid neurotransmitters predominate in the cortex, where they mediate both local and more distant communications. Gamma-aminobutyric acid (GABA) and glutamate are the most important examples of inhibitory (hyperpolarizing) and excitatory (depolarizing) neurotransmitters respectively. GABA is formed from glutamate through the action of glutamate decarboxylase. This enzyme is useful in histochemical localization. Glutamate must be synthesized via the Krebs cycle and transamination or by converting glutamine into glutamate via glutaminase.

The ligand-gated GABA$_A$ receptor contains multiple sites for binding different ligands including benzodiazepines, barbiturates, and GABA itself. Binding of different ligands alters the chloride ion conductance to produce hyperpolarization (Paul, 1995). GABA is highly concentrated in cerebral cortex.

Glutamate receptors include the N-methyl-D-aspartate (NMDA) subtype and the 3-hydroxy-5-methyl-4-isoxzole propionic acid (AMPA) subtype. The NMDA receptor regulates calcium ion permeable conductance while AMPA gates sodium and potassium ion flux. Projections of glutamate in the central nervous system originate in the neocortex and hippocampus.

Following a caudal-rostral sequence of development, cortical amino acid neurotransmitters appear later than the classical neurotransmitters synthesized by cells originating in the brain stem.

PEPTIDE NEUROTRANSMITTER SYSTEMS

Numerous peptide neurotransmitters exist. Among these many systems, the endogenous opiates, or endorphins, are of unique interest and serve to illustrate characteristics of other peptide neurotransmitter systems. The first of the opioid peptides discovered were the enkephalins (Hughes et al., 1975). Since that time, 3 families of opioid peptides have been described.

Up to this point we have dealt with neurotransmitters that are relatively small in terms of their molecular weight and that are created by enzymatically catalyzed reactions of relatively small substrates. Peptides, in contrast, are larger and are produced through cleavage from large precursor peptides having as many as 250 amino acid units. Beta-endorphin, for example, an endorphin neuropeptide, contains 31 amino acid units. The size and complexity of these amino acid sequences requires a synthetic route more sophisticated than simple enzymatic reactions.

Formation of Neuropeptides via Deoxyribonucleic Acid (DNA): The neuropeptides are smaller peptides cut from larger, inactive precursor peptides. The precursor peptide is formed through a multistep process beginning when the sense strand of the nuclear DNA is transcribed into heterogeneous nuclear ribonucleic acid (hrRNA) for processing into messengerRNA (mRNA). The mRNA enters the cytoplasm where ribosomes, either free or attached to endoplasmic reticulum, translate the mRNA nucleotide sequences into amino acid sequences. Translation must begin and end at specific sites on the mRNA, a process facilitated by 3 nucleotide sequences in the mRNA. Without the proper coding throughout the mRNA sequence, peptides would be improperly formed and function poorly as neurotransmitters.

The peptide formed as a result of mRNA translation is called a precursor peptide. The precursor peptide undergoes posttranslation processing, which cleaves this larger peptide into smaller, active forms as they are transported from their site of synthesis to the synapse (Liston et al., 1984). Several different types of neuropeptides may be created from one precursor peptide. The peptides are packaged and stored in secretory granules and eventually are released at the presynaptic site during neurotransmission.

Three Groups of Endogenous Opioid Neurotransmitters, Their Receptors, and Their Localization in the Central Nervous System: The precursor peptides exist in 3 forms, representing 3 families of opioid peptides. Enkephalin sequences appear not only in their own precursor peptide, proenkephalin, but in the other 2 precursor peptides as well. The precursor proopiomelanocortin derives its name from the 3 types of overlapping peptide sequences, beta-endorphin, melanocyte-stimulating hormone, and adrenocorticotropin (ACTH), of which it is composed. Because the sequences overlap, posttranslation processing drives the formation of certain peptides at the expense of others, a selectivity that can vary during development (Quinlan, 1989).

The opioid peptides have 3 receptor subtypes—delta, mu, and kappa—all of which are G-protein linked. The receptors can be described in terms of affinity to morphine and to the neuropeptides themselves. The mu receptor, for example, has a high affinity for morphine, while the delta receptor has a high affinity for enkephalins and less affinity for morphine. The kappa receptor has greater affinity for dynorphin than for morphine or enkephalin.

Enkephalin-containing cells are widely distributed through the central nervous system, both forming local circuits and projecting to distant areas in the brain. The proopiomelanocortin peptide–containing cells are found in the intermediate lobe of the pituitary, the hypothalamus, and the nucleus tractus solitarius. The dynorphin-containing cells are found in the hypothalamus and posterior pituitary and are extensively distributed elsewhere in the central nervous system (Khachaturian, et al., 1985).

The Ontogeny of Opioid Peptide Neurotransmitters: The enkephalin and dynorphin systems appear during gestation in the rat (Bayon, Shoemaker, Bloom, Mauss, & Guillemin, 1979; Pickel, 1980). Neurons have been identified from both systems showing continuous expression during postnatal development through the period of weaning (approximately postnatal day 21). Beta-endorphin appears in the arcuate nucleus at embryonic day 12 and reaches its peak at postnatal day 21.

COMMENTS ON ESSENTIAL NEUROTRANSMITTER SYSTEMS IN DEVELOPMENTAL PSYCHOPHARMACOLOGY

The belief that neurotransmitters are related to psychopathology has been a guiding dogma in the "Biological Era" of psychiatry. As a result, medication has become the primary focus of treatment for many severe psychiatric disorders. Child and adolescent psychiatry at first somewhat reluctantly followed this premise as well, although considerably less information about psychotropic drugs in children and adolescents is available. Clearly, though, the neurotransmitter systems in the maturing brain cannot be safely viewed as diminutive version of the adult central nervous system.

Pharmacokinetics in Developmental Psychopharmacology

Pharmacokinetics describes the effect the body has on medication through absorption, distribution, biotransformation, and excretion. Because these variables fluctuate over the course of development, dosing of medication for children and adolescents often cannot be readily predicted from adult dosing strategies.

ABSORPTION

For the vast majority of psychotropic medications used in children and adolescents, the predominant route of administration is oral with absorption in the gastrointestinal tract. Although transdermal preparations of clonidine; intramuscular preparations of anxiolytics, hypnotics, and antipsychotics; and the intranasal delivery of desmopressin circumvent the oral route, absorption can still be problematic. Factors that can influence drug absorption in children and adolescents include decreased gastric pH potentially reducing absorption of anticonvulsants, antidepressants, and amphetamine; increased gastrointestinal motility, potentially reducing absorption; and overall reduced flora in the gut, reducing metabolism of drugs absorbed. Some drugs, such as diazepam, are absorbed more rapidly in children than in adults; absorption, however, plays a relatively minor role in developmental changes in pharmacokinetics.

DISTRIBUTION

Distribution of medication in the body varies significantly during childhood and adolescence depending on the hydrophilic or lipophilic nature of the drug. The extracellular water content is an essential component of drug availability because drugs must distribute across this compartment in order to reach their target receptors. Extracellular water content is approximately 45% at birth and decreases to approximately 25% by early childhood. From childhood to midadolescence, the extracellular water content decreases another 5%, the most dramatic shifts taking place in early childhood and around puberty. By midadolescence the extracellular water content has reached adult levels (Friis-Hansen, 1961). The half-life of drugs that follow first-order kinetics can be decreased by a reduction in the volume of distribution (Rane & Wilson, 1976).

The percentage of lipid in adipose tissue increases from 35% in neonates to approximately 72% in adults (Friis-Hansen, 1971). Lean body mass increases during puberty for both sexes, but especially for males (Forbes, 1992). The distribution of fat in late puberty for males is 12% of body weight while in females it is 25% (Kreipe, 1992). In childhood, the sexes have similar body fat content. Gender differences in adolescent body composition thus can affect distribution of medications.

Factors influencing the distribution of medication in the body through protein binding in the circulatory system are similar in children and adults (Kearns & Reed, 1989). These factors include concentrations of total protein, plasma albumin, plasma globulin, unconjugated bilirubin, free fatty acids, blood pH, and alpha1-acid glycoprotein.

BIOTRANSFORMATION

Distribution is an essential step leading to biotransformation because, in most cases, the drug must reach the liver to be metabolized. Extrahepatic biotransformation occurs in some drugs, including methylphenidate (Hungund, Perel, Hurwic, Sverd, & Winsberg, 1979). For most psychotropic medications, however, the liver is the primary site of metabolism.

Biotransformation in the liver involves 2 processes. The first process includes phase I reactions, which metabolize most psychotropic medications and rely on the cytochrome P450 enzyme system. Phase I reactions convert the drug to a more polar state, typically inactivating the drug. Phase II reactions alter the drug by coupling it to another molecule to increase its water solubility and enhance its excretion. Phase II reactions also deactivate many psychotropic medications.

Phase I Reactions in Biotransformation: The cytochrome P450 system responsible for phase I reactions oxidizes molecules that are not normally found in the body, including carcinogens. The enzyme organization is extensive and has been categorized by a specific nomenclature of families, subfamilies, and individual enzyme. Cytochrome P450 2D6 is an enzyme that metabolizes an extensive number of psychotropic medications. The superfamily of all P450 enzymes is extensively described in Nelson (1993, 1996).

CYP	Represents the enzyme system itself. This system is found throughout the animal and plant kingdom. An enzyme can be shared between plants and animals. One enzyme found in fungi dates back to 3.5 billion years.
2	Identifies the family. Families 1 through 3 make up the bulk of cytochrome enzymes found in humans that metabolize medications. One through 5 are found in vertebrates.
D	Designates the subfamily of enzymes. If a gene is the sole member of the family, this specifies the member.
6	Designates the individual P450 enzyme when combined with the previous sequence.

Phase I reactions can have a dramatic influence on circulating levels of psychotropic medication, frequently causing adverse drug effects and interactions. Drug-induced effects can be due to impaired metabolism, leading to an overabundance of the drug, or to accelerated metabolism, resulting in rapid turnover and subtherapeutic plasma levels. Thus the biotransformational specificity of a drug for a particular cytochrome P450 enzyme or the inhibition of an enzyme by another drug can dramatically alter the rate of metabolism. The cytochrome P450 enzymes and the psychotropic medications they metabolize are as follows:

CYP1A2	Works predominantly through demethylation of the substrate. Dealkylates caffeine and theophylline. Induced by cigarette smoking and charcoal-broiled foods. Inhibited in in vitro studies by fluvoxamine. *Metabolizes acetamino-*

phen, amitriptyline, caffeine, clomipramine, clozapine, fluvoxamine, haloperidol, imipramine, and propanolol.

CYP2C19 Also predominately demethylates psychotropic medications. Inhibited in in vitro studies by fluoxetine and sertraline. *Metabolizes clomipramine, diazepam, and imipramine.*

CYP2D6 Metabolizes an extensive array of psychotropic medications. Has wide variability in activity and can be poorly active to nonactive in 3 to 10% of Caucasians. Inhibited in vitro by fluoxetine, paroxetine, and sertraline. *Metabolizes amitriptyline, clomipramine, clozapine, desipramine, fluoxetine, haloperidol, imipramine, n-desmethylclomipramine, norfluoxetine, nortriptyline, paroxetine, propranolol, reduced haloperidol, risperdone, thioridizine, and venlafaxine.*

CYP3A4 Metabolizes an extensive array of psychotropic medications. Inhibited by astemizole, fluvoxamine, ketoconazole, paroxetine, fluoxetine, nefazodone, and sertraline. *Metabolizes alprazolam, amitriptyline, carbamazepine, clomipramine, dexamethasone, imipramine, midazolam, nefazodone, sertraline, and triazolam.*

The cytochrome P450 enzyme system of the neonate has limited functioning. During the first year of life, this system dramatically increases in function. During childhood it becomes more efficient than the adult's system. Preadolescents can require up to twice as much medication as would be predicted from adult weight-based dosing schedules (Rodman, 1994). Limited information is available concerning the effect of puberty on cytochrome P450 enzyme activity (Rogers, 1994), although the system presumably begins to approach adult levels in adolescence.

The phenotypic expression of cytochrome P450 (CYP) enzymes can vary dramatically among the general population (Gonzalez, Skoda, & Kimure, 1988; Sachse, 1996). The CYP2D6 enzyme, for example, which may be involved in metabolism of 25% of psychotropic medications, has low activity in about 5 to 10% of Caucasians (Cholerton, Daly, & Idle, 1992). It has been implicated in drug toxicity and treatment failure of at least 40 drugs,

including neuroleptics and antipsychotics (Eichelbaum & Evert, 1996).

The mutation conferring low CYP2D6 activity is inherited as an autosomal recessive gene. At least 12 polymorphisms can result in complete loss of function, reduced activity, or increased activity. In 1 mutation, a guanine-to-adenine nucleotide substitution at a key site on the gene leads to a failure to synthesize the protein (Gonzalez et al., 1988; Heim & Meyer, 1992). In some cases, individuals with high 2D6 activity, requiring high doses of medication, have been misdiagnosed as nonresponders. In these individuals, the increased activity is due to gene amplification of the region coding for 2D6 (Bertilsson, Dahl, & Sjoquist, 1993; Johansson, Lundqvist, Bertilsson, & Dahl, 1993).

CYP2C19, which metabolizes diazepam, is another enzyme with a clinically significant polymorphism. The autosomal recessive trait affects 2 to 3% of Caucasians and 23% of Asians (Bertilsson, 1995). The defect results from a guanine-to-adenine nucleotide substitution, causing a premature splice in the sequencing read as a stop codon signal, leading to truncation of the enzyme transcribed (Goldstein & de Morias, 1994).

Limited information concerning these cytochrome P450 mutations in children and adolescents is available. The polymorphisms observed in adults presumably occur in children as well, but this bears further investigation.

Phase II Reactions in Biotransformation: The non-cytochrome P450 system metabolizes through a variety of processes, including acetylation, methylation, sulfation, glucuronidation, conjugation with amino acids (glycine), and glutathione conjugation.

These processes follow phase I reactions and increase the water solubility of the substance for excretion. Acetylation of primary amines, catalyzed by N-acetyl transferase, may be increased in younger individuals. Glucuronidation is another phase II reaction producing oxygen-glucuronide compounds through conjugation. The half-life of lorazepam metabolized in this reaction was found to be decreased in children under the age of 18 compared to adults (Crom, 1994). Sulfate conjugation is well developed in neonates, who metabolize some drugs typically metabolized through glucuronidation. Sulfate conjugation decreases in activity with age.

EXCRETION

After a drug has undergone biotransformation, it is eliminated through the gastrointestinal tract or renal system. Renal tubular excretion, described through the measurement of glomerular filtration rate, has been extensively studied in the pediatric population. The glomerular filtration rate in the neonate is less than half the rate of a 1-year-old. After 1 year, the glomerular filtration rate corrected for body surface area is similar in children and young adults.

COMMENTS ON DEVELOPMENTAL PHARMACOKINETICS

Special considerations in infants notwithstanding, older children and adolescents for whom psychotropic drugs are prescribed have, on the whole, more robust metabolisms than their adult counterparts. The range of factors contributing to drug disposition, however, makes a priori predictions in individual cases unreliable. Dosage based on surface area rather than on weight alone probably offers a better guide for initial treatment of a child. Dosing in children cannot be based simply on linear extrapolation downward from adult dosing recommendations.

Psychotropic Medications in Children and Adolescents

The first generation of theories of psychotropic drug effects was based on neurotransmitter deficit/excess models of psychopathology derived from the neuropathology and treatment of Parkinson's disease. Thus depression initially was hypothesized as a norepinephrine or serotonin deficit state, schizophrenia as a dopamine excess state, and hyperkinesis as a dopamine deficiency state. These early hypotheses were supported by known drug actions, which could be characterized according to their tendency to increase or decrease functional levels of monoaminergic activity.

The manner in which drugs influence neurotransmission therefore has been studied in depth. Drugs can alter communication at the synapse by changing the amount of transmitter available, by actions at the receptor, or by effects on second messengers. Concentration of transmitter in the synaptic cleft depends on the amount supplied by the presynaptic neuron from presynaptic pools, the rate at which the transmitter is metabolized, and the rate at which the transmitter is retrieved by the presynaptic cell for reuse (reuptake). Concentration of transmitter in the presynaptic cell, in turn, is influenced by the availability and cellular uptake of precursor. Drugs can have direct effects on receptors that imitate those of the neurotransmitter (agonist) or block those of the neurotransmitter (antagonist).

Psychotropic drugs used in children employ several of these mechanisms, including increased secretion into the synaptic cleft from presynaptic pools (amphetamine and possibly methylphenidate), reuptake blockade (tricyclic antidepressants and serotonin-specific reuptake inhibitors), postsynaptic receptor blockade (neuroleptics, beta-blockers), presynaptic receptor agonism (clonidine), reduced metabolism (monoamine oxidase inhibitors), and actions on second messengers (possibly lithium). Experimental treatment strategies, such as precursor loading with tyrosine or phenylalanine to increase synthesis of neurotransmitter, also have followed this model of neurotransmitter function.

If an excess or deficit of monoamine per se caused psychopathology directly, then remission of symptoms would be immediate upon institution of treatment that restored normal neurotransmitter levels. This indeed occurs in the treatment of Parkinson's disease with levodopa, attention deficit hyperactivity disorder with stimulants, and anticipatory anxiety with benzodiazepines.

Treatment of depression and schizophrenia, however, requires prolonged exposure to drugs affecting monoaminergic function. The current generation of theories about drug mechanisms in psychopathology seeks to explain this treatment latency through the concept of neural plasticity, introduced earlier in this chapter. Neural plasticity refers to relatively enduring changes within the cell, especially those occurring at the levels of gene expression and protein synthesis, that alter the way it responds to subsequent stimuli. Second messengers, such as cyclic AMP, effectively integrate intracellular information from multiple stimuli allowing intermediate-term responses mediated by protein phosphorylation and more enduring plastic changes at the genomic level.

In the following section we discuss the pharmacodynamics and pharmacokinetics of major psychotropic drug groups within a developmental framework. Pharmacodynamics describes effects the drug has on the body, including the mechanism of the drug's action and the patient's response to the medication. Pharmacokinetics, on the other hand, describes the effect the body has on the drug, its absorption, disposition, and elimination. It is beyond the scope of this chapter to review the literature concerning clinical drug trials establishing the efficacy and clinical effects of medications for specific psychiatric disorders. These are described elsewhere in the *Handbook*.

STIMULANTS

Although a broad range of sympathomimetic drugs have been used in children and adolescents with attention deficit hyperactivity disorder and narcolepsy, the most widely used agents are amphetamine derivatives, methylphenidate, and pemoline. These are among the few psychotropic drugs better studied in children than in older individuals, the treatment of adults with amphetamine having earned an unsavory reputation because of its popularity as a street drug.

Stimulant Pharmacodynamics: Amphetamine enhances catecholamine release and blocks its reuptake, in part through action on the catecholamine transporter. The catecholamine transporter, which ordinarily returns catecholamines from the synaptic cleft into the cell, works in reverse in the presence of amphetamine, a process referred to as exchange diffusion (Seiden, Sabol, & Ricaurte, 1993). Amphetamine also promotes release of catecholamine from the presynaptic storage vesicles and from newly synthesized pools of catecholamine. Methylphenidate acts on the storage vesicles but apparently not on the freshly synthesized pools of catecholamine. Whereas many antidepressants enhance noradrenergic activity through a reuptake mechanism, and to this extent resemble stimulants, only a few, such as bupropion and nomifensine, have significant dopaminergic effects. In these antidepressants dopaminergic effects are relatively weak by comparison with stimulants.

The mechanism of action of pemoline is unknown, but it too is thought to work through enhancement of catecholaminergic activity, including dopamine. Pemoline does not, however, appreciably elevate pulse or blood pressure, as do other sympathomimetics.

The dual effects of amphetamine on dopaminergic and noradrenergic function theoretically correspond to functional changes in activity level and attention/arousal respectively.

The dramatic and immediate response of hyperactive children to treatment with stimulants is consistent with a simple catecholaminergic deficit theory of the psychopathology of attention deficit hyperactivity disorder. Such a theory is also supported by a dopamine ablation model of attention deficit in the rat (Shaywitz, 1978) and by the occurrence of hyperkinesis in children smitten by von Economo's encephalitis, a disease that produces Parkinsonism in affected adults. Contradicting this view, however, it was long held that successful treatment with pemoline required weeks to achieve its full effects. Recent studies employing more objective measures and perhaps more aggressive dosing, however, have found pemoline to provide immediate effects comparable to the other stimulants. Similarly, the latency for tricyclic antidepressant effects on attention deficit hyperactivity disorder may be attributed to a delay in achieving adequate blood levels.

While the clinical benefits of stimulant medications occur rapidly and dramatically, addictive and psychotogenic phenomena arise insidiously over periods of weeks or months, suggesting an entirely different mechanism. Indeed, we have seen children in whom florid drug-induced psychoses went unnoticed for months because of the drug's salutary effects on hyperactivity.

Classical addictive phenomena are quite rare during stimulant treatment with prepubertal children, modal cases showing remarkable stability in dosage requirements over time. Brief rebound hyperactivity is common as part of withdrawal from stimulants and may persist for several days in unusual cases; withdrawal states characterized by depressed mood, anhedonia, and extreme fatigue are extremely uncommon.

Stimulant Pharmacokinetics: The commonly used stimulants, including short- and long-acting forms of dextroamphetamine and methylphenidate, dextroamphetamine elixir, and pemoline, are readily absorbed. The short-acting forms of methylphenidate and dextroamphetamine achieve peak plasma concentration at 1 to 2 hours. The elixir is more rapidly absorbed than the dextroamphetamine pill, while long-acting forms of both methylphenidate and dextroamphetamine are absorbed more slowly than the shorter-acting forms of the same drugs. The half-life of methylphenidate is about 2 to 4 hours; that of dextroamphetamine, about 6 to 8 hours; and that of pemoline, around 8 to 12 hours. Adults may require longer to eliminate the drugs and in practice often require much smaller weight-adjusted doses.

Pharmacokinetic studies of stimulant medications, especially methylphenidate, have shown only weak associations between plasma levels and clinical response. The plasma level vs. time curve rises steeply after administration of stimulants, with clinical effects occurring soon after administration and well before peak levels are achieved (Brown & Ebert, 1985). On the descending wing of the curve, however, similar blood levels are associated only with side effects such as insomnia and anorexia and perhaps with physiological effects such as growth hormone suppression.

ANTIDEPRESSANTS

Pharmacodynamics: Whereas attention deficit hyperactivity disorder responds immediately to stimulant treatment, mood disorders and many antidepressant-responsive anxiety conditions require weeks of treatment before benefits are evident. These disorders have forced scientists to look beyond the immediate monoamine-enhancing effects of the antidepressants in search of mechanisms that accord with the several weeks' course of treatment response. Changes in postsynaptic receptor density follow this time course and potentially implicate adaptations at the level of the gene in the mechanism of action of these drugs.

Antidepressants include monoamine oxidase inhibitors (MAOIs), tricyclic and heterocyclic antidepressants, serotonin-reuptake inhibitors, and other drugs that enhance mood. The monoamine oxidase inhibitors were the first antidepressants studied, following the serendipitous discovery of their mood-altering properties during treatment of patients with tuberculosis. They are rarely used

clinically in children and adolescents, owing to potential side effects, although there is some evidence of efficacy in attention deficit hyperactivity disorder and in adolescent depression. Monoamine oxidase maintains low cytoplasmic concentrations of monoamines, and monoamine oxidase inhibitors increase these concentrations.

Monoamine oxidase inhibitors gained some popularity in the 1980s in treating patients with atypical depressions characterized by mood reactivity and mild disturbances in vegetative function, often involving increased sleep and eating. Depression in adolescents likewise often is characterized by irritability and mood reactivity rather than by unremitting anhedonic depressive states, and changes in vegetative symptoms may be somewhat obscure if present. This fact has caused some to ask whether adolescent depression represents a distinct phase in the lifelong course of the disorder during which monoamine oxidase inhibitors used in adult atypical depressives would be more efficacious than tricyclic antidepressants. The advent of selective serotonin reuptake inhibitors may leave this question forever unanswered, however, as the newer drugs appear to be supplanting monoamine oxidase inhibitors for the treatment of adult atypical depression and certainly are preferred in children and adolescents.

The tricyclic antidepressants (TCAs), originally studied as a treatment for schizophrenia because of their structural similarity to phenothiazines, were found unexpectedly to elevate mood rather than ameliorate psychosis (Kuhn, 1958). The tricyclics are monoamine reuptake blockers with varying specificity for noradrenergic and serotonergic neurons. Blockage of the presynaptic catecholamine and serotonin transporters increases monoamine levels at the synapse.

Desipramine is the prototypical noradrenergic tricyclic antidepressant, while clomipramine is relatively serotonin-specific. Depressive and anxiety disorders, with the important exception of obsessive-compulsive disorder, respond equally well, on average, to any tricyclic, apparently not distinguishing between "noradrenergic" and "serotonergic" drugs. This nonspecificity fuels the argument that the *real* mechanism of drug action is somewhere downstream of the effect on monoamines.

Controlled studies of tricyclic antidepressants in child and adolescent depression, unfortunately, have consistently shown placebo responses and treatment failures. Several different hypotheses have been propounded to explain this observation, but the one of particular interest here is the possibility that tricyclic pharmacodynamics are fundamentally different in children and adults. This hypothesis has gained some support in studies of rats suggesting that juveniles have a reduced capacity to develop functional enhancement of serotonin systems following amitriptyline treatment (McCracken & Poland, 1995).

Pharmacodynamics encompasses not only drug actions that benefit the patient but also those that are harmful. This has been of special concern following the deaths of several children undergoing treatment with desipramine (Riddle et al., 1991). Opinion differs on whether these deaths are correctly attributed to the drug, but most clinicians have shied away from first- or second-line use of tricyclics in children as a result of these reports. Unfortunately, it is by no means clear that the effects in question are peculiar to children, as many adults receiving tricyclics expire without notice, their fates attributed to age or medical status. Whether children have any special vulnerabilities to these or other psychotropic drugs is uncertain.

In the last 10 years, the serotonin-specific reuptake inhibitors, including fluoxetine, sertraline, paroxetine, and fluvoxamine, accompanied by other "novel" antidepressants, such as bupropion, trazodone, venlafaxine, and nefazodone, have largely displaced the tricyclics as first-line treatments for depression and anxiety disorders. They have gained widespread use in children and adolescents with mood and anxiety disorders, and their indications have broadened—sometimes with little justification—to include disorders such as autism, attention deficit hyperactivity disorder, and conduct disorder.

The selective serotonin reuptake inhibitors block monoamine reuptake in a manner analogous to the tricyclics, but without appreciable effects on noradrenergic systems. The profile of venlafaxine is predominantly serotonergic, but, like the tricyclics, it enhances catecholaminergic systems as well.

Bupropion is unique in blocking reuptake of norepinephrine and dopamine without important effects on serotonin. More than any other clinically available antidepressant, its neurotransmitter profile resembles that of amphetamine, and

for this reason it has been employed extensively in treating attention deficit hyperactivity disorder.

Trazodone and nefazodone, triazolopyridine derivatives, are unique antidepressants. Developed from a theory that depression results from failure to integrate adverse emotional experiences, trazodone flunks the usual screening tests applied to putative antidepressants and also fails to down regulate beta-adrenergic receptors in rat cortex. Its effects on serotonin are complex. A selective inhibitor of serotonin reuptake, trazodone also displays serotonin receptor antagonism, while its active metabolite, m-chlorophenylpiperazine, is a serotonin receptor *agonist*. In contrast with selective serotonin reuptake inhibitors, which tend to be stimulating, trazodone is highly sedating, perhaps accounting for its popularity as a hypnotic.

Trazodone occupies a special niche in the treatment of aggression, especially in children, despite empirical support limited to a few case reports. The combination of serotonergic properties with sedation may explain its value in treating aggressive patients. For reasons that are unclear, children often tolerate extraordinarily high doses of trazodone without incurring excessive sedation, whereas adults often cannot achieve antidepressant doses while sustaining alertness. Differential metabolism across age groups could result in different ratios of trazodone to active metabolite and thus to modified side effect profiles.

Antidepressant Pharmacokinetics: The pharmacokinetic profiles of individual antidepressants are too numerous to review here, but some generalizations are possible. Tricyclics are metabolized more rapidly in children and adolescents than in adults owing to reduced protein binding and first-pass metabolism. Like other drugs undergoing first-pass hepatic metabolism, tricyclics are deactivated more rapidly in children than in adults because of the child's proportionately larger liver mass. Children and adults show considerable variability in plasma levels for a given tricyclic dose; this interindividual variability, attributable to cytochrome P450 polymorphisms, is more important than differences based on age and development.

Tertiary amines, such as imipramine, are demethylated to produce secondary amines, such as desipramine. Since the clinical profile depends in part on the relative proportion of these drugs, and since children execute the demethylation more rapidly than adults, side effects peculiarly associated with the tertiary amines, such as sedation, might be expected to be less prominent in children than in adults receiving imipramine or amitriptyline. This comports with clinical observation but lacks empiric substantiation.

The half-life of imipramine, which is proportional to the volume of distribution, rises from 11 to 42 hours in prepubertal children to 14 to 89 hours in adolescents (Branch, 1994). The short half-life implies a more rapid washout, possibly explaining the pronounced cholinergic rebound often noted in children abruptly withdrawn from tricyclic treatment.

Data concerning the pharmacokinetics of selective serotonin reuptake inhibitors and other novel antidepressants in children and adolescents are unavailable. In adults, selective serotonin reuptake inhibitors reach peak plasma levels within 1 to 8 hours after oral administration, while half-lives of the parent drugs range from 15 hours in fluvoxamine to 2 days in fluoxetine. Both fluoxetine and sertraline have active metabolites, norfluoxetine and desmethylsertraline, respectively, that prolong the drugs' effective half-lives. Norfluoxetine is a nonselective monoamine reuptake blocker, which could affect the drug's neurotransmitter profile in the context of vigorous metabolism. Sertraline's metabolite only weakly inhibits serotonin reuptake.

Because of the long half-lives, the selective serotonin reuptake inhibitors lend themselves to once-daily administration. Fluvoxamine, however, may require more frequent dosing, particularly in children.

Selective serotonin reuptake inhibitor biotransformation by and interaction with the P450 cytochrome system has received considerable attention recently. The P450 systems are well developed by the time children present for psychopharmacologic treatment and presumably are capable of producing the same range of complex drug interactions in children that have been described in adults.

ANTIPSYCHOTICS

Pharmacodynamics: Antipsychotics, which have a limited but important role in child and adolescent psychiatry, fall into 2 main groups: the traditional or typical neuroleptics, including the phenothi-azines, haloperidol, thiothixene, molindone, loxapine, and pimozide; and the atypical neuroleptics, including clozapine, risperidone, and olanzapine.

All antipsychotic drugs bind to dopamine receptors. Typical antipsychotics become clinically effective when about 80% of D2 receptors are occupied. Dopamine blockade triggers a temporary increase in the rate of firing and dopamine turnover, followed by a prolonged decrease in firing, called depolarization inactivation. Clozapine, which preferentially binds to D2 receptors in mesolimbic pathways, causes depolarization inactivation in mesolimbic but not in nigrostriatal cells. The timing of depolarization inactivation is thought to correspond to the time course of clinical benefits in schizophrenia, reflecting neuroplastic changes. The absence of this effect in nigrostriatal neurons following clozapine treatment would explain the low rate of extrapyramidal symptoms in patients treated with the drug.

In addition to dopamine blockade, atypical neuroleptics block 5-HT$_{2A}$ receptors involved in the regulation of dopamine pathways, suggesting that the unique effects of atypical antipsychotics could be attributable to the dual blockade of specific dopamine and serotonin receptors.

While treatment of adolescents with schizophrenia parallels the treatment of adults, neuroleptics frequently are given to children for different indications, including aggression and intractable hyperactivity; stereotypic and self-injurious behavior associated with autism and mental retardation; Tourette's disorder, and psychoses that, while nominally schizophrenic, are usually atypical. It is unclear whether the mechanisms of neuroleptic action in adolescent and adult schizophrenia, where considerable evidence supports the view of a dopamine-linked abnormality, are the same ones promoting tranquilization in children with nonschizophrenic disorders. Hyperkinesis and stereotypies are likely to be dopamine mediated, while a central role for dopamine in aggression and self-injurious behavior remains to be established.

Children appear to be susceptible to the development of movement disorders, especially transient withdrawal dyskinesias. This phenomenon may be attributable to pharmacokinetic factors or, alternatively, to the relatively higher concentration of dopamine receptors in brains of children vs. adults (Seeman et al., 1987).

Anitpsychotic Pharmacokinetics: Limited information is available on the pharmacokinetics of traditional neuroleptics in children and adolescents. Absorption is erratic following oral administration. Metabolism and elimination, when assessed, have been more efficient in children than in adults. The elimination half-life of chlorpromazine in children is only 8 hours, for example, compared to 31 hours in adults (Furlnaut et al., 1990). Similarly, the mean half-life of pimozide following a single 2 milligram (mg) dose was 66 hours in 4 children vs. 111 hours in 7 adults (Sallee, et al., 1987). Because of wide individual variability in drug disposition, plasma levels of haloperidol in autistic subjects reflect side effects but not dosage (Dugas et al., 1982). Relatively brief neuroleptic half-lives in children may account for the high rate of withdrawal dyskinesias observed following abrupt discontinuation of medication (Gualtieri et al., 1984).

ANXIOLYTICS

Perhaps on account of their reputation as drugs of abuse in adult patients, traditional anxiolytics—the benzodiazepines and related compounds—have been avoided in pediatric psychiatry except for sedating acutely agitated adolescents. The "abuse" rationale is not very compelling, however, inasmuch as drugs like diazepam, clonazepam, and cholorazepate have been employed as anticonvulsants for many years in epileptic children without major adverse consequences. Benzodiazepines also have earned a reputation for producing "paradoxical" excitation in some children, thought to range from 0 to 30% (Popper & Gherardi, 1996), although it is doubtful that this effect is any more troublesome than similar excitation from drugs such as diphenhydramine, methylphenidate, and clonidine. Theoretically, benzodiazepines could be extremely useful in treating acute anxiety in a variety of situations, including school avoidance, specific phobias, and trauma.

Anxiolytic Pharmacodynamics: The benzodiazepines block electroencephalogram arousal; suppress spinal reflexes, in part through effects at the reticular formation; and reduce the duration of limbic electrical after-discharge, accounting for their anticonvulsant effects. Specialized benzodiazepine receptors, detected in cerebral cortex and in the limbic system, part of the large macromolecular complex of the $GABA_A$ receptor, increase the frequency chloride ion channels opening which reducing the firing of the neuron. There is evidence that other mechanisms may be operative as well.

Experiments on infant monkeys separated from their mothers indicate that widespread behavioral and neuroendocrine stress responses can be mitigated by use of relatively high doses of alprazolam (Kalin, Shelton, & Turner, 1991). Since cortical development is still brisk early in life, pharmacologic interventions targeting developing GABA systems during infancy theoretically might have profound and enduring consequences for brain function and microanatomy later in development.

Buspirone, a $5-HT_{1A}$ pre- and postsynaptic blocker, has achieved considerable acclaim as an anxiolytic agent lacking the propensity for abuse associated with the benzodiazepines. Unfortunately, it also has no proven propensity for benefit in pediatric populations.

Anxiolytic Pharmacokinetics: Interpretation of benzodiazepine pharmacokinetics often is complicated by the presence of active metabolites and by the wide tissue distribution of liphophilic drugs such as diazepam. Benzodiazepines are highly protein bound. Absorption may be more rapid in children than in adults, with diazepam reaching peak concentrations in as little as 15 to 30 minutes; alprazolam, lorazepam, and clonazepam reach peak concentrations more slowly. Metabolism may be primarily hepatic, involving oxidation, hydroxylation, or demethylation, or extrahepatic, through transformation to glucuronide and sulfate conjugates for renal excretion. Lorazepam and oxazepam, which are metabolized extrahepatically, may be preferred in patients with impaired liver function. Benzodiazepines with shorter half-lives, such as alprazolam and lorazepam, produce more dramatic withdrawal states in adults and are considered to be more addictive. Addictive states in children are rarely if ever reported.

MOOD STABILIZERS

Pharmacodynamics: Lithium and anticonvulsants have been used extensively in children and adolescents both as mood stabilizers and as antiaggressive drugs. The anticonvulsants carbamazepine and valproic acid in particular have achieved acceptance in the treatment of bipolar disorder despite scant clinical literature, while phenytoin has fallen into disuse as a treatment for aggression.

No coherent theory of the mechanisms underlying mood-stabilizing properties of these drugs has been advanced, although considerable research has examined the effect of mood stabilizers, especially lithium, on the central nervous system. The antidepressant and antipsychotic drugs have shared properties, such as monoamine reuptake blockade and dopamine blockade, respectively, that point to a likely mechanism, steering attention away from the dozens of effects on different neurotransmitters and receptors documented for individual drugs. Lithium, on the other hand, as an elemental compound, is unique in structure and perhaps in mechanism.

Lithium has well-documented effects on all major neurotransmitter systems including monoamines, especially serotonin enhancement; amino acids; and opioid peptides; as well as on intracellular second messenger systems including the adenyl cyclase system and the phophatidyl-inositol cycle. The several-week response latency in patients with mood disorders suggests that lithium acts at the genomic level, perhaps involving expression of second messenger systems. Studies of lithium transport in red blood cells have been consistent with a theory of membrane stabilization as a mechanism of action. It is certainly possible that multiple mechanisms mediate lithium's mood-stabilizing and antiaggressive properties.

Still less is understood about the anticonvulsants valproic acid and carbamazepine, whose antiepileptic effects, which are immediate, may be mechanistically unrelated to their delayed mood-stabilizing properties. Both drugs have diverse effects on multiple neurotransmitter systems, among which GABA has received particular scrutiny. While carbamazepine binds to peripheral-type benzodiazepine receptors, valproic acid does not. Compared to most other anticonvulsants, carbamazepine impairs cognition only minimally; occasionally it has been suggested as a treatment for attention deficit hyperactivity disorder. Valproic acid has been associated with fatal liver toxicity in an apparently age-related phenomenon affecting primarily children under 2 years old, especially those receiving anticonvulsant polytherapy.

Mood Stabilizer Pharmacokinetics: Lithium is absorbed completely within 8 hours of administration. It is not bound to plasma protein and requires approximately a day to penetrate the central nervous system. Lithium is excreted in the urine and reabsorbed in the proximal tubules through a process that competes with sodium. Children, with proportionately larger kidneys than adults, eliminate lithium more readily and thus exhibit marginally shorter serum half-lives of about 18 hours (Vitiello et al., 1988).

Unlike most psychotropic drugs, the anticonvulsants have been used extensively in epileptic children, and dosing recommendations are well established in the pediatric literature.

Carbamazepine is well absorbed and about 60 to 80% protein is bound in plasma. Unbound drug concentrations probably can be modified by competitive protein binding, a factor to be considered when carbamazepine is administered in conjunction with another psychotropic drug. A major epoxide metabolite is active but usually is not measured.

Drug disposition of the anticonvulsants is complicated by autoinduction of enzymes of the P450 system. Thus chronic treatment with carbamazepine, in particular, frequently entails upward dosage adjustments after the first few weeks of therapy. The half-life is unstable for the same reason but usually falls in the range of 10 to 20 hours during chronic treatment. Structurally similar to the tricyclics, carbamazepine disposition probably is under similar genetic control, implying significant individual variability in dose-plasma level relationships that usually outweigh age-related considerations.

The pharmacokinetics of valproic acid also are relatively complicated. The drug is highly protein bound, but as plasma concentrations increase, the percent bound decreases. Several metabolites are active, and 2-propyl-2-pentenoic acid can accumulate to toxic levels. The half-life of valproic acid is in the range of 8 to 20 hours, but this can be reduced in the presence of other drugs.

Conclusion

The teratogenicity of psychotropic drugs such as lithium and valproic acid are accepted, if poorly quantified, risks in the treatment of women of childbearing age. Similarly, the notion of *delayed* teratogenic expression of subtle behavioral and cognitive abnormalities resulting from fetal exposure to drugs such as alcohol and cocaine has gained increasing acceptance in the last decade. To the extent that major organs substantially achieve their ultimate structural development by the second trimester of pregnancy, later exposure to teratogenic substances usually does not produce major structural anomalies. The brain develops more slowly than other organs, however, and the microanatomy of the central nervous system continues to develop in dramatic fashion long after parturition, presumably creating the neurological underpinnings for the complex psychodevelopmental events associated with human cognition and other phylogenetically advanced behavioral functions. At least theoretically, the potential for teratogenicity persists as long as the organ is actively developing; from this perspective, the first year of life may mean for brain development what the second and third months of gestation represent for, say, cardiac development. There is ample basis for speculating on how neurotrophic effects of neurotransmitters and neurohormones in conjunction with plasticity of receptor neurons may influence postgestational development, and there is no doubt that experience, in both behavioral and biochemical senses, mediates these events. It is fair to ask, then, what effects the administration of psychoactive drugs to a developing child may have in the long run, and whether these are beneficial or not. Unfortunately, the limited data bearing on this question provide no obvious answers, and the practical and ethical complexities of designing a study adequate to address such concerns definitively may be prohibitive.

Current drug therapy in psychiatry is intended to provide benefits that are immediate, or nearly so. Stimulants are given to reduce hyperactivity *now*, without the expectation that hyperactivity later (next week or next year) will be any better or worse. Treatment often is given in the hope that other aspects of development can be facilitated to have measurable effect years later; but, so far, there is only limited and imperfect evidence that this occurs.

Given the marked plasticity of the young brain, it is possible to imagine prophylactic drug therapy in infancy that would thwart the deleterious effects of environmental adversity or even facilitate the development of thinking and memory. It is also possible, however, that commonplace and accepted treatments will have lasting effects of which we are as yet unaware.

REFERENCES

Aitken, A. R., & Tork, I. (1988). Early development of serotonin-containing neurons and pathways as seen in whole mount preparations of the fetal brain. *Journal of Comparative Neurology, 274*, 32–47.

Bayon, A., Shoemaker, W., Bloom, F., Mauss, A., & Guillemin, R. (1979). Perinatal development of the endorphin and enkephalin-containing systems in the rat brain. *179*, 93–101.

Bertilsson, L. (1995). Geographical/interracial differences in polymorphic drug oxidation. Current state of the knowledge of cytochromes P450(CYP)2D6 and 2C19. *Clinical Pharmacokinetics, 29*, 192–209.

Bertilsson, L., Dahl, M. -L., & Sjoquist, F. (1993). Molecular basis for rational megaprescribing in ultrarapid hydroxylators of debrisoquine. *Lancet, 431*, 63.

Branch, R. A. (1994). Characteristics of drug disposition during childhood. In D. R. Rosenberg, J. Holttum, & S. Gershon (Eds.), *Textbook of pharmacotherapy for child and adolescent disorders* (pp. 7–16). New York: Brunner/Mazel.

Brown, G. L., & Ebert, M. H. (1985). Catecholamine metabolism in hyperactive children. In C. R. Lake & M. G. Ziegler (Eds.), *The catecholamines in psychiatric and neurologic disorders* (pp. 185–210). Boston: Butterworth.

Candy, J. M., Perry, R. H., Bloxham, C. A., Thompson, J., Johnson, M., Oakley, A. E., & Edwardson, J. (1985). Evidence for the early prenatal development of cortical cholinergic afferents from nucleus of Meynert in the human foetus. *Neuroscience Letters, 61*, 91–95.

Cholerton, S., Daly, A., & Idle, J. R. (1992). The role of individual human cytochrome P450 in drug metabolism and clinical response. *Trends in Pharm. Sci., 13*, 434–439.

Crom, W. R. (1994). Pharmacokinetics in the child. *Environmental Health Perspectives, 102*, 11, 111–117.

Diebler, M. F., Farkus-Bargeton, E., Wherle, R. (1979). Developmental changes of enzymes associated with energy metabolism and the synthesis of some neurotransmitters in discrete areas of human neocortex. *Journal of Neurochemistry, 32,* 429–435.

Dillon, J. E., Tsai, L. T., & Alessi, N. A. (1996). Child and adolescent psychopharmacology: A decade of progress. In F. Lieh Mak & C. C. Nadelson (Eds.), *International review of psychiatry* (Vol. 2, pp. 379–423). Washington, DC: American Psychiatric Association.

Dobbing, J., & Sands, J. (1979). Comparative aspects of the brain growth spurt. *Early Human Development, 3* (1), 79–83.

Dugas, M., Zarifian, E., Leheuzey, M. F., Regnier, N., Durand, G., Bianchetti, G., & Morselli, P. L. (1982). Surveillance des taux plasmatiques de psychotropes chez l'enfant, I. Taux plasmatiques d'haloperidol. *Nouv. Press Med. 11,* 2201–2204.

Ehringer, H., & Hornykiewicz, O. (1960). Verteilung von Noradrenalin und Dopamine im Gehirn des Menschen und ihr verhlten bei Erkrankungen des extrapyramidalen systems. *Klin. Wochenschr. 38,* 1236–1239.

Eichelbaum, M., & Evert, B. (1996). Influence of pharmacogenetics on drug disposition and response. *Clinical and Experimental Pharmacology and Physiology, 23,* 983–985.

Emerit, M. B., Riad, M., & Hamon, M. (1992). Trophic effects of neurotransmitters during brain maturation. *Biology of the Neonate, 62* (4), 193–201.

Finkelstein, J. W. (1994). The effect of developmental changes in adolescence on drug disposition. *Journal of Adolescent Health, 15,* 612–618.

Foster, G. A., Schultzberg, M., Goldstein, M., & Hokfelt, T. (1985). Differential ontogeny of three putative catecholamine cell types in the postnatal rat retina. *Developmental Brain Research, 22,* 187–196.

Friis-Hansen, B. (1961). Body water compartments in children: Changes during growth and related changes in body composition. *Paediatrics, 28,* 169–181.

Furlanut, M., Benetello, P., Baraldo, M., Zara, G., Montanari, G., & Donzelli, F. (1990). Chlorpromazine disposition in relation to age in children. *Clinical Pharmacinetics, 18,* 329–331.

Goldstein, J. A., & de Morias, S. M. F. (1994). Biochemistry and molecular biology of the human CYP2C subfamily. *Pharmacogenetics, 4,* 785–799.

Gonzalez, F. J., Skoda, R. C., & Kimura, S. (1988). Characterization of the common genetic defect in humans deficient in debrisoquine metabolism. *Nature, 331,* 442–446.

Gualtieri, C. T., Quade, D., Hicks, R. E., et al. (1984). Tardive dyskinesia and other clinical consequences of neuroleptic treatment in children and adolescents. *American Journal of Psychiatry, 141,* 20–23.

Heim, M. H., & Meyer, U. A. (1992). Evolution of a highly polymorphic human cytochrome P450 gene cluster: CYP2D6. *Genomics, 14,* 49–58.

Hughes, J., Smith, T. W., Kosterlitz, H. W., Fothergill, L. A., Morgan, B. A., & Harris, H. R. (1975). Identification of two related pentapeptides from the brain with potent opiate agonist activity. *Nature* (London), *258,* 577–579.

Hungund, B. L., Perel, J. M., Hurwic, M. J., Sverd, J., & Winsberg, B. G. (1979). Pharmacokinetics of methylphenidate in hyperkinetic children. *British Journal of Clinical Pharmacology, 8,* 571–576.

Hyman, S. E., & Nestler, E. J. (1993). *The molecular foundations of psychiatry.* Washington, DC: American Psychiatric Association.

Johansson, I., Lundqvist, E., Bertilsson, L., & Dahl, M. -L. (1993). Inherited amplification of an active gene in the cytochrome P450 CYP2D locus as a cause of ultrarapid metabolism of desbrisoquine. *Proceedings of the National Academy of Science* (USA), *90,* 11825–11829.

Johnston, M. V., & Coyle, J. T. (1980). Ontogeny of neurochemical markers for noradrenergic, GABAergic, and cholinergic neurons in the neocortex lesioned with methylazoxymethanol acetate. *Journal of Neurochemistry, 34,* 1429–1441.

Kalin, N. H., Shelton, S. E., & Turner, J. G. (1991). Effects of alprazolam on fear-related behavioral, hormonal, and catecholamine responses in infant rhesus monkeys. *Life Sciences, 49,* 2031–2044.

Kearns, G. L., & Reed, M. D. (1989). Clinical pharmacokinetics in infants and children. A reappraisal. *Clinical Pharmacokinetics, 17* (Suppl. 1), 29–67.

Kostovic, I. (1986). Prenatal development of nucleus basalis complex and related fibers systems in man: A histochemical study. *Neuroscience, 17,* 1047–1077.

Kreipe, R. E. (1992). Normal somatic adolescent growth and development. In E. R. McAnarney, R. Kreipe, D. P. Orr, et al. (Eds.), *Textbook of adolescent medicine.* Philadelphia: W. B. Saunders.

Kuhn, R. (1958). The treatment of depressive states with G22355 (imipramine hydrochloride). *American Journal of Psychiatry, 115,* 459–464.

Leret, M. L., & Freile, ___. (1985). Effect of gonadectomy on brain catecholamines during the postnatal period. *Comparative Biochemistry and Physiology, 81,* 405–409.

McCracken, J. T., & Poland, R. E. (1995). Reduced effect of antidepressant treatment on prolactin response to a serotonin antagonist in prepubertal rats. *Journal of Child and Adolescent Psychopharmacology, 5,* 115–120.

Nabin, A., & Bjorklund, A. (1973). Topography of the monoamine neuron systems in the human brain as revealed in fetuses. *Acta Physiologica Scandinavica* [Suppl.] *388,* 1–40.

Orosco, M., Trouvin, J. H., Cohen, Y., & Jacquot, C. (1986). Ontogeny of brain monoamines in lean and obese female zucker rats. *Physiol. Behav. 36,* 853–856.

Paul, S. M. (1995). GABA and glycine. In F. Bloom & D. Kupfer (Eds.), *Psychopharmacology: The fourth generation of progress* (pp. 87–94). New York: Raven Press.

Pickel, V. M., Sumal, K. K., Miller, R. J., & Reis, D. J.

(1981). Prenatal ontogeny of Substance P and enkephalin-containing neurons in the rat brain. Soc. Neurosci. USA [Abstr.] 6, 320.

Popper, C. W., & Gherardi, P. C. (1996). Anxiety disorders. In J. M. Wiener (Ed.), *Diagnosis and psychopharmacology of childhood and adolescent disorders* (pp. 293–348). New York: John Wiley & Sons.

Puig-Antich, J., Perel, J. M., Lupatkim, W. M., et al. (1987). Imipramine in prepubertal major depressive disorders. *Archives of General Psychiatry, 44*, 81–89.

Quinlan, P. E., & Alessi, N. E. (1991). Characterization of endorphin-related peptides in the caudal medulla oblongata and hypothalamus of the prenatal, postnatal and adult rat. *Developmental Brain Research, 62*, 1–5.

Rane, A., & Wilson, J. T. (1976). Clinical pharmacokinetics in infants and children. *Clinical Pharmacokinetics, 1*, 2–24.

Rodman, J. H. (1994). Pharmacokinetic variability in the adolescent: Implications of body size and organ function for dosage regimen design. *Journal of Adolescent Health, 15* (8), 654–662.

Sallee, F. R., Pollock, B. G., Stiller, R. L., et al. (1987). Pharmacokinetics of pimozide in adults and children with Tourette's syndrome. *Journal of Clinical Pharmacology, 27*, 776–781.

Seeman, P., Bzowej, N. H., Guan H. -C., Bergeron, C., Becker, L. E., Reynolds, G. P., Bird, E. D., Riederer, P., Jellinger, K., Watanabe, S., & Tourtellotte, W. W. (1987). *Human brain dopamine receptors in children and aging adults. Synapse, 1*, 399–404.

Seiden, L. S., Sabol, K. E., & Ricaurte, G. A. (1993). Amphetamine: Effects on catecholamine systems and behavior. *Annual Review of Pharmacology and Toxicology, 32*, 639–677.

Shaywitz, B. A., Anderson, G. M., & Cohen, D. J. (1985). Cerebrospinal fluid (CSF) and brain monoamine metabolites in the developing rat pup. *Developmental Brain Research, 17*, 225–232.

Simerly, R. B. (1989). Hormonal control of the development and regulation of tyrosine hydroxylase expression within a sexually dimorphic population of dopaminergic cells in the hypothalamus. *Molecular Brain Research, 6*, 297–310.

Smith Rogers, A. (1994). The role of the cytochrome P450 in developmental pharmacology. *Journal of Adolescent Health, 15*, 635–640.

Specht, L. A., Pickel, V. M., Joh, T. H., & Reis, D. J. (1981). Light-microscopic immunocytochemical localization of tyrosine hydroxylase in prenatal rat brain. I. Early Ontogeny. *Journal of Comparative Neurology, 199*, 233–253.

Vitiello, B., Behar, D., Malone, R., Ryan, P., Delaney, M. A., & Simpson, G. M. (1988). Pharmacokinetics of lithium carbonate in children. *Journal of Clinical Psychopharmacology, 8*, 355–359.

7 / Neuroimaging in Child and Adolescent Psychiatry

Kelly N. Botteron and Robert A. Kowatch

There has been a rapid expansion of neuroimaging technologies available for the study of in vivo brain structure and function over the past two decades. Many of these technologies, such as computed tomography (CT), magnetic resonance imaging (MRI), positron emission tomography (PET), single-photon emission computed tomography (SPECT), and magnetic resonance spectroscopy (MRS) have been embraced and at times widely applied to the study of psychiatric disorders in adults. Neuroimaging investigations in children have lagged significantly relative to the investigation of adults. A portion of this delay has been appropriate, secondary to safety concerns with some imaging modalities that involved exposure to radiation or were invasive. With the more recent development and refinement of MR technologies that are noninvasive and have no radiation exposure, a number of investigations examining children with psychiatric disorders have begun.

Neuroimaging methodologies relevant to the study of psychiatric disorders can be divided broadly into 3 main categories: structural, functional, and neurochemical. Structural techniques, including CT and MRI, are used to visualize and quantify specific brain regions. Techniques that examine central nervous system function, including PET, SPECT, and functional magnetic resonance imaging (fMRI), utilize different methods to examine blood flow or cerebral metabolism. Other techniques can quantify specific receptors or the chemical composition of specific regions through the use of PET or MRS. Each of these brain imaging techniques provides physiologically meaningful information about the central nervous system, and each has different inherent strengths and weaknesses.

Although neuroimaging currently has only limited clinical application in child psychiatry, these technologies are evolving rapidly and it is anticipated that they will become more clinically relevant over the ensuing decades. This chapter is intended to provide child psychiatrists with an overview and basic understanding of neuroimaging techniques currently available both clinically and as research tools. Each technology is briefly summarized along with a discussion of its advantages and disadvantages. In addition, because methodologic issues can be critical in the interpretation of reported results in the literature and in the comparison of results between different studies, select methodologic factors important to the interpretation of findings from research investigations are reviewed briefly. Finally, neuroimaging findings that have been reported to date for specific child psychiatric disorders are summarized.

Structural Neuroimaging

Two neuroimaging techniques are most relevant for examining brain structure—MRI and CT. Both of these techniques are useful for qualitative exams important in the clinical diagnostic evaluation of children and adolescents by neurologists and pediatricians. These tools are superb at identifying gross pathologic conditions such as tumors, infarctions, hemorrhages, or demyelinating disorders. However, currently they have much less relevance for clinical practice and patient evaluation for child psychiatrists. In general, child psychiatric conditions do not reveal gross neuropathologic changes that are evident or reported by pediatric neuroradiologists on MRI or CT scans. Despite the apparent lack of information on qualitative review, there is increasing evidence of clear quantitative differences in central nervous system structure between psychiatric and normal control populations. Neuromorphometry is defined as the quantification of cerebral structures, and current techniques are refining and potentially automat-

ing the process of neuromorphometric measures. Although currently they are applied only as research tools, within the next several decades neuromorphometric parameters probably will be important in clinical evaluations to provide information relevant to differential diagnosis, prognosis, course, and treatment response in child psychiatric patients. Prior to their clinical application, more extensive work needs to be done to define the normal variability in the structure of specific brain regions and to characterize the specific pattern of structural central nervous system changes associated with specific childhood psychiatric disorders.

COMPUTED TOMOGRAPHY

CT scanners revolutionized diagnostic medicine when they became available in the early 1970s. Their development allowed clinicians for the first time to examine soft tissues noninvasively. CT was the first tomographic imaging technique, later followed by MRI, PET, and SPECT. All of these techniques are based on the creation of 2-dimensional views of a tissue slice from a set of 1-dimensional projections taken at multiple angles. The contrast in a CT image is based on delineation of the differential attenuation of X rays by distinct tissue types. CT scanners are made up of a rotating X-ray beam surrounded by a ring of X-ray detectors. Images are acquired in a slice-by-slice fashion. Axial images of the brain parenchyma are created with a spatial resolution of around 1 millimeter. CT scans can be useful in the evaluation of central nervous system lesions such as tumors, infarction, and gross structural changes. Intravenous contrast agents are sometimes necessary with CT scanning to highlight areas of blood-brain barrier breakdown. However, there are drawbacks to CT scanning:

1. The scanning procedure involves exposure to ionizing radiation.
2. There is poor gray-white matter contrast resolution.
3. There is poor visualization of white matter disease.
4. CT is susceptible to artifacts in structures near bony surfaces and can obscure visualization of the basotemporal cortex and posterior fossa.
5. Patients may have allergic responses to the contrast agent.

CT's main advantages to date have been that it is less expensive than MRI and is superior for visualization of bony structure or disease.

MAGNETIC RESONANCE IMAGING

Background: MRI is currently the imaging method that provides the highest spatial and contrast resolution for neuroanatomical structures. In addition for children and adolescents, it is important to note that MRI is not associated with ionizing radiation and has no known biological risks, facilitating its use for the in vivo examination of brain structure. Structural MRI is the most common clinical application for MR scanners; however, a variety of magnetic resonance methods are available to provide chemical and functional information. These newer techniques, such as magnetic resonance spectroscopy (MRS), diffusion imaging and functional magnetic resonance imaging (fMRI), offer the potential for providing information that cannot currently be obtained in vivo by other methods. Several of these techniques are discussed in more detail later in this chapter.

Image Production: MR images are created based on inherent magnetic properties of atoms (most commonly hydrogen), which are amplified and enhanced for detection and visualization. A basic general description of the physical principles involved in the production and detection of an MR signal can provide an intuitive appreciation for the imaging technique and its potential flexibility and power. For interested readers, excellent reviews of the physical principles are available (Krishnan & MacFall, 1997; Newhouse & Wiener, 1991; Slichter, 1990). When elemental atomic nuclei have an odd number of electrons or protons, they are associated with a charge, which induces an inherent spin to the atom. The spinning of the charged molecule creates a minute magnetization—a magnetic dipole. Usually in the natural state, the randomly oriented dipoles cancel out each other's charges and there is no net magnetization of tissue. However, when the tissue is placed in a magnetic field, the nuclei will achieve their lowest energy state and align parallel to the field. This alignment produces a net positive magnetization of the tissue. MR scanners provide a strong magnetic field to facilitate this alignment. In their natural state, the nuclei spin evenly; however, nuclei within a magnetic field spin unevenly like a top, known as precession. The oscillation or precession of the nuclei occurs at a specific frequency—its Larmor frequency—which varies as a function of the nuclei examined and the strength of the magnetic field. The molecular precession releases energy in the form of a radio frequency, and these radio frequencies can be measured and localized by the MR scanner under appropriate conditions. In order to amplify the precession or resonance of the nuclei, the tissue is further excited through the application of an external radio frequency pulse, which shifts the nuclear dipoles out of the plane parallel to the magnetic field. When this radio frequency pulse is removed, the nuclei attempt to return to their lowest energy state, parallel to the magnetic field, in a process known as relaxation. Classically and in many clinical applications, the nuclei are shifted 90 degrees or perpendicular to the plane of magnetization. The receiver antenna detects the rate of relaxation and transforms this signal through a series of mathematical Fourier transformations to generate an MR image. Different types of relaxation parameters can be estimated—most commonly for clinical MR scanning, T1, T2, and proton density relaxation are measured. The images can be created in any plane of orientation, but the most common clinically used images are in the sagittal, coronal, and axial planes. (See Figure 7.1.)

Many nuclei can be imaged using MR technology, including phosphorous-31, carbon-13, sodium-23, and potassium-39; however, hydrogen is the most common nucleus targeted for clinical MRI. Tissues with different hydrogen concentrations and therefore different tissue relaxation parameters produce unique resonance signals, creating the characteristic appearance of cerebrospinal fluid, gray matter, white matter, tumor, and so on in MR images. Different types of relaxation parameters can be measured and manipulated at the time of image acquisition to alter and optimize the tissue contrast. For example, T1 weighted images often produce the clearest picture of cerebrospinal fluid in ventricular spaces while T2 weighted images are best for examining white matter pathology. (See Figure 7.2.) Initially, MR images were acquired in a slicewise fashion in a particular plane of orientation. However, newer 3-dimensional acquisitions acquire the volume of data in a simultaneous and 3-dimensional fashion,

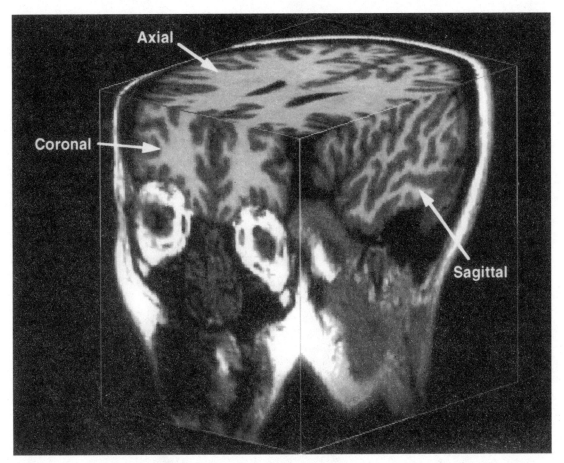

FIGURE 7.1.

Three-dimensional reconstruction of a 3D MPRAGE acquisition demonstrating the MR views commonly used in clinical applications—axial, coronal, and sagittal.

permitting visualization of the images obtained in any orientation desired. Many institutions now include 3-dimensional acquisitions in their clinical scanning protocols. Examples of such acquisitions include fast low-angle shots (FLASH), gradient recall acquisition in the steady state (GRASS), and magnetization-prepared rapid gradient echo (MPRAGE).

Standard clinical examinations vary depending on the question posed but usually include T-1 weighted axial or coronal images, T-2 weighted axial images, and at times T1 or T2 weighted 3-dimensional acquisitions. These sequences generally can be completed in 5 to 20 minutes, depending on the MR scanner. MR is sensitive to motion artifact so it is important for children to remain very still during each individual MR acquisition; some patients may require sedation. However, in general, many children over the age of 5 can lie quietly and complete a high-quality exam while awake and unsedated. Discussing the procedure in detail prior to an examination is helpful, and at many scanning centers a child can listen to a tape or CD with headphones or view a video with reflective glasses during an examination. Both of these distractors are quite helpful in achieving high-quality unsedated exams.

Advantages and Disadvantages: MRI has many advantages over CT principally related to its ability to acquire high-resolution images with superior gray to white matter contrast in any plane of orientation and its lack of radiation exposure. It provides superior detection for pathologic lesions in the white matter. MR avoids the bony artifacts associated with CT and thus is superior for visualizing the temporal lobes, posterior fossa, and

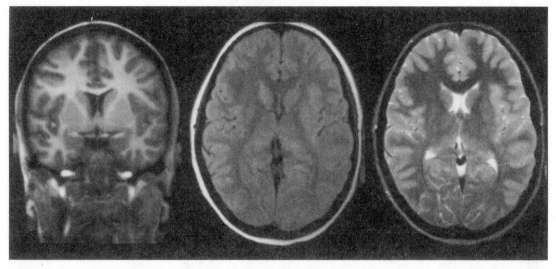

FIGURE 7.2.

Example of MR images demonstrating T1, proton density, and T2 weighting. The first panel is a coronal T1 weighted image; the middle, a proton density weighted axial image; the third image, a T2 weighted axial image. Note the differences in contrast between cerebrospinal fluid, gray matter, and white matter. The T1 image demonstrates cerebrospinal fluid CSF as black, gray matter as medium gray, and white matter as bright (similar to standard pathology specimens.) However, the T2 image demonstrated cerebrospinal fluid as bright, white matter as medium gray, and gray matter as a brighter gray. The proton density image is similar to the T2 weighting with the cerebrospinal fluid represented as darker than the white matter.

brain stem. There are no known clinical risks to normal individuals. Standard clinical MR scanners generally can achieve a spatial resolution of 1 to 2 millimeters; newer higher-power magnets (3–5T) can achieve microscopic resolution of around 300 μm.

Contraindications for MRI are related to the strong magnetic field of the scanner, which has the ability to dislodge metallic objects and interfere with the operation of mechanical devices. Thus intracranial or aneurysmal clips are a contraindication for scanning, and any history of intraocular metallic objects is a contraindication because potential movement of these metal fragments during MRI can cause blindness. Individuals at risk generally work in industrial situations or have a history of clear ocular trauma. The scanner can inactivate electric or magnetically operated devices such as cochlear implants or cardiac pacemakers. These contraindications are rarely limitations in children.

Image Analysis/Interpretation: MR images can be evaluated both qualitatively and with multiple quantitative techniques. In general, currently clinical images are interpreted only qualitatively.

However, advances in the automation of quantitative measures and the potential clinical knowledge that can be gained from these methods are bringing their clinical application nearer. Qualitative interpretations are adequate for gross structural abnormalities such as strokes, tumors, vascular malformations, or significant demyelinating disorders; however, they are insensitive to volumetric differences unless they are substantial and are unreliable for determining quantitative pattern differences. Quantitative image analytic techniques range from linear or area measures (e.g., the ventricular-to-brain ratio, which is calculated by determining ventricular area on the axial slice where the ventricles appear largest and dividing it by the area of the entire brain in that slice) to more sophisticated volumetric measures. Currently there are many neuromorphometric techniques available for measuring the volume of specific brain structures. Operator-dependent or manual methods generally rely either on manual outlining on sequential MR slices or stereological sampling (point counting methods). Quantitative volume measures using manual computer assisted techniques, semiautomated, and fully automated methods can reliably and validly quantitate specific brain structures and regions. Some automated and semiautomated methods have had significant limitations because they are based on analysis of differences in MR signal intensity. However, significant signal inhomogeneity across a volume of MR images can adversely impact automated measures and can be difficult to correct. Newer automated techniques that involve image warping or global deformation models reduce the dependence on pixel intensity by utilizing shape information. Such methods are in the final stages of development and are beginning to be applied in research situations (Haller et al., 1997). Currently, in child and adolescent populations there is insufficient knowledge to characterize specific structural differences associated with specific psychiatric disorders in comparison to normal controls.

Another significant methodologic issue in neuromorphometric quantification is related to boundary definition for specific brain structures or regions. The precise boundary of a structure can be difficult to determine in the MR image because, unlike a tissue section, each pixel has a signal intensity that reflects an average of the signals from all the tissue contained within the pixel, which can result in blurring of structural borders. This blurring or partial volume effect is much greater as the slice thickness increases, because more tissue types are included within and located adjacent to larger pixels. However, more recent studies with new-generation, high-field (1.0–1.5T) MR scanners routinely can produce 1.0 to 1.5 millimeter slices without interslice gaps, which provide high spatial resolution and significantly decrease this partial volume problem. These advances also have allowed for the reformatting of the images into standardized orientations, which improves the accuracy of area and volume measures. Without reformatting, significant variability in regional measures can be introduced related to small differences in head positioning. Volumetric measures obtained in individual laboratories often can vary substantially from other laboratories because the techniques used to obtain the measure as well as the definition of the structural boundaries of the region are uniquely defined. With the advent of thinner slices and the ability to identify small regional structures more accurately, regional definitions

are evolving toward true neuroanatomical definitions. Despite the differences present between laboratories, if measurements developed within a laboratory have good interrater and intrarater reliability, the results obtained for comparing subjects and controls within that individual lab can be valid and informative.

Clinical Indications: MRI can be a useful component of the child psychiatric evaluation in limited situations. There are no clearly established guidelines, and there is debate regarding the clinical utility of MRI in childhood psychiatric disorders. The decision for neuroimaging needs to be examined individually based on the clinical presentation, physical and neurologic examinations, and potential risk factors for gross central nervous system pathologic conditions. Conservative indications for neuroimaging in clinical practice in children should include first-onset psychosis; focal abnormalities on the neurologic examination, electroencephalogram, or possibly neuropsychologic testing; deteriorating cognitive abilities; and movement disorders of uncertain etiology. In the evaluation of children with autism, other pervasive developmental disorders, or mental retardation, MRI should be given consideration as a component of a comprehensive evaluation. Demaeral, Kingsley, and Kendall (1993) have demonstrated in a relatively large series of children with moderate to severe developmental disabilities that 30% demonstrated gross abnormalities on CT examination and 65% demonstrated abnormalities on MRI examination. MRI was clearly superior to CT in the detection of abnormalities, which included a significant number of problems with delayed myelination or white matter abnormalities. The abnormalities demonstrated are often nonspecific and do not necessarily point to specific etiologies; however, many times they are indicative of cerebral dysgenesis. Schaefer and Bodensteiner (1992) also have advocated that the presence of neuroimaging abnormalities suggesting dysgenesis characterizes a category of children with sporadic cases that do not confer increased genetic risk to the family and often display a nondegenerative course.

If structural developmental abnormalities, degenerative disorders, or sequelae from perinatal or neonatal insults are suspected, MRI is indicated. In addition, lesions in particular brain regions, including the frontal or temporal lobes, can be difficult to detect by neurologic examination and may present with psychiatric symptoms, including cognitive, motor, or behavioral disorders. For example, frontal lobe lesions often are associated with behavioral disinhibition, silly or apathetic affect, amotivation, and irritability. Thus MRI can be important in the evaluation of children who have atypical symptoms, including an atypical onset or course.

Functional Brain Imaging Techniques

SPECT

Background: Single-photon emission computed tomography (SPECT) is a nuclear medicine imaging technique that can measure regional cerebral blood flow (rCBF) or receptor density in vivo. SPECT imaging is based on the principle that normally there is a tight coupling between regional cerebral blood flow, glucose metabolism, and neuronal activity (Raichle, Grubb, & Gado, 1976; Sokoloff, 1981). The name SPECT, *single-photon computed tomography*, is used because the subject is injected intravenously with a compound composed of a flow tracer that is "bound" to a radionuclide. The radionuclide (commonly ^{99m}Tc) emits short-lived gamma rays called photons. This combination of a flow tracer such as hexamethylpropyleneamine oxime with a radionuclide produces a "radiopharmaceutical" capable of measuring either rCBF or receptor density. SPECT radiopharmaceuticals commonly used for measuring rCBF include ^{123}I IMP (Spectamine), ^{99m}Tc-HMPAO (Ceretec), and ^{99m}Tc-ECD (Neurolite). These radiopharmaceuticals have a "static distribution" as they remain stable within the brain for several hours. One of the first brain blood flow markers to be used for SPECT was the gas ^{133}Xenon, but, because Xenon diffuses out of the brain very rapidly and was able to obtain a spatial resolution of only 14 to 17 millimeters, X is not used as often as the stably distributed radiopharmaceutical agents just mentioned.

In practice, SPECT is a 2-stage process. During a typical brain SPECT study, the patient is injected intravenously with a radiopharmaceutical such as ^{99m}Tc-HMPAO. This compound perfuses into the subject's brain with arterial circulation and is trapped within 30 seconds of the initial injection in the brain, producing a "snapshot" of brain activity at the time of injection. This intravenous injection of radiopharmaceutical usually is done with the patients sitting quietly in a dimly lit room, but it is also possible to administer pharmacologic or cognitive "probes" during this injection period. Following this injection of radiopharmaceutical, the patient undergoes imaging 30 to 60 minutes later by lying with the head within a group of gamma cameras. The bound technetium in the radiopharmaceutical emits gamma rays for several hours after injection, which are detected by the gamma cameras rotating around the patient's head.

Unlike an MRI scan, a brain SPECT scan does not require the patient to lie in a tunnel and the scanning procedure is very quiet. It is possible to acquire excellent SPECT images using 50% of the standard adult dose of ^{99m}Tc-HMPAO, and a typical SPECT brain scan lasts 22 to 25 minutes. If necessary, it is also possible to sedate a patient after injection with a radiopharmaceutical or inhalation of a radiotracer and not affect the measurement of rCBF (Zilbovicius et al., 1992).

Image Production/Typical SPECT Images: SPECT images are produced by a process of "back-projection" where the exact origin of emitted gamma rays within the brain is determined by a reconstruction algorithm. This "raw" back-projected image is then processed through a series of image transformation steps, which include filtering and attenuation. The resultant images may be displayed as either 2-dimensional "slices," which are usually oriented in the transverse, coronal, and sagittal planes, or as a 3-dimensional representation of rCBF. Figure 7.3 shows several transverse SPECT images generated from a 16-year-old female with major depressive disorder using the Picker PRISM® SPECT system, which utilizes 3 rotating gamma cameras. This system is capable of spatial resolutions in the range of 6 to 8 millimeters.

Advantages/Disadvantages of SPECT: A major advantage of SPECT is that it is widely available within most hospital nuclear medicine departments and relatively affordable. The average cost of a SPECT brain scan is $400 to $600 per scan because the radioisotopes used for SPECT im-

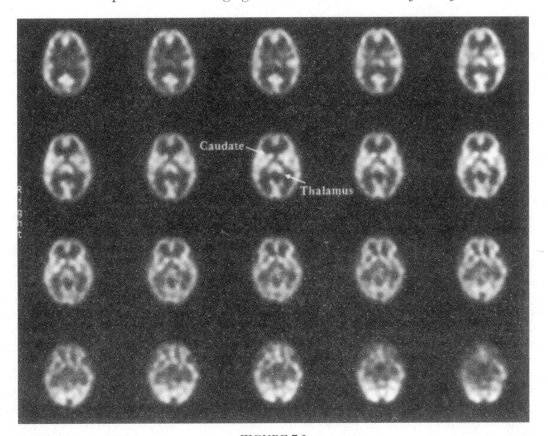

FIGURE 7.3.

Transverse sections from SPECT study of a 16-year-old female with major depressive disorder.

aging, unlike PET isotopes, do not require a cyclotron for their production and therefore are more affordable. Dedicated multiple-head SPECT acquisition units now are able to achieve spatial resolutions of 6 to 8 millimeters, and resolutions of 2 to 3 millimeters are expected to be achieved in the near future with improvements in image acquisition technology. Quantitative methods are available for measuring blood flow, and it is now becoming possible to study specific neurotransmitter receptors using SPECT (e.g., muscarinic, dopaminergic, adrenergic, GABAergic, and opiate receptors). These radioligands are currently under study in human trials.

Disadvantages of SPECT include extracranial contamination from background radiation, its inability to measure glucose metabolic rates, and our lack of both clinical and research experience using SPECT in children and adolescent with psychiatric disorders. Another major problem using SPECT for child psychiatry research is that the minimal dose of radiopharmaceutical necessary for a pediatric SPECT brain scan (approximately 10 millicurie) exceeds the recently revised Food and Drug Administration (FDA) radiation safety guidelines for research in pediatric subjects (Food and Drug Administration, 1995). Although there is no scientific evidence that radiation dosages in this range are harmful (Pollycove, 1995), the majority of institutional review boards will follow these guidelines, which limits the use of SPECT for child psychiatry brain research (Casey & Cohen, 1996).

Clinical Indications: Cerebral SPECT imaging is used in nuclear medicine to diagnose seizures, tumors, and some developmental abnormalities (O'Tuama & Treves, 1993). In child psychiatry there are no known clinical indications at this time for SPECT imaging. Although several research studies of attention deficit hyperactivity disorder using SPECT (discussed later in the chapter) have produced interesting results, there are not enough studies of normals or of children and adolescents with psychiatric disorders to support the use of SPECT diagnostically. SPECT's greatest promise for child psychiatry lies in the area of challenge studies, both cognitive and pharmacological, and for the measurement of specific brain receptor sites.

POSITRON EMISSION TOMOGRAPHY

Background: Positron emission tomography (PET) is one of the most powerful brain imaging techniques available in psychiatry today. Unfortunately, however, due to the high cost of creating and operating a PET facility, it is also one of the least available and affordable functional brain imaging methods. PET imaging uses a cyclotron to produce a short-lived isotope such as carbon (^{11}C), nitrogen (^{13}N), oxygen (^{15}O), or fluorine (^{18}F), which emit a short-lived particle called a positron. Using these positron-emitting radiopharmaceuticals, PET can measure cerebral blood flow and volume, oxygen or glucose metabolism, neuroreceptor binding, or water extraction across the blood-brain barrier. A variety of brain receptors may be imaged using specific PET radioligands, including D2 dopamine receptors, 5-HT2 serotonin receptors, opiate receptors, sigma receptors, N-methyl-D-aspartate (NMDA) glutamate and histamine receptors (Wong & Resnick, 1995).

Image Production/Typical PET Images: Similar to SPECT images, PET images are created by a process of back-projection followed by filtering and attenuation. During PET imaging, the injected radiotracer emits positrons within the brain, which collide with an electron producing 2 photons traveling in exactly opposite directions. A detector, called a coincidence circuit, will recognize this simultaneous ionization and create an image from these events by filtered back-projection methods. Spatial resolution for PET are usually in the range of 4 to 6 millimeters. One major difference between PET and SPECT is that with PET it is possible to determine absolute measures of rCBF if arterial sampling is used following the radioisotope injection; this is not possible with SPECT unless ^{133}Xenon is used.

Advantages/Disadvantages of PET: The advantages of PET are that it has a higher spatial resolution than SPECT, can image many specific neuroreceptors as well as quantify regional cerebral blood flow and glucose metabolism. Also, the dose of radiopharmaceutical used in pediatric PET research studies can be adjusted to be within current FDA radiation safety guidelines for research in children (Zametkin et al., 1993), although its research use in child and adolescent populations has been extremely limited. Disadvantages of PET scanning are that it is expensive and requires a cyclotron, which makes its availability to clinicians and researchers limited outside of major university research centers. Further disadvantages are radiation exposure and invasiveness of arterial line monitoring for some scanning procedures.

Clinical Indications: Both PET and SPECT have been used in pediatric patients with seizure disorders to identify focal areas of epileptogenesis. PET and SPECT studies typically reveal decreased cortical perfusion interictally and increased cortical perfusion ictally in regions of epileptic focus. PET also has been used in neurology as a diagnostic tool in selecting patients with partial epilepsy, particularly in the temporal lobes, for resective surgery. But the high cost of PET studies has limited its application in this area, while the low cost of SPECT has allowed it to be more widely used (Harvey & Berkovic, 1994; Wieser, 1994). Similar to SPECT, in child psychiatry there are no known clinical indications at this time for PET imaging, and it remains primarily a research tool.

FUNCTIONAL MAGNETIC RESONANCE IMAGING

Background and Image Production: Functional magnetic resonance imaging (fMRI) is an exciting functional imaging technology that is developing rapidly and is particularly suited for pediatric neuropsychiatric disorders. To date, functional imaging in children has been severely limited because of the limitations described earlier for techniques involving the use of radionuclides or radiopharmaceuticals. However, fMRI applications do not involve any exogenous chemicals or radiation exposure. Images in fMRI are based on image signals related to oxygen metabolism, blood volume, and blood flow. The most commonly applied fMRI technique is based on the fact that deoxyhemoglobin is paramagnetic, a property that causes it to suppress the MR signal from other substances in its immediate vicinity. The MR scanner can detect these shifts in local deoxyhemoglobin concentration to create images that detect local differences in blood flow. This effect has been called blood oxygenation level dependent contrast (BOLD) and was first demonstrated in humans by Kwong and colleagues (1992), who showed changes in cortical activation in the calcarine fissure of the visual cortex during a visual stimulation task. It has been demonstrated that when local neural activity increases, oxygen uptake, blood flow, and blood volume also increase locally. However, blood flow and volume increase more rapidly than actual oxygen utilization, causing deoxyhemoglobin concentration to decrease. This change in concentration results in a stronger local water signal indicating the brain regions activated by the experimental task.

Studies with fMRI now are beginning to identify similar regional changes for sensory or cognitive processing that have been previously identified in PET studies. Preliminary studies in adult psychiatric populations are providing promising results. These techniques are very early in their use with child psychiatric patients. However, they have been used to a limited extent in other pediatric disorders, such as in an examination of cerebral manifestations in children with sickle cell anemia (Tzika et al., 1993) and to assess language lateralization in epilepsy surgery planning (Hertz-Pannier et al., 1994).

Advantages/Disadvantages of fMRI: In addition to superior biosafety factors, fMRI has several other distinct advantages for blood flow imaging. fMRI provides spatial resolution of less than 1 millimeter and can provide temporal resolution as fast as 40 milliseconds. In fact, the temporal resolution exceeds the actual temporal resolution of hemodynamic changes, which may not be able to be differentiated in less than 0.5 seconds. As the images are acquired quickly, a number of activation tasks may be possible. The procedure is well suited for short- or long-term longitudinal investigations. In addition, fMRI is a less expensive technique, which can be performed on many standard MR scanners; thus it may be accessible to a greater number of researchers. However, fMRI currently has some disadvantages in comparison to PET; for example, BOLD contrast phenomena do not directly measure physiologic parameters such as absolute blood flow and it cannot currently assess neuroreceptor or transmitter systems.

MAGNETIC RESONANCE SPECTROSCOPY

Background: Nuclear magnetic resonance techniques also can be used to provide in vivo information about specific regional brain neurochemistry. Magnetic resonance spectroscopy (MRS) can assay atoms that possess a net charge such as ^{31}P, ^{1}H, ^{19}F, ^{13}C, ^{7}Li, and ^{23}Na if the molecules are present in sufficient concentration to produce an adequate signal. ^{31}P-MRS assays provide a measure of brain energy and membrane metabolism through quantification of adenosine triphosphate (ATP) and related metabolites including pH, Pi, adenosine diphosphate (ADP), adenosine triphosphate (ATP), phosphocreatinine (Pcr), phosphodiesters (PDE). PME and PDE are the precursors and breakdown products, respectively, of membrane phospholipids, and have been found to be altered in a variety of psychiatric disorders (Maier, 1995). ^{31}P-MRS techniques may be particularly useful for studying normal brain development and neuronal organization under normal and disease conditions. MRS can be used to tag (with ^{19}F labeling) certain substances, including specific medications, to investigate the distribution of these drugs in specific brain regions. However, MRS is technically demanding, requiring rigorous standardization and prolonged scanning times. The long scanning times currently limit its utility for imaging rapid changes in metabolism, but it can be used to compare individuals across longer time frames, such as within an episode of illness and later during remission.

Clinical Applications: Magnetic resonance spectroscopy also may prove to be of use in diagnosing central nervous system organic disorders. A recent imaging study compared 18 healthy children and 45 children with AIDS using structural MRI imaging and single-voxel H1 (proton) MRS (Lu et al., 1996). In this study, Lu and coworkers reported that 7 of the children with progressive encephalopathy and 8 with static encephalopathy had significantly lower mean N-acetyl aspartate (NAA)/creatine (Cr) ratios than age-matched control subjects ($p < 0.02$). Thirty patients without encephalopathy had normal NAA/Cr ratios but significantly lower choline/Cr ratios than age-matched control subjects. The authors concluded that proton MRS might be a more sensitive diagnostic technique than structural MRI in childhood AIDS encephalopathy. MRS may prove to be of particular use in studying child psychiatric disorders as it provides in vivo metabolic information different from that obtained by MRI, SPECT, or PET.

MRS has received only limited application in child psychiatric research. Some recent studies have examined normal brain development (Minshew & Pettegrew, 1996) and reported clear developmental changes in ^{31}P metabolic indices during adolescence and young adulthood. One small pilot study compared schizophrenic children to normals and reported a trend towards differences in choline-containing compounds in the schizophrenic children (Hendren et al., 1995). In addition, ^{31}P-MRS has been used in an investigation of the frontal cortex in high-functioning autistic subjects (Minshew, Goldstein, Dombrowski, Panchalingam, & Pettegrew, 1993).

Developmental Considerations in Brain Imaging

In child psychiatry, ongoing developmental processes (neural, cognitive, social, affective, etc.) are always relevant and important issues for clinical and research applications. Developmental factors also are critical to understanding and interpreting neuroimaging findings. Even clinical, qualitative interpretation of pediatric scans can reveal clear differences from similar scans in adults. For example, marked changes in brain tissue water content and changes in myelination profoundly alter the appearance of gray and white matter on MRI scans in infants and very young children. Despite its paramount importance in neuroimaging, there have been very few investigations quantifying normal developmental changes in children and adolescents. Most of our knowledge of structural brain development comes from neuropathologic studies of neonates and young infants. Recently a small number of studies have quantified regional structural development in normal children and adolescents. Our knowledge of functional brain development from functional neuroimaging stud-

ies currently is severely limited and based on small case series of children and adolescents who generally were undergoing SPECT or PET scanning for clinical indications, such as seizure investigations or cancer treatment planning.

NEUROMORPHOMETRIC DEVELOPMENT

It is increasingly clear from the few studies that have been completed using MRI to examine developmental structural changes that ongoing growth and remodeling is occurring in brain regions implicated in the pathogenesis of some child psychiatric disorders. Jernigan, Trauner, and Tallal (1991) were one of the first groups to quantify MRI changes in a small group of normal children and adolescents using a cross-sectional design. They reported changes including significant but slight increases in overall cerebral volume along with striking changes in the ratio of cerebral gray and white matter. They noted a decline in gray to white matter ratios from 1 to 8 in 8- to 10-year-old children to 1 to 3 in adults. The decrease in gray matter was parallel to and correlated with increases in ventricular and cortical cerebral spinal fluid. Subcortical basal ganglia and limbic structures, such as the caudate nucleus, putamen, globus pallidus, and thalamus, were found to decrease in volume from late childhood through adolescence. This observed decrease in the ratio of gray to white matter was hypothesized to correspond to known changes in synaptic pruning previously demonstrated in neuropathologic studies. Subsequent studies have examined similar regions using different imaging and image analysis techniques and also have reported increases in ventricular volume and decreases in subcortical structures over late childhood and adolescence. In the largest and most comprehensive cross-sectional study of normal developmental neuromorphometry, Giedd and colleagues (Giedd, 1997; Giedd, Rumsey, et al., 1996; Giedd, Snell, et al., 1996) computed structural volumes from 50 well-characterized normal children and adolescents between the ages of 4 to 18. They reported no significant change in cerebral or cerebellar volume in this age range. There were gender differences in developmental patterns of different structures. Lateral ventricular volumes increased significantly in males (only a trend for females) and more dramatically during puberty. In addition, caudate and putamen volumes decreased with age only in males. The midsagittal area of the corpus callosum increased significantly with age in both males and females (Giedd, Rumsey, et al., 1996a). Amygdala volume increased significantly in males but not females; however, for the hippocampus, there were significant increases over childhood and adolescence in females but not males (Giedd, 1997). It is clear that imaging studies with children and adolescents offer the opportunity to examine ongoing neural development and that studies of children and adolescents with psychiatric disorders will have to address and account for developmental factors.

FUNCTIONAL DEVELOPMENT

PET and SPECT studies also have found significant developmental and gender differences that must be taken into account when the brain of a child or an adolescent is imaged and compared to another individual. Several studies of the maturational changes of regional cerebral blood flow (rCBF) and local cerebral metabolic rates for glucose (ICMRGIc) in children and adolescents are available. Most of these studies have studied populations of children and adolescents referred for neurologic evaluation because of "transient neurologic difficulties," and many of these subjects were being treated with anticonvulsant medications when they were imaged. In 29 subjects (ages 5 days to 15 years) the studies reported that by the age of 2 years, absolute ICMRGIc for various gray matter regions (frontal, parietal, temporal, and occipital cortices) are similar to those of adults (Chugani & Phelps, 1991; Chugani, Phelps, & Mazziotta, 1987). LCMRGlc in most brain areas increased beyond adult values from age 2 years until the end of the second decade and then decreased to adult levels. In another functional imaging study that looked at "normal" children and adolescents using ^{133}Xe SPECT study, Chiron and colleagues (1992) studied 42 subjects (ages 2 days to 19 years) and reported global rCBF levels that were lower at birth than adult rCBF levels. These children's rCBF levels reached a maximum at 5 to 6 years, at which time they were 70% higher than adult levels and then decreased to adult levels after 15 years of age.

The imaging studies of brain development just summarized indicate that both age and gender effects must be controlled for before any comparisons can be made between populations with specific disorders and comparison controls using either structural or functional imaging techniques.

Brain Imaging Studies in Child Psychiatric Populations

DEVELOPMENTAL DISORDERS

Autism and other pervasive developmental disorders probably represent a heterogeneous group of disorders with distinct etiologies manifested by similar clinical presentations. Pervasive developmental spectrum disorders already have been demonstrated to be related at times to disparate but specific etiologies such as fragile X syndrome, other specific gross chromosomal abnormalities, congenital rubella, and others. Etiologic heterogeneity has been clearly demonstrated with another neuropsychiatric syndrome, Alzheimer's dementia, where multiple specific genetic mutations in at least 3 different genes have been identified so far for familial Alzheimer's disease in different pedigrees (Lendon, Ashall, & Goate, 1997). However, at this time clinical characteristics are not adequate for characterizing and distinguishing these populations. Autism may be a similar disorder with multiple etiologies impacting common neural pathways to produce an autistic phenotype. Neuropathology studies have suggested several cellular abnormalities, including a 50 to 60% reduction in Purkinje and granule cell numbers in the cerebellum, increased cell packing density, and reduced neuronal size in regions of the limbic system (Bauman, 1996; Ritvo et al., 1986). A number of early MRI studies focused on posterior fossa structures such as the cerebellum and brain stem in part because they were easy to visualize on midsagittal MR images. Courchesne and colleagues reported the first quantitative study indicating decreased area of cerebellar vermal lobules VI and VII (Courchesne, Yeung-Courchesne, Press, Hesselink, & Jernigan, 1988) (See Figure 7.4.) Subsequently they and other investigators, using improved imaging methodology and improved matching of controls, have replicated the finding of cerebellar vermian hypoplasia (Courchesne et al., 1994; Hashimoto et al., 1995). How-

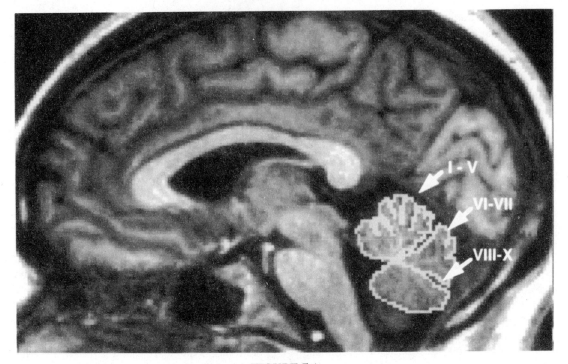

FIGURE 7.4.

A midsagittal T1-weighted image illustrating the cerebellar vermis lobules.

ever, a number of studies have not found significant differences (Filipek et al., 1992; Garber & Ritvo, 1992; Hashimoto, Tayama, Miyazaki, Murakawa, & Kuroda, 1992; Kleiman, Neff & Rosman, 1992; Piven et al., 1992; Ritvo & Garber, 1988). These studies are difficult to compare; often they involved small numbers of autistic subjects in different age ranges and levels of functioning. Comparison controls sometimes were not matched for gender, IQ, or socioeconomic status. In a recent study with very well matched controls for age, gender, socioeconomic status, and IQ, differences were not demonstrated in cerebellar structure between high-functioning children with autistic disorder and normal controls (Holttum, Minshew, Sanders, & Phillips, 1992). These investigators also suggested that the potential abnormalities could be less prominent in higher-functioning individuals such as those they studied. Courchesne and colleagues (1994) recently reported a meta-analysis of several of their own and other investigators' studies and concluded that there may be 2 distinct types of cerebellar abnormality in autism with approximately 85% of subjects demonstrating hypoplasia and 10 to 15% of

subjects demonstrating hyperplasia of the cerebellar vermi. This second group was not distinguishable in the individual studies with small numbers, but became more apparent when studies were grouped together. Increasing evidence is confirming the cerebellum's role in normal learning and cognition, which further supports the possible role of the cerebellum in the pathogenesis of autism. However, questions about specificity of cerebellar abnormalities to autism have been supported by a recent study by Schaefer and colleagues (1996) that demonstrates cerebellar vermal area differences in a variety of developmental disorders. They studied a population of 102 patients with a variety of neurogenetic abnormalities including autism and conditions associated with autistic behavior (Rett's, Sotos, fragile X, and Angelman's syndromes) and other neurodevelopmental disorders associated with mental retardation or specific cerebellar abnormalities. They reported that several neurogenetic disorders had relative hypoplasia in cerebellar lobules VI and VII.

A number of studies also have quantified brain stem regions with conflicting results. Several studies have reported that there is an increase in fourth ventricular size, decrease in the pons and midbrain (Courchesne et al., 1985; Gaffney, Kuperman, Tsai, & Minchin, 1988; Ornitz, Atwell, Kaplan, & Westlake, 1985) or medulla oblongata (Hsu, Courchesne, Courchesne, & Press, 1991). However, a nearly equivalent number of studies have reported no difference in the same regions (Garber et al., 1989; Kleiman et al., 1992; Rumsey, Creasey, & Stepanek, 1988). A smaller group of studies has reported cortical malformations including cortical atrophy of the parietal lobe (Berthier, 1994; Courchesne, Press, & Yeung-Courchesne, 1993) and polymicrogyria, macrogyria, or schizencephaly (Berthier, Starkstein, Robinson, & Leiguarda, 1990; Piven et al., 1990).

Increased total cerebral volume has been reported by 2 different groups (Filipek et al., 1992; Piven et al., 1995). Earlier area estimates of cerebral volume had not detected this difference (Gaffney, Kuperman, Tsai, Minchin, & Hassanein, 1987; Piven et al., 1992). Neuropathology studies have reported that brain weight of autistic subjects younger than age 12 was heavier than expected (100 to 200 grams) (Bauman, 1996) whereas in adult subjects it is less than expected (100 to 200 grams) (Bauman & Kemper, 1994).

Very few studies have attempted to correlate specific regional abnormalities with neuropsychological impairment. However, in at least 1 example a structural difference, parietal lobe atrophy, was correlated with an expected neuropsychologic deficit, poor performance on the Posner test of visual spatial attention (Courchesne et al., 1993).

Autistic disorder can be associated with clearly identified etiologies, such as neurofibromatosis, tuberous sclerosis, congenital rubella, or fragile X syndrome. Some of these distinct etiologies are characterized by specific neuroadiologic findings. For example, children with tuberous sclerosis exhibit classic findings of cortical tubers, white matter abnormalities, subependymal nodules, or subependymal giant cell astrocytomas. Neurofibromatosis often has characteristic nonneoplastic hamartomatous lesions and an increased incidence of specific central nervous system neoplasms. Children with congenital rubella often have delayed myelination, decreased total brain volume, and cortical and basal ganglia calcifications.

Several functional imaging studies have supported the hypothesis that autism is associated with abnormal hemispheric specialization and left-hemispheric dysfunction. Brain functional imaging using ^{133}Xe-SPECT was used to measure left/right asymmetry and absolute values of regional cerebral blood flow in 18 children with autism, ages four to 17 years, and 10 age-matched controls. The left-to-right indices, both hemispheric and regional, were positive in controls, indicating higher left than right rCBF values, but were negative in patients with autism. This inversion was statistically significant for total hemispheres, sensorimotor and language-related cortex and was explained by a significant decrease of the left absolute rCBF values in these regions in the patients with autism. The inversion was independent of handedness, sex and age. These results support the existence of left-hemispheric dysfunction in childhood autism, especially in the cortical areas devoted to language and handedness, leading to anomalous hemispheric specialization (Chiron et al., 1995). In another SPECT study that used ^{99m}Tc-HMPAO and high-resolution cameras (8.5 millimeter), Mountz, Tolbert, Lill, Katholi, and Liu (1995) reported abnormally low rCBF in the temporal and parietal lobes in a group of autistic children as compared to a group of normals. Further functional imaging studies of autistic subjects are necessary before any firm conclusions can be made about their rCBF patterns. However, these results support the existence of left-hemispheric dysfunction in childhood autism, especially in the cortical areas devoted to language and handedness, leading to anomalous hemispheric specialization (Chiron et al., 1995).

Minshew and colleagues (1993) used ^{31}P-MRS to study a small group of autistic subjects ($n = 11$); they reported significantly reduced levels of phosphocreatine and related products in the prefrontal lobe of autistic subjects as compared to normal controls matched for age, gender, race, IQ, and socioeconomic status. This finding was hypothesized to reflect lower synthesis and higher degradation of regional cell membranes. In this study, neuropsychological test performance on prefrontal lobe tasks in the autistic subjects was correlated with MRS metabolite levels.

Fragile X Syndrome: Fragile X syndrome is now identified as the second leading genetic cause of mental retardation. (Trisomy 21 is first.) The neuromorphometry of fragile X syndrome has been studied carefully in a small number of well designed controlled MR investigations. Reiss and colleagues (1994) have demonstrated differences in specific temporal lobe structures among individuals with fragile X, normal controls, and controls with other neurobehavioral and developmental disorders. Individuals with fragile X have larger hippocampal volumes along with an uncharacteristic age-related increase in hippocampal volume and an age-related decrease in superior temporal gyrus volume. Individuals with fragile X also have been reported to have hypoplasia of several posterior fossa structures, including cerebellar vermian hypoplasia (Reiss, Freund, Tseno, & Joshi, 1991). The differences in cerebellar structure demonstrated a dose-dependent effect of the fragile X mutation with males demonstrating the most deviation from controls and fragile X females intermediate to the fragile X males and normal controls.

Rett's Syndrome: There appear to be numerous brain structural abnormalities in girls with Rett's syndrome. Individuals with Rett's have been reported to have a general and significant reduction in overall cerebral volume accompanied by significant subcortical atrophy (Cassanova, Naidu, & Goldberg, 1991; Reiss et al., 1993). In comparison to normal controls specific regional neuroanatomic findings include a greater decrease in gray matter in comparison to white matter with profound losses in the frontal regions (Murakami, Courchesne, Press, Yeung-Courchesne, & Hesselink, 1989; Reiss et al., 1993). Subcortical structures such as caudate volume and midbrain structures are also significantly decreased (to a greater extent than overall brain volume decreases) (Reiss et al., 1993). Although the current studies have been limited to cross-sectional investigations, they do not clearly support a neurodegenerative process, which is in contrast to the clear clinical course with developmental regression over childhood. Future longitudinal studies beginning with and following younger subjects will help to clarify these issues.

Dyslexia: Dyslexia was one of the first developmental disorders studied with neuroimaging based on the hypothesis that anatomic abnormalities in the region of the planum temporale were related to reading disorders. Abnormalities in this region were first demonstrated by postmortem examination of several young adults with a history of reading disorders (Galaburda, Sherman, Rosen, Aboitiz, & Geschwind, 1985; Humphreys, Kaufmann, & Galaburda, 1990). The planum temporale is an important region for language processing and reading or phonologic processing located in the region of the posterior pole of the temporal lobe along the superior surface of the superior temporal gyrus. The left planum temporale is larger than the right in approximately 65% of normal brains. The individuals with reading disorders lacked the usual pattern of asymmetry in the planum temporale seen on visual inspection of the brain. In all cases, this was due to increased area on the right side rather than a reduction on the left side.

Early CT studies also demonstrated a lack of normal asymmetry in linear measures of the posterior occipital lobe (Haslam, Dalby, Johns, & Rademaker, 1981; Hier, LeMay, Rosenberger, & Perlo, 1978; Leisman & Ashkenazi, 1980). However, recent better-controlled MR studies have reported differing results in their examinations of the planum temporale region. Most of these studies have reported linear or, at best, area measures of the region. However, several have reported changes in asymmetry (Duara, Kushch, & Gross-Glenn, 1991; Larsen, Hoien, Lundberg, & Odebaard, 1990; Rumsey et al., 1986) with some investigators reporting greater right than left measures (Hynd, Semrud-Clikeman, Lorys, Novey, & Eliopulos, 1990), others reporting symmetry (Larsen et al., 1990), and a third group reporting greater left than right measures (Filipek et al., 1995; Schultz et al., 1994). Some of the discrepancy in reports may be related to difficulties in the definition of the region of the planum temporale and problems with reliability of measurements of this ill-defined region (Filipek, 1995). In addition, because most measures were linear or area measures, they are sensitive to differences in head positioning, which these early studies often did not account for. Most groups have used different analytic methods as well as different structural boundary guidelines to create their planum temporale estimates, and thus direct comparison of these studies is problematic. Recently Leonard and colleagues (1993) reported results from a well-designed study that included a 3-dimensional imaging acquisition and clear specification and reliability of their regional area measures. They measured both the temporal planum (traditional) and the parietal planum. They studied 9 young adult individuals with dyslexia in comparison to 10 of their first- and second-degree relatives and 12 normal controls, and concluded that the dyslexics demonstrated abnormalities in the region of the planum temporale with changes in asymmetry. Subjects with dyslexia had larger measures of planum temporale asymmetry and a shift of right planar tissue from the temporal to the parietal region. Additionally, they demonstrated a higher incidence of cerebral anomalies in this region; phonologic decoding scores correlated with these anomalies. Schultz and colleagues (1994) compared 17 children with dyslexia with 14 normal controls, also using fairly reliable convolutional surface area measures, and did not find differences between their groups. However, they did report strong effects of age and gender, which may have overshadowed any diagnostic effects. Significant gender differences in the region of the planum temporale have been reported in adult populations as well (Harasty, Double, Halliday, Kril, & McRitchie, 1997). These studies again underscore the importance of examining and accounting for developmental and gender effects on brain region measures.

Several other studies have examined asymmetry in different brain regions in individuals with dyslexia and also have reported significant findings in comparison to normal controls. Rumsey and colleagues (1986) reported loss of the usual left-greater-than-right asymmetry of lateral ventricles and right-greater-than-left asymmetry of the temporal lobes. Hynd and colleagues (1990) reported differences in the frontal cortex with the loss of right-greater-than-left asymmetry and overall size reduction in children with dyslexia. Several groups examining the corpus callosum have reported mixed findings with some demonstrating differences (Duara et al., 1991; Hynd et al., 1995; Rumsey et al., 1996) and other groups not finding significant differences (Larsen, Hoien, & Odegaard, 1992).

Several SPECT and PET investigations have been completed in adults with dyslexia. Rumsey and colleagues (1987) used a Xenon inhalation study with a semantic classification task and reported exaggerated asymmetry of blood flow in Wernicke's area in adults with a history of poor reading ability. [18]FDG PET studies have reported increased cerebral blood flow in dyslexic men performing reading tasks, including increased glucose utilization in the inferior occipital cortex when reading single words (Gross-Glenn et al., 1991) and increased glucose utilization in the medial temporal lobe bilaterally with a task requiring recognition of a target syllable (Hagman, Wood, Buchsbaum, 1992). Several O^{15} PET studies conducted by Rumsey and colleagues demonstrated differences in blood flow in temporal, parietal, and posterior temporal regions in dyslexic individuals in comparison to controls (Rumsey et al., 1992; Rumsey, Andreason, et al., 1994; Rumsey, Zametkin, et al., 1994).

ATTENTION DEFICIT HYPERACTIVITY DISORDER

Children with attention deficit hyperactivity disorder were among the first child psychiatric patients to be examined with early neuroimaging techniques. At the time of the initial studies with CT, established standardized diagnostic criteria were not available and the children investigated were reported to have minimal brain dysfunction, a characterization that included individuals who would now receive a diagnosis of attention deficit hyperactivity disorder. Several of these CT studies suggested that children with minimal brain dysfunction or adults with a history of minimal brain dysfunction demonstrated cerebral atrophy and/ or ventricular enlargement (Bergstrom & Bille, 1978; Caparulo et al., 1981; Nasrallah et al., 1986). However, not all investigators found these significant differences (Shaywitz, Shaywitz, Byrne, Cohen, & Rothman, 1983; Thompson, Ross, & Horwitz, 1980). Shaywitz and coworkers (1983) also noted a change in the asymmetry of the frontal lobes with the attention deficit disorder group demonstrating a smaller right than left frontal lobe width. This finding was opposite the expected asymmetry and observed asymmetry in the control group. These pioneering studies highlighted the possibility that there may be structural brain differences in children with minimal brain dysfunction or attention deficit hyperactivity disorder; however, they all had serious limitations, given the heterogeneity in diagnosis, the almost uniform lack of a normal control contrast group (secondary to the substantial exposure to ionizing radiation from CT), and limitations on the quantitative structural measures that could be obtained.

Several of the initial MRI studies in children with attention deficit disorder measured the corpus callosum on midline sagittal images. The corpus callosum is an easily visualized structure that can be measured fairly reliably and represents neural fibers crossing between the right and left hemispheres. Hynd and colleagues (1991) measured regional subdivisions of the corpus callosum in 7 children with attention deficit hyperactivity disorder in comparison to 10 normal controls. They reported significant differences in the corpus callosum using a 2-way ANOVA (diagnosis by region). The subjects with attention deficit hyperactivity disorder had smaller measurements in both the genu, most anterior segment, and the 2 posterior segments, including the splenium. Giedd and colleagues (1994) compared 18 boys with attention deficit hyperactivity disorder who also were comorbid for oppositional defiant disorder or conduct disorder to 18 normal controls matched for age, pubertal status, and handedness. They reported significant decreases in the rostral region of the corpus callosum in the attention deficit hyperactivity disorder subjects. There were no differences in total corpus callosum area between the groups. In addition, the reduction in rostral regions correlated with teacher and parent ratings of hyperactivity and impulsivity in the boys with attention deficit hyperactivity disorder. Semrud-Clikeman and colleagues (1994) examined regional corpus callosum areas in 15 males with attention deficit hyperactivity disorder in comparison to 15 normal controls matched for age, sex, handedness, and intelligence. They reported no significant difference in overall corpus callosum area or shape but did find the area of the splenium (most posterior portion) was significantly smaller in the group with attention deficit hyperactivity disorder. Most recently Baumgardner and colleagues (1996) reported on a study examining the corpus callosum in a group of children with Tourette's disorder and/or attention deficit hyperactivity disorder. Thirteen subjects had attention deficit only, 21 had both Tourette's and attention deficit, and 16 had Tourette's only; these groups were contrasted with 27 normal controls. The researchers also reported a significant decrease in the rostral region in the individuals with attention deficit. It was interesting that the individuals with Tourette's alone had significantly larger corpus callosal areas in all regions except the genu and that individuals with Tourette's and attention deficit appeared to have an additive effect with regional corpus callosal measures intermediate between the Tourette's-alone and attention deficit–alone groups. This finding points to the potential necessity of separate analysis for individuals with or without Tourette's or perhaps tics.

Recent MRI investigations have focused on prefrontal and striatal structures and are beginning to report consistent differences in these regions. Hynd and colleagues (1990) examined the prefrontal lobe by measuring the anterior width of both hemispheres and the posterior regions of the planum temporale in 10 subjects with attention deficit hyperactivity disorder in comparison to 10 subjects with reading disorders and 10 healthy controls. They reported that both patient groups had a smaller anterior width in the right hemisphere in comparison to the controls and that the patient groups did not demonstrate the expected right-greater-than-left asymmetry that the control group did. Subsequently they examined caudate asymmetry (Hynd et al., 1993) in 11 subjects with attention deficit hyperactivity disorder in comparison to 11 controls matched for age and handedness. They found no difference in midsagittal supratentorial area or in total caudate area (as measured on a single axial slice). However, they found a pattern of left-greater-than-right caudate asymmetry in 8 of 11 controls, which was reversed in 7 of 11 children with attention deficit hyperactivity disorder. Castellanos and colleagues (1994) estimated caudate volumes from thinner sliced (2-millimeter) T1 weighted coronal scans in 50 boys with attention deficit hyperactivity disorder in comparison to 48 normal control boys. The subject groups were not significantly different in age, weight, handedness, or pubertal stage. IQ estimates were higher in the controls. Total brain volume was reported to be 5.6% smaller in subjects with attention deficit hyperactivity disorder. The normal controls demonstrated a pattern of right-greater-than-left caudate asymmetry that was not present in the subjects with attention deficit hyperactivity disorder. Additionally, they reported that caudate volume did not decrease with increasing age in the boys with attention deficit hyperactivity disorder, as would be expected and was replicated in the control group. This study did not demonstrate any significant relationships between caudate changes and clinical features or standard continuous performance task measures. Subsequently Aylward and colleagues (1996) examined basal ganglia volumes in 16 boys with attention deficit hyperactivity disorder plus Tourette's, 10 boys with attention deficit hyperactivity disorder, and 11 normal controls. The first 2 groups were matched for age, handedness, and IQ; controls were matched for age and handedness. The caudate, putamen, and globus pallidus were measured on 3-millimeter axial sections. There were no group differences in estimated total brain volume. No significant differences were found in caudate or putamen asymmetries. When basal ganglia structures were controlled for overall brain volume (ANCOVA), the total and left globus pallidus volume in the attention deficit group was significantly smaller (21% reduction) than in controls. Right globus pallidus differences were substantial (18%) but did not reach significance. The comorbid group had globus pallidus volumes that were intermediate and did not differ significantly from either the attention deficit only group or control group. Recently Castellanos and colleagues (1994) enlarged their previous sample and added measures of the prefrontal lobe volume (see Figure 7.5: gray and white matter anterior to the corpus callosum demarcated by a coronal plane perpendicular to the AC–PC line) and volume measures of the globus pallidus and putamen. The sample included 57 boys with attention deficit hyperactivity disorder and 55 comparison normal control boys. They confirmed their previous findings of reduced total cerebral volume and loss of normal right-greater-than-left caudate asymmetry in the ADHD subjects. After adjusting for total cerebral volume with ANCOVA, they reported no differences in putamen volume or asymmetry between the groups, but significant effects of diagnosis and asymmetry in the globus pallidus (10.3% reduction on the right and 4.3% reduction of the left). Additionally, the right anterior prefrontal lobe was significantly smaller in the attention deficit group in comparison to controls. Subsequently, their group examined a subset of these children with several neuropsychology tasks designed to assess response inhibition (Casey et al., 1997). Twenty-six of the boys with attention deficit were compared to 26 normal control boys.

The 3 neuropsychology tasks were designed to examine unique components of inhibitory control during different stages of attentional processing: sensory selection, response selection, and response execution. Significant differences were reported in performance by children with attention deficit hyperactivity disorder in comparison to normal controls on all 3 tasks. Performance on the sensory selection and response selection task was significantly related to right prefrontal and right caudate volumes. Response selection and response execution performance were correlated with caudate symmetry and globus pallidus volumes. These data are some of the first to support a relatively robust relationship between specific neuropsychological tasks and a specific neuromorphometric parameter in a childhood psychiatric disorder.

Castellanos and colleagues (1994) also examined several other brain regions in this expanded study. They found that cerebellar volume was significantly decreased in subjects with attention deficit hyperactivity disorder and that left lateral ventricular volume, but not total ventricular volume, was significantly smaller in the attention deficit hyperactivity disorder subjects than control subjects. In control boys, lateral ventricular volume significantly increased with age whereas no significant age-related changes were noted in the boys with attention deficit hyperactivity disorder. There were no significant differences in overall temporal lobe volume.

Filipek (1996) subsequently reexamined the MR scans from 30 subjects from their corpus callosum study and using semiautomated thresholding techniques they segmented brain regions into gray matter and white matter. They subdivided the brain into 6 regions, both a superior and an inferior portion of precallosal, pericallosal, and retrocallosal regions, defined by coronal planes at the anterior and posterior boundaries of the corpus callosum. Using these methods, they did not find a significant difference in total cerebral volume (although attention deficit hyperactivity disorder subjects were 5% smaller than controls). The anterior superior pericallosal region was significantly smaller in the attention deficit hyperactivity disorder group with a significantly diminished right-greater-than-left asymmetry in those subjects. They also noted differences in the prefrontal lobe regions in the attention deficit sub-

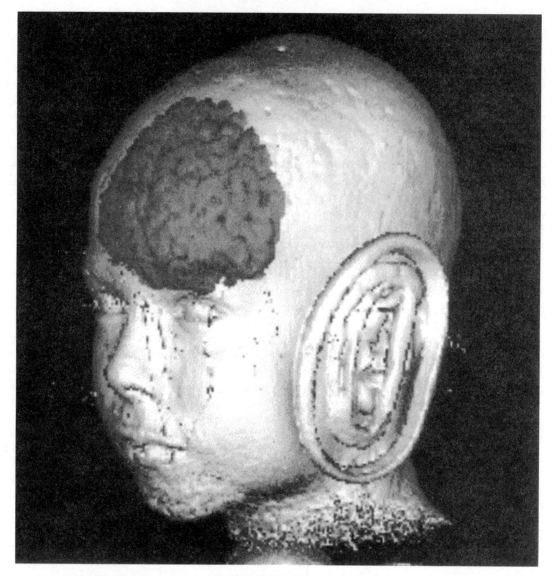

FIGURE 7.5.

Three-dimensional prefrontal lobe reconstruction created from 3D MPRAGE MR acquisition. Posterior boundary defined by the coronal plane just anterior to the genu of the corpus callosum.

jects. Subcortical regions, which included the caudate and other anterior basal ganglia, were significantly smaller in these subjects, and there were differences in asymmetry in them in comparison to the normal controls. A subsample of stimulant nonresponders demonstrated significant decreases in the superior retrocallosal region.

Several functional imaging studies used either PET or SPECT to study attention deficit hyperactivity disorder. Three of these earliest studies were by Lou and coworkers in Copenhagen, who used [133]Xenon SPECT to study mixed groups of children with either attention deficit disorder or attention deficit disorder with dysphasias vs. normal controls (Lou, Henriksen, & Bruhn, 1990; Lou, Henriksen, Bruhn, Borner, & Nielson, 1989; Lou, Henriksen, Bruhn, & Psych, 1984). In the first group, they found decreased blood flow to the striatal and posterior periventricular regions and increased blood flow in the primary sensory and sensorimotor cortex compared to their control group. Interestingly, they reported that this abnormal rCBF pattern in the striatal and periventricular regions was reversed by treatment with methylphenidate.

Zametkin and colleagues at the National Institute of Mental Health have used ^{18}F-PET to study adults and adolescents with attention deficit hyperactivity disorder. In their initial adolescent study, which compared a group of 10 adolescents with the disorder to a group of age- and gender-matched normal controls, they reported significant reductions of glucose metabolism in 6 of 60 specific brain regions studied (Zametkin et al., 1993). After the absolute glucose metabolic rates were normalized between subjects and controls, they found reduced glucose metabolism in the left anterior frontal area, right posterior temporal area, left posterior frontal area, right temporal area, left thalamus, and right hippocampus. This same group at the National Institute of Mental Health then expanded their sample to include 20 adolescents with attention deficit hyperactivity disorder and 19 normal controls and found no statistically significant differences in global or regional CMRglu between the groups. They did, however, find that the global CMRglu in girls with the disorder ($n = 5$; $p = 0.04$) was 15.0% lower than in normal girls ($n = 6$), while global CMRglu in boys with the disorder was not different from that in normal boys. Furthermore, global CMRglu in girls with the disorder was 19.6% lower than in boys with the disorder ($p = 0.02$) and was not different between normal girls and normal boys. These findings suggest that there may be important gender differences in attention deficit hyperactivity disorder that must be taken into account when functional imaging studies are performed (Ernst et al., 1994).

Taken together, these studies are beginning to demonstrate relatively consistent changes in the prefrontal lobe and basal ganglia in boys with attention deficit hyperactivity disorder. These results are consistent with hypotheses relating the pathophysiology of attention deficit hyperactivity disorder to dysfunction in frontal-striatal circuits. It remains to be demonstrated if these findings are present in girls with attention deficit hyperactivity disorder, if they are specific to this disorder, how they are affected by comorbidity, and how

these structural differences evolve over the course of development.

TOURETTE'S DISORDER

Several lines of evidence have suggested that the pathophysiology of Tourette's disorder is related to basal ganglia dysfunction. MR and functional studies completed to date further support this link. Investigations of children and adults have reported either decreased volumes on the left or an alteration in the normal asymmetry between right and left basal ganglia structures in the individuals with Tourette's in comparison to normal controls (Peterson et al., 1993; Singer et al., 1992). Several groups also have examined children with comorbid Tourette's and attention deficit hyperactivity disorder. Singer and colleagues (1992) demonstrated that these comorbid children had more extreme differences in globus pallidus lateralization compared to subjects with only Tourette's and normal controls. In fact, in the noncomorbid Tourette's group there were no significant differences in the basal ganglia from controls. (However, this study has a small number of subjects.) Hyde and colleagues (1995) completed volumetric caudate measurements in 10 monozygotic twin pairs with attention deficit hyperactivity disorder who were discordant for tic severity. They reported reduced right anterior caudate volume in the twin with more severe tics. These studies demonstrate the importance of assessing and accounting for attention deficit hyperactivity disorder symptoms and tic symptoms in populations of individuals with Tourette's and attention deficit hyperactivity disorder.

Studies of other brain regions also have supported alterations in lateralization in individuals with Tourette's, including differences in the corpus callosum (Baumgardner et al., 1996; Peterson, Leckman, & Duncan, 1994).

Several functional imaging studies of individuals with Tourette's also have supported the role of basal ganglia and prefrontal lobe dysfunction. Braun and colleagues (1993) completed a PET study demonstrating hypometabolism in the ventromedial caudate, nucleus accumbens, and left anterior putamen. These findings were consistent with an earlier report by Chase, Geoffrey, Gillespie, and Burrows (1986) demonstrating hypometabolism in the basal ganglia and in frontal cingulate and insular cortices. Several SPECT studies have reported similar results (George et al., 1992; Hall et al., 1990; Sieg, Buckingham, Gaffney, Preston, & Sieg, et al., 1993).

CHILDHOOD SCHIZOPHRENIA

Schizophrenia has been the subject of multiple neuromorphemetric studies in adults. It is relatively well established that adults with schizophrenia demonstrate enlargement of lateral and third ventricles, widened cortical sulci, and decreases in specific mesial temporal lobe structures (Shenton et al., 1997), specifically including reductions in the medial temporal lobe, superior temporal gyrus, hippocampus, and amygdala volumes. Several small studies of children with prepubertal-onset schizophrenia or schizotypal personality disorder recently have been reported. Because of the rarity of prepubertal-onset schizophrenia, only a handful of imaging investigations have been reported. A small study with 12 children with schizophrenia demonstrated decreased volume of the amygdala and temporal lobe cortex, decreased corpus callosal area, and differences in symmetry measures (Hendren et al., 1995). The National Institute of Mental Health Child Psychiatry Branch is conducting an ongoing study with national recruitment for individuals with prepubertal-onset schizophrenia. Some preliminary results have been reported on these subjects. The first report on 21 children in comparison to matched normal controls reported a lack of a normal right-greater-than-left asymmetry of the hippocampus, an increased asymmetry of the amygdala, and significantly smaller cerebral volumes. There were no significant differences in absolute temporal lobe, amygdala, hippocampus, or superior temporal gyrus volumes (Jacobsen et al., 1996). However, contrary to expectations, when regional volumes were adjusted for total cerebral volume, the superior temporal gyrus was larger than in the controls. Superior temporal gyrus volumes were, however, correlated with conceptual disorganization and unusual thought content. A second report on 24 subjects (Frazier et al., 1996) stated that schizophrenic children had an overall reduction in total cerebral volume and midsagittal thalamic area. It also reported larger caudate, putamen, and globus pallidus in the schizophrenics

and a trend toward increased lateral ventricular volume. Previous studies in adults have reported enlarged basal ganglia structures; however, it appears now that this may be a secondary effect from neuroleptic medication, and a follow-up study of a small subsample of these children who were maintained on the atypical neuroleptic clozapine supported this relationship (Frazier et al., 1996). Further examination of 29 of their subjects demonstrated a significant and robust relationship between negative symptoms and total cerebral volume in boys but not in girls (Alaghband-Rad, Hamburger, Giedd, Frazier, & Rapoport, 1997).

A small pilot study using ^{1}H MRS in children with prepubertal-onset schizophrenia has suggested that there may be differences between subjects and controls in NAA/Cr and choline containing compounds.

MOOD DISORDERS

Adults with major depressive disorder and bipolar affective disorder have been reported to have a variety of neuroanatomical changes, including increased incidence of subcortical white matter hyperintensities, increased ventricular size, decreased temporal lobe volume, decreased frontal lobe volume, and changes in basal ganglia structures. (For review, see Botteron & Figiel, 1997.) A pilot study of bipolar children and adolescents suggested similar changes with a 25% incidence of subcortical white matter hyperintensities (see Figure 7.6), changes in frontal asymmetry, and a trend toward increased ventricular size (Botteron et al., 1995). Subsequently a pilot study with depressed children demonstrated a loss of the normal prefrontal lobe volume asymmetry (right greater than left) in depressed children (see Figure 7.5) as compared to normal controls (Botteron, Geller, & Vannier, 1995).

Steingard and colleagues (1996) reported volumetric measures in 65 children and adolescents who were hospitalized for either major depressive disorder or dysthymia in comparison to 18 hospitalized psychiatric controls without a depressive disorder (11 conduct disorder/oppositional defiant disorder; 2 attention deficit hyperactivity disorder; 3 posttraumatic stress disorder; and 2 with an adjustment disorder). They retrospectively analyzed the volumes of 3 brain regions: the frontal lobes, the lateral ventricles, and the total cerebral

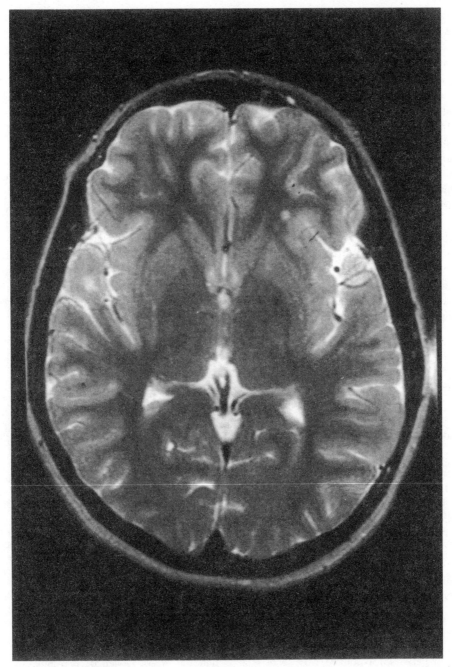

FIGURE 7.6.

T2-weighted axial image demonstrating a small confluent deep white matter hyperintensity in the left frontal lobe in a 10-year-old boy.

volume. They reported that their depressive group had a decrease in frontal lobe volume and an increase in ventricular volume when compared to their control group. This finding is similar to MRI findings in depressed adults with major depressive order, which also have demonstrated reduced frontal lobe volumes. Further controlled studies with normal age- and gender-matched controls are necessary before any conclusions can be made from these findings.

These preliminary studies are consistent with hypotheses from the adult literature that have suggested dysfunction and structural changes in frontal limbic circuit structures in both major depression and bipolar affective disorder. They add further support to the hypothesis of a neurodevelopmental etiology and offer exciting potential for future studies with child and adolescent populations to add significantly to our understanding of the pathophysiology of affective disorders, including early neurodevelopmental deviations and potential interactions with ongoing brain development during childhood and adolescence.

Conclusion

Neuroimaging in child psychiatry is still relatively undeveloped; however, over the past several years the number of reported investigations has expanded rapidly. Newer quantitative methods that are noninvasive and free of significant risk offer exciting potential for furthering our understanding of the pathophysiology of different child and adolescent psychiatric disorders. Investigations in several disorders, such as attention deficit hyperactivity disorder and Tourette's disorder, have demonstrated structural differences in specific brain regions consistent with a priori hypotheses implicating these neural circuits. Functional studies to date have been extremely limited; however, this is changing rapidly with the advent of fMRI. MRS studies are just beginning to describe the neurochemical correlates of childhood disorders. Although all imaging modalities currently are largely used for research, in the future they likely will have clinical application, influencing our treatment strategies, prognostic predictions, and differential diagnosis.

REFERENCES

Alaghband-Rad, J., Hamburger, S. D., Giedd, J. N., Frazier, J. A., & Rapoport, J. L. (1997). Childhood-onset schizophrenia: Biological markers in relation to clinical characteristics. *American Journal of Psychiatry, 154,* 64–68.

Aylward, E. H., Reiss, A. L., Reader, M. J., Singer, H. S., Brown, J. E., & Denckla, M. B. (1996). Basal ganglia volumes in children with attention-deficit hyperactivity disorder. *Journal of Child Neurology, 11,* 112–115.

Bauman, M. L. (1996). Brief report: Neuroanatomic observations of the brain in pervasive developmental disorders. *Journal of Autism and Developmental Disorders, 26* (2), 199–203.

Bauman, M. L., & Kemper, T. L. (1994). Neuroanatomic observations of the brain in autism. In M. L. Bauman & T. L. Kemper (Eds.), *The neurobiology of autism* (pp. 119–145). Baltimore, MD: Johns Hopkins University Press.

Baumgardner, T. L., Singer, H. S., Denckla, M. B., Rubin, M. A., Abrams, M. T., Colli, M. J., & Reiss, A. L. (1996). Corpus callosum morphology in children with Tourette syndrome and attention deficit hyperactivity disorder. *Neurology, 47,* 477–482.

Bergstrom, K., & Bille, B. (1978). Computed tomography of the brain in children with minimal brain damage: A preliminary study of 46 children. *Neuropaediatrie, 9,* 378.

Berthier, M. L. (1994). Corticocallosal anomalies in Asperger's syndrome. *American Journal of Roentgenology, 162,* 236–237.

Berthier, M. L., Starkstein, S. E., Robinson, R. G., & Leiguarda, R. (1990). Limbic lesions in a patient with recurrent mania [letter]. *Journal of Neuropsychiatry & Clinical Neurosciences, 2* (2), 235–236.

Botteron, K. N., Vannier, M. W., Geller, B., Todd, R., and Lee, B. C. (1995). Magnetic resonance imaging in childhood and adolescent bipolar affective disorder: A pilot investigation. *Journal of the American Academy of Child and Adolescent Psychiatry, 34* (6), 742–753.

Botteron, K. N., & Figiel, G. S. (1997). The neuromorphometry of affective disorders. In K. R. R. Krishnan & M. Doraiswamy (Eds.), *Brain imaging in clinicalpsychiatry* (pp. 145–184). New York: Marcel Dekker.

Botteron, K. N., Geller, B., & Vannier, M. W. (1995, October). *Prefrontal lobe volume in prepubertal major depression.* Paper presented at the annual conference of the American Academy of Child and Adolescent Psychiatry.

Braun, A. R., Stoetter, B., Randolph, C., Hsiao, J. K., Vladar, K., Gemert, J., Carson, R. E., Herscovitch, P., & Chase, T. N. (1993). The functional neuroanatomy of Tourette's syndrome: An FDG-PET study. I. Regional changes in cerebral glucose metabolism differentiating patients and controls. *Neuropsychopharmacology, 9* (4), 277–291.

Caparulo, B. K., Cohen, D. J., Rothman, S. L., Young, J. G., Katz, J. D., Shaywitz, S. E., & Shaywitz, B. A. (1981). Computed tomographic brain scanning in children with developmental neuropsychiatric disorders. *Journal of Abnormal Child Psychology, 20,* 338.

Casey, B., & Cohen, J. (1996). Letter to the editor. *Archives of General Psychiatry, 53,* 1059–1060.

Casey, B. J., Castellanos, F. X., Giedd, J. N., Marsh, W. L., Hamburger, S. D., Schubert, A. B., Vauss, Y. C., Vaituzis, A. C., Dickstein, D. P., Sarfatti, S. E., & Rapoport, J. L. (1997). Implication of right frontostriatal circuitry in response inhibition and attention-deficit/hyperactivity disorder. *Journal of the American Academy of Child and Adolescent Psychiatry, 36* (3), 374–383.

Cassanova, M. F., Naidu, S., & Goldberg, T. E. (1991). Quantitative magnetic resonance imaging in Rett syndrome. *Journal of Neuropsychiatry, 3,* 66–72.

Castellanos, F. X., Giedd, J. N., Eckburg, P., Marsh, W. L., Vaituzis, A. C., Kaysen, D., Hamburger, S. D., & Rapoport, J. L. (1994). Quantitative morphology of the caudate nucleus in attention deficit hyperactivity disorder. *American Journal of Psychiatry, 151,* 1791–1796.

Chase, T. N., Geoffrey, V., Gillespie, M., & Burrows, G. H. (1986). Structural and functional studies of Gilles de la Tourette syndrome. *Review of Neurology, 142,* 851.

Chiron, C., Leboyer, M., Leon, F., Jambaque, I., Nuttin, C., & Syrota, A. (1995). SPECT of the brain in childhood autism: Evidence for a lack of normal hemispheric asymmetry. *Developmental Medicine and Child Neurology, 37* (10), 849–860.

Chiron, C., Raynaud, C., Maziere, B., Zilbovicius, M., Laflamme, L., Masure, M. C., Dulac, O., Bourguignon, M., & Syrota, A. (1992). Changes in regional cerebral blood flow during brain maturation in children and adolescents. *Journal of Nuclear Medicine, 33* (5), 696–703.

Chugani, H. T., & Phelps, M. E. (1991). Imaging human brain development with positron emission tomography [editorial; comment]. *Journal of Nuclear Medicine, 32* (1), 23–26.

Chugani, H. T., Phelps, M. E., & Mazziotta, J. C. (1987). Positron emission tomography study of human brain functional development. *Annals of Neurology, 22,* 487–497.

Courchesne, E., Press, G. A., & Yeung-Courchesne, R. (1993). Parietal lobe abnormalities detected with MR in patients with infantile autism. *American Journal of Roentgenology, 160,* 387–393.

Courchesne, E., Saitoh, O., Yeung-Courchesne, R., Press, G. A., Lincoln, A. J., Haas, R. H., & Schreibman, L. (1994). Abnormalities of cerebellar vermian lobules VI and VII in patients with infantile autism. Identification of hypoplastic and hyperplastic subgroups by MR imaging. *American Journal of Roentgenology, 162,* 123–130.

Courchesne, E., Townsend, J., & Saitoh, O. (1994). The brain in infantile autism. *Neurology, 44,* 214–223.

Courchesne, E., Yeung-Courchesne, R., Hicks, G., &

Lincoln, A. (1985). Functioning of the brain-stem auditory pathway in non-retarded autistic individuals. *Electroencephalography and Clinical Neurophysiology, 61,* 491–501.

Courchesne, E., Yeung-Courchesne, R., Press, G. A., Hesselink, J. R., & Jernigan, T. L. (1988). Hypoplasia of cerebellar lobules VI and VII in infantile autism. *New England Journal of Medicine, 318,* 1349–1354.

Demaeral, P., Kingsley, D. P. E., & Kendall, B. E. (1993). Isolated neurodevelopmental delay in childhood: Clinicoradiological correlation in 170 patients. *Pediatric Radiology, 23,* 29–33.

Duara, R., Kushch, A., & Gross-Glenn, K. (1991). Neuroanatomic differences between dyslexic and normal readers on magnetic resonance imaging scans. *Archives of Neurology, 48,* 410–416.

Ernst, M., Liebenauer, L. L., King, A. C., Fitzgerald, G. A., Cohen, R. M., & Zametkin, A. J. (1994). Reduced brain metabolism in hyperactive girls. *Journal of the American Academy of Child and Adolescent Psychiatry, 33* (6), 858–868.

Filipek, P. A., Semrud-Clikeman, M., Steingard, R. J., Renshaw, P. F., Kennedy, D. N., Biederman, J. (1996). Volumetric MRI analysis comparing subjects having attention-deficit hyperactivity disorder with normal controls. *Neurology 48:* 589–601.

Filipek, P. A. (1995). Neurobiological correlates of developmental dyslexia—What do we know about how the dyslexics' brains differ from those of normal readers? *Journal of Child Neurology, 10* (Suppl. 1) (1), S62–S69.

Filipek, P. A. (1996). Brief report: Neuroimaging in autism: The state of the science 1995. *Journal of Autism and Developmental Disorders, 26* (2), 211–215.

Filipek, P. A., Pennington, B. F., Holems, J. F., Lefly, D., Kennedy, D. N., Meyers, J. M., Lang, J. E., Gayan, J., Galaburda, A. M., Simon, J. M., Eilley, C. M., Caviness, V. S., & DeFries, J. C. (1995). Developmental dyslexia: Cortical and subcortical anomalies by MRI-based morphometry [abstract]. *Annals of Neurology, 38,* 509.

Filipek, P. A., Richelme, C., Kennedy, D. N., & Caviness, V. S. (1994). The young adult human brain: An MRI-based morpohometric analysis. *Cerebral Cortex. 4* (4): 344–60.

Filipek, P. A., Richelme, C., Kennedy, D. N., Rademacher, J., Pitcher, D. A., Zidel, S. Y., & Caviness, V. S. (1992). Morphometric analysis of the brain in developmental language disorders and autism. *Annals of Neurology, 32,* 475.

Food and Drug Administration. (1995). 21 CFR Ch. I. *Code of Federal Regulations, 361.1,* 286.

Frazier, J. A., Giedd, J. N., Hamburger, S. D., Albus, K. E., Kaysen, D., Vaituzis, A. C., Rajapakse, J. C., Lenane, M. C., McKenna, K., Jacobsen, L. K., Gordon, C. T., Breier, A., & Rapoport, J. L. (1996). Brain anatomic magnetic resonance imaging in childhood-onset schizophrenia. *Archives of General Psychiatry, 53,* 617–624.

Gaffney, G. R., Kuperman, S., Tsai, L. Y., & Minchin, S. (1988). Morphological evidence for brainstem involvement in infantile autism. *Biological Psychiatry, 24,* 578–586.

Gaffney, G. R., Kuperman, S., Tsai, L. Y., Minchin, S., & Hassanein, K. M. (1987). Midsagittal magnetic resonance imaging of autism. *British Journal of Psychiatry* (151), 831–833.

Galaburda, A. M., Sherman, G. F., Rosen, G. D., Aboitiz, F., & Geschwind, N. (1985). Developmental dyslexia: Four consecutive cases with cortical anomalies. *Annals of Neurology, 18,* 222–223.

Garber, H. J., Ritvo, E. R., Chiu, L. C., Griswold, V. J., Kashanian, A., Freeman, B. J., & Oldendorf, W. H. (1989). A magnetic resonance imaging study of autism: Normal fourth ventricle size and absence of pathology. *American Journal of Psychiatry, 146,* 532–534.

Garber, H. J., & Ritvo, E. R. (1992). Magnetic resonance imaging of the posterior fossa in autistic adults. *American Journal of Psychiatry* (149), (2) 245–247.

George, M. S., Trimble, M. R., Costa, D. C., Robertson, M. M., Ring, H. A., & Ell, P. J. (1992). Elevated frontal cerebral blood flow in Gilles de la Tourette syndrome: A 99Tcm-HMPAO study. *Psychiatry Research (Neuroimaging),* 45 (3): 143–151.

Giedd, J. N., Castellanos, F. X., Casey, B. J., Kozuch, P., King, A. C., Hamburger, S. D., Rapoport, J. L. (1994). Quantitative morphology of the corpus callosum in attention deficit hyperactivity disorder. *American Journal of Psychiatry* 151:665–669.

Giedd, J. N. (1997). Normal brain development: Ages 4–18. In K. R. R. Krishnan (Ed.), *Brain imaging in clinical psychiatry* (pp. 103–120). New York: Marcel Dekker.

Giedd, J. N., Rumsey, J. M., Castellanos, F. X., Rajapakse, J. C., Kaysen, D., Vaituzis, A. C., Vauss, Y. C., Hamburger, S. D., & Rapoport, J. L. (1996). A quantitative MRI study of the corpus callosum in children and adolescents. *Developmental Brain Research, 91,* 274–280.

Giedd, J. N., Snell, J. W., Lange, N., Rajapakse, J. C., Casey, B. J., Kozuch, P. L., Vaituzis, A. C., Vauss, Y. C., Hamburger, S. D., Kaysen, D., & Rapoport, J. L. (1996). Quantitative magnetic resonance imaging of human brain development: Ages 4–18. *Cerebral Cortex, 6,* 551–560.

Gross-Glenn, K., Duara, R., Barker, W. W., Loewenstein, D., Chang, J. Y., Yoshii, F., Apicella, A. M., Pascal, S., Boothe, T., & Sevush, S. (1991). Positron emission tomographic studies during serial word-reading by normal and dyslexic adults. *Journal of Clinical and Experimental Neurophsychology, 13,* 531–544.

Hagman, J. O., Wood, F., Buchsbaum, M. S., Tallal, P., Flowers, L., & Katz, W. (1992). Cerebral brain metabolism in adult dyslexic subjects assessed with PET during performance of an auditory task. *Archives of Neurology, 49,* 734.

Hall, M., Costa, D. C., Shields, J., Heavens, J., Robertson, M., & Ell, P. J. (1990). Brain perfusion patterns with Tc-99mHMPAO/SPECT in patients with Gilles de la Tourette syndrome. *European Journal of Nuclear Medicine, 16,* 56.

Haller, J. W., Banerjee, A., Christensen, G. E., Gado, M., Joshi, S., Miller, M. I., Sheline, Y., Vannier, M. W., & Csernansky, J. G. (1997). Three-dimensional hippocampal MR morphometry with high-dimensional transformation of a neuroanatomic atlas. *Radiology, 202* (2), 504–510.

Harasty, J., Double, K. L., Halliday, G. M., Kril, J. J., & McRitchie, D. A. (1997). Language-associated cortical regions are proportionally larger in the female brain. *Archives of Neurology, 54,* 171–176.

Harvey, A. S., & Berkovic, S. F. (1994). Functional neuroimaging with SPECT in children with partial epilepsy. *Journal of Child Neurology, 9* (Suppl. 1), S71–S81.

Hashimoto, T., Tayama, M., Miyazaki, M., Murakawa, K., & Kuroda, Y. (1992). Brainstem and cerebellar vermis involvement in autistic children. *Journal of Child Neurology, 7,* 149–152.

Hashimoto, T., Tayama, M., Murakawa, K., Yoshimoto, T., Miyazaki, M., Harada, M., & Kuroda, Y. (1995). Development of the brainstem and cerebellum in autistic patients. *Journal of Autism and Developmental Disorders, 25,* 1–18.

Haslam, R. H. A., Dalby, J. T., Johns, R. D., & Rademaker, A. W. (1981). Cerebral asymmetry in developmental dyslexia. *Archives of Neurology, 38,* 679.

Hendren, R. L., Hodde-Vargas, J., Yeo, R. A., Vargas, L. A., Brooks, W. M., & Ford, C. (1995). Neuropsychophysiological study of children at risk for schizophrenia: A preliminary report. *Journal of the American Academy of Child and Adolescent Psychiatry, 34* (10), 1284–1291.

Hertz-Pannier, L., Gaillard, W. D., Mott, S., Cuenod, C. A., Bookheimer, S. Y., Weinstein, S., Conry, J., Theodore, W., & LeBihan, D. (1994,). *Pre-operative assessment of language by FMRI in children with complex partial seizures: Preliminary study.* Paper presented at the second annual meeting of the Society of Magnetic Resonance.

Hier, D. B., LeMay, M., Rosenberger, P. B., & Perlo, V. P. (1978). Developmental dyslexia. Evidence for a subgroup with a reversal of cerebral asymmetry. *Archives of Neurology, 35,* 90.

Holttum, J. R., Minshew, N. J., Sanders, R. S., & Phillips, N. E. (1992). Magnetic resonance imaging of the posterior fossa in autism. *Biological Psychiatry, 32,* 1091–1101.

Hsu, M., Courchesne, R. Y., Courchesne, E., & Press, G. A. (1991). Absence of magnetic resonance imaging evidence of pontine abnormality in infantile autism. *Archives of Neurology, 48,* 1160–1163.

Humphreys, P., Kaufmann, W. E., & Galaburda, A. M. (1990). Developmental dyslexia in women: Neuropathological findings in three patients. *Annals of Neurology, 28,* 727–738.

Hyde, T. M., Stacey, M. E., Coppola, R., Handel, S. F., Rickler, K. C., & Weinberger, D. R. (1995). Cerebral morphometric abnormalities in Tourette's syndrome: A quantitative MRI study of monozygotic twins. *Neurology, 45,* 1176–1182.

Hynd, G. W., Hall, J., Novey, E. S., Eliopulos, D., Black, K., Gonzales, J. J., Edmonds, J. E., Riccio, C., & Cohen, M. (1995). Dyslexia and corpus callosum morphology. *Archives of Neurology, 52,* 32–38.

Hynd, G. W., Hern, K. L., Novey, E. S., Eliopulos, D., Marshall, R., Gonzalez, J. J., & Voeller, K. K. (1993). Attention deficit-hyperactivity disorder and asymmetry of the caudate nucleus. *Journal of Child Neurology, 8,* 339–347.

Hynd, G. W., Semrud-Clikeman, M., Lorys, A. R., Novey, E. S., & Eliopulos, D. (1990). Brain morphology in developmental dyslexia and attention deficit disorder/hyperactivity. *Archives of Neurology, 47,* 919–926.

Hynd, G. W., Semrud-Clikeman, M., Lorys, A. R., Novey, E. S., Eliopulos, D., & Lyytinen, H. (1991). Corpus callosum morphology in attention deficit-hyperactivity disorder: Morphometric analysis of MRI. *Journal of Learning Disabilities, 24* (3), 141–146.

Jacobsen, L. K., Giedd, J. N., Vaituzis, A. C., Hamburger, S. D., Rajapakse, J. C., Frazier, J. A., Kaysen, D., Lenane, M. C., McKenna, K., Gordon, C. T., & Rapoport, J. L. (1996). Temporal lobe morphology in childhood-onset schizophrenia. *American Journal of Psychiatry, 153* (3), 355–361.

Jernigan, T. L., Trauner, D. A., Hesselink, J. R., & Tallal, P. A. (1991). Maturation of human cerebrum observed in vivo during adolescence. *Brain, 114,* 2037–2049.

Kleiman, M. D., Neff, S., & Rosman, N. P. (1992). The brain in infantile autism: Are posterior fossa structures abnormal? *Neurology, 42,* 753–760.

Krishnan, K. R. R., & MacFall, J. R. (1997). Basic principles of magnetic resonance imaging. In K. R. R. Krishnan (Ed.), *Brain imaging in clinical psychiatry* (pp. 1–12). New York: Marcel Dekker.

Kwong, K. K., Belliveau, J. W., Chesler, D. A., Goldberg, I. E., Weisskoff, R. M., Poncelet, B. P., Kennedy, D. N., Hoppel, B. E., Cohen, M. S., Turner, R., Cheng, H. M., Brady, T. J., & Rosen, B. R. (1992,). *Dynamic magnetic resonance imaging of human brain activity during primary sensory stimulation.* Paper presented at the National Academy of Sciences.

Larsen, J. P., Hoien, T., Lundberg, I., & Odebaard, H. (1990). MRI evaluation of the size and symmetry of the planum temporale in adolescents with developmental dyslexia. *Brain and Language, 39,* 289–301.

Larsen, J. P., Hoien, T., & Odegaard, H. (1992). Magnetic resonance imaging of the corpus callosum in developmental dyslexia. *Cognitive Neuropsychology, 9,* 123–134.

Leisman, G., & Ashkenazi, M. (1980). Aetiological factors in dyslexia: IV. Cerebral hemispheres are functionally equivalent. *International Journal of Neurology, 11,* 157.

Lendon, C. L., Ashall, F., & Goate, A. M. (1997). Exploring the etiology of Alzheimer's disease using molecular genetics. *Journal of the American Medical Association, 277* (10), 825–831.

Leonard, C. M., Voeller, K. K. S., Lombardino, L. J., Morris, M. K., Hynd, G. W., Alexander, A. W., Andersen, H. G., Garofalakis, M., Honeyman, J. C., Mao, J., Agee, O. F., & Staab, E. V. (1993). Anaomalous cerebral structure in dyslexia revealed with magnetic resonance imaging. *Archives of Neurology, 50,* 461–469.

Lou, H. C., Henriksen, L., & Bruhn, P. (1990). Focal cerebral dysfunction in developmental learning disabilities. *Lancet, 335,* 8–11.

Lou, H. C., Henriksen, L., Bruhn, P., Borner, H., & Nielson, J. B. (1989). Striatal dysfunction in attention deficit and hyperkinetic disorder. *Archives of Neurology, 46,* 48–52.

Lou, H. C., Henriksen, L., Bruhn, P., & Psych, C. (1984). Focal cerebral hypoperfusion in children with dysphasia and/or attention deficit disorder. *Archives of Neurology, 41,* 825–829.

Lu, D., Pavlakis, S. G., Frank, Y., Bakshi, S., Pahwa, S., Gould, R. J., Sison, C., Hsu, C., Lesser, M., Hoberman, M., Barnett, T., & Hyman, R. A. (1996). Proton MR spectroscopy of the basal ganglia in healthy children and children with AIDS. *Radiology, 199* (2), 423–428.

Maier, M. (1995). In vivo magnetic resonance spectroscopy. Applications in psychiatry. *British Journal of Psychiatry, 167* (3), 299–306.

Minshew, N. J., Goldstein, G., Dombrowski, S. M., Panchalingam, K., & Pettegrew, J. W. (1993). A preliminary 31P MRS study of autism: Evidence for undersynthesis and increased degradation of brain membranes. *Biological Psychiatry, 33* (11–12), 762–773.

Minshew, N. J., & Pettegrew, J. W. (1996). Nuclear magnetic resonance spectroscopic studies of cortical development. In R. W. Thatcher, G. R. Lyon, J. Rumsey, & N. Krasnegor (Eds.), *Developmental neuroimaging: Mapping the development of brain and behavior* London: Academic Press.

Mountz, J. M., Tolbert, L. C., Lill, D. W., Katholi, C. R., & Liu, H. G. (1995). Functional deficits in autistic disorder: Characterization by technetium-99m-HMPAO and SPECT. *Journal of Nuclear Medicine, 36* (7), 1156–1162.

Murakami, J. W., Courchesne, E., Press, G. A., Yeung-Courchesne, R., & Hesselink, J. R. (1989). Reduced cerebellar hemisphere size and its relationship to vermal hypoplasia in autism. *Archives of Neurology, 46,* 689–694.

Nasrallah, H. A., Loney, J., Olson, S. C., McCalley-Whitters, M., Kramer, J., & Jacoby, C. G. (1986). Cortical atrophy in young adults with a history of hyperactivity in childhood. *Psychiatry Research, 17,* 241–246.

Newhouse, J. H., & Wiener, J. I. (1991). *Understanding MRI.* Boston: Little, Brown.

O'Tuama, L. A., & Treves, S. T. (1993). Brain single-photon emission computed tomography for behavior disorders in children. *Seminars in Nuclear Medicine, 23* (3), 255–264.

Ornitz, E. M., Atwell, C. W., Kaplan, A. R., & Westlake, J. R. (1985). Brain stem dysfunction in autism. *Archives of General Psychiatry, 42,* 1018–1025.

Peterson, B. S., Leckman, J., & Duncan, J. (1994). Corpus callosum morphology from magnetic resonance images in Tourette's syndrome. *Psychiatry Research, 55,* 85–99.

Peterson, B. S., Riddle, M. A., Cohen, D. J., Katz, L. D., Smith, J. C., Hardin, M. T., & Leckman, J. F. (1993, May). Reduced basal ganglia volumes in Tourette's syndrome using three-dimensional reconstruction techniques from magnetic resonance images. *Neurology, 43* 941–949.

Piven, J., Arndt, S., Bailey, J., Havercamp, S., Andreasen, N. C., & Palmer, P. (1995). An MRI study of brain size in autism. *American Journal of Psychiatry, 152,* 1145–1149.

Piven, J., Berthier, M. L., Starkstein, S. E., Nehme, E., Pearlson, G., & Folstein, S. (1990). Magnetic resonance imaging evidence for a defect of cerebral cortical development in autism. *American Journal of Psychiatry, 147* (6), 734–739.

Piven, J., Nehme, E., Simon, J., Barta, P., Pearlson, G., & Folstein, S. (1992). Magnetic resonance imaging in autism: Measurement of the cerebellum, pons and fourth ventricle. *Biological Psychiatry, 31,* 491–504.

Pollycove, M. (1995). The issue of the decade: Hormesis. *European Journal of Nuclear Medicine, 22,* 399–401.

Raichle, M. E., Grubb, R. L. J., & Gado, M. H. (1976). Correlation between regional cerebral blood flow and oxidative metabolism: In vivo studies in man. *Archives of Neurology, 33,* 523.

Reiss, A. L., Freund, L. S., Tseno, J. E., & Joshi, P. K. (1991). Neuroanatomy of fragile X females: The posterior fossa. *American Journal of Human Genetics, 49,* 279–288.

Reiss, A. L., Lee, J., & Freund, L. (1994). Neuroanatomy of fragile X syndrome: The temporal lobe. *Neurology, 44,* 1317–1324.

Reiss, A. L., Naidu, S., Abrams, M., Beaty, T., Bryan, R. N., & Moser, H. (1993). Neuroanatomy of Rett syndrome: A volumetric imaging study. *Annals of Neurology, 34,* 227–234.

Ritvo, E., & Garber, J. H. (1988). Cerebellar hypoplasia and autism. *New England Journal of Medicine, 319,* 1152.

Ritvo, E. R., Freeman, B. J., Scheibel, A. B., Duong, T., Robinson, H., Guthrie, D., & Ritvo, A. (1986). Lower Purkinje cell counts in the cerebella of four autistic subjects: Initial findings of the UCLA-NSAC Autopsy Research Report. *American Journal of Psychiatry, 143,* 862–866.

Rumsey, J. M., Andreason, P., Zametkin, A. J., Aquino, T., King, A. C., Hamburger, S. D., Pikus, A., Rapoport, J. L., & Cohen, R. M. (1992). Failure to acti-

vate the left temporoparietal cortex in dyslexia. *Archives of Neurology, 49,* 527.

Rumsey, J. M., Andreason, P., Zametkin, A. J., King, A. C., Hamburger, S. D., Aquino, T., Hanahan, A. P., Pikus, A., & Cohen, R. M. (1994). Right frontotemporal activation by tonal memory in dyslexia, an 015 PET study. *Biological Psychiatry, 36,* 171.

Rumsey, J. M., Berman, K. F., Denckla, M. B., Hamburger, S. D., Kruesi, M. J., & Weinberger, D. R. (1987). Regional cerebral blood flow in severe developmental dyslexia. *Archives of Neurology, 44,* 1144.

Rumsey, J. M., Casanova, M., Mannheim, G. B., Patronas, N., DeVaughn, N., Hamburger, S. D., & Aquino, T. (1996). Corpus callosum morphology, as measured with MRI, in dyslexic men. *Biological Psychiatry, 39,* 769–775.

Rumsey, J. M., Creasey, H., & Stepanek, J. S. (1988). Hemispheric asymmetries, fourth ventricular size and cerebellar morphology in autism. *Journal of Autism and Developmental Disorders, 18,* 127–137.

Rumsey, J. M., Dorwart, R., Vermess, M., Denckla, M. B., Kruesi, M. J. P., & Rapoport, J. L. (1986). Magnetic resonance imaging of brain anatomy in severe developmental dyslexia. *Archives of Neurology, 43,* 1045.

Rumsey, J. M., Zametkin, A. J., Andreason, P., Hanahan, A. P., Hamburger, S. D., Aquino, T., King, A. C., Pikus, A., & Cohen, R. M. (1994). Normal activation of frontotemporal language cortex in dyslexia, as measured with oxygen 15 positron emission tomography. *Archives of Neurology, 51,* 27.

Schaefer, G. B., & Bodensteiner, J. B. (1992). Evaluation of the child with idiopathic mental retardation. *Pediatric Neurology, 39* (4), 929–943.

Schaefer, G. B., Thompson, J. N., Bodensteiner, J. B., McConnell, J. M., Kimberling, W. J., Gay, C. T., Dutton, W. D., Hutchings, D. C., & Gray, S. B. (1996). Hypopolasia of the cerebellar vermis in neurogenetic syndromes. *Annals of Neurology, 39,* 382–385.

Schultz, R. T., Cho, N. K., Staib, L. H., Kier, L. E., Fletcher, J. M., Saywitz, S. E., Shankweiler, D. P., Katz, L., Gore, J. C., Duncan, J. S., & Shaywitz, B. A. (1994). Brain morphology in normal and dyslexic children: The influence of sex and age. *Annals of Neurology, 35,* 732–742.

Semrud-Clikeman, M., Filipek, P. A., Biederman, J., Steingard, R., Kennedy, D., Renshaw, P., & Bekken, K. (1994). Attention-deficit hyperactivity disorder: Magnetic resonance imaging morphometric analysis of the corpus callosum. *Journal of the American Academy of Child and Adolescent Psychiatry, 33* (6), 875–881.

Shaywitz, B. A., Shaywitz, S. E., Byrne, T., Cohen, D. J., & Rothman, S. (1983). Attention deficit disorder: Quantitative analysis of CT. *Neurology, 33,* 1500–1503.

Shenton, M. E., Kikinis, R., Jolesz, F. A., Pollak, S. D., LeMay, M., Wible, C. G., Hokama, H., Martin, J., Metcalf, D., Coleman, M., & McCarley, R. W. (1997). Abnormalities of the left temporal lobe and thought disorder in schizophrenia. *New England Journal of Medicine, 327,* 604–612.

Sieg, K. G., Buckingham, D., Gaffney, G. R., Preston, D. F., & Sieg, K. G. (1993). HMPAO SPECT brain imaging of Gilles de la Tourette's syndrome. *Clinical Nuclear Medicine, 18,* 255.

Singer, H. S., Reiss, A. L., Brown, J. E., Aylward, E. H., Shih, B., Chee, E., Harris, E. L., Reader, M. J., Chase, G. A., Bryan, R. N., & Denckla, M. B. (1992). Volumetric MRI changes in basal ganglia of children with Tourette's syndrome. *Neurology, 43,* 950–956.

Slichter, G. P. (1990). *Principles of magnetic resonance.* Berlin: Springer-Verlag.

Sokoloff, L. (1981). Relationships among local functional activity, energy metabolism, and blood flow in the central nervous system. *Federal Proceedings, 40,* 2311.

Steingard, R. J., Renshaw, P. F., Yurgelun-Todd, D., Appelmans, K. E., Lyoo, K., Shorrock, K. L., Bucci, J. P., Cesena, M., Abebe, D., Zurakowski, D., Poussaint, T. Y., & Barnes, P. (1996). Structural abnormalities in brain magnetic resonance images of depressed children. *Journal of the American Academy of Child and Adolescent Psychiatry, 35* (3), 307–311.

Thompson, J. S., Ross, R. J., & Horwitz, S. J. (1980). The role of computed axial tomography in the study of the child with minimal brain dysfunction. *Journal of Learning Disabilities, 13* (6), 48–51.

Tzika, A. A., Massoth, R. J., Ball, W. S., Majumdar, S., Dunn, R. S., & Kirks, D. R. (1993). Cerebral perfusion in children: Detection with dynamic contrast-enhanced T2-weighted MR images. *Pediatric Radiology, 187,* 449–458.

Wieser, H. G. (1994). PET and SPECT in epilepsy. *European Neurology, 34* (Suppl. 1), S58–S62.

Wong, D., & Resnick, S. (1995). Neurotransmission. In H. Wagner (Ed.), *Principles of nuclear medicine* (pp. 590–594). Philadelphia: W. B. Saunders.

Zametkin, A. J., Liebenauer, L. L., Fitzgerald, G. A., King, A. C., Minkunas, D. V., Herscovitch, P., Yamada, E. M., & Cohen, R. M. (1993). Brain metabolism in teenagers with attention-deficit hyperactivity disorder. *Archives of General Psychiatry, 50* (5), 333–340.

Zilbovicius, M., Garreau, B., Tzourio, N., Mazoyer, B., Bruck, B., Martinot, J. L., Raynaud, C., Samson, Y., Syrota, A., & Lelord, G. (1992). Regional cerebral blood flow in childhood autism: A SPECT study. *American Journal of Psychiatry, 149* (7), 924–930.

SECTION II
Treatment

8 / Reader's Guide to Child and Adolescent Psychiatric (CAP) Treatment

Saul Isaac Harrison and Spencer Eth

Before we describe the format and suggest strategies for using the Treatments section of the *Handbook,* the P in CAP mandates linguistic precision. The terms *child* and *adolescent* require no explanation. But a sad relic of our field's rich traditions requires explanation that the word *psychiatry* is used in the clinical processes sections of the *Handbook* exclusively in its precise original meaning derived from the Greek words for mind and healing. In the clinical processes section, psychiatry refers to knowledge and skills; it does not refer to professionals. It has become acceptable over the years for the several professions schooled in psychiatric processes to be designated as mental health professions. But that euphemism does not seem to do justice to the rich mix of biopsychosocial knowledge and skills that comprise CAP treatments. Thus, in the pages that follow, references to child and adolescent psychiatry bespeak multidimensional, multidisciplined helping processes.

The foregoing explanation is necessitated by an unfortunate feature of our field's rich traditions. It denotes a deficiency of rational planning in the best interests of children, adolescents, and their families. It reflects, instead, a historical brew of economics, elitism, and politics combining to create and reinforce the formal educational and accreditational boundaries that delineate the several professions participating in child and adolescent psychiatry processes. Consistent with the arbitrary nature of the system we inherited, each of the professions possesses its own vertical career ladder with minimal, if any, horizontal permeability. For instance, if a nurse wishes to become a physician, he or she must start afresh and be educated as if no knowledge or skills had been acquired in the processes of qualifying and practicing as a nurse.

That this section on treatments is subdivided conceptually into distinct chapters focused on different aspects of therapeutic interventions reflects no more than the editors' organizational decisions. That obvious-sounding assertion is intended to underscore, as categorically as we can, that our editorial efforts to subdivide knowledge conceptually should be distinguished explicitly from what prevailed in our field in the 1960s and 1970s. Those decades were characterized by a dysfunctional balkanization into noncommunicating therapeutic parishes. The chapters that follow are designed for intercommunication to enrich one another and the effectiveness of therapeutic interventions with youngsters.

Thus, the separation of psychodynamic, cognitive, behavioral, and family interventions into distinct chapters in no way reflects the clinical needs, for example, of 6-year-old Victoria, who has devoted most of her life to cancer chemotherapy and related travails. Fortunately, her malignancy is controlled, but her behavioral adjustment in school is anything but.

Very likely, Victoria could benefit from cognitive and behavioral assessment and interventions to identify and to help her learn and practice alternatives to what had been both adaptive and useful in the hospitals, where she spent most of her life, but that are counterproductive in her school and community.

Perhaps Victoria would benefit also from sensitive psychodynamic attention to her individual means of coping with the years of pain and terror. In any other circumstance, what Victoria had to suffer would be considered abusive. The psychological sequelae inflicted by life-saving measures merit therapeutic attention. It is probable also that family systems interventions would contribute to healing the scars inflicted on her family.

Those are but a few of the chapters that might pertain to Victoria. In organizing the clinical processes sections in this volume and in Volume V, we conceived of the multiple chapters as building blocks available for constructing clinical processes for a particular patient.

Whether Victoria's therapeutic interventions will be the responsibility of a single clinician or of a coordinated team of clinicians will depend on a

169

range of circumstances. Nevertheless, it is vital that each of us remember that expanding our individual therapeutic range may require more than accumulating knowledge and skills. It also may entail attention to dexterity in therapeutic use of self.

Now for some global illustrations. Psychodynamically oriented interventions, for example, tend to postulate therapeutic change via a cognitive-affective reexperiencing of the internalized past. This reexperiencing occurs in the course of special kinds of interaction with the clinician, who endeavors to keep personal reactions under control while observing personal reactions. Clinical self-observation endeavors to discriminate objective professional reactions from those stimulated by the particular patient, and those reactions that stem from a clinician's own experiences and psychology.

Simultaneously, the patient is encouraged to look at self, explore the past, and study its effect on current life. The result is a deep and powerful encounter that has been compared to elements of the religious-magical interaction between shaman and patient. Psychodynamically oriented exploratory psychotherapy entails clinicians experiencing the patient through ourselves, almost as if we shared the patient's phenomenology.

In contrast, biological and behavioral interventions burden clinicians with different requirements by virtue of incorporating more of a naturalistic and scientific mode. It may be advantageous to maintain distance from the patient in order to maximize clinical objectivity. Prediction and control of the problem tend to be emphasized, perhaps at the expense of subjective understanding of the patient's inner experience.

Family treatments and other social interventions conceptualized and organized around systems perspectives tend to seek therapeutic effect by clinicians affiliating, so to speak, as professionals with the family or other social system. We may employ the relationship to alter individual roles in the dysfunctional transactional processes of the family system and its structural organization. Thus unlike in the foregoing characterizations, in systems interventions clinicians may not have to guard as vigorously against communicating spontaneous personal reactions. Generally, those reactions will be system-syntonic. If they are not, they can be employed as exploratory probes that contribute to establishing an affiliation with the family and experiencing its pressures in the course of effecting healthier solutions.

Before the foregoing global characterizations were understood in clinical practice, it was not uncommon for astute observers to aptly describe as "peek-a-boo" and "split brain" the efforts of American psychiatrists in the 1950s to add the new psychopharmacological interventions to the then prevailing American psychodynamic treatments.

The range of available building blocks are evident in the list of chapters. That the descriptions of treatments follows clinical assessment/intervention strategy planning in the preceding volume represents editorial reflection of clinical reality. But that in no way diminishes the inherent merit of the ancient professional wisdom about treatment beginning with the initial contact, that is, in the clinical assessment preceding therapeutic intervention, and that ongoing assessment should be an inherent and constant part of treatment.

In other words, readers focused on treatments are advised to peruse the building blocks available in volume five. Among those that could directly enrich treatment efforts are the series of decision trees about different presenting problems, the chapters about clinical communication, ethics, and the collection of clinical truths highlighted at the end of volume five's epilogue about clinical CAP's future.

9 / Crisis Intervention

Joseph J. Jankowski

A psychological crisis is defined as a disturbance in-thoughts, feelings, or behavior for which immediate intervention is required. Crisis intervention services proliferated in 1963, when the Community Mental Health Centers Act designated them to be one of 5 essential services in federally funded community mental health centers (Gerson & Bassuk, 1980). This act shifted the focus of mental health services from hospitals to less restrictive community-based intervention alternatives that required crisis intervention services to be provided within a variety of alternative settings.

Today crisis intervention remains a focal point of any mental health delivery system as patients often are seen initially in crisis and afterward referred for follow-up care. Crisis intervention may include one or several visits with the patient and/ or family, depending on patient needs, or may include referral to a program for further evaluation or short-term intervention to resolve the crisis. During such interventions the clinician often attempts to identify a central issue that has resulted in the patient's psychological disequilibrium. If this central issue cannot be readily identified or strategies developed for intervention, the patient might require admission to an inpatient unit, acute residential treatment facility, or remain at home with input from a team of outreach clinicians who will maintain the intensity and directiveness of crisis intervention. As the central issue is identified, appropriate intervention plans can be established to manage it, and other issues that might impact on the patient can be considered.

When a crisis arises, help may be sought in a variety of settings including the home, schools, pediatric outpatient clinics, pediatric inpatient units, outpatient psychotherapy offices, day care settings, and emergency rooms. The reasons for referral, dependent on the referring setting, are as follows:

Setting	Reasons for Referral
Home	Running away, school phobia, substance abuse, over-aggressivity, shoplifting
School	Overaggressivity, injurious to peers or self, school avoidance, truancy, physical and/or sexual abuse
Pediatric Outpatient Clinics	Noncompliance with medications, pregnancy, sexually transmitted diseases, physical and/or sexual abuse
Pediatric Medical Inpatient Units	Uncontrollable behaviors, organic vs. psychological problems, medication side effects, noncompliance with medications, physical trauma with loss of limb or disfigurement, death and dying, adverse effects of medical illness
Outpatient Psychotherapy Offices	Suicidal plan or attempts; sexual abuse; cannot be maintained at home, school, or community because of uncontrolled behavior; eating disorders, family violence
Day Care Setting	Physical and/or sexual abuse, severe developmental delay, neglect, hyperactivity, overaggressivity, injurious to peers
Emergency Room	Suicide plans and/or attempts, overaggressivity or assaultive behavior, runaway, substance abuse, arrests, physical and/or sexual abuse

171

Most referrals for crisis intervention result from a family problem rather than an intrapsychic crisis in the child (Burks & Hoekstra, 1964). Sixty percent of children and adolescents receiving crisis intervention reported that they had lost a parent or near relative through illness, hospitalization, marital separation, or death within 3 weeks of the onset of their symptoms (Morrison & Smith, 1975). Since family problems often play a major role in the onset of a psychological crisis for children and adolescents, the family becomes a major focus during the intervention.

Theory: Psychological Crises and Intervention

Lindemann (1944), considered the father of crisis intervention, reported on the Coconut Grove fire in Boston and made the following observations:

- Acute grief is a specific syndrome with psychological and somatic symptoms.
- It may occur right after a crisis or be delayed, be exaggerated, or even be absent in some patients.
- The response may appear as a distorted reaction unrelated to grief itself.
- By utilizing intervention techniques, such distorted reactions can be transformed into a normal grief reaction and resolved.

Caplan (1961) and Parad (1978) both describe homeostatic psychological mechanisms that maintain equilibrium in the individual and family. In their view, a crisis creates a psychological disequilibrium in the patient that changes the individual's and family's homeostatic mechanisms and thereby places the patient and family under unusual stress. They also discuss the "perceptual" meaning of crisis to the family: (1) the stressful event poses a problem that is by definition insoluble in the immediate future; (2) the problem overtaxes the psychological resources of the family since it is beyond their traditional problem-solving capability; (3) the situation is perceived as a threat or danger to the life goals of family members; (4) the crisis period is characterized by tension that mounts to a peak, then falls; (5) the crisis situation awakens unresolved key problems from both the near and distant past.

Parad and Caplan (1978) define crisis intervention as entering into the life situation of an individual, family, or group to alleviate the impact of a crisis-inducing stress in order to help mobilize the resources of those directly affected. "Individual-centered clinical observations" are not adequate to understand the etiology of a crisis, they believe, and they recommend the use of a 3-dimensional perspective that involves intrapersonal, interpersonal, and suprapersonal (or transactional) processes. They also recommend that the family be interviewed while its members are actively coping with the stressors that led to the crisis. They suggest that clinicians gather and analyze the data with the following issues in mind regarding the family: style, value system, communication, role system, problem solving, and need response pattern.

Family sociologist Hill (1978) reports that those factors conducive to a successful adjustment during a crisis include family adaptability, family integration, affectional relations among family members, good marital adjustment, companionable parent-child relationships, family council control and decision making, social participation of spouse/parents, and prior successful experiences with crises.

The dysfunctional aspects of a family often are not readily discernible. During the crisis, the child's presentation is highlighted; the family's involvement often is camouflaged by the "background noise" of the behavior that led to the referral for crisis intervention. The family's role must be clarified by interviewing family members and ancillary sources. Although it is seductive initially to consider the central cause of the crisis to be related principally to the child, more likely it is related to the family.

The goal of crisis intervention is to "rapidly assess and treat psychological disequilibrium within the natural social environment" (Eisler & Hersen, 1973). However, crisis intervention with children and adolescents should enable the entire family to function better but not at the expense of any 1 member (Berlin, 1970). Morrison (1969) recommends meeting with the families of suicidal children and adolescents as soon as possible. He notes that most of these children experienced family disruption with threatened or actual separation. Turgay (1982), on discussing psychiatric emergencies in children, reports that "the defensiveness of the individual and family against exploration and treatment is decreased when the patient is in an emergency." Therefore, in order to make inroads on the "family problem," the intervention must take place during this period of decreased psychological defensiveness. Once the crisis subsides, the family returns to its prior functioning and defensiveness until another incident occurs to indicate that the family problem still exists and requires intervention. The child or adolescent in crisis will continue providing signals, such as unhappiness, withdrawal, sadness, or avoidance of school. These signals, if unattended, will escalate to crisis behavior, such as dropping out of school, running away, taking an overdose, or making a suicide attempt. It is during this crisis period that the intervention team has an opportunity to observe and alter the dysfunctional system of the family for the patient's benefit.

During crisis intervention, several tasks must be accomplished with the family. These include:

1. Engaging the patient and family
2. Joining the family—being accepted within the inner circle of the family to view the dysfunctional aspects
3. Reframing or redefining the problem together with patient and family so that it is not only the patient's problem
4. Integrating change into the family's current functioning to help the patient.
5. Follow-up or continuity of care to help the family and patient maintain psychological homeostasis by improving family functioning

During this process, clinicians must work intensively to identify and alter those factors that led to the crisis. Relating the child's symptoms to the family's problems often frees the child from an untenable position within the family and alleviates the crisis. However, the family must be encouraged to complete the assessment and treatment to avoid recidivism.

Assessment

During crisis periods, parents are interviewed initially with the child to establish a data base of complaints, past medical and psychiatric illnesses, and prior treatments, and to identify those community-based agencies or persons involved previously.

A crisis assessment ideally is performed in a focused manner isolating the central issues leading to the crisis and contains the following components: engagement; anxiety reduction; clarification of the "real" complaint; traditional individual assessment tasks; family assessment; and social/educational/legal assessment.

ENGAGEMENT

Engagement of patient and family begins with the initial encounter. It is helpful initially to interview the patient and family together clarifying actions and behaviors and obtaining as reliable a history as possible regarding symptoms, past medical and psychiatric illnesses, and current functioning. A systems approach to assessing the patient and family can enhance engagement. This approach includes a clarification of the interpersonal dynamics that exist among and between individual family members and the family as a whole. Such an approach is also helpful in identifying the central issue of the child's crisis. For example, the child may have taken an overdose of medication in a suicide gesture as a mechanism to maintain the family in the face of the parents' troubled marriage.

A major function of engagement is to allow each family member, including the patient, to express themselves regarding the child's crisis. Engagement is invaluable for follow-up by enhancing patient and family's compliance during intervention.

REDUCING ANXIETY

Reducing anxiety avoids immobilization of the patient and family. Often the patient in crisis is brought for care because the level of anxiety generated has exceeded the family's tolerance. This anxiety can be reduced by (1) interviewing asymptomatic members of the family or social network to obtain an objective view; (2) focusing on real events; (3) using a direct interviewing style; (4) making empathic references to the difficulties experienced by the patient and members of the family and social network; (5) allowing these persons to learn more about each other; (6) avoiding blame; and (7) helping to prepare them for the task of problem solving and disposition which will now occur.

CLARIFY THE "REAL" COMPLAINT

Clarifying the real complaint is more difficult than it first appears. The initial complaint highlights the current central issue of the crisis but is usually not directly obvious. For example, a patient with an initial complaint of running away may be brought for services because of sexual abuse occurring in the environment. The parent and/or other family members may know about it but do not acknowledge it. Until this central issue is uncovered and intervention provided, the patient's crisis will most likely persist or recur regardless of the amount or intensity of intervention provided.

TRADITIONAL INDIVIDUAL ASSESSMENT TASKS

Traditional individual assessment tasks include psychiatric and medical diagnoses, impact of behavior on family and social network, safety issues, and mental status exam.

Psychiatric and medical diagnoses are determined by detailed history taking about past and current medical illnesses, medications, substance abuse, and injuries. If needed, medical tests can be obtained, such as serum and/or urine for toxicology screen, complete blood count, urinalysis, blood urea nitrogen/creatinine, liver and thyroid function, electroencephalogram, magnetic resonance imaging/computed tomography scans, and X rays.

The impact of the patient's crisis behavior on family members and social network often reaches a threshold beyond which the individuals involved cease their denial of the problem and/or realize they cannot manage it safely. At that point, the child is brought in for care. This impact must be acknowledged and discussed during the assessment phase.

In assessing safety issues, the clinicians must consider homicidality, suicidality, fire setting, accidents, and assaultiveness. During the assessment of safety, new and painful material may be brought to awareness. If this is followed by rebuttal, anger, hostility, or rejection by the family or social network, the patient's safety risk may increase. However, if the individuals are compassionate, understanding, and accepting and if communication is enhanced, the patient's safety risk will likely decrease.

Often the assessment worker must decide whether the patient can go home. In that case, it must be known whether the caregiver can provide for the safety of the patient. If the caregiver is understanding, firm, and reliable in monitoring the child's behavior at home and in the community, the patient can be sent home. However, if safety remains in question, arrangements must be made either to hospitalize the child psychiatrically or place him or her in an alternative or temporary living arrangement. This is especially relevant in cases involving sexual and/or physical abuse. In such cases, a child abuse petition will need to be filed immediately. If the caregiver cannot provide for the patient's safety, alternative arrangements for the child's care will need to be made through the court and the child placed elsewhere.

A mental status examination is performed throughout the entire evaluation, including interview data from the patient, family, and social network. Major aspects of the mental status exam are obtained when the evaluator meets alone with the patient. However, by interviewing the patient with family and/or social network members, the examiner obtains valuable supplementary data, including whether the patient is aware of his or her impact on others; whether the patient reveals disturbed thinking; whether he or she is properly oriented to events, issues, and dates; and whether the patient is depressed or manic in the presence of others.

In group interview sessions with the patient, family, and/or others, themes of paranoia, suspiciousness, obsessiveness, inappropriateness, repression, depression, anxiety, and phobias may be expressed that might not otherwise be mentioned when interviewing the child or adolescent alone.

FAMILY ASSESSMENT

Family assessment includes those family members who are immediately present and with whom the evaluator can communicate. Understanding how the family perceives the patient's problem usually helps the clinician to frame the crisis in a specific and practical context, allowing him or her to classify and acknowledge the response more easily. Also, although the child or adolescent is the designated patient, other family problems may be driving the request for services or creating the crisis.

Development of a genogram utilizing past and present medical and psychiatric illnesses within the family, including prior attempts at treatment, can be helpful in the diagnostic and planning course of intervention. Other data to be obtained include a chronology of past life events, alliances, level of functioning, and communication styles in the family. This information will help the clinician assess potential strengths and weaknesses that will aid in reunifying the child and family once the crisis is over.

It is also helpful to determine the family's agenda. How do they present the child's problem and what do they expect from the intervention? Do they intend to extrude the patient from the family or reunite with the patient? Are they expecting psychiatric hospitalization, day treatment, or outpatient follow-up? What type of psychiatric service has been provided previously, and was it beneficial or unsuccessful? What does the family expect from this crisis intervention? Frequently family members expect intervention to be "magical" and fantasize that long-standing, chronic problems will be ameliorated. It is important for the clinician to point out that the central issue that is related to the current crisis will be identified and intervention provided. Other agendas, such as long-standing anger and hostility directed at family members, not attending school or substance abuse, will require longer-term intervention as follow-up to this episode of crisis intervention.

SOCIAL/EDUCATIONAL/LEGAL ASSESSMENT

Social/educational/legal assessment includes the child's involvement with and success/failure in dealing with peers, teachers, and community agencies. The data required for this part of the assessment includes the family's prior involvement with governmental agencies, including social services, welfare, foster care, police, youth services, and the courts. Are the child and family isolated from the mainstream of society, or do they have access through formal/informal groups and activities? Is the family interested/involved in educational matters? Does the family obey the laws of society? Children often mirror the pattern of the

family; if the family is socially involved, educationally minded, and obey the laws of society, the children are likely to do the same.

Intervention Plan

The assessment of a crisis must generate an intervention plan, the development and implementation of which involves a number of considerations, such as basic factors, types and levels of intervention programs, and categories of psychiatric treatment provided.

BASIC FACTORS

During assessment, the clinician obtains information about a variety of problems. Some will require immediate intervention and others, intermediate or longer-term psychiatric follow-up. Not all of the problems can be solved during the crisis intervention. The clinician attempts to identify the central problem that can be practically resolved to reduce the impact of the crisis and return the patient to a functional level.

In crisis intervention, a number of practical problems need to be addressed.

Daily Care and Basic Functioning: What is the patient's capacity or need for self-care? Will he or she accept the care of others without undue resistance or lack of compliance? For example, will the patient accept food and medication and abide by the basic laws of hygiene such as washing, toileting, and dressing?

Safety of Patient and Others: Safety issues concern whether the patient can be trusted not to injure self or others or if the family/social network can ensure this. Will the patient require 24-hour observation and containment?

Acceptability to Family: Can family members tolerate the patient's aberrant behavior, work with him or her in changing behaviors, and not feel threatened or attacked by the patient? Can the patient remain living in the family?

Tolerance of Community: Community tolerance depends on its capacity to accept the patient's behavior, for example, stealing, fire setting, perpetration of sexual/physical abuse, selling drugs, destruction of property, and violence toward others. The community may be more tolerant of some types of behavior than others. If the community is not tolerant, the patient may require placement in another setting.

Role of Agencies: How does the patient's problem impact on a variety of agencies, such as Department of Social Services, courts, and school? For example, the Department of Social Services might be concerned about an escalating level of aberrant behaviors, which could cause the child to be extruded from foster or residential care. Another example is the court's concern about repeated delinquent acts that lead to arrests and incarceration. On the other hand, the school is likely to be concerned about failing grades, truancy, and disruptive behavior in the classroom.

Need for Alternative Placement: The need for alternative placement is a major factor to be considered at any time during crisis intervention. Whether a placement outside of the home is required depends on the answers to the following questions:

1. Is the psychopathology of the child/adolescent and/or family so debilitating that the patient will require a therapeutic environment outside the home?
2. Is the patient safe in his or her current environment?
3. Can the home/family or current placement provide for his or her immediate physical and emotional care?
4. Have several other attempts at crisis intervention failed?
5. Has it been impossible to delineate the central issue with the child and family while the patient remains in the home?

The type of alternative placement depends on information obtained during the assessment and intervention phases of crisis intervention. A patient who is acutely suicidal or homicidal during assessment might require inpatient psychiatric hospitalization on a locked or staff-secure unit. However, a patient may manifest behaviors that might require alternative placement during the intervention phase. These include running away or a continuation of self-destructive acts. If sexual/physical abuse by a perpetrator living at home is discovered, the patient may require placement in an acute residential treatment facility or a therapeutic foster home. The placement of a child might be accompanied by an abuse/neglect petition (report) as well as placement of the child in the legal custody of the state.

TYPES AND LEVELS OF INTERVENTION PROGRAMS

When an intervention plan is created while the child is living at home, the targets for behavioral change and expectations of the intervention must be made clear to the patient, family, and others. Clinical problems often require stratification of acute, intermediate, and long-term intervention goals. Crisis intervention usually requires meeting immediate and intermediate goals.

Acute intervention goals must be specific—for example, prevent patient from running away, maintain safety of patient and others, provide protection in child abuse cases, manage acute psychiatric decompensation, and provide 24-hour care for patient unable to care for self due to, say, delirium. These goals are verbalized clearly to the patient, family, and others because these problems require a rapid response, either immediately or within 24 hours.

Intermediate goals require a lengthier period of intervention. They may include treating severe depression, psychosis, organic brain disorders, and severe anxiety. Additional intermediate interventions require removing weapons from the home, obtaining treatment for substance abuse, and dealing with psychiatrically disturbed parent(s), including a parent who abuses a spouse. Also, if the patient has a learning or cognitive disorder, he or she will require neuropsychological testing and perhaps a rearrangement of educational objectives. Intermediate goals require intervention from 24 hours to 30 days.

Long-term goals usually include patients with pervasive developmental disorder, Tourette's disorder, anorexia nervosa, schizophrenia, bipolar disorder, recurring substance abuse, and organic brain disorders. These more chronic disorders, although at times needing acute or intermediate intervention, generally require interventions of longer duration.

Acute Intervention Services: These are provided rapidly to the patient in need—within 24 hours. They include the 24-hour hot line, emergency room services, and mobile teams.

The *24-hour hot line* allows patients to telephone a trained person immediately to whom they can express their problem and gain advice or be directed to obtain help. These hot lines are staffed by individuals who are trained and receive ongoing supervision to handle emergencies over the telephone.

Emergency room services are available on a 24-hour basis to accept patients in crisis. They are staffed with highly trained medical and psychiatric providers who can deal with a wide range of problems. Generally, patients remain in such a setting for less than 24 hours. The intervention can be intense but is usually short-lived. Follow-up care needs to be arranged on discharge or transfer. Such units have assumed the role of psychiatric evaluator, not only as triage. Such services also can provide for medical evaluations and tests concurrently with psychiatric evaluation. This is especially helpful in cases where there is concern about toxicity of medications, overdose, substance abuse, injuries, or other medical/psychiatric problems.

Approximately two-thirds of patients going to an emergency room for crisis intervention require medical intervention, including blood tests for alcohol levels, urine and blood tests for toxic screens, induced vomiting after ingestion, and treatment of superficial wounds. Also, children who have been physically abused can receive X rays to reveal fractures; those who have been raped or sexually abused can receive appropriate genital exams, cultures, and blood tests for sexually transmitted diseases, including HIV testing. The provision of this type of service ranges from a walk-in service within a community mental health center to an emergency room in a general hospital.

Mobile teams include staff who, within 30 to 60 minutes, arrive on-site at the patient's home, community agency, school, court, or general hospital to provide emergency services. They usually are directed via telecommunications to the patient's current location. The mobile clinician can call for further help, such as police or ambulance, as needed. Additionally, the mobile clinicians have immediate access to a central clinical supervisor with whom they can discuss the case, including diagnosis, intervention, and disposition. They also might have access to a patient data base including past medical/psychiatric records and current placement availability at a variety of participating programs.

Intermediate Intervention Services: These services often require the utilization of staff and programs other than the initial crisis assessment team itself. These intervention services include a 24- to 72-hour holding unit, brief hospitalization, acute residential treatment, day treatment, family crisis teams, and detoxification units.

A *24- to 72-hour holding unit* may be used in managing a patient who is in an acute crisis. The 5 most common uses of such a unit include assessing suicide potential, gathering further history, assessing dangerousness, ensuring medical stability, and linking with other agencies to find alternate placements. This service site reduces hospitalization rates and overall costs to the mental health system. Hospitalization rates drop from 52% to 36% when using such a holding unit for crisis intervention (Gillig et al., 1989). It has been demonstrated that one-fourth of all psychiatric patients seen in an emergency room can be managed well in a holding unit (Ianzito, Fine, Sprague, & Pestana, 1978).

The holding unit provides containment for patients who may be under the influence of substances, are suspected of having a head injury, have been traumatized by sexual/physical abuse and cannot immediately return to their prior living arrangement, or where their clinical condition requires more stabilization before a final disposition plan can be made. Often these units are attached programmatically to an emergency room in a general or psychiatric hospital. They are helpful in allowing a lengthier period of observation/ evaluation of a patient in order to develop a more refined intervention plan, thereby avoiding a more restrictive or intense treatment. Since these patients cannot be discharged at the point of evaluation in the emergency room, if such a unit were not available, the patient would need to be admitted to an inpatient psychiatric unit for basically the same service reasons.

Brief hospitalization (3 to 5 days), increasingly conceptualized as crisis management, is used for patients who require further diagnostic clarification, recommendations for further care, and psychiatric stabilization, which often includes a psychopharmacologic plan. This intervention allows the patient to be better stabilized and the intervention plan to be more clearly directed, for example, to include family therapy and psychopharmacologic interventions. There is better assessment of the patient's potential to harm self or others. Such hospitalization is also helpful for the family to regain its coping capacity vis-à-vis the patient and to be aided regarding continued management at discharge. Such a unit will provide medical backup, intense staffing, and containment. Therefore, it can accept patients who are difficult to manage, have serious underlying medical and/or psychiatric problems, or have comorbid psychiatric disorders—for example, eating disorders and major depression, organic mood disorders, anxiety disorder and learning disability, or posttraumatic stress disorder and major depression.

Acute residential treatment (7 to 21 days) is used for emotionally troubled children and adolescents who require placement out of the home but do not need the intensive clinical stabilization provided by an inpatient psychiatric unit. These units provide less containment and less specialized staffing, and are helpful for children with posttraumatic stress disorder, substance abuse, conduct disorder, and adjustment disorders.

Day treatment programs (10 to 21 days) are helpful as step-down programs from inpatient and acute residential units. Patients who are recidivistic and have recurrent crises can be managed in a day treatment program, which provides more intense intervention and stabilization than outpatient care. Children generally enter this type of program at 9:00 A.M. and leave at 5:30 P.M. for 5 days per week. Their day includes individual, group, and family psychotherapy as well as recreational and educational interventions. They serve children with eating disorders, anxiety disorders, posttraumatic stress disorder, bipolar disorder, and pervasive developmental disorder with comorbid features.

The *family crisis team* (21 to 22 days) provides home visits to stabilize the entire family. It can be used as a step-down plan after psychiatric hospitalization or admission to an acute residential treatment center. It also can be used as an adjunct to outpatient therapy or in lieu of inpatient hospitalization after an emergency room evaluation.

Staff members of this team visit the home 3 times per week, extending the evaluation period, arranging for outpatient care, providing crisis intervention on site in the community (home, school, day care center, boy's/girl's club). Their emphasis generally is on the family, and they im-prove the child's functioning by helping the family integrate around family or social network members who are better functioning and supportive. Children with posttraumatic stress disorder, phobias, school avoidance, conduct disorders, and adjustment disorders respond well to this form of intervention.

Detox units (3 to 5 days) for adolescents are becoming commonplace due to the high prevalence of substance abuse in this population. Substance-abusing patients are difficult to evaluate clinically on a crisis basis unless the therapist can arrange for detoxification. Detox centers serve as crisis intervention centers because patients often come there in emotional turmoil, requiring stabilization and reunification with their families. These patients often have been out of school and not participating in their communities. Unfortunately, detox units do not keep children for more than 3 to 5 days. However, in many cases this is the only place to engage the substance-abusing adolescent and his or her family, directing them into needed longer-term intervention. As a result, although the detox center is important in getting the child temporarily off substances, its more vital task is one of engagement, providing for acute care and arranging for intermediate crisis intervention, such as day treatment program or a family crisis team.

After-care is needed regardless of the type of acute or intermediate intervention service provided, because usually follow-up transition care from one of the specialized intervention units back to the community is needed. After-care providers are critical in maintaining patients in their own environment following intervention in a more restrictive setting.

After-care services support the efforts of the patient and family to resolve their crisis within the family. They also assist community agencies or resources that made the referral to continue providing ongoing treatment/management (Youthdale Psychiatric Service, 1987).

TYPES OF PSYCHIATRIC TREATMENT PROVIDED

The types of psychiatric treatment utilized in crisis intervention include social network therapy, psychopharmacology, family therapy, individual therapy, and supportive group therapy.

Social Network Therapy: This type of therapy

includes all human relationships that have a lasting impact on the life of the individual. In social network therapy, the focus tends to be on nuclear family members, kin, neighbors and friends (Speck & Attneave, 1973). Its therapeutic approach relies on the concept that shared psychopathology exists in the social milieu of the patient and that treating the network is vital to the patient's recovery. Most models of social network therapy rely on creating new support systems (Greenblatt, Becerra, & Serafetinides, 1982).

Network therapy identifies psychopathology as within the social network. Therefore, a major therapeutic goal is altering the network to benefit the patient by making it more responsive to the individuals within it. Such therapy, of course, requires becoming familiar with as many individuals within the patient's community as possible.

Psychopharmacology: Medications have been used extensively in crisis intervention to help stabilize patients so they are more manageable and accepted by family and community. They are used during crises primarily for anxiety, mania, depression, psychosis, and delirium. During the acute intervention phase, short-acting benzodiazepines can be used for anxiety and mania and neuroleptics for psychosis and delirium. Since depression cannot be treated rapidly with antidepressants, a benzodiazepine can be used to alleviate agitation secondary to depression.

During the intermediate intervention phase, other medications can be used as follows:

- Selective serotonin reuptake inhibitors for anxiety and/or depression
- Neuroleptics for psychosis
- Antiseizure medications (valproate, carbamazepine) for manic behavior or bipolar cycling
- Lithium for overaggressivity, dangerous behavior, bipolar disorder

Family Therapy: Family therapy is a vital treatment modality in crisis intervention. Working with the family is valuable and necessary for acute and intermediate problems, as mentioned earlier. During the acute intervention phase, the family needs to feel included, be part of the decision for a particular form of treatment, and have a role in managing the patient when he or she returns to the community. Family needs and requirements must be considered and maintained throughout the patient's treatment.

Also, as noted previously, families are more receptive to acknowledging problems and accepting intervention during a crisis. Often, before seeking help, the family and patient may have tried a number of unsuccessful ways to cope with the problem.

During intermediate intervention, family therapy becomes progressively more intense. Issues within the family that relate to the patient's psychiatric problems—genetic, psychological, substance abuse, or child abuse—usually surface and require intervention.

Throughout the treatment of families in crisis, the clinician needs to stress the family's singular importance, the need for family members to be involved if the treatment is to work, and the importance of the information family members have about the problem (Perlmutter, 1983).

During crisis intervention, the tasks of family therapy include: (1) increasing the capacity of family members to handle future crises; (2) avoiding scapegoating the identified patient; (3) reducing long-term morbidity; (4) identifying precipitating stressors; and (5) educating family members regarding potential treatment to help with future crises (Langsley & Kaplan, 1968; Richman, 1979; Rubinstein, 1972).

Individual Therapy: This type of therapy begins with the engagement of the patient during the first meeting, whether at home, at school, or in the emergency room. The emphasis of intervention is on the here and now, attempting to acknowledge the existence of an acute crisis, identifying precipitating stressors, and determining the availability and cooperation of "significant others"—parents, teachers, other agencies. The major goal is to create an impact on the patient, alleviate the crisis in a realistic manner, and help the patient resume a homeostatic level of functioning.

Patient cooperation is needed to obtain clinical information to make decisions about further care. If the patient cannot provide such information, it must be obtained from others.

During the acute intervention phase, the clinician must engage the patient and obtain his or her trust. Communication, understanding, and empathy are vital tools of the individual crisis intervention clinician during this phase.

Once the patient passes into the intermediate intervention phase, the individual therapy takes on a different approach but retains many of its prior characteristics. The goal remains to stabilize the patient emotionally and to prepare him or her for discharge from one of the specialized crisis intervention units.

During all phases of crisis intervention, the patient uses the psychotherapist as a support when negotiating with family members, outside agencies, and the community, placing the therapist in the role of an ombudsman. Throughout, the therapist must maintain an objective and practical stance vis-à-vis patients and the environment, not doing for patients what they could do for themselves. Patients must be encouraged to do things for themselves to help reentry into their network—for example, attend school or be compliant with medications and special educational approaches.

Cognitive, behavioral, and reality-oriented techniques are especially helpful during the crisis intervention phase of individual psychotherapy.

Supportive Group Therapy: This therapy allows the patient to join others in a group to discuss the sharing of crisis impact, alternative solutions, coping mechanisms, avenues of support, information about psychiatric disorders, and preventive techniques so the problem does not recur. In this setting, the patient does not feel alone and can share experiences with others.

Group experiences also are structured to help the patient in negotiating issues with family members who may be projecting their own problems onto the patient or responsible for a dysfunctional environment. In acute residential treatment and brief hospitalization experiences especially, family members are included in the groups. They are particularly well suited for working on family problems in a controlled setting. Patients can explore dysfunctional family constructs more easily in a group setting, where they feel the support of their therapist and the other patients.

Follow-up

Follow-up care, a component of crisis intervention, begins at the moment the patient presents with the crisis. The type of follow-up will vary depending on the service initially provided. For example, a patient who utilizes a hot line will not give a name or phone number, but the receiver of the call can obtain clinical information about the caller that will help to identify him or her if another call is made. If another call is made, the patient can be identified from the prior data and an attempt made to further engage or recommend face-to-face care.

If the patient goes to the emergency room, follow-up care begins after completion of the crisis assessment. Follow-up care can be assured by either a formally assigned case manager or a clinician from one of the involved service units. Contact can be maintained with the patient and family by telephone and home visits as crisis intervention proceeds.

Follow-up is expected to continue the treatment/process initiated during crisis assessment; provide medical and psychological support to patient and family; enhance treatment compliance by monitoring close contact with the patient and family; and maintain contact with and sustain the roles of those within the patient's social network.

Acute and intermediate intervention often can provide only a portion of the total intervention plan required by the patient and family. It can defuse the crisis and stabilize the patient and family, but longer-term therapeutic inputs usually are needed. Without follow-up beyond the acute and intermediate stages, the recidivism rate of patients is considerable.

Staffing Issues

Specific staffing issues for crisis intervention programs relate to task and functions; training; safety; burnout; information/telecommunications; and role of the child and adolescent psychiatrist.

TASKS AND FUNCTIONS

Staff providing crisis intervention must provide a rapid response, assess the degree of severity of the problem, assess dangerousness, engage the patient and family, determine the type of intervention required, and provide a holding environment for the patient if needed by means of inpatient, acute residential treatment, or partial/day hospitalization. Staff may be assigned to fixed units, such as emergency centers, or to roving teams that evaluate the patient in the community.

TRAINING

Training is critical to help develop a new pool of potential staff and maintain existing staff. Trainees of many disciplines frequently are placed in crisis intervention settings because it is felt that this type of experience is valuable. Case supervision is provided and supplemented with a specific curriculum.

Staff members require continuing education in such issues as assessment of families, management of the dangerous patient, seclusion/restraint, substance abuse, screening for toxic substances, head injury, physical/sexual abuse, trauma, psychopharmacology, dispositional alternatives, and stress on the clinicians themselves.

SAFETY

The very nature of crisis intervention presupposes patients who have become psychologically destabilized and cannot be tolerated or managed in their environment by family or others. Such patients might be verbally threatening or physically assaultive towards others. Some are dangerous in terms of possessing suicidal or homicidal thoughts, plans, or actual attempts to act.

It is helpful for staff members to have training in defusing dangerous patient behavior so it does not proceed to fully expressed behaviors where someone is injured. Security staff members need to be familiar with the function and needs of the crisis intervention team so they can respond rapidly and effectively when called.

BURNOUT

Occupational burnout may occur due to the excessive stress associated with crisis intervention work. Symptoms of such stress—depressive feelings, cynicism, dread of returning to work, disillusionment, strong negative attitudes, and feelings about specific patients or patient types—can af-

fect the clinician's intrapersonal feeling of well-being. Problems in interpersonal relationships also may arise, causing avoidance, delays in responding, irritability, overt resentment, hostility, and reduced effectiveness at work. Burnout can be diminished or avoided by a reorientation to treatment focusing on less tense, pressured interactions with patients and providing services that are more fulfilling for patient and staff. Sharing of problems, discussing stress, presenting suggestions for change, and negotiating solutions to problems foster cohesion and improve morale (Pines & Maslach, 1978).

Since the crisis intervention team interfaces with a wide variety of other medical and psychiatric providers, it is helpful to include them in discussions about shared responsibilities, teaming, and dispositional alternatives.

INFORMATION/TELECOMMUNICATIONS

Information/telecommunications includes a data base about patients as well as a telecommunications system. A data base regarding patient demographics, diagnoses, and prior treatment is helpful in assessing and managing patients who are undergoing crisis intervention. Ideally such a data base would be available to all providers within a regional network. All providers should have access to existing data and be able to add new data for each patient or during an encounter.

A telecommunications system can allow any staff person or trainee to access a child and adolescent psychiatrist for clinical consultation, backup, and supervision on an immediate basis. In such a system, the provider could interact with clinical supervisors or specialists by utilizing audio or video equipment. This is particularly helpful to mobile teams that engage the patient and family in the community. The team may need to summon the clinical supervisor or specialist, police, ambulance, hospital or medical personnel, and needs access to existing patient information.

ROLE OF CHILD AND ADOLESCENT PSYCHIATRIST

This person has a variable role within a crisis intervention team, serving as program director, clinical supervisor, specialist, or provider. Since a majority of child and adolescent patients requiring crisis intervention also require medical attention, the child and adolescent psychiatrist is well suited to help make decisions regarding medical/psychiatric problems. This is especially important with patients involved with substance abuse, the ingestion of toxic substances, medication side effects, physical/sexual abuse, and head or other trauma.

Additionally, the child and adolescent psychiatrist is helpful in considering other potential medical problems that may relate to the deviant behavior, such as encephalitis, neuroleptic malignant syndrome, meningitis, or brain tumor.

REFERENCES

Berlin, I. N. (1970). Crisis intervention and short-term therapy—an approach in a child psychiatric clinic. *Journal of the American Academy of Child Psychiatry, 9,* 595–606.

Burks, H. L., & Hoekstra, M. (1964). Psychiatric emergencies in children. *American Journal of Orthopsychiatry, 34,* 134–137.

Caplan, G. (1961). *Prevention of mental disorders in children.* New York: Basic Books.

Eisler, R., & Hersen, M. (1973). Behavioral techniques in family oriented crisis intervention. *Archives of General Psychiatry, 28,* 111–116.

Gerson, S., & Bassuk, E. (1980). Psychiatric emergencies: An overview. *American Journal of Psychiatry, 137,* 1–11.

Gillig, P., Hillard, J., Bell, J., Combs, H., Martin, C., & Deddens, J. (1989). The psychiatric emergency service holding area: Effect on utilization of inpatient resources. *American Journal of Psychiatry, 146,* 369–372.

Greenblatt, M., Becerra, R., & Serafetinides, E. (1982). Social networks and mental health: An overview. *American Journal of Psychiatry, 139,* 977–984.

Hill, R. (1978). Generic features of families under stress. In H. J. Parad (Ed.), *Crisis intervention* (pp. 32–52). New York: Family Service Association of America.

Ianzito, B., Fine, J., Sprague, B., & Pestana, J. (1978). Overnight admission for psychiatric emergencies. *Hospital and Community Psychiatry, 29,* 728–730.

Langsley, D. G., & Kaplan, D. M. (1968). *The treatment of families in crisis.* New York:

Lindemann, E. (1944). Symptomatology and management of acute grief. *American Journal of Psychiatry, 101,* 141–148.

Morrison, G. C. (1969). Approaches to suicidal children and adolescents. *Journal of the American Academy of Child Psychiatry, 8,* 140–153.

Morrison, G. C., & Smith, W. R. (1975). Child psychiatric emergencies: A comparison of two clinic settings and socioeconomic groups. In G. C. Morrison (Ed.), *Emergencies in child psychiatry* (pp. 107–114). Springfield, IL: Charles C Thomas.

Parad, J. H. (1978). *Crisis intervention.* New York: Family Service Association of America.

Parad, J. H., & Caplan, G. (1978). A framework for studying families in crisis. In H. J. Parad (Ed.), *Crisis intervention* (pp. 53–74). New York: Family Service Association of America.

Perlmutter, R. (1983). Family involvement in psychiatric emergencies. *Hospital and Community Psychiatry, 34,* 255–257.

Pines, A., & Maslach, C. (1978). Characteristics of staff burnout in mental health settings. *Hospital and Community Psychiatry, 29,* 233–237.

Richman, J. (1979). The family therapy of attempted suicide. *Family Process, 18,* 131–142.

Rubinstein, D. (1972). Rehospitalization versus family crisis intervention. *American Journal of Psychiatry, 129,* 715–720.

Speck, R., & Attneave, C. (1973). *Family networks: Retribalization and healing.* New York: Pantheon.

Turgay, A. (1982). Psychiatric emergencies in children. *Psychiatric Journal of the University of Ottawa,* 254–260.

Youthdale Psychiatric Crisis Service. (1987). Stabilizing teens in crisis and fortifying their support network. *Hospital and Community Psychiatry, 38,* 1211–1214.

10 / Foundations of Child and Adolescent Psychopharmacotherapy

Charles W. Popper

Since the early 1980s, the psychopharmacological treatment of children and adolescents has moved from a controversial fringe of child psychiatry and neurology to a routine and central part of clinical psychiatric and pediatric practice. Drawing strength from biological psychiatry, developmental neurosciences, clinical pharmacology, quantitative psychology research, and treatment outcome assessment, the field of child and adolescent psychopharmacology is making rapid gains toward providing relief from the emotional and behavioral symptoms, the associated physiologic disturbances, and, through early pharmacological intervention, the developmental and psychosocial complications of the biopsychiatric disorders of youth.

The practice of child and adolescent psychopharmacology is challenged and growing in response to many forces. The lingering taboos that "protect" children from medical research and treatment innovations are receding. Older theoretical frameworks are beginning to incorporate biochemical, physiologic, and genetic concepts. Reductionist brands of psychopharmacology are coming to terms with the critical roles of personal and family psychodynamics and of sociocultural factors in the presentation of child psychopathology and in the daily clinical practice of psychopharmacology with youngsters. And underdeveloped models of cost containment and fragmented financial approaches are being challenged to integrate the basic elements of scientific and clinical medicine.

Changing Clinical Presumptions

THE HISTORICAL TREND TOWARD INCREASINGLY RAPID ADVANCES

Psychostimulant treatment of behavioral disorders in children was originally described 60 years ago (Bradley, 1937). From its inception, this highly effective treatment received a mixed reception by physicians and parents alike. Theoretical and philosophical concerns limited its clinical use, the nascent field remained frozen for years, and no major innovations were spawned in child psychopharmacology until the pioneering studies of Barbara Fish and Magda Campbell in the 1950s. It remained until the 1980s for the new array of psychopharmacological treatments, developed by the "biological revolution" in adult psychiatry beginning in the 1960s, to generate the rapid "biological explosion" in pediatric psychiatry.

In the early 1990s, empirical trials of numerous and diverse psychopharmacological therapies in youngsters moved beyond the confines of university clinics and have proceeded on a widespread basis in many outpatient and inpatient settings. Simultaneously, isolated pharmacotherapy of children and adolescents with psychiatric problems is being encouraged by economic forces, for better and for worse, because of its presumed cost-saving value. These changes are likely to lead to more rigorous and naturalistic comparisons of isolated pharacotherapies and combined biopsychosocial interventions in community settings.

During this period of rapid change, the increasing popularity of psychopharmacological treatments for youngsters has far outpaced the availability of sound clinical research. Many commonly used treatments are supported only by case reports and preliminary findings from uncontrolled studies. Clinical decisions often are based on the practitioners' judgment, experience, background, and training site. But the pace of research is quickening.

Psychopharmacological research is no longer rare in children and adolescents below the age of 17. Well-controlled studies in pediatric psychopharmacology are becoming more available, with a sharp rise in the number of double-blind placebo-controlled studies published annually since 1994. Several multisite drug research studies, which were rare in the early 1980s, are currently in progress. There are indications of increased flexibility in the consideration of research paradigms that are viewed as scientifically valid and clinically useful (Arnold, 1993; Jensen, 1993; Rudorfer, 1993; Vitiello & Jensen, 1995b). Perhaps most crucially, increasing interest in "naturalistic" studies has facilitated more extensive investigation of psychopharmacological treatments on the basis of clinical practice methodologies rather than relying exclusively on traditional clinical trial protocols. This is particularly important in pediatric psychopharmacology, where patient recruitment of "pure" research populations has been all but impossible for some common clinical disorders.

Moreover, the Food and Drug Administration (FDA) in the U.S. government has undertaken a general initiative to foster child-oriented research on all new drugs and to expand package insert information regarding pediatric uses for all commercially released medications (FDA, 1992; Jensen, Vitiello, Leonard, & Laughren, 1994).

Despite these forward steps, new psychopharmacological research in youths remains quite limited. About 80% of all clinical articles in child and adolescent psychopharmacology are published in just 2 journals: the *Journal of Child and Adolescent Psychopharmacology* and the *Journal of the American Academy of Child and Adolescent Psychiatry*. Thus family practitioners, pediatricians, child neurologists, and general psychiatrists who apply these treatments in their practices must go beyond their usual journals and seek subspecialty journals.

Through the various channels of information spread in medicine, knowledge from a small bank of researchers has been generating advances in pediatric psychopharmacology that are changing the routine clinical practice in a variety of medical specialties.

THERAPEUTIC EMPIRICISM

The empirical clinical approach consists of trying nonestablished treatments and judging them on the basis of observed failure or success in the clinical setting. The increasingly routine use of empirical drug trials in pediatric psychopharmacology has led to a new tradition in selecting the clinical indications, dosing regimens, and target age ranges for these treatments. Rather than relying on the medical literature for making treatment decisions, trial-and-error empirical treatments in child and adolescent psychopharmacology are proceeding on the basis of what scientific or clinical documentation is available, with assessment of the unknowns and uncertainties of the treatment, and with consideration of the specific circumstances and needs of individual children.

The use of an empirical approach is hardly an innovation in medicine and often represents the natural, typical, and necessary approach when scientifically based medical knowledge is inadequate. The time-honored principles underlying empirical medicine have been fueled in pediatric psychopharmacology by several factors. First and foremost, the availability of "almost relevant" findings from adult psychopharmacology and the clinical exigencies of today's young patients have contributed to the current prominence of therapeutic empiricism in pediatric psychopharmacology. Furthermore, despite the advances of the nosology and diagnostic criteria in psychiatry and child psychiatry, many clinicians treating youths have come to view the making of a diagnosis to be an act of faith, and so the selection of a diagnosis-based pharmacological treatment has come to be seen by some physicians as a leap of faith. The "Just try it and see if it works" approach to managing emotional and behavioral problems in youngsters is common and currently has a large measure of acceptance among clinicians. This approach frequently is encouraged and rewarded by economic forces, particularly for psychopharmacological treatments.

As therapeutic empiricism has become the standard of practice in child and adolescent psychopharmacology, the clinical application of untested treatments has, in certain domains of treatment, increasingly become the rule rather than the exception. Untested clinical treatments are now freely discussed at national meetings by many physicians, bringing psychopharmacology into the mainstream of the medical specialties. Numerous treatments, and perhaps the majority, are well known and commonly employed by practitioners before being subjected to rigorous assessment. Often clinicians appear to be ahead of researchers in identifying effective psychopharmacological treatments for children and adolescents.

This empirical strategy might be defended as a

way of generating hypotheses for subsequent investigation using scarce research resources, but it is not difficult to identify important questions for child and adolescent psychopharmacological research without putting some children at risk. The legal and ethical requirements of these trial-and-error treatments entail particularly sound permission and understanding of the treatment by patient and family. But even with understanding and permission, there is compelling logic in the goal of assessing safety and efficacy of new treatments before their general application.

The empirical approach in child and adolescent psychopharmacology brings help to many children whose medical conditions are only speculatively treatable, but also exposes many children to potential medical risks. The common use of unproven and novel treatments is periodically dampened by sobering new findings: the repeated failure of tricyclic antidepressants to produce statistically significant antidepressant effects in controlled trials in children and adolescents, the unexpected appearance of sudden death as a putative side effect of psychotropic medication, and ambiguous data regarding the safety of certain drug combinations in youngsters.

The aggressive use of weakly documented treatments poses clinical, ethical, legal, and economic dilemmas for which data-based solutions are sorely needed. But in the view of many parents and physicians, many children and adolescents in the current generation cannot wait until these treatments have undergone rigorous evaluation.

DIAGNOSTIC AMBIGUITIES

The basic medical principle of "Diagnose, then treat" has been challenged by the confounding fact that many children and adolescents do not fit neatly into discrete diagnostic categories. Fully half of children in outpatient psychiatric clinics do not fit into the accepted diagnostic categories (American Psychiatric Association [hereafter APA], 1994). Furthermore, the high rate of neuropsychiatric comorbidity in youngsters makes the use of a single diagnosis or even a set of medical diagnoses into a simplistic distortion that ignores the complexity of interacting diagnoses, family and developmental factors, and circumstance.

The dominant nosologies, spearheaded by the American Psychiatric Association and the World Health Organization, are riddled with tentative solutions to controversial issues. In both systems, diagnostic criteria and even full syndromal definitions often are overlapping. The series of conditions that are labeled as attention-deficit/hyperactivity disorder result from a broad range of genetic and environmental etiologies, and the clinical presentations of the disorder are mimicked by an extensive list of psychiatric and medical conditions. All of the symptoms of attention-deficit/hyperactivity disorder are often a part of bipolar disorder in youths. Psychotic disorders in children can appear without the overt symptoms typically seen in adults. Childhood anxiety disorders can be defined individually and categorized by the formal nosologies, but in nature they tend to occur in clusters that at least cast doubt on their identity as distinct entities.

Despite all of the major progress afforded by the systematization of diagnoses, the field trials, the detailed modifications based on expert consensus, and increasingly scientific rigor of the current nosologies, numerous examples of inconsistency, incompleteness, and ambiguity in the diagnostic systems persist and limit their clinical applicability to children and adolescents with emotional and behavioral disorders.

Even if the diagnostic definitions were optimized, the current nosologic categories do not correspond in a simple manner to psychopharmacological treatments. Certain drugs can be used to treat a very wide variety of disorders in children and adolescents. For example, the so-called antidepressants are prescribed for enuresis, attention-deficit/hyperactivity disorder, bulimia, pain, and perhaps depressive and anxiety disorders. Most emotional and behavioral disorders of youths can be treated by a very wide variety of medications. (See Chapter 11.) Some childhood disorders can be treated by seemingly opposing treatments; for example, both psychostimulants and neuroleptics can be used to treat attention-deficit/hyperactivity disorder, despite their opposing dopamine effects; both selective serotonin reuptake inhibitors and atypical neuroleptics seem to help children with autistic and other pervasive developmental disorders, despite some opposing serotonin effects.

From a psychopharmacological viewpoint, current nosologic systems seem primative, are neither chemically nor physiologically oriented, and do not constitute an effective basis for drug selection decisions.

SYMPTOM-ORIENTED TREATMENT

Instead of targeting recognizable diagnoses, psychotropic medications often are prescribed to treat a specific symptom or cluster of symptoms. Symptomatic or syndromic treatment is valid and even necessary at the current level of knowledge. However, these treatments are often disguised and presumably glorified by attempts to view them as treatments of a "working diagnosis" or an uncategorized disorder. That is, the "not otherwise specified" (NOS) disorders of *Diagnostic and Statistical Manual of Mental Disorders,* Fourth Edition (*DSM-IV*) (APA, 1994) are not contained within the well-defined part of the diagnostic system and can be viewed as nosologically classified only in name. Used in such a way, a "working diagnosis" or "NOS diagnosis" is a clinical pretense, adapted to generate a sense of order or simplicity, to clarify communication, to create a feeling of scientific validity in the clinical setting, and to satisfy economic overseers. It obscures the fact that it is a symptomatic treatment, similar to many other valid treatments in child and adolescent psychiatry and psychopharmacology.

Once a specific symptom or syndrome is promoted as a "working diagnosis," a clinician might be more inclined to aim drug treatment at a "false target" diagnosis, to overemphasize the significance of the patient's minor symptoms that are a part of the "false target" disorder, to gloss over the absence of the other diagnostic criteria, to overinterpret the prognosis, and to close off other treatment options. For example, symptoms such as motor hyperactivity or depressed mood have countless causes and provide a weak basis for drug selection. It is closer to the mark, and fosters more appropriate clinical application of scientific findings, to perceive the treatment as essentially symptomatic rather than in pseudodiagnostic terms.

There are remarkably few symptom-oriented studies in pediatric psychopharmacology, and even fewer pharmacological studies are based on syndromes; for example, treatment of suicidal behavior presenting in association with aggressive behavior, stereotypies with and without obsessional symptoms in pervasive developmental disorders. Such studies can be as scientifically rigorous and meaningful as disorder-based studies, so there is little to be gained from attempts to disguise symptomatic treatments as diagnosis-based in order to lend scientific or economic credibility to a particular treatment.

In clinical practice, even diagnosis-based treatments often resemble symptomatic therapies because of the confounding effects of concurrent psychopathology. Child and adolescent patients who are treated in psychiatric outpatient clinics have a mean of 2 concurrent *DSM* diagnoses, and youths treated in psychiatric hospitals have a mean of 4 concurrent *DSM* diagnoses. The complex interactions among comorbid disorders can require a prioritizing of the most problematic symptoms and the use of multiple concurrent medications aimed at different pieces of the symptom complex—sometimes without much clarity about whether a particular symptom results from one or several disorders. Even in children with 2 clearly identified disorders, interactions among the disorders and among the symptoms of the disorders often renders pharmacotherapy an essentially symptomatic treatment.

It is legitimate to make pediatric psychopharmacological decisions based on symptomatic, syndromic, diagnostic, or multidiagnostic thinking. It is a significant failing, though, to believe that the findings of drug research conducted on patient samples selected for "purity" of diagnosis have a simple and direct relevance to the common symptomatic and syndromic presentations seen in clinical practice.

The clinical correctness of a symptomatic or syndromic treatment is judged, as all treatments are, by the subsequent finding of whether the symptoms improved. However, it is incorrect to infer that a working diagnosis was accurate because it led to a successful treatment outcome, just as it is inappropriate to infer that a child had a tension headache (instead of migraine or a brain tumor) because of improvement on aspirin. Similarly, it cannot be induced that a patient has bipolar disorder because of a therapeutic response to lithium or, more generally, that a diagnosis can be inferred from a drug response. A successful treatment can show that a treatment was appropriate, not that the diagnosis was appropriate.

The Context of Child Psychopharmacological Decisions

Not diagnoses, or symptoms, or syndromes—nor their severity, duration, or intensity—nor comorbid medical or neurologic disorders—provide a sufficient basis for making decisions about the selection of proper medications, especially in treating the behavioral disorders of youths. This is consonant with the more general principle, propagated throughout Volume 5 of this *Handbook,* that such factors are not sufficient in themselves to dictate clinical decisions about treatment planning.

Numerous "extraneous" or seemingly extraneous factors can impinge on virtually every clinical decision in psychopharmacology. Psychosocial events, such as a grandmother's visit, a morning at church with mother, father's salary change, new teacher, a friend's move away, or a summer with an uncle can alter the expression of clinical symptoms or apparent adverse effects in a way that might be falsely attributed to medications. Various treatment-related variables, such as prior adherence to prescribed treatments, past treatment failures, hope and expectation for change, concurrent treatment modalities, and clinician's departures, can alter the timing, drug selection, or general management of pharmacotherapy. Such clinical judgments also will be influenced by medical factors, such as concurrent medications or chronic illness. Another influential factor is the child's physiologic state, such as changes that accompany transient dehydration, pregnancy, and certain maturational changes such as menarche. Similarly, these judgments will necessarily be responsive to age-related experiences and activities, such as alcohol and drug experimentation, and to variations in exercise, such as involvement in sporting events and dance classes. Additional factors concern sleep patterns, which can vary around exam periods and with television schedules, and also eating patterns, which may lead to variations in dietary salt and fluid intake.

These "extraneous" factors, which are largely determined by environmental influences, at times can have a stronger influence on drug and dose selection than diagnosis. An adolescent who is diagnosed as having attention-deficit/hyperactivity disorder but who is also suspected of having a depressive disorder might appear to be a straightforward candidate for a psychostimulant or antidepressant trial. However, a stimulant (whose effects can be quickly assessed) rather than an antidepressant (whose effects would take several weeks or months to evaluate) might be preferred if the child will be going away on vacation in 2 weeks. A tricyclic antidepressant might be selected if the child is going to spend the summer vacation with a substance-abusing uncle, but a psychostimulant might be preferred if the uncle abuses alcohol and not other substances. The usefulness of the medication during the summer might be overestimated if the child is supportively stabilized by accompanying the uncle to meetings of Alcoholics Anonymous or to religious services. The value of the medication also might be overestimated if the summer heat causes persistent dehydration (and elevated plasma drug levels) or if the uncle does not reliably report the presence of problematic behaviors. More generally, doses might be elevated inappropriately if a mother's anxiety disorder leads her to exaggerate descriptions of the problematic behaviors. Doses might need to be increased only temporarily if a child's vacation from competitive athletics leads to a reduction in exercise (and dehydration), if situational stress and altered sleep patterns during an examination period leads to a time-limited increase in irritability or impulsivity, or if the child eats a large amount of chocolate (caffeine) during winter holidays.

In actual clinical practice, many of these "extraneous" factors operate outside of a clinician's awareness. These distracting and confounding variables often make it difficult to evaluate the effects of a treatment rigorously or even adequately. In drug research, these variables are willfully conceptualized as placebo factors. Because they are essentially uncontrolled, these factors sometimes are disparaged as if they are unimportant occasional confounders of science. However, these "extraneous" factors can easily modify treatment outcome or the perception of treatment outcome, and thereby influence current and future clinical impressions about drug effects and alter decisions in psychopharmacological treatment planning.

USE OF TREATMENT GUIDELINES IN CLINICAL PRACTICE

To improve the quality of care and sometimes to foster more cost-effective care, various forms of treatment guidelines have been promulgated. Within a health care institution, for example, a pharmacy committee might articulate maximal permissible doses for children and perhaps indicate requirements for a pre-treatment workup. These guidelines are intended to document the specific elements of good patient care in order to protect patients, clinicians, and institutions from treatment errors and aberrations as well as lawsuits.

There is also a recent movement toward the development of treatment guidelines by some national clinically oriented professional organizations. These guidelines typically are focused on selection of treatment modality and are primarily based on diagnosis, although they generally have accommodations for concurrent symptoms (suicidality) or circumstances (available resources for monitoring treatment). Treatment guidelines for a particular diagnosis usually cover the various intervention approaches, including psychosocial and alternative nonpharmacological treatments. They also can include specific psychopharmacological guidelines, including contraindications, psychiatric and medical workup, laboratory testing, dosing regimens, drug sequences, and treatment monitoring.

Nationally based treatment guidelines usually are developed by a consensus of medical experts, often both clinicians and researchers. A key characteristic of good treatment guidelines is the recognition that a general principle or expert recommendation not only can but should be modified according to the needs of the individual patient and circumstance. Advocates of guidelines should not promote the notion that they can anticipate every possible exigency that might arise or provide recommendations for every patient. At their heart, treatment guidelines should be understood to be generalized recommendations that operate primarily as educational material for clinicians by giving specific step-by-step directions. If properly framed, they are instructive and can provide order and clarity, but they are not rigid instructions or coercive in tone or intent.

Clinically appropriate guidelines give general instructions and leave the decision making to individual clinicians and patients. They are intended to strengthen, not replace, clinical judgment in patient care.

Despite their potential to support good treatment, there are some potentially severe drawbacks to treatment guidelines. Attempts to view treatment guidelines as invariant, complete, or final do not reflect an understanding of treatment involving individual patients. Furthermore, past attempts at standardization of clinical methods have a dismal history of being systematically abused. An obvious and indefensible example is the application of diagnostic criteria listed in the *DSM-IV* as economic determinants of the distribution of health care. Treatment guidelines will be abused in a similar manner. Undoubtedly some corporate officials already are chomping at the bit for the chance to abuse treatment guidelines, especially if it means lowering their costs by restricting care to "established" treatments.

"OFF-LABEL" USE OF MEDICATIONS

Sound clinical judgment often leads to use of medication treatments that also do not conform to the apparent limitations promulgated by governmental regulatory agencies. Commonly used and generally accepted treatments involve drug choices and dosing regimens that do not conform to the wording of the FDA, as contained in the *Physicians' Desk Reference* (*PDR*) and on package labels and inserts in the United States. Furthermore, the information contained in the *PDR* (1997) and package inserts is misleading and unhelpful for child and adolescent psychopharmacology, so there is substantive reason to depart from the *PDR* wordings in clinical practice.

Such off-label treatments are employed routinely throughout all of medicine. Off-label usage is accepted as legitimate and viewed as routine by the FDA, but it can create tension in certain clinical situations if a clinician believes that there is something dubious about prescribing outside of FDA advertising regulations, misinterprets them as having some legal or regulatory influence on the practice of medicine, or views them as treatment guidelines.

Contrary to many clinicians' understanding, the

FDA does not attempt or have any interest in limiting clinical treatment regimens. The FDA limitations are issued solely to regulate commercial advertising by pharmaceutical manufacturers. The information contained in package inserts does not and was never intended to govern the prescribing practices of clinicians. If a clinician believes that a particular drug or dose is appropriate for a child, that judgment takes precedence and the clinician is free and expected to pursue that regimen (FDA, 1982; also see foreword to the 1997 *PDR*).

FDA "approval" indicates that government panels have found that there is sufficient scientific evidence to indicate that the drug is *safe* and *effective* for managing a specified *disorder* in a specified *drug regimen* in a specified *population*. This FDA "approval" permits the medication to be released commercially in the United States, allowing it to be distributed in pharmacies, under certain limitations on manufacturing and marketing. The FDA limitations on manufacturing generally are concerned with quality control, including purity, bioavailability, shelf life, and protection of controlled substances from theft or abuse.

The FDA limitations on marketing require that drug advertisements and product-related materials (package inserts, patient education forms, the *PDR*) make no claims about the safety or effectiveness of a drug except with regard to the specifically approved conditions (indication, regimen, and population). Under these legal requirements, the pharmaceutical manufacturer can make no written or verbal endorsement about the use of a product except as approved by the FDA.

The validity of off-label treatment has never been in any doubt. U.S. courts invariably have upheld that, once a drug is commercially released, clinical decisions about its use are to be made by clinicians and patients for the benefit of individuals in their specific circumstances—for treatment of any disorder, at any dose, and at any age—without regard to arbitrary, external, or pre-defined limits.

Apart from having the unintended effect of limiting some clinicians' prescribing habits, the treatment regimens described in the *PDR* are sometimes actively misleading, unhelpful, or outdated. Especially in pediatric psychopharmacology, the stated regimens would be drastic and peculiar

limitations. If taken seriously, they would result in treatment failures on a massive scale.

Many psychopharmacological agents are described in the *PDR* without dosing statements relevant to children or, worse, the pharmaceutical companies have simply taken the liability-limiting step of having the *PDR* indicate that their drugs should not be used in children. It is not surprising, then, that many dosing statements in the *PDR* have only a tenuous connection to appropriate pediatric dosing.

For example, the *PDR* (1997) indicates that depression and enuresis are approved (i.e., not off-label) uses of imipramine and notes that doses "of 2.5 mg/kg [milligrams per kilogram] daily should not be exceeded in childhood." This dose range is somewhat applicable in the treatment of enuresis but not to treatment of childhood depression. Virtually all sources in the medical literature for over 15 years have recommended doses up to 5 mg per kg for treatment of major depression in children and adolescents. More recently, although tricyclic antidepressant treatment of childhood depression has been demonstrated to be ineffective in many double-blind, placebo-controlled studies, tricyclic antidepressant treatment of childhood depression remains listed as an approved use in the *PDR*.

This is not an isolated example. In adult psychiatry, the use of lithium for patients who never had a full manic episode, trazodone for sleep induction, and carbamazepine or beta blockers for any behavioral disorder are "off label." In child psychiatry, off-label treatments include the use of neuroleptics for pervasive developmental disorder, chlorpromazine or thioridazine for Tourette's disorder, or lithium for patients less than 12 years old. Approved uses of medications in child psychiatry that have never been supported by rigorous controlled trials include treatment of bipolar disorder with mood stabilizers, antidepressant treatment of mood disorders, conventional neuroleptics for impulsivity and agitation, or sedatives for preoperative anxiety.

The FDA and its written word in the *PDR* serve legal and governmental regulatory purposes that often are misunderstood as having clinical relevance. The FDA and *PDR* do what they can to prevent this misunderstanding, but some clinicians continue to practice with the uninformed view that the *PDR* is a source of standard dosing regimens for child and adolescent psychopharmacology.

Developmental Pharmacosciences

Although certain principles of adult psychopharmacology can be applied to children and adolescents, some basic principles are genuinely different. There are numerous examples of substantive differences between psychopharmacological treatment in adults and children.

DEVELOPMENTAL PHARMACOKINETICS

Throughout childhood and adolescence, developmental changes can be observed in the speed and extent of drug absorption, peak plasma levels, rates and pathways of biotransformation, protein binding, hemodynamics, properties of the blood-brain barrier, body fat composition, volume of distribution, movement into water and lipid compartments, and hepatic and renal clearance of different drugs. Quantitatively, these developmental pharmacokinetic changes vary greatly among children (as among adults), depending heavily on the specific characteristics of the drug (or drugs) administered to the child.

The complexity, variability, and at times unpredictability of pharmacokinetics in youths is due to the multiplicity of biochemical and physiological processes involved in the pharmacokinetic handling of drugs. These processes mature at different rates, interact in different ways, and shift in relative importance through time. These age-related changes—in drug absorption, distribution, metabolism, and elimination—have a profound influence on clinical management of pediatric psychopharmacological treatments in individual patients (Jatlow, 1987; Vitiello & Jensen, 1995a).

Birth to Age 3 Years: The dramatic pharmacokinetic changes during infancy and toddlerhood are the most rapid and extensive of postnatal life. The first 3 years entail extensive and simultaneous developmental changes in every pharmacokinetic dimension and parameter. For example, the overall activity of the hepatic drug-metabolizing enzymes is low during the early postnatal weeks and then builds in fits and starts over the first 3 years.

Due to the extreme complexity of these changes, psychopharmacological treatment of children below age 3 should be approached cautiously (if at all) and coordinated closely with a specialist in pediatrics or pediatric pharmacology.

Ages 3 Years to Puberty: The overall rate of hepatic drug biotransformation reaches a lifetime maximum at age 3 and then declines rapidly over the next 10 to 15 years, and then decreases gradually with age throughout life. The developmental changes in hepatic biotransformation rate involve the drug-metabolizing enzymes of the P450 cytochrome system as well as non-P450 mechanisms. The different enzyme families and individual isoenzymes appear to follow semi-independent developmental courses, but a detailed picture of the developmental changes in activity of the various drug-metabolizing enzymes has not yet been carefully delineated in the liver. Similarly, there is little developmental description of the drug-metabolizing enzymes in the intestinal lumen, circulating blood, or brain. Partly because of the changing activity of the drug-metabolizing isoenzymes, clinical drug effects and drug interactions are considerably less predictable in children than in adults. Developmental variations in metabolite profiles can result in age-related changes in the profile of adverse drug reactions. Likewise, a medication might produce different therapeutic effects in children, adolescents, and adults.

The developmental pharmacokinetic changes that continue after age 3 are clinically simpler than the massive and largely unpredictable changes of the earlier years. Dosage calculations can be based on body weight and no longer require the more cumbersome indices such as surface area. Weight-adjusted doses can be expressed in simple milligram-per-kilogram (mg/kg) figures.

The major reason for this simplification is the emergence of liver biotransformation as the predominant factor influencing drug elimination and therefore the main determinant of weight-adjusted drug doses in children after age 3 years.

The faster hepatic metabolism of drugs is clinically evident in the higher weight-adjusted drug doses that are required to treat children in comparison to adults. That is, children need higher mg/kg doses of liver-metabolized drugs in order to overcome their more rapid drug clearance, which is primarily related to the high quantity and efficiency of their hepatic biotransformation. Compared to adults, children have a faster hepatic metabolism of psychostimulants, tricyclic antidepressants, anticonvulsants, antipsychotic drugs, and antianxiety agents, generally converting these drugs more quickly and completely into their active and inactive metabolites.

Depending on the particular drug, adolescents typically need doses that are about 50% higher than in adults, pre-adolescents may need doses that are 75% higher than in adults, and preschool children often need doses that are 100% higher than in adults.

The influence of the high hepatic biotransformation rate is particularly striking in view of the fact that several other developmental pharmacokinetic changes would lead to the expectation that children require *lower* weight-adjusted doses than adults. For example, children have an increased gastric emptying time and intestinal motility, so drug absorption is greater than in adults. Children often have higher plasma concentrations of the free (unbound) fraction of drugs; for imipramine, plasma protein binding is 81% at age 8 and 89% in adults. Children have a greater distribution of drugs into their aqueous compartments; they generally have less adipose tissue and provide a smaller depot for lipophilic drugs. Each of these factors would lower the dose requirements in children (3 years old and older) in comparison to adults.

Despite all of these factors, the mg/kg doses required for treating children tend to be significantly higher than adults' doses, primarily because of the greater activity of the hepatic drug-metabolizing enzymes and more rapid drug clearance in young people.

Adolescence: The slow reduction in the rate of drug metabolism, which starts at age 3 years, is interrupted just prior to puberty. A transient acute reduction in the drug biotransformation rate appears several months before puberty, as sex hormones increase in plasma concentration and compete for hepatic enzyme sites. At that time, plasma drug levels may rise rapidly without a change in body weight or dose (Pippinger, 1980). Dose reductions may be required when a nearly pubertal child shows a sudden increase in side effects on a stable drug regimen. Over the following 6 to 12 months, unpredictable hormonal surges and ebbs may lead to intermittently inadequate symptom control and to several changes in drug dosing. In

some cases, it is helpful to measure plasma drug levels every few weeks as a child enters puberty.

As body weight increases and spurts, absolute doses (milligrams daily) reach their lifetime maximum during adolescence. Body weight typically doubles between ages 10 and 18, so doses may need frequent adjustment (perhaps every 6 to 12 months) continuing past the period of the adolescent growth spurt and into late adolescence. With both increased weight and still relatively rapid drug biotransformation, the average-size teenager can require a larger absolute (milligram total) dose of an antidepressant than the parent.

By late adolescence, both liver metabolic rates and weight-adjusted drug doses decline into the adult range.

In addition to their more rapid hepatic clearance, renal clearance is faster in youths than in adults. Many drugs (including lithium) and drug metabolites are eliminated by the kidneys.

Both faster hepatic drug metabolism and faster renal clearance lead to shorter drug elimination half-lives in children and adolescents than in adults. The faster drug clearance in youths has significant clinical implications, including some modifications of the "standard" dosing regimens developed in adults.

As a result of the faster clearance, the clinical duration of many drug effects is briefer in children than adults, especially in younger children. To counter the effects of rapid clearance in children and adolescents, it is sometimes necessary to give individual dosages more frequently and at shorter intervals during the day. For example, tricyclic antidepressants sometimes are administered to young children in 2 or 3 divided doses daily (rather than once daily typically prescribed for adults).

The shorter elimination half-lives in youths also implies that steady-state concentrations are reached sooner (blood levels of a drug reach equilibrium in approximately 5 half-lives) and that plasma drug levels drawn for therapeutic drug monitoring can be sampled sooner in children than in adults. Based on current pharmacokinetic data in children (Vitiello et al., 1988), plasma lithium levels can be generally sampled after 3 to 4 days in children (compared to 4 to 6 days in adults) and at about 8 to 10 hours after last dosing (rather than 10 to 12 hours in adults). In order to refine current drug management parameters for youths, pharmacokinetic studies in youths are needed for each drug.

Pharmacokinetic studies of psychotropic drugs in children or adolescents are rare. Even for the psychostimulants, which have received the most examination, many pharmacokinetic questions remain unanswered. Virtually no studies have investigated the clinical effects of a psychopharmacological treatment at various ages, especially within a single protocol or by a single research team, and none has made proper corrections for developmental pharmacokinetic changes. Few treatment outcome studies are large enough to compare the pharmacokinetic characteristics of drug responders and nonresponders. No studies are available that adequately clarify dose-response relationships at different ages: The usual research protocols that examine only 1 or 2 doses are likely to miss (or misinterpret) an age-related change in the dose required to produce a treatment effect (i.e., a lateral shift in the dose-response curve).

Therapeutic drug monitoring (i.e., following plasma drug levels during clinical treatment) is commonly conducted with some psychopharmacological agents. However, the actual utility of plasma drug monitoring is commonly overestimated and rarely assessed in naturalistic studies. The studies on these methods usually describe population averages and are almost never examined in terms of the ability of these methods to enhance the quality of care of individuals (i.e., in a series of subjects using single-case design methods).

In brief, then, most psychopharmacological agents (including hepatically metabolized agents and renally cleared lithium) need to be administered in higher weight-adjusted doses and sometimes with more frequent dosages to young patients than to adults, simply in order to overcome their more rapid hepatic drug biotransformation and renal clearance of youth. Children typically require doses of psychotropic agents that are 50 to 100% higher than adult doses, when corrected for body weight. Stated differently, a child treated with a "full adult dosage" typically receives only two-thirds of the actual dose requirement. The use of adult psychopharmacological regimens in children leads systematically to underdosing and undertreatment. At two-thirds of a proper dose, the child may show a partial clinical response that may not be recognized as undertreatment.

The limited knowledge of developmental pharmacokinetics in child and adolescent psychopharmacology places an undue burden on the use of empirical trial-and-error approaches for optimizing dose regimens for individual patients.

DEVELOPMENTAL PHARMACODYNAMICS

In addition to the developmental changes in the pharmacokinetic movement of drugs and drug metabolites around the body, there are also developmental changes in drug effects that result from changing physiologic and biochemical characteristics of the target organs and target sites of action. That is, even after correcting for developmental pharmacokinetic changes, children and adolescents may have different therapeutic effects and side effects with psychiatric medications because, for example, of developmental changes in receptor sensitivity at the sites of drug action in the body or brain (Teicher & Baldessarini, 1987; Vitiello & Jensen, 1995a).

Several examples of pharmacodynamic responses that change with age have been proposed in child and adolescent psychopharmacology (Teicher & Baldessarini, 1987). A possible increase in neuroleptic-induced akathisia during late adolescence (compared to adulthood) and an increased susceptibility to drug-induced seizures in youths have been supported by some experimental data. Other proposed developmental pharmacodynamic effects are more hypothetical, including claims of reductions (in youths relative to adults) in susceptibility to tardive dyskinesia, mood changes induced by steroids, euphoric effects of psychostimulants, arousal effects of amphetamine (based on developmental studies in animals), and therapeutic effects of tricyclic antidepressants on major depression. There is also speculation of a possibly increased susceptibility of youths to the side effect of agitation during carbamazepine treatment.

Developmental pharmacodynamic effects will be explainable by a huge array of possible developmental changes in the physiology or chemistry of a brain region or neurophysiologic mechanism, such as age-related changes in the functional activation of different neurotransmitter systems, maturation of receptor mechanisms (types, number, and sensitivity), age-related changes in membrane physiology (reuptake and release mechanisms, membrane permeability, sodium-potassium AT-Pase pump and other pump mechanisms, membrane stability), presence of natural inhibitory substances, and the virtually uncountable intracellular sites of drug action as well as interactions with developmental changes in neighboring cells (e.g., glial and vascular structures).

Although such developmental changes in drug target site mechanisms could explain age-related differences in therapeutic effects and adverse reactions of medications, the existence and clinical significance of such drug effects are largely speculative at present. No clinically relevant developmental pharmacodynamic-effects have yet been convincingly demonstrated in child and adolescent psychopharmacology, but examples will certainly be identified as more is learned about the development of biochemical structures and mechanisms in the brain.

BIOCHEMICAL DEVELOPMENT OF THE BRAIN

Neurotransmitter and neuromodulator systems in the human brain have been described only partially, but their development is the subject of major research efforts (Vitiello & Jensen, 1995a). Only a tiny fraction of the potentially relevant neurochemicals have been studied developmentally with respect to their anatomic distribution, chemical activity, or functional significance.

Although major aspects of brain development are believed to be governed by complex gene homeobox structures, developing biochemical processes and structures in the brain are highly responsive to environmental influences and experiences. Neurotransmitters appear to exert trophic effects on brain structures and other neurotransmitter systems during development and thereby may produce lasting changes in the anatomical and biochemical organization of the brain.

In the human fetus, the developing neocortex has region-specific rates and time courses of change; that is, different parts show different developmental courses (Diebler, Farkas-Bargeton, & Wehle, 1979). Within each region, specific neurotransmitters show distinct rates and time courses of developmental change.

These region- and neurotransmitter-specific changes in brain development generally follow the caudal-to-rostral sequence that is characteristic of brain development (Coyle, 1987).

The particulars of these region-specific and neurotransmitter-specific maturational changes in each individual create an enormous diversity in the details of structures, connections, neurochemical activity, and receptor sensitivities in each part of the brain among different people. These details themselves change through time, partly in response to neuronally mediated stimulation and experience and partly in response to physiologic feedback and corrective reorganizations as the brain continues to mature.

Biochemical development of the human brain continues at least into late adolescence and merges into the slowly evolving neurochemical and neurophysiologic changes of adult life. There is no end point or completion date of neurochemical development (Popper, 1987b). It is impossible to specify an age or developmental level beyond which drugs become "safe."

DEVELOPMENTAL TOXICOLOGY AND NEUROTOXICOLOGY

A vulnerability to short-term side effects or long-term toxic effects of psychotropic medications persists throughout life. Concerns about potential long-term adverse effects of psychotropic drugs are magnified in children (Herskowitz, 1987) because unforeseen drug-induced effects on brain and body development are theoretically possible, and perhaps even likely.

Medications that are safe in adults can be dangerous in children. However, looking across the broad range of drugs used employed in psychiatry, neurology, and general medicine, only 5 examples of drug effects on brain or body in children were not and probably could not have been predicted from adult studies. That is, surprisingly few examples have been described of drugs that act on biologic development processes or that act specifically during postnatal biological development: the slowing of body growth by psychostimulants, the induction of Reye's syndrome by aspirin, the discoloration of body organs by tetracyclines, the impairment of myelin formation by hexachlorophene bathing of premature infants, and valproate-induced hepatotoxicity.

These developmental effects of drugs range from mild to severe. The only known postnatal drug effect that is exerted on the development of the central nervous system occurs exclusively in premature infants. But what is striking is that there are so few examples throughout all of medicine. Children's bodies and brains do not appear to be particularly more sensitive than the bodies and brains of adults to the toxic effects of drugs—except during the uniquely vulnerable period of intrauterine development, when teratogenic effects are apparent with numerous drugs. Therefore, when assessing the safety of psychopharmacological treatments in children, the adult toxicological model appears more applicable than the intrauterine teratogenic model.

In general, the track record of a medication in adults can serve as a reasonable estimate or first approximation of its likely adverse effects in children and adolescents. In this respect, pharmacological research in adults can yield information that allows clinicians to reduce safety risks to children. If a drug has a good track record of side effects in adults, it is likely to be comparably safe in children. But there is no substitute for direct studies of these medications in children and adolescents.

Toxicological studies on developing animals could be conducted in laboratories to assess possible "developmental" effects of medications. However, the usual preclinical toxicological studies examine the effects of drugs on laboratory animals during adulthood only, searching for carcinogenic, cytotoxic, and gross anatomical pathology (e.g., Dunnick & Hailey, 1995). Interestingly, at present, no studies—not even animal studies—are required by the FDA to identify possible *developmental* effects of new psychotropic agents prior to their commercial release.

The standard clinical tests that are conducted mainly in adults by a pharmaceutical manufacturer on a new drug prior to its commercial release are relatively extensive. However, subtle or infrequent adverse effects can easily be missed, because the premarketing studies generally involve only a few thousand patients. Often it takes several years of large-scale clinical use of commercially released drugs before rare or unusual side effects begin to be recognized. When chemically novel agents are prescribed in adults for some years before their introduction for routine use in children, unexpected problems due to short-term side effects and even long-term developmental toxicity generally would be expected to be quite low.

For newly released medications and especially those with novel chemical structures, it is strongly advisable that physicians delay or deemphasize their use in children until after the accumulation of a substantial multi-year track record of their use in adults.

This careful approach creates a dilemma, though, when a new drug offers a major therapeutic opportunity that is not otherwise available. The technical advance may lead to a relatively "early" extension of these treatments to children. For example, many clinicians were willing to treat children with new antidepressants (selective serotonin reuptake inhibitors, bupropion) and "atypical" neuroleptics (clozapine, risperidone) soon after their commercial release and before a multi-year track record in adults had accumulated to allow a large-scale assessment of potential risks and toxicity of these medications in adults.

While the benefits of these new drugs were sizable, the uncertainty regarding their risks must be considered sizable as well. In the same manner that tooth discoloration by tetracycline in children could not be anticipated from previous knowledge, it is possible—and even likely—that the new "comfort" with using novel psychotropic agents to treat children before having an adult track record will lead to some surprises in the future.

Clinical Decision Making in Pediatric Psychopharmacology

UNKNOWN EFFECTS OF DRUGS AND DISEASES

Just as clinicians, parents, and youths need sound scientific information about the short-term and long-term effects of drug treatments, they also need substantive knowledge about the short-term prospects, expectable course of illness, and long-term prognosis of psychiatric disorders in children and adolescents. Balanced information about drug treatments, alternative treatments, and disease characteristics are essential for any informed decision making in treatment planning.

Unfortunately, the course and prognosis are unknown for most emotional and behavioral disorders of childhood and adolescence. Apart from studies of attention deficit hyperactivity disorder (Schachar & Tannock, 1993), long-term follow-up studies on most of these biopsychiatric disorders of youths are few number, uncontrolled, contradictory, or seriously incomplete. Moreover, the complexities of comorbidity, family environment, and community response limit the capacity to make even short-term predictions about the future development of individual children.

As rudimentary as the knowledge of the side effects of child psychopharmacological treatment may be, there is even less precise description of the unintended consequences ("side effects") of most other treatment modalities. Dependency reactions, termination effects, and parental divorce are not unusual effects of psychosocial treatments of children and adolescents. Negative therapeutic reactions to most treatment modalities generally are not researched systematically, making it difficult to provide adequate description to inform a consent process or to assess the adverse treatment effects of pharmacotherapy in comparison to other treatments for youths with biopsychiatric disorders.

In addition to the enormous lack of knowledge about the developmental aspects of the safety and efficacy of psychotropic drug effects, there are serious inadequacies in current knowledge about psychopathology in youths and its prognosis. These knowledge gaps—about childhood psychiatric disorders, their treatment in general, and child psychopharmacological treatment—have direct implications for clinical decision making.

Uncertainties about potential drug effects and potential disease effects do not cancel each other out. Some physicians and families do not feel justified in proceeding with drug treatment in the face of these uncertainties. At times, these significant areas of unknowns and uncertainty seem to create impasse and can lead to the avoidance of valid biological treatments of biopsychiatric disorders.

This potential impasse usually can be resolved by weighing the unknowns about drug treatments against the unknowns about developmental psychopathology. In most cases, the largely unknown risks associated with the biopsychiatric disorders of youngsters (regarding course and prognosis) probably are more dangerous than the largely un-

known risks of their treatments. Even with the unknown potential for "developmental" drug side effects, the biopsychiatric disorders of youths probably have more serious consequences. For example, the prognosis in childhood-onset bipolar disorder appears more serious than in adult-onset cases, perhaps due to the greater genetic loading of early-onset disorders in psychiatry. In view of the 15% risk of mortality from suicide alone in adult-onset bipolar disorder, childhood-onset bipolar disorder would be expected to carry an even higher risk of mortality. In the absence of direct long-term developmental data, it seems that the risk of short-term and potentially long-term adverse developmental effects of lithium (or other mood stabilizers) is unlikely to approach the degree of risk associated with the natural course of childhood-onset bipolar disorder (Popper, 1987a).

The potential impasse in treatment posed by multiple levels of medical uncertainty can be surmounted. Even unknown risks can be thoughtfully weighed against each other.

In the face of incomplete data-derived knowledge, physicians still can base their judgments on available knowledge, balanced assessment of the known risks, a reasoned assessment of the unknown risks, and individual circumstances. The application of the medical knowledge base to actual clinical situations is rarely a simple process and itself requires considerable judgment. The uncertainties involved in clinical decision making require that the parent's informed consent (permission) and the child's assent for treatment be secured in a manner that promotes clinical understanding (American Academy of Pediatrics, Committee on Bioethics, 1995; Krener & Mancina, 1994; Popper, 1987a; Stine, 1994; also see Chapter 11 herein). Especially in pediatric psychopharmacology, a well-conducted process of consent/assent that deals with both information and patient attitudes to drug treatment can be expected to enhance compliance and thereby increase the likelihood of a successful therapeutic outcome (Bastiaens, 1995).

THE ROLE OF BASIC RESEARCH IN MAKING PSYCHOPHARMACOLOGICAL RECOMMENDATIONS FOR YOUTHS

Despite the recent appearance of increasingly specific neuropharmacological agents, most clinically used psychopharmacological medications still have numerous pharmacological effects. None of the psychopharmacological treatments are "clean" interventions. Clinically available medications do not act on a single neurotransmitter and instead have effects on several (or many) of the over 150 putative neurotransmitters and neuromodulators. No psychotropic agent has yet been assessed for its effects on all known neuroreceptor subtypes in all known transmitter systems.

Dextroamphetamine, for example, has at least 6 distinct biochemical mechanisms of action, each operating minimally at 35 locations in the human brain. Even a hypothetical agent that could produce a highly specific neuropharmacologic effect on a single receptor still would exert its influence at multiple sites corresponding to the regional distribution of the receptor throughout the brain and body.

The actual site or sites of action have not yet been fully determined for any therapeutic effect of a psychotropic drug in humans. This situation is likely to change, as new genetic techniques allow a more molecular picture of the physiologic or chemical mechanisms underlying medical disorders, which in turn may clarify sites and mechanisms of drug action.

Some sophisticated and insightful proposals have been generated to provide tentative explanations for the interplay of drug effects, psychiatric disease processes, and biologic development (Deutsch, Weizman, & Weizman, 1990; Rogeness, Javors, & Pliszka, 1992; Teicher, Andersen, Glod, Navalta, & Gelbard, 1997). However, our current knowledge of developmental psychopharmacology is quite embryonic and is not sufficient to offer clinicians more than simple and general concepts. And it would be quite remarkable if all neuropsychiatric diseases and psychotropic drugs were explicable in terms of the very few transmitters that have been examined so far.

The most useful contribution of basic science to clinical psychopharmacology remains the technological generation of new drugs. However, despite all of the current advances in technology and biology, the therapeutic effectiveness of psychotropic drugs for children and adolescents is still determined empirically in the clinical setting.

THE ROLE OF CLINICAL RESEARCH IN MAKING PSYCHOPHARMACOLOGICAL RECOMMENDATIONS FOR YOUTHS

Pediatric psychopharmacology, like most medical specialties, bridges a major gap between pharmacological research and clinical practice. Researchers examine a treatment under controlled conditions in patients with defined psychopathology, whereas clinicians conduct several treatments simultaneously under "naturalistic" conditions for patients with diverse psychopathology and comorbidity. Researchers often describe clinical change in predominantly statistical terms using numerical ratings derived from standardized scales that focus on targeted symptoms (Rapoport, Conners, & Reatig, 1985), whereas clinicians usually place primary emphasis on the impressionistic comments of a child and family, honed clinical judgment, and quality-of-life variables. The presence or absence of controls does not sufficiently characterize the strengths and weaknesses of these different approaches. Each has its own limitations and, when used singly, does not provide adequate answers to some fundamental questions about clinical drug treatment.

Finding drug *effectiveness* (a clinically significant therapeutic effect emerging during a drug treatment) in a clinical setting does not demonstrate that the mechanism of change was pharmacological, because multiple factors could explain an apparent improvement. So controlled research remains necessary to demonstrate (and quantify) the pharmacological component of the therapeutic change. Conversely, a medication with statistically demonstrable *efficacy* in controlled research studies may produce no clinically meaningful change in the patient's target symptoms, general functioning, or quality of life (especially in the context of comorbidity and life setting), or a medication may produce occasional or delayed adverse effects that do not appear in the controlled drug studies. Thus, systematic naturalistic studies are almost always required to demonstrate drug effectiveness. In rare cases, the naturalistic research might not be essential if a drug produces very large drug-placebo differences in the efficacy studies and overwhelmingly obvious clinical effects in uncontrolled settings. But this situation is rare in treating emotional and behavioral disorders, especially in youngsters. Naturalistic studies almost always are valuable for evaluating adverse drug effects in pediatric psychopharmacology.

Both controlled and naturalistic studies are essential to advance knowledge in child and adolescent psychopharmacology, because the advantages of each approach cannot be replaced by the other. Studies under controlled conditions always will have tight limits on their generalizability, while studies that lack placebo controls are inherently unable to prove treatment "efficacy." Both approaches are needed to demonstrate clinical mechanism and clinical value.

In a shift from nearly total reliance on controlled "efficacy" research for evaluation in clinical pharmacology, new "effectiveness" studies are starting to emerge based on clinical treatments conducted in naturalistic settings. The National Institute of Health is beginning to fund different research designs for drug evaluation in children (American Academy of Pediatrics, Committee on Drugs, 1995; Arnold, 1993; Elliott, 1995; Jensen, 1993; Rudorfer, 1993; Vitiello & Jensen, 1995), and the Food and Drug Administration also is showing some interest in using less traditional data sources in its drug approval process (Jensen et al., 1994). In part, these changes are occurring because treatments with apparent *effectiveness* in naturalistic clinical settings may not stand up once their *efficacy* is compared to placebo, and treatments that look "efficacious" in research settings may not be particularly "effective" in clinical settings.

The efficacy and effectiveness approaches seem associated with contrasting values and cultures, even for clinician researchers who strive to bridge the gap. At times, it seems as if different standards of "truth" lie at the heart of these 2 approaches, with the researchers upholding "knowledge" and clinicians endorsing "judgment" (Popper, 1995). Should treatments with demonstrated efficacy always be used first? Should a clinician use only treatments with demonstrated efficacy? Is it an advantage or disadvantage for patients if their clinician's decisions are based on a synthesis of "knowledge" of controlled research and "understanding" gained from other sources, with a critical eye toward both systems of belief? In child and adolescent psychopharmacology, where very few treatments have demonstrated efficacy or effec-

tiveness, these questions come up daily at virtually every step in clinical practice.

The few and therefore overvalued protocol studies in child and adolescent psychopharmacology leave many uncertainties, and the naturalistic studies are open to diverse interpretations. Most clinicians seem to lean toward a balanced combination of "evenly hovering" skepticism, gentle faith, and nonfinal judgment. Some researchers who have found a lack of treatment efficacy in their controlled studies continue to use those medications in their clinical practices, because they value their clinical as well as their research observations.

The notion that clinical decision making is "unscientific" can be quite misleading, since good science itself is not based exclusively on logic or empirical "knowledge." Intuition, interpretation, inductive thinking, weighing of uncertainties, and inferences from unreplicable circumstances play a part in the formation of scientific "knowledge" as much as in clinical "judgment." Bringing the findings of scientifically controlled clinical research into clinical psychopharmacological practice requires sophisticated disciplined thinking.

THE BIOPSYCHOSOCIAL-FINANCIAL MODEL IN PSYCHOPHARMACOLOGY

The biopsychosocial approach has been the dominant concept underlying the evaluation and treatment of emotional and behavioral disorders in recent decades. The more recent serious consideration of financial costs (Burke, Silkey, & Preskorn, 1994) has, at times, felt like an unwelcome addition and even an inappropriate intrusion, but most physicians have long worked to find ways to save money for patients when medically possible.

The traditional medical model of clinical pharmacological decision making has emphasized the balancing of risks and benefits of treatment. In an era when treatment costs are becoming relevant to clinical decisions, clinicians need to compare both risks and benefits to treatment costs. We need to replace our traditional evaluation of risks vs. benefits with a more updated examination of risks vs. benefits vs. costs.

The "risk-benefit-cost-ratio" has become a crucial clinical parameter. In addition to cost efficiency ("cost-sensible effectiveness"), we want medications whose greater safety is not excessively more costly ("cost-sensible safety").

The risk-benefit-cost ratio could be an essential factor in determining whether a new pharmacological agent constitutes an advance over traditional agents. A shift toward routine systematic risk-benefit-cost evaluation can be justified both in psychopharmacological research and in clinical practice.

At times, financial resources will set limits on what clinical research can do. Such limitations can make it difficult to obtain data that are needed as a basis for some important psychopharmacological decisions. For example, the use of multiple concurrent psychopharmacological treatments ("polypharmacy") in children is widespread and often clinically appropriate (see Chapter 11 in this volume; Wilens, Spencer, Biederman, Wozniak, & Connor, 1995), but systematic controlled research on drug combination treatments is almost unfeasible because of the size and technical complexity of "polypharmacy" studies. Complete studies would require the recruitment of at least 4 sizable comparison groups (without and without 1 drug, with and without the other drug) and so can cost as much as 2 or more other pharmacological studies. In an era of scarce resources, such expensive studies are not readily funded, so that funding can instead go to several competing research projects. Except for a very small number of crucial combined drug treatments (Carlson, Rapport, Kelly, & Pataki, 1995), most commonly used drug combinations in pediatric psychopharmacology are unlikely to be evaluated systematically in the foreseeable future.

The triumph of financially managed clinical care poses a potential threat to pediatric psychopharmacological practice. Although drug treatment of behavioral disorders sometimes is viewed as the preferred choice when simple cost-cutting is the primary goal, medication treatments need to be protected from overuse and indiscriminate use. By underemphasizing other treatment options, or failing to provide balanced multimodal treatments of these multidimensional biopsychosocial disorders, excessive cost-cutting can ask for too much from pharmacotherapy. On the positive size, the ascendance of therapeutic empiricism, the expansion and increasing sophistication of the scientific evaluation of clinical drug effects, and the growing academic interest in the cost effectiveness of psychopharmacological treatments are important historical forces that herald the likelihood of more effective biopsychosocial-financial techniques for helping children and adolescents afflicted by neuropsychiatrically based behavioral and emotional disorders.

Despite some lingering large and complex problems, nothing is more difficult in the field of pediatric psychopharmacology than discerning the proper relative roles of medication treatment and other types of therapeutic intervention. The split between these camps has been bridged successfully by many clinicians, but some still remain focused on providing primarily psychosocial or primarily biological treatments, not because of training and skills but because of a belief that one treatment orientation is superior to the other. These clinicians appear to operate with the belief that treatment can be polarized and focused on just the body or just the mind. These physicians are likely to provide poorly integrated care because their conceptions of their patients are unscientifically split.

The biopsychosocial-financial model is here to stay, and it challenges physicians to continued to learn new techniques in a fast-growing field. Clinicians can keep ready for future developments by reading tomorrow's journals. As technological advances offer more chemically sophisticated means to help these children, it will remain a clinical necessity to look at a child, see the disorder, see the illness around the disorder, and to treat them all.

REFERENCES

American Academy of Pediatrics, Committee on Bioethics. (1995). Informed consent, parental permission, and assent in pediatric practice. *Pediatrics, 95,* 314–317.

American Academy of Pediatrics, Committee on Drugs. (1995). Guidelines for the ethical conduct of studies to evaluate drugs in pediatric populations. *Pediatrics, 95,* 286–294.

American Psychiatric Association. (1980). *Diagnostic and statistical manual of mental disorders* (3rd ed.). Washington, DC: Author.

American Psychiatric Association. (1994). *Diagnostic and statistical manual of mental disorders* (4th ed.). Washington, DC: Author.

Arnold, L. E. (1993). A comparative overview of treatment research methodology: Adult vs. child and adolescent, psychopharmacological vs. psychosocial treatment. *Psychopharmacology Bulletin, 29,* 5–17.

Bastiaens, L. (1995). Knowledge, attitudes and compliance with pharmacotherapy in adolescent patients and their parents. *Journal of Child and Adolescent Psychopharmacology, 5,* 39–48.

Bradley, C. (1937). The behavior of children receiving Benzedrine. *American Journal of Psychiatry, 94,* 577–585.

Burke, M. J., Silkey, B., & Preskorn, S. H. (1994). Pharmacoeconomic considerations when evaluating treatment options for major depressive disorder. *Journal of Clinical Psychiatry, 55,* 42–52.

Carlson, G. A., Rapport, M. D., Kelly, K. L., & Pataki, C. S. (1995). Methylphenidate and desipramine in hospitalized children with comorbid behavior and mood disorders: Separate and combined effects on behavior and mood. *Journal of Child and Adolescent Psychopharmacology, 5,* 191–204.

Coyle, J. T. (1987). Biochemical development of the brain: Neurotransmitters and child psychiatry. In C. W. Popper (Ed.), *Psychiatric pharmacosciences of children and adolescents* (pp. 3–26). Washington, DC: American Psychiatric Press.

Deutsch, S. I., Weizman, A., & Weizman, P. (1990). Application of basic neuroscience to child psychiatry. New York: Plenum Medical Book Company.

Diebler, M. F., Farkas-Bargeton, E., & Wehle, P. (1979). Developmental changes of enzymes associated with energy metabolism and the synthesis of some neurotransmitters in discrete areas of human neocortex. *Journal of Neurochemistry, 32,* 429–435.

Dunnick, J. K., & Hailey, J. R. (1995). Experimental studies on the long-term effects of methylphenidate hydrochloride. *Toxicology, 103,* 77–84.

Elliott, G. R. (1995). The National Plan for Research on Child and Adolescent Disorders: A report card at the midway point [editorial]. *Journal of Child and Adolescent Psychopharmacology, 5,* 87–91.

Herskowitz, J. (1987). Developmental toxicology. In C. W. Popper (Ed.), *Psychiatric pharmacosciences of children and adolescents* (pp. 83–123). Washington, DC: American Psychiatric Press.

Food and Drug Administration, Department of Health and Human Services, United States Government. (1992, October 16). Specific requirements on content and format of labeling for human prescription drugs; Proposed revision of "Pediatric Use" subsection in the Labeling [21 CFR Part 201]. *Federal Register, 57* (201), 47423–47427.

Jatlow, P. I. (1987). Psychotropic drug disposition during development. In C. W. Popper (Ed.), *Psychiatric pharmacosciences of children and adolescents* (pp. 29–44). Washington, DC: American Psychiatric Press.

Jensen, P. S. (1993). Development and implementation of multimodal and combined treatment studies in children and adolescents: NIMH perspectives. *Psychopharmacology Bulletin, 29,* 19–26.

Jensen, P. S., Vitiello, B., Leonard, H., & Laughren, T. P. (1994). Child and adolescent psychopharmacology: Expanding the research base. *Psychopharmacology Bulletin, 30,* 3–8.

Krener, P. K., & Mancina, R. A. (1994). Informed consent or informed coercion? Decision-making in pediatric psychopharmacology. *Journal of Child and Adolescent Psychopharmacology, 4,* 183–200.

Licamele, W. L., & Goldberg, R. L. (1989). The concurrent use of methylphenidate and lithium in a child. *Journal of the American Academy of Child and Adolescent Psychiatry, 28,* 785–787.

Physicians' Desk Reference, 51st edition. (1997). Montvale, N.J.: Medical Economics Co., Inc.

Pippinger, C. E. (1980). Rationale and clinical application of therapeutic drug monitoring. Pediatric Clinics of North America 27, 891–895.

Popper, C. W. (1995, April). Balancing knowledge and judgment: A clinician looks at new developments in child and adolescent psychopharmacology [review]. *Child and Adolescent Psychiatric Clinics of North America, 4,* 483–513.

Popper, C. W. (1987a). Medical unknowns and ethical consent: Prescribing psychotropic medication for children in the face of uncertainty. In C. W. Popper, *Psychiatric pharmacosciences of children and adolescents* (pp. 127–161). Washington, DC: American Psychiatric Press.

Popper, C. W. (Ed.). (1987b). *Psychiatric pharmacosciences of children and adolescents.* Washington, DC: American Psychiatric Press.

Rapoport, J. L., Conners, C. K., & Reatig, N. (1985). Rating scales and assessment instruments for use in pediatric psychopharmacology research. *Psychopharmacology Bulletin, 21,* 714–1124.

Rogeness, G. A., Javors, M. A., & Pliszka, S. R. (1992). Neurochemistry and child and adolescent psychiatry. *Journal of the American Academy of Child and Adolescent Psychiatry, 31,* 765.

Rudorfer, M. V. (1993). Challenges in medication clinical trials. *Psychopharmacology Bulletin, 29,* 35–44.

Schachar, R., & Tannock, R. (1993). Childhood hyperactivity and psychostimulants: A review of extended treatment studies. *Journal of Child and Adolescent Psychopharmacology, 3,* 81–97.

Stine, J. J. (1994). Psychosocial and psychodynamic issues affecting noncompliance with psychostimulant treatment. *Journal of Child and Adolescent Psychopharmacology, 4,* 75–86.

Teicher, M. H., Andersen, S. L., Glod, C. A., Navalta, C. P., & Gelbard, H. A. (1997). Neuropsychiatric disorders of childhood and adolescence. In S. C. Yudofsky and R. E. Hales (Eds.), *American Psychiatric Press textbook of neuropsychiatry* (3rd ed.). Washington, DC: American Psychiatric Press, 1997, pp. 903–940.

Teicher, M. H., & Baldessarini, R. J. (1987). Developmental pharmacodynamics. In C. W. Popper (Ed.), *Psychiatric pharmacosciences of children and adoles-*cents (pp. 47–80). Washington, DC: American Psychiatric Press.

Vitiello, B., Behar, D., Malone, R., Delaney, M. A., Ryan, P. J., & Simpson, G. M. (1988). Pharmacokinetics of lithium carbonate in children. *Journal of Clinical Psychopharmacology, 8,* 355–359.

Vitiello, B., & Jensen, P. S. (1995a). Developmental perspectives in pediatric psychopharmacology. *Psychopharmacology Bulletin, 31,* 75–81.

Vitiello, B., & Jensen, P. S. (1995b). Psychopharmacology in children and adolescents: Current problems, future prospects: Summary notes on the 1995 NIMH-FDA conference. *Journal of Child and Adolescent Psychopharmacology, 5,* 5–7.

Wilens, T. E., Spencer, R., Biederman, J., Wozniak, J., & Connor, D. (1995). Combined pharmacotherapy: An emerging trend in pediatric psychopharmacology. *Journal of the American Academy of Child and Adolescent Psychiatry, 34,* 110–112.

11 / Clinical Aspects of Child and Adolescent Psychopharmacotherapy

Charles W. Popper

Many currently dominant techniques in child and adolescent psychopharmacology are not legitimatized by controlled clinical research. Instead, the "standard of care" floats on a surface of tradition, clinicians' training (often many years in the past), physicians' observations and recollection of their experiences, clinical rumor ("This is how we do it at the University Clinic"), the seemingly established knowledge contained in textbooks, and the fluidly changing medical literature consisting of anecdotal reports, case series, pilot investigations, original naturalistic and controlled research, the occasional confirmation of findings from a prior research study, and speculation. The term *standard of care* imparts an air of authority and summons a mythical image of scientifically demonstrated and time-tested clinical knowledge.

The field of general psychopharmacology has blossomed into a huge enterprise, with international distribution of modern treatment methods and grand research primarily focused on adults. In comparison, child and adolescent psychophar-macology is a small but growing puppy. About 80% of the new research in pediatric psychopharmacology is published in just 2 journals, the *Journal of Child and Adolescent Psychopharmacology* and the *Journal of the American Academy of Child and Adolescent Psychiatry.* Several excellent textbooks on pediatric psychopharmacology are available (Green, 1995; Riddle, 1995; Rosenberg et al., 1994; Theesen, 1995; Werry & Aman, 1993). But knowledge that guides clinical decision making for youngsters still is quite rudimentary (see Table 11.1) and consists substantially of "hand-me-down" information derived from adult psychopharmacology.

Even if the contents of this chapter could be based predominantly on a knowledge base consisting of efficacy and effectiveness studies conducted in youths (see Chapter 10), it is recommended that readers understand that this interpretation of current techniques in child and adolescent psychopharmacology is offered with a tentativeness befitting beliefs that require further

TABLE 11.1

Indications for Psychopharmacological Treatment in Children and Adolescents

Psychopharmacological Treatment	Established[a]	Probable[b]	Proposed[c]
Psychostimulants	Attention deficit hyperactivity disorder	Inattentiveness Impulsive behavior Hyperactivity Agressive behavior	Oppositional defiant disorder Emotional lability SSRI-induced apathy
Heterocyclic Antidepressants	Enuresis Attention deficit hyperactivity disorder Bulimia nervosa	Major depressive disorder Panic disorder Phobic disorder School absenteeism Sleep terror disorder	Dysthymic disorder Separation anxiety disorder Sleepwalking disorder Aggressive behavior
Selective Serotonin Reuptake Inhibitors	Obsessive-compulsive disorder	Major depressive disorder Dysthymic disorder Panic disorder Bulimia nervosa Pervasive developmental disorder Selective mutism Phobic disorder School absenteeism	Self-injurious behavior Attention deficit hyperactivity disorder Separation anxiety disorder Body dysmorphic disorder Aggressive behavior
Venlafaxine		Attention deficit hyperactivity disorder Obsessive-compulsive disorder Major depressive disorder	Dysthymic disorder Pervasive developmental disorder SSRI-induced apathy Selective mutism Separation anxiety disorder
Clomipramine	Obsessive-compulsive disorder Attention deficit hyperactivity disorder	Pervasive developmental disorder	Major depressive disorder Stuttering
Bupropion		Attention deficit hyperactivity disorder Bulimia nervosa Major depressive disorder	Dysthymic disorder SSRI-induced apathy
Monoamine Oxidase Inhibitors		Bulimia nervosa Attention deficit hyperactivity disorder	Major depressive disorder Enuresis Panic disorder
Valproate		Bipolar disorder	Conduct disorder with aggressive behavior Rage outbursts Schizophrenia Seizure-related behavioral disorders
Carbamazepine	Attention deficit hyperactivity disorder	Bipolar disorder	Conduct disorder with aggressive behavior Rage outbursts Major depressive disorder Seizure-related behavioral disorders

TABLE 11.1

Continued

Psychopharmacological Treatment	Established[a]	Probable[b]	Proposed[c]
Lithium	Overt mania	Bipolar disorder Major depressive disorder Antidepressant augmentation Conduct disorder with aggressive behavior	Aggressive behavior Rage outbursts Cyclothymic disorder Emotional lability Self-injurious behavior
Neuroleptics	Schizophrenia Mania Organic psychosis Delusional disorder Tourette's disorder Pervasive developmental disorder Agitation Preoperative sedation Extreme situational anxiety	Aggressive behavior Impulsive behavior Destructive behavior Attention deficit hyperactivity disorder	Emergency control of agitation (PRN dosing or chemical restraints)
Benzodiazepines	Anxiety Neuroleptic-induced akathisia Psychosis (as supplement to neuroleptics) Lithium-induced tremor	Extreme situational anxiety Pre-operative sedation Sleep induction Panic disorder Phobic disorder Night terror disorder	Tic disorders Generalized anxiety disorder Separation anxiety disorder Sleepwalking disorder Head-banging
Antihistaminic Sedatives	Neuroleptic-induced extrapyramidal symptoms	Peroperative sedation Sleep induction	Emergency control of control agitation or anxiety (PRN dosing or chemical restraints)
Buspirone			Generalized anxiety disorder Agitation or impulsivity associated with brain injury
Clonidine		Stimulant-induced insomnia Some drug withdrawal syndromes	Tic disorders Attention deficit hyperactivity disorder Oppositional defiant disorder Stuttering Hyperexcitement Self-injurious behavior Post-traumatic stress disorder Anxiety Anxiety disorders

TABLE 11.1

Continued

Psychopharmacological Treatment	Established[a]	Probable[b]	Proposed[c]
Beta Blockers	Lithium-induced tremor Neuroleptic-induced akathisia	Anxiety Rage outbursts Agitation associated with brain injury or mental retardation	Attention deficit hyperactivity disorder Impulsive behavior Anxiety disorders
Desmopressin	Enuresis		
Piracetam		Developmental reading disorder	

[a]Established: Supported by (1) well-controlled studies or (2) long-standing tradition with apparent effectiveness.
[b]Probable: In author's opinion, likely to prove effective in future studies.
[c]Proposed: Supported by uncontrolled data or anecdotal evidence; clinical value is uncertain but empirical trials are reasonable. [This is not a complete list of reasonable indications for empirical trials.]

examination. At best, the knowledge base in child and adolescent psychopharmacology remains quite limited—especially from the point of view of children and families whose lives we can improve only to a mild or moderate degree with current psychopharmacological techniques.

Future and probably imminent advances in this field will overtake the clinical methods described here. Techniques will be improved, extended, and supplanted as new drugs, new concepts, new studies, and new clinical observations are contributed. The speed with which the current techniques are supplanted will be a direct measure of medical progress.

Psychopharmacological treatments today are rarely the sole or even primary treatment for most children and adolescents with emotional and behavioral disorders. Instead, these drug treatments typically serve as one of several components in a developmentally oriented multimodal treatment.

Occasional patients are suitably treated with pharmacotherapy alone, but they are the exceptions. Clinicians are unlikely to encounter these children, who present with a "pure" biopsychiatric disorder that is unaccompanied by developmental complications of illness, neurocognitive deficits, disruptive stress in the home environment, or personality or family factors that interfere with securing and complying to treatment regimens. The unusual children with "pure" biopsychiatric illness, once treated with medication, do not show significant emotional or behavioral problems, de-

velopmental impairments, or residual deficits that require long-term, multimodal, or intensive interventions.

These patients constitute an atypical but theoretically important subgroup because their clinical presentations highlight the symptoms of the "core" biological disorder, unobscured the usual complications. The "core" symptoms help us define the essential features of the disorder, see which common symptoms are not directly related to the metabolic and physiologic mechanisms underlying the illness, and more readily recognize presenting symptoms or even diagnostic criteria of the illness that may instead relate to family and circumstance.

These unusual children can be managed appropriately with pharmacotherapy, education of the child and family about the illness and its treatment, instructions about early warning signs of potential relapse, brief communications with pediatrician and school, periodic medical monitoring with ongoing attention to the knowledge and attitudes of the child and family to the illness and treatment, and perhaps follow-up visits every 6 to 24 months after drug discontinuation to help maintain perspective on the illness and facilitate future help-seeking. These exceptional children may even have a severe form of the illness but, if they respond to psychopharmacological treatment, have a good prognosis.

In contrast, the vast majority of children with biopsychiatric disorders have developmental causes and consequences of their biopsychiatric disturbances that justify or require additional therapeutic interventions. In these children, the "core" biological symptoms have become embedded within a system that reflects problems of the past, the frailties of family members (often biopsychiatric frailties), the strengths and weakness of family structures and supports, the barriers and opportunities in the community, traumatic experiences, the consequences of financial or environmental poverty, the accumulating developmental deficits (academic, cognitive, social, affective, somatic), impaired intrapsychic competences (loss of self-discipline, hope, self-esteem, motivation), ineffective self-care and self-management, among others.

In most children and adolescents, psychopharmacotherapy works in concert with psychotherapeutic, cognitive, behavioral, psychosocial, educational, and other medical interventions aimed at establishing or re-establishing developmental success.

Managing Medication Treatments in Youths

GENERAL MEDICAL PROCEDURES

Prior to starting any drug treatment, a medical history and physical examination should be conducted. Not all drugs require pretreatment laboratory testing, but a thyroid screen, complete blood profile (hematocrit, white blood count and differential, platelet count), liver function tests (transaminases and total bilirubin), and perhaps renal tests (serum creatinine, blood urea nitrogen) generally are useful to rule out physical conditions that might exacerbate or conceivably cause biopsychiatric symptoms, and also for comparison in the event of untoward drug reactions. Neurologic evaluation and other consultations (psychology, neuropsychology), electroencephalogram, and neuroimaging should depend on individual circumstances. Baseline data are needed on height, weight, heart rate, and blood pressure (with pediatric cuff). Observations to identify any baseline tics or dyskinesias should be made directly by the prescribing physician. School nurses should be informed in writing of medication treatments, including a statement of anticipated side effects and a request for periodic feedback concerning therapeutic and adverse effects observed at school.

Many adolescents will experiment with the ingestion of alcohol (whatever the legal drinking age may be) and other banned recreational substances. Recognizing this aspect of reality, many physicians choose to advise some adolescent psychiatric patients about "pharmacologically safe" limits of alcohol use in the context of their psychotropic treatment—while emphasizing the legal, medical, and interpersonal (family, friends) risks. This approach is controversial. For those physicians who employ this approach, some pharmacological generalizations can be relevant. In general, once medication doses have been steady for 2 weeks, a responsible adolescent may be allowed to drink in moderation, drive a car, or use machinery in shop class. With most adolescents, safe limits for the use of alcohol are two glasses of wine or beer, or one glass of whiskey or other spirits (1.2 ounces of 80-proof liquor), per evening. Regarding other substances of abuse (with the possible exception of marijuana), ingestion at any dose in combination with psychopharmacotherapy is prohibitively dangerous. A history of impulsivity or poor judgment or a significant risk of unmoderated alcohol or substance use (especially in drug-prone or conduct-disordered youth) can prevent safe medication treatment in some cases. In other cases, though, the risks of not using a medication may exceed the risks of its use.

Every 3 to 6 months at a minimum, children should have redocumentation of their height, weight, blood pressure, pulse, tics, and dyskinesias. A physical examination, a repeat of baseline blood tests (hematology, thyroid, liver, kidney), and perhaps an electrocardiogram (depending on the drug) should be obtained annually for any child on long-term drug treatment. Twice-yearly dental care should be ensured, especially for children receiving medications with anticholinergic properties, because mouth dryness can accelerate plaque formation and the development of caries (tooth cavities).

DOSAGE MANAGEMENT

When initiating drug treatment, it is worthwhile to start with a small test dose, in order to be certain that the individual is not an extremely slow metabolizer of that agent. Subsequently, gradual changes in doses usually can minimize adverse effects. Doses should be reevaluated every 6 to 12 months with trials of both higher and lower doses. If lower doses are tolerated, a trial off medication may be considered. When stopping a treatment, all psychotropic medications except lithium should be tapered slowly and monitored for possible withdrawal effects and symptom recurrence.

Dose requirements of a drug can change over time in response to the evolution of the behavioral or emotional disorder, developmental shifts in pharmacokinetics and pharmacodynamics, puberty, psychosocial maturational crises, psychological stress at home and school, physical exercise (sometimes a dose reduction on the day of competitive athletic event is necessary to avoid toxicity during dehydration), variable eating patterns (skipped meals), diet (caffeine, salt, fluids), alcohol and drug experimentation, exposures to toxins and environmental chemicals, seasonal and circadian changes (temperature, light), and intercurrent illness (upper respiratory infections may require temporary dose decreases of anticholinergic agents, which can be overly drying to mucosal membranes).

THERAPEUTICALLY APPROPRIATE POLYPHARMACY

Multiple concurrent use of psychotropic drugs—combination treatments—is often appropriate and necessary. A large variety of combined treatments now in common use (Wilens, Spencer, Biederman, Wozniak, & Connor, 1995). When 2 drugs produce therapeutic effects through different mechanisms, usually it is expected that their combined use would increase the overall therapeutic effect. However, 2 drugs do not necessarily produce a better outcome, even when side effects and drug interactions are not problematic. Although the combination of a psychostimulant and a tricyclic antidepressant is commonly used to treat attention deficit hyperactivity disorder, it appears under well-controlled conditions to offer only modest benefits over treatment with a single agent (Carlson, Rapport, Kelly, & Pataki, 1995; Pataki, Carlson, Kelly, Rapport, & Bincaniello, 1993; Rapport, Carlson, Kelly, & Pataki, 1993).

The prescribing physician must anticipate and sometimes manage drug interactions. Drug combinations can act additively in producing cognitive impairments, anticholinergic side effects, and cardiovascular reactions.

Drug-induced cognitive impairments in children are quite common and generally mild but often are overlooked. Such impairments typically include word-finding difficulty, forgetfulness, difficulty in focusing on detail, impaired concentration, mind racing or mind slowing, clouding of consciousness ("fogginess"), or mild confusion-like states (cognitive "scrambling").

CONSENT AND ASSENT FOR TREATMENT

Informed consent or "permission" (American Academy of Pediatrics, Committee on Bioethics, 1995) for treatment is provided by parents, and assent of the child is essential for clinical (as well as legal) reasons.

Informed consent is based on substantive disclosure of the goal, nature, costs, and risks of treatment as well as reasonable alternative treatment approaches. For most treatments in pediatric psychopharmacology, informed consent also should imply an explicit awareness that there may be unknown risks in young people.

Children are legally presumed to be unable to provide consent, so the notion of assent has been developed (Krener & Mancina, 1994; Popper 1987). Obtaining assent is a sensible clinical step that helps the clinicians and parents be aware of the hesitations and concerns of the child. What constitutes appropriate "assent" depends on the child's capacity for understanding and is best approached in a manner that respects the individuality of the child.

Although a child will need education about the pharmacotherapy at the start of the treatment, multiple opportunities to ask questions and express concerns about the psychopharmacological treatment are essential throughout the course of treatment. Written information sheets, prepared to be reader-friendly for children and adolescents, have been published (Bastiaens & Bastiaens, 1993; Dulcan, 1992) and have been shown to be effective in enhancing knowledge about, attitudes toward, and feelings concerning psychotropic medication treatments (Bastiaens, 1995). Especially for treatments that persist over several years, children can make use of periodic discussions about the nature and purpose of their medication treatment. Such discussions allow children to update and expand their knowledge about their treatment, keeping pace with their increasing cognitive abilities. Although it is obviously valuable to enhance adolescents' knowledge of these treatments, their attitudes and feelings toward psychotropic medications appear to be better predictors (than their knowledge) of compliance to psychopharmacological treatment (Bastiaens, 1995). Ongoing attention to the knowledge, attitudes, and feelings of youths toward their medication treatments can be expected to improve clinical outcome.

For a variety of reasons, some parents say "The doctor knows best" and turn their decisions over to the judgment of the doctor, but these parents are attempting to avoid emotional involvement and responsibility for their decisions. Especially for "unproven" treatments, parents should "wrestle" emotionally with the decision to start a medication treatment, because usually some conflicting considerations need to be weighed against each other. If a parent cannot provide such full "emotional consent," treatment sometimes has to proceed with the disadvantages of the "best available consent" and of the parent's ongoing ambivalence toward the treatment, which the child usually can feel.

Recommendations for psychopharmacological treatment of children sometimes evoke special alarm. Even some professionals view drugs as dangerous, particularly when the illness or treatment is a new concept for them. It is best to expect some emotionally charged reactions or irrational concerns to arise and require management. Some community-based resistance is based on realistic limitations; for example, where schools do not have nurses to provide safe administration, residential programs do not have full medical coverage, and homes do not have consistent parental supervision. At times, it is best to defer drug therapy until other interventions permit effective environmental support for the treatment.

To reduce the risk of the child being exposed to nonsupportive comments from influential people, all parents (and sometimes other caregiving figures) should be directly involved in the treatment (Krener & Mancina, 1994). When a divorced parent lives in another state, even one phone call a month can generate turmoil if that parent tells the child not to take the medication or voices doubt. This parent should given the opportunity for direct contact with the prescribing physician. The physician should be prepared to explain the treatment to the faraway parent in detail, and answer questions, as a routine part of the child's treatment. Other influential caregivers (e.g., the babysitting grandmother, the soccer coach) might involved as well and can be kept informed by the parents.

Similarly, all sibs should be informed and given the chance to ask questions of the parents, in order to forestall the possibility of inappropriate teasing or counterproductive remarks.

DOCUMENTING CONSENT FOR TREATMENT

Documentation of consent and assent in the medical chart is a crucial aspect of physicians' legal protection. Its primary clinical value is that it helps the physician conceptualize the treatment structure. Both initial notes and progress notes are essential components of chart documentation of the consent and assent process for a child or adolescent in psychopharmacological treatment. The first such clinical note in the medical record should document the initial consent and assent for medication treatment. It should contain:

1. Date when caregiver's consent (permission) and patient's assent (agreement) were provided initially.
2. A clinical description of the parents' and child's responsiveness in the consent/assent process, including a statement about their cognitive involvement in the consent process and an estimate of their degree of understanding.
3. Diagnoses and/or target symptoms for medication treatment.
4. Drug name, starting dose, estimated rate of increase, and estimated maximal dose.
5. Comorbid psychiatric, neurologic, or medical conditions that may interact with the drug.
6. Clinician's observations of relevant baseline physical parameters (e.g., height, blood pressure, tics) and significant baseline laboratory findings.
7. Possible sources of medication abuse in the child's situation. Progress notes in the medical chart should document changes in items 2 through 5 during the course of treatment.

It is desirable but not essential to record explicit information regarding the treatment goal, process, costs, and risks, and the possible alternative treatment approaches, as described to the parents. While it is also not required to list all adverse effects that were mentioned in the consent discussions, it is useful to name the most serious side effects that were discussed and, for newer treatments or those newly introduced for children, to note that some side effects in children are likely to be unknown. At times, it is worthwhile commenting on some of the environmental obstacles to treatment that the child might encounter.

Written consent forms are commonly used, largely for legal reasons, but these forms have little value. In court, they mainly serve to prove that the signer was present at the time of starting treatment. The signed forms do not prove that the treatment was appropriately explained or that the signer understood what was said or written. Indeed, many studies show that adults frequently misunderstand the content of such forms. Written consent can reinforce a belief that pharmacotherapy is more important or powerful than psychosocial interventions, which are rarely tied to written permission. The signing of a consent form might give the appearance, to physician and parent, that the consent process has been completed, whereas genuine consent requires an ongoing process throughout treatment of increasing awareness and understanding by patient and family. Most important, the signing of a consent form does not in any way substitute for good verbal explanations and multiple meetings at which the parents can ask questions of the prescribing physician. Chart notes that describe the consent process are a clinically and legally stronger form of consent.

PSYCHOSOCIAL INTERVENTIONS WITH PHARMACOTHERAPY

Pills are a form of help, and, to many children and adults, they carry an aura of power. These 2 characteristics tend to evoke rapid and sometimes strong emotional, cognitive, and behavioral reactions from patients and families toward the pills (and the clinician). These reactions can be helpful and aid in focusing the patient and family toward making good use of the medication treatment. However, the reactions also can be directed *against* the drug treatment and interfere with its effectiveness. Treatment noncompliance, lowered expectations for improvement, and increased complaints regarding minor side effects are examples of how these patient reactions and family interactions can interfere with treatment.

It is quite typical for such reactions against drug treatment (involving both mental and behavioral obstacles, to both the pills and the prescribing clinician, by both the child and family members) to parallel the "resistances" seen in the psychosocial interventions. In traditional technical language, clinicians have an opportunity to use the pharmacologic treatment process as an arena for "transference" work. However, because pills are tangible, the patient's and families' disruptive reactions to pharmacotherapy often can outline more clearly and concretely the emotional, cognitive, and behavioral reactions that may appear more slowly and be more difficult to identify and manage in psychosocial treatments. The prescribing psychopharmacologist must be ready to handle these reactions, in coordination with the psychotherapist and treatment team. Dealing with the obstacles and reactions to pharmacologic treatment allows rapid access to personal psychologic reactions and family interactions, and thereby can have far-ranging impact on the child's use of medication, psychosocial interventions, and help in general.

The addition of a pharmacotherapy to ongoing psychosocial treatment can sometimes feel awkward to both patients and therapists. To initiate a medication-oriented evaluation or treatment in the midst of ongoing psychosocial interventions, it is helpful to state explicitly "I would like to take another look . . ." or "I want to take another approach" as an introduction to reviewing some parts of the history or asking questions that might cover new ground (hallucinations, details of sleep, etc.).

Medication treatments can enhance or interfere with the effectiveness of other treatment modalities. The influence of other therapies can lead to over- or underestimating the effectiveness of medications, and pharmacotherapy can exaggerate or obscure the influence of psychosocial interventions.

INFORMATION FLOW AROUND THE PRESCRIBING PHYSICIAN

A clinician's use of a pharmacotherapy is based largely on experience, including experience with a particular psychopharmacological agent and with management aspects of these treatments. The physician's sense of comfort and familiarity is essential to avoid certain iatrogenic adverse effects in the clinical process and to optimize its impact. For new clinical treatments, this comfort often is achieved through consultation and direct supervision. Due to the developmental stage of scientific knowledge in this field, the application of many current child psychopharmacological treatments brings each clinician into an innovative position in carrying the products of psychopharmacology research into pediatric practice. In the absence of established drugs of choice for most of these disorders, even the clinician's selection of first-choice and subsequent choice agents involves thoughtful innovation. (See Table 11.2.)

At times the potential anxiety of managing new treatments can lead to avoidant underprescribing or, alternatively, to aggressive overprescribing. The best interests of children are served by the waning of the mistakenly "protective" taboos and the "admiring" idealizations placed on their psychopharmacological treatment (and research). Empirical studies of the relative contributions, risks, and interactions of psychopharmacological and psychosocial treatments are needed to refine the scope of our scientific imagination and to define the actual contributions and limitations of these medical techniques.

In a fast-changing pharmacological world of child and adolescent psychopharmacology, the "established" drug treatments may not be so established. Psychopharmacologists, working with changing tools in clinical practice, often are evaluating "partially studied" drugs and "barely studied" drugs in children.

The "standard of care" now includes some novel drug treatments that are not established at all and perhaps have never been examined systematically. Significant progress is being made by the Food and Drug Administration (United States Government) in promoting pharmacokinetic studies in children prior to marketing, encouraging postmarketing studies of children, and expanding information on treatment of children contained in package inserts (Food and Drug Administration [hereafter FDA], 1992). But bupropion, venlafaxine, nefazodone, fluvoxamine, and perhaps moclobemide are arriving on the scene before child psychopharmacologists have sorted out heterocyclic antidepressants vs. selective serotonin reuptake inhibitors (SSRIs). We appear to be entering an era in which attractive new pharmacological options might become outdated before adequate safety and efficacy data can be secured in children.

PARENTS AND SIBLINGS

Many children with biopsychiatric disorders have parents who themselves carry significant emotional and behavioral pathology. When a parent who is troubled by psychosis or depression exerts a major influence on the child and the child's environment, the pharmacologic evaluation and treatment of a parent's biopsychiatric disorder is an essential component of the child's treatment.

The recognition that many parents have drug-treatable disorders has had a major impact on the traditional model of treatment for youngsters with emotional and behavioral disorders. With the integration of the biological approach into pediatric practice, parents are taking the explicit role of patient as well as the role of child caregiver. Such parents formerly might have believed that they were seeking help for "parent counseling" only, or viewed their related psychosocial treatment under the guise of parent guidance, but parents cannot receive pharmacotherapy without explicitly taking the patient role.

Taking a medication makes it clear to parents that they are not merely seeking professional help "for the sake of the child." It forces them to confront their own biopsychiatric disorder and into an active position in seeking personal change in their emotional and behavioral symptoms. But it does not undercut parents' treatment to emphasize the impact of their own potential change on the potential development of the child.

The clinical task of helping parents contemplate this significant conceptual shift usually is facilitated by a simple and frank statement about the genetics of the child's disorder. For example, "Whenever we find a child who has this type of drug-responsive biomedical disorder, we often (or usually) find a parent who has a related medical condition with drug-treatable symptoms." Exactly the same point needs to be made to help parents realize that other siblings also might need a similar evaluation.

TABLE 11.2

Drugs for Neuropsychiatric Disorders of Children and Adolescents:
A View of Preferential Order for Empirical Drug Trials

These suggestions describe my personal order of preference for specific drug trials to be used in treating different emotional and behavioral disorders in youths. It provides a reasoned view of drug sequences for the treatment of imaginary patients and would be altered in response to actual individual characteristics of real patients, such as therapeutic and adverse responses to prior medication trials, comorbid biopsychiatric disorders, comorbid symptoms (suicidality, substance abuse, lethargy, etc.), concurrent medications, age, family history of response to medications, parental supervision, financial resources, child and family preference, among many other factors. Moreover, this abstracted list of medications does not portray augmentation strategies (except for heterocyclic antidepressants [HCAs] plus selective serotonin reputake inhibitors [SSRIs] to offset SSRI-induced apathy) or other forms of therapeutically appropriate polypharmacy.

Disorder or Condition	Medication Sequence
Acute stress	Benzodiazepines, antihistamines
Aggressive conduct disorder	Valproate, lithium, olanzapine, risperidone, trazodone
Attention deficit hyperactivity disorder	Dextroamphetamine, methylphenidate, Adderall®, bupropion, venlafaxine, imipramine, nortriptyline
Bipolar disorder	Valproate, controlled-release lithium, carbamazepine, conventional neuroleptics, clozapine
Bulimia nervosa	HCA, SSRI with an HCA
Enuresis	Imipramine, nortriptyline, desmopressin
Extreme situational anxiety	Conventional neuroleptics, benzodiazepines
Major depressive disorder	Venlafaxine, SSRI with an HCA, bupropion, imipramine
Obsessive-compulsive disorder	SSRI with an HCA, clomipramine
Organic psychosis	Risperidone, olanzapine, conventional neuroleptics
Overanxious disorder	Benzodiazepines, buspirone risperidone, olanzapine
Panic disorder	SSRI with an HCA, benzodiazepines, MAOI monoamine oxidase inhibitor
Pervasive developmental disorder	Venlafaxine, SSRI with an HCA, risperidone, valproate
Post-traumatic stress disorder	SSRI with an HCA, nadolol, clonidine
Schizophrenia	Risperidone, olanzapine conventional neuroleptics, clozapine
Selective mutism	SSRI with an HCA
Tourette's disorder	Risperidone, olanzapine pimozide, conventional neuroleptics

GENERATING HOPE

The seriousness of a biopsychiatric diagnosis and the severity of the disorder are no longer the key determinants of prognosis in most youngsters. With the growing availability of effective child psychopharmacological treatments, it appears that most children can achieve somewhat successful management of their biopsychiatric symptoms through the available relatively primitive treatments.

Increasingly, the limiting factor in disease progression and prognosis is the child's and family's ability to seek professional help, to overcome their "resistances" to treatment, to learn to use medications properly, and to perceive warning signs of returning symptoms.

It is important for youths and parents to feel their influence on the course of the illness. A child who has a very severe bipolar disorder might, if able to obtain and stay involved in effective pharmacotherapy and psychosocial treatments, have a future that shows minimal effects of the biological illness. In contrast, a child with a mild mood disorder but who does not seek treatment may have lifetime course of chronic underachievement, underemployment, and underfulfillment.

When children and families are confronted with difficult news concerning diagnosis and biological severity, it is crucial for them to understand that—realistically—the future course of the illness does not lie outside of their hands: They need to be informed directly that the *learnable* ability to *recognize* the illness and to *get* care promptly is the major determinant of the future course for most of these young patients.

The development of help-seeking behaviors, both by the child and the family, can be promoted by helping the child and family build a realistically hopeful perspective on the future. This includes a clear sense of the extent of their ability to modulate their symptoms and physician-aided awareness of ways to improve their own help-seeking behavior.

Even in this early era of pediatric psychopharmacology, and despite the limitations imposed by the current biopsychosocial-financial model of medicine, most youngsters with major emotional and behavioral illnesses can be helped significantly by available treatments. Basic medical management of youths and families afflicted by the biopsychiatric disorders entails promoting their development of help-seeking skills and realistic hope.

Psychotropic Medications in Youths

The specific drug treatment techniques are presented in this section as if it were possible to provide a simple abstract description of these treatments in isolation. These crystallized descriptions do not do justice to the actual complexities and interactions among the various components of multimodal treatments of children with emotional and behavioral disorders.

In this chapter, when evidence supporting the value of a treatment is based primarily on uncontrolled studies and case reports, it is stated that the effect *appears* or *seems* to be helpful. *Well-controlled* studies typically refer to double-blind, placebo-controlled clinical research, which also might involve use of additional methods to increase the rigor of the findings. However, especially for double-blind and placebo-controlled studies conducted before 1980, *controlled* research in pediatric psychopharmacology did not usually employ randomization, structured diagnostic instruments, or standard outcome measures.

Psychostimulants

Psychostimulant treatments are controversial and misunderstood, even though they (1) have been used successfully to treat behavior disorders in youths for nearly 60 years; (2) remain the most commonly used medications in pediatric psychopharmacology; (3) have demonstrated efficacy in treating attention-deficit/hyperactivity disorder (ADHD) in over 175 double-blind, placebo-controlled studies in youths; (4) are more effective than alternative treatments of the attentional components of ADHD; and (5) are now widely used to treat adults with ADHD.

Clinical Uses: In addition to treating the "core" ADHD symptoms of inattention and hyperactive/impulsive behavior defined in the *Diagnostic and Statistical Manual of Mental Disorders* (DSM-IV, American Psychiatric Association, 1994), psychostimulants have a beneficial influence on both nonverbal and verbal aggressive behavior associated with ADHD (Murphy, Pelham, & Lang, 1992). Psychostimulants often are used to treat ADHD-like symptoms in youngsters with pervasive developmental disorders (PDD) such as autistic disorder (Quintana et al., 1995), mental retardation (Aman, Kern, McGhee, & Arnold, 1993), and traumatic brain injury. Stimulants also can be helpful for treating narcolepsy in youths (Dahl, Holttum, & Trubnick, 1994).

The presence of most comorbid disorders does not generally alter the likelihood of clinical response to stimulants, but comorbid disorders can influence compliance with and outcome of stimulant therapy. The presence of psychotic disorders clearly can alter outcome, especially if psychotic symptoms are induced or aggravated by the stimulant treatment. Also, comorbid anxiety disorders with ADHD may alter the effects of stimulant treatment. In children with ADHD and internalizing symptoms, there are suggestions that stimulants may cause symptom aggravation (DuPaul, Barkley, & McMurray, 1994) or may work in a different manner (Urman, Ickowicz, Fulford, & Tennock, 1995), less well (Tannock, Ickowicz, & Schachar, 1995), or at different optimal doses (Livingston, Dykman, & Ackerman, 1992).

Psychostimulants do not appear helpful for treating ADHD symptoms associated with right hemisphere disorder, conduct disorder in the absence of ADHD, or oppositional disorder in the absence of ADHD, and they are not helpful for treating learning disorders (as defined in *DSM-IV*). Stimulants might be less effective for ADHD in preschool children than in older children or may show a wider range of responsiveness, varying from mild to robust (Spencer et al., 1996). Alternatively, preschool children might require a different dosing regimen of psychostimulants, such as more frequent dose administrations.

Few youths become symptom-free as a result of stimulant treatment (Dulcan, 1990). Over the course of years, stimulants remain effective in treating the core symptoms of ADHD and thereby have a direct beneficial effect on long-term outcome (Schachar & Tannock, 1993). However, extended stimulant treatments seem to have little effect on "associated features" such as self-esteem, peer relationships, academic achievement, and general conduct (Schachar & Tannock, 1993), for which psychosocial interventions appear to be appropriate.

Clinical Implications of Pharmacokinetics: The clinical effects of amphetamines and methylphenidate appear in 30 minutes, last for 3 to 8 hours, and then might be followed by symptom rebound (ADHD symptoms returning and exceeding baseline severity) at 10 to 20 hours. These short-acting stimulants typically require 2 or 3 dose administrations daily. The "acute dosage pharmacokinetics" of d-amphetamine and methylphenidate implies that patients never achieve the steady-state pharmacokinetics seen with most psychopharmacological treatments. The clinical effects of dextroamphetamine and methylphenidate tend to have a prominent on-off pattern during the course of the day; that is, symptom control can be quite variable despite multiple dosings. Rapid metabolizers of amphetamines and methylphenidate may experience both cognitive toxicity during peak drug action and rebound hyperactivity during drug offset.

The magnitude and duration of clinical effects are correlated only weakly to plasma stimulant levels and seem better correlated to the rate of rise (slope) of the plasma levels during the onset phase of drug action. This "ramp effect" may explain why slow-release formulations of d-amphetamine and methylphenidate generally have a shorter and weaker action than regular tablets. In most patients (a rough estimate might be 75 to 85%), the slow-release forms of dextroamphetamine and methylphenidate do not provide a longer duration of clinical effects and offer no benefit over the less expensive regular formulations. In some patients, though, these preparations do provide a marginally longer clinical duration, although perhaps not enough to justify the added expense. The slow-release formulations, if used at all, must be swallowed rather than chewed in order to avoid sudden drug release and potentially toxic reactions.

A commercial mixture of dextro- and levoisomers of amphetamine (Adderall) appears to be more reliable in producing a longer duration of action than dextroamphetamine or methylphenidate. In general, once- (or sometimes twice-) daily dosing of Adderall is sufficient. This preparation might be helpful in some patients who do not have an adequate duration of clinical response to dextroamphetamine (or methylphenidate). Its other clinical properties have not been well characterized (Popper, 1994).

Methamphetamine (Desoxyn®) also can be a reasonable choice when once-daily administration is desired, but it is often avoided due to the stigma of "speed" abuse and its very high cost.

Magnesium pemoline (Cylert®) has a substantially different chemistry and pharmacology from the other stimulants. Pemoline has immediate clinical effects that appear within 1 to 2 hours and last for at least 6 hours (Pelham, Swanson, Furman, & Schwindt, 1995). Its beneficial changes can endure throughout the day, so that pemoline usually can be given once daily each morning and still provide more steady control of symptoms (i.e., less on-and-off effect) and fewer rebound symptoms than shorter-acting dextroamphetamine and methylphenidate. There might be a further increase in therapeutic effects after 2 to 8 weeks, although this does not appear to be generally observed. Clinical effects of pemoline can persist for several days after drug discontinuation; this can be a disadvantage if side effects require stopping the medication or an advantage if the patient frequently misses taking the daily dose. The primary problem posed by pemoline is a 3% risk of hepatotoxic metabolite formation.

Adverse Effects: Adverse effects of dextroamphetamine and methylphenidate are comparable. Although some reports suggest an association of a specific side effect with 1 or another drug, these claims are unreplicated.

The symptom rebound (aggravation of hyperactivity/impulsivity and inattention) is associated mainly with amphetamine and methylphenidate. Rebound tics also can emerge during the "offset" phase of stimulant action. Rebound symptoms can be managed by shortening the time interval between dose administrations or by using a longer-acting once-daily medication.

There has been some controversy about the existence and clinical significance of putative stimulant-induced tics (Gadow, Sverd, Sprafkin, Nolan, & Ezor, 1995). Unlike rebound tics, these tics appear during drug onset. Psychostimulants have been found to induce or aggravate tics or dyskinetic movements at an overall incidence of 9% in children with ADHD, regardless of specific stimulant drug (Lipkin, Goldstein, & Adesman, 1994). The tics might become more apparent over several weeks of treatment (Riddle et al., 1995).

Excessive stimulant dosing can impair cognitive functioning, by inducing either attentional overfocusing or mild cognitive scrambling (distinct from more frank confusion or delirium). The circumstances and possible mechanisms that give rise to cognitive disruption remain unclear and debated (Douglas, Barr, Desilets, & Sherman, 1995; Tannock & Schachar, 1992).

The most common of the acute adverse effects of psychostimulants in children are decreased appetite and weight loss (typically 2 to 10 pounds),

sleep impairment, headache, dysphoria, irritability, and sedation (Ahmann et al., 1993) and may require dose adjustment, drug change, or supplemental treatment. Stimulants also may induce or aggravate psychosis, presumably in genetic vulnerable patients.

Psychostimulants carry a particularly high risk of abuse of various kinds. Both methylphenidate and the amphetamines are contraindicated in patients who are involved in or at risk for recreational substance abuse (Dulcan, 1990). Even when the possibility of substance abuse seems remote, any child who carries (or has easy access to) these pills can be subjected to coercion or violence by peers (or elders) involved in drug abuse or drug dealing. In addition, psychostimulants often are implicated in "medication abuse," such as indiscriminate prescribing, sale or use of stimulants for weight control, or overuse for behavioral control by caregivers. Stimulant abuse, in these various forms, can pose significant threats to patient, family, peers, and community.

The additional risk of chemical hepatitis is associated only with pemoline. Drug-induced hepatocellular injury in children usually is due to idiosyncratic toxic metabolites rather than to the cholestasis or immunologic hypersensitivity that typically causes drug-induced hepatotoxicity in adults. About 3% of pemoline-treated children develop significant liver signs. The prevalence of pemoline hepatotoxicity in adults is unclear. Plasma levels of liver transaminases may begin to increase gradually after 6 months of pemoline treatment, but the child usually remains asymptomatic. Following drug discontinuation, the transaminases usually reduce after a delay but may not return back to baseline levels (suggesting some persistent fibrosis). Some cases proceed to chronic liver disease. Acute hepatic failure has resulted in death in rare instances, averaging less than 1 case every 2 years in the United States since the release of pemoline in 1975. Monthly blood checks generally would detect this change but are justifiable only if there is concurrent liver disease. Transaminase levels should be obtained yearly at the annual physical examination or in the event that symptoms of hepatitis (decreased appetite, fatigue, nausea, or stomach "fullness") emerge after several months or years of pemoline therapy.

There is good evidence that stimulant side effects do not include clinically significant cardiovascular changes in healthy children (Safer, 1992), increased seizure risk, physical addiction, psychological dependence, or subsequent overreliance of medications for solving somatic problems. Although psychostimulants are abusable, and substance abuse appears to be highly prevalent in adults with ADHD, the medicinal use of psychostimulants during childhood does not seem to be associated with an increased tendency to experiment with recreational drugs or to become involved in substance abuse during adolescence or young adulthood (Weiss & Hechtman, 1986).

The safety of psychostimulants for patients who remain on them for many years has not been well evaluated, but it is known that a reduction or delay in height growth sometimes is observed with long-term use (Safer, Allen, & Barr, 1972). This effect usually is small in magnitude and clinically insignificant, and the height may rebound after the stimulant treatment is discontinued (Safer, Allen, & Barr, 1975). Typically, the growth delay has a minimal effect on eventual height, affecting less than 2% of the variance in adult height outcome (Gittelman & Mannuzza, 1988). This minor height loss generally is acceptable when considered in the context of a child's total emotional, social, and academic growth. In rare cases when growth retardation or delay is judged problematic, dose reduction or drug holidays can help. Permanent effects on height generally can be avoided by minimizing use during the period of epiphyseal closing, which can range in different adolescents from age 13 to 18.

Other questions have been raised about the possible risks of long-term stimulant treatment in light of concerns about "amphetamine psychosis," cardiovascular changes, depression, and carcinogenesis. In a study of 11 adults with narcolepsy whose excessive daytime sleepiness was treated with extremely high doses of methylphenidate (mean 200 milligrams [mg] daily) for a mean of 22 years, no evidence of psychosis was evident except in 2 patients with predisposing factors (Pawluk et al., 1995). Hypertension was not overrepresented (mean age 55). However, depressive disorders were more prevalent than in the general population, despite the concurrent treatments of cataplexy with antidepressants. Such depressive symptoms might be due to drug, disease, or chronicity of illness. The potential relevance of these findings to ADHD is speculative. Although no elevated risk of mood disorders has been ascribed to chronic stimulant treatment in patients with ADHD, the potential for behavioral toxicity after decades of stimulant treatment has not been evaluated in such patients.

In human pharmacoepidemiologic studies of chronic psychostimulant treatment, methylphenidate did not have carcinogenic effects and instead was associated with a below-expected prevalence of cancer. In animals, no cytotoxic effects have been observed, and both increases and decreases were found in cancer rates, depending on the type of cancer and the species (Dunnick & Hailey, 1995). The other psychostimulants have not been investigated for potential cellular toxicity as systematically.

Drug Selection: Dextroamphetamine (Dexedrine® or generic) and methylphenidate (Ritalin® or generic) generally are comparable in overall efficacy, but individuals may show a better response to a particular drug, with respect to both beneficial effects and adverse effects.

Dextroamphetamine generally is preferable as the stimulant of first choice because, after correcting for potency (dextroamphetamine 5 mg = methylphenidate 10 mg), it is considerably less expensive than methylphenidate. At the 1997 wholesale costs paid by pharmacies to their pharmaceutical suppliers in the United States, both generic dextroamphetamine and brand-name Dexedrine were less costly than equivalent doses of either generic methylphenidate or Ritalin. These wholesale costs are lower than pharmacy prices to consumers; however, some local pharmacies set equal prices on both drugs by charging methylphenidate prices for dextroamphetamine products. The specific costs cited pertained only to the United States. In other countries, the manufacturing costs, wholesale costs, and local pharmacy prices can be structured very differently.

In addition to cost, dextroamphetamine carries the additional advantages over methylphenidate of slightly longer duration of action as well as availability in a liquid formulation. However, certain pharmacies may not carry dextroamphetamine because of concerns about substance abuse; most pharmacies dispense these medications when directly requested to do so by a physician.

Both dextroamphetamine and methylphenidate are excellent drug choices for ADHD because

TABLE 11.3

Clinical Treatment with Psychostimulants in Youths

	D-amphetamine	Methylphenidate	Pemoline
Dosage and Regimen			
Starting dose	2.5–5 mg each morning	5–10 mg each morning	18.75–37.5 mg each morning
Rate of dose elevation	2.5–5 mg every 3 days	5–10 mg every 3 days	18.75–37.5 mg every 5 days
Typical full dose	10–40 mg daily	20–80 mg daily	1 mg/pound (0.45 mg/kg)
Number of daily dosages	2 (AM, noon)	2 (AM, noon)	1 each morning
Delayed clinical response	No	No	No
Length of full trial	5 days at full dose	5 days at full dose	3 weeks at full dose
Duration of treatment	Indefinite	Indefinite	Indefinite
Available Strengths			
	5, 10 mg—generic Oral elixir—brand[a] Sustained-release 5, 10, 15 mg— brand only	5, 10, 20 mg—generic Sustained-release 20 mg—brand only	18.75, 37.5, 75 mg— brand only

Major Adverse Effects

Initial insomnia
Anorexia
Weight loss or less than developmentally expected gain
Irritability
Abdominal pain
Dysphoria, weepiness, clinging regressive behavior
Rebound hyperactivity
Rebound tics
"Overfocusing," similar to "excessive" concentration
Tics
Slowed growth in height
Increased heart rate
Mild blood pressure elevation
Psychotic symptoms
Risk of recreational abuse and drug dealing.
Pemoline only: hepatotoxicity

Precautions

For potential drug abusers, use tricyclic antidepressants.
Avoid pemoline in liver disease.
Administer after meals to minimize anorexia and weight loss.
Use drug holidays to minimize height loss.
Avoid use with sympathomimetics to minimize psychosis.

Toxicity

Either: Withdrawn, quiet, overfocused, spacey, or slow
Or: Agitated, anxious, irritable

Relative Contraindications

Psychosis, tic disorders, substance abuse (patient or family), hypertension, some cardiac disorders

TABLE 11.3

Continued

Initial Medical Workup

Height, weight, blood pressure, heart rate
Observe for involuntary movements, including tics.
Check family history regarding tics, involuntary movements, and psychotic disorders.
For pemoline, liver function tests

Ongoing Medical Monitoring

Follow involuntary movements (including tics), psychotic symptoms, weight closely.
Measure height every 3 to 4 months.
For pemoline, liver function tests after 10 weeks, then every 3 to 6 months.

ᵃAvailable only in brand-name formulation; ie, no generics are manufactured.

they have a stronger effect on attentional symptoms than alternative treatments. However, these agents can be used only if the risk of substance abuse is deemed low and if multiple daily dose administrations are feasible and realistic.

For once-daily dosing (or sometimes twice), slow-release forms do not generally provide longer clinical effectiveness and are approximately 25% more expensive than the regular forms of dextroamphetamine and methylphenidate. Methamphetamine (Desoxyn®) is stigmatized and more expensive. Pemoline has no generic formulation, is markedly more expensive and occasionally causes chemical hepatitis. The commercial mixture of 4 dextro- and levo-amphetamine salts (Adderall) might be preferred among the longer-acting stimulant preparations, although the specific clinical properties of this salt mixture are still under investigation. Its cost is more expensive than dextroamphetamine and Dexedrine and comparable to the price of Ritalin.

A first stimulant trial (e.g., dextroamphetamine) typically does not provide an adequate clinical response in about 25% of children with ADHD, and a trial with a second short-acting stimulant (e.g., methylphenidate) is then helpful in about 25% of those cases. There are little data to support any further steps for stimulant selection strategy, but again cost and adverse effects can be decisive. Adderall probably is a reasonable third-choice stimulant, despite the generally sparse characterization of its clinical properties, because of its much lower cost than pemoline. However, there are no data regarding the chances of a therapeutic response to Adderall following treatment failures with dextroamphetamine and methylphenidate.

The use of Adderall or pemoline (despite its hepatotoxicity and very low risk of fatality) probably could be justified before going onto the much more expensive methamphetamine. The therapeutic yield with the slow-release psychostimulant preparations is low. In general, it is probably sensible and perhaps advisable to try (at least) a third psychostimulant formulation before proceeding to alternative treatments of ADHD, which are less likely to help the patient's inattention.

Clinical Monitoring: No specific laboratory testing is essential prior to starting stimulant treatment, except for liver function tests for pemoline (Dulcan, 1990). Blood pressure and heart rate should be measured to rule out a preexisting vulnerability, but they do not need to be followed in routine cases (Safer, 1992). Height and weight should be documented and subsequently monitored. The main baseline evaluation, required because risks of stimulant induction or aggravation, is careful assessment of any baseline tics, dyskinesias, or psychotic symptoms.

Once the psychostimulant dose is stabilized, it is advisable to reevaluate the dose requirements of a patient every 6 to 12 months by trials of both higher and slower doses. The common practice of maintaining a child on invariant doses over several years is hardly ever appropriate.

Two recent studies of children with ADHD, designed to examine the interaction of stimulant medications with other treatments, yielded consistent and perhaps unexpected results. One study examined stimulants and behavioral modification (Ialongo et al., 1993), and the other examined interactions with cognitive-behavioral therapy (Pelham et al., 1993). In both studies, stimulants were more effective than the behavioral methods, and their combined use was not significantly more efficacious than stimulant therapy alone. These treatment responses did not appear to depend on the presence or absence of comorbid conduct disorder (Pelham et al., 1993). Although other types of intervention (parent, school, social skills) still might prove demonstrably useful in combination with stimulants, it was noteworthy that there was surprisingly little evidence to support the use of these popular multimodal treatments over pharmacotherapy alone.

Antidepressants

HETEROCYCLIC ANTIDEPRESSANTS

Clinical Uses: Heterocyclic antidepressants are established but not first-choice treatments of ADHD and enuresis (bedwetting). The efficacy of heterocyclic antidepressants in the short-term treatment of bulimia nervosa has been demonstrated in several well-controlled studies. These drugs also have been widely used to treat major depression in youths, but their clinical value is questioned by the failure of numerous controlled trials to demonstrate efficacy (Ambrosini, Bianchi, Rabinovich, & Elia, 1993; Jensen, Ryan & Prien, 1992; Jensen & Elliott, 1992; Kutcher et al., 1994). HCA treatment of anxiety disorders is not currently supported by controlled studies in youths, but investigation continues.

Eleven different investigative groups, starting over 30 years ago, have demonstrated the efficacy of imipramine, desipramine, and amitriptyline for treating ADHD in double-blind, placebo-controlled studies (Biederman, Baldessarini, Wright, Knee, & Harmatz, 1989; Biederman et al., 1989; Donnelly et al., 1986; Garfinkel, Wender, Stoman, & O'Neill, 1983; Gualtieri & Evans, 1988; Krakowski, 1965; Kupietz & Balka, 1976; Rapoport, Quinn, Bradbard, Riddle, & Brooks, 1974; Singer et al., 1995; Waizer, Hoffman, Polizos, & Engelhardt, 1974; Werry, Aman, & Diamond, 1980; Winsberg, Bialer, Kupietz, & Tobias, 1972; Yellin, Spring, & Greenberg, 1978; Yepes, Balka, Winsberg, & Bialer, 1977). Uncontrolled studies suggest that nortriptyline (Wilens et al., 1993A; Wilens et al., 1993B) and clomipramine (Gordon,

State, Nelson, Hamburger, & Rapoport, 1993) can be beneficial as well. These agents, and probably any of the heterocyclic antidepressants, are reasonable alternatives (i.e., after 2 or more stimulant trials have failed) for managing the impulsive and hyperactive symptoms of treatment-resistant cases of ADHD. Despite their generally robust behavioral and weaker cognitive effects in treating ADHD, HCAs often leave a significant residue of attentional symptoms.

Enuresis is commonly treated with imipramine, and this treatment is well supported by controlled trials (Fritz, Rockney, & Yeung, 1994). HCAs customarily are employed for nocturnal enuresis only after behavioral methods have failed. Standard behavioral methods include fluid restriction before bedtime; awakening the child during the night before the usual time of the enuresis; and a "bell alarm" blanket that can be used at night either to awaken the child during the wetting episode or (more effectively) to awaken the parents who in turn awaken the child. For the less common presentations of daytime enuresis, imipramine is an appropriate first-line treatment.

Bulimia nervosa has been shown to respond to various heterocyclic antidepressants in numerous well-controlled but short-term studies (Agras, Dorian, Kirkley, Arnow, & Bachman, 1987; Alger, Schwalberg, Bigaouette, Michalek, & Howard, 1991; Mitchell et al., 1990; Pope, Hudson, Jonas, & Yurgelun-Todd, 1983; Walsh, Hadigan, Devlin, Gladis, & Roose, 1991). However, the clinical response is typically incomplete, and there is a high rate of relapse within several months (Walsh et al., 1991). The presence or absence of depressive disorders does not appear to alter the likelihood of a response to HCAs in bulimia, so the antibulimic effect appears to be independent of any possible antidepressant effect of the HCAs.

Clinical Implications of Pharmacokinetics: HCA clearance rates vary markedly between individual children (elimination half-life range of imipramine is 4 to 20 hours in children), but HCA clearance is generally faster in youths (mean elimination half-life of nortriptyline is 14 hours in children and 28 hours in adults). Like other liver-metabolized drugs, hepatic biotransformation of heterocyclic antidepressant is more rapid in children than adults and is responsible for their faster clearance. HCA withdrawal symptoms can emerge between dosages, especially when administered on once-daily regimens. In young children, it may be necessary to administer in 2 to 3 divided doses to avoid daily withdrawal symptoms and to reduce adverse effects at peak blood levels (Geller et al., 1987).

Dosing: HCA dosing regimens for children typically emphasize starting at low doses, increasing gradually, and respecting a firm maximal dose equivalent to imipramine 5.0 milligram per kilogram (mg/kg) daily. The gradual dose elevation in youths reduces the adverse effects but also can result in a weaker or delayed antidepressant response. Following the documented case of a young child who died suddenly during treatment with imipramine 15 mg/kg (Saraf, Klein, Guttelman-Klein, & Greenhill, 1978), the firm maximal dose of 5.0 mg/kg daily is maintained because of concerns about cardiovascular (and seizure) risks. However, some occasional cases require slightly higher doses, which might be considered at times but certainly only with a record of excellent patient compliance to the prescribed drug regimen, full informed consent with assent, and absolutely consistent supranormal treatment monitoring.

Catastrophic Effects: Overdose Lethality and Sudden Death: Heterocyclic antidepressants are associated with high rates of lethality following overdose and are one of the most common causes of poisoning deaths, especially from accidental ingestion by young children (Frommer, Kulig, Marx, & Rumack, 1987). Deaths from HCAs in children also result from suicidal overdose and iatrogenic overmedication. Even if suicidal overdose is viewed as unlikely in a particular child, the risks to young siblings or potentially suicidal family members must be considered. The problems presented by accidental, suicidal, and iatrogenic overdose require clinical management that exceeds casual attention.

There are now 5 published cases of children and adolescents who have suddenly collapsed and died during the course of seemingly routine clinical treatment with desipramine (Norpramin®), without evidence of overdose or other medical explanation (Abramowicz, 1990; Popper & Zimnitzky, 1995; Riddle, Geller, & Ryan, 1993). The available clinical detail in these cases generally is sketchy and insufficient to establish a causal relationship, but some disturbing patterns have emerged (Abramowicz, 1990; Biederman, 1991;

Elliott & Popper, 1991; Elliott, Popper, & Frazier, 1990; Popper & Elliott, 1990; Popper & Zimnitzky, 1995; Riddle et al., 1991b; Riddle et al., 1993). All 5 cases involved desipramine. Four of the 5 cases had ADHD. Three of the 5 cases involved a known personal or family history of unusual cardiac problems.

One adolescent had a congenital anomaly of a coronary artery, which may have interacted with desipramine to precipitate the death (Popper & Zimnitzky, 1995). This cardiac vulnerability was asymptomatic, would not be evident on physical examination or electrocardiogram, and could not have been identified prior to autopsy, except perhaps by angiography. The possibility that a major risk factor for sudden death might be not be known to the prescribing physician, despite a thorough baseline workup, implies that desipramine treatment will not be averted in a small number of dangerously vulnerable children.

A role of desipramine in causing sudden death in children has not been proven definitely. The risk of sudden death during desipramine treatment appears to be extremely small (Biederman et al., 1993; Biederman, Thisted, Greenhill, & Ryan, 1995), but it is noteworthy that similar deaths have not been documented with other HCA treatments.

It is not obvious why desipramine would constitute a significantly higher risk than other HCAs. It is especially puzzling that imipramine, which is chemically similar and metabolically transformed into desipramine, and is used very commonly, has not been linked to sudden death in children. However, there is a significantly higher risk of lethality following overdoses on desipramine than overdoses on other HCAs, including imipramine, in children (Popper, 1994) and adults (Cassidy & Henry, 1987; Kapur, Mieczkowski, & Mann, 1992).

It cannot be assumed that the high lethality following desipramine overdose is related to the unexplained sudden deaths at apparently therapeutic doses, but the mechanisms of these catastrophic effects might be connected. For example, desipramine appears to cause a greater sympathetic-to-parasympathetic imbalance than imipramine in youths (Walsh, Giardina, Sloan, Greenhill, & Goldfein, 1994), and thereby might increase autonomic instability and consequently the risks of many medical problems (Bartels et al.,

1991; "Neural mechanisms," 1991; Walsh et al., 1994). Alternatively, both types of death might result from prolonged QT syndrome, reflecting drug-induced cardiac conduction slowing that can lead to potentially fatal polymorphous ventricular tachyarrhythmias (Riddle, Nelson, et al., 1991). Interestingly, in careful studies, prolonged QTc intervals (greater than 440 milliseconds) were found in 20% of 71 youths during desipramine treatment (Biederman et al., 1993) and 0% of 23 imipramine-treated children (Fletcher, Case, Sallee, Hand, & Gillette, 1993). Also, 11% of desipramine-treated children and 0% of imipramine-treated children showed evidence of supraventricular tachycardia (Biederman et al., 1993; Fletcher et al., 1993).

About 5 to 10 deaths from desipramine overdose in youths have been reported each year during the 1990s to the national poison control network in the United States (Litovitz, Clark, & Soloway, 1994). This figure includes only deaths related to single drug overdoses in 6 to 16-years-olds, and so does not include the numerous accidental poisonings in toddlers. This count is an underestimate of actual desipramine-related deaths in youths, because it does not include deaths due to polydrug overdose (which are the majority) or deaths not reported to poison control centers. By comparison, only 5 cases of sudden death in desipramine-treated children have been identified over the 10 to 15 years that the drug has been in common use in pediatrics. It appears that deaths resulting from desipramine overdose are much more common than the seemingly sudden deaths putatively linked to desipramine therapy.

The high fatality rate following a desipramine overdose (about 1%) is a legitimate clinical concern. In the past, this type of concern led to the historical shift away from the use of barbiturates and toward benzodiazepines. This putative link between desipramine treatment and sudden death is still under investigation, but its clarification is not necessary to establish that heterocyclic antidepressants in general and desipramine especially are potentially dangerous.

Adverse Effects: Apart from the catastrophic effects, the HCAs are associated with a variety of "merely" adverse effects. The chief concerns are cardiovascular changes and seizures.

All HCAs cause some degree of cardiac conduction slowing. Mean changes can be observed in all electrocardiogram intervals (PR, QRS, QTc) axis after 5 weeks of treatment (Leonard et al., 1995) and might increase progressively during the first few weeks on a stable dose. These changes in cardiac function generally are not problematic in HCA-treated children who are appropriately monitored, but without adequate monitoring they can potentially result in heart block or arrhythmia.

HCAs cause an *increase* in blood pressure in children and adolescents (Kuekes, Wigg, Bryant, & Meyer, 1992), in contrast to their typically hypotensive effects in adults. Also, the tricyclic antidepressants cause sinus tachycardia in perhaps one-third of children and adolescents (Leonard et al., 1995). The increase in blood pressure is not clinically significant in most cases, but routine monitoring is advisable.

Estimates of the prevalence and extent of conduction slowing, hypertension, and tachycardia vary markedly among studies and may depend on dose, duration of treatment, and specific HCA agent. The comparative risks of the different HCAs have not been adequately studied in children.

The risk of HCA-induced seizures appears to be similar in youths and adults. As in adults, the increased risk of drug-induced seizures may be reduced by gradual dose increases; if a seizure emerges during treatment (and the subsequent neuromedical workup is negative), HCA treatment generally can proceed along with concurrent anticonvulsant prophylaxis (Ryan, 1990).

HCA withdrawal symptoms, either between dosages or upon rapid dose reduction, can include headache, gastrointestinal symptoms (abdominal pain, nausea, vomiting, anorexia), malaise, drowsiness or excitation, sleep disturbance, and tearfulness.

Patients and physicians also must contend with the usual litany of side effects associated with traditional antidepressants, including anticholinergic side effects, weight gain, sedation, anxiety, and irritability. HCAs have been shown induce switches into acute manic episodes using an ABABA clinical design (2 drug withdrawals and reinstatements) in children (Briscoe, Harrington, & Prendergast, 1995), but there is doubt about whether HCA treatment predicts conversion to bipolar disorder in children (Geller, Fox, & Fletcher, 1993; Geller, Fox, & Clark, 1994).

Clinical Monitoring: The workup prior to starting heterocyclic antidepressants involves the obligatory baseline electrocardiogram, measurement of heart rate and blood pressure, and some standard blood tests for general medical screening. Personal and family history of seizures, cardiovascular disorders, and cardiac problems (including sudden death) should be obtained.

Treatment response for enuresis and ADHD typically appears within 2 to 5 days of attaining proper dosage. The duration of these treatments depends on symptom persistence but typically runs months to years. For childhood depression, response latency (time to attain clinical improvement) and treatment duration are speculative in the absence of a controlled demonstration of efficacy. Major depressive disorder appears to takes a longer time to respond to current HCA treatment protocols in youths (if it responds at all) than in adults, so that empirical clinical trials could sensibly be extended from 2 to 4 weeks to 6 to 10 weeks and perhaps longer in treating chronic illness (Ambrosini, Bianchi, Metz, & Rabinovich, 1994).

EKG Monitoring. Electrocardiogram monitoring is an absolute requirement for heterocyclic antidepressant treatment of children under the age of 16. Both baseline and on-drug testing is essential to identify children with preexisting or HCA-induced cardiac conduction slowing, heart block, or arrhythmia. Even if electrocardiogram monitoring is unable to identify children at putative risk for sudden death with desipramine, cardiac conduction slowing is a relatively common side effect of HCAs and must be followed. Several lawsuits are filed each year regarding the deaths of children who did not receive electrocardiogram monitoring during their HCA treatments.

There is general agreement on the necessity for a baseline electrocardiogram and for some subsequent monitoring. The range of opinion is quite wide concerning the advisable frequency of monitoring during HCA treatment, with some specialists recommending a repeat electrocardiogram after each 25 mg dose increase (Ryan, 1990). As a reasonable minimum, an electrocardiogram should be obtained prior to the start of treatment, again at about half the anticipated maximum dosage, and again at the full dosage. In view of recent suggestions that these abnormalities may develop after some weeks (Leonard et al., 1995), it is sensible to obtain another electrocardiogram after 3 months at full dosage and conceivably every 4 to 6 months thereafter. At a minimum, subsequent electrocardiograms should be obtained once yearly at the annual physical examination for children on long-term treatment.

In monitoring HCA treatment, electrocardiograms should be obtained at least 48 hours after the last dose increase, in order to allow time for most drug-induced changes to be expressed. These tests should be interpreted by physicians trained in reading pediatric electrocardiograms.

Current standard electrocardiogram limits for children, beyond which HCA dose increases usually require pediatric cardiology consultation, are uniformly consistent (Biederman, 1991; Elliott & Popper, 1991; Popper & Elliott, 1990; Riddle, Nelson, et al., 1991; Riddle et al., 1993; Ryan, 1990; Tingelstad, 1991):

PR interval	≤ 0.21 seconds
QRS interval	≤ 0.12 seconds (or $\leq 30\%$ over baseline QRS interval)
QTc interval	≤ 0.450 seconds

These limits may be exceeded occasionally following careful pediatric cardiology consultation.

Blood pressure and heart rate monitoring. In following for possible hypertensive (and occasional hypotensive) changes, a pediatric cuff should be used when appropriate. This monitoring should be obtained at each visit with a physician, minimally every 6 weeks. The recommended clinical limits for blood pressure and heart rate during HCA treatment in youths are:

Systolic blood pressure	≤ 130 mm Hg
Diastolic blood pressure	≤ 85 mm Hg
Heart rate	≤ 130 beats per minute

The routine use of therapeutic *plasma drug level monitoring* is another area of debate. A therapeutic range for treating depression in youths cannot be defined in the absence of a demonstrable therapeutic effect, and plasma level monitoring generally is not conducted in treating ADHD or enuresis. The correlations of plasma levels and therapeutic responses are only weak to moderate ($r = 0.4$–0.7, depending on the clinical indication) and are more meaningful for describing drug effects in patient populations than for influencing routine dose adjustments for individuals.

Plasma HCA monitoring is probably most useful to assess mild cognitive deficits in HCA-treated youths (Preskhorn, Weller, Jerkovich, Hughes, & Weller, 1988), specifically when excessive plasma levels are associated with central nervous system toxicity that is too subtle to be identified readily; for example, with an adolescent whose word-finding difficulty or mild "forgetting" might be related to excessive HCA levels.

Steady-state levels of most HCAs are achieved (in 5 half-lives) within 1 to 5 days in children, so plasma drug levels may be sampled sooner than the 5 to 7 days required in adults.

Drug Selection: The choice of a particular heterocyclic antidepressant for an initial drug trial may be based on expected side effects, costs, and pharmacokinetic properties. Each agent has its own profile of predominant side effects, but most of the side effects are shared among all HCAs and are generally similar in children, adolescents, and adults.

All of the tricyclic antidepressants and older HCAs are available in generic form, except for protriptyline. However, contrary to common belief, the costs of these generic HCAs have not appreciably lower than the corresponding brand products and are comparable to the pill cost of the newer antidepressants. Just counting the cost of the pills themselves, and not counting the additional costs of laboratory testing and medical monitoring required with HCAs, the average price of the clinical treatment of a child or adolescent at typical doses is about $4 daily with nortriptyline or amoxapine; more than $2 daily with desipramine, maprotiline, or protriptyline; over $1 daily with doxepin and trimipramine; and about $0.50 to $0.75 daily with imipramine and amitriptyline. These prices are rendered at wholesale prices (cost to the pharmacist) and so underestimate the costs to consumers.

Of the 2 low-cost HCAs, imipramine has fewer anticholinergic (dryness of mouth and nasal passages, blurred vision, constipation, urinary hesitation) and antihistaminic effects (sedation) than amitriptyline. Imipramine generally is preferred to amitriptyline because of its more favorable profile of side effects. Imipramine is usually well tolerated in children and is relatively well studied, and so it is a good first drug choice for starting HCA treatment.

If using generic imipramine or any other generic drug, it is advisable to be certain that a patient consistently uses the products of a single manufacturer. It is not sufficient for a patient to use only generic pills distributed by a particular generic drug house, because some generic drug firms distribute (rather than manufacture) pills and may obtain pills of different strengths from different manufacturers that use different industrial chemical processes. In this way, even pills of varying strength that are distributed under the name of a single generic drug house may generate clinical problems relating to bioequivalence. A patient's pharmacist can be asked to check and ensure that the manufacturing sources of the dispensed generic pills are consistent across different dose strengths. Without this step, the patient will not be protected from variations in bioequivalence when switching between pill strengths as doses are increased.

Protriptyline has a notably longer elimination half-life (undetermined in children, 120 hours in adults) than most tricyclic antidepressants (20–40 hours in adults) and so can be particularly useful for noncompliant children or families. However, in the event of a major protriptyline overdose, the risk of cardiovascular collapse is high because of the extended period of physiologic stress.

Most drug failures in psychopharmacology are related to (1) nonadherence to the prescribed regimen, which may reflect child or family noncompliance; (2) the use of inadequate doses; or (3) inadequate trial durations, such as stopping after 4 rather than 6 to 10 weeks of treatment (Ambrosini et al., 1994). If a fully adequate trial of a first HCA is not helping, it is reasonable to try another HCA agent but speculatively more helpful to choose a different chemical class of antidepressants for the second drug trial.

Clinical Comment: The heterocyclic antidepressants have provided helpful clinical treatments for almost 4 decades but now are being challenged by a variety of newer antidepressants. The minor cost savings that might derive from using the generically available HCAs is undercut by the extensive medical monitoring that they require. Even the least expensive of the HCAs do not fair well in cost competition with the newer antidepressants. But the HCAs remain the best understood of the antidepressants, and they have

TABLE 11.4

Clinical Treatment with Heterocyclic Antidepressants in Youths

Dosage and Regimen

Doses are expressed in imipramine milligram equivalents.

Starting dose	25–50 mg nightly at beddtime
Rate of dose elevation	25 mg every 3–5 days
Typical full dose	Enuresis: 1–3 mg/kg nightly ADHD: 1–3 mg/kg at bedtime, although sometimes up to 5 mg/kg at bedtime Major depressive disorder: 4–5 mg/kg at bedtime
Number of daily dosages	1 for adolescents, 2 for pre-adolescents, 3 for pre-schoolers
Delayed clinical response	Enuresis: 1–3 days ADHD: 1–3 days Major depressive disorder: 2–10 weeks
Length of full trial	Enuresis: 10 days ADHD: 10 days Major depressive disorder: 6–12 weeks
Duration of treatment	Enuresis: As long as needed, often years ADHD: As long as needed, often years Major depressive disorder: 3–12 months, sometimes several years, or indefinitely

Available Strengths

Imipramine	10, 25, 50 mg	generic
Nortriptyline	10, 25, 75 mg	brand only
Maprotiline	25, 50, 75 mg	generic
Amitriptyline	10, 25, 50, 75, 100, 150 mg	generic
Desipramine	10, 25, 50, 75 mg	generic

Major Adverse Effects

High rate of death following overdose
Cardiac conduction slowing, involving all electrocardiogram intervals, with potential for heart block or arrthymia
Tachycardia
Increased blood pressure
Irritability, agitation, rage, or psychosis
Insomnia, nightmares
Sedation
Weight gain
Lightheadness, especially orthostatic
Anticholinergic effects
Mild confusional state, with word-finding difficulty, "forgetting"
Tics or minor neurologic symptoms
Seizures
Caries
Rash
Medically unexplained sudden death (putative)—desipramine only

Precautions

Avoid dehydration.
Administer at bedtime to minimize daytime sedation.
Give child and family repeated reminders to watch for irritability and mild confusion.

TABLE 11.4

Continued

Toxicity

Sedation, fatigue, or "sick" feeling, cognitive scrambling, irritability
In dangerous overdose: arrhythmias, tachycardia, hypotension, fever, sweating, seizures, involuntary movements
  or rigidity, stupor, cardiovascular collapse, death

Relative Contraindications

Bipolar disorder, psychosis, hypertension, seizures, family history of sudden death
Concurrent treatment with monoamine oxidase inhibitor

Initial Medical Workup

Physical exam to assess cardiac, cardiovascular, and neurologic status
Blood pressure, heart rate, electrocardiogram [see text regarding evaluation]
Observe for baseline tics.
Family history of psychosis, sudden death, serious or unusual cardiac abnormalities, hypertension, seizure
  disorders, tic disorders

Ongoing Medical Monitoring

Repeated electrocardiograms [see text]: minimally, at half dose, at full dose, and then every 6 months thereafter.
Follow blood pressure, heart rate, weight, involuntary movements (including tics).
Height and weight every 3 to 4 months
Routine dental care every 6 months

the important long-term track record of generally adequate safety that aids in long-term risk assessment, especially for growing children.

These "old" medications have some bothersome adverse effects and serious safety issues. Although most HCAs are not even putative causes of sudden death, they still carry the cardiovascular risks associated with suicidal, accidental, and iatrogenic overdoses and, in addition, the risk of seizures.

Desipramine is a special case. The lengthening string of sudden deaths putatively related to desipramine treatment in children is raising appropriate concern, with no evidence that extensive electrocardiogram monitoring could have prevented any of the deaths. However, the more common danger of overdose lethality is the main factor that weakens the grounds for using HCAs in general and desipramine in particular.

The 2 major safety concerns associated with desipramine—the 1% lethality rate following overdose and the putative link to rare sudden deaths—suggest that desipramine in children and adolescents should be used sparingly if at all. In view of the many available HCA alternatives that appear safer, the routine use of desipramine in treating nonlethal disorders (such as enuresis and ADHD) is especially questionable. Despite the risks of suicidal overdose, its use in treating youngsters with potentially lethal conditions such as major depressive disorder might be more defensible in very treatment-resistant cases.

There are plenty of alternative heterocyclic agents whose use can be justified in treating ADHD and enuresis. If HCAs are useful to treating depressive disorders in youths, it seems that current criteria for major depressive disorder may not be the optimal way to identify candidates for HCA therapy. Speculatively, developmentally variant criteria are needed to identify such children, or perhaps HCAs would be more effective for youngsters with dysthymic disorder. Perhaps the study designs were compromised by any of many potential technical limitations. But some researchers who conducted rigorous controlled studies showing no efficacy continue to use HCAs to treat depressed youths in their clinical practices.

Clinicians have received quite a rude awakening from their previous comfort and sense of familiarity with the HCAs. If the safety or efficacy of commonly used treatments had ever been accepted complacently, the desipramine story will help maintain a healthier vigilance.

SELECTIVE SEROTONIN REUPTAKE INHIBITORS

As concerns about the heterocyclic antidepressants have mounted, the selective serotonin reuptake inhibitors (SSRIs) arrived on the psychopharmacological scene and were met with both zealotry and controversy. Prozac® (fluoxetine) became the Valium of the early 1990s, mainly because of its relative freedom from the worst HCA side effects. SSRI-associated suicidality and violence were officially dismissed by several major scientific bodies as disease-related and not drug-related, but it is nonetheless likely that some individuals develop obsessive (Teicher, Glod, & Cole, 1990) or agitated suicidality or self-destructive behavior (King et al., 1991) as a genuine reaction to SSRI treatment. Despite such controversies, the availability of SSRIs has profoundly altered clinical practices in treating what used to be called "neurotic" and what Kramer (1993) has called "psycho-cosmetic" problems in adults.

SSRIs also appear to be changing the treatment philosophy of specialists in child and adolescent psychopharmacology. Almost as quickly as these drugs became available, physicians began to prescribe them to adolescents and children for a variety of presumed indications. Unlike the cautious approach characteristic of the past, large numbers of youngsters were treated with these new agents from the start—despite the lack of a lengthy track record to demonstrate their safety in adults. Their common use by American college students, high schoolers, and younger ones led to the emergence of the Prozac Generation, a phenomenon both hyped and questioned by the public media (Wertzel, 1994).

Whatever their merits may turn out to be, and whatever long-term and short-term liabilities emerge, selective serotonin reuptake inhibitors have led many physicians to feel comfortable in prescribing antidepressants for children. In breaking this barrier, there is a risk that physicians could become blasé or even numbed about playing with newly found fire.

Clinical Uses: The antiobsessional and antibulimic properties of SSRIs in children are better demonstrated than the still-unproven antidepressant properties. Several well-designed studies demonstrate a substantive though partial benefit of SSRIs in youths with obsessive-compulsive disorder (OCD) and with obsessive-compulsive symptoms associated with Tourette's disorder (Kurlan, Como, Deeley, McDermott, & McDermott, 1993; Riddle, Hardin, King, Scahill, & Woolston, 1990, Riddle et al., 1992).

SSRIs have been shown in controlled studies to be efficacious in treating bulimia (Fluoxetine Bulimia Nervosa Collaborative Study Group, 1992; Goldbloom & Olmstead, 1993; Goldstein, Welson, Thompson, Potvin, & Rampey, 1995) but not anorexia nervosa (Biederman et al., 1985; Halmi, Eckert, LaDu, & Cohen, 1986). Fluoxetine treatment of bulimia was found to be significantly more effective at doses of 60 mg than 20 mg (Fluoxetine Bulimia Nervosa Collaborative Study Group, 1992; Goldbloom & Olmstead, 1993), with improvements noted in binge-eating, vomiting, carbohydrate craving, pathological eating attitudes, and depression (Fluoxetine Bulimia Nervosa Collaborative Study Group, 1992). A significant treatment response can be observed within 1 week. Thus it appears that fluoxetine is faster but requires higher doses to treat bulimia than to treat adult major depressive disorder, and the presence or absence of depression does not appear to modify the likelihood of a therapeutic response (Walsh & Devlin, 1995).

Without controlled data even suggesting antidepressant properties in children, SSRIs became widely advocated among specialists as the first-line treatment for major depressive disorder in children and adolescents (Ambrosini, Emslie, Greenhill, Kutcher, & Weller, 1995), and several open-label cases series have reported good effectiveness of fluoxetine and sertraline in depressed youth (Apter et al., 1994; Boulos, Kutcher, Gardner, & Young, 1992; Colle, Bélair, DiFeo, Weiss, & LaRoche, 1994; Jain, Birmaher, Garcia, Al-Shabbout, & Ryan, 1992; McConville et al., 1996; Nguyen et al., 1994; Tierney, Joshi, Llinas, Rosenberg, & Riddle, 1995). However, the only published double-blind, placebo-controlled study reported no antidepressant effect of fluoxetine in adolescents. A large well-controlled but unpublished study found statistically significant fluoxetine-placebo differences in children and adolescents with major depressive episode, but the study design was selected to minimize the effects of naturalistic factors that ordinarily would elevate placebo response rates (Ambrosini et al., 1995; Emslie, 1995).

The efficacy of SSRIs in treating panic disorder in adults in well established, but no studies are yet available in youngsters with anxiety disorders. The use of fluoxetine in selective mutism is supported by 1 well-controlled (Black & Uhde, 1994) and 1 open-label study (Dummit, Klein, Tancer, Asche, & Martin, 1996). Preliminary data in patients with autistic disorder and other pervasive developmental disorders suggest that SSRIs might reduce perseverative and obsessive-compulsive symptoms, stereotypies, and self-injurious behavior (Bass & Beltis, 1991; Cook, Rowlett, Jaselskis, & Leventhal, 1992; Epperson et al., 1994; King, 1991; McDougle, Price, & Goodman, 1990).

SSRIs also have been reported to be helpful in open-label treatments of body dysmorphic disorder in adolescents (El-khatib & Dickey, 1995; Phillips, Atala, & Albertini, 1995).

The effects of SSRIs in ADHD are currently a matter of debate. Open-label clinical trials in children with ADHD have suggested some benefit of SSRIs, either alone (Barrickman, Noyes, Kuperman, Schumacher, & Verda, 1991) or in combination with psychostimulants (Bussing & Levin, 1993; Findling, 1996; Gammon & Brown, 1993). However, fluoxetine and sertraline have been reported frequently to aggravate impulsivity, hyperactivity, and inattention in children with ADHD (Riddle et al., 1991a). It is unclear whether SSRIs offer genuine benefits to children with ADHD or whether behavioral deterioration is a typical response of ADHD children to SSRI treatment. (In the author's clinical practice, fluoxetine or sertraline appear generally problematic for children with ADHD, and paroxetine seems more helpful.)

Adverse Effects: Various studies and case series confirm that fluoxetine can induce behavioral deterioration in children with obsessive-compulsive disorder, depression, or ADHD. Although symptoms of "behavioral activation" were found in 50% of children and adolescents when fluoxetine doses of 20 mg daily were reached early in treatment (Riddle et al., 1991a), behavioral deterioration can be seen at lower doses and also with sertraline (Tierney et al., 1995). Suicidal and self-destructive changes also have been noted in children whose fluoxetine doses were raised rapidly (King et al., 1991). The phenomenology of SSRI-induced behavioral deterioration in youths is still being clarified but appears to involve motor hyperactivity

and restlessness, excited feelings, agitation, sleep disturbances, and social disinhibition (Riddle et al., 1991a). At least some cases of SSRI-induced mania have been identified in youths (Minnery, West, McConville, & Sorter, 1995; Rosenberg, Johnson, & Sahl, 1992). and it is difficult to discern whether some examples of behavioral activation are actually mild or incipient hypomanic episodes (Tierney et al., 1995). Possible mechanisms of SSRI-induced behavioral deterioration include disinhibition (similar to benzodiazepines), manic switch, irritability, sleep disruption, extrapyramidal akathisia, and neurotoxic delirium.

SSRIs also have been reported to induce cognitive impairments in the therapeutic dose range (Bangs, Petti, & Janus, 1994) and to exacerbate LSD (lysergic acid diethylamide) flashback syndrome in adolescents (Markel, Lee, Holmes, & Domino, 1994) and adults.

Apart from the apparently increased risk of behavioral side effects in youths, SSRI adverse effects and their management are generally similar in children and adults. If a dose reduction is not clinically feasible, sleep interference (initial, middle, or late insomnia) usually responds to trazodone 50 to 200 mg or nortriptyline 25 to 75 mg nightly. Headaches generally respond to mild analgesics. Nausea usually can be managed with over-the-counter agents (such as Pepto-Bismol® or Gaviscon®) and be discontinued after several days. Sexual dysfunction in adolescents can be countered by the concurrent use of low doses of bupropion, although amantadine, cyproheptadine, or yohimbine also can be considered. SSRI-induced "wired" feelings and anxiety are generally well controlled with benzodiazepines.

The *serotonin syndrome* can appear during treatment with SSRIs, typically when used in combination with other serotonergic agents. In its subtle presentations, perhaps only 1 or 2 symptoms might be seen, such as nausea, abdominal cramps, sweating, diarrhea, restless behavior, insomnia, hyperreflexia, and myoclonus. When several symptoms of serotonin syndrome appear, immediate treatment should be initiated with cyproheptadine (4 mg, with repeats to 12 mg), preferably in a hospital because of some fatalities reported in adults.

The *SSRI withdrawal syndrome* (malaise, fatigue, headache, nausea, sedation, agitation) is relatively common following dose reduction or drug discontinuation, even after brief treatments at low doses.

SSRI Amotivational Syndrome: This frequent adverse effect has not received adequate attention, especially in children (Popper, 1995a; Walkup, 1994). Diminished motivation and disinclination to engage in effortful activity can emerge after several weeks or months of SSRI treatment, with or without clinical improvement in obsessive-compulsive or depressive target symptoms.

The clinical picture in adults involves apathy, decreased initiative, and indifference, including a lack of concern about the apathy (Hoehn-Saric et al., 1991; Hoehn-Saric, Lipsey, & McLeod, 1991). I first observed this problem in SSRI-treated children who showed a satisfactory resolution of their target symptoms but had an actual decline in their school grades, despite an apparent improvement in their cognitive processing and mental clarity. In more typical cases, a child becomes more content but is uncharacteristically unmotivated and uninvolved. A previous "straight arrow" might start to use marijuana (which further aggravates the motivational problem) or choose new friends with a low interest in self-growth, activities that involve good self-esteem, achievement, or the future.

Rather than having a depressive "I don't care" attitude, these children tend to have an indifferent "I care but it doesn't bother me" attitude. Similarly, adults describe a lifting of their target symptoms but a growing feeling of "Anything is okay with me" as chores pile up at home and incomplete work accumulates at the office. This phenomenon is distinct from depressive anhedonia, because these patients can again experience their former interests and pleasures, while important tasks that require effort or motivation are postponed or avoided without concern.

This type of apathy is easily overlooked or tolerated, particularly in patients whose behavioral symptoms are reduced, mood is improved, and preoccupations are minimal. Family and physician may view the "relaxed" attitude as a positive change or postulate that the patient is taking a well-needed mental vacation after the illness. When asked, a child can report some awareness of the amotivational change, but child (or adult) patients typically do not volunteer this side effect until the clinician inquires specifically about the symptoms.

This amotivational/apathetic syndrome is associated with other subtle cognitive effects, such as a decline in long-term memory, a hard-to-define impairment in attention, and decreased planning for the future.

These SSRI-induced changes have been compared to the "apathy" and "la belle indifference" of patients with frontal lobe deficits (Hoehn-Saric et al., 1990, 1991). A young adult, reported to have developed amotivational symptoms during fluoxetine treatment, showed neuroimaging evidence of diminished blood flow in the frontal cortex and changes on neuropsychological testing that are usually observed in frontal lobe dysfunction. The frontal abnormalities in this patient resolved after drug discontinuation (Hoehn-Saric et al., 1991).

Both apathy and disinhibition are classically associated with frontal lobe syndrome (Stuss & Benson, 1986). It has been speculated that both the behavioral activation (Riddle et al., 1992) and the self-destructive behavior (King et al., 1991) in children during SSRI treatment might result from frontal dysfunction (Walkup, 1994). That is, both frontal apathy and frontal disinhibition may be adverse effects of SSRI treatment.

In my clinical practice, the prevalence of SSRI-induced frontal changes appears to increase with the duration of treatment. Disinhibition seems to appear sooner than apathy (days to weeks vs. weeks to months), but apathy is the more frequent side effect, appearing in the majority of children treated with SSRIs (at typical doses for obsessive-compulsive disorder or depression) within 6 months. Fluoxetine, sertraline, and paroxetine appear comparable in producing these effects, and venlafaxine seems to have a lower risk. No other antidepressant agents (including HCAs, lithium, and trazodone) or drug categories appear to induce a similar amotivational state, as assessed in a nonblind screening of patients in my practice. There appears to be no reduction in either the drug-induced apathy or disinhibition over time; instead both may worsen progressively while doses are kept steady. SSRI discontinuation leads to improvement within several days or weeks.

Dose reduction can improve the apathy and disinhibition while preserving therapeutic effects for some patients (Hoehn-Saric et al., 1990). In my practice, these dose reductions seem to be helpful only temporarily. The frontal apathy typically reappears after several weeks or months at

TABLE 11.5

Clinical Treatment with Selective Serotonin Reuptake Inhibitors in Youths

Dosage and Regimen

Doses are expressed in fluoxetine milligram equivalents.

Starting dose	5 mg each morning
Rate of dose elevation	5 mg every 4–7 days
Typical full dose	20–30 mg daily
Number of daily dosages	1 (each morning for fluoxetine and sertraline, qhs for paroxetine)
Delayed clinical response	Major depressive disorder: 2–10 weeks
Length of full trial	Major depressive disorder: 6–12 weeks
Duration of treatment	Major depressive disorder: 6–12 months, sometimes several years, or indefinitely

Available Strengths

Fluoxetine	10, 20 mg—brand only
	Oral solution—brand only
Sertraline	50, 100 mg—brand only
Paroxetine	20, 30 mg—brand only

Major Adverse Effects

Amotivational syndrome, apathy, decreased productivity
Behavioral disinhibition
Anxious, agitated, or "wired" feelings
Insomnia
Psychosis
Anorexia, stomachache, feeling of stomach fullness, nausea
Diarrhea, loose stools
Weight loss
Sedation
Headache
Mild cognitive interference: word-finding, "forgetting"
Sexual dysfunction (reduced drive, decreased performance)
Suicidal ideation
Violent behavior (?disinhibition)
Sweating, tremor
Serotonin syndrome
Serotonin withdrawal syndrome

Precautions

Avoid multiple concurrent serotonergic agents (re neuroleptic malignant syndrome).
Give child and family repeated reminders to watch for irritability and mild confusion.

Toxicity

Tremor, sweating, apathy, agitation, violence, suicidality

Relative Contraindications

Migraine
Heavy concurrent marijuana use (re amotivational syndrome)
Bipolar disorder, psychosis
Concurrent MAOI treatment

TABLE 11.5

Continued

Initial Medical Workup

Body weight
Observe for tremor.
Family history of psychosis

Ongoing Medical Monitoring

Follow motivation, initiative, productivity, and task completion.
Initiate questions concerning sexual dysfunction.
Check weight every 3 to 4 months.

the lower dose. Instead, careful supplementation with a noradrenergic agent (e.g., heterocyclic antidepressants or stimulants) appears to reduce or eliminate the frontal side effects of SSRIs.

These SSRI-induced frontal effects have been described in only a few reports (Hoehn-Saric et al., 1990, 1991; Popper, 1995a; Walkup, 1994), and probably would not have been identified in protocol-based research studies, because standard interviews and rating scales do not include the items relevant to assessing apathy, indifference, or frontal amotivational states. Identification of SSRI-induced apathy and indifference requires exploration of a patient's experiences with particular attentiveness to quality of life and without bias derived from apparent improvements in the patient's target symptoms.

Controlled studies are needed to determine whether children are at greater risk than adults for SSRI-induced apathy or disinhibition. It would not be surprising if frontal lobe functioning were more readily compromised by medications in youths (frontal lobe functions mature relatively late in development) or in ADHD (which involves frontal dysfunction).

Clinical Monitoring: No premedication workup or ongoing laboratory monitoring is required for the SSRIs, so clinical attention can be focused on identifying adverse effects. The appearance of the frontal effects of disinhibition and apathy is often sufficiently gradual that it can be difficult to identify the onset or even to perceive the change in behavior as it is happening.

In treating depressive disorders, therapeutic effects of SSRIs might emerge after a longer duration of treatment in children than adults. Preliminary findings, similar to suggestive findings with

HCAs (Ambrosini et al., 1994), suggest that the clinical response to SSRIs in depressed youths might take more than 2 to 4 weeks to become apparent and could take to 10 weeks or more (Colle et al., 1994). In treating depressed youngsters, a routine 10- to 12-week course of SSRI (or HCA) treatment might be sensible before declaring a treatment failure. The required length of SSRI treatment for major depressive disorder in youths is uncertain.

Overall, the SSRIs have some clear clinical uses in children with obsessive-compulsive bulimia, and probably selective mutism, and might be useful in pervasive developmental disorders and body dysmorphic disorder. Their effects in youngsters with depressive and anxiety disorders need further evaluation.

Especially because some clinicians have put these drugs on the "fast track" for use in children, possible adverse effects of the SSRIs in youths need to be evaluated with controlled studies. These chemically novel agents may have important side effects that are not yet known. Enthusiasm for SSRI treatments of children and adolescents should be tempered by current suggestions of frontal apathy and disinhibition and should remain tempered until a more extensive clinical track record of their properties has accumulated in adults.

OTHER ANTIDEPRESSANTS

Venlafaxine: Venlafaxine (Effexor®) is the first marketed agent to inhibit the neuronal reuptake of both norepinephrine and serotonin selectively, a mechanism that speculatively might help a wider spectrum of depressed patients than the selective serotonin reuptake inhibitors. Its adverse effects are generally predictable from its shared properties with the heterocyclic antidepressants and SSRIs, but its occasional hypertensive effect in adults indicates that blood pressure should be carefully monitored in venlafaxine-treated children.

Controlled studies of venlafaxine in youths are not yet available. Early anecdotal observations in children and adolescents suggest that venlafaxine might be useful for treating obsessive-compulsive or perseverative symptoms, mood, anxiety, agitation, cognitive clarity and speed, and ADHD-like symptoms in patients with major depression, obsessive-compulsive, ADHD, anxiety disorders, and pervasive developmental disorders.

In my clinical practice, venlafaxine appears to be a particularly promising for treating youths with major depressive disorder. Venlafaxine seems to have a higher rate of response than SSRIs in treating depressed youths, and its effects on blood pressure appear to be minimal. Moreover, venlafaxine seems to have a lower risk of frontal apathy and disinhibition than SSRIs, perhaps because of the protective effects of its norepinephrine properties. Venlafaxine also seems more reliable than the SSRIs in treating ADHD.

Clomipramine: Clomipramine (Anafranil®) is another nonselective serotonin uptake inhibitor, but it has the chemical structure and many adverse effects of a tricyclic antidepressant. In contrast to the SSRIs and more than most other HCAs, clomipramine carries a relatively high risk of inducing seizures in adults (1.5% annually).

In well-controlled studies of children with obsessive-compulsive disorder, clomipramine was found more efficacious than desipramine (Leonard et al., 1989; Leonard et al., 1991) and placebo (DeVeaugh-Geiss et al., 1992; Flament et al., 1985; Leonard et al., 1989; Leonard et al., 1991). Although the SSRIs may have fewer obvious side effects, clomipramine appears more effective than .the SSRIs for treating obsessive-compulsive disorder in adults; if not used in preference to the SSRIs, it should be considered when this disorder in youths does not respond adequately to SSRIs.

In a well-controlled study of children with autistic disorder (ages 6 to 23 years), clomipramine was found effective in treating stereotypies, angry outbursts, and compulsive ritualized behaviors, whereas neither desipramine nor placebo re-

duced these symptoms (Gordon et al., 1993). The finding that clomipramine may be efficacious is consistent with initial reports that the SSRIs appear helpful for treating some features of pervasive developmental disorder (Bass & Beltis, 1991; Cook et al., 1992; Epperson et al., 1994; King, 1991; McDougle et al., 1990). However, in an open-label study conducted in younger children (ages 3 to 8 years) with autism, adverse effects and clinical changes predominated (Sanchez et al., 1996). Self-injurious behavior in patients with pervasive developmental disorder (or mental retardation) also has been reported to respond to clomipramine, with observed improvements in 14 out of the 15 patients treated in 2 studies (Garber, McGonigler, Slomka, & Monteverde, 1992; Gordon et al., 1993).

In a double-blind, placebo-controlled study of school absenteeism, depressive symptoms were incidentally found to reduce on a clomipramine dose of 75 mg daily (Berney et al., 1981). The efficacy of clomipramine in treating childhood depression has not yet been examined systematically using current methodology.

Similar to venlafaxine, clomipramine is worth investigating for its possible antidepressant effects and other therapeutic properties in youths, without assuming that it provides merely a simple summation of SSRI and HCA effects.

Bupropion: Buproprion (Wellbutrin®) represents a substantively novel pharmacologic approach to the treatment of depression, speculatively involving some undetermined antidepressant mechanism. Its dopaminergic effects are established, but its serotonergic and noradrenergic properties seem minimal in comparison to other antidepressants. No reports have been published on bupropion treatment of depression in youths.

Successful bupropion treatment of ADHD in adults has been described (Wender & Reimherr, 1990), but findings in children with ADHD are mixed (Casat, Pleasants, Schroeder, & Parler, 1989; Clay, Gualtieri, Evans, & Gullion, 1988; Conners, 1994; Simeon, Ferguson, & Van Wyck Fleet, 1986). In a direct comparison with methylphenidate, bupropion produced comparable but consistently weaker therapeutic effects (Barrickman et al., 1995). In that study, fewer patients experienced adverse effects with methylphenidate and, after the study, more patients preferred to continue on methylphenidate than bupropion.

Bupropion has been reported in a well-controlled study to substantially reduce the symptoms of bulimia nervosa (Horne et al., 1988). However, its use in anorexia nervosa is relatively contraindicated because of a possibly increased risk of seizures in such patients.

Bupropion has been reported to aggravate tics in youth with comorbid ADHD and tic disorders (Spencer, Biederman, Steingard, & Wilens, 1993). An unexpectedly high incidence of severe skin rash has been described in 2 studies of bupropion-treated children. The increased risk of seizure induction may be reduced by gradual dose increases; if a dose of 450 mg daily is exceeded, concurrent treatment with a anticonvulsant medication is recommended.

Other adverse effects of bupropion are quite minimal and manageable. It has an unconfirmed reputation for having a low rate of manic switching in adults with bipolar disorder. If a low switch rate and anti-ADHD properties are demonstrated in youngsters, bupropion could become a valuable option for treating comorbid bipolar disorder and ADHD.

Bupropion might become an attractive agent, especially because of its minimal weight gain and sexual dysfunction, but current information is scanty on its safety and efficacy in youths. Controlled trials in children and adolescents are needed for major depressive disorder, ADHD, and bulimia nervosa.

Moclobemide and Other Monoamine Oxidase Inhibitors: Moclobemide has not been approved for commercial release in the United States, but it has been well received in Canada and Europe for treating depressed adults. This new monoamine oxidase inhibitor (MAOI) is reversibly and selectively able to target monoamine oxidase A (MAO_A). Because of its selectivity and reversibility, moclobemide has fewer side effects and does not require the dietary restrictions associated with conventional MAOIs. These features could allow safer use of MAOIs in children and adolescents who might not reliably adhere to the required rigorous diet (Ryan, Puig-Antich, et al., 1988).

Moclobemide has been reported to be effective in children with depression or ADHD in open trials (Trott, Elliger, & Nissen, 1990; Trott, Friese, Menzel, & Nissen, 1992). Controlled studies suggest the efficacy of brofaromine (Kennedy et al., 1993) and phenelzine (Rothschild et al., 1994;

Walsh et al., 1988) in treating bulimia nervosa. Uncontrolled reports suggest some value for ADHD and for depressed, enuretic, or phobic children (Frommer 1972; Trott et al., 1992). Except in treating bulimia, the traditional nonreversible MAOIs are rarely used to treat children with mental disorders in the United States.

Moclobemide can be prescribed in the United States, obtained from a foreign pharmacy, and imported for medical treatment under the Personal Importation Policy of the Food and Drug Administration (FDA) of the United States Government (FDA, 1988). This policy reflects a decision by the FDA not to rigorously enforce existing regulations that prevent importation and medical treatment with drugs it has not approved, under the conditions that the medication be used in the direct clinical treatment of a single patient monitored by the prescribing physician. This policy was adopted several years ago to allow some flexibility for certain drugs, including clomipramine and some anti-AIDS drugs, that were available in neighboring countries but unapproved in the United States. The provisions of the Personal Importation Policy do not encourage or allow research, treatment of several patients, or sale of the drug. No prior approval or governmental involvement is needed, and no limits are set on the patient's age. Procedurally, the physician writes a prescription, the patient makes telephone arrangements with a foreign pharmacy and mails the prescription with payment, the medication is mailed directly to the patient, and the physician has the usual responsibility for proper clinical treatment. The U.S. government retains the right to seize the medication at the border, but, under the provisions of the Personal Importation Policy, typically does not enforce this right.

In the context of persisting questions about the safety and efficacy of the HCAs and SSRIs in treating major depressive episodes in youths, and the increasing availability of "improved" MAOI options, the new breed of diet-friendly MAOIs might receive renewed clinical and research interest.

At this time, under very unusual clinical circumstances involving repeated treatment failures on numerous drug categories, moclobemide might be considered a possible alternative to electroconvulsive therapy in youths (Ghaziuddin et al., 1996; Kutcher & Robertson, 1995). The scarcity of experience with moclobemide in children, though, should make physicians reluctant to proceed with its use in children.

Mood Stabilizers

VALPROATE

In adults, valproate has been displacing lithium as the treatment of choice for bipolar disorder, especially since a large-scale, randomized, double-blind, placebo-controlled study of acute mania demonstrated that valproate and lithium were equally efficacious in adults but that the adverse effects of valproate were better tolerated (Bowden, et al., 1994).

The case for valproate (Depakene® or generic; Depakote®) as the treatment of choice for acute mania in youths is becoming quite strong. The extensive experience with valproate treatment of seizure disorders provides very substantial data on its safety in children. By comparison, there is virtually no documentation regarding the safety of lithium therapy in youths. In the absence of adequate controlled studies and efficacy data on either lithium or valproate in treating bipolar disorder in youngsters, clinical decisions regarding empirical drug trials can be based on safety considerations. Thus the first-line use of valproate for empirical treatment of acute mania in children and adolescents is justified by available data on safety rather than efficacy.

Valproate is far from harmless and, at times, even can be life-threatening. However, its adverse effects are well delineated in children, and serious problems with valproate generally can be avoided with systematic monitoring of liver and blood indices. Deaths from acute liver failure have been reported mainly in children under 2 years of age with seizure disorders and receiving multiple anticonvulsants, especially in children with mental retardation and somatic anomalies (Bryant & Dreifuss, 1996; Dreifuss et al., 1987; Rothner, 1981; Zafrani & Berthelot, 1982; Zimmerman & Ishak, 1982). Valproate-induced hepatic fatalities have been reported in 1 in 600 children younger than 2 years old (Bryant & Dreifuss, 1996). Beyond age 2 years, the risk of major liver toxicity on valproate monotherapy is estimated at 1 in 45,000 cases (Dreifuss, 1987). This risk is considerably lower

for patients above age 11, and extensive monitoring generally is not required.

With appropriate monitoring and clinical observation, serious difficulty is rare. Under ordinary clinical circumstances, basic liver and blood indices can be monitored on a weekly basis for the first month, on alternate weeks during the second month, and monthly thereafter. There are no adequate long-term data to support the discontinuation of monthly monitoring at a later point in treatment, nor are there data to show the cost-effectiveness of indefinite monitoring. Extensive monitoring is needed only if valproate is prescribed in the presence of hematologic or hepatic disorders.

The other adverse effects of valproate are considerable. At times, valproate (like other anticonvulsants) can induce behavioral deterioration characterized by excitation, agitation, or even psychosis (Trimble, 1990). Especially in youths, weight gain can be a significant problem, potentially leading to noncompliance and discontinuation. Sedation and gastrointestinal discomfort (including nausea and vomiting) are the most frequent problems. If gastrointestinal distress is accompanied by actual pain, assessment for possible valproate-induced pancreatitis should be initiated rapidly.

Even in adults, the efficacy of valproate for treating bipolar disorder remains open to considerable uncertainty. The current data showing a clinical advantage of valproate over lithium is restricted to treatment of mania during the acute phase. Unlike lithium, valproate does not appear to have antidepressant properties and has not yet been adequately examined in adults for prophylaxis of manic episodes.

Valproate has not been examined systematically in the treatment of any behavioral or emotional disorder of youths. In open clinical trials (Kastner, Friedman, Plummer, Ruiz, & Henning, 1990; Papatheodorou & Kutcher, 1993; West, Keck, & McElroy, 1995; West et al., 1994), adolescents with acute mania appeared relatively responsive to valproate, perhaps because of the high prevalence of mixed episodes in bipolar disorder of youths. Controlled data in youths on valproate treatment and prophylaxis of bipolar disorder are sorely needed.

Until new research identifies specific clinical advantages of lithium over valproate, valproate

TABLE 11.6

Clinical Treatment with Valproate in Youths

Dosage and Regimen

Starting dose	15–20 mg/kg, in 2–3 divided doses
Rate of dose elevation	
250 mg	every 3 days
Typical full dose	30–60 mg/kg daily, with plasma concentration at 80–100 mcg/ml (but blood levels may not be clinically meaningful or valid)
Number of daily dosages	2–4
Delayed clinical response	4–10 days
Length of full trial	3 weeks at full dose
Duration of treatment	Minimally 12 months, as long as needed, often years

Available Strengths

Valproic acid:	250 mg—generic
	Oral syrup—generic
Divalproex:	125, 250, 500 mg—generic
	"Sprinkles" that may be placed on food—brand only

Major Adverse Effects

Weight gain
Stomachache, nausea, vomiting
Diarrhea
Sedation
Tremor
Behavioral excitation or hyperactivity
Peripheral neurotoxic symptoms
Irregular or absent menstruation
Alopecia
Leukopenia, thrombocytopenia
Hepatotoxic metabolite formation, potentially fatal
Pancreatitis

Precautions

Alert patient and family to watch for symptoms of chemical hepatitis, agranulocytosis, and aplastic anemia.

Toxicity

Sedation, confusion, vomiting, tremor, weakness, ataxia

Relative Contraindications

Liver disease, bone marrow suppression, severe leukopenia, thrombocytopenia

Initial Medical Workup

Physical exam to assess cardiac and neurologic status
Complete blood count, with differential
If platelet count is low normal, get manual count.
SGOT, SGPT, bilirubin.
Blood urea nitrogen, creatinine.
Optional: Serum iron [increases in bone marrow suppression]

Ongoing Medical Monitoring

White blood count, platelet count, SGOT, SGPT, and bilirubin should be obtained weekly for the first month.
Subsequently they (and perhaps serum iron) should be obtained monthly for children under 10 years old and every 4 to 6 months for older patients.
If platelet count is low normal, get manual count (not computerized).
Check weight every 3 to 4 months.

---

may be considered to fill the clinical void as the mood stabilizer of choice for youths—at least for short-term treatment of acute manic episodes.

LITHIUM

Despite extremely meager available data supporting its safety and efficacy in youths, there is widespread use of lithium to treat children and adolescents with psychotic and nonpsychotic behavior disorders.

Clinical Uses: No well-controlled studies of adequate size are available that evaluate lithium treatment of bipolar disorder in adolescents or children for anti-manic, prophylactic, or antidepressant properties. An uncontrolled but careful study found a good clinical response to lithium in 10 out of 10 preadolescent children with overt psychotic mania (Varanka, Weller, Weller, & Fristad, 1988). A very large literature regarding open-label lithium treatments, described in case reports and small case series, suggests that lithium can be helpful for managing bipolar disorder. However, the diagnostic criteria for bipolar disorder used in these reports are quite diverse (Alessi, Naylor, Ghaziuddin, & Zubieta, 1994; Youngerman & Canino, 1978).

Two open-label reports suggest that lithium augmentation of heterocyclic antidepressant can be helpful in treating about 30 to 40% of cases of major depression in youths (Ryan, Meyer, Dachille, Mazzie, & Puig-Antich, 1988; Strober, Freeman, Schmidt, & Diamond, 1992). However, the degree of improvement often was not impressive (Strober et al., 1992).

Nonpsychotic children with "behavior disorders"—but not identified as having bipolar disorder—have been reported to respond to lithium in some controlled studies and a large literature of uncontrolled case series and case reports. These patients have presented with a wide range of mental and behavioral symptoms, including impulsivity, temper tantrums/rage, assaultiveness, social intrusiveness, emotional lability (Alessi, Naylor, Ghaziuddin, & Zubieta, 1994; Brumback and Weinberg 1977; McKnew et al., 1981; Youngerman & Canino, 1978) as well as "overly strong" (almost "violently strong") feelings, and nonpsychotic euphoria with obliviousness to the harsh realities of their circumstances and problems.

Lithium has been shown to be particularly helpful for treating certain forms of impulsive and aggressive behavior. Double-blind, placebo-controlled studies indicate some efficacy of lithium in treating aggressive behavior in hospitalized children with conduct disorder (Campbell et al., 1984; Campbell, Adams, et al., 1995; Campbell, Kafantaris, & Cueva, 1995). Lithium has appeared useful in treating impulsive behavior disorders in several reports that utilize double-blind placebo-controlled single-case design methods in a small number of patients (DeLong, 1978; Dyson & Barcai, 1970; McKnew et al., 1981; Rifkin, Quitkin, Carrillo, Blumberg, & Klein, 1972) and in uncontrolled case series (Davis, 1979; DeLong, 1978; DeLong & Nieman, 1983; Lena, Surtees, & Maggs, 1978; Siassi, 1982; Vetro, Szentistvanyi, Pallag, Varga, & Szilard, 1985). Lithium has been reported to be helpful for managing self-injurious behavior in some patients with developmental disabilities (Winchel & Stanley, 1991). In 1 controlled study (Rifkin, Quitkin, Carrillo, Blumberg, & Klein, 1972) and many case reports, the symptom of emotional lability was noted frequently and appeared to respond to lithium treatment.

In all of these reports, bipolar disorder was not diagnosed, but an underlying or comorbid bipolar disorder usually cannot be excluded. It remains to be determined, both in youths and in adults, whether lithium is efficacious treatment for symptoms completely unrelated to bipolar disorder, or whether certain nonpsychotic behavior disorders constitute a subdiagnostic, precursor, or childhood variant form of bipolar disorder.

Pre-school children with nonpsychotic behavior disorders also have been described to respond to lithium treatment (Feinstein & Wolpert, 1975; Vetro et al., 1985). Children with severe temper tantrums, impulsive behavior, emotional lability, vegetative symptoms, and a family psychiatric history of manic-depressive illness have been identified as young as 2 years of age and have been demonstrated to be lithium responsive as young as age 4 (DeLong & Aldershof, 1987).

The majority of lithium-responsive youths do not present with overt psychosis or have predominant symptoms of bipolar disorder. However, when treated without pharmacotherapy, these youths generally are viewed as strenuously "difficult" cases in outpatient clinics and frequently require psychiatric hospitalization.

Comments on Childhood Behavior Disorders and Bipolar Disorder: Sometimes nonpsychotic children with behavior disorders are in fact labeled as carrying a diagnosis of bipolar disorder. The diagnosis of bipolar disorder seems to be placed on children with nonpsychotic (or psychotic) behavior disorders especially when they (1) have family members with bipolar disorder, (2) present with some neurovegetative symptoms, or (3) are found to respond to lithium or another mood stabilizer. The diagnosis (or "working diagnosis") of bipolar disorder in these situations is controversial, especially because all 3 of these characteristics can be seen in children who do not have bipolar disorder. These children highlight the question of whether the diagnostic boundaries (and criteria) for bipolar disorder need to be drawn differently in youths and adults.

Most of these youngsters fulfill criteria for ADHD, although it would be very misleading to view these children as having the disorder. ADHD itself does not improve with lithium treatment and often is aggravated by lithium (Greenhill, Rieder, Wender, Buchsbaum, & Zahn, 1973; McKnew et al., 1981; Whitehead & Clark, 1970). In some cases, genuine ADHD may present comorbidly with bipolar disorder and be treated with a lithium-psychostimulant combination (Licamele & Goldberg, 1989).

Many of these children also fulfill criteria for conduct disorder, but their course is typically more stormy. Among a sample of adolescents whose conduct disorder is sufficiently severe to require hospitalization, 25% may have fulfilled criteria for bipolar disorder (Arredondo & Butler, 1994). In contrast, major depression was not over-represented in this sample. These findings suggest that hospitalized adolescents with conduct disorder could be reasonably treated with mood stabilizers, and that they may not respond to antidepressants any more (or less) frequently than other hospitalized adolescents (Arredondo & Butler, 1994).

An over-representation of bipolar disorder among hospitalized adolescents with conduct disorder is consistent with the likelihood that bipolar disorder makes the course of conduct disorder more problematic. Thus, some youths with "conduct disorder" (especially those hospitalized) appear to have bipolar disorder. An over-representation of bipolar disorder among hospitalized adolescents with conduct disorder could account for the apparent responsiveness of "aggressive conduct disorder" to lithium treatment (Campbell et al., 1984; Campbell, Adams, et al. 1995; Campbell, Kafantaris, et al., 1995). Some adolescents show a major improvement or even resolution of their conduct disorder symptoms when treated with lithium. Bipolar disorder should be suspected in any case of "episodic conduct disorder."

Generally, youths with bipolar disorder seem to present with fewer and less severe psychotic symptoms than adults. Over time, the nonpsychotic symptoms of childhood often are overshadowed by psychotic symptoms in adolescence. These youths, both as children and adolescents, appear to follow a more severe and chronic course than youths with other behavior disorders. Interestingly, their mood and behavioral symptoms only sometimes suggest cyclic or periodic change, and they tend to present with mixed manic episodes more frequently than adults with bipolar disorder.

Despite the controversy about viewing these youths as having "prepsychotic" or "subpsychotic" conditions, empirical evidence is mounting that at least some of these youngsters with nonpsychotic behavior disorders respond to mood stabilizers and go on to have bipolar disorder as adults. Like major depressive disorder in youths, it is speculatively possible that the current diagnostic criteria for bipolar disorder might not be a clinically precise, reliable, or vivid characterization of its presentation in youths.

Clinical Implications of Pharmacokinetics: The pharmacokinetics of lithium carbonate is quite distinct from the kinetics of other psychopharmacological agents, because lithium is neither metabolized by the liver nor protein-bound. Lithium clearance is largely determined by the rate of renal clearance, which (like hepatic clearance) is more rapid at younger ages. As a result, plasma lithium levels decrease more rapidly after a dosage in youths than adults. The 2-phase elimination half-lives of lithium in preadolescent children are 6 and then 18 hours (Vitiello et al., 1988), compared to a mean elimination half-life of 18 hours in adolescents, 24 hours in adults, and 33 hours in geriatric patients.

The implications of fast lithium clearance could include some changes in the procedures for monitoring plasma lithium levels in children. For example, plasma sampling conducted 10 to 12 hours after lithium administration (as in adults) would appear to be 2 to 4 hours late for most children and adolescents. Also, steady-state plasma lithium levels could be sampled on average after 3 days in preadolescents, 4 days in adolescents, and 5 days in adults. More comprehensive pharmacokinetic data are needed in adolescents and children (examining carbonate, citrate, and each of the 2 slow-release formulations separately), so that systematic underdosings and overdosings can be avoided.

Other age-related factors should be considered when monitoring and adjusting plasma lithium levels. Children and especially adolescents are subject to abrupt changes in diet, exercise, and physical activity. Mild toxicity symptoms can emerge during periods of dehydration associated with missed meals, summer heat, exercise or exertion (competitive sports, cramming for exams), or illness (fever, diarrhea, vomiting). A meat-containing meal can produce a transient 40% increase in lithium clearance in children (DeSanto et al., 1991). A dietary salt load also can cause a rapid transient reduction in plasma lithium levels and a breakthrough of lithium-responsive symptoms; because of the high salt content of some mass-marketed foods, DeLong has dubbed this phenomenon "taco tantrums." Physicians should be aware that children and some parents are unfamiliar with the high salt content of pizza, Asian food, and common hamburgers. A low-salt diet is unnecessary and potentially risky during lithium therapy, but reasonably regular salt intake should be advised.

As in adults, a premenstrual reduction in plasma lithium levels is present during adolescence (Conrad & Hamilton, 1986). In pregnant teenagers (and adults), plasma lithium levels decrease progressively (increased renal clearance) and then increase abruptly after childbirth. To prevent lithium toxicity in the postpartum mother and in the neonate (whose renal clearance is slow), lithium doses should be reduced by 50% about 7 to 10 days before delivery.

Dose tolerance and dose requirements may decrease as the severity of symptoms reduces during treatment, so that relatively higher blood levels of lithium typically are needed when a child is overtly manic than when slightly "behavior disordered" (mildly irritable, hypomanic) or when euthymic.

Are Youths Less Responsive to Lithium?: Early-onset bipolar disorder has been reported to be less responsive to lithium than the later-onset disorder (Strober et al., 1988). If this age-related differential response to lithium were confirmed, it could be explainable by several (not necessarily independent) mechanisms:

1. Earlier-onset of a biopsychiatric disorder usually is associated with a stronger genetic loading and a more severe course of illness, so the early-onset cases might be generally treatment-resistant.
2. Lithium is less effective in treating "mixed" bipolar episodes, which are especially common in youths with bipolar disorder.
3. A longer treatment duration appears to be needed for HCA and SSRI treatment of major depressive disorder in youths than in adults (Ambrosini et al., 1994; Colle, Bélair, DiFeo, Weiss, & LaRoche, 1994), so clinical trials of lithium similarly might need to be extended beyond the 10 days usually needed to see therapeutic effects of lithium in adults.
4. The faster renal clearance of lithium in children (Vitiello et al., 1988), a pharmacokinetic difference from adults, would be associated with a more "sawtooth" pattern of serum lithium levels and more variable symptom control.
5. The higher transmembranal pump (Na,K-ATPase) activity in children than adults, a pharmacodynamic difference, would reduce the effect of lithium on neuronal excitability in youths (El-Mallakh, Barrett, & Wyatt, 1993).

The latter 3 explanations imply that the apparently weaker response to lithium in younger children possibly could be overcome by age-specific modifications in lithium treatment regimens. Specifically, by using a longer duration of empirical trials, a controlled-release formulation of lithium, and a slightly higher therapeutic range of plasma lithium levels, the apparent effectiveness of lithium in youths might speculatively be enhanced.

In my experience, the use of a controlled-release formulation of lithium (such as Eskalith CR® 450 mg or Lithobid® 300 mg) is more frequently and fully effective in youths than the usual carbonate pills or citrate elixir. Multiple small daily administrations of lithium carbonate also seem more effective than once-daily dosing, but this regimen can engender multiple daily skir-

234

mishes between caregivers and noncompliant patients, so treatment with controlled-release lithium is far more feasible.

No therapeutic range of plasma lithium levels has been defined for treating bipolar disorder in youths, because therapeutic efficacy in youngsters has not been established. However, it appears that most youngsters can be treated within the therapeutic range developed in and used for adults.

Although most children are well treated in the "adult" therapeutic lithium range, a small number of children with psychotic mania show neither adverse effects nor therapeutic effects at the upper end of the "adult" therapeutic range. In my experience, these children can respond to slightly higher plasma lithium levels. Such aggressive use of "above-maximum" plasma lithium levels has not been documented as safe or effective, is applicable exclusively to youths with neither adverse effects nor therapeutic effects when treated with lithium at the top end of the adult therapeutic range, requires specific consent, and demands very cautious monitoring.

Finally, in my experience, empirical lithium trials of 3 to 4 weeks rather than 5 to 10 days are particularly valuable in treating youths with acute mania if aggressive dosing is not pursued.

Adverse Effects: The safety of lithium in children and adolescents has not been adequately examined in short-term or long-term studies. It is clear that lithium treatment is cumbersome because of its many side effects and the need for periodic blood sampling. Moreover, adverse clinical changes observed in lithium-treated children tend to be incorrectly interpreted and systematically overly ascribed by clinicians to lithium side effects (Silva et al., 1992), a bias that leads to additional management complications.

Two well-conducted studies report a similar profile of adverse lithium effects in adults and children (Hagino et al., 1995; Varanka et al., 1988), but there is a range of opinion regarding whether children have a high prevalence of adverse effects (Campbell et al., 1991; Hagino et al., 1995; Silva et al., 1992), are similarly prone to lithium side effects as adults (Varanka et al., 1988), or have generally fewer side effects than adults (Annell, 1969; DeLong & Aldershof, 1987; Siassi, 1982). The misattribution of medical disorders and incidental symptoms to lithium (Silva et al., 1992) may contribute to the discrepancies between observers and to misjudgments in clinical treatment of youths. Whatever the prevalence of adverse effects in the lithium-treated child population, it is clear that they require considerable monitoring.

The antithyroid effects of lithium are a particular concern in children because of the potential influence on body growth, especially in long-term treatments. Lithium-induced hypothyroidism is commonly associated with elevated levels of thyroid-stimulating hormone (TSH). If hypothyroid symptoms are not clinically apparent, this TSH elevation is considered evidence of "chemical" hypothyroidism and typically is not treated in adults. If lithium-treated adults with chemical hypothyroidism develop fatigue or other symptoms of "clinical" hypothyroidism, thyroid supplementation can be considered. Generally, endocrinologists do not attempt thyroid supplementation in such cases unless the TSH level has risen to 2 times the upper limit of normal. (This limit varies between laboratories, depending on chemical assay methods.) In contrast, psychiatrists often conduct a trial of thyroid replacement to treat lithium-induced fatigue, even if there is no TSH elevation.

In children, no data are available regarding lithium effects on body growth, so it is difficult to know whether lithium-induced chemical hypothyroidism (in concert with other metabolic effects of lithium) would have a significant effect on growth. To minimize the theoretical risks during lithium treatment, the author recommends monitoring the plasma TSH levels every 3 months (in contrast to every 6 to 12 months, which is customary in adults).

As an additional attempt to minimize any possible lithium effect on body growth, the author has administered thyroid supplementation to correct small but persistent deviations in TSH levels above the normal range during lithium treatment. For example, if a child's TSH level rises just beyond the laboratory limit of normal, measurement of TSH level is repeated on a different blood sample. If the elevation is persistent, I have taken the approach of starting L-thyroxine at a dose of 25 micrograms each morning. After two weeks, if the TSH is still elevated (on a single sample), then the daily morning dose of L-thyroxine is increased by 25 micrograms, and the 2-week cycle is repeated until the TSH level is stably within normal limits.

It is my impression that this approach to thyroid supplementation has enhanced the clinical effectiveness of lithium on its target behavioral symptoms, even in cases where neither fatigue nor other hypothyroid symptoms were apparent. In addition, this procedure perhaps has helped avoid clinically apparent effects on height growth. These small thyroxine doses rarely cause any symptoms of hyperthyroidism. As in adults, thyroid functioning springs back reliably after the dose of lithium is tapered, even after years of lithium treatment. However, there are no controlled data to support the need, efficacy, or safety of this form of thyroid supplementation during lithium treatment of youths.

This unproven approach to minimizing hypothetical lithium effects on body growth is distinct from standard thyroid augmentation of lithium treatment that is commonly used in adults to enhance therapeutic effects. Standard augmentation in youths often appears to involve higher doses of thyroxine than needed for "thyroid protection." At times, standard augmentation sometimes can require doses that approach full thyroid replacement, which in children is about 150 to 300 micrograms daily.

In addition to elevating TSH, lithium can induce increases in plasma levels of parathyroid hormone, potentially leading to calcium mobilization and lithium deposition in bones. Again, this is a theoretical concern, and altered calcium metabolism has not led to any reported clinical problems in youths.

Acne and weight gain are adverse effects that may be particularly distressing to adolescents. Lithium-induced aggravation of acne responds to routine dermatological interventions, but noncompliance with acne treatment is common in this population, so extra attention may be required to prevent facial and body scarring. Dietary directives to counteract weight gain are unlikely to be followed during a manic or hypomanic episode, and often it is advisable to wait until behavioral symptoms are stabilized before dealing with this side effect.

Few systematic studies have been conducted on the adverse effects of lithium in youths (Campbell et al., 1991; Platt, Campbell, Green, & Grega, 1984; Silva et al., 1992). Cognitive interference has appeared minimal in the available studies (Platt et al., 1984). Similarly, no enduring effects on kidney function have been reported in the pediatric literature, but available data are very limited (Khandelwal, Varma, & Srinyasa Murthy, 1984; Wood, Parmelee, & Foreman, 1989). Clinical vigilance is appropriate regarding both cognitive and renal effects of lithium treatment in youths.

Other common side effects of lithium, such as tremor and polyuria/polydipsia, seem to be identical in children and adults. Some data suggest that children might be more prone to lithium-induced diabetes insipidus and nocturnal enuresis than adults (Silva et al., 1992; Wagner, Teicher, & Popper, 1992). No data are available concerning the frequency of seizures in children, but lithium has significant seizurogenic potential in adults. The few reports on lithium toxicity suggest that the symptoms are similar in children and adults (Fitz-Simons & Keane, 1981; Goetting, 1985).

Clinical Monitoring: The pretreatment "lithium workup" is identical in children and adults. The primary difference in clinical monitoring procedures during the course of treatment is the more frequent measurement of TSH levels, which might be obtained every 3 months in children and growing adolescents. Plasma lithium levels often can be reduced by about 20% after several months of symptomatic control.

Appropriate duration of lithium treatment has not been determined. It is unknown whether most lithium-responsive children need to maintain their medication treatment for extended periods of time. It is also unknown whether most youths with bipolar disorder need chronic treatment. In the absence of data-based guidelines, it is reasonable to maintain a child on lithium therapy for 6 to 24 months, or longer if necessary for developmental changes or the passage of time to permit a tapering of the medication. Some lithium-responsive children need to have their medication maintained for at least several years.

Over the months or years, the lithium dose may need to be increased periodically to manage re-emerging or new symptoms and lowered periodically to reduce adverse effects. It appears that the lithium dose requirement might change cyclically, most likely in parallel with an underlying bipolar illness. Lithium can remain clinically efficacious for years (DeLong & Aldershof, 1987), as in adults, assuming that varying dose requirements are met.

TABLE 11.7

Clinical Treatment with Lithium in Youths

Dosage and Regimen

Starting dose	300 mg two or three times daily
Rate of dose elevation	300 mg every 3–4 days
Typical full dose	900–2,100 mg daily
Number of daily dosages	3–4, or 2 for controlled-release formulations
Delayed clinical response	4–10 days
Length of full trial	3 weeks
Duration of treatment	12–24 months, sometimes several years, or indefinitely

Available Strengths

150, 300, 600 mg—generic
Oral syrup—generic
300, 450 mg controlled-release formulation—brand only

Major Adverse Effects

Hypothyroidism (?effect on growth)
Weight gain
Sedation
Tremor
Stomachache or upset, nausea
Acne
Diabetes insipidus—polyuria, polydipsia, low urine specific gravity
Diarrhea
Enuresis, stress incontinence
Cognitive interference, with word-finding and memory impairment
Rash
Caries
Hypokalemia
Seizures

Precautions

Warn patient and family about risks of dehydration (exercise, exertion, summer heat, fever, fluid loss).
Maintain good hydration throughout day (especially before, during, and after exertion).
Avoid excessive or irregular salt intake.

Toxicity

Vomiting, ataxia, diarrhea, slurred speech, muscle twitching or weakness, rigidity, lethargy, nystagmus, confusion, fever, seizures, arrhythmias, circulatory collapse

Relative Contraindications

Thyroid dysfunction
Seizure disorder
Severe acne
Pregnancy or breast-feeding
Hyponatremia or patients on low-salt diet
Cardiovascular or renal disease

Initial Medical Workup

Physical exam to assess cardiac and neurologic status
Observe for any baseline tremor.
Weight
Complete blood count with differential

TABLE 11.7

Continued

Initial Medical Workup

Thyroid battery, including thyroid stimulating hormone (TSH)
Creatinine
Calcium if under age 12
Electrolytes
Electrocardiogram
Urinalysis on first morning sample, no oral intake after 10 P.M. on previous evening (to assess renal
  concentrating ability)
Pregnancy test

Ongoing Medical Monitoring

Follow for hypothyroid symptoms.
Plasma lithium levels—weekly during dose adjustment, then monthly; if very stable, every 2 to 3 months
Thyroid-stimulating hormone (TSH) every 3 to 4 months
Weight every 3 to 4 months
Plasma creatinine and first morning urine specific gravity every 6 months
Routine dental care every 6 months
Electrocardiogram every year

It cannot be assumed that a lithium-responsive child has bipolar disorder. Lithium is employed to treat various conditions in adults, including bipolar I and II disorders, recurrent depression, rapid-cycling disorder, cyclothymic disorder, premenstrual mood disorder, and aggressive behavior, among others. A lithium-responsive child might speculatively have any of these illnesses or a precursor form thereof. Alternatively, such a child might have a distinct time-limited childhood version of any of these disorders that does not emerge again in later life. Some lithium-responsive disorders are general medical conditions, such as leukopenia, the syndrome of inappropriate antidiuretic hormone secretion (SIADHS), or herpes infection.

More generally, a mental or behavioral diagnosis cannot be inferred from a positive response to a drug therapy. It should be evident that a lithium-responsive child could have any of a variety of disorders, might not have bipolar disorder, and might not develop bipolar disorder in the future. Until long-term follow-up studies are available, the developmental implications of lithium-responsiveness in a child will remain speculative. However, the limited follow-up studies have made it clear that some lithium-responsive children, including nonpsychotic children with behavior disorders, will develop a form of bipolar disorder in the future.

CARBAMAZEPINE

Like valproate, carbamazepine (Tegretol® or generic) has been shown to be effective for treating bipolar disorder in adults. Unlike valproate, carbamazepine has antidepressant properties (presumably due to its tricyclic structure) that might be valuable in managing some patients with ADHD, depressive and perhaps anxious symptoms, but it can be destabilizing (via manic switch) to other patients.

Carbamazepine has been shown in several studies to be effective in treating ADHD (Silva, Munoz, & Alpert, 1996), although its potential toxicity makes it an undesirable option for uncomplicated ADHD. Early reports have described improvement in impulsive and aggressive symptoms in children with mixed behavior disorders, with (Jacobies, 1978) and without seizure disorders (Evans, Clay, & Gualtieri, 1987; Groh, 1976; Kuhn-Gebhart, 1976; Puente, 1976; Remschmidt, 1976). A well-controlled study using more modern methodology found no significant effects of carbamazepine in treating the aggressive or rageful behavior of hospitalized children with conduct disorder (Cueva et al., 1996). No controlled studies are available regarding carbamazepine treatment of bipolar disorder in adolescents and children.

Carbamazepine has been used extensively in

TABLE 11.8

Clinical Treatment with Carbamazepine in Youths

Dosage and Regimen	
Starting dose	100 mg
Rate of dose elevation	100 mg/weekly
Typical full dose	10–50 mg/kg daily, with trough serum levels at 9–12 micrograms/ml
Number of daily dosages	2–3
Delayed clinical response	5–14 days
Length of full trial	4 weeks at full dose
Duration of treatment	Minimally 12 months, as long as needed, often years

Available Strengths

100 (chewable), 200 mg—generic
Oral suspension—brand only

Major Adverse Effects

Psychosis
Agitation, behavioral excitation, hyperactivity
Sedation
Weight gain
Lightheadness, especially orthostatic
Nausea
Anticholinergic effects
Caries
Ataxia
Blurred vision
Nystagmus
Peripheral neurotoxic symptoms
Skin rash, including Stevens-Johnson syndrome
Leukopenia, agranulocytosis, aplastic anemia
Hepatotoxicity
Syndrome of inappropriate secretion of antidiuretic hormone (SIADH)—hyponatremia, water intoxication; sedation, fluid retention, frequent urination, nausea, headache, weakness

Precautions

Alert patient and family to watch for and immediately report symptoms of agranulocytosis and aplastic anemia.

Toxicity

Dizziness, nystagmus, vomiting, peripheral neurotoxic symptoms, confusion

Relative Containdications

Bone marrow suppression, severe leukopenia, thrombocytopenia, liver or kidney disease

Initial Medical Workup

Complete blood count, with differential
If platelet count is low normal, get manual count.
SGOT, SGPT, bilirubin.
BUN, creatinine.
Optional: Serum iron [increases in bone marrow suppression]

Ongoing Medical Monitoring

Repeat initial tests after 4 weeks and then every 3 to 6 months thereafter.
If platelet count is low normal, get manual count.
Check weight ever 3 to 4 months.
Routine dental care every 6 months

children with seizure disorders, so its adverse effects and the required medical monitoring of liver and hematologic indices are well defined (Trimble, 1990). Neuropsychologic effects of carbamazepine are usually minimal in both children (Evans et al., 1987) and adults. At times, carbamazepine can worsen seizure control (Leviatov, Veselovskaja, Marienko, & Chtchegoleva, 1976).

Carbamazepine, even in monotherapy, can induce behavioral deterioration in children (Evans et al., 1987; Silverstein, 1982). Like valproate and other anticonvulsants, carbamazepine appears to cause a kind of excited or agitated state with behavioral deterioration (American Academy of Pediatrics, Committee on Drugs, 1995). One component of this behavioral deterioration seems to operate through a poorly defined neurotoxic effect. Another source of behavioral deterioration, which appears more specific to carbamazepine, is induction of hypomania.

I believe that behavioral deterioration is caused much more commonly by carbamazepine than valproate in children, despite its "mood-stabilizing" properties, presumably because of the antidepressant effects of carbamazepine (which valproate does not seem to have). Furthermore, I believe that carbamazepine-induced behavioral deterioration is more common in children than adults. In the absence of efficacy data on these drugs, these 2 reasons suggest that valproate may be preferable to carbamazepine for managing behavior disorders in children (perhaps including bipolar disorder).

OTHER ANTICONVULSANTS

Phenytoin (Dilantin® or generic) has been employed in empirical trials to treat rage episodes in adults and some behavior disorders in youths, but it seems useful for behavioral control primarily when abnormalities are present on neurologic examination or electroencephalogram. Clinical attempts to treat behavior disorders with phenytoin in the absence of demonstrable neurologic findings have not yielded specific criteria for predicting its effectiveness.

Barbiturates and primidone (which forms phenobarbital as a major metabolite) now are rarely recommended for emotional and behavioral indications, because of their danger in overdose. They have been helpful sporadically in open-label trials for treating behavioral disorders, but these effects may result from their sedative rather than anticonvulsant properties. These agents require careful monitoring in children at risk for drug-induced disinhibition.

At present, there is little evidence to support the use of phenytoin or primidon for treating emotional or behavioral disorders in youths. As more neurochemically novel anticonvulsants (such as lamotrigine, gabapentin, and felbamate) become available, their hypothetical mood-stabilizing properties will be assessed while initial track records of their safety are accumulating. The example of clobazam, an effective benzodiazepine anticonvulsant that is marketed outside of the United States and that has been found to induce severe behavioral deterioration at low doses in 11% of children (Sheth, Goulden, & Ronen, 1994), can serve as another reminder that familiar drug categories can still carry surprises.

Neuroleptics

After a lengthy lull in the field of neuroleptic development, a major new series of medications has been developed that appears to incorporate some important technologic advances. Clozapine and risperidone share an "atypically" weak affinity for dopamine D_2 receptors and have strong antagonist effects at dopamine D_4 and serotonin $5HT_{2A}$ (and $5HT_{1C}$) receptors, although other properties also may be critical to their antipsychotic action.

In adults, these *atypical* neuroleptic agents are providing substantial advantages over the *conventional* neuroleptics in both safety and efficacy. The new agents produce many fewer extrapyramidal symptoms and may carry a lower risk for tardive dyskinesia in adults. In adults with schizophrenia, they reduce the negative symptoms that had been poorly responsive to conventional neuroleptics and also have stronger effects on the positive symptoms.

It remains to be seen whether these gains seen in adults will translate to a significant clinical advantages for children, either in terms of safety or effectiveness. However, comparable advantages in youths could be reasonably expected in view of the similarity of the actions of the conventional neuroleptic agents in children and adults, with a generally comparable range of indications, adverse effects, and precautions.

With both the old and new neuroleptics, neuroleptic malignant syndrome and tardive dyskinesia remain major concerns. As data accumulate on the atypical neuroleptics, it appears that these drugs may not be as free of extrapyramidal symptoms as originally believed, and perhaps especially in children. Unlike the newer agents, the conventional neuroleptics remain better understood and have a long track record of use in children and adults.

CONVENTIONAL NEUROLEPTICS

Clinical Uses: As in adults, conventional neuroleptics are employed in youths to treat schizophrenia, schizoaffective disorder, mania and hypomania, psychotic depression, delusional disorder, psychosis due to a general medical condition, dangerous aggressivity, agitation, and extreme situational anxiety (presurgery, postrape, postassault). In low doses, neuroleptics are also helpful in Tourette's disorder (for which pimozide appears more effective than other neuroleptics), some types of impulsivity associated with subpsychotic or prepsychotic conditions, certain symptoms in children with mental retardation or pervasive developmental disorder, and (as a very last resort) ADHD. Single or sequential doses of conventional neuroleptics often are employed in emergency or inpatient settings, either as "chemical restraints" to control unmanageable or dangerous behavior or, alternatively, in "as needed" (PRN) doses to prevent disruptive behavior from escalating into unmanageable behavior.

Except in treatment of schizophrenia, Tourette's disorder, and pervasive developmental disorders, none of these common clinical uses has been rigorously demonstrated to be efficacious.

The empirical use of low doses of neuroleptics for managing impulsive or aggressive behavior is common and valid, even (or especially) if a more specific diagnosis has not yet been determined. It is my experience that sedating neuroleptics (chlorpromazine, thioridazine, loxapine) are more effective in such situations than nonsedating agents (haloperidol, perphenazine) and, further, that divided dosing in this situation allows the use of a lower total daily dose than once-daily administration. For example, chlorpromazine 10–50 mg 4 times daily may be used to treat impulsive or aggressive behavior for several weeks until more specific pharmacologic treatment can be initiated.

The use of neuroleptics for nonpsychotic disorders sometimes is criticized excessively despite their often crucial role in treating youngsters with Tourette's disorder, pervasive developmental disorders, severely impulsive and aggressive behavior, and the extremes of situational anxiety.

Clinical Implications of Pharmacokinetics: The few available pharmacokinetic data on the conventional neuroleptics indicate that their disposition and metabolism is more rapid in youths than adults, consistent with more rapid hepatic biotransformation in younger patients. Higher weight-adjusted doses are needed in youths than adults, but dose requirements vary with the specific condition being treated and its severity.

Adverse Effects: The common side effects of the conventional neuroleptic agents, including postural hypotension and anticholinergic effects, are generally similar in children and adults. Adolescents tend to become particularly distraught about weight gain, acne, easy sunburning, galactorrhea, retrograde ejaculation (mainly with thioridazine), and changes in alertness (Teicher & Glod, 1990). Potentially lethal conditions, such as cardiac conduction delay and agranulocytosis, are seen but rarely with conventional neuroleptics and do not require routine monitoring—except for electrocardiogram monitoring with pimozide.

Cognitive blunting and sedation are distinct problems with conventional neuroleptics. Both adverse effects can become troublesome at low doses, even when sufficiently subtle to escape easy clinical detection. Chronic drowsiness, cognitive slowness, and academic impairment should not be dismissed routinely as residual mental symptoms or psychological complications of illness. Instead, these cognitive "symptoms" routinely should receive consideration as possible neuroleptic effects. The sedative properties of these medications increase the risk of "management abuse" by family and institutional caregivers. In addition to cognitive blunting and sedation, conventional neuroleptic agents (especially haloperidol) also can induce depressivelike symptoms, including dysphoria, anxiety, separation anxiety disorder, school absenteeism, and social phobia.

Conventional neuroleptics can increase the vul-

TABLE 11.9

Clinical Treatment with Conventional Neuroleptics in Youths

Dosage and Regimen

Doses are expressed in chlorpromazine milligram equivalents. That is, chlorpromazine 100 mg is equivalent to about haloperidol 1.1 mg, pimozide 2 mg, thiothixene 3 mg, perphenazine 10 mg, or loxapine 15 mg.

Starting dose	25 mg
Rate of dose elevation	25 mg every 1–5 days In emergency, 25 mg every 3 hours until sedated
Typical full dose	300–600 mg daily for psychosis; 50–200 mg for nonpsychotic disorders
Number of daily dosages	Usually once daily, but can be up to 4 daily (or more in crisis)
Delayed clinical response	2–10 days for psychosis; otherwise, 1–2 days
Length of full trial	2–4 weeks for psychosis
Duration of treatment	As needed

Available Strengths

Chlorpromazine	10, 25, 50, 100, 200 mg—generic 30, 75, 150, 200, 300 mg sustained-release spansules—brand only Oral concentrate—generic Injectable—brand only
Haloperidol	0.5, 1, 2, 5, 10, 20 mg—generic Oral concentrate—generic Injectable—generic Decanoate injectable for extended effect—brand only
Pimozide	2 mg—brand only
Thiothixene	1, 2, 5, 10, 20 mg—generic Oral concentrate—generic Injectable—brand only
Perphenazine	2, 4, 8, 16 mg—generic Oral concentrate—generic Injectable—brand only
Loxapine	5, 10, 25, 50 mg—generic Oral concentrate—brand only Injectable—brand only

Major Adverse Effects

Withdrawal dyskinesia
Tardive dyskinesia
Neuroleptic malignant syndrome (NMS)
Sedation
Cognitive interference—dulling, blunting
Fatigue or malaise
Hypotension
Weight gain
Extrapyramidal motor symptoms:
   Akathisia
   Acute dystonic reactions
   Parkinsonian tremor, rigidity, akinesia, masklike fascies
   Laryngeal dystonia (potentially lethal)
Photosensitization.
Irregular or absent menstruation, galactorrhea, lactation, gynecomastia, impotence
Dysphoria, separation anxiety, school absenteeism—mainly with haloperidol and pimozide
Seizures

TABLE 11.9

Continued

Major Adverse Effects

Cardiac conduction disturbance, especially with pimozide
Agranulocytosis
For thioridazine: retrograde ejaculation
                        pigmentary retinopathy

Precautions

Use sunblock in sun.
Keep diphenhydramine on hand in case of sudden emergence of parkinsonian or dystonic reaction.
For chlorpromazine, advise slow standing and sitting up when first starting on the drug.

Toxicity

Sedation, hypotension, dystonia, parkinsonian symptoms, fever, confusion, seizures

Relative Contraindications

Neuroleptic malignant syndrome (NMS)
Withdrawal dyskinesia
Tardive dyskinesia
Agranulocytosis
Cardiac conduction defects, including prolonged QT syndrome
Coma or obtundation

Initial Medical Workup

Liver function tests
Weight
For pimozide, electrocardiogram

Ongoing Medical Monitoring

Follow for emergence of tardive dyskinesia.
Monitor weight.
For pimozide, electrocardiogram during period of dose increase

nerability to certain types of seizures while decreasing the clinical risk of other types of seizures, depending on the particular neuroleptic. Following a neuroleptic-induced seizure (or any drug-induced seizure), immediate neuromedical assessment is needed along with evaluation of possible drug interactions; then neuroleptic treatment usually can be continued safely in conjunction with an anticonvulsant agent (Teicher & Glod, 1990).

Acute motor side effects of conventional neuroleptics (dystonic reactions, akathisia, and parkinsonian tremor, rigidity, akinesia, drooling) are quite common and similar in adults and children, although some evidence suggests that older adolescents may develop more akathisia than adults (Keepers, Clappison, & Casey, 1983).

Neuroleptic withdrawal dyskinesia and also tardive dyskinesia (Wolf & Wagner, 1993) seem phenomenologically similar in youths and adults, and both populations appear equally vulnerable to these motor side effects. Withdrawal-emergent dyskinesias sometimes emerge after only several weeks or months of treatment at relatively low doses. Permanent tardive dyskinesia has not yet been reported in youths, although 1 child has been reported to have dyskinetic symptoms that persisted for almost 5 years.

It can be difficult to identify withdrawal or tardive dyskinesias when they appear in the context of Tourette's disorder, but these conditions can be distinguished by monitoring features such as the premonitory urges of Tourette's disorders and symptom changes during mental distraction (Silva et al., 1993). The theoretical possibility of cognitive or affective symptoms appearing during drug withdrawal or in a "tardive" manner also might be considered.

Neuroleptic malignant syndrome (NMS) has been described in over 50 adolescents and children. The syndrome has been identified in children as young as 3 years of age, and even after single dosages (Latz & McCracken, 1992; Steingard, Khan, Gonzalez, & Herzog, 1992). It is essential for clinicians to respond immediately in the event of fever (present in all or virtually all pediatric cases of neuroleptic malignant syndrome), autonomic instability, changes in consciousness, parkinsonian rigidity or catatonia, and increased blood levels of creatine phosphokinase (CPK) or myoglobin. CPK levels can be grossly elevated for a variety of reasons apart from neuroleptic malignant syndrome, including recent use of physical restraints, so the clinical picture needs to be evaluated in full. Although the clinical presentation of the syndrome in adults and children is similar, a higher mortality rate has been reported in children than in adults, perhaps because of reduced suspicion, delayed diagnosis, and the added difficulties of differential medical diagnosis in children (Peterson, Myers, McClellan, & Crow, 1995; Riddle, 1992).

Clinical Monitoring: For any patient starting treatment with conventional neuroleptics, it is essential to obtain predrug and periodic reassessments of extrapyramidal motor status. Periodic reevaluations of neuroleptic dose requirements are essential throughout treatment, with the intent of avoiding unnecessarily large doses that increase the risk of tardive dyskinesia. These precautions are especially critical for children whose treatments might become long term, such as children who have pervasive developmental disorder or who are chronically institutionalized.

ATYPICAL NEUROLEPTICS

Unlike the conventional neuroleptics, clozapine (Clozaril®) and risperidone (Risperdol®) appear to treat the negative as well as the positive symptoms of schizophrenia in adolescents. The risk of extrapyramidal symptoms is lower than with conventional neuroleptics but, with both agents, extrapyramidal symptoms may be more common in children than in adults.

Clozapine: Clozapine treatment in adults has been limited by concerns about its hematological toxicity, the associated requirement for weekly monitoring of blood indices, and the increased risk of seizures. Its cost is relatively high in comparison to many other medications, but not in comparison to residential treatment or hospitalization.

Several case series of open-label treatment involving over 200 adolescents with schizophrenia (Amminger, Resch, Reimitz, & Friedrich, 1992; Braun-Scharm & Martinius, 1991; Frazier et al., 1994; Kowatch et al., 1995; Remschmidt, Schulz, & Martin, 1992, 1994; Schmidt, Trott, Blanz, & Nissen, 1990; Siefen & Remschmidt, 1986) are supplemented by numerous letters and cases reports on clozapine treatment of early-onset schizophrenia (Birmaher, Baker, Kapur, Quintanu, & Ganguli, 1992; Csik & Molnár, 1994; Freedman, Wirshing, Russell, Bray, & Unutzer, 1994; Jacobsen, Walker, Edwards, Chappell, & Woolston, 1994; Mandoki, 1993; Mozes et al., 1994; Towbin, Dykens, & Pugliese, 1994). Nearly all of the uncontrolled reports suggest that clozapine can be helpful in treating adolescent schizophrenia. In a clozapine-haloperidol comparison study without placebo in adolescents, clozapine was found to be more effective in improving both the positive and negative symptoms of schizophrenia in adolescents, with a stronger effect on the positive symptoms (Kumra et al., 1996), similar to the findings in adults.

Bipolar disorder also can be reasonably treated with empirical trials of clozapine (Fuchs, 1994; Kowatch et al., 1995). In my experience, clozapine is generally more effective than conventional neuroleptics in treating adolescents with severe bipolar disorder (or with schizophrenia). Due to its serious adverse effects and cumbersome monitoring requirements, clozapine is reserved for management of treatment-resistant psychosis.

About 10 to 16% of adolescents receiving clozapine develop akathisia or tremor (Remschmidt et al., 1994; Schmidt et al., 1990; Siefen & Remschmidt, 1986), so these side effects may appear more commonly in youths than adults. Clozapine also induces abnormal electroencephalogram patterns in 33 to 78% of treated adolescents (Braun-Scharm & Martinius, 1991; Remschmidt et al., 1994; Schmidt et al., 1990; Siefen & Remschmidt, 1986) and might be associated with a higher incidence of seizures in youths than in adults (Freedman et al., 1994; Remschmidt et al., 1994; Siefen & Remschmidt, 1986). Moreover, the postmarketing data collected in the United States sug-

TABLE 11.10

Clinical Treatment with Clozapine in Youths

Dosage and Regimen

Starting dose	12.5 mg daily
Rate of dose elevation	25–50 mg daily every 1–2 days
Typical full dose	100–500 mg daily
Number of daily dosages	2–4
Delayed clinical response	2–10 days for psychosis; otherwise, 2–4 days
Length of full trial	2–4 weeks for psychosis at full dose
Duration of treatment	As long as needed

Available Strengths

25, 100 mg—brand only

Major Adverse Effects

Neuroleptic malignant syndrome
Agranulocytosis
Seizures and electroencephalogram changes
Sedation
Weight gain
Orthostatic hypotension
Anticholinergic effects
Tachycardia
Hypersalivation
Fatigue or malaise
Electrocardiogram changes

Precautions

Advise patient and family to report any infection, fever, sore throat, weakness, lethargy.
Advise slow standing and sitting up when first starting medication.

Toxicity

Tachycardia
Hypotension
Hypersalivation
Sedation
Confusion
Seizures
Respiratory depression
Cardiac arrythmias

Relative Contraindications

Prolonged QT syndrome
Leukopenia <3,500/mm^3
Neutropenia <1,500/mm^3
Cancer chemotherapy
AIDS
History of agranulocytosis or bone marrow suppression
Seizure disorder
Hypotension, including orthostatic
Tachycardia

TABLE 11.10

Continued

Initial Medical Workup

Complete blood count with differential
Electroencephalogram
Electrocardiogram
Blood pressure, heart rate
Weight
Registration in clozapine distribution system

Ongoing Medical Monitoring

Weekly complete blood count with differential
Electrocardiogram on full dose, then yearly
Blood pressure, heart rate
Weigh every 3 to 4 months.
Advise patient and family to report any infection, fever, sore throat, weakness, lethargy.
Monitor white blood counts under the auspices of the clozapine distribution system.

gest that the risk of agranulocytosis may be significantly greater in patients under age 18 than in 20- to 40-year-olds (Alvir, Lieberman, Safferman, Schwimmer, & Schaff, 1993).

It is advisable that clozapine use in adolescents and especially children be approached cautiously until controlled studies regarding safety and efficacy are available in youth. Also, an electroencephalogram and assessment of neuromotor signs should be obtained routinely prior to starting clozapine treatment.

Risperidone: Risperidone is the first neuroleptic available in the United States that is comparatively free of neuromotor side effects and does not require invasive monitoring. At present, controlled trials of risperidone have been conducted only in adults with schizophrenia. Its potential for inducing neuroleptic malignant syndrome (NMS), tardive dyskinesia, and even extrapyramidal symptoms has yet to be adequately assessed in adults.

The few and uncontrolled reports on risperidone in youths are encouraging for treatment of schizophrenia, bipolar disorder, and organic psychosis (Dryden-Edwards & Reiss, 1996; Mandoki, 1995; Quintana & Keshavan, 1995; Simeon, Carrey, Wiggins, Milin, & Hosenbocus, 1995; Zimnitzky, DeMaso, & Steingard, 1996). Risperidone appears helpful for youths with tic disorders (Lombroso et al., 1995; Mandoki, 1995) and for pervasive developmental disorder in youths (Fisman & Steele, 1996; Simeon et al., 1995) and adults (McDougle et al., 1996; Purdon, Lit, La-Belle, Jones, et al., 1994). Risperidone has been

reported to help (Lombroso et al., 1995) and aggravate (Dryden-Edwards & Reiss, 1996) patients with obsessive-compulsive disorder.

Preliminary reports on risperidone suggest that acute motor side effects may not be unusual in youths (Lombroso et al., 1995; Mandoki, 1995). To help minimize possible neuromotor effects, risperidone doses can be started at 0.25 to 0.5 mg twice or even 4 times daily, increased gradually, and when possible kept to a maximal dose of 2 mg twice daily (Mandoki, 1995; Simeon et al., 1995).

Risperidone is relatively expensive when used in full antipsychotic doses (over $6 daily for 2 mg BID at 1997 wholesale prices). However, at lower doses, risperidone would be less financially burdensome and still might be helpful for managing pervasive developmental disorders, Tourette's disorder, or impulsive/aggressive behavior disorders.

Speculatively, risperidone might someday become the neuroleptic of choice for Tourette's disorder, replace conventional neuroleptics in managing certain patients with pervasive developmental disorder or mental retardation, and perhaps challenge valproate and lithium as first-line agents for treating bipolar disorder. It might turn out to be a reasonably safe generalized treatment of impulsive or aggressive behavior. Risperidone seems quite useful for treating anxiety disorders, although a less anxiety-inducing risperidone-like agent might be more helpful.

Additional studies on risperidone and future risperidone-like agents will be needed in youths and adults. Despite the absence of a substantial

TABLE 11.11

Clinical Treatment with Risperidone in Youths

Dosage and Regimen

Starting dose	0.25 mg daily
Rate of dose elevation	0.25 mg every 2–5 days
Typical full dose	0.5–4 mg daily
Number of daily dosages	2–3
Delayed clinical response	2–10 days for psychosis; otherwise, 2–4 days
Length of full trial	2–4 weeks for psychosis at full dose
Duration of treatment	As long as needed

Available Strengths

1, 2, 3, 4, mg—brand only

Major Adverse Effects

Neuroleptic malignant syndrome (NMS)
Parkinsonian symptoms
Akathisia
Sedation
Weight gain
Orthostatic hypotension
Agitation
Insomnia
Dizziness
Nasal congestion

Precautions

Keep diphenhydramine on hand in case of sudden emergence of parkinsonian symptoms.
Advise slow standing and sitting up when first starting medication.

Toxicity

Tachycardia
Hypotension
Akathisia
Parkinsonian symptoms
Sedation

Initial Medical Workup

Electrocardiogram
Blood pressure, heart rate
Weight

Ongoing Medical Monitoring

Weight
Blood pressure, heart rate
Electrocardiogram once on full dose, then yearly

track record of risperidone use in adults, the technical advantages of a neuroleptic with apparently few neuromotor and hematologic side effects are very alluring to apply in both psychotic and non-psychotic disorders.

A WARNING ABOUT BETTER NEUROLEPTICS

As the risk-benefit ratios of neuroleptics improve through time, the spectrum of their potential indications is likely to widen. Ironically, "safer" neuroleptics could present a serious threat of abusive overprescribing practices, encouraged by anxious caregivers and fueled by cost-focused third-party payers.

In the past, concerns about tardive dyskinesia helped curb excessive use of conventional neuroleptics, especially in children (Wolf & Wagner, 1993). With the appearance of "safer" neuroleptics, overly zealous financial "management" of medical care might lead to systematic and indiscriminate use in children and adolescents, particularly for the nonspecific control of disruptive or impulsive behavior disorders.

Despite the current expense of the atypical neuroleptics, managed care consultants might come to believe that long-term use of risperidone-like drugs is more cost effective than providing comprehensive child mental health evaluations, appropriately targeted pharmacotherapy, or psychosocial treatment.

Risperidone is probably not the "overprescribable" drug that will break this barrier and generate a new "Safe Neuroleptic Generation." Independently of their profile of motor and hematologic side effects, all currently available neuroleptics run the risk of causing neuroleptic malignant syndrome (Latz & McCracken, 1992; Steingard et al., 1992). Indiscriminate nonspecific treatment of behavior disorders with current neuroleptic agents is still obviously inadvisable, even in the short term (i.e., not counting tardive dyskinesia), most compellingly because of the serious concerns raised by neuroleptic malignant syndrome alone. For now, we may be spared routine neuroleptic treatment abuse by health care institutions, but we should be ready for the day when a truly nontoxic neuroleptic becomes available.

Antianxiety Agents

BENZODIAZEPINES

In view of the risks of recreational abuse, behavioral disinhibition, interactions with alcohol and recreational substances, physical or psychologic dependence, and drug withdrawal, it may seem remarkable that benzodiazepines are used to treat children at all. Despite the risks, the very few controlled studies, and the reluctance of some physicians' to medicate "mere" anxiety, benzodiazepines can be employed safely and sensibly in youths in a variety of clinical situations (Coffey, 1990).

Clinical Uses: Benzodiazepines can be appropriately employed in youths to manage posttraumatic agitation (extreme situational anxiety following rape or severe physical assault) or to reduce preoperative anxiety and physiologic stress prior to surgery. Adjunctive use of clonazepam and lorazepam with neuroleptics is routine in treating psychosis. Separation anxiety disorder, generalized anxiety disorder, panic disorder, and phobic disorder often are treated with benzodiazepines, either alone or as adjuncts to other medications (Birmaher et al., 1994; Graae, Milner, Rizzotto, & Klein, 1994). School absenteeism ("school phobia") is improved to a clinically satisfactory degree only occasionally by benzodiazepines alone, but the anticipatory anxiety around returning to school can be helped.

Anxiety-related sleep problems such as difficulty in falling asleep, nightmares, and midsleep awakenings generally do not require medical treatment. If sufficiently severe, though, benzodiazepines can be used briefly (up to 2 weeks) before they lose their effectiveness for these symptoms. If the anxiety-related symptoms persist, a more thorough neurobehavioral and medical evaluation is appropriate: Anxiety symptoms can be part of a serious or pervasive biopsychiatric picture that requires specific diagnosis and treatment.

Sleepwalking (somnambulism) and night terrors (pavor nocturnus) in children reflect neurodevelopmentally immature arousal mechanisms regulating Stages 3 and 4 sleep during the first 3 hours of sleep and usually are not associated with emotional problems. (These symptoms are more likely to be associated with psychopathology in late adolescents and adults.) A brief course of benzodiazepines may be useful if sleepwalking is dangerous or night terrors are frequent (more than once weekly).

Rhythmic motor behaviors during sleep (head banging, head rolling, or body rocking) of infants and toddlers persist in 3% of children after 3 years of age. When these symptoms are severe enough to interfere with social activities, such as family va-

TABLE 11.12

Clinical Treatment with Benzodiazepines in Youths

	Alprazolam	Lorazepam	Clonazepam
Dosage and Regimen			
Starting dose	0.25–0.5 mg daily	0.5–1 mg daily	0.25–0.5 mg twice daily
Rate of dose elevation	0.25–0.5 mg every 3–4 days	0.5–1 mg evert 2–3 days	0.25–0.5 mg evert 2 days
Typical full dose	0.5–4 mg daily	1–8 mg daily	1–8 mg daily
Number of daily dosages	3–4	3–6	2–4
Delayed clinical response	None	None	None
Length of full trial	1–3 weeks	1–2 weeks	1–3 weeks
Duration of treatment	As long as needed, but typically not more 3 months		
Available Strengths			
	0.25, 0.5, 1, 2 mg—generic	0.5, 1, 2 mg—generic	0.5, 1, 2 mg
	Injectable—brand only	Injectable—brand only	

Major Adverse Effects

Similar for all benzodiazepines:
    Substance abuse
    Physical dependence
    Psychological dependence
    Sedation, fatigue, weakness
    Cognitive interference, including memory or mild delirium—during treatment or withdrawal
    Slow reflexes, motor dyscoordination
    Rebound insomnia and anxiety
    Behavioral disinhibition, including rage
    Anticholinergic effects
    Seizures, mainly in drug withdrawal
    Hallucinations—during treatment or withdrawal.
    Respiratory depression (mainly when used in combination with other drugs)

Precautions

Taper dose gradually with slower taper for longer treatments.
Warn patient and family about risks of substance abuse, dependence, withdrawal, disinhibition.
Advise strongly against alcohol use, especially during period of dose elevation.

Toxicity

Sedation, ataxia, slurred speech, tremor, confusion or delirium, bradycardia, slowed reflexes, and (mainly in combination with other drugs) respiratory depression

Relative Contraindications

Alcohol or substance abuse, past or present (or in immediate family)

Initial Medical Workup

Perhaps confirm normal liver and kidney function
Perhaps blood screen for abused or toxic substances

Ongoing Medical Monitoring

Follow with attention to alcohol and substance abuse.

cations or overnights, benzodiazepines can be helpful temporarily, but symptoms usually return after several days or weeks.

Little documentation supports use of benzodiazepines to treat impulsive behavior or conduct disorders. Especially with these diagnoses, the risks of substance abuse, noncompliant use, and perhaps disinhibition might be particularly relevant.

Clinical Implications of Pharmacokinetics: The various benzodiazepines have different metabolic breakdown pathways, hepatic clearance rates, and durations of action (Coffey, Shader, & Greenblatt, 1983). Due to rapid hepatic metabolism, the clearance in children is faster (apparent elimination half-life is 17 hours in children and 24 hours in adults for diazepam), and so dose requirements run higher in youths (generally about 50% above weight-adjusted adult dosages). The durations of the clinical effects of the different benzodiazepines have not been examined systematically in children.

Adverse Effects: Benzodiazepines generally seem quite safe for children and adolescents who manage to steer clear of substance abuse and dependence, interactions with alcohol and other abusable substances, disinhibition, iatrogenic dependence, drug interactions, and drug withdrawal. These agents can be problematic for adolescents who, though not substance abusers themselves, might still be at risk for dealing in drugs or being "strong-armed" by peers who want drugs. Mere access to benzodiazepines places parents, siblings, and other family members at risk for abuse-related problems.

Benzodiazepine-induced disinhibition or excitation seems phenomenologically similar to the disinhibitory effects of alcohol or light general anesthesia (second-stage delirium). The frequency of disinhibition reactions in children is undetermined, but rates reported in clinical studies of children have run as high as 30%. Claims of an increased risk for benzodiazepine disinhibition in children with ADHD have never been substantiated.

Clinical Monitoring: When stopped suddenly or when rapidly tapered after long-term use, even low doses of benzodiazepines (e.g., diazepam 5 mg daily) entail risks of potentially dangerous withdrawal symptoms (including seizures) and rebound symptoms (anxiety, insomnia). The withdrawal effects might be particularly worrisome in young patients who might not recognize warning signs that call for medical management.

These agents are generally safe and easy to use, but the potential dangers of benzodiazepines are sufficient to discourage casual use until stronger safety and efficacy data are available in children and adolescents.

OTHER ANTIANXIETY AGENTS

Buspirone: Several open-label reports have suggested a beneficial effect of buspirone (Buspar®) for children with anxiety disorders (Simeon et al., 1994), but controlled data are needed to demonstrate the clinical significance of these antianxiety effects. Buspirone also might be helpful in controlling impulsivity in some children with traumatic brain injury (Mandoki, 1994). A more extensive track record of safety and efficacy in adults is desirable before buspirone treatment in youths become routine (Coffey, 1990).

Antihistaminic Sedatives: Although diphenhydramine and hydroxyzine commonly are used in pediatric medicine at individual doses of 25 to 50 mg every 4 to 6 hours, no controlled studies have demonstrated clinical efficacy or safety in children treated with doses required to control major behavioral or mental symptoms. Unlike the benzodiazepines, these medications have little risk of drug dependence, disinhibition, recreational abuse, or dangerous interactions with alcohol.

Diphenhydramine and hydroxyzine have a long history of use for inducing sleep in short-term treatments and for calming acute distress in children. In addition, these medications often are employed on inpatient units to control agitated, assaultive, or destructive behaviors in children. Used in single doses of 25 to 75 (occasionally to 150) mg, these agents generally have little value in psychotic adolescents and appear more useful in nonpsychotic children below age 8 years old (Coffey, 1990).

At doses relevant to treatment of behavioral and emotional symptoms, several dosages of diphenhydramine or hydroxyzine may be associated with persistent daytime sleepiness and with a cognitive and affective hangover. These acute side effects seem better tolerated by young children than by adolescents, but they are problematic at any age.

In the absence of adequate studies, the antihistaminic sedatives appear to carry significant limitations in both safety and efficacy for treating children with behavioral disorders.

Barbiturates: These agents, discussed earlier under anticonvulsants, now are rarely used for anxiety or behavioral disorders in children. Along with psychostimulants, barbiturates were the dominant medication treatments in child and adolescent psychiatry in the 1950s. They are now obsolete—and they symbolize genuine medical progress.

Alpha$_{2A}$ Adrenergic Agonists

CLONIDINE

Clonidine is a clinically useful antihypertensive agent (Lowenthal, 1980; Lowenthal, Matzek, & MacGregor, 1988) that reduces noradrenergic transmission through presynaptic alpha$_2$ adrenergic autoreceptor agonism. It is used widely to treat a variety of behavioral and some emotional conditions in children, despite weak documentation of its effectiveness and safety in that age group.

Clinical Uses: Clonidine initially was used in pediatric psychopharmacology to treat Tourette's and other chronic tic disorders (Cohen, Detlor, Young, & Shaywitz, 1980) and of ADHD (Hunt, Cohen, & O'Connell, 1982). Other neurobehavioral uses of clonidine in youths have included management of aggressive behavior not associated with ADHD, oppositional behavior, insomnia induced by psychostimulants, self-injurious behavior, certain forms of drug withdrawal, anxiety and anxiety disorders, and other hyperexcited states including posttraumatic stress disorder (Hunt, Capper, & O'Connell, 1990).

Clonidine treatment of Tourette's and other tic disorders is only weakly supported by available data. The well-controlled studies have had conflicting findings, suggesting efficacy (Borison, Ang, Hamilton, Diamond, & David, 1983; Leckman et al., 1991), no efficacy (Goetz et al., 1987; Singer et al., 1995), and modest transient efficacy (Jaselskis, Cook, Fletcher, & Leventhal, 1992). Improvements, if any, appear to include simple and complex motor tics, phonic tics, and some associated behavioral symptoms. As an aggregate, these controlled efficacy studies suggest partial or minimal clinical effects that are weaker and less consistent than the effects of neuroleptics.

There are no well-controlled studies of adequate size regarding clonidine monotherapy of ADHD. Controlled but small studies of children with ADHD have demonstrated clonidine-placebo differences (Hunt, 1987; Hunt, Minderaa, & Cohen, 1985, 1986), but all other data are either open-label or retrospective studies (Comings et al., 1990; Hunt, 1987; Kemph, DeVane, Levin, Jarecke, & Miller, 1993; Schvehla, Mandoki, & Summer, 1994; Steingard, Biederman, Spencer, Wilens, & Gonzalez, 1993). According to these reports, clonidine may be helpful in ADHD for treating the behavioral symptoms of hyperactivity and impulsivity as well as associated aggressive behavior and insomnia. Clonidine appears less useful for treating attentional symptoms.

Attempts have been made to determine whether clonidine would be more beneficial for treating ADHD in the presence of comorbid tic disorders. A chart review found that clonidine helped 95% of children with comorbid ADHD and tic disorders but only 53% of children with ADHD in the absence of tic disorders (Steingard et al., 1993). While this retrospective study suggests that the putative anti-ADHD effect of clonidine might be specific to treating ADHD with comorbid tic disorders (or ADHD presenting as part of a tic disorder), a well-controlled study of children with both ADHD and tic disorders found that clonidine was no different from placebo in treating impulsivity/hyperactivity, inattention, and tics (Singer et al., 1995).

Overall, the few available studies suggest that clonidine has little or no effect on tic disorders or ADHD. Other uses of clonidine for other emotional and behavioral problems in youths have not been systematically examined.

Clinical Implications of Pharmacokinetics: Expectably, clonidine clearance is more rapid in youths. Following oral administration, the elimination half-life is 12 to 16 hours in adults, 8 to 12 hours in adolescents, and 4 to 6 hours in preadolescents. It has no active metabolites and low plasma protein binding.

Adverse Effects: The safety (and efficacy) of clonidine for treating children with hypertension has not been examined.

The side effects of clonidine vary with the time

TABLE 11.13

Clinical Treatment with Clonidine in Youths

	Oral	Transdermal Therapeutic System
Dosage and Regimen		
Starting dose	0.025 mg QID	TTS-1 patch (delivers 0.1 mg daily for 5 days); replace every 5 days
Rate of dose elevation	0.025 mg daily	Increase by one-half of a TTS-1 every 5–7 days
Typical full dose	0.1–0.4 mg daily	1 TTS-1 patch to 2 TTS-2 patches
Number of daily dosages	3–4	Change patch every 5 days
Delayed clinical response	No	2–3 days
Length of full trial	4–6 weeks	4–6 weeks
Duration of treatment	As long as needed	As long as needed
Available Strengths		
0.1, 0.2, 0.3 mg—generic		TTS-1, TTS-2, TTS-3—brand

Major Adverse Effetcs

Sedation
Hypotension
Bradycardia
Rebound hyperactivity, hypertension, and tachycardia
Nightmares and midsleep insomnia
Electrocardiogram changes and potential arrhythmias
With patch: local skin irritation and inflammation
Depression
Anticholinergic effects
Stomachache, nausea, vomiting
Headache
Raynaud's phenomena
Blood sugar elevation

Precautions

Advise patient and family against sudden discontinuations in dose administration, sudden dose reductions, and noncompliant use (risk of rebound hypertension, etc.).
With patch, rotate patch site with each change of patch; if skin is inflamed, change site daily

Toxicity

Hypotension, bradycardia, sedation, dizziness, syncope; or rebound hypertension and tachycardia

Relative Contraindications

Current or past history of depression
Blood pressure or heart rate abnormalities
Certain cardiac conditions, especially arrhythmias
Certain cardiovascular conditions, including Raynaud's
For patch, dermatological conditions

Initial Medical Workup

Blood pressure, heart rate
Electrocardiogram
Fasting blood sugar, electrolytes, and perhaps thyroid screen

Ongoing Medical Monitoring

Check blood pressure and heart rate weekly for 1 month following dose elevation, then every 1 to 2 months.
Electrocardiogram after full dose for 1 week
If drowsiness or depression reappear, obtain blood pressure and heart rate.

following last dosage. During the first several hours, while clonidine is exerting its direct receptor effects, the major adverse effects are bradycardia, hypotension, and sedation. After 4 to 8 hours, during the period of drug offset (withdrawal), the main problems are rebound hypertension, tachycardia, behavioral hyperactivity, and central nervous system hyperexcitation (anxiety, headache, insomnia, nightmares, hyperarousal). Both the hypotension/bradycardia phase and the hypertension/tachycardia phase can be potentially dangerous.

Sedation and rebound motor hyperactivity are particularly prominent at the start of clonidine treatment. The sedation often limits dose elevation and can take several weeks to subside. Rebound hyperactivity presents with increased hyperactive behavior (relative to predrug baseline), overly excited emotional reactions, and a hyperarousal state.

Clonidine-induced bradycardia and hypotension are typically benign but can result in syncope. Rebound tachycardia and hypertension in children (Whelan & Dearlove, 1995) can be observed between dosages (shortly before the next scheduled dosage) or if clonidine is abruptly discontinued (e.g., patient runs out of pills), especially after chronic use.

These problems result from overly sharp increases and decreases in clonidine blood levels that result from children being treated with dosing regimens developed for adults. Both the hypotension/bradycardia/sedation and the rebound hypertension/tachycardia/excitation symptoms are dose-dependent and time-dependent, and they can be minimized by starting treatment with small multiple daily doses rather than with the twice-daily regimen often used in adults. The smaller doses reduce the peak blood levels and associated side effects, and the multiple daily dosing reduces extent of the withdrawal effects. Without careful management using such methods, the short-acting effects of orally administered clonidine can produce striking variations in blood pressure, heart rate, arousal, and symptom control.

Electrocardiogram conduction changes have been reported in 3 out of a sample of 60 children treated with clonidine for behavioral and emotional indications (Chandran, 1994). These 3 children experienced only dizziness or were asymptomatic, but the cases were complicated by concurrent treatments with an heterocyclic antidepressant or neuroleptic agent. Their conduction patterns reflected anterior ischemic changes and nonspecific intraventricular conduction delays. This preliminary study raises the possibility that cardiac as well as vascular changes of clonidine might be clinically significant in children.

Clonidine can induce or exacerbate depression, dysphoria, or irritability during the treatment of hypertension, and this risk is likely to be elevated in psychiatric populations. Other adverse effects include increased appetite and weight, stomach discomfort, headache, and rash (Hunt, Capper, & O'Connell, 1990), and possibly precocious puberty (Levin, Burton-Teston, & Murphy, 1993).

Transdermal administration of clonidine, which continuously releases the drug from a bandaidlike "patch," seems to produce fewer toxic and rebound effects on target symptoms, cardiovascular parameters, and arousal. Skin irritation and inflammation emerge in about half of patch-treated children (Hunt et al., 1990). This problem can be mitigated by daily patch relocations and, if necessary, topical steroids. Also, the patch may fail to adhere reliably to moist skin because of sustained sweating (in summertime and warm climes) or lengthy soaking (swimming or bathing for more than 20 minutes).

Hypothetical Drug Interaction with Methylphenidate: Combined clonidine-methylphenidate treatment has been commonly used in the management of ADHD symptoms and stimulant-induced insomnia (Prince, Wilens, Biederman, Spencer, & Wozniak, 1996) for 10 years. About 40% of children who received clonidine treatment for ADHD in 1994 were concurrently treated with psychostimulants (Swanson et al., 1995).

The United States national data base of adverse drugs reactions, which are spontaneously reported to the Food and Drug Administration (United States Government) after medications are marketed commercially, has received reports of 3 fatalities and 1 life-threatening reaction in children who were treated with a combination of clonidine and methylphenidate (Fenichel, 1995). The 3 fatalities were confounded by potentially lethal preexisting and concurrent medical factors, so the deaths could not be attributed to clonidine, methylphenidate, or their combined use. The life-threatening reaction involved bradycardia and hypotension, which are known effects of clonidine alone (Hunt et al., 1990; Lowenthal, 1980; Lowenthal et al., 1988; *Physicians' Desk Reference,* 1997; Whelan & Dearlove, 1995). The FDA came to the valid conclusion that these cases do not raise any new concerns about the risk of these medications, either alone or in combination (Fenichel, 1995), beyond highlighting the known cardiovascular risks of clonidine (Popper, 1995b).

Despite its common use, the clonidine-methylphenidate combination has never received controlled study to evaluate its safety or efficacy. Only 2 studies are available concerning its use in open-label treatment of children (Hunt, 1989; Prince et al., 1996). The use of this drug combination is based on clinical rather than scientific grounds.

Speculatively, the cardiovascular effects of clonidine and methylphenidate could be additive, depending on the relative timing of the drug administrations. Hypertension and tachycardia might be accentuated if methylphenidate is given during a period of clonidine (withdrawal) rebound, or hypotension and bradycardia might be increased if clonidine is given during methylphenidate rebound. The nighttime use of clonidine to induce sleep in a child treated with psychostimulants during the day could induce both of these additive interactions (around 8 A.M. and 9 P.M.). These concerns about additive effects are purely theoretical, and actual clinical problems with blood pressure or heart rate involving such interactions have not been reported.

The currently published cases give no reason for clinicians to discontinue use of the clonidine-methylphenidate combination but have served to underscore the known problems and monitoring requirements that pertain to clonidine treatment of children.

Clinical Monitoring: Clinicians are advised to monitor blood pressure and heart rate before and during any treatment involving clonidine, alone or in combination with other drugs. Electrocardiograms are not commonly used to follow clonidine treatment but nonetheless might be considered in view of the preliminary data suggesting a 5% risk of cardiac conduction slowing in clonidine-treated children (Chandran, 1994). It is essential to warn patients and families about the risks of improper administration or sudden discontinuation of clonidine. Particular caution is appropriate if clonidine-methylphenidate treatment is prescribed in combination with additional medications, is administered inconsistently, or is given to a patient with cardiac or cardiovascular problems (Swanson et al., 1995).

By starting oral clonidine at a dose of 0.025 mg four times daily (one-quarter of the smallest available 0.1 mg pill) and each day increasing the total daily dose by 0.025 mg to side effect tolerance, the problematic side effects of sedation and rebound phenomena are minimized in most patients. Therapeutic effects of clonidine, if any, might become apparent clinically only after several weeks.

Transdermal administration of clonidine (via the patch) is useful primarily when rebound symptoms are limiting dose elevations or when patient noncompliance is interfering with proper administration. The patch should be placed away from sweaty areas on a hairless skin surface, such as on the lower back (off center). The patch typically requires replacement every 4 to 5 days in children.

When discontinuing clonidine treatment, the dose should be tapered over 1 to 2 weeks, or longer following long-term treatment, in order to avoid rebound hypertension.

Overall, clonidine can be viewed as a drug that is generally not problematic but certainly capable of causing clinically important and potentially dangerous cardiovascular effects. Its clinical effectiveness for neurobehavioral conditions is uncertain.

GUANFACINE

This alpha$_{2A}$ adrenergic agonist is different from clonidine in that guanfacine has weaker effects at alpha$_1$, alpha$_{2B}$ or $_{2C}$, and beta-adrenergic, histamine, serotonin, beta-endorphin, and possibly dopamine receptors. The greater receptor specificity explains the fewer adverse effects observed with guanfacine than clonidine. Rebound hypertension and hyperactivity, hypotension, and sedation appear to be less problematic. Guanfacine also has longer duration of clinical action, so fewer daily dose administrations are required (1 to 2 vs. 3 to 4 for clonidine).

Guanfacine has been introduced as a treatment of behavioral and emotional disorders (Hunt et al., 1995) only recently, and few studies are currently available. In open studies of children with ADHD (Horrigan & Barnhill, 1995; Hunt, 1995), guanfacine appeared to improve hyperactivity, impulsive behavior, aggressivity, inattention, cognition, frustration tolerance, affect modulation, and social behavior. An open-label study of comorbid ADHD and Tourette's disorder in youths (Chappell et al., 1995) suggested improvements in attention, impulsivity, and tics. Adverse effects were common in children (25 to 30%) but minimal and transient. Sedation was mild, and blood pressure changes were not problematic.

Optimal dose regimens for guanfacine have not been determined for neurobehavioral indications in children. Similar to clonidine, both safety and efficacy are under investigation.

Other Agents

BETA BLOCKERS

Beta-adrenergic blocking agents appear to be helpful for treating certain anxiety states and agitation, and for rage episodes in adults, especially in brain-damaged patients (Coffey, 1990).

There are no controlled studies to support these uses in youths (Connor, 1993). Open-label studies of propranolol in children suggest therapeutic effects on rage and aggressive behavior associated with mental retardation, brain damage, or other central nervous system pathology (Kuperman & Stewart, 1987; Williams, Mehl, Yudofsky, Adams, & Roseman, 1982). Propranolol also was found helpful for children in open-label trials for treating the anxiety and aggressivity associated with posttraumatic stress disorder (Famularo et al., 1988).

As in adults, the beta-adrenergic blocking agents are relatively contraindicated in children with depression, asthma, diabetes, bradycardia, and some other cardiac conditions.

PEPTIDERGIC AGENTS

Despite some initial hope that naltrexone (Trexan®) might be useful for children with autistic disorder in treating symptoms that do not respond to neuroleptics, more recent controlled studies have provided only mixed support for the efficacy of this opiate receptor blocker in children with autism (Campbell et al., 1993; Kolmen, Feldman, Handen, & Janosky, 1995). Patients with bulimia showed no improvement in the 2 well-controlled studies of naltrexone (Alger et al., 1991; Mitchell et al., 1989). Self-injurious behaviors actually may worsen in response to naltrexone (Benjamin, Seek, Tresise, Price, & Gagnon, 1995; Willemsen-Swinkels, Buitelaar, Nijhof, & van Engeland, 1995).

Desmopressin, an arginine-vasopressin analog that is administered by nasal spray, is an alternative drug treatment of enuresis. The 18 randomized controlled trials of desmopressin generally support its efficacy, which appears comparable to the efficacy of imipramine (Thompson & Rey, 1995). However, the mean wholesale cost of desmopressin is over $4.50 daily in 1997 wholesale prices, compared to about $0.25 daily for imipramine, so heterocyclic antidepressants are preferred as first choice when medications are indicated (i.e., after behavioral methods have failed).

CALCIUM CHANNEL BLOCKERS

Calcium channel blockers have received essentially no attention in child and adolescent neuropsychiatry. In view of the calcium channel blocking properties of tetracycline, initial use of these agents in children less than 7 years old should involve close monitoring for the possible side effect of tooth graying, a manifestation of more generalized organ discoloration in tetracycline-treated youths.

PIRACETAM

Piracetam is a derivative of gamma-aminobutyric acid (GABA) that has been used for 25 years in many countries (not the United States) for treating cognitive changes in the elderly. Piracetam does not have psychostimulant effects and does not produce changes in alertness or arousal. In adults, it increases the power parameters on the electroencephalogram in the left hemisphere in comparison to the right hemisphere. Neuropsychologic tests have found that piracetam-induced improvements are found primarily in left hemisphere (verbal) functions.

In numerous double-blind, placebo-controlled studies with standardized reading tests among the outcome measures, this agent has been found to improve learning in children with developmental reading disorder (Wilsher & Taylor, 1994). The changes induced by piracetam in children are modest but consistent and statistically significant in the majority of studies. The longer studies (5 to 9 months) showed more pronounced improvements in reading.

These results in children with dyslexia are consistent with 5 double-blind placebo-controlled studies in adults. This first putative noötropic agent (to improve memory or learning) agent in child neuropsychiatry deserves further study.

NEWER TREATMENT APPROACHES

Steroids have been found useful in treating certain cases of Tourette's disorder that appear to be precipitated by antistreptococcal antibodies that cross-react with dopamine receptors in the basal ganglia (Allen, Leonard, & Swedo, 1995; Kies-sling, Marcotte, & Culpepper, 1993; Matarrazo, 1992; Swedo, 1994).

Pharmacologic treatment of stuttering is becoming feasible, with promising results in well-controlled studies of clomipramine (Gordon et al., 1995) and clonidine (Althaus, Vink, Minderaa, Goohuis-Brouwer, & Oosterhoff, 1995). Some positive findings regarding sertraline are preliminary (Costa & Kroll, 1995).

Other encouraging preliminary reports have concerned disulfiram for treating alcohol abuse in adolescents (Myers, Donahue, & Goldstein, 1994) and desipramine for cocaine craving in adolescents (Kaminer, 1994). In developmentally disabled children and adolescents, successful treatments have been described using psychostimulants for treating pica (Singh, Ellis, Crews, & Singh, 1994), transdermally administered scopolamine for drooling (Lewis, Fontana, Mehallick, & Everett, 1994), and melatonin for sleep symptoms (Jan, Espezel, & Appleton, 1994).

REFERENCES

Abramowicz, M. (1990). Sudden death in children treated with tricyclic antidepressant. *The Medical Letter on Drugs Therapeutics, 32,* 53–54.

Agras, W. S., Dorian, B., Kirkley, B. G., Arnow, B., & Bachman, J. (1987). Imipramine in the treatment of bulimia: A double-blind controlled study. *International Journal of Eating Disorder, 6,* 29–38.

Ahmann, P. A., Waltonen, S. J., Olson, K. A., Theye, F. W., Van Erem, A. J., & LaPlant, R. J. (1993). Placebo-controlled evaluation of Ritalin side effects. *Pediatrics, 91,* 1101–1106.

Alessi, N., Naylor, M. W., Ghaziuddin, M., & Zubieta, J. K. (1994). Update on lithium carbonate therapy in children and adolescents. *Journal of the American Academy of Child and Adolescent Psychiatry, 33,* 192–304.

Alger, S. A., Schwalberg, M. D., Bigaouette, J. M., Michalek, A. V., & Howard, L. J. (1991). Effect of a tricyclic antidepressant and opiate antagonist on binge-eating in normal weight bulimic and obese, binge-eating subjects. *American Journal of Clinical Nutrition, 53,* 865–871.

Allen, A. J., Leonard, H. L., & Swedo, S. E. (1995). A new infection-triggered, autoimmune subtype of pediatric OCD and Tourette's syndrome. *Journal of the American Academy of Child and Adolescent Psychiatry, 34,* 307–311.

Althaus, M., Vink, H. J. F., Minderaa, R. B., Goorhuis-Brouwer, S. M., & Oosterhoff, M. D. (1995). Lack of effect of clonidine on stuttering in children. *American Journal of Psychiatry, 152,* 987–1089.

Alvir, J. M. J., Lieberman, J. A., Safferman, A. Z., Schwimmer, J. L., & Schaff, J. A. (1993). Clozapine-induced agranulocytosis: Incidence and risk factors in the United States. *New England Journal of Medicine, 329,* 162–167.

Aman, M. G., Kern, R. A., McGhee, D. E., & Arnold, L. E. (1993). Fenfluramine and methylphenidate in children with mental retardation and attention-deficit hyperactivity disorder: Clinical and side effects. *Journal of the American Academy of Child and Adolescent Psychiatry, 32,* 851–859.

Ambrosini, P., Bianchi, M. D., Metz, C., & Rabinovich, H. (1994). Evaluating clinical response of open nortriptyline pharmacotherapy in adolescent major depression. *Journal of Child and Adolescent Psychopharmacology, 4,* 233–244.

Ambrosini, P. J., Bianchi, M. D., Rabinovich, J., & Elia, J. (1993). Antidepressant treatments in children and adolescents. I. Affective disorders. *Journal of the American Academy of Child and Adolescent Psychiatry, 32,* 1–6.

Ambrosini, P. J., Emslie, G. J., Greenhill, L. L., Kutcher, S., & Weller, E. B. (1995). Selecting a sequence of antidepressants for treating depression in youth. *Journal of Child and Adolescent Psychopharmacology, 5,* 233–240.

American Academy of Pediatrics, Committee on Bioethics. (1995). Informed consent, parental permission, and assent in pediatric practice. *Pediatrics, 95,* 314–317.

American Academy of Pediatrics, Committee on Drugs. (1995). Behavioral and cognitive effects of anticonvulsant therapy. *Pediatrics, 96,* 538–540.

American Psychiatric Association. (1994). *Diagnostic and statistical manual of mental disorders* (4th ed.). Washington, DC: Author.

Amminger, G. P., Resch, F., Reimitz, J., & Friedrich, M. H. (1992). Nebenwirkungen von Clozapin in der Therapie psychotischer Zustandbilder bei jugendlichen: Eine retrospektive kinische studie. *Zeitschrift für Kinder-und-Jugendpsychiatrie, 20,* 5–11.

Annell, A. L. (1969). Lithium in the treatment of children and adolescents. *Acta Psychiatrica Scandinavica, 207* [Suppl.], 19–30.

Apter, A., Ratzoni, G., King, R. A., Weizman, A., Iancu, I., Binder, M., & Riddle, M. A. (1994). Fluvoxamine open-label treatment of adolescent inpatients with obsessive-compulsive disorder or depression. *Journal of the American Academy of Child and Adolescent Psychiatry, 33,* 342.

Arredondo, D. E., & Butler, S. F. (1994). Affective comorbidity in psychiatrically hospitalized adolescents with conduct disorder or oppositional defiant disorder: Should conduct disorder be treated with mood stabilizers? *Journal of Child and Adolescent Psychopharmacology, 4,* 151–158.

Bangs, M. E., Petti, T. A., & Janus, M. D. (1994). Fluoxetine-induced memory impairment in an adolescent. *Journal of the American Academy of Child and Adolescent Psychiatry, 33,* 1303–1306.

Barrickman, L., Noyes, R., Kuperman, S., Schumacher, E., & Verda, M. (1991). Treatment of ADHD with fluoxetine: A preliminary trial. *Journal of the American Academy of Child and Adolescent Psychiatry, 30,* 762–767.

Barrickman, L. L., Perry, P. J., Allen, A. J., Kuperman, S., Arndt, S. V., Herrmann, K. J., & Schumacher, E. (1995). Bupropion vs. methylphenidate in the treatment of attention-deficit hyperactivity disorder. *Journal of the American Academy of Child and Adolescent Psychiatry, 34,* 649–657.

Bartels, M. G., Varley, C. K., Mitchel, J., & Stam, S. J. (1991). Pediatric cardiovascular effects of imipramine and desipramine. *Journal of the American Academy of Child and Adolescent Psychiatry, 30,* 100–103.

Bass, J. N., & Beltis, J. (1991). Therapeutic effect of fluoxetine on naltrexone-resistant self-injurious behavior in an adolescent with mental retardation. *Journal of Child and Adolescent Psychopharmacology, 1,* 331–340.

Bastiaens, L. (1995). Knowledge, attitudes and compliance with pharmacotherapy in adolescent patients and their parents. *Journal of Child and Adolescent Psychopharmacology, 5,* 39–48.

Bastiaens, L., & Bastiaens, D. K. (1993). A manual of psychiatric medications for teenagers. *Journal of Child and Adolescent Psychopharmacology, 3,* M1–M59.

Benjamin, S., Seek, A., Tresise, L., Price, E., & Gagnon, M. (1995). Paradoxical response to naltrexone in treatment of self-injurious behavior. *Journal of the American Academy of Child and Adolescent Psychiatry, 34,* 238–242.

Berney, T., Kolvin, I., Bhate, S. R., Garside, R. F., Jeans, J., Kay, B., & Scarth, L. (1981). School phobia: A therapeutic trial with clomipramine and short-term outcome. *British Journal of Psychiatry, 138,* 110–118.

Biederman, J. (1991). Sudden death in children treated with a tricyclic antidepressant. *Journal of the American Academy of Child and Adolescent Psychiatry, 30,* 495–498.

Biederman, J., Baldessarini, R. J., Goldblatt, A., Lapey, K. A., Doyle, A., & Hesslein, P. S. (1993). A naturalistic study of 24-hour electrocardiographic recordings and echocardiographic findings in children and adolescents treated with desipramine. *Journal of the American Academy of Child and Adolescent Psychiatry, 32,* 805–813.

Biederman, J., Baldessarini, R. J., Wright, V., Knee, D., & Harmatz, J. S. (1989). A double-blind placebo controlled study of desipramine in the treatment of ADD: I. Efficacy. *Journal of the American Academy of Child and Adolescent Psychiatry, 28,* 777–784.

Biederman, J., Baldessarini, R. J., Wright, V., Knee, D., Harmatz, J. S., & Goldblatt, A. (1989). A double-blind placebo controlled study of desipramine in the treatment of ADD: II. Serum drug levels and cardiovascular findings. *Journal of the American Academy of Child and Adolescent Psychiatry, 28,* 903–911.

Biederman, J., Herzog, D. B., Rivinius, T. H., Harper, G. P., Ferber, R. A., Rosenbaun, J. F., Harmatz, J. S., Tondorf, R., Orsulak, P. J., & Schildkraut, J. J. (1985). Amitriptyline in the treatment of anorexia nervosa: A double-blind, placebo-controlled study. *Journal of Clinical Psychopharmacology, 5,* 10–16.

Biederman, J., Thisted, R. A., Greenhill, L. L., & Ryan, N. D. (1995). Estimation of the association between desipramine and the risk for sudden death in 5- to 14-year old children. *Journal of Clinical Psychiatry, 56,* 87–93.

Birmaher, B., Baker, R., Kapur, S., Quintana, H., & Ganguli, R. (1992). Clozapine for the treatment of adolescents with schizophrenia. *Journal of the American Academy of Child and Adolescent Psychiatry, 31,* 160–164.

Birmaher, B., Waterman, G. S., Ryan, N., Cully, M., Balach, L., Ingram, J., Simeon, J. G., Knott, V. J., Du-Bois, C., Wiggins, D., Geraets, I., Thatte, S., & Miller, W. (1994). Buspirone therapy of mixed anxiety disorders in childhood and adolescence: A pilot study. *Journal of Child and Adolescent Psychopharmacology, 4,* 159–170.

Black, B., & Uhde, T. W. (1994). Treatment of elective mutism with fluoxetine: A double-blind, placebo-controlled study. *Journal of the American Academy of Child and Adolescent Psychiatry, 33,* 1000–1006.

Borison, R. L., Ang, L., Hamilton, W. J., Diamond, B. I., & David, J. M. (1983). Treatment approaches in Gilles de la Tourette syndrome. *Brain Research Bulletin, 11,* 205–208.

Boulos, C., Kutcher, S., Gardner, D., & Young, E. (1992). An open naturalistic trial of fluoxetine in adolescents and young adults with treatment-resistant major depression. *Journal of Child and Adolescent Psychopharmacology, 2,* 103–111.

Bowden, C. L., Brugger, A. M., Swann, A. C., Calabrese, J. R., Janicak, P. G., Petty, F., Dilsaver, S. C., Davis, J. M., Rush, A. J., Small, J. G., Garza-Trevino, E. S., Risch, S. C., Goodnick, P. J., & Morris, D. D. (1994). Efficacy of divalproex versus lithium and placebo in the treatment of mania. *Journal of the American Medical Association, 271,* 918–924.

Braun-Scharm, H., & Martinius, J. (1991). EEG-Veranderungen und Anfalle unter Clozapinmedikation bei schizophrenen Jugendlichen. *Zeitschrift für Kinder-und-Jugendpsychiatrie, 19,* 164–169.

Briscoe, J. J. D., Harrington, R. C., & Prendergast, M. (1995). Development of mania in close association with tricyclic antidepressant administration in children: A report of two cases. *European Child and Adolescent Psychiatry, 4,* 280–283.

Brodsky, M. (1994). Fluoxetine for childhood anxiety disorders. *Journal of the American Academy of Child and Adolescent Psychiatry, 33,* 993–999.

Brumback, R. A., & Weinberg, W. A. (1977). Mania in childhood. II. Therapeutic trial of lithium carbonate and further description of manic-depressive illness in children. *American Journal of Diseases of Children, 131,* 1122–1126.

Bryant, A. E., & Dreifuss, F. E. (1996). Valproic acid hepatic fatalities: III. U.S. experience since 1986. *Neurology, 46,* 465–469.

Bussing, R., & Levin, G. M. (1993). Methamphetamine and fluoxetine treatment of a child with attention-deficit hyperactivity disorder and obsessive compulsive disorder. *Journal of Child and Adolescent Psychopharmacology, 3,* 53–58.

Campbell, M., Adams, P. B., Small, A. M., Kafantaris, V., Silva, R. R., Shell, J., Perry, R., & Overall, J. E. (1995). Lithium in hospitalized aggressive children with conduct disorder: A double-blind and placebo-controlled study. *Journal of the American Academy of Child and Adolescent Psychiatry, 34,* 445–453.

Campbell, M., Anderson, L. T., Small, A. M., Adams, P., Gonzalez, N. M., & Ernst, M. (1993). Naltrexone in autistic children: Behavioral symptoms and attentional learning. *Journal of the American Academy of Child and Adolescent Psychiatry, 32,* 1283–1291.

Campbell, M., Kafantaris, V., & Cueva, J. E. (1995). An update on the use of lithium carbonate in aggressive children and adolescents with conduct disorder. *Psychopharmacology Bulletin, 31,* 93–102.

Campbell, M., Silva, R. R., Kafantaris, V., Locascio, J. J., Gonzalez, N. M., Lee, D., & Lynch, N. S. (1991). Predictors of side effects associated with lithium administration in children. *Psychopharmacology Bulletin, 27,* 373–380.

Campbell, M., Small, A. M., Green, W. H., Jennings, S. J., Perry, R., Bennett, W. G., & Anderson, L. (1984). Behavioral efficacy of haloperidol and lithium carbonate. *Archives of General Psychiatry, 41,* 650–656.

Carlson, G. A., Rapport, M. D., Kelly, K. L., & Pataki, C. S. (1995). Methylphenidate and desipramine in hospitalized children with comorbid behavior and mood disorders: Separate and combined effects on behavior and mood. *Journal of Child and Adolescent Psychopharmacology, 5,* 191–204.

Casat, C. D., Pleasants, D. Z., Schroeder, D. H., & Parler, D. W. (1989). Bupropion in children with attention deficit disorder. *Psychopharmacology Bulletin, 25,* 187–201.

Cassidy, S., & Henry, J. (1987). Fatal toxicity of antidepressant drugs in overdose. *British Medical Journal, 295,* 1021–1024.

Ceseña, M., Lee, D. O., Cebollero, A. M., & Steingard, R. J. (1995). Behavioral symptoms of pediatric HIV-1 encephalopathy successfully treated with clonidine. *Journal of the American Academy of Child and Adolescent Psychiatry, 34,* 302–306.

Chandran, K. S. K. (1994). ECG and clonidine [letter]. *Journal of the American Academy of Child and Adolescent Psychiatry, 33,* 1351.

Clarvit, S. R., Graae, F., Piacentini, J., Tancer, N., Gitow, A., DelBene, D., Davies, S., Jaffer, M., & Liebowitz, M. (1994). Double-blind, placebo-controlled study of fluoxetine for child and adolescent obsessive-compulsive disorders [abstract]. Scientific Proceedings presented at the annual meeting of American Academy of Child and Adolescent Psychiatry. Philadelphia, Pennsylvania.

Clay, T. H., Gualtieri, C. T., Evans, R. W., & Gullion, C. M. (1988). Clinical and neuropsychological effects of the novel antidepressant bupropion. *Psychopharmacology Bulletin, 24,* 143–148.

Coffey, B. J. (1990). Anxiolytics for children and adolescents: Traditional and new drugs. *Journal of Child and Adolescent Psychopharmacology, 1,* 57–83.

Coffey, B., Shader, R., Greenblatt, D. (1983). Pharmacokinetics of benzdiazepines and psychostimulants in children. *Journal of Clinical Psychopharmacology, 3,* 217–225.

Cohen, D. J., Detlor, J., Young, J. G., & Shaywitz, B. A. (1980). Clonidine ameliorates Gilles de la Tourette syndrome. *Archives of General Psychiatry, 37,* 1350–1357.

Colle, L. M., Bélair, J. F., DiFeo, M., Weiss, J., & LaRoche, C. (1994). Extended open-label fluoxetine treatment of adolescents with major depression. *Journal of Child and Adolescent Psychopharmacology, 4,* 225–232.

Connor, D. F. (1993). Beta blockers for aggression: A review of the pediatric experience. *Journal of Child and Adolescent Psychopharmacology, 3,* 99–114.

Conners, C. K. (1994). Multi-site bupropion clinical

trial in children: Methods and problems [abstract]. Scientific proceedings presented at the annual meeting of American Academy of Child and Adolescent Psychiatry, Philadelphia, Pennsylvania.

Conrad, C. D., & Hamilton, J. A. (1986). Recurrent premenstrual decline in serum lithium concentration: Clinical correlates and treatment implications. *Journal of the American Academy of Child and Adolescent Psychiatry, 25,* 852–853.

Cook, E. H., Rowlett, R., Jaselskis, C., & Leventhal, B. L. (1992). Fluoxetine treatment of children and adults with autistic disorder and mental retardation. *Journal of the American Academy of Child and Adolescent Psychiatry, 31,* 739–745.

Costa, A. D., & Kroll, R. M. (1995). Sertraline in stuttering [letter]. *Journal of Clinical Psychopharmacology, 15,* 443–444.

Csík, V., & Molnár, J. (1994). Possible adverse interaction between clozapine and ampicillin in an adolescent with schizophrenia. *Journal of Child and Adolescent Psychopharmacology, 4,* 123–128.

Cueva, J. E., Overall, E., Small, A. M., Armenteros, J. L., Perry, R., & Campbell, M. (1996). Carbamazepine in aggressive children with conduct disorder: A double-blind and placebo-controlled study. *Journal of the American Academy of Child and Adolescent Psychiatry, 35,* 480–490.

Dahl, R. E., Holttum, J., & Trubnick, L. (1994). A clinical picture of child and adolescent narcolepsy. *Journal of the American Academy of Child and Adolescent Psychiatry, 33,* 834–841.

Davis, R. E. (1979). Manic-depressive variant syndrome of childhood: A preliminary report. *American Journal of Psychiatry, 136,* 702–706.

DeLong, G. R. (1978). Lithium carbonate treatment of select behavior disorders in children suggesting manic-depressive illness. *Journal of Pediatrics, 93,* 689–694.

DeLong, G. R., & Aldershof, A. L. (1987). Long-term experience with lithium treatment in childhood: Correlation with clinical diagnosis. *Journal of the American Academy of Child and Adolescent Psychiatry, 26,* 389–394.

DeLong, G. R., & Nieman, G. W. (1983). Lithium-induced behavior changes in children with symptoms suggesting manic-depressive illness. *Psychopharmacology Bulletin, 19,* 258–265.

DeSanto, N. G., Anastasio, P., Coppola, S., Barba, G., Jadanza, A., & Capasso, G. (1991). Age-related changes in renal reserve and renal tubular function in healthy humans. *Child Nephrology and Urology, 11,* 33–40.

DeVeaugh-Geiss, J., Moroz, G., Biederman, J., Cantwell, D., Fontaine, R., Greist, J. H., Reichler, R., Katz, R., & Landau, P. (1992). Clomipramine hydrochloride in childhood and adolescent obsessive-compulsive disorder: A multicenter trial. *Journal of the American Academy of Child and Adolescent Psychiatry, 31,* 45–49.

Donnelly, M., Zametkin, A. J., Rapoport, J. L., Ismond, D. R., Weingartner, H., Lane, E., Oliver, J., Linnoila, M., & Potter, W. Z. (1986). Treatment of childhood hyperactivity with desipramine: Plasma drug concentration, cardiovascular effects, plasma and urinary catecholamine levels, and clinical response. *Clinical Pharmacology and Therapeutics, 39,* 72–81.

Douglas, V. I., Barr, R. G., Desilets, J., & Sherman, E. (1995). Do high doses of stimulants impair flexible thinking in attention-deficit hyperactivity disorder? *Journal of the American Academy of Child and Adolescent Psychiatry, 34,* 877–885.

Dreifuss, F. E. (1987). Fatal liver injury in children on valproate. *Lancet, 1,* 47–48.

Dreifuss, F. E., Santilli, N., Langer, D. H., Sweeney, K. P., Moline, K. A., & Menander, K. B. (1987). Valproic acid hepatic fatalities: A retrospective review. *Neurology, 37,* 379–385.

Dryden-Edwards, R. C., & Reiss, A. L. (1996). Differential response of psychotic and obsessive symptoms to risperidone in an adolescent. *Journal of Child and Adolescent Psychopharmacology, 6,* 139–145.

Dulcan, M. K. (1990). Using psychostimulants to treat behavioral disorders of children and adolescents: Traditional and new drugs. *Journal of Child and Adolescent Psychopharmacology, 1,* 7–20.

Dulcan, M. K. (1992). Information for parents and youth on psychotropic medications. *Journal of Child and Adolescent Psychopharmacology, 2,* 81–102.

Dummit, E. S., Klein, R. G., Tancer, N. K., Asche, B., & Martin, J. (1996). Fluoxetine treatment of children with selective mutism: An open trial. *Journal of the American Academy of Child and Adolescent Psychiatry, 35,* 615–621.

Dunnick, J. K., & Hailey, J. R. (1995). Experimental studies on the long-term effects of methylphenidate hydrochloride. *Toxicology, 103,* 77–84.

DuPaul, G. J., Barkley, R. A., & McMurray, M. B. (1994). Response of children with ADHD to methylphenidate: Interaction with internalizing symptoms. *Journal of the American Academy of Child and Adolescent Psychiatry, 33,* 894–903.

Dyson, W. L., & Barcai, A. (1970). Treatment of children of lithium-responding parents. *Current Therapeutic Research, 12,* 286–290.

El-khatib, H. E., & Dickey, T. O. (1995). Sertraline for body dysmorphic disorder. *Journal of the American Academy of Child and Adolescent Psychiatry, 34,* 1404–1405.

Elliott, G. R. (1995). The national plan for research on child and adolescent disorders: A report card at the midway point. *Journal of Child and Adolescent Psychopharmacology, 5,* 87–91.

Elliott, G. R., & Popper, C. W. (1991). Tricyclic antidepressants: The QT interval and other cardiovascular parameters. *Journal of Child and Adolescent Psychopharmacology, 1,* 187–189.

Elliott, G. R., Popper, C. W., & Frazier, S. H. (1990). Tricyclic antidepressants: A risk for 6–9 year olds? *Journal of Child and Adolescent Psychopharmacology, 1,* 105–106.

El-Mallakh, R. S., Barrett, J. L., & Wyatt, R. J. (1993). The Na,K-ATPase hypothesis for bipolar disorder: Implications of normal development. *Journal of Child and Adolescent Psychopharmacology, 3,* 37–52.

Emslie, G. (1995, May 31–June 3). A double-blind, placebo-controlled study of fluoxetine in depressed children and adolescents [abstract]. Paper presented at the symposium on SSRIs in children and adolescents. Program Book, Annual Meeting of the New Clinical Drug Evaluation Unit (NCDEU), Orlando, FL.

Epperson, C. N., McDougle, C. J., Anand, A., Marek, G. J., Naylor, S. T., Volkmar, F. R., Cohen, D. J., & Price, L. H. (1994). Lithium augmentation of fluvoxamine in autistic disorder: A case report. *Journal of Child and Adolescent Psychopharmacology, 4,* 201–207.

Evans, R. W., Clay, T. H., & Gualtieri, C. T. (1987). Carbamazepine in pediatric psychiatry. *Journal of the American Academy of Child and Adolescent Psychiatry, 26,* 2–8.

Famularo, R., Kinscherff, R., Fenton, T. (1988). Propranolol treatment for childhood posttraumatic stress disorder, acute type: A pilot study. *American Journal of Diseases of Children 142,* 1244–1247.

Feinstein, S. C., & Wolpert, E. A. (1975). Juvenile manic-depressive illness: Clinical and therapeutic considerations. *Journal of the American Academy of Child and Adolescent Psychiatry, 12,* 123–136.

Fenichel, R. R. (1995). Combining methylphenidate and clonidine: The role of post-marketing surveillance. *Journal of Child and Adolescent Psychopharmacology, 5,* 155–156.

Fichter, M. M., Leibl, K., Rief, W., Brunner, E., Schmidt-Auberger, S., & Engel, R. R. (1991). Fluoxetine versus placebo: A double-blind study with bulimic inpatients undergoing intensive psychotherapy. *Pharmacopsychiatry, 24,* 1–7.

Findling, R. L. (1996). Open-label treatment of comorbid depression and attentional disorders with co-administration of serotonin reuptake inhibitors and psychostimulants in children, adolescents, and adults. *Journal of Child and Adolescent Psychopharmacology, 6,* 165–175.

Fisman, S., & Steele, M. (1996). Use of risperidone in pervasive developmental disorders: A case series. *Journal of Child and Adolescent Psychopharmacology, 6,* 177–190.

FitzSimons, R. B., & Keane, S. (1981). Severe lithium intoxication in a child. *European Journal of Pediatrics, 137,* 353–354.

Flament, M. F., Rapoport, J. L., Berg, C. J., Sceery, W., Kilts, C., Mellstrom, B., & Linnoila, M. (1985). Clomipramine treatment of childhood obsessive-compulsive disorder. *Archives of General Psychiatry, 42,* 977–983.

Fletcher, S. E., Case, C. L., Sallee, F. R., Hand, L. D., & Gillette, P. C. (1993). Prospective study of the EKG effects of imipramine in children. *Journal of Pediatrics, 122,* 652–654.

Fluoxetine Bulimia Nervosa Collaborative Study Group. (1992). Fluoxetine in the treatment of bulimia nervosa: A multicenter, placebo-controlled, double-blind trial. *Archives of General Psychiatry, 49,* 139–147.

Food and Drug Administration, Department of Health and Human Services, United States Government. (1982). Use of approved drugs for unlabeled indications. *Food and Drug Administration Drug Bulletin, 12,* 4–5.

Food and Drug Administration, Department of Health and Human Services, United States Government: Import Operations Branch. (1988). *Regulatory Procedures Manual,* Chaps. 9–71, Exhibits X9-71-1 and X9-71-2.

Food and Drug Administration, Department of Health and Human Services, United States Government. (1992, October 16). Specific requirements on content and format of labeling for human prescription drugs; Proposed revision of "pediatric use" subsection in the labeling [21 CFR Part 201]. *Federal Register, 57* (201), 47423–47427.

Frazier, J. A., Gordon, C. T., McKenna, K., Lenane, M. C., Jih, D., & Rapoport, J. L. (1994). An open trial of clozapine in 11 adolescents with childhood-onset schizophrenia. *Journal of the American Academy of Child and Adolescent Psychiatry, 33,* 658–663.

Freedman, J. E., Wirshing, W. C., Russell, A. T., Bray, M. P., & Unutzer, J. (1994). Absence status seizures during successful long-term clozapine treatment of an adolescent with schizophrenia. *Journal of Child and Adolescent Psychopharmacology, 4,* 53–62.

Fritz, G. K., Rockney, R. M., & Yeung, A. S. (1994). Plasma levels and efficacy of imipramine treatment for enuresis. *Journal of the American Academy of Child and Adolescent Psychiatry, 33,* 60–64.

Frommer, D. A., Kulig, K. W., Marx, J. A., & Rumack, B. (1987). Tricyclic antidepressant overdose: A review. *Journal of the American Medical Association, 257,* 521–526.

Frommer, E. A. (1972). Indications for antidepressant treatment with special reference to depressed preschool children. In A. L. Annell (Ed.), *Depressive states in childhood and adolescence* (pp. 449–454). New York: John Wiley & Sons.

Fuchs, D. C. (1994). Clozapine treatment of bipolar disorder in a young adolescent. *Journal of the American Academy of Child and Adolescent Psychiatry, 33,* 1299–1302.

Gadow, K. D., Sverd, J., Sprafkin, J., Nolan, E. E., & Ezor, S. N. (1995). Efficacy of methylphenidate for attention-deficit hyperactivity disorder in children with tic disorder. *Archives of General Psychiatry, 52,* 444–455.

Gammon, G. D., & Brown, T. E. (1993). Fluoxetine and methylphenidate in combination for treatment of ADD and comorbid depressive disorders. *Journal of Child and Adolescent Psychopharmacology, 3,* 1–10.

Garber, J. H., McGonigle, J. J., Slomka, G. T., & Monteverde, E. (1992). Clomipramine atreatment of stereotypic behaviors and self-injury in patients with developmental disabilities. *Journal of the American Academy of Child and Adolescent Psychiatry, 31,* 1157–1160.

Garfinkel, B. D., Wender, P. H., Sloman, L., O'Neill, I. (1983). Tricyclic antidepressants and methylphenidate treatment of attention deficit disorder. *Journal of the American Academy of Child and Adolescent Psychiatry, 22,* 343–348.

Geller, B., Cooper, T. B., Schluchter, M. D., Warham, J. E., & Carr, L. G. (1987). Child and adolescent nortriptyline single dose pharmacokinetic parameters: Final report. *Journal of Clinical Psychopharmacology, 7,* 321–323.

Geller, B., Fox, L. W., & Clark, K. A. (1994). Rate and predictors of prepubertal bipolarity during follow-up of 6- to 12-year-old depressed children. *Journal of the American Academy of Child and Adolescent Psychiatry, 33,* 461–468.

Geller, B., Fox, L. W., & Fletcher, M. (1993). Effect of tricyclic antidepressants on switching to mania and on the onset of bipolarity in depressed 6 to 12 year olds. *Journal of the American Academy of Child and Adolescent Psychiatry, 32,* 43–50.

Ghaziuddin, N., King, C. A., Naylor, M., Ghaziuddin, M., Chaudhary, N., Giordani, B., DeQuardo, J. R., Tandon, R., & Greden, J. (1996). Electroconvulsive treatment in adolescents with pharmacotherapy-refractory depression. *Journal of Child and Adolescent Psychopharmacology, 6,* 259–271.

Gittelman, R., & Mannuzza, S. (1988). Hyperactive boys almost grown up. III. Methylphenidate effects on ultimate height. *Archives of General Psychiatry, 45,* 1131–1134.

Goetting, M. G. (1985). Acute lithium poisoning in a child with dystonia. *Pediatrics, 76,* 978–980.

Goetz, C. G., Tanner, C. M., Wilson, R. S., Carroll, V. S., Como, P. G., & Shannon, K. M. (1987). Clonidine and Gilles de la Tourette's syndrome: Double-blind study using objective rating methods. *Annals of Neurology, 21,* 307–310.

Goldbloom, D. S., & Olmsted, M. P. (1993). Pharmacotherapy of bulimia nervosa with fluoxetine: assessment of clinically significant attitudinal change. *American Journal of Psychiatry, 150,* 770–774.

Goldstein, D. J., Wilson, M. G., Thompson, V. L., Potvin, J. H., & Rampey, A. H. (1995). Long-term fluoxetine treatment of bulimia nervosa: Fluoxetine Bulimia Nervosa Research Group. *British Journal of Psychiatry, 166,* 660–666.

Gordon, C. T., Cotelingam, G. M., Stager, S., Ludlow, C. L., Hamburger, S. D., & Rapoport, J. L. (1995). A double-blind comparison of clomipramine and desipramine in the treatment of developmental stuttering. *Journal of Clinical Psychiatry, 56,* 238–242.

Gordon, C. T., State, R. C., Nelson, J. E., Hamburger, S. D., & Rapoport, J. L. (1993). A double-blind comparison of clomipramine, desipramine, and placebo in the treatment of autistic disorder. *Archives of General Psychiatry, 50,* 441.

Graae, F., Milner, J., Rizzotto, L., & Klein, R. G. (1994). Clonazepam in childhood anxiety disorders. *Journal of the American Academy of Child and Adolescent Psychiatry, 33,* 372–376.

Green, W. H. (1995). *Child and adolescent clinical psychopharmacology* (2nd ed.). Baltimore, MD: Williams & Wilkins.

Greenhill, L. L., Rieder, R. O., Wender, P. H., Buchsbaum, M., & Zahn, T. P. (1973). Lithium carbonate in the treatment of hyperactive children. *Archives of General Psychiatry, 28,* 636–640.

Groh, C. (1976). The psychotropic effect of Tegretol in non-epileptic children, with particular reference to the drug's indications. In W. Birkmayer (Ed.), *Epileptic seizures—behaviour—pain.* Baltimore, MD: University Park Press.

Gualtieri, C. T., & Evans, R. W. (1988). Motor performance in hyperactive children treated with imipramine. *Perceptual and Motor Skills, 66,* 763–769.

Hagino, O. R., Weller, E. B., Weller, R. A., Washing, D., Fristad, M. A., & Kontras, S. B. (1995). Untoward effects of lithium treatment in children aged four through six years. *Journal of the American Academy of Child and Adolescent Psychiatry, 34,* 1584–1590.

Halmi, K. A., Eckert, E. D., LaDu, T. J., & Cohen, J. (1986). Anorexia nervosa: Treatment efficacy of cyproheptadine and amitriptyline. *Archives of General Psychiatry, 43,* 177–181.

Hammock, R. G., Schroeder, S. R., & Levine, W. R. (1995). The effect of clozapine on self-injurious behavior. *Journal of Autism and Developmental Disorders, 25,* 611–626.

Hoehn-Saric, R., Harris, G. J., Pearlson, G. D., Cox, C. S., Machlin, S. R., & Camargo, E. E. (1991). A fluoxetine-induced frontal lobe syndrome in an obsessive compulsive patient. *Journal of Clinical Psychiatry, 52,* 131–133.

Hoehn-Saric, R., Lipsey, J. R., & McLeod, D. R. (1990). Apathy and indifference in patients on fluvoxamine and fluoxetine. *Journal of Clinical Psychopharmacology, 10,* 343–345.

Horne, R. L., Ferguson, J. M., Pope, H. G., Hudson, J. I., Lineberry, C. G., Ascher, J., & Cato, A. (1988). Treatment of bulimia with bupropion: A multicenter controlled trial. *Journal of Clinical Psychiatry, 49,* 262–266.

Hughes, P. L., Wells, L. A., Cunningham, C. J., & Ilstrup, D. M. (1986). Treating bulimia with desipramine: A double-blind, placebo-controlled study. *Archives of General Psychiatry, 43,* 182–186.

Hunt, R. D. (1987). Treatment effects of oral and transdermal clonidine in relation to methylphenidate: An open pilot study in ADD-H. *Psychopharmacology Bulletin, 23,* 111–114.

Hunt, R. D. (1989, October). *Treatment effects of clonidine and methylphenidate* [abstract]. Paper presented at the annual meeting of the American Academy of Child and Adolescent Psychiatry, New York.

Hunt, R. D., Capper, L., & O'Connell, P. (1990). Clonidine in child and adolescent psychiatry. *Journal of*

Child and Adolescent Psychopharmacology, 1, 87–102.

Hunt, R. D., Cohen, D. J., & O'Connell, P. (1982). Strategies for study of the neurochemistry of attention deficit disorder in children. *Schizophrenia Bulletin, 8,* 236–252.

Hunt, R. D., Minderaa, R. B., & Cohen, D. J. (1985). Clonidine benefits children with attention deficit disorder and hyperactivity: Report of a double-blind placebo-crossover therapeutic trial. *Journal of the American Academy of Child and Adolescent Psychiatry, 24,* 617–629.

Hunt, R. D., Minderaa, R. B., & Cohen, D. J. (1986). The therapeutic effects of clonidine in attention deficit disorder and hyperactivity: A comparison with placebo and methylphenidate. *Psychopharmacology Bulletin, 22,* 229–236.

Ialongo, N. S., Horn, W. F., Pascoe, J. M., Greenberg, G., Packard, T., Lopez, M., Wagner, A., & Puttler, L. (1993). The effects of multi-modal intervention with ADHD children: A 9-month follow-up. *Journal of the American Academy of Child and Adolescent Psychiatry, 32,* 182–189.

Jacobies, G. (1978). Alertness and scholastic achievement in young epileptics treated with carbamazepine (Tegretol). In H. Meinardi & A. Rowan (Eds.), *Psychology and new diagnostic approaches.* Amsterdam: Swets and Zeitlinger.

Jacobsen, L. K., Walker, M. C., Edwards, J. E., Chappell, P. B., & Woolston, J. L. (1994). Clozapine in the treatment of a young adolescent with schizophrenia. *Journal of the American Academy of Child and Adolescent Psychiatry, 33,* 645–650.

Jain, U., Birmaher, B., Garcia, M., Al-Shabbout, M., & Ryan, N. D. (1992). Fluoxetine in children and adolescents with mood disorders: A chart review of efficacy and adverse effects. *Journal of Child and Adolescent Psychopharmacology, 2,* 259–265.

Jan, J. E., Espezel, H., & Appleton, R. E. (1994). The treatment of sleep disorders with melatonin. *Developmental Medicine and Child Neurology, 36,* 97–107.

Jaselskis, C. A., Cook, E. H., Fletcher, K., & Leventhal, B. L. (1992). Clonidine treatment of hyperactive and impulsive children with autistic disorder. *Journal of Clinical Psychopharmacology, 12,* 322–327.

Jensen, P. S., Ryan, N. D., & Prien, R. (1992). Psychopharmacology of child and adolescent major depression: Present status and future directions. *Journal of Child and Adolescent Psychopharmacology, 2,* 31–45.

Jensen, P. S., & Elliott, G. R. (Eds.). (1992). Why don't antidepressants seem to work for depressed adolescents? [Special Section] *Journal of Child and Adolescent Psychopharmacology, 2,* 7–45.

Kaminer, Y. (1994). Cocaine craving [letter]. *Journal of the American Academy of Child and Adolescent Psychiatry, 33,* 592.

Kapur, S., Mieczkowski, T., & Mann, J. J. (1992). Antidepressant medications and the relative risk of suicide attempt and suicide. *Journal of the American Medical Association, 268,* 3441–3445.

Kastner, T., Friedman, D. L., Plummer, A. T., Ruiz, M. Q., & Henning, D. (1990). Valproic acid for the treatment of children with mental retardation and mood symptomatology. *Pediatrics, 86,* 467–472.

Keepers, G. A., Clappison, V. J., & Casey, D. E. (1983). Initial anticholinergic prophylaxis for acute neuroleptic induced extrapyramidal sundromes. *Archives of General Psychiatry, 40,* 1113–1117.

Kemph, J. P., DeVane, C. L., Levin, G. M., Jarecke, R., & Miller, R. L. (1993). Treatment of aggressive children with clonidine: Results of an open pilot study. *Journal of the American Academy of Child and Adolescent Psychiatry, 32,* 557–581.

Kennedy, S. H., Goldbloom, D. S., Ralevski, E., Davis, C., O'Souza, J. D., & Lofchy, J. (1993). Is there a role for selective monoamine oxidase inhibitor therapy in bulimia nervosa? A placebo-controlled trial of brofaromine. *Journal of Clinical Psychopharmacology, 13,* 415–422.

Khandelwal, S. K., Varma, V. K., & Srinyasa Murthy, R. (1984). Renal function in children receiving long-term lithium prophylaxis. *American Journal of Psychiatry, 141,* 278–279.

Kiessling, L. S., Marcotte, A. C., & Culpepper, L. (1993). Antineuronal antibodies in movement disorders. *Pediatrics, 92,* 39–43.

King, B. H. (1991). Fluoxetine reduced self-injurious behavior in an adolescent with mental retardation. *Journal of Child and Adolescent Psychopharmacology, 1,* 321–329.

King, R. A., Riddle, M. A., Chappell, P., Hardin, M. T., Anderson, G. M., Lombroso, P., & Scahill, L. (1991). Emergence of self-destructive phenomena in children and adolescents during fluoxetine treatment. *Journal of the American Academy of Child and Adolescent Psychiatry, 30,* 179–186.

Kolmen, B. K., Feldman, H. M., Handen, B. J., & Janosky, J. E. (1995). Naltrexone in young autistic children: A double-blind, placebo-controlled crossover study. *Journal of the American Academy of Child and Adolescent Psychiatry, 34,* 223–231.

Kowatch, R. A., Suppes, T., Gilfillan, S. K., Fuentes, R. M., Grannemann, B. D., & Emslie, G. J. (1995). Clozapine treatment of children and adolescents with bipolar disorder and schizophrenia: A clinical case series. *Journal of Child and Adolescent Psychopharmacology, 5,* 241–253.

Krakowski, A. J. (1965). Amitriptyline in treatment of hyperkinetic children: A double-blind study. *Psychosomatics, 6,* 355–360.

Kramer, P. D. (1993). *Listening to prozac.* New York: Viking Press.

Krener, P. K., & Mancina, R. A. (1994). Informed consent or informed coercion? Decision-making in pediatric psychopharmacology. *Journal of Child and Adolescent Psychopharmacology, 4,* 183–200.

Kuekes, E. D., Wigg, C., Bryant, S., & Meyer, W. J. (1992). Hypertension is a risk in adolescents treated with imipramine. *Journal of Child and Adolescent Psychopharmacology, 2*, 241–248.

Kuhn-Gebhart, V. (1976). *Behavioural disorders in non-epileptic children and their treatment with carbamazepine.* Baltimore, MD: University Park Press.

Kumra, S., Frazier, J. A., Jacobsen, L. K., McKenna, K., Gordon, C. T., Lenane, M. C., Hamburger, S. D., Smith, A. R., Albus, K. E., Alaghband-Rad, J., Rapoport, J. L. (1996). Childhood-onset schizophrenia: A double-blind clozapine-haloperidol comparison. *Archives of General Psychiatry 53*, 1090–1097.

Kuperman, S., & Stewart, M. A. (1987). Use of propranolol to decrease aggressive outbursts in young patients. *Psychosomatics, 28*, 315–319.

Kupietz, S., & Balka, E. (1976). Alterations in vigilance performance of children receiving amitriptyline and methylphenidate. *Psychopharmacology, 50*, 29–33.

Kurlan, R., Como, P. G., Deeley, C., McDermott, M., & McDermott, M. P. (1993). A pilot controlled study of fluoxetine for obsessive-compulsive symptoms in children with Tourette's syndrome. *Clinical Neuropharmacology, 16*, 167–172.

Kutcher, S., Boulos, C., Ward, B., Marton, P., Simeon, J., Ferguson, H. B., Szalai, J., Katic, M., Roberts, N., DuBois, C., & Reed, K. (1994). Response to desipramine treatment in adolescent depression: A fixed-dose, placebo-controlled trial. *Journal of the American Academy of Child and Adolescent Psychiatry, 33*, 686–694.

Kutcher, S., & Robertson, H. A. (1995). Electroconvulsive therapy in treatment-resistant bipolar youth. *Journal of Child and Adolescent Psychopharmacology, 5*, 167–175.

Latz, S. R., & McCracken, J. T. (1992). Neuroleptic malignant syndrome in children and adolescents: Two case reports and a warning. *Journal of Child and Adolescent Psychopharmacology, 2*, 123–129.

Leckman, J. F., Hardin, M. T., Riddle, M. A., Stevenson, J., Ort, S. I., & Cohen, D. J. (1991). Clonidine treatment of Gilles de la Tourette's syndrome. *Archives of General Psychiatry, 48*, 324–328.

Lena, B., Surtees, S. J., & Maggs, R. (1978). The efficacy of lithium in the treatment of emotional disturbance in children and adolescents. In F. N. Johnson & S. Johnson, *Lithium in medical practice* (pp. 79–83). Baltimore, MD: University Park Press.

Leonard, H. L., Meyer, M. C., Swedo, S. E., Richter, D., Hamburger, S. D., Allen, A. J., Rapoport, J. L., & Tucker, E. (1995). Electrocardiographic changes during desipramine and clomipramine treatment in children and adolescents. *Journal of the American Academy of Child and Adolescent Psychiatry, 34*, 1460–1468.

Leonard, H. L., Swedo, S. E., Lenane, M. C., Rettew, D. C., Cheslow, D. L., Hamburger, S. D., & Rapoport, J. L. (1991). A double-blind desipramine substitution during long-term clomipramine treatment in children and adolescents with obsessive-compulsive disorder. *Archives of General Psychiatry, 48*, 922–927.

Leonard, H. L., Swedo, S. E., Rapoport, J. L., Koby, E. V., Lenane, M. C., Cheslow, D. L., & Hamburger, S. D. (1989). Treatment of obsessive-compulsive disorder with clomipramine and desipramine in children and adolescents: A double-blind crossover comparison. *Archives of General Psychiatry, 46*, 1088–1092.

Leviatov, V. M., Veselovskaja, T. D., Marienko, G. P., & Chtchegoleva, A. P. (1976). Psychoses au Tegretol des epileptiques. *Annals of Medical Psychology, 1*, 473.

Levin, G. M., Burton-Teston, K., & Murphy, T. (1993). Development of precocious puberty in two children treated with clonidine for aggressive behavior. *Journal of Child and Adolescent Psychopharmacology, 3*, 127–131.

Lewis, D. W., Fontana, C., Mehallick, L. K., & Everett, Y. (1994). Transdermal scopolamine for reduction of drooling in developmentally delayed children. *Developmental Medicine and Child Neurology, 36*, 484–486.

Liebowitz, M. R., Hollander, E., Fairbanks, J., & Campeas, R. (1990). Fluoxetine for adolescents with obsessive-compulsive disorder. *American Journal of Psychiatry, 147*, 370–371.

Lipkin, P. H., Goldstein, I. J., & Adesman, A. R. (1994). Tics and dyskinesias associated with stimulant treatment in attention-deficit hyperactivity disorder. *Archives of Pediatric and Adolescent Medicine, 148*, 859–861.

Litovitz, T. L., Clark, L. R., & Soloway, R. A. (1994). 1993 annual report of the American Association of Poison Control Centers Toxic Exposure Surveillance System. *American Journal of Emergency Medicine, 12*, 546–584.

Livingston, R. L., Dykman, R. A., & Ackerman, P. T. (1992). Psychiatric comorbidity and response to two doses of methylphenidate in children with attention deficit disorder. *Journal of Child and Adolescent Psychopharmacology, 2*, 115–122.

Lombroso, P. J., Scahill, L., King, R. A., Lynch, K. A., Chappell, P. B., Peterson, B. S., McDougle, C. J., & Leckman, J. F. (1995). Risperidone treatment of children and adolescents with chronic tics: A preliminary report. *Journal of the American Academy of Child and Adolescent Psychiatry, 34*, 1147–1152.

Lowenthal, D. T. (1980). Pharmacokinetics of clonidine. *Journal of Cardiovascular Pharmacology, 2* (Suppl. 1), S29–S37.

Lowenthal, D. T., Matzek, K. M., & MacGregor, T. R. (1988). Clinical pharmacokinetics of clonidine. *Clinical Pharmacokinetics 14*, 287–310.

Mandoki, M. (1993). Clozapine for adolescents with psychosis: Literature review and two case reports. *Journal of Child and Adolescent Psychopharmacology, 3*, 213–221.

Mandoki, M. (1994). Buspirone treatment of traumatic brain injury in a child who is highly sensitive to adverse effects of psychotropic medications. *Journal* of Child and Adolescent Psychopharmacology, 4, 129–139.

Mandoki, M. (1995). Risperidone treatment of children and adolescents: Increased risk of extrapyramidal side effects? Journal of Child and Adolescent Psychopharmacology, 5, 49–67.

Markel, H., Lee, A., Holmes, R. D., & Domino, E. F. (1994). LSD flashback syndrome exacerbated by selective serotonin reuptake inhibitor antidepressants in adolescents. Journal of Pediatrics, 125, 817–819.

Matarazzo, E. B. (1992). Tourette's syndrome treated with ACTH and prednisone: Report of two cases. Journal of Child and Adolescent Psychopharmacology, 2, 215–226.

McCarthy, M. K., Goff, D. C., Baer, L., Cioffi, J., & Herzog, D. B. (1994). Dissociation, childhood trauma, and the response to fluoxetine in bulimic patients. International Journal of Eating Disorders, 15, 219–226.

McConville, B. J., Minnery, K. L., Sorter, M. T., West, S. A., Friedman, L. M., & Christian, K. (1996). An open study of the effects of sertraline on adolescent major depression. Journal of Child and Adolescent Psychopharmacology, 6, 41–51.

McDougle, C. J., Brodkin, E. S., Yeung, P. P., Naylor, S. T., Cohen, D. J., & Price, L. H. (1996). Risperidone in adults with autism or pervasive developmental disorder. Journal of Child and Adolescent Psychopharmacology, 5, 273–282.

McDougle, C. J., Price, L. H., & Goodman, W. K. (1990). Fluvoxamine treatment of coincident autistic disorder and obsessive compulsive disorder: A case report. Journal of Autism and Developmental Disorders, 20, 537–543.

McKnew, D. H., Cytryn, L., Buchsbaum, M. S., Hamovit, J., Lamour, M., Rapoport, J. L., & Gershon, E. S. (1981). Lithium in children of lithium-responding parents. Psychiatry Research, 4, 171–180.

Minnery, K. L., West, S. A., McConville, B. J., & Sorter, M. T. (1995). Sertraline-induced mania in an adolescent. Journal of Child and Adolescent Psychopharmacology, 5, 151–153.

Mitchell, J. E., Christenson, G., Jennings, J., Huber, M., Thomas, B., Pomeroy, C., & Morley, J. (1989). A placebo-controlled, double-blind crossover study of naltrexone hydrochloride in outpatients with normal weight bulimia. Journal of Clinical Psychopharmacology, 9, 94–97.

Mitchell, J. E., Pyle, R. L., Eckert, E. D., Hatsukami, D., Pomeroy, C., & Zimmerman, R. (1990). A comparison of antidepressants and structured group psychotherapy in the treatment of bulimia nervosa. Archives of General Psychiatry, 47, 149–157.

Mozes, T., Toren, P., Chernauzan, N., Mester, R., Yoran-Hegesh, R., Blumensohn, R., & Weizman, A. (1994). Clozapine treatment in very early onset schizophrenia. Journal of the American Academy of Child and Adolescent Psychiatry, 33, 65–70.

Murphy, D. A., Pelham, W. E., & Lang, A. R. (1992). Aggression in boys with attention deficit-hyper-activity disorder: Methylphenidate effects on naturalistically observed aggression, response to provocation, and social information processing. Journal of Abnormal Child Psychology, 20, 451–466.

Myers, W. C., Donahue, J. E., & Goldstein, M. R. (1994). Disulfiram for alcohol use disorders in adolescents. Journal of the American Academy of Child and Adolescent Psychiatry, 33, 484–489.

Neural mechanisms in sudden cardiac death: Insights from long QT syndrome. (1991). Lancet [Editorial], 338, 1181–1182.

Nguyen, N., Whittlesey, S., Bui, B., DiGiacomo, D., Scarborough, A., & Bui, T. (1994). Pattern analysis of fluoxetine in childhood depression: Preliminary findings [abstract]. Scientific proceedings presented at the annual meeting of American Academy of Child and Adolescent Psychiatry.

Papatheodorou, G., & Kutcher, S. P. (1993). Divalproex sodium treatment in late adolescent and young adult acute mania. Psychopharmacology Bulletin, 29, 213–219.

Pataki, C. S., Carlson, G. A., Kelly, K. L., Rapport, M. D., & Biancaniello, T. M. (1993). Side effects of methylphenidate, desipramine alone and in combination in children. Journal of the American Academy of Child and Adolescent Psychiatry, 32, 1065–1072.

Pawluk, L. K., Hurwitz, T. D., Schluter, J. L., Ullevig, C., & Mahowald, M. W. (1995). Psychiatric morbidity in narcoleptics on chronic high dose methylphenidate therapy. Journal of Nervous and Mental Disease, 183, 45–48.

Pelham, W. E., Carlson, C., Sams, S. E., Vallano, G., Dixon, M. J., & Hoza, B. (1993). Separate and combined effects of methylphenidate and behavior modification of boys with attention deficit hyperactivity disorder in the classroom. Journal of Consulting and Clinical Psychology, 61, 506–515.

Pelham, W. E., Swanson, J. M., Furman, M. B., & Schwindt, H. (1995). Pemoline effects on children with ADHD: A time-response by dose-response analysis on classroom measures. Journal of the American Academy of Child and Adolescent Psychiatry, 34, 1504–1513.

Peterson, S. E., Myers, K. M., McClellan, J., & Crow, S. (1995). Neuroleptic malignant syndrome: Three adolescents with complicated courses. Journal of Child and Adolescent Psychopharmacology, 5, 139–149.

Phillips, K. A., Atala, K. D., & Albertini, R. S. (1995). Body dysmorphic disorder in adolescents. Journal of the American Academy of Child and Adolescent Psychiatry, 34, 1216–1220.

Physicians' desk reference (51st ed.). (1997). Montvale, NJ: Medical Economics Co.

Pippinger, C. E. (1980). Rationale and clinical application of therapeutic drug monitoring. Pediatric Clinics of North America, 27, 891–925.

Platt, J. E., Campbell, M., Green, W. H., & Grega, D. M. (1984). Cognitive effects of lithium carbonate and haloperidol in treatment-resistant aggressive children. *Archives of General Psychiatry, 41,* 657–662.

Pope, H. G., Hudson, J. I., Jonas, J. M., & Yurgelun-Todd, D. (1983). Bulimia treated with imipramine: A placebo-controlled, double-blind study. *American Journal of Psychiatry, 140,* 554–558.

Popper, C. W. (1992, May). *Desipramine deaths may be adrenergic* [abstract]. New Research Program and Abstracts presented at the annual meeting of the American Psychiatric Association.

Popper, C. W. (1994). The story of four salts. *Journal of Child and Adolescent Psychopharmacology, 4,* 217–23.

Popper, C. (1995a). Balancing knowledge and judgment: A clinician looks at new developments in child and adolescent psychopharmacology [Special issue]: *Pediatric Psychopharmacology II,* edited M. A. Riddle. *Child and Adolescent Psychiatric Clinics of North America, 4,* 483–513.

Popper, C. W. (1995b). Combining methylphenidate and clonidine: Pharmacologic questions and news reports about sudden death. *Journal of Child and Adolescent Psychopharmacology, 5,* 157–166.

Popper, C. W., & Elliott, G. R. (1990). Sudden death and tricyclic antidepressants: Clinical considerations for children. *Journal of Child and Adolescent Psychopharmacology, 1,* 125–132.

Popper, C. W., & Zimnitzky, B. (1995). Sudden death putatively related to desipramine treatment in youth: A fifth case and a review of speculative mechanisms. *Journal of Child and Adolescent Psychopharmacology, 5,* 283–300.

Preskorn, S. H., Weller, E. B., Jerkovich, G. S., Hughes, C. W., & Weller, R. A. (1988). Depression in children: Concentration-dependent CNS toxicity of the tricyclic antidepressants. *Psychopharmacology Bulletin, 24,* 275–279.

Prince, J. B., Wilens, T. E., Biederman, J., Spencer, T. J., & Wozniak, J. R. (1996). Clonidine for sleep disturbances associated with attention-deficit hyperactivity disorder: A systematic chart review of 62 cases. *Journal of the American Academy of Child and Adolescent Psychiatry, 35,* 599–605.

Puente, R. M. (1976). The use of carbamazepine in the treatment of behavioural disorders in children. In W. Birkmayer (Ed.), *Epileptic seizures—behaviour—pain.* Baltimore, MD: University Park Press.

Purdon, S. E., Lit, W., LaBelle, A., & Jones, B. D. W. (1994). Risperidone in the treatment of pervasive developmental disorder. *Canadian Journal of Psychiatry, 39,* 400–405.

Quintana, H., Birmaher, B., Stedge, D., Lennon, S., Freed, J., Bridge, J., & Greenhill, L. (1995). Use of methylphenidate in the treatment of children with autistic disorder. *Journal of Autism and Developmental Disorders, 25,* 283–294.

Quintana, H., & Keshavan, M. (1995). Risperidone in children and adolescents with schizophrenia. *Journal of the American Academy of Child and Adolescent Psychiatry, 34,* 1292–1296.

Rapoport, J. L., Quinn, P. O., Bradbard, G., Riddle,

K. D., & Brooks, E. (1974). Imipramine and methylphenidate treatments of hyperactive boys: A double-blind comparison. *Archives of General Psychiatry, 30,* 789–793.

Rapport, M. D., Carlson, G. A., Kelly, K. L., & Pataki, C. S. (1993). Methylphenidate and desipramine in hospitalized children: II. Separate and combined effects on cognitive function. *Journal of the American Academy of Child and Adolescent Psychiatry, 32,* 333–342.

Remschmidt, H. (1976). The psychotropic effect of carbamazepine in non-epileptic patients, with particular reference to problems posed by clinical studies in children with behavioural disorders. In W. Birkmayer (Ed.), *Epileptic seizures—behaviour—Pain.* Baltimore, MD: University Park Press.

Remschmidt, H. Schulz, E., & Martin, M. (1992). Die Behandlung schizophrener Psychosen in der Adoleszenz mit Clozapin (Leponex). In D. Naber & F. Muller-Spahn (Eds.), *Clozapin. Pharmakologie und Klinik eines atypischen Neuroleptikums: Eine kritische Bestandsaufnahme* (pp. 99–119). New York: Schattauer.

Remschmidt, H., Schulz, E., & Martin, P. D. M. (1994). An open trial of clozapine in thirty-six adolescents with schizophrenia. *Journal of Child and Adolescent Psychopharmacology, 4,* 31–41.

Riddle, M. A. (1992). Neuroleptic malignant syndrome in children and adolescents: Time to stop, look, and listen. *Journal of Child and Adolescent Psychopharmacology, 2,* 155–156.

Riddle, M. A., Geller, B., & Ryan, N. (1993). Another sudden death in a child treated with desipramine. *Journal of the American Academy of Child and Adolescent Psychiatry, 32,* 792–797.

Riddle, M. A., Hardin, M. T., King, R., Scahill, L., & Woolston, J. L. (1990). Fluoxetine treatment of children and adolescents with Tourette's and obsessive compulsive disorder: Preliminary clinical experience. *Journal of the American Academy of Child and Adolescent Psychiatry, 29,* 45–48.

Riddle, M. A., King, R. A., Hardin, M. T., Scahill, L., Ort, S. I., Chappell, P., Rasmusson, A., & Leckman, J. F. (1991). Behavioral side effects of fluoxetine in children and adolescents. *Journal of Child and Adolescent Psychopharmacology, 1,* 193–198.

Riddle, M. A., Lynch, K. A., Scahill, L., deVries, A., Cohen, D. J., & Leckman, J. F. (1995). Methylphenidate discontinuation and reinitiation during long-term treatment of children with Tourette's disorder and attention-deficit hyperactivity disorder: A pilot study. *Journal of Child and Adolescent Psychopharmacology, 5,* 205–214.

Riddle, M. A., Nelson, J. C., Kleinman, C. S., Rasmusson, A., Leckman, J. F., King, R. A., & Cohen, D. J. (1991b). Sudden death in children receiving Norpramin®: A review of three reported cases and commentary. *Journal of the American Academy of Child and Adolescent Psychiatry, 30,* 104–108.

Riddle, M. A., Scahill, L., King, R. A., Hardin, M. T., Anderson, G. M., Ort, S. I., Smith, J. C., Leckman,

J. F., & Cohen, D. J. (1992). Double-blind, crossover trial of fluoxetine and placebo in children and adolescents with obsessive-compulsive disorder. *Journal of the American Academy of Child and Adolescent Psychiatry, 31,* 1062–1069.

Riddle, M. A. (Ed.). (1995). Pediatric psychopharmacology I and II. *Child and Adolescent Psychiatric Clinics of North America, 4* (1, 2), 1–520.

Rifkin, A., Quitkin, F., Carrillo, C., Blumberg, A. G., & Klein, D. F. (1972). Lithium carbonate in emotionally unstable character disorder. *Archives of General Psychiatry, 27,* 519–523.

Rosenberg, D. R., Holttum, H., & Gershon, S. (1994). *Textbook of pharmacotherapy for child and adolescent psychiatric Disorders.* New York: Brunner/Mazel.

Rosenberg, D. R., Johnson, K., & Sahl, R. (1992). Evolving mania in an adolescent with low-dose fluoxetine. *Journal of Child and Adolescent Psychopharmacology, 2,* 299–306.

Rothner, A. D. (1981). Valproic acid: A review of 23 fatal cases. *Annals of Neurology, 10,* 287.

Rothschild, R., Quitkin, H. M., Quitkin, F. M., Stewart, J. W., Ocepek-Welikson, K., McGrath, P. J., & Tricamo, E. (1994). A double-blind placebo-controlled comparison of phenelzine and imipramine in the treatment of bulimia in atypical depressives. *International Journal of Eating Disorders, 15,* 1–9.

Ryan, N. D. (1990). Heterocyclic antidepressants in children and adolescents. *Journal of Child and Adolescent Psychopharmacology, 1,* 21–31.

Ryan, N. D., Meyer, V., Dachille, S., Mazzie, D., & Puig-Antich, J. (1988). Lithium antidepressant augmentation in TCA-refractory depression in adolescents. *Journal of the American Academy of Child and Adolescent Psychiatry, 27,* 371–376.

Ryan, N. D., Puig-Antich, J., Rabinovich, H., Fried, J., Ambrosini, P., Meyer, V., Torres, D., Dachille, S., & Mazzie, D. (1988). MAOIs in adolescent major depression unresponsive to tricyclic antidepressants. *Journal of the American Academy of Child and Adolescent Psychiatry, 27,* 755–758.

Safer, D. J. (1992). Relative cardiovascular safety of psychostimulants used to treat attention-deficit hyperactivity disorder. *Journal of Child and Adolescent Psychopharmacology, 2,* 279–290.

Safer, D., Allen, R., & Barr, E. (1972). Depression of growth in hyperactive children on stimulant drugs. *New England Journal of Medicine, 287,* 217–220.

Safer, D., Allen, R., & Barr, E. (1975). Growth rebound after termination of stimulant drugs. *Journal of Pediatrics, 86,* 113–116.

Sanchez, L. E., Campbell, M., Small, A. M., Cueva, J. E., Armenteros, J. L., & Adams, P. B. (1996). A pilot study of clomipramine in young autistic children. *Journal of the American Academy of Child and Adolescent Psychiatry, 35,* 537–544.

Saraf, K. R., Klein, D. F., Gittelman-Klein, R., & Greenhill, P. (1978). EKG effects of imipramine treatment in children. *Journal of the American Academy of Child and Adolescent Psychiatry, 17,* 60–69.

Schachar, R., & Tannock, R. (1993). Childhood hyperactivity and psychostimulants: A review of extended treatment studies. *Journal of Child and Adolescent Psychopharmacology, 3,* 81–97.

Schmidt, M. H., Trott, G. E., Blanz, B., & Nissen, G. (1990). Clozapine medication in adolescents. In C. N. Stefanis, A. D. Rabavilas, & C. R. Soldatos (Eds.), *Psychiatry: A world perspective* (Vol. 1, pp. 1100–1104). Proceedings of the 8th World Congress of Psychiatry, Athens, October 1989. New York: Excerpta Medica.

Schvehla, T. J., Mandoki, M. W., & Summer, G. S. (1994). Clonidine therapy for comorbid attention deficit hyperactivity disorder and conduct disorder: Preliminary findings in a children's inpatient unit. *Southern Medical Journal, 87,* 692–695.

Sheth, R. D., Goulden, K. J., & Ronen, G. M. (1994). Aggression in children treated with clobazam for epilepsy. *Clinical Neuropharmacology, 17,* 332–337.

Siassi, I. (1982). Lithium treatment of impulsive behavior in children. *Journal of Clinical Psychiatry, 43,* 482–484.

Siefen, G., & Remschmidt, H. (1986). Behandlungsergebnisse mit Clozapin beischizophrenen Jugendlichen. *Zeitschrift für Kinder-und-Jugendpsychiatrie, 14,* 245–257.

Silva, R. R., Campbell, M., Golden, R. R., Small, A. M., Pataki, C. S., & Rosenberg, C. R. (1992). Side effects associated with lithium and placebo administration in aggressive children. *Psychopharmacology Bulletin, 28,* 319–326.

Silva, R. R., Magee, H. J., & Friedhoff, A. J. (1993). Persistent tardive dyskinesia and other neuroleptic-related dyskinesias in Tourette's disorder. *Journal of Child and Adolescent Psychopharmacology, 3,* 137–144.

Silva, R. R., Munoz, D. M., & Alpert, M. (1996). Carbamazepine use in children and adolescents with features of attention-deficit hyperactivity disorder: A meta-analysis. *Journal of the American Academy of Child and Adolescent Psychiatry, 35,* 352–358.

Simeon, J., Carrey, N., Wiggins, D., Milin, R., & Hosenbocus, S. (1995). Risperidone effects in treatment-resistant adolescents: Preliminary case reports. *Journal of Child and Adolescent Psychopharmacology, 5,* 69–79.

Simeon, J. C., Dinicola, V. F., Ferguson, H. B., & Copping, W. (1990). Adolescent depression: A placebo-controlled fluoxetine treatment study and follow-up. *Progress in Neuro-Psychopharmacology and Biological Psychiatry, 14,* 791–795.

Simeon, J. G., Ferguson, H. B., & Van Wyck Fleet, J. (1986). Bupropion effects in attention deficit and conduct disorders. *Canadian Journal of Psychiatry, 31,* 581–585.

Singer, H. S., Brown, J., Quaskey, S., Rosenberg, L. A., Mellits, E. D., & Denckla, M. B. (1995). The treatment of attention-deficit hyperactivity disorder in Tourette's syndrome: A double-blind placebo-controlled study with clonidine and desipramine. *Pediatrics, 95,* 74–81.

Singh, N. N., Ellis, C. R., Crews, W. D., & Singh, Y. N. (1994). Does diminished dopaminergic neurotransmission increase pica? *Journal of Child and Adolescent Psychopharmacology, 4*, 93–99.

Spencer, T., Biederman, J., Steingard, R., & Wilens, T. (1993). Bupropion exacerbates tics in children with attention-deficit hyperactivity disorder and Tourette's syndrome. *Journal of the American Academy of Child and Adolescent Psychiatry, 32*, 211–214.

Spencer, T., Biederman, J., Wilens, T., Harding, M., O'Donnell, D., & Griffin, S. (1996). Pharmacotherapy of attention-deficit hyperactivity disorder across the life cycle. *Journal of the American Academy of Child and Adolescent Psychiatry, 35*, 409–432.

Spencer, T., Biederman, J., Wilens, T., Steingard, R., & Geist, D. (1993). Nortriptyline treatment of children with attention-deficit hyperactivity disorder and tic disorder or Tourette's disorder. *Journal of the American Academy of Child and Adolescent Psychiatry, 32*, 205–210.

Steingard, R., Biederman, J., Spencer, T., Wilens, T. E., & Gonzalez, A. (1993). Comparison of clonidine response in the treatment of attention-deficit hyperactivity disorder with and without comorbid tic disorders. *Journal of the American Academy of Child and Adolescent Psychiatry, 32*, 350–353.

Steingard, R., Khan, A., Gonzalez, A., & Herzog, D. B. (1992). Neuroleptic malignant syndrome: Review of experience with children and adolescents. *Journal of Child and Adolescent Psychopharmacology, 2*, 183–198.

Strober, M. (1992). The pharmacotherapy of depressive illness in adolescence: III. Diagnostic and conceptual issues in studies of tricyclic antidepressants. *Journal of Child and Adolescent Psychopharmacology, 2*, 23–29.

Strober, M., Freeman, R., Schmidt, S., & Diamond, R. (1992). The pharmacotherapy of major depression in adolescence. II. Effects of lithium augmentation in nonresponders to imipramine. *Journal of the American Academy of Child and Adolescent Psychiatry, 31*, 16–20.

Strober, M., Morrell, W., Burroughs, J., Lampert, C., Danforth, H., & Freeman, R. (1988). A family study of bipolar I disorder in adolescence: Early onset of symptoms linked to increased familial loading and lithium resistance. *Journal of Affective Disorders, 15*, 255–268.

Stuss, D. T., & Benson, D. F. (1986). *The frontal lobes.* New York: Raven Press.

Swanson, J. M., Flockhart, D., Udrea, D., Cantwell, D., Connor, D., & Williams, L. (1995). Clonidine in the treatment of ADHD: Questions about safety and efficacy. *Journal of Child and Adolescent Psychopharmacology, 5*, 301–304.

Tannock, T., Ickowicz, A., & Schachar, R. (1995). Differential effects of methylphenidate on working memory in ADHD children with and without comorbid anxiety. *Journal of the American Academy of Child and Adolescent Psychiatry, 34*, 886–896.

Tannock, R., & Schachar, R. (1992). Methylphenidate and cognitive perseveration in hyperactive children. *Journal of Child Psychology and Psychiatry, 33*, 1217–1228.

Teicher, M. H., & Glod, C. A. (1990). Neuroleptics drugs: Indications and guidelines for their rational use in children and adolescents: Traditional and new drugs. *Journal of Child and Adolescent Psychopharmacology, 1*, 33–56.

Teicher, M. H., Glod, C., & Cole, J. O. (1990). Emergence of intense suicidal preoccupation during fluoxetine treatment. *American Journal of Psychiatry, 147*, 207–210.

Theesen, K. A. (1995). *The handbook of psychiatric drug therapy for children and adolescents.* New York: Haworth Press.

Thompson, S., & Rey, J. M. (1995). Functional enuresis: Is desmopressin the answer? *Journal of the American Academy of Child and Adolescent Psychiatry, 34*, 266–271.

Tierney, E., Joshi, P. T., Llinas, J. F., Rosenberg, L. A., & Riddle, M. A. (1995). Sertraline for depression in children and adolescents: Preliminary clinical experience. *Journal of Child and Adolescent Psychopharmacology, 5*, 13–27.

Tingelstad, J. B. (1991). The cardiotoxicity of the tricyclics. *Journal of the American Academy of Child and Adolescent Psychiatry, 30*, 845–846.

Towbin, K. E., Dykens, E. M., & Pugliese, R. G. (1994). Clozapine for early developmental delays with childhood-onset schizophrenia: Protocol and 15-month outcome. *Journal of the American Academy of Child and Adolescent Psychiatry, 33*, 651–657.

Trimble, M. R. (1990). Anticonvulsants in children and adolescents. *Journal of Child and Adolescent Psychopharmacology, 1*, 107–124.

Trott, G. E., Elliger, T. J., & Nissen, G. (1990). Moclobemide: First experiences in children and adolescents. In C. N. Stefanis, A. D. Rabavilas, & C. R. Soldatos (Eds.), *Psychiatry: A world perspective, Vol. I: Proceedings of the VIII World Congress of Psychiatry, Athens, October 1989.* (pp. 1096–1099). New York: Excerpta Medica.

Trott, G. E., Friese, H. J., Menzel, M., & Nissen, G. (1992). Use of moclobemide in children with attention deficit hyperactivity disorder. *Psychopharmacology, 106*, S134–S136.

Urman, R., Ickowicz, A., Fulford, P., & Tannock, R. (1995). An exaggerated cardiovascular response to methylphenidate in ADHD children with anxiety. *Journal of Child and Adolescent Psychopharmacology, 5*, 29–37.

Varanka, T. M., Weller, R. A., Weller, E. B., & Fristad, M. A. (1988). Lithium treatment of manic episodes with psychotic features in prepubertal children. *American Journal of Psychiatry, 145*, 1557–1559.

Vetro, A., Szentistvanyi, I., Pallag, L., Varga, M., & Szilard, J. (1985). Therapeutic experience with lithium in childhood aggressivity. *Neuropsychobiology, 14*, 121–127.

Vitiello, B., Behar, D., Malone, R., Delaney, M. A.,

Ryan, P. J., & Simpson, G. M. (1988). Pharmacokinetics of lithium carbonate in children. *Journal of Clinical Psychopharmacology, 8,* 355–359.

Wagner, K. D., Teicher, M. H., & Popper, C. W. (1992). Efficacy and safety of long-term lithium treatment in hospitalized aggressive children. *Houston Med, 8,* 71–75.

Waizer, J., Hoffman, S. P., Polizos, P., & Engelhardt, D. (1974). Outpatient treatment of hyperactive school children with imipramine. *American Journal of Psychiatry, 131,* 587–591.

Walkup, J. T. (1994). A different diagnosis of the adverse behavioral effects of fluoxetine. *American Academy of Child and Adolescent Psychiatry News, 25,* 28–30.

Walsh, B. T., & Devlin, M. J. (1995). Eating disorders. In M. A. Riddle (Ed.), *Pediatric Psychopharmacology II* [Special issue], *Child and Adolescent Psychiatric Clinics of North America, 4,* 343–347.

Walsh, B. T., Giardina, E., Sloan, R., Greenhill, L., & Goldfein, J. (1994). Effects of desipramine on autonomic control of the heart. *Journal of the American Academy of Child and Adolescent Psychiatry, 33,* 191–197.

Walsh, B. T., Gladis, M., Roose, S. P., Stewart, J. W., Stetner, F., & Glassman, A. H. (1988). Phenelzine vs. placebo in 50 patients with bulimia. *Archives of General Psychiatry, 45,* 471–475.

Walsh, B. T., Hadigan, C. M., Devlin, M. J., Gladis, M., & Roose, S. P. (1991). Long-term outcome of antidepressant treatment for bulimia nervosa. *American Journal of Psychiatry, 148,* 1206–1212.

Weinberg, W. A., Brumback, R. A. (1976). Mania in childhood: Case studies and literature review. *American Journal of Diseases of Children 130,* 380–385.

Weiss, G., & Hechtman, L. T. (1986). *Hyperactive children grown up: Empirical findings and theoretical considerations.* New York: Guilford Press.

Wender, P. H., & Reimherr, F. W. (1990). Bupropion treatment of attention-deficit hyperactivity disorder in adults. *American Journal of Psychiatry, 147,* 1018–1020.

Werry, J. S., Aman, M. G., & Diamond, E. (1980). Imipramine and methylphenidate in hyperactive children. *Journal of Child Psychology and Psychiatry, 21,* 27–35.

Werry, J. S., & Aman, M. G. (Eds.). (1993). *Practitioner's guide to psychoactive drugs for children and adolescents.* New York: Plenum.

Wertzel, E. (1994). *Prozac nation: Young and depressed in America.* Boston: Houghton Mifflin.

West, S. A., Keck, P. E., & McElroy, S. L. (1995). Oral loading doses in the valproate treatment of adolescents with mixed bipolar disorder. *Journal of Child and Adolescent Psychopharmacology, 5,* 225–231.

West, S. A., Keck, P. E., McElroy, S. L., Strakowski, S. M., Minnery, K. L., McConville, B. J., & Sorter, M. T. (1994). Open trial of valproate in the treatment of adolescent mania. *Journal of Child and Adolescent Psychopharmacology, 4,* 263–267.

Whelan, R., & Dearlove, O. R. (1995). Management of clonidine overdose in a child with Tourette's syndrome [letter]. *Developmental Medicine and Child Neurology, 37,* 469.

Whitehead, P. L., & Clark, L. D. (1970). Effect of lithium carbonate, placebo, and thioridazine on hyperactive children. *American Journal of Psychiatry, 127,* 824–825.

Wilens, T. E., Biederman, J., Geist, D. E., Steingard, R., & Spencer, T. (1993a). Nortriptyline in the treatment of attention-deficit hyperactivity disorder: A chart review of 58 cases. *Journal of the American Academy of Child and Adolescent Psychiatry, 32,* 343.

Wilens, T. E., Biederman, J., Spencer, T., & Geist, D. E. (1993b). A retrospective study of serum levels and electrocardiographic effects of nortriptyline. *Journal of the American Academy of Child and Adolescent Psychiatry, 32,* 270–277.

Wilens, T. E., Spencer, R., Biederman, J., Wozniak, J., & Connor, D. (1995). Combined pharmacotherapy: An emerging trend in pediatric psychopharmacology. *Journal of the American Academy of Child and Adolescent Psychiatry, 34,* 110–112.

Willemsen-Swinkels, S. N. H., Buitelaar, J. K., Nijhof, G. J., & van Engeland, H. (1995). Failure of naltrexone hydrochloride to reduce self-injurious and autistic behavior in mentally retarded adults: Double-blind placebo-controlled studies. *Archives of General Psychiatry, 52,* 766–773.

Williams, D. T., Mehl, R., Yudofsky, S., Adams, D., & Roseman, B. (1982). The effect of propranolol on uncontrolled rage outbursts in children and adolescents with organic brain dysfunction. *Journal of the American Academy of Child and Adolescent Psychiatry, 21,* 129–135.

Wilsher, C. R., & Taylor, E. A. (1994). Piracetam in developmental reading disorders: A review. *European Child and Adolescent Psychiatry, 3,* 59–71.

Winchel, R. M., & Stanley, M. (1991). Self-injurious behavior: A review of the behavior and biology of self-mutilation. *American Journal of Psychiatry, 148,* 306–317.

Winsberg, B. G., Bialer, I., Kupietz, S., & Tobias, J. (1972). Effects of imipramine and dextroamphetamine on behavior of neuropsychiatrically impaired children. *American Journal of Psychiatry, 128,* 1425–1431.

Wolf, D. V., & Wagner, K. D. (1993). Tardive dyskinesia, tardive dystonia, and tardive Tourette's syndrome in children and adolescents. *Journal of Child and Adolescent Psychopharmacology, 3,* 175–198.

Wood, I. K., Parmelee, D. X., & Foreman, J. W. (1989). Lithium-induced nephrotic syndrome. *American Journal of Psychiatry, 146,* 84–87.

Yellin, A. M., Spring, C., & Greenberg, L. M. (1978). Effects of imipramine and methylphenidate on behavior of hyperactive children. *Research Communications in Psychology and Psychiatry Behav 3,* 15–25.

Yepes, L. E., Balka, E. B., Winsberg, B. G., & Bialer, I.

(1977). Amitriptyline and methylphenidate treatment of behaviorally disordered children. *Journal of Child Psychology and Psychiatry, 18,* 39–52.

Youngerman, J., & Canino, I. A. (1978). Lithium carbonate use in children and adolescents. *Archives of General Psychiatry, 35,* 216–224.

Zafrani, E. S., & Berthelot, P. (1982). Sodium valproate in the induction of unusual hepatotoxicity. *Hepatology, 2,* 648–649.

Zimmerman, H. J., & Ishak, K. G. (1982). Valproate-induced hepatic injury: Analysis of 23 fatal cases. *Hepatology, 2,* 591–597.

Zimnitzky, B. M., DeMaso, D. R., & Steingard, R. J. (1996). Use of risperidone in psychotic disorder following ischemic brain damage. *Journal of Child and Adolescent Psychopharmacology, 6,* 75–78.

12 / Electroconvulsive Therapy

Charles H. Kellner, Mark D. Beale, and Hilary J. Bernstein

Electroconvulsive (ECT) therapy remains a standard treatment for a limited range of serious psychiatric illnesses in adults. Its use in children and adolescents is more restricted, largely because the conditions for which the treatment is effective occur much less commonly in this age group. Nonetheless, electroconvulsive therapy is an important treatment modality to have available when the clinical situation warrants its use, and age is not a contraindication.

The prejudice against the use of electroconvulsive therapy in children stems largely from the absence of compelling data about its safety, not from data demonstrating that it is unsafe. Indeed, a growing body of case report material suggests that this treatment is likely to have a similar safety profile in children as in adults. In this chapter, we present a general overview of the use and technique of electroconvulsive therapy and a discussion of issues specific to its use in children.

Indications

The indications for the use of electroconvulsive therapy in children and adolescents should closely parallel those in adults (American Psychiatric Association [hereafter APA], 1990). Thus it generally should be reserved for those patients with severe mood disorders who have not responded to more conventional therapies (psychotherapy, medications). Electroconvulsive therapy also can be very helpful in cases of acute psychosis or catatonia, due to primary mood or thought disorders.

Literature describing the experience in treating children with electroconvulsive therapy whether is limited to case material; there are no controlled studies comparing it and medications in the young. In 1989 Bertagnoli and Borchardt (1990) reviewed the literature on the use of electroconvulsive therapy in children and adolescents, and found 149 cases (ages 5 to 19) of depression, mania, or "schizophrenia" so treated since 1947. Of these, 140 were reported to have improved after receiving the treatment. Additionally, 1 patient with anorexia nervosa was reported to be improved and 1 with Tourette's disorder unchanged after electroconvulsive therapy. However, because of imprecision in earlier psychiatric diagnostic categories, it is hard to draw firm conclusions from these cases regarding modern indications for the use of electroconvulsive therapy in children.

Recently other reports documenting its successful use in the young have appeared. Schneekloth, Rummans, and Logan (1993) described 20 adolescents (ages 13 to 18 years), 13 of whom improved after electroconvulsive therapy. Those with mood disorders responded at a higher rate than those with schizophrenia or schizoaffective disorder. Kutcher and Robertson (1995) reported on 22 adolescents (identified by a review of hospital records over 8 years) who were offered electroconvulsive therapy either for depression ($n = 11$) or mania ($n = 11$). The 16 patients who elected to have electroconvulsive therapy had better treatment outcomes and shorter hospital stays than those who elected to continue standard pharmacotherapy. Two reports detail the successful treatment with electroconvulsive therapy of catatonia in children (one an 8-year-old girl, the other a 13-year-old boy) (Cizadlo & Wheaton, 1995; Powell, Silveira, & Lindsay, 1988). Moise and Petrides (1996) reported their experience with electroconvulsive therapy in 10 adolescents between the ages of 16 and 18 who also were identified by retrospective chart review. Ten out of the 13 were considered responders; consistent with other reports, those with affective illness, psychosis, or catatonia benefited the most. Follow-up was available for 8 patients, 5 of whom remained asymptomatic for at least 3 years and 3 of whom had relapsed within 1 year despite maintenance pharmacotherapy. No patient reported persistent memory disturbance nor was there any evidence of neurological impairment. These authors concluded that, in their experience, electroconvulsive therapy was as safe and effective in adolescents with severe psychiatric illnesses as it was in adults.

Additional reports of the successful use of ECT in adolescents include that of Ghaziuddin, King, Naylor, Ghaziuddin, Chaudhary, and Greden (1995) (for refractory depression, n = 7), Cohen, Paillére-Martinot, and Basquin (1997) (for major depression, n = 10, mania, n = 4, and schizophrenia, n = 7), Nolen and Zwaan (1990) (for lethal catatonia, n = 1). Hill, Courvoisie, Dawkins, Nofal, and Thomas (1997) reported the successful use of ECT in two 7-year old boys with intractable mania.

The APA Task Force Report on electroconvulsive therapy (1990) provides specific guidelines for the treatment of children and adolescents. The report recommends that in children 12 years or younger, electroconvulsive therapy be used only when "other viable treatments have not been effective or cannot be safely administered." Furthermore, 2 psychiatric consultants who are experienced in the treatment of children, and not otherwise directly involved in the care of the patient, should provide documented agreement with the recommendation for electroconvulsive therapy. For adolescents ages 13 to 17, the recommendation is less stringent; only 1 psychiatrist experienced in treating adolescents needs to document agreement with the treatment plan. The Task Force Report also points out that the anes-

thetist for electroconvulsive therapy should be experienced in anesthetic delivery to children.

There are no absolute contraindications to administering electroconvulsive therapy in adults or children, and children are less likely to have many of the medical conditions, such as heart and lung disease, that increase the risks of electroconvulsive therapy and general anesthesia. However, a thorough medical examination is required to rule out any condition that would necessitate modifications in electroconvulsive therapy technique. Prior to treatment, each patient should undergo a physical exam, complete blood count measurement of serum electrolytes, and urinalysis. Those with psychosis or catatonia probably should receive a computerized tomography (CT) or magnetic resonance imaging (MRI) scan of the brain to rule out a space-occupying lesion or hydrocephalus. Further studies and consultations should be performed on those with a positive cardiac or neurologic history or physical findings suggestive of organic disease. There is no evidence that seizures induced by electroconvulsive therapy are harmful to the developing central nervous system.

Procedure

Electroconvulsive therapy usually is performed in a specially equipped suite with the capability to provide anesthesia and emergency support. Oxygen and suction as well as a fully stocked emergency cart must be available. Such suites may be located on a psychiatry inpatient unit or in a general ambulatory care facility or even in a general hospital recovery room setting. Appropriate waiting and recovery areas should be available. The team of health care professionals who administer electroconvulsive therapy usually consists of the psychiatrist, the psychiatric nurse, and an anesthesiologist or nurse anesthetist. Additional recovery area personnel are present in larger services.

Once it has been decided that a course of electroconvulsive therapy is to be given, and informed consent has been obtained, the patient is instructed to come to the suite having had nothing to eat or drink for the previous 8 to 12 hours. An intravenous needle is inserted into an arm vein for administering the standard medications as well as any additional ones that may be required. The electrodes (now available as stick-on, disposable pads) are applied either for bilateral or right unilateral placement, and electrocardiogram, electroencephalogram, pulse oximetry, and nerve stimulator leads are attached. An automatic blood pressure cuff is used to monitor vital signs; a second manual blood pressure cuff is placed on the patient's right ankle, in order to exclude the succinylcholine from the right foot so that the motor manifestations of the seizure may be observed in the foot.

The treatment sequence begins with the administration of an anticholinergic premedication (either glycopyrrolate or atropine) to prevent bradycardia (some practitioners consider this optional) followed by the anesthetic methohexital in a dose of 1 milligram (mg) per kilogram (kg). As the patient becomes unconscious over the next 30 to 45 seconds, the anesthetist takes control of the airway and ventilates with 100% oxygen throughout the procedure. When unconsciousness is assured, succinylcholine in a dose of 0.75 to 1.0 mg/kg is injected to relax the patient's muscles. The blood pressure cuff on the right ankle is inflated just before the succinylcholine is given. Muscle relaxation occurs over the next 1 to 2 minutes and is confirmed by the loss of reflexes, cessation of fasiculations (caused by the succinylcholine), and loss of response to the nerve stimulator. A specially designed rubber bite block is then inserted into the patient's mouth to protect the teeth and tongue, and is held firmly in place as the electrical stimulus is delivered. The subsequent seizure is observed in the cuffed right foot and electroencephalogram tracing. A typical seizure lasts 30 to 60 seconds and ends spontaneously with cessation of motor manifestations followed by a flat electroencephalogram tracing. The anesthetist assists ventilation as needed for the next several minutes, and the patient is allowed to awaken in as unstimulating an environment as possible. Most patients are ready to leave the suite within 30 minutes.

Particular attention should be paid to the electrical stimulus dose given to children. It is well established that younger patients have lower seizure thresholds and a tendency to have longer seizures (Beale, Kellner, Pritchett, Bernstein, & Burns, 1994; Sackheim, Devanand, & Prudic, 1991). Thus stimulus doses should be much lower in children than in adults and the practitioner should be

prepared to terminate a prolonged seizure pharmacologically, either with additional anesthetic or anticonvulsant medication (APA, 1990).

Informed Consent

The process of obtaining informed consent for electroconvulsive therapy is a crucial and integral part of the treatment procedure for patients of any age. Because electroconvulsive therapy is used infrequently in children and because there may be heightened concerns about the appropriateness of its use, this process takes on even greater significance in this patient group. Consent should be obtained from the patient and a parent (or both parents) or legal guardian. If the patient is unable to give consent (e.g., in the case of a catatonic child), local guidelines for the process of substituted consent should be followed, including appropriate involvement of the court system. The APA Task Force on ECT (1990) has guidelines for the appropriate procedure for informing a patient about electroconvulsive therapy and for obtaining informed consent.

The informed consent document should be written in layman's terms that are understandable to the person providing consent. Videotapes about electroconvulsive therapy can be helpful aids to enhance understanding of the treatment, particularly for young patients, but cannot be used in lieu of a formal consent process.

The APA Task Force Report suggests that the following topics be included in the consent form: (1) a description of the procedure; (2) an explanation of why the therapy is being recommended and by whom; (3) treatment alternatives; (4) major and minor risk factors associated with the treatment; (5) a description of behavioral restrictions associated with the treatment before, during, and after the, procedure; (6) a statement that consent for electroconvulsive therapy is voluntary and may be withdrawn at any time; and (7) and the name of a contact person who will be available to answer questions about the treatment at any time (APA, 1990, p. 68). The report also suggests that individual facilities develop policies for the use of electroconvulsive therapy consistent with state and federal laws, including consent procedures for minors. The policies should specify when children may be considered adults for purpose of consent for medical procedures.

Conclusion

Electroconvulsive therapy is an effective and safe treatment for children and adolescents with severe affective and psychotic disorders. Patients with depression or mania respond at a higher rate than those with schizophrenia, and those with catatonia may respond dramatically. Careful attention to consent issues and documentation is essential. Additional research (as called for in Editorials by Fink (1993), and Kellner (1995)) is needed to further define the role of electroconvulsive therapy in the treatment of children and adolescents.

REFERENCES

American Psychiatric Association. (1990). *The practice of electroconvulsive therapy: Recommendations for treatment, training and privileging.* Washington, DC: Author.

Baker, T. (1994). ECT and young minds (letter). *The Lancet, 345,* 65.

Beale, M. D., Kellner, C. H., Pritchett, J. T., Bernstein, J. H., & Burns, C. M. (1994). Stimulus dose-titration in ECT: A two-year clinical experience. *Convulsive Therapy, 10* (2), 171–176.

Bertagnoli, M. W., & Borchardt, C. M. (1990). A review of ECT for children and adolescents. *Journal of the American Academy of Child and Adolescent Psychiatry, 29* (2), 302–307.

Cizadlo, B. C., & Wheaton, A. (1995). Case study: ECT treatment of a young girl with catatonia. *Journal of the American Academy of Child and Adolescent Psychiatry, 34* (3), 332–335.

Cohen, D., Paillère-Martinot, M. L., Basquin, M. (1997). Use of Electroconvulsive Therapy in Adolescents. *Convulsive Therapy, 13* (1), 25–31.

Cook, A., Scott, A. (1992). ECT for young people (letter). *Br J Psychiatry, 161,* 718–719.

Fink, M. (1993). Electroconvulsive Therapy in Children and Adolescents (editorial). *Convulsive Therapy, 9* (3), 155–157.

Ghaziuddin, N., King, C., Naylor, M., Ghaziuddin, M., Chaudhary, N., and Greden, J. (1995). Electroconvulsive treatment (ECT) in refractory adolescent depression. *Biol Psychiatry, 37,* 595.

Hill, M. A., Courvoisie, H., Dawkins, K., Nofal, P., and Thomas, B. (1997). ECT for the Treatment of Intractable Mania in Two Prepubertal male Children. *Convulsive Therapy, 13* (2), 74–82.

Kellner, C. H. (1995). Is ECT the Treatment of Choice for First-Break Psychosis? *Convulsive Therapy, 11* (3), 155–157.

Kutcher, S., & Robertson, H. A. (1995). Electroconvulsive therapy in treatment-resistant bipolar youth. *Journal of Child and Adolescent Psychopharmacology, 5* (3), 167–175.

Martin, B. A., & Bean, G. J. (1992). Competence to Consent to electroconvulsive therapy. *Convulsive Therapy, 8* (2), 92–102.

Moise, F. N., & Petrides, G. (1996). Case study: Electroconvulsive therapy in adolescents. *Journal of the American Academy of Child and Adolescent Psychiatry, 35* (3), 312–318.

Nolen, W. A., Zwaan, W. A. (1990). Treatment of lethal catatonia with electroconvulsive therapy and dantrolene sodium: a case report. *Acta Psychiatr Scand, 82,* 90–92.

Powell, J. C., Silveira, W. R., & Lindsay, R. (1988). Prepubertal depressive stupor: A case report. *British Journal of Psychiatry, 153,* 689–692.

Sackeim, H. A., Devanand, D. P., & Prudic, J. (1991). Stimulus intensity, seizure threshold, and seizure duration: Impact on the efficacy and safety of electroconvulsive therapy. *Psychiatric Clinics of North America, 14,* 803–843.

Schneekloth, T. D., Rummans, T. A., & Logan, K. M. (1993). Electroconvulsive therapy in adolescents. *Convulsive Therapy, 9,* 158–166.

13 / Phototherapy

William A. Sonis

Seasonal changes in the photoperiod (light-and-dark cycle) are a ubiquitous part of life. For thousands of years, physicians and other observers of the human condition have noted a relationship between the seasons and mood. Araetus (2nd century A.D.) first recorded use of light to treat depression, but this treatment was "lost" to the European medical community until in the 19th century, Frederick Cook, an insightful ship's physician, noted that his crew became lethargic in the dark days of the Arctic winter and treated their languor with bright artificial light (Wehr, 1989).

The current era of phototherapy began with a single case study using bright, full-spectrum light to treat a patient with recurrent winter depression successfully (Lewy, Kern, Rosenthal, & Wehr, 1982). This form of recurrent depression, the symptoms of which occur only in the winter and resolve with light therapy, has been called seasonal affective disorder (SAD) (Rosenthal et al., 1984), but more technically, it is a specific form of recurrent major depression, winter type (American Psychiatric Association [hereafter APA], 1994). Since the original case study by Lewy et al. (1982), over 550 patients with seasonal affective disorder have been treated successfully with phototherapy at multiple centers using different types of treatment paradigms and experimental designs. Furthermore, winter depressive symptoms appear to be a broadly distributed human trait (Terman, 1989), and up to 20% of surveyed adolescents may experience a mild form of seasonal affective disorder (Sonis, 1989). Despite the potentially large numbers of children and adolescents who may experience recurrent seasonal symptoms, there is little systematic information about either seasonal symptoms or phototherapy for children and adolescents.

However, seasonal patterns of mood clearly occur in children and adolescents; these generally follow the patterns observed in adults. A sizable minority of schoolchildren and adolescents experience seasonal symptoms—seasonal changes in mood and behavior—although no sex differences have been reported. Symptoms occur more frequently in the North than the South (Carskarden & Ascebo, 1993, Sonis, 1989).

The literature about light treatment for seasonal affective disorder in children and adolescents is also very sparse. Maghir and Vincent (1991) reported the adjunctive use of phototherapy in a 16-year-old girl with recurrent winter depression; Rosenthal et al. (1986) reported the disorder in 7 children and adolescents and treated 6 of them with phototherapy; Sonis, Yellin, Garfinkel, and Hoberman (1987) compared phototherapy with relaxation treatment in 5 adolescents with and 15 subjects without seasonal affective disorder; Teicher and Glod (1990) used phototherapy and alprazolam in a 16-year-old boy; while Sonis (1991) compared morning against evening phototherapy in 7 children and adolescents with the disorder. These studies are reviewed in detail later in this chapter.

The Nature of Phototherapy

Light is a form of radiant energy and belongs to the same class of physical phenomena as radio waves, heat waves, X rays, and cosmic rays. Radiant energy is described either by its wavelength or frequency (which is the inverse of wavelength). Wavelengths of radiant energy can be very short (e.g., cosmic waves, $<10^{-10}$ meters) or very long (e.g., broadcast waves, > 1 meter). The wavelengths of visible light are between 380 to 770 nanometers (10^{-9} meters).

The intensity of visual light as perceived by the human eye is called illuminance and is measured in lux. Lux is the amount of luminous flux per meter squared (lumens/m²). Examples of different levels of illuminance are: 200 to 300 lux for ordinary room lighting; 2,500 lux at sunrise in the springtime; and 100,000 lux at noon on a sunny summer day. Levels of illumination used in phototherapy vary between 2,500 and 10,000 lux, well within the range of human exposure to natural levels of illumination.

Light must be visually perceived in order to relieve depressive symptoms (Rosenthal, 1989). As it enters the eye, light is conducted through the cornea and the lens to the retina, where it stimulates the visual rods and cones. The resultant nerve impulses are conducted through the retino-hypothalamic tract to the suprachiasmatic nucleus, which is thought to be the pacemaker for most circadian rhythms. The specific mechanism by which light relieves depressive symptoms is unknown, although several hypotheses have been proposed.

Mechanism of Action of Light Therapy

There is no general agreement about the specific mechanism by which light relieves depressive symptoms of seasonal affective disorder. Rosenthal and the National Institute of Mental Health research group proposed the "melatonin hypothesis." According to this view, bright light was effective in treating seasonal affective disorder because it shortened the duration of melatonin production. After testing this hypothesis, its authors concluded that it is probably not correct and proposed an alternative formulation, the "photon-counting hypothesis." According to this hypothesis, only the intensity and duration of light treatment (i.e., the number of photons received), not timing, are crucial in reversing the symptoms of winter depression. Unfortunately, this hypothesis does not propose a specific mechanism that can be validated experimentally. Yet another hypothesis, the "phase-shift" hypothesis, has been proposed by Lewy and his research group. According to this theory, individuals with seasonal affective disorder are biologically "phase-delayed" (meaning that their circadian rhythms occur later than expected) in the winter. Lewy and his research group have tested this approach systematically using dim light melatonin onset (DLMO) as a marker of circadian phase position. In their stud-

ies, morning phototherapy "phase advances" DLMO (i.e., shifts it earlier in time), thus alleviating depressive symptoms. Furthermore, clinical studies have demonstrated that morning is superior to other times of day to treat the symptoms of seasonal affective disorder with phototherapy. Although the evidence in support of this hypothesis is strong, the "phase-shift" conception has not gained unanimous acceptance at the present time (Blehar & Lewy, 1990).

There are interesting phenomenologic parallels between the symptoms of recurrent winter depression and mammalian hibernation. However, substantial physiological differences exist between animals and humans in respect to reproduction, sleep and temperature regulations, carbohydrate craving, and synchronization of body rhythms, all of which limit the use of hibernation as an animal model (Zucker, 1989).

In summary, no one hypothesis clearly accounts for the effect of light in relieving the symptoms of seasonal affective disorder. The "phase-shift" hypothesis is the most promising theory, although it has yet to be validated and accepted.

Diagnosis of Seasonal Affective Disorder

ASSESSMENT

A thorough and complete psychiatric evaluation is crucial prior to initiating phototherapy for seasonal affective disorder. The evaluation should include a history of present illness, specifically inquiring about seasonal allergies and seasonal psychosocial variables (above and beyond the school year), any of which may influence affective symptoms. The evaluation should include a past psychiatric history, including any medication trials, and a family psychiatric history specifically inquiring about seasonal affective disorder and other affective disorders. Although there are no published family history studies of children and adolescents with this disorder, we found that as many as 33% of our subjects had a first-degree relative with a major affective disorder, often with a seasonal pattern. The mental status exam often reveals a youngster with depressed affect, low energy, variable psychomotor slowing, difficulty concentrating, and sleep problems (both hyposomnia and/or hypersomnia). Suicide attempts or psychotic thinking are rare without comorbid Axis I or II disorders. A medical history and physical examination with an ophthalmologic examination are necessary. Basic screening laboratory blood tests (complete blood count, UA, chemistry profile, thyroid function tests) are important, as seasonal fluctuations in thyroid function may or may not be reflected in subclinical conditions.

CLINICAL FEATURES

According to the fourth edition of the *Diagnostic and Statistical Manual of Mental Disorders* (*DSM-IV*) (APA, 1994), the diagnostic criteria for seasonal affective disorder in children and adolescents are essentially the same as for adults. The individual must meet *DSM-IV* criteria for either a bipolar or a recurrent major depressive disorder, and there must be a regular temporal relationship between the symptom onset and offset in a particular 60-day period of the year. There must have been at least 3 episodes of mood disturbance in 3 separate years that demonstrated the previously defined temporal seasonal relationship, with at least 2 consecutive years of mood disturbance. Finally, seasonal episodes of mood disturbance should outnumber any nonseasonal episodes of such disturbance by more than 3 to 1.

There are several important clinical differences between criteria used to diagnose seasonal affective disorder in adults and the same diagnosis in children and adolescents. According to the *DSM-IV*, since most adults live in a relatively aperiodic context, depressed adults are not considered to have seasonal mood patterns if their mood disturbance is related to seasonal psychosocial stressors. That is, most adults maintain more or less the same schedule all year except for relatively brief vacations. In this respect, the lives of children and adolescents are significantly more seasonal than adults. The imposition of a 9-month school schedule and a 3-month summer vacation in children and adolescents each year, makes the diagnosis of seasonal affective disorder more difficult, but not impossible. In general, children and adolescents with this disorder begin and end the school year without significant depressive symptoms. The symptoms of seasonal affective disorder tend to begin when daylight saving time ends in the fall after school has started and often remit when daylight savings time begins again in the spring before school ends.

Rosenthal's classical description of adults with seasonal affective disorder requires that the individual could not meet criteria for any other Axis I psychopathology. In contrast to this, children and adolescents with seasonal affective disorder are often comorbid for anxiety disorders as well as attention deficit hyperactivity disorder.

There are also several differences in seasonal affective disorder sex distribution and clinical presentation between adults on the one hand and children and adolescents on the other. Children and adolescents have a 1 to 1 male/female ratio rather than the 1 to 4 ratio described for adults with the disorder. In the 2 studies of youngsters with the disorder, the average number of cycles prior to presentation for treatment was 6.0 Sonis (1989) compared 30 children and adolescents with seasonal affective disorder to 125 adults with the disorder and found that hypersomnia and hyperphasia were not central features of the disorder in the younger population, but anergia was. Over 70% of 30 adolescents with seasonal affective disorder reported sadness, fatigue, poor quality of sleep, irritability, anhedonia, anxiety, and difficulty with concentration in schoolwork. Compared to the adults significantly fewer ($p < 0.05$) children and adolescents with this condition reported seasonal changes in activity and sadness, while significantly more ($p < 0.05$) adolescents reported decreased sleep. Fewer children and adolescents with the disorder than adults reported anxiety and increased appetite, while more children and adolescents reported irritability than was true for affected adults. These differences approached but did not reach significance (Sonis, 1989).

DIFFERENTIAL DIAGNOSIS

The differential diagnosis of seasonal affective disorder in children and adolescents includes: nonseasonal major depressive disorder, attention deficit hyperactivity disorder with depressed mood, and symptomatic normal mood and energy variation (subsyndromal seasonal affective disorder). By definition, children with major depressive disorder without seasonal variation do not have the typical seasonal waxing and waning of depressive symptoms year after year. The average nonseasonal depressive episode lasts longer than the average depressive episode of seasonal affective disorder ($m = 5$ months). Nonseasonal depressives may report an exacerbation of symptoms in the winter, but symptoms fail to remit in the spring or summer. Individuals with attention deficit hyperactivity disorder can present with depressed mood and often meet criteria for a major depressive episode. However, they usually do not report the waxing and waning constellation of depressive symptoms (especially the psychomotor retardation) reported by individuals with seasonal affective disorder. Finally "normal" children or adolescents may experience a seasonal pattern of neurovegetative variation without the severity of mood symptoms reported by individuals with the full-blown condition.

Developmental Considerations

The natural history of the disorder in children and adolescents has not been studied. However, like the depressive disorders in general, it may be assumed that once a child or adolescent is diagnosed with having seasonal affective disorder, the individual remains at risk for continued depressive episodes. Despite the absence of prospective data, developmental continuity with repeated winter depressive episodes is likely, since 33% of adults with the disorder reported the onset of symptoms in adolescence and 9% reported the onset of symptoms before 11 years of age (Rosenthal et al., 1986).

In children under 8 years old, the safety and efficacy of phototherapy for alleviation of depressive symptoms is unknown. (The youngest patient to receive phototherapy in our treatment studies was 8 years old.) Younger children are unlikely to be able to sit for the time required for phototherapy, or to tolerate wearing a hat unit. Because of this, phototherapy for seasonal affective disorder is not recommended for children younger than 8 years old, but it may be attempted depending on the child's development and ability to tolerate the procedure.

Goals and Objectives

The goal and objective of phototherapy is the relief of depressive symptoms, particularly the neurovegetative symptoms of disturbed psychomotor activity, sleep, and appetite, with secondary improvement in mood.

Interaction With Other Modalities

Phototherapy has been used to potentiate antidepressant response in adults, although no studies report combined phototherapy and antidepressant use in children and adolescents. However, interactions between phototherapy and other medications do exist. See the section entitled "Contraindications and Risks" for more information. Phototherapy can be integrated easily with psychotherapy and behavior modification programs.

Qualifications of the Clinician

Since the treatment paradigms for psychopharmacology and phototherapy are similar, it is important that the treating clinician have experience assessing child and adolescent psychopathology and using psychopharmacolgic approaches with children and adolescents.

The dangers of self-treatment with light are minimal but nonetheless present. Eager parents may try to self-diagnose seasonal affective disorder in their children, often on the basis of inaccurate or sketchy press reports. Popular articles about phototherapy often contain little or no information about the timing, dose, and duration of light treatment, nor the circumstances under which light treatment is optimal. Without supervision, the parent may not deal effectively with the side effects of phototherapy, including changes in sleep/wake cycles and, in bipolar depressives, possible swings to mania or hypomania. The efficacy of light treatment is difficult to self-monitor without the tempering observations of clinical supervision. Furthermore, self-treatment with light may influence parents to avoid or delay necessary professional assessment of other serious psychiatric disorders. Unsupervised use also must be discouraged in cases of ocular or retinal pathology (cataracts, glaucoma, retinal detachment, retinal degeneration, or the predisposing factor of diabetes), skin cancer, or for brief periods of insomnia or depression (Terman, Reme, Rafferty, Gillin, & Terman, 1990).

Equipment and Technological Considerations

Several different types of phototherapy units are available. Phototherapy boxes are available as free-standing upright or table models. The intensity of commercially available boxes vary from 2,500 to 10,000 lux. Boxes can be equipped with both full-spectrum and cool white fluorescent bulbs. Because of the additional risk of exposure to ultraviolet radiation, full-spectrum bulbs, are neither necessary nor as safe as cool white bulbs. Boxes should be equipped with a Plexiglas diffuser, which are used in boxes with full-spectrum bulbs, to decrease ultraviolet radiation and, in boxes with cool white bulbs, to diffuse the glare. The differences in illumination (2,500 or 10,000 lux) produced by phototherapy units is determined by the number of bulbs and the type of reflective backing in the box. The unit should have a multiple position switch to allow for different light intensities and should be approved by the Underwriters Laboratory (UL) for safety.

When using a light box, the individual receiving treatment is asked to position the phototherapy box at eye level and to sit approximately 3 feet away from a 2,500 lux light box or approximately 18 inches from a 10,000 lux unit. Initially patients were asked to glance directly at the light intermittently, but more recent data suggest that this is not necessary. However, the patient's eyes must be open, and the patient must be looking in the direction of the lights in order to achieve the therapeutic effect.

In addition to phototherapy boxes, several versions of "hat" phototherapy units have been developed and currently are being tested in various re-

search centers. Although portable, hat units tend to cause significant eye strain and discomfort in addition, they have not demonstrated the same robust clinical efficacy as the other units. There are no reports of children or adolescents using the "hats."

Description of the Process

After establishing the diagnosis of seasonal affective disorder, ruling out specific contraindications and discussing the benefits and risks of phototherapy with the patient and family, treatment should begin as soon as possible. Unless the seasonal pattern is established and the time of symptom remission is well known by the patient and family, initiating phototherapy in the spring should be discouraged. Without an adequate baseline, the effect of phototherapy may be confused with the typical seasonal waning of symptoms, and the patient may be treated unnecessarily. Phototherapy can be administered on either an inpatient or outpatient basis, either at a facility or at home. Some manufacturers and treatment centers rent phototherapy units to allow patients to determine if they are treatment responders, before asking them to purchase a phototherapy unit.

Phototherapy can be initiated either in the morning or the evening, depending on the patient's schedule and the type of phototherapy unit used. Two hours of 2,500 lux exposure is the treatment standard for adults with seasonal affective disorder, but many adolescents and virtually all children find that sitting in one place for 2 hours is very difficult. Furthermore, 2 hours of morning treatment is virtually impossible for adolescents and children, who would need to arise between 4:00 and 5:00 A.M. to get to school on time. However, since Terman (1989) demonstrated that 30 minutes of exposure to 10,000 lux is as effective as 2 hours of exposure to 2,500 lux in producing remission of seasonal affective disorder symptoms, morning treatment has now become feasible for children and adolescents and is the treatment of choice. Dawn simulation is an emerging technology that should simplify treatment immensely. In dawn simulation treatment, the phototherapy box is placed next to the bed and attached to a timer that gradually increases the light intensity of the phototherapy box to simulate dawn (Avery et al., 1993). Once again, the effectiveness of this treatment has been demonstrated in adults, but there are no reports of its use in children or adolescents.

Once treatment has begun, response is usually rapid, and symptoms often begin to resolve within a week. A full treatment effect usually is achieved within 1 to 2 weeks with virtually complete symptomatic relief. Patients report that sleep improves first, followed by an increase in energy and then improved mood.

Customizing treatment is crucial both to avoid side effects and to decrease conflict between the parents and the child about compliance. Evening treatment should not be initiated after 7:00 P.M. because the patient may experience phototherapy as energizing, and then have difficulty falling asleep. Morning treatment should begin by 7:00 A.M. and, if at all possible, its initiation should be advanced gradually to an earlier point in the morning, so that it ultimately begins somewhere between 6:00 and 6:30 A.M. Initiating treatment using morning phototherapy can be a problem, because the symptomatic morning hypersomnia often interferes with the patient's starting treatment sessions on time. To minimize this problem, treatment may begin in the evening and then switch to morning after the patient's symptoms begin to remit and the hypersomnia decreases.

When discontinuing phototherapy, symptom reappearance is more variable than symptom relief. Most patient's symptoms return 1 to 2 weeks after discontinuing phototherapy, but in some individuals, it may take up to 4 weeks before the full symptomatic picture reappears. The gradual return of symptoms after stopping phototherapy allows the individual to customize treatment. For example, one 16-year-old patient achieved full remission of his symptoms after 1 week of 2 hours of 2,500 lux evening phototherapy. Since his symptoms did not begin to return until he had missed 2 consecutive evening treatments, he found that he could maintain full treatment response even if he skipped treatment every third day.

Once the desired therapeutic response has been obtained, and the patient has determined the effect of stopping or missing treatments, minimal clinical supervision is needed for individuals with uncomplicated seasonal affective disorder. It is, however, recommended that when initiating and stopping phototherapy each year, psychiatric consultation be obtained, as in some years symptoms may be minimal and treatment may not be necessary. When seasonal affective disorder occurs along with other Axis I or II disorders, or if the clinical picture is complicated by educational, family, or social factors, multimodality treatment is indicated.

Side Effects

Phototherapy is a relatively safe treatment with few side effects. Major side effects include central nervous system stimulation and ophthalmologic problems.

Central nervous system side effects include irritability, headaches, insomnia, and hypomania. Insomnia is most likely to occur when patients use lights late at night. Irritability and hypomania are most likely to occur in individuals with either bipolar illness or a family history of bipolar illness. A few cases of florid mania in individuals with a bipolar illness have been reported in adults (Rosenthal, 1989), although none has been reported in children and adolescents. If this is a concern, mania can be prevented with the addition of lithium to the treatment program.

Eye strain often is reported when phototherapy is initiated, but usually it is transient. No serious ophthalmologic problems have been reported over the past decade with the use of 2,500 lux phototherapy. Although no short-term lesions to the eye have arisen during 10,000 lux therapy (Terman et al., 1990), the potential long-term (e.g., decade range) effects of using light of this intensity are unknown. Therefore, each clinical center or individual practitioner should engage an ophthalmologic consultant to provide appropriate advice about any problems that arise.

Side effects can be reduced by altering the intensity, duration, or timing of treatment. Phototherapy intensity can be modified by changing either the number of bulbs illuminated or the distance from the light source to the patient. For example, when using a 3-bulb, 10,000 lux unit with a 3-position switch, initial eye strain and irritability can be minimized by gradually increasing the number of bulbs illuminated (1, 2, then all 3 bulbs) over several days, allowing the patient gradually to become accustomed to approximately 3,000, then 6,500 and finally 10,000 lux. Alternatively, the patient can begin sitting 3 to 4 feet away from a 10,000 lux phototherapy unit and gradually shorten the distance to approximately 18 inches as comfort allows with all 3 bulbs illuminated. Furthermore, exposure time can be shortened (10 to 15 minutes) and gradually increased to 30 minutes as tolerated. Finally, the timing of treatment may be modified to minimize side effects. For example, if evening phototherapy initiated at 7:00 P.M. is too stimulating and produces insomnia, the start time could be shifted to 5:00 or 6:00 P.M., depending on the patient's schedule.

Indications

There are 2 primary and 2 secondary indications for the use of phototherapy in children and adolescents. The 2 primary indications are seasonal affective disorder and the subsyndromal disorder. Secondary indications include delayed sleep-phase syndrome and nonseasonal recurrent depression. While there are no published studies of the efficacy of phototherapy for children or adolescents with these problems, phototherapy has been demonstrated to be effective in adults with these disorders (Rosenthal, 1989).

Contraindications and Risks

The only contraindication for phototherapy are specific ophthalmologic conditions such as cataracts, glaucoma, retinal detachment, or diabetes.

Risks of phototherapy are minimal and include the side effects described previously as well as possible lenticular and retinal damage in individuals taking other medications known to increase retinal photosensitivity. Examples of such medications are antidepressants, phenothiazines, psoralens, antimalarials, antirheumatics, sulfonamides or tetracyclines, and possibly lithium as well as other photosensitizing medications (Terman et al., 1990).

Duration, Termination, and Restarting Phototherapy

One a therapeutic response is obtained, treatment should be continued until the period of expected seasonal symptom remission. At the end of the winter, phototherapy can be decreased by shortening exposure time, increasing the distance from the light, or decreasing the intensity by decreasing the number of bulbs used. If the treatment exposure is maintained at full intensity until after seasonal symptom remission, phototherapy can be stopped abruptly with minimal discomfort.

Many patients with seasonal affective disorder begin treatment each fall at the earliest indication of symptoms. Others choose to wait until their symptoms peak in order to determine if treatment is, in fact, necessary. Although most patients with the disorder do indeed experience a depression each season, the severity of the depression varies, and some individuals may not need treatment each year. This can vary with weather conditions or changes in personal or other environmental factors.

Economic, Ethical, and Social Considerations

The economic issues associated with phototherapy are minimal. Costs associated with phototherapy are limited to psychiatric consultation and the purchase of the phototherapy unit. Current prices for the units vary between $250 to $500. Depending on the patient's insurance, if purchased with a prescription, up to 80% of the cost of the unit may be reimbursed. The Society of Light Treatment and Biologic Rhythms (P.O. Box 478, Wilsonville, OR 97070; 503–694–2404) provides an informational packet about phototherapy for patients to submit to their insurance carrier.

Other than the discussion of benefits/risks

expected from the use of phototherapy, there are no ethical considerations in prescribing this treatment.

Although more theoretical than real, the social implications of seasonal affective disorder and phototherapy are important. Since many children and adolescents report winter depressive symptoms, sufficient ambient school lighting and increased sunlight exposure for children and adolescents are important (Carskarden & Ascebo, 1993; Sonis, 1989).

Outcome Studies

There have been only 2 case reports (Maghir & Vincent, 1991; Teicher & Glod, 1990) and 3 treatment studies on the use of phototherapy with children and adolescents (Rosenthal et al., 1986; Sonis, 1991; Sonis et al., 1987); these involved a total of 20 subjects.

Rosenthal et al. (1986) reported the successful use of phototherapy in 6 children and adolescents with seasonal affective disorder. In this study, 6 of 7 subjects with the disorder agreed to participate in an open trial of 2,500 lux phototherapy. The diagnosis was made using Rosenthal's criteria (Rosenthal et al., 1984). Duration and timing of phototherapy varied, and no structured evaluations or rating scales were used to determine outcome. However, according to both the parents and the children, mood and schoolwork improved dramatically.

Teicher and Glod (1990) treated a 16-year-old boy who suffered from recurrent winter depression with low-dose alprazolam. He had had an equivocal response to a trial of 2,500 lux phototherapy but had then responded to a tropical vacation. Unfortunately, the article did not include details of the trial of phototherapy, which limits readers' ability to determine the adequacy of the phototherapy trial. With 0.25 mg of alprazolam 3 times per day, the boy's HAM-D and seasonal addendum scores decreased to within the normal range.

Maghir and Vincent (1991) used 1 hour of morning phototherapy (intensity of phototherapy not specified) to treat the depressive symptoms of a 16-year-old girl with recurrent winter depression.

Sonis et al. (1987), in a single blind, randomized cross-over study with a 1-week washout between conditions, compared 2 groups. One consisted of 5 children and adolescents with seasonal affective disorder attention deficit hyperactivity disorder who received 2 hours of evening 2,500 lux phototherapy at sundown with systematic relaxation at the same time period. The other included 14 comparison subjects (4 with nonseasonal recurrent depression, 5 with without dysphoria, and 5 with subsyndromal seasonal affective disorder). The diagnosis of seasonal affective disorder was made using a structured interview and modifying Rosenthal's criteria, as described earlier. A structured clinical depression interview was the primary dependent measure. We found that 100% of the subjects with seasonal affective disorder improved on phototherapy and relapsed in the alternative condition. In the subjects with seasonal affective disorder on phototherapy there was a 30% decrease from baseline level of depression and no difference between baseline and relation therapy. Subjects with nonseasonal recurrent depression improved during relaxation treatment but not on phototherapy. Children with attention deficit hyperactivity disorder and the subsyndromal disorder did not improve in either condition. This effect was both statistically and clinically significant ($p < 0.01$). There was also a specific pattern of symptom relief that was unique to the subjects with seasonal affective disorder. The subjects reported improvement in neurovegetative symptoms (sleep, appetite, fatigue, psychomotor activity, and speech latency) that increased over baseline during washout and relaxation treatment. These symptoms were similar to the neurovegetative factor identified in a separate sample of highly seasonal adolescents (Sonis, 1989) and may represent the central elements of seasonal disorder.

In a more recent study of 7 subjects with the disorder, Sonis (1991) compared 30 minutes of 10,000 lux morning phototherapy with evening phototherapy. This study used a randomly assigned, single-blind cross-over design with a variable washout period between conditions, and it sought to test the hypothesis that morning treatment would be more effective than evening treatment. All subjects met *DSM-III-R* criteria for major depression, recurrent, winter seasonal pattern using the K-SADS-E. The dependent measure was the CDRS-R. Subjects entered the study when their CDRS-R score was ∈ 40. Although neither morning or evening light was superior to the other, both treatments decreased depressive symptoms to between 30 to 40% below baseline. All subjects responded to phototherapy, but only 80% experienced greater than a 30% decrease in symptoms.

Phototherapy is significantly more effective than antidepressants in the treatment of adolescent depression. Although only a small number of subjects have been studied, phototherapy appears to be a highly effective treatment for specific individuals who meet criteria for seasonal affective disorder.

Clinical Standards

Phototherapy is an established but as yet not completely proven treatment for seasonal affective disorder in children and adolescents. It appears to have significant promise in the treatment of many aspects of the syndrome in children and adolescents, but further studies are needed to establish its efficacy in individuals with the full syndrome. Phototherapy for delayed sleep-phase syndrome in children and adolescents may be practiced in the community but is not mainstream and has not been reported in the literature.

REFERENCES

American Psychiatric Association. (1994). *Diagnostic and statistical manual of mental disorder* (4th ed.). Washington, DC: Author.

Avery, D., Bolte, M., Dager, S., Wilson, L., Weyer, M., Cox, G., & Dunner, D. (1993). Dawn simulation treatment for winter depression: A controlled study. *American Journal of Psychiatry, 150,* 113–117.

Blehar, M., & Lewy, A. (1990). Seasonal mood disorders: Consensus and controversy. *Psychopharmocological Bulletin, 26* (4), 465–494.

Carskaden, M., & Acebo, C. (1993). Parental reports of seasonal mood and behavior changes in children. *Journal of the American Academy of Child and Adolescent Psychiatry, 32* (2), 264–269.

Lewy, A. J., Kern, H. A., Rosenthal, N. E., & Wehr, T. A. (1982). Bright artificial light treatment of a manic-depressive patient with a seasonal mood cycle. *American Journal of Psychiatry, 139,* 1494–1498.

Maghir, R., & Vincent, J. (1991). Phototherapy of seasonal affective disorder in an adolescent female. *Journal of American Academy of Child and Adolescent Psychiatry, 30,* (3), 440–442.

Rosenthal, N. E. (1989). Light therapy. In *Treatments of psychiatric disorders: A task force report of the American Psychiatric Association,* (Vol. 3, pp. 1890–1896) AP Washington, DC: American Psychiatric Association.

Rosenthal, N. E., Carpenter, C. J., James, S. P., Perry, B. L., Mendelson, W. B., Tamarkin, L., & Wehr, T. A. (1986). Seasonal affective disorder in children and adolescents. *American Journal of Psychiatry,* 143 (3), 356–358.

Rosenthal, N. E., Sack, D. A., Gillin, C. J., Lewy, A. J., Goodwin, F. K., Davenport, Y., Meuller, P. S., Newsome, D. A., Wehr, T. A. (1984). Seasonal affective disorder. *Archives of General Psychiatry, 41,* 72–80

Sonis, W. A. (1989). Seasonal affective disorder of childhood and adolescence: A review. In N. E. Rosen-thal & M. C. Blehar (Eds.), *Seasonal affective disorders and phototherapy* (pp. 46–54)). New York: Guilford Press.

Sonis, W. A. (1991). Morning vs. evening phototherapy of SAD on adolescents. Proceedings for Papers and New Research Posters, American Academy of Child and Adolescent Psychiatry, 6

Sonis, W. A., Yellin A. M., Garfinkel, B. D., & Hoberman, A. H. (1987). The antidepressant effect of light in seasonal affective disorder of childhood and adolescence. *Psychopharmacology Bulletin, 23,* (3) 360–363.

Teicher, M. H., & Glod, C. A. (1990). Seasonal affective disorder: Rapid resolution by low-dose alprazolam. *Psychopharmacology Bulletin, 26,* 197–202.

Terman, M. (1989). On the question of mechanism in phototherapy for seasonal affective disorder: Considerations of clinical efficacy and epidemiology. In N. E. Rosenthal, & M. C. Blehar (Eds.), *Seasonal affective disorders and phototherapy* (pp. 357–376). New York: Guilford Press.

Terman, M., Reme, C., Rafferty, B., Gillin, P., & Terman, J. (1990). Bright light therapy for winter depression: Potential ocular effects and theoretical implications. *Photochemistry and Photobiology, 51,* (6), 781–792.

Terman, M., Terman, J. S., Quitkin, F. M., McGrath, P. J., Stewart, J. W., & Rafferty, B. (1989). Light therapy for seasonal affective disorder: A review of efficacy. *Neuropsychopharmacology, 2,* 1–22.

Wehr, T. A. (1989). Seasonal affective disorders: A historical overview. In N. E. Rosenthal & M. C. Blehar (Eds.), *Seasonal affective disorders and phototherapy* (pp. 11–32). New York: Guilford Press.

Zucker. (1989). Seasonal affective disorder: Animal models non fingo. In N. E. Rosenthal & M. C. Blehar (Eds.), *Seasonal affective disorders and phototherapy* (pp. 149–167). New York: Guilford Press.

14 / Nutritional Interventions

Patricia Novak and Marion Taylor Baer

Diet has long been used in the treatment of psychiatric disorders. While some dietary modifications have proven to be effective, such as the use of a low-phenyalanine diet in phenylketonuria to prevent mental retardation, others have been shown to be ineffective or controversial at best, as the use of vitamin B6 in the treatment of autism (Kozlowski, 1993).

Effects of Diet on Behavior

It is generally accepted that protein, energy, or iron deficency in utero or in early childhood may lead to developmental delays, possibly as a result of reduced brain cell number or inadequate myelination (Cravioto, 1979). Some delays may be ameliorated with good nutrition and adequate stimulation, yet deficits not addressed prior to age 3 are thought to be permanent (Walter, de Andvaca, Castillo, Rivera, & Cobo, 1990).

Lead intoxication is known to produce a syndrome similar to attention deficit hyperactivity disorder as well as speech problems, ataxia, and learning disorders; universal screening is now recommended (Needleman, Schell, Bellinger, Leviton, & Allred, 1990). Both lead intoxication and iron deficiency should be considered in the differential diagnosis of attention deficit hyperactivity disorder, autism, and pervasive developmental disorder (Galler, Ramsey, Golimano, & Lowell, 1983).

Severe vitamin deficiency syndromes can cause psychiatric symptoms. While the dementia associated with niacin deficiency (pellegra) has been eliminated as a public health concern, thiamin deficiency, secondary to high carbohydrate and low protein intakes, is still seen, although primarily in alcoholics (Kanarek & Marks-Kaufmann, 1991).

Other links between nutrition and behavior are more controversial. Orthomolecular medicine has championed megavitamin therapy to treat psychiatric conditions, mental retardation, and attention deficit hyperactivity disorder (Kozlowski, 1993). The B vitamins frequently are discussed due to their role as cofactors in the synthesis and breakdown of neurotransmitters. Controlled studies have not universally supported orthomolecular claims (Lipton, Mailman, & Nemeroff, 1979). It is well known that autism, attention deficit hyperactivity disorder, and mental retardation may have various etiologies. Accordingly, the possibility has been raised that a small subgroup in each of these diagnostic categories might respond to vitamin/mineral use as an adjunct to other therapies (Kanarek & Marks-Kaufmann, 1991).

Feingold (1975) proposed that attention deficit hyperactivity disorder is caused by a reaction to food additives and natural salicylates. Several studies have failed to support this hypothesis; others, however, suggest that while the Feingold diet is an ineffective treatment, certain children do display behavioral changes in response to specific food additives (Rowe & Rowe, 1994). The National Advisory Committee on Hyperkinesis and Food Additives has issued a report-regarding the Feingold diet. It recognizes the possibility of a beneficial placebo effect from use of a modified diet (Wender & Lipton, 1980). Additionally, there are no negative results from limiting or removing food additives from the diet; in fact, most diets are improved. Therefore, a supervised trial may be warranted for interested families.

It is a common perception that sugar may cause hyperactive behavior in children with and without the diagnosis of attention deficit hyperactivity disorder. Numerous double-blind studies have found no relationship between sugar and hyperactive behavior (Kruesi et al., 1986). It has been suggested that the anecdotal reports of a sugar-behavior relationship results from a misperception caused by the context within which consumption of sugar-rich foods takes place. This behavior tends to occur at stimulating, unstructured events, the increased activity being a function of the situation, not the diet (Kanarek & Marks-Kaufmann,

1991). Another variable is the concomitant and obligatory replacement of more nutrient-dense foods by sugar. A lack of essential nutrients may have been observed rather than a direct effect of sugar. A link between sugar, resulting reactive hypoglycemia, and criminal behavior or depression has been suggested; yet studies have failed to support this view sufficiently (Gray, 1989).

A global explanation of the connection between diet and behavior relates altered brain concentrations of the neurotransmitters serotonin, acetylcholine, and norepinephrine to changes in dietary amino acid intake, particularly tryptophan and tyrosine (Fernstrom & Wurtman, 1974). Alterations in the metabolism of serotonin or catecholamines have been documented in individuals with such psychiatric disorders as attention deficit hyperactivity disorders, autism, and eating disorders. Although biochemical and behavioral changes have been documented in response to dietary manipulation, the extent of actual neurotransmitter control and functional change remains controversial (Kanarek & Mark-Kaufmann, 1991).

Nutrition Intervention

Psychiatric disorders are multifactorial and benefit from intervention planned by a multidisciplinary team. Such a group would include a registered dietitian, trained in pediatrics. Following the psychiatric assessment, the nutritional component details goals that are integrated into the treatment or education plan of the child. The nutrition plan is designed to consider the child's diagnosis, developmental skills, and the family's cultural and economic needs and to define meal frequency and food types (Ekvall, 1993).

Nutritional rehabilitation may facilitate psychological therapy in disorders such as anorexia, bulimia, or failure to thrive, where poor nutritional status is compromising cognition. With eating disorders, weight gain through self-feeding is encouraged. If oral feedings are refused initially and weight loss is severe, tube feeding may be necessary (Rock & Yager, 1987).

The dietitian's role includes aiding the family in translating behavioral goals into mealtime practice and using techniques set forth by the therapist to alter inappropriate habits that may affect nutrition. Such habits include textural aversion, rumination or vomiting, inability to attend to meals, prolonged bottle use, or inability/refusal to breast-feed (Ekvall, 1993). The dietitian also supervises the use of the special diets so frequently prescribed for this population. Specified diets that may potentially improve symptomatology include: the ketogenic diet to reduce seizures, additive-free diets to reduce hyperactive behaviors, weight-control diets to reduce obesity, or low amino acid diets to prevent or reduce mental retardation in genetic disorders of amino acid metabolism.

REFERENCES

Cravioto, J. (1979). Malnutrition, environment and child development. In D. A. Levitsky (Ed.), *Malnutrition, behavior and development.* (pp. 28–38). Ithaca, NY: Cornell University Press.

Ekvall, S. W. (Ed.). (1993). *Pediatric nutrition in chronic diseases and developmental disorders: Prevention, assessment and treatment.* New York: Oxford University Press.

Feingold, B. F. (1975). Hyperkinesis and learning disabilities linked to artificial flavors and colors. *American Journal of Nursing, 75,* 797–803.

Fernstrom, J. D., Wurtman, R. J. (1974). Nutrition and the brain. *Scientific American, 230,* 84–91.

Galler, J. R., Ramsey, F., Golimano, G., & Lowell, W. E. (1983). The influence of early malnutrition on subsequent behavioral development: Classroom behavior. *Journal of Child Psychiatry, 22,* 8–15.

Gray, G. E. (1986). Diet, crime and delinquency: A critique. *Nutrition Review, 44* (Suppl), 89–93.

Kanarek, R. B., & Marks-Kaufmann, R. (1991). *Nutrition and behavior: New Perspectives.* New York: Van Nostrand Reinhold.

Kozlowski, B. W. (1993). Megavitamin treatment of mental retardation in children: A review of effects on behavior and cognition. *Journal of Child and Adolescent Psychopharmacology, 2,* 307–320.

Kruesi, M. J. P., et al. (1986). Effects of sugar and aspartame on aggression and activity in children. *American Journal of Psychiatry, 144,* 944–945.

Lipton, M. A., Mailman, R. B., Nemeroff, C. B. (1979). Vitamins, megavitamin therapy and the nervous system. In R. J. Wurtman & J. J. Wurtman (Eds.), *Nutrition and the brain* (Vol 3, pp. 183–264). New York: Raven Press.

Needleman, H. L., Schell, A., Bellinger, D., Leviton, A., & Allred, E. N. (1990). The long-term effects of exposure to low doses of lead in childhood: An 11-year follow-up report. *New England Journal of Medicine, 322,* 83–88.

Pollitt, E., Viteri, F., Saco-Pollitt, C., Leibel, R. L. (1982). Behavioral effects of iron-deficiency anemia in children. In, E. Pollitt & R. L. Leibel (Eds.), *Iron deficiency: Brain biochemistry and behavior,* (pp. 195–208). New York: Raven Press.

Rock, C., & Yager, J. (1987). Nutrition and eating disorders: A primer for clinicians. *International Journal of Eating Disorders, 6,* 267–280.

Rowe, K. S., & Rowe, K. J. (1994). Synthetic food coloring and behavior: A dose response effect in a double blind placebo controlled, repeated measures study. *Journal of Pediatrics, 125,* 691–698.

Walter, T., de Andvaca, I., Castillo, M., Rivera, F., & Cobo, C. (1990). Cognitive effect at 5 years of age in infants who were anemic at 12 months: A longitudinal study. *Pediatric Research, 28,* 295.

Wender, E. H., & Lipton, M. A. (1980, October). *Final Report to the Nutrition Foundation.*

15 / Speech, Language, and Communication Interventions

Christiane A. M. Baltaxe

Communication delays and impairment come in a number of types and severities and are associated with a variety of risk and causative factors. These include environmental deprivation, intellectual deficiency, and etiological categories such as autism or brain injury, seizure disorder, or fetal alcohol syndrome. Language intervention is needed whenever a child displays communication skills that are not commensurate with chronological age. A child with a serious communication problem often requires intervention over a period of many years. Successful intervention is contingent on accurate identification, assessment, and planning. Children whose linguistic skills are below their skills in nonverbal cognitive areas may show more dramatic changes in language growth than youngsters where both linguistic and nonlinguistic skills are significantly below age level. Intervention usually is provided by a specialist, such as a speech-language pathologist, but it also may be implemented by a teacher, parent, or caregiver or other persons involved with the child's development.

Intervention begins with feedback to parents or caregivers and identification of community resources for the family. Feedback should provide information about the nature, scope, and severity of the youngster's communication problems and their impact on daily living skills, school performance, peer relationships, and the like. Some home environments reduce the opportunities for language use; others do not facilitate the youngster's better ways to communicate. Often parents anticipate their child's needs and adopt their own interpretations of their child's unconventional or delayed linguistic behavior. The clinician must teach parents and caregivers about the ways in which children communicate verbally and nonverbally, and identify the specific goals and procedures that are critical to their child's acquisition of linguistic skills. They must help parents maximize the opportunities and experiences that are conducive to linguistic and cognitive growth and the development of appropriate social interaction.

When planning intervention we must consider the age of the child; the child's attention span and frustration level; possible additional motor, visual, auditory, and cognitive deficits; as well as such factors as behavior and emotional problems. All these may affect the type of goals selected, the strategies and procedures used, and the time schedule projected for intervention. Whenever possible, cooperation with other disciplines is recommended.

In setting up therapy goals, we need to consider the normative sequences of language acquisition and where the youngster fits in. We also need to consider what features are shared with other youngsters with this specific disability and what are this youngster's specific needs. Patterns of normal development are the most reliable guide to determining aspects of language that the child is best equipped to learn at any given time. Therefore, we need to be cognizant of the general patterns and sequences of development. Whenever possible, developmental steps in normal acquisition should be mimicked. Within that context, however, the emphasis may be on speech, language, or communication (Lahey, 1988; Rosetti, 1995). Yet even when following a developmental model, we must address those communication behaviors that are considered linguistically deviant or at least unusual. For example, intervention with an autistic child must take into consideration the presence of immediate and delayed echolalia. The current approach is to consider the echolalia a source of strength and use it in developing the child's language by gradually breaking down the echolalic pattern. A child's linguistic strengths always should be used to build on when addressing communication weaknesses.

Most current intervention programs are designed on a deficit model. The clinician compares the youngster's linguistic skills with normal developmental expectations and identifies those elements that are deficient. A reliable baseline is important in order to provide a picture of the communication behaviors that the youngster is capable of and to measure the effects of a variety of intervention procedures. We as clinicians also will be called upon to decide what constitutes mastery of a particular linguistic behavior and when intervention should be terminated. For some language-impaired children, the acquisition of an adultlike linguistic system may not be a realistic goal. We must consider when the cost of intervention outweighs its benefits. Follow-up always should be part of the intervention plan, and when necessary, therapy should be resumed.

Intervention is most effective when the procedures are specific to the causes associated with the impairment. While similar goals may be pursued in teaching children with hearing impairment and autism, special techniques such as amplification, speech reading, cued speech, and/or manual sign-ing may be required for the hearing-impaired child to reach these goals. For autistic children, behavior modification techniques and reward systems may be needed. Since it is not always possible to find specific causes for communication problems, an accurate identification and description of the youngster's communication behaviors or lack thereof must provide the basis for intervention planning.

Therapy can be provided on an individual or group basis, and intervention can be clinician or child directed. In the adult-directed approach, targets for intervention as well as the stimuli and contextual controls are in the hands of the clinician. For example, in articulation therapy, the clinician selects the sounds and sequences of sounds and their positions in a word to be worked on. In the child-directed approach, the clinician determines what the child needs, but then the child takes the lead in selecting the linguistic and extra-linguistic contexts. The adult acts as a facilitator and guides the child in the language learning process. Hybrid approaches combine aspects of both. For example, the child may produce a contextual plural for nouns in a social interaction, without, however, providing the plural marker /-s/. The clinician may then repeat the child's utterance including the plural marker for the noun and then find additional examples to further elicit plural occurrences. Child-directed and hybrid approaches can be used by parents an teachers without disrupting the child's daily routines as well as in group or classroom settings. The emphasis is on target forms in meaningful naturally occurring contexts of interest to the child.

When selecting targets we should focus on those aspects of speech, language, and communication that interfere the most with effective communication. When considering comprehension or expression as a focus of intervention, we need to recognize that a great deal of evidence indicates that a child's spontaneous use of a language form, such as a sentence or a word, does not ensure the child can *always* comprehend this same form. This is common in young children. Likewise, autistic children often use language forms they do not comprehend (Baltaxe & Simmons, 1997; Chapman, 1992). There is some evidence that children learn to produce and use, although not necessarily comprehend, new lexical items more quickly and easily when the sounds and sound sequences in the new words are already established in the phonological repertoire.

Another consideration in intervention planning is the teachability of a particular linguistic target. Are the stimuli used demonstrable or picturable? Can the stimulus materials be organized easily? Are target forms evokable with meaningful questions and comments? Do occasions for the use of a specific linguistic or pragmatic structure occur frequently and naturally in the activities in which the child is engaged? Target behaviors and goals that are more teachable are also presumed to be learned more quickly by the child (Lahey, 1988).

Language Intervention

EARLY LANGUAGE INTERVENTION

When intervention focuses on the age range between 0 and 3 years, intervention usually involves at-risk infants and toddlers. Early intervention with at-risk children is crucial. Children who are identified early as presenting confirmed developmental delay or are at risk for displaying later delay and receive intervention early do better than those who are identified at later stages. The other factor that significantly contributes to the effectiveness of early intervention is the involvement of parents and caregivers (Rosetti, 1997). Therefore, we must do everything possible to increase the likelihood of early identification and parental involvement.

Infant stimulation programs for at-risk infants can be delivered at home or in developmental centers. Before they can take an active role in intervention, parents and caregivers need assistance in identifying communicative target behaviors. Although parents modify their input to the child, without guidance, they generally do not change it as effectively or as consistently as clinicians do to meet the child's needs (Manolson, 1992). Research has shown that communication development in normal children can be enhanced by specific strategies mothers use when talking to their infants (Rosetti, 1995). Effective mothers use short sentences and simplified grammar and keep within the parameters of a small core vocabulary that is relevant to the child's needs and is object centered. Their conversational interaction with their child is limited to the here and now, that is,

what a child can see and experience directly. These mothers also use heightened facial expressions and gestures in communicating. They make frequent use of questions and greetings. There is meaningful interactive turn-taking and prolonging of the communicative interchange between mother and child as well as the use and practice of verbal rituals associated with daily routines. All of these strategies are recommended in intervention with infants and toddlers identified with a delay or at risk for a delay in communication.

LANGUAGE INTERVENTION IN THE PRESCHOOL PERIOD

There are several current approaches to language intervention with preschoolers. One focuses on vocabulary building and improvement in sentence structure, with grammar playing a central role. An alternative approach stresses the social use of language, with grammar and vocabulary being incidental to the enhancement of social communication. In this pragmatic approach the clinician needs to make sure that there are opportunities for the child to use communication meaningfully. The child learns grammar and vocabulary as well as the rules of conversation all as part of pragmatic therapy. Familiar routines, such as birthday parties, food preparation, washing dishes, playing games, and going shopping or for a walk, can be structured in such a way as to demand increasing linguistic specificity. Thus, when a young child is developmentally at the 1-word level, the clinician needs to follow the child's attentional leads and use the words already in the child's vocabulary, gradually adding and expanding these to multiword utterances. Questions intended to encourage particular communicative functions may be asked, such as greetings or comments on topics.

Language-impaired children, just as normally developing children, learn better when there is novelty involved in the learning. For example, changing the color, size, and texture of items increases their novelty or informativeness. With children in the early stages of language development, self-talk and parallel talk also can be useful techniques implemented during facilitative play. Self-talk and parallel talk are particularly useful when children are shy or reluctant to interact verbally, since they make no demands on the child while at the same time providing a language model. Using simplified grammar the clinician, in self-talk, talks about his or her own actions while engaged in an activity with the child. In parallel talk the clinician talks about the child's actions, pairing his or her language with the child's actions and objects of interest.

Other useful techniques with children during the preschool period are the use of expansions, expatiations, recasting utterances, and buildups and breakdowns. In using expansions, we take the child's utterances and add relevant grammatical detail to what the child has said. In *expatiations* we comment on the child's initial utterance and extend some aspect of its meaning by contributing some new but relevant information. For example, when the child says "baby sleep," the clinician may say "yes the baby is tired, she needs a nap, time for the baby to go to sleep." In observational investigations of the verbal interactions of mothers and their young children, expansions and expatiations are typically among the features of adult input that are most strongly correlated with indices of linguistic growth (Fey, 1986). *Recasting* is a specific form of expansion. Instead of repeating the child's utterances and filling in missing grammatical and semantic details, recast utterances change the basic sentence type. For example, the child says "the baby is sick" and the clinician recasts the utterance into "Is the baby sick?" In *buildups* the clinician goes from a simple word in his or her own utterance to an utterance that is more complete. For example, the clinician may offer the child a pencil and say "here." He or she then may repeat the utterance and say "here, take the pencil." In *breakdowns* the clinician simplifies the earlier, more complete utterance. The clinician may say "eat your food" and then repeat "eat." In studies with normal children, both buildups and breakdowns were significantly associated with accelerated language growth (Fey, 1986; Lahey, 1988).

There is little doubt that an adult's utterances to young children in the initial stages of language development should be simplified along grammatical and semantic parameters and with developmental expectations in mind to meet the child's communication needs. What is not clear is whether communication directed toward language-deficient children should consist of very short, simple utterances that lack certain gram-

matical details or whether simple but grammatically well-formed utterances are better for the child's progress. Clinicians usually prefer to use simple, grammatically well-formed sentences instead of telegraphic speech.

INTERVENTION AT THE LATER PRESCHOOL AND KINDERGARTEN PERIOD

As the child progresses intervention begins to rely less on visual stimuli and the here and now and more on auditory stimuli, language processing, and the development of narrative skills. Narrative skills are addressed in story-based teaching. This technique introduces a series of self-developed or preprogrammed stories appropriate to the child's linguistic level, with familiar characters and events. These can be used in association with objects, videotapes, and picture stimuli. Children learn to sequence events and elaborate about characters and events.

A child with more advanced linguistic skills may be encouraged to talk about things not present in the immediate context with few or no props. Topics of interest to the child may be used to elicit linguistic target behaviors. For example, false assertions may be effective to get the child to produce particular types of linguistic structures in a spontaneous fashion, and various interchange techniques may be used to help the child correct errors in the use of target forms. The clinician may want to use schemata of familiar events or routine actions to predict events as well. Open questions, such as "What will your mom do tomorrow?" can be used to train temporal sequences and verb tense markers (Lahey, 1988).

LANGUAGE INTERVENTION DURING THE SCHOOL YEARS

In school-age youngsters there is more demand for auditory language processing and abstract language skills. Auditory processing relates to auditory memory, figure-ground discrimination, and auditory discrimination of sounds (Sloan, 1991). Poor auditory language processing skills frequently are associated with language impairment and also with attention deficit hyperactivity disorder. Deficits in abstract language represent language disabilities in the older child and can be found in autism, psychosis, and a variety of other disorders. These deficits affect school performance and the use of language in a social context.

Perhaps leave of heading *Intervention for auditory language processing and abstract language* With auditory language processing problems, usually the child is unable to follow directions. Intervention strategies and activities should be designed to improve the child's ability to remember, organize, and categorize tasks and instructions. For example, the youngster can be taught that tasks can be broken down into the following 6 steps: (1) What do I have to do? (2) Can I do it? (3) Do I have everything I need? (4) Is there a better way to do this? (5) Have I done what I am supposed to do? (6) What am I supposed to do after I am finished?

Background noise at home and at school should be kept at a minimum. Lengthy directions should be broken up into several simple ones. Teachers and parents need to speak at a slower rate with more expression in their voices. New concepts and new information should be rephrased and restated and the child given additional time to respond. The child also should be asked to repeat directions or concepts or silently rehearse the instruction until a task is completed. Whenever possible, the child should be given assignments in writing and allowed to use a tape recorder.

Suggested activities are having the child recount a movie, a favorite story, or television program, with emphasis on plot development, sequence of events, who the main characters are, what the child thinks about them, and possible alternative endings, or having the clinician tell or read a story followed by a series of related questions. Encouraging the child to listen for words that give cues about the order of events such as *now, later, after,* and *before* helps the child remember sequences of events. Memory games such as add-on games and games that require logic, strategies, and problem solving are also useful.

Visualization techniques are useful to encourage a child to make a mental picture or form an image of an activity, concept, or abstract idea. The child may need to learn how to organize time and activities in advance. The child should do homework assignments at a certain time every day without background noise (radio or TV), finish regular chores around the home at a particular time, and plan for the clothes to wear for the next day. Mak-ing written lists for chores and homework also helps the child to develop planning and organizational skills.

In the classroom it is a good idea to make sure that the child sits close to the teacher and the chalkboard. Establishing a buddy system, where a fellow student is available to answer questions and provide help when instructions are missed or forgotten, is very useful.

To improve auditory language processing skills and develop compensatory strategies, progressions (building on previously recalled sequences), memory games and expanded stories, and delayed or deferred recall activities are excellent techniques. In addition, the child should be encouraged to develop note-taking skills and to use mnemonic devices (Kelly, 1995; Sloan, 1991).

We also need to address problems with abstract language where the child has difficulties comprehending verbal asurdities, metaphors, synonyms, and/or the multiple meaning of words as well as solving problems and understanding inferences (Edwards & Lahey, 1996; Wiig & Semel, 1984). Since both auditory processing and abstract language skills interact with social communication skills, the latter should also be looked at closely and included in therapy whenever necessary. At home, the youngster should be encouraged to participate in family conversations and parents and caregivers should make it a point to include the youngster's daily activities and interests in such conversations (Brinton, 1989; Naremore, 1995; Norris, 1993).

Intervention with Speech Problems

The motor aspect of speech is operationally defined as including articulation, fluency, voice, and prosody or melody of speech. The type of intervention chosen depends on the type of identified deficit, age of the child, and other variables.

ARTICULATION

In articulation therapy the clinician assesses and identifies the sounds, sound combinations, and positions of sounds in a syllable or word for which the child shows delayed or deviant behaviors and then addresses these in remediation. As with language intervention, a developmental approach is used whenever possible. Sound patterns and regularities are important in articulation therapy. The phonological or sound system of a language is viewed as internally related and rule governed, with sets of sound more closely related to each other than to other sounds. For example, sounds such as /p/, /t/, and /k/ all are stop consonants, produced with total closure in the oral cavity and are characterized by labial, alveolar, and palatal or velar closure respectively. These sounds (/p/, /t/, /k/) are also unvoiced, that is, they are produced with vocal folds separated. The only feature that distinguishes them from /b/, /d/, and /g/ is a voicing feature. In the latter sounds the vocal folds are brought together. Commonalities in sounds are important in articulation therapy since they allow us to address groups of related sounds simultaneously. The positioning of sounds—that is, initial, medial, and final word positions—are equally important in identifying regularities. Commonalities among sounds and regularities in sound positioning can be reduced to simple rules, which form the basis for articulation therapy. Articulation therapy is generally clinician directed and includes drill exercises, kinesthetic and proprioceptive training relating to sound placement, and auditory training to improve auditory attention to and perception of specific speech sounds and auditory discrimination between and among sounds. Gradual shaping and approximations of speech sounds as well as self-monitoring of speech sound production is also important. In the drill exercises, the child may be required to practice the targeted sound or groups of sounds many times in isolation, in syllables, in words, and in a variety of phonetic contexts, with contexts becoming increasingly more complex and progressing from isolated sound productions to conversational speech.

When a child is nonverbal initially, oral motor exercises, such as blowing pieces of paper, and the use of a mirror to observe lip rounding may precede training of, say, the /f/ sound (Hodson, 1986; Hodson & Paden, 1991).

MOTOR SPEECH DISORDERS (DYSARTHRIC AND APRAXIC SPEECH)

Dysarthric Speech: Intervention with children expected to develop motor speech disorders can begin as early as 2 months of age (Love, 1992). The goals of early intervention frequently focus on feeding problems, prelinguistic skills, and stimulating language development. Dysarthric problems can range from mild deficits in speech sound production to totally unintelligible speech. Surgery, such as pharyngeal flap surgery, sometimes is considered a medical option for dysarthric speech in order to decrease velopharyngeal insufficiency and hypernasality and increase intelligibility. Prosthetic devices such as a palatal lift, an orthodontal device, also must be considered in treating severe dysarthria of speech (white, 1996).

Strengthening exercises to improve skills in respiration, phonation, resonance, and articulation often are part of the intervention program with dysarthria. Heightened awareness of correct articulation placement can be achieved through over-articulation, that is, exaggerated movement of the articulators (lips, tongue, velum). Repetitive drill exercises can be useful and should include verbal, visual, and/or instrumental feedback; the clinician's modeling of sounds and speech patterns also is useful. Helping youngsters make speech motor movements as conscious as possible is also useful in improving articulation and intelligibility in those with dysarthric speech, as are teaching self-correction and self-monitoring. When breath control is inadequate, breathing exercises often help to prolong breath control and increase control of expiratory breathing. Speech intelligibility may be improved by having children control their speech rate and use short phrases and timed inhalations. Phonation problems frequently relate to too much or too little tension in the vocal folds, resulting in pitch that is too high or too low or a voice that is breathy or harsh. Resonance problems can be treated through improving velopharyngeal function by therapy or through surgery and prothetics. When dysarthria is severe, alternative modes of communication also must be considered. Currently available augmentative communicative devices include a wide range of picture boards and electronic equipment that substitute for or supplement the youngster's primary method of language expression (Brookshire, 1992; Love, 1992; McNeil, 1997).

Apraxic Speech: In apraxia of speech, motor programming of speech is impaired. Intervention for apraxic speech generally involves intensive and systematic drills involving speech production and a variety of stimuli organized in a hierarchy of difficulty. An 8-step continuum approach which moves from limited, clinician assisted speech to volitional, purposeful speech productions is advocated by Rosenbek (1985). A task continuum that leads the youngster through a series of levels of difficulty are widely used. When setting up a task continuum for a particular youngster, the clinician must consider the phonetic features of target sounds, the frequency of occurrence of words or sounds, the position of target sounds or words within an utterance, utterance length and utterance complexity as well as stress characteristics. Love and Fitzgerald (1994) suggest that in developmental apraxia, the emphasis should be on phonetic placement of sounds through a combined use of auditory, visual, and tactile stimulation, such as listening to the sound, self-observation in the mirror while producing the targeted sounds, and feeling the contacts made by the articulators (lips, teeth, alveolar ridge, palate, velum, and tongue). Through repeated practice and exercises, the youngster with an apraxia of speech may move from nonspeech sounds or isolated speech sounds to syllables and words before moving to drills consisting of phrases and sentences or connected speech (e.g., moving from consonant to consonant-vowel, to consonant-vowel-consonant combinations, etc). The use of starter or carrier phrases, sound approximations and prolongations, drills in sound sequencing, alternating stress patterns, and silent rehearsal all are techniques used in the elimination of apraxic speech. Other approaches to apraxia include melodic intonation therapy, where words and sounds are produced melodically. Also used are gestures paired with speaking, tapping in rhythm to speech production, and pacing speech with a metronome as well as reading and using visual imagery. Other techniques include· relaxation and bio-feed-back. Techniques often are used in combination. Compensatory strategies and alternative systems may be needed when other approaches fail. Writing, gesturing, or the use of communication boards or electronic systems are alternatives to intervention (Moore, Yokston, Beukelman, 1991).

Dysfluency: The most commonly described feature of stuttering is its variability. Some environments and situations increase severity and frequency while others do not. In designing a program, we need to know when the child stutters most and to assess the severity of the stuttering. We need to deal with many aspects of the child's life that might possibly cause or exacerbate the stuttering. We may intervene with the child directly on a one-to-one basis, in a small group, or indirectly through the parents. Work with the child should be done in such a way that the youngster is unaware that speech is the focus of the interaction. Play situations and a calm and low-key atmosphere are recommended. Other activities with young children include talking while drawing, telephoning, echoing reading, picture naming, and speaking with puppets. Word games and card games also may be used to facilitate fluency.

A comprehensive approach, including stress monitoring and desensitization procedures, focuses on reducing conditions in the child's life that may exacerbate or maintain stuttering. Parent counseling and education can address improving parental listening practices and interactions with the child in an effort to reduce stress from speaking situations. Since speech rate and utterance length and complexity appear to be associated with stuttering, the child should be trained to speak at a somewhat slower than normal rate of speech. Intervention should progress from a requirement of single and 2-word utterance responses to longer and more complex utterances and responses in the context of the therapy situation and also include turn-taking practices.

"Easy" speech is a special technique for reduction of stuttering. For "easy" speech or "loose contacts" to occur, the tension in the articulators is reduced so that lips and tongue make light contact with any opposing surface during speech. In vowel production, easy onset of vowels can be trained by having the child feel a little breath escape prior to vowel production. Easy-onset vowels then can be shaped into actual words, such as "I" and "and," that young children frequently stutter. Making clear the difference between "hard" or "bumpy" (tensed articulators) and easy speech (articulators in light contact) helps the youngster monitor speech production. Using a slightly slower rate of speech and paying attention to hard and easy speech production can help a child overcome or improve stuttering blocks. Stuttering blocks consist of repetitions and prolongations of sounds, syllables or words that the stutterer is trying to avoid.

When there is marked physiological involvement, respiration and phonation also must be addressed and breathing patterns regulated. The youngster should be told to use a slower speech rate and be taught speech breathing and speech phrasing—how to coordinate speaking and breathing. Speech phrasing allows the youngster time at appropriate points in the utterance to take a breath and to organize linguistically and physiologically for the next part of the sentence.

In contrast to preschool children, school-age children are more aware of their problem and also may show more resistance to intervention. Stuttering blocks may be more prominent and youngsters habitually may use word substitutions or circumlocutions to avoid a stuttering block. Secondary characteristics in the form of tension of facial, neck, and trunk muscles also may be present in older youngsters with stuttering problems. The clinician uses the same techniques as with younger children, but play is now replaced by face-to-face interaction with the clinician and question-and-answer sessions about topics of interest. Spontaneous conversations, particularly with older school children, become a valuable tool for the practice of loose contact speech and ultimately to practice any stuttering modification strategies. Choral reading, rhythmic stimulation, masking, successive readings, altered inflection, singing, and whispering all have been used in approaches to remediate stuttering (Conture, 1990; Ham, 1986, 1990).

Voice and Prosody: Voice disorders come in a wide variety of etiologies. When a voice disorder is identified, consultation with a specialist, such as an otolaryngologist, becomes important. Intervention in voice disorders is divided into medical surgical and behavioral voice therapy. Medical surgery procedures are sometimes required. when indicated by the nature of the voice problem. Voice therapy by a specialist such as a speech-language pathologist is indicated postoperatively after a period of total voice rest.

Behavioral voice therapy, in cases where surgery is not required or postoperatively, focuses on teaching the child "vocal hygiene," that is, teaching the child about the functions of the larynx and strategies for altering various aspects of voice production. Children who have polyps removed from their vocal folds need to be taught how to be less abusive of their vocal mechanism to prevent a recurrence, which often is the result of the shouting or screaming but also of habitual coughing and throat clearing and talking over loud noise. In these vocal activities the vocal cords are slammed together with excessive force. Excessive effort and muscular strain in phonation and force of vocal fold closure can be reduced through several techniques. As with stuttering, children need to be trained to produce an "easy" onset of voice, to prevent "hard" glottal attacks at voice initiation, and to use a slightly breathy quality at voice initiation. A yawn-sigh technique to relax laryngeal tension and a chewing technique aimed at muscle relaxation (exaggerated jaw movement and exaggerated chewing movement) also can be used to maintain a healthy vocal apparatus and a healthy voice.

In some voice disorders the vocal folds do not come together (adduct) with sufficient force, which results in a weak and breathy-sounding voice. These disorders may have psychological and/or physical causes, such as vocal cord paralysis. For these conditions, intervention techniques are the reverse of those just described and are aimed at increasing the force of vocal fold closure. Isometric exercises, such as pushing down strongly on a chair while simultaneously phonating, using a hard glottal attack to initiate phonation, or using coughing or throat clearing as preparatory to phonation are effective strategies. Techniques to improve vocal endurance include warm-up and cool-down exercises and stress breathing exercises to optimize vocal output.

When there is excessive loudness and pitch modulation, relaxation techniques in association with biofeedback techniques can be very helpful (Boone & McFarlane, 1988; Wilson, 1987). Excessive loudness and pitch modulation affect prosody or the melody of speech as well. When prosodic disturbances are present, modeling by the clinician, drill exercises, and self-monitoring are important. Visual feedback is a useful technique. Pitch, loudness, and durational features of the youngster's speech are acoustically extracted and visually displayed on a screen, with the clinician simultaneously modeling and displaying the pitch, loudness, and durational features of the same speech output. Self-monitoring and gradual approximations are used in the process (Andrews, 1988).

Intervention for Language and Speech with Hearing Impaired Youngsters: Hearing loss in a youngster can range from mild to severe. When hearing impairment is severe, assistive listening devices, hearing aids, cochlear implants, and vibro-tactile devices as well as manual or total communication approaches should be considered.

Many factors must be considered in planning intervention, including type and degree of hearing loss, age at which hearing loss occurred, rapidity of onset, and such individual factors as intelligence and personality, family life, educational background, ethnic background, as well as the presence of other disabling conditions (Northern & Downs, 1991). The complex relationship between the use of residual hearing and motor development of speech forms the basis for any speech-language intervention programs for children with hearing impairment, Hearing impaired youngsters commonly also have problems in respiration, phonation, resonation, and articulation, which must be also be addressed. Intervention must address auditory training and use of residual hearing for the auditory perception of speech sounds, the production of meaningful speech, and the use of other modalities, such as visual or kinesthetic to establish speech representation. The use of alternative methods of communication when necessary is important. If the youngster wears a hearing aid, care must be taken that it is working. Very young children with impaired hearing should receive language stimulation. The multisensory syllable-unit approach is the approach most widely used with hard-of-hearing children (Ling, 1989). This approach uses structural learning whenever possible within the developmental model, using a variety of sensory modalities (auditory, visual, and tactile) in speech training stimulation. The syllable is the basic unit of stimulation, and the child learns through imitation of speech patterns. Speech sounds are introduced gradually in a predetermined order. The first sounds taught—those thought to be easiest to learn—are the labial consonants. A hierarchy of planned teaching usually begins at the syllable level and progresses to the production of spontaneous meaningful speech.

Another approach, the auditory global approach, rests on the assumption that a child will develop a great deal of intelligible speech spontaneously, if he or she receives sufficient auditory input in the form of fluent connected speech. The child learns by reproducing the speech patterns heard. Success depends on the age level at which the intensive auditory stimulation begins as well as on the child's hearing level (Calvert & Silverman, 1983).

When hearing is severely impaired, other methods of teaching language include a sign language, such as American Sign Language (ASL). In American Sign Language, hand shapes and gestures represent words, phrases, and ideas. Facial expressions and other body movements are used to indicate differences in meaning. Fingerspelling uses hands and fingers to form different shapes to represent letters of the alphabet to spell out words and sentences. Speech-reading or lip-reading as well as cued speech, a system of hand shapes representing spoken sounds to improve speech reading (Hyde & Power, 1991), all are methods of communication for hard-of-hearing children. In a total communication approach, all available avenues are used including spoken language, body language, signing, and written language. Assistive mechanical devices, such as telecommunication devices, help deaf individuals communicate over telephone lines. Other devices allow deaf individuals to read captions for television dialogues. Newly developed artificial ears also can help hard-of-hearing individuals who cannot benefit from the use of hearing aids.

Conclusion

Providing intervention for speech, language, and communication skills is a complex process that requires specialized knowledge and training. When linguistic deficits are suspected, referral to a speech language specialist should be a first stop. Adequate speech, language, and communication are crucial components in a child's development. Optimal success rests on early identification and early intervention.

REFERENCES

Andrews, M. (1988). *Voice therapy for adolescents.* Boston: Little, Brown.

Baltaxe, C. (1997). Communication behaviors associated with psychiatric behaviors. In T. Ferrand & R. L. Bloom (Eds.), *Organic and neurogenic disorders of communication* (pp. 51–83). Boston: Allyn & Bacon.

Boone, D. R., & McFarlane, S. C. (1988). *The voice and voice therapy* (4th ed). Englewood Cliffs, NJ: Prentice-Hall.

Brinton, B. (1989). *Conversational management with language impaired children: pragmatic assessment and intervention.* Rockville, MD: Aspen.

Brookshire, R. H. (1992). *An introduction to neurogenic communication disorders* (4th ed). Englewood Cliffs, NJ: Prentice-Hall.

Calvert, D. R., & Silverman, S. R. (1983). *Speech and deafness* (rev. ed). Washington, DC: Alexander Graham Bell Association for the Deaf.

Chapman, R. (1992). *Processes in language acquisition and disorders.* St. Louis, MO: C. V. Mosby.

Conture, E. G. (1990). *Stuttering* (2nd ed.). Englewood Cliffs, NJ: Prentice-Hall.

Edwards, J., Lahey, M. (1996). Auditory lexical decisions of children with specific language impairment. *Journal of Speech and Hearing Research, 39* (6); 1263–1273.

Fey, M. (1986). *Language intervention with young children.* Needham, MA: Allyn & Bacon.

Ham, R. (1986). *Techniques for stuttering therapy.* Englewood Cliffs, NJ: Prentice-Hall.

Ham, R. (1990). *Therapy of stuttering: preschool through adolescence.* Englewood Cliffs, NJ: Prentice-Hall.

Hodson, B. (1986). *The assessment of phonological processes.* Danville, IL: Interstate Press.

Hodson, B. W., & Paden, E. P. (1991). *Targeting intelligible speech: A phonological approach to remediation* (2nd ed.). Austin, TX: PRO-ED.

Hyde, M. B., & Power, D. J. (1991). Teachers' use of simultaneous communication. *American Annals of the Deaf, 136,* 381–387.

Kelly, D. (1995). *Central auditory processing disorder.* San Antonio, TX: Communication Skill Builder.

Lahey, M. (1988). *Language disorders and language development.* New York: Macmillan.

Ling, D. (1989). *Foundations of spoken language for hearing-impaired children.* Washington, DC: A. G. Bell Association for the Deaf.

Love, R. (1992). *Childhood motor speech disability.* New York: Maxwell Macmillan International.

Love, R. J. (1992). *Motor speech disability.* Columbus, OH: Merrill Publishing.

Love, R. J., & Fitzgerald, M. (1994). Is the diagnosis of developmental apraxia of speech valid? *Australian Journal of Human Communication Disorders, 12,* 170–178.

Manolson, A. (1992). *It takes two to talk.* Toronto: Haven Center.

McNeil, M. R., Rosenbek, J. C., & Aronson, A. E. (Eds.) (1985). *The dysarthrias: Physiology, acoustics, perception, management.* San Diego: College Hill Press.

McNeil, M. (1997). *Clinical management of sensorimotor speech disorders.* New York: Thieme.

Moore, C., Yokston, K., & Beukelman, D. (1991). *Dysarthria and apraxia of speech: perspectives on management.* Baltimore, MD: P. H. Brookes Pub. Co.

Naremore, R. (1995). *Language intervention with school-aged children: conversation, narrative and text.* San Diego: Singular Publishing Group.

Norris, J. (1993). *Whole language intervention for school-age children.* San Diego: Singular Publishing Group.

Northern, J. L., & Downs, M. (1991). *Hearing in children* (4th ed.). Baltimore, MD: Williams & Wilkins.

Rosenbek, J. C. (1985). Treating apraxia of speech. In D. Johns (Ed.), *Clinical management of neurogenic communication disorders.* Austin, TX: PRO-ED.

Rosetti, L. (1997). Epidemiology of risk and socio-communicative development in medically fragile children. In C. T. Ferrand & R. L. Bloom (Eds.), *Organic and neurogenic disorders of communication* (pp. 9–28). Boston: Allyn & Bacon.

Rosetti, L. (1995). *Communication intervention: Birth to three.* San Diego: Singular Press.

Sloan, C. (1991). *Treating auditory processing difficulties in children.* San Diego: Singular Press.

White, P. (1996). *Taking time to talk: a resource for apraxia therapy, esophageal speech training, aphasia therapy, and articulation therapy. 2d ed.* Boston: Butterworth-Heinemann.

Wilson, D. K. (1987). *Voice problems in children* (3rd ed.). Baltimore, MD: Williams & Wilkins.

Wiig, E. H., & Semel, E. (1984). *Language assessment and intervention for the learning disabled* (2nd ed.). Columbus, OH: Charles Merrill Publishing.

16 / Family Treatment

Allan M. Josephson and Frank J. Moncher

Family treatment includes any intervention that focuses on altering the interactions between or among family members with the intent of improving the functioning of the family as a unit and the functioning of the individual members who comprise the family. Family treatments provide ways to alter the patterns of interaction between family members that cause distress within them. When such distress within children and adolescents becomes clinically significant, family therapy becomes an important component in the treatment of the resulting psychiatric disorder.

This chapter emphasizes an intergrated approach to the practice of family treatment. It focuses on providing a conceptual basis for intervention and a clinical guide toward effective interventions with families. "Family treatment" refers to the numerous ways in which clinicians can intervene with families: with the entire family system, with dyadic subgroups, or with individual members. Any such intervention—behavioral, psychological, or educational—directed at impacting change in the symptoms of a child or adolescent with a psychiatric disorder is subsumed under family treatment. The term *family therapy* is utilized in certain instances to enhance readability, yet the broader view connoted by the term *family treatment* is the focus of this chapter.

Formats for these interactions include conjoint family treatment, concurrent family treatment, and multiple family groups. Conjoint family treatment refers to sessions in which all family members are treated in the same room simultaneously. Concurrent family treatment refers to family therapy and individual therapy conducted concurrently, either by the same clinician or different clinicians. Finally, multiple family groups are meetings of several families, all of whom have an individual member with a specific problem. In each of these varieties, sessions are typically held once a week and can last as long as 2 hours, although there is wide variation in terms of the frequency of encounters.

All family therapies share a key assumption:

Families must be involved in clinical interventions with children and adolescents because they can directly contribute to the worsening or amelioration of their child's symptoms. There are different views of the family's role in the evolution of a child's psychopathology. Family functioning can be categorized as contributing to the emotional and behavioral disorders of children or, alternatively, as attempts to respond to the disorders. In some situations it may be a complex combination of both directional effects. A child with a biologic vulnerability may stress a family environment, which may, at the same time, respond in ways that either worsens or improves the condition. Effective family interventions are based on a thorough data base of history and observations that leads to a rational and empathic approach to the family and its role in psychopathology.

Family therapy shares some characteristics with other treatments. Concepts in individual psychotherapy, such as developing an alliance, working through, and dealing with resistance, are helpful in conducting effective family interventions. Family therapy also includes a clear behavioral emphasis. Clinicians observe specific behaviors and design plans to alter them through intervening in interactional patterns associated with these behaviors. Family therapy shares characteristics with group therapy. Pragmatically, there is more than one individual receiving clinical attention. Conceptually, individuals are viewed as performing functions for the group as a whole. In family therapy, however, roles and hierarchies do not evolve solely out of group interactions but also are assigned by biologic relationship of parent to child and sibling to sibling. Further, the shared history of participants is clearly more influential than that experienced by group therapy members. Finally, because family interactions observed in therapy reflect enduring patterns outside the therapy experience, they indicate a pervasive effect on the internalized world of its members, in contrast to the less pervasive effects of group therapy interactions on its members.

Antecedents

The development of family therapy in this century has been fostered by the work of many influential figures and has gone through several phases. In the early part of this century, child guidance clinics recognized that the problems of children were embedded in a family context, yet the primary focus of clinical intervention remained the mind of the child. The psychiatrist treated the child, while the mother or parents were seen by a social worker.

In the 1940s and 1950s, clinicians who had psychoanalytic orientations were increasingly dissatisfied with individual treatments. They either believed the treatments ineffective or observed effective treatments being undermined by families that were having difficulty adjusting to therapeutically induced changes in their children. Many of these individuals experimented with seeing the entire family simultaneously and, while not disbanding psychodynamic notions entirely, began to take a broader view of the psychodynamic process. Their efforts at improvement were typified by Nathan Ackerman (1958). This pioneering work merged with a revolutionary period in psychotherapy during which the family became defined as a system, a group whose interactions were seen as interdependent on each other member. A wave of clinicians began applying the concepts of general systems theory (Von Bertalanffy, 1968) to clinical work with families, including Carl Whitaker, Donald Jackson, and Salvador Minuchin.

Child and adolescent psychiatrists and family systems clinicians interacted minimally. The acceptance of family treatments by the general medical community was impeded by a prevailing view in which systems theorists saw medicine as linearly reductionistic, reducing complex phenomena to single causes. This climate added to the difficulties associated with a paradigm shift from a dyadic patient-therapist relationship to a complex group, interactive process (McDermott & Char, 1974). Psychiatrists experienced the cognitive challenge of mastering a new approach and the affective challenge of questioning much of their individually oriented training. Such challenges precluded an easy transition to systems thinking for most psychiatrists.

In the last decade, a shift toward eclecticism has occurred in which systemic perspectives are being integrated with individual psychodynamic, educational, and behavioral approaches to assess and treat the psychiatric disorders of children and adolescents. Family treatments now include parent training and education and individual work with parents and children as logical continuations of the initiations of family treatments. Family treatments are no longer characterized by one specific approach or school of family therapy but emphasize a pragmatic eclecticism, utilizing specific approaches for specific problems. (See also Chapters 17 and 21.)

This brief overview of the antecedents of current family treatments can be supplemented by consulting reviews (Broderick & Schrader, 1991; Silver & Liebman, 1986) and textbooks on family therapy (Barker, 1992; Levant, 1984; Nichols & Everett, 1986).

Conceptual Frameworks

An integrated approach to family treatment must include not only the systemic and psychodynamic perspectives but also must consider developmental issues and behavioral theories (Pinsof, 1995). The systemic perspective states that individuals in a family system are viewed as interdependent. No change occurs in a family without everything else changing accordingly, and, in any change process, the family desires to maintain homeostasis or equilibrium. In clinical situations, symptoms are viewed as serving a purpose for the family, and each family member is presumed to act in a way that would oppose symptomatic improvement in the presenting patient. In addition to the clinician's conscious efforts at change, natural developmental changes can have a destabilizing effect on a family system, such as the youngest child in the family leaving home. The principle of homeostasis suggests that a family might act in a way to resist the child's independence. Therapeutic interventions at such times manage the tension inherent in such change, try to prevent families from reverting to old patterns, and try to help families achieve a new equilibrium, as parents without dependent children but with functioning young adults. Family therapy approaches that share some of the characteristics of the systemic view are the structural approach (Minuchin, 1974) and the strategic approach (Madanes, 1991).

An integrated view of family treatment also emphasizes the individual development and unique life experience of each family member. This perspective presumes that a child's life experience in family relationships becomes internalized. These internalizations prepare the way for choice of a life partner and new family formation. When a parent's family-of-origin life experiences are negative, such as physical abuse, parental intrusiveness, or parental overprotectiveness, they predispose the individual to pathologic family interaction. In some measure, they predict how a parent will negotiate the transitions of the family life cycle in the next generation. The family's negotiation of life cycle tasks and the interactions that accompany it contribute to the definition of the inner world of the developing child. Treatments that have elements of this approach are object relations family therapy (Scharff & Scharff, 1987), intergenerational family therapy (Bowen, 1978) and contextual family therapy (Boszormenyi-Nagy & Ulrich, 1991).

An integrated approach to family treatments also requires an understanding of behavioral elements, such as the parents' use of behavioral management strategies. Child behavior is a function of environmental contingencies—positive reinforcement, negative reinforcement, and punishment—with parents being the primary sources of such contingencies. Family treatment often reveals deficits in parenting skills that may respond to parent training and education regarding child development and behavior management. Behavioral approaches to family treatment include behavioral family therapy (Griest & Wells, 1983) and functional family therapy (Barton & Alexander, 1981).

CASE EXAMPLE

Karen Jones, a 14-year-old with anorexia nervosa, is the eldest of 2 children. Mrs. Jones, a dependent woman, regularly gets advice from her mother, who is quite critical of her parenting of Karen. Mr. Jones is a controlling and, at times, tyrannical man who has difficulty with intimacy. Mr. and Mrs. Jones initially met each other's needs but problems developed in the childbearing years. Mr. Jones withdrew, becoming overly involved in work, while Mrs. Jones became invested in her young child as a source of emotional support.

From a systems view, Mother's overinvolvement with her daughter is a response to a conflicted marriage. Karen's symptoms allow the rift in the marriage to go unexplored and detour potential conflict. Father's excessive involvement in work is a response to his failure to negotiate an intimate relationship with his wife, who is emotionally close to her family of origin and to her daughter.

From a psychodynamic view, Mrs. Jones's overinvolvement with Karen and her marriage to a dominant man are related to her own sense of ineffectiveness, shaped by an intrusive parent-child relationship in her family of origin. Mr. Jones's withdrawal arises from his own sense of inadequacy with its own developmental origins. He attempts to shore up this deficit through business success. Karen, the recipient of a great deal of maternal attention, does not develop internal mechanisms for self-esteem regulation and is excessively dependent on the external environment to enhance her self-regard. Her response to her sense of ineffectiveness is to restrict her food intake and lose weight. Mother's overinvolvement with Karen and Father's detachment from family life prevent them from being aware of, and altering, their developmentally based inner models of self.

From a behavioral viewpoint, Karen's lack of eating receives positive reinforcement from Mother through attention, while also being negatively reinforced by allowing her to avoid normal adolescent developmental activities such as dating and driving. Also, Mrs. Jones's misinterpretation of some of Karen's autonomous strivings reflects an inadequate knowledge base regarding adolescent development.

In addition to clinical rationale, findings from theoretical and research activity offer support for the integration of systemic and individual treatments. Family theorists such as David Reiss (1989) and child development researchers such as Robert Emde (1983) have described how the development of mental representations, or the child's inner world, is generated from a relational context. Prominent clinical models in psychiatry, the biopsychosocial (Engel, 1977) and the goodness of fit (Thomas & Chess, 1980), have emphasized that biologically vulnerable individuals develop symptoms only in certain interactional contexts. Finally, the psychodynamic perspectives of object relations and self psychology include family interaction as part of their theory building, although not directly applied in clinical practice.

We now move from background material relevant to family treatments to describing the treatments and their various aspects. First we review the clinical task—what we do and who does it. This is followed by a description of clinical process, the different phases that often occur in family treatment. Then we review specific methods, or techniques, of intervention—how we do family treatment.

The Clinical Task

GOALS OF FAMILY TREATMENT

A family usually becomes involved in treatment through the presentation, by the parent(s), of a symptomatic child or adolescent. Family treatment is recommended because a clinical formulation has indicated the need to address family factors. The first goal of family treatment must be the relief of the child's presenting symptoms. Family treatment involves other goals, but all other goals are derivatives of the attempt to address the presenting symptom, usually described as residing within an identified patient. To meet these goals, the clinician must develop an alliance with the family and thereby enlist their efforts in supporting the needs of the identified patient.

Symptoms often are associated with disturbed family functioning in the areas of family: structure, communication, belief, and regulation of child development. Family treatment attempts to alter these underlying processes and, as a result, ameliorate presenting symptoms. When individual motivations, unfinished developmental tasks, and psychodynamic factors give rise to problematic family interactions, our goals include altering those factors.

A core tenet of family treatment is that any intervention in the family has the potential to benefit other, asymptomatic members. As therapy proceeds, its scope naturally broadens to where the individual needs of all family members are understood and addressed. This broader outcome is an implicit goal in all family treatments, one with preventive implications.

INDICATIONS

Treatment of the family always is indicated, because the family is so critically a part of children's lives. The questions become: "Should work proceed with subgroups or the whole family?" "What sequence of intervention is appropriate?" "What will be the impact of working with individual, subsystem or whole group?" The most important consideration is how the clinician shall approach the family. The nature of the approach depends on whether the family is etiologically important in the onset and evolution of the disorder, in which case the clinician *empathically explores* and elucidates the role of family conflict in a child's disorder, or whether family interactions are seen as a response to illness within the child. In this instance, the clinician educates and *empathically supports* the family.

Neurologic disorders such as mental retardation and autism, medical disorders such as cystic fibrosis and diabetes, and psychiatric disorders with strong biologic components such as schizophrenia, require empathic support of families. The stresses faced by families of such ill children are unique and, often, overwhelming. Education, family support groups, respite care for children, and linkage with relevant agencies are all important adjuncts to supportive family treatment.

In the following instances, more intensive family treatment should be offered. With empathic exploration and persistent application of treatment efforts, symptoms in the child and family will improve.

The Clinical Presentation Is an Interactional Problem: Problems such as a child running away from home, the physical and sexual abuse of a child, aggression directed toward a parent, and separation anxiety all present as interactional problems. In addition, virtually any childhood behavior problem requires healthy parenting responses, and such problems are indications for working with the family. Treatments range from basic parent education to formalized family therapy.

Parental Psychopathology Precludes Effective Parenting: Parental psychopathology, such as substance abuse or aggressive behavior, often is unmasked by the challenge of a child's developmental needs. If a child is of a difficult temperament, the stress is magnified. Family treatment can address parent-child mismatch of temperament and recognize the contribution of parental psychopathology to the interactional problem.

Psychiatric Disorders with Identified Family Contributions: As research in developmental psychopathology progresses (Rutter & Rutter, 1993), family concomitants of disorders are being more clearly defined. The disorders for which there is the most empirical support for family treatments include separation anxiety, eating disorders, substance abuse, conduct disorders, and psychosomatic disorders (Diamond, Serrano, Dicky, & Sonis, 1996).

Psychiatric Disorders with a Secondary Family Emphasis: Major depression and attention deficit hyperactivity disorders are examples of disorders in which biologic factors are given primary etiological emphasis. The biologic vulnerabilities in these disorders, however, can be ameliorated or exacerbated by family response. (Barkley, 1990) The presence of significant psychosocial vulnerabilities in these children also suggests that intervention with families could facilitate adjustment.

The etiology of many child and adolescent disorders remains poorly understood. As a result, both types of family intervention, empathic support and empathic exploration, frequently are necessary in the same case. This broad approach may be necessary in families whose child has both a distinct biological and psychological dysfunction. It is possible, for example, for a family with a child with a neurologically based learning disorder to demonstrate overprotective behaviors.

QUALIFICATIONS OF CLINICIANS

An individual providing family treatments also should be trained in individual therapy. Family therapy is a type of psychotherapy, and the clinician should build on the basic constructs of psychotherapy. As an example, many clinicians acknowledge that treating families mobilizes significant countertransference and must guard against their own, personal family situation from intruding upon the therapeutic process. With this

foundation, the clinician then can develop an understanding of systems thinking. The techniques that are learned in studying systems should be integrated into a theoretical base that considers individual, intrapsychic development. A clinician with such a background is trained to provide an effective, integrated approach to family treatment. Cross-cultural exposure also would be an important component of a clinician's qualifications because the diversity of presentation of families is strongly influenced by culture.

The Clinical Process

The following description of a sequential, integrated approach to family treatment is offered as a clinical guide. The predominant approach to the family will be one of empathic exploration, attempting to address family processes associated with pathology. The interventions described in that approach are technically more difficult than those involved supporting the family of an ill child. Family treatments may not utilize all phases, and each phase, when experienced, may not occur in the order offered. The clinical process described is an attempt to cover the complex phenomena of family treatments.

STABILIZE THE CRISIS

Clinical disorders often present acutely, as crises. In order to stabilize a crisis, interventions with family and other systems often are needed, which may include removing a child from the home for a psychiatric hospitalization. Clinicians may need to utilize community resources, such as shelters for runaway children, emergency foster care, or other family members, to help stabilize a situation. Acute pharmacologic interventions may accompany these systems interventions.

CASE EXAMPLE

Kristen was receiving psychotherapy for depressive symptoms. She and her mother had a hostile, dependent relationship, and, after an argument about Kristen's boyfriend, her mother demanded she leave the home. She yelled, "You'll never come back here again," took all of Kristen's clothes, and threw them out in the front yard, locking her out of the house. Kristen called her doctor saying "I don't know where to go." After crisis intervention, it became clear that Kristen had an older brother who had recently married and was willing to care for her, at least on a short-term basis.

Frank, a husky 16 ½-year old, was admitted for evaluation of aggression. He stated, "I want to kill my father." The crisis assessment revealed that Frank and his father had an increasingly fractious relationship over the previous 3 years. His father believed in corporal punishment and continued to attempt to discipline his son in this manner. This only increased Frank's noncompliance. Frank's mother begged his father to stop this type of discipline, to no avail. On the night of admission to hospital, Frank and his father got into a physical altercation during which Frank struck his father and left the house, looking for a gun. His mother called the police, who brought him to a psychiatric unit for evaluation. He was admitted and, after a brief evaluation, it was determined he should not return home but should go live with his uncle.

Merrilee MacGregor, a 15-year-old female, was referred by her maternal grandmother with whom she was living. She had been expelled from school, been increasingly oppositional, and demonstrated depressive symptoms with a suggestion of suicidal ideation. Merrilee would return to her mother's home for periods of time only to get into conflicts with her mother, Mandy, and her mother's live-in boyfriend, Bob. Mandy and Bob had two younger boys, Jacob, 4 years, and Jeremy, 6 years. Merrilee was hospitalized to ensure safety, complete a diagnostic evaluation, and initiate pharmacotherapy. An effort was made to have her return home to be parented by her mother and Bob.

PARENT EDUCATION

Clinical problems may present less acutely and, in these instances, as well as when crises resolve, an educative approach gives parents immediate direction. Here we offer suggestions regarding child management that can be understood and implemented readily by many parents. Parent training and education may be sufficient to interrupt behavioral problems, particularly when the problems are mild or parents are merely inexperienced. Problems related to limit-setting, fostering a child's independence, and understanding a child's developmental needs often respond to didactic interventions and behavioral plans.

CASE EXAMPLE

Mr. and Mrs. Fleming brought their son for evaluation. They believed he had attention deficit hyperactivity disorder, obsessive-compulsive disorder, and Tourette's disorder. The clinician, in evaluating the symptoms, found the parents had trouble setting limits on him. They attributed his saying "Shut up" and "I hate you" to attention deficit disorder. When the clinician assured the parents that such disorders did not absolve their son from individual responsibility, Mr. Fleming offered, "You know, my parents have been telling us that. They think he can control this." A subsequent review of parenting revealed the parents had been infertile for a number of years and treated their son in a special manner. The parents welcomed guidance and directions about being more consistent and expecting behavioral compliance. In 2 brief follow-up sessions, they described much improved behavioral control of their 6-year-old.

When education is partially effective or completely ineffective, the clinician likely has observed parental psychopathology or marital conflict underlying the inability of parents to respond to education. This information prepares for intervention in family interaction.

CASE EXAMPLE

During Merrilee's hospitalization and in the following course of outpatient treatment, her mother, Mandy, and mother's boyfriend, Bob, were instructed in providing Merrilee consistent discipline. In addition to offering behavioral management techniques, the treating clinician discussed how a nurturant stance can facilitate a child's acceptance of limits. They were unable to implement changes. Mandy related to her daughter as a sister would, indulging her when consistent discipline was indicated. Efforts to get Mandy and Bob to work together to set limits on Merrilee were unsuccessful, as she accurately perceived that Bob had no sanctioned role in the family. Merrilee's tyrannical, aggressive behavior toward her 6-year-old half brother necessitated an intervention in family process.

INTERVENTION IN FAMILY PROCESS

At this point, the clinician sees the entire family and notes patterns of interaction that are maintaining the clinical problem. The clinician challenges the family to utilize new patterns of interacting and challenges the individuals in the family to adopt new coping mechanisms. Altering interaction through the use of some of these techniques may eliminate some family problems and provide opportunities for improved adaptation by all family members. Often, however, these interventions are met with resistance; the system desires homeostasis, and individual family members have their own reasons for resisting change. An intervention in family process may then lead to a review of the clinical needs of the individuals in the family.

CONSIDERING THE INDIVIDUAL PERSPECTIVE

When techniques to alter family interaction are not successful, the most common reason is the individual motivation of a family member or members. By considering the internalized world of family members and using individual interviews to explore this world, a clinician can understand resistances and plan effectively for them. It is not uncommon at this stage for family treatment to broaden to individual interventions with the symptomatic child, either parent, or the marriage. (See also Chapter 21.) A caveat in this broadening of effort is to avoid the risk of being drawn in to pathologic family processes, such as "scapegoating" an individual member.

CASE EXAMPLE

Mother, Jill, asked to see the clinician after a family treatment session that explored her separation from Kristen, her 14-year-old daughter with anorexia nervosa, and her relationship with her husband. In the individual session, Jill immediately launched into a vivid personal narrative. "The thing that I've become aware of is that I rely on Kristen a lot. I'm dependent on her. She's always there for me and aware of what my needs are. I know this isn't healthy. From the moment I conceived her, she has been important to me. She was the baby I wanted more than anything else and, right now, I love her more than anything else in the world."

This revealing interview communicated to the clinician that a renegotiation of the marital relationship was indicated and that any intervention effort would have to attend to Jill's need for acceptance, which she had fulfilled through her close relationship with Kristen. Concomitantly, the effects of this close, special relationship on Kristen's development included her dependency and selflessness, which required the clinician's individual attention.

MARITAL THERAPY

A clinician may notice an evolution toward parents considering their relationship after the family intervention. Such an evolution is usually an indication of a deepening process of family treatment. Developmental histories prior to marriage, issues surrounding the choice of a partner, and the nature of the family life cycle come into a new perspective for individuals who are considering their child difficulties. This stage typically unfolds later in treatment when a child's disorder is stable, permitting parents to reflect on their possible contributions to the clinical problems, but they also may occur earlier in the treatment sequence.

CASE EXAMPLE

Fourteen-year-old Mary is hospitalized for noncompliant behavior and suicide risk. The first family session includes her mother and stepfather as well as her grandmother. The themes shift quickly from Mary's depressive symptoms and behavior problems to marital conflict, with Father leaving the session early, in anger related to Mother's indifference.

One of the clinicians follows the distraught man into the hall and listens to his angry venting. The other clinician remains in the room, processing with the family what had happened, asking each why they thought he had left and how to handle his return. As stepfather is able to calm himself and return, the clinicians structure the session by stating that, in addition to Mary's problems, it is apparent the parents also are having some difficulty. Grandmother and Mary are asked to leave to allow the parents to talk alone. It becomes clear that the viability of the marriage is tenuous and requires further intervention. Subsequent marital treatment bolsters the marriage and nuclear family unit by increasing Father's involvement in the family and decreasing Grandmother's involvement.

DEALING WITH SIBLINGS

Family treatment may reveal problems with other siblings. Improvement in one family member affects other members and requires their adaptation. Adaptation required of siblings may reveal that the family interactive process has been toxic to their development as well. Patterns of sibling symptomatology may differ related to such variables as a child's sex, temperament, intelligence, and birth order.

CASE EXAMPLE

Neil Thompson, a 36-year-old lawyer, was involved in family treatment of his 15-year-old son, Rodney. His wife, Nell, and 12-year-old son, Brian, were also in attendance. Much of the treatment dealt with Father, who had very high expectations for Rodney, athletically and academically. Rodney was rebelling against these expectations, on the verge of dropping out of school, and had recently left the high school's swim team. In the process of treatment, the clinician noted that Rodney, while very angry, made a compelling case that he felt he was living his life for his father rather than himself. As treatment proceeded, Brian appeared submissive, tentative, and insecure and became of more concern to the clinician. Brian's mother volunteered that she was more concerned about Brian as well.

Treatment continued to foster Rodney's own development, and he was able to convince his father to respect his needs for autonomy. His grades improved and, while he did not rejoin the swim team, his relationship with his father stabilized. Efforts shifted toward treating Brian's depression. Mr. Thompson's aggressive, assertive style tended to intimidate his quiet, younger son. The next phase of treatment focused on increasing the directness and clarity of Brian's self-expression when communicating with his father and increasing Mr. Thompson's ability to listen to his son.

The need to treat siblings may occur before parents consider their individual and marital issues. It is important to determine whether the onset of symptoms in another child is diverting our attention from another family problem, such as marital pathology, or a statement of individual vulnerability. In the former instance, family treatment should address the problem from which attention is diverted. In the latter situation, treatment directed toward the needs of the sibling, or siblings, should be undertaken.

DURATION AND TERMINATION

The duration of family treatment varies according to the level of dysfunction within a family. Longer-term treatments are required for families whose interactional problems are pervasive and have persisted over time. The duration of family treatment can range from a brief, focused intervention for a specific problem to a longer-term relationship characterized by intermittent contacts around different problems, often posed by differ-ent family members. While the frequency of treatment for some families is intermittent due to economic or other practical constraints, a long-term relationship with a clinician who has a comprehensive understanding of the family is invaluable. Termination initiated because of the cessation of symptoms in one child often leads to a new phase of treatment when symptoms arise in another family member. For such multiproblem families, termination does not occur formally. The treatment of such families typically includes several, if not all, of the previously described phases.

The clinical processes just reviewed, beginning with stabilizing a crisis and ending with termination, characterizes an integrated approach to family treatment. The chronologic sequence is offered as a guide of a typical unfolding of therapy. In the clinical setting, the actual sequence varies according to clinical need, and the various treatment components of treatment evolve over time. Some families may require only a few components of this sequence whereas the most troubled could receive intervention at any level. The principle we wish to emphasize is that coordinated family treatment may involve an intervention with the entire system or with parts of the system. In the following discussion, we have placed greater emphasis on treatment techniques because of their fundamental importance in family intervention and because work with components of the family, such as parents, is covered elsewhere in this *Handbook*.

Techniques of Family Treatment

The following discussion describes some family therapy techniques and approaches to family problems commonly observed in clinical practice.

MIMESIS

The technique of mimesis is analogous to the individual psychotherapist's attempt to develop an alliance through empathic understanding. In family treatment, the therapist adopts the cultural style and understanding of the family as an effort gain their acceptance and confidence. The therapist makes every attempt to adopt family rules and perspectives as a way of gaining their trust and minimizing resistance to treatment.

CASE EXAMPLE

Ms. Jones began her description of parenting problems with an open statement of her intermittent drug abuse. She seemed embarrassed by this and implied that the clinician would be no longer interested in working with her and her 3 children. She stated, "The kids' teachers think I'm just a drug user." The clinician spent a good bit of time in the early treatment sessions consolidating the therapeutic alliance by describing how psychiatrists, at times, are also misunderstood and people do not think they are "good for anything either." Ms. Jones chuckled softly as the psychiatrist mentioned his profession's problems.

JOINING

This technique refers to the clinician joining the family as an agent of change. The clinician emphasizes aspects of his or her own personality that are syntonic with the family. This process can be active and overt or indirect and covert. In either instance, we must communicate that we are in relationship with each family member and understand each person's views. This process, much like mimesis, often determines whether a family continues in treatment. It is particularly important to join with fathers in order to facilitate their ongoing participation in family treatment.

CASE EXAMPLE

Mr. and Mrs. Stone were seen in family treatment related to the conduct problems of their eldest, 14-year-old Matthew. He did not respect his father and disregarded his mother's expectations for his behavior. Family treatment revealed a distant, ineffective father and a mother who responded enthusiastically to the clinician's comments, saying "You understand Matthew so well, Doctor. I think you really know what's going on with him." Whenever she would make these statements, Mr. Stone visibly withdrew, appeared tense, and his involvement in the session decreased. The clinician, recognizing this interaction, made every attempt to support Father's opinions and validate his involvement in treatment. This approach was associated with his continuation in therapy and, eventually, more effective interaction with his son.

Mr. and Mrs. Martin began family treatment reluctantly. Their son, Lance, age 15 had been caught with drugs on the school campus and had deteriorating school grades. Lance had been defying their limits and recently had made physical threats toward his mother. The parents' inconsistency in coming for treatment seemed related to the fact that Mr. Martin had a history of substance abuse and had trouble maintaining a job. In the first several sessions, Lance freely described how his father had set limits on him by being physically aggressive.

In a sensitive response to all parties concerned, the clinician noted that while Father had been inappropriate in his limit setting, Lance was clearly out of control and extremely difficult to live with at the present time. This open acknowledgment of the unacceptability of Lance's behavior enabled Mr. and Mrs. Martin to join the treatment process and be more open about their own difficulties.

REFRAMING

Reframing is a verbal intervention, akin to clarification in individual psychotherapy, whereby the therapist provides an alternative way to perceive a behavior. Often it is utilized in taking problematic behaviors and giving an adaptive, positive connotation to them. At times, the clinician will describe the reframe in terms that reveal a child's behavior as having adaptive qualities.

CASE EXAMPLE

Seven-year-old Joey is developing a history of behavior problems at school and home. His parents have recently separated, are planning to divorce, and the son's misbehavior begins to escalate. Joey states, "I hate my daddy" and "I want to kill him." Mother attempts to calm Joey by telling him "No, you don't."

Joey's behavior is reframed by the clinician as a reaction to the uncertainty of the marital relationship. It is explained to Mother that Joey may be concerned about losing her and is attempting to show his loyalty to her. In addition, it is suggested that he may feel uncertain of how to respond to his father because of his awareness that his parents are having difficulty with each other. The clinician restates Joey's comments: "It seems Joey is very confused about how to feel toward his father and wants you to feel he is on your side." The mother is encouraged to state that "Even though your father and I are having difficulty, you can love us both." Mother eventually is able to begin to see the relationship of marital difficulty to Joey's distress and behavior problems.

CIRCULAR QUESTIONING

By circular questioning, we do not directly confront the symptomatic individual but explore or track patterns of communication within the family as problems are discussed with family members. We encourage each participant to express his or her perspective on interactions between 2 other members of the family. This intervention often produces many other family responses and thereby reveals a great deal more information on the family.

CASE EXAMPLE

Fifteen-year-old Doug is impulsive, oppositional, and openly rude to his parents in family sessions. He speaks loudly and frequently interrupts his parents' attempts to explain their view of a situation. As Mother attempts to describe why she and his father decided not to allow him to go on a trip with friends, he verbally explodes, tells her that she is "wrong" and "stupid," ending his tirade by telling her to "shut up." Father, clearly upset by the way his son is treating his wife, attempts to intervene, stating that if this behavior continues "Someday I'm going to beat you so badly you won't get up."

At such times it is most useful to communicate with the family member most likely to remain calm in response to our questions, in this case the mother. We ask, "How can your husband support you without threatening Doug?" This may gently make a point regarding nonviolence to the emotionally labile family members but not require a response from them. As Mother talks about her need for support, observation of Doug and Father can cue us to whether either can be gently confronted on the source of their affect. Asking Doug to acknowledge that his statements toward his mother were inappropriate can help assuage Father. Alternatively, Father may be able to begin discussing the background of his intense reaction—his upbringing by parents who while loving and caring, demanded absolute respect for their authority—and its relationship to his current behavior.

FAMILY ENACTMENT

In this situation, the clinician promotes an enactment of a family problem in order to understand its interactional and structural aspects. The clinician has an opportunity to offer alternative responses by directing family members to resolve conflicts evident in the consulting room. Enactments have the dual intent of exposing the problem and assisting the family to find ways to ameliorate its effects.

CASE EXAMPLE

Fifteen-year-old Hannah, who had a long history of learning problems, developed depressive symptoms and behavior problems. She frequently stated in sessions that her mother did not listen to her. The night before a session, she and her cousin had, with Mother's permission, gone on a group date. They were late in returning. Mother appropriately responded by setting a limit and restricting her from further such activity for the next week. However, when Hannah began to explain why they were late, her mother refused to listen.

The clinician attempted to have the problem, an unempathic response from Mother, enacted within the session. Hannah was asked to attempt again to communicate her account of the evening to her mother. Mother reacted quickly saying "I'm not going to change the punishment." The clinician intervened by supporting, in front of Hannah, Mother's consequence as given, but then asked Hannah to explain her reasons for being tardy to him. Mother needed to be urged to listen on several occasions, by the clinician nonverbally indicating the need for her to wait and let her daughter finish speaking. When Hannah had finished, the clinician explained that although the consequence for the behavior would not change, the process of Mother listening to daughter was an important one. Hannah seemed relieved.

Fifteen-year-old Sarah had a long history of learning problems and struggled with depression. She frequently had stated in sessions that her mother did not listen to her. Sarah arrived at one treatment session in tears because her uncle had molested her girlfriend the night before the session, during a sleepover. Mother responded by questioning the validity of the accusation; thereafter Sarah began sobbing to the extent she could not speak.

The clinician attempted to have the unempathic response from Mother corrected in the session. The clinician asked Mother, "What do you think Sarah needs from you right now?" Mother persisted in defending her brother, and the clinician again asked, rephrasing "What might a child need from her mother when she is crying?" Mother was able to respond that the child would likely need nurturing, but explained that in her family of origin, not much affection was shown to the children. She described that she had felt uncomfortable with expressing emotion "my whole life." The clinician urged some demonstration that the mother cared for her daughter, regardless of what was true regarding the events. Sarah's mother was able to caress her daughter's back, which eventually enabled her talk during the session.

PRESCRIBED TASKS

Prescribed tasks are behaviorally oriented interventions by which families are given instructions to approach a conflicted area and attempt to master it away from the session ("homework"). The family members bring the results of the prescribed task back to the family session and reviewed by the clinician. Successes and failures are explored with new potentials for change offered.

CASE EXAMPLE

Mr. Williams, a 37-year-old businessman, was angry because his 9-year-old son was noncompliant at his bedtime, usually the time Mr. Williams arrived home from work. Sensing that his son only wanted more time from his father, the clinician instructed Mr. Williams to spend 15 minutes each day with his son, as soon as he returned from work, and to write down his experiences of these 15 minutes. After several weeks, Mr. Williams returned to the clinic with an amazed look on his face as he recounted how pleasant the interactions had become with his son and how he looked forward to spending time with him. This led to an exploration of his emphasis on career and how other relationships, including those with his wife and friends, had suffered.

PARADOXICAL INTERVENTIONS

In a paradoxical intervention, the clinician makes an unusual or contrary demand of a family, such as a request to exaggerate a symptomatic family pattern. If a family refuses or is unable to meet this demand, new potentials for change are experienced. If complied with, the paradoxical directive at the least facilitates a family's alliance with the therapist and also may open up potentials for change. This technique is likely not to be successful when used with individuals who are cognitively and emotionally not able to process nuance.

CASE EXAMPLE

Mrs. Ronning was observed to be an overprotective, overinvolved mother by the clinician evaluating her 15-year-old son's depression. Her son, Elvin, was the youngest of her 4 children; her husband was frequently gone on business trips. As it became clear that Mrs. Ronning was overinvolved in her son's life, the clinician stated, "I think you should try to find out more about your son and what's going on in his life. I think you need to spend more time with him." Several weeks later in sessions, Mrs. Ronning said in exasperation, "I think it's impossible to know everything about my son and, you know what, I have a life to live too." In this instance the clinician's paradoxical directive led to Mother's recognition that overinvolvement in her son's life was compromising her own experience as well.

REALIGNING BOUNDARIES

Family boundaries define family roles and help differentiate between parents, siblings, and subsystem groups. These boundaries protect families from intrusions within the family and help define exchanges with other groups of individuals. Boundaries can be too rigid, denying exchange; too permeable, making exchange too easy; and misaligned, facilitating inappropriate exchange.

CASE EXAMPLE

Twelve-year-old David is beginning puberty and reports feeling embarrassed when his mother discusses this development with his friends' parents. David's stepfather, who has been absent from many sessions and often is unavailable in the home, begins speaking about his understanding of David's feelings.

The clinician takes this opportunity to amplify the developmental need for a son to identify with his father by encouraging the father's narrative of his own adolescent development. The clinician reinforces the importance of the stepfather's role in raising David and in teaching him to become an adult. This discussion leads to a consideration of Mother's feelings related to David's developing autonomy.

Merrilee is a noncompliant 15-year-old who rejects the limit-setting efforts of Bob, her mother's boyfriend. Bob is not supported by Mandy, Merrilee's mother, and Merrilee takes advantage of this fact, often commenting "You are not my father." Mandy frequently joins her daughter in berating Bob, which exacerbates family tension. This structural problem makes effective behavioral control of Mandy impossible. It appears that Bob and Mandy are minimally committed to each other.

The clinician attempts to help Bob and Mandy strengthen their relationship and identifies a fundamental problem for them: They will be unlikely to effectively parent Mandy and their 2 young boys until they can support each other. The clinician also suggests that Mandy's acceptance of her mother's daily offer to care for her 2 boys confuses them about who has ultimate authority in the family.

EXPLORING FAMILY BELIEF

Family belief refers to the fact that families have a type of memory function that goes beyond the beliefs and memories of each of its members. Family belief relates to the family as a whole and its multigenerational functioning. After some period of treatment, apparently puzzling family behavior is seen to be perpetuated by family beliefs that cross the generations.

CASE EXAMPLE

Merrilee married a young man with a history of conduct and legal problems. Her mother appeared to take some pleasure at his difficulties and predicted doom for the marriage. The clinician, over several treatment sessions, determined that Merrilee's grandfather had been incarcerated for significant crimes, Merrilee's father abandoned the family and also had legal difficulties, and her mother's common-law husband was a drug abuser who did not gainfully support the family. As the clinician worked toward problem solving and dealing with male-female relationships, he recognized that the starting point was to identify a core family belief: Males are unworthy and unsupportive and, therefore, should not be respected and little should be expected of them. This family belief was tenacious, not easily changed, but of critical importance for the clinician to understand.

FACILITATING ATTACHMENT TO CAREGIVERS

Attachment behavior is an instinctive bonding behavior a child utilizes in establishing relationships with persons encountered in his or her environment from birth onward. It is a fundamental building block of personality formation and can be facilitated, or frustrated, by parental behavior. When parents are either unavailable or too readily available for the child, significant developmental problems can unfold. A family intervention redirects the family's regulation of attachment behavior, facilitating the child's disengagement or engagement with caregivers.

CASE EXAMPLE

Fourteen-year-old Robert is experimenting with drugs and alcohol, which results in family treatment with his mother and stepfather. Assessment indicates that Robert's family has a history of depressive disorder, Robert's biological father abandoned the family and later died, and Robert's previous stepfather was physically abusive. His current stepfather initially appears concerned but, after the crisis of Robert's drug use is over, ceases attending sessions. Mother and Robert report a great deal of anger at him, and the therapeutic goal becomes establishing his availability to Robert, an adolescent with a long history of unstable attachments to fathers.

In this case, it would be useful to allow Robert to express his anger regarding his stepfather's absence from the sessions and from other areas of his life. While this could be accomplished in his mother's presence, it would be important to prevent her from criticizing her husband in front of her son. It may be necessary to meet with her alone to allow her to deal with her feelings of frustration. Next we might review ways in which Robert can talk with his stepfather about his concerns. If this appears too imposing for Robert, we could encourage Mother to ask her husband to attend sessions. Should this fail, our direct contact with the stepfather could explore his reasons for withdrawal from the intervention process. When the stepfather next comes to the clinic, it is important to avoid directly confronting his absence but instead to encourage his expression of concerns he may have for Robert. In this way, he can begin to experience the value of participating in treatment. We should encourage his willingness to be involved in his stepson's life, including not only monitoring Robert's activities but also in spending enjoyable time with him. The importance of these involvements for Robert's identity formation and self-confidence should be made clear to the stepfather.

Fifteen-year-old Michael had developed problems of runaway behavior, truancy, and drug usage. He was the youngest of 3 boys, separated by 10 years from his next brother. Michael had a special relationship with his parents, particularly his mother, because she had been advised to abort him during her pregnancy due to a gynecological tumor. She chose to carry the pregnancy to term and had seen his existence as special from that time onward. The family responded to Michael's every need and had a great deal of difficulty setting limits. When he was 12 and had run away from home for 10 days, the family expressed no anger upon his return, only relief. In fact, his mother made his favorite dinner upon his return.

When Michael began to tyrannize the family, the clinician advised his parents to spend less attention on him in order to facilitate his independence. During this work, his parents stated that they had been too available to him in his development. His parents' emotional distancing was associated with Michael's increasing depression and anger toward them. He did respond later with an acknowledgment of personal responsibility for his actions and requested individual therapy.

UNBALANCING

In the unbalancing technique, the clinician attempts to change the hierarchical relationship of the members of a family subsystem. In many instances, the developmental process of the family life cycle facilitates this shifting of hierarchical roles. When this occurs, the clinician does not need to initiate the unbalancing as much as identify it and help the family understand its familial and interpersonal consequences.

CASE EXAMPLE

Janice Brown was a 29-year-old mother of a 6-year-old, first-grade child, Nancy, who was born prematurely and had several medical complications earlier in her development. As a result of Nancy's medical complications, Janice resigned from her teaching position and stayed home to facilitate her adjustment. Her husband, Ron, was promoted to a position as a bank vice president and traveled frequently. When Nancy had difficulty attending school and developed psychosomatic symptoms, she was referred for treatment. After 2 months of behavioral interventions and help from the school, Nancy attended school without resistance and her performance improved. Subsequent to this development, Janice developed depressive symptomatology and began to use alcohol.

In the family intervention, the clinician attempted to identify the meaning of Nancy's attending school and the effect Janice's parent role had in filling an emotional void she experienced in her marriage to Ron. As Nancy's need for Mother's support decreased, the clinician assisted Janice in facing the problems in her marriage and her sense of loss related to the interruption of her career.

The techniques just reviewed are not ordered to suggest relative importance or frequency of occurrence, or to imply a suggested sequence of treatment interventions. There is overlap in the elements described in some of the techniques. A great many more techniques exist than those just described, the reader is referred elsewhere for their elaboration (Gurman, & Kniskern, 1981; Haley, 1976; Miermont, 1995; Minuchin & Fishman, 1981).

Complications and Difficulties in Family Treatment

Clinical progress in family treatment occurs when there is a reduction of the child's or adolescent's presenting symptoms. There are also 2 less direct indicators of improvement: The family as a system develops a clear, hierarchical structure and is clearer in communication patterns and articulation of family beliefs and values; also individuals within the family make internal adjustments that are associated with improved adaptation in family relationships and relationships in the broader social world.

When progress does not occur, the presence of one, or several, of the common impediments to successful family treatment should be suspected.

1. Minimal father involvement in treatment. Mothers may bring children for treatment with fathers passively or actively resisting the process of intervention. In single-mother families, fathers often are physically unavailable to supplement treatment efforts. When fathers are involved in treatment, progress is not assured but a major roadblock to success is removed.

2. A poorly defined role for siblings. Many siblings do not understand their need to come to therapy and, by their lack of involvement, facilitate the idea that the identified patient is the only problem in the family.

3. The relative neglect of the problems of the identified patient. At times, other family members may have more immediate needs than the identified patient, which may distract the clinician from treating the diagnosed concern.

4. An inaccurate formulation of the family's role in the child's disorder. Progress is delayed when a family receives a supportive therapy approach for a disorder resulting from family interactions which need alteration. On the other hand, progress is frustrated when family interactions are seen as accounting for a disorder that is primarily biologically based and largely outside the family's control.

5. Inattention to a relationship that has the potential to be an important resource for the child. Such relationships include, but are not limited to, an estranged biologic parent and a father's girlfriend.

6. The entire family has not been evaluated. It is justifiable to determine that ongoing family treat-

ment does not require all the family members to be present. On the other hand, if the clinician has never interviewed certain family members, the treatment process may be, without the clinician's knowledge, undermined by those members' behavior. In addition, the unevaluated member could be an asset to family treatment.

7. The clinician's issues are intruding on the treatment process. Family issues often mobilize significant countertransference responses. Marital roles, child-rearing practices, and human sexuality are examples of the emotionally laden material with which clinicians themselves may be dealing in their personal lives. Undetected attitudes on the part of the clinician may negatively affect the treatment process.

8. Communicating inadequately with divorced biological parents. Most divorced parents who do not have legal custody of their children continue to have the legal right of access to medical information about their child's health status. The clinician conducting a family-based treatment of the child must communicate with the non custodial parent regarding the child's condition when requested to do so.

Interaction with Other Interventions

Interaction with other interventions—individual, group, behavioral, marital, pharmacologic, and other systems—is a common occurrence, and these interventions may be implemented simultaneously. Successful integration with other treatments is based on a biopsychosocial understanding of a child's vulnerabilities and on several guiding principles.

PRINCIPLES GUIDING INTERACTION WITH OTHER INTERVENTIONS

Follow the Patient: Individual family members may request attention to their individual needs. This request should be taken seriously and not as merely diverting from family interaction. At times the clinician may discern an individual need that is impeding family treatment and may recommend the initiation of individual therapy.

Use Formulation as a Guide to Intervention

Choice: A complete, accurate case formulation allows a clinician to choose rationally which other interventions should supplement family treatment. A formulation that includes a mother's overprotectiveness and a father's emotional distance may lead to marital therapy, individual therapy with either the mother or father, or the expectation of father's physical presence at family therapy sessions. Also, an accurate formulation protects the clinician from becoming part of a pathologic family interaction. Shifting to individual therapy may be helpful in treating the depression of a mother but, at the same time, may inappropriately identify her as the family member with the most problems.

Think Sequentially: Certain interventions are not effective if they precede other interventions. The return of a child who has been placed outside the home will be unsuccessful until individual factors within the child and the family environment have been stabilized. Similarly, a couple with ineffective limit-setting techniques may require marital therapy before behavioral interventions with their child will succeed.

Prioritize Interventions: The clinician must determine which factors are of most current significance. The vegetative signs of depression, an unremediated learning disorder, the overprotectiveness of the mother, or emotional unavailability of the father may all be relevant. The clinician must judge which factors are most directly impeding clinical progress and sequence interventions accordingly. The clinician who considers the biological, psychological, and social factors of each clinical problem is best equipped to make these judgments.

COMMON INTERACTIONS

Pharmacotherapy: It is important to identify when family members are on medication and determine the family's understanding of the role medication plays in the treatment of the individual. Families vary in their views, from ascribing to medication the potential for total remediation of problems, to devaluing any possible benefit from it. The clinician may be asked by a parent to provide medication for him or her, or the clinician may judge such an intervention necessary. The practicality of parents and child being treated by one physician is an important advantage. On the other hand, it requires that the physician simultaneously maintain the perspective of treating individuals and the family as a whole.

Behavioral Treatments: Homework assignments and contingency planning are an important component of family treatment, especially in the early stages of treatment. In the initial sessions, the clinician reviews parents' consequences for a child's behavioral problems, with positive and negative reinforcement schemes developed. In subsequent treatment sessions, target symptoms response to the behavioral intervention is reviewed and modifications in the behavioral program suggested.

Individual Therapy: Intervening in family interaction often reveals deficits parents brought to their relationship and intrapsychic deficits children possess as a result of family interaction. When the clinician judges that problematic family interactions have receded, it may be an appropriate opportunity for the vulnerabilities of individual family members to receive attention.

Marital Therapy: Effective family therapy leads couples to view their relationship in a new perspective and may foster a desire for improved marital adjustment. For couples unsure about the viability of their relationship, marital therapy is a necessary prelude to family therapy.

Other Systems Interventions: Aggressive, externalizing disorders, psychotic disorders, and life-threatening situations, such as eating disorders and suicidal behavior, require a residential intervention. Hospitalization is the most typical of these interventions, although limitations on economic resources may necessitate other settings. Group therapy is helpful for children with socialization difficulties and becomes increasingly important with age, as the family's role as primary socializing agent lessens. School collaboration is indicated for children with learning difficulties; family cooperation with school personnel maximizes educational success. Children with conduct disorder frequently are involved with the courts. This involvement can be therapeutic in that it can assist families in limit-setting efforts with which they have been unsuccessful. Families that have difficulty setting limits can benefit through collaboration with probation officers and court workers. This collaboration is important in that psychotherapeutic interventions with such children and families are devalued if there are no behavioral consequences for breaking the law.

Ethical Issues and Contraindications to Treatment

The most important ethical considerations in family treatment are related to issues of confidentiality. When a family is seen, the simplest of questions—Who is the patient?—becomes problematic. Therapy is planned initially for the identified patient but, as work proceeds, the concerns and, at times, disorders of other members of the family become a focus for treatment. By empathically exploring the concerns of one family member, the clinician is at risk of coming into conflict with the needs of other family members. Healthier families can tolerate this apparent unfairness and seeming lack of responsiveness to their concerns. Families whose members have been traumatized by each other are less likely to be patient when one member appears to be benefiting most directly from the clinician's intervention. One approach to this ethical dilemma is for the clinician to make a deliberate attempt to relate to all family members. Drawing on a therapeutic alliance with the whole family, the clinician makes explicit that, over time, each family member will have his or her perspective heard and taken into account.

CONTRAINDICATIONS

The main areas that indicate a contraindication to family treatments involve ethical and legal issues. If it is not clear whether family treatment is indicated, a therapeutic trial may be necessary to determine the appropriateness of the intervention. In the following relative contraindications to family treatment, the clinician is likely to be unsuccessful by:

1. Repeatedly involving those individuals who are not consistently involved in a child's life. Some family clinicians advocate work with extended family networks; these contacts can assist the assessment and formulation of problems. It is contraindicated to actively involve individuals who do

not have generational authority to make caregiving decisions for children. In fact, such sustained blurring of intergenerational boundaries often fosters a continuation of a psychopathologic family interaction.

2. Continuing to work jointly with parents who are divorced. Once a couple has divorced, to see them together exacerbates tensions and confuses children. A session to clarify both parents' relationship to the clinician may be necessary, including such things as how information about a child's disorder is to be communicated. Ongoing work with each parent, and new family unit, should be conducted separately to reflect the new legal definition of family.

3. Conducting family therapy that escalates the potential for harm of family members, especially physical harm. Some parents have too many deficits to safely, and effectively, set limits on their child's behavior. In such families, in-session interaction may predispose the family to violence; discerning clinical judgment is required to determine when to resist exploring family conflicts.

Developmental Considerations

The clinician conducting effective family treatment considers how therapy differs according to the constellation of ages presented by the family in treatment. As the family is the developmental setting, the family therapist must consider how family interaction facilitates or frustrates the individual development of each of its members.

AGE CONSIDERATIONS

The younger the child, the more likely that the problems of an individual parent or difficulties in the parents' relationship will determine the nature of clinical presentation. Parental caregiving practices are the prime determinants of the clinical presentation in infants and toddlers, except in instances of obvious biologic disability. Families of school-age children are dealing with issues of success and competence; mastery of this stage requires the availability of parents to foster the success of their children. Adolescent children question parental values, test the stability of the parents' marriage, and the strength of each parent's sense of self. The adolescent's emotional and

geographic moving away from family taxes the resources of both parent and adolescent. The potential serious consequences of high-risk behaviors involving sexuality, drugs, and motor vehicles brings an urgency to many family treatments of adolescent patients.

Over arching these age-specific issues are the tasks and stages of the family life cycle, an orienting principle for family clinicians. The broad concerns of families with children not yet in school and families of children on the verge of becoming young adults are very different. Consideration of the family life cycle and most issues of normal development are complicated by alterations in family structure influenced by divorce, single parenting, remarriage, and stepfamily formation.

DEVELOPMENTAL PROCESS CONSIDERATIONS

The tasks and behaviors that help define the stages of a child's developmental need to be regulated. To illustrate, a child's developmental need for an attachment to caregiving person serves as the basis for future developmental successes. Deprivation, neglect, and variants of unavailable parenting underregulate a need for attachment. Overprotective, indulgence, and excessively available parents overregulate the need for attachment. Both patterns are associated with the development of clinical problems, analogous to physical states of starvation and obesity, and are evidence of unempathic parenting. The developmentally sensitive family clinician must consider: How does this family regulate the developmental needs of its children? What intervention in the regulatory process will have most effect on the child's symptoms and development? To what extent do inappropriate regulations, such as parental overprotectiveness, reflect unfinished developmental tasks within the parent or parents? Developmental process considerations guide the initial choice of intervention and sequencing of later interventions in family treatment.

Outcome Studies

In the last several decades, as family treatments have become more accepted, empirical approaches have been developed and applied to family treatment outcome and family process evaluation. There is general support for the efficacy of family treatments in patient samples with a variety of diagnoses and increasing support for the efficacy of family treatment in a few specific populations, such as drug abusers, delinquents, and adolescents with eating disorders. Research in schizophrenia suggests family treatment plays a powerful adjunctive role and the family treatment of affective disorders appears promising. Meta-analytic studies have shown family treatments better than no treatment, more effective than some alternative treatments, and comparative to behavioral and cognitive behavioral treatments in a variety of disorders (Diamond, et al., 1996). There are several areas of consensus regarding outcome research of family treatments:

1. No one method, or school, of treatment has established overall superiority in effectiveness.
2. Individual diagnosis or clinical problem remain the preferred way to organize treatment groups as currently there is no universally accepted method of family diagnosis.
3. The growth in the epidemiology of family risk factors suggests numerous areas where family interventions are clinically justifiable, such as anxiety disorders and personality pathology, even though not yet empirically verified as effective.
4. Even with advances, there remain significant limitations in the ability of current research efforts to measure the complex components of family treatments.
5. Dysfunctional family processes typically apply to more than one diagnostic grouping. Family enmeshment occurs in eating disorders and separation anxiety; poor parental supervision occurs in conduct disorders and substance abuse.

In summary, outcome research in family treatments is developing sophistication and breadth. It is supplemented by family treatment process research that does not examine the results of treatment models but rather assesses how the processes of treatment determine outcome. Process researchers are beginning to assess the effects of techniques of family therapy. Linking process measures to outcome studies has potential for the further development of rational family treatments.

Social and Cultural Issues

Norms with respect to expected family development and child-rearing practice vary according to culture and, within cultures, socioeconomic level. At the same time, there are cross-cultural continuities with respect to healthy family functioning and clinical problems. It is imperative for clinicians who are treating families to understand the cultural background of the family in treatment and to modify family treatment accordingly. As treatment proceeds, clinicians can ask the family to educate them regarding family customs and culturally related values. If language and cultural barriers are too imposing, enlisting the assistance of a cotherapist, either from the family's culture or conversant in matters related to it, can facilitate treatment.

The effective family clinician keeps informed regarding societal changes in basic family structures. In North America, experienced clinicians note that the families they treat seem to have problems that are more severe and more numerous than those of a previous generation (Achenbach & Howell, 1993). Alternative family treatments and programs to support families, such as in home treatments, are evolving to meet the needs of families. The fluidity of contemporary family structure is a social issue with important implications for all clinicians conducting family treatments.

Future Directions

An integrated approach to family treatment is the cornerstone of family interventions: The family clinician works with family process but identifies the needs of the individual. Newer perspectives will likely refine this integrated perspective. The development of the narrative approach in the last decade, which emphasizes the personal story of each family member and the personal construction of life events, is an example of such a refinement (Freedman & Combs, 1996). On the other hand, current neuroscience emphases in psychiatry run the risk of viewing the impact of families solely as purveyors of genes and not of social experience. Whether these scientific developments result in a balanced view of the biological and experiential contributions by families to their children remains a question to be answered.

Rapid cultural shifts in the definition of the family, alterations in family structure, and psychosocial stressors impacting the family will continue to affect family treatments. Clinicians will have to develop flexibility and utilize other resources to support their work with families. The clinician's relationship with the family will remain the foundation for all interventions, but other systems will be critical in meeting the multiple needs of families. The generic term *family treatment*, used in this chapter, is consistent with the likely broadening of emphases to include interventions beyond the consulting office.

As the field of family treatment evolves, there will be efforts to define relationship disturbances and attempts to develop relationship diagnoses in order to target treatment more rationally. Whether relationship diagnoses become accepted in clinical practice as primary diagnoses or continue as related descriptors of individual diagnoses is uncertain.

More than ever, the future will need clinicians who recognize the power of the family to facilitate a child's development and ameliorate a child's symptoms and clinicians who implement effective treatments of the family.

REFERENCES

Achenbach, T. & Howell, C. (1993). Are American children's problems getting worse? A 13-year comparison. *Journal of the American Academy of Child and Adolescent Psychiatry, 32*, 1145–1154.

Ackerman, N. (1958). *The psychodynamics of family life: Diagnosis and treatment of family relationships.* New York: Basic Books.

Barker, P. (1992). *Basic family therapy* (3rd ed.). New York: Oxford University Press.

Barldey, R. (1990). Attention deficit hyperactivity disorder: A handbook for diagnosis and treatment. New York: Guilford Press.

Barton, C., & Alexander, J. (1981). Functional family therapy. In A. Gurman, & D. Kniskern, (Eds.), *Handbook of family therapy*, (Vol. 1, pp. 403–443). New York: Brunner Mazel.

Boszormenyi-Nagy, I., & Ulrich, D. M. (1991). Contextual family therapy. In A. S. Gurman & D. P. Kniskern (Eds.), *Handbook of family therapy*, (Vol. 1). (pp. 200–300) New York: Brunner Mazel.

Bowen, M. (1978). *Family therapy in clinical practice.* New York: Jason Aronson.

Broderick, C. B., & Schrader, S. S. (1991). The history of professional marriage and family therapy. In A. S. Gurman & D. P. Kniskern (Eds.), *Handbook of family therapy*, (Vol. 2). (pp. 3–40) New York: Brunner mazel.

Diamond, G., Serrano, A., Dicky, M., & Sonis, B. (1996). The current status of family based outcome and process research. *Journal of the American Academy of Child Psychiatry, 35*, 6–16.

Emde, R. N. (1983). The prepresentational self and its affective core. *Psychoanalytic Study of the Child, 38*, 165–192.

Engel, G. (1977). The need for a new medical model: A challenge for biomedicine. *Science, 196*, 129–136.

Freedman, J. & Combs, G. (1996). *Narrative therapy: The social construction of preferred realities.* New York: W. W. Norton & Company.

Griest, D., & Wells, K. (1983). Behavioral family therapy for conduct disorders in children. *Behavior Therapy, 14*, 37–53.

Gurman, A. S., & Kniskern, D. P. (Eds.). (1991). *Handbook of family therapy*, (Vol. 2). (pp 65–476) New York: Brunner Mazel.

Haley, J. (1976). *Problem solving therapy.* San Francisco: Jossey-Bass.

Levant, R. (1984). *Family therapy: A comprehensive overview.* Englewood Cliffs, NJ: Prentice-Hall.

McDermott, J. F., & Char, W. F. (1974). The undeclared war between child and family therapy. *Journal of the American Academy of Child Psychiatry, 13*, 422–436.

Miermont, J. (1995). *The dictionary of family therapy,* ed. H. Jenkins Cambridge: Blackwell Publishers.

Minuchin, S. (1974). *Families and family therapy.* Cambridge, MA: Harvard University Press.

Minuchin, S., & Fishman, H. C. (1981). *Family therapy techniques.* Cambridge, MA: Harvard University Press.

Madanes, C. (1991). Strategic family therapy. In A. Gurman & D. Kniskern (Eds.), *Handbook of family therapy*, (Vol 2), (pp 396–416). New York: Brunner Mazel.

Nichols, W. C., & Everett, C. A. (1986). *Systemic family therapy: An integrative approach.* New York: Guilford Press.

Pinsof, W. (1995). Integrative problem-centered therapy: A synthesis of family, individual and biological therapies. New York: Basic Books.

Reiss, D. (1989). The represented and practicing family: Contrasting visions of family continuity. In A. Sameroff & R. Emde (Eds.), *Relationship disturbances in early childhood: A developmental approach* (pp. 191–220). New York: Basic Books.

Rutter, M., & Rutter, M. (1993). *Developing minds: Challenge and continuity across the life span.* New York: Basic Books.

Scharff, D., & Scharff, J. (1987). *Object relations family therapy.* Northvale, NJ: Jason Aronson.

Silver, M., & Liebman, R. (1986). Family oriented treatment of children and adolescents. In A. Solnit, D. Cohen, & J. Schowalter (Eds.), *Psychiatry: Child psychiatry,* (Vol. 6). (pp 457–468) Philadelphia: J. B. Lippincott.

Thomas, A., & Chess, S. (1980). *Dynamics of psychological development.* New York: Brunner Mazel.

Von Bertalanffy, L. (1968). *General system theory: Foundations, development, applications.* New York: George Braziller.

17 / Parent Training

James M. Briesmeister

The Nature of Parent Training

At its core, the family is a social unit. Within this structure, the parents have traditionally offered guidance, direction, discipline, and influence as well as love, warmth, and nurturance. The parents are responsible for the care, education, and growth of their children. They are not only the role models and agents of change for their children, they prepare them for their place within the larger culture. Indeed, the word *parenting* may be used interchangeably with the term *socialization*. In the rearing of children within the family setting, parents prepare the children for the roles and expectations of the social group into which they were born. One of the major tasks of parenting is to design an environment in which the children can learn appropriate and responsible social behavior.

Since parents and early childhood experiences within the family are crucial variables in the development and behavior of a child, it follows that the parenting role is essential to the overall welfare of individuals and society. At its best, the family develops and evolves in a constructive and socially responsible direction. Family members learn mutual acceptance and respect, and children acquire personal and social skills that will make them productive members of society. Love, trust, and reciprocity emerge, and children learn to how to generalize these skills outside the confines of the family.

Unfortunately, these ideal acquired skills are not always the norm for all families. There are times when negative and disruptive behaviors emerge from within the family unit. These dysfunctional behaviors certainly can impinge well beyond the immediate family structure. They may have damaging consequences for the extended family members, those who come into direct contact with the family members, and the community at large. As such, the maladaptive behaviors warrant and demand positive modifications. As proposed by Braswell and Kendall (1988), children and their behavioral problems are deeply embedded within a social context. The notion of parent training is essentially a behavioral approach that is grounded in the philosophy that social beings mold and shape each other's behaviors, actions, and reactions. This mutual and oftentimes reciprocal sculpting of behaviors follows certain logical and empirical patterns rooted in the principles of social learning theory and behavioral management. The more thoroughly parents understand and employ these systematic principles, the more effectively will they function as agents of change for their children.

One of the key tenets of applied behavioral analysis is that a child's behavior, whether appropriate or inappropriate, adaptive or maladaptive, is a product of the youngster's past and current interactions with people and circumstances. In view of the parent's responsibilities as primary caregivers, managers, disciplinarians, instructors, protectors, and behavior models for their children, the concept of educating parents in the basic and most effective principles of behavioral and social learning techniques is a logical and expedient process in child management and child development. Still further, if we seek to modify a child's behavior, it also may be necessary to change the behaviors of significant people in that child's life. Parent training is, in essence, a form of behavioral family intervention. It seeks to establish the conditions necessary to maintain and generalize desirable behaviors and reduce the frequency of undesirable behaviors within the family structure. Consequently, educating parents in effective child-rearing and parenting procedures is an invaluable intervention strategy that may positively affect the behaviors of the parents as well as the child. Parent training as a systematic approach to the intervention and remediation of problems continues to evolve and influence the fields of child and family therapies.

Parent training consists of educating parents in various techniques of behavioral management that are effective in remediating children's behavioral problems. In accord with the limits stipulated by a child's developmental level, parents must acquire 2 sets of skills. Many behavior deficits or excesses can be modified if the parents have the appropriate mastery skills. On the other hand, some behavioral deficits or excesses are age-appropriate. These usually cannot be changed. In fact, they are part and parcel of the child's developmental stage. Consequently, the parents may need to learn appropriate coping strategies. Parental mastery and coping skills may, of course, overlap. If, for example, the parents are confronted with problems at bedtime, such as the child's refusal to go to bed, procrastinating in getting ready for bed, and crying and bartering for a later sleep time, the parents may need to acquire a number of different but interrelated child management and coping skills. The parents may be taught how to handle bedtime by setting firm limits, establishing a consistent bedtime, providing structured preparatory activities that are preliminary to bedtime, and refraining from nagging or bartering. The parents, however, must be capable of providing these parenting skills within the lim-

its imposed by the child's developmental level. For instance, the parents must learn what bedtime rituals are appropriate for the child's age. They must learn that the child may not like or accept limits. Hence, the parents must learn ways of coping with the child's resistance.

Some Historical Antecedents of Parent Training

A review of the literature (Braswell & Kendall, 1988; Dangel & Polster, 1984; Kendall & Braswell, 1985; Briesmeister & Schaefer, 1997) indicates that the explicit inclusion of parents in the therapy of their children has been the exception rather than the rule. Historically, most intervention strategies focused on the internal cognitions, dynamics, and related inner processes of the target child. Including the parents and parent training as essential components within the therapy is a relatively contemporary conception. Although it has been primarily within the past 2 decades that the behavioral training approach has surfaced as a formidable topic for scientific research and application, the technique is not completely novel. One of the earliest recorded cases of therapeutic intervention involving a child was reported at the turn of the century. Freud (1909/1995) presented the analysis of one of his patients, Little Hans, a boy who was less than 5 years of age. It is particularly noteworthy that within the discussion and analysis of this classical case, Freud did not treat Little Hans directly. He instructed the youngster's father in techniques for resolving and modifying Hans's underlying phobic impulses. A significant amount of time elapsed before we find similar recorded cases of parent training as a supplement to therapy.

The role of the parents as educators and agents of therapeutic and social change in their children has a long tradition. We need only go back to the post–World War II era to uncover the burgeoning popularity of Benjamin Spock and the impact of his child care manuals. Already by that time parenting information and instructional maneuvers were making their mark on the parents, physicians, therapists, and educators of our culture.

Parent training and the mastery of effective behavioral skills continued to be influential. The significance of educating parents about the importance of altering antecedents and consequences of behaviors in order to effect positive changes in their children became increasingly apparent.

Definition and Some Applications of Parent Training

Traditionally, therapists have attempted to effect change directly with their young patients. Within the parent training format, however, the therapist educates the parents in those techniques and intervention strategies that elicit socially desirable and acceptable changes in negative and/or disruptive behavioral patterns. Indeed, parent training is a collaborative venture in which the parents are trained to be effective agents of positive change in their child. As Braswell (1991) proposed, the perception of patient-client relationships as a collaborative effort is a major tenet of the behavioral and the cognitive-behavioral approaches. Indeed, this collaborative alliance is reaffirmed by actually involving the parents in the intervention strategy planning and process. Parents are no longer on the outside looking in at the therapeutic encounters taking place between their child and the child's therapist. They are now invited to be an integral part of the therapeutic process. Parental involvement is essential to the success of the entire therapeutic endeavor. Within the scope of parent training, the target child's social and familial environment is not incidental. An understanding of the child's environment is essential if the therapeutic intervention is to be effective.

By its very nature, parent training is primarily educational. Parents are trained in techniques that will help them to identify, assess, and modify disruptive and dysfunctional behaviors, faulty communication patterns, and harmful styles of relating. Despite the multiplicity of approaches to parent training, one of the basic assumptions that remains is the underlying conviction that a child's behaviors, constructive or destructive, can be affected by environmental circumstances. Within the child's environment, the parents employ a system of rewards and punishments. They also use significant verbal and nonverbal communications and various forms of social interaction to discipline the child and ensure that the youngster becomes a productive member of society at large. There is little doubt that parent's are the most important social agents and the most influential environmental force that most children encounter (Crane, 1995). Typically, these are the people with whom the child interacts the most. More to the point, the parents are in a position to distribute or withhold various rewards and punishments. The parents not only nurture, they also educate their child. The parents have greater access to the child than any therapist or agent of change outside of the immediate family structure. Given these considerations, it is not surprising that some researchers, such as Graziano (1977) in his review of child intervention strategies, proposed that training parents to effect positive changes in their children and their behaviors may be one of the most significant achievements in the field of child therapy.

In the parent training format, the therapist and parents identify the child's behavioral problems that need to be addressed. Typically, these may include such things as noncompliance, acting out, inappropriate or dysfunctional behavioral responses, faulty peer interactions (social withdrawal or bullying behaviors), bedtime hassles, mealtime problems, concerns surrounding toilet training, disruptive classroom behaviors, and academic difficulties. Once the problems are identified, the severity or degree of conflict is assessed. The parent training strategies are prescriptive. That is to say, the approach that is selected is specific and tailored to the target child and the particular undesirable behaviors. The parents and child are trained in the acquisition of new skills. Furthermore, since the skills are essentially therapeutic, the distinction between skill training and therapy may be blurred.

The parent training format, then, involves various approaches all of which are child-focused interventions aimed at remediating specific problematic deficits or excesses. Parent training usually takes place in a controlled learning environment, such as the therapist's office or a group therapy or classroom setting, in which empirically based parenting skills are taught to parents by way of didactic instruction, modeling, and role playing, to name but a few approaches. Parents, for example, may be trained in the correct use of parent-child contingency contracting, a contract that clearly states that rewards will be given contingent upon appropriate behaviors. The details of the specific occasions and behaviors that will be rewarded and those in which reinforcements will be withheld may be set in writing. The behaviors that merit rewards will be clearly delineated for the child. Depending on children's age and capabilities, they may be allowed some input regarding the types of rewards that will be used. The expectations for reinforcements can be determined. For example, will the child receive a monetary reward (an allowance) or extra privileges, such as extended playtime, for desirable behaviors? This, of course, is also a function of the child's age and developmental level. Similarly, the contract should explain what specific privileges or rewards will the child risk losing if undesirable behaviors occur?

The parents also may be instructed in the appropriate use of a "time-out" period. If the child engages in unacceptable behaviors, time-out may be imposed. This procedure involves assigning the child a given amount of time in which he or she is removed from provocative environmental stimuli or circumstances, such as sitting in a chair or going to his or her room for 15 minutes in order to calm down following a fight with a playmate, thereby separating the child from the conflictual stimulus and affording the youngster time to consider (relearn) positive alternative behaviors, actions, or responses that will elicit a reward.

The parents may be trained in the best use of contingency schedules. For instance, will the child be rewarded each and every time the desirable behavior occurs (continuous reinforcement schedule), or will the reinforcement be applied on a sporadic basis (intermittent reinforcement schedule)? During the behavioral-educational process of parent training, the parents can be instructed in the most effective use of schedules of reinforcement. Should the child be rewarded every time he picks up his toys and she cleans her room, or should the rewards be administered on an every-other-occasion or a weekly basis? The principles of behavior modification suggest that learning that takes place on a partial or intermittent schedule of reinforcement tends to be more persistent and, in general, more effective. Once again, however, in any determination of the nature and schedule of reinforcements to be used, the in-

dividual child and the specifics of the problem and situation must be considered.

In some parent training formats, the parents may be offered guided practice in or modeling of the correct parent-child interactions, communications, or applications of behavioral principles. The therapist, for example, may model the way in which a request for desired behaviors can be clearly explained to the child. Indeed, given the child's age and level of cognitive understanding, the professional can help the parents to determine which requests are appropriate. The parents are able to learn the correct application of social learning and behavioral principles as well as which expectations are appropriate and consistent with the target child's age by watching the mental health professional in action. This modeling and demonstration may, of course, be presented in video form and/or in person. Not only will this procedure offer the parents guided practice in the application of the behavioral management principles, it also presents an opportunity for corrective feedback. This ensures that the parents will learn the new therapeutic skills in the most systematic and effective manner. Not only do they acquire the necessary parenting skills and behavioral modification techniques, they also witness the practical and correct application of these strategies. In turn, the parents can model appropriate behaviors and responses in the home setting. The principles that the parents have discussed, learned, and practiced in the therapy session or in the classroom are now generalized into the home. The parents then are able to model what they have learned for their child. By means of modeling, the parents, in effect, teach the child by example. They relay a message to the child that, in essence, states, "Do as I say *and* do as I do."

Parent training can offer the parents an opportunity to learn appropriate limit-setting strategies for the child. The parents can learn the most effective and time-tested methods for helping their child to achieve objectives by fostering a better understanding of age-appropriate roles, expectations, boundaries, and limits. When the expectations and requests are reasonable and in accord with the child's developmental level, the youngster's chances for success and accomplishment are increased. This affords the child, as well as the parents, a sense of competence. It also makes the child a more pleasant and acceptable member of the family, the classroom, the playground, and society in general. Furthermore, when the child's desirable behaviors far outweigh the undesirable behaviors, this offers occasion for fostering the youngster's self-esteem and sense of self-worth.

Developmental Considerations

Parent training focuses on imparting to parents the scientifically researched and most effective principles of behavior modification and social learning theory. Parents are taught how to apply basic behavioral concepts, such as the principle of contingency of reinforcements, time out, the setting of limits and boundaries, and effective parent-child communications. Whatever the parent training approach, it is essential that any attempts at prescriptive problem-solving must, of course, be relevant and appropriate to the developmental stage of the target child or adolescent. Any and all intervention strategies must be age-appropriate. Therapeutic techniques that are too complex and detailed may certainly elude a very young child. Overly sophisticated or abstract procedures may exceed the youngster's cognitive, emotional, and social development and comprehension. In a similar manner, if the intervention strategy plan is too naive or childlike, it may bore or even anger the adolescent who is at a higher level of development. Clearly, any effective parent training format must be in keeping with the age and developmental level of the target child.

Interactions with Other Intervention Approaches

The impact of a child's dysfunctional, undesirable, or disruptive behaviors is certainly not restricted to the confines of the immediate family. The child is a member of a larger community. Therefore, the negative effects of the dysfunctional behaviors reverberate well beyond the scope of the immedi-

ate family unit. They are felt within the extended family, the neighborhood, the school system, and the community at large. As such, the positive effects of any parent training intervention strategy should benefit the family in particular and society in general. In order to broaden the range of its impact, parent training may be combined with other intervention modalities.

By its very nature, parent training focuses on the child's social and interpersonal relationship styles as well as on behavioral responses. In addition to modifying faulty behavioral patterns, it also seeks to enhance social skills and peer interactions, improve social comprehension and judgments, establish appropriate impulse controls, and decrease negative and inappropriate behaviors. It also can be instrumental in improving the child's academic skills and classroom behaviors, such as eliminating disruptive classroom behaviors or comments, increasing attention and concentration, or improving the child's study habits. The educational, behavioral management, and social learning strategies employed in parent training can be readily coupled with individual child therapy approaches, the collateral treatment of parent and child, and family systems interventions. They also can be combined effectively with school and academic programs as well as community training and related educational objectives.

Extensive discussions, reviews, and evaluations of various parent training procedures and the ways in which they can be combined with other educational, therapeutic, child-rearing, and child discipline approaches have been presented in Dangel and Polster (1984) and Briesmeister & Schaefer, 1997). They offer detailed discussions of both parent training as a viable intervention strategy and, in addition, the effective combination of parent training with other modalities. Examples of only a few possibilities include parent training combined with cognitive-behavioral intervention approaches for the treatment of enuresis, oppositional defiant behaviors, and the elimination of tics and stuttering. Furthermore, parent training approaches have been combined with group therapy to modify antisocial behaviors (Ruma, Burke, & Thompson, 1996; Serketich & Dumas, 1996).

Parent training approaches also have been employed in conjunction with family systems approaches to modify the disruptive and manipulative behaviors of children within the family. In a similar manner, the parent training modality can offer parents as well as the child new and therapeutic skills. Parents, for example, can be taught anger control and stress reduction techniques in order to lessen the risks of of child abuse. Parenting training can be employed as an efficient means of changing a troubled parent's aversive reactions to an oppositional child. Parents also can learn alternative and nonabusive ways of controlling the child's undesirable behaviors, such as the use of time-out, withholding of rewards, appropriate and positive social skills training, and modeling, to name but a few.

Qualifications of the Clinician

The techniques of parent training may be offered by a wide variety of trained professionals, including, but not limited to: pediatricians, psychiatrists, pediatric nurses, psychologists, social workers, educators, child and family therapists, child care providers, and those entrusted with the rearing and education of children and adolescents. As mentioned, parent training can be applied in and of itself or in combination with other therapuetic and educational formats. Therefore, the training process can be presented by a wide spectrum of professionals. Practitioners in the fields of human development, education, and mental health are typically trained in the precepts of social learning and the application of systematic behavioral research. The principles of social learning and behavior management as well as knowledge about child development are available to those who specialize in child and adolescent therapy, education, and care.

In addition to a thorough body of knowledge and experience regarding the empirical concepts of behavior modification and social learning, the skilled parent training professional also must be aware of the realistic constraints as well as strengths of this intervention strategy. For instance, clinicians must remain alert to the fact that few variables are completely within their control. When practitioners work directly with children or adolescents, they are able to manipulate some factors to the overall well-being of the child and family. However, by using parent training the professional instructs the parents who, in turn, work with the children. The parents certainly have more controls, for greater periods of time, over the child's environment and behaviors. Despite the professionals' level of expertise or experience, they cannot determine the consequences of the parents' actions and responses to the child's behaviors. The clinician, of course, must consider the parents' level of personal, cognitive, and social awareness. The clinician, then, must tailor the parent training techniques in accord with the parents' as well as the target child's abilities, resources, and levels of understanding.

The qualified professional must train the parents in the essential and appropriate child management skills. The parenting skills typically are presented in a didactic style, discussed, modeled, analyzed, reviewed, and evaluated by the parents and the mental health practitioner. If the parenting techniques are not working, they can be revised. The therapist's primary focus is on accurately identifying and assessing problem areas, thoroughly considering all relevant developmental issues, and prescribing the most effective treatment procedures. The professional is not only responsible for training the parents in the proper child modification techniques but also must instruct them in how to measure and assess their child's progress. For example, parents may be given rudimentary charts and rating scales. Parents, as well as the child, can be taught how to measure the successful acquisition of appropriate and effective behaviors on a simple 1 to 10 rating scale, from least desirable (1) to most desirable (10). Similarly, parents can learn how to use basic techniques for tallying or keeping an account of a child's positive actions and responses. The child may receive stars or points on a chart. For every fifth star (intermittent reinforcement schedule), for example, the child can earn a reward, such as extra play time with a favorite playmate and/or toy. Any and all parenting techniques, of course, are in keeping with the target child's level of development and specific problems. Furthermore, the parents must be trusted to comply reasonably and correctly with the provisions of the parent training intervention strategies.

Equipment and Technological Considerations

Behavioral-social parent training affords a variety of styles and techniques. The format is limited only by the imagination of the professionals and the parents involved. Strategic intervention plans include the use of video equipment in order to give parents and children feedback on the performance and communication styles. Training also includes television, movies, and books as learning devices that can reflect and model correct parenting styles. Tape recorders frequently are used. Playground and playroom equipment also are commonly utilized.

Written instruments, such as self-rating, parent-rating, and teacher-rating reports, are also frequently a part of parent training. These evaluations can be used to diagnose the problems, assess the level or intensity of the problems, and determine whether any significant improvements have occurred following the parent training intervention.

Whether the parent training intervention plan employs technical electronic equipment; nontechnical toys, games, and charts; or rating scales and reports depends, of course, on the nature of the problem and the intervention strategy. The parents' and childrens' abilities and competencies in operating and understanding equipment and rating scales, for instance, must be considered. The availability of equipment and resources must enter into the overall considerations.

Indications and Contraindications

Whether parents can be educated to apply parent training strategies in an effective and appropriate manner is contingent on a variety of factors, such as the competencies of the parents and children, the professional's experiences, a diagnosis and analysis of the problem behaviors, and the application of appropriate modification and intervention modalities. Several variables have been studied in order to determine the feasibility of

parent training as a viable intervention manuever. Wahler (1980), for example, clarifies the relationship between familial isolation and failures to comply with the parent training process in an effective manner. If the parents have little or no social support or social contact, it is unlikely that they will be able to follow through with the training process. In particular, this may be the case if the training involves encouraging the child to increase acceptable social contacts and interactions.

In addition, Blechman (1984b) presents a discussion of parental competency and the impact this has on the successful achievement of parent training goals. A functional definition of "competence" denotes the possession or acquisition of adequate skill at a specific task, such as parenting or communicating with others. It should be noted, of course, that the notion of "competence" is not equated with "personal worth" or a genuine love and caring for one's children. Parents who, for whatever reasons, are unable to comprehend or master the fundamental principles of behavioral management or social learning would certainly not be good candidates for parent training programs.

The obvious indicator that an individual can benefit from parent training is the presence of some measure of motivation and competence. Parents must be able to set realistic expectations and structures for their children. The parents must have the personal, cognitive, emotional, and social resources necessary to identify and cope with their children's problems. They also must be able to comprehend and persist in a viable parent training program. The parents must be cautioned to avoid either overestimating or underestimating their children's skills and abilities. In addition, the parents must be able to generalize the newly acquired social learning and behavioral skills. They must be able to recognize the similarity or the links among various behavioral components.

We stated earlier that parent training tends to be prescriptive. As such, it focuses on specific target behaviors and specific techniques for ameliorating these behaviors. The strategy that the parents learn must be specific enough to address particular problems. However, it also must be open-ended enough to allow for possible applications to other similar problems. That is to say, the parenting skills must be generalizable, otherwise the parents would have to retrain for each and every problem that arises during the course of the child's development. For example, if parents have learned to encourage their child to engage in age-appropriate peer interactions and play in order to overcome the youngster's social shyness and isolation, they also must be able to apply these learned skills to related social and interpersonal behaviors, such as teaching the child to respond more in class or to initiate conversations with other children. The parents, with the help of the professional, also must be able to recognize that these skills can be used to address and modify the child's self-doubts, social fears, and bullying or submissive behaviors. In a very real sense, parent training skills are of value only to the degree that they can be generalized and applied to similar yet distinct behaviors and circumstances. Indeed, if taught and acquired effectively, these parenting skills should be of long-term value and applicable in a number of situations.

Various researchers have investigated a number of other factors that might directly or indirectly affect parental competencies to master parent training techniques. Some researchers—for example, Blechman (1984a) and Eyberg and Johnson (1974)—have reviewed the impact of low-income and single-parent status on success and persistence in parent training and therapeutic endeavors. It has been suggested that this population may not have the resources to follow through with proper training procedures. They conclude, however, that family income did not prove to be a strong or consistent variable for predicting success in parent training programs. These researchers also studied the number of parents involved in the process, educational background, and occupational prestige. They concluded that occupational prestige was the only variable that proved to have any predictive value. In considering some of these variables, however, we must be cautious and avoid perpetuating presumptions and misconceptions. The majority of single parents are women, and, historically, the occupational prestige of women has not matched that of men. In our culture there has been a tendency to assume that 2-parent families have a higher social status than 1-parent families. As such, 2-parent families may be more likely to comply with therapeutic intervention. These presumptions are not always valid or in accord with research findings.

Obviously, some measure of competence corre-lates with success in the learning and application of parent training. There are cases, however, when basic competence is lacking. Parents who have marked intellectual-cognitive deficits, psychological and personality inadequacies, or severe mental health problems may find it difficult to comprehend the procedural instructions and to apply the intervention plans correctly or effectively. Similarly, parents who have chronic and incapacitating physical disorders may not have the stamina necessary to persist in an extensive training program. For a number of reasons, some parents do not have the personal, emotional, or cognitive resources necessary to identify, remediate, or cope with their offspring's problems.

A final consideration as to the advisability of a parent training intervention strategy focuses on those children who may be in a hospital, residential, or related treatment facility, which typically involves relatively long-term care. If the child is in such a treatment facility, the parents may be included in that agency's intervention plans, including participating in diagnostic issues, a discussion of the rationale and expectations of various treatment options, evaluative team meetings, and preparations for participation in a viable follow-up program. Even in situations that consist of severe and long-term care, parents can be trained to become part of the therapeutic milieu. They can be taught to recognize and resolve those behaviors and interactions that, in the long run, may be destructive to the well-being of all involved. By instructing the parents in appropriate parent training methods, the therapeutic structure can be replicated within the family and home setting. Therefore, progress continues without any significant disruption when the youngster is home on a weekend visit or eventually discharged from the hospital or residential program. In parent training, the parents and family members as well as the home environment they provide become an integral part of the child's ongoing intervention process.

Progress in Parent Training

As we have noted, the effectiveness of parent training as a viable technique in modifying or remediating a child's disruptive behaviors and enhancing coping mechanisms and social skills has been well documented. The efficacy of modeling appropriate behaviors, social and interpersonal skill training, the constructive use of guided practice, the positive impact of verbal and communication cues, and the appropriate use of reinforcement contingencies to foster or extinguish certain behaviors have all been extensively recorded. (See Dangel & Polster, 1984; Schaefer & Briesmeister, 1989.) The issue of generalizability certainly comes to the fore whenever we discuss the progress made in the realm of parent training. Research and application in the field has progressed from the specific and prescriptive approach to a more global application.

Contemporary parent training procedures and applications consist of a growing technology of practical know-how based on empirical research that can be used by clinicians, counselors, and educators. The research and application of parenting skills has evolved from a one-on-one parent training program occurring in the professional's office to home-, school-, and community-based programs. The understanding, familiarity, and implementation of the scientific principles of social-learning theory and behavioral modification have extended beyond the realm of the mental health professional and the clinician's office. Even further, parent training has expanded from the confines of the immediate family and home into the classroom, day care, playground, residential treatment facility, and overall community.

Progress in the research and application of parent training formats is also seen in the inclusion of an additional facet of treatment outcome, namely, "social validity" (Kazdin, 1977). This aspect refers not only to the generalization of parent training but also evaluates therapeutic changes that are important to the psychological and social well-being of the target child or adolescent. Growth and progress can be measured by the impact parent training has on other didactic and therapeutic programs. It supplements and increases the intervention strategies, gains, and options that are offered in formal child and adolescent therapy and in child-rearing, child-management, and educational programs. Whether in isolation or in combination, each of these intervention approaches makes for happier and better-adjusted children, parents, and families.

Future Directions

Ongoing challenges confront professionals who work in the field of parent-child relationships and parent training. The highest priority is accorded the quality of parent training. Investigators and practitioners must continuously strive for more thorough, systematic, and heuristic research and theory construction. Future research and empirically grounded studies also must remain bidirectional. The focus must remain on both the capacities and concerns of the child and the impact these have on the parents, as well as the resources and concerns of the parents and their impact on the child. We must continue to investigate procedures that foster adaptive changes in parental attitudes and behaviors based on an increased repertoire of knowledge about social learning theory and skills in behavioral child management.

The concept of behavioral change involves 3 sequential stages: the acquisition, maintenance, and generalization of adaptive skills and prosocial behaviors. Future progress in parent training depends on continued advances in techniques for establishing all 3 aspects of behavior modification in the parents as well as the children. Still further, these must be researched, developed, and applied against the backdrop of contemporary developmental theory.

The research in parent training must continue to focus on prevention. Just as the prescriptive approach designates different intervention strategies for specific problems, so too different preventive training programs must be designed to meet the needs of parents and children. Future research in parent training must aim not only to remediate problems but also to prevent the recurrence of future maladaptive behaviors, such as troubled children or parents who are abusive, neglectful, or merely unenlightened as to proper parenting procedures. Equally as important, parent training and intervention must take place before any problems within the family occur. By establishing a healthy, nurturing, and adaptive family structure as well as constructive relationship and communication patterns, the risks for potential problems can be reduced significantly. Instructional courses on parenting skills can be offered at the high school level. More sophisticated and involved parenting skills training programs that anticipate some of the more common needs of parents can be developed. For example, pediatric hospitals and prenatal care units could offer parents, especially new parents, instructions, directions, and practical tips on the use of contingency and reinforcement schedules, positive parenting skills, and developmental milestones and expectations, to name but a few approaches to improved child management and understanding. With continued research, preventive programs, expanded application, and mounting interests, the future of parent training appears promising.

REFERENCES

Blechman, E. A. (1984a). Are children with one parent at psychological risk?: A methodological review. *Journal of Marriage and the Family, 44,* 179–195.

Blechman, E. A. (1984b). Competent parents, competent children: Behavioral objectives of parent training. In R. F. Dangel, & R. A. Polster (Eds.), *Parent training: Foundations of research and practive* (pp. 34–63). New York: Guilford Press.

Braswell, L. (1991). Involving parents in cognitive-behavioral therapy with children and adolescents. In P. C. Kendall (Ed.). *Child and adolescent therapy,* 316–351. New York: Guilford Press.

Braswell, L., & Kendall, P. C. (1988). Cognitive-behavioral methods with children. In K. Dobson (Ed.). *Handbook of cognitive-behavioral therapies* (pp. 167–213). New York: Guilford Press.

Briesmeister, J. M., & Schaefer, C. E. (Eds.). (1997). Handbook of parent Training: Parent as co-therapists for children's behavior problems, 2nd. Ed. New York: John Wiley & Sons.

Crane, D. R. (1995). Introduction to behavioral family therapy for families with young children. *Journal of Family Therapy, 17,* 229–242.

Dangel, R. F., & Polster, R. A. (Eds.). (1984). *Parent training: Foundations of research and practice.* New York: Guilford Press.

Eyberg, S. M., & Johnson, S. M. (1974). Multiple assessment of behavior modification with families: Effects of contingency contracting and order of treated problems. *Journal of Consulting and Clinical Psychology, 42,* 594–606.

Freud, S. (1955). The analysis of a phobia in a 5-year-old boy. In J. Strachey (Ed. & Trans.), *The standard edition of the complete psychological works of Sigmund Freud* (Vol. 10, pp. 149–289). London: Hogarth Press. (Original work published 1909.)

Graziano, A. M. (1977). Parents as behavior therapists. In M. Hersen, R. M. Eisler, & P. M. Miller (Eds.). *Progress in behavior modification* (Vol 4, pp. 223–266). New York: Academic Press.

Kazdin, A. E. (1977). Assessing the clinical or applied importance of behavior change through social validation. *Behavior Modification, 1,* 427–452.

Kendall, P. C., & Braswell, L. (1985). *Cognitive-behavior therapy for impulsive children.* New York: Guilford Press.

Ruma, P. R., Burke, R. V., & Thompson, R. W. (1996). Group parent training: Is it effective for children of all ages? *Behavior Therapy, 27,* 159–169.

Serketich, W. J., & Dumas, J. E. (1996). The effectiveness of behavioral parent training to modify antisocial behavior in children: A meta-analysis. *Behavior Therapy, 27,* 171–186.

Wahler, R. G. (1980). The insular mother: Her problems in parent-child treatment. *Journal of Applied Behavior Analysis, 13,* 207–219.

18 / Conjoint Parent-Child Interventions, Infancy through Three Years

Saul L. Brown and Helen Reid

Background for Referral

While self-referral by the parents may be the starting point for a conjoint parent-child intervention, more often it follows upon referral from a professional who has observed or assessed the child, or from the staff in a setting where the interactions between child and parent are perceived to need such help. Day care and nursery schools are the most common sites where the need for this kind of intervention becomes apparent. Although problematic child-parent interactions may not be directly observed in a pediatric office, family physicians, pediatricians, or their professional associates may nevertheless discern problematic interactions between the child and parent based on questions raised by the parent or on description of events at home.

Situations likely to cause the parents themselves to initiate a request for conjoint help are those in which a disruption of child care has occurred because of disabling physical or mental illness in a parent or the death or sudden departure of one parent or of a primary caregiver, or when the parent feels overwhelmed or even, in some instances, out of control.

Sequential Assessment and Conjoint Parent-Child Intervention

While an initial individual assessment of the child is desirable, it is not always a realistic option. The life circumstances of many families may not lend themselves easily to a series of initial individual assessments or to an extended series of sessions. For this reason, entry of the very young child into the clinical sphere often proceeds in an evolutionary fashion, with the line between formal assessment and intervention somewhat blurred.

Conjoint parent-child sessions therefore may be viewed as a pragmatic and flexible mode of intervention that includes assessment and intervention, and that is responsive to the social and economic situation of the family. In summary, in relation to the very young child, the conjoint modality may be characterized as *sequential assessment* extended over time.

Problematic Relationships

The premise underlying conjoint parent-infant (usually mother-child) interventions is that the relationship between the parents and their infant/toddler or 3-year-old is in some ways failing or faulty. This premise has evolved from important clinical research and direct observations made by many individuals in the past several decades. Perhaps the most influential has been John Bowlby in England who, in a series of papers published in the 1950s, described what he designated as the "attachment" process and the associated phenomenon of separation anxiety between mother and the very young infant. (See Bowlby, 1969.) He and an associate, Mary Ainsworth (1985), subsequently have carried out and stimulated widely recognized research relating to issues surrounding the phenomena of separation and reunion between young child and parent and to the psychopathology that can be traced to those aspects of the parent-infant relationship.

From a somewhat different perspective, the psychoanalytic studies and writings of Donald Winnicott in England in the 1940s and thereafter have been of profound significance for illuminating the exquisite sensitivity of mother-infant interaction in the earliest months, drawing on the inner fantasies of mother and of the child.

Of equal significance for clinical practice and theoretical understanding has been the clinical research of Margaret Mahler and her associates, published in the 1960s. Her written and filmed presentations of the developing mother-child relationship in the second year relating to early child independence and the evolution of an autonomous sense of self have created both a theoretical and clinical basis for conjoint interventions for this age group.

Various researchers have demonstrated how pathologic events may occur in the parent-child interaction. An outstanding study in the 1950s using films was carried out by Sylvia Brody, showing modes of feeding of the child in the first year. (See Brody, 1956.)

Relationship Disturbances in Early Childhood, A Developmental Approach, edited by Arnold Sameroff and Robert Emde (1989) has contributed to the theoretical basis for a definitive diagnosis of "relationship disorder." The work of Daniel Stern, Arnold Samerof, and L. Alan Sroufe published in that volume, is of noteworthy importance for conjoint parent-child interventions in very early childhood.

The many detailed descriptions of early childhood pathology and the techniques for interventions with parent and child offered by Stanley Greenspan are of signal importance for conjoint work.

Finally, relative to the diagnosis of relationship disorders, the publication of a diagnostic manual, *Zero to Three,* by the National Center for Clinical Infant Programs, in 1994, creates a framework for employing the conjoint parent-child intervention for this age group.

Introducing the Parent(s) to the Conjoint Intervention

In order to establish a productive working relationship, the clinician needs to make clear to the parents that it is not the intent of the sessions to seek for an ultimate source for the problem they are experiencing; instead, it is first to discern what in their current interaction with their child causes the problem to continue and prevent its resolution, and then to find alternative behaviors for them and for their child. Bringing them to this understanding requires discussion of the nature of reciprocal process in parent-child relationships. While many parents arrive already psychologically sophisticated about this, others are focused solely on their child's behavior, viewing this as the problem to be solved. Still others may be filled with self-condemnation, believing themselves to have failed as parents. These feelings in parents, which tend to paralyze their ability to manage their child's behavior effectively, require empathetic response from the clinician together with a firm problem-solving orientation.

Reasons for Intervention— First 12 Months

Problematic interactions are not always discrete from one another. These may be subtle and difficult to recognize in a short clinical observation. They may at times be more evident in the behavior of the infant and at other times more easily seen in the parent's behavior. Following are some examples.

PROBLEMATIC ATTACHMENT

What may be most evident of poorly established attachment is the infant's looking away or avoidance of eye contact with the parent. In the slightly older infant a repetitive tendency to crawl away without looking back or checking for the parent's reactions may be observed. This has been dramatically demonstrated in a video study developed by Robert Emde (1989). In some infants there is a noticeable increase in tension when the parent makes contact with the baby. In others what is notable is a marked resistance to separation from the parent's—usually the mother's—body sometimes including an obsessive attachment as in clinging to the mother's hair or breast. An impassive or joyless reaction in the infant at moments of reunion with the parent is a marked indicator of problematic attachment.

PARENTAL INSENSITIVITY TO THE INFANT'S EXPERIENCE

Parental behaviors that represent significant insensitivity include imprecise reading of the infant's immediate needs such as prolonged overfeeding; excessive comforting; misjudging when the infant needs to be put down or picked up; handling the baby awkwardly or too abruptly; introducing changes that are disruptive to the baby's natural rhythms; holding or turning the baby in a direction that does not allow for comfortable eye contact with the parent or visualization of each other's facial expressions.

Other examples include a relative absence of reciprocal communications as in failing to echo the baby's sounds and vocalizations, or to respond expressively or in an appropriately timed fashion to its non-verbal gestures. These phenomena have been elaborately studied by Daniel Stern among others (1985), imposing excitatory or overly stimulating actions upon the infant as in tickling or throwing into the air or jiggling too vigorously.

A significant kind of insensitivity that may be observed in parents is their failure to recognize the infant's normal reactions to separation episodes and their tendency to misinterpret the baby's discomfort or agitation at times when leaving without having prepared the infant for this through comforting, talking about what is about to occur, waving good-bye and the like. Often related to this is a lack of awareness in the parents of the importance to the baby of some kind of transitional object such as a favorite soothing blanket or soft object or a pacifier. Donald Winnicott has been particularly articulate in discussing these attachments as fundamental components in the infant's transition from the early merging with the mother (1971).

Affective dissonance may be observed in the parent-infant interaction when the infant's irritability or restlessness or, on the other hand, impassivity and lack of vitality evoke impatience, or distancing or mechanical responses from the parent.

INFANTS WITH DEFINITIVE DEVELOPMENTAL DEFICITS

Infants with congenital or genetic or posttraumatic developmental deficits present particularly poignant difficulties for the infant-parent interaction and relationship. These fall into a major category of parent-infant intervention. Issues represented in the foregoing examples may apply in many of those situations and add to their complexity.

Reasons for Interventions—Parents with Toddlers Through Age 3

The following examples of relationship problems between child and parents are in some instances similar to those described for the first 12 months.

PROBLEMATIC ATTACHMENT

Observable in the parent and or child are behaviors that reflect problems of attachment. The studies by Mary Ainsworth have been particularly illustrative of these behaviors. They may include emotional or affective distancing in either or both; denial by the child of a normal need for comforting; psuedo-independence on the child's part; unremitting or inconsolable crying or complaining; extreme clinging by the child to the mother; reluctance on the mother's part to grant or encourage age appropriate independent activities.

PROBLEMATIC SEPARATION AND REUNION

Evidence for this may overlap with the observable attachment issues noted above. Margaret Mahler's film studies of the toddler's evolving capability to move away in small increments from the mother's immediate space with a resulting sense of individual autonomy and curiosity have illuminated both the normal and the potential pathology in this phase of parent-toddler relating (1980). In some relationships what may be observed is a relative absence or diffuseness about saying good-bye at times of separation, or a failure to definitively prepare the toddler for imminent parental departures or separations. Noteworthy in some interactions is an absence of affectively expressive greetings by the parents at times of reunion with the infant.

UNEVEN USE OF PARENTAL AUTHORITY

What may be observed in parents is confusion and or inconsistency in setting age-appropriate limits for the toddler, or in defining personal boundaries such as invasions of the body privacy of others, as in unlimited and overly excitatory crawling onto or wrestling with parents or siblings.

PARENTAL FAILURE TO APPROPRIATELY MIRROR THE TODDLER'S BEHAVIORS

This complex interactional process initially formulated by Donald Winnicott (1971) represents the profound need for empathic mirroring of the toddler's feelings and positive behaviors in order to stabilize an authentic sense of self. Evidence of a problematic parent-toddler relationship may occur in the behavior or attitudes of a toddler who is not genuine in affective expressions, who tends to over-demand attention through disingenuous behaviors, or who, on the other hand, appears to have "given up" and is severely shy or withdrawn.

INAPPROPRIATE ROLE-CASTING OF THE TODDLER

Not unusually difficult parent-toddler relationships can be observed when the parents impose early negative characterizations on their child's personality, such as "the little fighter," "the manipulator," "the greedy one," "the passive one," and the like. Even more problematic are these kinds of attributions that parents may link to a family member, for example, an unsuccessful sibling or an unlikable grandparent. (See the work of Zeanah and Benoit, 1995).

RESPONSES TO PREGNANCY

Within the parent-child relationship there is a profound sensitivity to the imminent or actual displacement of the toddler by a new sibling. Prior to the birth are the toddler's reactions to the pregnant body of the mother. The relationship becomes vulnerable at these times and insensitive parental responses to the toddler may be seriously disruptive of the toddler-mother emotional bond.

BIOLOGICALLY DETERMINED DEFICITS

Self-evident is the possibility and even the probability that problematic parent-toddler relationship issues will occur that are reflective of the deep emotional wound to the parents when their toddler manifests significant developmental deficits or delays. These unfortunate and often tragic situations are particularly needful of conjoint parent-child intervention.

The Clinician's Function in Conjoint Parent-Child Interventions

The task for the clinician varies according to whether the problematic issue is primarily one of relationship or whether it is secondary to but nevertheless interwoven with one or more specific deficits or traumata. Since a clear line cannot always be drawn between what are primary causative factors and what are secondary, the clinical effort with the child and parent is essentially a "here-and-now" one. It is focused intensively on the interpersonal behaviors and interactions as they unfold in each session.

Conjoint sessions typically require frequent and rapid shifts of the clinician's attention and interventions, directed now to the child and now to the parents. These may vary from interactive play with the child, to modeling of constructive ways of being with and communicating with the child, to brief commentaries directly to the child or to the parents about what feelings they may be experiencing in a specific interaction, to suggestions to the parents of a specific action to carry out in the session or at home.

With infants, the clinician may model physical handling of the baby, always being careful to quickly return the baby to the parent once the purpose of the specific intervention has become clear, thereby reaffirming the parent's role and encouraging competence. Interventions in this phase generally are educative for the parent and aim to demonstrate attuned and empathic parenting. This is the case regardless of the specific behavior of the infant—that is, whether it shows developmental delay from whatever source or problematic attachment.

Often the relationship difficulties are associated with depression or ambivalence in the mother. In some instances severe psychopathology, addictions, or abusive inclinations are operant. In these situations, while the conjoint intervention is essential, individual therapy for the mother is equally necessary.

In conjoint therapy with toddlers, modeling or demonstrating ways to interact with their child in each session should, whenever feasible, include the nature of verbal acknowledgment of the parents' authority and encouragement for them to "take over" once the nature of the specific intervention is clear. The clinician typically remarks to parent and/or to child about what is happening between them as behaviors or interactions occur in the session. Comments addressed directly to the child usually are intended to affirm what he or she is trying to do or may be feeling at a given moment. Comments to the parent are intended to educate about the meaning of the child's actions but also seek to awaken the parent's awareness of his or her own feelings in response to what the child is doing and to encourage reflection about what is happening between them. This encouragement for reflection should occur only for brief interludes and should not dominate the session.

While the clinician needs to offer authoritative leadership to both the child and parents, the basic ambiance of the sessions should be one of comfortable mutuality and cooperative exploration. Creating this ambiance may require several sessions to accomplish. The exact mode of intervention varies according to the age of the child, the adaptability of the parent(s), and the receptivity of both the child and the parent(s) to the experience. The clinician gradually builds on the experiences of each·session so that repetitive behaviors become subject to increasingly precise interventions. For example, a mother who becomes immobilized and is at a loss for setting limits when her child is provocative is reminded, each time that this occurs, that she can institute some action, while the child is reminded of what the "rules" are.

When the 2- or or 3-year-old actively resists involvement in the sessions or becomes hyperactive or overly excited or aggressive, the parent needs to be prompted to take control. Occasionally the clinician may initiate direct encounters with the child, in essence provoking a small interactional crisis. Doing so may be necessary if the child persistently ignores the clinician. It is most typical with very provocative or oppositional children who are compelled to test a situation. At times it reflects an undercurrent negativity or resistance in the parent about the intervention experience.

Goals for the Conjoint Parent-Child Intervention

The principal clinical goal for the parent-child intervention is to reduce or ameliorate behavioral symptoms in the child from whatever cause. Other goals that inevitably accompany this goal are to: (1) increase parental knowledge about child development and reinforce their feelings of competence as a parents; (2) facilitate age-appropriate behaviors in the child and parental responses to them; (3) deepen the parents' understanding of the normative separation-individuation process in both the child and themselves; and (4) reinforce parental sensitivity and empathic responses to their child's feelings.

Summary

Parents whose infant or very young child is not functioning at an age appropriate level are wounded and frightened. Even as they seek help they are likely to be defensive in the beginning and wary of the clinician who they may fear will displace them in their parental role. Moreover, the parents may be divided about whether professional help is in fact needed. Marital conflict, which often includes undercurrent blame about each other's parenting, may cause them to delay seeing help for considerable lengths of time. Finally, both shame and guilt are the perennial shadows that follow parents whose very young child is failing to develop in an age appropriate fashion.

These feelings evoke ambivalence in the parents about seeking help and they often make the initial act of referral difficult for clinicians. Pediatricians, family physicians, pediatric neurologists, nursery school teachers, day care providers, or special educators often find that referring parents for conjoint intervention is a delicate process that typically requires maximum tact and tolerance.

The signal challenge for the clinician who undertakes conjoint parent-child intervention is to focus firmly but supportively upon the interaction between the child and parent (see Lieberman, 1992 and 1993) while dealing only tangentially or indirectly with the manifest individual psychopathology in either or both parents.

REFERENCES

Ainsworth, M. D. S. (1985). Patterns of infant-mother attachments: Antecedents and effects on development. *Bulletin of the New York Academy of Medicine, 61,* 771–791.

Bowlby, J. (1988b). Attachment, communication, and the therapeutic process in J. Bowlby (Ed.), *A secure base: clinical applications of attachment theory.* London: Routledge.

Brody, S. (1956). Patterns of mothering: maternal influence during infancy. New York: University Press.

Emde, R. N. (1989). The infant's relationship experience: Developmental and affective aspects. In A. J. Sameroff & R. N. Emde (Eds.), *Relationship disturbances in early childhood* (pp. 33–51). New York: Basic Books.

Greenspan, S. I. (1988). The development of the ego: Insights from clinical work with infants and children. *Journal of the American Psychoanalytic Association, 36* (suppl), 3–55.

Lieberman, A. F. (1992). Infant-parent psychotherapy with toddlers. In *Development and Psychopathology,* Vol. 4, pps. 559–574.

Lieberman, A. F., & Pawl, J. H. (1993). Infant-parent psychotherapy. In Zeanah (Ed.), *Handbook of infant mental health.* New York: Basic Books.

Mahler, M. S. (1980). Rapprochement subphase of the separation-individuation. In R. Lax, S. Bach & J. A. Burland (Eds.), *Rapprochement: The critical subphase of separation-individuation* (pp. 3–19). New York: Jason Aronson.

Stroufe, L. A. (1989b). Relationships and relationship disturbances. In A. J. Sameroff & R. N. Emde (Eds.), *Relationship disturbances in early childhood* (pp. 97–124). New York: Basic Books.

Stern, D. N. (1985). *The interpersonal world of the infant.* New York: Basic Books.

Winnicott, D. W. (1971). Mirror-role of mother and family in child development. In *Playing and reality.* New York: Basic Books.

Zeanah, C. H., & Benoit, D. (1995). Clinical applications of a parent perception interview in infant mental health. In Minde K. (Ed.), *Infant psychiatry, child and adolescent psychiatry clinics of North America.* Philadelphia: Saunders.

19 / **The Therapeutic Nursery**

Eva Sperling

This chapter describes the therapeutic nursery, its functions, and the major issues and problems that commonly arise in the use of this form of treatment. Readers will find this chapter useful in designing a therapeutic nursery and in understanding how children benefit from this treatment.

The therapeutic nursery represents an integration of the cumulative contributions of the great educators, psychologists, and psychoanalysts of the 19th and 20th centuries, whose views in turn were rooted in earlier humanistic philosophy. (Elkind, 1996) Their ideas brought about a revolution in both the vision and care of children. It became evident that the minds of young children are constantly at work and that children's development is shaped by their own experience and actions. With this recognition, early childhood education gained its place as a separate profession.

Children's inner lives then became the focus of the psychoanalytic movement. Anny Katan, coming from Anna Freud's Hempstead Clinic in London, established a therapeutic nursery in Cleveland in which treatment of mothers and children was closely coordinated. (Furman, 1957) This work was described in a landmark book, which inspired the development of therapeutic nurseries throughout the country. (Furman, 1969)

Since then major advances in the knowledge about child development and pathology have been achieved. Neuropsychology, new imaging techniques, genetic studies, and cognitive studies all have contributed to a more empirically validated understanding of the child. These new findings also have changed the view of the parents' role in the genesis of certain childhood psychopathologies and developmental disorders. These advances have influenced the way therapeutic nurseries work with the children and their families and have generated new forms of treatment, such as the behavior therapies, sensory integration, and pharmacotherapy.

Definition

The therapeutic nursery is a unique and complex form of treatment that has the capacity to offer the best of early childhood education in combination with a wide variety of interventions on a long-term, intensive, and highly individualized basis. Historically the line between education and psychological therapies has been a fine one, but nowhere is that line more fluid than when applied to the development of young children. This fluidity and merging of approaches is fundamental to the therapeutic nursery, which is at once both nursery school and day treatment for children under 5.

During the past 30 years this modality has flourished, its definition has broadened, and it is being used for many different, often specialized, target populations, such as children of homeless families, children of psychotic mothers, abused children, autistic children, and language-impaired children. (Zelman, 1996) Although some therapeutic nurseries may concentrate on providing diagnostic evaluations and/or rapid intervention for

children who may attend for only a few weeks, most offer a much longer course of intervention.

As a group, therapeutic nurseries usually share the following characteristics:

- Classes usually are divided according to age: preschool (3- to 5-year-old) and toddler (2- to 3-year-old) groups.
- Children attend several-hour sessions, several times per week, for 1, 2, or even 3 years.
- As compared to a regular nursery, the number of children in the class is small (5 to 10) and the adult-child ratio large (1 to 4 or even 1 to 2).
- Parents or other major caregivers are actively involved in the nursery effort, whether they participate within the classroom on a regular basis or not.
- Service to the children and families is planned and provided by an interdisciplinary team using an integrated psychoeducational strategy that, in addition to specially trained teachers, includes the disciplines of child psychiatry, psychology, language pathology, social work, and occupational therapy. Referrals are made to pediatric neurology and other specialties as indicated.

Since there are many permutations of the features, this chapter concentrates on issues of general applicability and interest to the entire spectrum of therapeutic nursery models.

Indications

Most often young children are brought for evaluation and service for the following presenting problems:

- Severe problems in managing the routines of daily living, when the efforts of the family and the pediatrician have been unsuccessful. These may include problems with sleeping, eating, or toileting. Often these symptoms have seriously disrupted family functioning.
- Unsuccessful attempts to attend another preschool or to benefit from other interventions.
- Failure to achieve age-appropriate development of language, communication, social interaction with peers or adults, control of aggression, impulsivity, ability to play, and ability to separate.
- Primary and secondary prevention for children experiencing severe or unusual stresses.

- Physical conditions that have contributed to a major disruption of the child's affect and behavior, such as asthma, arthritis, or congenital anomaly.
- Diagnostic clarification. (Katan, 1959)

The underlying causes of all these presenting problems may be acute or chronic environmental stresses, biologically based developmental delays or deficits, or the potentiating combination of both. Environmental problems include parental drug or alcohol dependence, neglect, abuse, domestic violence, multiple foster placements, or poor parenting skills. Reactions to loss, serious illness in the family, or other traumatic events are also appropriately treated in a therapeutic nursery. It is important to note that children who have been severely stressed may appear delayed in their intellectual development even when their innate cognitive abilities are intact. (Zelman, 1985) For these children, who require simultaneous attention to their emotional and educational needs, placement in a therapeutic nursery is an excellent option since it offers the combination of a small, nurturing, and cognitively stimulating setting. Underlying biological conditions, such as autistic spectrum disorders, disorders of language development, attention deficit hyperactivity disorder, motor delays, mood disorders and cognitive deficits, often have not been recognized in these children prior to their entry into the therapeutic nursery.

Sources of referral include nursery schools, Head Start programs, day care centers, social welfare agencies, adoption agencies, pediatricians, mental health professionals, school systems, and parents.

Criteria for Enrollment

Four decisive factors determine which children are suitable for admission: First is the type of child the nursery is designed to serve; for example, some programs specialize in the treatment of homeless children or autistic children. Second is the severity of the child's problems: Does the child's condition warrant this level of intervention?

A third factor to be considered is the desired balance of children within the class so that (1) staff can provide the optimal level of care for each child; (2) children and parents benefit from each other's presence; and (3) balance in age, developmental level, gender, and/or ethnic or racial distribution is achieved. A class in which both hyperactive, aggressive and shy, withdrawn children are included may be preferable to one in which all the children are behaviorally similar. Nonverbal and verbal children grouped together will be more interactive and more helpful to the less communicative children than a group composed entirely of nonverbal children.

Finally, since the role of the caregiver is crucial in the treatment of the child the availability of a parental figure with whom the potential for a working alliance exists is of paramount importance.

Characteristics of the Therapeutic Nursery

HOW THE THERAPEUTIC NURSERY DIFFERS FROM REGULAR PRESCHOOLS

As many important aspects of early education and early therapeutic interventions are shared and overlap, the ultimate goals of therapeutic nurseries and regular preschools are similar. The therapeutic nursery stands as a bridge between early education and psychiatric treatment in its capacity to integrate the principles of both. In both settings, the children attend often, regularly, and over a long period. It becomes possible to know the children well as individuals and to understand their abilities, both cognitive and social. Particularly in the early years, the teacher's mission is to educate in the broadest sense, to awaken, and to nurture all the potential in the young personality. Experience in the nursery can have an impact on all areas of the children's growth. This is the period of life that presents the challenge of being with peers and adults outside the family, of responding to the interactive demands of free play, of accommodating to the structure of group activities (being able to wait, to share, to listen), of learning about and becoming tolerant of differences, of meeting the outside world as a separate, autonomous entity. Good schools encourage curiosity, exploration, experimentation, expression of needs and wishes, both in reality and in the fantasy of play.

For children requiring therapeutic nursery intervention, many of these challenges are far too difficult. These children cannot manage tasks that are taken for granted in a regular preschool program. For example, one child may not be able to understand instructions, another may provocatively refuse to comply with them, another has no concept of sequence, while yet another is unrelated and seems not to hear. Even the best educational approach will not be effective for these children unless it is combined with expertise that specifically addresses the developmental and psychiatric problems that these behaviors represent.

The therapeutic nursery combines elements of good nursery practice with therapeutic attitudes in a number of ways. For example, in the therapeutic nursery, emphasis is on understanding rather than judging the child's communications and problem behaviors. Staff members encourage all sorts of communications. The child's expressions and actions are seen as having both manifest and personal symbolic meaning. At any moment, a window may open to reveal the child's perception and misunderstanding of events.

Parents and staff meet regularly in and out of the class in order to create a working alliance and continuity of care between home and nursery.

In-depth knowledge of the child's history and current life experience outside of school, on a day-to-day basis, allows the staff to understand and respond to the child's behavior as it relates to life at home. It is then possible to connect affect to its source, feeling to behavior, and to further the child's reality testing.

Staff members can allow, even encourage, the problems of the child and of the parent-child dyad to surface to their full extent because maintaining a smoothly running class is not the primary concern. In order to work on the problems, staff members need to observe and experience them. For example, because of her anxiety, Debra cannot let her mother leave the room. When observing this dyad, the nursery staff notices the mother's contribution to the separation problem: She is indecisive, gives Debra mixed messages, asks her permission to leave, and is untruthful about how long she will be away.

Pressure to conform is reduced because there are sufficient staff members to work with the child both in and out of the group.

The child can be nurtured according to individual needs rather than according to chronological age. Personal attention and physical warmth from staff members beyond what is possible in a larger nursery group offer important restitutive experiences, especially for children who have been starved for affection and for whom affection and abuse have been linked. When a child capable of behaving age appropriately takes on a more infantile role in play, the teacher has both the time and the understanding of the child's particular circumstances to use this play in a therapeutic way. For example, coping with the loss of her mother, Annie repeatedly curled up in the carriage to be nurtured as a baby by her teacher therapist, who, within the play, acknowledged the child's sadness and longing and then helped her to grow up gradually to become her 4-year-old self again.

Staff members are available constantly to help the children negotiate interactions, which are difficult for them.

Limit setting can be carried out in a more supportive and personal way. For example, when a child needs to be separated from the group or to be physically restrained, a teacher is available to stay with the child to help him or her regain control and composure.

Because of the personal relationship established between child and teacher, behavior can be modified more easily with incentives that are social, such as an activity, a smile, or praise, rather than with material rewards.

In this age group, it is prudent to be wary of drawing rapid diagnostic or prognostic conclusions. It takes time for the picture to come into focus, to delineate the extent of the child's deficits, strengths, or intellectual potential. Initial anxiety, deprivation, trauma, and the characteristic "honeymoon" reaction may all confound the picture. Because of its ability to provide prolonged treatment, the therapeutic nursery is ideally suited for undertaking an evaluation while providing intensive intervention.

BENEFITS SPECIFIC TO THE GROUP FORMAT OF THE THERAPEUTIC NURSERY

For assessment as well as intervention, seeing a child daily for 2 to 3 hours offers an in-depth opportunity. Staff members can observe the child in the presence and absence of the parent, arriving and departing, after a week at school, and following a weekend at home. The child can be observed interacting with a teacher or playing house with other children. Staff members see the child during free play, story time, snack time, music, painting, on the tricycle, and on the climber. Many of the child's social difficulties would not emerge when alone with an adult. Arousal of sibling rivalry, low frustration tolerance, and inability to wait all would not be seen to their full extent outside of a group setting. Further, there is the opportunity to intervene on the spot, at the very moment of the experience itself. Staff members also can refer back to the event that they and the child, and perhaps the parent, experienced together. The staff can see the child through the eyes of several adults and from the perspectives of several disciplines. It is a great asset to have a team that can discuss and refine the view of the child and family. Such intensive and longitudinal care promotes more reliable evaluation of development and pathology and provides a better base for designing a treatment strategy.

For the child, the presence of other children offers both challenges and advantages. With each other, children are often freer and more expressive in their play. They enact their actual experience and emotionally charged perceptions in rich detail thereby reliving and mastering aspects of their lives. They also express their conflicts and experiment with troubling issues in more disguised ways in their symbolic play. Children stimulate and elaborate each other's play. "You be the baby and I'll be the mommy" is often more exciting and immediate, especially at this age, than representing the same scene with little dolls in a doll house. With its varied spaces and many props, a well-equipped nursery encourages expressive play. There are big blocks, fabrics, dress-up clothes, a carriage large enough for a child, and more. Children stimulate imitation, competition, and rivalry in each other. Since many children who are referred either have had no group experi-

ence or have had unsuccessful ones, it is important for expert help to be constantly available for them to meet this challenge.

Even very young children recognize each other's difficulties and alter their responses accordingly. For example, Robert, an autistic child, hits out at Matt. Matt recognizes the different meaning of this behavior and does not retaliate as he would if another child did the same. Children can be caring and helpful to each other, with positive effects on both the giver and the receiver. Children notice and cheer the achievements of a more disabled child: "Emma can pour her own juice now," or "Look at Peter playing Lotto!" A child with a missing forearm was constantly "lent" a hand by others in the group. As part of a group, children will take risks that they would not attempt alone. Children who are struggling with similar burdens may join forces in their attempts at mastery. For example, two unrelated girls, both of whose mothers had been murdered, repeatedly set out in their toy boat, which they equipped with food, blankets, and other supplies for survival, declaring that they needed no one and could manage on their own.

Parents as well as professionals are concerned about children learning undesirable behaviors from peers whose symptoms are more overt and socially unacceptable. In working with the parents, it is helpful to anticipate that some unwanted imitation will indeed occur. Some children are particularly vulnerable in this respect. However, even in mainstream education, children are not safe from such exposure. It can be argued that it is better to deal with this issue in the earliest years and to do so in a setting where it can be handled expertly. Helping the parents to extinguish such behavior at home is an essential part of such intervention. Parents who are worried about their child learning bad habits from classmates often have to be helped to see that their child's own behavior is what is most stigmatizing and that the copied behaviors are likely to be transient and of less importance.

Having said this, it is important to recognize that both selection of the children to form a group and placement of a child in a group require careful consideration. For example, a child with pervasive developmental disorder has made good progress in cognitive and language skills, but the class of similarly impaired children offers no opportunities for modeling appropriate socialization skills that this child is now ready to acquire. It would be advantageous to move this child to a class in which some children's social skills are intact.

Parents and the Therapeutic Nursery

The success of intervention is greatly influenced by the extent to which a working alliance can be formed with the major parenting figures in the child's life. Clinicians must attempt to predict which parent will or will not be able to form such a helpful partnership. Making the decision about which child and family can best benefit from this intensive and expensive form of treatment remains a humbling task. The parents' degree of psychopathology and their educational or their socioeconomic level is not necessarily a reliable predictor of their ability to change their interactions with their child.

The value of being able to work with a family over the period of a year or 2 cannot be overemphasized. Trust and openness develop slowly as crises are tackled, misunderstandings resolved, achievements celebrated, as life experience unfolds and is shared by parents and staff. The therapeutic nursery offers a holding environment for the parents as much as for the child.

Because there is a natural tendency in our society to view the mother as the primary caregiver, the team may tend to engage mainly with the mother. To resist this tendency, it is important to involve fathers as early as possible. After the family problems have already been presented from the mother's point of view, it is more difficult for the father to join in the work. Once the mother's skills in dealing with the child's problems have improved, the father feels even further disadvantaged and excluded.

For parents, bringing their child to the therapeutic nursery raises great hopes but also may raise fears that threaten their self-esteem and sense of autonomy. Parents may be reluctant to enroll their child for fear of the stigma of a special nursery, fear of being seen as an inadequate parent, and because of anxieties that their child may be influenced by the "bad" or bizarre behavior of the other children. They worry that the nursery will not support the family's standards of behavior. In response to the child's difficulties, parents may feel overwhelmed by feelings of hopelessness and despair and may even develop symptoms of a clinical depression for which psychiatric treatment should be sought. It is crucial for staff members to be sensitive to the parents' vulnerable position especially when the parents behave in provocative ways. In offering their expertise, staff members must avoid being perceived as trying to be a better parent to the child.

In the nursery setting, parents may feel rivalrous for the attention and love of staff members and feel competitive with their own children and with other parents. Since these socially unacceptable reactions are usually not conscious, they are expressed in disguised forms. Information about the parents' own life history may be especially helpful here (Fraiberg, 1975).

Often parents are not yet able to face the extent of their child's deficits or pathology. They prefer to think of the nursery as just a school, not a therapeutic milieu where several treatment modalities are used. For example, they may hold onto the idea that their autistic child is only a little learning disabled or somewhat delayed in acquiring language. Since the children are very young, denial of the severity of their problems is still possible. In addition, parents do not yet understand the importance of their own role in helping their child. Fixing the problem is the school's job.

It is essential for all staff members to be in close communication with each other and to coordinate their responses to the parents' questions, particularly about their children's diagnosis and prognosis. Parents often ask the same questions of different staff members. The timing and the advantages and disadvantages of sharing emotionally loaded information with parents must be carefully weighed.

Parents may react by being extremely critical, demanding, or uncooperative toward staff members. Toward their child they may be neglectful, overly controlling, and even overtly hostile. All this fuels strong negative feelings in staff members. They experience a sense of helplessness, overidentification with the child, and develop rescue fantasies. One such case can become the focus of staff energy, interfere with morale, and may even disrupt the smooth functioning of the entire nursery group. Furthermore, although the identified patient is the child, not the parent, it is important to keep in mind that the parent nevertheless will have reactions quite similar to anyone in a patient-therapist relationship, including powerful positive or negative transference feelings. These must be understood as such but must be handled without stepping across mutually agreed upon boundaries, that is, without making the parent into a patient.

The therapeutic nursery helps parents move toward a greater sense of mastery and control in many ways. Foremost is the daily opportunity to discuss problems, obtain expert advice, and try out new parenting strategies. With such steady support parents gradually feel more secure and hopeful. Training parents in practical management techniques makes daily routines more pleasant and improves the quality of life for the whole family. The therapeutic nursery also teaches parents as much as possible about their child's condition. Such knowledge, and a greater understanding of their child's experience, enables parents to better confront a painful reality and to become active intermediaries and advocates for their children within the family, the school, and the world at large. Staff members share their expertise with the parents, for example, by including parents in language therapy sessions.

Some parents can be taught best by modeling rather than by more direct instruction. Some parents have never played and need to be offered a chance to enjoy playing themselves before they can learn to play with their children. Attending to the parents' needs, emotional and physical, is often a key to enhancing their parental roles. Doing so may take the form of bringing them coffee while they are sitting on the couch, celebrating their birthdays, arranging respite care or baby-sitting, accompanying them to a doctor's appointment, helping them to obtain entitlements or improved housing, or connecting them to a food pantry at the end of the month, when the next check is still days away. Once their children are enrolled in the therapeutic nursery, parents are not alone with their problems.

During individual sessions with a teacher therapist, social worker, or other mental health professional, parents have the opportunity to discuss personal issues as parents rather than as patients. Staff and parents understand that the content of these sessions remains confidential except for

events or feelings experienced by the child. Such information is shared with the team to allow an appropriately informed response to the child's reactions. Home visits are often helpful.

Many therapeutic nurseries have regular parents' group meetings that cover topics of child care or issues specific to certain disorders, or are conducted in a more open-ended way. For parents facing similar problems both in and out of the nursery, being part of a group provides a special dimension of support as well as a source of new ideas. Members often form friendships that lead to contacts outside the nursery such as arranging play dates for their children attending conferences together, and mobilizing support for services for their children.

These close relationships enable parents and staff to weather the difficult times inherent in this work. Staff members must acknowledge these close bonds and respond with care to the reactions of parents that accompany the ending of this collaboration.

Staff Members and the Nursery

For staff members, the therapeutic nursery is a social unit in which the constant smooth teamwork, the intimate as well as stressful nature of the work, all lead to a strong sense of mutual support and closeness. This closeness tends to promote blurring of boundaries between private and professional relationships, which can become troublesome when a hierarchical position has to be used to make decisions.

Because the work is so personal, intense, and prolonged, an additional challenge for staff members is to maintain the appropriate professional distance from the families, especially when members of the staff resemble the parents in age and socioeducational background.

CASE EXAMPLE

Tommy, a 3 year old boy, presented with an almost total failure to develop expressive or receptive language. His mother reported management problems in every aspect of daily living. He did not respond to his name and used little gestural communication. Tommy, curious, energetic, and enthusiastic as he flitted from one activity to another, seemed in a world of his own. He was generally unrelated and avoided eye contact even with his mother for whom, in other ways, he showed a positive attachment.

Tommy's mother had been unable to provide the structure and limits he needed to organize himself in the face of his severe deficits. Their life together was one of chaos: Tommy ate where, what and when he wanted. He was in constant motion. Joyous when allowed free reign, he reacted with panic and tantrums to any attempts to redirect him. Eight months of twice weekly language therapy had produced little gain.

Initially, Tommy attended the nursery with his mother. Although able to leave his mother's side, he refused to look at or listen to his teachers and reacted to all adult direction with anxiety and opposition. He was allowed to observe the routines and activities at his own pace and it soon became clear that once he experienced and lived through a situation, he understood, remembered and could predict the sequence of events. At first, Tommy refused to sit at the table for snack and there was no way to explain to him that he could return to playing later. After several days of watching these activities, he happily came to the table on his own. With many such experiences, he gradually developed a sense of comfort and trust, allowed himself to be helped, and became a full participant in nursery activities. Once his teachers and his language therapist had his cooperation and his attention, the work on communication started to progress; he was now motivated to look at the gestures and facial expressions which accompanied their words. The therapeutic nursery had provided a clear structure and consistent positive thrust to his development which had previously been missing at home. The world was now more predictable and less threatening.

The medication Tommy received for his symptoms of attention deficit and hyperactivity proved to be very helpful. Neuropsychological testing with non-verbal instruments, showed him to be of at least average intelligence. As his behavior came under better control and his anxiety decreased, his contact also improved. Tommy's mother, both through her presence in the class and in regular individual conferences, learned to understand and handle her son's behavior. While working to come to terms with his deficits, she also came to appreciate and enjoy his strengths.

Tommy was a child with a pervasive developmental disorder which included a severe central language disorder, attention deficit hyperactivity disorder, poor relatedness, and mild motor and balance problems. His mother could not leave him in anyone else's care and he could not have been maintained in a regular preschool or daycare facility. During Tommy's second year

of attendance in the nursery, his mother was able to resume her career.

The therapeutic nursery, with its capacity to provide multi-modal intensive, long term interventions which in Tommy's case included neuropsychological testing, psychotherapy, education with group participation, language therapy, psychopharmacology and in depth parent counseling, offered a coordinated approach to a very difficult and complex problem.

Evaluation of the Modality

The therapeutic nursery is regarded as a powerful form of treatment for the psychiatric problems of young children and their families most of whom are at risk for continuing severe dysfunction.

Outcome studies of childhood disorders and syndromes are appearing more frequently in the literature but as yet there are no global systematic studies of treatment results from therapeutic nursery interventions. However, anecdotal reports and personal communications indicate that for many children this form of treatment is successful in promoting healthy child development and in improving the quality of life for the family. For those children whose biologically based conditions impose limitations on aspects of their development, impressive improvements also can be achieved.

The children treated in a therapeutic nursery are often the most troubled subgroup of at-risk children. (Carnegie Task Force, 1994) They often are referred to the therapeutic nursery as a treatment modality of last resort.

In evaluating the therapeutic nursery as a treatment modality it is important to note that although studies of Head Start have convincingly demonstrated the powerful impact of early intervention, they also have shown that its benefits cannot be sustained unless psychological and social supports are continued into the later years.

The therapeutic nursery is also recognized as a milieu eminently suited for the teaching of early child development and psychopathology. Trainees can learn about the children and their treatment in great detail and over a long period while simultaneously benefiting from the observation of multidisciplinary teams at work.

REFERENCES

Carnegie Task Force on Meeting the Needs of Young Children (1994). The Quiet Crisis. *Starting Points* 2–22. Carnegie Corporation of New York

Elkind, D. (1996). Early childhood education. *Child and Adolescent Psychiatry*, Lewis M., (Ed), 1092–97, Williams and Wilkins, Baltimore, MD

Fraiberg, S., Adelson, E., & Shapiro, V. (1975) Ghosts in the nursery: a psychoanalytic approach to the problems of impaired infant-mother relationships. J. Am. Acad. Child Psychiatry, 14:3, 387–421

Furman, E. (1957). Treatment of under-fives by way of their parents. *Psychoanalytic Study of the Child*, 12, (250–261)

Furman, R., & Katan, A. (Eds.). (1969). *The therapeutic nursery school,* New York: International Universities Press

Katan, A. (1959). The nursery school as a diagnostic help to the child guidance clinic. *Psychoanalytic Study of the Child, 14*, 250–264

Zelman, A. B., Lopez, T., Balter, N. et al (Eds.) (1996), Cornerstone: A therapeutic nursery for severely disadvantaged children, in *Early Intervention with High-Risk Children*, 23–84, E. Jason Aronson, Northvale, NJ

Zelman, A. B. Samuels, S., & Abrams, D. (1985). I Q changes in young children following intensive long term psychotherapy. American Journal of Psychotherapy, 39: 215–227

20 / Principles of Psychodynamic Interventions

Steven Marans and E. Kirsten Dahl

The guiding principle of any psychodynamic intervention is that throughout development, there is a complex interaction between internal and external demands and children's unfolding capacities to meet these demands. The goal of psychodynamic psychotherapy is to help children find alternative solutions to conflicts that have given rise to symptoms that interfere with current functioning and progressive development. Psychodynamic intervention is based on the notion that symptoms and problematic behavior that have not yielded to time or changes in the external world derive from a complex matrix of constitutional, developmental, and environmental factors that find representation in children's fantasies and theories about themselves, their expectations of the world, and their adaptation to it. In this context, symptoms are seen as a result of children's best efforts both to resolve and to express in disguised keep between form solutions to conflicts among their wishes, the demands of external reality, and their developmental capacities.

First and foremost, psychodynamic intervention recognizes that any defensive maneuver, regardless of how disruptive to the children's lives it may appear, is felt by the children to be necessary.

On that basis, the central task of intervention is to learn in what way symptoms serve to protect children from and help them adapt to unconscious conflict aroused by the demands of development and of everyday life. The therapist's capacity to decode children's presentation in play, activity, and discussion occurs in the context of a relationship that provides a safe forum for the communication of feelings, impulses, and ideas that children have about their life, self, and others. As the relationship between a child and therapist deepens, the child becomes better able to tolerate and be curious about his or her inner life and the multiple ways internal conflicts may compromise development and daily functioning.

The clinician's choice of dynamic psychotherapy may be made when considering a range of presenting clinical situations. In addition to being the treatment of choice for children suffering internal conflict (Glenn, 1987), a dynamic perspective also may be appropriate for a diverse range of clinical presentations in which internal conflict appears to be absent, such as conduct disorders (Kernberg, 1979). In conjunction with pharmacologic, educational, and behavioral management interventions, psychodynamic psychotherapy may be the treatment of choice in working with a child who is coping with chronic illness or a matrix of constitutional, cognitive, and developmental deficits (Cohen & Leckman, 1991; Moran & Fonagy, 1987; O'Brien, 1992) or with a child who has experienced acute or cumulative trauma (Marans, 1994; Pynoos, Steinberg, & Wraith, 1995; Shengold, 1989; Wallerstein, 1983). In each of these clinical situations, the dynamic psychotherapist's are to learn the language of the child and to develop a relationship that provides a forum in which the child can explore his or her experience of self and others while trying on new solutions to difficulties that have blocked the path to optimal development.

Psychodynamic interventions may be employed in a broad range of contexts, including intensive psychotherapy with several sessions per week over a long period of time, weekly psychotherapy, brief psychotherapy, structured sessions, and parent-child guidance. What distinguishes a psychodynamically oriented intervention from other types of clinical intervention is the therapist's conviction that children's behavioral difficulties have as their source the complex interplay between the wishes and fears inherent to children's inner world, their maturational capacities, the pressures of progressive development, and the demands of external reality.

Developmental Frames of Reference

The notion of unconscious conflict is central to any conceptualization of psychodynamic intervention. The "unconscious" refers to the dynamic interaction of thoughts, feelings, memories, bodily experiences, and thought processes that operate outside of an individual's conscious awareness while exerting influence on patterns of behavior, interactions with others, perceptions of the world, and feelings about the self. Many behavioral symptoms of childhood reflect children's attempt to ward off dangers experienced as originating in the intensity of their urges and wishes, in the severity of internal moral judgment about the self, or in the prohibitions and demands from the environment.

CASE EXAMPLE

Seven-year-old Sally was referred for psychodynamic psychotherapy because she was frequently in trouble in school with the other girls of her age. The other girls in Sally's class complained that Sally was "mean" to them. The teacher noticed that Sally frequently made derogatory comments under her breath to whatever girl happened to be sitting next to her while they were doing work. Although Sally was an intelligent and imaginative child, her teacher felt that Sally expended a good deal of intelligence and energy in hurting other children's feelings. When the teacher pointed this out to Sally or in any way reprimanded her, Sally complained that she was being "unfair." After a careful evaluation, Sally was referred for once-a-week psychodynamic psychotherapy. Gradually, in talking and playing with Sally, her therapist began to understand that the girl was extremely critical of herself, feeling that nothing she did was able to measure up to her own very high standards. Sally's critical attitude toward her classmates was an attempt to ward off her own self-critical feelings, in essence saying "There's nothing wrong with me—it's that other girl who is stupid, ugly, and so on."

The conflict between children's desires and the inherent limitations imposed by the demands of reality in the form of moral prohibitions, external controls, and rules is a ubiquitous phenomenon that motivates children's exploration of alternative forms of expression and satisfaction that meet acceptable internal and external standards. Children search for a compromise that is acceptable to themselves and others between their own wishes and environmental expectations. The form the compromise solution takes is shaped by the specific age-typical wishes in conjunction with the children's capacities as determined by endowment, maturation, and level of development. Children's unfolding intellectual and physical competencies; experiences and opportunities in the home, school, and community; and ability to postpone gratification, tolerate delay, and accept substitute gratifications all contribute to their ability to create a compromise between the competing demands of their inner world and external reality. As such, "symptoms" also may reflect children's efforts to negotiate developmentally expectable conflicts on the way to attaining mastery, self-sufficiency, pleasure, and pride in the world of increasing demands, delayed gratifications, disappointments, and real dangers.

Sam, a very bright 8-year-old, had frequent temper outbursts at school in which he loudly mocked his teacher and refused to follow directions. Although at other times he demonstrated rather mature social skills, when he lost control he bullied and humiliated his teacher in such a way that she felt she "had" to be extremely controlling of him. Behavior management strategies proved ineffective in the long term, although changes in classroom management of Sam always produced a short-term effect. After a careful evaluation that ruled out depression as well as attentional deficits and hyperactivity, Sam was referred for intensive dynamic psychotherapy. In the beginning of his therapy Sam repeatedly demonstrated how competitive he was: He wanted to be the best at everything! Because of his superior endowment, Sam was able to realize this wish much of the time. Sam also felt very strongly that it was important to "be the goodest person you can be." It emerged that being competitive was *not* being "good" because it implied that one saw oneself as superior to others. Sam repeatedly disavowed any competitive feelings, insisting he didn't want to be "better" than anyone else, just the best he could be. Although this was certainly a very mature attitude, it was clear from his behavior that Sam valued winning more highly than he could tolerate acknowledging. When he was unable to meet his inappropriately high performance standards, which was often, Sam felt very bad about himself, saying that he was "stupid" and "no good." As he worked with his therapist, it also became clear that for Sam winning meant not only being "the best" but being "the only one." His daydreams were resplendent with competitions in which he won brilliantly, making everyone else feel little and humiliated. Sam and his therapist began to understand that when Sam started to have his being-no-good, being-too-little feelings, they were intolerable and he felt he *had* to get rid of them. Although mocking and humiliating his teacher got Sam into serious trouble, inside he felt very big and powerful: *No one* could be *his* boss! Sam got rid of his painful feelings and restored his sense of being the "winner" by turning everything around so that his teacher felt little and out of control and Sam felt that he was the "big, bad boss."

At each phase of development there tend to be nodal conflicts, as detailed in other volumes, that inevitably give rise to crises and symptoms of childhood that evoke concern in the adults who are most involved with children. While the tantrums, separation anxiety, and difficulties in sleeping and eating typical in toddlerhood are troublesome to caregivers, they do not necessarily indicate deviation from normal trends in development. These developmentally expectable symptoms are especially salient during the time of children's emerging recognition that they are individuals, separate and different from their parents, whom the children wish to please in their expectations of more mature behavior. Similarly, the nighttime fears, transient phobias, and defiance of 4- to 6-year-old children do not automatically represent psychopathology but, rather, reflect their active attempts to negotiate conflicts between normal feelings love, hate, jealousy, and competition. Senior preschoolers or early grade school children have ambivalent feelings about establishing a greater sense of autonomy. These mixed feelings may be expressed in testing rules, tattling on others, social difficulties, rapid shifts in mood, or heightened concerns about bodily changes; they do not automatically signal the need for clinical intervention. Additionally, above and beyond the symptomatology of normal development, children's behavior or mood may change in direct response to clear external precipitants, such as moving to a new house, changing schools, parental discord and divorce, acute illness, exposure to exceptional, traumatic incidents, or it may reflect the stress of coping with cognitively based learning difficulties. Children undergoing such external stressors may require supports or interventions that are informed by an appreciation of the dynamic interaction of multiple contributions, but they do not necessarily warrant extensive individual psychotherapy. Where conflicts and attendant symptoms are primarily reactive in nature, work with parents and teachers to alter a child's environment or to increase adult appreciation for the nature of developmental struggles may be sufficient. Such intervention, when based on psychodynamic principles, can help a child mobilize adequate resources to achieve a more adaptive set of responses and so resolve the immediate crisis. Alternatively, when a careful evaluation reveals a history of a child's failure successfully to negotiate previous developmental tasks and when presenting difficulties have not yielded to environmental manipulation, the severity and persistence of symptoms may reflect a relatively intransigent adaptation to internalized conflict that the child experiences as protective but that actually exacts a high price for both the child and those around him or her. In this situation, the adult's logic, suggestions, and admonitions are at exasperating odds to the child's counterproductive albeit best attempts to resolve the internal conflicts that seem to elude conscious recognition and rational response. In such a case, the psychotherapeutic task with the child is to provide a new and very different setting in which the therapist and patient can develop a language for exploring, revealing, and understanding what has heretofore been unknown to both. A therapist should decide to engage a child of any age in dynamic psychotherapy based on a careful evaluation of the patient's presenting difficulties; dynamic psychotherapy is called for when the child's difficulties reflect a failure to negotiate conflicts that are at once an essential part of every phase of development and at the same time have become elaborated, and permanent, requiring an expenditure of psychic energy that impedes rather than promotes developmental progression.

Aims of Dynamic Psychotherapy

Fantasy is both a testing ground—trial in thought—and a refuge from the disappointments of reality and the demands of others. When wishes and urges are unable to yield to reality or when alternative modes of satisfaction are not available or facilitated in children's environments, fantasy can serve as a retreat from the current demands of external reality and advances in phase development. As such, fantasy can serve as a respite and as a staging ground in which new responses to demands and new solutions to conflicts can be tried and practiced.

CASE EXAMPLE

During the month before he was to begin kindergarten, 5-year-old Josh told his mother that he was very worried that he wouldn't be "ready" to go; he didn't think he could learn to read "in time." Although his mother tried to reassure him that he didn't need to know how to read before he went to school, that in fact he would *learn* how to read when he went to school, Josh seemed unable to make use of her reassurances. He seemed quite anxious, sometimes ruminating over what school would be like. Occasionally he woke up in

the middle of the night saying he had had a bad dream. Around this time, his mother noticed an upsurge in Josh's imaginative play. He built elaborate cities with his blocks, positioning his toy soldiers so that the city was guarded from attack. Josh staged various assaults on his city, sometimes sneaky solo "destroyers" and other times, vast armies. However, *his* soldiers were always much more clever than the attackers and always were successful in warding off the danger. Josh experimented with all sorts of martial strategies, checking out which were most likely to make his soldiers victorious. He communicated his great pleasure in this imaginative play. On several occasions he described to his mother the various maneuvers of his soldiers, emphasizing that they had to work very hard to be clever enough to repulse their enemies, but they liked to work hard and they felt "really great" when once again they "got rid" of the enemy. Over a period of several days Josh gradually seemed to relax; he seemed cheerier and more industrious. His mother was surprised at his readiness to take on new tasks around the house and his greater intellectual curiosity. Josh's imaginative play appeared to give representation to the satisfying and reassuring fantasy that if you worked hard and were well prepared, you would "win."

When fantasy is not able to support children's ability to develop appropriate strategies for mastery, children may be unable to give up the fantasies, which may become the basis for continuing internalized conflict. In this situation, children cling to the maladaptive fantasied "solution," unable to accept any compromise that would help them develop a solution in reality. Unable to use new developmental competencies to mediate and express impulses and feelings, the children's earlier wishes may retain their force and urgency while being experienced as unacceptable; the attending unconscious conflicts find expression in symptoms and behavior. For all of these reasons, Freud's guiding principle of "making the unconscious conscious" remains central to the psychotherapeutic task of alleviating symptomatic presentation and helping children return to the path of optimal development. Psychodynamic intervention provides a forum in which children can become more observant of their feelings and fantasies, of the conflict between what they wish for and the demands of reality; with the therapist's help, children can try out new solutions in an effort to find a compromise that permits some realization of their wishes while simultaneously adapting to the constraints of reality.

Whatever the underlying cause, academic difficulties, constant fights with peers, siblings and parents, soiling, enuresis, disturbed sleep and eating, social isolation, drug and alcohol abuse, avoidant behavior and phobias, and depressive withdrawal may cause a great deal of discomfort to patients and families. However, seen from a psychodynamic perspective, each of these symptomatic difficulties represents an individual's attempt both to defend against wishes and urges that are experienced as unacceptable and dangerous *and* to give expression to them in a disguised form. Where symptomatic behavior and age-inappropriate functioning serve children as the best available means of representing internal distress, these symptoms can be viewed as highly condensed modes of communication that no one—not parents, teachers, or patients themselves—have been able to translate fully and understand. Simply put, the aim of psychodynamic psychotherapy is to provide a setting in which patients can increasingly experience safety in exploring previously "unknowable" aspects of their inner world that give rise to conflict, defense, and maladaptive ways in which they negotiate daily life.

From a psychodynamic perspective, difficulties that bring children into treatment represent attempts to avoid or modulate the experience of internal conflict or threats to their sense of well-being. Although it is common to attribute loss of self-esteem to failures in external reality, it is equally possible that the threat to self-esteem stems from internalized conflicts involving the guilt and shame associated with internal moral judgment. Children may condemn wishes and feelings as well as their representation in fantasy because their realization is perceived as unacceptable or impossible. For example, by the late preschool years, children recognize that their destructive wishes toward parents or siblings are incompatible with their intense loving feelings and need for these same people. The little boy who wants to vanquish all competition from the field, particularly his father or older brother, at the very same time loves his father, wants to be like him, and needs to feel that his father loves and approves of him. The child may experience the intensity of the contradiction between his loving and hating feelings for his father or other significant person as so painful that he wants to avoid any recognition of his feelings. While such conflicts occur naturally in development, they may be exacerbated by multiple and interweaving contributions from children's lives, such as: (1) a history of risk of realization of attack, either emotional or physical, by parents or other caregivers in response to the child's expression of developmentally appropriate needs; (2) the failure of age-expectable capacities to regulate impulses and needs that lead to feeling flooded and overwhelmed. Children may fear being overwhelmed by impulses and needs when: (a) their capacities for self-regulation are centrally compromised—via constitutional hypersensitivities, inadequate visual-motor apparatus, chronic illness, disordered language and cognitive development, skeletal or neuromusculature abnormalities; or (b) the capacities that are in place are not able to reduce the level of environmental overstimulation—for example interpersonal violence in the home and in the neighborhood; the absence of external order as represented by consistent parental rules and expectations; exciting exposure to parental nudity or sexual activity; or (3) a history of repeated failure of satisfaction of children's basic needs—such as poor bodily and physical care with the associated somatic distress, discontinuous and unreliable presence of the caregiver, or inconsistent and unpredictable communication of affection.

Whatever the prominence or combination of specific risks to children's ability to sustain an age-appropriate sense of control, their capacity to mediate these stresses is determined by whether their defenses allow them to maintain a sense of equilibrium, a conviction that their needs will be met in a timely fashion (Mahler, Pine, & Bergman, 1975), and their sense of effectiveness in achieving satisfaction and pleasure with an increasingly broad and sophisticated array of activities. The most basic human endeavors of ensuring safety and securing pleasure guide children's attempt to guard against danger and helplessness. When the dangers and threats are primarily externally based and current, interventions first must focus on remedying or alleviating the immediate and persisting risks to children (e.g., mandated referrals to protective services when a child is neglected, abused, or sexually exploited; intensive work with parents, educators, social services in altering the child's milieu). Similarly, where neurophysiological and other impairments of the physical and cognitive apparatus can respond to pharmacologic interventions or remedial assistance, these approaches need to be considered as central to the overall treatment plan. Often, however, even with changes in the environment or children's physical and cognitive profiles, the history of environmental failures or the contributions of deficient regulatory and processing capacities will have had an impact on developing capacities for conflict resolution and defensive configurations that lead to optimal adaptation. At the point when children enter into psychotherapy, their defensive strategies to avoid internal pain and external discomfort are not up to the task without requiring a high price in the form of symptoms, unhappiness, and failure.

Unlike the adult who seeks out psychotherapy, most frequently it is parents who make the decision for treatment for their children and adolescents. Often children are told that they are going to see this very different kind of doctor because of worries and difficulties that suggest unhappiness. For school-age children and adolescents, regardless of their suffering, nothing magical or immediate about seeing a therapist decreases the need to maintain defenses/adaptations against the unknown and unknowable dangers that give rise to the problems that bring them into treatment.

Finding alternative forms of expression and alleviating the necessity of adhering to current modes of response require the development of a new setting, a new relationship, and a new language in which the dynamic interaction between what is internal and what is experienced in daily life can be explored. Over time, psychotherapy sessions provide a setting in which the child and a relatively neutral adult can examine the themes and consistent patterns of play, discussion, modes of expression, and interpersonal interactions. The clinician's goal is to understand children's internal life, to relate this to their behavior inside and outside of the therapeutic situation, and to try to alter inner or outer functioning through helping children to become better and more understanding observers of their experiences, feelings, thoughts, and life. The psychotherapeutic intervention provides a stage on which, over time, the language of the unconscious—fantasies, conflicts, defenses and symptoms—can be played out imaginatively, in games and through discussion, thereby becoming observable and translatable, and gradually understood. To this end, the psychotherapist engages in the process as an observer, a participant, and an anchor in reality, helping children clarify what they are thinking and feeling as well as noticing repetitive themes and patterns, making connections between themes and feelings for children. Interpretations assist children in understanding and mastering thoughts, feelings, and behaviors of which they previously had been unaware and that have given rise to the current difficulties. The therapist uses verbalization, clarification, and interpretation in the context of a relationship that includes elements of transference, displacement, and therapeutic alliance. The psychotherapist engages in the process as an observer and participant in an ongoing discussion led by the children.

Therapeutic Tasks

In the course of treatment and in the context of a developing therapeutic relationship, the clinician may make observations about the unfolding stories that emerge in the play activities and what they reveal about children's conflicts, defenses, and consequent behaviors and modes of relating. For some therapists, children's play affords not only a window into the inner life but is the material that bears interpreting for the purpose of increasing children's conscious awareness of and insight into the relationship between unconscious conflict, defenses, and manifest behavior and symptoms (Kennedy, 1978; Kennedy & Yorke, 1982; Klein, 1958). For others (Neubauer, 1987; Winnicott, 1965) children's capacity to play and talk freely in the presence of another and to develop multiple narratives that give expression to underlying conflicts, interests, and concerns is therapeutic in and of itself. Particularly with regard to young children, this conceptualization emphasizes the action of play as serving the function of mastery through repetition and elaboration of central themes in their lives, trying on new solutions to problems as well as practicing and expanding the modes of representing them. In this model, the goal of interpretive work is not to create or enhance children's insight per se but rather to decrease the anxiety and defensive operations that disrupt or interfere with the expansion and unfolding of the play and/or discussion itself.

Transference

Children's manifest attitudes toward the therapist comprise one central marker of the transference and are an essential ingredient in considering their ability or inability to play or engage in discussion with analyst. This is especially the case at the beginning of a treatment, when children's expectations of what will occur in the sessions are not determined by specific past experiences of contact with the therapist but rather by expectations that derive from habitual modes of relating, current relationships, and past experiences with others.

Transference is the term used to describe or characterize patient's attitude toward the therapist. The term derives from psychoanalytic treatment with adults and refers to the ways in which patient's perceptions of and relationships with significant figures from childhood are expressed in current perceptions, thoughts, fantasies, feelings, attitudes, and behavior in current relationships. In the clinical situation, transference refers specifically to the ways in which these experiences from the past are organized around and expressed within the relationship with the therapist (Sandler et al., 1980). A major difference in considering this phenomena in work with children lies in the fact that, unlike adults, children continue to live with and rely on parents. Much of what children bring to the treatment situation reflects not only a transference of aspects of relationships from the past but significant aspects of current experiences, fantasies, perceptions, feelings, and attitudes from current relationships—particularly those with parents and other family members (Sandler et al., 1980).

In an attempt to clarify the phenomena of transference, particularly as it is observed in the treatment of children, Anna Freud and her colleagues developed a topology of transference of: (1) habitual modes of relating (2) current relationships, (3) past experiences, and (4) transference neurosis (Sandler et al., 1980). The first type refers to fixed ways of relating to others that, while deriving from earlier relationships, have now been applied to the world at large or to whole categories of people with whom children have contact. The second category refers to the transfer or displacement of current preoccupations with real situations in children's lives or with aspects of current developmental challenges. The emphasis here is on the distinction between a revival of past experiences vs. the displacement of current ones that can be observed in children's relationships with the analyst. The third category involves children's attitudes, fantasies, and memories from the past that were previously repressed and that are now manifested in the current relationship with the therapist as it develops during regular contact over a sustained period of time. In the last category, there is a "very special intensification of the transference involving an externalization of a major pathogenic internal conflict onto the therapist, so the conflict is felt by the patient to be between himself and the therapist" (Sandler et al., 1980 pg. 92). In child psychotherapy, it is much less common to see as much evidence of the transference neurosis as occurs in the analysis and psychotherapy of adults. When it emerges, there is a significant shift in the patient's attention, interests, and preoccupations to a focus on the interaction with the therapist.

The notion that children's attitudes to the therapist tell us something about their internal frame of reference or internal configurations of experience, urges, feelings, and fantasies would seem to suggest that the encounter with the new person—the therapist—is *mainly* a reflection of children's lives outside the consulting room. This notion assumes that the therapist's presentation and modes of relating to children have no or only minimal bearing on the ways in which the children present themselves in this particular setting. The opposite view suggests that the therapist's demeanor and the particular circumstances of the encounter have everything to do with children's presentation and therefore skew the nature and significance of their attitude to the clinician as a prominent source of data or window into their inner world. These two views reflect the extremes in considering the extent to which children's manifest attitudes toward the therapist are a pure reflection of their inner life or of their day-to-day experiences outside of the consulting room. That is, children's attitudes in isolation from other aspects of the fuller presentation of themes and emotional presentation may, in fact, tell the therapist very little about the children's central interests, fantasies, concerns, and modes of regulating and communicating them. In addition, even when considering children's attitudes in the broader context, initial impressions may not be borne out as the fuller picture of the children emerges over the course of the psychotherapy treatment. Rapid shifts in children's presentation may occur, from friendly, positive engagement to attitudes of hostility, disappointment, and fear. It is important to remember that children's attitudes to the therapist develops in the context of a unique setting and special relationship. As such, their attitudes the clinical as data emerges from an observational approach that manifestly involves 2 people in the room who set the stage for understanding the children's experiences of themselves in relations to the many others who have and have had significance in both inner and daily life.

The Therapist-Child Interaction

Children's comfort in the room with the therapist and their experience of their interaction with the therapist will be a key determinant of the play, discussion, and activities that occur in a given hour. Children's attitudes toward the therapist suggest their feelings about being with an adult other than the parent. At most, the attitude children present in this particular setting may reflect a generalized set of expectations and modes of relating that have referents *outside* of the consulting room, in the children's daily lives—from the present or the past. At the very least, the attitude presented may reflect aspects of children's expectations of the current situation in the consulting room itself. A central focus of the clinician's observations is the way in which children relate to him or her, from the first introduction in the waiting area to the myriad shifts in attitude presented in the consulting room throughout the course of psychotherapy. From a psychodynamic perspective, ways of relating to the therapist reveal a great deal about children's attitudes to the most important people in their daily lives and suggest observable surface markers for a range of internal configura-

tions involving their fantasies about those people. Representations of self and others as reflected in play and discussion reveal the organization of the variety of composite images of self and others that children have constructed on the basis of experiences, urges, and feelings. These representations of the self and others, although never fully conscious, are reflected in children's ever-changing conscious fantasies, attitudes, and behavior. In other words, the children's attitudes, suggested by the way they relate to others, reveal an internal frame of reference that draws on (1) their experience of interacting with similar figures and their awareness of an expectable set of social conventions; (2) the status of specific urges and the relative balance between the pleasure gained from their expression vs. fear of potentially negative consequences in the form of shame, guilt, anxiety, or actual danger that might result from a clash with either internal or external expectations; and (3) the developmental status of a sense of self, that is, an appreciation for personal abilities that are now experienced as autonomous in relation to the parents.

Unlike other approaches to clinical interviews with children (Costello, Edelbrock, & Costello, 1985; Schaffer, 1989), psychodynamic technique eschews structured questions that aim at eliciting "mental status" on the basis of verbal responses and verbal information regarding attitudes and interests. Instead, it is felt that children are most likely to reveal their interests, attitudes, and capacities in a situation that can become most familiar and comfortable. The sense of familiarity and comfort can best be established by children themselves as they become acclimated to the therapeutic setting. The therapist is in the best position to observe what children brings to the sessions if the therapist's ideas and demands—in the form of questions, suggested activities, directing of play narratives, and the like—are kept to a bare minimum. When the session is not directly shaped by themes that the therapist introduces, children will bring to therapy their own versions of personal experiences that are configured and represented in play, activities, and discussion. This does not mean that the therapist must remain inactive, silent, or vacant in his or her presentation but rather that he or she should convey a friendly interest and respect for children by attending to what children themselves introduce in the session.

The Interview Setting

In the clinical situation, the child psychotherapist has the task of introducing the consulting room and the psychotherapy as a safe situation in which the therapist and children together have an opportunity to explore and work through the difficulties that have brought children into treatment. Children's sense of safety will vary according to what is uppermost in their mind at any given time, but it also is influenced by the ways in which the therapist conveys appreciation for the dangers children confront throughout the process. At the beginning of any treatment, the therapist's knowledge of children's developmentally phase-specific concerns contributes to his or her ability to set the stage for the development of a therapeutic atmosphere in which therapist and child can learn about and work on the dynamic intersection between inner life and the external world of the particular child.

Preschool children experience, the sense of safety in the familiarity and pleasure of the imaginative play with a friendly adult who can follow their lead while maintaining effective limits on potentially dangerous or overly exciting behavior. Safety also will be experienced in the comfort or confidence the parents convey in their attitude toward the therapist and by their availability before, after, and, at times during the session. Children will begin to develop a sense of safety as they discover that the therapist will do no harm—whether in response to provocative behavior or to any thoughts, fantasies, or feelings that may emerge.

These same issues may be equally prominent for school-age children. However, there is now an additional burden for the children. They are invited to reveal aspects of their inner life at a time in development when the need to renounce the open expression of infantile longings is paramount. School-age children's increased interest in privacy and secrets; games with rules; cause-and-effect thinking; engagement with peers and activities outside the home; curiosity and learning; and bodily self-care are products of newly emerging mental structures, in concert with advances in both cognitive and physical capacities. These interests reflect children's ability and need to move away from their earlier dependence on parents and from a fantasy life in which the parents figured prominently as direct objects of sexual and aggressive impulses as well. In many ways these new developmental acquisitions compound the expectable challenges to establishing a psychotherapeutic relationship. For school-age children, anxiety is aroused that the intimacy of the relationship with the therapist will reawaken old, now-unacceptable dependent longings as well as stimulate the emergence of wishes and fantasies experienced as dangerously regressive.

For adolescents, the dangers of yielding to a resurgence of longings and interactions that resonate with earlier phases of development are now intensified by physiologic and endocrinologic maturation. Asking for or being sent for psychotherapy may confirm adolescents' worst fears that their fluctuations in mood, preoccupations with sexual and aggressive fantasies and feelings, and anxiety about negotiating aspects of daily life are indications that they are crazy, infantile, and incompetent (Marans & Cohen, 1996).

In therapeutic work with each of these age groups, children's sense of safety will, in large part, derive from the therapist's and their own recognition of the specific dangers that are evoked for them by the introduction of the psychotherapeutic situation and from their appreciation of the importance of the defenses that are called into play.

Developing the Therapeutic Process

The first meeting with children usually is preceded by meetings with the parents in which the presenting difficulties and developmental and family history are discussed. These meetings with the parents are conducted either by the child therapist or by a colleague. This background information will provide a context for direct observations made by the therapist over the course of 2 or 3 evaluative sessions. In the context of these meetings, it is suggested to parents of young children that they be told in simple terms that they will be meeting with someone who helps children who are having worries. The parents can introduce to their child the idea of meeting with the therapist by saying that they know that their child has been having troubles and that they would like to help so that the child can feel happier and free of the worries that are making life so difficult. Additionally, parents may briefly describe the nature of the contact with the therapist by telling the child that they will have a chance to play and talk, get to know the therapist over time and slowly figure out worries with the help of the therapist. While the details of what parents tell their child may vary, parents of children younger than 5 years of age are counseled to keep the explanation brief and to follow the child's lead through questions and statements regarding how elaborate the explanation about the consultation should be. For example, in response to the child's questions, parents may distinguish the difference between the kind of doctor who does examinations and gives shots and the doctor who helps children through play activities and/or words.

Children 6 years and younger may feel most comfortable if a parent accompanies them and the therapist into the consulting room for the initial meeting. Young children frequently make verbal and nonverbal requests—by holding onto a parent's hand, climbing onto the parent's lap, or leaning up against the parent's body—that the familiar adult remain in the consulting room for some time. The therapist's initial communications—a verbal introduction of him- or herself and intentions (i.e., "We are going to a room where we can play and talk"); regard for children's wishes about the timing of separating from the parent; and friendly but low-key invitation to children to explore the contents of the playroom and to use the toys and drawing materials—are meant to convey and demonstrate that the setting and the therapist *are,* in fact, safe and free of real, external demands or threats that might prove overwhelming.

Just as the parents of young patients have introduced them to the idea of seeing the therapist, the clinician also may say tell children that he or she is there to help them with their worries. Some psychotherapists prefer to say more, describing in greater detail the schedule as well as the nature of their work; others say very little, preferring initially to learn from children their beginning ideas about the treatment.

The choice of play materials should reflect the developmental age of each child and invite the child's imaginative use of them. For younger children, the use of small animal and human figures,

puppets, a doll house, toy cars, paper and markers all serve as relatively neutral objects that they can use in developing play themes and narratives. Alternatively, using toys that derive from television shows may evoke scripts that even when personally elaborated by children were originated in the imagination of someone else and therefore confuse and diminish their projective and communicative value in the therapeutic process. Similarly, too many toys or activities that increase the potential for regression and direct enactment of impulses—play with water, paints, swords, and guns with projectiles—may succeed in engaging children in the room but may be overstimulating for many children who come to experience the consulting room and the therapist as a dangerous.

CASE EXAMPLE

A psychotherapist just beginning her work with a 5-year-old girl expressed surprise and some anxiety as she reported in supervision on the first 3 psychotherapy hours with the girl. The therapist reported that the girl, Yvonne, had been referred because of chronic battles with her mother, frequent nightmares, fights with kindergarten classmates, and obstinate refusal to refuse her teacher's requests to join in group activities. There were no immediate external precipitants to these difficulties, which had been apparent in varying degrees for the previous 18 months. Her history was unremarkable except for her mother's acknowledgment that both she and her husband were perhaps overly strict, demanding compliance to their expectations that, from age 2, Yvonne should behave like a "little grown-up." Mother reported that prior to the current difficulties, both she and her husband as well as other adults frequently had commented on how well behaved and mature their daughter seemed—"she was such a sweet, good little girl . . . maybe too good."

The therapist went into some detail in describing the first 3 sessions and her consternation about the dramatic fluctuations in Yvonne's presentation. In the first hour, the girl had separated easily from her mother, was friendly and seemed comfortable accompanying the therapist into the consulting room. However, once in the room, Yvonne stood in one corner, finger in her mouth, eyeing the therapist and the contents of the room quietly. After several minutes the therapist invited her to explore, in sequence, the doll house, human figures, and finally the crayons and paper. Yvonne stood her ground and quietly shook her head. The therapist posed several questions about favorite toys and activities, to which Yvonne gave brief responses. After 30 minutes in the room, Yvonne walked over to the doll house and explored it for the next several minutes. She ignored or did not respond to any of the therapist's attempts to engage her but remained seated in front of the doll house fingering the figures and furniture inside. Suddenly, 40 minutes in the session, Yvonne looked up at the therapist and announced, "I'm done," and walked out of the room with the therapist trailing behind her. She was not interested in the suggestion that perhaps it might feel more comfortable to have Mom in the room with them and instead informed both therapist and mother that it was time to go home.

The second session began in a similarly quiet fashion. However, the therapist had decide to become more active in this meeting and to bring more play materials that might be of more interest to the girl. She equipped the room with an easel, paints and brushes as well as several cans of Play-Do, and several different size dolls. The therapist described her demeanor as more upbeat, for example, greeting Yvonne with a buoyant announcement that she had a number of surprises waiting for her in the room. Yvonne declined the offer to have Mother in the room. Again she stood for several moments surveying the room as the therapist began unpacking Play-Do, mixing paints, and describing what fun they might have playing with these items. After several moments, Yvonne did engage in painting, at first slowly and carefully on the paper and then with less care, which then culminated in a frenzy accompanied by wild giggles as she flung paint onto the paper, the walls, and the floor. Before the therapist had any time to comment, Yvonne went to the Play-Do, which she rolled in balls and excitedly threw against the wall while darting about the room, glancing in a challenging way at the therapist. And so the session continued as the therapist spoke of the need to keep her patient safe through, the rules for being able to continue to use the materials, and so on— all accompanied by the therapist's frozen smile and strained attempts to retain her composure. The session ended abruptly when Yvonne gleefully ran out of the room screeching her way down the hall until she reached her mother and again grew quiet as she looked out from behind Mother's dress, gazing at the therapist who had finally caught up with her.

The third hour presented yet another picture of Yvonne and a new set of challenges for the therapist as her young patient was now terrified of entering and then remaining in the consulting room. Yvonne insisted on having Mother in the room and sat quietly on her lap for the entire session. The therapist hypothesized that her eagerness to engage Yvonne in exciting activities was an attempt at seduction that had been too overwhelming for a child whose threshold for excitement and retaining self-control is especially low. The therapist and the sessions themselves had become the focus of fear as they represented the invitation to give full rein to impulses that Yvonne found both exciting and dangerous. In subsequent hours, the therapist verbalized how excited and frightened Yvonne had become and how important it was for her to feel safe again. In addition to inviting Mother into the room, the therapist eliminated the more stimulating paints and Play-Do while assuming a more low-key and patient approach to Yvonne. After several sessions Yvonne was again comfortable being alone with her therapist and continuing, at her pace, the exploration of this new setting and the struggle over expression of impulses that brought her into treatment.

In contrast to the younger child, many school-age children are well aware of the troubles that have prompted their referral for treatment. With children of this age, the therapist will need to discuss more directly the children's and therapist's ideas about why children are coming for psychotherapy. When appropriate, the therapist may want to negotiate directly with older school-age children such issues as the scheduling of sessions and elicit something of their interest to inform the therapist's choice of materials available in the room. The goal here is to create a bridge, or neutral ground, in which children can begin to describe directly or in displacement their experience of themselves internally and in relation to others in day-to-day life. Although school-age children may choose the same materials as younger children, such as play figures, puppets, a doll house, markers and paper, older children may prefer activities less clearly associated with their younger selves. A deck of cards, checkers or chess, and models to be constructed may all play a role in the psychotherapy of older school-age children. Children may employ such activities as "something to do" while they talk, or children may use them in the service of representing their difficulties around aggressive, competitive, and super-ego conflicts.

CASE EXAMPLE

John was a 10-year-old, highly constricted boy who shied away from engaging with peers or attending to his schoolwork when referred for evaluation and subsequent psychotherapy. Over the course of his 18-month treatment, the theme of competition became increasingly linked to danger as he developed play and written stories about armies fighting over a country and the affections of its ruler, the queen. The sessions often would end with each of the armies being decimated. As the therapist eventually commented on how dangerous the battles seemed for both sides, John replied outside of the play, "Well, that's what can happen when you want something too badly." During the work, John could reveal through play and discussion the extent to which his wish to be the best at everything preoccupied him. This longing was accompanied by intense rivalrous and destructive fantasies—first toward his father and siblings for his mother's exclusive attention and, by extension, toward peers for the teacher's—that were unacceptable morally *and* in conflict with his positive attachments to the same figures. For John, any competitive strivings engendered the same massive superego repudiation, guilt, and accompanying anxiety that greeted his unconscious fantasies and the conviction that his destructive wishes would come true. As John became more conscious of the link between his fantasies and his symptomatic avoidance of any show of competence and competition, his academic and peer involvement significantly improved. Exploring the origins of intensely rivalrous feelings through play and talk led to a greater tolerance for himself and an increased sense of safety in the fact that, as he put it, "Wishes are only wishes, you know."

The use of elaborate board games, while reflecting age-appropriate interests, often narrow the focus of the therapeutic work to the task of mastering specific rules and strategies, thereby closing off other avenues of representation and communication that might be expressed and observed more easily in a less demanding game. The repetitive and circumscribed nature of more elaborate games may, in fact, serve the defensive function of avoiding conscious awareness of fantasies and associated troubling feelings. In addition to the tasks of listening, observing, and exploring the contents of the imaginative play, games, or discussions, the therapist must be able to appreciate the importance of children's defensive operations in order to assist in developing a safe enough forum in which fantasies and feelings can be elaborated. In some treatments, such as John's, the original use of displacement (or the expression of conflictual themes and feelings via characters in play, narratives accompanying drawings, or discussion of the lives of "others") may lead to greater insight, conscious recognition, and verbalization of the links between inner life and patterns of behaviors. In many other treatments, however, the use of displacements themselves may provide just the opportunity children need to work through new

solutions to conflicts that have given rise to the symptoms and troubles that have brought them into psychotherapy. Verbalizing formulations that reflect hard-won insight into the presenting problems may be more of a need for the therapist than for such children.

Similarly, the developmental tasks of adolescence demand a very different approach from preschool and school-age children—usually from the moment of referral. Although young and midadolescents may come for treatment primarily at the instigation of parents or school, usually they have a very clear idea of why others think they are in trouble. It is important in the beginning work for the therapist to recognize that adolescents' protests that it is parents or others who have the real problems does not determine or predict the extent to which they will be able to engage in the psychotherapeutic process. Instead, adolescents may have a very different agenda concerning psychotherapy from the adults who have encouraged, or required, them to seek help. Although the therapist may want to make some effort to negotiate with adolescents the differences between their agenda and that of the adults, if adolescents are to be engaged successfully in their own treatment, the therapist must acknowledge and, when possible, accept their agenda as the central psychotherapeutic task.

Unlike preschool or school-age children, adolescent patients may be much more comfortable sitting and talking—"like an adult"—rather than playing. However, the psychodynamic, developmentally informed therapist understands that the operative word here is "like," not "as." Young to midadolescents, although wishing to appear adultlike, often are not able to sustain for long the sort of introspective, self-reflective stance that characterizes many adults seeking treatment. Adolescents may feel most comfortable about their life with peers and interests or about the failings of their parents; often they are very reticent to engaging in or reveal the self-reflection and troubling affects that may accompany such "neutral" topics that are seemingly so distant from internal experiences. It is the therapist's task gradually to introduce adolescents to a more self-reflective stance and to help them to sustain such a stance during sessions. Because it is the central developmental task of the young to midadolescence to achieve greater psychological independence and separation from parents, adolescents experience any thoughts, fantasies, or feelings that they associate with earlier developmental levels as a dangerous move backward toward earlier childhood feelings (i.e., regression); therefore, they go to great pains to avoid them. When adolescents experience the psychotherapeutic process as exerting a regressive pull toward psychological reengagement with the parent of childhood, they are most likely to flee psychotherapy in the service of reestablishing what they are convinced is a developmentally necessary separation and attainment of greater autonomy. For these reason, it is the therapist's task to approach the inner conflicts of adolescents, which inevitably carry with them this regressive valence, with great tact and developmental understanding. Young to midadolescents may be most comfortable "chatting" during their hours about sports, apparently superficial peer relationships, or television shows and characters. During the early phase of treatment, the therapist may have to work almost exclusively through the displacements afforded by such seemingly bland topics, which, over time, may help both to establish a feeling of control and safety in sessions as well as to provide his or her version of the bridge to discussing more directly increasingly relevant personal material.

In attempting to make adolescents feel comfortable, the therapist may make the mistake of trying to present him- or herself as a "hip" pal by initiating conversation that adolescents experience as dangerously seductive or intrusive (e.g., presenting as knowledgeable and "up" on culturally current topics, such as the latest sports or cultural figures and popular music). Adolescents in treatment are most comfortable with a therapist who is clearly an adult, but one who is an especially careful and thoughtful listener. Young adolescents often will become more comfortable as they feel confident that the therapist will not intrude on their burgeoning sense of psychological autonomy by moving to intolerably "deep" levels too quickly or making interpretations that they experience as "wild" and tactless. For adolescents who have the greatest difficulty in tolerating any verbal engagement or face-to-face contact that increases the sense of being scrutinized, the offer of simple games (e.g., card games, checkers, chess, etc.) may provide a more neutral basis of interaction. Again, adolescents' experience of control and

of the therapist as nonintrusive may allow them to feel safer revealing themselves in their own good time and guided by *their* own wish to feel relief from struggles that have brought them to treatment.

The choice of materials, scheduling, and frequency of meetings is crucial in setting the tone of the therapeutic relationship. These decisions should be informed by the therapist's understanding of the patient's developmental level. For preschool children, a minimum of twice-a-week appointments usually is necessary to provide the continuity in which psychodynamic lens can be employed usefully. Although older children may be able to develop a sense of therapeutic continuity in a once-a-week treatment, here, too, more frequent weekly appointments help therapist and children to cultivate a sustained "therapeutic atmosphere" in which the material of sessions can be understood by both participants to reflect the children's inner world with its conflicts and defenses. This therapeutic atmosphere, which includes the even, observing attention of the therapist to children's underlying conflicts and defenses as they are revealed in their play, behavior, and talking, permits children and therapist to develop a shared therapeutic language.

Working with Parents as an Adjunct to Treatment

Collaborative work with parents is an especially crucial component of the psychodynamic treatment of preschool and school-age children. Children are not able to present a full picture of their daily lives and behavior and, in particular, may wish to avoid reporting events from outside their hours of which they fear the critical judgment of the therapist. Meetings with parents during which they can report on events in children's daily lives are important for filling out the therapist's understanding of the children. Here we offer a few guidelines and warnings.

Collaborative work with the parents is critical to the psychodynamic treatment of children under 6 and under. Unless parents share information concerning a child's daily life and behavior with the therapist, his or her capacity to understand the referents of the child's play may be severely compromised. In addition, parents of young children brought for treatment frequently are quite anxious or confused about how to handle their children's behavior. Developmental child guidance attuned to the needs of the specific family and child can be extremely useful not only in ensuring the parents' continuing support of the treatment but, when necessary, in helping the parents understand why they should alter their approaches to the child and in helping them to develop these new strategies. Children younger than 5 have not yet developed a firm cognitive understanding of privacy or secrets and expect that the significant adults in their life share a mutual concern for their well-being; for these reasons, children under 5 usually are quite comfortable with the idea of meetings between parents and therapist.

Children over 5, however, have begun to develop a strong sense of privacy and secrets and may be much less comfortable with the notion that material from their sessions might be shared with parents. For this reason, the therapist of school-age children must not only assure the children of the confidentiality of material from sessions but must in fact be careful during parental child guidance sessions that the material children wish to have kept private is not revealed.

Parental meetings should be scheduled often and regularly enough that parents understand their importance as a tool in conveying significant information about their child's ongoing life. Frequency and regularity of contact between parent and therapist also helps parents recognize that they have a critical contribution to make to the success of their child's treatment; under such circumstances, parents are less likely to retain the magical notion that they can turn their child over to the therapist to be "fixed." In addition, parental meetings underpin the development of sufficient trust in the therapist for the parents to utilize any development child guidance that is offered. Finally, such meetings permit the therapist to gain adequate understanding of the parents' personalities to know whether it would be useful to the success of the child's treatment to refer one or both parents for their own treatment. If such a referral is indicated, the therapist who has developed a collaborative relationship with the parents will have an adequately informed working alliance through which he or she can decide how to best approach the question.

Although it is usually the parent of adolescents initiate the contact with the therapist and undoubtedly pays for any treatment undertaken, collaboration with parents of children of this age is more difficult. Because adolescents are moving toward greater psychological emancipation from their parents, they may experience any collaboration with their parents as infantilizing; collaboration thereby runs the risk of compromising the usefulness of the treatment to the adolescents. In general, adolescents are also better reporters of their daily lives and behavioral difficulties than younger children. For these reasons, parental contacts should be infrequent in the treatment of adolescents, in most cases they should not occur without the adolescents. Often, however, parents of adolescents feel most confused and upset about how to handle their child's behavior; thus they may be most desirous of increased contact with the therapist as a way of allaying their own anxieties and of developing new ways of handling their child. During the initial contact with the parents, the therapist must make clear the developmental reasoning behind the necessary restriction of contact between parents and him or her. Often treatment of adolescents is enhanced or successful only when the parents are seen on regular or as-needed basis by a colleague. With information about the parents and their contributions to family interactions alongside of reports from the adolescent's therapist, the collaborating clinician will be in a good position to help parents develop and assess new ways of understanding and responding to their adolescent more effectively while helping to maintain the confidentiality of the adolescent's treatment itself.

Conclusion

It is difficult to conceive of a psychological affliction where psychodynamic intervention would not be useful. All psychodynamic interventions focus on the dynamic interplay between internal agencies of the mind, the child's inner world, and how the demands of external reality are experienced. Psychodynamic intervention may take a variety of forms: intensive long-term psychotherapy, weekly play therapy, brief treatment, semistructured sessions, and consultation with parents. The multiplicity of methods of psychodynamic intervention are linked by a set of shared principles:

1. The individual has an "inner world" that includes representations of central wishes and fears, associated feelings, characteristic modes for avoiding discomfort, displeasure, and tension (defenses) as well as for obtaining pleasure.
2. Aspects of the inner world are unconscious.
3. Conflict is inherent within the inner world between wishes, within and between psychic structures, and between the inner world and the demands of reality.
4. Conflict within the inner world may either stimulate or impair developmental progression.
5. The inner world unfolds developmentally, supported, enhanced, or compromised by constitutional givens and environmental responses.
6. Behavioral symptoms reflect the child's efforts at finding a compromise solution to conflict.

7. The nature of the child's inner world can be understood through observations of play, verbalizations, behavior, and relationship to the therapist and significant others.

The data used for making intervention decisions are derived from observations of the child in the consulting room—modes of relating, thematic content, regulation of emotions, activity levels, and self-observation capacities—as well as what is reported about the child's life outside of the consulting room. The form of the psychodynamic intervention is determined by the child's developmental level, the nature of environmental stresses and supports, and the child's constitutional endowment. The fundamental techniques employed are influenced by the child's level of developmental organization but are likely to include imaginative play; discussion; observation of behavior and feelings; and exploration, verbalization, clarification of wishes, fears, and feelings.

REFERENCES

Cohen, D., & Leckman, J. (1991). Tic disorders. In M. Lewis, (Ed.), *Child and adolescent psychiatry: A comprehensive textbook.* Baltimore, MD: Williams & Wilkins.

Costello, E. J., Edelbrock, C. S., & Costello, A. J. (1985). Validity of the NIMH Diagnostic Interview Schedule for Children: A comparison between psychiatric and pediatric referrals. *Journal of Abnormal Child Psychology, 13,* 579–595.

Furman, E. (1995). *Pre-schoolers: Questions and answers—Psychoanalytic consultations with parents, teachers and caregivers.* New York International Universities Press.

Glenn, J. (1987). Supervision of child psychoanalysis. *Psychoanalytic Study of the Child, 42,* 575–596.

Kennedy, H. (1978). The role of insight in child analysis: A developmental viewpoint. *Journal of the American Psychoanalytic Association, 27,* 9–28.

Kennedy, H., & Yorke, C. (1982). Steps from outer to inner conflict viewed as superego precursors. *Psychoanalytic Study of the Child, 37,* 221–228.

Kernberg, P. (1979). Psychoanalytic profile of the borderline adolescent. *Adolescent Psychiatry, 7,* 254–256.

Klein, M. (1958). On development of mental functioning. *International Journal of Psychoanalysis, 39,* 84.

Mahler, M., Pine, F., Bergman, A. (1975). *The psychological birth of the human infant.* New York: Basic Books.

Marans, S. (1994). Community violence and children's development: Collaborative interventions. In C. Chiland & J. Gerald, (Eds.), *The Monograph Series of the International Association for Child and Adolescent Psychiatry and Allied Professions.* NJ: Jason Aronson.

Marans, S., & Cohen, D. (1996). Psychoanalytic theories of development. In M. Lewis (Ed.), *Child and adolescent psychiatry: A comprehensive textbook.* Baltimore, MD: Williams & Wilkins.

Moran, G., & Fonagy, P. (1987). Psychoanalysis and diabetic control. *British Journal of Medical Psychology, 60,* 357–372.

Neubauer, P. (1987). The many meanings of play: Introduction. *Psychoanalytic Study of the Child, 42,* 3.

O'Brien, J. D. (1992). Children with attention deficit hyperactivity disorder and their parents. In J. D. O'Brien, et al. (Eds.), *Psychotherapy with children and adolescents: Adaptation to the psychodynamic process.* Washington, D.C.: American Psychiatric Press.

Pynoos, R. S., Steinberg, A. M., & Wraith, R. (1995). A developmental model of childhood traumatic stress. In D. Ciccetti & D. Cohen, (Eds.), *Manual of developmental psychopathology.* New York: John Wiley & Sons.

Schaffer, D. (1989). *The Diagnostic Interview Schedule for Children (DISC-2): Its development and administration.* Paper presented at the annual meeting of the American Academy of Child and Adolescent Psychiatry, New York.

Sandler, J., Kennedy, H. Tyson, R., 1980. Technique of Child Psychoanalysis: Discussions with Anna Freud. Cambridge: Harvard University Press. pg. 92.

Shengold, L. (1989) Autohypnosis and soul murder: Hypnotic evasion, autohypnotic vigilance and hypnotic facilitation. In H. Blum, E. Weinshel, & F. Rodman, (Eds.), *The psychoanalytic core* (pp. 187–206). Madison, CT: International Universities Press.

Wallerstein, J. S. (1983). Children of divorce: Stress and developmental tasks. In N. Garmezy, M. Rutter, (Eds.) *Stress: Coping and development in children* (pp. 265–302). New York: McGraw-Hill.

Winnicott, D. W. (1965) *The maturational process and facilitating environment.* New York: International Universities Press.

---

21 / Individual Planned Time-Limited Treatment

Karen Belinger Peterlin and Richard Sloves

Over the last 50 years, time-limited treatment has gone from an abbreviated form of long-term psychodynamic psychotherapy to a distinctive yet methodologically diverse modality with its own particular point of view. It is no longer the "second-best" intervention used for patients who are seen as unsuitable for the emotional and intellectual rigors of long-term treatment. It is no longer considered a domain that should be left to the unskilled clinician, the outcomes of which are regarded as patient flights into health. The fact is that time-limited treatment, in all its incarnations (individual, family, and group), is currently the predominant format employed in psychotherapeutic treatment. Two-thirds of all patients who receive psychiatric treatment are seen for an average of 6 sessions or less, and only 10% attend for more than 25 sessions.

Several factors inspired the ascendancy of time-limited interventions. These treatments represent an effort to address such deficiencies as the rising cost of health care, the emphasis on crisis-oriented treatment, and the long waiting lists, all of which are inherent in the existing mental health care delivery system. Costly broken appointments and expensive, time-consuming diagnostic sessions resulted in some clinician's interest to develop briefer treatments. Contemporary modalities tend to be more health-oriented than their predecessors, a fact that appears due, in no small part, to a general loss of enthusiasm for the theoretical models that emphasize major structural or personality change. This function of treatment is being replaced with the idea that times of crisis or periods of psychological and social disequilibrium are an inevitable consequence of living. With the demands for immediate access to treatment, long-term modalities have the disadvantage of unacceptably high rates of attrition that may be due to patients being frustrated or inconvenienced by interminable attendance.

Brief interventions provide new tools with which to address a patient's needs without the prolonged absences from school and/or work and the accumulated expense of the longer treatments. The brief modalities meet the request for help more immediately and directly, as a result patient remain in treatment for the duration with fewer cancellations or "no-show" appointments. Other advantages include sharpening the focus on the major therapeutic issues, decreasing patient resistances, and increasing patient expectations of success. Additionally, brief interventions minimize the amount of time that any family member is assigned to the "sick" or "bad" role. Finally, as a means of fostering a progressive momentum, time-limited treatment avoids excessive dependence on the clinician, which can weaken the essential child-parent attachment.

Historical Antecedents

Brief focused interventions for children emerged within the psychodynamic models of long-term treatment. It is perhaps ironic that Freud's first work should come closest to the modern, time-limited modalities. However, as Freud developed the psychoanalytic theory of neurosis, his interventions became lengthier, an attribute that his students (with the exception of Otto Rank, Sandoe Ferenczi, and Franz Alexander) did little to change. It was during the 1960s that Habib Davanloo, David Malan, James Mann, and Peter Sifneos developed an open-ended psychodynamic model of brief treatment for adults, with only Mann and Malan emphasizing the importance of a fixed end point. In contrast, brief interventions for children were an outgrowth of pediatric-liaison services and advanced clinical social casework, all nurtured within both the child guidance and community mental health movements. Evidence mounted that traditional diagnostic procedures and treatment not only alienated patients from the process but rendered them passive and inactive. Procedures were devised to engage the families by giving them a feeling that they had something to say about how and what was to be changed. This led to what Bertha Reynolds called the short contact and single-interview intervention. In addition, as early as 1949, 5- to 6-session child psychiatric treatment was in place. The major child guidance clinics of that decade began to substitute a 1- to 2-session intake procedure for the existing costly, time-consuming battery consisting of a separate intake as well as psychological and psychiatric evaluations.

The direct involvement of parents and children in their own treatment is accepted in contemporary psychotherapeutic interventions. Forty years ago, however, the concept was innovative and generated many new and creative ideas, such as allowing the child's active participation in the treatment experience. The goal was to help children overcome the harmful effect of trauma, reduce their overdependence on adults, and assert their individuated status. This approach led to changes at the Philadelphia Child Guidance Clinic and the Buffalo Children's Hospital Guidance Clinic, where treatments consisted of 6 to 7 sessions over the course of 5 to 6 weeks. Also at this time, brief treatment techniques were devised to help parents in the immediate management of their medically ill children. Limited goals were used, and the focus was exclusively on those factors that interfered with compliance and with the ultimate success of a medical treatment program.

The development of crisis theory laid the groundwork for the time-limited treatments that were to follow. Both draw on a common theoretical and clinical thesis, one based on the contributions of Gerald Caplan, Erich Lindemann, and Howard J. Parad and Libbie G. Parad. They share a highly focused orientation and use a variety of intervention strategies so that the clinician can establish as quickly as possible a positive relationship with the patient, while avoiding, at all costs, the development of any negative feelings (anger, doubt, or belligerence) on the patient's part. Brevity became possible with the development of problem-focused and learning-based approaches, the description of a systems perspective, and the evolution of sophisticated and effective techniques for biological assessment and intervention. Goals are set that the patient can realistically accomplish. More recently, concern for the emotional well-being of physically abused, sexually abused, and other traumatized children gave rise to the development of focused, problem-oriented interventions tailored to the needs of this specific population. Other interventions such as Ericksonian, behavioral, cognitive, and strategic family therapies are inherently brief interventions, although they do not pay homage to the issue of time.

There is general agreement that drawing a sharp distinction between crisis intervention and time-limited treatment serves no real purpose, because both modalities operate within a limited time frame. In fact, Parad and Parad (1968) note that whenever crisis intervention attempts to change a patient's fundamental mechanisms for coping with stress, it comes closer to time-limited treatment. This said, important distinctions do exist. Crisis intervention is applied when there is an imminent danger of psychological decompensation from internal or external stress. Therefore, crisis intervention is concerned primarily with establishing stability. The goal is to return the patient to the precrisis level and to do so as quickly as possible. Forces are brought to bear to reduce and contain the patient's strong emotions, because, if let unchecked, they have the potential to flood, overwhelm, and thus destabilize the psychological system.

In contrast, time-limited interventions attempt to immunize the patient from the source that gave rise to the crisis and that rendered him or her susceptible to the decompensation in the first place. The goal of time-limited treatment is to help patients modify their views of the world and of themselves, to help them identify internal strengths and external supports, so that the normal strategies for coping can operate. In order to accomplish this, at times it is important in the brief treatments to *increase* rather than decrease a patient's subjective experience of anxiety, discomfort, or distress. Crisis interventions are brief and close-ended because most crises are inherently self-limiting, whereas time-limited interventions are concise because brevity is thought to promote and facilitate active patient participation and rapid change. Time-limited treatment of children and adolescents targets symptom removal and the acquisition of both adaptive coping and improved parenting skills. In addition, it helps prepare the family for events that might destablize the youngster in the future.

Conceptual Framework

Time-limited treatment with children and adolescents exists within a progressive developmental framework. This framework distinguishes it from schools of time-limited treatment that focus primarily on historical, genetic, and structural aspects of conflict, defense, and symptomatology. This developmental orientation serves to acknowledge those biological, social, cognitive, academic, and affective experiences that are unique to children. As children mature, they move toward increased organizational complexity, efficiency, and productivity. The developmental model takes into consideration the changing nature of tasks and problems in the cognitive, social, educational, and familial domains as a function of developmental progression. For example, the same task or challenge at one age takes on completely different meaning at another, not merely because the child is now older. The model takes note of the intermittent nature of problems and of how progress occurs in fits and starts. Periods of success and mastery are interspersed with episodes of conflict, stress, imbalance, and psychosocial destabilization. The more disabling the psychopathology, the more likely emotional growth is

stalled, diverted or delayed. That young patients retain a remarkable capacity for growth in spite of negative social and familial forces is one of the major contributors to the swift effectiveness of this intervention. A developmental approach recognizes the innate, biological pressures that drive children and adolescents toward more elaborate levels of integration, toward becoming their own person, and toward separating themselves as individuals from their family. Time-limited interventions take into account the child's dependence on the goodwill of adults, the child's vulnerability to dislocation and loss, and the child's need for limit setting and external structure.

Technique is predicated on the assumption that many patients have experiences that put a strain on their development but that they do not require extensive psychiatric treatment or major structural change to resume forward momentum. Assuming that neither the child nor family is grossly dysfunctional, it is most likely that the child will be brought for psychiatric treatment when the child and/or family are in the midst of a crisis, such as divorce, birth of a sibling, death of a family member or close friend, or change in domicile. These reactive, psychosocial disturbances of childhood represent a departure from normal development and arouse primitive feelings, such as fears of loss (death), separation (divorce), dependency (illness and/or hospitalization), helplessness (parental job loss), or social isolation (relocation). At these moments, children usually feel frustrated, victimized, or frightened by external circumstances as they strive to maintain existing ways of dealing with life and attempt to emulate the autonomous or self-reliant functioning of their elders. Moreover, there are times when children fail to hit the mark set by a developmentally defined objective; this may lead to what Simon Budman and Alan Gurman labeled "developmental dyssynchrony." The failure to meet a specific benchmark can lead to a sense of dislocation, separateness, and isolation.

A child's or adolescent's first response to stress may become the model of subsequent reactions to later psychosocial stressors. During a period of crisis, the youngster will repeat the original response to the first trauma, especially if this first counteraction was more or less effective. Intervention is therefore, offered in response to the patient's developmental vulnerabilities; these operate as psychological fault lines that continue to be sensitive to stress or trauma over time. The goal of time-limited treatment is to return the patient to healthy developmental pathways and to open avenues for further progress. If there were one superordinate task, it would be to induce a sense of autonomy in the child and family and to assist them in negotiating a particularly difficult developmental transition point. Moreover, it is important to do this before therapy is ended so that treatment can continue even after termination, in other words, outside of the "therapy hour." Target symptoms are reduced or eliminated from the patient's repertoire while adaptive problem-solving skills are strengthened. The aim is to have both children and adolescents gain a more objective view of themselves and a greater appreciation of their own role in bringing about the difficulties at hand, as well as for them to acquire healthier ways of handling life's conflicts. Time-limited treatment takes as one of its goals the child's greater acceptance of a role as a separate and special person. Treatment therefore must culminate in the surrendering of any pathological attachments (fear, anger, or overdependency) to parents or to other significant adults.

CASE EXAMPLE

From her earliest memories, Brenda recalls her parents arguing. Sometimes the arguments would escalate to the point where her father would storm out of the house, slamming the door on his way out. Her sobbing mother would isolate herself in her bedroom. Brenda said she remembers feeling scared, helpless, and alone. She recalls that at these times she would sing to herself as "loud as she could" any song she could think of and would sing it over and over again to try and block out the yelling that would continue in her brain even after her father had left the house.

Later, Brenda would use the radio and turn it on full volume. When she received a Walkman for her twelfth birthday, it became her favorite and constant companion that she used to block out all unwanted thoughts or feelings. As she said, the Walkman was her security blanket, she wore it constantly, even attempting to shower with it under her shower cap. She stated she was "addicted to it," and could not fall asleep without it on.

Brenda blocked out her parents' arguments as a very young child by singing, later she used the same blocking out mechanism to protect herself from any potential unpleasantness, upsetting situations, pain, angry feelings, etc.

The clinician examines complexes of symptoms to determine the degree and extent to which they represent deviations from normal development. The clinician identifies how and by what means a specific stage of development is being diverted and assesses the disparity between children's resources and the requirements of the environment. The therapist need not accompany children all the way to their destination. Rather, he or she uses a variety of methods to help children regain their footing and negotiate a difficult developmental transition, where upon the therapist withdraws. The clinician helps patients to be less afraid to separate from sustaining figures of authority. Coincidentally, these aims happen to be at the core of many maturational/developmental conflicts experienced by children and adolescents. It is a process of shedding a dependent, fearful self by looking for less ambivalently held role models in order to shape an emerging grown-up self, a self that is substantively different from that of the parents. Children and adolescents struggle daily to defend assaults on their self-esteem, autonomy, and emotional separateness. Treatment makes an explicit alliance with patients' potential for mastery and for realizing their "true self." It does this by gaining access to children's and adolescents' potential rather than allowing them to be frustrated by their interactions with others. Time-limited treatment is organized in such a way as to complement and reinforce independence and self-directedness, while it provides a blanket of security against any perceived loss of self-control. The format of treatment strives for meaningful change as well as for the acquisition of new and purposeful ways of acting.

The fixed-session approach for adults advocated by of James Mann (1973) has wide appeal in the field of child and adolescent treatment. Mann came to the conclusion that the most critical goal of brief treatment is providing the time and space for the patient to individuate psychologically from the family and to do this within a maximum time frame of 12 sessions. The termination date, in this model, is predetermined at the onset of treatment. By holding the number of sessions to 12, Mann is able to create a predicable flow in the treatment, through 3 sharply demarcated stages: beginning, middle, and termination. Mann does not provide direct guidance about how to adjust the time-limited model to work with children.

This task was left to Proskauer (1969) and Drisko (1978), who developed concrete techniques to convey time's passage to children in what was essentially an insight-oriented, psychodynamic intervention. They conclude that a close-ended intervention with a specified last session date is ideally suited for children, because of its focus on the here-and-now crisis of separation rather than on the resolution of neurotic conflicts from the distant past. Diagnostic and structured play techniques as well as written therapeutic contracts were added later (Sloves & Peterlin, 1994). This, in turn, was integrated into a strategic model that was influenced by the focused problem resolution approach of Watzalwick, Weakland, and Fisch (1974). In current practice, the total number of sessions varies from one 2- to 3-hour-long "single-session" intervention to as many as 26 sessions.

Basic Characteristics

DEFINITION

Time-limited interventions, known under a variety of rubrics that include short-term, short duration, focal or focused, planned, time-managed, or brief treatment, refer to a broad range of interventions that use restricted, rationed, and strategically allocated time to propel the treatment toward its stated goals and objectives. Time-limited interventions are common to all the major psychiatric treatment modalities, including family, marital, and group treatment. They can take place in virtually any setting, including schools, community mental health clinics, outpatient and short-stay in-patient psychiatric hospitals, or in the field when a disaster or tragedy strikes a neighborhood or community. A set of common principles and techniques are applicable to all modalities, because they represent more of a strategic approach to helping people change than a unified theoretical point of view. Mina Dulcan (1984) offers a comprehensive survey of the available repertoire of short-term therapies available for children and families.

Success is dependent on the clinician's assertive management in maintaining both an adherence to the time schedule that was set between both clinician and child before the first treatment session and maintaining a selective focus once a target symptom, core conflict, or a central dynamic theme is identified. Time-limited treatment relies heavily on the child's ability to learn enough in a few sessions so as to continue to learn and improve after the intervention has ended. In longer, open-ended procedures, most if not all of the remediation and change is expected to take place in the presence of the clinician and is, therefore, treatment-bound.

When treatment goes on beyond 6 months, time begins to have an a less commanding influence, the intervention loses most if not all of its distinctiveness, and the process starts to resemble a traditional long-term treatment. An outer limit of 26 sessions is consistent with both clinical experience and research, which indicate that the benefits decrease as the number of sessions increase. When rates of improvement for patients in long-term and short-term treatment are plotted as a function of the time spent in treatment, approximately one-half of the patients show significant improvement by the eighth session and three-fourths by the 26th session (Howard, Kopta, Krause, & Orlinsley, 1986). This fact suggests that regardless of the type of intervention, patients maximize the benefits around the same time and do so relatively early in the intervention process. The total number of sessions can be presented in temporal proximity to one another or they may be unevenly distributed over time to maximize their impact and effect. The total number of appointments can be set at the beginning, with the time between sessions varying. This schedule is especially useful when the intensity of the clinician-patient relationship needs to be diluted in order to reduce the likelihood of the emergence of anger and ambivalence. Sometimes patients need a break to rest, reflect on their progress, analyze what is getting in the way of progress, or enjoy the fruits of their labor before plunging back into the work.

THE CONCEPT OF INTERMITTENCY

Time-limited treatment can be conceived as brief, intermittent, and episodic installments of psychiatric treatment that meet recurring crises. A short-term intervention is rarely terminated in the conventional sense, rather, it is interrupted.

This brings to the fore the powerful notion of rationed yet unlimited availability of treatment throughout the patient's life. A family's eventual return is taken as a positive identification with the treatment institution and as a sign of satisfaction with their previous intervention. Time-limited treatment reduces the stigma of failure that is often experienced by a family forced by life circumstances to return for an additional intervention at some later date. Time-limited treatment takes the view that reactive disturbances are both inevitable and potentially constructive opportunities rather than solely negative traumatic events.

In the majority of instances, when children are under psychological stress, a serialized, sequenced course or "dose" of time-limited treatment rather than one uninterrupted period of therapy makes the most sense. The function of this strategy is to concentrate the intensity of intervention. In this approach, the therapist recognizes that the present symptoms are not all that require treatment and that traumatic events will have different or additional meaning to children as they mature. When the therapist can anticipate a particularly difficult phase in development, sessions are arranged before problems reach crisis proportions. Regularly scheduled checkups, taking the form of brief psychotherapeutic "booster shots," provide a useful adjunct to the intervention proper. The intervention progresses more intensely and smoothly because the usual issues of separation and loss that in long-term therapies have such potential to distract, disrupt, or sabotage the ongoing work toward the end are absent. Children do not have to create new symptoms to prolong their attachment to the therapist as their "special friend." Whatever feelings of loss are engendered by the leave-taking are more than made up for by the therapist's assurances that the child can return in the future.

THE UNIQUE EXERCISE OF TIME

Time sets the treatment into motion and provides a kind of psychodynamic "heat" that brings home to patients the need to focus on the work at hand. Time, as a metaphor, communicates the prevailing pressure cooker atmosphere and affects the speed of activity that impregnates the treatment. Rationed time, whether it is embodied in a written contract or conveyed orally, is used to

sustain momentum, to forestall dependency, and to assuage the fear held by many patients that the clinician has designs on their newly acquired autonomy. When patients know approximately when the intervention is to end, they have fewer reasons to be concerned with feelings of rejection. Patients work harder when they understand that there is a finite amount of time available. Parents, and especially adolescents, have a positive reaction to time-limited interventions, because not only is the purpose of treatment clear, but because the time limit also provides assurances that a solution to the presenting problem is attainable and very much within their grasp. Children are less afraid in situations when it is made clear that they need not fear psychological engulfment and that their precious reserve of autonomy is not only respected but augmented by the therapeutic work. (Peterlin & Sloves 1985).

Rather than regard time as a constraint, as a symbol for the inevitability of loss, it is embraced as an ally. Time limits provide a structure wherein family members can gauge their progress and their own healing. The imposition of time limits is predicated on the assumption that the clinician can determine with a *reasonable* degree of clinical certainty how long it will take to bring the presenting problem, target symptom, or central dynamic conflict to a reasonable conclusion. Emphasis is on the word *reasonable,* and this in turn suggests that both patient and clinician need to set realistic goals. Time proscriptions are not imposed arbitrarily, and patients are not forced to accept a prescribed package of time. The clinician does not set a time limit and then decide on what can and cannot be accomplished within this time frame. Limits are chosen so that the passage of time becomes a vital component of the treatment with useful psychodynamic and developmental ramifications. The central paradox of this treatment is that while its brevity inspires confidence in patients, who feel reassured that their concerns are treatable, it places the clinician under considerable pressure to plan, maintain, manage, and monitor the therapeutic process.

RAPID ENGAGEMENT

Brief interventions are called instant access therapy because treatment begins the minute the clinician and patient meet. It begins before any of

355

the environmental, psychological, and/or familial forces that brought the family into treatment begin to dissipate, and the motivation for treatment begins to decline. At this juncture, the motivational level is at its peak, and the forces that can obstruct change are at their weakest. Thereafter, the clinician's influence declines precipitously, and the family's willingness to endure the inconvenience entailed by the intervention decreases. The fact that during the early stages of the treatment premature withdrawals increase with the dissolution of the presenting symptom makes it all the more important for the clinician to maintain the motivational level for the duration of the intervention. Unlike crisis intervention, the initial action taken by the clinician is not calculated to reduce the family's or child's distress. Time-limited interventions seek to structure and channel the patient's debilitating response to anxiety into a commitment to the work of the treatment. Efforts to reduce or eliminate this vital source of energy too early in the process inevitably deprive the treatment of a principal ally: the family's desire for change.

THERAPEUTIC PRAGMATISM

There was a time when one of the most derogatory epithets ascribed to a psychiatric model of treatment was that it was eclectic in theory or methodology. Eclecticism was thought to signify fuzzy thinking, the random or haphazard application of technique, the dominance of technique over theory, and the predominance of action over introspection. In response to the theoretical and methodological model characterized by a single paradigm, Arnold Lazarus advocated "technical eclecticism," and, in so doing, helped the concept attain a new level of respectability. In this ecumenical view, the clinician is free to draw upon a wide array of methods derived from various and, at times, conflicting viewpoints. It is a form of developmental pragmatism and clinical flexibility that draws from the best techniques, methods, and conceptual frameworks so long as they are derived from scientific and clinical empiricism. It is for this reason that brief interventions are problem-oriented rather than treatment-focused. The clinician borrows, without bias or discrimination, from any number of conceptual frameworks and is more concerned with helping people

change than with what Malan reproached as "psychotherapeutic perfectionism."

SELECTIVE FOCUS

Time-limited treatment is further characterized by its clarity of purpose, its tenacious pursuit of treatment goals, and its active collaboration with the patient. Rationed time does not mean that there is less intervention; it means a more efficient intervention, where specific symptoms, problems, and sectors of disturbance are targeted. The selected focus has a present-centeredness, dealing with the problem at hand rather than dealing with historical and open-ended issues. Time-limited clinicians prefer to work in a relatively circumscribed focal area. For this to be effective, both clinician and patient need to negotiate a contract in which the treatment goals are attainable. All too often, the participants have unrealistic, utopian goals. Perhaps the most challenging and most important decision that is made in time-limited treatment is the determination of what specific problem area will be chosen for the central theme. In essence, the entire success of time-limited treatment depends on how well the clinician can find and hold to a focus. A single theme or target symptom is selected from what may be a profusion of presenting problems. If the theme formulated is broad enough to encompass the patient's need for the symptom, the intervention is in a position to free the patient to continue growing in the direction of normal development. Such a focus contributes to a sense of control because it encourages the development of positive, adaptive coping behaviors. The theme comes to symbolize the patient's need to gain mastery over the environment as well as any internal fears, worries, and anxieties. A child's or adolescent's experience of loss, real or imagined, concrete or metaphorical, is an excellent foundation on which to base and construct a central dynamic theme.

CASE EXAMPLE

Albert is a sad 9-year-old boy who developed a complex motor tic shortly after his father's death 2 months ago. The tic that involved the upper torso, arms, and face, bore a striking resemblance to the seizures that characterized the terminal stage of his father's illness. Albert disclosed that he daydreams and does not pay attention in school because "I try real hard to remember what my father looks like," and he expressed the belief that "I will forget what he looks like," if he should stop and pay attention to what is going on around him.

The clinician said, "Since your father died, you have been working very hard to keep him alive in your mind and in your body. You think about him in school, because Dad was going to school (community college) just before he got sick. You saw Dad have 4 seizures, and so you have borrowed them. For the next 10 weeks, you and I, with the help of your mother, are going to find ways for you to remember him without feeling sick all the time. You will put a little bit of your father into everything you do, and that way, wherever you go and whatever you do, he will be there. Let's start now. Here are a doll family, doll house, and furniture. Show me what you and your dad did together."

Another common focus emerges from the precipitating events (a suicide note, an assault against a peer, or school avoidance) that brought the family into treatment. However, there are times when symptomatology alone is not the central focus. This is especially true when dysfunctional relationships exist or there are recurrent patterns of maladaptive behavior. Another general principle in deciding on a focus is to choose an area that has the potential for progressive rather than regressive functioning; to use any past and present accomplishments, successes and interests, that the clinician feels will give the most therapeutic leverage.

CASE EXAMPLE

A 7-year-old girl who rarely showed her anger except for refusing to go to school was told that during treatment sessions we would work on ways she could say what she felt without having to worry that she would be in trouble. In this case, the focus was not directed to her school refusal nor to the conscious or unconscious reasons why she refused.

CLINICIAN ACTIVITY

In long-term treatment, patients begin where they want to and tell their story in their own time. In time-limited approaches, a directive and active approach is employed in order to elicit relevant material when it does not emerge spontaneously. A primary feature of this approach is that the responsibility falls on the clinician to plan a strategy for solving the patient's problems. It makes no sense to pretend that anyone other than the clinician is in charge of the process. With the patient's agreement, the clinician steadfastly pursues the agreed-upon clinical goals despite the patient's natural and, at times, vigorous efforts to avoid the sense of dislocation that comes with all change. The clinical messages have to be sufficiently clear, vivid, and intense to be both heard and felt above the roar of the patient's pain, fears, and uncertainty. Above all else, the clinician is motivated by the need to provide relief from feelings of emotional distress and helplessness.

A direct intensive pursuit of a central issue dictates an unusually high level of clinician activity; serves to nurture and sustain a positive tone and relationship with the patient throughout the entire length of treatment. The idea of therapeutic activity means that, in addition to being animated, the clinician is intellectually active in keeping the patient focused on what really matters, and does so by either passively ignoring or actively discouraging discussions that only serve to sidetrack the vigorous pursuit of the central issue.

CASE EXAMPLE

Ronald is an intellectually gifted 10-year-old boy with congenital lymphodema. He is in almost constant medical crisis that requires 24-hour nursing care. Because of the school's concern about his medical condition, they do not allow him to play outside with peers, sit with them in class, or eat lunch with them. He was referred because "I don't want to go to school anymore. I just want to stay home and play video games. I said that I wanted to kill myself and that's the truth. I mean, what's the use?"

During the initial interview the clinician used the word *special* to describe some aspects of Ronald's functioning. To this he responded with uncharacteristic anger and contempt. "Special? Special? I hate that word because it means that I'm not . . . I'm not normal."

At some point during the second visit, Ronald struggled as he tried to maneuver a small play object in his swollen hands. Finally he turned to the clinician, and, in an exasperated and plaintive tone, said, "Help me."

The clinician replied, "Now you are asking me to treat you like a special person. You are actually upset with me because I am *not* treating you like a sick, sad, and helpless person. I want you to know that this is the one place where you won't be treated special. This is the one place where you can count on being treated like a normal kid."

357

The clinician's demonstrated activity tends to raise the patient's positive expectations. With children, more than intellectual activity is required: Physical activity and a lively presentation are necessary. During the assessment stage, the clinician's singleminded effort to define the problem and delineate goals is accomplished through focused interviewing, trial therapy, and diagnostic play. Once the intervention begins, the clinician takes charge and makes interpretations, uses structured play, issues directives and paradoxical injunctions, spins metaphors, confronts unrealistic expectations, and assigns homework. Directives must be laden with support, encouragement, and, at times, a good dose of drama and enthusiasm lest the hard work of treatment frighten the child and/or activate the defenses of passivity, avoidance, or flight. Even missed appointments are dealt with assertively. When the patient fails to show at the appointed time, the clinician immediately calls to reschedule, preferably within the same week. This communicates to the family that the clinician takes the problem as seriously as they do. Further, it gives the message to the family that the psychotherapist is assuming that they are committed to having their child "get better" and are therefore obligated to complete the treatment contract.

FAMILY EMPOWERMENT

The ability of the clinician to form a close bond with the adult members of the family is the first alliance of note, and any improvements made in the parent/child relationship will promote the easing up of conflicts in other relationships. Weekly contacts in person or by phone with significant adults increase the scope of the work of treatment; they ensure that everything possible is being done to reinforce each positive effort by the patient. Second, they address behavior by the family that might undermine, sabotage, or otherwise deter the child's new learning. Because the central work, the length of treatment, the manner in which the process will unfold, and the responsibilities of each of the participants is discussed openly, there is little hidden, mysterious or vague about the treatment process. The clinician's early withdrawal conveys a message to the family members that they are competent to handle most of life's problems. And it is precisely because the treatment is experienced by family members as

brief, to the point, and an empowerment of themselves that there is an increase in the likelihood that they will return for further treatment at a time of their own choosing. The family has learned that problems are sometimes better handled with treatment, and there is no threat to their autonomy in seeking it out.

STRUCTURED PLAY THERAPY

While an occasional child and a fair number of preadolescents prefer to sit and talk directly with the clinician, the vast majority need the medium of play to communicate their thoughts, ideas, and feelings. In other words, because it is a safe place to practice without dire or negative consequences, play is the primary avenue of influence and change for school-age children. Play serves as a bridge between reality and fantasy, a psychological staging area where what is real or pretend, social or private, external or internal are all given a voice, where information is exchanged and a "new" reality can take shape. When play is a healthy expression of the child's experiences, fantasies, and feelings, it becomes an opportunity for mastery. It is an occasion for living out those memories or experiences that are just outside of consciousness as well as a protected site for wish fulfillment and social intercourse. However, the use of play in time-limited treatment necessitates a considerable modification of technique and a thoughtful examination of many assumptions that govern more traditional, open-ended treatment formats. Several major characteristics of childhood shape the structure and technique of time-limited play treatment and necessitate the use of a highly focused and organized approach. This is essential so that the child's interest and motivation for change are held at a consistently high and beneficial level throughout the process. The child's predilection for immediate gratification, spontaneity, and uncensored expression demands a structured format that at once prohibits regression and limits dependency. This and a child's passion and need of action make it impossible to be inactive, or "just talk," in treatment; an active, play-oriented treatment is therefore required. Children need to externalize and validate their experiences through a manipulation of objects. In fact, the technique of time-limited play with children represents a progressive movement away

358

from what was the predominant method of treatment, what is commonly referred to as "free play," toward what we now know as "structured play." The free-play guidelines advocated by Virginia Axline and later incorporated into the paradigm employed by virtually all insight-oriented child treatments contain several admonitions that run counter to the process of time-limited treatment. For example, the clinician is charged not to direct the child's actions or conversation in any manner and is advised to do nothing to hurry the treatment along. The child leads the way, the clinician follows. No two principles could be more at variance with the effective practice of time-limited treatment with children.

Structured play therapy is based on the premise that when time is limited, play is not free. While the ability of children to solve problems in their own way is respected, they are not allowed to do it in their own time. Because this format of play limits and, to some extent, controls the range and intensity of emotions and behaviors expressed, children feel assured and protected. They thrive in situations that are organized, because they know what is expected of them and that they will be protected, should they become overwhelmed. Rather than assume a posture of detachment, the clinician's role is both directive and facilitative. Structured play is used to focus attention on specific issues that the clinician deems relevant to symptom relief, to the resolution of psychological conflict, and/or to dramatize or illustrate a particular thought, feeling, or interpersonal interaction that is not easily communicated with words. It represents a safe, familiar language system to initiate children into the treatment process.

As a technique, modern structured play is an outgrowth of the play interview techniques of David Levy, Jacob Conn, and Erik Erikson. Levy was perhaps the first to use what is now known as structured, preplanned, or problem-oriented play therapy. Originally, children were provided with materials and toys aimed at helping them recreate traumatic events in play, and were left free to decide just how to use them. In this way, their play becomes the basis for treatment, which addresses children's problems by exploiting the very methods that all children use to "treat themselves." The central proposition of this method is that children might indeed benefit from the free, cathartic expression of feelings in play. But they

do so most effectively within a series of situations to be constructed by the clinician using play materials optimized to mirror specific psychological, social, and relational conflicts. Later refinements directed children to play with toys that are arranged to resemble the anxiety-provoking life situations but where limits are set on the expression of strong emotions that might cause emotional disorganization. This technique became known as active or guided play therapy (Hambridge, 1955; Solomon, 1955). Language-based interventions were later formalized in the "mutual storytelling technique" of Richard Gardner (1971), wherein the clinician introduces a new, more adaptive ending that reframes the child's verbalized or acted-out play. The narrative of the play is shaped by the historical context and the current relationships that influence the child's difficulties. In the "corrective denouncement" technique by Terr (1991), the clinician dramatizes for the child an alternative way that the traumatic event might have been handled. Play-in-Progress (Sloves & Peterlin, 1993) is an inclusive term that describes the process by which guided fantasy, mutual storytelling, cognitive restructuring, and symbolic work are integrated into structured play therapy. Here the clinician sets the stage and arranges the play materials into a scene *before* the child enters the room. In other words, the clinician develops a strategy for each session, designs specific play scenarios, selects the appropriate play materials, introduces the major players, and sets it in train with an opening narrative.

In order to prevent each session from becoming a series of endless new beginnings, structured play pushes the central theme to the forefront of each session, so that an entirely different or conflicting subtheme does not emerge. Clinician and child do not begin each session with a tabula rasa, because the opening gambit is planned in such a manner as to keep previously articulated issues alive in the current session. The selected story line contains the overriding theme as well as the specific details that emerged during the previous session. In this regard, the clinician is the repository of the treatment memory. With the kind of thematic continuity provided by structured play, it is a relatively easy task for the child and clinician to pick up from where they left off at the last session. Instead of many situational and essentially irrelevant events dictating the pace and direction of the work, it is the shared consciousness of the child and clinician that takes charge and directs the process. It is the clinician who helps recall what has transpired, who connects the play directly to the child's extratherapeutic experiences. The clinician gives voice to the child's intuitive, experiential self; articulates emotional states and cognitive processes that are intuitively sensed by children but lie just beyond their linguistic and conceptual powers. Watching the clinician play, the child becomes at once both an interested observer and active participant in the process of problem clarification and conflict resolution. This improvisational switching of roles helps children reflect on their thinking and allows them to become critical observers of their own thoughts and feelings.

In the choice of play materials and construction of a play scenario, several factors are taken into consideration, these include the stage of treatment and what happened in the preceding session. Specific play materials are used, while others are strictly avoided. Puppets, dolls, doll houses and furniture, action figures, toy animals and vehicles, wooden building blocks, and water-soluble drawing materials are the primary tools of treatment; they are chosen for their ability to dramatize thoughts, feelings, and behaviors. At the same time, any play activity that is too cumbersome, takes too much time to set up or to be played out or offers the child sanctuary from the treatment focus is avoided. Board games are not used, no matter what their therapeutic intent, because they are inherently dependent on fixed rules of engagement that limit spontaneity, constrict fantasy, and force potential allies to assume an adversarial relationship. Only materials that help a child to feel age appropriate are used. Finger paints, Play Do, water play, and other primitive materials are not used, as they can cause regressive behavior in the child. This can create conflicts over control between the clinician and child instead of the freedom of expression that is desired.

Toward the end of the assessment stage and at the end of each subsequent meeting, children are asked to bring in those dolls, action figures, toy vehicles, and other possessions that they think will help the clinician understand their worries better. This is particularly useful with traumatized children, because much of their play is usually secret, especially that which centers around an unresolved core issue such as what is addressed in the

central theme. This request for children's own toys accelerates the work and makes for the efficient use of time. Unlike the toys in the clinician's playroom, children's toys are already imbued with the unique and distinctive aspects of the children's past and present experiences. They come replete with an abundant and fertile psychosocial subtext.

CASE EXAMPLE

Jamie, a 6-year-old girl, was in the midst of a complicated bereavement that followed the death of her father 6 months earlier. She brought to her first session a life-size stuffed doll she named Samantha.

Jamie: Daddy got me Samantha before he got sick but Mommy said I can't take her everywhere with me. Like school and stuff.
Dr. S.:   It's okay here. I bet she has seen and heard a lot of things. Now Samantha can tell us why you are so very upset with everyone.

Description of the Process

FORMAT

Brief interventions are organized into several different formats that can vary in duration and intensity. Brief interventions are either open or close ended. An intervention is open ended when the exact number of sessions or a specific time frame is not specified, and work stops whenever the goals are achieved. It is close ended when the total number of sessions, the frequency of contact (daily, weekly or monthly), or the overall length in weeks or months is made explicit to the family. Clinicians who want to insert a heightened sense of urgency into the proceedings usually inform the patient that they have limited time in which to accomplish their goals. But the clinician can start the intervention with no clear end date in mind and wait to impose it when it serves a clear strategic purpose, such as to accelerate an intervention that has hit a dry patch, or to jump-start a stalled but otherwise viable intervention, or to help a patient who has accomplished his or her goals but who is having difficulty in leaving treatment.

When the family is not expected to return, it is

a single-dose intervention. When a resumption of treatment is anticipated, the clinician and family prearrange the return appointment (planned reengagement). Alternatively the date of return can be left to the family or adolescent (elective reengagement). When the intervention is envisioned as only the first stage of what could well be a recurrent healing experience, it is (according to Beverly James) developmentally sequenced or serialized. In the latter case, the end date simply marks a temporary deferment in the treatment to some time in the future. Return sessions are scheduled and distributed over time to coincide with the patient's particular developmental vulnerabilities. For example, a sexually abused preadolescent girl was asked to return when she reaches puberty, a young boy was given an appointment 2 weeks before the first anniversary of his father's death, while another who was physically assaulted on the school bus returned shortly before he entered a high school that required him to use the subway during rush hour.

PROCESS

The process begins at the assessment stage, during which the clinician has the task of judging the family's appropriateness for treatment as well as of assessing any collateral interventions that can expedite the treatment process. Treatment begins as quickly as possible, because, as the span between assessment and treatment increases, so does the likelihood of premature withdrawal. In the case of school-age children, individual sessions are rarely offered without some family intervention. An active, direct manipulation of relationships within the family is a fundamental component. This is not always the case with adolescents, who often travel to their sessions without parental assistance, who are capable of providing reasonably accurate information, and who might need treatment to facilitate their separation from the family. Whether the intervention progresses through an opening, middle, and end stage or not depends on the length of the treatment. With 6 or less sessions, the middle and end stages may collapse into the predominant opening stage with its feverish pitch of activity, heightened concentration, and defined focus. In some cases, one or another stage never appear; on the other hand, one or more stages may appear several times during the treatment. As the length of treatment increases, the 3 stages become more clearly delineated.

In the opening stage, the clinician nourishes the relationship with the child, offering an empathic umbrella as shelter from the interpersonal and intrapsychic storms that have brought the patient into treatment. At this stage, the goal is to cast the clinician in the role of the all-comprehending special friend or ally; it is a time when children learn how to adapt the intervention to their needs. It is in the middle stage that the patient's motivation begins to wane, as the child comes to the realization that the clinician is not going to do all of the work, is not an appropriate parental substitute, and has no special powers to make things right. On the contrary, the clinician is someone who actually makes patients feel uncomfortable, who may ask them to struggle with and, at times, to accomodate to the demands of reality. In this stage of treatment, the patient begins to sort out realistic and beneficial options to deal with the problems. In the end stage, the clinician continues the work of helping the child to choose between magical wishes and tangible, real sources of gratification. Moreover, the therapist helps the patient to understand that to be relatively happy and able to cope with stress, he or she must let go of expecting and demanding constant protection from the rub of reality. Children, tend to form faster and more intense relationships with the clinician than do adolescents; accordingly, they may need help to separate and reconnect with parent or parental surrogates in the natural environment. Follow-up contacts are an integral component of the intervention, and they are routinely scheduled at 6-month intervals for at least 18 months after the last treatment session.

ASSESSMENT STAGE

The vigorous nature of time-limited treatment and the unique pressures it brings to bear on all the participants give the assessment a significantly more intense and probing quality than is true for a patient being evaluated for long-term treatment. The selection process is a calculated exercise in prediction, and most treatment failures are traceable to this stage—that is, they arise when the clinician miscalculates the good-enough fit between patient, clinician, and the treatment modality. The assessment process differs substantially from the standard psychodiagnostic evaluation in that the task is the identification and isolation of a single, predominant central theme or core conflict. It is not primarily an assessment of individual or family psychopathology that, albeit present, might obscure rather than highlight their combined strengths.

The clinician has a number of goals. The first is to determine whether both the identified patient and family require an intervention other than time-limited treatment. Second, the clinician must identify any psychodynamic, systemic, situational, or environmental factors that will hamper or sabotage the intervention. The patient's capacity, willingness, and interest in forming a positive working relationship with the clinician are central. With school-aged children, it is their capacity for symbolic play, and for adolescents, their perception that the clinician is a suitable ally in the struggle for identity vis-a-vis the family, that make rapid change possible. A determination must be made of the necessity for collateral psychological and/or medical interventions. Toward the end of the final assessment session, the central theme, crafted into a coherent and functional clinical hypothesis, is presented to the family, and the treatment contract is drafted.

Timeliness in assessment is of central importance. In all modalities of psychiatric treatment, there comes a time when the clinician must shift from an emphasis on data collection to a focus on remediation. In the time-limited approach, the therapeutic intervention begins sooner rather than later. The assessment is conducted quickly in order to maintain and concentrate rather than to dilute the family's level of motivation. Brief interventions borrow the concept of rapid case formulation. This approach is widely practiced in the psychiatric emergency room and short-stay inpatient psychiatric hospitals, where assessment and crisis intervention take place almost simultaneously. The main point to keep in mind is that protracted assessments are to be avoided at all costs, because they carry with them increased clinical risk. If spread out over a considerable period of time (3 weeks or more), the very forces that originally motivated the patient to seek relief begin to decline at a precipitous rate, and there is an increased likelihood of a premature withdrawal. Whenever possible, the initial consultations are scheduled for consecutive days or in such close proximity to one another as to optimize the clinician's influence. Experience suggests that for maximum therapeutic effect, the same clinician should conduct both the assessment and the treatment. When this is done, continuity between assessment and intervention is assured, the clinician does not have to waste time getting to know the patient, going over questions already answered and thereby risking patient alienation. This sense of familiarity and intimacy empowers the clinician to, in the words of Simon Budman (1981) "hit the ground running."

There are 2 general yet opposing approaches to assessment. In the first approach, advocated for only the most experienced clinician, the boundary between evaluation and intervention is seamless, and the 2 processes are virtually indistinguishable from one another. Here the intervention is said to begin as soon as the patient walks in the door. In the second, more conservative approach, the boundaries are more sharply demarcated, and the distinction between the 2 is made clear to patients, so that they understand that what is to follow is substantively different from that which has occurred. Patients are told that the intervention will begin promptly with the *next* appointment, and, if a time limit is part of the contract, then the countdown to the last session begins from there.

PATIENT SELECTION

When adult time-limited treatments were in their infancy, the selection criteria for them bore a striking resemblance to those criteria commonly used to describe a patient suitable for long-term insight-oriented treatment: a single focal dynamic conflict; acute onset; psychological mindedness; at least one stable, meaningful interpersonal relationship in the past or present; and a high level of motivation. Currently, these criteria are thought to be too narrowly conceived and defined. Because children and adolescents learn and adapt faster than their adult counterparts, time-limited intervention strategies cast a far broader net than when employed with adults; children's capacity for change is greater and the parental influence extends rather than limits the clinician's range of influence.

It is recommended that in the absence of specific contraindications, time-limited interventions be considered as the intervention of choice. In other words, it is suggested that, rather than specify who is most appropriate for time-limited treatment, it might be better to assume that every child or adolescent is appropriate until proven otherwise. If a child should return to treatment, the clinician can renew the original contract, shift the emphasis, turn attention to a fresh problem, add colateral intervention, or substitute an entirely new intervention.

This said, there are nonetheless selection criteria for time-limited treatment. Clinical experience indicates that for children and adolescents to be successful in time-limited treatment, they need to have experience a sustained and affectionate relationship with an adult, either in the recent past or in the present. It is not necessary that this relationship be with the birth parent. For example, children who are in reasonably stable foster care placements or who are in a well-structured group home setting are responsive to time-limited treatment, but only when a positive relationship exists between child and caregiver. An equally critical component is whether the children are willing to immerse themselves in a positive relationship with the clinician and are able to tolerate this relationship, which can be, at times, both challenging and confrontational. Children's suitability for treatment is directly related to a capacity for basic trust, a desire to work rather than oppose or obstruct, and a willingness to take some ownership for the problems that will be addressed in treatment.

Oppositional-based relationships are far less problematic with adolescents because their level of cognitive development allows for the use of paradoxical and strategic techniques to avoid the appearance of a power struggle. Homework assignments for both individual and collective members of the family are an excellent means by which to gauge their commitment to the work. The homeworks serves also as a reminder that the family has accepted responsibility for their own treatment. The appearance of a target symptom, focal dynamic issue, or central theme, preferably related to separation or loss, is an important contributor to success. The more vague and nebulous the presenting problem—such as "I want him to listen to me" or "I want them [the parents] to leave me alone"—the more futile will be this form of treatment. Clinicians describe the best candidates

as willing to engage in symbolic and imaginative play or to speak directly about problems in daily living. When working with school-age children and early adolescents, the clinician needs as an ally, an adult authority figure who is and will be sufficiently supportive and flexible to adapt and accommodate the changes as they occur in patients. This treatment cannot work with an identified parental figure who will collude with children's pathology or undermine their effort to experiment with new solutions. On the other hand, although many children and even more adolescents experience their problems as caused by inappropriately high or unrealistic parental expectations, the assessment must not implicate the caregivers as malevolent or pathologically motivated.

While symptoms of recent onset are more easily remedied, chronicity alone does not disqualify a patient, especially when a symptom is relatively stable over time. It is now recognized that time-limited treatments are of value to children and adolescents with other than reactive disorders. Many children, burdened with extensive conflicts that go back many years, are able to marshal sufficient inner strengths to make a sound adaptation. However, a single potent psychosocial stressor or several stressors in close temporal proximity to one another may be enough to impair patients' ability to maintain an equilibrium. Stress can re-open closed traumatic chapters in patients' lives but expose them so that they are displayed in a different way. What is important is the stability of children's coping mechanisms before the traumatic event that led to initiating treatment. Consequently, many patients with a difficult history and presenting symptomatology have been treated successfully by means of the brief treatment modalities. For instance, good results are being achieved with institutionalized patients who have histories of fire setting and destructiveness, or who are diagnosed with obsessional or narcissistic personality disorders as well as those having a borderline diagnosis.

The majority of children with conduct disorders are appropriate. However, a history of persistent violence or sociopathy as well as the presence of masochistic or self-destructive behavior would preclude a patient from time-limited treatment. Acute phobias, with or without psychophysiological reactions, are treatable with one caveat: Parents must experience the symptom as a highly noxious or as a disruptive irritant lest they collude with the child to maintain the disorder. Children with diagnoses of posttraumatic stress disorder are suitable for time-limited play. However, children who have witnessed an especially violent physical assault on a family member are not. It should come as no surprise that the entire category of transitory or adjustment disorders lend themselves to time-limited treatment because the diagnosis rests on a presumption of an underlying adaptive character structure. Also, the time-limited approach is beneficial to children whose parent has recently died, especially those whose death has come after a chronic or long illness.

There are several serious situations where the need for long-term interventions are apparent from the onset. Any parent, child, or adolescent who cannot fully participate in this unusually intense and occasionally confrontative treatment must be ruled out. For this reason, psychotic, antisocial, or sociopathic patients require alternative treatments. Likewise, profoundly depressed adolescents are equally unsuitable because they have limited resources to invest in the process and because the risk of suicide is a significant factor. Excluded as well are children with multiple and/or significant losses, children with numerous psychiatric hospitalizations, and those with chronic, residual psychosis. These children rarely can form the immediate, positive, and trusting relationship that is essential in the briefer treatments. Frequent changes in domicile such as those caused by homelessness or by multiple and short-lived foster care placements require reconstitutive work. These children are not able to tolerate the anxiety of separation and loss inherent in the time-limited approach. Instead, they will either refuse to engage with the clinician or will experience the ending of treatment as yet another abandonment. While patients with moderate to profound developmental retardation require family-oriented interventions, those with borderline or mild mental retardation take quite readily to this approach.

CENTRAL THEME AND THERAPEUTIC CONTRACT

When the clinician has sufficient information to understand and to begin to do something about the problem, a therapeutic contract is drafted. Patients provided with *written* contracts have higher rates of participation along with fewer canceled and no-show appointments than those who do not. Treatment contracts make explicit to both parent and child that the clinician has fully understood what they hope to derive from the process. Further, the participants have a clear sense of where they are going and approximately how long it will take them to get there. The contract answers, in a very tangible way, a question on the mind of most patients, which is "What is wrong with me and how long will it take for me to feel better?" The activity of both the clinician and patient working out the goals and time frame increases the patient's motivation as it reduces resistance: a tendency to avoid the work of treatment as the work itself becomes more difficult. It is easier to endure a painful yet necessary process when one knows when it will end.

In a procedure that differs significantly from long-term treatment, the dynamic or strategic formulation is always shared directly with the family, this increases each participant's understanding of the problem and gives him or her a starting point as to how to supplement the work of treatment at home. A clear focus tends to restrict grandiose thinking or the contemplation of utopian goals, not only for the child and family but for the clinician as well. The contract contains a statement of the central theme in jargon-free language intelligible to all participants and, in most cases, the total length of treatment and the date of the last session. The family is told what they can expect at each stage of treatment because symptom remission during the early stage can give a false impression that the major issues have resolved themselves; symptom recurrence during the end stage might then precipitate a loss of confidence in the procedure. School-age children need concrete, graphic, and mnemonic devices such as contracts and calendars to push time to the forefront of their consciousness. Furthermore, the time limit is a way for children to know when to expect the disappointment of ending. With school-age children, in addition to the contract, a calendar is used which marks the date of each session. As they mark off the date each and every time a session is attended, this highlights the brevity of the treatment. They can thus actually see time passing as the end date becomes increasingly prominent and indisputable.

CASE EXAMPLE

The clinician's first encounter with Elijah was when he marched into the office, urging Ms. D., whom he called Mother D. or Mom, to hurry up so they could "get this over with and go home." The family was referred by the school who threatened Elijah with expulsion if help was not obtained. As Ms. D. articulated her concerns for this 8-year-old boy, her frustration with him, and her disapproval of his behavior, she also communicated a warmth and belief in him: Things could get better with "God's and Elijah's help."

Elijah is a handsome, sturdily built child of mixed Afro-American, Hispanic, and Caucasian background. At the time of referral, his mother was incarcerated for prostitution as well as using and selling narcotics. Elijah lived with his 44-year-old maternal great-aunt, Ms. D., with whom he had been since birth, when he was diagnosed with fetal alcohol syndrome. Elijah entered public school at age 6, was retained in the first grade, and, at the time of referral, was attending special education placement for children who were learning disabled and "emotionally disturbed." A year ago the consulting psychiatrist prescribed a regimen of psychostimulants because Elijah was aggressive and defiant in school. His teachers and Ms. D. reported that this had "helped some," but he continued to fail in most of his studies and remained provocative toward peers. Ms. D. stated that she could manage him at home without too much difficulty because she tolerated "no stepping out of line from him." She stated she welcomed the clinic's help as she was at her wit's end.

When alone with the clinician, Elijah stated that he got into fights because the other kids teased him about his mother. He stated that the teacher never took his side, he felt picked on, undefended. He liked his ability to fight, his strong arms and legs, his deftness at karate kicks. He agreed that his fighting did get him into trouble, not only with his teacher but also with Mother D. He had no friends, hated the "stupid" school and wished his birth mother could get herself together so they could move down South.

To develop a theme for Elijah, the clinician took into account his experiences of repetitive loss: the suddenness and frequency of the birth mother's arrivals and departures, an absent birth father, his failure in several areas—to make friends, to succeed academically, and to sustain himself in a "regular" class. Elijah had lost control of himself and had alienated the significant people around him. His many strengths were not left out of the equation: his strong and positive attachment to Ms. D. who was involved and committed to his welfare, his ability to focus and articulate his feelings to the clinician, and his willingness to assume responsibility in making things better for himself. With these variables in mind, a central theme was worked out by the clinician and presented to Mother D. and Elijah.

CASE EXAMPLE

"You are a very powerful and strong 8-year-old, Elijah, who has done a splendid job in taking care of yourself and Mother D at home. However, you seem to be unable to get your teacher and classmates to see just how smart and clever and strong you are. They see you only as angry and often not fun to be with. Together, you and I, will find a way to let everyone know just how special you are, so they can appreciate you for being so smart, strong and good looking, and fast and wonderful. Together we will convince them and we will do it in 12 times of seeing each other. We will begin our first time next week.

TIME-LIMITED TREATMENT
WITH ADOLESCENTS

A time-limited treatment is the preferred modality for adolescents precisely because it is congruent with the main goals of this developmental phase, a phase that essentially includes an emotional and physical separation from the family, the consolidation of an identity, and the establishment of a coherent value system. The more the adolescent displays the capacity to generalize and abstract, and to generate and assume alternative views and perspectives, the less the adult time-limited technique needs to be modified. A principal goal of the treatment is to aid and promote the adolescent's effort to achieve a relatively stable sense of self. The clinician acts quickly and decisively to join the youngsters in their distress and thereby to dissociate him- or herself from those other adults in the adolescents' world who, rightly or wrongly, demand conformity, compliance, and accommodation. In the opening stages of treatment, the goal is to identify those factors that interfere with coping in the present. For this process to go forth smoothly, the clinician must be fully conversant with the society that forms the basis of the given adolescent's value system.

Where the theme focuses on interpersonal interactions, it is recommended to use a here-and-

365

now approach with a minimum of contemplation of historical events. Early events are explored only when they appear to be actively thwarting adaptation in the present. Overcoming present fears and failures is more important than knowing the events that led to them. Adolescents are most defenseless to the destabilizing effects of regression when they are forced to reflect on their childhood. Therefore, the emphasis in treatment is on the need to restore and support a phase-specific level of autonomy and self-regulation. However, this is not meant to imply that the adolescent is treated gingerly, for to do so is a condescension that is destined to breach the clinician-patient relationship. Emotionally confrontative techniques are used to engage the adolescent in the process of self-awareness but always in an atmosphere of support and respect. For the most part, adolescents respond negatively to emotional aloofness and distrust adults who are perceived as authoritarian.

For the adolescent, a fixed time-limit rather than an open-ended contract is a powerful tool. A fixed end date provides the adolescent with reassurance that the transient clinician has no designs on the patient's autonomy or sense of control, nor is the clinician plotting to change the personality of the adolescent. The end date provides a built-in escape clause, as it establishes an uncompromising limit. The clinician negotiates the total number of sessions, provides a written "guarantee" as to its length, and leaves it up to the adolescent to seek a renewal of the contract as the end date approaches. There are occasions when a treatment contract and fixed end session are a perfect foil for oppositional or defiant adolescents who feel they are in treatment against their will. Adolescents such as these spend most, if not all, of their time in either passive or active resistance to the very idea that they need any help. Faced with such a dysfunctional level of opposition, the clinician might consider a shift to a time-limited approach.

CASE EXAMPLE

Fifteen-year-old Jerome spent the better part of the first 4 sessions of treatment arguing with the clinician. The appointment was at an inconvenient time, arrangements for transportation were problematic, and besides "I don't have to come here anymore because I'm not doing it anymore." Whether Jerome arrived on time or, more often, late, he began to negotiate for the session's end as soon as he was seated, if not as he came storming into the office. Very little work was being accomplished, so, at the beginning of the fifth session, and before Jerome had a chance to complain, the clinician advanced the following proposition:

"For the past four weeks you have tried to convince me that you don't need therapy, that it's a waste of your time, that you have better things to do, and besides, you are no longer getting into any difficulties in school, so what's the point?

"I want to make a deal with you. Whether you think you have a problem or not, we both know that you do. The problem is that your parents insist that you come to see me and if you don't come you are going to be in big trouble. Here is what I suggest. If you promise to come on time for the next 6 sessions, we will stop at the end of session number 6. There is only one other condition. Besides you promising to come on time, you must promise to stop complaining about what a pain it is to come here. After the sixth session I will continue to see you only if you insist."

OPENING STAGE

At this beginning stage, every effort is made to nurture the clinician-patient relationship and the parental alliance, so that the patient feels understood. This is accomplished by the clinician making a direct appeal to that aspect of the patient that craves security and support without dependency and yearns for the triumph of defending the self without fear of retaliation. The task that is first and foremost on the clinician's agenda is to demonstrate to the patient, by example, how treatment takes effect and how the central work can get accomplished within the time frame specified. The sooner patients are acclimated to the process, the faster they are free to explore the central issue. Children, and, for that matter, most adults, know little more about treatment than "you play" or "you talk." But just how talk and play relate to improved functioning in the family and the community at large will remain a mystery until someone takes the responsibility to explain it to them. In long-term interventions, the question of who does what to whom is gradually revealed, as the clinician-patient relationship evolves slowly and takes on a life of its own. Short-term work requires that the clinician educate the child about the rules of engagement, the work ethic that pervades the process, and, in the case of school-age children, the notion that play is a problem-solving tool and not a recreational activity. Children are not given time to discover the implicit rules that govern the intervention. The clinician gives them a helping hand.

The clinician has certain fixed and immutable responsibilities that are emphasized in the beginning of treatment and that remain constant and unrelenting right through to the end. The clinician is above all else the objective and psychological timekeeper, the one who experiences most comprehensively the effect of time's passage on the treatment. It is the clinician who conveys time's passage to the patient, who keeps the treatment pointed in the right direction, who screens out or reframes distractions in positive terms, and who holds the central theme in the foreground. In order to keep the child focused on the central work of treatment, each session begins the same way. First, the child checks off the current session date on the treatment contract. Then the clinician verbalizes the passage of time: "Today is session number 3, we now have 9 sessions to go." Also, at the beginning of each session, the clinician reads the central theme from the contract. The session ends on a similar note: "Today we finished session 3, and next week is session 4. That means we have 9 sessions to go."

With school-age children especially, the clinician uses symbolic play, metaphors, analogies, life stories, and parables to address the issues that the central theme conveys. The clinician also comments on the process and acts as an outside observer to the process by providing a sense of continuity and flow, not only during a particular session but also between sessions. When momentary setbacks threaten to undermine the patient's confidence, accomplishments are reinforced and encouragement is provided. Resistances to the treatment are interpreted wherever and whenever they occur, because time-limited interventions cannot work in the presence of hostility, negativism, or disinterest.

CASE EXAMPLE

During the second session, Elijah mentioned in passing that he did not have a fight all week and that his teacher had let him water the plants yesterday. In the play, he declared that the action figure that he was playing with didn't need his muscles anymore, that he could outsmart the enemies with his brains. The clinician was quick to compliment the action figure for discovering he had a wonderful brain but was also quick to point out that muscles had good parts to them too, and perhaps Elijah and she could figure out together how the action figure could put both strength and brains to good use. Now that he could use his head to keep him safe, he didn't need his arms and legs to fight.

At this opening stage of treatment, a significant number of patients discard their presenting symptoms and behave as if the clinician-patient relationship alone is sufficient to obviate the need for the very maladaptive coping system that brought them together. Symptom reduction is attributed to the clinician's empathic exploration of the central issue and by the process of bringing into consciousness memories and feelings that heretofore, were outside awareness. Further, the promotion of positive feelings about the self causes different and more constructive behavior in the patient, and this is underscored by positive feedback about the new behaviors from family, friends, and teachers. The calm, purposeful manner in which the core conflict is explored tends to desensitize patients to whatever powerful and frightening feelings may have caused them to avoid problem-solving in the past.

MIDDLE STAGE

When the intervention extends beyond 4 or 5 sessions, a middle stage may emerge. At this juncture, several factors can affect the rate and course of the process. The work may accelerate as gains accrued earlier in the process encourage and reinforces more change. On the other hand, the opening stage can bring such dramatic and significant relief that the whole process can run out of steam within a few sessions. A third possibility is that the work may languish as the patient realizes he or she will have to give up this supportive and mutually accepting relationship. In those instances where both the presenting symptomatology and motivation are on the decline, it is the clinician's role to maintain the treatment momentum by being both more interpretive and more confrontational. Regardless of the patient's response, the clinician, trading on the goodwill established in the opening stage, more directly challenges the patient's maladaptive responses to psychosocial conflict. New alternative responses are developed and practiced.

Not surprisingly, as the clinician and patient begin to spend more time together, the therapeutic alliance begins to change. As they become more comfortable with one another, a certain level of optimal tension is lost to the relationship. Whereas in the opening stage, the clinician may represent the fantasy of the all kind, all-sustaining parent, a more fully formed, positive but more reality-based relationship evolves during this second stage of treatment. Disappointed in finding that the clinician has no magical quick fix, the patient may feel torn between feelings of disillusionment, sadness, irritability, or anger. If left untreated, the emergence of negative feelings toward the clinician is the single most destructive event that can ensue, and it can sabotage a brief intervention. Therefore, whenever it appears, decisive action by the clinician is required. The clinician is also alert to any shift in the clinician-patient alliance in order to avoid becoming embroiled in an unproductive struggle for control. Because it is so important to maintain a positive relationship with the patient, the clinician must first determine whether emotional withdrawal, passive resistance, or outright oppositionalism is a reenactment of a past relationship with a significant other, an effort to distract the clinician from some issue, or a valid criticism of the psychotherapist at that moment in time. Finally, the clinician must evaluate whether this is simply an act on the child's part of age-appropriate self-assertiveness. Disagreements over power must be avoided because they almost always lead to the perception of the clinician as impotent or inadequate.

CASE EXAMPLE

Elijah rushed into the office on his fifth visit, made a dash for the contract which was on the desk, signed his name as having come to the session, and then dumped the contents of his backpack onto the floor. What tumbled out was a most marvelous collection of miniature dinosaurs. The clinician had constructed a fort out of wooden blocks in anticipation of Elijah's arrival, but she chose to use the dinosaurs because Elijah was sending a signal that they had special meaning for him and could be easily integrated into the story line that was planned. The story evolved around a character, human or animal, who would be slightly older than Elijah, and who would struggle to be close to the authority figure in the story.

A fort or any block-built structure is an excellent metaphor to use with children because it can be made to represent so many things. Walls contain within them powerful thoughts, feelings, and memories as they defend against real or imagined assaults from without. Further, they serve a defensive purpose, offer a staging area from which offensive forces are marshaled, and provide a differential line between the internal and external world. Play can collapse a structurally weak fort and thus provide an opportunity for clinician and child to problem-solve around the nature of the enemy and what steps need to be taken to strengthen it against future attack. Solutions are always kept within the bounds of reality, with no help from magical or supernatural forces implied. Therefore, a building engineer or a soldier who invented very strong cement could be enlisted to help, but a cartoon character or superhero such as Superman could not.

CASE EXAMPLE

In the middle of the shared storytelling, Elijah jumped up and retrieved his notebook that lay on the floor. He stated he needed to do his homework, but was vague as to what it was to be about. The clinician saw this as an avoidance of the issues that were being acted out in the play. She reminded Elijah that they had a different kind of work to do, here, and that she was keeping her part of the bargain, and expected that he was strong enough to keep his part. She reminded him that they had a deal, and only seven more times were left to get the job done. With that, Elijah scowled, thought a bit and returned to the therapeutic play.

END STAGE

An end stage is inevitable when the intervention has forged such a significant emotional bond between the participants that the act of leaving is painful. A majority of adolescents and adults greet the end stage with a mixture of relief, positive anticipation, and a sense of accomplishment. Whatever sadness they may feel is mitigated by a sense that the worst is now behind them, that they have regained a semblance of control over their lives, and, from this point on, they can pick up where they left off. They have found within themselves the resources to confront and cope with a terrifying moment in their lives. Often they feel a sense of gratitude and respect toward the clinician for the support and understanding offered and received.

Children, on the other hand, find it difficult to step back, reflect on their experiences, and disengage, without a deep sense of regret and the feeling that something valuable is about to be lost. Children perceive the clinician and the intervention as one and the same: The clinician becomes the embodiment of the process of change. Whereas an adolescent or adult can differentiate between the clinician and the skills imparted in the relationship, children are unable to do this without obvious and explicit help from the clinician. It is especially difficult for those children who have experienced grievous losses due to parental abandonment, divorce, or death, because the end stage may reawaken strong emotions associated with these events. It is not surprising that most children try to remain with the clinician, and they use an exquisite array of techniques in an attempt to hold on to what they fear they might lose. These techniques include denial, negation, anger, bargaining, and symptom substitution. Some will intentionally or "accidentally" damage or destroy the written therapy contract in the hope the clinician will forget that the end is close at hand. Others may claim that the clinician has miscounted the number of sessions remaining or insist that it was some other child who last week checked off the date on their contract. Some children try to make time stand still, as was the case when Roberta threw the clock out of the window, or when Wayne unplugged the clinician's electronic clock, plugged it back in, and, as it flashed 12 o'clock, said with a smile, "See, now we have more time left." Children may develop an entirely new problem or lapse back into the original symptom that was in remission for a good part of the intervention, all in an effort to give the intervention a rationale for continuing. On the other hand, children can come up with an infinite number of manifestly legitimate excuses of why they cannot attend the last few sessions. Perhaps it is a classroom project that is suddenly due on the same day as the last session, or they may develop a somatic complaint such as a headache or stomachache that accomplishes the same purpose.

Parents are not immune to their own tactics. Concerned that they cannot match the clinician's skill in either maintaining their child's progress or fearful that they will not know what to do should a new problem arise, they too may find reasons to prolong the contact. School-age children usually are brought to therapy by their parents, so that any resistance to coming to the sessions can be anticipated and worked out with the parents. With adolescents, who may come to the sessions on their own, cancellations or a no-show appointment demand vigorous intervention. When they fail to appear, the clinician must call immediately and reschedule the missed appointment within a day or 2. Every minute that the clinician waits weakens the therapeutic impact of the treatment's ending and leaves unresolved the reason for the patient's failure to appear. The patient is not allowed to leave prematurely without a good fight.

In a time-limited intervention, successful management of the ending of treatment is of the highest priority as it stabilizes the gains made earlier in treatment. It is the clinician's primary responsibility to help the child to navigate this stage in a way that enhances the child's sense of power, mastery, and autonomy. The clinician helps children to understand that although they may be leaving the person of the clinician, they possess the capacity to internalize and thereby take with them the clinician's problem-solving powers. Whether the patient is expected to return or not, the work continues unabated right up to the final minute. The task, at this final stage of treatment, is to hold the course: to continue to address the unfinished work and to express confidence in the patient's ability to confront the future with confident expectations.

Some clinicians see this stage of leave-taking as an ideal time for the patient to work through painful losses experienced in the past. In this view, separation from the clinician is experienced as a process filled with enormous pain and ambivalence. A successful separation from the clinician can inspire an internal awareness of separateness, which in turn leads to the acquisition of a distinct and unique individuality. Therefore, the clinician actively discourages patients from the belief that they will have any future contact. Patients are asked to make an explicit, existential choice. They can leave treatment in a way that replicates earlier unsatisfactory losses or separations; however, this will only preserve and perpetuate an emotionally conflicted past. Technically, this means patients must begin to relinquish the prospect of the return of a lost-forever relationship; this was the case with a boy who had to make peace with the idea that his drug-addicted father would not return and make him feel whole. Patients are quite naturally frustrated by this predicament, and it is another source of much of their acting-out during this final stage of treatment. The clinician responds with empathy but holds firm to the end date, because to concede to a request for "a few more sessions" is a tacit admission that the clinician shares with patients the belief that they are too weak or helpless to graduate. To act in accordance with patients' wishes is to reinforce the most maladaptive needs: to remain dependent, to remain in permanent fusion with a significant other, and to stay rooted in infinite time. Infinite time represents the fantasy of living forever, of never losing anything, of never having to say good bye. However, emotional support at this point is not enough. The clinician expresses an appreciation of the idea that while it is perfectly acceptable to feel dissatisfaction or disillusionment with one's caregivers, patients have available a wide assortment of peers, siblings, teachers, neighbors, and relatives who are far better substitutes. Further, the clinician underlines children's own unique store of inner resources and strengths. As mastery and self-esteem are enhanced, the ability to tolerate separateness is simultaneously strengthened. For children with a history of especially traumatic separations, the end stage should be kept as uncontaminated as possible by other separations. Therefore, the clinician should try to schedule the last session so that it will not coincide temporally with any anticipated separations. For example, the last session is not usually planned so that it comes at the beginning of summer vacation. Failure to pay attention to the timing of the end date may encourage children to believe that treatment simply is being postponed, only to resume when school starts up again.

CASE EXAMPLE

Elijah smiled as he entered the office for his 11th visit, stating "I have a deal that you cannot resist." He said that the school was talking about phasing him into regular class, but if he had but one fight, he would return to special education. Elijah reasoned he needed to stay in treatment because he did not want "to blow it," and the clinician simply would have to renew the contract to help him. She had said many times, after all, that they would do this together.

The theme in the play for the session stressed how the protagonist's mother had died, but how the hero found a stepmother who lived in the same apartment building and who, although not the "real" mother, was more than good enough. It was further stressed how the hero was more able to do for himself, how much he had learned, how strong and more powerful he was than even one year ago.

A few words need to be said about when *not* to end an intervention that has a predetermined end date. No contract is ever inviolate or set in stone. The end date is always renegotiable when life events demand it, and it is postponed whenever the patient or family is faced with a significant loss such as the serious illness or death of a loved one or even a beloved pet.

Clinician Qualifications

Time-limited interventions make intense emotional and technical demands on the clinician and require an active approach that require an inordinately high degree of skill and organizational and planning ability. It is a relatively unforgiving and demanding intervention requiring a great deal of specialized training to gain competence.

Time-limited clinicians must possess an improvisational style, flexibility, and decisiveness, along with a willingness to take risks and to engage in intense, short-lived relationships. Clinicians need the psychiatric emergency room skills of rapid assessment and crisis intervention in order to extract a theme quickly from a vast array of data and know where they want to go with the treatment. They must be able to exclude interesting material that is not pertinent to the central theme and be willing to adopt modest and reasonable goals. Finally, time-limited clinicians must be able to speak the language of play. At first glance, the directive, active stance assumed by the time-limited clinicians may be misunderstood as manipulative, while the structured approach to play is seen as paying insufficient respect to children's autonomy and independence. Time-limited clinicians must be comfortable and able to tolerate frequent losses and repeated separations. Treatments begin, end, and then begin again in rapid succession.

Clinicians must prove themselves repeatedly as they face such issues as: Will this patient like me, will I be able to help, will I be able to facilitate change in this patient, will I understand the dynamics correctly, and will I be able to formulate a theme that is personal and yet central enough?

Consideration also must be given to the process of selecting the best match of clinician, patient, and type of therapy. While clinicians must adhere to the basic guidelines about self-disclosure, it is clear that because of the intense, directive nature of this treatment, more of the clinicians is revealed than is the case in the more lengthy treatments. In a classically oriented, long-term treatment, the clinician's personality becomes less and less important as the patient places onto the clinician whatever issues or needs might be on the treatment table. With children in time-limited therapy, clinicians must be willing to get their hands dirty, to play and be engaged in a furious give-and-take milieu. It requires a display of utmost confidence in the possibility of rapid change and a conviction that the patient, whom they are treating, is capable of it.

Outcome Studies

Several independent variables have been used in studies that examine the efficacy of time-limited strategies. These include both clinician and patient satisfaction at treatment end, dropout rates in brief vs. long-term treatments, rates of medical use, and the relative effectiveness of time-limited vs. long-term modalities. However, most of the studies failed to meet current methodological standards. This said, clinical effectiveness seems related to the proper selection of a suitable patient, the delineation of a workable and appropriate focus of treatment, an expertise in setting up a structurally clear therapeutic approach, and a high degree of staff commitment.

Pediatric medicine, with its brief, intermittent yet intensive interaction with families, generated a number of early studies that supported the claim that time-limited treatments were effective. In fact, findings indicate that the majority of cases in pediatric practice could be handled satisfactorily, at least on a symptomatic level, with a very brief type of treatment. Hare (1966) reviewed 119 treatment cases that were limited to a single diagnostic interview followed by a psychoanalytically oriented treatment that consisted of individual sessions with the child and conjoint parent-child meetings. The rate of improvement was 72% at discharge and 81% at the 2-year follow-up. Eisenberg (1967) found significantly more improvement among 80 children who received a 5-session regimen than among those placed in a no-treatment control group. In what is perhaps the largest and most comprehensive study of its kind, Parad and Parad (1968) surveyed 98 agencies that offered point-of-entry time-limited services to families. A total of 1,656 cases were examined from outcome ratings complied by the clinicians; three-quarters of the families were judged improved. Those patients who were given a prescribed time limit were more likely to remain in treatment until completion than they were to withdraw prematurely.

The relationship between patient and clinician variables and treatment outcome in a 6-week brief therapy with 210 children was assessed by Wurmser (1973). Of all the outcome criteria, the best predictors were a measure of the patient's initial level of functioning and a measure of the amount of change expected by the clinician. Leventhal and Weinberger (1975) found that for some 945 cases who received only brief treatment, only 9.73% became readmissions. When a comparison was made, 77% of cases in time-limited vs. 66% in long-term treatment were rated by the clinician as improved. Time-limited treatment (with a mean of 8.6 treatment sessions) provided in a health maintenance organization resulted in a 60% reduction in medical use for the 5 years following the intervention (Cummings, 1977). Finney, Riley, and Cataldo (1991) evaluated medical use among 93 children who belonged to a health maintenance organization and who were provided with a brief, psychological consultation that lasted from 1 to 6 visits. Partial or complete resolution of the presenting problem was found in 74% of the children along with a reduced rate of acute primary care visits throughout the following year.

A comparison of the relative effectiveness of 6-week and 12-week time-limited treatments to those families on a waiting list revealed the 6-session treatment to be as effective as was a considerably longer course of therapy, (Fisher, 1980). There was no evidence of deterioration and no significant changes reported on a follow-up 1 year later. The dropout rate for patients in time-limited treatment (32%) is one-half the dropout rate for patients in brief treatment (67%) as opposed to those in long-term, individual treatment (61%) (Sledge, Moras, Hartley, & Levine, 1990). Within the setting of a psychiatric hospital, favorable results have been reported when treatment duration was held to less than 4 weeks. Findings indicate quicker recovery, fewer readmissions, and better medical compliance among those patients who participated in brief treatment (Doherty, Manderson, & Carter-Ake, 1987; Gold, Heller, & Ritorto, 1992; Ney, Mulvihill, & Hanna, 1984).

REFERENCES

Alexander, F., & French, T. M. (1946). *Psychoanalytic therapy*. New York: Ronald Press.

Axline, J. (1947). *Play therapy*. Boston: Houghton-Mofflin.

Budman, S. H. & Gurman, A. S. (1983). The practice of brief-psychotherapy. *Professional Psychology, 14*, 277–292.

Budman, S. H. (Ed.). (1981). *Forms of brief therapy*. New York: Guilford Press.

Caplan G. (1964). *Principles of Preventive Psychiatry*. New York: Basic Books.

Conn, J. H. (1989). Play interview therapy: Its history, theory and practice-A fifty year restrospective account. *Child Psychiatry and Human Development, 20*, 3–13.

Cummings, N. A. (1977). Prolonged (ideal) versus short-term (realistic) psychotherapy. *Professional Psychology, 8*, 491–501.

Davanloo, H. (Ed.). (1980). *Short-term dynamic psychotherapy*. New York: Jason Aronson.

Doherty, M. B., Manderson, M., & Carter-Ake, L. (1987). Time-limited psychiatric hospitalization for children. *Hospital & Community Psychiatry, 1*, 643–647.

Drisko, J. W. (1978). Time-limited therapy with children. *Smith College Studies in Social Work, 48*, 107–131.

Dulcan, M. K. (1984). Brief psychotherapy with children and their families: The state of the art. *Journal of the American Academy of Child Psychiatry, 23*, 544–551.

Eisenberg, L. (1967). Treatment for disturbed children: A follow-up study. *Mental Health Program Reports*, PHS Publication #1568. Bethesda, MD: National Institute of Mental Health.

Erickson, E. (1968). *Identity, Youth and Crisis*. New York: W. W. Norton.

Ferenczi, S., & Rank, O. (1956). *The development of psycho-analysis*. (C. Newton, Trans.) New York: Dover. (Original work published in 1925.)

Finney, J. W., Riley, A. W., & Cataldo, M. F. (1991). Psychology in primary health care: effects of brief targeted therapy in children's medical care utilization. *Journal of Pediatric Psychology, 16*, 447–461.

Fisher, S. G. (1980). The use of time-limits in brief psy-

chotherapy: A comparison of six session, twelve session, and unlimited treatment with families. *Family Process, 19*, 377–392.

Gardner, R. A. (1971). *Therapeutic communication with children: The mutual story telling technique*. New York: Science House.

Gold, I. M., Heller, H., & Ritorto, B. (1992). A short-term psychiatric inpatient program for adolescents. *Hospital and Community Psychiatry, 43*, 58–61.

Hambridge, G. (1955). Structured play therapy. *American Journal of Orthopsychiatry, 25*, 601–617.

Hare, M. (1966). Shortened treatment in a child guidance clinic: The results in 119 cases. *British Journal of Psychiatry, 112*, 613–616.

Howard, K. I., Kopta, S. M., Krause, M. S. & Orlinsky, D. E. (1986). The dose-effect relationship in psychotherapy. *American Psychologist, 41*, 159–164.

James, B. (1989). Treating traumatized *children: New insights and creative interventions*. Massachusetts: Lexington Books.

Lazazus, A. A. (1967). In support of technical eclecticism, *Psychological Report, 21*, 415–416.

Levy, D. (1939). Release therapy. *American Journal of Orthopsychiatry, 9*, 713–737.

Leventhal, T., & Weinberger, G. (1975). Evaluation on a large-scale brief therapy program for children. *American Journal of Orthopsychiatry, 45*, 119–133.

Lindemann, E. (1944). Symptomatology and management of acute grief. *American Journal of Psychiatry, 101*, 141–148.

Malan, D. H. (1963). *A study of brief psychotherapy*. New York: Plenum.

Mann, J. (1973). *Time-limited psychotherapy*. Cambridge, MA: Harvard University Press.

Ney, P. G., Mulvihill, D., & Hanna, R. (1984). The effectiveness of child psychiatric inpatient care. *Canadian Journal of Psychiatry, 29*, 26–30.

Parad, H. J., & Parad, L. G. (1968). A study of crisis-oriented planned short-term treatment: Part I. *Social Casework, 49*, 346–355.

Peterlin, K. B., & Sloves, R. (1985). Time-limited psychotherapy with children: Central theme and time as major tools. *Journal of the American Academy of Child Psychiatry, 24*, 788–792.

Proskauer, S. (1969). Some technical issues in time-limited psychotherapy with children. *Journal of the American Academy of Child Psychiatry, 8* (1), 154–169.

Sifneos, P. E. (1972). *Short-term psychotherapy and emotional crisis.* Cambridge, MA: Harvard University Press.

Sledge, W. H., Moras, K., Hartley, D., & Levine, M. (1990). Effect of time-limited psychotherapy on patient dropout rates. *American Journal of Psychiatry, 147,* 1341–1347.

Sloves, R., & Peterlin, K. B. (1993). Where in the world is my father: A time-limited treatment of video game addiction. In T. Kottman & C. Schaefer (Eds.), *Play therapy in action: A casebook for practitioners.* New York: Jason Aronson 301–346.

Sloves, R., & Peterlin, K. B. (1994). Time-limited play therapy with children. In K. O'Connor & C. Schaefer

(Eds.), Handbook of play therapy (Vol. 2). New York: John Wiley & Sons 27–59.

Solomon, J. C. (1955). Play technique and the integrative process. *American Journal of Orthopsychiatry, 25,* 591–600.

Terr, L. C. (1991). Childhood traumas: An outline and overview. *American Journal of Psychiatry, 148,* 10–20.

Watzlawick, P., Weakland, J. H., & Fisch, R. (1974). *Change: Principles of problem formation and problem resolution.* New York: W. W. Norton.

Wurmser, J. H. (1973). *The relationship among patient variables, therapist variables and outcome in brief psychotherapy with children.* Unpublished doctoral dissertation, Teachers College, Columbia University, New York.

22 / **Behavioral Interventions**

Stephanie Sergent Daniel, David B. Goldston, and Jeffrey A. Smith

Behavioral interventions are a class of clinical interventions that are based on the principles of learning theory. Generally these interventions are based on the principles of classical conditioning, the principles of operant conditioning, or a combination of the 2 models of learning.

The classical conditioning models of learning focus on the role of the environment in triggering or eliciting behavior. These models were developed in the tradition of Ivan (1927) Pavlov who, in his work with dogs in the early 1900s, (1927) noticed that after repeated pairing of a previously neutral stimulus (e.g., tone) with food, the dogs would salivate at the signal of the tone, similar to the manner in which dogs responded when the food itself was presented. The dogs apparently "learned" from the repeated contiguous association of the food and the tone that the tone signaled the presentation of food.

In a similar manner, John Watson and Rosalie Rayner (1920) demonstrated the learning of fear

reactions with 11-month-old Albert B. Initially the infant was not afraid of a white rat that had been presented to him. However, after being deliberately startled with a loud noise as he touched the rat, Albert cried and avoided the rat when it was presented to him again. That is, the boy learned to associate the rat with the noxious noise and began to exhibit anxiety and avoidance behavior in response to the previously innocuous environmental cue.

In contrast to classical conditioning models of learning that focus on the role of the environment in eliciting or cueing behavior, operant models focus on the consequences from the environment that occur after the behavior and serve to increase or decrease the likelihood of behavior recurring. These models were developed in the tradition of Thorndike's (1913) Law of Effect. By observing the escape of cats from puzzle boxes, Thorndike suggested that behavior with rewarding consequences will tend to recur more frequently than behavior with unsatisfying consequences.

B. F. Skinner (1953) more specifically pointed out that the rate or frequency with which organisms emit behavior is dependent in part on the frequency or consistency with which conse-

Preparation of this chapter was supported in part by a Faculty Scholar Award to Dr. Goldston by the William T. Grant Foundation. We thank Stephen Rapp, Ph.D., for his helpful comments and suggestions.

quences follow the behavior. In an experimental setting, for instance, the rate at which a rat will press a lever to obtain food is dependent on the frequency or consistency with which the food is presented to it.

Regardless of whether behavioral interventions are based on the principles of classical or operant conditioning, virtually all of these interventions are predicated on several common assumptions. First, observable behavior change is the most important goal of behavioral interventions and the criterion by which treatments should be evaluated. Although other outcomes often are acknowledged to have value, overt behavior change is traditionally the focus of behavioral interventions. Second, specific and current environmental factors are assumed to affect the likelihood that a behavior will occur. Third, aspects of the environment thought to influence the behaviors should be able to be objectively and precisely defined. Fourth, behaviors chosen to be the focus of a behavioral intervention should be able to be quantified or measured, most typically in terms of duration, frequency, and/or intensity.

Behavioral Assessment and Behavioral Intervention

An integral part of behavioral intervention is the process of behavioral assessment, which is used to identify and quantify the behaviors that ultimately will be the focus of treatment. That is, behavioral assessment is used to determine whether the behaviors of concern are occurring too much (*behavioral excess*) or too little (*behavioral deficits*), or may be inappropriate for the situation or context (*behavioral anomalies*) (Walker, Hedberg, Clement, & Wright, 1981).

Behavioral assessment also is used to evaluate the efficacy of behavioral interventions in altering the behaviors of concern. Behavior is assessed prior to the beginning of treatment in order to establish a baseline level of functioning and is measured repeatedly thereafter in order to determine whether changes in the intervention need to be made.

In addition, the behavioral assessment enables the clinician to formulate hypotheses about the events that trigger the behavior of interest and the consequences that follow the behavior. In this context, the behavioral assessment is referred to as a functional analysis, referring to the role of function of the environment in controlling the behavior of interest. The systematic framework used as the basis of functional analysis is summarized by the acronym S-O-R-C, which stands for stimulus-organism-response-consequence (Goldfried & Sprafkin, 1976).

The first component of the S-O-R-C model, the stimulus, refers to the antecedent events in the environment that trigger or provide the setting within which the behavior of concern occurs. Organismic variables are those differences among individuals in physiology, genetic makeup, and learning histories that in part influence whether a behavior occurs in a particular setting. The response or target behavior is the behavior that has been systematically identified through behavioral assessment as being in need of enhancement or reduction. Consequences, the last component of the S-O-R-C model, are the environmental events that occur subsequent to the target behavior and that either increase or decrease the likelihood that the behavior will reoccur.

The Behavioral Interventions

A variety of behavioral procedures have been employed in the treatment of child and adolescent behavior problems. Some of these procedures focus on altering consequences to modify behavior, some focus on altering the association between antecedent environmental cues and behavior, and some rely on a combination of these techniques. Different behavioral interventions can be employed one at a time or in conjunction with other behavioral interventions.

In contrast to many other psychotherapeutic techniques, behavioral interventions often are designed to take place in the home setting or the setting in which the behavior typically occurs. In fact, several studies note the importance of parental and/or family participation in the success of various behavioral interventions for children and adolescents (Bry & Krinsley, 1992; Crane, 1995; Epstein, Valoski, Wing, & McCurley, 1994; Knox, Albano, & Barlow, 1996; Piacentini, Gitow, Jaffer, Graee, & Whitaker, 1994). Caregivers' consistency in the administration of the behavioral techniques is especially important. Without consistency, children learns that the contingencies in their natural environment are not predictable and cannot be well understood. In turn, their behavioral problems may be inadvertently reinforced or strengthened rather than ameliorated.

CONTINGENCY MANAGEMENT

Contingency management refers to the systematic application of consequences, both reinforcement and punishment, to change behavior. By definition, the term reinforcement refers to consequences that increase the likelihood of behavior, whereas punishment refers to consequences that reduce the likelihood of behavior. The systematic administration of reinforcement or punishment is always made contingent upon the occurrence of the target behavior.

Two types of reinforcement and punishment are used in contingency management procedures, depending on whether consequences are administered or withdrawn from the environment. *Positive reinforcement* occurs when a consequence is presented following the occurrence of a behavior and increases the likelihood that the behavior will occur again in the future. A mother's verbal praise, for instance, is a positive reinforcer if this praise results in her child using the word "please" more often when making requests of others. *Negative reinforcement* occurs when a consequence is removed following the occurrence of a behavior and increases the likelihood that the behavior will occur again in the future. To illustrate, a child may engage in a desired behavior, such as helping his younger brother with homework, after being told that if he does so, he will not have to wash dishes after dinner. In this case, not washing dishes is a negative reinforcer that increases the probability that the older child will help the younger child with his homework.

In an analogous manner, *positive punishment* refers to the application of an aversive consequence following the occurrence of a behavior that decreases the likelihood that a behavior will occur again in the future. A young autistic child who receives extremely mild electric shock after engaging in self-injurious behavior such as head banging is receiving positive punishment (Duker & Seys, 1996). *Negative punishment*, in contrast, refers to the removal of a consequence that results in a decrease in the likelihood that the behavior will recur in the future. A teenager who is forbidden to go to a party with peers from school because of poor grades on a report card has received negative punishment.

Punishment by itself may be used to reduce or eliminate a behavior, but it does not facilitate the learning of any new, more appropriate behaviors to take the place of the old behavior. Therefore, punishment and positive reinforcement often are used in tandem to change behavior. To illustrate, a parent may punish an undesired behavior, such as temper tantrums, while rewarding and praising a child for engaging in more desirable behaviors, such as compliance with the parent's requests.

Reinforcers can be applied following every instance of a target behavior or less often. The frequency with which reinforcers are applied is referred to as a schedule of reinforcement. Different schedules of reinforcement are known to produce different effects on behavior. A schedule of reinforcement in which children receive a reward every time that they exhibit a behavior will result in very quick learning of that behavior. However, if the reward is suddenly removed, children will discontinue the behavior quickly. On the other hand, if a behavior is rewarded intermittently, children may learn the behavior more slowly than if they were rewarded for its every occurrence. However, following the removal of the intermittent reward, children will continue to exhibit the new behavior for a longer time than if the behavior had been rewarded at every occurrence. Therefore, a common strategy with contingency management procedures is to facilitate the learning of new behaviors by rewarding every or nearly every occurrence of the target behavior, but then to gradually shift to an intermittent schedule of reinforcements, so that the behavior will be more likely to persist on those occasions when the originally administered reward is not available.

In addition, reinforcers and punishers must be selected on an individual basis. A consequence that is rewarding to one child may have no effect or promote the opposite effect for another child. Therefore, at the outset of any behavioral intervention that relies on contingency management, it is important to assess which consequences are reinforcing for a particular child. Often this can be accomplished simply by asking children about their preferences for reward. Reinforcers can be tangible (food, money, stickers, toys), or intangible (praise, smiles, nods), or may consist of access to desirable activities (e.g., privileges).

Token Economies and Response Cost: For some children and adolescents, intangible reinforcers may not be effective in changing behavior. Therefore, clinicians or parents may implement a system in which tangible reinforcers are given for appropriate behaviors. One method for providing tangible reinforcers is the use of a *token economy system.* The token economy system requires a child's caregivers to work in conjunction with the therapist to specify the target behaviors that need to be elicited to earn tokens, the means for monitoring target behaviors, and the number of tokens required to earn a larger reinforcer, referred to as a *backup reinforcer.* Backup reinforcers can be objects, such as small toys or trading cards, special foods or treats, or they can be privileges or activities. A variety of items can be used as tokens, including stickers, stars, points, check marks, and poker chips. For young children, tokens such as colorful stickers may be reinforcing in and of themselves, but they also will assume a reinforcing quality because of their association with the backup reinforcer and because of the caregiver's praise, which often accompanies the earning of tokens.

Charts or posters often are used to keep track of the earned tokens. It is important that the points or tokens be displayed prominently so that children as well as the caregivers responsible for monitoring the target behavior and administering the tokens can see and assess progress. The display of tokens can serve as a cue to remind children to act in a desired manner and as a cue to caregivers to comment on the children's behavior. Token economy systems can be used in the home, at school, or in a facility such as a psychiatric unit.

Token economy systems also can stipulate the loss of a token for misbehavior. This procedure is referred to as *response cost* and is an example of negative punishment. Response cost can be used to underscore the fact that certain particularly egregious behaviors, such as assaultive behavior, will not be tolerated. However, response cost is not recommended as a primary method of behav-

ior modification for 2 reasons. First children who lose points after they have put forth effort to earn them may become angry or frustrated, and may lose motivation to continue earning additional tokens following response cost. Second, like other forms of punishment, response cost can be used to decrease undesirable behaviors but cannot be used by itself to facilitate the development of new or alternative behaviors to the undesirable behaviors.

Shaping and Differential Reinforcement: In instances in which the goal is to teach children complicated or difficult behaviors, reinforcers can be used to reward successive approximations to the desired behavior or target behavior. This process is referred to as shaping. Shaping often is used when children or adolescents have the ability to perform part but not all of a desired behavior. The clinician or parents initially can use physical or verbal prompts as needed to direct or guide the children through the target behavior or response and then gradually decrease the involvement as the children begin to respond independently.

In addition to the shaping procedure, clinicians and other adults in the environment of the child can *differentially reinforce* or pay attention to desired and undesired behaviors. That is, undesired behaviors can be ignored or punished, while competing or desired behaviors can be responded to with positive reinforcement. Differential reinforcement is illustrated by the parent who ignores a child's whining when something is wanted but praises a child after a polite request without whining.

Time-out Procedures: Just as positive reinforcers can increase desired behavior, the removal of positive reinforcers can decrease unwanted behavior. The removal of positive reinforcers is referred to as *time-out from positive reinforcement.* The time-out procedure involves removing children from situations in which reinforcing stimuli are available and placing them in an environment that lacks such stimuli following the occurrence of an unacceptable behavior.

The time-out procedure yields the most successful results if it is introduced after steps have been made to ensure that children's normal environment is sufficiently reinforcing. In particular, time-out often works best if it is implemented after a parent already has started to reward a child regularly for appropriate behavior. Stated differently, the time-out procedure may not be effective if a child does not receive much positive reinforcement, such as attention or rewards for appropriate behavior in the environment. In this case, removal from the child's normal environment does not eliminate opportunities for reinforcement because the child does not receive reinforcement outside the context of time-out.

A number of considerations are worth noting in the use of time-out procedures. First, the location of the time-out is an important consideration in the successful use of the procedure. Often parents send children to their room after they have engaged in undesirable behaviors. However, in their rooms, children often have access to multiple potential sources of reinforcement, such as a telephone, radio or stereo, toys, books, games, and a comfortable bed. Therefore, although children may protest being sent to their room against their wishes, in fact, often multiple sources of reinforcement are available to them there. Particularly with younger children (for whom it is more feasible), time-out procedures are generally more efficacious when the time-out location is in the corner of a room or in a similarly nonreinforcing environment.

Time-out can be used effectively in the home and at school, and with special considerations, the procedure can be used in public settings (Forehand McMahon, 1981). Nonetheless, time-out should be implemented in public settings only after parents or caregivers have consistently demonstrated successful use of the procedure in the home. Parents are more likely to have greater control of the environment in the home than in public.

When using time-out in a public setting, such as a grocery store, a young child can be removed from the setting and can be placed in the backseat of the family car for several minutes while the parent or caregiver either remains beside the car or sits in the front seat of the car. Following the time-out period, the child can return to the public setting, and should be reinforced by the caregiver for more appropriate behavior. Time-out also can be used while riding in the car, as the caregiver may pull off of the road and ignore the undesired behavior until the child stops engaging in it.

The time-out procedure is *not* intended to remove a child from a situation for extended periods of time. The amount of time recommended for a

child or adolescent to spend in time-out depends on the age of the individual, with younger children requiring less time and older children tolerating somewhat longer periods.

A second consideration in the use of time-out is to ensure that children know or have been informed about what specific behavior is being punished. Parents should be cautioned, however, against engaging in lengthy or prolonged discussions with children about why the behavior is inappropriate before children go to time-out. In providing lengthy explanations about misbehavior, adults inadvertently pay attention to the inappropriate behavior, and children may learn to elicit attention or postpone punishment by engaging adults in lengthy discussions.

Third, it is important for adults to follow through with sending children to time out consistently rather than allowing "one more chance." If children are given additional chances to comply rather than consistently being sent to time-out, they learn that they can wait until they have already been warned or are actually being sent to time-out before they actually have to comply with adult commands.

Fourth, upon leaving time-out, children should be asked to perform the behavior that led to being placed in time-out. Children's failure to do so should signal a need for a return to time-out. In this way, children learn that they cannot have the option of choosing time-out in lieu of engaging in an undesired activity or chore.

Fifth, it is important that caregivers avoid affective displays, such as shouting or appearances of exasperation, when sending children to time-out. Such displays inadvertently give additional attention to the misbehavior. Additionally, once children have been sent to time-out, their tantrum behavior and displays of anger or upset generally should be ignored as long as the children stay in time-out. Otherwise, children learn that they can receive additional attention by engaging in tantrum behavior while in time-out. Such additional attention defeats the purpose of the time-out from positive reinforcement procedure in that children are supposed to be placed in an environment devoid of reinforcement, including attention.

When a learned behavior begins to decrease in frequency or intensity as reinforcement for the behavior is removed, the behavior is said to be in the process of *extinction*. Initially, however, when a parent begins sending children to time-out consistently as a consequence for inappropriate behavior, children commonly exhibit what is referred to as an extinction burst before the target behavior actually begins to decrease. That is, the children's misbehavior may not automatically decrease in response to time-out but may increase temporarily as they try even harder to elicit attention. If the parent remains consistent in administering time-out, the extinction burst is temporary and will subside as children learn that they will not receive reinforcement for each occurrence of the inappropriate behavior. However, if parents are not instructed to expect this temporary escalation of behavioral problems, they may mistakenly and prematurely conclude that the time-out procedures being used are not effective, and they may discontinue their use.

Overcorrection (Restitution and Positive Practice): Overcorrection is a behavioral technique predicated on the assumption that children or adolescents should overcorrect the consequences of misbehavior. Two types of overcorrection procedures are available. One procedure is referred to as restitution. Restitution requires children or adolescents not only to return the environment back to the original condition in which it was found prior to the misbehavior but actually to improve it. For example, the child who breaks a window for fun by throwing a rock through it might be required to make restitution for the damage by paying for the cost of a new window and agreeing to wash the interior side of all windows in the house.

A second overcorrection procedure is referred to as positive practice. Positive practice requires children or adolescents to practice repeatedly a more appropriate way to respond in the situation in which the misbehavior occurred. For example, the child who engages in tantrum behaviors, such as slamming doors or stomping up or down stairs, might be required to practice several times closing the door gently or walking up and down the stairs without stomping.

Parent Training: Parent training is intended to assist parents to reinforce more effectively appropriate behaviors and decrease problem behaviors through ignoring and punishment. A variety of parent training approaches and models are in use, each of which supports different assumptions about the nature of parent and child interactions

and relationships (e.g., Barkely, 1987; Forehand & McMahon, 1981). Some programs are intended for parents who may be experiencing difficulties in responding to more common misbehaviors in children, whereas other programs are more specialized and intended for parents of children with special needs (e.g., children or adolescents diagnosed with attention deficit hyperactivity disorder). Many programs incorporate some of the behavioral procedures already described, such as contingency management, positive reinforcement, differential reinforcement of appropriate and inappropriate behaviors, token economy systems, and time-out. Parent training classes are offered through a variety of sources including school systems, mental health centers, social service or human resource departments, medical and child guidance centers, and private practice offices.

BEHAVIORAL CONTRACTING

Behavioral contracting is the process of discussing and agreeing on a behavior that children or adolescents will perform and outlining the consequences for performing or not performing the agreed-upon behavior. Behavioral contracts explicitly specify both the behaviors to be modified and the consequences that will result if the behavior occurs. In addition, behavioral contracts specify the specific situations in which the target behavior is expected to occur or not occur.

Individual differences must be considered in deciding whether to use a behavioral contract and in developing one. Behavioral contracts should be used only with individuals who are capable of understanding the consequences of their behavior and who have the cognitive abilities necessary to enter into an agreement with another person. In addition, behavioral contracts are easiest to implement with youths who have demonstrated some capacity for reliably living up to others' expectations for their behavior. Behavioral contracts are more difficult to implement with youths who have limited attention spans or cognitive capacities or are very impulsive. Older or more mature youths or those with capacity for sustained attention may be able to agree to more complex or a greater number of behaviors and may not require as frequent a schedule of reinforcement.

Behavioral contracts are more effective if they focus more on behaviors to be performed rather than behaviors to be eliminated. If a behavioral contract specifies that a particular behavior not be performed, the contract also should specify the alternative behaviors that are desired of the child. In this context, it is essential that the contract focus on behaviors that the child already has learned or demonstrated the capacity to perform. A behavioral contract that focuses on behaviors the youth has never performed may not be effective because the child may lack the requisite skills for performing the desired behavior. Illustrated clinically, an adolescent desiring to make new friends after moving with the family to a new neighborhood may agree with parents to try to meet 1 new peer in a week. However, if the teenager lacks the appropriate skills for approaching and entering groups, or for initiating and maintaining conversation (i.e., the teenager has "social skills" deficits), the contract, however well intentioned, is not likely to be effective.

Behavioral contracts can be verbal or written agreements between either the parent and the child or adolescent or between the clinician and the child or adolescent. It is also possible to assist school personnel, such as teachers, in developing a behavioral contract for a student who may be having academic or behavioral difficulties at school. Behavioral contracts are of particular use in creating potential "win-win" scenarios with children in which parents are able to get their children to perform a behavior, while children are able to earn desired activities or rewards. Written contracts often are advantageous in that they render different retrospective accounts of the contractual agreement moot. However, like the token economy system, behavioral contracts require that someone monitor the behavior to be performed and administer the agreed-upon consequences for the behavior.

SYSTEMATIC DESENSITIZATION

Systematic desensitization is a behavioral technique that is used to reduce anxiety associated with specific feared stimulus cues. These techniques can be used to reduce anxiety associated with both with overt stimulus cues, such as objects or situations to which children are afraid, or they can be used to reduce anxiety associated with certain mental images. In systematic desensitization, children are gradually and systematically exposed to the anxiety-provoking stimulus cues while steps are taken to reduce the anxiety usually associated with those cues.

In these procedures, the clinician and the patient first develop a hierarchy of anxiety-provoking stimuli ranging from minimally anxiety-provoking to extremely anxiety-provoking. The process of determining which stimuli are least and most anxiety-provoking is facilitated by asking the individual to assign a number from 1 (least anxiety-provoking) to 100 (extremely anxiety-provoking) to each stimulus to indicate the degree of anxiety associated with each particular stimulus. The number the individual assigns to the stimulus is referred to as a subjective unit of distress, or SUDS value.

In the second step of systematic desensitization, children are taught a response that is incompatible with anxiety, such as relaxation. To learn how to relax, children engage in relaxation training. Relaxation training assumes that individuals can be taught to relax various muscle groups and, thereby, reduce their experience of anxiety (Jacobson, 1970). More detailed information about relaxation techniques is contained in Chapter. Several types of relaxation training are available. One of the most common types employed is the tense-relax method. This method requires the clinician to direct the individual to tense a particular muscle group and then to relax the same muscle group until all of the major muscle groups of the body have been tensed and relaxed. This method is especially useful in teaching individuals to identify or notice the differences between feelings of tension and relaxation. Once individuals are able to identify the differences between feelings of tension and relaxation, they can continue to use similar relaxation techniques without using the tense component.

In the third step of systematic desensitization, the clinician begins to expose individuals to the least anxiety-provoking stimulus and gradually increases the anxiety-provoking quality of the stimuli to which the patient is exposed. Contemporaneously with this exposure, patients use the relaxation techniques to reduce the anxiety response to the phobic stimulus. This process is then repeated until patients are able to relax instead of feeling anxious in the presence of the phobic stimulus. The notion of engaging in a response that is incompatible with the anxiety response is referred to as reciprocal inhibition (Wolpe, 1969).

In the next step of systematic desensitization, the clinician exposes patients to the next highest anxiety-provoking stimulus on the hierarchy (i.e., the stimulus with the next highest SUDS value). The process of repeated exposures combined with relaxation (steps 3 and 4) is repeated until individuals are able to tolerate exposure to the new phobic stimulus without the anxiety response. These steps are repeated until relaxation is achieved in the presence of the phobic stimuli associated with the greatest amount of distress or discomfort.

Systematic desensitization is more efficacious with persons who have very specific and circumscribed fears or phobias; it is not as effective with individuals who have generalized anxiety or multiple fears. Moreover, systematic desensitization may not be as effective with individuals who are extraordinarily fearful or anxious as it is with persons who are somewhat less easily aroused. Additionally, on occasion, some individuals experience anxiety because they do not know how to perform a new behavior that they want or need to perform. In this situation, systematic desensitization and relaxation techniques may be used to reduce anxiety but will need to be complemented by interventions to teach them how to perform the desired behavior.

Finally, it should be recalled that it is developmentally appropriate to exhibit different fears at different ages. For example, younger children normally have fears of being separated from their parents, and older youths often have fears focused on safety issues. Some of these fears may have an adaptive quality, such as cueing youths to avoid potentially dangerous situations. Clinical interventions should be utilized only when the phobic behaviors have become so intense that they have resulted in very significant distress or functional impairment for the youths.

IMPLOSION AND FLOODING

Implosion and flooding are 2 additional behavioral procedures that are used to reduce or eliminate avoidance behavior in response to an anxiety-provoking situation. Implosion requires patients to imagine true-to-life and/or unrealistic and exaggerated instances of anxiety-provoking situations. The anxiety-provoking stimuli used in implosion may represent observable, objective threats or may consist of anxiety-eliciting stimuli that are unobservable (e.g., thoughts about childhood trauma or conflicts). In contrast to implosion techniques, flooding procedures require that patients be exposed to objective environmental cues that are associated only with increased anxiety.

Similar to systematic desensitization, in both flooding and implosion procedures, a hierarchy of feared situations often is utilized in a series of graduated exposures. However, unlike systematic desensitization, in these techniques the exposure to feared situations is not paired with relaxation. Instead, during the period of increasing exposure to anxiety-provoking stimuli, patients are prevented from escaping from the situation of using avoidance behaviors. The process of preventing avoidance behaviors in response to the feared stimuli is referred to as response prevention. Rather than avoiding the fear-provoking stimuli, patients simply are exposed repeatedly to increasingly fear-provoking situations until the anxiety subsides. Anxiety is typically very high at the beginning of the exposure but becomes attenuated with repeated exposure to the threatening stimuli. Through this process, patients learn that no untoward or aversive consequences necessarily accompany the anxiety-provoking stimuli. This, in turn, is associated with a decrease in the likelihood that anxiety and avoidance behavior will continue to occur in the presence of these stimuli.

Although implosion techniques and flooding are not frequently used in the treatment of many childhood disorders, they have been used successfully in the treatment of obsessive-compulsive disorder. In clinical practice, a teenager with obsessive-compulsive behavior may be exposed to situations feared to be associated with germs or dirt but prevented from engaging in compulsive behaviors used to ward off these feelings of contamination. Flooding techniques recently have been reported to be used in the treatment of children and adolescents diagnosed with posttraumatic stress disorder (Richards, Lovell, & Marks, 1994; Saigh, 1992; Saigh, Yule, & Inamdar, 1996). A primary consideration in deciding to use these techniques is whether patients will be able to tolerate the intense arousal associated with the repeated exposures and whether the behaviors of concern are sufficiently problematic to warrant this type of intervention.

MODELING

Modeling refers to the behavioral technique in which children learn by observing another individual perform a particular behavior. The children then attempt to engage in the behavior through the process of imitation. Observations can take place during or outside of the therapy session and can involve live models or videotapes of models.

Models can be peers or adults. As a general rule, however, models that are similar to patients are generally more effective than models perceived as dissimilar. Moreover, coping models are generally more effective than mastery models. Coping models are models who may struggle with or have difficulty with a task but eventually are able to cope with the situation at hand. Mastery models are models who perform the desired behavior to perfection on the first attempt.

Modeling procedures can range from simple observation or imagination of another individual engaging in the target behavior to participant modeling. In participant modeling procedures, children not only observe the target behavior being performed but also are guided through the steps of engaging in the behavior. The youths receive feedback, prompting, and support, until they are able to perform the behavior autonomously.

When participating in a modeling procedure, children may observe the actor(s) receiving positive reinforcement for demonstrating the desired behavior. In this way, the children are able to observe the possible contingencies that might occur when they perform the behavior. When children initiate the behavior, they receives feedback and praise for the efforts from peers and adults. Once the behavior starts to occur automatically in the natural environment, it is assumed that the natural contingencies including attention and praise from peers will maintain the new behavior.

SOCIAL SKILLS TRAINING

Social skills training involves efforts to teach new or more appropriate behavior(s) that are required for social interaction. Examples of social skills targeted in social skills and assertiveness interventions include the ability to: maintain appropriate eye contact with others, enter a play group or peer group appropriately, respond to a peer or other in a nonaggressive manner, use appropriate manners, and share and cooperate with others. In social skills training procedures, youths may be instructed on how to perform the desired behaviors, they may discuss alternative ways of handling problematic situations, and they may observe the desired behavior being modeled.

In addition, a commonly used procedure for training social skills among children and adolescents is *role playing* or *behavioral rehearsal*. With role-playing procedures, children are able not only to practice and rehearse new skills with guidance and feedback (similar to participant modeling), but they also can role-play new or novel situations in which they might be required to perform the targeted behaviors. This procedure provides a safe environment for the youths to practice a particular behavior and enables the clinician or peers in a group setting to provide direct feedback regarding their performance. As part of the behavioral rehearsal, it is common for a clinician to use shaping procedures and to divide complex social skills into their component skills for practice until the entire skill can be performed.

To illustrate this procedure clinically, consider an 8-year-old child who is referred for behavioral intervention due to difficulties interacting with peers. During the first stage of therapy, it is recommended that the child watch a brief video, such as the one pioneered by Meichenbaum and Goodman (1971), which depicts children thinking about joining other children in an activity, deciding to do so, and then experiencing positive consequences. If a video is unavailable, the therapist can play the role of the socially reluctant child and verbalize the child's desire to participate and fears about negative outcomes, the ensuing internal debate, and ultimate decision to join in the activity. After watching the model, the child practices many of the routine social behaviors observed, including practicing the skills of greeting, making eye contact, asking to be included, information sharing, and leaving the group. During this guided practice, the therapist may play or act out the role of another student in the child's class, giving the child additional opportunities for practicing the new skills.

Social skills training can occur in individual sessions with a clinician or in groups with peers. Social skills training in groups is particularly advantageous in that it provides opportunities for youths to see peers coping with some of the same difficulties they are experiencing. In social skills groups, the peers also can act out some of the roles in the behavioral rehearsals and can gain practice in giving appropriate feedback and support to peers.

Historical Trends in Child and Adolescent Behavioral Interventions

Behavioral interventions generally have been based on the principles of classical and/or operant conditioning. In one of the first therapeutic interventions relying on the principles of classical conditioning, Mary Cover Jones was able to demonstrate that the acquired fears of young children could be unlearned as well as learned. In her pioneering work, she found that the fear response learned by an infant could be "unconditioned" by gradually and repeatedly presenting the previously innocuous stimuli to the infant in the absence of the accompanying noxious stimuli and under more neutral or pleasant environmental conditions (e.g., during the child's lunch or snack time). Thus, just as Watson and Rayner (1920) demonstrated that fear reactions could be conditioned or learned via association in young children, Jones illustrated that fears could be eliminated or deconditioned in the same manner (Watson, 1978).

In the late 1950s and early 1960s, Wolpe (1958; Wolpe & Lazarus, 1966) extended these early experiments by developing interventions to replace existing stimulus-response relationships with new stimulus-response associations. These interventions used the methods of reciprocal inhibition, described earlier in this chapter. Stated simply, these interventions were predicated on the notion that the acquired response of anxiety to a set of threatening environmental cues could be systematically replaced with a new acquired response of relaxation.

Flooding and implosion techniques, introduced in the 1950s (Malleson, 1959; Stampfl & Levis, 1967), but also not popularized until the mid-1960s to the 1970s, also focused on problematic emotional and behavioral responses triggered by environmental cues. In contrast to systematic desensitization methods, however, these techniques were designed to extinguish avoidance and anxiety-related behaviors via repeated exposure to the anxiety-eliciting stimuli rather than relying on relaxation techniques to directly compete with or reduce the anxiety.

Operant models, in contrast to classical conditioning models of learning, focused on the environmental consequences that influenced behavior. Following principles delineated by B. F. Skinner (1953), the principles of operant conditioning were used with a variety of previously difficult-to-treat populations in the 1950s and 1960s. The use of token economies in the treatment of adults with schizophrenia and other chronic mental illnesses was commonly reported in the literature (e.g., Ayllon & Azrin, 1968; Ullman & Krasner, 1969). These early interventions focused in part on extinguishing "inappropriate speech," such as the verbal descriptions and reports of delusions and hallucinations by psychotic individuals, and on reinforcing socially appropriate behavior.

Lovaas (1966) and others also began to use reinforcement and punishment contingencies to reduce or extinguish self-destructive behaviors, and to facilitate learning and discrimination among youths with autism and mental retardation. In an early demonstration, Lovaas and Simmons (1969), for example, administered painful electric shocks to mentally retarded psychotic children when they engaged in self-destructive behavior such as head-banging.

In the 1960s and 1970s, contingency management and time-out procedures also were described in the treatment of tantrums and defiant behavior. The first contingency management and time-out procedures were taught in laboratory or office settings. However, with increasing concern about the generalizability of behavior change, clinicians began training teachers and parents to be "therapists," or agents of change in children's natural environments. In an early report, Zeilberger, Sampen, and Sloane (1968) taught a parent to use a combination of reinforcement and time-out procedures in the home to modify 4-year-old child's yelling and tantrum behavior. Subsequently a variety of integrated parent training packages were developed that focused on the uses of reinforcement, punishment, time-out, token or point systems, and the most effective ways of stating commands to elicit compliance from children (Barkley 1987; Forehand & McMahon, 1981; Patterson & Gullion, 1968).

In the 1960s and 1970s, Bandura (Bandura & Walters, 1963) described observational learning and the therapeutic uses of modeling. Modeling procedures have been demonstrated to have utility in the teaching of complex prosocial behaviors and have been included as central components of multifaceted social skills training groups and procedures that could be implemented in clinic- or school-based settings (Goldstein, Spraskin, Gershaw, & Klein, 1980; McGinnis, 1984).

Current Trends in Child and Adolescent Behavioral Interventions

Since the 1970s, and particularly through the 1980s and 1990s, behavioral methods have been used increasingly in pediatric medical settings and in health promotion programs. Behavioral techniques, for instance, have been used to reduce anxiety of physically ill children in an effort to increase their tolerance of painful medical procedures and/or the experience of pain associated with various medical conditions. A variety of medical conditions, including burns (Tarnowski, Rasnake, & Drabman, 1987), cancer (Van Dongen-Melman & Sanders-Woudstra, 1986), cystic fibrosis (Spirito, Russo, & Masek, 1984), asthma (King, 1980), and scoliosis and kyphosis (Birbaumer, Flor, Cevey, Dworkin, & Miller, 1994) have been addressed using behavior interventions by persons in pediatric behavioral medicine. Behavioral interventions also have been employed in the treatment of somatic complaints that are asso-

ciated with, but not primarily attributable to, medical conditions, in an attempt to minimize the likelihood that such symptoms will interfere with medical treatment and recovery (Larson, 1992; Luiselli, Haley, & Smith, 1993; Masek, Fentress, & Spirito, 1984). In addition, interventions using reinforcement have been employed in a number of settings for increasing children's compliance with their medical regimens (Lalli, Mauk, Goh, & Merlino, 1994).

In addition to expanding the application of behavioral interventions to pediatric medical settings, several other trends have been identified in their use. The use of traditional behavioral interventions has broadened in both the range of clinical problems addressed and in the focus of the intervention. Skills training and behavioral rehearsal have been used to assist youths in dealing with peer pressure to engage in substance use or sexual behavior. Behavioral interventions continue to be employed in the treatment of individual behavioral problems, but they also are increasingly applied in the treatment of system and community-focused interventions (Franks, 1984). There also has been increasing consideration of developmental factors in the design of behavioral interventions (Forehand & Weirson, 1993). A final trend in the application of behavioral interventions is an increasing willingness to use such interventions in tandem with others (e.g., pharmacotherapy) to promote behavioral change (Engeland, 1993).

In sum, behavioral interventions tend to be short-term interventions, with durable and generalizable effects that are easily demonstrated via the procedures of behavioral assessment. In a managed health care environment in which cost-effective interventions with documentable outcomes are valued, behavioral interventions likely will continue to be increasingly utilized, both by themselves and in tandem with nonbehavioral interventions.

REFERENCES

Ayllon, T., & Azrin, N. (1968). *The token economy: A motivational system for therapy and rehabilitation.* New York: Appleton-Century-Crofts.

Bandura, A., & Walters, R. (1963). *Social learning and personality development.* New York: Holt, Rinehart, & Winston.

Barkley, R. (1987). *Defiant children: A clinician's manual for parent training.* New York: Guilford Press.

Birbaumer, N., Flor, H., Cevey, B., Dworkins, B., & Miller, N. E. (1994). Behavioral treatment of scoliosis and kyphosis. *Journal of Psychosomatic Research, 18,* 623–628.

Bry, B. H., & Krinsley, K. E. (1992). Booster sessions and long-term effects of behavioral family therapy on adolescent substance use and school performance. *Journal of Behavior Therapy and Experimental Psychiatry, 23,* 183–189.

Crane, D. R. (1995). Introduction to behavioural family therapy for families with young children. *Journal of Family Therapy, 17,* 229–242.

Duker, P. C., & Seys, D. M. (1996). Long-term use of electrical aversion treatment with self-injurious behavior. *Research in Developmental Disabilities, 17,* 293–301.

Engeland, H. V. (1993). Pharmacotherapy and behaviour therapy: Competition or cooperation? *Acta Paedopsychiatrica: International Journal of Child and Adolescent Psychiatry, 56,* 123–127.

Epstein, L. H., Valoski, A., Wing, R. R., & McCurley, J. (1994). Ten-year outcomes of behavioral family-based treatment for childhood obesity. *Health Psychology, 13,* 373–383.

Forehand, R., & McMahon, R. (1981). *Helping the noncompliant child: A clinician's guide to parent training.* New York: Guilford Press.

Forehand, R., & Weirson, M. (1993). The role of developmental factors in planning behavioral interventions for children: Behavioral interventions for children: Disruptive behavior as an example. *Behavior Therapy, 24,* 117–141.

Franks, C. M. (1984). Behavior therapy with children and adolescents. *Annual Review of Behavior Therapy: Theory and Practice, 10,* 236–290.

Goldfried, M., & Sprafkin, J. (1976). Behavioral personality assessment. In J. Spence, R. Carson, & J. Thibaut (Eds.), *Behavioral approaches to therapy* (pp. 295–321). Morristown, NJ: General Learning Press.

Goldstein, A., Spraskin, R., Gershaw, N., & Klein, P. (1980). *Skillstreaming the adolescent: A structured learning approach to teaching prosocial skills.* Champaign, IL: Research Press.

Jacobson, E. (1970). *Modern treatment of tense patients: Including the neurotic and depressed with case illustrations, follow-ups, and EMG measurements.* Springfield, IL: Charles C Thomas.

King, N. J. (1980). The behavioral management of asthma and asthma-related problems in children: A critical review of the literature. *Journal of Behavioral Medicine, 3,* 169–189.

Knox, L. S., Albano, A. M., & Barlow, D. H. (1996). Parental involvement in the treatment of childhood compulsive disorder: A multiple-baseline examination incorporating parents. *Behavior Therapy, 27,* 93–114.

Lalli, J. S., Mauk, J. E., Goh, H., & Merlino, J. (1994). Successful behavioral intervention to treat children who are reluctant to ambulate. *Developmental Medicine and Child Neurology, 36,* 625–629.

Larsson, B. (1992). Behavioural treatment of somatic disorders in children and adolescents. *European Child and Adolescent Psychiatry, 12,* 68–81.

Lovaas, O. I. (1966). A behavior therapy approach to the treatment of childhood schizophrenia. In J. Hill (Ed.), *Minnesota Symposium on Child Psychology, Volume 1* (pp. 108–159). Minneapolis: University of Minnesota Press.

Lovaas, O. I., & Simmons, J. Q. (1969). Manipulation of self-destruction in three retarded children. *Journal of Applied Behavior Analysis, 2,* 143–157.

Luiselli, J. K., Haley, S., & Smith, A. (1993). Evaluation of a behavioral medicine consultative treatment of chronic, ruminative vomiting. *Journal of Behavior Therapy and Experimental Psychiatry, 24,* 27–35.

Malleson, N. (1959). Panic and phobia: A possible method of treatment. *Lancet, 1,* 225–227.

Masek, B. J., Fentress, D. W., & Spirito, A. (1984). Behavioral treatment of symptoms of childhood illness. *Clinical Psychology Review, 4,* 561–570.

McGinnnis, E. (1984). *Skillstreaming the elementary school child: A guide for teaching prosocial skills.* Champaign, IL: Research Press.

Meichenbaum, D., & Goodman, J. (1971). Training impulsive children to talk to themselves: A means of developing self-control. *Journal of Abnormal Psychology, 77,* 115–126.

Patterson, G., & Gullion, M. (1968). *Living with children: New methods for parents and teachers.* Champaign, IL: Research Press.

Pavlov, I. P. (1927). *Conditioned reflexes: An investigation of the physiological activity of the cerebral cortex* (G. V. Anrep, Trans). New York: Dover Publications.

Piacentini, M., Gitow, A., Jaffer, M., Graae, F., & Whitaker, A. (1994). Outpatient behavioral treatment of child and adolescent obsessive compulsive disorder. *Journal of Anxiety Disorders, 8,* 277–289.

Richards, D. A., Lovell, K., & Marks, I. M. (1994). Posttraumatic stress disorder: Evaluation of a behavioral treatment program. *Journal of Traumatic Stress, 7,* 669–680.

Saigh, P. A. (1992). The behavioral treatment of child and adolescent posttraumatic stress disorder. *Advances in Behaviour Research and Therapy, 14,* 247–275.

Saigh, P. A., Yule, W., & Inamdar, S. C. (1996). Imaginal flooding of traumatized children and adolescents. *Journal of School Psychology, 34*, 163–183.

Skinner, B. F. (1953). *Science and human behavior.* New York: Free Press.

Spirito, A., Russo, D. C., & Masek, B. J. (1984). Behavioral interventions and stress management training for hospitalized adolescents and young adults with cystic fibrosis. *General Hospital Psychiatry, 6*, 1–8.

Stampfl, T. G., & Levis, D. J. (1967). Essentials of implosive therapy: A learning-theory-based psychodynamic behavioral therapy. *Journal of Abnormal Psychology, 72*, 496–503.

Tarnowski, K. J., Rasnake, L. K., & Drabman, R. S. (1987). Behavioral assessment and treatment of pediatric burn injuries: A review. *Behavior Therapy, 18*, 417–441.

Thorndike, E. (1913). *Educational psychology: The psychology of learning.* New York: Teachers College.

Ullmann, L. P., & Krasner, L. (1969). *A psychological approach to abnormal behavior.* Englewood Cliffs, NJ: Prentice-Hall.

Van Dongen-Melman, J. E. W. M., & Sanders-Woudstra, J. A. R. (1986). Psychosocial aspects of childhood cancer. *Journal of Child Psychology and Psychiatry, 27*, 145–180.

Walker, C., Hedberg, A., Clement, P., & Wright, L. (1981). *Clinical procedures for behavior therapy.* Englewood Cliffs, NJ: Prentice-Hall.

Watson, J. B., & Rayner, R. (1920). Conditioned emotional reactions. *Journal of Experimental Psychology, 3*, 1–14.

Watson, R. I. (1978). *The great psychologists* (4th ed.). Philadelphia: J. B. Lippincott.

Wolpe, J. (1969). *The practice of behavior therapy.* New York: Pergamon Press.

Wolpe, J. (1958). *Psychotherapy by reciprocal inhibition.* Stanford, CA: Stanford University Press.

Wolpe, J., & Lazarus, A. (1966). *Behavior therapy techniques: A guide to the treatment of the neuroses.* New York: Pergamon Press.

Zeilberger, J., Sampen, S. E., & Sloane, H. N., Jr. (1968). Modification of a child's problem behaviors in the home with the mother as therapist. *Journal of Applied Behavior Analysis, 1*, 47–53.

---

23 / **Cognitive Behavioral Interventions**

Kevin D. Stark, Anne Reysa, Cynthia A. Kurowski, and Susan M. Swearer

Cognitive-behavioral therapy is not a unitary model; rather, it is a general perspective that encompasses many treatment models that are based on a number of common underlying principles highlighted and illustrated through case examples in this chapter. The broad spectrum of treatment models that comprise cognitive-behavioral therapy vary in the extent to which they emphasize change in cognition (automatic thoughts, attributions, expectancies, distortions in information processing, and schemata) and/or behavior (acquisition of self-control, coping, or social skills) as the goal of therapy. They also vary in the extent to which they use cognitive (cognitive restructuring, self-instructional training) and/or behavioral procedures (environmental contingencies) to achieve therapeutic goals. Included among these models, as they apply to children and adolescents, are such approaches as traditional behavior therapy (Ollendick & Cerny, 1980), rational emotive therapy (RET; Ellis & Bernard, 1983), cognitive therapy (Reinecke, Dattilio, & Freeman, 1996), self-control training (Kendall & Braswell, 1993), and coping skills training (Stark, 1990). The focus of this chapter is on the general principles and application of cognitive-behavioral therapy with youths.

Most early work in the development of cognitive-behavioral therapy was with adults (Beck, 1967; Ellis, 1962; Mahoney, 1974; Meichenbaum, 1977). Historically, this work has served as the basis for the development of the therapy with youngsters as clinicians and researchers have translated adult treatments for use with children and adolescents. As research and clinical practice progressed, child-specific treatments were developed (although they still clearly have their roots in adult treatments), and there has been a greater recognition of the need to create developmentally sensitive treatment programs that reflect the differ-

Table 23.1

Examples of Childhood Disorders Treated with Cognitive-Behavioral Therapy and Exemplary References

Psychological Disorder	References
Aggression	Camp, Blom, Herbert, and van Doornick (1977)
Anxiety	Kendall (1991)
Attention deficit hyperactivity disorder	Braswell and Bloomquist (1991)
Autism	Caracciolo, Moderato, and Perini (1985)
Bulimia nervosa	Agras, Schneider, Arnow, Raeburn, and Telch (1989)
Chronic illness	Walco and Varni (1991)
Depression	Stark (1990)
Food phobias	Singer, Ambuel, Wade, and Jaffe (1992)
Interpersonal difficulties	Halford (1983)
Learning disabilities	Wong, Harris, and Graham (1991)
Mental retardation	Whitman, Scherzinger and Sommer (1991)
Obesity	Foreyt and Kordo (1983)
Oppositional defiant disorder	Stein and Smith (1990)
Pain	Jay, Elliott, Katz, and Siegel (1987)
Separation anxiety	Ollendick, Hagopian, and Huntzinger (1991)
Social phobia	Keroack (1987)

ences in cognitive, behavioral, interpersonal, and physical functioning of youths. The translation of developmental principles into clinical practice has been slow in its realization, perhaps due to the difficulty of the process. Nevertheless, procedures have been developed for treating youngsters who are experiencing a variety of serious psychological problems. Some examples are noted in Table 23.1. Since cognitive-behavioral therapy was initially conceived, it has grown from primarily an individual treatment model to a model for treating groups (Elkin, 1983), couples (Epstein, 1983), families (Epstein, Schlesinger, & Dryden, 1988), and for creating a cognitive-behavioral hospital milieu for treating inpatients (Wright, Thase, Beck, & Ludgate, 1993).

Cognitive-behavioral therapy with children recognizes that the successful psychological treatment of children, seemingly regardless of the disorder, involves concurrent work with the youngster's parents and/or family. The work with the parents may take a myriad of forms, including education, parent training, marital counseling, in-

dividual therapy for one or both parents, and teaching a parent to be a cognitive-behavioral therapist for the child (to teach the child problem solving). Thus, because the individual treatment of the youngster is supported by and integrated with a parallel and supportive intervention with the parents and/or family, both are discussed in this chapter. The specific parent or family interventions that are used with a child are individualized to meet the youngster's needs and to address the disturbances in family functioning.

Background

Cognitive-behavioral therapy grew out of changes that occurred within the field of behavior therapy and events that were occurring within the field of psychology in general (Mahoney & Arnkoff, 1978). Within behaviorism, at least 3 critical developments are evident that each led to a greater inclusion of cognitive/mediational constructs and procedures in traditional behavior therapy and learning theories (Kazdin, 1978). As behavior therapy developed and the clientele changed from severely disturbed and/or disabled inpatients to less disturbed outpatients, the techniques changed and were more centered on using the client as the change agent rather than focused on changing behavior through alteration of contingencies within the patient's environment. The assumption that an individual's behavior was determined by the environment was weakened by the development and empirical evaluation of models of self-control (Kanfer, 1970) and Bandura's (1974) cognitive interpretation of learning principles, including the concept of reciprocal determinism. Behaviorists were beginning to recognize that humans exert some personal control over behavior and can influence, and to some extent shape, their environments. Concurrently, the targets of behavioral intervention were changing from overt behaviors to thoughts (Cautela, 1967; Homme, 1965).

Outside of the field of behaviorism, psychology in general was experiencing a cognitive revolution (Dember, 1974). This overall interest in, and study of, cognitive variables had an influence on clinical practice as research supported a mediational model of human functioning. As the field of psychology in general was becoming more cognitively focused, 2 cognitive models of clinical practice emerged that garnered both popular and empirical support. The emergence of rational emotive therapy (Ellis, 1962) and cognitive therapy (Beck, 1976), which hypothesized that disturbances in cognition were at the heart of psychopathology and have cognitive variables as their primary focus for intervention, had a major impact on the practice of behavior therapy (Meyers & Craighead, 1984).

Description of Process and Variations

The practice of cognitive-behavioral therapy is based on a model of human functioning that guides assessment and provides the therapist with a conceptual framework from which targets of intervention can be identified. This model it forms

the backdrop for the design of an effective treatment program. Common principles that underlie cognitive-behavioral therapy with children (Kendall & Braswell, 1993) include:

1. Children respond primarily to mental representations of events and their environment rather than to objective reality. The representations develop from learning experiences that the children have.
2. Cognition, behavior, affect, and biochemistry are causally interrelated. If one is altered, the other also will be affected.
3. Cognitive variables are important in understanding child psychopathology and the process of psychological change.
4. It is desirable to combine cognitive and behavioral procedures in therapeutic programs.

The cognitive-behavioral model of human functioning is integrationist; it emphasizes the human's information-processing capabilities while recognizing the mutual importance and reciprocal influence of other child (behavior, affect, and biological factors) and environmental variables (contingencies, parental pathology, distal variables such as parental stressors, etc.). Reciprocal influence means that each variable in the model influences every other variable. For example, the child's behavior is affected by the contingencies in the environment at the same time that the child's behavior is helping to construct and shape these contingencies. Thus the influence goes in both directions simultaneously. For example, parents of children with attention deficit hyperactivity disorder give more commands and more often have negative, punitive exchanges with their children. These exchanges affect the child's behavior, emotions, and sense of self. In turn, when such a child is placed on an effective medication, the parents give fewer commands and the interactions are more positive. Thus the environment affects the child's behavior and the child's behavior affects the environment.

As noted, the cognitive-behavioral model emphasizes the human's information processing capabilities. Children are information seekers who actively derive meaning and learn from life experiences. Youngsters' environments are hypothesized to impact their information processing and their behavior through the learning experiences that they provide. Each event, each interaction, represents a learning experience for children. During the first 6 to 8 years of life, while children are especially egocentric, the experiences are interpreted against and form the children's budding sense of self. For example, being angrily shaken communicates the message "I'm unlovable," "I'm bad," and "Other people hurt me." Repeated learning experiences that communicate these messages and the associated affect lead to the development of a negative sense of self. Thus the foundation of children's senses of self is formed through early learning experiences. As the sense of self crystallizes, it colors the way that new information is interpreted and incorporated into the existing cognitive structure. In addition to these psychological mechanisms, parents provide children with genetic predispositions that represent a diathesis for the development of a variety of disorders. Significant others in the environment, especially family members, also provide children with learning experiences through modeling, the behavioral contingencies and the affective tone that they establish, the behavior they enact, and direct education.

The contingencies, or lack thereof, within the environment do not automatically and mechanistically impact the children's behavior. Rather they provide children with information about the relationship between actions and consequences that eventually coalesce into rules about the relationship between specific behaviors or classes of behavior and consequences. Once a rule is established, this sets the stage for expectations about the outcomes of the behaviors. For example, a 7-year-old boy is watching television and does not want to leave the program, so he ignores his mother's directive to put his jacket and backpack away. Most of the time the mother thinks that she has so much to do that it is easier just to go ahead and put them away rather than go back and ask him to do it. Sometimes the mother gets frustrated ("I do everything around this house! No one ever helps me and I am tired of it!") and scolds the child for not doing what he is told to do. The scolding has led to an additional delay in having to follow the directive; other times it leads to the parent leaving in anger without following through on the directive or associated threats. The child learns from repeated experiences that he can delay doing what he is told to do or avoid doing things that he does not want to do by ignoring his mother. If this does not work, he can get his mother so frustrated

that she eventually gives up and does it herself or drops the directive. The child develops the expectation that low-level coercion leads to escape from having to do unwanted things, and the mother develops the expectation that the child will not do what he is asked to do, so why bother to tolerate the unpleasantries: "So I might as well do it myself." In the following sections each of the major components of the model are described briefly.

Cognition

Humans are hypothesized to be active constructors of reality through their information-processing capabilities. Children are presumed to respond primarily to their cognitive representation of the environment rather than to the environment as it actually exists. In other words, children respond to their environment as they perceived it rather than to how it actually is. Children's construction of the environment is the product of a combination of what is actually happening and, as a result of a feed-forward mechanism (Mahoney, 1982), their interpretation of events, which is based on internal models and rules that are derived from previous learning experiences. The feed-forward mechanism is a cognitive process through which a schema directs information processing, both what is attended to and how it is perceived, at a preattentive level. For example, a person who has a self-schema of unworthiness will attend to environmental events that confirm this sense of self and will construct incoming information to conform to his or her sense of unworthiness. Due to this feed-forward mechanism, the individual will seemingly seek information that is schema-consistent and ignore schema-inconsistent information.

The primary source of learning experiences that shape children's schemata is the family. Thus the cognitive-behavioral therapist is continually eliciting children's perceptions through the interview and using deductive reasoning to form hypotheses about what may have or may be leading to the development and maintenance of maladaptive perceptions. In addition, the therapist is evaluating children's perceptions to determine whether they are veridical and reflect an unhealthy situation or whether they reflect a distortion in information processing.

Here we define the cognitive variables of central importance to the cognitive behavioral model, including schema (plural schemata), cognitive products, and cognitive operations. Schemata, also referred to as cognitive structures in the literature, are hypothesized to underlie the consistency that is observed in an individual's behavior, emotions, and thinking (Meichenbaum, 1977). A schema is comprised of structure, which is referred to as the cognitive structure, and content, which is referred to as a proposition. The cognitive structure stores information. It is not a physical structure; rather it is a functional unit that stores information such as long-term memory (Ingram & Kendall, 1986). Each proposition is comprised of memorial representations of a domain, including general knowledge and specific exemplars, and a specification of relationships among the primary attributes of the domain (Turk & Salovey, 1985). Schemata have been referred to as "filters" and "templates" (Kendall, 1985) because they directly influence the way an individual derives meaning from the environment, both internal and external. Schemata affect what the individual attends to, perceives, recalls, and views as important (Kendall, 1985). They direct the focus, structure, and sequence of encoding, and the storage and retrieval of information (Turk & Salovey, 1985) Thus they provide the guidelines for processing information.

Schemata are presumed to develop out of repeated learning experiences. As children have repeated learning experiences in a particular domain, they begin to develop a set of rules about the domain as well as examples of it. These rules and examples become progressively more elaborate and detailed over the course of development as a result of additional learning experiences. Mahoney (1982) hypothesizes that schemata are hierarchically organized based on developmental primacy. Those that develop earliest are referred to as core schemata; they may shape the formation of related schemata that develop later. Schemata are organized in interrelated clusters based on similarity in content, and they are interconnected through a web of cognitive operations. The most core schema is the self-schema, which is comprised of a youngster's rules about the self.

Due to the central role of schemata in guiding information processing, oftentimes they are the primary focus of treatment. It is hypothesized that schematic change is necessary to produce meaningful and lasting improvement. If an error in assessment occurs and the focus of treatment is at the level of automatic thoughts, for example, and not on the schemata that give rise to these thoughts, then the problem may surface in an alternative form. In addition, it is hypothesized that schematic change creates more of a ripple effect. In other words, changing a schema changes a host of automatic thoughts, information-processing errors, and related behavior. Oftentimes the schema that underlies a maladaptive way of thinking does not become evident until late in treatment as the client learns to trust the therapist and open up. In addition, often it takes time to gather enough related information to be able to tie it together as a means of defining the underlying rule.

Cognitive products are thoughts, images, symbolic words, and gestures that occur in children's streams of consciousness and can be made conscious through introspection. These cognitive events are the products of the interaction of environmental information, cognitive operations, and schemata (Ingram & Kendall, 1986). Cognitive products have been referred to as cognitions, automatic thoughts, and self-statements in the cognitive-behavioral literature. These terms are used synonymously in this chapter. As noted earlier, a disturbance at the level of cognitive products may take the form of a deficit or a distortion. A deficit is a failure to engage in adaptive information processing while a distortion is a misinterpretation of information. The distortion may be in the direction of being unrealistically positive or negative. Early cognitive-behavioral interventions were designed to intervene at the level of cognitive products. Thus the interventions were designed to change an individual's conscious thoughts. For example, self-instructional training was used as a means of teaching anxious children to say to themselves "Stay calm, you are in control and have nothing to worry about." A test-anxious child may have been taught to think "Relax and focus on the test. Ignore all other distractions." An impulsive child may have been taught to say "Stop and think." Interventions that are directed at this level of cognitive products may be effective when a deficit in information processing underlies the youngster's difficulties, but they fail to address the maladaptive schema that may underlie a distortion in information processing. This oversight may limit the immediate efficacy of the intervention and may lead to a failure to maintain treatment gains as the schema continues to guide the child's misperceptions and actions because it has not changed.

Cognitive operations, also referred to as cognitive processes in the literature, are the rules for processing information that shape and transform information into cognitive products. They also serve as the procedures that enable the components of the system to interact. Cognitive operations are both driven and shaped by schema, and they construct the cognitive representations that comprise the proposition (cognitive content). Cognitive operations determine how incoming information is encoded, stored, combined, and altered with respect to information and structures already in the system, and how the existing structures are engaged, disengaged, or altered (Hollon & Kriss, 1984). When maladaptive schema are operating, errors are evident in the rules that are guiding information processing.

From the preceding discussion it is evident that cognitive-behavioral therapists conceptualize client issues on multiple levels of cognitive functioning. During the assessment process, an attempt is made to identify the nature of the cognitive disturbance as well as the client behaviors and environmental events that have led to the development and maintenance of the cognitive disturbance. The client's schemata, automatic thoughts, and cognitive operations are evaluated to determine whether a cognitive deficit or distortion underlies, or contributes to, the presenting problem. Depending on the nature of the disturbance, a variety of intervention strategies would be directed at the maladaptive cognitions and the behaviors and environmental events that maintain them.

Behavior

The quintessential characteristic of behavior therapy is that the goal of psychological intervention is change in overt behavior. This remains a goal of behavior therapy. However, the view of behavior and the underlying mechanisms for change are different between behavior therapy and cognitive-behavioral therapy. Commonly, the pure behaviorist attempts to identify the behavioral excesses and deficits as well as the antecedents and consequences of those behaviors. From this perspective, a behavioral excess is a behavior that occurs too frequently or too intensely for the situation. A behavioral deficit is characterized either by a complete absence of the behavior or when the behavior does not occur with adequate frequency or intensity. A third primary behavioral disturbance is in stimulus control. The youngster exhibits a behavior at an acceptable frequency and intensity, but it is enacted at an inappropriate time or in an inappropriate situation. The cognitive-behavioral therapist will be equally concerned with, and have as a target of intervention, these behavioral disturbances. However, the cognitive-behavioral therapist also will be concerned with the cognitions that initiate, support, and follow the problem behavior. In addition, he or she will be concerned with the cognitive rules or schemas that underlly maladaptive behavior.

From a cognitive-behavioral perspective, behavior is viewed as both a product and an initiator of cognition and environmental events. It is a product in the sense that the child's behavior is the result of the way that he or she interprets environmental events and in the sense that it may be guided by the child's cognitions. It is an initiator of cognition in that the behavior produces environmental changes and perceivable reactions that serve as information that the youngster then processes. The child's behavior impacts the environment both in a physical sense and by contributing to the perceptions of others. Other people in the child's environment react to the child's behavior; their reactions in turn affect the way they then behave toward the child.

Emotion

Emotional processes, both those that we are aware of and those that are outside of awareness, impact behavior and cognition and vice versa. From the cognitive-behavioral perspective, emotions are viewed as the product of automatic preattentive information processing (Greenberg &

Safran, 1984). Emotion it is "a unified, phenomenal, conscious human experience, constructed by an information-processing system from subsidiary components that are themselves not in awareness (p. 570, Greenberg & Safran, 1984). Emotions are generated by combining the initial perception of the environmental stimulus with the resulting expressive motor reaction. Since some disorders are characterized by affective disturbances, for example, anxiety and depressive disorders, these emotions become targets of treatment. Such interventions as pleasant-events scheduling and relaxation training may be used to target the unpleasant emotions directly. Other indirect methods may be used, such as cognitive restructuring or changes in the affect that characterizes the family environment. Pharmacologic interventions also may be used to enhance mood.

Environment

The child's environment is a critical determinant of behavior. However, the environment does not necessarily have a direct-mechanical affect on behavior. It affects behavior through a number of avenues. The significant others in the child's environment establish the contingencies for the child's behavior. These contingencies provide the child with learning experiences about appropriate and inappropriate behavior as well as information about the self and the world. Significant others serve as models for a variety of behaviors, rules, beliefs, and emotional reactions. They also directly impart information through the things they tell the child. Family members constantly are sending messages to the child about the self, the world, and the future through their actions and the things they say. It is equally important to note that children are active constructors of their environment through their behaviors. These behaviors impact the environment and the perceptions of others within the environment.

The environment also may be the source of stress that interacts with a genetic diathesis and leads to the development and expression of a disorder. Current research suggests that a variety of stressors, including major life events, chronic strains, and daily hassles, have both a direct effect on the expression of various symptoms of psychological disturbance and an indirect effect on the development of a disorder through the impact they have on the information-processing system. A variety of interventions may be employed to impact environmental disturbances. Most commonly, parent training is used to teach the parents child management procedures for changing environmental contingencies. In addition, they may be taught how to support desirable behaviors. They may learn how to change interactions that support maladaptive schema. Family therapy, couple's therapy, or individual therapy with a parent may become one of the adjunctive forms of treatment.

Biological Variables

Biological variables are an equally important component of the cognitive behavioral-model that has been, for the most part, underrepresented within the literature. Clearly the child's behavior, cognitions, and affect are related to biochemical variables. In fact, Beck (1976) refers to neurochemical reactions and cognitions as opposite sides of the same coin. The youngster's physical and neurological abilities establish limits and constraints on what the child can and cannot do and achieve. Biochemical disturbances are associated with a number of psychological disorders, and there is strong evidence for a genetic link to psychological disturbances of childhood. At an entirely different level, the child's appearance and physical abilities are primarily biologically determined and affect the way the child is perceived by others.

Case Conceptualization

ASSESSMENT

The model of human functioning just described guides the assessment and intervention efforts of the cognitive-behavioral therapist. Each of the broad domains of functioning alone or in combination represents possible areas of disturbance that may underlie the presenting problem. In addition, results of the assessment guide treatment.

The cognitive-behavioral interventions are problem and symptom focused. In other words, they are designed to remediate the current difficulties that youngsters are experiencing. Consequently, the therapist works with a child and significant others, including parents and teachers, to collaboratively identify the presenting problems. Once the presenting problems have been identified, an assessment of the child, significant others, and the primary environment in which the child functions is initiated. An ongoing hypothesis-generation and testing procedure is followed to identify the variables, both child and environmental (broadly defined), that led to the development and maintenance of the presenting problem. The assessment is ongoing as the therapist and child continually uncover information about the thoughts, behaviors, emotions and interaction patterns that contribute to the problems. In addition, as old hypotheses are tested, the results lead to the development of new hypotheses.

Assessment of the child will go beyond the delineation of psychiatric symptoms to include an evaluation of the youngster in the cognitive, behavioral, emotional, and physiological domains. Since the cognitive-behavioral model embraces the principle of reciprocal determinism, each domain in isolation as well as in combination with each other domain is evaluated. For example, if a behavioral disturbance is identified as the target of change, then the behavior itself would be evaluated to determine whether it was an excess, deficit, or a problem with stimulus control. Similar to traditional behavior therapy, the antecedents and consequences (immediate and distal) associated with the problematic behavior are evaluated. In addition, distal variables that might impact the behavior of significant others who are enforcing the contingencies are evaluated. For example, environmental stressors such as work or financial problems may cause a parent to become irritable, which leads to angry verbal reprimands as well as other forms of punishment.

The cognitions that might lead to, guide, maintain, and reflect the impact of the behavior would be assessed and possibly become targets of intervention. The behavioral disturbance may be related to or cause an emotional reaction. For example, the angry child reacts in an oppositional fashion toward parents. The parents respond with coercive behaviors, which leads the child to think

that "It's not fair," which produces more anger and behavioral retribution. The behavior may be a result of a biochemical or organic disturbance, but this disturbance is exacerbated by the maladaptive behavior. For example, a youngster may be experiencing an organic brain disorder that leads to an excessive emotional reaction in response to frustration and thoughts of unfairness, which leads to inappropriate behavior, such as throwing things around. This damages belongings and escalates his or her emotional reaction. In addition, other people in the child's environment respond to his or her anger with anger and attempts to bring the aggressive behavior to a halt. This leads to additional anger and aggressive behavior.

As noted earlier, assessment would be designed to determine the nature of the cognitive disturbance that is associated with the identified problem. Once again, this portion of the assessment would be directed at the child and significant others. Typically through an interview, the therapist determines whether the maladaptive behavior is due to a cognitive deficit or distortion. A deficit would exist if the child's problems were due to a failure to think before, along with, or after the problem behaviors. Similarly, the interview would reveal whether the cognitions that preceded, accompanied, or followed the maladaptive behavior were a misinterpretation of environmental or interpersonal events. A distortion is evident when the youngster's interpretations of events are discrepant from objective facts. After gathering information about the cognitive products that are associated with the identified problem, the therapist begins trying to identify the schemata and processing errors that support and give rise to these cognitions. Through deductive reasoning, the therapist develops hypotheses about the schemata that may exist and explain or account for the consistencies and themes in the youngster's thinking and behavior. If a cognitive disturbance exists, then the therapist develops hypotheses about the learning experiences, interaction patterns, and relationships that would lead to and maintain the schemata. Interaction patterns may be observed during family meetings as a means of evaluating the hypotheses.

As noted earlier, the assessment of cognitions is not limited to the child. It is equally important for therapists to assess the cognitions of caregivers and other family members. This assessment includes the cognitions that interfere with effective parenting and give rise to affect that prevents effective parenting. In an earlier example, the parent thinks that she is unfairly burdened with work, which leads to anger that causes her not to follow through on directives or consequences. Another class of cognitions that are assessed in significant others are the cognitions that may support the child's cognitive disturbance. Sometimes a child's schemata, attributional style, or processing errors may parallel a parent's. For example, a parent may believe that it is okay to take what you want and that others do not have a right to prevent you from obtaining what you want. This premise guides their parent's behavior, and the child learns the same beliefs through daily exposure to them. Similarly, a parent may believe that life is an arduous undertaking full of pain and that death represents the only respite from the pain. After hearing this belief verbalized through subtle and not-so-subtle statements as well as parental actions that may make the youngster's life painful, the child incorporates this view of life.

Assessment of the child's behavior is consistent with that described in texts on behavioral assessment. The difference from the cognitive-behavioral perspective is that the concomitant cognitive and affective disturbances are assessed as well. The therapist performs a functional analysis of the maladaptive behavior by directly observing the behavior and by interviewing significant others. In addition, a task analysis may be completed of the desired behavior that would identify not only the behaviors that must be enacted for success but the cognitions that must occur for the child to be successful at enacting the desired behaviors. The therapist uses results of the functional analysis and the task analysis to guide the intervention.

The youngster's emotions are the targets of assessment in their own right and as they impact behavior and cognition. The assessment would include information gathered through an interview, self-report measures, observation, responses to projectives, and parent report forms.

The final broad area of assessment is in the physical realm. As part of the assessment, the therapist may request a medical evaluation to determine whether a physical condition is contributing to the youngster's presenting problems. Furthermore, a psychiatric consultation may be recommended to evaluate the appropriateness of pharmacological intervention.

TREATMENT

Based on the results of a comprehensive assessment, an intervention plan is developed and implemented. The overarching objective of treatment is long-lasting symptom relief and improvement in adaptive behavior. It is believed that this is accomplished through (1) changing behavior, (2) changing the associated cognitive disturbances, (3) providing relief from unpleasant emotions, (4) altering the maladaptive environmental events that lead to and maintain the targets of treatment, (5) changing the cognitive disturbances that impede the parent's ability to effectively parent the child, (6) changing family interactions that support maladaptive cognitions of the child, and (7) using appropriate and supportive adjunctive therapies, including pharmacological interventions where appropriate.

While the objective of this chapter is to describe cognitive-behavioral therapy with children, any description of the treatment approach is going to be arbitrary as the actual intervention employed is tailored individually to meet the youngster's specific needs as identified through assessment. Some general principles that are followed in most cases are described to help define the approach.

The cognitive-behavioral treatment of children takes place within the interpersonal context of the therapeutic relationship. The therapeutic relationship is an important and often overlooked ingredient of cognitive-behavioral therapy. Much therapeutic work is completed within this interpersonal context. The relationship provides the therapist with a window to the interpersonal experiences of significant others in the child's life. The therapist experiences the "walking on eggshells" experience of parents of children with oppositional defiant disorder or an explosive disorder as the youngster behaves in a passive-aggressive and coercive fashion, continually trying to draw the therapist into the coercive cycle of defiance and explosive affect. When playing a game with a child, the therapist has the opportunity to experience what the child's peers experience when they play with the youngster. In short, the therapeutic relationship provides the therapist with a microcosm of the child's interpersonal behaviors. It enables the therapist to gain a deep empathic understanding of the child, which leads to trust and guides treatment.

The therapeutic relationship provides the child with an opportunity to experience, and learn from, a healthy relationship. The therapist provides the youngster with a safe environment in which he or she can explore the presenting problems and the associated affect, cognitions, and behaviors. It serves as a source of motivation for the child to try to change. It also provides the child with new learning experiences that can lead to the development of new adaptive schemata or counter existing maladaptive schemata. The child's self-schemata is enhanced through positive supportive feedback and the more basal experience of having someone genuinely care. This positive, healthy experience can counter maladaptive self-schema such as "No one cares about me" and "I'm not likable." Within the therapeutic relationship, the therapist models appropriate interpersonal behavior and provides the youngster with objective, nonthreatening feedback about his or her interpersonal behavior. For example, while playing a game, the therapist models good sportsmanship, conflict resolution skills, and how to be complimentary.

As the therapeutic relationship is being established, the therapist educates the child about his or her problem and its cognitive-behavioral formulation. Through education and other procedures, the therapist attempts to get the youngster and significant others motivated for change. Since the child is going to be responsible for carrying out much of the intervention, it is critical that he or she is motivated for change; as all clinicians know, change is a difficult and often anxiety-provoking process. Concurrently, the therapist identifies thoughts and beliefs of the child and significant others that might impede change and attempts to restructure these thoughts.

Typically, the next stage of treatment involves helping the child to "try on" the conceptualization of the presenting problem through teaching the youngster to self-monitor the occurrence of the targets of treatment. If the target of treatment was an affective state, for example, anxiety, then the youngster would be taught to use an increase in the experience of anxiety as a cue to self-monitor the subjective severity of the anxiety, thoughts,

and images that precede, co-occur, and follow anxiety, and the situational context in which it occurs. This information provides the therapist and child with a better understanding of the nature of the problem, the triggers for anxiety, and the role that others might play in the problem.

Similarly, a child who is experiencing an externalizing disorder would be taught to self-monitor his or her problematic behavior, the associated thoughts, images, affect, and situational context. Concurrently, parents and teachers would be taught to monitor the child's target behaviors and the antecedents and consequences of those behaviors. In addition, the parents may be instructed to self-monitor the thoughts they experience surrounding the problem behavior and their reaction to it. This information then would be used to guide the development of the treatment program.

The next stage of treatment involves teaching the child skills for remediating the problem. The child may be taught any of a variety of self-control and coping skills. The self-control skills typically include self-monitoring, self-evaluation, use of self-instructions, and self-reinforcement. Coping skills are a much broader category of skills that exceeds the scope of this chapter. Examples include problem-solving training, relaxation, distraction strategies, anger management strategies, assertion, conflict resolution skills, and so on. The skills are typically taught through education, modeling, guided practice, feedback, and completion of within-session activities, and the skills are applied through therapeutic homework assignments.

Earlier sections highlighted the cognitive aspects of psychological functioning. These cognitive disturbances would be modified using a variety of procedures. If the misperceptions reflected a cognitive deficit, then the youngster would be taught when and how to use compensatory new cognitions to guide his or her thinking and behavior. In contrast, when the perceptions reflect a distortion in thinking, then the maladaptive cognitive products, schemata, or processing errors would become the focus of intervention. If the negative cognitions were the objective reflection of an unfortunate situation, then the therapist would help the youngster develop plans and skills for changing the situation or for coping and adjusting to it.

The primary procedure used for remediating a deficit in thinking is self-instructional training, a procedure that helps the youngster internalize any set of cognitions. It is aimed at the level of cognitive products. The procedure involves a series of steps beginning with the therapist overtly modeling the use of the self-instructions while completing the task. Next the child is coached in the overt use of the self-instructions while completing the task. Subsequently the therapist models the faded use of the self-instructions. The child also fades out the overt use of self-statements. Then the therapist completes the task while covertly using the self-instructions. Finally the child covertly uses the self-instructions while completing the task.

Cognitive restructuring procedures are used when the cognitive disturbance is characterized by a distortion in thinking. The most powerful cognitive restructuring technique appears to be behavioral experiments. When a behavioral experiment is used, the youngster and the therapist state the child's maladaptive schema or cognition in an objective and testable fashion and then they discuss the evidence that would support or refute the schema. Subsequently they develop a behavioral experiment that involves the child doing something that directly tests the cognition. Finally the therapist and child evaluate the outcome of the experiment against the preestablished criteria. A number of other cognitive restructuring techniques, including counters. What's the evidence? What if? and alternative interpretation may be used. All of these techniques and examples of their implementation are described in Stark (1990).

As noted earlier, the schemata that are of greatest clinical importance are the core schemata and in particular the self-schema because they direct the overall information-processing system. Cognitive restructuring procedures are used to change these schemata. Cognitive restructuring is an ongoing process as the more central a schema, the longer it has been in existence; due to information-processing biases, it has an extended history of evidence to support it. Thus multiple learning experiences over an extended period of time are required to change the existing schema or build a more adaptive one. It also is important to note that the objective of therapy is to help the youngster learn how to identify his or her own maladaptive cognitions, schemata, and processing errors, and then to apply the cognitive restructuring procedures to them. It is not easy for children to learn to do this. Doing so takes a good deal of self-

FIGURE 23.1.

Problem solving homework form

reflection, ongoing effort, and introspective ability. Thus the therapist models the cognitive restructuring process for the child and provides in-session exercises and extra-therapy homework assignments to give the child independent practice at applying the techniques.

Once the child has learned the therapeutic skills, the next phase of therapy, skills application, is begun. Throughout treatment, the therapist strives to make the process and learning experiences "real" for the child. The therapist and child work together to bring the child's everyday experiences into the therapy session. The skills are taught within the context of the child's life experiences. During the skills application stage, the therapist blends the child's experiences with the teaching process to help the youngster learn how to apply the skills to his or her real problems. In addition, the therapist, child, and in some instances the parents collaboratively develop therapeutic homework assignments that help the youngster apply the skills in vivo. The homework assignments may be highly or only modestly structured. For example, Figure 23.1 is an example of a homework form that we use to help youngsters apply problem solving. This form is part of a structured workbook of therapeutic activities and homework assignments. A less structured homework assignment would involve instructing the child to remember a time when he or she used problem solving over the week. In most cases, it is important to work with the child's parents and teachers to develop a reward system that encourages the child to complete the therapeutic homework.

PARENTAL INVOLVEMENT

Concurrent to working with the child, the therapist devises and implements an integrated parent training program that supports the work that is being completed with the child. In some cases, the parents will be taught behavior management skills that reflect the results of the functional assessment. In other instances, the parents will become collaborators in treatment who are taught behaviors, attitudes, and interaction patterns that will support the intervention with the child. This may involve educating the parents and having them monitor their child's progress. In other instances, parents may be taught to establish contingencies that will motivate the child to enact the skills and new ways of thinking that are being taught during therapy. The therapist and child may teach the parents the same skills and cognitions that the child is learning as well as strategies for helping their child master and apply the strategies. For example, the child may be asked to teach the parents the 5 step problem-solving strategy that he or she has been learning. The therapist then would teach the parents when and how the child is supposed to apply problem solving, and the parents would be encouraged to help their child do so correctly. Parents often can cue the child that a problem exists and then help the youngster to work through the steps to solving it. Early in treatment, a child may not be aware of the cues that he or she is experiencing certain emotions. The parents may be taught to cue the child and then help the child apply various coping strategies. For example, parents of a child with an anger management problem may be taught a humorous signal that they can use to cue their child that he is becoming angry. Subsequently, they can suggest that it would be a good time to use some anger reducers. A child who is withdrawing and becoming depressed may be cued to write down his or her thoughts in a diary and then asked to join in a pleasant activity with a parent, such as playing a board game, shooting baskets, going for a walk. A parent might recognize that a child is becoming anxious. This would be the cue to go to the youngster's diary and use a 2-column technique to dispute the anxiety-engendering thoughts. Or the child may verbalize a negative self-statement. The parent would help the child recognize the thought and ask the child for the evidence that supports and refutes it. The child may come home from playing complaining about being mistreated. If the parent thinks that the child may have misperceived the situation, the parent would ask the child for alternative explanations for why the friend acted in the upsetting fashion. As is evident from these examples, in an integrated treatment plan, the parents are taught how to create a healthy cognitive, affective, behavioral, and interpersonal mileu at home that facilitates the therapeutic change process.

FAMILY THERAPY

The goal of family therapy within a cognitive-behavioral framework is to identify and help the family alter interaction patterns, communications, and family rules that support the child's maladaptive behavior, information processing, and schemata. Treatment of a family begins with helping members understand how their family fits into the cognitive-behavioral formulation of their child's disorder. The therapist joins the family and observes them for examples of maladaptive interactions while he or she is establishing a therapeutic relationship. The therapist explores the thoughts and beliefs that underlie the maladaptive interactions of family members, sometimes using cognitive restructuring procedures. The family, like the identified patient, is given specific homework assignments to work on between meetings.

The therapist looks for clues as to what within the family might be producing and maintaining the child's maladaptive behavior and cognitive disturbances. Based on this information, the therapist looks for interaction patterns, messages, schemata, and family rules exhibited by family members, especially parents, that may have led to the development and currently the child's disturbances. Once identified, the therapist may use therapeutic directives, education, coaching, modeling, feedback, behavioral rehearsal, and contracting to help the family change. The family may be taught a variety of skills, such as communication skills, conflict resolution skills, problem solving, empathic listening, self-esteem enhancement techniques, decision-making skills, frustration tolerance skills, recreation skills, and the like. The guiding objective is to develop a family environment that supports the healthy affective, cognitive, behavioral, and interpersonal development of the child.

Variations

As noted throughout this chapter, no singular model of cognitive-behavioral therapy exists; rather it is a general perspective. Thus there different therapists employ different treatment models. However, the general principles that guide treatment and its progression will be quite similar. The type and degree to which cognitive techniques are incorporated into the intervention will vary according to the training of the therapist, as will the degree to which parent training and family therapy components are integrated into the overall treatment plan. The cognitive models of Beck and Ellis have had a major impact on professional psychology as a whole and have been central to the cognitive-behavioral perspective. While theoretical differences exist—and these differences are significant—in practice some of the principles and procedures from each of the major models are combined and applied to the treatment of youths. We provide a brief summary of these 2 models and how they are applied as an illustration of the ways that cognitive-behavioral therapists vary in their practice based on the different training.

The objective of cognitive therapy (Beck, 1976) is to use a combination of cognitive and behavioral procedures to produce a change in the child's distorted thinking, which is presumed to underlie the youngster's psychological symptoms. Thus the principles and procedures of cognitive therapy appear to be most applicable to disorders that have a distortion in information processing at their core. The internalizing disorders are characterized by such disturbances. However, it is apparent that distortions in information processing also

may be evident in externalizing disorders. For example, youths with a conduct disorder diagnosis tend to perceive the actions of others as representing a personal affront or provocation.

The therapeutic objective, from the cognitive therapy perspective, is to change the youngster's unrealistic and negative perceptions as well as the processing errors that support these faulty views. To accomplish this, typically the intervention program begins with behavioral interventions that are designed to produce symptom relief as well as to provide the child with some distance from his or her thinking. In the case of the depressed youth, activity scheduling, mastery and pleasure experiences, and graded task assignments will be used to elevate mood. In the case of the anxious youngster, relaxation training may be used to reduce physical tension. With a conduct-disordered youth, social skills training may be the initial target of intervention. As therapy progresses, children are taught to identify their negative thoughts and information processing errors as well as themes in their negative thinking. As distortions in thinking are identified, they are stated in terms of hypotheses, and cognitive restructuring procedures are used to test the validity of the negative thoughts. When a negative thought is shown to be unsupported by the objective evidence, more positive and realistic thoughts are identified and incorporated into a youngster's thinking. Similarly, behavioral assignments are given that help the youngster test the validity of the negative thoughts that underlie his or her distorted thinking. The overarching goal is to alter the automatic thoughts, processing errors, and schemata that underlie the youngster's symptoms.

Rational emotive therapy (Ellis, 1962) is similar to cognitive therapy as it is based on the assumption that an individual's psychological problems stem from a disturbance in thinking. However, the nature of the disturbance differs between the 2 perspectives. Within rational emotive therapy, it is hypothesized that individuals create their own emotional and behavioral disturbances by believing in irrational beliefs. Recognizing the risk of being overly simplistic, the central thesis of the therapy is that an individual causes his or her own emotional and behavioral consequences by strongly holding certain maladaptive beliefs. The impact that an activating event (A) will have on an individual's emotions or behaviors (C) is mediated by his or her beliefs (B). If the person is exhibiting some sort of emotional or behavioral disturbance, it is due to holding irrational beliefs. Thus a child's symptoms would be assumed to be the result of faulty and irrational beliefs.

The first goal of rational emotive therapy is to help the child understand the relationship between emotions and the irrational beliefs (B) he or she holds concerning various activating events (A). Once this rationale has been taught, the youngster and therapist identify the various irrational beliefs that the child holds. Subsequently, the child is taught to replace the irrational beliefs with more adaptive ones through the use of disputation (D). (Disputing is another term for cognitive restructuring.) The child is taught to use 4 cognitive restructuring procedures to replace the maladaptive beliefs, including detecting, debating, discriminating, and semantic defining (Ellis, 1962). In addition to using cognitive restructuring procedures, the therapist uses rational-emotive imagery and shame-attacking exercises as well as behavioral homework assignments. The goal of therapy is to produce deep philosophical change in the youngster's belief system, which is referred to as a new effect (E).

Developmental Considerations

When devising a treatment plan for a child from a cognitive-behavioral perspective, one of the first developmental considerations is the child's level of cognitive development. This variable is the primary determinant of (1) the mix of cognitive and behavioral procedures that are going to be used with the child and (2) the extent to which the child or the child's parents/family are going to be the primary agent of change. A prerequisite for the effective use of cognitive procedures is that the child has the metacognitive ability to be aware of what he or she is thinking. In other words, the child must be able to monitor his or her own consciousness to be able to identify maladaptive thoughts when they occur. Furthermore, with some of the cognitive restructuring procedures the child must be able to evaluate maladaptive thoughts and counter them with more adaptive and realistic ones. To accomplish this, the thera-

pist can build some crutches for the less cognitively mature child by helping him or her to learn to recognize internal and external cues that are associated with the target thoughts, thus making it easier for the child to recognize that it is time to introspect and listen to his or her cognitive stream. In addition, the child and therapist can develop a menu of cognitive counters that the child can write down on an index card to read outside of the session when the target thought appears.

The child's cognitive development also determines the type of cognitive restructuring procedures that will be used. With the less mature youngster, self-instructional training (SIT) is used instead of the cognitive restructuring techniques associated with cognitive therapy (What's evidence?). Self-instructional, training (Meichenbaum, 1977) is a procedure that is used to help a client internalize a set of cognitions that guide his or her behavior or help moderate his or her emotions. The child learns the self-statements through a multistep process of observing the therapist modeling the self-instructions, being coached while verbalizing the self-instructions out loud, and gradually fading to the covert use of the self-instructions. In addition, the child's self-statements are matched with the relevant behaviors. This cognitive restructuring procedure requires basic memory strategies and abilities and less abstract thinking and evaluation.

With the less cognitively mature child, more emphasis is placed on using behavioral procedures. Similarly, emphasis is placed on parent training or family therapy rather than on using cognitive procedures to alter the child's thinking and thus the disturbance in mood or behavior. This seems to stem from the fact that the disturbance in thinking is still being formed by interactions within the family and with peers.

Another challenge to the cognitive-behavioral therapist is designing intervention programs that are engaging and match youngsters' developmental levels. To accomplish this, we have found it necessary to create games that help younger children acquire therapeutic skills and learn how to apply the therapeutic procedures to their own problems. In addition to using games, we have developed an illustrated skills book that helps concretize the concepts being taught and helps the youngsters remember what they are learning in therapy (Stark & Kendall, 1996). This illustrated book includes numerous paper-and-pencil activities that help the children acquire the therapeutic skills and cartoon sequences that illustrate the concepts being taught.

faculties to be able to use the cognitive-behavioral strategies. In some cases, the medication may take the edge off emotional experiences, which enables children to use the coping strategies to manage the symptoms.

Interaction with Other Interventions

To intervene successfully with some childhood disorders and certain clinical situations, cognitive-behavioral therapy has to be combined with other forms of treatment. Typically this means combining it with a pharmacological intervention. To date, there has been very little empirical evaluation of the combination of cognitive-behavioral therapy with psychotropic medications. The treatment of attention deficit hyperactivity disorder has received the most attention. A few studies have evaluated the effectiveness of cognitive-behavioral therapy with and without psychostimulant medication for treatment of attention deficit. Based on their review of the literature, Braswell and Bloomquist (1991) have concluded that psychostimulant medication is critical for effective treatment of attention deficit hyperactivity disorder. They argue that the medication gives children the cognitive/attentional ability to use the cognitive and behavioral strategies that the therapist is trying to help them and their parents acquire.

While there is a paucity of research of the interactive effects of cognitive-behavioral therapy and pharmacological interventions, they do appear to work together. The pharmacological interventions, through their biochemical actions, appear to help some youngsters to gain distance from their maladaptive thinking patterns, which helps them to look at these thoughts more objectively. Doing so seems to diminish some of the believability of the thoughts, which helps the youngsters to counter and restructure them. In other cases, medication may slow down the emotional reaction enough that youngsters have a foothold to begin to use the coping strategies to manage the affect and other symptoms. The medication also might provide children with the energy necessary to utilize the psychological procedures. It may normalize their sleep patterns and other vegetative functions so that they have the necessary physical

Indications

Identifying the child variables that are predictive of successful treatment with a particular intervention is highly desirable. When this is possible, it maximizes the potential for devising effective treatment plans. One of the hallmarks of behavior therapy was the very precise matching of a specific problem, conceptualized as a behavioral excess or deficit, and a specific intervention for that problem. In addition, each intervention was individually tailored to meet the needs of the child client and his or her environment. Variation in child characteristics were incorporated into the behavior management program automatically. Due to this idiographic approach, behavior therapy was applied successfully to many children with a wide variety of disturbances as long as the environment provided the therapist with control over relevant consequences. This emphasis on individualizing the treatment program and matching intervention strategies to problems is a characteristics of cognitive-behavioral therapy as well. However, unlike behavior therapy, cognitive-behavioral therapy relies more on the client's own efforts to produce change to be effective. Thus there is more of a need to determine whether any client characteristics predict treatment success.

It is imperative that an empirical approach is taken to identifying the child variables that are predictive of successful treatment with cognitive-behavioral therapy. At the most basic level, such research should be designed to determine which childhood disorders respond to the therapy. As noted earlier, a good deal of this research has been conducted. Another level to this research that has not been realized is to identify specific child variables that might predict success in treatment. In one of the few existing relevant studies, Bugental, Whalen, and Henker (1977) found that children with an internal locus of control responded better to self-control strategies whereas children with an external locus of control responded better to a behavioral intervention that consisted of manipulating environmental contingencies.

Given this paucity of research, we will turn to our clinical experience to identify variables that appear to predict successful treatment with cognitive-behavioral therapy. Some of these variables are true for successful treatment of children in general. One of the things commonly heard when receiving a referral from the community is "This child would be perfect for you. He (She) is bright, very verbal, motivated, and conscientious." These sound like characteristics of a child client that would be ideal for any approach to psychological therapy. However, given the emphasis on changing cognitions, it is commonly believed that more intelligent youngsters respond better to such an approach. To some extent this is a myth, as cognitive-behavioral therapy has been applied successfully to youngsters with very limited intellectual ability (Whitman, Scherzinger, & Sommer, 1991). On the other hand, oftentimes it is these very bright students who are best able to introspect, verbalize, and evaluate their own thinking. In addition, given the collaborative nature of the approach, such youngsters are readily able to understand the rationale for treatment. The comment about the child being highly verbal stems from the perception that cognitive-behavioral therapy is more of a "talk therapy" than other forms of child therapy, such as play therapy. Once again, this is partially true and depends on both child and therapist characteristics. With younger and less verbal child clients, often it is necessary to use a process other than the traditional interview to conduct therapy. The more creative and skillful cognitive-behavioral therapist can use play as the medium for conducting therapy.

The extent to which the child is experiencing overwhelming emotions seems to determine the appropriateness and effectiveness of cognitive procedures. When the child is experiencing overwhelming dysphoria or anger, we believe that behavioral and self-control procedures should be used prior to trying cognitive procedures. Having the angry child attend to his or her angry thoughts seems to foment the anger. Likewise, having the very depressed youngster attend to his or her depressive cognitions can lead to greater dysphoria. As the youngster begins to experience some relief and control over the emotions, he or she can gain some distance from the experience and the related cognitions, which enables the child to restructure maladaptive cognitions. Thus, in the beginning of treating depressed youths, we rely more on behavioral procedures such as pleasant activity scheduling and self-monitoring. Similarly, if the dominant and overwhelming emotion is anger, the child is taught to use anger reducers as a means of controlling anger and gaining some distance from the related cognitions. If the behavioral procedures do not have the desired impact, then a regimen of psychotropic medication may be indicated and used as a means of providing the child with a base of relief for helping him or her develop behavioral and cognitive strategies.

Cognitive-behavioral therapy is based on a collaborative client-therapist relationship. Thus, for it to be effective, the child must first be able to establish a therapeutic relationship with the therapist. If the child cannot trust the therapist and the relationship does not enable the child to feel safe enough to try on the new ways of perceiving things and behaving, then change is not going to take place. In addition, the child must be open to self-exploration. Furthermore, the child must be capable of verbalizing his or her thoughts, feelings, emotions, concerns, and in general what is happening in his or her life. It takes much longer to produce the desired change with more defensive youngsters, because they are not able to provide themselves and the therapist with access to such treatment relevant information.

Since cognitive-behavioral therapy is based so heavily on the premise that the youngster is the change agent, the child must be motivated to change. This certainly is not true in many instances. For example, aggressive children often get their immediate desires met through their aggressive acts. The child who is acting out at home often can coerce his or her way into getting what he or she wants.

Contraindications and Risks

To date, there has been a minimum of empirical evaluation of the effectiveness of cognitive-behavioral therapy with children or adolescents who are psychotic. Consequently, presence of such a disturbance may be a contraindication for its use. Children who are experiencing an organic disturbance or a severe learning disability in addition to an emotional disorder are more difficult to treat with cognitive-behavioral therapy, perhaps because their neurological disturbances get in the way of acquiring cognitive strategies for overcoming the emotional disturbance. For example, the children may not have the attentional ability to complete the problem-solving sequence. Or other thoughts might intrude and prevent them from being able to complete a cognitive restructuring process. Some of these children have such serious language disabilities that the verbally laden cognitive-behavioral therapy procedures are ineffective. With such youngsters, an alternative mode (e.g., visual/imaginal) of presentation or treatment may prove more effective. Risks of using cognitive-behavioral therapy appear to be quite minimal.

Measures of Clinical Progress

Ongoing measurement of progress in treatment was one of the hallmarks of methodological behaviorism and is one of the defining characteristics of cognitive-behavioral therapy. The specific instruments used to measure change are dependent on the child's disturbance and the targets of intervention. Typically, this assessment will involve a measure of symptom presence and severity completed by the child as well as a significant other, an observational measure of change, and measures of the cognitive, behavioral, mood, and family variables that are the targets of change. Some of the measures that might be used appear in Table 23.2.

Duration and Termination

One of the definitive characteristics of cognitive-behavioral therapy is that it is designed to be problem-oriented, time-limited, and thus short term in nature. Within the literature, treatment typically lasts between 10 and 16 sessions. How-

ever, it is important to note that this time frame is specific to treatment outcome *research* and may not reflect actual treatment practices. In the case of research, the decision to terminate treatment is based on experimental considerations rather than on the basis of demonstrated amelioration of the psychological disturbance. In actual practice, children vary greatly in the number of sessions required for treatment. The number of sessions required for successful treatment depends on child and family characteristics, type of presenting disorder, presence of co-occurring disorders, history of physical or sexual abuse, presence of parental psychopathology, substance abuse in the family, presence of environmental stressors, degree of parental involvement in therapy, degree of child involvement in therapy, success at getting the child and family to complete homework assignments, simultaneous use of pharmacologic intervention, presence of other psychologically disturbed family members, stability of the marital relationship as well as other variables. Thus while cognitive-behavioral therapy is designed to be short term in nature, not all cases present themselves in a fashion that can lead to a short-term remedy. However, treatment can be terminated when the child, parents, and family have acquired and are using the skills that are necessary for maintaining change.

Outcome Studies

As noted in Table 23.1, cognitive-behavioral therapy has demonstrated efficacy with a wide variety of disorders. In fact, a relatively large number of outcome studies have been conducted over the past 20 years.

Clinical Standards

Any approach to psychological treatment is going to be defined in part according to the procedures that are associated with it. In Tables 23.3, 23.4, and 23.5, we list the procedures and their current clinical status. Most of these procedures are described in detail in Stark (1990).

Table 23.2

Sample Assessment Tools That Can Be Used to Evaluate Treatment Effectiveness

Target of Treatment	Possible Assessment Tools
Cognitive disturbance	
Deficit	Matching Familiar Figures Test (Kagan, Rosman, Day, Albert & Phillips, 1964)
Distortion	Cognitive Triad Inventory for Children (CTI-C; Kaslow, Stark, Printz, Livingston, & Tsai, 1992)
	Automatic Thoughts Questionnaire for Children (Stark, Humphrey, Laurent, Livingston & Christopher, 1993)
	Cognitive Bias Questionnaire for Children (Haley, Fine, Marriage, Morretti, & Freeman, 1985)
	Projectives (e.g., Thematic Apperception Test, Rorschach, drawings)
Negative expectancies for the future	Hopelessness Scale for Children (Kazdin, French, Unis, Esveldt, Dawson, & Sherick, 1983)
Self-control deficits	
Self-monitoring	Pleasant and Unpleasant Events Schedules for Children
	Automatic Thoughts Questionnaire for Children (Stark et al., 1993)
	Projectives such as TATs
Self-evaluation	My Standards Questionnaire-Revised (Stark, 1990)
	Self-Esteem Inventory (Coopersmith, 1967)
Self-reward	(Kaslow, Rehm, & Siegel, 1984)
Social skills	Matson Evaluation of Social Skills for Youths (Matson, Rotatori, & Helsel, 1983)
	Observation of free play
Assertiveness skills	Observation of social interactions

1. Children respond primariliy to mental representations of events and their environment rather than to objective reality. The represntations develop from learning experiences that the children have.
2. Cognition, behavior, affect, and biochemistry are causally interrelated. If one is altered, the others also will be affected.
3. Cognitive variables are important in understanding child psychopathology and the process of psychological change.
4. It is desirable to combine cognitive and behavioral procedures in therapeutic programs.

Unresolved Problems and Future Directions

Cognitive-behavioral therapy is a promising approach to treating the psychological problems of childhood. However, much continued development is needed if this approach is going to remain viable and one of the most commonly practiced. Thankfully, the therapy has embraced the empirical rigor and self-evaluation principles and methodology of methodological behaviorism (Mahoney, 1974). Thus ongoing empirical evaluation of cognitive-behavioral models and methods will ensure continued evolution that is based on scientific results.

While advances have been made in the development of empirically based cognitive-behavioral formulations of various childhood disorders, it is our belief that existing cognitive-behavioral models in general are too unidimensional (focusing solely or almost exclusively on the disturbances of the child) and fail to discuss the important contribution, and the reciprocal impact of the child's disturbance on, the family. While it is self-evident that the family plays a significant role in the development and maintenance of psychological distur-

Table 23.3

Accepted and Useful Cognitive-Behavioral Procedures

Cognitive	Behavioral
Visual imagery	Token systems
Journals and diaries	Self-monitoring
What's the evidence?	Self-evaluation
Alternative interpretation	Self-reinforcement
What if it happens?	Reinforcement
Reframing	Behavioral contracts
Problem solving	Relaxation
Self-instructional training	Time out
Guided discovery	Social skills
Reattribution training	Assertiveness skills
Decatastrophizing	Role-playing
Use of coping statements	Modeling
Cognitive modeling	Activity scheduling
	Homework

Table 23.4

Established but Unproven Cognitive-Behavioral Procedures

Perceptual shifting
Environmental practice
Paradoxical procedures
Biofeedback

Table 23.5

Nonmainstream Cognitive-Behavioral Procedures

Shaming techniques
Use of altered states such as hypnosis

bances, the many mechanisms through which this occurs and leads to, or interacts with, the child's cognitive, behavioral, affective, and biochemical disturbances must be explored. We also would concur with Mahoney and Nezworski (1985) who argue for incorporating concepts from object relations theory into cognitive-behavioral formulations of the development of the child's self-schemata.

Most existing cognitive-behavioral interventions appear too simplistic and overly reliant on adult treatment models for their methods and procedures. They fail to recognize the basic developmental characteristic of youths—they are immersed within the family and school environments, both of which have a profound effect on them. An example of the simplicity is the current literature that leaves the reader with the impression that problem-solving training is a panacea for childhood disturbances. While problem-solving skills are related to adjustment, many other variables may contribute to healthy adjustment or the lack thereof. However, a more recent and promising trend in the literature seems to grow from the recognition that more encompassing interventions that include integrated treatment components for the child, family, and classroom are necessary to produce long-lasting and meaningful change (Braswell & Bloomquist, 1991; Stark, 1990). This expansion of the targets of intervention and the use of significant others in the child's environment needs to be a focus of continued development.

Our own clinical experience indicates that the field also would be well advised to continue to work toward developmentally sensitive treatment programs. While this statement holds true across age groups, 2 age groups in particular have been overlooked: very young children who typically are treated through play therapy and children of middle school age. Very little attention has been paid to the merging of play and cognitive-behavioral therapies. Meichenbaum (1977) provides the reader with one of the few relevant descriptions. Middle school children have unique needs. This is a time of great disparity in development, as some youngsters are clearly pubescent while others lag far behind. At this time some of a youngster's first expressions of adolescent independence appear, which require an adjustment on the part of the family. These youngsters typically see themselves as "too cool" for the intervention programs that have been developed for children while they are not cognitively mature enough to maximally benefit from the interventions designed for older adolescents. A major developmental concern that has received inadequate attention is the description of methods for creating developmentally sensitive and thus engaging methods for delivering cognitive-behavioral ther-

apy. Children often view traditional procedures as "boring," and many times the concepts are too complex for youngsters to understand fully. In our treatment program for depressed youths, we have been developing and piloting illustrated cartoon or comic books that facilitate understanding and acquiring various therapeutic skills. We also have been working on the creation of a variety of games that children can play that teach them therapeutic skills or concepts.

A major concern both conceptually and from a treatment standpoint is comorbidity. It is becoming apparent that children commonly experience multiple psychological disorders at one time. The implications for theory and practice are great. For example, what are the cognitive, behavioral, affective, and environmental differences between a depressed youngster with and without a co-occurring oppositional defiant disorder? What would be the difference in treatment programs for these children and their families? The development of empirically based and integrated treatment programs will be necessary to address the needs of these youngsters successfully.

REFERENCES

Agras, W. S., Schneider, J. A., Arnow, B., Raeburn, S. D., & Telch, C. F. (1989). Cognitive-behavioral and response-prevention treatments for bulimia nervosa. *Journal of Counsulting and Clinical Psychology, 57,* 215–221.

Bandura, A. (1974). Behavior theory and the models of man. *American Psychologist, 29,* 859–869.

Beck, A. T. (1967). *Depression: Clinical, experimental, and theoretical aspects.* New York: Harper & Row.

Beck, A. T. (1976). *Cognitive therapy and the emotional disorders.* New York: International Universities Press.

Braswell, L., & Bloomquist, M. L. (1991). *Cognitive behavior therapy with ADHD children: Child, family, and school interventions.* New York: Guilford Press.

Bugental, D. B., Whalen, C. K., & Henker, B. (1977). Causal attributions of hyperactive children and motivational an interactionist position. *Child Development, 48,* 874–884.

Camp, B. W., Blom, G. F., Herbert, F., & van Doornick, W. J. (1977). "Think aloud": A program for developing self-control in young aggressive boys. *Journal of Abnormal Child Psychology, 5,* 157–169.

Caracciolo, E., Moderato, P., & Perini, S. (1985). On childhood autism: A few methodological punctualization and intervention prospects. First International Convention on the Social Learning of Psychotics: Elimination of the psychiatric hospital—Utopia or reality? *Rivista Sperimentale di Freniatria e Medicina Legale delle Alienazioni Mentali, 109,* 1381–1387.

Cautela, J. R. (1967). Covert sensitization. *Psychological Reports, 20,* 459–468.

Coopersmith, S. (1967). *The antecedents of self-esteem.* San Francisco: Freeman.

Dember, W. (1974). Motivation and the cognitive revolution. *American Psychologist, 29,* 161–168.

Ellis, A. (1962). *Reason and emotion in psychotherapy.* New York: Lyle Stuart Press.

Ellis, A., & Bernard, M. E. (Eds.). (1983). *Rational-emotive approaches to the problems of childhood.* New York: Plenum Press.

Elkin, A. (1983). Working with children in groups. In A. Ellis & M. E. Bernard (Eds.), *Rational-emotive approaches to the problems of childhood* (pp. 485–508). New York: Plenum Press.

Epstein, N. (1983). Cognitive therapy with couples. In A. Freeman (Ed.), *Cognitive therapy with couples and groups* (pp. 107–124). New York: Plenum Press.

Epstein, N., Schlesinger, S. E., & Dryden, W. (1988). Concepts and methods of cognitive-behavioral family treatment. In N. Epstein S. E. Schlesinger & W. Dryden (Eds.), *Cognitive-behavioral therapy with families* (pp. 5–83). New York: Brunner/Mazel.

Foreyt, J. P., & Kordo, A. T. (1983). Cognitive and behavioral treatment of childhood and adolescent obesity. In A. E. Ellis & M. E. Bernard (Eds.), *Rational-emotive approaches to the problems of childhood* (pp. 241–270). New York: Plenum Press.

Greenberg, L. S., & Safran, J. D. (1984). Integrating affect and cognition: A perspective on therapeutic change. *Cognitive Therapy and Research, 8,* 559–578.

Haley, B. M. T., Fine, S. L., Marriage, K., Moretti, M. M., & Freeman, R. J. (1985). Cognitive bias and depression in psychiatrically disturbed children and adolescents. *Journal of Consulting and Clinical Psychology, 53,* 535–537.

Halford, K. W. (1983). Teaching rational self-talk to help socially isolated children and youth. In A. E. Ellis & M. E. Bernard (Eds.), *Rational-emotive approaches to the problems of childhood* (pp. 241–270). New York: Plenum Press.

Hollon, S. D., & Kriss, M. R. (1984). Cognitive factors in clinical research and practice. *Clinical Psychology Review, 4,* 35–76.

Homme, L. E. (1965). Perspectives in psychology: XXIV. Control of coverants, the operants of the mind. *Psychological Record, 15,* 501–511.

Ingram, R. E., & Kendall, P. C. (1986). Cognitive clinical psychology: Implications of an information processing perspective. In R. E. Ingram (Ed.), *Information processing approaches to clinical psychology* (pp. 3–21). New York: Academic Press.

Jay, S. M., Elliott, C. H., Katz, E., & Siegel, S. E. (1987). Cognitive-behavioral and pharmacologic interventions for childrens' distress during painful medical procedures. *Journal of Consulting and Clinical Psychology, 55,* 860–865.

Kagan, J., Rosman, B. L., Day, D., Albert, J., & Phillips, W. (1964). Information in the child: Significance of analytic and reflective attitudes. *Psychological Monographs, 78* (1,).

Kanfer, F. H. (1970). Self-regulation: Research, issues, and speculations. In C. Neuringer & J. L. Michael (Eds.), *Behavior modification in clinical psychology,* (pp. 178–220). New York: Appleton-Century-Crofts.

Kaslow, N. J., Rehm, L. P. & Siegel, A. W. (1984). Social-cognitive and cognitive correlates of depression in children. *Journal of Abnormal Child Psychology, 12,* 605–620.

Kaslow, N. J., Stark, K. D., Printz, B., Livingston, R., & Tsai, S. (1992). Cognitive Triad Inventory for Children: Development and relationship to depression and anxiety. *Journal of Clinical Child Psychology, 21,* 339–347.

Kazdin, A. E. (1978). *History of behavior modification: Experimental foundations of contemporary research.* Baltimore, MD: University Park Press.

Kazdin, A. E., French, N. H., Unis, A. S., Esveldt-Dawson, K., & Sherick, R. B. (1983). Hopelessness, depression, and suicidal intent among psychiatrically disturbed inpatient children. *Journal of Consulting and Clinical Psychology, 51,* 504–510.

Kendall, P. C. (1985). Toward a cognitive-behavioral model of child psychopathology and a critique of related interventions. *Journal of Abnormal Child Psychology, 13,* 357–372.

Kendall, P. C. (1991). *Child and adolescent therapy: Cognitive-behavioral procedures.* New York: Guilford Press.

Kendall, P. C., & Braswell, L. (1993). *Cognitive-behavioral therapy for impulsive children.* New York: Guilford Press.

Keroack, J. (1987). Behavior therapies for social phobia. *Revue de Modification du Comportement, 17,* 152–178.

Mahoney, M. J. (1974). *Cognition and behavior modification.* Cambridge, MA: Ballinger.

Mahoney, M. J. (1982). Psychotherapy and human change processes. In P. Pliner, K. R. Blankstein, & M. M. Parks (Eds.), *Psychotherapy research and behavior change* (pp. 73–122). Washington, DC. American Psychiatric Press.

Mahoney, M. J., & Arnkoff, D. (1978). Cognitive and self-control therapies. In S. L. Garfield & A. E. Bergin (Eds.), *Handbook of psychotherapy and behavior change* (Vol. 2, 689–722). New York: John Wiley & Sons.

Mahoney, M. J., & Nezworski, M. T. (1985). Cognitive-behavioral approaches to children's problems. *Journal of Abnormal Child Psychology, 13,* 467–476.

Matson, J. L., Rotatori, A. F., & Helsel, W. J. (1983). Development of a rating scale to measure social skills in children: The Matson Evaluation of Social Skills with Youngsters (MESSY). *Behavioral Research and Therapy, 41,* 335–340.

Meichenbaum, D. (1977). *Cognitive-behavior modification: An integrative approach.* New York: Plenum Press.

Meyers, A. W., & Craighead, W. E. (Eds.), (1984). *Cognitive behavior therapy for children.* New York: Plenum.

Ollendick, T. H., & Cerny, J. A. (1980). *Clinical behavior therapy with children.* New York: Plenum Press.

Ollendick, T. H., Hagopian, L. P., & Huntzinger, R. M. (1991). Cognitive-behavior therapy with nighttime fearful children. *Journal of Behavior Therapy and Experimental Psychiatry, 22,* 113–121.

Petti, T. A., Bornstein, M., Delamater, A., & Conner, C. K. (1980). Evaluation and multimodality treatment of a depressed prepubertal girl. *Journal of the American Academy of Child Psychiatry, 19,* 690–702.

Reinecke, M. A., Dattilio, F. M., & Freeman, A. (1996). *Cognitive therapy with children and adolescents.* New York: Guilford Press.

Singer, L. T., Ambuel, B., Wade, S., & Jaffe, A. C. (1992). Cognitive-behavioral treatment of health-impairing food phobias in children. *Journal of the American Academy of Child and Adolescent Psychiatry, 31,* 847–852.

Stark, K. D. (1990). *Childhood depression: School-based intervention.* New York: Guilford Press.

Stark, K. D., Humphrey, L. L., Laurent, J. L., Livingston, R., & Christopher, J. C. (1993). Cognitive, behavioral, and family factors in the differentiation of depressive and anxiety disorders during childhood. *Journal of Consulting and Clinical Psychology, 61,* 878–886.

Stark, K. D. & Kendall, P. C. (1996). *Treating depressed children: Therapist manual for "Action".* Ardmore, PA: Workbook Publishing.

Stein, D. B., & Smith, E. D. (1990). The "REST" program: A new treatment system for the oppositional defiant adolescent. *Adolescence, 25,* 891–904.

Turk, D. C., & Salovey, P. (1985). Cognitive structures, cognitive processes, and cognitive-behavior modification: I. Client issues. *Cognitive Therapy and Research, 9,* 1–17.

Walco, G. A., & Varni, J. W. (1991). Cognitive-behavioral interventions for children with chronic illnesses. In P. Kendall (Ed.), *Child and adolescent therapy: Cognitive behavioral procedures* (pp. 209–244). New York: Guilford Press.

Whitman, T. L., Scherzinger, M. F., & Sommer, K. S. (1991). Cognitive instruction and mental retardation. In P. Kendall (Ed.), *Child and adolescent therapy: Cognitive behavioral procedures* (pp. 276–315). New York: Guilford Press.

Wong, B. Y. L., Harris, K. R., & Graham, S. (1991). Academic applications of cognitive-behavioral programs with learning disabled students. In P. Kendall (Ed.), *Child and adolescent therapy: Cognitive behavioral procedures* (pp. 245–275). New York: Guilford Press.

Wright, J. H., Thase, M. E., Beck, A. T., & Ludgate, J. W. (1993). *Cognitive therapy with inpatients.* New York: Guilford Press.

---

24 / Hypnotherapy

Anthony Spirito and Scott Powers

There are many different definitions of hypnosis and many theories, which emphasize a variety of underlying mechanisms, such as physiologic, learning, cultural, and cognitive, each postulated to explain the efficacy of hypnotherapy. (See Lynn and Rhie [1991] for a more complete description of the different theoretical stances.) The abundance of theories and definitions reflects the many different opinions about what hypnosis is, whether it is helpful, and even whether a subject is in a hypnotic state or not. Nonetheless, there are certain commonalities across most theories (Lynn & Rhie, 1991): (1) the context created by the interpersonal interaction between hypnotherapist and subject is key to the response; (2) subjects may have little awareness of their behavior under hypnosis—that is, there is some degree of self-deception by hypnotic subjects; (3) subjects find very creative ways to respond to suggestions; and (4) no simple determinant, whether social, cognitive, or psychological, can adequately account for behavior as complex as that seen under hypnosis.

Clinicians commonly cite Erickson's (1958) definition of hypnosis: "a state of intensified attention and receptiveness and increased responsiveness to an idea or set of ideas." Hypnotherapy is a treatment approach that takes place once the hypnotic trance is entered, during which either the therapist or the patient (i.e., self-hypnosis) delivers therapeutic techniques. After entering a hypnotic trance, the patient is more open to suggestion, which in turn, can then lead to behavior change. The purpose of this chapter is to acquaint the reader with the technique of hypnotherapy and symptoms that might be best addressed via hypnotherapy. A good overview of hypnosis can be found in Crasilneck and Hall (1985).

Background

Hypnosis can be traced back to ancient times when the use of suggestion and entry into trance states were common in religious rituals and ceremonies as well as in the healing arts. In some of the original work by Mesmer in the 18th century, which marked beginnings of the modern history of hypnosis, children were occasional subjects. By the end of the 19th century, evidence had accumulated that children could be hypnotized, and hypnosis was being used for both medical and psychological problems. Interested readers may consult both detailed (Tinterow, 1970) and concise (Gardner & Olness, 1981) histories of hypnosis with children.

Developmental Considerations

Gardner and Olness (1981) have summarized a number of variables believed to affect the success of child hypnotherapy. Gender differences have not been found. Age is an important characteristic, with findings indicating that peak susceptability is between 7 and 14 years of age. There is a modest positive relationship with intelligence. Children in the stage of concrete operations (using Piagetian terminology) are presumed to be more susceptible, because they are less easily concerned with abstract issues.

Therapist-Directed vs. Self-hypnosis

One major difference in the technique of hypnosis is whether a self-hypnosis or therapist-directed procedure is used. In a self-hypnosis procedure, the original hypnotherapy session between therapist and child usually is tape-recorded and then the child is asked to listen to the tape—must often on a daily basis—to reinforce the suggestions used in the original session. In a therapist-directed procedure, hypnosis is induced only by the therapist during 1 or more scheduled sessions.

Indications/Contraindications

Hypnotherapy has been suggested as an appropriate intervention technique for a variety of medical and psychological problems in childhood. Clinicians should consider relaxation training and biofeedback as comparable techniques and select the procedure most applicable to the particular symptom and patient. Similarly, individual psychotherapy and/or family therapy may be more appropriate interventions than hypnosis, depending on the specific circumstances of a case.

Hypnotherapy is particularly useful for conversion disorders, including such symptoms as hysterical coughing, sneezing, and hiccups. Anxiety disorders, including specific phobias, may be appropriate targets for hypnotherapy, although relaxation training alone often is sufficient to address anxiety problems. Pain secondary to medical procedures and/or disease is a common medical problem addressed via hypnotherapy. (See Hilgard and Hilgard [1983] for overview). Asthma and dermatologic problems, including eczema and warts (Spanos, Stenstrom, & Johnston, 1988), are other conditions often addressed via hypnotherapy. Hypnosis sometimes is used to uncover hidden conflicts and memories that have been repressed by the patient; however, work with uncovering techniques is relatively uncommon and done only by skilled hypnotherapists.

There are several important contraindications when using hypnotherapy with children. First, in many instances another form of psychotherapeutic treatment is a more appropriate first choice. Second, if secondary gain maintains the symptom, hypnotherapy will not be effective because of predictable patient resistance. The child's environment may maintain the symptom inadvertently, and in any cases the child will not want to give up the symptom, so motivation will be low. Third, if the child or adolescent has particular concerns about control, and this issue has not been adequately addressed in preparing the patient for hypnotherapy, then resistance may be encountered or a negative reaction will occur. Fourth, children who are very anxious, have unusual thought patterns, or a formal thought disorder are not good candidates for hypnosis, because they may feel they are being controlled by the therapist in a way that will increase their anxiety.

Process of Hypnotherapy

PATIENT PREPARATION

It is very important to speak with parents first to allay misconceptions and fears regarding hypnosis, or else the treatment approach will not be successful. Common misperceptions to examine include believing that hypnosis means a loss of consciousness, that only weak-willed persons can be hypnotized, that it is possible to get "stuck" in a trance, and that subjects will tell secrets or be made to do something they find distressing. Those who are afraid of losing control often stare "I can't be hypnotized" is this belief should also be addressed, if necessary.

It is also important to assess both the parent's and child's motivation for hypnotherapy and to reassure the child regarding its efficacy. In most cases, it is helpful to take an entire session to review the symptoms and explain how hypnosis will help for the presenting problem. Once the hypnotherapist explain why it will work, then it is important to describe the different steps involved in hypnotherapy in order to address any unstated fears or concerns. Often it is helpful to schedule the appointment to conduct the hypnotherapy session a few days after the initial session. The waiting period may increase motivation and enhance expectancy effects.

Take, as an example, a 12-year-old child who, after having been evaluated by a number of medical specialists who ruled out any organic basis for the symptoms, was referred for treatment of coughing, which occurred continuously every 5 to 10 seconds over a 1-month period. After deciding that hypnotherapy was an appropriate intervention, the hypnotherapist explained the reasons why people cough to the child, including the idea of a "cough center" in the brain. It is much more important to give an understandable, simplified rationale than a complex albeit complete discussion of the origins of a symptom. A sample introduction in this particular case might be as follows:

The problem you have is that the switch which turns on your cough center is stuck in the 'on' position. It originally got turned on for a good reason, such as a foreign body or a virus, but for some reason, in your case, it got stuck 'on.' You've taken a lot of different medicines that usually make coughs stop. Since they didn't work, we need to do something to make your cough center turn off. There are no medicines that turn off the cough center; it's in your brain. So hypnosis is the only way that doctors have to turn off the cough center.

When using hypnotherapy with children, it is very important to establish rapport and make them feel at ease. It is important to present hypnotherapy as an enjoyable but novel experience. Finally, it is important to tell children that the therapist will serve as a teacher; the greater their motivation and the harder they try, the greater the likelihood of symptom removal occurring in a short time.

INDUCTION TECHNIQUES

There are 3 basic components to hypnotherapy: hypnotic induction, deep relaxation, and suggestion. An *induction procedure* typically is used to initiate the hypnotherapy. Induction techniques refer to methods used to achieve a trance state. The induction technique sets the stage for the entire procedure and is one of the main distinguishing features between relaxation and hypnosis. Resistance is sometimes encountered in this stage. Consequently, the hypnotherapist must have a wide variety of induction techniques ready for use if resistance is encountered. The induction techniques used depends both on patient variables and therapist preference and experience. However, direct techniques such as eye fixation typically are used with children. Eye fixation refers to fixating eyes on some point or object, such as a coin, so that the eyeballs are rolled forward in their sockets and eventually will close due to gravity. Any number of other visual images or auditory images can be used as induction techniques. For a thorough discussion of different induction techniques for children of different ages, see Gardner and Olness (1981). Although highly hypnotizable persons can be hypnotized without formal induction, successful induction usually increases the efficacy of the entire procedure, especially responsiveness to suggestion. Some hypnotherapists prefer to eliminate direct induction procedures when using a self-hypnosis approach.

Once the hypnotic induction procedure has taken place and a trance state has been achieved, any number of *relaxation and deepening procedures* can be used as the next step in hypnotherapy. Questions regarding imagery and the ability to relax should be asked first to devise the best relaxation procedures for the child. The various relaxation and deepening techniques discussed in Chapter 25 also can be used during hypnotherapy.

Once relaxation is evident, *hypnotic suggestions* can be made. The depth of the relaxed/

trance state and the specific suggestions used depend on the child's presenting problem. The depth of the trance can vary during the course of the hypnotic procedure and gives the clinician an idea on how well the session is proceeding. In a light trance state, the eyelids flutter, posture is relaxed, lips are slightly parted, and the child reports a dry mouth (because of breathing through the mouth). Light levels of a hypnotic trance are very comparable to having performed a relaxation exercise. In a medium state, slow, audible breathing is evident and the hand and arm are droopy if picked up by the therapist. In a deep trance, partial or complete posthypnotic amnesia may be evident, as is "glove anesthesia." The likelihood of inducing a deep level of hypnotic trance varies according to the subject's hypnotic susceptibility and the therapist's goals and skills. Deeper trance states are necessary in addressing certain symptoms. For example, if trying to achieve anesthesia in order to help a child with a painful medical procedure, then a deep trance state should be induced before suggestions are made.

When making a suggestion, it is important for the therapist to state that something will happen as a result of the hypnotherapy; when exactly it will occur is the only question. Most times the therapist states very clearly what symptom will be worked on and what suggestions will be used. Only rarely should a posthypnotic suggestion be used without a child's knowledge. Open-ended suggestions should be used to maximize the chances of success. Experienced hypnotherapists enhance suggestions with a number of techniques, including modulating voice tone and pace of the speech, emphasizing key words, using simple words in the present tense, frequent pauses, and repetition. A range of suggestions for different symptoms can be found in Gardner and Olness (1981) as well as in the work published by the American Society of Clinical Hypnosis (1973).

The following suggestion might be used with the hysterical cougher described earlier:

Now that you are in a very deeply relaxed state, we can talk to your unconscious mind [pause] to shut off your cough center. [pause] There's no longer any need for it to remain on. [pause] Picture the cough center in your mind as a switch that is stuck in the "on" position. [pause] Now just imagine the switch very slowly moving down to the "off" position—[pause] just picture the switch moving slowly downward [pause], very slowly, al-most imperceptibly. [pause] Know that it will eventually move all the way to the "off" position and turn totally off—it may be right now, or later today [pause], tomorrow, or next week [pause], but it will turn off.

To end a hypnotherapy session, guidelines suggested in Chapter 25 for relaxation should be followed. Also, children should be told they will remember everything about the hypnotherapy session in order to help them achieve symptom relief.

CLINICAL PROGRESS/DURATION

A typical session lasts from 20 to 45 minutes. The course of treatment varies according to the presenting problem and the response to the first session. For some children, symptom removal will occur after the initial session; for others, the procedure must be repeated over several weeks to gain the full effect. Where appropriate, a tape can be made of the procedure, and the child can be asked to practice the technique at home (i.e., self-hypnosis).

INTERACTION WITH OTHER INTERVENTIONS

Often an overlap exists among the procedures called hypnotherapy, self-hypnosis, relaxation, and meditation. The labels used depend, at least in part, on the clinician's training and preferences. As discussed previously, hypnotherapy is just one tool in the therapeutic array from which the clinician should choose in developing a comprehensive treatment plan for a particular child.

QUALIFICATIONS OF THE CLINICIAN

Use of hypnosis, whether with children or adults, requires special training and supervision. Workshops vary in quality, but those routinely offered by the American Society of Clinical Hypnosis and the Society for Clinical and Experimental Hypnosis are typically of high quality. Training itself does not guarantee success as a hypnotherapist; some clinicians are better than others at this specialty. In addition, practice and experience in hypnotherapy are needed in order to increase the hypnotherapist's confidence and skill. A background in relaxation training is particularly useful, because deep relaxation plays such an important role in hypnotherapy.

EQUIPMENT/TECHNOLOGICAL CONSIDERATIONS

There are no equipment considerations when using hypnotherapy. A quiet room with a comfortable chair is most useful.

OUTCOME STUDIES

A large number of case studies of hypnotherapy exist for a wide range of presenting problems. (See Gardner and Olness [1981]). Very few studies, however, use multiple subjects of children or adolescents. One example is a study of 12 adolescents with cancer, in which hypnosis was used to reduce postchemotherapy vomiting. Eight of the subjects improved significantly (Zeltzer, Kellerman, Ellenberg, & Dash, 1983). Group design outcome studies of hypnosis with children are even rarer, and the results are mixed. In one study on pain and anxiety associated with invasive medical procedures with childhood cancer patients, Zeltzer and LeBaron (1982) found the hypnosis group was slightly superior to the nonhypnotic intervention group. Another study (Katz, Kellerman, & Ellenberg, 1987) compared hypnosis with a nondirective play comparison group and found equal improvements in pain and anxiety in both groups. Thus, at the present time, hypnotherapy is a practiced technique, but it is not mainstream. The future of hypnosis and hypnotherapy will depend on the results of carefully designed outcome studies.

REFERENCES

American Society of Clinical Hypnosis. (1973). *A syllabus on hypnosis and a handbook of therapeutic suggestions.* Privately published.

Crasilneck, H., & Hall, J. (1985). *Clinical hypnosis: Principles and applications* (2nd ed.). New York: Grune & Stratton.

Erickson, M. H. (1958). Hypnosis in painful terminal illness. *American Journal of Clinical Hypnosis, 1,* 117–121.

Gardner, G. G., & Olness, K. (1981). *Hypnosis and hypnotherapy with children.* New York: Grune & Stratton.

Hilgard, E. R., & Hilgard, J. R. (1983). *Hypnosis in the relief of pain* (rev. ed.). Los Altos, CA: William Kaufmann.

Katz, E., Kellerman, J., & Ellenberg, L. (1987). Hypnosis in the reduction of acute pain and distress in children with cancer. *Journal of Pediatric Psychology, 12,* 379–394.

Lynn, S. J., & Rhie, J. W. (1991). Theories of hypnosis: An introduction. In S. Lynn & J. Rhie (Eds.), *Theories of hypnosis—Current models and perspectives.* New York: Guilford Press.

Spanos, N. P., Stenstrom, R. J., & Johnston, J. C. (1988). Hypnosis, placebo, and suggestions in the treatment of warts. *Psychosomatic Medicine, 50,* 245–260.

Tinterow, M. M. (1970). *Foundations of hypnosis: From Mesmer to Freud.* Springfield, IL: Charles C Thomas.

Zeltzer, L., Kellerman, J., Ellenberg, L., & Dash, J. (1983). Hypnosis for reduction of vomiting associated with chemotherapy and disease in adolescents with cancer. *Journal of Adolescent Health Care, 4,* 77–84.

Zeltzer, L., & LeBaron, S. (1982). Hypnosis and nonhypnotic techniques for reduction of pain and anxiety during painful procedures in children and adolescents with cancer. *Journal of Pediatrics, 101,* 1032–1035.

25 / Relaxation Training

Scott Powers and Anthony Spirito

Relaxation training is used to help children and adolescents who display a variety of presenting problems, particularly disorders that involve negative emotional and/or physiological arousal states, such as anxiety and pain. Such training involves teaching the child a skill that, when used, results in a sensation that is incompatible with or counteracts these negative emotional and/or somatic states. Relaxation skills can be conceptualized as pragmatic, self-directed, and active coping strategies. Mental health professionals who work with children often have opportunities to use this treatment technique within the context of a comprehensive, individualized therapeutic program.

This chapter describes the use of relaxation training for the practicing child clinician and discusses the types of relaxation skills that can be learned, how patients should be prepared for training, and how to decide which skills to teach for different presenting problems. The chapter also covers the use of relaxation training with other treatments. Emphasis is placed on application as opposed to basic mechanisms of action or theory. Readers interested in a scientific review of relaxation training can refer to other sources (e.g., Lichstein, 1988).

Background and Conceptual Framework

Although the exact origins of the use of relaxation to manage negative emotional states are difficult to ascertain, Edmund Jacobson (1938) often is credited with initiating the formal use of progressive muscle relaxation training. Since his original procedure was introduced, a number of variations of the technique have developed. Active debate continues regarding the mechanisms of action in the relaxation response. Current frameworks focus on a physiologically mediated response, a cognitively mediated response, or a combination of the 2. Physiological conceptualizations highlight the actual somatic changes characteristic of the relaxed state, including decreased muscle tension, heart rate, and oxygen consumption. Cognitive conceptualizations suggest that perceived success at relaxation results in feelings of self-control and self-efficacy, which, in turn, lead to better and more frequent efforts to cope with an actual or perceived stressor (Bandura, 1977).

Indications/Contraindications

PRESENTING PROBLEMS

Relaxation training has been employed for a wide variety of presenting problems of children and adolescents, sometimes as the primary mode of intervention and sometimes as an adjunct to another intervention (Richter, 1984). The problems that seem to respond best to relaxation training include anxiety-based disorders and stress-related symptoms occurring secondary to medical problems (Gagnon, Hudnall, & Andrasik, 1992; Walker, 1979). Anxiety-based disorders include specific phobias, sleep disorders secondary to anxious mood, social anxiety, and more generalized anxiety conditions. Examples of stress-related symptoms include migraine and/or tension headaches, recurrent abdominal pain, fear and distress in reaction to invasive medical procedures, and concomitants of chronic illnesses such as nausea and vomiting in cancer patients secondary to chemotherapy.

DEVELOPMENTAL CONSIDERATIONS

Relaxation training is used most often with children 7 years old or older. However, with developmentally appropriate adjustments to the training procedures, relaxation training procedures, especially those emphasizing imagery, have been used successfully with intellectually limited children as well as preschoolers (Harvey, 1979; Koeppen, 1974). Because of the cognitive, attentional, and social-emotional demands of the treatment, the use of standard relaxation training protocols is best suited for older children. Children need to be able to understand the rationale of using relaxation to combat feelings such as fear or pain. They also must be able to concentrate on their bodily sensations for an extended time and have the social-emotional maturity and self-directedness to learn both how to manage stress and how to sustain the practice necessary to acquire and maintain the relaxation skills. In most instances, a child who has not reached a developmental level consistent with these cognitive, emotional, and behavioral demands will not succeed with standard relaxation training.

CONTRAINDICATIONS

It is quite rare for a child to have untoward effects from learning relaxation. The one exception involves a child becoming emotionally upset because of the novelty of the sensation of relaxation (Heide & Borkovec, 1984). This sensation might be especially problematic for a child who has experienced a number of traumatic events that are "relieved" in a state of relaxation.

Preparation for Initiating Treatment

QUALIFICATIONS OF THE CLINICIAN

The process of teaching a child to relax is relatively straightforward; it is easily acquired by a trained clinician, especially when working with older children and adolescents. However, in choosing what type of relaxation procedure fits the individual client's developmental level, presenting problem, and coping style, the clinical decision making involved is more complex. Indeed, tailoring the treatment for the child is a key to its effectiveness; a clinician will need supervision when learning how to decide which form of relaxation training to use with children who exhibit different problems, temperaments, physiologic responses, and imaging abilities.

EQUIPMENT AND TECHNOLOGICAL CONSIDERATIONS

For standard relaxation training, the only equipment needed is a tape recorder. Tape-recording relaxation procedures helps improve both compliance with home practice (which typically is recommended) as well as more focused training in the procedure, especially at the start of training. After the child has used the procedure for a number of weeks and can demonstrate that he or she knows how to complete the relaxation procedure without a tape, the child can be weaned from the tape to practice alone. Clinicians also would benefit from accumulating a number of standard relaxation scripts from various sources. This collection of scripts (and its continued growth) helps in tailoring treatment to the child's needs. In addition, it keeps the clinician up to date on innovations in the use of relaxation training with children and adolescents. Scripts can be found in sources such as Bernstein and Borkovec (1973), Cautela and Groden (1978), Gardner and Olness (1981), and Koeppen (1974).

Description of Process and Variations

TYPES/CATEGORIES

Relaxation training typically involves one or more of the following techniques: progressive muscle relaxation, diaphragmatic or meditative breathing, autogenic training, or imagery. Progressive muscle relaxation training involves alternate tensing and relaxing of various muscle groups throughout the body (Jacobson, 1938). Its goal is to teach the child the contrast between tension and relaxation via systematic physical manipulation (i.e., tensing a specific muscle group and then relaxing it) along with concentration on the associated sensations. Meditative breathing involves systematic inhalation and exhalation (Benson, 1975). Again, the child learns the relationship between tension and relaxation by attention to breathing, which produces somatic changes in a systematic fashion. Autogenic training relies on a cognitive means of producing the sensation of relaxation (Luthe, 1969). By repeating specific words or phrases such as "relax" or "calm," the child experiences sensations of relaxation. With sufficient practice, a conditioned response can develop such that simply repeating the word can result in relaxation. Imagery also relies on a more passive, cognitive means of producing a state of relaxation. In this procedure, the child visualizes a pleasant scene or favored activity, such as playing in the woods or taking a ride on a favorite amusement park adventure, in order to achieve a state of relaxation (Gardner & Olness, 1981).

PREPARATION OF THE PATIENT

When preparing a child for relaxation training, it is important to give an age-appropriate explanation of the technique. One goal is to have the child distinguish between "relaxing" and "relaxation." Often it is helpful to explain to the child that sitting at home watching television is a relaxing activity but there is no physiologic effect. However, when one is relaxed after doing a relaxation exercise, there is an actual physical effect. Depending on the child's age, the therapist can describe the fact that, with relaxation, there is a decrease in muscle tension throughout the body, a slight decrease in heart rate, a decrease in the amount of oxygen consumption, and an increase in blood flow or peripheral temperature.

It is important for the therapist to explain in easily understandable terms how the physical effects of relaxation will help the child's particular symptoms. For example, if the symptom is a muscle contraction headache, the therapist can describe how a relaxation procedure can have a direct effect on the muscle tension in the child's forehead that is contributing to the headache. Spending sufficient time on the rationale ensures that the child has a good understanding of both relaxation on the one hand and the link between the relaxation procedure and the particular symptom on the other. It is helpful to explain the procedure with both parents and child present, so that parents also can ask questions and understand the rationale for this approach. Then, if resistance occurs at home, or if the child has questions about the technique, the parent will be better able to address them.

A second goal in preparing a child for relaxation is to assess the relaxation procedure best suited to him or her. As discussed, there are a number of different ways to induce relaxation. The efficacy of relaxation for any particular problem is directly related to the clinician's ability to tailor the relaxation procedure to the child in question. The following is one assessment approach that we have found helpful.

First, the child is asked to make a fist with the right hand, hold it as tightly as possible, feel the tension and pressure in the arm as it is held (approximately 10 seconds), and then relax (opening the fingers of the hand and resting the arm on the chair). After having done so, the child is asked several questions, including "How does that feel?," (to see if the child describes the experience in a positive way) and "Does it feel better now that you let go than when you were tensing it?" In almost all cases, the child will say yes. Progressive muscle relaxation probably is contraindicated if the child says no. The child is asked to describe the feeling in the hand and arm. If it cannot be described, the clinician should present a series of statements, such as "Some people say it feels 'tingly' after they tense and loosen their arms"; "Some people say it feels 'warm' (or cold)"; and "Some people say it feels 'heavy' (or light)." These questions should help the clinician determine whether this was an enjoyable experience for the child and what particular adjective he or she uses to label a pleasant and relaxed state, for example, "tingly," "warm," "heavy." These adjectives are important because they will be the descriptors employed when making the relaxation tape for this child.

In next step in the assessment process, the child is asked to shut his or her eyes and to imagine a feeling of relaxation in the left hand using the following description: "Imagine a kind of relaxation that starts in your fingertips and moves slowly up the fingers, making all the muscles [use the appropriate words which the child has chosen, e.g., "making all the muscles warm, limp, tingly, etc."]. Imagine that feeling moving up through your fingers past your knuckles into the palms of your hands. Let the palms of your hands become _____ (e.g., "warm and tingly").

Following this procedure, which lasts about 10 seconds, the child is asked if he or she was able to imagine the sensations described. Then the child is asked to describe the sensations experienced or if any different words would better describe them. Finally, the child is asked which procedure felt better, the imagery-based procedure just completed or the tensing and relaxing of the right hand. Based on the child's preference, the clinician decides whether to use a progressive-muscle whole-body relaxation procedure or an imagery-based whole-body relaxation procedure.

In the third step in the procedure, the child is asked to take a deep breath and hold it as long as possible. This provide the therapist some ideas of the child's lung capacity knowledge of which is helpful if mediative breathing technique are used. By so doing, the therapist will know approximately how long to ask the child to hold his breath during the procedure. This is especially important when working with children with asthma or other lung diseases.

Fourth, it is important to assess a child's imaging abilities. One easy way to do this is for the therapist to ask children to shut their eyes and describe their room. Differences between children who describe in detail the colors and objects in their room vs. those who offer a relatively brief and nonspecific description are obvious. The therapist can probe for imaging ability by asking children such questions as "What is the color of your bedspread?; The posters or pictures on the walls in your room?" And so on. It is also helpful to ask a child's favorite color. The spontaneity and the completeness of the descriptions suggest whether a focus on imagery is appropriate in the relaxation procedure vs. other techniques.

Finally, it is helpful to ask children if they have a favorite place. The most common response is Disney World or another amusement park. Sometimes young children will describe vacations they've had with their families. One relaxing image that some children describe is going to their grandparents' house; if it can be evoked, this is often a very powerful image. The images children describe are often quite different from those of adults, who tend to focus on the beach and mountains. Many children seem to select action images as their relaxing scene. This does not pose a problem, because the involvement of the child in the image, as opposed to the actual content of the image, seems to be the active component in achieving a relaxing effect.

RELAXATION TRAINING

Based on the assessment procedure just described, a relaxation procedure integrating the most appropriate techniques can be devised. Before making an audiotape of the procedure, the therapist should describe the different parts of the procedure that will be used. This helps prepare children for the procedure that is to follow. A sample procedure follows. It is a compilation of different techniques that have been taught over many years. By now it is difficult to cite any of the original sources; the authors' apologies are offered to anyone who recognizes their ideas in this script:

Lie back with your arms at your sides and get yourself in as comfortable a position as you can easily find. [pause] It helps if you close your eyes. [pause] I want you to start by taking a deep breath and holding it . . . feel the tension in your chest as you hold it . . . and then slowly let your breath out. Note the difference between the tension and relaxation. [Repeat twice]: This is a *simplified meditative breathing technique.* Now imagine a feeling that starts in your toes that is warm and relaxing. Imagine that feeling moving slowly past the balls of your feet [pause], through the arches of your feet [pause], through the entire foot [pause], and up past your ankle.

Note: If the child has identified a favorite color, an alternative procedure to enhance the *imagery-based whole-body relaxation* is to ask him or her to imagine the color moving up the body as follows:

Now I also want you to imagine this feeling of relaxation like a wave of color moving up your body, starting down in your toes with your favorite shade of red (or blue, pink, etc.), slowly moving up through the balls of your feet [pause], the wave moving up past your ankle into your calf muscles [pause], all the tension draining away [pause], your muscles getting loose and relaxed and moving up now past your knees into your thighs. [pause] Just imagine that wave of color moving up and, as that wave hits your thigh muscle, you notice those muscles beginning to feel loose, warm, and relaxed. [*Note:* We are assuming that the words used by the child to describe relaxation are warm, loose, relaxed]. [pause] Just notice now how your lower body is feeling more relaxed and comfortable [pause], a pleasant feeling. [pause]

Now imagine that feeling moving up past your hips into your stomach—that wave of red moving up, all the tension draining away [pause], muscles loose and relaxed [pause], the relaxing feeling moving up into your chest—any pain or tension, any discomfort just draining away, feeling yourself relaxed and calm [pause], and then up into your shoulders—all the tension draining away again. Notice a relaxed feeling as you imagine that wave of red moving through your shoulder muscles [pause], down your upper arms [pause], relaxed and calm [pause], down past your elbows into your forearms—a warm, relaxing feeling. [pause] That wave of red moving past your wrists into the palms of your hands, warm and relaxed [pause], down to your fingertips, relaxed and calm [pause], making your whole body relaxed.

Now that you've seen how to make your whole body relaxed, we can do the same for your neck and face by just imagining that wave moving up now through your neck muscles [pause], loose and warm [pause] past your chin [pause], the wave of red moving up past your lips and nose, all the tension draining away [pause], warm and comfortable, as it moves up past your eyes and forehead [pause], warm and relaxed, warm and comfortable over the top of your head [pause], your whole body is relaxed and calm.

Note: It is important to pace the whole-body relaxation procedure so that the child responds most beneficially. As the therapist recites the procedure, he or she can note whether the child stays engaged in the procedure or starts to have difficulty attending to the instructions. If the latter is true, it may be helpful to speed up the process a little bit and not focus so much on the relaxation in order to maintain the child's attention and interest in the procedure.

Now that you've made your whole body relaxed and calm, we can improve on these feelings of relaxation in the following way: I want you to just imagine yourself in your bedroom at home and about to walk down the stairs to watch some TV. You're barefoot and the stairs have very thick, deep, comfortable carpeting, and it feels very pleasant on your feet. Walk down the stairs very slowly because it feels so good as you walk through this thick carpeting. [pause] Count the stairs as you go along [pause], and, with each step you count, you'll become more and more relaxed.

Note: This procedure is known as a *deepening technique* and is commonly used in order to achieve a deep state of relaxation during a hypnotic procedure. It is a worthwhile technical addition when working with an attentive child. The assumption here is that this particular child has a bedroom on the second floor. Many children will be able to count exactly the number of stairs they have at home; and the therapist should use this

number. There are other ways to use a deepening procedure, such as counting trees on a walk through the forest, or counting waves as one sits on the beach. Once again, in the initial assessment procedure, the therapist must decide whether to use deepening and the best way to use it.

Count the first step—one—and notice your body getting loose and relaxed. [pause] Now two, calm and comfortable [pause], three, feelings of warmth and relaxation throughout your body.

Note: The therapist should continue this procedure, up to the chosen number of steps. There are many guidelines about how to enhance the deepening effect. Some simple ones for the therapist to keep in mind are that there should be a sufficiently long pause between the numbers and that the tone and the loudness of the voice should vary.

Now you are about to take your last step, and when you do so, a wave of relaxation will move throughout your entire body and you will feel your whole body totally relaxed and comfortable. And now the last step, ten. Feel that wave of red move up through your entire body as you become totally relaxed and comfortable. [pause] Now use your imagination and see yourself slowly moving over to a comfortable chair near your TV and taking the remote control. This is a special remote control that shows your own relaxing thoughts and images on the TV. Today your thoughts and images are of calm, relaxing places, the kinds we talked about earlier—being at your grandmother's house (going to the beach, etc.). [The child's chosen images are described.] The images will come on the TV. [pause] You can control the image with your thoughts. [pause] Try to stay on one image for a little while, but you can switch images if you find one more relaxing. Just use your imagination for the next few moments. [pause] As you do so, notice how your body becomes more and more relaxed.

Note: This imagery-based procedure is directed by the child him- or herself. The length of time the therapist allows the child to engage in the imagery varies, depending on the child's age and involvement in the relaxation procedure up to this point. However, it is better for the child to use the image in a short period of silence rather than too long a period during which time the child becomes distracted. In most cases, 30 seconds to a minute is long enough for this type of technique. Because this is self-directed, external noises and internal thoughts can disrupt the relaxation procedure very easily. Thus, it is also helpful to use the following statement before the child starts the self-directed imagery.

While you are relaxing, if you hear any noises they will not bother you. [pause] Just let them fade in and out, in and out, as you continue to focus on your relaxing image. [pause] If you have any thoughts that seem to distract you, just let them fade in and out, in and out, as you focus on this relaxing, calm image. [pause] Let's do so for the next few moments, being very relaxed and calm.

Note: After the tape has run for about 30 seconds, or if the child is squirming or having difficulty paying attention, this part of the procedure should be stopped.

The therapist can end the relaxation procedure with the following statement:

Now that you have been able to make yourself very relaxed and calm, you can count silently to yourself from 5 down to 1, and when you reach 1 you will feel alert and refreshed, almost as if you've taken a pleasant nap, and you can return to any activities feeling relaxed and comfortable and calm.

Note: As the tape recorder runs, the therapist counts, slowly (and silently) from 5 down to 1 and observes how slowly the child counts from 5 down to 1. The tape recorder is stopped when the child slowly begins to move around and open his or her eyes.

An alternative ending to this procedure can be used for children with sleep problems. In cases in which the child might use this tape during the day and also at night, the following statement can be added: "Now you have a choice; if you'd like [pause], you can drift off to sleep, a deep, peaceful, relaxing sleep [pause], or, if you prefer, you can count from 5 down to 1." [Repeat the above procedure.]

CLINICAL PROGRESS AND DURATION OF INTERVENTION

Both the measurement of clinical progress and the length of treatment are dependent on the particular presenting problem—its intensity, duration, frequency—and/or related disorders and on the effects of relaxation training on associated symptoms. Hence, while a minimum amount of direct training and practice is necessary to learn

such a new skill, the exact length of treatment for a given child is quite variable. The best gauge is a continuous assessment of clinical progress and of the effects of relaxation training on the presenting problem.

Measurements of clinical progress should be made frequently; typically, they include a self-report rating of relaxation by the child before and after a practice session (skill acquisition measure) and a rating of presenting problem frequency and/or intensity (treatment outcome measure). A skill acquisition rating can be made on a 0 to 10 scale, where 0 = "total relaxation" and 10 = "most tense possible" (or a descriptor specific to a presenting symptom). Skill acquisition also is judged by the child's ability to use the relaxation procedure without the audiotape. Treatment outcome ratings, such as headache frequency and intensity or the frequency of anxious episodes, also should be made on a daily basis. It is useful to give the child index cards with spaces for ratings each day at the end of each session. Also, the therapist should reinforce a child's practice efforts, for example, ending sessions with office computer games if the child has practiced the relaxation skills.

Outcome Studies

Mounting empirical evidence suggests that children can learn various forms of relaxation skills and actually can use such strategies in an effort to cope with physiological and psychological stressors (Masek, Spirito, & Fentress, 1984; Richter, 1984). Most of these research studies include relaxation training as part of a comprehensive treatment package. While not as plentiful or conclusive as research studies with adults, investigations that focus on relaxation training as the primary treatment for specific presenting problems such as pediatric headache (Masek & Hoag, 1990), painful medical procedures (Dahlquist, 1992), and anxiety (Powers & Rickard, in press) are increasing in number. At present, relaxation training with children is accepted and proven effective, especially when utilized as part of a comprehensive treatment package.

Interactions with Other Treatment

Relaxation is an integral part of 2 related treatment modalities, biofeedback (see Chapter 26) and hypnotherapy (see Chapter 24). Additionally, relaxation training often is one part of a comprehensive intervention package, combined with cognitive, behavioral, psychodynamic, and other therapeutic interventions.

REFERENCES

Bandura, A. (1977). Self-efficacy: Toward a unifying theory of behavioral change. *Psychological Review, 89,* 191–215.

Benson, H. (1975). *The relaxation response.* New York: Morrow.

Bernstein, D. A., & Borkovec, T. D. (1973). *Progressive relaxation training: A manual for the helping professions.* Champaign, IL: Research Press.

Cautela, J. R., & Groden, J. (1978). *A comprehensive manual for adults, children, and children with special needs.* Champaign, IL: Research Press.

Dahlquist, L. M. (1992). Coping with aversive medical treatments. In A. M. LaGreca, L. J. Siegel, J. L. Wallander, & C. E. Walker (Eds.), *Stress and coping in child health.* New York: Guilford Press.

Gagnon, D. J., Hudnall, L., & Andrasik, F. (1992). Bio-feedback and related procedures in coping with stress. In: A. M. LaGreca, L. J. Siegel, J. L. Wallander, & C. E. Walker (Eds.), *Stress and coping in child health.* New York: Guilford Press.

Gardner, G., & Olness, A. (1981). *Hypnosis and hypnotherapy with children.* New York: Grune & Stratton.

Heide, F. J., & Borkovec, T. D. (1984). Relaxation-induced anxiety: Mechanisms and theoretical implications. *Behavior Research and Therapy, 22,* 1–12.

Jacobson, E. (1938). *Progressive relaxation.* Chicago: University of Chicago Press.

Koeppen, A. S. (1974). Relaxation training for children. *Elementary School Guidance and Counseling, 9,* 14–21.

Lichstein, K. J. (1988). *Clinical relaxation strategies.* New York: John Wiley & Sons.

26 / **Biofeedback**

Scott W. Powers and Anthony Spirito

Introduction and Nature of the Modality

The goal of this chapter is to provide a brief overview of biofeedback as it relates to children and adolescents. The information presented should be used along with the detailed coverage of relaxation training in Chapter 25. Biofeedback involves the electronic monitoring, measurement, and display of physiological processes, such as muscle tension and blood flow, which are normally beyond conscious awareness but which when observed, can come under voluntary control. In biofeedback physiological information is displayed in an easily understandable form—for example, as a line graph on a monitor—as a means of teaching self-regulation (Schwartz, 1987).

Biofeedback is most often used as an adjunct to relaxation training for reducing problems that involve pain and anxiety. Instrumentation is used to monitor the physiological effects of relaxation and/or facilitate the learning of relaxation skills by providing visual or audio feedback about actual changes in otherwise invisible bodily processes. These changes are thought to counteract and/or be incompatible with negative emotional or somatic states. When described in this manner, it is evident that biofeedback itself is not a treatment modality. Rather, biofeedback instrumentation is used to enhance self-control training. Alternatively, biofeedback has also been used by specialists in pediatric behavioral medicine to address specific disorders, such as fecal incontinence (this will be discussed later). Both applications of biofeedback are discussed in this chapter, with an emphasis on the former.

Background and Conceptual Framework

Biofeedback is a relatively new treatment modality. As a clinical procedure, it evolved from laboratory research on controlling, by operant conditioning, autonomic nervous system responses in animals. It was the product of a combination of efforts initiated by learning theorists, psychophysiologists, biomedical engineers, and professionals interested in behavioral medicine. The mechanisms of biofeedback are the subject of debate; how and why it works is not clear. The interested reader is referred to Olson and Schwartz (1987) for an overview of the history and various theoretical models of biofeedback. Holroyd et al. (1984) describe a model of biofeedback that has particular appeal for clinicians and provides the conceptual framework for the discussion in this chapter. Holroyd et al. (1984) suggest that, in some cases, individuals learn to control a physiologic response, such as muscle tension, via biofeedback training and then use that control, as needed, to reduce symptoms. In most cases, cognitive change is a more important result of biofeedback. That is, individuals perceive that they are successful in biofeedback training, and this perception improves their overall feeling of self-efficacy. An enhanced feeling of self-efficacy leads to more successful coping efforts, lower stress, and improved symptoms.

Indications and Contraindications

PRESENTING PROBLEMS

Biofeedback has been used with children and adolescents to treat pain disorders—particularly tension and migraine headaches as well as other presenting problems, including asthma and insomnia, that have an anxiety component. Any problem that lends itself to treatment with relaxation is a candidate for treatment with biofeedback, which may enhance the effects of relaxation. Specific pediatric behavioral medicine applications have included fecal incontinence, urinary incontinence, spasmodic torticollis, and rumination syndrome (see Russo & Varni, 1982, for examples).

DEVELOPMENTAL CONSIDERATIONS

Biofeedback is most often used with children 7 years old and older. As with relaxation training, the cognitive and attentional demands of the treatment, make biofeedback best suited for older children. Children need to be able to understand the rationale of using biofeedback equipment for their problem. They must also be able to maintain attention and concentrate on their bodily sensations for an extended time and have the social-emotional maturity and self-directedness to want to learn about their own psychophysiologic responses. Clinical reports have suggested that children and adolescents may actually respond more favorably to biofeedback than do adults (Blanchard & Andrasik, 1985). The better performance by children than adults is probably related to the youngsters' greater enthusiasm and comfort with computer technology; their willingness to think of biofeedback training as a challenging game; and their acceptance of the biofeedback concept, without challenging the assumptions (e.g., children accept the fact that there may not be a one-to-one relationship between psychophysiologic control and symptom abatement).

CONTRAINDICATIONS

It is quite rare for a child to have untoward effects from exposure to biofeedback equipment per se. Clinicians must be cautious to allay any apprehension the child has about the equipment. It is necessary to offer clear, developmentally appropriate, and repeated explanations of the procedures and devices to both children and parents. Frightening terms such as *conductance, electrodes,* etc., should be avoided, and the child assured that the equipment cannot give him or her

418

an electrical shock. In addition, if a parent wants the child to be treated but the child has no motivation, the treatment will not be successful.

Preparation for Initiating Treatment

QUALIFICATIONS OF THE CLINICIAN

Because of equipment and technological considerations, specialized training in the use of biofeedback instrumentation is necessary. Clinicians must learn how to introduce biofeedback to children and their families and how to integrate physiologic findings into the overall treatment protocol.

EQUIPMENT AND TECHNOLOGICAL CONSIDERATIONS

At a basic level, biofeedback involves a sensor, a receiver, and a translation and feedback device. A bathroom scale is an example of a simple biofeedback device. The scale "senses" the amount of weight on it when a person steps on, receives the information, and translates it to a gauge that "feeds back" the information, using understandable terminology, (pounds). In order to use biofeedback with children and adolescents, specific and oftentimes expensive equipment is needed. Most biofeedback systems in use today utilize computer technology. Peek (1987) provides an understandable introduction to biofeedback instrumentation for the interested reader. With children, the use of computers and active, colorful feedback mechanisms akin to video games can be helpful and, with current technological advances, are becoming readily available.

Description of Process and Variations

WHAT TO MONITOR AND FEED BACK?

Two parameters considered correlates of physiological arousal are the most commonly used in biofeedback training with children and adolescents. The first is electromyographic (EMG) activity, electrical discharge in the muscle fibers, a correlate of skeletal muscle tension. EMG activity is measured in microvolts. The second is skin temperature monitoring. Skin temperature, a correlate of vasomotor control mechanisms, is measured in degrees Fahrenheit. Galvanic skin response (GSR) a correlate of sweat gland activity, is sometimes used as a general indication of arousal, but it is much more commonly employed with adults, as are blood pressure and heart rate. The feedback is usually given via a visual display. For adults, a line graph is a typical display; displays for children are usually gamelike, utilizing graphics and audio feedback.

PREPARATION OF THE PATIENT

Because biofeedback involves equipment, children may perceive it as a medical procedure and fear that biofeedback could hurt. Thus, it is important to describe to the child just what happens in biofeedback—do this before attaching the sensors. Describe how the sensors will be attached and make sure the child understands that the wires running to the forehead will not cause an electric shock. One of the most typical sensor placements is bifrontal EMG. This placement is often used for headache patients; it is commonly involved as well when using biofeedback to assist in relaxation training.

Peripheral finger temperature is another general physiologic indicator of the stress response; hence, the second most common physiologic monitoring done with children is measuring peripheral temperature by placing a thermister on a finger. At the same time, it can be used as a training technique for children with vascular headaches. Once again, the success of the feedback treatment will depend, at least in part, on the ability of the clinician to explain why monitoring finger temperature is important. Monitoring finger temperature is described as an indirect way of measuring blood flow which, in turn, is related to stress and/or migraine headaches.

BIOFEEDBACK-ASSISTED RELAXATION TRAINING

The detailed description of various relaxation techniques in Chapter 25 provides the basis for biofeedback-assisted relaxation training. The primary difference lies in the additional communication of actual physiologic data to the child. This feedback provides the child with confirmation of the physical effects of relaxation.

Biofeedback instrumentation is used in the treatment process to accomplish three goals: to make the child *aware* of physical responses, to teach *control* of these responses, and then to teach ways to *transfer* (generalize) these skills to everyday life. First, when monitoring physiologic responses initially, a child is not given any feedback regarding his or her performance. In typical situations, a baseline evaluation is conducted first to assess the physiologic parameters of interest. The child is asked to sit quietly in a room without moving too much (to avoid movement artifact) for a 5-minute period to assess resting levels of, for example, EMG frontalis activity and peripheral finger temperature. Second, a very common assessment application is to present some sort of cognitive stressor, such as difficult math problems to be done without pencil and paper, to see any changes in physiologic response. For clinical purposes, it is also helpful to pick a stressor that is related to the child's life, such as having a test in school the next day, having a fight with a sibling, etc. Third, after the child has been taught a relaxation procedure, the child's physiologic responses are monitored while he or she is relaxed. As a result of the training, there is usually a decrease in muscle tension and sometimes an increase in finger temperature.

Ideally, the pattern would show somewhat elevated baseline readings, followed by an increase in the readings in the stressful direction when the child is stressed, and a subsequent decrease in the stress response when relaxing. After each one of these trials—the baseline trial, the stressor trial, and the monitored relaxation trial—computer programs save the data and display it in some user-friendly fashion. It is then helpful for the clinician to review the results of these sessions with the child to highlight the relationship between stress and physiologic responses and/or relaxation and physiologic response.

When biofeedback equipment is used for monitoring, the clinician gains a better understanding of the degree to which the child being monitored is psychophysiologically reactive under stress. When the equipment is used over a series of sessions in this manner, the clinician is able to gauge whether there are changes in baseline over time

and/or improvement in physiologic responses as a result of using the relaxation techniques at home and in biofeedback sessions over a number of weeks and months. In most sessions, it is helpful to have the child relax for the therapist and then to determine whether there is an improvement over time in the physiologic responses during relaxation. Since the relaxation procedures themselves may become boring after a while, this kind of information is helpful in keeping the child practicing relaxation at home on a regular basis. Achieving a goal set by the therapist, such as reducing frontalis EMG by 1 microvolt, is often intrinsically reinforcing. Although children may be willing to work for the sounding of an audio signal from the biofeedback equipment, it is also useful to provide extrinsic reinforcement, such as permission to play computer games as a reward for attaining a specific goal. Motivation to practice decreases if the child's symptoms begin to improve; such lagging often needs to be countered by using a reinforcement procedure.

In addition to monitoring, feedback trials can be used to improve the child's relaxation response and to control symptoms. In the feedback trial, unlike the monitoring trials described previously, the child is given immediate access to his or her physiologic readings (feedback). In the most typical scenario, while a child is relaxing, a visual cue (usually on a TV screen) or audio signal is provided to the child. The child is typically instructed to try to relax and then to look toward the screen occasionally or listen to the tone to determine the efficacy of the relaxing. If the feedback indicates the child is not relaxing well, then that is the signal to try other approaches to relaxation. For example, if a child is using a meditative breathing technique, shifting to imagery-based relaxation might be a way to improve the physiologic responses. In turn, the feedback from the TV screen or the audio signal tells the child if the shift in relaxation has helped improve the physiologic response.

Some children find the feedback very helpful and enjoyable, and like to spend a good deal of the session using feedback trials to improve their skills. Others find that either the audio or visual signal is a distraction from relaxation and does not enhance their ability to relax. Consequently, they are unenthusiastic about the feedback and, in many cases, say they would rather just relax and have their trial monitored than receive feedback during the trial. Some children and adolescents become upset during a feedback trial if they are unable to produce results (e.g., a lowering of the EMG frontalis level). In most of these cases, frustration causes a significant rise in muscle tension or drop in finger temperature. Thus, the physical effects of the stress response are demonstrated quite readily to the child and the ensuing expectations for achievement become a topic for discussion and work in sessions.

The other major way to use feedback in biofeedback-enhanced relaxation training is to run a stress trial with feedback. In these instances, a situation that usually exacerbates the symptoms—such as a surprise quiz in school—is role-played. In response to this stressor, the child is then asked to perform some abbreviated relaxation exercise that will lower physiologic responsiveness. This kind of application training helps both to generalize the skills taught in the lab and to promote mastery.

DIRECT APPLICATIONS OF BIOFEEDBACK

When biofeedback is applied directly to treat disorders such as fecal or urinary incontinence, feedback is the primary active treatment modality employed. For example, in the case of fecal incontinence, a special internal probe inserted into the rectum is used to measure anal sphincter pressure. A representation of the pressure, some auditory or visual signal, is then fed back to the child. The child is instructed to try various methods of tensing the sphincter to determine which one produces the best effect. Thus, if a child is able to move the pelvic floor muscles or tighten the buttocks in a way that has a direct effect on the sphincter, feedback makes understanding that relationship possible. Once the physical maneuver—say, tightening the buttocks in a certain way—is determined to affect sphincter control, further training sessions are used to teach the child how to make the movements on a regular basis so that, by tightening the anal sphincter, the youngster can eliminate soiling on a daily basis. This approach has been used with a fair degree of success for children with spina bifida (see Whitehead et al., 1986). In these instances, in order to affect the changes in sphincter control, for most patients biofeedback technology is mandatory.

This is not true with other relaxation techniques, in which the effects can be obtained without the equipment (such as stress management or teaching a child relaxation when biofeedback is used merely to enhance the effects.)

Clinical Progress and Duration

The number of sessions of biofeedback training varies according to the symptom. For example, a typical headache treatment protocol is 8 to 12 sessions over a 3- to 4-month period. One approach is to conduct treatment until the symptom abates. Those who advocate this approach want to achieve a treatment effect. On the other hand, some experts maintain that it is the patient's ability to control body functions, that is critical, hence, they believe treatment should continue until a specified physiologic outcome—such as the ability to lower EMG 2 microvolts or raise finger temperature to 95 degrees—is achieved, even if symptoms have already been eliminated. Those who hold this view want to achieve a training effect. Of the two approaches, the latter is ideal but not always practical.

Outcome Studies and Clinical Standards

Research has shown that biofeedback-assisted relaxation is often efficacious in cases of childhood headache (Fentress, Masek, Mehegan, & Benson, 1986; Larsson & Melin, 1988); asthma-related symptoms (Kotses et al., 1991); painful medical procedures, such as cardiac catheterization (Campbell, Clark, & Kirkpatrick, 1986); and other problems that involve anxiety. However, the addition of biofeedback may not increase the effectiveness of standard relaxation (see Fentress et al., 1986). Biofeedback-assisted relaxation is an accepted intervention that has proven effective for specific problems, most notably tension and migraine headaches.

Interaction with Other Interventions

As discussed, with children and adolescents biofeedback is most often used as an adjunct to relaxation training, either as part of an overall stress management program or to address a specific symptom. Of course, other treatment modalities, such as family therapy or individual therapy, are often used as part of the overall treatment approach for a given symptom.

Conclusion and Future Directions

Biofeedback has proven to be a valuable tool in the hands of well-trained clinicians skilled in the treatment of stress-related disorders. Further research on treatment of specific problems in children and adolescents needs to be conducted to draw firm conclusions about whether biofeedback increases treatment effectiveness beyond that of standard behavioral intervention protocols.

SUGGESTED READING

Blanchard, E., & Andrasik, F. (1985). *Management of chronic headaches: A psychological approach.* New York: Pergamon Press.

Campbell, L., Clark, M., & Kirkpatrick, S. (1986). Stress management training for parents and their children undergoing cardiac catheterization. *American Journal of Orthopsychiatry, 56,* 234–243.

Fentress, D. W., Masek, B. J., Mehegan, J. E., & Benson, H. (1986). Biofeedback and relaxation-response training in the treatment of pediatric migraine. *Developmental Medicine and Child Neurology, 28,* 139–146.

Holroyd, R., Penzien, D., Hursey, K., Tobin, D., Rogers, L., Holm, J., Marcille, P., Hall, J. R., & Chila, A. G. (1984). Change mechanisms in EMG biofeedback training: Cognitive changes underlying improvements in tension headache. *Journal of Consulting and Clinical Psychology, 52,* 1039–1053.

Kotses, H., Harver, A., Segreto, J., Glaus, K., Creer, T., & Young, G. (1991). Long-term effects of biofeedback-induced facial relaxation on measures of asthma severity in children. *Biofeedback and Self-Regulation, 16,* 1–21.

Larsson, B., & Melin, L. (1988). Psychological treatment of recurrent headache in adolescents—short-term outcome and its prediction. *Headache, 28,* 187–195.

Olson, R. P., & Schwartz, M. S. (1987). An historical perspective on the biofeedback field. In M. S. Schwartz (Ed.), *Biofeedback: A practitioner's guide* (pp. 3–16). New York: Guilford Press.

Peek, C. J. (1987). A primer of biofeedback instrumentation. In M. S. Schwartz (Ed.), *Biofeedback: A practitioner's guide* (pp. 73–127). New York: Guilford Press.

Russo, D. C., & Varni J. W. (1982). *Behavioral pediatrics: Research and practice.* New York: Plenum Press.

Schwartz, M. S., & Associates (1987). *Biofeedback: A practitioner's guide.* New York: Guilford Press.

Whitehead, W. E., Parker, L., Bosmajian, L., Morrill-Corbin, E. D., Middaugh, S., Garwood, M., Cataldo, M. F., & Freeman, J. (1986). Treatment of fecal incontinence in children with spina bifida: Comparison of biofeedback and behavior modification. *Archives of Physical and Medical Rehabilitation, 67,* 218–224.

27 / Pair Therapy

Dennis J. Barr, Michael J. Karcher and Robert L. Selman

Introduction

For most children and adolescents, friendships are vital contexts promoting social, cognitive, emotional, and moral development (Selman and Schultz, 1990; Piaget, 1965; Sullivan, 1953). Youths who lack adequate interpersonal competencies, however, enter into vicious cycles of rejection and isolation, often losing critical developmental opportunities. Further, poor peer relationships in childhood and adolescence are a risk factor for future psychopathology and adult criminality (Parker and Asher, 1987). Therapy with dyads of children who have had chronic and severe difficulties relating with peers can foster the growth of the interpersonal competencies they need to make and sustain friendships and, consequently, to participate more fully and successfully in their social world.

The one-therapist–two-children therapeutic modality has a surprisingly short history. The first documented efforts to conduct dyadic therapy did not appear until the mid-1970s (Mitchell & Levine, 1982; Fuller, 1977; Bender, 1976; Birnbaum, 1975). These early approaches derived from principles of individual child psychotherapy; for example, children with similar traumatic issues were paired with the hope that each would gain support and insight through the sharing of personal histories (Antze, 1976). Over the past 20 years, a handful of reports have emerged describing variants of dyadic therapy called duo-therapy and peer psychotherapy. These variants are used with specific age groups and in particular settings, such as day care centers or child guidance clinics (Appelstein, 1993; Mitchell & Levine, 1982; Mehl & Petersen, 1981). In general, these models extend psychodynamic, cognitive-behavioral, or information processing theories to a dyadic therapy.

One form of dyadic therapy, called pair therapy, has been relatively well documented and successfully implemented in multiple contexts, with a broad spectrum of children and adolescents manifesting a variety of disorders (Selman, Watts, & Schultz, 1997; Selman & Schultz, 1990). In contrast to forms of duo-therapy that rely on adult-directed discussions, social skills training, or psychoeducation, pair therapy focuses on the interpersonal competencies youths employ during sessions as they develop a relationship with one another over time. This dyadic modality is overviewed in this chapter.

The Goals and Applications of Pair Therapy

The primary goal of pair therapy is to foster the growth of the interpersonal competencies, in both thought and action, that children need to form and maintain healthy, close relationships throughout life. The modality is especially suited for promoting the capacity to coordinate social perspectives, a social cognitive capacity that underlies such skills as resolving conflict, sharing experiences, cooperating, empathizing, and collaborating (Selman & Schultz, 1990).

The nature of the everyday social functioning of the children referred for pair therapy suggests the starting point and goals for each pair. For children with severe disorders, such as residual autism or broad-spectrum developmental delays, pair therapy is primarily a skill-building approach, helping them become less impulsive in their interactions. Such children need the most basic friendship skills: the ability to work and play in a shared space, to restrain egocentric and aggressive impulses, and to both tolerate and enjoy the presence of a peer.

For children who are less constrained by the limitations of severe cognitive and communicative deficits, but who nevertheless have great difficulties making and keeping friends, pair therapy is used to foster complex interpersonal understanding and skills, such as reciprocity and mutuality. In general, the pair therapist fosters progressively accurate and more caring perceptions of and balanced concerns for the needs and wishes of both the self and the other peer.

The specific goals of pair therapy also depend on the context in which the treatment is offered. In the residential treatment setting, for example, pair therapy may have the additional goal of positively influencing the social climate of the therapeutic milieu by fostering the psychosocial development of the youths in residence.

In public school settings, pair therapy (also known in schools as pair counseling) may be adapted as an early intervention for youth who do not yet have psychiatric disorders but who are nevertheless showing early signs of school failure, conduct disorder, and problematic interpersonal relationships. The challenge for such youths may not be learning how to make friends under ordinary circumstances, but rather how to manage and make sense of their friendship in relation to dangerous and risky environmental conditions (e.g., violent neighborhoods, easy access to addictive substances, health threats such as AIDS, etc.) (Selman et al., 1992). With such children, pair therapy can operate as a preventive intervention against negative life consequences that result from risk-taking behaviors such as dropping out of school, fighting with peers, using drugs and alcohol, engaging in unsafe sex, etc.

Pair therapy can also be employed strategically to support children during specific transitions or in relation to certain social forces. The move from elementary to junior high school or from junior high to high school, for example, are points of vulnerability in development, and pair therapy can strengthen the readiness of youth to manage what will certainly be the upheaval in their social supports during such transitions. Finally, pair therapy can help children take the perspective of children from other cultural, class, or religious groups in order to ameliorate group-based prejudices, hatred, and intergroup misunderstandings (Karcher & Nakkula, in press).

Indications and Treatment Planning

In day and residential treatment settings, pair therapy is indicated for children, with a wide range of disorders, who have marked difficulties getting along with and are relatively isolated or withdrawn from peers. Children who lag behind their peers in their ability to coordinate social perspectives and to resolve interpersonal conflicts, who tend to be overly aggressive or passive in their interactions with peers, and who lack basic communicative competencies are likely to benefit from this modality. In addition, children who can make friends but generally cannot sustain friendships are good candidates for pair therapy.

For children with severe psychiatric disorders, pair therapy is not a substitute for individual or family therapy or other interventions, but can be an important piece of a broader treatment plan. Individual therapy, which may address thoughts and feelings about peer relationships, does not provide direct assistance with social functioning with peers. Children's interpersonal problems are typically manifest when young people are in therapy *with* a peer, and pair therapy can thus complement the more reflective individual work with the specific goal of promoting interpersonal competence.

The decision as to which type of socially based intervention a child may need—group or pair therapy—requires an assessment of the social capacities and needs of the referred child. Like group therapy, pair therapy offers the therapist the opportunity to observe the child's relational difficulties and strengths directly as they happen. Therefore, the therapist can intervene when difficulties arise. Pair therapy differs from group work, however, in a variety of important ways. Pair therapy is better suited than is group therapy for helping children learn how to participate in relatively intense peer relationships, which are not generally developed in group therapy. In pair therapy, children experience each other's actions or lack of action directly, and have repeated opportunities to gain perspective on themselves through the eyes of another. Conflicts and misunderstandings, for example, have a direct impact on a specific relationship, not on a number of relationships or, in the case of group therapy, the whole group.

On a more functional level, pair therapy provides a therapeutic structure that is particularly well suited for children who are overstimulated or overwhelmed by group therapy. These children may find pair therapy a manageable interpersonal context, despite its intensity. Certainly not all children require pair therapy; some—for example those who need a group setting to work on such skills as group decision making and social problem solving—may benefit more from group therapy.

Matching Pair Partners

When matching pair partners, therapists take into account the gender; interpersonal maturity; interpersonal style; existing relationship between the children; and, to a lesser extent, their personal interests. Children are almost universally matched with same-sex partners because through early adolescence children normatively develop the capacities for making and maintaining intimacy in relationships in close, same-sex friendships (Sullivan, 1953). Furthermore, the different ways in which boys and girls manage intimacy and autonomy needs in childhood (Watts, 1997) can add a level of complexity to pair therapy, which is already complicated by the individual relational difficulties of the participants.

The next consideration in matching is the interpersonal maturity of the candidates for pair therapy. The goal is to identify and pair children who function at roughly the same levels of interpersonal thought and action in peer relationships. The therapist assesses the children's reflective capacity to coordinate social perspectives and to regulate their needs for intimacy and autonomy in relationships. Social perspective coordination involves differentiating and integrating the points of view of self and a significant other person through an understanding of the thoughts, feelings, and wishes of each person. Research on social development has revealed five perspective coordination levels, ranging from undifferentiated, global perspectives on self and other to differentiated and hierarchically integrated perspectives on self and other. These levels are: Undifferentiated/Egocentric, Differentiated/Subjective, Second

Person/Self-Reflective, Third Person/Mutual, and Interdependent (Selman, Watts, & Schultz, 1997).

Perspective taking is a necessary condition for adaptive social behavior but not a sufficient one. Children often act at levels that are below their social-cognitive competency to understand social situations. In order to match children in pair therapy, therefore, it is necessary to assess the range and predominant levels of their interpersonal action. In brief, two fundamental social processes characterize an individual's interpersonal actions: *Intimacy processes* foster closeness and connectedness between self and the other; *autonomy processes* foster clear boundaries delineating the needs of self and other as separate and distinct. Intimacy and autonomy functions are operationalized in the constructs of *shared experience* and *interpersonal negotiation strategies*, respectively. Research has identified five levels of shared experiences and interpersonal negotiation strategies that correspond to the perspective-taking levels mentioned previously: Impulsive, Unilateral, Reciprocal, Compromise, and Collaborative (Selman & Schultz, 1990). Matches for pair therapy are made with children with roughly the same range and predominant levels of interpersonal skills.

The final key consideration in matching pairs is the children's predominant interpersonal styles. Children referred for pair therapy tend to have trouble making friends either because they are overly aggressive and bully others or because they are overly submissive or withdrawn and tend to be victimized. Children with these opposing styles are paired because the tension between contrasting interpersonal orientations usually becomes a catalyst for growth toward a more balanced interpersonal orientation. Neither child can remain rigidly assertive or submissive if the relationship is to be sustained, and thus both must learn new strategies and gain flexibility in their use.

In general, it is not advantageous to pair children who already have a solid relationship, although pairing children with shared interests sometimes helps children feel motivated to start pair therapy and helps them form an initial bond with one another. Conversely, children who have a long history of conflict or who are unlikely to find anything they would like to do together are not an ideal match. In this respect, pair therapy differs from peer mediation, a technique gaining popularity in public school conflict-resolution programs.

The Initial Session and Activities in Pair Therapy

It can be very useful to have a brief individual meeting with each child prior to the first pair session. In this meeting the therapist describes pair therapy and its goals, explains why the child was referred, to tells the child who the pair partner will be. Also, the therapist answers questions. When the pair is brought together for the first session, the pair therapist explains that pair therapy can be a lot of fun, but that it is not always easy because it involves working out problems with one another. The therapist explains that several rules are necessary for pair therapy: (1) The pair must stay together during sessions and throughout the planned course of treatment (i.e., until the end of the school year or for a specified number of session) (2) the pair cannot use physical force with one another or the therapist and (3) they cannot destroy property. Other rules may pertain to the specific site where pair therapy is being conducted, and the children may wish to generate some rules of their own. The pair therapist explains confidentiality—the agreement that whatever is said or done in pair therapy remains private to the three participants and the therapist's supervisor. Finally, the children should be informed that, if one of them is absent on a given day, the other child may meet with the therapist so that one child does not lose out because of the other's absence.

Pair sessions are typically of the same duration as individual therapy sessions (i.e., 50 minutes), but the length of a session may be shortened, depending on the quality of the interactions. Most pair therapy sessions start off in the therapy room with the selection of an activity, as the following interchange illustrates.

T.J.:   I want to play Legos.
Paul: Uh-uh, I'm gonna draw.
Therapist: Remember, we promised to decide together what we would do. How can you two work this out so that you both get to do something you want to do?
Paul: Maybe we should do something different that we both like.
T.J.:   Well, I'll play Legos today if we can draw next time.
Therapist: Paul are you willing to draw next week if we play Legos today?
Paul: Yeah.
Therapist: I really like how you were able to work that out, and T.J. that was very nice of you to offer to let Paul choose the game for this week. The Legos are in the game box.

From the standpoint of the therapeutic process, the actual activity that is chosen by the pair is less important than the way the pair decides on activities. The choice of an activity is the first context for negotiation during the pair session, one of many opportunities to develop and refine critical interpersonal competencies. The therapist may intervene during this process by using the techniques described in the next section. In addition, the therapist ensures that the activity chosen is safe and within the guidelines already outlined. Beyond that, the only limits to activities are the imagination of the participants and their capacity to engage in them together.

In pair therapy, children may play board games, do athletic activities, create artwork, watch videos, go on outings, spend their time talking, and so on. Over time, most pairs tend to find a favorite activity that they enjoy together and return to. This is especially the case when, in their relationship, the pair has been exploring anxiety-provoking interpersonal territory.

Most games may be used in different ways, depending on the children's interpersonal maturity and styles and their history with one another. Positive shared experiences, reflection, and interpersonal skill development are the priorities rather than competence at any particular activity or specific rules for play. The key for the therapist is to meet the children where they are and help them move toward increasingly mature, verbal, organized, and controlled activity.

Depending on the maturity of the pair, special activities, such as field trips, can afford opportunities for some pairs to plan together and to experience their relationship in the world beyond the therapy room. The therapist must first assess whether the partners can manage such an activity and consider whether it would be a useful experience. If the pair wishes to do something together outside the therapy room, the activity should be planned in advance and be an activity they can agree upon and do together. Meeting in the therapy room to touch base with one another and meeting again at the end of the session to discuss how things went is also helpful. These guidelines keep the focus on working together, organizing behavior, reflecting on interactions, and ensuring safety.

Therapeutic Processes and the Therapist's Role

The process of pair therapy, given adequate time and proper supervision, evolves through a series of phases. Initially the children try to figure out how to interact in the pair. So they begin by sizing each other up and, typically, settle quickly into a pattern in which one of the children is the leader. This creates a temporary equilibrium, which later breaks down when conflicts arise between them. When the more passive child feels safe enough in the pair to assert his or her needs, these assertions, with the support of the therapist, typically lead to a restructuring of the pair's power relationship. This cycle may repeat many times over the course of a year, with the goal being that the children become able to establish an increasingly effective and balanced pattern of functioning.

The pair therapist focuses his or her attention on these dynamics between the pair partners. It can be challenging for some therapists trained in individual psychotherapy to shift their focus from the adult-child relationship to an emphasis on the peer relationship. New pair therapist often report initially that they feel their role is peripheral as the children develop their relationship. Pair therapists, however, are critically important to the process of relationship development. Children who have had chronic difficulties getting along with peers require the careful guidance and support of the adult therapist to benefit from peer interactions that would generally sour outside the structured pair therapy context.

The pair therapist's first task is to set a positive tone and to explain the goals and guidelines of pair therapy so that the pair partners feel it will be a safe and enjoyable experience. Some troubled children find it difficult to simply tolerate being with a peer and an adult in a novel situation. The therapist helps the partners find initial activities, if necessary, to help the youth tolerate their anxiety. Throughout the course of pair therapy, the therapist helps mediate conflicts that might otherwise become overwhelming for the youths. There may be times when the partners refuse to return to pair therapy and, if so, it is critically important that the therapist understand the dynamics so that he or she can facilitate the return to the pair. In these ways, the therapist acts to hold the partners together until they are capable of doing so themselves.

In general, pair therapists strive to help the partners recognize and acknowledge one another's points of view and to translate that understanding into correspondingly mature actions. The therapist's goal is not to provide solutions to conflicts between the partners, but rather to have the partners develop strategies for resolving their own conflicts. The therapist does this by helping the children work just beyond their current level of functioning. The therapist's role evolves, therefore, in tandem with the pair's shifts toward more complex perspective taking, new social competencies, and greater caring for one another. Specifically, depending on the maturity of the pair and the children's needs the moment, the therapist uses such techniques as *empowering* the children; *linking* their perspectives; and *enabling* them to see a shared point of view, which typically means helping the partners see what is best for their relationship. These three techniques will be described in detail in the sections that follow.

EMPOWERING

The therapist can empower children who tend to interact impulsively with others by helping them to identify and articulate their own beliefs, desires, goals, and feelings. That is, the therapist helps the children to identify personal points of view (rather than simply to engage in unreflective action) and to see how their different perspectives (i.e., desires, interests, and beliefs) affect their own behaviors. By helping the children see how their desires relate to their actions or lack of action, therapists help children to gain a sense of efficacy and control and learn to take responsibility for their actions.

How does empowering look in practice? When a therapist sees a power imbalance—such as one child always bossing the other—he or she will call the child's attention to this pattern. Therapists may want to allow time for the pair to modify their own relationship if the imbalance presents no immediate risks, but the therapist must be sure to communicate his or her perspective on their behavior. As the children may not hold their own perspective clearly, the therapist must carefully select times to share ideas about how each child may have experienced an interaction. In sum, the therapist's reflections on the children's individual needs, interests, and beliefs empowers them to gain a more differentiated view of their own points of view, making possible the next level of maturity in interactions. On one hard, a therapist should avoid critiquing and directing the children's every interaction; on the other, he or she must avoid reinforcing ineffective or abusive behavior by saying nothing.

LINKING

Once a child is able to understand that he or she has unique wishes and interests, the therapist encourages the child to understand the partner's perspective and then links each child's perspective or behavior to the other's. The therapist can do this by helping Partner A tell Partner B how Partner A is feeling, what made Partner A feel that way, and what Partner A would like to happen next time. Sometimes therapist may need to articulate this for the pair; for example, by saying, "Tom's feelings seem to be hurt because you haven't allowed him to select a game in several weeks. I think he would like to choose the game today. Is that right Tom?" Teaching and modeling these assertive statements by describing feelings, identifying the problem, and suggesting concrete solutions helps the children communicate and negotiate more effectively on their own.

When linking, the therapist's primary focus is to help each child hear, acknowledge, and respect the other's opinions, desires, experiences, and feelings. The therapist links the children's per-

spectives by helping them see conflict as a shared concern that they must work out together in a way that satisfies them both. The therapist facilitates cooperation, therefore, by helping the partners with reciprocal negotiating, problem solving, and sharing.

In times of conflict, the therapist will help the partners by breaking down the steps of problem solving and encouraging the children to follow them. He or she will model the process of identifying or agreeing on a goal, then help the children generate various possible ways of resolving the conflict. Lastly, the therapist helps them choose and implement a strategy both agree on. When successful, the therapist will praise the children's work, describe how both got their own needs met in the situation, and encourage them to think about other ways to cooperate.

ENABLING

Enabling is the third structuring tool available to the pair therapist, and it is used when children cooperate well but still maintain self-serving goals, not seeing what is best for their relationship with their peer over time. Although successful coordination of one's needs and wants with the needs and wants of a peer is an important skill—one that is certainly a considerable advancement over fight or flight strategies—lasting relationships require the capacity to consider the impact of present interactions on the relationship over the long run. Enabling entails helping children see that their relationship will strengthen if they balance their *individual interests* with the *needs of the relationship* over time. This is a particularly difficult task because, in many societies, it is a skill that is neither taught, practiced, nor modeled regularly. Furthermore, it is not a skill that normally develops prior to early adolescence. Nevertheless, the capacity to collaborate, to establish a "we" perspective in a close relationship based on mutuality and shared reflection, is the keystone for developing close friendships and romantic relationships.

Pair therapists can enable this mutuality in relationships by helping the children gain perspective on their friendship and think about their actions in terms of the consequences for the friendship itself, not just in terms of each child's immediate needs. Therapists help the children review their shared history, remind them how they have settled similar past disputes, and help them think about the ramifications of their different ways of settling conflict. The pair therapist also helps them recognize times when they have been able to collaborate, coming up with ideas and interests benefiting them both. The therapist's primary focus is to enable the children to see the importance of their relationship and to foster their ability to care for, support, and respect the other person.

A Typical Pair Therapy Session in a Day Treatment School

What does pair therapy look like? The following is a brief description of a typical pair therapy session, or the activities of a pair therapist from the time he meets the children until they return to class.

Each week the pair therapist shows up at the door of either Kenny or Carl's classroom and goes with that child to get his partner. The three walk to the therapy room. During the entire 50-minute class period this day, the pair of students will work and play together in the therapy room.

The room is familiar and all three take their usual seats, corner, or space. The pair therapist waits a short while for spontaneous conversation before touching base with the kids, briefly asking how they are. He does this to discover if there are any pressing issues that either boy might need to address before beginning the work, whether the work will be talking, playing, planning, or disagreeing. On this particular day, the boys do not say anything; they would rather get right to their favorite activity, Monopoly.

As they prepare to play the game, the pair therapist shares his thoughts about how the last session went. During the previous session, Kenny caught Carl cheating at Monopoly, but Kenny said nothing about it to Carl. This is consistent with a pattern of interacting that has emerged between the two, so the pair therapist encourages the boys to talk about it. He wants the boys to express their thoughts on this issue before they play Monopoly

again so that they can both recognize the power imbalance they perpetuate. He hopes that empowering them to articulate their perspectives will lead to more honest game play. After the pair therapist reviews what happened the last time they played and the boys discuss what the cheating means to them, the boys resume their activity.

The boys play for much of the hour, talking throughout, but the last 5 or 10 minutes are spent reviewing how they played with each other. The boys evaluate themselves and their day's work. They talk, for example, about the fact that neither boy cheated, and they discuss whether this is a better way to play. The pair therapist identifies moments of conflict and compliments the boys on how they handled the situations. He asks them if they would do anything differently next time; they say no, they liked the way they played together today.

Before returning to their classrooms, the boys and the pair therapist talk about what they might do next week. Kenny says he wants to throw a football outside. Carl says he has one he can bring, and the pair therapist encourages Kenny to remind Carl to bring it the following week. He also reminds the boys that, since there are only 2 months left in the school year, they might consider what they might like to do or accomplish in pair therapy during that time. He also points out some progress they have made so far and helps Kenny and Carl describe the changes they have observed in their relationship and think about ways each might be a better friend to the other. This does not take long because the kids do not contribute much. Nonetheless this ritual is an important wrap-up for the day, reminding them of the purpose of their time together and setting the tone for the next meeting. All three leave, and the pair therapist walks the boys back to their classes.

Practical Considerations

Various institutional factors—including scheduling issues, billing, and the availability of facilities and equipment—have an impact on pair therapy. Pair work, when delivered in treatment-oriented institutions (i.e., day and residential treatment centers) is usually complemented by other services, such as individual and group psychotherapy, speech and language therapy, and academic remediation (McCullough, Selman, & Wilkens, 1997). The scheduling of pair therapy in those settings, therefore, must be coordinated with that of other services. Residential treatment settings may offer great flexibility in scheduling, given the availability of after-school and evening hours. Games and other activities for use in pair therapy are usually readily available in these clinical settings, since the settings are likely to be used for a variety of purposes.

It is essential in public school contexts for the principal and teachers to understand and fully support the goals of a pair therapy program and for parents to give informed consent for their child's participation in pair therapy. Principals generally welcome pair therapy because of the negative impact of severe interpersonal problems on academic achievement and school climate and because few, if any, other services are available to deal with these problems. Nevertheless, resources for pair therapy (i.e., time, space, and equipment) may be limited. Scheduling must be carefully and sensitively coordinated with teachers so that the coming and going of children from the classroom is not overly disruptive to others or stigmatizing for the children receiving services.

Conclusion

Children and adolescents develop their capacity to engage in caring, intimate relationships through their involvement in peer relationships. Many troubled children and adolescents, however, never develop their potential to participate in close peer relationships and, instead, participate in exploitative and abusive relationships as victim, victimizer, or both. Sadly, these relational patterns often persist into adulthood, becoming a legacy for future generations. Pair therapy is based on the assumption that children—even those who are severely dysfunctional in their relationships with peers—can learn how to become friends, to trust and be trustworthy, and to take care of themselves while caring for others. When these lessons are learned, cycles of abuse, social isolation, and rejection can be broken.

Pair therapy, a relatively well-documented dyadic therapy, assumes that it is through corrective interpersonal experiences in peer relationships that troubled youth learn how to care for and get along with peers in healthful ways. This assumption, at the heart of the pair therapy approach, differentiates it most clearly from individual psychotherapy, where there is no peer with whom to practice relational skills (such as conflict resolution and experience sharing) or to build and maintain an ongoing relationship.

Managing conflicts and the feelings that they can engender is paramount in the relationship-building process in pair therapy, just as in any intense, long-term relationship. The pair therapist supports the participants in staying together and working through conflicts in increasingly mature ways. These experiences in pair therapy may contrast with what the participating children experience personally in other relationships or witness in the media where intimidation, aggression, fleeing, and abandonment are commonplace strategies for managing difficult feelings and accomplishing ends. If so, pair therapy offers troubled youths a critical alternative template for engaging in relationships that can help them begin to fulfill their deepest personal yearnings for both closeness with and secure independence from others.

SUGGESTED READING

Antze, P. (1976). The role of ideologies in peer psychotherapy organizations: Some theoretical considerations and three case studies. *Journal of Applied Behavioral Science, 12* (3), 323–346.

Appelstein, C. D. (1993). Peer helping peer: Duo therapy with children in residential care. *Residential Treatment for Children and Youth, 10* (4), 33–53.

Barr, Dennis J. (1997). Friendship and belonging. In R. L. Selman, C. L. Watts, & L. H. Shultz (Eds.), *Fostering friendship: Pair therapy for treatment and prevention.* Hawthorn, NY: Aldine deGruyter, 19–30.

Bender, B. (1976). Duo therapy: A method of casework treatment of children. *Child Welfare, 55,* 95–108.

Birnbaum, M. (1975). Peer pair psychotherapy. A new approach to withdrawn children. *Journal of Clinical Child Psychology, 4,* 13–16.

Fuller, J. S. (1977). Duo therapy case studies: Process and techniques. *Social Casework, 58* (2), 84–91.

Karcher, M. J., & The Group for the Study of Interpersonal Development. (1996). *The pair counseling manual.* Cambridge, MA: The Group for the Study of Interpersonal Development, Harvard Graduate School of Education, 615 Larsen Hall, Appian Way, 02138.

Karcher, M. J., & Nakkula, M. J. (1997). Multicultural pair counseling and the development of expanded world views. In R. L. Selman, Watts, C. L., & Schultz, L. H. (Eds.), *Fostering friendship: Pair therapy for treatment and prevention.* Hawthorn, NY: Aldine deGruyter, 207–227.

Lieberman, S. N., & Smith L. B. (1991). Duo therapy: A bridge to the world of peers for the ego-impaired child. *Journal of Child and Adolescent Group Therapy, 1* (4), 243–252.

McCullough, A., Selman, R. L., & Wilkens, G. (1997). Pair therapy in a residential treatment center for children and adolescents. In R. L. Selman, C. L. Watts, & L. H. Schultz (Eds.), *Fostering friendship: Pair therapy for treatment and prevention.* Hawthorn, NY: Aldine deGruyter, 101–120.

Mehl, L. E., & Petersen, G. H. (1981). Spontaneous peer psychotherapy in a day care setting: A case report. *American Journal of Orthopsychiatry, 51* (2), 346–350.

Mitchell, C. (1976). Duo therapy—an innovative approach to the treatment of children. *Smith College Studies in Social Work, 45* (3), 236–47.

Mitchell, C., & Levine, B. (1982). Duo therapy in a residential program. *Residential Group Care and Treatment, 1* (2), 31–49.

Parker, J. G., & Asher, S. R. (1987). Peer relationships and later personal adjustment: Are low-accepted children "at-risk"? *Psychological Bulletin, 102,* 357–389.

Piaget, J. (1965). *The moral judgment of the child* (M. Gabain, trans.). New York: Free Press.

Schultz, L. H., & Selman, R. L. (1989). Bridging the gap between interpersonal thought and action in early adolescence: The role of psychodynamic processes. *Development and Psychopathology, 1* (2), 133–152.

Selman, R. L. (1980). *The growth of interpersonal understanding.* New York: Academic Press.

Selman, R. L. (1993). Assessment of personality development: Which analysis when? *Psychological Inquiry, 4* (1), 49–53.

Selman, R. L., & Demorest, A. (1984). Observing troubled children's interpersonal negotiation strategies. Implications of and for a developmental model. *Child Development, 55,* 288–304.

Selman, R. L., & Schultz, L. H. (1990). *Making a friend in youth: Developmental theory and pair therapy.* Chicago: University of Chicago Press.

Selman, R. L., Schultz, L. H., Nakkula, M., Barr, D., Watts, C., & Richmond, J. (1992). Friendship and fighting: A developmental approach to the study of risk and prevention of violence. *Development and Psychopathology, 4,* 529–558.

Selman, R. L., Schultz, L. H., & Yeates, K. O. (1990). Interpersonal understanding and action: A development and psychopathology perspective on research and prevention. In Cicchetti and S. L. Toth (Eds.), *Rochester symposium on development and psychopathology* (Vol. 3). Hillsdale, NJ: Earlbaum, 289–329.

Selman, R. L., Watts, C. L., & Schultz, L. H. (Eds.). (1997). *Fostering friendship: Pair therapy for treatment and prevention.* Hawthorn, NY: Aldine deGruyter.

Sullivan, H. S. (1953). *The interpersonal theory of psychiatry.* New York: W. W. Norton.

Watts, C. L. (1997). The growth of an intimate relationship between preadolescent girls. In R. L. Selman, C. L. Watts, & L. H. Schultz (Eds.), 1997, *Fostering friendship: pair therapy for treatment and prevention.* Hawthorn, NY: Aldine deGruyter, 77–100.

28 / Group Therapy with Children

Seth Aronson

Introduction

Peer groupings enact a significant and readily apparent role in the personality development of children. For the world of children is indeed a network of groupings ranging from loose play groups in the schoolyard or street to special-purpose clubs, athletic teams, and cliques. Even among preschoolers perceptions of self and social conduct are rooted in actual play-group experiences and built on a sense of being either accepted and liked or excluded and disliked (Barkow, 1977). As for elementary school–age children, Erik Erikson (1959) noted that ". . . at no time is the individual more ready to learn quickly and avidly, to become big in the sense of sharing obligation, discipline, and performance rather than power . . . and he is able and willing to profit fully by the association with teachers and ideal prototypes" (p. 81). In addition, Harry Stack Sullivan (1953) discussed the broadening of social/interpersonal awareness that occurs as a result of exposure to group life outside the home and the subsequent establishment of ingroups and out-groups in childhood society. The importance of these children's group life, of organized games and of manual activities for the expression of emotions, for identity formation, and for the learning of social skills, has been stressed in the child development literature. Additionally, the organic links between group experiences, self-esteem, and self are well known (Grunebaum & Solomon, 1987).

Historical Background

The ready responsiveness of children to group experiences was first used for therapeutic purposes in the early 1930s by S. R. Slavson (1943) and Fritz Redl (1944). These new approaches were especially welcome in child guidance clinics, where clinicians had learned how difficult it was to elicit verbal communications and introspection in elementary school–age children in a one-to-one treatment context (Scheidlinger, 1982). As its name implies, Slavson's *activity group therapy* (AGT) stresses the expression of feelings and of fantasies through action, manual activities, and play. A permissive environment with an accepting adult in charge promotes a benign regression that can function as a corrective emotional experience. The interactions of the children with each other and with the therapist constitute the major therapeutic ingredients.

Later clinicians—in contrast to Slavson, who advocated a nonverbal model of activity group therapy—demonstrated the value of talking groups for children (Charach, 1983; Sugar, 1974).

Assessment groups, as developed by Redl, contain rich opportunities for detailed observation of dysfunctional children. As Anthony (1957) put it, should the dyadic child therapist ". . . by chance, place a child in a children's group for a period long enough to let him warm up after his clinic experience, he will observe him opening out like a Japanese flower in water, suddenly full of color and spontaneity" (p. 232). While early efforts described in the literature entailed about four diagnostic sessions, more recently, a two-session observation series built into the regular evaluation program has been described (Kernberg & Liebowitz, 1986). With a therapist in charge, the children—mixed in age, sex, and diagnoses—met in a playroom equipped with a variety of crafts materials, toys, games, etc. Unknown to each other, they had been told beforehand that these two sessions were designed to see how they played and related to each other. This two-session diagnostic intervention has the advantages of brevity and the use of the group modality, a developmentally syntonic way for children to feel comfortable, which may lead to their displaying presenting problems in full relief.

Redl extended his original work with diagnostic groups to major models of group work with conduct-disordered youth in outpatient and in residential settings (1966). Slavson's "classical" model was extended by his students to include interpretive techniques for use with adolescents (Gabriel, 1939) as well as therapeutic play groups for preschoolers (Schiffer, 1969). Saul Scheidlinger (1960) and Margaret Frank (1976) offered adaptations that made the original method suitable for severely disturbed elementary school–age youngsters (a well-known population to those who work in municipal and state-funded facilities in the public sector). A conceptual model applying object-relations theory, utilizing children's group therapy for correction of early deficits, was developed by Soo (1985). Virginia Axline (1947) developed a play-group model built on the "nondirective" treatment theories of Carl Rogers (1942), a theory later expanded by Haim Ginnott (1961).

Distinct from psychoanalytic approaches and based on principles of behavior modification, behavioral group treatment models were developed that initially stressed a clear delineation of specific maladaptive behavior and the employment of objective procedures such as contracting, rehearsal, modeling, desensitization, and extinction. As depicted by Rose (1972), behavioral group therapy proceeds toward a succession of goals, with the beginning phases requiring maximum control and reinforcement by the group therapist. Subsequently, responsibility is shifted to the group member; in the final stage group members apply the newly gained social skills to the world outside. An extended "multi-method" group approach encompassing operant conditioning, modeling, and cognitive restructuring as well as relaxation training was described by Rose and Edelson (1987).

Currently, then, group treatment modalities for children cover a wide range of theoretical bases, including psychodynamic, behavioral, and object relations, among others.

Classifications of Child Treatment Groups

In this chapter, a general framework will be maintained wherein children's *clinical psychotherapy groups* will be differentiated from *psychoeducational* and from *support groups,* based on Scheidlinger's (1985) conceptual model of types of adolescent groups. Thus, group psychotherapy proper will always entail a group practitioner working with a carefully balanced small group, each child-patient having been judged suitable for group therapy on the basis of a diagnostic assessment. The other two categories (i.e., psychoeducational and support groups), in contrast—though invariably aimed at some kind of preventive intervention, remediation, or enhancement of optimal functioning—are not necessarily conducted by mental health professionals, need not be carefully balanced, and do not have the avowed purpose of "repairing" pathology. The issue here is not whether any one category of group to help children is superior to any other, but rather to maintain their differences in the interest of conceptual clarity.

Developmental Considerations in the Choice of Group Interventions

In the determination of the most suitable group modality, each child's age, gender, stage, and developmental level need to be considered. Thus, for preschoolers who are as yet unable to verbalize their thoughts and feelings, play groups such as those described by Ginnott (1961) and Schiffer (1969) would be indicated. Preschoolers relate with ease in coeducational groups and accept the authority of adults of either sex. With elementary school children, verbalization skills are becoming more fully developed, as are the capacities for abstract thinking and for self-awareness. The peer group now constitutes a major support in the beginning emancipation from the family and serves as a prime source of self-esteem. Games, sports, crafts, and other creative efforts become the essential building blocks for a sense of identity. Accordingly, an activity therapy group is uniquely suited to act as a normative environment for the elementary school–age child. Processes of identification and modeling are greatly facilitated when these groups comprise peers and therapists of the same gender. Furthermore, an equilibrium of ethnic, racial, and educational characteristics (what Slavson [1943] termed the "balance" necessary for a treatment group) is an important consideration. Sophistication levels and life experiences (i.e., how "streetwise" and savvy a youngster might be) are often more important than age or school grade placements. Some degree of homogeneity is necessary. The best rule of thumb is to examine the presenting difficulties (and diagnoses) of the children and then structure the group accordingly. For example, a group containing many children with severe behavioral difficulties would fare better with highly structured, planned activities led by an active, firm group leader. In contrast, those children who are initially more constricted and withdrawn will do better in a less restrictive group led by an adult who may have a quieter, gentle leadership style.

A comprehensive scheme relating children's developmental phases and differential diagnoses to varied group treatment models was proposed by Schamess (1986). In organizing a group for children according to their developmental needs, it is necessary that the group contain the following elements:

1. A safe physical environment that facilitates peer interaction
2. Furnishings and play materials that are both developmentally appropriate and serve to evoke meaningful communication
3. The planned use of group equipment either to promote internal organization or to encourage controlled regression.
4. A clearly defined therapist-leader to help the group members individually and as a whole master specific developmental tasks

Groups for more seriously disturbed children tend to be experiential and restitutive rather than insight-oriented in their goals and methodology. Thus, the corrective experience of being in a setting in which anxiety is tolerable, limits are set, and the children feel contained and nurtured will be more therapeutically efficacious for these children than any verbal interventions aimed at insight awareness. For those children who present with less disturbance, groups that are geared toward talking will have a more beneficial outcome; these children may, in fact, even grow a bit impatient with too much activity and make their need

for talking known to the group leader in a loud and clear manner!

Indications and Contraindications

The literature has shown that most children—ranging from the conduct-disordered (Kernberg & Chazan, 1991) to abused children (Mandell & Damon, 1989; Kitchur & Bell, 1989) to those who witness domestic violence (van Dalen and Glasserman, 1997) to the chronically ill (Williams & Backer, 1983)—can gain therapeutically from a group experience. However, each clinician is faced with determining which group is indicated for which child and with which therapist. A screening appointment with the child (and parent) can help determine the suitability of the match of the child with the group. During this interview, the group leader can ascertain the child's motivation, degree of sophistication, intelligence, diagnosis, and level of impulsivity, as well as other factors. This meeting also permits the beginning formation of a therapeutic alliance and may also provide an opportunity to formulate an individualized treatment plan. The child's questions and concerns regarding joining a group can be addressed.

This initial interview allows the group therapist to balance the prospective group. This entails a careful consideration of who the group members will be based on developmental factors and presenting difficulties as well as race, sex, SES, etc. Balancing the group maximizes the therapeutic effect and potential cohesion of the group. Thus, placing a highly constricted, shy 8-year-old Latino girl in a group full of impulse-disordered 10-year-old Caucasian boys is probably a recipe for disaster, which can be averted by screening and thoughtful balancing.

As for contraindications, extremely fragile and anxious children are best seen individually or in duo-therapy (to be discussed later in this chapter) prior to placement in a larger group. Children who are highly impulsive, extremely paranoid, or actively psychotic are generally poor candidates for group therapy.

Since it is often hard to predict how questionable group candidates will perform in the group, some clinicians have found it useful to invite a prospective group member to come to an ongoing group as a visitor. Some children will benefit from group placement provided that they receive concurrent drug therapy (e.g., Ritalin for children with attention deficit disorder) or family therapy. Pfeifer and Spinner (1985) have prescribed combined individual and group therapy by the same therapist—often recommended for many adolescent and adult patients—for children. This can be extremely beneficial to the therapist because combined therapy provides the leader with important in vivo experience of the child's interaction with peers, which is often quite different from behavior within an individual session.

Anthony, age 9, was referred for treatment because of violent outbursts in school, during which he flung chairs at students and teachers alike. In individual sessions over the course of several months, he was extremely polite, soft-spoken, and cooperative (to the point that the therapist was beginning to doubt the almost weekly reports from the school of Anthony's temper). Anthony's second group session was characterized by an alteraction with another group member over a second helping of a snack; Anthony lost control to the extent that he needed to be restrained by the male leader.

The Group Setting

Group size and balance, as well as the location and furnishings of the group room, are all critical factors in setting up a group. A small, crowded room will precipitate frustration because it does not allow expressive movement or activity. Similarly, a conference room with a plush carpet and expensive furniture invites trouble, as does a location near the clinic's waiting area (where high decibel levels will be quickly noticed).

If the group is held in a room where adult groups are conducted, other issues may arise.

During one group session, Alan discovered a discarded Alcoholics Anonymous pamphlet on the floor. He wondered if "groups for drunk people" were held in the room. Bobby wondered if the purpose of the boys' group was to keep them from becoming alcoholics. The co-therapists realized the significance of even seemingly peripheral materials in the group room.

The materials and games should be chosen for their therapeutic intent and age appropriateness. Elementary school–age boys, for example, will respond enthusiastically to arts and crafts materials as well as to controlled games such as dodgeball or around the world (using sponge balls). They will also value competitive board games. Girls will enjoy crafts materials such as beads to make jewelry and tend to favor board games with clear and distinct rules. Preschoolers are best served by projective toys such as dollhouses, puppets, telephones, etc.

Snacks and food are used widely in childrens' groups. Simple refreshments—that is, cookies or fruit and juice, with pizza and soda for special parties (such as a farewell session)—can be a means of real and symbolic feeding. In the real sense, food offered in a session to children from deprived and abusive backgrounds provides needed nutrition. In a symbolic sense, food is nurturing and as such is one way of helping to create a positive attachment to the group. The charged interactions induced by the food serve very often as sources for significant assessment data and as subjects for verbal interventions in fostering self-awareness.

In a time-limited group for bereaved children, the group members often began each session in silence. However, as soon as the snacks were distributed, as if by magic, the children began to talk. The group leaders quickly realized the value of food in allaying fear and anxiety, soothing these bereft children enough for them to begin to speak and participate in the sessions.

It is generally a good idea to run a children's group for at least one full hour, and ninety minutes (an hour and a half) if possible. This length of time allows for a warm-up period and permits full emergence and exploration of issues during the course of the session.

Although the child group therapy pioneers, such as Slavson (1943) and Redl (1944), utilized one therapist for each group, in recent years there has been a growing use of the co-therapy model with a male-female team in charge. Although the original idea of one group leader emerged, in part, because of theoretical notions (e.g., the nature of the transference), today's children's groups often call for individual attention to overly impulsive or "hard-to-reach" children. Two leaders can give more individual attention than one can. There is also a teaching advantage to having a trainee conduct (and simultaneously observe) a group with a senior practitioner. Additionally, in a two-therapist model, the therapists can provide each other with welcome opportunities for support, discussion, postsession processing, and relief through humor. Careful selection of co-therapists should team therapists who have complementary personality characteristics. In addition, a two-therapist team may provide the advantage of serving as a parental model.

After the co-therapists debated the merits of allowing a former group member to return to the group after a hiatus, Jennifer exclaimed, "I don't get it! Don't you ever get mad? You two are talking so calmly. In my house, somebody always ends up punching a wall!" We explained that, although two adults could, in fact, disagree, there were nonviolent ways to resolve differences and negotiate a compromise.

Finally, if a child needs to be briefly removed from a group, the co-therapy model allows one clinician to be with the child while the other covers the group.

A disadvantage of the co-therapy model is that it may prompt children to pit one therapist against the other, but this can be discussed both in the group or in collegial consultation (Soo, 1986, 1991; Schamess, Streider & Connors, 1997).

Therapist Qualifications

Therapists working with children in groups must be prepared for a variety of tasks. In most groups, it is necessary to set limits and provide structure. However, this must be done in such a way that firmness, not punitiveness, is communicated. It is easy for a children's group to force a therapist into the role of harsh disciplinarian.

Any therapist working with children must demonstrate respect for and warmth and sensitivity toward children. The ability to communicate verbally and nonverbally with children is also crucial, particularly because these groups often involve both talk and play. Although children's group leaders must be able to participate creatively in play, they need also to be able to contain overly regres-

sive behavior. Absorbing aggression without personalization is also important because children may, at times, taunt and tease each other and the leaders. In order for group members to learn that adults can withstand and contain their aggression, the adult must be able to tolerate such behavior, remaining relatively calm all the while.

The group therapist must be able to focus on relationships within the group, supporting and facilitating communications. At the same time, a consistent, predictably safe atmosphere must be established so that expression and exploration of feelings can occur. An awareness of each child's social, ethnic, and cultural background is integral. Sensitivity will help the therapist tailor the interventions for each group.

The leader must not rely on the group for much personal gratification. Often, children's groups can be frenetic—at times, chaotic. If a therapist's identity is too connected to the success or failure of the group, the group and therapist will not flourish.

Finally, a sense of humor is an important factor in keeping a perspective on the therapeutic work.

The group leader must be cognizant of many of the pitfalls of working with children: pressure from parents for instant changes, overidentification with the children, and the quandry of gaining respect and authority while not being overly permissive. Spontaneity; flexibility; playful creativity; and an ability to set firm, consistent limits are all important characteristics for a child group therapist (Azima, 1986).

Stages of Group Development

Various schemata have been proposed for the progressive phases in children's therapy groups. Thus, Garland, Jones, & Kolodny (1973) postulated a detailed five-stage model beginning with a *Pre-affiliation-Approach and Avoidance Stage,* moving through stages of *Power and Control,* then *Intimacy,* and ultimately *Differentiation,* and *Termination.* During the Pre-affiliation phase there is considerable anxiety, with concerns about "How do I fit in?" foremost in the children's minds. The adult becomes the center of attention as children test the limits of what is acceptable.

Introducing new members is easiest in this stage, where there is much fluidity and a minimum sense of "groupness." Having decided that the group might be gratifying and even beneficial, the children move to a stage where issues of *power and control* are dominant. A struggle for status now ensues with much conflict, resulting eventually in a relatively stable pecking order, although this may fluctuate depending on the activity. For example, when intellectual skill is required, a less-coordinated boy who is academically inclined may be sought after; when sports are in ascendance, this boy may give way to the athlete of the group. Deviant behavior may appear as a way of testing the therapist's and the group's limits. The Intimacy phase is characterized by a noticeable personal involvement of the members with each other and with the group as a single entity. A family-like feeling grows, accompanied by evidence of sibling rivalry. The children may begin to refer to the group as a prized unit. The stage of Differentiation entails the emergence of separate individuals who value the now-cohesive group experience. The frequent experiences of the earlier two phases, in which the children relate to the adults and other children as figures from their own lives, now yield to more reality-based perceptions of peers and of the leader. There emerges too, a clarity of the group purpose, good communication, and an atmosphere of trust. The Termination stage involves a moving apart—with sadness and mourning—that may evoke temporary regressions and recapitulations of the entire group history, demanding understanding and mastery of the conflicted feelings. Group members may reminisce and wax nostalgic over the group's history and their experiences.

Even though these stages were initially outlined for long-term groups, short-term therapy groups undergo similar but accelerated developmental stages.

The recent development of short-term group therapies, whose length may be 8 to 12 weeks, forces the leaders to pay particularly careful attention to patient selection, group composition, and the establishment of realistic achievement goals. Furthermore, as noted by Scheidlinger (1984) in his overview of short-term group therapy for children, these groups can emphasize and focus on adaptation, competency, strength, and growth. The child-patient's active participation in the shortened change effort becomes essential. Short-term groups tend to work best with those children who have a focal issue, suffer from situational distress, demonstrate mild behavioral difficulties, and have relatively strong familial supports in place. No matter what the term of the group is, the indications and contraindications and various factors noted previously are critical to the group's success.

Within the category of short-term approaches, duo-therapy is a uniquely promising group method where children are treated in pairs. It can be a useful preparatory step for group therapy in larger groups, for children who are either too fearful or too undersocialized for the usual group experience. It has also been valuable for the short-term, concentrated handling of severe instances of sibling rivalry (Lieberman and Smith, 1991).

Parent Groups

Recognizing the need to reinforce the effects of child group therapy by work with the parents, Slavson (1950) introduced Child-Centered Guidance Groups for Parents. Since then, conjoint parent groups have grown in popularity because they help to foster the gains made by the children in their own groups (Kernberg & Chazan, 1991; Arnold, Rowe, & Tolbert, 1978). In conducting parents' groups designed to focus on understanding their children and on parental roles, the group experience can lead individual parents to seek psychotherapy (individual or group) for themselves. The advantages of parent groups can include (1) enhanced motivation in supporting the child's group work, (2) information sharing regarding the children's daily functioning, (3) increased understanding of the part the parent plays in the child's difficulties, (4) learning new parental skills, (5) emotional support.

Given the difficulties involved in getting parents to attend group meetings, some clinicians have relied on single or occasional get-togethers to obtain information (however minimal) about the childrens' functioning and to dispel parental misconceptions about the group treatment. This can be particularly useful in work with children from dysfunctional, chaotic families. Such a connection with the parent or caregiver is crucial because the child often relies on the adult for transportation to the appointments; without the parent's involvement, the child cannot attend the group. It is also important to clarify for the parent that snacks and enjoyable activities notwithstanding, the group is a necessary *therapeutic* component and attendance should not be viewed as a reward or punishment.

Interaction with Other Interventions

Because some children might benefit from but are not yet ready to enter a group, individual and/or family treatment may be indicated initially. The child who is treated in individual or family and group therapy may have one therapist or two. Issues of confidentiality and information sharing relative to the two treatments arise. This is also relevant to very young children's groups, which often have a parental component, either in the form of regular parent meetings or a separate parallel group. Obviously, information learned in a group session may be extremely beneficial in individual or family work, but the therapist must exercise caution and clinical judgment about sharing such information. He or she must obtain permission where permission is required.

Conclusion

Given the economic realities of today, which include managed care, group therapy is likely to expand in tandem with the mental health field's shift toward increasingly pragmatic and cost-effective treatment methods. New methods will also reflect the mental health field's preference for pluralistic, systems-oriented, and problem-focused approaches.

The long-term group therapy models first developed by the pioneers in the field of children's groups are likely to be replaced further by short-term clinical models. In schools and in pediatric departments of hospitals, psychoeducational groups and support groups will probably grow in popularity, because they are proven, valuable treatment modalities for such disparate populations as children of divorce (Kalter, Pickar, & Lesowitz, 1984), children with chronic medical conditions, youths who have lost a parent to AIDS (Aronson, 1994), children with chronic medical conditions (Williams & Backer, 1983), and those from alcoholic and abusing families.

In this age, in which families and communities seem less able than in the past to provide children with support, planned children's groups can serve as an important resource in providing youths with major restitutive experiences, paving the way for a more normative developmental course.

SUGGESTED READING

Anthony, E. J. (1957). Group analytic psychotherapy with children and adolescents. In S. H. Foulkes & E. J. Anthony (Eds.), *Group psychotherapy* (pp. 186–232). Baltimore: Penguin.

Arnold, L. E., Rowe, M., & Tolbert, H. A. (1978). Parent groups. In L. E. Arnold (Ed.), *Helping parents help their children* (pp. 114–125). New York: Brunner Mazel.

Aronson, S. (1994). Group intervention with children of parents with AIDS. *Group, 18* (3), 133–140.

Axline, V. (1947). *Play therapy*. Boston: Houghton-Mifflin.

Azima, F. J. (1986). Countertransference: In and beyond child group psychotherapy. In A. E. Riester & I. Kraft (Eds.), *Child group psychotherapy: Future tense* (pp. 139–156). Madison, T: International Universities Press.

Barkow, J. H. (1977). Human ethology and intra-individual systems. *Social Science Information, 16*, 133–145.

Charach, R. (1983). Brief interpretive group psychotherapy with early latency-age children. *International Journal of Group Psychotherapy, 33*, 349–364.

Erikson, E. (1959). *Identify and the life cycle*. New York: International Universities Press.

Frank, M. G. (1976). Modifications of activity group therapy: Responses of ego-impoverished children. *Clinical Social Work Journal, 4*, 102–103.

Gabriel, B. (1939). An experiment in group treatment. *American Journal of Orthopsychiatry, 9*, 146–169.

Garland, J., Jones, H., & Kolodny, R. (1973). A model for stages of development in social work groups. In S. Bernstein (Ed.), *Explorations in group work* (pp. 17–71). Boston: Milford House.

Ginnott, H. (1961). *Group psychotherapy with children.* New York: McGraw-Hill.

Grunebaum, H., & Solomon, L. (1987). Peer relationships, self-esteem and the self. *International Journal of Group Psychotherapy, 37,* 475–513.

Kalter, N., Pickar, J., & Lesowitz, M. (1984). School-based developmental facilitation groups for children of divorce: A preventive intervention. *American Journal of Orthopsychiatry, 54,* 613–623.

Kernberg, P. F., & Chazan, S. L. (1991). *Children with conduct disorders: A psychotherapy manual.* New York: Basic Books.

Kernberg, P. F., & Liebowitz, J. H. (1986). Diagnostic play groups for children: Their role in assessment and treatment planning. In A. E. Riester & I. Kraft (Eds.), *Child group psychotherapy: Future tense* (pp. 71–82). Madison, CT: International Universities Press.

Kitchur, M., & Bell, R. (1989). Group psychotherapy with preadolescent sexual abuse victims: Literature review and description of an inner-city group. *International Journal of Group Psychotherapy, 39,* 285–310.

Lieberman, S. N., & Smith, L. B. (1991). Duo therapy: A bridge to the world of peers for the ego-impaired child. *Journal of Child and Adolescent Group Therapy, 1,* 243–252.

Mandell, J. G., & Damon, L. (1989). *Group treatment for sexually abused children.* New York: Guilford Press.

Pfeifer, G., & Spinner, D. (1985). Combined individual and group psychotherapy with children: An ego developmental perspective. *International Journal of Group Psychotherapy, 35,* 11–36.

Redl, F. (1944). Diagnostic group work. *American Journal of Orthopsychiatry, 14,* 53–67.

Redl, F. (1966). *When we deal with children.* Glencoe, IL: Free Press.

Rogers, C. R. (1942). *Counseling and psychotherapy.* Boston: Houghton-Mifflin.

Rose, S. D. (1972). *Treatment of children in groups—a behavioral approach.* San Francisco: Jossey-Bass.

Rose, S. D., & Edelson, J. S. (1987). *Working with children and adolescents in group: A multimethod approach.* San Francisco: Jossey-Bass.

Schamess, G. (1986). Differential diagnosis and group structure in the outpatient treatment of latency-age children. In A. E. Riester & I. Kraft (Eds.), *Child group psychotherapy: Future tense* (pp. 29–70). Madison, CT: International Universities Press.

Schamess, G., Streider, F. and Martel Connors, K. (1997). Supervision and staff training for children's group psychotherapy: General principles and applications with cumulatively traumitized, inner city children. *International Journal of Group Psychotherapy, 47(4),* 399–425.

Scheidlinger, S. (1960). Experiential group treatment of severely deprived latency-age children. *American Journal of Orthopsychiatry, 30,* 356–368.

Scheidlinger, S. (1982). The concept of latency: Implications for group treatment. In S. Scheidlinger (Ed.), *Focus on group psychotherapy—clinical essays* (pp. 125–132). New York: International Universities Press.

Scheidlinger, S. (1984). Short-term group psychotherapy for children: An overview. *International Journal of Group Psychotherapy, 34,* 573–585.

Scheidlinger, S. (1985). Group treatment of adolescents: An overview. *American Journal of Orthopsychiatry, 55,* 102–111.

Schiffer, M. (1969). *The therapeutic play group.* New York Grune & Stratton.

Slavson, S. R. (1943). *An introduction to group therapy.* New York: International Universities Press.

Slavson, S. R. (1950). *Child centered group guidance for parents.* New York: International Universities Press.

Soo, E. S. (1985). Applications of object relations concepts to children's group psychotherapy. *International Journal of Group Psychotherapy, 35,* 37–47.

Soo, E. S. (1986). Training and supervision in child and adolescent group psychotherapy. In A. E. Riester & I. Kraft (Eds.), *Child group psychotherapy: Future tense* (pp. 157–172). Madison CT: International Universities Press.

Soo, E. S. (1991). Strategies for success for the beginning group therapist with child and adolescent groups. *Journal of Child and Adolescent Group Therapy, 1,* 95–106.

Sugar, M. (1974). Interpretive group therapy with latency-age children. *International Journal of Group Psychotherapy, 13,* 646–666.

Sullivan, H. S. (1953). *The Interpersonal Theory of Psychiatry.* New York: W. W. Norton.

van Dalen, A. and Glasserman, M. (1997). My father, Frankenstein: A child's view of battering parents. *Journal of the American Academy of Child and Adolescent Psychiatry, 36:7,* 1005–1007.

Williams, K., & Backer, M. (1983). Use of small groups with chronically ill children. *School Health, 3,* 205–207.

29 / Group Psychotherapy with Adolescents

Max Sugar

Group psychotherapy with adolescents has been a well-recognized therapeutic modality for many decades. This chapter offers a perspective on it, beginning with its history and value. The chapter then discusses the indications that suggest group psychotherapy may be effective, and it describes types of group treatment; practical considerations, such as group composition and specific techniques; and therapeutic factors.

Historical Considerations

Group psychotherapy began in Boston in 1905 as a class for adult patients with tuberculosis. The class was based on an inspirational approach pioneered by Dr. Joseph Pratt. In 1908 Emerson used the same method with undernourished children. In 1911, Moreno and separately Slavson, treated adolescents in a group. Adler used group therapy with adolescents in 1918. Aichorn used groups to deal with delinquent adolescents in the 1920s.

In his work with delinquent adolescents, Redl focused on leadership and group formation, particularly in the residential setting. Others involved in the early efforts with adolescent group therapy were Gabriel, Bender, Waltman, Ackerman, Curran, Wollan, and Spotnitz (Rachman & Raubolt, 1984). *The Journal of Child and Adolescent Group Therapy,* which began in 1991, was the first journal dealing with group work involving children and teens. Books on group psychotherapy and adolescents first appeared in the 1970s; relevant authors include Sugar (1975), Brandes and Gardner (1973), Berkovitz (1972), and MacLennan and Felsenfeld (1970).

The burgeoning of adolescent group therapy began in the '60s, with the growth of community mental health centers. It is now one of the most widely used of all psychotherapies for adolescents, since it is used extensively (about 28 hours per week) for inpatients and routinely in outpatient mental health, guidance, and university clinics, as well as in private practice.

The Value of Group Therapy for Adolescents

A therapeutic group is particularly appropriate for adolescents since it is consonant with parents, as a source of emotional support. The unique feature in group therapy is the catalytic effect that patients can have on each other. With the group therapist to guide the process, patients learn to verbalize rather than act on their feelings, they hear what others feel about the expression of these emotions, and they can then consider new ways to manage their problems. In time they may even learn how their difficulties originated.

In the therapy group the teenager soon realizes he is not the only one with problems. This may boost his self-esteem, and the youngster may feel "not crazy" and "not weak," especially in regard to the therapist. Despite positive feelings toward the therapist in individual therapy, the adolescent may still see him/her as a frightening or critical parent surrogate. The presence of the others may make the therapist seem less imposing. This may lead to audaciousness and openness, and later to trust in the therapist.

Adolescents have a need to idealize and then derogate the authority figure; this evokes a fantasy of retaliation by the therapist, which in turn arouses anxiety. In the group, however, the youngster feels strong and protected by peers. The group of peers provide some relatively healthy ego functions and can offer observations that may be helpful to the individual. In the therapy group adolescents may also learn something about nonexploitative relationships. Therefore, an adolescent often engages in group therapy more easily than in individual therapy.

Indications

For adolescents group therapy is used to enhance ego functioning, improve social competence, modify behavioral patterns, adapt to chronic illness or severe environmental difficulties, and develop some understanding of their own unusual or inappropriate feelings and behavior.

For a youngster who is so closed off or avoidant that individual therapy is unproductive, group therapy may offer successful treatment approach. A minimal indication arises for the youngster who relates fairly well in individual therapy but withholds at times, has some meaningful group associations, and whose degree of disturbance is not severe. The youngster whose problems fall in between these polarities may be offered and choose individual, family, or group therapy.

Outpatient adolescent group psychotherapy is contraindicated in cases of overt psychosis, severe narcissistic and borderline personality disorder, antisocial personality disorder, persistent negative attitude to therapy, panic, marked impulsivity, and proselytizing (Sugar, 1986). However, some patients with these problems may be helped in a homogeneous group composed of others with the same diagnosis.

Types of Groups

HETEROGENEOUS GROUPS

Heterogeneous groups contain patients with a variety of diagnoses. Diagnostic groups of 2 to 4 sessions are often used to decide whether group treatment or some other form of therapy is most suitable for a given cluster of outpatients.

Long-term or brief outpatient groups can be useful in treating mood, anxiety, mild personality, and a few schizoid or borderline personality disorders. These groups may also be used to treat some eating and conduct disorders (Sugar, 1975). A developmental language–disordered or mildly retarded youngster may be included in the outpatient group but will require extra support from the therapist. An inpatient group is usually heterogeneous and may include patients with borderline and narcissistic personality disorders, schizophre-

nia, bipolar disorder, severe separation anxiety disorder, eating disorders, and substance abuse.

Aftercare groups are also heterogeneous, since different diagnoses apply to the patients. The patients are all posthospital and have a similar set of recent experiences, however; these common characteristics enhance group cohesiveness.

HOMOGENEOUS GROUPS

Homogenous therapy groups are those in which the same diagnosis applies to all the patients. Homogeneous groups stimulate less apprehension within members than do heterogeneous groups, since all the patients have the same condition. The patients therefore feel more empathy from the others, less vulnerability to them, and may be more open about their feelings. Such therapy groups may be helpful to patients with bipolar disorder, schizophrenia, language disorder, mental retardation, asthma, eating disorders, substance abuse disorders, post-traumatic stress disorder, cancer, or head injury. Homogeneous groups may also be helpful to adolescents with divorced parents or those suffering from sexual or physical abuse. Youngsters who are inept, shy, and withdrawn, and who need help with social activity, may best be treated in homogeneous groups.

INSTITUTIONAL GROUPS

The term *institution* includes hospitals and residential centers and guidance, mental health, and university clinics. For example, some institutions require co-therapists and observers; in others, the therapist functions alone. In some institutions, group therapy is done routinely and with all patients unless group therapy is specifically contraindicated. The purpose and policies of the institution will affect the form and function of therapy groups conducted within it.

INPATIENT GROUPS

An adolescent is usually admitted to an inpatient setting against his/her wishes. The patient usually has a negative attitude about therapy. Since such patients consider the hospital as rejection or a jail sentence, they often try to manipulate an early discharge.

Since inpatient group consists of patients who

feel "captive" they usually display the behaviors in response to coerced feeling: defiance, projection, blaming, scapegoating and attempts to escape are common. Inpatient groups meet frequently, 5 or 6 days per week. Since other kinds of group meetings occur daily for inpatients, therapy group–related exchanges may not end when the group therapy session is over. This may lead to lapses in confidentiality and remarks that are inappropriate when expressed outside the group. When confidentiality is broken, the matter should be discussed openly in the next group session.

CRISIS GROUPS

Some homogeneous groups are designed to offer therapy for only a brief period or organized to deal with a crisis. College entrance, teen pregnancy, or physical illness are examples of such crises. Another group arrangement—called adolescent peer group, or office network, therapy—involves only one adolescent and his or her friends. This may be a helpful therapy to deal with suicidal feelings, marked resistance° to therapy, or to avoid hospitalization. °Resistance is defined here as an obstacle to therapy. It may involve resistance to change, and change could involve learning, unlearning, or facing unpleasant feelings. To form this special group, the patient—say, a teenage boy—brings as many of his friends as he wishes to his individual sessions. He does this for as long as he chooses, making it a group of his own selection and size, to help him with his problem. His friends are asked to discuss the patient from their perspective, but they are not treated (Sugar, 1975).

Transference

Transference is a universal mental mechanism, a special kind of displacement seen, in therapy, in the form of unrealistic roles or identities that the patient unconsciously imputes to the therapist, along with the patient's reactions to this misrepresentation, which derives from earlier experiences with significant people. In group therapy with adolescents, the focus is mostly on the here and now so that there is relatively little work done on trans-

ference, and only when necessary. However, awareness of the transferences in group therapy is necessary to understand the group process, the group as a whole, and the situation of the individuals.

A wide array of transferences is possible in group therapy, and there may be multiple transferences toward group members. Transferences are based on various specific past or present important figures in patients' lives. There may be a transference to the group as a family or to the group as a parent. There may be erotic, affectionate, or sibling transference to the therapist. Several different transferences may occur simultaneously from patients to the therapist or to other group members, or from the therapist to a patient or patients. The patients may experience ambivalence, rivalry, hostility, affection, and affiliation to each other based on their transferences. For example, as part of a parental or sibling transference, a patient may seek approval by being overly compliant to the therapist or to another patient. With this spread of transferences in group therapy, most of which are directed to peers, there is relatively little direct transference to the therapist (Sugar, 1986).

CASE EXAMPLE I

A talented white male therapist became hostile toward a black male adolescent in his group. Over a period of time this caused the therapist increasing discomfort, and he could not understand the basis of his hostility. In the course of supervision it became clear that the resident had an erotic transference to the patient's mother whom he saw for infrequent guidance sessions. She reminded him of the maid his family had employed when he was a youngster and his erotic feelings to her. In the present situation he viewed his adolescent patient as a rival and, therefore, felt hostile. He experienced this as inappropriate and interfering with the therapy. When the source of his hostility became clear, he felt relieved and his hostility ceased.

Countertransference

The many definitions of *countertransference* include (1) a response to the patient's transference, and (2) the totality of the therapist's feelings about a patient. All the definitions involve concern about whether these feelings interfere with the therapist's functioning.

Countertransference may be viewed as having two components. One part is the communication that emanates from the patient's fantasies. The other component is the therapist's inappropriate response to such communication, regardless of whether it arises from the patient's stimulus or the therapist's problem. For example, a therapist's excessive talking may be due to anxiety or a rivalrous sibling transference to a patient. Stepping over the therapist-patient boundary with inappropriate personal revelations may be due to the therapist's transference to the group as a whole (that is, to the group as a family) or a countertransference response or (it may reflect a wish to be in group therapy).

In the group the therapist may have a countertransference reaction to one patient or to the group as a whole. When the therapist becomes aware of an irrational or strange fantasy or feelings but allows the fantasy to continue, she will presently realize that it derives from the fantasies of the patient or the group as a whole to the therapist. This awareness helps the therapist understand the communication of the patient or group, and may provide some notion about the current transference attitude of the patient or group.

When the whole group attacks the therapist for some behavior or comment, she should view the attack as a possible countertransference issue. For example, if the therapist recognizes that during a session he voiced an inappropriate response to the group or a patient and the group perceived it, he should acknowledge the error and compliment group members for their accurate perception. Then he should try to understand what occurred. If he recognized the error long after the fact, then he can assume that the group managed it or reacted to it in some way and went on in spite of it. The therapist's recollection of events surrounding the inappropriate response may help clarify the group's reaction to the therapist's countertransference.

Some common countertransference occurrences are calling a patient by another patient's name; feeling bored, sleepy, or intensely angry when a patient recounts an event; experiencing lapses in empathy or attention; and being unable to recall ongoing session material.

CASE EXAMPLE II

In a late-adolescent group the therapist fantasized having a female patient sit in his lap. He felt ashamed and distressed by this fantasy and tried to avoid it and her by becoming very active with the other patients. When he considered these feelings and behavior in connection with the patient's earlier material, he became more aware of her intense rivalry with the other patients. As he listened to her, he felt he understood her fantasies and eventually her wish to be special to him. She then said that she wanted to sit in his lap and not share him with the other group members.

CASE EXAMPLE III

In an early-adolescent group of boys, the therapist's bias led him to view the patients as unfortunate, needy youngsters and as much younger than they were. This led to holding the group sessions in a room containing children's toys and extra chairs with rollers. Refreshments, including soft drinks, were provided. When the patients became anxious about some issue, several of them began to play with the toys, disrupting the group. A subgroup emerged simultaneously; these patients jostled one another in the roll-around chairs, as if they were involved in a cavalry charge. The group responded to limit-setting efforts each time these events occurred, but the disruptions continued. On several occasions the youngsters' hostile feelings were not contained, and they sprayed their soft drinks onto the ceiling and walls. This led to considering the therapist's contribution to the problems and, ultimately, to discontinuing the food and removing all toys and rolling chairs, and all toys leaving only one chair per patient. After voicing many objections to the changes, the group settled down and became a very good working group.

Arranging the Group

PREPARATION AND ARRANGEMENTS

Before entering an outpatient therapy group, the youngster needs some introductory individual therapy. He/she should have positive feelings about and a working relationship with the therapist prior to group therapy.

The therapist explains the indications for group therapy after the patient is comfortable with the therapist. If the youngster—a boy, in this case— is interested, the arrangements are described and questions are invited and answered. Confidentiality and the consequences of breaking it (removal from the group) along with the limits (that no one is allowed to hurt anyone or anything in the group room) should be explained.

The invitation to say anything he wishes in the group is clarified so that he understands that he may be silent if he chooses. Silence is often a patient's way of not saying something that seems unkind, but the therapist explains that a therapy group is not a social group in which he is trying to make friendships. The patient's only goal is trying to help himself. Therefore, by saying whatever comes to mind, he is doing his job, and by doing it he may also help the other patients. Some therapists do not allow group members to socialize with one another while they are patients in the group. The therapist explains this restriction if it applies. The therapist also makes clear the fact that courtesy, the form of allowing others to finish their sentences, is expected.

Patients frequently wish to discontinue group therapy prematurely. The therapist discusses this in the preparatory period as something to be expected and makes sure the patient understands that such a wish may be due to fear of exposing some unpleasant feelings. Then the patient should agree to discuss this wish in the group whenever it occurs and for at least two consecutive sessions before discontinuing group therapy. Such efforts may lead to an understanding of the obstacles the patient is facing and prevent premature termination.

The therapist responds to the youngster's anxiety about group therapy, which may be evident in his appearance and questions, by exploring, explaining, and reassuring. During this preparatory period the therapist explains the goals, schedule, and administrative details to the patient's parents and answers their questions.

COMPOSITION

Number, Age and Sex: Early-adolescent groups include a single sex; mid- and late-adolescent groups may include both sexes. A mid- or late-adolescent group contains a maximum of 10 patients. Six patients should probably be the limit in an early-adolescent group, since these youngsters tend to express feelings physically and be verbally disruptive. Some therapists advocate inviting 12 to 16 adolescents with the hope that 6 to 8 will remain in the group. This may send the youngsters the message that they would not be missed if absent, leading them to feel unimportant and thus discourage regular attendance.

An age spread of 3 years may be optimal for early- and mid-adolescent groups, but in the late-adolescent group it may be up to 5 years; for example, a late-adolescent group could include patients from 19 to 24 years old. When all patients in an inpatient group, balancing the group (discussed later) and controlling the age spread are difficult. The result may be isolates or some who gain little from group therapy initially. In the following case it was apparent in retrospect that the youngster should not have entered the inpatient group.

CASE EXAMPLE IV

A very mature-looking, tall 12-year-old boy attended an inpatient therapy group in which the other patients, male and female, were ages 14 to 17. He was asynchronous in developmental stage and, although very bright, was unable to follow the others' material. His anxiety increased markedly, as did his misconduct and disruption of the group. This led to his removal from the group.

Besides the diagnosis, the therapist's considerations in selecting a youngster for a particular group involve the adolescent's physical, social, chronological, and academic levels. These should be within close range for all of the youngsters in a group. The clinical picture of each youngster should be viewed as a distinct and individual matter. Each potential member must be viewed in terms of how he or she might fit with the other patients being considered. Attention needs to be given to the makeup of the group as a whole so that it has more verbal than nonverbal patients, and patients whose diagnoses represent a mixture of affective, anxiety, and personality disorders.

Each patient in the group should have something in common with at least one other patient to avoid having isolate or anyone so deviant that he/she cannot relate to someone about something. Occasionally an isolated youngster may have a very productive group experience in which the patient gives and receives help from similar group member. Such youngsters may complicate the group process, since initially the therapist may need to be more actively supportive to them than the other patients, in order to protect them from rejection. These activities by the therapist stimulate jealousy among the other group members, along with hostility to the therapist.

CASE EXAMPLE V

In a heterogeneous early-adolescent outpatient group of boys, a depressed 15-year-old with a reading disability had difficulty with peer acceptance. He blamed this on his slight enunciation difficulty. His intelligence, abstract-thinking, and mechanical-task capabilities were above average. Due to low self-esteem he rarely initiated any comments. The therapist often supported or protected him from the others' hostility. This led to jealous feelings toward the patient and hostility toward the therapist.

When a 13-year-old gifted, isolated, depressed boy with poor peer relations entered the group, the boys soon rejected him because of intellectualization, compulsive talking, and disdain for others. To gain the approval of the other patients, he tried being the group comedian and bringing them gifts of food.

As therapy progressed, the two unaccepted youngsters found themselves allies on the basis of being rejected. Their mutual difficulty led to an acceptance of each by the other and, eventually, of both by the other patients. This culminated in a rewarding, growth-promoting, and successful group therapy experience for both.

Balancing the Group After the therapist has established the physical, social, chronological, and academic criteria for group members and considered the desirable clinical mix, he/she must consider a wide range of characteristics and try to compose a group in which opposing characteristics balance each other. This is called balancing the group. It is part of composition and it is especially important in working with outpatient adolescents because even with similar diagnoses, they are unique. They also have such a great potential for action and differences in its expression. The characteristics a therapist must consider in this phase of composition include level of maturation, judgment, reality testing, type of defenses, ease of losing control, and level of and threats to integration. In balancing, pairs of patients with characteristics (which are representative, but not the totality, of) such as the following may be considered for inclusion: shy-aggressive, loosely-controlled–tightly controlled, imaginative-conventional, relaxed conscience–rigid conscience, demanding-compliant, gregarious-withdrawn, leader-follower, minimizer-exaggerater, and action-oriented–introspective. These groupings may reflect diagnostic categories, but not precisely. Such pairings provide the potential for interstimulation, for balancing different modes of emotional expression, and for reducing anxiety in the early phase of the group.

ADMINISTRATION

The therapist needs to plan for the group according to the prospective members' developmental and therapy needs. Accordingly, attention to the following items may be helpful in organizing the group.

DURATION OF SESSIONS

Early-adolescent sessions may be an hour in length; mid- or late-adolescent sessions can last for 90 minutes. If youngsters cannot concentrate for an hour, 45-minute session is preferable.

DURATION OF THERAPY

In open-ended groups for outpatients, the individual is in therapy for as long as needed. There is no contract except for discharge, and that is based on a consensus with the other patients and therapist. Some adolescent groups are scheduled to last 3 or 6 months, or 20 sessions. Groups with a fixed end date are called closed groups. Some therapists arrange for patients to attend group for a minimum of 6 months or for an academic year. The patients may continue with a new group afterward.

THE PHYSICAL SETTING

A group therapy room should be soundproof. It should be locked on the inside to prevent intrusions, but patients should be able to exit easily. During early-adolescent sessions some therapists use a slide bolt on the door to prevent youngsters from leaving impulsively. The room should have no distractions, such as toys, and be large enough to accommodate all the group members comfortably. Some simple drawing materials should be available. The chairs should be arranged in a circle so that the view between therapist and patients is unabstructed. Seats are unassigned.

The Group Therapist's Functions

The management of the site, administration regarding fees and contract, and decisions about session duration and meeting time are the responsibility of the therapist. The therapist must foster a positive relationship with parents and provide guidance as needed. For inpatients, the hospital administration usually sets some limits due to school and other schedules, but the therapist has much to contribute to and coordinate with the administration.

The group therapist:

- Determines the initiation and termination of the group
- Introduces new members
- Is directive
- Promotes or decreases interactions
- Focuses on feelings and issues
- Clarifies material
- Provides stimulation of topics
- Enlarges the scope of topics
- Respects defenses
- Interprets group emotion nearest the surface
- Supports
- Sets limits
- Confronts
- Manages resistance
- Manages the transference
- Manages countertransference
- Universalizes
- Uses 'going around'
- Protects a group member by changing the subject
- Deflects to decrease anxiety
- Compliments patients on their memories, ideas, linkages, suggestions, and improved function
- Reflects and rewords; e.g., "The group seems to be saying . . ."
- Summarizes
- Notes and correlates the patients' behavior and feelings

The therapist may heighten group interaction by asking patients to express their feelings about a topic or encourage them to speak without interruption. After the peak of interaction he or she may make interpretive or generalizing comments. The therapist may lower interaction to reduce extreme anxiety or decrease excess excitement by making a supportive or universalizing comment or a group interpretation. He or she may universalize by saying, for example, "This would be upsetting to everyone."

Going around, refers to asking each member of the group to discuss his or her feelings about a particular event, another patient, the therapist, or feelings about the group as a whole. This may provide different views that may lead to a majority, or consensus, opinion, or highlight new ideas about the issue. It is used to deal with problems such as increased anxiety, scapegoating, long silences, or resistance.

Some major cautions for the therapist are to listen carefully, avoid rushing in when there is a silence, and notice his or her own feelings and fantasies during the session.

Since the therapist in an adolescent group has a more active role than in an adult group or in individual therapy, he/she may try to behave, dress, or look like the adolescents. To do this is to ignore the recommendation to maintain boundaries between patient and therapist. However, using the patients' vernacular is appropriate.

Techniques

The composition, particular issues, and dynamics of the group and whether patients are in an inpatient or outpatient group affect the choice of techniques the therapist uses.

FOR ANXIETY

To decrease anxiety, the therapist may universalize, change the topic, deflect the focus, or "go around" about the patients' thoughts.

THERAPEUTIC COHESION

This may be fostered by pointing out how well the group is working on a problem or that the members are all attentive and sympathetic to the problems of the index patient.

PAIRING

Pairing is encouraged in the beginning phase by pointing out similarities between the problems the patients face. This may help patients relate to each other.

PERSONAL SYMBOLS AND OBJECTS

Poetry, drawings, songs, letters, diaries, or photos by the patients and are accepted enthusiastically since they provide an opportunity to deal with a representation of great personal significance to the patient. The youngster may need guidance from the other patients and the therapist to verbalize his thoughts about the objects and connect them with relevant issues or events. Eventually, these may lead to some insight.

GROUP OFFICERS

In some groups members select a member, weekly or monthly, to be the secretary. At the beginning of the session, the secretary gives a synopsis of the preceding session. A member may also volunteer for the job. A president may be elected by the group on a similar rotating basis to guide productivity, discussion, or topic selection. Having such rotations may help the patients to observe the others and their interaction more closely with others become more responsible in the group.

THE CLONES

Creating and using clones in adolescent inpatient and outpatient group therapy has been useful in dealing with low self-esteem, scapegoating, avoidance, or denial. This may also be used with outpatients. A clone in this case, is a full-sized cardboard cutout that each patient draws, and then cuts out of him- or herself. On one side is a drawing that shows the good or positive aspect of the patient; on the other side is a drawing their reflecting negative or undesirable aspect. These are expressed by the colors, clothes, posess, facial expression, or makeup. The clone is brought to every session and used as a stimulus to discuss various components of the youngster's behavior. The youngster may be asked by the other patients or the therapist to turn the clone to the side that reflects the patient as perceived currently by the others. The patient is then asked to discuss what the clone represents at that particular time in reference to the patient's behavior. A clone may also be made of the parents by the youngster and used similarly to focus feelings about them.

The youngster's negative feelings may be reflected by refusing to create a cloner, delaying the drawing, forgetting the clone, to sessions or tearing it up. However, since the clone soon takes on the aura of "a part of me," the youngster becomes very protective of it and treats it as a valuable object. Destruction of the drawing can be viewed as self-destructiveness. As youngsters change and improve their view of themselves, they often make new clones to reflect their improvement. They then discuss the two 'clones' and how the change in the drawings reflect change in themselves.

GOAL SETTING

Goal setting presses group members to focus on problem solving. After setting goals patients review what is attained every week or month. In therapy groups of short duration reviews may occur in each session. In approaches the therapist summarizes, whenever he/she thinks it is indicated, progress toward the stated goals.

ROLE-PLAYING

Role-playing can be very useful in separating the patient's feelings from those of others important to him; it may involve many group members. Specific roles, remarks, or themes may be assigned by the index patient, the therapist, or the others. Those involved in the role-playing then participate in portraying a specific scene or theme by verbalizing what they think is called for in that role. After this the patients share their observations and feelings about the portrayal.

VIDEOTAPING

Unstructured videotaping has been very useful in group therapy. Taping is stopped whenever the patient or therapist wish to focus on some behavior or comment made in the group, and playback occurs immediately. This leads to a discussion of the issue which, since it involves all the members, may enhance understanding of both that topic and the group process.

The self-reporting or reflection the tape may elicit usually focus on a patient's specific difficulties, such as avoidance, denial, or blaming. Initially, the result may be discomfort and anxiety for a patient in the "hot seat," but the therapist can allow verbalization of these issues on both aspects of the patients self the "good me" and the "bad me." This leads toward integration of the accepted and derogated parts of the personality.

FRIENDS

Occasionally, after obtaining permission from other patients, a patient may bring or be invited to bring a friend to a group session to discuss a particular problem. The friend is not treated as a patient but as a helper to the patient, someone who brings a peer's view of the patient in daily life. These data may help amplify the group's positive view of the patient as well as focus scrutiny on undesirable behavior or traits.

PARADOXICAL INTENTION

Spotnitz (1969) described paradoxical intention—that is, joining with the patient's negative attitude or behavior as a device to deal with it. In this approach the patient is complimented on his particular negative behavior or symptom as an asset. The patient usually questions this strange view, feels unsettled, and may begin considering what the behavior or symptom might mean or allow him or her to avoiding or meaning. This may be used limit impulsive or inappropriate behavior in the group.

FAMILY NIGHT

Some therapists have family night once a month. On that night one patient's family (on a rotating basis) interacts with the group and discusses their views of the youngster's problems. Sometimes a large-group session is held, in a room of appropriate size, with all the families and patients.

GENOGRAMS AND DRAWINGS

Genograms are often used to help a youngster describe multiple generations in his or her family. First the patient focuses on supplying names and relationships. Drawings of family members may be used similarly, and the patient may indicate likes and dislikes by adding smiles and frowns. The therapist asks the patient to elaborate on these feelings.

STORYTELLING

Storytelling is especially useful with early adolescents. In this the therapist focuses on feelings of anxiety or depression by asking patients to "go around" and report "the most scared time I ever had," "the most scary movie I ever saw," "the saddest day in my life," "the weirdest I ever felt," or the like.

Problems in Adolescent Group Therapy

NEGATIVE FEELINGS

Negative feelings about therapy are universal but may be greater in adolescent group therapy than in groups with patients of other ages. This may be due to adolescents' developmental issues and anxieties, such as the drive toward independence, ambivalence to authority, along with feeling strong enough in the group to express it. When the patients attack the therapist verbally, someone in the group usually comes to his/her defense unless the therapist has made an error. In group therapy other patients do not usually allow a patient's negative attitude to linger long. They attack it frontally, confronting or challenging the index patient's rationalizations, denial, etc.

PREMATURE TERMINATION

The premature dropout rate in adolescent groups is 15 to 25 percent even when well-prepared, beforehand. Therefore, it is useful to have other patients continually in preparation for entry into an openended outpatient group, or to be ready to start a new closed one. If a youngster's problems seem to be more than can be managed in the group and the patient is ambivalent about group therapy but the therapist feels the group is helpful nonetheless, then concomitant individual, family, or peer network therapy might be offered to keep the patient from dropping out.

SYMBIOTIC PAIRING

Symbiotic pairing is a special problem that may become a major resistance, especially when the pair involves patients with borderline or narcissistic personality disorders. A symbiotic pair forms a subgroup that tries to be impervious to therapeutic efforts. Each of the two speaks for, supports, and protects the other from the comments of the therapist and other group members. Clarification, labeling, confrontation, limit setting, and paradoxical intention techniques in a supportive-interpretive approach may be very helpful in such a case (Sugar, 1991).

CONFRONTING THE THERAPIST

With direct questions to and provocations of the therapist, adolescents may be more challenging in group therapy than in individual therapy. Their questions may be about very personal or intimate matters. They may ask the therapist to join them in drug abuse, such as smoking pot during the session. Or patients may insult the therapist's spouse or children; deride the therapist's appearance clothes; or denigrate the furniture, decorations, etc. The therapist should expect such attacks and deal with them as communications.

Therapeutic Factors in Group Therapy

Although all therapies offer hope, the therapy group offers universality also. With universality the patient no longer feels that he is the only one who has ever had such feelings; he can observe the others and hear similarities, and the others can empathize with his feelings. There is also information to be gleaned. For example, socializing techniques can be imparted from one patient to another. Another significant therapeutic factor in group therapy is the patient's feeling that he/she is accepted by peers.

From the beginning, in preparation for the group, altruism is stressed. In actual group ses-

sions altruism is often expressed by one member to another. The therapist can set an example by complimenting the youngsters on good work in a session or for achieving some insight remembering some detail that helps clarify something, for another patient, or their progress in therapy.

The group may also take on some aspects of a good family by providing a feeling of comfort. This enables the youngsters to feel more free to talk about personal matters. In a modified fashion this also allows for a corrective recapitulation of the primary family group.

A good deal of imitative behavior might occur. Since each member observes the behavior of the other youngsters as well as that of the therapist, he/she may copy it. On the other hand, peers may tell the index patient of some irritating personal habits or gestures. The youngster may then make efforts to modify these to gain approval.

The positive aspects of group interactions are derived from identification; mutual support; reduction of defenses; multitransferences; and, through the leader's example, the reduction of conscience harshness. Interpersonal learning occurs in the group through transference and insight about behavior and feelings. Interstimulation of the group members is a regular, helpful feature that promotes the therapy. Working on, or overcoming, a problem helps the patient feel the group is valuable and increases hopefulness and therapeutic cohesiveness for all the members. This helps the individuals feel that they are learning and that, eventually, they will be able to manage themselves without therapy.

The First Group Session

The first session in group therapy can be a very uncomfortable experience for both therapist and patients. For the therapist it is a test: It is the culmination of efforts to bring together strangers he hopes will work well together therapeutically. For the patients, the new experience elevates their apprehension and adds discomfort to whatever other problems they have. When all have arrived, the therapist asks patients to "go around" by introducing themselves and giving a summary of the problems that bring them to the group.

Usually the most anxious patient begins verbalizing. If there is a silence, the therapist may wait a short time and then make a universalization, such as "We're all nervous in here today." Patients often ask each other questions about school, grade, and interests as a way of getting to know each other. They may not return to their initial problems for the rest of the session, but they have made contact emotionally and their group therapy has begun.

At the end of that session, there is usually great relief apprehension has disappeared, and they feel the group is a great success. Additionally, the patients may have learned that may be helpful to express personal facts and feelings in this special setting.

Outcome

The outcome of group treatment, no matter which specific theory is applied, depends on the patient population; diagnoses; composition; balance; and the therapist's skill.

All theories of group therapy contain some common elements including: relation or transference, catharsis, insight and/or ego strengthening, reality testing, and sublimation.

There is a great need for but still a short supply of research on group psychotherapy with teenagers. However, extant outcome studies show good results for the majority of patients (Sugar, 1993).

Conclusions

Some therapists avoid group therapy with adolescents due to insufficient exposure to the significant therapeutic benefits and satisfaction that may be derived from such efforts. This chapter presents some fundamentals and guidelines to assist in planning for group therapy with adolescents, as well as considerations that may avoid problems in the endeavor. Hopefully, this material provides some clear direction that will stimulate further interest in, and use of, this modality. For therapists who are engaged in this enterprise, this chapter may enhance and broaden their approach.

SUGGESTED READINGS

Azima, F. K. & Richmond, L. C. (1989). *Adolescent group psychotherapy.* Madison, CT.: International Universities Press.

Berkovitz, I. H. (1972). *Adolescents grow in groups.* New York: Brunner/Mazel.

Brandes, N. S., & Gardner, M. L. (1973). *Group therapy for adolescents.* New York: Jason Aronson.

MacLennan, B. W., & Felsenfeld, N. (1970). *Group counseling and psychotherapy with adolescents.* New York: Columbia University Press.

Rachman, A. W., & Raubolt, R. R. (1984). The pioneers of adolescent group psychotherapy. *International Journal of Group Psychotherapy, 34,* 387–413.

Spotnitz, H. (1969). *Modern psychoanalysis of the schizophrenic patient.* New York: Grune & Stratton.

Sugar, M. (Ed.). (1975). *The adolescent in group and family therapy.* New York: Brunner/Mazel.

Sugar, M. (1986). Transference in adolescent group therapy. In M. Sugar (Ed.), *The adolescent in group and family therapy* (2nd ed., pp. 283–294). Chicago: University of Chicago Press.

Sugar, M. (1991). Symbiotic pairing in adolescent inpatient group psychotherapy. In S. Tuttman (Ed.), *Psychoanalytic group theory and therapy.* Madison, CT: International Universities Press. pp. 221–235.

Sugar, M. (1993). Research in child and adolescent group psychotherapy. *Journal of Child and Adolescent Group Therapy, 3,* 207–226.

30 / Multifamily Group Therapy

Lawrence G. Hornsby

After an existence of nearly 25 years, the multifamily group therapy modality remains an infant of ambiguous parentage. The practitioners of the therapy have yet to agree on its name: Should it be multiple family group therapy or multiple family therapy? Although some authors use these terms interchangeably, others claim that the two terms define different approaches. Since the literature shows little justification for distinguishing two terms, in this chapter they are considered interchangeable. Both describe a modality in which two or more families work together under the guidance of a trained mental health professional. In the remainder of the chapter, this approach will be called multifamily group therapy.

History of Multifamily Group Therapy

Multifamily group therapy arose in inpatient settings as an attempt to minimize the disintegrating effects that the psychiatric hospitalization of a family member was overling on the involved families. Originally, the homogeneity among these families was based to a large extent on the index patient's diagnosis (e.g., schizophrenia, or substance abuse) or age. In recent years, multifamily group therapy has been used in a variety of outpatient settings, with heterogeneous populations. Given the diverse antecedents of multifamily therapy, it follows that no solid, consistent conceptual framework exists. The strategy appears to be a blending of the techniques of family therapy and group psychotherapy.

Process Issues

Multifamily group therapy involves a highly variable process that depends on many factors. These include such elements as homogeneity of index patients, group purpose, sessions available for therapy, theoretical orientation of the therapist, and the presence or absence of specific goals and objectives. For example, in a group involving conduct-disordered adolescent index patients, the process would include such tactics as affect modulation, limit setting, boundary definition and violation, and development of a common language for dissipating positive energy. The process for a group of substance-abusing adolescent index patients, on the other hand, would include the tactics found in the conduct-disordered group as well as tactics for avoiding problem substances.

In more heterogeneous groups, especially those in which the index patients are primarily neurotic children or adolescents, the vital issues in the process of psychotherapy are developmental considerations. In this type of group, the members' clear understanding of the distinctive characteristics of various developmental processes, stages, and milestones are necessary for empathic communication among group members. This need for understanding suggest that the first stage of therapy be didactic so that all members receive a common information base.

The following vignette describes an actual case and demonstrates the need for common developmental understanding.

In the initial meeting of a multifamily group with high-functioning, pervasive developmentally disordered index patients, some family members were new to psychotherapy. These participants, who had not received information about normal child development and pervasive developmentally disordered child development, were visibly astonished at the calmness and relative ease of parents who had worked with their children in filial therapy. The informed parents were able to manage their children's behavior and understand their seemingly bizarre verbalizations. Discussion about the psychotherapy helped the "new" parents feel supported and it helped the therapists overcome formidable ambivalence and resistance on the part of some newly involved parents.

Goals and Objectives

Most clinicians agree that goals and objectives should be a part of all therapeutic endeavors. In multifamily group therapy, these goals and objectives will vary widely, reflecting the wide variety in the groups' makeups.

For example, in groups of the families of schizophrenic patients, goals and objectives can be narrowly focused on acquisition of social skills and reduction of isolation and withdrawal. Conversely, in heterogeneous groups of families with neurotic patients, major restructuring of the "family personality" may become the necessary focus of the goals and objectives.

Since multifamily group therapy embraces many of the therapeutic aspects of other modalities, a relatively short course of treatment will frequently utilize a multitude of interventions. Insight gained through identification with other families or family members is a distinctive feature of this therapy. The following vignette is from a multifamily group made up of families of both inpatients and discharged patients, in which the adolescent patient is hospitalized from 4 to 8 weeks.

Brittany, an attractive 15-year-old with a strong will, attended multifamily group weekly during her 5-week hospitalization. She had been living with her mother since she was 7 years old, and had not desired contact with her alcoholic father since her parents' divorce 8 years before Brittany's hospitalization. She had been admitted to the hospital after about 18 months of bouts of stealing, sexual promiscuity, and running away. Her mother, powerless and fearful of her daughter's destructive behavior, hospitalized her. During hospitalization, Brittany refused to make concessions to her mother, vowing that she would much rather live away from home than follow any of her mother's rules. The numerous attempts made to improve their communication and respect for one another failed; Brittany continued her belligerent attitude toward her mother and claimed she was looking forward to placement in a residential treatment center. She was discharged to residential treatment.

Three weeks after discharge to the residential center, Brittany, showing very different demeanor, returned to the group with her mother. She appeared depressed, speaking in a low, serious tone. After revealing her previous fantasies about residential treatment, she described how she had found it in reality. She felt she was in a miniprison—no negotiations regarding rules, and a cold, rigid atmosphere. She spoke profusely of missing her mother and the loss of a "sense of family."

Beth, another teenager in the group with her parents, appeared to be in awe during Brittany's revelations. During the time the two were in the hospital together, Beth had given up any hope of working things out with her family so she could return home. After hearing Brittany's revelations, Beth spoke up, telling her surprise at the change in Brittany's attitude and her resultant decision to open herself up to a commitment to serious family work. Beth's decision provoked further conversation in the group families. They cited numerous examples of work they had done or were doing in family therapy to improve home life for all the family's members.

Clinical Skills

Ideally, the clinician using multifamily group therapy is highly proficient in several of the forms of family and group therapy and has had training in and an understanding of dynamic individual therapy. Perhaps the ability to do quick, expert crisis intervention is one of the most essential skills for the clinician, since rapid development of highly charged affect is not uncommon in multifamily group therapy. The therapist must be prepared to deal with such a situation; indeed, because of the affective unpredictability of some multifamily groups, many clinicians choose to involve a cotherapist.

Settings

Multifamily group therapy should be carried out in a comfortable, sound-conditioned room with a minimum of distractions. Videotaping is valuable for a range of interventions: video clarification and confrontation, making patients aware of important but often unconscious nonverbal communications, recall of previous sessions, etc. Assigning different group members to be camera operator can focus group discussion on why the operator selected specific interactions to videotape.

Indications

Most clinicians and authors agree that the indications for multifamily group therapy are nonspecific and that it is an adjunctive form of therapy to be used along with other more targeted treatments. Some clinicians use multifamily group therapy as the sole treatment modality, without stating therapeutic indications vis-à-vis other forms of therapy.

Major contraindications to multifamily group therapy are certain types of families, such as those prone to explosive physical violence and loss of affective control. Reclusive or paranoid families are included with caution. Other poor-risk candidates are demanding, "entitled" families and families with a history of noncompliance with other forms of therapy.

Measures of Progress

Clear-cut behavioral goals and objectives and a basis for measurement of progress are primary tools. Periodic reviews and updates of the goals and objectives are necessary in an extended group. Affective measures include discussion of reduction in major problems experienced by each family, and group feedback on observed progress of one family each session. Clinical observations of the accepted indications of progress used in other modalities are also useful in evaluating progress.

Multifamily group therapy varies widely in regard to number of sessions. The number depends on the group's purpose. Sessions of a group focused on adolescent substance abuse may be limited in number; a group of families of schizophrenic patients may need long-term support.

Multifamily groups have typically been disparate in their makeup and duration; however, as with other modalities, duration parameters are increasingly influenced by the external organizations that manage mental health care.

Current Status

Multifamily group therapy has become increasingly widespread. This increase appears to have less to do with any proven efficacy than with economic and related factors.

Conclusion and Future Needs

One formal outcome study by McFarlane demonstrates a reduction in symptom levels and rehospitalization with family group therapy. Many clinicians find it a useful form of intervention and feel that further research about its efficacy and validity should be done, perhaps by employing some of the methodology used in family therapy and group therapy research.

Although multifamily group therapy has no official clinical standards or guidelines, it is generally accepted and thought to be effective despite the lack of researched conclusions. The modality appears to be a useful adjunct to other therapies, though it is not apparent at this time that it should be used to replace more standard forms of treatment.

To become a modality with its own place in the therapeutic armamentarium, multifamily group therapy will require research study results supporting it.

SUGGESTED READING

Anderson, C. M. (1983). A psychoeducational program for families of patients with schizophrenia. In W. R. McFarlane (Ed.), *Family therapy in schizophrenia* New York: Guilford Press.

Asen, K., George, E., Piper, R., & Stevens, A. (1989). A systems approach to child abuse: Management and treatment issues. *Child Abuse and Neglect, 13* (1), 45–57.

Atkinson, J. A., Coia, D. A. (1995). Families Coping with schizophrenia: A Practitioner's Guide to family groups. New York: John Wiley & Sons.

Benningfield, A. B. (1978). Multiple family therapy systems. *Journal of Marriage and Family Counseling, 4,* 25–34.

Eliot, A. O. Group coleadership: A new role for parents of adolescents with anorexia and bulimia nervosa. *International Journal of Group Psychotherapy, 40* (3), 339–351.

Falloon, I. R. H., & Lieberman, R. P. (1983). Behavioral family interventions in the management of chronic schizophrenia. In W. R. McFarlane (Ed.), *Family therapy in schizophrenia*. New York: Guilford Press.

Garfield, S. & Bergin, A (Eds.) (1994). *Handbook of psychotherapy and behavior change.* Fourth edition. New York: John Wiley & Sons.

Ghuman, J. W. (1993). An integrated model for intervention with infants, preschool children, and their maltreating parents. *Infant Mental Health Journal, 14* (2), 147–165.

Hofman, A., Honig, A. & Vossen, M. (1992). Bipolar depression: An educational multi-family group program approach. *Tijdschrift Voor Psychiatrie, 34* (8): 549–558.

Laquer, H. P. (1980). The theory and practice of multiple family therapy. In L. R. Wolberg & M. L. Aronson (Eds.), *Group and family therapy.*

Luber, R. F., & Wells, R. A. (1997). Structured, short-term multiple family therapy: An educational approach. *International Journal of Group Psychotherapy, 27,* 43–58.

McFarlane, W. R. Multiple family therapy in the psychiatric hospital. In H. Harbin (Ed.), *The psychiatric hospital and the family.*

McFarlane, W. R., Link, B., Dushay, R., Marchal, J. (1995). Psychoeducational multiple family groups:

Four-year relapse outcome in schizophrenia. *Family Process, 34* (2): 127–144.

McFarlane, W. R., Lukens, E., Link, B., Dushay, R. (1995). Multiple-family groups and psychoeducation in the treatment of schizophrenia. *Archives of General Psychiatry, 52* (8): 679–687.

O'Shea, M. D., Bicknell, L., & Wheatley, D. (1991). Brief multifamily psychoeducation programs for schizophrenia: Strategies for implementation and management. *American Journal of Family Therapy, 19* (1), 33–44.

O'Shea, M. D., & Phelps, R. (1985). Multiple family therapy: Current status and critical appraisal. *Family Process, 24* (4), 555–582.

Raasock, J. W. (1981). Multiple family therapy. In R. J. Corsini (Ed.), *Handbook of innovative psychotherapies.* New York: John Wiley & Sons.

Satin, W., La Greca, A. M., Zigo, M. A., & Skyler, J. S. Diabetes in adolescence: Effects of multifamily group intervention and parent simulation of diabetes. *Journal of Pediatric Psychology, 14* (2): 259–275.

Schwartzben, S. H. (1992). Social work with multifamily groups: A partnership model for long term care settings. *Social Work Health Care, 18* (1), 23–28.

Singh, N. (1982). Notes and observations on the practice of multiple family therapy in an adolescent unit. *Journal of Adolescence, 5,* 319–332.

Sprenkle, D. H., & Bischof, G. P. (1994). Contemporary family therapy in the United States. Special issue: Developments in family therapy in the USA. *Journal of Family Therapy, 16* (1), 5–23.

Streinick, A. H. (1977). Multiple family group therapy: A review of the literature. *Family Process, 16,* 307–534.

Szymanski, L. S., & Kiernan, W. E. (1983). Multiple family group therapy with developmental disabled adolescents and young adults. *International Journal of Group Psychotherapy, 33,* 521–534.

Zarski, J. J., Aponte, H. J., Bixenstine, C., & Cibik, P. (1992). Beyond home-based family intervention: A multi-family approach toward change. *Contemporary Family Therapy: An International Journal, 14* (1), 3–14.

31 / Self-Help, Mutual-Help, and Peer Helping Services

Milton F. Shore and F. Vincent Mannino

Self-help has begun to play a significant role in the area of mental health/service delivery to children and youth. However, it is important to distinguish what we mean by self-help (in which a person uses self-care methods to effect self-improvement), mutual help (in which individuals with common problems assist one another), and peer help (in which a nonprofessional such as a young person is trained to help a peer). Despite their similarities, it is essential to separate these three areas (which are frequently lumped together as self-help), particularly when we are dealing with services delivered by children and youth.

Although self-help, mutual help, and peer help have been actively proliferating, and are coming to be viewed more and more as significant additions to the adult mental health system, there are relatively few such activities designed for children and youths. The overall picture of those that do exist is not, in great measure, one of a planned, organized effort to develop and evaluate such programs, but rather one of a scattered collection of diverse efforts involving young people who assist themselves or their peers.

A significant development over the last two decades has been the rapid growth of self-help clearinghouses, which offer information on self-help groups. Several years ago, the President's Commission on Mental Health (President's Commission on Mental Health, 1978) set the stage for linking formal health care systems with informal helping networks by recommending the formation of resource centers to collect and disseminate information on self-help groups. Many of these centers are now known as self-help clearinghouses. There are currently over seventy such centers in the United States and Canada. More recently we have witnessed the development of networking organizations at a national level (Borkman, 1990).

Combined with the Surgeon General's Workshop, (Surgeon General's Workshop on Self-Help and Public Health, 1988), these groups have been responsible for developing links among self-help groups and professionals. They have also served to increase the visibility and credibility of self-help groups. One particularly valuable resource for professionals in the health and mental health fields, is the *Self-Help Source Book,* (White and Madara, 1995). This volume presents updated contacts and descriptions of hundreds of national and model self-help groups and provides ways of contacting dozens of self-help clearinghouses worldwide. The authors list over seventy-five national toll-free helplines, and, for the computer literate, provides information regarding self-help on-line where there are thousands of different networks, e.g., The Internet, American-on-Line, Compu Serve, which provide worldwide health information and peer-support. Indeed, online networks may represent one of the most powerful new elements in the future of self-help, (Madara, 1997). What follows are examples of activities for children and youths. The examples are drawn from the three areas described previously: self-help, mutual help and peer help.

Self-Help

One example of a self-help activity for young people is the behavioral self-help manual used to curtail the drinking behavior of incarcerated youth (McMurran & Boyle, 1990). An increasingly common form of self-help is the promotion of psychological wellness through the use of books, tapes, CDs, and videos in areas such as physical fitness and relaxation training. A means of delivery more recent than manuals and books is computer programs, which are very popular among children and youths. One such program for teens identifies health risks and makes suggestions about behavioral change (Centers for Disease Control, 1983). Another computer program attempts to help youths deal with smoking, alcohol, nutrition, exercise, drug use, stress management, sexuality and family communication (Families and Telematics, 1983). The program focuses on specific aspects of a youth's problem and even assists in locating helping resources. When more than one person views the program, it can stimulate dialogue on problem related topics, thus linking self-help to social supports and helping services. Of course, the advent of online has made dialoguing possible in ways never thought of before, with one result being the rapid development of online mutual help groups, thus adding to the already present self-help activities.

However, one must be wary of the ever increasing use of computers by children and youths. Take caution or the widespread belief in the authority of the computer can promote a belief that any information obtained from one must be true. In the absence of professional guidance, individuals may make wrong decisions that could damage or aggrevate mental health problems. Moreover, the potential danger of exploitation related to developing online mutual help activities is another area of grave concern.

Mutual Help

The most well-known example in the area of mutual help is the Alateen program for teenage alcoholics and children of alcoholics. Founded in 1957 and based on Alcoholics Anonymous model, it uses the 12 steps and 12 traditions overlaid by the spiritual beliefs that are the foundation of Alcoholics Anonymous (See White & Madara, 1995).

There are also mutual help programs in which autistic children help each other (Krantz, Ramsland, & McClannahan, 1989), behavior disordered children help each other (Franca, Kerr, Reitz & Lambert, 1990), hospitalized impulsive boys assist one another (Nelson & Behler, 1989), and underachieving students help other underachieving students via reciprocal peer tutoring (Fantuzzo, Polite, & Grayson, 1990). In a new model of reciprocal peer tutoring which stems from the helper therapy principle, Riessman & Carrol (1995) have all students participate in giving and receiving help and make being a tutee a prerequisite for becoming a tutor. The goal is the development of student-centered peer focused

schools which can lead to such additional peer opportunities as peer mentoring, peer mediation, peer education, and peer helping. Another example of mutual help is the Encourage program of Children's Hospital in St. Paul, Minnesota (Schuchman, 1997) in which teens with chronic or life-threatening illnesses help each other. Professionals train adolescents and young adults with certain illnessess to provide support to other young people with a similar illness. Support emphasizes strengths and competencies, as well as helping with problems. The adolescent helpers maintain contact with their peers through hospital visits, discussions and social activities, sharing their experiences in coping with their mutual illness (McGraw-Schuchman, 1994). Referrals are made by the teenager, by family members or friends, or by a peer making contact with the young person or a member of the teenager's family.

A uniquely innovative approach concerns the *Time Dollar Youth Court* in Washington D.C. Operating under the authorization of the Superior Court and the Prosecutor's Office, juvenile first offenders with nonviolent offenses are brought before a jury of high school youths who impose sentences consisting of community service, restitution, and jury duty. For their participation, the jurors earn Time Dollars for which they can purchase recycled computers or gain preferential access to summer jobs (Cahn, E.S., 1997).

A classic study of mutual help is that of Halpern (1982). She studied a recreational setting that was not created for the purpose of helping children with issues of orphanhood. Over time, however, Halpern found that fatherless young people developed mutual helping networks spontaneously. She noted that the children established the same kind of helping networks and supports that are evident in adult mutual help groups.

PEER HELP

Of self-help, mutual help and peer help, peer help is the most popular in the context of children and youths. Peer tutoring and peer counseling are particularly popular. In these programs children and adolescents who do not have the same problems as those they will help are trained to assist peers with problems. Such programs provide alcohol education (Perry, Grant, Ernbereg & Florenzano, 1989); math tutoring for autistic children (Kamps, Locke, Delquadri, & Hall, 1989); tutoring for students with behavioral disorders (Campbell, Brady, & Linehan, 1991); peer modeling for overcoming shyness (Booth, 1980); group counseling for students at risk of suicide (Herring, 1990); and, more recently, counseling groups for students at risk for AIDS (Rickert, Jay, & Gottlieb, 1991).

In addition to these "mainstream" programs is a type of peer-help that has grown rapidly over the past 15 years: peer mediation in educational settings. Young people in elementary and secondary schools are trained to resolve conflicts among their peers. Not only does peer mediation resolve conflict, but it can also be viewed as a way of preventing violence (Prothrow-Stith, 1987). Prothrow-Stith sees it as an element in the planning of antiviolence programs. Recent research examining the impact of conflict-resolution and peer mediation training on students in grades six to nine, found that the students increased their use of integrative negotiations and had more positive and less punitive attitudes toward conflict (Dudley, B., Johnson, D. & Johnson, R., 1996). Mediation programs have recently expanded onto college campuses. In fact, it has been found that the impetus for the initiation of college mediation programs has come from those who were trained as mediators in junior and senior high schools (Warters, 1991). Mediation programs appear to be more organized than programs in other areas of peer help. This may be due to their promotion by the National Institute for Dispute Resolution, which absorbed the National Association of Mediation in Education (NAME) and has maintained a clearinghouse for the field, holds annual conferences and regional meetings, supports theory and research, and publishes a bi-monthly newsletter.

In summary, peer help has taken two directions: (1) the more traditional which focuses on ongoing behavior problems, symptoms and diagnostic categories; and (2) training in mediation and conflict resolution.

Summary

A review of self-help, mutual-help, and peer help highlights two features: (1) there are few pro-

grams for the young in contrast to the number of such programs for adults; and (2) there appears to be little direction, planning or organization in the development of child and youth programs in general. However, the main difference between self-help, mutual-help, and peer help for adults in contrast to such programs for children and youths, is that the latter are usually initiated, developed, and monitored by adults and sometimes supervised by them. At the same time we see occasions where mutual help groups have arisen without adult intervention (Halpern, 1982). What has not been addressed is how much adult involvement is necessary? When young people develop child and youth services by themselves the potential for harm exists. How well we know that gangs develop "support systems" and "mutual-help services" as part of their destructive ethos, (e.g. kangaroo courts, scapegoating and victimizing others and at times even their fellow members). Do we yet know what the conditions are that foster constructive mutual help by children and youth? Are there developmental issues that need to be taken into account? For example, no one would expect 5 or 6 year olds to participate in mutual help groups. But what about preadolescents or adolescents? What is appropriate to expect from different age groups? As we understand more about the formation and use of groups by children and youths of different ages, we will better understand how groups can benefit the members. A more general problem is the lack of research and evaluation regarding self-help, mutual help, and peer help groups for adults, children and youths (Humphreys, 1997). These groups sometimes are seen as alternatives to traditional treatments. At other times they are seen as adjuncts to standard services. Anecdotal evidence has shown that self-help and mutual help groups assist adults in developing support networks and aiding recovery and/or adjustment. We need to determine whether exactly the same purposes are served in such groups for children and youths. Perhaps such groups for young people can serve an educational purpose as well, as children and youths develop a sense of community out of their interpersonal relationships, a sense that contributes to their overall growth as caring and responsible adults.

Conclusion

When used appropriately, self-help, mutual help and peer help have great potential for reaching youths, especially hard-to-reach youths, at all levels in their natural settings. Such groups can provide unusual opportunities for intervening early, appropriately, and effectively. They also can help us understand how they assist children and youths in both helper and recipient roles toward healthy growth and development. Indeed, they should be viewed, not as substitutes, but as an integral part of a total community service network.

SUGGESTED READING

Booth, R. (1980). A short-term peer model for treating shyness in college students: a note on an exploratory study. *Psychological Reports*, 66, 417–418.

Borkman, T. (1990). Self-Help groups at the turning point: Emerging eqalitarian alliances with the formal health care system? *American Journal of Community Psychology*, 18, 321–332.

Cahn, E. (1997). The co-production imperative. *Social Policy*, 27, 62–67.

Campbell, B., Brady, M., & Linehan, S. (1991). Effects of peer mediated instruction on the acquisition and generalization of written capitalization skills. *Journal of Learning Disabilities*, 24, 6–14.

Centers for Disease Control (1983). Teen Health Risk Appraisal. Atlanta: Author.

Dudley, B., Johnson, D., & Johnson, R. (1996). Conflict-resolution training and middle school students' integrative negotiation behavior. *Journal of Applied Social Psychology*, 26, 2038–2052.

Families and Telematics. (June, 1983). *American Family*. 6, 8–9.

Franca, V., Kerr, M.M., Reitz, A. & Lambert, D. (1990). Peer tutoring among behaviorally disordered students: Academic and social benefits to tutor and tutee. *Education and Treatment of Children*. 13, 109–128.

Halpern, E. (1982). Children's support systems in coping with orphanhood: Child helps child in a natural setting. *Series in Clinical and Community Psychology: Stress and Anxiety*. 8, 261–266.

Herring, R. (1990). Suicide in the middle school: Who said kids will not? *Elementary School Guidance and Counseling*. 25, 129–137.

Humphreys, K. (1997). Individual and social benefits of mutual aid/self-help groups. *Social Policy*. 27, 12–19.

Kamps, D., Locke, P., Delquadri, J., & Hall, R. (1989). Increasing academic skills of students with autism using fifth grade peers as tutors. *Education and Treatment of Children*. 12, 38–51.

Krantz, P., Ramsland, S., & McClannahan, L.E. (1989). Conversational skills for autistic adolescents: an autistic peer as prompter. *Behavioral Residential Treatment*. 4, 171–189.

Madara, E. (1997). The mutual-aid self-help online revolution, *Social Policy*. 27, 20–26.

McGraw-Schuchman, K., (1994). The encourage program: peer-helping for adolescents with chronic illness. *The Peer Facilitator Quarterly*. 11, 21–23.

McMurran, M., & Boyle, M. (1990). Evaluation of a self-help manual for young offenders who drink: a pilot study. *British Journal of Clinical Psychology*, 29, 117–119.

Nelson, W., & Behler, J., (1989). Cognitive impulsivity training: The effects of peer-teaching. *Journal of Behavior Therapy and Experimental Psychiatry*. 20, 303–309.

Perry, C.L., Grant, M., & Florenzano, R. (1989). WHO collaborative study of alcohol education and young people: Outcomes of a four country pilot study. *International Journal of The Addictions*, 24, 1145–1171.

President's Commission on Mental Health: Task Panel on Community Supports (1978). Vol. 2. Washington, D.C. US Government Printing Office.

Prothrow-Stith, D. (1987). *Violence Prevention: Curriculum for Adolescents*. Newton, Ma: Education Development Center.

Rickert, V., Jay, M. & Gottlieb, A. (1991). Effects of a peer counseling AIDS education program on knowledge, attitudes, and satisfaction of adolescents. *Journal of Adolescent Health*, 12, 38–43.

Riessman, F. & Carroll, D. (1995). Redefining self-help. San Francisco: Jossey-Bass.

Schuchman, K. (1997). Feminist approaches to working with adolescents: Acknowledging competencies and developing alternative interventions. *Women and Therapy*. The Hayworth Press, 20, 101–110.

Surgeon General's Workshop on Self-Help and Public Health. (1988). Washington, D.C. DHHS, Public Health Service, Health Resources and Services Administration, Bureau of Maternal and Child Health and Resource Development.

Warters, B. (1991). Mediation on campus: A history and planning guide. *The Fourth R*. 33, 4–5.

White, B. and Madara, E. (Eds) (1995). *The Self-Help Source Book* American Self-Help Clearing House. Danville, New Jersey: Northwest Covenant Medical Center.

32 / Twelve-Step Group Treatment

Steven L. Jaffe

Twelve-Step groups employ the group recovery process for chemical dependency treatment that began with the development of Alcoholics Anonymous, (AA). This has been the strongest group movement of the 1980s. There are almost two million members in 63,000 groups (Robertson, 1988), and membership doubles every ten years.

Historical Development of Alcoholics Anonymous

Alcoholics Anonymous dates its beginnings to 1935 and is rooted in the struggle of Bill Wilson against alcohol. At the time, a prominent physician, Dr. William Silkworth, believed alcoholism was caused by a physical allergy rather than a moral defect. In an attempt to end his "allergy" to alcohol, Bill Wilson became involved in the Oxford Group. This group was started by a Lutheran minister at Oxford University, and although the group strove to help people stop drinking and live a better life, it had no specific theology. The program involved absolute honesty, purity, unselfishness, and love. Members surrendered their will to that of God, took a personal moral inventory, confessed past crimes, made amends to those they had harmed, and helped others without thought of financial reward. While trying to practice the principles of the Oxford Group, Wilson went on another drinking binge and was hospitalized for the fourth time. During alcoholic withdrawal and while medicated with narcotics and cathartics (including belladonna), Wilson experienced an overwhelming religious exaltation that changed his life. Although he suffered many subsequent depressions, he never drank again.

Through the Oxford Group Wilson had found that trying to help other alcoholics often saved him from taking another drink. In such a way he was introduced to Dr. Robert Smith, a physician who was also struggling with alcoholism. These two men helped a third alcoholic, and the movement began. A cover article in a 1941 edition of the popular magazine *Saturday Evening Post* doubled AA membership. In 1951, AA received the Lasker Award from the American Public Health Association. Over the following years, AA has extended to 114 countries and two million people. One third of the U.S. membership is now female. During the past 10 years, there has been a sharp increase in the membership of teenagers and young adults. These younger members are often addicted to drugs in addition to alcohol, and attend meetings of Narcotics Anonymous or Cocaine Anonymous as well as AA meetings.

The Twelve Steps and the AA Meeting

The remarkable growth and effectiveness of AA is related to clear guidelines detailed in Bill Wilson's *Twelve Steps and Twelve Traditions*. AA owns no property, does no fund raising, and avoids all politics. No living member may give more than $1,000 to AA in any year, no outside contributions are accepted, and no one person speaks for AA. A board of trustees and a nonprofit corporation (AA World Services) publishes its literature (written by anonymous members) and serves the thousands of individual groups. Membership is open to anyone who wants to stop drinking. This open, decentralized structure enables AA to avoid the problematic issues of wealth and politics, and no powerful leader can emerge to corrupt its purpose. Individual groups pay for coffee and the space they rent by passing a basket for anonymous donations at each meeting. The chairperson for meetings is rotated frequently.

Meetings begin on time with a member reading the AA Preamble. Only first names are used, and the confidentiality of what members reveal is essential. "Birthdays" (time periods of sobriety) are announced and newcomers are welcomed. Speakers' stories are followed by open or topic discussion. Closed meetings are for alcoholics only; open meetings may be attended by family and friends. There is no pressure for someone to speak up, just lots of support for honest sharing of thoughts and feelings. Position and achievements are not important; only one's struggles not to drink and to live a good life. Empathic understanding, tears and laughter, as well as older members sharing what worked for them are prominent. After 60 minutes, the meeting ends with the Serenity Prayer:

> God grant me the serenity
> To accept the things I cannot change;
> Courage to change the things I can;
> And the wisdom to know the difference.

Relationships with those who have been in the program a long period of time are encouraged. These contacts help participants stay sober "one day at a time." One of these contacts becomes a special (always nonromantic) same-sex friend and guide who is called a sponsor. These special relationships and frequent attendance at AA meetings help the individual to take the steps to recovery.

The Twelve Steps were written in 1938 by Bill Wilson, and with only slight modifications after discussion with the early AA groups, were published in 1939 in *Alcoholics Anonymous* (also called The Big Book). The concepts in the Twelve Steps come from the principles of the Oxford Group and also from William James's *The Varieties of Religious Experience: A Study in Human Nature*. James's descriptions of a person experiencing total collapse and then finding relief in a self-surrender experience were incorporated into the steps (Walle, 1992). A copy of the steps is placed on a wall at every AA meeting:

1. We admitted we were powerless over alcohol—that our lives had become unmanageable
2. Came to believe that a Power greater than ourselves could restore us to sanity
3. Made a decision to turn our will and our lives over to the care of God as we understand Him
4. Made a searching and fearless moral inventory of ourselves
5. Admitted to God, to ourselves, and to another human being the exact nature of our wrongs
6. Were entirely ready to have God remove all these defects of character
7. Humbly asked Him to remove our shortcomings
8. Made a list of all persons we had harmed, and became willing to make amends to them all
9. Made direct amends to such people wherever possible, except when to do so would injure them or others
10. Continued to take personal inventory and when we were wrong, promptly admitted it
11. Sought through prayer and meditation to improve our conscious contact with God as we understood Him, praying only for knowledge of His will for us and the power to carry that out
12. Having had a spiritual awakening as the result of these Steps, we tried to carry this message to alcoholics, and to practice these principles in all our affairs

The steps are the guide for the changes in actions, thoughts, feelings, and beliefs that an individual addict slowly undergoes in order to abstain from drinking. This complex psycho-social-spiritual treatment path is to be individualized as it makes sense to each addict in his or her struggles to live an honest, quality life without alcohol or drugs.

Twelve Steps for Adolescents

Recently, modifications in the application of the steps have been developed to enhance their meaningfulness for adolescents (Jaffe, 1990). In a workbook the adolescent writes answers to specific questions. This presses the teenager—a boy, for example—to commit himself to looking at his life and experiences. In the First Step, the teenager examines the effects of alcohol and drugs on his life. If his life—including school, family, and friends—is impaired because of alcohol and drugs and he cannot use in moderation, then total abstinence is needed. In adolescent treatment, it is emphasized that an addict is powerless if he uses alcohol or drugs. If he does not use alcohol or drugs, then he has the power to have a life. Another helpful concept for teenagers working a First Step is that the teenager may be "on the way to becoming an addict." Here the teenager recognizes that if he continued with his alcohol- and drug-abusing patterns, he will develop all the problems of chemical dependency. A detailed accounting of his life history enables the teenager to define what in his life he wishes were different and what is out of his control.

The Second Step involves the teenager developing a belief in something positive beyond himself (a Higher Power). Teenagers often have difficulty with this step because they have not dealt with the severe traumatic events related to their early parental figures who are their childhood Higher Powers. Mourning the pain and sadness from the disappointments of their childhood Higher Powers enables them to begin to develop a sense of something positive in the universe that they can turn to for help. The Higher Power concept is not a religious belief, but a spiritual feeling that one can trust something positive (i.e., the group, another person, nature, etc.) to take care of those aspects of one's life that one cannot control. One controls one's own behavior but not what others say or do. The belief system developed when using alcohol and drugs (a system imbued with dishonesty, lying, abuse of self and others) is then compared to the positive belief system of people working Twelve-Step programs (honesty, responsibility, caring about self and others).

The Third Step involves making a decision to *commit* to working the steps and having a positive spiritual higher power. The teenagers are helped to recognize that they turned over their lives to alcohol and drugs. Now they are being asked to turn their lives over to a positive program.

In the Fourth Step, the teenagers answer numerous detailed questions covering all aspects of their early life, family life, school life, anxieties, image, sexuality, actions, and jobs. Here the teenagers process the many other problems (e.g., depression, learning problems, family instability, or physical or sexual abuse) that chemically dependent people have.

The Fifth Step consists of the cathartic experience of verbalizing this inventory to another person.

Steps Six through Eleven involve changing behavior, making amends, continuing the personal inventory, and enhancing spirituality. The important Twelfth Step involves helping other addicts who are trying to work the Twelve-Step program. Leading a Twelve-Step meeting and serving as a contact or sponsor for others is extremely fulfilling

and enhances self-esteem for any teenager whose life had deteriorated into chemical dependency. Twelve-Step groups provide a nonusing, recovering peer group. Such a group is essential for adolescents as they try to abstain from using alcohol and drugs.

Twelve-Step Groups and Substance Abuse and Dual-Diagnosis Disorder Programs for Adolescents

Twelve-Step programs are frequently integrated into after-school, day, residential and in-patient treatment programs for adolescents. As part of many programs, staff take teenagers to Twelve-Step meetings so the young people can become comfortable with the format and make an attachment with some aspect of attendance. Teenagers at the "preoccupation with use" stage of substance abuse or chemical dependency cannot use alcohol or drugs in moderation; they require an abstinence program. Twelve-Step programs for adolescents, which are abstinence programmer, consist of:

1. attending Twelve-Step community meetings (groups)
2. working the steps
3. developing a sponsor
4. developing a recovering (abstinent) peer group

Usually, a special daily alcohol or drug treatment group is conducted where step work is presented and meeting attendance or sponsorship is developed. Jaffe's *The Step Workbook for Adolescent Chemical Dependency Recovery* (1990) gives a structure for teenagers to work their steps and present their work treatment group. The teenager is given a workbook and writes the answers to the questions of the First Step. Individual reviews encourage the adolescent to provide numerous details, such as how many times he or she drove drunk, with how many people were in the car, each time, and how many accidents and near misses occurred. The group discusses the risks and negative consequences of the drug or alcohol use. Hopefully, the teenagers become honest about their amount of drug use and the emotional consequences of their experiences. This process of working the First Step is essential for beginning recovery; it helps the teenager realize how badly drugs or alcohol has messed up his or her life and that abstinence is needed. In a similar manner, a life story and Steps three and four are written and presented. Step four is presented to a staff member as part of step five. Program staff help the adolescent to call and meet with a temporary sponsor. This is someone in good recovery, with usually at least one year of sobriety, who helps the adolescent work their Twelve-Steps. The adolescent learns to call the sponsor frequently, often goes to meetings with him or her, and develops a relationship that will continue for a long time. At groups and Twelve-Step meetings, the adolescent also develops a recovering peer group. Returning to peers that use and abuse drugs and alcohol is the most frequent cause of relapse for adolescents. Twelve-Step groups and meetings are a very positive way for adolescents to connect with other adolescents who are committed to an abstinence program. The child and adolescent psychiatrist involved in these programs needs to understand and help integrate the Twelve-Step program components into the other psychiatric aspects of the program.

The Twelve Steps are also used in Narcotics Anonymous and Cocaine Anonymous as well as in self-help groups for other addicts (e.g., Gamblers Anonymous). Co-dependency groups for the relatives of addicts (e.g., Alanon, Alateen, and Adolescent Children of Alcoholics) frequently use a modified version of the steps. Overeaters Anonymous (OA) uses the Twelve-Step structure relating it to the abuse of food as an addiction. In this view, anorexia nervosa and bulimia are addictive diseases, and many administrators integrate OA groups into recovery program for for those with severe chronic eating disorders.

Follow-up Studies

Although there is little follow-up research, two major objective studies indicate the importance of Twelve-Step groups in the treatment of chemically dependent teenagers. The CATOR report (Harrison, & Hoffman, 1987) indicates that those teenagers who attended two or more meetings per week were almost six times more likely to report abstinence than those who never attended. A series of follow-up studies of posttreatment recovery patterns (Brown, 1993) revealed that teens with the poorest drug use outcome at one year posttreatment had the greatest exposure to alcohol or drugs in their posttreatment environment and had the least continued involvement in self-help groups. Although a small number recovered without the help of Twelve-Step groups, the larger proportion that were functioning well one year posttreatment had regularly attended self-help groups.

Conclusion

From its humble origins in the late 1930s—as an adult male–dominated, Christian-based group movement for the treatment of alcoholics—Twelve-Step groups have evolved into a nondenominational worldwide movement that includes many women and teenagers, and has extended into the treatment of other addictions. Keeping to their original nonpolitical, no-fee, decentralized tradition has enabled Twelve-Step groups to continue pursuing their sole purpose: helping the addict who wants to stop. The basic Twelve Steps, as modified and individualized for different groups, continues to be an important therapeutic modality in the treatment of chemically dependent individuals.

SUGGESTED READINGS

Brown, S. A. (1993). Recovery patterns in adolescent substance abuse. In J. S. Baer, G. A. Marlott, & R. J. McMahon (Eds.), *Addictive behaviors across the lifespan: Prevention, treatment and policy issues.* Beverly Hills, CA: Sage Publications.

Harrison, P. A. & Hoffman, N. G. (1989). CATOR report: Adolescent treatment completers one year later. St. Paul, MN: Ramsey Clinic.

Jaffe, S. L. (1990). *Step workbook for adolescent chemical dependency recovery: A guide to the first five steps,* Washington, DC: APA Press.

Robertson, N. (1988). *Getting better—inside Alcoholics Anonymous.* New York: William Morrow.

Walle, A. H. (1992). William James' legacy to Alcoholics Anonymous: An analysis and a critique *Journal of Addictive Diseases, 11* (3), 91–99.

33 / Day Treatment or Partial Hospitalization for Children

Stewart Gabel

Introduction

Day treatment, also known as day hospitalization and partial hospitalization, has been a recognized psychiatric treatment modality for adults for decades. Although it has demonstrated both treatment benefits and cost-effectiveness, day treatment is still far less common than its advantages would suggest (Parker & Knoll, 1990). Parker and Knoll (1990) report that the proponents of day treatment have had to (1) define day treatment and clarify confusing terminology, (2) standardize selection criteria and models of treatment, (3) establish that day treatment is a valid modality with therapeutic and economic benefits, and (4) explain why this modality has been poorly utilized.

Day treatment for children and adolescents has been a viable option for more than 25 years (Zimet and Farley, 1991; Doan and Petti, 1989). Although day treatment for children may be viewed within the context of day treatment generally, research demonstrating the advantages of day treatment for children and adolescents is far less advanced than that regarding day treatment for adults. This places additional burdens on advocates of day treatment for children, since this modality, while it is less expensive than comparable inpatient treatment, is far more expensive than usual outpatient treatment.

In this chapter the first section will discuss types and characteristics of day treatment programs for children, including typical staffing patterns, and types of patients. The second section will review research dealing with the question of outcome in children's day treatment. This section will note important issues in day treatment, such as patient selection criteria, models of treatment, and the development of assessment protocols that are now recognized as being crucial for professional acceptance and sometimes for accountability and third-party reimbursement. The third section will emphasize the potential of day treatment as a therapeutic modality and highlight a number of the strengths of day treatment. It will also describe the various organizational and clinical problems typical of day treatment. Quite often the issues and challenges faced in day treatment involve concerns different than those associated with common outpatient or inpatient settings. This discussion will take a somewhat experiential approach in an attempt to illustrate the complexity of day treatment for children as a treatment modality.

Terminology should be clarified at the outset. As with partial hospitalization for adults, there is confusion about terminology in partial hospitalization for children and adolescents as contrasted to day treatment. While day treatment and partial hospitalization usually imply treatment for psychiatrically disturbed children and adolescents in a hospital-based setting; day treatment includes the notion of day hospitalization. However, it commonly refers as well to day treatment programs in less restrictive environments, such as schools in the community and in other types of mental health settings.

In general, day hospitalization indicates a more restrictive level of care and probably a more intensive treatment program than is provided in community-based day treatment programs. Hospital based programs usually serve patients who are more psychiatrically disturbed than those in day treatment, although data about different populations in different types of day treatment settings are limited. In this chapter the term *day treatment* will be employed in its most inclusive sense. It will refer to day hospitalization and partial hospitalization, as well as other types of community- and school-based day treatment programs.

Reviews of day treatment often survey designed programs that serve children and those that serve adolescents. Some programs restrict the age range of youth served; others serve both children (defined for the purposes of this chapter as youngsters of elementary school age, i.e. 5 to 12 years of age) and adolescents. This chapter will emphasize day treatment for children. The reader should refer to the chapter on day treatment for adolescents for discussion of programs for that age group.

Programs, Characteristics, and Patients

The types of children served in day treatment programs, as well as the programs themselves and their treatment orientations, are diverse. Important goals for those involved in day treatment, whether for children or adults (Parker & Knoll, 1990), include clarifying the types of patients, programs, staffing patterns, and therapies that are offered (and needed) in response to various patient characteristics, treatment goals, etc. Important attempts in this direction have been made (see, e.g., American Academy of Child and Adolescent Psychiatry, unpublished; Block et al., unpublished).

Kiser, Pruitt, McColgan, Ackerman and (1986) surveyed child and adolescent day treatment programs to learn about particular programs, patient, staff, and funding patterns and about clinical as-

pects of the programs. They found that the typical day treatment program was generally in operation 5 days a week. Children attended for 6 to 7 hours each day. Groupings by age, in the "typical program," were from ages 5 to 12 and from 12 to 18. The majority of programs did not have affiliations with inpatient units. The most frequent diagnostic category found in the child (and adolescent) population was conduct disorder. Attention deficit disorder diagnoses were found frequently in programs for children. Children (and adolescents) on average remained in day treatment for about 16 months.

Day treatment programs frequently utilize multidisciplinary teams that include psychiatrists, psychologists, social workers, and educators, along with various types of counselors and aides (Kiser, Pruitt, McColgan, and Ackerman, 1986). The programs had low staff-to-patient ratios, indicating the intensity of the services provided. Compared to inpatient units, the staffing patterns in day treatment programs reflect the relatively decreased influence of medical and psychiatric involvement. Only about 10 percent of the programs employed a full-time psychiatrist, although most had psychiatric consultation on a part-time basis.

The majority of programs utilized individual therapy, although group therapy and family therapy were also important. About 33 percent of the day treatment programs considered their theoretical framework to be eclectic. About as many emphasized behavioral approaches. Few used an analytic approach. Nearly all programs included milieu therapy and a level or token system in their overall treatment approach.

Kiser, Pruitt, McColgan, and Ackerman argue that their survey confirms that, although "a typical program can be described, programs show little consistency in length and hours of operation, number of children served, affiliation or non affiliation with an inpatient service" (p. 250). Heterogeneity in staffing patterns, clinical approaches, and funding patterns also seemed to be common.

Doan and Petti (1989) surveyed 18 child and adolescent day treatment programs in Pennsylvania. About 75 percent of the patients were white and about the same percentage were male. About 70 percent of those enrolled were relatively poor, with funding achieved through Medicaid or county mental healthy or mental retardation funds. The most common diagnoses in the children's group were conduct disorder (26 percent), attention deficit disorder with hyperactivity (25 percent), oppositional disorder (13 percent), and adjustment disorders (11 percent). In all of these categories, males outnumbered females by large margins. Externalizing disorders (defined as conduct disorder, attention deficit disorder with hyperactivity, or oppositional disorder) were extremely common, accounting for nearly 66 percent of the patients. Disorders such as autism, pervasive developmental disorder, and schizophrenic spectrum disorders accounted for only 9 percent of the total patients in the 3- to 12-year old group. Compared to adolescents, children were significantly more likely to receive a diagnosis of externalizing disorder and significantly less likely to be viewed as having an affective disorder.

Prior mental health involvement for youngsters in day treatment was common. Almost 50 percent had had prior psychiatric hospitalization. About 66 percent had had some form of outpatient mental health treatment.

Forty percent of patients who were discharged from day treatment had attained some treatment goals, but about the same percentage were discharged because of lack of improvement or deterioration.

As part of a study to determine the relationship between several preadmission variables and outcome, Gabel, Swanson, and Shindledecker (1990) provide additional data to indicate the diversity of programs and children found in day treatment programs. They reviewed the records of patients discharged from three-day treatment programs— two were hospital-based programs and one was community-based. All of the programs had more male than female patients. Minority patients were the largest group at the two hospital-based day treatment programs; white patients were more common in the community program.

Conduct disorder and attention deficit disorder with hyperactivity were common in the three programs, although these externalizing disorders were more common in the day hospital groups and less common in the community program. The prevalence of parental substance abuse, suicidality, severe aggressive or destructive behavior, and suspected child abuse or maltreatment as preadmission variables varied. The variables were most common in the hospital-based programs and

less common in the community-based program. Recommended discharge disposition to an "in home" (community) setting or to an "out of home" (inpatient or residential) setting varied also and seemed to be associated with the degree of family dysfunction and child behavior disorder.

Research Regarding Children's Day Treatment

One of the most important areas of research in child and adolescent mental health involves the study of outcome in treatment. Literature on outcome in child and adolescent psychiatric inpatient hospitalization is relatively sparse. Literature on outcome in children and adolescent day treatment is even more limited. A number of reviews have been done in recent years, however.

Gabel and Finn (1986) reviewed the literature on outcome in children's day treatment. They found available literature to be more descriptive or clinical than empirical. In general, the literature suggested that many children benefited from day treatment, especially children who were young when entering treatment. The gains were often modest but included improvement in both academic and behavioral areas. Some evidence suggested that greater improvement occurred with family involvement in treatment. Day treatment seemed to be effective in reducing the need for inpatient hospitalization or residential placement and appeared to facilitate the return of some children to school placements that were less restrictive.

The review by Baenen, Parris Stephens, and Glenwicks (1986) included both child and adolescent studies. They found that most programs reported improvement in treatment groups. "When clinical observations, behavior ratings, or psychological tests are used to assess behavioral outcome, about 80% are considered improved" (p. 265). Behavioral improvement seemed to be greater than academic gains. Parental psychopathology appeared to be prominent among the children treated, and clinical services to the family, as well as aftercare for these children, seemed important in overall outcome.

Kiser's (1991) review of the literature on child and adolescent studies also suggests that many patients benefit and return successfully to community-based schools. Family functioning is an important factor in improvement. Younger children showed greater benefits than children who are older.

One increasingly important area of outcome research involves comparisons of children treated in day treatment and children served in either inpatient programs or in residential settings. Some preliminary work along these lines has been done, with findings indicating comparable outcome for children in day treatment and children in residential treatment (Prentice-Dunn, Wilson, & Lyman, 1981).

Research involving outcome and program effectiveness should involve the development and utilization of systematic assessment procedures and a comprehensive database, without which adequate comparisons are impossible. Kiser (1991) and Kiser, Heston, Millsap, & Pruitt (1991) have implemented standardized assessment protocols as well as standardized treatment approaches for particular problems with which patients and families enter day treatment. These types of efforts are important not only for future studies in day treatment, but also for studies of the outcome and effectiveness of other treatment modalities.

Day Treatment: Strengths, Potential, and Challenges

Although utilized relatively infrequently until recently, day treatment is now recognized as a major component in the continuum of care for children. The theoretical benefits of day treatment are numerous. Many children with moderate to severe behavioral and emotional disorders may be maintained in an outpatient setting rather than in an inpatient or residential program, thus providing them with a "less restrictive" and more normalized environment.

The same groups of children, residing for long periods in residential centers or on inpatient units, have little or no chance to manifest their problem areas and conflicts outside these unique; highly structured; and, often, closed settings. Children in day treatment exhibit their emotional and behavioral problems in a "more usual" family and environmental context. It is in the family context that most of the problems of children in day treatment have arisen, and it is in this context that, for many, the problems may be adequately assessed and treated.

Day treatment is the major outpatient treatment modality for severely disturbed children who need intensive supervision several hours per day to be able to benefit from educational services and to receive intensive psychotherapeutic services. The latter may include individual, group, or family therapy. Ongoing, multidisciplinary therapeutic and educational services for children with moderately severe to severe disorders are far less costly in day treatment setting than in inpatient care. This makes day treatment a major benefit to the family and to the society.

Day treatment also offers the potential to stabilize and keep together many dysfunctional families, since it is able to provide intensive, ongoing, and frequently monitored therapeutic services to children and to their families.

Despite the numerous potential benefits of day treatment, it is important to recognize that day treatment differs significantly from both inpatient treatment and outpatient treatment. Day treatment is not a modality that should be considered "in the middle" on the continuum of treatment approaches. Some clinical and organizational issues are unique to the day treatment setting.

The success of a day treatment program requires careful consideration of criteria for admission, length of stay, discharge, etc. Without appropriate program design, day treatment programs may not be able to provide needed services to children with various problems, such as aggressive behavior. The same might be true for children with other conditions. Acutely suicidal children, for example, are not candidates for day treatment, although children without imminent risk for self-harm who chronically have some suicidal ideation might be appropriate candidates.

Staffing patterns also merit careful thought. It is common in milieu- and program-oriented treatments to emphasize the inclusion of several mental health disciplines and to utilize a team approach to treatment planning and decision making. Multidisciplinary teams have been praised for the variety of perspectives members bring to individual cases and for the array of treatment options the team offers. They have been criticized for their slowness in arriving at decisions, for the need to include so many perspectives that decisions lose focus and action becomes inefficient, for being expensive, and for providing overlapping services. In an era of aggressive utilization management and cost control, day treatment administrators must clearly define treatment goals and the disciplines needed to reach them. Administrators must recognize that, because of cost, all children may not be able to receive the multiplicity of educational and therapeutic services available in the day treatment setting. Eliminating the inefficiencies and expense of multidisciplinary teams while bringing together broad services and multiple perspectives when needed will remain a challenge.

Safety is another important issue in a day treatment program. Unlike the commonly locked and/or highly secure inpatient setting, day treatment is a modality that provides structure and security for only part of the 24-hour day. Day treatment staff commonly address these clinical questions: Is sending the child home safe for the child and for others? Will the child become overtly suicidal or aggressive in the face of his or her own internal stresses—perhaps in combination with an indifferent, hostile, or potentially abusive home? Day treatment programs must provide the mechanism to bring together appropriate staff at the appropriate time (often toward the end of the day) to evaluate these or other questions, and to develop alternative plans if the child's or family's safety is in question.

Appropriate on-call mechanisms must be set up to monitor the child at home during evenings and weekends, given the severe nature of the child's psychopathology and the often-severe dysfunctionality in his or her family. Home visitation, off-hours visits to a clinical site, and frequent clinical monitoring by telephone are important treatment components to include in program planning.

Clarification of goals and treatment focus is essential in day treatment. As noted earlier, many programs consider their treatment orientation to be "eclectic". Sometimes this designation offers the possibility of carefully considering the individual clinical case and applying the particular treatment orientation necessary for that particular situation and child. At other time times, the term "eclectic" has come to indicate a lack of theoretical rigor in the determination of the types of services provided to a particular patient. In these cases, "eclectic" programs may offer the child a whole gamut of individual, group, and family therapies, sometimes without adequately considering the child's needs. The current economic climate requires more treatment focus, reduced staffing, and clarity about what is essential for the patient.

The current emphasis in inpatient treatment is on early discharge to day treatment. This haste to discharge children often seems prompted by cost, not clinical evaluation. The trend toward day treatment may be helpful for many children, even if not based entirely on clinical objectives. However, the same emphasis on cost will probably result in an emphasis on early discharge from day treatment to outpatient or home-based services. Day treatment administrators must ask important questions. What is essential to accomplish during the child's potentially shorter-than-desirable day treatment? What can be left to less restrictive and less costly outpatient services?

Day treatment has often been considered a preferred treatment cost because of the desire to maintain children in their homes and in the community. Clinical experience confirms, however, that a large percentage of severely disturbed children with externalizing disorders have extremely dysfunctional parents and families. In some cases the parents are not amenable to treatment themselves, to family therapy, or to parent-centered guidance or counseling. Should children in these homes be treated in day treatment rather than in residential settings? If they are treated in day treatment, what are the goals of day treatment for them? Can they be helped to deal with their chronically indifferent, neglectful, or sometimes-abusive parents?

We currently do not have systematically organized treatment approaches for such children, who likely will be under some form of social service, mental health, or juvenile court supervision for many years. Yet, as clinical experience and the previous reviews suggest, these youngsters compose a group of chronic patients who are likely to remain in day treatment for extended periods.

Program planners must decide if their day treatment programs will undertake short-term or long-term treatment. Short-term programs have an average length of stay of 1 to 6 weeks. They often function to stabilize acutely impaired children who might otherwise need inpatient hospitalization, or provide a brief transition from inpatient hospitalization to less intensive outpatient services. The milieu orientation, focus, staff and peer relationships, and expectations in short-term programs are different from those in longer-term programs, whose lengths of stay may be 1 to 2 years.

As noted, day treatment is often considered an important, sometimes preferred, treatment modality for chronically impaired youths with externalizing disorders. It is a very appropriate long-term treatment option for such youths. Economic realities may require a redefinition of this day treatment role as the pressure toward less costly alternatives increases. In this context, intensive outpatient treatment or home-based treatment may come to be used more for treatment of chronically impaired youth than is now the case, a situation that ironically may result in day treatment itself being considered too costly. This pressure may force very much shorter lengths of stay in some day treatment programs and require the development of conceptual and treatment models that recognize this reality.

Day treatment, like other care modalities, is faced with the challenge of linking its services with those of others along the continuum of care. Stand-alone and unaffiliated programs, which are numerous, may be less efficient and clinically effective for severely disturbed children than are programs, that are clearly part of a continuum of care. Programs should provide ready access to both more and less restrictive treatment setting options for individual children. Programs that refer to inpatient or to outpatient settings based on the child's changing needs provide more clinically appropriate services than do programs that hesitate to refer children to other settings or define treatment on a set schedule (such as the school year).

Staff stress is another major challenge in day treatment. Children in inpatient treatment are often extremely disturbed psychiatrically and come from extremely dysfunctional home environments, but they remain in a contained and supervised environment for 24 hours a day. Children in typical outpatient treatment, along with their families, are generally less disturbed and receive treatment once per week or more often, depending on clinical needs. Day treatment (especially hospital-based day treatment) often involves caring for extremely disturbed children from disturbed families who, after several hours per day spent in the structured environment of school classrooms and treatment, return to their dysfunctional homes. Day treatment staff is continually frustrated because of the repeated trauma experienced by children from homes where violence, abuse, and physical and emotional neglect are the rule. Progress for many of these children is extremely slow, consistent with the severity of their own disturbances and the emotional and social difficulties of their parents. Dealing with frequent crises regarding the child's behavior, parent-child interactions, change of caretakers, change in residence, and child neglect and abuse can be a major stressor for day treatment staff.

Another issue that arises in day treatment programs (and in inpatient and residential settings) involves interdisciplinary relationships. As noted, day treatment programs are often organized according to a team model. The psychiatrist is not usually the team leader, although the team is heavily influenced by psychiatric recommendations. Psychiatry, psychology, social work, therapeutic activities, and nursing all have somewhat discrete functions and overlapping areas of interest. The different backgrounds of team members, combined with the stress of dealing with severely disturbed children and dysfunctional families, raises questions of boundaries and difficulties in coordination and communication.

Coordination with teaching staff presents additional challenges. Educational personnel, in many programs, are not under the direct leadership of the clinical director; but they may report to local school authorities. Conflicts concerning the perceived needs of the child (e.g., time in the classroom versus psychotherapy time) may surface at various points.

A good deal of time in day treatment programs seems to be spent on maintaining communication and clarifying structure and roles for staff and then also for children and families. The numerous disciplines involved in the program, the potentially differing agendas of the disciplines, the highly disturbed nature of the patients, and the dysfunctional nature of the families all necessitate the development of a carefully defined structure for the program as a whole and for the staff, children, and families who participate in it. The sensitive development of organizational structure, boundaries, and roles in this highly complex treatment modality is very helpful in maintaining staff morale and cohesion, as well as in enhancing patient and family satisfaction and in supporting the clinical improvement noted in many of the children.

Conclusions

With the apparently increasing number of day treatment programs in the United States and with growing recognition of the importance of this modality, those involved in day treatment for children will need to devote greater attention to the tasks described by Parker and Knoll (1990) and presented at the beginning of this chapter. These efforts should further integrate day treatment into the overall mental health delivery system for children and adolescents with severe emotional and behavioral problems.

SUGGESTED READING

American Academy of Child and Adolescent Psychiatry. *Child and adolescent psychiatric illness: Guidelines for treatment resources, quality assurance, peer review and reimbursement.* Unpublished manuscript.

Baenen, R. S., Parris Stephens, M. A., & Glenwick, D. S. (1986). Outcome in psychoeducational day school programs: A review. *American Journal of Orthopsychiatry, 56,* 263–270.

Block B. M., Arney K, Campbell D. J., Lefkoviz, P. M., Speer S. K., Kiser L. J. and titled Standards and Guidelines for Partial Hospitalization Child and Adolescent Programs, Second Edition. Alexandria, Virginia. American Association for Partial Hospitalization, 1995.

Doan R. J., & Petti, T. A. (1989). Clinical demographic characteristics of child and adolescent partial hospital patients. *Journal of the American Academy of Child and Adolescent Psychiatry, 28,* 66–69.

Gabel, S., & Finn, M. (1986). Outcome in children's day treatment programs: Review of the literature and recommendations for future research. *International Journal of Partial Hospitalization, 3,* 261–271.

Gabel, S., Swanson, A. J., & Shindledecker, R. A. (1990). Outcome in children's day treatment: Relationship to preadmission variables. *International Journal of Partial Hospitalization, 6,* 129–137.

Grizenko, N (1997). Outcome of Multimodal Day Treatment for Children with Severe Behavior Problems: A Five-Year Follow-up. Journal of the American Academy of Child and Adolescent Psychiatry, 36:989–997.

Grizenko N, Papineau D, Sayegh L (1993). Effectiveness of a Multimodal Day Treatment Program for Children with Disruptive Behavior Problems. *Journal of the American Academy of Child and Adolescent Psychiatry, 32:127–134.*

Kiser LJ, Millsap P. A., Hickerson S, Heston J. D., Nunn W, Pruitt D. B., Rohr M. (1996). Results of Treatment One Year Later: Child and Adolescent Partial Hospitalization. *Journal of the American Academy of Child and Adolescent Psychiatry, 35:81–90.*

Kiser, L. J. (1991). Treat-effectiveness research in child and adolescent partial hospitalization. *The Psychiatric Hospital, 22,* 51–58.

Kiser, L. J., Heston, J. D., Millsap, P. A., & Pruitt, D. B. (1991). Treatment protocols in child and adolescent day treatment. *Hospital and Community Psychiatry, 42,* 597–600.

Kiser, L. J., Pruitt, D. B., McColgan, E. B., & Ackerman, B. J. (1986). A survey of child and adolescent day-treatment programs: Establishing definitions and standards. *International Journal of Partial Hospitalization, 3,* 247–259.

Parker, S., Knoll, J. L. III. (1990). Partial hospitalization: An update. *American Journal of Psychiatry, 147,* 156–160.

Prentice-Dunn, S., Wilson, D. R., & Lyman, R. D. (1981). Client factors related to outcome in a residential and day treatment program for children. *Journal of Clinical Child Psychology, 10,* 188–191.

Zimet, S. G., & Farley, G. K. (1991). *Day treatment for children with emotional disorder* (Vol. 1). New York: Plenum Press.

Zimet, S. G., Farley, G. K., Silver, J., Hebert, F. B., Robb, E. D., Ekanger, C., & Smith, D. (1980). Behavior and personality changes in emotionally disturbed children enrolled in a psychoeducational day treatment center. *Journal of the American Academy of Child Psychiatry, 19,* 240–256.

34 / Adolescent Day Treatment

Gordon K. Farley and Sara G. Zimet

In this chapter, we will trace the history and development of adolescent day treatment and describe its models, treatment philosophy, and staffing patterns. Next we will discuss some of the important issues associated with its present status, issues concerned with the place of adolescent day treatment in a continuum of mental health care, age segregation, and program planning. The research on treatment outcome and its predictors will be summarized. Finally, we will examine future directions for this treatment modality.

The History and Development of Adolescent Day Treatment

Day treatment for adolescents is a relative newcomer on the psychiatric treatment scene. Although information was available on the history of day treatment for adults and for children, we were unable to find any publications that chronicled the inception and early development of day treatment for adolescents in the United States. The likelihood is that day treatment for adolescents followed a path similar to that for adults and for children, although at a different pace. It was largely an offshoot of inpatient or residential treatment, a treatment modality established by the early 1960s. Placing adolescents in treatment settings with adults was customary. As adolescence was recognized in the broader society as a separate developmental stage, however, a gradual shift occurred: younger adolescents were placed with child patients, and older adolescents with adult patients. This practice remains today, particularly in residential and hospital settings. Adolescents-only programs are most commonly found in public school settings. In 1985, the *Directory for Exceptional Children* listed 206 private and 36 state and public facilities that offered day psychiatric treatment to adolescents. It is likely that the total number is larger now.

In the United States, the Mental Health Acts of 1963 and 1965 provided a stimulus to the development of day treatment facilities for all age groups. Through the funding of construction and staffing costs of community mental health centers, the possibility for a continuum of care was assured by statute. Treatment in the least restrictive and optimally intensive setting was also affirmed. The acts made five services in every community mental health center: inpatient hospitalization, outpatient treatment, consultation-liaison services, emergency psychiatric services, and day or partial hospital services.

The Federation of Partial Hospitalization Study Groups, which later became the American Association for Partial Hospitalization (AAPH), was established in the 1970s, and its first annual conference was held in 1976. Its founding members were all professionals in the field of partial hospitalization for adults. It wasn't until 1987 that a special-interest group focusing on children and adolescents emerged within the organization. As a result of the subgroup, the AAPH broadened its goals and objectives. Four years later, the AAPH published its standards for child and adolescent facilities (Block et al., 1991). This document was a first attempt at establishing guidelines for defining programs for patients 21 years old and younger.

Criteria for Admission

According to the standards recommended by AAPH, criteria for admission to day psychiatric treatment should incorporate the following clinical indicators:

1. The patient is at risk for exclusion from normative community activities or residence.
2. The patient exhibits psychiatric symptoms, chemical dependency, behavioral problems, and/or developmental delays of sufficient severity to bring about significant or profound impairment in day-

to-day educational, social, vocational, and/or interpersonal functioning.

3. The patient: (a) has failed to make sufficient clinical gains within a traditional outpatient setting or has not attempted such outpatient treatment and the severity of presenting symptomology is such that success of traditional outpatient treatment is doubtful, and (b) is ready for release from an inpatient setting but is judged to be in continued need of ongoing intensive therapeutic intervention in order to make the appropriate transition toward full community activities.

4. The patient's family, guardian, or custodian: (a) is able and willing to provide the support and monitoring of the patient, enabling adequate control over behavior; and (b) is involved in treatment.

5. The patient has the capacity to benefit from the therapeutic interventions provided.

Criteria for admission have been described by several other writers as well. Of special interest is the scale developed by Kiser and her co-workers (Kiser, Heston, Millsap, & Pruitt, 1991), which attempts to consider dimensions of impulse control, family functioning, suicide risk, substance abuse, and elopement or runaway risk. Conditions usually taken into account in these scales include danger to self or other(s), serious psychological impairment, and motivation for treatment.

Demographic and Clinical Characteristics of Adolescents Accepted for Day Treatment

A number of studies examined profiles of populations enrolled in day treatment or of those who had completed treatment. Researchers compared the profiles to those of patients in more intensive treatment settings, such as private psychiatric hospital, a state psychiatric hospital, and a residential treatment setting. The conclusion drawn from these studies was that the adolescents in all of these treatment settings were more similar than they were different in both demographic and clinical characteristics. Apparently, local practice, insurance benefits, and professional training in the use of day treatment influence who is referred and accepted for treatment.

Models of Adolescent Day Treatment

PHILOSOPHY OF TREATMENT

Theoretical models for day psychiatric treatment can be categorized as psychodynamic, behavioral/cognitive, developmental/psychobiological, or systems theory–based. These categorizations are not mutually exclusive, nor are they at the same level of discourse. Programs that are systems theory–based often encompass all other philosophies. Other programs are described as eclectic, usually meaning that many different theoretical bases are included with an emphasis on practical application. Family work has also achieved increasing prominence and has been incorporated into a variety of models, including behavioral, systemic, strategic, and structural.

Behavioral/cognitive treatment programs are organized around the view that psychopathology represents a maladaptive habit pattern, involving either thought or behavior. Cognitive/behavioral approaches are part of nearly every treatment program and are particularly important in disorders such as obsessive-compulsive disorder, unipolar depression, bipolar disorder, anxiety disorder, adolescent schizophrenia, and eating disorders. Behavioral/cognitive treatments are likely to be combined with psychopharmacological treatments, especially when there is a striking biological contributor to the disorder. This combination of treatments could come under the rubric of systems treatment or developmental psychobiological treatment. Many programs include individual child psychotherapy as an important part of the therapeutic intervention. Family psychotherapy of a dynamic, structural, or strategic type is also part of most treatment programs and is particularly important for adolescents locked in conflict involving issues of rebellion, emancipation, and separation and individuation.

PATIENT EVALUATION

The first order of business upon admission to day treatment is a comprehensive evaluation. Data gathered at this point vary from sparse to extensive, but information from a variety of sources—such as the adolescent, the family, and the school—should be included. Some of

TABLE 34.1

Evaluation and Treatment of the Day Patient

| | Sources of information | | |
| | Present | Past | |
	Descriptive	Developmental genetic	Treatment
Biological	Physical exam Laboratory tests Diagnostic procedures	History of genetic and other constitutional factors History of physical illness, injuries, operations, abuse, and medications	Psychoactive medication Medication for physical illnesses Somatic thearapies Other medical treatments
Psychological	Mental status exam Psychological assessment Applied behavioral analysis Home behavior checklists	Developmental factors and experiences in infancy, childhood, adolescence, and adulthood	Individual psychodynamic child psychotherapy Individual parent psychotherapy Group child psychotherapy Family therapy Behavior modification programs Parent groups
Educational	Achievement testing School behavior checklists Classroom observations Perceptual-motor evaluations	Educational history	Milieu Educational programming Special-education techniques Developmental learning materials Integrated curriculum Speech and language therapies
Sociocultural	Social support assessment Psychosocial stressor assessment	Family history Racial, religious, cultural, and socioeconomic background	Enhancing social supports Employment assistance Financial counseling

these sources of information are shown in Table 34.1.

Several programs have designed their patient assessment and treatment-monitoring process for use in program evaluation efforts (Zimet, Farley, & Avitable, 1987). These endeavors are laudable and are being reported with increasing frequency.

STAFFING PATTERNS

From one day treatment center for adolescents to another staffing patterns differ considerably, depending on whether the center is private, public, or hospital-affiliated. Increasingly, adolescents with major psychiatric disorders are being treated in day hospitals rather than inpatient units. Thus, psychopharmacological treatment is required for

more patients than in the past. The program director is often, but not necessarily, a child or adult psychiatrist. The director may also have a background in psychology, social work, psychiatric nursing, or special education. If the director is not a psychiatrist, the Joint Commission on the Accreditation of Health Care Organizations specifies that either a medical director who is a physician or a regular medical consultant be available.

Those who have daily frontline responsibility for patient care are special educators; teacher aides; and, sometimes, psychiatric nurses and mental health technicians or mental health aides.

PROGRAM ACTIVITIES

The emphasis on educational diagnosis and remediation varies from setting to setting. It may range from being quite limited, meeting only the minimal requirements of the local school district, to being quite intensive and the principal focus of the program. The amount of improvement in academic achievement has been noted to be modest (Gabel, Swanson, & Shindledecker, 1990; Zimet, 1990), an outcome that may be related to the time spent on instruction.

The schedule of activities varies greatly from program to program, but programs usually include the traditional school subjects of mathematics, reading, language arts, literature, science, social studies, history, art, music, and career education. Time must be allocated for group, family, and individual psychotherapy, socialization, physical education, and occupational therapy.

Naturally, there should be flexibility to respond to the needs and interests of the patient population. The usual day for an adolescent day treatment unit is 6 to 7 hours. Common hours of operation are between 8:00 A.M. and 5:00 P.M.. Many programs have afternoon and evening hours, and some even have weekend hours. Individual psychotherapy sessions are spaced throughout the week. Other services—such as speech and language assessments and therapy, psychological assessments, art therapy, and occupational therapy—are arranged as needed. Some programs, depending on interests and location, have special emphasis on sports, outdoor education, technical arts, or computers. Vocational training and career education are particularly important and are discussed later. Field trips, both within and outside the surrounding community, are often arranged for a day or a half day.

Group psychotherapy, because peer issues are so important to adolescents, is part of nearly every program. In some programs, there may be as much as 90 minutes of group psychotherapy per day, and it may be strategically placed at the very beginning of the day.

Family psychotherapy is commonly recognized as a cornerstone of psychotherapeutic work with adolescents. A recurring problem is the assurance of parent participation. One innovative but not surprising approach to this has been to meet with families in their homes. This approach resulted in changing a family dropout rate of 90 percent to a family participation rate of 90 percent.

Issues in Adolescent Day Treatment

AGE SEGREGATION

Although there is not complete agreement on this point, many clinicians feel that adolescent day hospitals should be separate from adult facilities. Advocates of separate facilities maintain that adolescents face a number of specific issues that are different in both type and degree from those adults face. Adolescents tend to be noisy, disruptive, intrusive, inconsiderate, and self-centered, and these qualities do not wear well on an adult day treatment unit. Those making a counterargument maintain that mixing adults and adolescents on the same unit contributes to adolescent socialization, increased ability to take another's perspective, and perhaps even an activation of lethargic adults.

Children have been placed with adolescents in hopes of evoking more mature behavior on the part of the children. What is more likely to happen, however, is that the younger children exert a downward pull on the adolescents, who are poor models for the children. In practice, therefore, adults, adolescents, and children have been kept separate whenever possible.

ACCESSING SERVICES

Ideally, a day treatment unit for adolescents should exist as an integral part of a complete continuum of care. There should be ready access to more intensive treatment, such as inpatient and residential treatment, as well as to less intensive psychotherapeutic treatment, such as outpatient treatment, in order to ensure that lengths of stay are not longer than necessary. Other services—such as respite care, group and individual foster homes, therapeutic foster homes, and necessary medical treatment and consultation—should be adjuncts to all services so that they, too, are easily available.

BEHAVIORAL MANAGEMENT

A successful treatment program for adolescents often rests on the adequate control, sublimation, and appropriate expression and transformation of sexual and aggressive energies and impulses. Adolescents present special problems in these areas in that they have the bodily needs and urges of adults but often the impulse control and judgment of children. Aggression is the most common reason for referral of an adolescent for mental health treatment; therefore, the management of aggression in the day treatment setting is critical. Central, in this regard, is a set of clear rules and clearly defined consequences regarding the violation of and adherence to these rules. Consequences usually derive from some kind of behavioral program involving assessment and graded responses to rule violations. Several comprehensive behavioral management systems, thoughtfully conceived and tested, have been developed. Three of note include the Social Learning Approach to Family Intervention (Patterson, Reid, Jones, & Conger, 1975), the Brewer-Porch Children's Center approach (Lyman & Prentice-Dunn, 1991), and the Achievement Place Program (Phillips, Phillips, Fixsen, & Wolf, 1971). Combinations of these treatment approaches have recently been termed, *multimodal* (Grizen Ko, 1997).

Kiser and her co-workers (1991) developed guidelines for deciding which difficult adolescents can be admitted for treatment and for whom more intensive treatment is required. They described special treatment procedures for programs that care for patients who use drugs, are suicidal, assaultive, or combative.

INSURANCE COVERAGE AND FUNDING

Most day treatment settings are dependent on a mixture of funds. This mixture usually includes public funds (federal, state, county, and municipal); third-party payments; and, to a minor degree, out-of-pocket private payments. Since adolescent day treatment includes education, funds from local, state, and federal sources are often available for the educational portion.

DEVELOPMENTAL ISSUES CONCERNING ADOLESCENTS

Identity Formation and Separation from the Family of Origin: Tumultuous struggles around identity formation are characteristic of adolescence. Group psychotherapy sessions on adolescent day treatment units frequently focus on the questions Who am I? and How am I different from my family? Individual psychotherapy is the most common therapeutic modality offered, and in most programs it is done at a frequency of once or twice a week. Identity formation includes formation of sexual identity, occupational identity, and cultural identity and is often linked with emancipation and separation from the family of origin. In many programs, a significant percentage of patients leave the day hospital and do not return to their family setting. For these patients, the principal issue in treatment is the negotiation of this transition. This issue, therefore, is likely to be addressed in all psychotherapeutic modalities.

Education and Occupational Choice: Since two of the developmental tasks of adolescents are continuation of education and beginning occupational choice, educational assessment and diagnosis assume increased importance on an adolescent day treatment unit. The striking comorbidity of conduct disorders and learning disabilities (or academic underachievement) makes an academic evaluation to identify undiagnosed learning problems critical. Since selection of and gaining the necessary skills to compete and succeed in an occupation are important tasks of adolescence, vocational or prevocational skills should be emphasized more than they currently appear to be except where programs are conducted within public school settings. Classroom time may range from the minimum required by local law (as little as 1 hour per day) to a complete educational program. The range of abilities and future aspirations of these adolescents is likely to be large, from unskilled laborer to college-bound scholar. In order to take this variation into consideration and to meet this developmental task of adolescence, individual planning with patients is a critical part of any treatment program.

With older adolescents, (16 to 18 years old), there has been some interest in using a psychoeducational approach to teaching "life skills." Lazarus (1973) has developed such a program, which includes such topics as assertiveness training, verbal and nonverbal communication, depression, weight control, human sexuality, stress management, relaxation, dance, physical education, ceramics, vocational exploration, money management, and food preparation.

Drug and Alcohol Abuse: In some programs, as many as 60 percent of the admissions relate to drug or alcohol abuse. In such settings, drug education is considered an important part of the treatment. In addition, a program involving urine monitoring, begun at admission or with random "tox screens" during treatment, is useful as an aid to detection and abstinence.

Sexuality and AIDS: Sexual interactions among the adolescents in day treatment units deserve important attention because of potential damage to the patients and because of risk-management issues for the institution. As a result, most units have firm rules prohibiting sexual contact. Similarly, rules regarding sexual contact between patients and staff members are strictly enforced. Many localities have laws prohibiting sexual contact and require statements from mental health personnel to patients, announcing their understanding of the illegality of these acts and of the professional ethics involved.

The high likelihood of sexual activity among adolescents requires that sex education be an integral part of any program. This apparent need becomes even more compelling in view of the large number of pregnant teenagers and the threat of AIDS and other sexually transmitted diseases. Many curricula are available for sex and AIDS education. Two of the best are the Teenage Health Teaching Modules on AIDS and on Sexuality, both produced by the Rocky Mountain Center for Health Promotion and Education (1990). Included in these modules is discussion of refusal skills, instructions on safe sex, prevention of rape, and responsible sexual practices.

SPECIALIZED ADOLESCENT DAY TREATMENT SETTINGS

Units dedicated to the treatment of specific psychiatric and health disorders are becoming increasingly common. The growth of these units are attributed to efforts to seek the best treatment approaches for specific conditions. Thus, units now exist for treating drug and alcohol abusers; pregnant teenagers; juvenile offenders; and those with conduct, dissociative, eating, and affective disorders. Boys and girls may be separated within these groups or in the units by themselves.

Another recent phenomenon is the development of medical-psychiatric, or med-psych, day treatment units. As the name implies, these settings treat adolescents who are both mentally and physically very ill.

Outcome of Treatment

Seventeen studies concerned with the outcome of day treatment for adolescents were reviewed. They spanned 28 years, from 1968 to 1996, and differed from one another in terms of the age and diagnostic composition of the group, the type and philosophy of the program, and in the variables examined. Some studies examined good versus poor outcome per se; others attempted to identify predictors of the effects of treatment. In general, all of the studies reported improvement in academic functioning, behavior, or both. A positive outcome was strongly related to a high rate of attendance in the treatment program by adolescents alone or with their parents, starting treatment at an early age, less severe psychopathology at the start of treatment, the absence of drug and alcohol use, no trouble with the law, steady employment, and a sustained relationship with a nonfamily member for at least six months. Furthermore, locus of control was the sole variable predicting attrition; those with an external locus of control were not as likely to drop out of treatment as were those with an internal locus. It seems that adolescents who are developmentally involved in issues of separation, autonomy, and independence but have an external locus of control are more likely to submit to treatment suggested by an external authority. A recent study has shown that most of these positive changes, including improvement in daily functioning, remain evident one year following discharge.

Conclusion: Current and Future Trends

AN INCREASE IN THE USE OF DAY TREATMENT

The research has indicated that day treatment for adolescents is comparable or superior to inpatient or residential treatment. In addition to clinical efficacy, studies have also found day treatment to be financially more efficacious than are more restrictive treatment settings. There is every likelihood, therefore, that there will be a significant reduction in inpatient beds and residential placements and an increase in day treatment chairs.

AN INCREASE IN SERIOUSLY DISTURBED PATIENTS

As pressure increases to reduce the length of hospital stays and to eliminate hospital beds, more seriously disturbed patients are likely to be entering day treatment facilities than is currently the case. This will lead to an increased use of psychopharmacological approaches.

A SHORTER LENGTH OF STAY

Efforts to contain the cost of all mental health services will result in pressure to reduce the length of day treatment and to transfer patients to outpatient care. In effect, there is likely to be a rapid assessment of comorbidity. What once was regarded as a simple conduct disorder will more likely be seen as a manifestation of an affective disorder, such as a bipolar disorder or major depression; an obsessive-compulsive disorder; an attention deficit hyperactivity disorder; or temporal lobe epilepsy. In these cases, appropriate pharmacological treatment will quickly be instituted, and the monitoring of complex medication regimens carried out. Carefully structured behavioral, cognitive, family, and rehabilitative approaches are likely to be integrated with pharmacological approaches in the treatment of these complex disorders. Consequent to these changes, there will probably be a decreasing emphasis on psychodynamic approaches; administrators will carefully select patients who can benefit most from specific therapies. Along with more aggressive treatment of the adolescent, there will be an increased emphasis on more intensive work with families.

In order to optimize a shorter length of stay, efforts will be made to deliver treatment earlier, building on the evidence that the younger the adolescent starts treatment, the better the outcome. Furthermore, there is likely to be an increase in collaborative patient-staff goal setting and in the monitoring of these treatment goals.

OTHER THERAPEUTIC INTERVENTIONS

Group psychotherapy will continue to be emphasized along with other approaches that foster improved peer and adult relationships. In addition, assessment of learning disabilities, educational remediation, and vocational or occupational training will become more prominent in treatment planning. More attention also will be given to teaching about human sexuality and AIDS and to the monitoring of alcohol and drug use.

SPECIALIZED PROGRAMS FOR SPECIFIC PROBLEMS

There is likely to be an increase in day treatment programs for adolescents with specific problem types, possibly but not necessarily segregated by gender. Programs for adjudicated youngsters will probably increase, particularly if the programs demonstrate long-lasting, positive treatment outcomes.

A CHANGE IN STAFFING PATTERNS

Highly trained mental health professionals (i.e., those with doctoral and master's degrees) will be used as consultants and/or supervisors, and less expensive professionals (i.e., certified personnel and those with bachelor's degrees) will carry out the treatment interventions.

TRAINING AND RETRAINING MENTAL HEALTH PROFESSIONALS

As patients are referred less often to inpatient and residential treatment, those in child and adolescent psychiatry residency programs; clinical psychology internship programs; and programs to train psychiatric social workers, psychiatric nurse, and other mental health workers are likely to receive training in day treatment as a mandatory part of their professional education. For example, 4 to 10 months of full-time inpatient training is now required in child psychiatry residency training programs, but there is no requirement for day treatment experience the programs will probably contain a day treatment component in the near future. Likewise, those professionals currently working in more restrictive treatment settings will need to be retrained to apply their skills to day treatment.

REFERENCES

Armstrong, H. E., Jr., Tracy, J. J., Rock, D. L., & Hays, V. L. (1981). The life skills program: A psychoeducational approach to psychiatric day care. *International Journal of Partial Hospitalization, 1,* 141–149.

Block, B. M., Arney, K., Campbell, D. J., Kiser, L. J., Lefkovitz, P. M., & Speer, S. K. (1991). American Association for Partial Hospitalization Child and Adolescent Special Interest Group: Standards for child and adolescent partial hospitalization programs. *International Journal of Partial Hospitalization, 7,* 13–21.

The directory for exceptional children (10th ed.). (1985). Boston: Porter Sargent Publishers.

Farley, G. K., & Zimet, S. G. (Eds.). (1991). *Day treatment for children with emotional disorders: Vol. 2, Models across the country.* New York: Plenum Press.

Fink, E., Longabaugh, R., & Stout, R. (1978). The paradoxical underutilization of partial hospitalization. *American Journal of Psychiatry, 135,* 713–716.

Gabel, S., Swanson, A. J., & Shindledecker, R. (1990). Outcome in children's day treatment: Relationship to preadmission variables. *International Journal of Partial Hospitalization, 6,* 129–137.

GrizenKo, N. (1997). Outcome of multimodal day treatment for children with severe behavior problems: a five-year follow-up. *Journal of the American Academy of Child and Adolescent Psychiatry, 36,* 989–997.

Kiser, L. J., Heston, J. D., Millsap, P. A., & Pruitt, D. B. (1991). Testing the limits: Special treatment procedures for child and adolescent partial hospitalization. *International Journal of Partial Hospitalization, 7,* 37–53.

Kiser, L. J., Millsap, P. A., Hickerson, S., Heston, J. D., Nunn, W., Pruitt, D. B., & Rohr, M. (1996). Results of treatment one year later: Child and adolescent partial hospitalization. *Journal of the American Academy of Child and Adolescent Psychiatry, 35,* 81–90.

Lazarus, A. A. (1973). Multimodal behavior therapy: Treating the "BASIC ID." *Journal of Nervous and Mental Disease, 156,* 404–411.

Lyman, R. D., & Prentice-Dunn, S. (1991). A behavioral model of day treatment. In G. K. Farley & S. G. Zimet (Eds.), *Day treatment for children with emotional disorders: Vol. 2, Models across the country* (pp. 97–116). New York: Plenum Press.

Patterson, G. R., Reid, J. B., Jones, R. R., & Conger, R. E. (1975). *A social learning approach to family intervention: Vol. 1, Families with aggressive children.* Eugene, OR: Castalia Publishing Company.

Phillips, E. L., Phillips, E. A., Fixsen, D. L., & Wolf, M. M. (1971). Achievement place: Modification of the behaviors of predelinquent boys within a token economy. *Journal of Applied Behavior Analysis, 4,* 45–59.

Rocky Mountain Center for Health Promotion and Education. (1990). *Healthy sexuality: A module for middle school.* (Available from 7525 West 10th Avenue, Lakewood, CO).

Zimet, S. G. (1990). Does partial hospitalization for children with emotional disorders mean partial education? *International Journal of Partial Hospitalization, 6,* 81–94.

Zimet, S. G., & Farley, G. K. (Eds.). (1991). *Day treatment for children with emotional disorders: Vol. 1, A model in action.* New York: Plenum Press.

Zimet, S. G., Farley, G. K., & Avitable, N. (1987). Establishing a comprehensive data base in a day-treatment program for children. *International Journal of Partial Hospitalization, 4,* 1–15.

35 / Residential Treatment

Martin Irwin

Residential treatment is a multidisciplinary, multimodality treatment that combines various aspects of milieu therapy, individual psychotherapy, collateral treatment with parents (casework), and family therapy. All these therapies can employ an eclectic mix of psychodynamic, behavioral, cognitive, and psychoeducational approaches. It is estimated that close to 20,000 children under the age of 18 are in residential treatment. Despite the advances in home- and community-based treatments for children, the number of youngsters in residential treatment continues to grow and the waiting lists remain long.

The vast majority of children admitted to residential facilities are among the most disturbed youngsters. They are likely to have already received and "failed" the multiple interventions available from local mental health and child welfare systems. Once admitted, residential treatment helps children to become aware of long-standing patterns of behavior, interpersonal relationships, and feelings and to develop a more adaptive set of behaviors to deal with their feelings, needs, and problems. The goal of treatment is for children to improve to the point where they can successfully reintegrate into home and community settings and be discharged to lower levels of mental health services.

Milieu Therapy

A cornerstone of residential treatment is the therapeutic use of residence, the use of the milieu as an agent to bring about change in children. A milieu in a residential treatment center is a highly structured and consistent environment specifically designed to allow a child to establish a sense of security, to provide a variety of human relationships, to promote appropriate interactions that allow the child to develop satisfying interpersonal relationships, and to provide meaningful academic and nonacademic activities through which the child develops adaptive behaviors and achieves an emerging sense of competence and self-esteem. To reach these goals, milieu therapy as currently practiced tends to combine traditional psychodynamically based techniques (aimed at enhancing human connectedness with group) with psychoeducational, behavioral, and cognitive approaches (which are geared toward behavior management and the teaching of adaptive skills). There are four broadly based models for organizing milieus: interpersonal/psychodynamic, behavioral, psychoeducational, and group/peer culture. Although many residential treatment centers may emphasize one particular approach, most utilize principles and techniques from some or all of the models.

INTERPERSONAL/PSYCHODYNAMIC MODEL

In milieu treatment the therapeutic relationships that form between child and staff are vehicles for change. In this model, a child's mistrust of adults and the resulting affective and behavioral expression can be changed through the transference potential that is unique to a milieu. The child will relive, reenact, and reexperience all of his significant problems in the residential setting and in relation to its staff. Children in residential treatment are likely to behave toward staff with the long-standing maladaptive patterns with which they related to most adults in the past. In return, they expect that staff will react toward them as adults in their past did. If the staff do not react with anger, punishment, retaliation, rejection, or abandonment but instead provide warmth, nurturance, and understanding, the child's underlying feelings, conflicts, and needs may cease to find symptomatic expression. Instead they may manifest themselves interpersonally. Once the feelings are expressed interpersonally and the child has a trusting relationship with a staff member, the staff can begin to help the child express feelings more directly and deal more realistically with conflict. Over the course of treatment, if this interactive pattern persists, the child begins to experience the adults in his present life as different from those in the past; to modify his or her world view and misperceptions of reality; and to feel secure enough to attempt different, more adaptive modes of relating.

Expanding on the interactional approach, milieus for school-aged children may focus on fostering discriminant attachments. All interventions are evaluated from the perspective of whether they help the child get to know the staff member with whom he or she is interacting; help the individual staff member get to know the child; and promote appropriate, positive, and discriminant attachments between the two. Milieu activities are structured to actively and quickly build a large base of shared positive experiences on which discriminate attachments can be formed. The assignment of a primary staff member for a child is never done at admission and is not arbitrary, based on who is next in a rotation. Instead, children are asked to choose staff members with whom they would like to spend time. Likewise, when children need to go for appointments outside the treatment center, they chose the staff member who will accompany them. As much as possible, children are encouraged to share experiences with staff members they like and trust. When children run errands, such as fetching a meal from the dining room for a child who is unit-restricted, the errand is regarded as a special time when a child can share the task with an adult the child chose. Similarly, if staff members go out to rent a movie for the weekend, the task becomes a group activity shared with children who have earned that level of privilege. Children are discouraged from going to school or the dining room alone, even when they have earned the privilege of doing so. Instead, children are encouraged to define their privileges as special time shared with favorite staff. During community meetings, younger children are encouraged to sit on a staff member's lap so that they can use the security of the relationship to begin to explore intense affect and highly charged conflicts. The older children are asked to sit next to a favorite staff member. Once a child begins to form positive relationships with some of the staff members, these attachments need to be used therapeutically for the child to work through the difficulties and strong negative affects that occur in these relationships. When children become upset, a staff member with whom the child has a close relationship (as opposed to any available staff member) is the most likely to become the recipient of the child's anger and aggressive behaviors.

To keep the focus and theme of residential treatment consistently on issues of human connectedness, in this model the content of most verbal interventions must be constructed in terms of attachment. For the child who always sits away from the group in community meeting, an intervention might be "Sam, you seem to be pushing us away by always wanting to sit by yourself. We think you are trying to reject us because you are convinced we'll ultimately reject you." A staff member, working through an episode of aggression with a youngster might say, "You seem to want to get close to adults, but many times you get uncomfortable when you get too close too quickly. So you hit and spit and push us away again." With psychotic children, issues might be stated in terms of the children's discomfort with relationships in the real world; therefore, the children feel they must withdraw into a fantasy world.

BEHAVIORAL MODEL

In milieus organized according to a behavioral model, children's maladaptive behaviors are viewed as the central problem. Treatment focuses on changing specific targeted behaviors, not nec-

essarily their emotional underpinnings. Treatment involves a host of techniques aimed at reducing negative behaviors and/or increasing positive behaviors. In the implementation of behavior modification, rewards and punishments are used as contingencies. Rewards can consist of privileges, such as late bedtimes; extra phone calls, visits, television, or playground time; toys, snacks, or other physical objects; or points, stars, tokens, or the like that can be accumulated or cashed in. In some programs, the positive reinforcer is awarded for every appearance of the targeted prosocial behavior. In other programs, a reward is earned based on the presence of a targeted positive behavior and or the absence of a targeted negative behavior during a preselected unit of time, which can range from minutes to hours. Punishments can include loss of privileges, fun activities, or takens or points; room restrictions; early bedtime; or isolation. As with positive reinforcement, punishment is dispensed whenever a child displays a targeted negative behavior or after a preselected unit of time in which the child engaged in the negative behavior and/or did not engage in a targeted positive behavior.

Behavior modification programs may be individualized or constructed for groups of children. An individualized program targets the most problematic behaviors that interfere with a specific child's day-to-day functioning. In addition, certain positive prosocial behaviors that are incompatible or may substitute for the negative behaviors (such as verbal communication of strong dysphoric affect or asking staff for help) may also be identified. In group programs, rules, expectations, and contingencies are developed for all children on a unit. Instead of targeting only a few of the most serious behaviors of a specific child, consequences apply to the individual child for infractions of unit rules that cover most aspects of group residential life. Offenses can range from hitting and talking out of turn in school to mealtime misbehavior and not making one's bed in the morning. Similarly, rewards are given for compliance with a general set of prosocial behaviors that are expected of all children on the unit.

The level system is a variation on formal behavior modification programs that is especially suited to the residential treatment setting. The progression of treatment is defined in terms of a certain finite number of levels, each with its own specific set of privileges and restrictions. Early in treatment or during periods of regression, a child will be placed on a lower level with greater restrictions, a high degree of staff supervision, and few privileges—especially those involving trust and independent activity. In theory, as a child begins to make progress, especially as discharge nears he or she is at a higher level with few restrictions, age-appropriate supervision, a high degree of staff trust, and ample opportunity for independent activity. Children move up or down the level system based on how successfully they meet individual behavioral goals or the general unit-wide expectations that are preset for each level. Those expectations may include differing levels of behavioral and emotional control, individual responsibility, and/or appropriateness of the child's relationships to peers and staff. Levels are frequently assigned during weekly review meetings attended by both staff and all the children on the unit.

Other behavioral interventions are also commonly used in residential treatment. A very effective way of dealing with maladaptive behaviors is through the use of short periods of "time out" from pleasurable activity. When a child is crossing a unit limit, not responding to verbal cues, or beginning to escalate toward out-of-control behavior, a time-out is given. Upon receiving a time-out, the child must sit down in a place designated by staff and remain silent for a specified period of time, usually 1 to 5 minutes. During a time-out, the child is not permitted to interact either verbally or physically. If the child talks, the time starts over. The length of time a child receives is determined by several factors, including age, maturity, severity of the child's disturbance, ability to appreciate the situation sufficiently to benefit from the time-out, and the nature of the infraction. Usually, the child receives a single warning so he or she can choose to stop the problematic behavior receiving the time-out.

Seclusion, or isolation, rooms are another common intervention. The room is usually padded and without furniture. Windows and light fixtures are screened with unbreakable material. The room should be constructed so that a child, no matter how out of control, will be safe from self-injurious behavior. Seclusion rooms are used as a safe, low-stimulus environment where children who are exhibiting dangerous behavior can discharge strong feelings until they calm down and

begin to work on the problem constructively. Seclusion is also used as the highest level of negative contingency in behavioral programs, especially those designed to deal with noncompliant behavior. Although seclusion rooms can be an effective intervention, arbitrary and punitive use diminishes their therapeutic value. Because of this, some treatment programs do not use seclusion.

PSYCHOEDUCATIONAL MODEL

As part of the therapeutic process of residential treatment, a child may need to experiment with new patterns of interaction, behavior, and affect to replace patterns of symptomatic behavior. Children can be taught new adaptive skills, especially in the areas of interpersonal social behavior, expression of affect, coping, and problem solving. Psychoeducational techniques—such as social skills training, cognitive behavior modification, recreational therapy, anger control therapy, and social problem solving—can easily be incorporated into a residential treatment program.

Many residential centers employ these approaches in special treatment hours scheduled separately in the child's program and led by therapists who are off the unit and not involved in daily child care functions. An alternate approach is to build the techniques of these adjunctive therapies into the hour-by-hour, day-to-day programming of the therapeutic milieu. Instead of art therapy or recreational therapy per se, regularly scheduled activities such as art and sports can be designed to provide therapeutic benefit for children. The child care staff can be taught the skills they need to help children improve expression of affect, social skills, and social problem solving.

The regular day-to-day programming that incorporates skills training can have tremendous therapeutic impact. For example, art can be used as a vehicle for teaching effective communication. Sports activities are an excellent venue for working with competition, cooperation, and frustration tolerance. The dining room can serve as laboratory for modeling, teaching, and trying out new social and conversational skills. Bedtime provides an excellent opportunity for staff and children to work on anxiety reduction, relaxation, and self-soothing.

Through the use of psychoeducational techniques, the important skills children need for success after discharge can be effectively taught within the cohesive and integrative environment of the milieu. (Another advantage to this approach is that child care staff feel like empowered members of the child's treatment team, not just functionaries in a custodial role. The result is an increase in staff morale.)

A use of the psychoeducational approach specifically designed for residential treatment is the life-space interview (Redl, 1959). If a child becomes upset or acts inappropriately, any staff member who is part of the experience will try to convert these everyday issues into a therapeutic interaction. In time and space the interaction should occur as close to the action as possible.

In a variation of the life-space interview, time-outs are coupled with processing of the event leading to the time-out. After sitting quietly for the prescribed time-out, the child is expected to say how she earned the time-out, thereby helping her identify patterns of maladaptive behavior. Next, staff help the child learn that misbehavior usually indicates that the child is feeling something. Staff then encourage the child to identify the feeling, see the misbehavior as an expression of that feeling, and teach the child appropriate ways to communicate about the feeling. Alternate behaviors are also explored. After this process is completed, the consequence is over and the child is free to join the group.

GROUP/PEER CULTURE MODEL

The group/peer culture model emphasizes the use of group process to catalyze change in behavior. Peer influence is very significant to children. Through frequent group meetings and peer control over the level system and privileges, children can exert significant support for positive behavioral change in each other. During group discussions confrontation about negative behavior, verbal reinforcement of positive behavior, and almost continuous feedback from peers may serve as a powerful tool to bring about change. Gradually a caring, adaptive, and prosocial group culture may be created that can further encourage positive change in its members. Staff facilitate the process and help to ensure that the group processing does not become abusive.

An extension of the group process approach uses group limits instead of individual conse-

quences for inappropriate behavior that involves more than one child. Instead of reinforcing the notion that the individual child's behavior is symptomatic and requires an individual consequence, group limits emphasize that difficulties occur in the interpersonal context of children living together and getting along with one another. Unit problems are handled by maintaining group restrictions until the group can work through difficulties. For instance, when a number of children are being physically aggressive, the whole group of children are restricted to the unit. Initially, all the children may be placed in their rooms, where they are expected to play quietly with their roommates. When this goal is accomplished, each set of roommates discusses with a staff member the unit's difficulties and their roles in the problems. Next, small group of children are given the chance to interact in a common area. Finally, a special community meeting takes place. Only when the group can successfully negotiate all these steps can the children resume their usual daily schedule. Although similar to group behavior modification programs a group limits program focuses on using group process and peer culture to influence group behavior. The behavioral restriction is used only as a means to bring about group discussion.

Education as a Treatment Element

A good intramural school (i.e., a school in the treatment facility) is an essential part of residential treatment. Since children admitted to residential treatment are typically 2 years behind academically and are likely to have had unsatisfactory school experiences, a meaningful educational experience is crucial. Youngsters in residential treatment have come to associate school in general and learning in particular with failure. It is therefore important that the child's intramural educational program does not repeat this pattern.

The function of the classroom teacher is to structure the child's academic tasks so that he or she experiences pleasure and success and avoids failure. This creates an atmosphere of positive expectancy in which the child comes to anticipate success instead of failure. A positive classroom experience in residential treatment can serve as yet another corrective emotional experience for the child.

The interface between the school and the milieu is important. School, as the part of the residential treatment program that most resembles the "real" outside world,—which is defined by rules, expectations, and limits—offers an important frame of reference for observing a child's intellectual and social functioning in a peer group. Therefore, teachers should be included in the interdisciplinary treatment team. Similarly, the handling of a child's classroom behavior needs to be part of the total approach for the child, an approach tailored by the interdisciplinary team with input from both teaching and child care staff.

During the transitional phase, preceding discharge from residential treatment, the child often begins to attend a school outside the residential center. The goal is to prepare the child for reintegration into the community and give him or her the experience of working alongside "normal" children.

Not all residential centers use intramural schools. Some programs believe that the normalizing environment of an outside school is more beneficial than an intramural school program.

Psychotherapy

Although psychotherapy is an important and commonly employed modality in residential treatment, the process of psychotherapy in residential and outpatient settings are different. The children in a residential setting are very aware of who their therapist's other patients are. They may compete with the other children for the therapist's attention. Children of various therapists may be in competition as to whose therapist is better. Because of involvement with the milieu, the therapist in a residential setting is more likely than the outpatient therapist to be involved in active decision making about the patient's real life outside the therapeutic hour. There is a vastly increased amount of collateral information available to the residential therapist. Finally, residential psychotherapy is inherently less confidential than it would be in an outpatient practice. Because of staff turnover in residential treatment, there is

also an increase in the likelihood that there will be disruptions in therapy and that a child in long-term treatment may have successive therapists.

Traditional psychotherapeutic methods of interpretation which are to lead to the working-through process, are less likely to be effective with children in residential treatment than in outpatient treatment. This is a consequence of the likelihood that the child is action-oriented and impulsive and has developmental, cognitive, language, and learning deficits.

Given the differences in psychotherapy in outpatient and residential settings, it is not surprising that modifications in the traditional practice of conducting therapy need to be instituted. Because of their lack of trust and need for constant action, children in residential treatment may be unable to spend a full session confined to an office talking about their problems to a relative stranger. Therefore, early in treatment, in order to build a therapeutic relationship, the therapist must take an extremely active role in engaging the child. Relationship-building activities—such as a walk on grounds, a trip to the snack shop, or a visit to the gym—can be substituted until the child can tolerate a longer time in the therapist's office with child and therapist talking. Before this can happen, the child must have had enough positive experience with the therapist to sustain him or her when negative transference issues emerge. If child can recall liking the therapist, he or she will be able to work the issues through.

Other modifications on the therapist's part may be needed. The goal for psychotherapy for children in residential treatment should be modified to emphasize reality testing and the formation of meaningful relationships. The child's repetitive patterns of behaving, expressing emotion, and getting needs met—patterns that occur over and over again in the milieu—may be the focus and major content of the individual therapy sessions.

Lastly, the role of the therapist vis-à-vis the milieu needs to be clarified. The therapist may be the case administrator and team leader, the person who formulates, coordinates, and directs the management of the child's case. The therapist is also responsible for shaping and directing the milieu treatment. Milieu therapy and psychotherapy are closely integrated. However, confidentiality is not absolute and the child's communication with the therapist is likely to be influenced by the child's knowing that the content of therapy will have a major influence on privileges on the unit. An alternative that attempts to address these difficulties is a model in which the therapist is not the case administrator, although the therapist maintains frequent contact with the treatment team and milieu staff.

In most institutions today both individual psychotherapy and milieu therapy are important components of residential treatment. On the other end of the spectrum, there is the rare institution that does not provide individual psychotherapy at all or where there is a fusion of caregiving, case management, and therapy components (Bettelheim & Sanders, 1979). It is the counselor, the child care worker who ministers to the child's daily needs and is intimately involved in the child's management, who becomes the child's individual therapist.

Family Involvement

A small number of residential centers discourage contact between child and parents. The administrators feel it is best that the parents be uninvolved if they can tolerate the separation (Bettelheim, 1950). Clinical staff at most residential centers believe that work with families is a crucial component of residential treatment. The word *family* need not include biological parents only. It may be appropriate to work with foster families, adoptive parents, preadoptive placements, grandparents, or other relatives, depending on a given child's situation. Among the vast array of services offered to families are collateral treatment with parents with the child's therapist or a different therapist, family therapy, parent's group, family or parent education classes, therapeutic visitation, and parental participation in milieu therapy. Regardless of which services or combination of services are offered at a particular treatment center, the goals of work with the families of children in residential treatment are often the same: increased expression of feelings, increased communication, more distinct boundaries, better relatedness among family members, improved behavior management, empowerment of families,

reframing of symptoms, understanding of family developmental issues, and resolution of individual issues that affect family functioning. Many of these goals, and therefore many of the techniques used, are similar to those of outpatient practice. However, removing the child from a family and placing him or her in residential treatment clearly calls for many changes in the parameters of working with families. Special attention needs to be paid to the unique feelings that families experience as a result of the placement of their child. Families feel like utter failures and suffer from mixed emotions. They experience guilt because they feel they caused their child's illness; rage at having the child placed; shame because of the stigma involved in the placement; jealousy as a result of the strong relationships that develop between staff and patients; and envy of the nurturance, caregiving, and positive experiences their child may be having in residential treatment. In addition, family members also experience a tremendous amount of relief: They no longer have to deal with a problematic child on a day-to-day basis. This relief may engender further guilt and denial. Parents frequently do not get in touch with these feelings until well into their child's and their own treatment. If any of these feelings and conflicts are not dealt with appropriately, they can result in families unconsciously sabotaging their child's treatment and even lead to premature discharge.

Although community-based treatment facilities tend to encourage both regular weekly visits and regularly scheduled weekly therapy appointments, many centers, because they are far from the child's home, have families visit about once a month for a 1- to 3-day period. The visit typically includes family sessions with a therapist. Occasionally, when children are placed in different sections of the country at very great distances from the family, the parents visit even more infrequently but stay for several days of intensive multiple therapy sessions and visits with their child.

Since visits are an important opportunity for parents and children to interact with one another, they can be the ideal laboratory for understanding and changing long-standing dysfunctional patterns. Such patients may relate to interaction, behavior, emotional expression, communication, problem solving, or relatedness of child and parent. Graduated therapeutic visitation is an attempt to use visits as a therapeutic and psychoeducational intervention. A facilitator or therapist actively participates in visits, helping the family to clarify and understand chronic dysfunctional patterns and develop new, adaptive interactions and solutions. The patient and the family practice the new patterns in subsequent visits. Issues of nurturance, limit setting, discipline, emotional expression, communication, appropriate understanding of developmental expectations, and other difficulties are dealth with as they occur naturally during the course of the visit. There is no set curriculum or course guide. Each plan is individualized to the needs and difficulties of the family. Initially visits are held in the same location, usually an area that is part of the child's living space. The early visits should be short, in order to increase a sense of mastery. Before change begins to occur, visits tend to become chaotic if they are too long. Such visits result in the family experiencing a sense of failure. The facilitator, if not a therapist, can be any member of the treatment team. In many instances, it is the nurse, counselor, or child care worker. As parents show increased skills in parenting, communication, relatedness, and other issues specific to each family, the duration of visits is gradually increased. The visits may move to different locations in a graduated fashion—for example, from the grounds of the residential center, to 1 hour at a restaurant, to longer and less structured time in other venues, to 1 hour at home, to one half day at home, to a full day at home, to an overnight visit. As visits increased and progress continues, supervision gradually decreases accordingly. However, all visits involve (1) clear plans and goals for the visit, (2) practicing new skills, and (3) feedback and processing of the visit immediately after its conclusion. Moving to the next stage of graduated therapeutic visitation requires mastering the skills required in the current stage.

In the beginning of residential treatment, much of the content of family therapy sessions relates to family conflicts, strong negative affect, and difficult behaviors during contact of parents and children. Planning for visits, anticipating difficulties, dealing with feelings both before and after the visits, communicating needs during the visit, and going over the difficulties that occured provides the material the therapist uses to help the family understand difficulties, learn new adaptive skills, and better relationships. The problems that arise in regard to visits and passes are likely to parallel the difficulties parents and their children have had in the past. Using visits as the raw data for therapy with families serves as a jumping-off point for discussion of general issues that affect family functioning. When modified appropriately, work with families becomes an important component of residential treatment.

Conclusion

Residential treatment is a comprehensive treatment for seriously disturbed children who suffer primarily from severe developmental disruptions in their ability to form discriminant, trusting, and meaningful interpersonal relationships; to regulate their affect; and to modulate their behavior. Since children in residential treatment are removed from their families and their communities for long periods and have in most cases already "failed" acute short-term psychiatric hospitalizations, residential treatment is the highest level of psychiatric care available for the most disturbed youngsters. When viewed as part of the continuum of care, with provisions made for adequate aftercare, the outcome for many youngsters is favorable. Given the severity of the youngsters' problems, the likelihood that they have not responded to all lower levels of care, and the poor prognosis for youngsters with this degree of psychopathology, residential treatment can be beneficial and effective. It can offer hope to otherwise hopeless youngsters and is deserving of continued support as one element in the continuum of mental health services.

REFERENCES

Alt, H. (1960). *Residential treatment for the disturbed child.* New York: International Universities Press.

Bettelheim, B. (1950). *Love is not enough.* New York: Free Press.

Bettelheim, B., & Sanders, J. (1979). Milieu therapy: The Orthogenic School model. In J. D. Noshpitz (Ed.-in-Chief) *Basic handbook of child psychiatry* (vol. 3, pp. 216–230). New York: Basic Books.

Browning, R. M., & Stover, D. O. (1971). *Behavior modification in child treatment.* Chicago: Aldine Publishing.

Curry, J. F. (1991). Outcome research on residential treatment: Implications and suggested directions. *American Journal of Orthopsychiatry, 61;* 348–357.

Fahlberg, V. (1990). *Residential treatment: A tapestry of many therapies.* Indianapolis, IN: Perspectives Press.

Irwin, M., Kline, P. M., & Gordon, M. (1991). Adapting milieu therapy to short-term psychiatric hospitalization of children. *Child Psychiatry and Human Development, 21;* 193–202.

Lyman, R. D., Prentice-Dunn, S., & Gabel, S. (1989). *Residential and inpatient treatment of children and adolescents.* New York: Plenum Press.

Phillips, E. L., Phillips, E. A., Fixsen, D. L. & Wolf, M. M. (1974). *The teaching-family handbook.* Lawrence, KS: University Printing Service.

Redl, F. (1959). Strategy and techniques of the life space interview. *American Journal of Orthopsychiatry, 29;* 1–18.

Redl, F., & Wineman, D. (1951). *Children who hate.* Glencoe, IL: Free Press.

Redl, F., & Wineman, D. (1957). *The aggressive child.* Glencoe, IL: Free Press.

Reid, J., & Hagan, H. (1952). *Residential treatment of emotionally disturbed children.* New York: Child Welfare League of America.

Schulman, J. L., & Irwin, M. (1982). *Psychiatric hospitalization of children.* Springfield, IL: Charles C Thomas.

Small, R., Kennedy, K., & Bender, B. (1991). Critical issues for practice in residential treatment: The view from within. *American Journal of Orthopsychiatry, 61,* 327–338.

Trieschman, A. E., Whittaker, J. K., & Brendtro, L. K. (1969). *The other twenty three hours.* Chicago: Aldine Publishing.

Vorrath, H. H., & Brendtro, L. K. (1985). *Positive peer culture* (2nd ed.). Hawthorne, NY: Aldine Publishing.

36 / Inpatient Treatment

Gordon Harper

Definition

Inpatient psychiatric treatment is the most intensive psychiatric treatment, providing round-the-clock care and more intensive intervention than is possible outside the hospital. It is used for clinical problems that cannot be treated at less intensive levels of care. Inpatient treatment means *hospital* treatment; residential treatment is discussed in Chapter 35.

Until the 1990s, inpatient treatment lasted for months or years, with the goals of producing personality change or providing long-term custodial care for impaired children. Indeed, the term *inpatient treatment* was often used for nonhospital, residential treatment. In some settings and in some countries, long-stay inpatient treatment still occurs. In the United States in particular, however, inpatient treatment, as the most expensive as well as the most intensive treatment, has now been assigned a more focused goal: to bring about, as expeditiously as possible, those changes in the problem that led to hospitalization that will allow the patient to be treated at a less intensive level of care. Lengths of stay, formerly months to years, are now measured in days to weeks.

The key to this contemporary definition of inpatient treatment is the emphasis on what *must* be done at this level of care, not on what *can* be done.

History

Like child psychiatry as a field, inpatient psychiatric treatment of children and adolescents is a phenomenon of the 20th century, one that has been developed to greatly varying degrees in different parts of the world.

Inpatient treatment began in Western Europe and the United States in the 20th century. It grew out of the orphanages, training schools, and specialized institutions for the retarded developed in the 19th century. The impetus to create a new kind of institution to treat troubled children, rather than to contain or punish them, came from child advocates, progressive educators, and psychoanalysts, who treated children.

The history of inpatient treatment can be divided into four phases. In the 1920s and 1930s, innovators like August Aichhorn, in Austria (see Aichhorn, 1935), and Charles Bradley, in the United States (see Bradley, 1938), founded the first "inpatient," or residential units. Most of these were developed outside hospitals or in freestanding psychiatric hospitals. An exception was the unit established in the 1920s at Bellevue, in New York City, to treat children suffering the consequences of encephalitis lethargica.

Between the 1940s and the 1970s, many inpatient units were established by child welfare organizations, teaching hospitals, and government departments of mental health. Many of the children were being treated for disruptive behavior disorders; some had psychotic or borderline psychotic disorders. Many books and articles described the theory and practice of intervening with these children and set standards for residential (and, to a lesser degree, hospital) treatment (see, e.g., Stone, 1979; Zinn, 1979; American Psychiatric Association, 1957). The idea that disturbed children should receive inpatient treatment and that the state should be the "treater of last resort" became accepted as part of a modern society's obligation to the most vulnerable.

In the 1980s, particularly in the United States, the number of inpatient units and the number of children and adolescents treated rose rapidly, both in general hospitals and in the for-profit sector. Inpatient treatment came to be seen as a potentially profitable business, attracting investors seeking opportunities for profits. Many of the adolescents hospitalized in these units were not as severely disturbed as other psychiatric inpatients. Stretching of the indications for admission, along with resulting ethical problems, caused considerable public doubt about inpatient treatment of children and adolescents. While public doubt was increasing, many state officials were questioning the state's role in providing treatment of last resort; some replaced the direct provision of care by the state with private contracting or with attempts to shift the state role to private insurance. At the same time, a movement arose to shift the treatment of seriously disturbed youth from institutional treatment (both hospital and residential) far from home to community-based systems of care in which the child's family played a larger role in treatment.

In the 1990s, several trends produced rapid change, at first in the United States but, increasingly, elsewhere as well. The use by insurers of managed health care, including managed behavioral health care:

- created a new industry overseeing inpatient treatment
- brought new parties to the decision-making table, alongside clinician, parent, and child
- greatly reduced utilization of inpatient services, resulting in the closing of many units and the reduction of length of stay in others
- stimulated the creation of additional interventions along the continuum of care (e.g., acute residential programs and in-home family treatment) to which patients otherwise likely to be hospitalized were diverted or to which hospitalized patients were discharged earlier than before

Compared to their counterparts in the 1980s, children and adolescents who receive hospital care now are likely to be more disturbed and stay a shorter time in the hospital. The development of systems of care for disturbed children offers the promise, as yet only partially realized, of more coordinated care in a less restrictive setting. In regard to this development, much less consensus exists than formerly—not only about how care should be provided, but about what, in a modern society, constitutes a standard of care for disturbed children.

In the United States and Western Europe, care for seriously disturbed children has gone, in three generations, from the undeveloped; through the variably developed; to the variably overdeveloped,

486

to a transitional, some would say involutional, phase.

Current changes in inpatient treatment have to be considered against the background of the state of services for disturbed children throughout the world. To whatever extent mental health services for children have been implemented in any given country, the fact remains that for most seriously disturbed children in most of the world, recognition that clinical services can make a difference, let alone the provision of such services, remains a distant goal (see Desjarlais, Eisenberg, Good & Kleinman, 1995).

The Ingredients of Inpatient Treatment

THE CONCEPTS

Sympathetic Support: The concept underlying sympathetic support is that treatment heals by caring for the child; sympathetically validating the child's experience; affirming the good in the youngster; and adopting a nonblaming, nonpunitive attitude to the child's emotional needs and symptoms.

This idea is central to all inpatient treatment. It has three components: attention to the child's own experience and point of view (what Healy [1915] called the child's "own story"); nonblaming acceptance (children do the best they can, and their symptoms represent not just trouble but a solution to some as-yet-poorly-understood dilemma); and openness to taking a fresh look at the child's needs, emotional and developmental. This sympathetic attitude contrasts with the idea that children with troubling behavior need to be "straightened out" and that they are hospitalized to "teach them a lesson."

Institutionalizing a sympathetic attitude is not easy. Hospitalized children have experienced much punishment and abuse; many of their symptoms are very disturbing to others; and many of the patients (and some adults as well) see their hospitalization as punishment, not help. Their behavior can elicit unsympathetic and punitive responses as well as the fantasy of "rescue" (for a classic description, see Ekstein, 1966).

Despite these obstacles, a sympathetic attitude is necessary. It must be expressed in the ways problems are defined and interventions offered, in the language staff use when talking about and to children, and in the staff's behavior. Relevant staff include *all* those with whom the child has contact—from doctors, nurses, and social workers to the dietary and housekeeping staff.

The physical design of the ward must also express a sympathetic attitude. Deprived and disturbed children have learned to hate their own needs and doubt their own worth. What message do they receive from bare or drab bedrooms, dining rooms, and bathrooms? In contrast, attractive and pleasant decor, furnishings, and tableware say to the child, "You are a valued person, a person for whom we as a staff, as an institution, and as a society, have hope. Your eating, learning, even bathing should occur in positive, affirming circumstances" (Cotton & Geraty, 1984; Bettelheim, 1974).

Sometimes this sympathetic attitude, along with the "fresh start" it gives the child, is remembered as a key ingredient in inpatient treatment. Such was the case of a 12-year-old who was admitted after he became enraged, destroyed property, and assaulted two classmates and a teacher. At both school and home he had been regarded as having a "bad attitude," being ungrateful and argumentative, and having a "chip on his shoulder." Looking back on his 10-day admission, he said the most important intervention was that people took a fresh, sympathetic look at him. "Everybody wasn't on my case; they thought I had something good to say. That was a big change."

Containing: The concept underlying containing is that treatment helps the child by blocking the use of destructive action to ward off painful feelings while acknowledging the child's pain and providing new avenues for expression and new methods of coping.

The inpatient unit, by "containing" behavior harmful to the patient or to others, serves both a protective and a psychotherapeutic purpose. Having the ability and the readiness to protect the patient and others from harm is the first, nonnegotiable way that inpatient units help patients. This ability must be evident to all—patients, family members, visitors, staff. The physical means to provide protection are discussed in the paragraphs that follow.

The most restrictive forms of protection are seclusion and restraint. These interventions have been described, on the one hand, as efforts to control the child's behavior for others' convenience and, on the other hand, as a key ingredient of treatment (Garrison et al., 1990; Cotton, 1989; Gair, 1989). Control can take the form of seclusion, physical restraint (being held by a person), mechanical restraint (leather limb restraints), or pharmacotherapy used as a chemical restraint. From a developmental point of view, containment is seen as providing external control so that the child who assaults others when overcome with fear, shame, or rage may feel safely in control with help from others as a first step on the path toward being able to manage feelings and actions autonomously.

Special care should be taken when using external control with children who have survived physical or sexual abuse. These children may experience being restrained as a repetition of earlier trauma. To minimize the risks of retraumatization, the use of physical restraint should be avoided wherever possible. Alternatives include inviting the child to be a partner in self-management (i.e., by developing his or her own "anger management plan"); paying careful attention to the technique and the spirit with which restraint, when necessary, is practiced; and repeating verbal statements, in language the child can understand, of the differences between past injuries and current efforts to help.

Containing has psychological as well as a physical dimension. Blocking self-destructive action and holding the child physically and psychologically allow healing to begin. Interventions in the child's daily world, which Fritz Redl (1959) called "life-space interviews," exploit crises in the dining room, on the playing field, or in the activity group to help the child stop, reflect, and begin to practice more adaptive responses.

Sometimes a patient experiences the locked ward itself as psychologically containing and reassuring. This was the case for a 17-year-old girl who was repeatedly hospitalized for a restrictive eating disorder and depression. She was transferred from an open to a closed setting after impulsively ingesting a bottle of aspirin while on a brief visit in the community. She later described her admission to the closed unit as a turning point: "I was always thinking, There's some place, some other place, where things would be different, and I wouldn't have to change. Well, here I saw I wasn't going *any*where. I had to work on my problems myself."

Remaking: The concept underlying remaking is that treatment brings about personality restructuring by helping the child develop more mature defenses, including the capacity to bear ambivalent feelings and to manage impulses, mood, and interpersonal relations better.

These ideas—developed by Rudolph Ekstein, Robert Wallerstein, Joseph Noshpitz, Saul Harrison, John McDermott, James Masterson, Donald Rinsley, and others—have given treatment in public and private institutions a strong therapeutic orientation. The therapeutic model provided an encompassing theory of personality development, psychopathology, and treatment. It reflected an ambitious therapeutic agenda that defined a field, inspired high ideals, and was personally and professionally gratifying.

Even during a short inpatient stay, a key intervention is giving a child the *idea* that modification of seemingly entrenched responses is possible. For example, in a short inpatient admission, a teenager can be helped to recognize that drug use, running, or other action defenses have been leading to negative consequences. The teen can then learn to appreciate that these patterns, though well established, can be examined and modified with professional help. Although the teenager will not *develop* those alternatives during an acute admission, let alone have a chance to practice them, the patient may nonetheless accept the goal of doing that work in the next, less intensive level of treatment.

Focal Intervention: The concept underlying focal intervention is that inpatient treatment should change the problem that required hospitalization so that it can be managed out of the hospital. Such a change will be brought about by modifying the *factors* contributing to the crisis or impasse. Factors are identified in a biopsychosocial formulation (Harper, 1989).

This way of organizing the work of inpatient treatment has several sources. In *crisis intervention theory,* crises—times of disequilibrium in personal or social systems—are seen as points at which people and systems can change more rapidly than at other times. In *family systems theory,* the identified patient's symptoms are seen as the expression of nonadaptive family interactions; the family is seen as the relevant unit of change. In *life-cycle developmental theory,* points of disequilibrium are considered to be natural events in the life cycle and opportunities for growth. The *"remedicalization" of child psychiatry* sparked new interest in the classification of childhood disorders and in disorder-specific biological treatments. The concept of *stabilization goals* defined the work of hospitalization as the restoration of a stable, precrisis status quo. *Constructivist* theory saw the meanings parents make of the child and of the child's symptoms as a fertile field for focused intervention. *Ecological* theory emphasized the social field in which symptoms occur and supported an out-of-hospital focus for intervention.

Focal treatment requires the inpatient clinician to identify a specific problem requiring hospitalization, a problem that may include but is not limited to a categorical diagnosis. Agreement should be sought among clinicians, patient, and parents as to the definition of the problem requiring intervention. After the problem has been identified, the clinician identifies factors that contribute to that problem—factors that are amenable to change and that, once changed, will modify the problem.

The following case illustrates this way of organizing an intervention.

Bob, a 16-year-old boy with moderate mental retardation, was referred after outbursts of kicking, punching, head banging, and grabbing. These outbursts were so severe that three adults had to restrain him. Other symptoms included increased motor activity, decreased appetite, and insomnia. In addition, restraint terrified Bob. Admission had been sought close to home, but his retardation, agitation, and explosive assaultiveness led to referral to a tertiary center where he had been admitted on another occasion. History and clinical presentation suggested bipolar disorder. Chlorpromazine was given, later replaced by lithium carbonate. Neuroleptics were introduced rapidly to avoid use of restraints if possible, since restraints were likely to be experienced as a new trauma. To prevent the regression seen during previous admissions, familiar caregivers attended Bob on the ward, reassuring him frequently. He was gradually introduced into the ward community. On discharge, a week after admission, his foster mother was eager to get him home.

The *focal problem* was defined on referral as unmanageable aggression and assaultiveness in a teenager with mental retardation. By discharge, the focal problem had been changed to manic episode in a teenager with mental retardation and previously undiagnosed bipolar disorder. Modifiable *factors* were identified as (1) untreated manic episode, (2) exhaustion or depletion of caregivers, and (3) panicky reaction to restraint and seclusion.

In this approach, the focal problem, goal, and factors are stated in jargon-free, user-friendly language that can be shared with patient and family, encouraging a respectful, collaborative attitude toward the family and eliminating professionals' use of a private, in-group language that keeps patient and family in the dark.

Focal treatment requires the clinician, while aware of many problems, to identify the specific problem in need of immediate help and to abstain from addressing the others, except for helping families define future work and develop alliances with treaters at the next, less intensive, level of care. A focused approach should not be used to justify a simplistic approach to treatment—for instance, treatment limited to symptom reduction and a reliance on pharmacological or behavioral interventions that fail to engage the child as a person. Such an approach would deprive the sickest children of the best in clinical resources.

Defining treatment as preparing the patient for the earliest possible resumption of his or her nonhospital life connects the inpatient team to the world outside. It changes inpatient treatment from the hoped-for "definitive treatment" to the phase in which acute symptoms are treated. To those with longer term responsibility for the patient, focal treatment offers a consultation. The consultation should take into account both vulnerabilities evident in the hospital and strengths evident out of the hospital. Inpatient and outpatient treaters can then jointly generate an operational approach to the patient's problems.

PROGRAM DESIGN

After consensus is reached on the mission of the inpatient unit (see Harper & Geraty, 1985), the implementation of an inpatient program starts with organizational and physical design.

Unit Organization: Formal structure refers to the formally defined roles and relationships represented on the organizational chart. Inpatient units tend to have complex formal structures, with multiple disciplines and multiple lines of accountability—for instance, nursing staff may be accountable to both Nursing and Psychiatry. A matrix design is often used to represent these doubly accountable positions.

Informal structure refers to the relationships that develop within a program that make it possible for people to work together. Like the formal structurer, the informal structure of the unit is complex. It changes continually as staff and trainees come and go. Clarity of the formal structure and smooth operation in the informal structure, important for all organizations, are especially important for inpatient services. An ambiguous formal structure or problems in informal relationships create the risk of regression in individual patients or in the ward group as a whole.

Formal and informal structures must foster a healthy tension between central control and individual staff autonomy. Individual staff members should be able to exercise mature, independent judgments in dealing with patients and parents. The details of particular interactions can never be fully anticipated, so personal maturity and a high degree of professionalism are required. But autonomy must be balanced with mutual accountability and coordination of overall effort. Uncoordinated individual actions with a patient, known as solo flying, raise the risk of the antitherapeutic pattern known as splitting, in which different members of the treatment team become polarized in the patients' and in their own views. Team members work at cross-purposes, with one member being sympathetic while the other is punitive, for instance, or one being indulgent while the other is strict. Undetected or unaddressed splitting defeats the purposes of treatment and exposes patient and staff to the risk of injury.

Physical space design guarantees *physical safety* and *therapeutic space*. Physical safety requires a design that protects patients from self-harming behavior and from unauthorized intruders. These requirements are usually met by keeping the unit locked. Unlocked units have advantages (less stigma, encouragement of patients' ability to manage themselves), and some programs (particularly long-stay programs) have developed effective "staff-secure" arrangements. However, most contemporary hospital units with high patient turnover and high acuity (in terms of suicidal or assaultive behavior) provide safety by

maintaining a full-time locked door. The locked perimeter also gives the staff control over visitors' arrival. This helps staff members check patients who are being admitted or returning from visits off the ward. The staff look for objects that should not be brought onto the ward, such as substances of abuse, unauthorized medications, or articles that might be used for self-harm. In addition, state licensing authorities and insurers often require that a hospital unit intended to treat the most acutely disturbed children be kept locked. The negative impact of the locked door can be mitigated by the liberal use of (reinforced) glass in the doors to the ward.

The inpatient unit should provide adequate differentiated *space for adaptive activities* (physical recreation, therapeutic arts, school) and *privacy* for individual, group, and family meetings. Specialized architectural consultation is needed to translate the program mission into a workable design. In addition to minimizing the opportunities for self-harming behavior, the design should minimize the risk of patients finding places where contraband can be secreted. The unit should also include a "quiet room" that can protect, contain, and encourage self-control (Cotton & Geraty, 1984).

The *staffing design* includes direct-care staff and other staff. Direct-care staff includes nurses and child care workers. One fourth to one third of the total direct-care staff are registered nurses. Units with patients with comorbid medical disorders have a higher proportion of nurses. The other direct-care staff are called child care workers or group-care workers. They often bring to the unit a gift for working with children. Many have acquired special expertise over years of working with disturbed young people. For some youngsters, child care work is a waystation on the road to further formal professional training. For others, it is a life's work; their career ladder leads to more responsible positions in therapeutic child care.

In terms of nurses and child care workers, there should be one staff person for every 3 to 4 children on the day and evening shifts, amounting to 1.6 to 1.8 full-time equivalents (FTEs) per occupied bed.

Other staff bring specialized knowledge and skills from disciplines such as therapeutic recreation, education, occupational therapy, and art therapy. These professionals work with the children individually and in groups. Child psychiatrists, psychologists, and social workers conduct interviews individually with children and parents, assess children "in the midst of things" on the ward, and preferably share in leading groups along with the nursing staff. A pediatrician or pediatric nurse practitioner and a nutritionist should be members of the unit team, not just consultants. A full range of subspecialist consultants should be available from—among others, experts in pediatric neurology, neuropsychology, and endocrinology.

The *daily program* should support adaptive functioning, provide diagnostic information about the child's ways of coping in a variety of activities (this information constitutes an "assessment over time"), and give the children opportunities to learn new ways of coping. The daily schedule should provide a balance of therapeutic, educational, and recreational groups. Recreational activities can use simple, inexpensive materials, alternatives to television and other passive entertainment, to give children experience with new media or games, to have fun, and to practice prosocial behaviors. Unscheduled time should be deliberately prescribed, not just used to fill a void.

Groups may be devoted to such topics as conflict resolution, "choices" (i.e., decision making), alcohol and substance abuse, psychoeducation regarding psychiatric disorders and medication, dealing with the consequences of abuse or molestation, and dealing with foster care and state agencies. Group discussions on conflict resolution, parent-child negotiation, and violence prevention can be based on a developed curriculum, not just a reaction to patients' expressed concerns.

A system of *privileges* that patients earn by working on specific goals is an essential part of the daily program. The goals for each patient include prosocial behaviors in general as well as specific behaviors related to the problem that led to admission. Individual goals might be "to learn to take time-out when I am angry," or "to speak up in family meetings," or "to work with others in group without losing my temper." The choice of goals should be made by patient and staff together.

Grouping: Patients should have sleeping quarters and programs arranged by age and gender. Developmentally appropriate programming requires a deliberate decision regarding which age groups the unit will serve, daytime scheduling that meets the recreational and educational needs of the groups selected, and appropriate recruitment and training of staff (Berlin, 1978).

Admission Criteria: As mentioned, inpatient treatment is increasingly reserved for seriously impaired children. This level of care is being saved for crisis intervention, as opposed to long-term treatment. Admission criteria written in 1989 by the American Academy of Child and Adolescent Psychiatry stipulated that inpatient treatment should be used when a child has significant risk of self-harm, harm to others, or impaired functioning in two or more areas of life and when less restrictive forms of treatment have been tried unsuccessfully or are judged unlikely to be effective.

Legal Status: The treatment of children and adolescents is authorized not by the patient but by his or her parents or guardian. In a crisis involving a seriously disturbed child, at risk of harm to self or others, and parents who balk at admission, admission can occur on the basis of a commitment paper—regardless of the parents' wishes. (The parent must always first be given the option of admitting the child voluntarily.) The age at which an adolescent can sign him- or herself in or out varies from one jurisdiction to another. In the United States, most children are admitted to the hospital on what is called a conditional voluntary basis. This means that a parent, if wishing to discharge the child before the responsible physician deems the child ready, must sign a note indicating an intention to remove the child in 3 days. During that time the hospital team must decide whether to initiate a commitment hearing. If parental action places the child at risk, local protective services may seek a care-and-protection order. The hospital team's commitment decision or a care-and-protection order can override a parent's wishes.

When patients with criminal charges pending are referred, many clinicians insist that psychiatric admission not take the place of the judicial process, but that the child be arraigned regardless. This practice reduces the risk that avoiding the judicial system will become a covert motive for hospital stay.

Child Protection: Preferably, and most often, the child's parent or guardian authorizes the child's treatment, providing the basis for a therapeutic alliance between parents and clinicians. In one third to one half of inpatient cases, however, the treating team must also take a protective position on behalf of the child. The team's position may be at odds with a parent's stated wishes and with his or her definition of what needs to be done. Inpatient clinicians should be prepared to balance protective practices, with efforts to work with and on behalf of the child's parents (Harper & Irvin, 1985).

Protective intervention may arise before admission, through a previously filed protective report; through a service plan developed by a protective agency with the parent; or through a court order finding the child in need of state care and protection. It may also arise during an inpatient admission, when signs or symptoms of abuse or molestation are recognized or when a child makes a disclosure of abuse or molestation. The form of protective intervention varies and may include one or more of the the following:

- Education. "Your child needs to have treatment; not providing it would constitute neglect."
- Admonition. "If you withdraw your child from the hospital against advice, without a plan for helping with his or her depression, we would be required under law to make a protective report."
- Protective reporting. "Your child has reported sexual molestation; we are required . . . ."
- Use of a commitment paper. "Because of your child's depression and stated wish to kill his or her father, your child meets criteria for involuntary treatment, regardless of your wishes."
- A petition for state custody, sometimes on an emergency basis. ("Your plan to discharge your daughter against medical advice while your companion who molested her and has threatened to kill her is still in the home presents an immediate danger to her life. Accordingly, we are going to petition the Court for a Temporary Restraining Order which will temporarily override your rights as a parent.")
 (Such a petition be known as a temporary restraining order.)

When children admitted for psychiatric symptoms (especially suicidal risk or severely disorganized behavior or psychosis) are found to be suffering unrecognized abuse or molestation, protective acknowledgment and intervention is the key to psychiatric recovery. Acknowledgment takes the form of action and of affirmative statements to the child: "You have been hit (or exploited sexually). That is wrong. No one, including you, should be hit (or exploited sexually). [Blank] (naming the perpetrator, if known) may be a good person in other ways, but he (or she) has a problem with (managing temper, controlling his [or her] hands, using children when it's not right, etc.). We (and the relevant protective services) will work to ensure that you are not hit (or exploited) again."

Protective intervention, including protective acknowledgment, should be made with respect to the victimized child's place in the progression from submission to abuse or identification with the abuser to a self-protective and self-affirming position.

These cases require a liaison between the hospital child-protection team and the hospital attorney. Protective intervention should be combined with a respectful and sympathetic attitude toward the parent (the protective report is filed on behalf of the child, not "against the parent"), including an acknowledgment that the parent has a problem (with impulse control, with depression, with substance use, etc.). Self-scrutiny is always indicated in the protective process. For example, administrators should always look for ways to work on behalf of the child that may not be initially apparent (Harper & Irvin, 1985). The goal is to help the family and child identify the child's protective needs and implement appropriate protection. This goal is not always achievable during an acute admission. In such a case, depending on the nature of the risk to the child, the child may be discharged to an alternative living environment, with a protective family member or in an out-of-family placement.

MILIEU THERAPY

In the 1940s Bruno Bettelheim and Emmy Sylvester recognized that, for disturbed children, (as for severely disturbed patients of all ages), "therapy" should not be limited to what happens in the therapist's office. Optimally, therapeutic interventions should *surround* the child in a pattern of deliberately designed and integrated care. An inpatient program limited to housing the child while office-based therapies are carried out is insufficient. The terms *milieu therapy* and *therapeutic milieu* express these ideas. Fritz Redl, used the term *life-space interviews* for the therapeutic encounters taking place in the setting where the child learns, plays, and has friendships. Redi also used the term *life space* to describe space that was not the therapist's office space. Today milieu therapy and life-space interviews are a key part of all inpatient treatment, both short- and long-term.

This section discusses the ways that all aspects of the child's hospital environment can be used therapeutically.

A Total Therapeutic Environment: In a therapeutic milieu, every element of design and every interaction with the child supports the therapeutic aims of the program. The pictures on the walls, the unit's privilege system, the ways the children spend their days, and the ways staff work with each other and with the child and parents, are all used therapeutically. Nothing "just happens"; nothing is the concern of only one or two isolated staff members. A shared approach to the child—by therapist, child care worker, teacher, cafeteria staff—is necessary. Through such a shared approach, the program helps the fragmented child begin to see that he or she can be whole, can "make sense" as a person.

Coordination and Communication: Everything done by child care staff, therapists, parent workers, and even consulting medical subspecialists should reflect a shared understanding of the nature of the child's problem and of the therapeutic goal. Such a consensus is not achieved just by developing a written care plan available to all. A shared approach requires both a written plan *and* face-to-face communications in scheduled meetings (rounds, team meetings, case conferences) and in unplanned, ad hoc conversations throughout the course of the day.

Treatment planning should integrate the data arising from the life space with the assessments and interventions of the child psychiatrists, psychologists, and social workers. The data come from many people; the daily program should be arranged to permit those with direct observations to participate in rounds and other planning meetings. Rivalrous feelings arise easily along the interface between child and family clinicians, on the one hand, and child care workers and nurses on the other. For their part, child psychiatrists and psychologists have to make an effort to come up with a language of description and analysis that works for the whole staff and the child and family.

Such a language puts the concepts of adaptive ego psychology into the language of the everyday.

Clinical Administration

Clinical administration is an essential ingredient of all inpatient treatment and a clinical specialty in itself. The term *clinical administration* encompasses administrative activities on behalf of the individual patient and clinical leadership of the unit as a whole.

THE UNIT AS A SOCIAL SYSTEM: ITS FUNCTIONS

The psychiatric unit is both the site of treatment for individual patients and a social entity with its own natural history, homeostatic functions, and vulnerabilities to dysfunction. All clinicians, those responsible for individual patients as well as those responsible for the whole unit, must be aware of the unit as a social organization.

As discussed, the unit must have the physical resources to contain dangerous behavior and the psychological readiness to contain emotional anguish. Contributing to these capabilities are the developmental stage of the unit; the degree of consensus about the mission of the unit; formal and informal organizational structures; and staff skill level, which itself is a product of staff selection and in-service training. Consensus should exist regarding the goals and objectives for each patient as well as the overall mission of the unit (Harper, 1989). It is vital to discuss nonconsensus; hiding it renders it toxic.

Reaching consensus requires that disagreeing parties express their points of view to each other. Risk arises when the differences are not acknowledged, a pattern known, after the psychiatrist and sociologist who first described it, as the Stanton-Schwartz phenomenon. Inpatient work requires that members of the team agree to work together, even if they still have disagreements.

The patient-staff *community* has considerable power that can be used therapeutically or antitherapeutically. Even on short-stay units, a cohesive therapeutic community promotes group and individual responsibility, peer support, and adaptive coping. Clinicians should understand their patient's behavior in the context of the entire ward group in order to mobilize support for the patient and to help the patient take responsibility for his or her behavior, verbalizing conflict rather than expressing it through action.

MANAGING THE UNIT

On behalf of the unit as a whole, the clinical administrator balances the perspective of those working most closely with the patient with a broader and longer view. The clinical administrator stimulates integration of diverse program elements for a given patient into a cohesive whole, coordinates treatment efforts undertaken on behalf of individual children with those of the other patients, and fosters the therapeutic efficacy of the ward as a whole. Leadership must relate each component of a patient's treatment (e.g., individual therapy, pharmacotherapy, child management, parent assessment, or protective intervention) to the others and to what is happening on the ward. Failure to integrate all these elements exposes staff and patients to the risk of therapeutic stagnation or even injury.

Like any therapeutic team, the unit group (including staff and students) needs time and permission to acknowledge significant events, including staff changes, losses, and adverse outcomes. Appropriate bearing and sharing of their own experiences helps the staff and the other patients to be open to the pain of the individual patient. Unacknowledged staff feelings—resentment at a departing leader or doubt about a new leader or example—interfere with treatment. Acknowledgment is facilitated by providing time on a regular basis for such work and by leaders who value open communication, especially when what needs to be shared are hard-to-express feelings like disagreement, dissatisfaction, and demoralization.

MANAGING COMPLICATIONS OF TREATMENT

The administrator must be familiar with the risks of inpatient treatment. In "adoption," the unit takes over parental functions, acting as if the child had no parents. Loss of alliance with parents can also occur, independent of adoption. In scapegoating, a patient, or staff member, parent, outside treater, or state agency is blamed for problems that arise elsewhere—in the system as a whole or as a result of fate. In fatigue, unrecognized staff exhaustion or burnout limits the efficacy of the unit and increases the risk of injury or death. In loss of task orientation, the unit group becomes preoccupied with external enemies, internal politics, other people's jobs, or its own feelings of deprivation, not noticing that the treatment of the child has slipped from view. In punitive or angry responses, unobserved emotional reactions to the patient dominate. Sexual excitement—in which the unit group becomes preoccupied with the real or fantasized sexual activities of patients, patients' parents, or staff—can accompany loss of task orientation. Self-absorption occurs when the ward group loses touch with the communities from which patients come and to which they will return. A related risk is pathocentricism, in which the team loses sight of the child's (or family's) strengths and think he or she has nothing but weaknesses. The opposite of pathocentricism is rescue (or sentimentalism), in which the child's symptoms are seen solely as the result of environmental adversity and the unit or a staff person is seen as the "good parent" who can, just by being with the child, make the trouble go away.

When inpatient stays are short, new risks arise: that the inpatient unit, no longer doing a comprehensive assessment, will base intervention on inadequate assessment; that coercion will replace collaboration, as treatments done to children and families supplant those done with them; that the child's voice, the child's inner life, will not be sought or heard; and that the inpatient unit will be co-opted by insurance carriers and managers of benefits and lose the capacity for independent judgment, assessment, and advocacy.

The ward administrator must be alert to detect and to help the group detect any of these treatment complications, to let the problem come into discussion, and to foster corrective measures.

PLANNING AND GOALS

The administrator is not only facilitator of the treatment team; he or she must also help the group develop goals. Goals may involve quality improvement and strategic planning, and in the case of nonclinical administrators, monitoring progress toward the goals.

The Unit Spirit

Hope, respect, and respectful playfulness should characterize inpatient treatment. Hope includes the belief that the child has capacities for growth and self-management that have not been apparent amid negative symptoms and mutual frustration. Such faith in the child is balanced by a developmentally informed appreciation of his or her need for help from others—optimally, in a mutually gratifying partnership.

Respect for others is conveyed in the ways people are referred to and addressed (e.g., by referring to and addressing adults in the forms they prefer), in appreciating that patients and parents have faced unusual and severe challenges, and in consensual (as opposed to unilateral) development of the treatment plan. Respect extends to the program's readiness to bear emotional pain, to model for patients and families a readiness to be open to sadness, hopelessness, and terror—especially when these have been difficult to acknowledge.

Respectful playfulness characterizes the creative spirit that the unit brings to bear on the child's problems. The unit will not heal children by forcing them into a mold or a category (even a diagnostic category). Respectful playfulness informs therapeutic creativity and belief in the child's capacity for restorative play.

Implementation: Individual Treatment Planning

Individual treatment planning begins with the definition of the problem requiring intervention at this level of care (the focal problem) and development of a corresponding goal. Factors that contribute to the focal problem are then identified; those that lend themselves to intervention that will change the focal problem are selected (Harper, 1989). The focal problem, the goal, and the selected factors are stated in jargon-free language that all parties—clinicians, patient, parents, case managers—can agree on and that can be shared with (or, better, developed jointly with)

parents. Such language includes sympathetic terms conducive to the development of a treatment alliance.

DEFINING THE PROBLEM REQUIRING TREATMENT

In inpatient treatment, the categorical diagnosis (that is, the diagnosis given in the *Diagnostic and Statistical Manual of the American Psychiatric Association*, 4th edition [DSM-IV], 1994 is usually not enough to explain why a particular child has been admitted, much less to guide treatment. For this reason, a separate statement of the problem requiring admission is sought.

The patient was a 9-year-old girl with marginally compensated congenital heart disease and disruptive behavior (tantrums in which she barked like a dog). Her physicians were uncertain about the child's cardiac status, given the agitation with which her mother, a highly anxious person, reported the child's symptoms at home. Each party—mother, doctors, child—stated the reason for admission differently. The mother denied that the child had emotional problems and sought admission to "show the doctors once and for all" how physically compromised the child was. The cardiologists, stymied by the agitation with which the mother described these episodes, hesitated to pronounce the child physically well and wanted an admission for assessment. The child, inhibited except during her tantrums, offered no opinion of her own, but acceded to the plan that she should come to the hospital.

REACHING CONSENSUS ABOUT THE PROBLEM

The problem requiring hospitalization is often stated first in general terms, allowing, as in the case of the 9-year-old girl, the parties to continue to hold their own views of the problem while agreeing on the plan for admission. Thus, the focal problem was defined in this way.

Agitated and possibly life-endangering behavior in a child with partially repaired heart disease and without consensus regarding her physiological and emotional status and indicated treatment.

DECIDING HOW TO INTERVENE

Intervention follows an analysis of the factors in the child's life that contribute to the problem requiring admission and a selection of those factors believed changeable. For instance, in this case, the contributing aspects of the child's medical and psychosocial background were summarized by three factors:

the child's unexpressed resentment at many aspects of her life, including exercise restrictions enforced by her mother but with dubious medical authorization

the mother's poorly acknowledged anxiety and grief, making it hard for her to distinguish "bad" behavior from physiologically dangerous behavior

the doctors' uncertainty regarding the child's physiological status

Each of these factors lent itself to intervention.

COORDINATING THERAPEUTIC MANAGEMENT AND THERAPY

Inpatient treatment offers a unique opportunity to coordinate interventions in the office (with child or parent) and therapeutic management in the life space. The case of the 9-year-old girl illustrates this coordination.

On the ward the child tried previously forbidden behavior and elicited responses different from the ones she received at home. Simultaneously, her mother, sharing her experience of having repeatedly "nearly lost" the child, received validation for her fears, her frustration with the child and with doctors, and her grief about the "easy" child she didn't have. Her anxiety, though well known to doctors, had never before been recognized as a clinical problem. In office interviews, the child told the story of a magic dragon "with a bad heart" who secretly resented exercise restrictions and wished for a freer life.

LEARNING WHILE APART, COMING TOGETHER

Many children benefit from a three-phase model of inpatient treatment, in which child and parent take advantage of the separation provided by the hospital stay to try out alternative responses that would have felt impossible or too dangerous at home. Parent and child later come together to try out with each other what they have learned with professionals.

In this case, the child performed for her mother the story she had created of the dragon with the bad heart.

Her mother was surprised to learn, through the play, that her outwardly compliant daughter aspired to a less restricted life. Both mother and daughter used the interruption of their mutually frightening interactions to expand their repertoire of ways to deal with their own feelings and with each other.

FACTORS IN THE TREATMENT SYSTEM

Inpatient treatment offers consultation about and often provides an opportunity to make changes in the services that have been holding (or failing to hold) the child as an outpatient. It is possible to state as contributing factors, and then to intervene in, aspects of the case in which the clinicians themselves play a part. In the case being discussed, as the child became more active, without cardiac decompensation, the cardiologists reassured the mother (and themselves) about the child's cardiac capacity.

THE CHILD'S (AND FAMILY'S) STRENGTHS

The treatment plan should recognize and list explicitly the strengths of the child and family, strengths easily lost sight of in the crises that lead to psychiatric hospitalization. In this case, the child's creativity and the mother's determined advocacy for her child were emphasized, with benefit for child and mother, who had lost touch with the other's strengths. Emphasis on family strengths also benefited the team, who could easily have fallen into the trap of focusing on the visible pathology.

PROBLEMS IN TREATMENT PLANNING

Maintaining an Adaptive Focus: Helping patients to return to a less restrictive level of care as soon as possible requires that the inpatient team focus on the child's adaptation in the community rather than an effort to uncover pathology to be worked through in the hospital. Emotional problems are addressed to the extent required to allow the patient to leave acute care.

An adaptive focus is enhanced by the maintenance of community ties and by the integration of elements of the outside world into the ward. The elements include family, school, religion, and ethnicity (Hendren & Berlin, 1991). When hospitalized patients lack families, specific interventions can validate their different status, acknowledge their losses, and build relevant competencies. An example of such an intervention for children in state custody is called a psychoeducation group Learning About State Agencies.

Managing the Burden of Trauma: In all but name, most child and adolescent inpatient units are de facto trauma units. Increasingly, inpatient treatment is dealing with patients' burdens of traumatic experiences—exposure to violence, physical abuse, or sexual molestation. Program planners are developing special groups for trauma survivors. These groups offer the child validation, peer support, and a chance to develop a positive role as an abuse survivor and advocate. In addition, program planners are replacing restraint procedures, such as physical holding or mechanical restraint, by methods less likely to be experienced traumatically. The methods used depend on the child and his or her trauma history.

The staff must be aware of the effects of working with traumatized patients. One effect is secondary retraumatization, traumatization of clinicians that occurs as a result of "reliving" events with trauma survivors (Lyon, 1993). Another effect is staff polarization, which occurs when team members disagree about whether trauma has occurred and what role it plays in the patients problem.

The possibility of trauma can rivet the attention of the inpatient team, resulting in one-factor formulations, as in the case of a 6-year-old girl referred for severe fighting, yelling, defiance, and sexual provocativeness. Case discussions repeatedly focused on whether she had been, or was now being, abused or molested, as if possible abuse were all that mattered. Such a focus represented serious underassessment of the child, omitting factors such as her ego vulnerability, with poor impulse control, reality testing, and affect management; her identification with abusive caregivers, reactivated when threatened; and her hypervigilance and suspicion of men. Aspects of her environment were also at risk of underassessment, including her foster parents' limited understanding of her needs, their ambivalence about caring for her, and their strained relationship with the care agency. Too narrow a focus cannot always be prevented; alertness to such a condition makes early acknowledgment and correction possible.

DEVELOPING A TREATMENT PLAN

Hearing the Child's (and Family's) Voice: The treatment plan should give voice to the actual experience and point of view of the child and family. Having the child attend and be interviewed in rounds, team meetings, or case conferences is useful. In such meetings or in one-on-one conversations, children can be asked for their own understanding of the reason for admission. A clinician can usually do this by asking, "Whose idea was it for you to come to the hospital?" Such a question may elicit the child's own language for symptoms, as well as the patient's ideas about what will help. The clinician can also elicit the child's view of what must change to allow a return home. Looking further, the team can ask questions to determine if the patient has hope for the future or a personal ambition or dream. Data from such direct inquiries can be combined with inferences made from the child's play, drawings, and projective tests to create an empathic diagnosis, a statement in ordinary language of how the child feels and of how the world feels to the child.

The treatment plan should make explicit the best diagnostic thinking available regarding the child, including the child's own point of view; an awareness of the child's efforts to master inner and outer challenges; and a sense of the child as a growing person, with potentials as yet unrealized.

Language and Play: Because inpatient treatment removes a child from home, it is easy for inpatient treatment systems to develop their own language, not easily understood (often, not meant to be understood) by outsiders. This tendency should be avoided. Treatment plans should be stated in words that patient, parents, and community providers can understand. Language should support the positive self-regard of the patient and parents and promote the treatment alliance.

Similarly, because of the important role of impulse control in inpatient treatment, inpatient unit staff can easily overemphasize control and be suspicious of spontaneity, creativity, and play. The treatment plan, like the program in general, should make room for creative use of language as well as art, music, drama, dance, and the other means children use to feel good, join with others, and create something of their own.

The Hospital and the Community: Finally, the treatment plan should express the aim of the contemporary child psychiatric unit to be closely tied to the child's community—past, current, and potential. A "discharge picture" that the team can believe in should inform the treatment plan and express this commitment to helping the child grow and move on. A discharge picture answers these questions about the child's life after discharge:

Where will the child live?
With whom will he or she live?
What services, including protective services, will the current patient receive?
What symptoms will remain?
In what school program will the child be enrolled?
When will the child leave the hospital?

The Scope of Inpatient Psychiatry: The Place of Hospital Treatment In The Life of the Child

The following five cases illustrate how hospitalization can occur at very different places in a child's life as a patient.

INPATIENT PSYCHIATRIC INTERVENTION IN A CRISIS

A 12-year-old boy became agitated and suicidal in his pediatrician's office after the diagnosis of diabetes mellitus. He was admitted to a psychiatric ward, where he expressed anger, then cried, then began to learn about diabetes and its management. Concurrent family meetings reviewed the meanings of loss of good health, chronic illness, and diabetes in a family proud of a son who had seemed "perfect." Meetings also addressed the family's fear of the heritage of the mother's grandfather, who had died a slow death from peripheral vascular disease exacerbated by adult-onset diabetes. After the 12-year-old was discharged, the patient's pediatrician followed up.

CRISIS RESULTING IN INTRODUCTION TO MENTAL HEALTH TREATMENT

A 13-year-old disclosed to his mother, then to his pediatrician, that he had been preoccupied for months with suicidal and homicidal thoughts, including visions of hanging himself from a flagpole at school and of get-

ting a gun and killing people at random. Auditory hallucinations precipitated some of these thoughts. Inpatient treatment with psychoeducation, neuroleptic, and antidepressant medication was followed by outpatient treatment.

REPEATED CRISES, PUNCTUATING TREATMENT

A 16-year-old with repeated admissions for anorexia nervosa and depression made gains with each admission, becoming more able to observe and manage her mealtime anxiety and to maintain an alliance with outpatient treatment. She eventually settled into outpatient treatment, stabilized her weight, and went on to college.

DEFINING CRISIS, WATERSHED TREATMENT

A 14-year-old girl's two brief admissions represented a turning point. Admitted first after 2 years of intractable bulimic symptoms, she was readmitted a week after discharge with negligible bingeing but with new symptoms: intense depression with suicidal thoughts. The family then acknowledged previously undiscussed problems, including paternal alcohol abuse, marital strain, and financial strain. Integration of these subjects into the outpatient treatment resulted in a decrease of the girl's bulimic and depressive symptoms.

CRISIS RESULTING IN TRANSITION TO MORE RESTRICTIVE TREATMENT

A 14-year-old boy's long-standing isolation, secretive manner; intermittent, unprovoked, explosive behavior; and paranoid thinking responded only partially to neuroleptic and antidepressant treatment. Repeated attempts to discharge to home and day hospital were followed by readmission after the patient assaulted a sibling. The patient was readmitted with a plan for transition to residential treatment.

Efficacy

The efficacy of psychiatric hospitalization for children and adolescents has been difficult to demonstrate. Follow-up studies show better outcomes in patients with higher intelligence, intact central nervous system, healthier diagnosis, and family resources (Pfeiffer & Strzelecki, 1990; Blotcky,

Dimperio, & Gossett, 1984) Following long-term hospital treatment, gains made often erode, particularly when aftercare is not obtained (Lewis et al., 1980). There are few truly comparative studies that examine outcomes in similar groups in hospital or residential treatment versus nonhospital treatment (Sherman et al., 1988). Researchers are just beginning to integrate the effect of important variables like ethnicity into outcome studies.

The field has not yet begun to grapple with a set of questions specific to short-term treatment. For example, once the goal of hospitalization shifts from symptomatic change in the individual patient to improved functioning of child, family, and treaters together (Woolston, 1989), evaluation research must be directed at how well the child, family, and services fit together—a metavariable that goes beyond change in any one of the parties by itself.

Beyond such questions, which apply to outcomes of treatment in specific programs, are questions relating to children's fate not just in single institutions, but in systems of care (Burns & Friedman, 1990). Future studies should examine what is the least restrictive and most effective intervention that will help with a given problem and which arrays of services, in what kind of network, best support family ties and decrease the chance that a disturbed child will have to leave home and school. These questions take on new urgency and relevance in the context of the likely reorganization of all health services into networks of affiliated services of different degrees of intensity and restrictiveness.

Conclusion: The Future of Inpatient Psychiatry

INPATIENT TREATMENT IN CONTEXT

Everything about inpatient treatment—including the goals, the way the problem is formulated, the way an operational plan is developed, and even the number of inpatient beds needed—depends on the arrangements of care outside the hospital. The more components of the continuum of care available in a given community, the smaller the need for hospital-based treatment will be.

Where alternative resources are not available, more inpatient treatment resources will be necessary.

Resources will increasingly be vertically integrated, whether in the private sector, under the initiatives of managed care, or in the public sector, in the models developed in Ventura County (Jordan & Hernandez, 1990) and under the Child & Adolescent Service System Program (CASSP) initiatives and the R. W. Johnson Foundation projects (England & Cole, 1992). Social and economic pressure not to place children out-of-home will counteract the residual tendencies in the field toward parent blaming; models more supportive of families will benefit. Family support, in turn, needs to be balanced with realistic assessment of outcomes. Family preservation must not be used as a slogan with which to dismantle child protection.

Despite a spirit of partnership with parents, tension will continue between those who focus on the disorder in the child and those who emphasize the contributions of all factors. As hospitals are used more sparingly and as rapid patient turnover produces a more transient ward community, inpatient units will become "hospitals without walls," collaboratively connected to community services.

OVER- AND UNDERUTILIZATION, REPEATEDLY INTERRUPTED RELATIONSHIPS

Overutilization occurred in the 1980s; we must ensure that the converse does not happen in the 1990s and beyond. There is a tendency, in moving away from overreliance on long-term hospitalization, to replace inpatient services with those offered by long-term nonhospital facilities. These facilities may be staffed by nonpsychiatric personnel without the background to diagnosis or treat serious psychiatric disorders. Enthusiasm for cutting costs must not interfere with the hospital treatment some children and adolescents need. The present generation of inpatient clinicians and administrators, as custodians of the experience of several generations of clinicians, have an obligation to see that shorter and less restrictive innovations do not deprive children and their families of the benefits of clinical understanding developed in the past five decades.

Another danger is that seriously disturbed children, like seriously disturbed adults caught in "revolving door" admissions, will go from one brief admission to another not receiving effective help and missing the rudiments of stability (including relationships and school) that all children, and especially the most disturbed, need. In such circumstances, children end up having to apply their youth and resilience, while trying to manage serious emotional disturbance, to coping with an ever-unsettled world of changing services and placements.

In seeking more efficient ways, including the use of competitive systems borrowed from the private sector, to provide for the most needy children, society must find ways to reconcile the goals of efficiency with the traditional goals of protecting, fostering, and advocating for children.

HUMANE TREATMENT AND A SHARED LANGUAGE FOR TREATMENT

Humanistic treatment of psychologically vulnerable children has had to overcome adults' fear of children's rage and despair, the counteraggressive responses easily elicited by dangerous behavior and by symptoms that do not respond to treatment, the dearth of advocates that comes with social as well as psychological disadvantage, and society's tendency to skimp on resources for children whose distress make us all uncomfortable. In addition to these age-old threats, disturbed children today face the new risks of psychological distancing inherent in a taxonomy that can lose the child in the disorders and the risks of powerful pharmacotherapy capable of misuse as well as causing great benefit.

Against these dangers, the protections offered by professionalism and state regulation are now supplemented by consumer empowerment and by the movement to link inpatient services to outpatient services, breaking down the walls. In this regard, a new language of treatment planning that empowers by providing a common way to describe problems, goals, and objectives will make a significant contribution.

REFERENCES

Aichhorn, A. (1935). *Wayward youth*. New York: Viking Press.

American Academy of Child and Adolescent Psychiatry. (1989). *Inpatient hospital treatment of children and adolescents: policy statement*. Washington, DC: Author.

American Psychiatric Association. (1957). *Psychiatric inpatient treatment of children*. Baltimore, MD: Lord Baltimore Press.

American Psychiatric Association. (1994). *Diagnostic and statistical manual of mental disorders* (4th ed.). Washington, DC: Author.

Barker, P. J. (Ed.). (1974). The residential psychiatric treatment of children. New York: John Wiley & Sons.

Berlin, I. (1978). Developmental issues in the psychiatric hospitalization of children. *American Journal of Psychiatry, 135*, 1044–1048.

Bettelheim, B. (1974). A *home for the heart*. New York: Knopf.

Bettelheim, B., & Sylvester, E. (1948). A therapeutic milieu. *American Journal of Orthopsychiatry, 18*, 191–206.

Blotcky, M. J., Dimperio, T. L., & Gossett, J. T. (1984). Follow-up of children treated in psychiatric hospitals: A review of studies. *American Journal Psychiatry, 141*, 1499–1507.

Bradley, C. (1938). A pioneer hospital for children's behavioral disorders. *Modern Hospital, 50*, 68–72.

Burns, B. J., & Friedman, R. M. (1990). Examining the research base for child mental health services and policy. *Journal of Mental Health Administration, 17*, 87–98.

Cotton, N. S. (1989). The developmental-clinical rationale for the use of seclusion in the psychiatric treatment of children. *American Journal of Orthopsychiatry, 59*, 442–450.

Cotton, N. (1993). *Lessons from the lion's den: Therapeutic management of children in psychiatric hospitals and treatment centers*. San Francisco: Jossey-Bass.

Cotton, N., & Geraty, R. D. (1984). Therapeutic space design: Planning an inpatient unit. *American Journal of Orthopsychiatry, 54*, 624–636.

Dalton, R., & Forman, M. (Eds.). (1992). *Psychiatric hospitalization of school-age children*. Washington, DC: American Psychiatric Press.

Desjarlais, R., Eisenberg, L., Good, B., & Kleinman, A. (1995). *World mental health: Problems and priorities in low-income countries*. Oxford: Oxford University Press.

Ekstein, R. (1966). Children of time and space, impulse and action. New York: Appleton-Century-Crofts.

Ekstein, R., Wallerstein, J., & Mandelbaum, A. (1959). Countertransference in residential treatment of children. *Psychoanalytic Study of the Child, 14*, 186–218.

England, M. J., & Cole, R. F. (1992). Building systems of care for youth with serious mental illness. *Hospital and Community Psychiatry, 43,* 630–633.

Gair, D. S. (1989). Psychiatric restraint of children and adolescents: clinical and legal aspects. Chap. 21 pp 345–378. In R. Rosner & H. I. Schwartz (Eds.), *Juvenile psychiatry and the law.* New York: Plenum Publishing.

Garrison, W. T., Ecker B, Friedman M, Davidoff R, Haeberle K, Wagner M. (1990). Aggression and counteraggression during child psychiatric hospitalization. *Journal of the American Academy of Child and Adolescent Psychiatry, 29,* 242–250.

Harper, G. P. (1989). Focal inpatient treatment planning. *Journal of the American Academy of Child and Adolescent Psychiatry, 28,* 31–37.

Harper, G., & Cotton, N. S. (1991). Child and adolescent treatment. Chap. 12 pp 320–337. In L. I. Sederer (Ed.), *Inpatient psychiatry* (3rd ed.). Baltimore, MD: Williams & Wilkins.

Harper, G. P., & Geraty, R. D. (1985). Hospital and residential treatment. Chap. 64 pp 1–20. In J. Cavenar & R. Michels (eds.), *Psychiatry.* Philadelphia: J. B. Lippincott.

Harper, G. P., & Irvin, E. A. (1985). Alliance formation with parents: limit-setting and the effect of mandated reporting. *American Journal of Orthopsychiatry, 55,* 550–560.

Harrison, S. I., McDermott, J. F., Jr., & Chethik, M. (1969). Residential treatment of children: The psychotherapist-administrator. *Journal of the American Academy of Child Psychiatry, 8,* 385–410.

Healy, W. (1915). The individual delinquent: A textbook of diagnosis and prognosis for all concerned in understanding offenders. Boston: Little, Brown.

Hendren, R. L., & Berlin, I. N. (Eds.). (1991). Psychiatric inpatient care of children and adolescents: A multicultural approach. New York: John Wiley & Sons.

Jordan, D. D., & Hernandez, M. (1990). The Ventura planning model: A proposal for mental health reform. *Journal of Mental Health Administration, 17,* 26–47.

Lewis, M., Lewis, D. O., Shanok, S. S., Klatskin, E., & Osborne, J. R. (1980). The undoing of residential treatment: A follow-up study of 51 adolescents. *Journal of the American Academy of Child Psychiatry, 19,* 160–171.

Lyon, E. (1993). Hospital staff reactions to accounts by survivors of childhood abuse. *American Journal of Orthopsychiatry, 63,* 410–416.

Masterson, J., (1992). Treatment of the borderline adolescent: A developmental approach. New York: John Wiley & Sons.

Noshpitz, J. D. (1962). Notes on the theory of residential treatment. *Journal of the American Academy of Child Psychiatry, 1,* 284–296.

Palmer, A. L., Harper, G., & Rivinus, T. M. (1983). The "adoption process" in the inpatient treatment of children and adolescents. *Journal of the American Academy of Child Psychiatry, 22,* 286–293.

Pfeiffer, S. I., & Strzelecki, S. C. (1990). Inpatient psychiatric treatment of children and adolescents: A review of outcome studies. *Journal of the American Academy of Child and Adolescent Psychiatry, 29,* 847–853.

Redl, F. (1959). A strategy and technique of the life-space interview. *American Journal of Orthopsychiatry, 29,* 1–18.

Rinsley, D. B. (1980). Principles of the therapeutic milieu with children. In P. G. Sholevar, R. Benson, & B. Blinder (Eds.), *Treatment of emotional disorders in children and adolescents.* New York: SP Medicine and Scientific.

Sherman, J., Barker, P., Lorimer, P., Swinson, R., & Factor, D. C. (1988). Treatment of autistic children: Relative effectiveness of residential, out-patient, and home-based interventions. *Child Psychiatry and Human Development, 19,* 109–125.

Stanton, A. H., & Schwartz, M. S. (1954). The mental hospital: A study of institutional participation in psychiatric illness and treatment. New York: Basic Books.

Stone, L. A. (1979). Residential treatment. In S. I. Harrison (Ed.), J. D. Noshpitz (Ed.-in-chief), *Basic handbook of child psychiatry* (Vol.3, Chap. 15 pp 231–262). New York: Basic Books.

Treischman, A. E., Whittaker, J. K., & Brendtro, L. K. (1969). The other twenty-three hours. Chicago: Aldine Publishing.

Woolston, J. (1989). A transactional risk model for short and intermediate term psychiatric inpatient treatment of children. *Journal of the American and Academy of Child and Adolescent Psychiatry, 28,* 38–41.

Zinn, D. (1979). Hospital treatment of the adolescent. In S. I. Harrison (Ed), J. D. Noshpitz (Ed.-in-chief), *Basic handbook of child psychiatry,* (Vol. 3, Chap 16 pp. 263–288). New York: Basic Books.

37 / Crisis Residence

W. Douglas McCoard and Roger J. Minner

Crisis residence provides short-term respite, crisis intervention, and clinical support services 24 hours a day, 7 days a week, for youth in psychosocial crisis who need a temporary, structured, supportive residential setting. Such care can be used as an alternative to a hospital or detention center when those levels of intervention or structure are not required. When hospital intervention is necessary, however, a crisis residence can serve as an access point for the youth to receive the necessary assessment and gain admission to this setting. Crisis residences include runaway and homeless youth shelters, specialized foster homes, crisis respite programs, and small group homes. The purpose for using a crisis residence is the reunification of youths with their family in a short time, using community-based supports to assist the reunified family to remain together. Using a crisis residence permits the family to gain some perspective on the problem. It also provides the family and caregivers a chance to begin a planning process, identify needs, and identify the strengths as well as the individuals who can assist the family to get through this period. Because the goal is family reunification, a crisis residence should not be used as a transitional placement for imminent residential treatment; this would serve only to confuse the youth and confound the staff providing the service.

By definition, crisis is time-limited. Crisis residences, therefore, should be designed for short-term stays and quick turnaround from admission to discharge. Also, because family stability is upset during a crisis, there is an opportunity to effect greater change during the episode than is often possible through longer-term services once a family returns to equilibrium. Consequently, the setting in which the intervention occurs is inextricably woven into the efficacy of crisis intervention. (Please refer to the "Suggested Reading" section for more information on crisis intervention.) An atmosphere that allows the youth to begin to feel comfortable and regain control over a situation is essential. This is achieved through the physical facility, the decor, and the approach used by staff from the initial greeting and throughout the youth's stay at the residence.

Accessibility

A crisis residence should always be accessible and should be perceived as accessible to those who use it. For this reason it is preferable to be located as part of a community. For example, a home in a neighborhood or even a separate building on the campus of a residential treatment center is more desirable than a wing of a larger institution. The more normal the setting, the quicker the youth will feel in control and regain stability. Being in a safe place that can be reached by public transportation and near community activities is important. In this way, young people and families can get to the residence when a crisis occurs and not necessarily have to wait for official sanction from an outside entity. Making the choice to use the service is a particularly helpful aspect in gaining the trust of the youth.

Location

Location is important in designing crisis residence as the ability of the users to maintain their typical day-to-day activities. Youths who are enrolled in school should attend classes with minimal disruption. They should continue any job or extracurricular activities in which they take part.

A crisis residence should always be accessible and should be perceived as accessible to those who use it. For this reason it is preferable to be located as part of a community. For example, a home in a neighborhood or even a separate building on the campus of a residential treatment center is more desirable than a wing of a larger institution. The more normalized the setting, the quicker the youth will feel in control and regain stability. Being in a safe place which can be reached by public transportation and near community activities is important. In this way, young people and families can get themselves to the residence when a crisis occurs and not necessarily have to wait for official sanction from an outside entity. Also, a youth in crisis who has left home or is considering leaving home should have options available to assist with the problem. For this reason a crisis residence should be open to any youth seeking help. Making the choice to use the service is a particularly helpful aspect in gaining the trust of the youth, and enhances the ability of engaging those with whom the youth is in conflict.

Depending on their age and input from their guardians, youths can take responsibility for getting to these places using public transportation. In the same way, getting to appropriate leisure activities is a typical adolescent activity and can be maintained if the location of the residence permits. Of course, a parent or guardian has the ultimate authority and responsibility for where young people may go and what activities they may do, and the limits must be negotiated at admission. However, permitting the youths some voice over these aspects of daily living grants them control and decision-making power, both important ingredients in successful crisis intervention. In this way location of the crisis residence is important to the outcome of the stay.

Decor

In addition to location and accessibility, another facet of the physical facility that enhances the service is the interior design. Stressing the distinction between hospitals and other institutions by keeping the facilities unpretentious and comfortable will assist in building trust between the staff and the youths. Consideration should be given to privacy and leisure activity in setting up the residence. Sleeping and eating arrangements also must be taken into account. Again, avoiding the institutional look is the goal, but allowing for adequate space is a reality. For this reason, many crisis residences look more like adapted family homes than community institutions. While much of the relationship building and other important interactions can happen in any milieu, it is important to have formal interview space included in the design of the residence. Meetings between youths and their parents can become highly emotional, and they should have the ability to meet in private.

Staff

The staff of a crisis residence is key to its success in becoming the short-term respite that allows families the time to adapt and/or learn new coping mechanisms to the crisis which caused them to use the facility. While it is necessary to have some staff professionally trained in crisis intervention techniques, not all those working in a crisis residence need to have degrees or licenses. However, all those staff having direct contact with youths and families using the facility should have some common skills. First, they should have good assessment skills to determine the intensity of the crisis being presented. For example, being able to distinguish between shyness, uncomfortableness, and depression when observing a youth's isolation within the facility is critical. Crisis residential staff also need to have the ability to connect quickly with youths and families in crisis. They need to be flexible and adaptable; they need to be able to work with people from a wide variety of backgrounds, cultures, and lifestyles; they need to have a high level of skill and competence. Good crisis residential staff have a high energy level and commitment and a strong sense of confidence and self-esteem. They must allow the crisis to be defined by the person seeking help. They must be able to be totally involved with youths and families and then be able to focus quickly the family into the family's natural support environment. As mentioned, it is important to have professionally trained personnel as part of the crisis residence staff. Proficiency in diagnostic assessment for both mental health and alcohol and other drug issues is necessary. Having a physician on staff is not obligatory, but having access to physician and psychiatric consultation is critical.

A crisis residence is open 24 hours; therefore, the staffing configuration and support is important to consider. Ideally, a professional staff member greets any parent or guardian who brings in a child for respite. The crisis resolution process can advance quickly if the professional takes advantage of this initial meeting. However, when no professional staffer can meet with the family on intake, a backup system for consultation with the professional and supervisory staff is necessary. Also, regular access to case-related supervision is needed.

Additionally, and perhaps more basic than these characteristics, is the value-base necessary for successful crisis residence staff. How one person views another person experiencing a crisis will dominate the approach taken to alleviate the effects of that crisis and is more of an intrinsic quality than a learned skill. Since assisting youths to regain control and permitting them to make decisions is key to the crisis resolution process, it is crucial that staff members can identify common ground between themselves and the families they are serving, and identify their strengths. Each family must be assessed and a plan developed with them that is tailored individually to their specific needs, builds on their own inherent strengths, and uses their own natural supports as much as possible.

Approach

In a similar way, there can be no rigid policies and procedures that lay out the approach and answers questions posed by young people; this would serve only to disempower the youths and put the staff in a one-up position. Rather, staff members must be willing to struggle with the issues raised and take the opportunity to explore each interaction, thus building youths' self-esteem and confidence in their own mastery in problem solving. The ability of staff members to "operate in the gray area" takes self-discipline and a great deal of support. As such, staff members must be supported and covered with a comprehensive on-call and backup plan.

Crisis residence activities must be immediate and concrete. The initial goal is to engage youths into the crisis resolution process. Thus, it is important to understand the nature of the crisis. While not all presenting situations may look like a crisis to the staff, the crisis is defined by the person seeking help. It is equally important to understand the importance of establishing a helping relationship between the person using the residence and the staff. These very intentional trust-building activities in crisis residence programs may include informal introductions to other youths in the facility, getting the person something to eat or drink, and talking in an open area (dining room, front steps) rather than moving too quickly into the formal interview space. This milieu interview process can help acclimate youths in crisis to recognize the supports the crisis residence can provide to assist in problem resolution rather than seeing the crisis residence staff as trying to control them.

The crisis residence also serves as gatekeeper for more acute services. It is not uncommon for youths entering a crisis residence to need a more secure level of intervention. While family, formal, and natural supports believe short-term respite with crisis intervention services will be sufficient to bring their situation under control, during the assessment process and with some observation, it may be determined that continued use of the crisis residence is contraindicated. In these cases, a close working relationship with hospital pre-screeners and/or other residential programs is helpful.

Conclusion

Crisis residences are community-based alternatives to unnecessary, more restrictive settings such as hospitals. They are used to provide respite and assist the family to get an effective reunification and after-crisis service plan in place. Because of the short-term nature of the service, it is important to build trust as quickly as possible. Ways this is accomplished include providing a homelike setting and having the youths who use the residence maintain as much of their daily routine as possible. Skilled and value-based staff are key in building a successful crisis residence.

The future of crisis residences looks bright. With the current trend toward reducing youth institutionalization and increasing community-based care, there will be many opportunities to develop or provide this type of service.

REFERENCES

Dixon, S. L. (1987). *Working with people in crisis.* Columbus, OH: Merrill.

Gilliland, B. E., James, R. K. (1993). *Crisis intervention strategies.* Pacific Grove, CA: Brooks/Cole Publishing.

Goldman, S. K. (1988). *Series on community-based service for children & adolescents who are severely emotionally disturbed: Volume 2: Crisis services.* Washington, DC: CASSP Technical Assistance Center, Georgetown University Child Development Center.

Stroul, B. A., & Friedman, R. (1986). *A system of care for severely emotionally disturbed Children & Youth.* Washington, DC: CASSP Technical Assistance Center, Georgetown University Child Development Center.

38 / Group Homes

Janet M. Demb

Children are removed from their families for a variety of reasons, and there is a spectrum of services has been designed to meet their needs. The most severely disturbed are served by hospitals or residential treatment facilities. For those youngsters who do not require the level of containment or the specialized services these provide, a group home becomes the treatment of choice. A group home lies lying between the formal institution and the family.

Group homes are facilities that provide congregate care for individuals in need, be they adults or children. Group homes for children are designed to provide care for youngsters whose families are not able to parent them. These youngsters have been either neglected or abused by their families and need a safe haven in which to grow until such time as they can be managed in some other way. In some instances, they safely returned to their families, in others they reach an age and level of development that allow them to: care for themselves; be adopted; or, move to a facility for adults in need of care.

Physical Plant

Facilities of various sizes and configurations have been designated as group homes. They may be in urban or rural settings, some with their own schools and recreational facilities, others making use of neighborhood schools and recreational facilities. Some have the flexibility to provide all necessary services for those children who require more than routine care. This flexibility includes the capacity to offer changing levels of care suitable to the changing needs of a child. For example, a group home may include special units to manage crises and less respective settings for older children who are getting ready to function independently. For a child capable of living in a traditional family setting, a group home may offer preparation for a move to a foster family. There is also movement in the other direction, from foster to group home, depending on a child's current need.

Staff

Some group homes have house parents, a couple who lives at the home full-time and acts in loco parentis. Or there may be house counselor, who work in shifts to provide for the children, and a supervisor who ensures consistent service delivery and communication among the various workers. Although house parents or house counselors are hired specifically to provide direct services to the children, virtually all of the contacts experienced by the children become a part of their life experience and, potentially, can be therapeutic—or countertherapeutic. An emotionally available and nurturing handyman, cook, or housekeeper can have a profound effect upon a child, for better or for worse, and this should be considered when such positions are filled.

In addition to those who provide the direct care, there is often an array of other professionals. The list may include psychiatrists, psychologists, pastoral counselors, social workers, educational consultants, nurses, and pediatricians. Some homes provide more "in house" services while others may rely more heavily upon the community to provide for ancillary needs of the children.

Entry into the Group Home

A child's first contact with a group home is important and can facilitate a positive attitude and positive adjustment. Regardless of the actual family circumstances in a child's life it is rare for group homes to be chosen by a child as the place they would prefer to live. Even abuse or extreme neglect is very often preferred to the anonymity that results from being removed from family, neighborhood, school, and, in short, from all that is known and familiar. A positive introduction during which children can be reassured about who will be caring for them, what the rules will be, and what ways there are for them to make their needs known is essential. Such an introduction should result in a child feeling confident that he will have not only a place to sleep food to eat and clothing to wear, but also adults (most often social workers) who will be available and who will facilitate the maintenance of ties to family.

A child should visit and tour the home in which he or she will live and have an opportunity to meet both staff and residents. Unfortunately, referrals are often made at a time of crisis, obviating the possibility of an orderly transition from home to group home. A holding area, a place in which a new arrival can wait until a more permanent setting is identified and the child can be received in a controlled and welcoming fashion, is beneficial.

Once a child has physically been placed in a house, there may be a period of relative calm of-

ten ensues. In this period the staff tries to get to know the child and the child tries to get to know the staff. During this early phase it is not uncommon for those with a history of defiant and oppositional behavior or antisocial activity to be mild mannered and cooperative. On the other hand, some children who immediately defy staff. Defiance may take the form of nothing more serious than leaving the house without permission and coming home late. All children, whether they appear cooperative or defiant at the time of admission, should receive a clear, early statement about how transgressions will be addressed. These children put off serious acting-out behavior until they feel more at home at which point the problems that have been described by family or school staff resurface in the group home. What follows are some interventions that have been used successfully in addressing problems that arise in a group home.

Team Meetings

Consistency is important in well-functioning families and even more important in group homes. Sincea child may interact with a dozen different people, much opportunity for confusion, and distortion exists. Therefore, staff must confer about children on a regular basis. In many group homes conferring takes the form of weekly team meetings attended by at least one member of the group home staff as well as representatives from other disciplines, e.g. mental health, education. These meetings provide a forum in which information about children can be shared and team members can provide information about their interaction with residents. Seeing a child from the perspective of providing for direct care can flesh out the material gathered through the more artificial setting of a clinical interview, while insight derived from theoretical constructs can provide the necessary distance not always available to those who must deal directly with a child. More concretely, it provides the opportunity for each member of the team to learn more about the child. A youngster who seems to be going to school each morning may have accumulated four school absences in a week. A child who politely extorts bus fare each morning may, in fact, have already been issued a bus pass. A child who allegedly has weekend visits with family may be discovered to be spending that time with a friend instead. A child who appears tough and insensitive during the day may be observed by night staff to be crying in bed. Besides sharing such basic information, staff will learn if a child has been trying to privileges from one staff members that have already been denied by another, much as in a family a mother and a father may be divided and manipulated. Like good parents, group home staff need to provide a united front.

Team meetings also often an opportunity to air feelings. When confronted with angry and needy children, it is only human for staff to take the anger and demands of the children personally. It is helpful to establish and reiterate that the behavior displayed by a child in a group home is being displaced from family members and that, in the absence of an abusing or depriving parent, whomever is handy will be assigned the parental role by the child. Not to take a child's anger personally is a lesson that must be learned and relearned for it is difficult to avoid doing personal reaction when a youngster is cursing or physically lashing out against staff. A professional staff must learn techniques for dealing with such behavior, techniques that do not entail retaliation or repetition of the behavior exhibited by the child's family. All team members benefit from being repeatedly directed to the issues of deprivation and loss that characterize the lives of the residents and the demanding and angry behavior which results.

Behavioral Interventions

Having basic rules and regulations are essential and must apply to all children who exhibit specific behaviors. It is easier for both residents and staff to be dispassionate in the face of a regulation that is publicly known and unchanging. For example, rules may specify that children required to must attend school, do certain chores, and keep certain hours.

Along with establishing rules it is necessary to allow children the opportunity for greater freedom when it becomes clear that they can handle it. Many group homes have incorporated level systems whereby children may move from the lowest level at which they begin upon entry, to increasingly higher levels as a function of their performance. As they move up the levels, residents receive more freedom in the form of later curfew, a greater amount of discretionary time away from the group home and larger allowances. Rewards in the form of a special privilege may be awarded too, for example, all residents with one month of perfect school attendance, could attend an amusement park or have dinner out. Some children will need rewards that are more immediate such as being taken out for an ice cream cone at the end of an entire day with no fights. In addition to the formal rewards and punishments which are instituted by group homes, there are naturally occurring interactions with staff that may frustrate or gratify a group home resident. Children quickly become aware of who cares about them, who is tough, who is fair, who is easily angered, and who will stick by them in hard times. As a result it is not uncommon for children to behave differently when different staff members are on duty.

Although positive rewards may be helpful in motivating some youngsters, others may not have the self control to be able to conform to house rules. At times feelings will escalate and a child may go beyond verbal attack and direct physical aggression against another resident or a staff member. For this reason group homes should require that staff be trained in the proper application of restraint should that become necessary. This include an opportunity when the crisis has passed, for the child to discuss what it was that pushed him to violence and what alternative measures might be taken to avoid such an outbreak in the future. Having extra staff in the form of a crisis worker can help to provide the necessary external controls at times when a child's internal controls are unavailable. In addition to allowing the rest of the patient group to continue to function during crises. In addition, the child who has been restrained receives the message that he or she will be helped to deal with his rage and his potentially dangerous impulses. This can be highly reassuring.

Even when behavior does not escalate to the point of physical violence, acting out can be detrimental to the running of a group home. When children steal, break furniture, etc., their disruptive behavior must be addressed. Children can be given additional chores for which they are paid in order to defray the cost of damages or, if they are able to do so, they can be asked to help in making necessary repairs.

Counseling and Psychotherapy

Rewards and punishments along with consistent expectations can have a salubrious effect on some children but in other instances this is insufficient to help them modify their behavior. Sometimes providing a staff member to listen to a child's grievances and help address them can be helpful. House meetings in which residents can air their grievances both with other residents and staff should be conducted regularly and this too provides an opportunity for residents to ventilate their problems and perhaps avoid explosive outbursts.

There are times when problems are of such a nature that the direct and sometimes ongoing intervention of a mental health professional is indicated to help get at the root causes of a child's behavior and try to change it.

Specialized Group Homes

For those children who present very specific and challenging problems there are specialized home, e.g., for firesetters (Dalton, Haslett & Daul, 86), for those with mental retardation (Denkowski & Denkowski, 83) or for those at risk for suicide (Lothian, 91).

Problems

It is important to keep in mind that while group homes provide important services for youngsters in need of a safe and supportive setting in which to grow, such settings are not families. Children are acutely aware of this and a commonly heard rejoinder from a child being asked to do something by a staff member is "you are not my mother/father." Trying to create an environment that approximates a family in the absence of a family tie is invariably experienced as second best. Moreover, older children often feel additionally stigmatised by the onus of having to live in a group home.

Just as group homes are not families and cannot provide what is best provided by a good family, neither are they psychiatric hospitals with the services that would be available in such a specialized setting. Without locked doors, "quiet rooms", intravenous medication, and a high ratio of staff to residents, some circumstances cannot be managed. It is therefore not surprising that when a youngster having major psychiatric illness, dangerously violent behavior, or an inability to follow even basic rules is referred to a group homes not just does the youngster suffers. So too do the other residents, whose problems are eclipsed. Financial pressures including the lack of the availability of more appropriate and services and can diminish the effectiveness with which group homes are able to function.

Future Considerations

Group homes do not readily lend themselves to rigorous, scientific study. Nonetheless, specific questions remain unanswered and call for exploration: What are the advantages of single sex versus mixed sex homes? Do siblings do better together or apart, and under what circumstances? How effective are level systems in improving behavior and how can they be best implemented? What training enhances service delivery? Is there an optimum size for a group home, and what ratio of staff to resident is necessary? How do physical amenities affect the functioning of a group home? What outcome measures should be used to gauge effectiveness? Implementation of information derived from studying such issues could lead to changes that would have a positive effect on services provided by group homes.

SUGGESTED READING

Dalton, R., Haslett, N., & Daul, G. (1986). Alternative therapy with a recalitant fire setter. *Journal of the American Academy of Child Psychiatry, 25,* 713–717.

Denkowski, G. C., & Denkowski, K. M. (1983). Group home designs for initiating community-based treat-ment with mentally retarded adolescent offenders. *Journal of Behavior Therapy and Experimental Psychiatry, 14,* 141–145.

Lothian, C. (1991). Working with suicidal adolescents and their families. *Journal of Child and Youth Care, 6,* 1–9.

39 / **In-Home Treatment**

John Mordock

Nature of the Modality

In-home treatment is an intervention delivered to children and their families in the families' homes and surrounding community. Those who work in this modality share a commitment to maintaining children in their homes and to meeting families' needs for concrete, supportive, and objective-specific therapeutic services.

Type of Child Served

In-home treatments were developed to serve a variety of children. They include those who need linkage with community agencies (to be able to profit from community-based mental health programs, such as clinics and day treatment programs), those who are at risk of placement outside the home, and those faced with immediate removal from the home. In addition, in-home treatment benefits those needing less intensive services, such as youths who are receiving community-based mental health services and whose progress would be facilitated by additional concrete services in the home or community. In-home treatment embraces such interventions as periodic respite for parents or help for parents in enrolling a child in a summer camp for disturbed children.

Among those needing more intense services would be youngsters in homebound schooling, on waiting lists for residential treatment facilities, or those failing to respond to day-patient care. Weekly visits by the practitioner might include helping the family to develop consistent discipline practices, taking a child to an afternoon recreational program, or assisting the recreational staff to manage a child's inappropriate behavior. If two children from a practitioner's caseload display similar social needs, the practitioner might take them both to a Friday-night church-sponsored youth group. If successful, the practitioner might then arrange for the two sets of parents to meet and take turns driving the children to the youth group.

Youngsters needing the most intensive services would be those presenting at psychiatric emergency rooms or placed in temporary shelters to await foster care placement. In such cases the practitioner is available to the family on a 24-hour basis and may make daily visits to the home to assist a parent concretely with some task, such as helping the mother get a reluctant child on the school bus each school day.

Families of the Children Served

Family problems of enrolled children are precipitated by a combination of complex environmental and interpersonal family conditions. Such problems include poverty, poor health care, inadequate housing, violent communities, poor nutrition, child behavior problems, lack of parenting skill, domestic violence, and educational failure.

Indications

The responsible parent and, in some cases, the child, must agree that in-home services will help implement the treatment plan developed for the child. Where the youth is at risk of placement or when placement is imminent, both the child and the family must want to avoid placement. The family has to recognize that the child's problems affect the family and that all family members need help managing the child, their own reactions toward the child, and the problems the child creates for other family members.

In programs designed to avoid psychiatric hospitalization, the family and the child have to agree in the emergency room to complete, as soon as possible, certain tasks that will keep the child or the family safe from harm. If they are unwilling to do so, the child should be hospitalized.

Contraindications and Risks

Because the large majority of children requiring in-home treatment are from multiproblem families, the major risk is that the parents can become dependent upon the practitioner to perform responsibilities that should be theirs; such dependency can eventually undermine their executive role.

The parents and the child should actively participate in the finding, planning, and utilization of services the family needs to assist the child. Such involvement helps to promote the growth of both parent and child, foster their ability to plan more effectively, and enhance their self-esteem. When concrete services are provided outside this context, strong regressive tendencies are encouraged and only temporary and sporadic relief occurs. Herein lies the danger of intensive home-based

services, be they crisis or long-term programs. The danger is heightened by the availability of supplemental funds. Before offering a concrete service, the worker needs to be sure that the service will not interfere with the realistic goal of increasing the executive function of parent or child. Consider the situations that follow.

- An adolescent girl who has been sexually abused calls her case manager at 11:30 P.M. from a shopping mall. She asks for a ride home.
- A mother calls in the morning, asking for cab fare to take her son to school. She feels he is too upset to take the bus.
- A mother who works until 5:00 P.M. asks the worker for money so she can arrange for a cab to take her son to Little League practice at 3:00.

The decision to meet these requests could result in a lost opportunity to increase parental or child executive functioning and to an increase in dependency on outside resources.

Historical Background

Early in the development of the social work profession, social services were routinely provided to families in the home. Thus, the "friendly visitor" was an early model of intervention (Hancock & Pelton, 1989). Early in this century, in-home mental health services were available to adult patients discharged from mental hospitals. In the late 1960s, mental health professionals demonstrated the value of treating a family in crisis in the home rather than by hospitalizing the adult "patient," but these methods were not immediately utilized to help a family with a child in crisis.

Models for Existing Programs

Stimulated by the success of aggressive outreach programs for adults with serious mental illness, in the 1970s selected communities established funds to develop similar services for children. These services were called case management, and they were established with common principles in mind. These principles included a problem-solving orientation that addressed specific life issues, no matter how mundane; provision of some services directly rather than referral to other programs; and case managers with very small caseloads, enabling the client to access services at almost any time.

Initially, case managers for children were most often brokers of services rather than direct service providers. They were not clinicians trained in the delivery of verbal or behavioral therapies. Nevertheless, practitioners helped both the child and the family to deal with the day-to-day issues of life in the community. Early programs were established to serve children at risk for hospitalization or institutionalization, and discretionary funds were made available to the case managers to meet unmet needs of the child or to provide experiences that would enhance the child's functioning.

A model for another type of in-home service came from programs designed to prevent foster care of children. The most influential program was called Homebuilders and was developed in Tacoma, Washington, in 1974. The Homebuilders program was based on the premise of earlier programs: Alternative community-based approaches should be tried before removing a child from the home to foster care. The program included a strategy of intensive, time-limited intervention to prevent family dissolution (Kinney, Madsen, Fleming, & Haapala, 1977). Practitioners, not all of whom were trained clinicians, served small numbers of families at any one time and provided services for a maximum of 6 weeks.

Working from crisis resolution theory, the practitioners helped the family to alleviate the conditions that led to the seeming need for placement. Upon termination, practitioners left the family with the skills needed to prevent the conditions from recurring. Because of the aggressive marketing efforts of the program's developers, policy makers began to advocate for more such programs.

Process and Variations

The three types of in-home programs developed to date

- Case management. Services at this level of intensity are usually offered in conjunction with other mental health or social services and may continue after these services have been completed.
- Intensive case management. This type of treatment is typically offered to families for an indefinite period to help alleviate and/or prevent the appearance of those conditions that could lead to a referral for out-of-home placement.
- Time-limited crisis management. Often referred to as home-based crisis intervention, this type of treatment is designed to ameliorate the immediate conditions that have led to a child's referral either to a psychiatric emergency service for hospitalization or to a temporary shelter to await a foster home placement.

The section that follows will present the unique features and advantages of in-home treatment for children and families, regardless of program type.

SERVICES COMMON TO IN-HOME PROGRAMS

Case Management: Case management designates those services provided to individual children and their families. Such services include assessment, planning, linkage, monitoring, advocacy, and planned use of discretionary funds to assist in meeting needs of the child or the family to enhance the child's functioning. A functional analysis of case management services would reveal that the tasks involved include systems coordination; program and resource development; service coordination, crisis intervention, supportive outreach; basic necessities assurance; and advocacy.

Case management practice is guided by concern with service integration, continuity of care, individualized planning, and meeting the multiple needs of individuals. Effective case management requires the availability of a strong service system. If the community lacks essential services, case management programs will be ineffective.

Assessment: Assessment focuses both on the factors that interfere with the child's successful adjustment in the community and on developing a treatment plan to address these factors. Although practice is guided by knowledge of problems related to personality maladjustment—that is, the child's mood disturbances, thought distortions, value confusions, behavior problems, or any combination of these factors—the practitioner scrutinizes existing problems in the child's interactional and sociocultural systems, problems that may contribute more to the child's current difficulties than the level of individual psychopathology. Two children, both with similar levels of depression, might function quite differently in different environments. Assessment involves considering the family's communication, marital, parental, child-rearing, alienation, and societal problems.

In-home practice enhances assessment because it allows the practitioner to observe the family's natural environment, interaction regarding real problems, environmental resources, and home management skills. The in-home practitioner can learn firsthand about the geographic world of the family. He or she is likely to meet family, friends, and others and can discern their roles and potential as social supports. The practitioner learns about cultural values and beliefs, religious practices and rituals, home governance and leadership, spoken and unspoken family rules, and child-rearing practices. (For example, single-parent families often have to rely on routines that would be unacceptable in many two-parent families.) Home visits to blended and reconstituted families provide a wealth of information about coalitions and alliances within these clusters of unrelated children and their different extended families. Sometimes it's a family member's behavior or even the absence of a family member during an evening home visit that brings an issue to light.

An 11-year-old's highly sexualized behavior was a puzzle until the practitioner inquired about the aged grandfather, who lived in separate quarters and interacted minimally with the family. In examining these quarters the practitioner learned that the grandfather had a collection of pornographic magazines. Discussion with the parents revealed that grandfather's reading of this literature was a "family secret" that was not only tolerated but tacitly approved: "After all, he has no other outlets with Grandma dead, and he's a virile old guy." The family took a different view, however, after the practitioner explored this situation further and the patient revealed that grandfather had been secretly reading these magazines with him for some time.

In-home assessment allows the practitioner to determine the extent and influence of alcohol and substance abuse in the home. Denial of substance abuse is less likely, when the practitioner has opportunity to observe and to talk with both family and extended family members.

Because case managers can spend up to a full day with a family at any one time, the family can become comfortable enough to reveal family secrets quickly. This fact may significantly alter the intervention strategy developed by the treating facility.

Toward the end of a 6-hour observation and interview day, a mother confessed that she had moved to the area to avoid arrest in another state and that the fear of discovery significantly influenced her family life. Grandparents could not be visited, old friends could not be contacted, and new friends could not be trusted.

In-Home Intervention: When case management is a planned service response of an outpatient intervention strategy, then the case manager takes direction from the agency treatment team. Nevertheless, even if the case manager's role is to provide a concrete service, such as linking a parent to a support group, all case managers employ skills in relationship building and service contract management. Active listening, support, values clarification, and limited advice giving about child development and child management issues are techniques most practitioners employ.

If the practitioner is also trained to deliver direct treatment, in-home treatment has the advantage of increasing the likelihood that all family members will be involved and, most importantly, that the interventions will be tailored to the particular environmental or situational obstacles faced by that family.

In one three-generation, single-parent family, the grandparent was critical of her daughter's child-rearing practices. The practitioner observed, however, that the grandparent was no more skilled than the child's mother. The real problem lay in both "parents'" unfulfilled needs. The practitioner, who the family came to view as someone who really cared, was able to get these two parents to work together.

In-home treatment allows practitioners to engage hard-to-reach, isolated families. The willingness of practitioners to extend themselves beyond the usual practice sites can make a favorable impression on these families, many of whom experience real difficulties in getting to traditional clinic settings.

Once the needs of the child and the family have been assessed and interventions planned, some programs make extensive use of unrestricted dollars to supplement existing services. Funds can be used to enroll a child in a summer camp for disturbed children, employ a tutor, obtain a taxi to transport a child or a parent to an activity, take several children on outings to develop positive peer relations, provide periodic respite care to parents, or pay parent advocates to assist parents in dealing with public schools and other agencies involved with the child.

PROGRAMS PROVIDING MORE THAN CASE MANAGEMENT

Intensive Case Management: Intensive case management services are services provided by experienced clinicians to the family of a seriously disturbed child. The clinician typically carries a small caseload, perhaps ten clients, and the services the clinician provides include many of the same services provided by case managers: assessment, planning, linking, monitoring, advocacy, and allocation of funds to purchase special services. Unlike the case manager, however, the trained clinician who serves as an intensive case manager needs less supervision in the assessment process and provides direct treatment to the child and family. This treatment can include one of the verbal therapies—individual, family, or group—or behavior therapy or behavior modification techniques. The intensive case manager can also provide short-term respite, recreation, and social skill–building activities to patients and their families. Typically, the child and other family members who require intensive case management services are more disturbed than are the clients served by the case manager.

In-Home Crisis Services: In-home crisis services, most often referred to as home-based crisis intervention, are designed to prevent the immediate placement of a child outside the home. The targets of these intervention programs are youths who present at emergency rooms and who are thought to need hospital-level psychiatric care and those about to be removed from home and placed in foster care. Clinicians are on call 24 hours a day for 4 to 6 weeks for each family. Each clinician works with only two or three families at a time. If treatment is required beyond the 6-week maximum, the family is linked with other community programs, including case management services.

Studies suggest that children in home-based crisis intervention programs, as opposed to intensive case management programs, suffer more from anxiety and depression, with the majority appearing at emergency rooms for suicidal behaviors (Armstrong, Huz, & Evans, 1992). Nevertheless, many children also display aggressive behaviors. For example, a child may make a suicidal gesture following suspension from school for attacking another child or for holding a gun to another child's head.

Home-based crisis intervention programs are guided by several overriding principles. First, these programs were specifically designed to prevent removal from home, by providing services directly, at the point when removal is being recommended. This purpose contrasts with that of case management programs, which emphasize linking and coordinating ongoing services to prevent a possible placement. Although institutionalization is not avoided at any cost, clinicians in crisis-intervention programs are in a better position than the referral source to assess whether removal from the home is really needed. Because the patient-to-clinician ratio permits direct provision of most services, rather than the brokering of services, clinicians are more confident of their ability to divert the child's placement. Because each clinician takes the ultimate responsibility for the well-being of clients, with a "drop everything" attitude toward service delivery, a quick resolution of the crisis is expected.

The second principle that guides crisis-intervention programs is the belief that families make the best use of skills taught when the teaching happens within the "environment of need." Services delivered in surroundings chosen by the clients themselves are better received. Clinicians focus on training families to make use of techniques to prevent the emergence of crises and, perhaps more importantly, to do better with the management of unavoidable crises.

The third principle is emphasis on family advocacy. Family members are active participants in defining problems and setting goals. The primary unit of intervention is the whole family, not just the identified child. Clinicians concentrate their early intervention efforts on making each family member feel understood and communicating that the clinician will make every effort to help the family improve the quality of their intrafamily relationships. The clinician actively demonstrates this belief by the willingness to help the family deal with the practical problems of everyday life. No problem is considered too small or beneath the training of the clinician.

The fourth principle is that the patient's intrapsychic, learning, and personality problems are not precipitants of the crisis. Energy is directed at assessing problems in the patient's interactional and sociocultural systems to determine what prompted the perceived need for out-of-home placement.

The initial therapeutic techniques employed borrow heavily from general crisis management procedures developed to manage suicidal behavior and episodes of periodic dyscontrol (Linehan, 1981; Harbin, 1977). These crisis management techniques are

1. Active listening to each family member, with the goal that each family member's feelings and views will be understood by the clinician.
2. Communication of hope and optimism that the crisis can be resolved without hospitalization.
3. Provision of factual information about how the program operates if family and child want diversion.
4. Formulation of the present problem situation. (E.g., Bill, a teenager, responds to frustration by escalating his blaming of family members for his difficulties. Parental consequences follow. Bill refuses to comply and makes suicidal gestures.) Formulation of possible immediate responses to the problem. (Parents and sibling will ask Bill to call the clinician when Bill's blaming behavior escalates. Then they will leave the house.)
5. Prediction of the future consequences of various courses of action.
6. Working out a specific contract with the client, in which a course of action is agreed upon when feelings are aroused that could lead to the high-risk behaviors (e.g., frustration and anger).
7. Working out a contract with the family about courses of action to take if the client appears to exhibit behaviors that could weaken the resolve to keep the contract (e.g., open hostility followed by suicidal threats).
8. Helping the family to identify changes they feel are needed that will contribute to resolution of the child's problems. (E.g., Bill needs to develop more mature responses to frustration and, until he does, family members need to learn how to manage him when his blaming gets out of control and he vents hostility at all family members.)

9. Helping the family to identify goals related to changes they would like to achieve (e.g., Bill will manage his frustration without blaming others) and short-term objectives they think would help them to reach these goals (e.g., Bill will make a list of frustrating situations).
10. Getting the family committed to taking certain concrete actions immediately that will help them to reach the first objective. (Bill will identify a family member to help him make his list.)
11. Giving advice and concrete suggestions that will help the child or family perform the agreed-upon concrete actions.
12. Reemphasizing the 24-hour availability of help to meet concrete goals. (Bill will call the clinician when he feels his anger escalating in response to frustration.)

Once the initial reaction to the crisis has passed, clinicians help families to develop problem-solving and communication skills. Problem-solving techniques are applied to day-to-day problems that interfere with managing the identified patient. The problem-solving sequence includes the following components: (1) identifying and personalizing the problem from the perspective of each family member, (2) actively listening to one another, (3) considering strategies for coping with and solving the problem, (4) evaluating and weighing alternative solutions, (5) implementing the strategy, (6) evaluating the effect of the implemented strategy. Communication skills include the following components: (1) active listening, (2) active expression of positive feelings and praise for others; (3) stating expectations as positive, direct requests; (4) stating negative feelings in a rational, purposeful, and productive manner. Therapeutic work with the individual child relies heavily on cognitive-behavioral techniques. The child is helped to identify situations that led to the feelings that precipitated suicidal or aggressive behaviors and strategies are taught to help manage these feelings. Anger management is one of the skills taught to many youngsters.

In hospital diversion programs attached to child guidance clinics (which historically work with families), clinicians tend to follow up crisis management techniques with procedures developed by family therapists. The family is helped to focus attention on identifying the key factors that led to the child's regressed and symptomatic behavior.

Developmental Considerations

Since in-home treatment focuses primarily on developing individualized family and community supports designed to meet the unique needs of each family, neither the age nor developmental attainments of the identified child are a factor in selecting the modality for use. In-home services can be modified to meet the developmental needs of each client.

Qualifications of Practitioners

To provide case management services, agencies typically employ staff with a background in the social sciences and then provide extensive in-service education both prior and subsequent to working with clients. Those who provide intensive case management and home-based crisis intervention services are licensed mental health professionals whose background includes skill in the delivery of verbal therapies. Emergency room psychiatrists typically see hospitalization as the treatment of lesser risk. They are less anxious turning a patient over to the staff of a diversion program when staff members are well-trained clinicians. All practitioners of in-home treatments (regardless of academic preparation) are provided in-service training in active listening, behavioral contracting, crisis management, and anger management techniques for use by parents and children. Practitioners are taught to make extensive use of positive reframing techniques so that parents feel supported and not blamed for their child's difficulties.

Measures of Clinical Progress and Outcome

Because of the emphasis on the cost savings realized by reducing institutional placements, few agencies have utilized any standard measures to assess for treatment-related changes in either family or child functioning.

Reviews of evaluative studies indicate that, despite methodological weaknesses in many studies, home-based treatments prevent, delay, or reduce the length of placement of children and enhance the functioning of children and parents. Youths who avoided placement were those with less delinquent behaviors, those from accepting families, and those whose treatment plan significantly addressed the development of social supports.

Studies of children receiving intensive case management services reveal minor changes on measures of child symptomatology, and parents showed changes only in their acceptance of their child's difficulties. Parents showed no changes in their ability to manage their child's problematic behavior, and only one third of the families showed evidence of achieving objectives set for changes in their parenting behavior. Objectives that were met in many cases were those related to linking the child to community activities and keeping the child in school and in school-related activities. Over one third of children served were eventually placed in some out-of-home program (Huz, Evans, Rahn, & McNulty, 1993).

Evaluation of home-based crisis intervention programs based on the Homebuilders model indicates that over 90 percent of the at-risk children receiving services remained with their families or relatives at termination of services. In addition to avoidance of placement, improvements in child and family functioning were also noted (Pecora, Fraser, & Haapala, 1992).

Unfortunately, follow-up studies indicate that, within a year of termination of services, a significant number of cases are placed out of the home. This demonstrates the need for continuing high-quality substitute care and treatment programs for children from vulnerable families.

In-home services are less effective with children from neglectful families. Nearly twice as many children from neglectful families are placed during in-home intervention than are children from abusive families. These services are also less effective with youths who display a pattern of severe, long-standing and multiple emotional and behavioral problems with a prior history of previous placements. Such youths tend to reside in families where all children are scapegoated by overwhelmed parents who are in alliance against the children and where a tyrannical stepfather typically rules the household. The parents display "murky" and "unclear communications," and sexual abuse dominates both the family's and the youths' background as well as the present situation (Bath & Haapala, 1993; Werrbach, 1992).

Economic, Ethical, and Social Issues

Home-based interventions have been lauded because they are more cost-effective than out-of-home care and because they keep families together. Although the primary goal of in-home treatment is the prevention of placement, wholesale adoption of this outcome is unwarranted. Economic benefits, such as the cost savings of avoiding placement, should not be the only criterion used to evaluate a program's effectiveness. Advocates for in-home treatment should emphasize other outcomes that have been achieved. For example, family functioning may improve but that of the identified patient may not (Werrbach, 1992). Studies should also evaluate the effects of the removal of a child from home on both the family and the larger community. The removal of a child may have positive effects on some families; therefore, temporary or even long-term removal may be of benefit to a family.

Unfortunately, the type of child for whom in-home services are inappropriate tends to make minimal progress in hospital settings. Perhaps a therapeutic group home or long-term family-based residential treatment is more appropriate for children and families with long-standing histories of parental neglect, psychiatric difficulty, and substance abuse.

Conclusion: Future Directions

There is a need to refine existing models of in-home treatment for the more difficult and challenging family situations (Werrbach, 1992). One of the most significant challenges is changing drug- and alcohol-affected family systems. Creative ways must be found to bring substance abuse services directly into the family home or into community settings such as schools or work. Some combination of in-home and in-school services needs to be developed. Blended families also merit considerable attention, as do families marked by sexual abuse. Research efforts should be directed at utilizing current measures of family functioning to assess changes in the family system following intervention and at defining outcomes in terms broader than simple avoidance of placement, decreases in the number of placements, or in length of stay.

Overuse of any treatment modality distracts from that modality's effectiveness. The effects of in-home treatment should be compared with those of other possible treatments (this type of comparison is often referred to as systematic utilization review), and models of in-home treatments should be compared.

Home-based interventions clearly have a significant place in the continuum of services for emotionally disturbed children, but they should not be viewed as a panacea for all the problems of children or their families.

REFERENCES

Adams, P. (1994). Marketing social change: The case of family preservation. *Children and Youth Services Review, 16,* 417–432.

Armstrong, M. I., Huz, S., & Evans, M. E. (1992). What works for whom: The design and evaluation of children's mental health services. *Social Work Research and Abstracts, 28,* 35–41.

Bath, H. I., & Haapala, D. A. (1993). Intensive family preservation services with abused and neglected children: An examination of group differences. *Child Abuse and Neglect, 17,* 213–226.

Fahl, M. A., & Morrissey, D. (1979). The Mendota model: Home community treatment. In S. Maybanks & M. Bryce (Eds.), *Home based services for children and families: Policy, practice, and research.* Springfield, IL: Charles C Thomas.

Hancock, B. L., & Pelton, L. H. (1989). Home visits: History and functions. *Social Casework: The Journal of Contemporary Social Work, 70,* 21–27.

Harbin, H. T. (1977). Episodic dyscontrol and family dynamics. *American Journal of Psychiatry, 134,* 1113–1116.

Huz, S., Evans, M. E., Rahn, D. S., & McNulty, T. L. (1993). *Evaluation of intensive case management for children and youth: Third year final report.* New York: Bureau of Evaluation and Services Research, New York State Office of Mental Health, Albany.

Kinney, J., Haapala, D., & Booth. (1991). *Keeping families together: The homebuilders model.* New York: Aldine de Gruyter.

Kinney, J. M., Madsen, B., Fleming, T., & Haapala, D. S. (1977). Homebuilders: Keeping families together. *Journal of Consulting and Clinical Psychology, 45,* 667–673.

Linehan, M. M. (1981). A social-behavioral analysis of suicide and parasuicide: Implications for clinical assessment and treatment. In H. G. Glazer & J. F. Clarkin (Eds.), *Depression: Behavioral and directive intervention strategies* (pp. 229–294). New York: Garland Publishing.

Pecora, P. J., Fraser, M. W., & Haapala, D. A. (1992). Intensive home-based family preservation services: An update from the FIT Project. *Child Welfare, 71,* 177–188.

Stroul, B. A. (1988). *Series on community based services for children and adolescents who are severely emotionally disturbed, Volume 1: Home-based services.* Washington, DC: CASSP Technical Assistance Center, Georgetown University Child Development Center.

Werrbach, G. B. (1992). A study of home-based services for families of adolescents. *Child and Adolescent Social Work Journal, 9,* 505–523.

---

40 / Respite Care Services for Families

Mayu P. B. Gonzales and Vincent J. Fontana

Respite care services provide temporary child care to families with disabled, chronically or terminally ill children, or children who are at risk for abuse or neglect. The goal of such intervention is to relieve families from their caregiving responsibilities, thereby sustaining their efforts at maintaining family integrity and preventing out-of-home placement.

In the United States, respite care services emerged in the 1960s as previously institutionalized individuals were returned to their families and communities. The philosophy of providing better care for the severely disabled in their own environment is based on the theory of normalization. Overtime, the theory caused dramatic shifts in intervention from institution to both community and home-based services. Poor and abusive treatment of children in some institutions and the high costs of institutional care encouraged the movement further. The practice of returning institutionalized children to their families and communities is called deinstitutionalization.

The Theory of Normalization

The theory that children with disabilities "normalize"—that is, establish and maintain more culturally normative behaviors and achieve more normal functioning by living at home in as regular circumstances as possible—implies that the youngsters will encounter the "normal" ways and rhythms of families and society in general. Normalization grew out of a view that the developmentally disabled youngster is a human being with feelings and a potential for growth and is entitled to the same rights as other young people. Normalization and institutionalization were incompatible. As severely disabled and chronically ill children returned home, the burden of child care on the families, particularly the mothers, increased significantly. In this environment respite care became essential and emerged as one of the most basic components in the continuum of family support services.

Several judicial decisions supporting the disabled and their families allowed deinstitutionalization to continue. These laws reinforced the obligation of each state to all its citizens. Amendments to the Social Security Act contributed greatly to establishing funds for a wide range of services to a broad population of disabled and at-risk children and adults unable to protect their own interests. The Rehabilitation Act of 1973 provided protection against discrimination of the handicapped in any federally funded program. PL 94–142, The Education for All Handicapped Children Act of 1975, mandated education regardless of severity of disability. In 1986 the U.S. Congress passed the Temporary Child Care for Children with Disabilities and Crisis Nurseries Act, which established federal funding for crisis nursery and respite care demonstration projects. A crisis nursery is a respite programs established to prevent child abuse and/or neglect. Generally, respite care programs are incorporated within a larger system of care in the community or state, thereby forming a natural collaborative network among the various disciplines.

Most societies have organized family and community support services that are legislated and regulated by governmental agencies. In some countries, respite care services are provided informally, through familial and community networks with minimal state involvement.

The theoretical basis for understanding normative stressors in families and family developmental stages is well documented and covered in the chapters on family treatment. These chapters provide the background needed to appreciate adaptation and coping mechanisms in families that are burdened by the disability of a member or other psychosocial stressors.

Stress in families is caused by multiple factors and can be viewed as the product of an interaction among personal, familial, and community variables. Poverty and other socioeconomic factors are important stressors. The structural and functional adaptations required to maintain family stability can be compromised under stress. Parents who lack adequate coping strategies because of poor integration, organization, low frustration tolerance, and social isolation probably have poor adaptive responses. These can be taxed by a handicapped or even a nonhandicapped child. In families with chaotic relationship patterns and poor delineation of roles, the demands of parenting may put children at risk for abuse and neglect. Other factors that contribute to parental stress include family size (a large family increases the demands on parental time, energy, and finances); single parenthood with diminished emotional and financial supports; and nonexistent family ties or social isolation. Purely external environmental factors that cause a need for formal respite are uncommon but do occur during situational emergencies. Such emergencies are job relocation, sudden death of a spouse, hospitalization or imprisonment of a parent, and similar disruptive circumstances.

The primary objective of respite care is to support the integrity of the family by reducing familial and environmental stress. This can be achieved by various patterns of caregiving. The goal of relieving families from their caregiving responsibilities is accomplished by providing child care. Families can be emotionally or physically exhausted by the demands of child rearing. Respite care may be required by families who have children with mental retardation; developmental disability; emotional, behavioral, or learning disorder; traumatic brain injury; chronic or terminal illness; or other handicapping condition. The awesome responsibility of rearing a disabled or troubled child can leave parents depressed and anxious. Feelings of guilt, shame, and failure and the resort to blaming behavior may accentuate tension between parents, diminishing parental effectiveness. This affects both the family as a whole and individual family members. A lack of familial and social supports can lead to child or spousal abuse, marital discord, substance abuse, loss of employment, truancy, delinquency, psychiatric disorders, and other difficulties. The result is further compromised functional adaptation.

In addition to providing child care, respite care services serve a primary preventive function by promoting mental health. Respite care services reinforce the family's strengths by decreasing the members' isolation, improving their ability to cope with other responsibilities, and providing them opportunities to enjoy leisure activities.

Variations of Respite Care Services

Long before formal respite care programs became available, volunteers provided informal respite to families of the developmentally disabled. This respite came in the form of friends, neighbors, and relatives. More organized volunteer programs developed under the sponsorship of communities, churches, or other organizations.

An innovative concept developed by United Cerebral Palsy Associations, Inc., is an expansion of volunteerism whereby the private sector and respite care programs form a partnership. The partnership requires a business establishment—such as a hotel, entertainment, or recreational facility—to provide a family with lodging, food, or recreational activities while a respite program provides respite care.

The definition of *respite* as temporary, intermittent child care to relieve families reflects a shift from child-centered to family-centered service provision. There are many variations in the scope, time period, nature, and purpose of these services. The nature of the service and its duration are dictated by client needs and financial considerations in conjunction with other family supports. Service can be provided in an emergency or on a regular, planned basis. The most basic distinction between these variations is whether the service is delivered in the family home or out of the home.

IN-HOME RESPITE SERVICES

These services are provided by individuals who come to the family's home. Caregivers for in-home services may be provided by:

- Homemaker services. Provided by a trained homemaker and available through a home health agency.
- Sitter or companion services. Offer respite in the same manner as homemaker services, with the distinction that a specific caregiver is matched with a family or a child to provide continuity of care. Such a relationship, allows continued implementation of training and goals during respite.
- Parent-trained services. Utilize individuals from the family's own support network. These may include friends, relatives, or neighbors who are recruited and trained to provide respite. In this model, parents participate in all aspects of training and recruitment, allowing them to share specific information and strategies that may be helpful to them and their children.

OUT-OF-HOME RESPITE SERVICES

These services are provided in home or facility outside the family home. Some models of out-of-home respite can serve more than one individual at a time; others provide congregate care. Out-of-home respite services include

- Family care service. A model where beds in the homes of licensed family care providers are allocated for the purpose of respite.
- Parent cooperative service. A variation in which families agree to care for each others' dependent member reciprocally, in their own homes.
- Respite provider home services. Rendered in the private, nonlicensed home of the person providing the respite.
- Day drop off. Uses space in the community to provide respite. The space may be in a community center, school, church, temple, shelter, treatment program, or any other community space. In this model, care is usually provided during particular hours on a regular basis, such as after school, during evenings, or on weekends.
- Intermediate care facility or a community residence. Provides respite care for a day, overnight, or on an extended basis. These facilities are usually for the develop mentally disabled.
- Institutional care services. Provide respite on an emergency basis or as a regular program of an institution. Some state institutions or developmental centers have allocated an area or a number of beds for respite care services.
- Respite residence. Provides residential services for respite care. These state-licensed residences offer services 24 hours per day throughout the year. The residential model frequently offers a variety of family support–related programs, such as placement, substance abuse prevention and treatment, and parent education.

Secondary sources of respite provide caregiving relief to families, but their main goal is other than caregiving. It may be education, rehabilitation, or recreation and may be a part of a school, vocational, or treatment program.

Advantages and Disadvantages of Various Models

The various models of respite present distinct advantages and disadvantages that need to be considered in matching family needs to respite care services. Any good program involved in providing respite care has a process of recruitment, selection, training, supervision, and ongoing support to ensure the effectiveness of the caregiver in providing respite. In-home respite services provide minimal disruption to a child and family. But, such a service may be inappropriate for children with specialized medical or behavioral needs, or children who can benefit from increased socialization with peers. These children may be particularly appropriate for center- or facility-based programs. Other factors to take into consideration include the level of training and supervision required of caregivers, the frequency and predictability of the need for respite, and the costs.

To address some of the issues of diverse needs, level of training necessary for caregiver, and economic feasibility, respite care programs have been developed to provide services to a specific population for specific circumstances or functional capacity. Crisis nursery programs provide respite for children up to 12 years old who are at risk or who have experienced abuse or neglect. Programs may provide services to a particular age group (infancy, preschool, school age, or adolescence) or to those with a particular disability or illness (e.g., HIV-related conditions, autism, mental retardation, or medical fragility). This specialization requires that staff be highly trained in a limited area rather than versatile and ready to meet varying needs of different clients.

Standards of Care

The qualifications cited most frequently by parents as being essential for caregivers are patience, understanding, dependability, special training, and experience. An adequate supply of qualified, well-trained, and nonjudgmental caregivers is an important determinant in the success of a respite care program and will profoundly influence a family's decision to use respite as an alternative to institutionalization or other out-of-home placement.

Training can be given through in-service workshops focused on providing general information. Workshops can increase the trainees' knowledge base, improve attitudes toward family needs and demands, and teach general and advanced child care skills.

The various skill areas can be assigned to one of three categories:

- Preparation. Prior to entering the family system caregivers must gather adequate information and interact to appropriately maintain the relationship that exists between the child and family members.
- Ongoing competency. Caregivers must manage the child physically, behaviorally, and medically in a manner appropriate to the disability or risk situation.
- Crisis competency. Caregivers must know how to manage crises and emergencies.

Beyond providing physical care in the form of feeding, toileting, and bathing, caregiving skills include a variety of interactions that require attunement, empathy, and responsiveness. These enable caregivers to provide a safe environment for the children and a supportive, nonpunitive resource for the parents. Such skills are applicable to the variety of situations and conditions that require respite.

If respite care services are regulated, respite caregivers may require certification. In such situations a standard process of certification and training protocol is required. Without certification quality assurance and monitoring are left to the agency, program, or family that arranges the respite services. If care is given through an agency outside the family home, the site—be it a family care home, day care, foster care, residence, or respite care program—may require licensure. License requirements vary, depending on the level of care. They mandate adherence to health and safety codes and specify the qualifications and training of caregivers.

Interaction with Other Service Providers

The continuum of family support services includes case management or service coordination, financial subsidy, legal assistance and advocacy, housing, home management training, behavior management training, information about and referral to medical or dental care, parenting education, support groups, and counseling. Interaction with these services is generally indicated to meet the needs of families that require respite. Collaboration between the pediatrician, psychiatrist, psychologist, special educator, developmental specialist, social worker, caregiver, and parent is essential because prescriptions for medical and auxiliary services may be part of the goals during respite. Auxiliary services may include speech, movement, and occupational therapy. Family support services help families sustain their efforts in keeping their children home, providing a quality of life that is otherwise not possible without some supports.

Despite the existence and use of respite care as part of the continuum of family support services, there are times when families appear to lack the recuperative power to integrate. This may happen when the cumulative effects of life stressors drain the family and produce chronic unresolved conflicts. In such situations active follow-up and coordinated services may promote the family's recovery from the crisis. It may also serve as a transition to a higher level of in-home care or for long-term intervention outside the home.

Funding

In the United States, despite the deinstitutionalization movement and the economic imperatives of institutional care (institutional care costs 7 to 10 times more than care in the natural family), fiscal and legal systems have lagged in actively supporting in-home care. A large proportion of the funds available for the care of the once-institutionalized population is still earmarked for the vast improvement of institutional care; only a small portion is allocated for residential services within the community. In view of the lack of funding, priority is given to those who cannot remain with their families. Such funding and spending priorities prove to be a disincentive to families who want to keep a family member at home. The families are in a bind, being told that children do not belong in institutions but not being given the resources to keep them out of institutions.

The responses to legislative initiatives over the past decade have been uneven. In some states a variety of family support services, including respite care, are available. In others, respite care programs charge families a sliding fee that may be reimbursable through private insurance or a public entitlement program. Cash vouchers or service subsidies to reduce the financial burdens on families are available in some states. The idea of tax credits or deductions for respite care and other in-home services for the severely disabled has gained support in others. A sliding-fee schedule is in place in many respite programs. The fee schedule may be based on a person's care level, from light to heavy in physical/medical and behavioral/psychological areas, and or the family's ability to pay.

Conclusion

Although research in respite care is limited, there is evidence of the necessity of respite care services in the community. Respite is used most often by extremely needy families in which the burden of child care is heavy and the familial support system is weak. It plays an important role in reducing family stress, maintaining and improving the mental health of parents, stabilizing the family, preventing psychiatric disorder or its escalation, and reducing the likelihood of long-term out-of-home placement. The amount and array of respite alternatives are important variables in measuring respite care effectiveness in improving family functioning. Studies in the form of surveys show that families prefer in-home services to out-of-home services but report a definite need for out-of-home care. Ongoing studies and research need to provide convincing evidence of the positive impact of respite care on family functioning and as an effective investment of limited funds.

Respite care service was originally designed for families of the developmentally disabled. It has proven to have great potential in preventing family breakdown in a number of other situations involving long-term stress. These situations involve the frail elderly, the chronically or terminally ill, and the mentally ill. Families with a potential for abuse, compose a population for which respite care is critical. Respite care for children at risk for neglect or abuse is a service of value. A policy of providing integrated and coordinated community respite care services to support families is clearly indicated. Hopefully, societal concerns about family stability, its preservation, and the provision of family support services will keep respite care in the policy agenda of public and private agencies at all levels.

REFERENCES

ARCH National Resource Center for Crisis Nurseries and Respite Care Services. (1933). General information about respite care. *Child Welfare Report, 1* (1), 1–4.

ARCH National Resource Center for Crisis Nurseries and Respite Care Services. (1994). General information about crisis nursery care. *Child Welfare Report, 2* (3), 1–3.

Cohen, S., & Warren, R. D. (1985). *Respite care: Principles, programs & policies.* Austin, TX: Pro. Ed., Inc.

Salibury, C. L., & Intaglia, J. (1986). *Respite care: Support for persons with developmental disabilities and their families.* Baltimore, MD: Paul H. Brookes.

41 / Therapeutic Foster Placement

Mario I. Rendon

Introduction

In the United States *foster care* has a generic meaning that includes, besides placement with a family, other forms of congregate care and specialized placements. In its more specific sense, however, *foster care* means planned temporary placement, of a child, with a family other than that of origin (usually through social services agencies) to improve the child's quality of life and provide the child's family with support toward the goal of reunification. If reunification is impossible, the usual goal is termination of parental rights, with continued foster care, adoption, or independent living—the "resolution" depends, among other things, on the child's age.

Therapeutic foster care—also called foster family–based treatment and specialized foster care—is a treatment approach that combines family-based care with the gamut of specialized treatment interventions. These are provided through specialized foster family training, individualized planning, coordination of services with community resources, therapeutic teamwork, close monitoring through clinical supervision, and appropriate discharge planning. It is the least restrictive of the residential placements, and it is a relatively new treatment modality that has gradually evolved and is indicated for the treatment of severely emotionally disturbed children and adolescents.

Background, Epistemology, and Conceptual Framework

Therapeutic foster care has developed as a result of the rights movement that advocates the least restrictive setting possible in the treatment of special populations, of the development of behavioral and social learning theories and techniques, of the development of family and systems theories and techniques, and of postmodern philosophical currents that promote cultural understanding. The political and legislative actions that resulted from these trends have also played a role in the growth of therapeutic foster care.

In preindustrial societies child placement was a response to orphanhood, poverty, or the need for labor; the child was often seen as a small adult. In England placement was institutionalized in the 14th and 15th centuries by poor laws enacted to suppress vagrancy and begging. Almshouses for persons of all ages were gradually replaced by orphanages specifically for children. It is only during the present century that social reform and the development of child welfare and psychiatry led to different types of institutions for children with special needs. Hospitalism and other ill effects of institutionalization led to a search for alternatives.

The Residential Treatment Center was a product of the 1940s, when the number of orphan children decreased and there was a dramatic increase of children with absent fathers. Therapeutic foster care came into existence in the 1950s, at the same time that the National Association for Retarded Children started its drive toward integration of exceptional persons into the community. In the 1960s, federal payments to families with dependent children were extended to foster care, and the number of these children grew to a peak of over half a million in the 1970s. By 1980 child welfare agencies were mandated to develop permanency plans. External citizen and judicial review were created to monitor, among other things, excessive lengths of stay in foster care.

Most children with serious emotional disturbance were receiving little or no treatment, however, and many were receiving inappropriately restrictive care because of lack of community-based services (Knitzer, 1982). In 1984 the Child and Adolescent Service System Program (CASSP) from the National Institute of Mental Health was instituted and has since contributed to develop systems of care. In 1990 the Robert Wood Johnson Foundation awarded grants to eight state-community partnerships to develop systems of care for mentally ill children and adolescents. Therapeutic foster care is fashioned on this model (Stroul, 1989).

The community psychiatry and deinstitutionalization movements reflected in the Community Mental Health Centers Construction Act of 1963 are essential ingredients in the evolution of foster care. Mainstreaming exceptional children in public schools was a similar development reflected in Public Law 94–142, the Education for All Handicapped Children Act. In regard to child welfare, a federal court ruling in the case of *Gary* vs. *The Louisiana Department of Health and Human Resources* in 1974 applied the principle of least restrictive setting to the placement of handicapped children.

The first therapeutic foster care programs were transitional or supplemental to residential treatment centers. In the late '60s their transformation into the modern therapeutic foster care home took place. An outgrowth of behavior modification theory, Achievement Place, was an educational family model that proved to be an important factor in spearheading the new treatment modality. By 1977 the first National Teaching Family Association was founded, a welcomed source of technical support. Differentiation from traditional foster care grew as the roles of both foster parents and caseworkers were redefined. During the 1980s many new programs appeared, and the self-definition of this therapeutic approach was achieved.

The passage of the Community Mental Health Centers Act represented a significant shift in the philosophy of the delivery of mental health services. The essence of this shift was the inclusion of communities in the planning and delivery of services and the participation of patients in their treatment planning. The new epistemology gave the patient the status of partner in the planning of his or her care. This important modification shifted to the postmodern trend of sharing culturally divergent definitions of reality. It often called for a consensus among parties from quite diverse socioeconomic, ethnic, ideologic, and cultural backgrounds.

Process and Variations

The principle that a family environment is the most therapeutic milieu possible is the core belief in therapeutic foster care. If separation from the natural family is essential, the next-best atmosphere is the one most similar to the family of origin. Besides family living, therapeutic foster family homes provide a range of specialized services that in the past were only obtained through institutionalization in hospitals or residential treatment facilities.

No monolithic approach exists in therapeutic foster care. Some programs are designed along behavioral theory principles; others are psychodynamically oriented. Family systems theory offers a solid foundation that is embraced by most programs, although in differing degrees. Some programs have a highly specific orientation and others are eclectic. The programs designed according to behavioral models have the advantage that clearer protocols for dealing with specific behaviors have been developed. Family systems–based approaches, on the other hand, provide excellent tools to facilitate interactions between the two families involved—that of origin and that of placement—as well as with the agencies and larger institutional systems that are necessarily part of this type of intervention.

A clear emphasis is on continuity of care. For the most part, a child remains with the foster family regardless of type of problem. In contrast to institutionalization, this is a treatment modality that facilitates behavioral generalization. The failure of prior institutionalization models in this regard is reflected in the high number of homeless persons with histories of placement during childhood. Essential family-based learning was lost for this population. Consequently, the foster parents are the primary therapists in this model and their attitude, knowledge, and skills become the central therapeutic issue of quality of care.

The administrators of foster care programs follow a series of steps from recruitment to ongoing program maintenance to ensure a continued blend of highly competent and motivated professional foster parents. These steps are recruitment, pretraining, monitoring and supervision, in-service training, institution of support measures, empowerment and professionalization, and appropriate remuneration. The techniques of foster parent recruitment have become more and more sophisticated, and they include creative use of relevant local media, presentations at community organizations, brochures, posters, mailings, booths at fairs and malls, finder's fees for professional parents and agency staff, etc. A very simple and effective recruitment method has been—and continues to be—word of mouth from existing foster parents.

Foster parents with fulfillment needs—such as personal frustrations, rescue fantasies, or excessive mothering needs—and those seeking to obtain peers for their children are less successful than those with a clear job-oriented motivation. When such motivation exists, it is very important that both members of the therapeutic couple share it and that they both participate in foster care activities, particularly training. Other considerations are foster parents' confidence, types of discipline applied to their own children, beliefs about child rearing and children's disabilities, and awareness of personal responsibility in children's behavior. Additionally, foster family size and composition, ages of all members; and socioeconomic, ethnic, and cultural backgrounds are factors in the match between foster family and placed children (Stroul, 1989).

Agencies vary widely in regard to the types of screening procedures used. Procedures range from family interviews, observation of parent-child interactions, and letters of reference, to specific instrument-driven assessments of motivation, attitudes, personality, knowledge, and prior experience with disabling conditions or foster placement. Of course selectivity depends heavily on the size of the applicant pools.

Training varies in intensity, breadth and the sponsoring agency's philosophy. The administrators of some agencies, for example, believe that the environment of a basically sound family unit, along with the appropriate attitude, is the essential therapeutic ingredient. Other administrators place great emphasis on various forms of knowledge and skills. Areas of knowledge range from child development and behavior modification principles to psychopathology and the understanding of family and other encompassing social systems. Obviously, the understanding of the most common problems leading to placement and a grasp of their management are important for the prospective parents. In addition, they should be provided with anticipatory guidance about predictable crises and complications, such as legal issues and self-protection. A frequent focus of training is behavior modification, with some agencies implementing a wide range of techniques that extend from point systems and full token economies to quite sophisticated individualized behavioral contingency plans. Finally, a basic understanding of the theory and principles of the family and systems approach is quite useful not only for foster families, but also for the clinician team, supervisory staff, administrators of child welfare agencies, family judges, educators, and others. One such type of program philosophy is described by P. Minuchin (1995), and a training manual based on it has been developed by her group (Minuchin et al., 1990). Parental skills training manuals have also been developed (Bryant et al., 1986) and a host of other educational materials, including audiovisuals, are presently available to agencies for training purposes (National Resource Center on Family Based Services, 1995).

Careful and continued monitoring of therapeutic services, as well as continuous in-service training and support for therapeutic foster parents, are essential. These are either provided or coordinated by the immediate supervisor of the foster parents, who is usually a social worker with access to the other professionals in the multidisciplinary team. The social worker is available most of the time for emergencies and consultations, and he or she visits the home frequently. Besides in-service training, supervision, and on-call availability, the foster parents must be provided with other sources of support in order to avoid burnout. These are, for example networking opportunities, workshops, recreational activities, and respite placement services geared to foster parent holidays. Some programs have created small networks of couples fashioned after the extended family model. These supports are essential to the morale and enthusiasm of those who implement this most challenging therapeutic modality. Careful criteria-based recruitment, intensive training, and salary enhancements all contribute to the professional status of the therapeutic foster parents. Some programs have even granted therapeutic foster parents the status of municipal employees.

In spite of all efforts, placement at times cannot be continued as planned. Some of the reasons are

the specific problem behaviors of the child, which prompt the family to request removal; discovery by new licensed parents that they do not want to continue being foster parents; problems of discord in the foster home; and sustained requests for replacement by the child (Meadocroft & Trout, 1990). In this regard, ongoing treatment parent evaluation and support are important components in the maintenance of a program.

Few agencies place more than one or two children per therapeutic family. These families often have their own children. Some of the children placed in therapeutic foster homes are not expected to go back to their natural parents; in such instances forming a stable emotional bond in the new home is essential. In these cases successful adjustment to independent living becomes the final goal. Services are increasingly individualized as the quality of the foster program improves. Unless clearly contraindicated, therapeutic inclusion of families of origin as well as maximization of participation with them are part of the therapeutic plan.

Referral requirements include detailed information about the need for placement, history and family history, psychological and psychiatric assessments, testing, school records, etc. A team or committee reviews this information. If the child is considered eligible, the crucial process of child-family matching ensues. Final outcome is often contingent on this important variable, and it is during this step that the skill of the program staff is put to a test. The team must carefully consider the child's problem as well as characteristics of the family of origin and foster family. The geographic distance between family of origin and foster family may be an important factor, depending on if the placement is considered permanent. The treatment family's composition, cultural preferences, and religious orientation must be taken into consideration in the matching process. Prospective families fitting the particular characteristics are sorted, and the top-ranking treatment family selected. They may be given information first or allowed to observe the child in a videotape or through a one-way mirror to avoid labeling bias. An initial contact may then follow, either as a home visit or as a meeting in a neutral place. Short stays may be the next step. The child and family of origin are allowed to participate in varying degrees as clinically indicated. Once there is reasonable assurance of a proper child-family fit, placement takes place.

As in any other therapeutic modality, intervention starts with assessment and planning. Any missing assessment needs are the early focus; all strategic questions must be answered. An individualized intervention strategy plan is then developed. This becomes the foundation of the therapeutic process. The plan clearly identifies assets, problems, measurable long- and short-term goals, and discrete methods of addressing the issues singled out for intervention. These plans are comprehensive and include activities within and outside the family. Expectations are defined and include rules about behavior on visits with natural families, at school, in the neighborhood, etc. As in any therapeutic milieu, home activities may include participation in specific family functions and schedules, behavior modification protocols, and strategies designed to eliminate problem behaviors and reinforce desired ones. Although in principle parents implement most of the therapeutic plans, it is possible that the foster children may be involved in additional individual, group, or family therapy either with professional team members or by contract with professionals from the community. Agency or contractual staff may be assigned to provide therapeutic interventions at the home on a full- or part-time basis. Treatment plans are evaluated periodically by a team, and they are considered a contract with the youngster and his or her family. In some models, the therapeutic family is trained for and expected to provide some degree of education or treatment interventions for the family of origin; in others, professional staff provides most of these services, from counseling and casework to education and sharing in the therapeutic process. At times special liaison with schools or other agencies may be undertaken by education specialists or other specially designated personnel. Crises are frequent as could be expected in these therapeutic arrangements. They vary from minor disciplinary violations to dangerous behaviors to accusations of abuse. In this area education and anticipatory guidance are of paramount importance, and most agencies provide around-the-clock on-call staff for consultation and intervention. The frequency of crisis is one of the reasons therapeutic families need respite periods. These may be provided by child visits to family of origin, respite visits with currently unassigned therapeutic families, or specialized respite homes. Summer programs, recreational holiday programs, etc. are all part of therapeutic planning, and they also provide needed support and respite to the therapeutic parents. How much therapeutic parents undertake and how much is provided by agency or community personnel in terms of ancillary services varies. Duties can be negotiated as the parents become more skilled. There is a great deal of flexibility according to agency, parent, and community characteristics.

Developmental Considerations

Of course age is an overarching consideration in terms of placement planning. Children have been placed in therapeutic foster homes from birth to late adolescence. In infants and younger children, temperament and quality of bonding are of paramount clinical importance, as are genetic and perinatal vulnerabilities and appropriateness of stimulation. Separation and individuation issues become extremely important later and through early childhood. Socialization, school, cognitive, and learning issues become more important as the child grows. During preadolescence and adolescence maturation, quality of peer relations, and moral development are areas that need special attention. Regardless of level of psychopathology, quality of object relations and family loyalty are fundamental issues.

Multiple levels of readiness for placement occur according to the child's development. These are of course mirrored by the family of origin and come to resonate in the foster family and reverberate throughout the entire system. During the early phases of the AIDS epidemic, there was a resurgence of hospitalism—that is, abandoning infants by leaving them at hospitals. Therapeutic foster care was of particular usefulness for many of these children (Rendon, Gurdin, Bassi, & Weston, 1989; Gurdin & Anderson, 1987).

Although foster parents may accept very young children more easily than they would older children, the very young often have special silent needs in the areas of bonding. As a child grows older, the child and natural parents work out emotional and behavioral sequences and accommodations that become entrenched. He or she becomes less adaptable in a sense, so a good initial fit with a foster family becomes more and more important the older the child becomes. In summary, age-related developmental tasks and deficits must be considered in assessment and planning, and foster parents must be trained to address the tasks and deficits.

Independent of age, severity of psychopathology and level of disruption of the family of origin are important factors in the success of the placement and prognosis. Recent media-publicized family reunification court battles illustrate the clinical and ethical complexities involved in this type of care. Clinical assessments and ethics must drive the development of realistic goals and objectives for the child.

Goals and Objectives

From a clinical point of view, the methodology for setting goals and objectives in therapeutic foster placement does not differ from that in other settings. It must be focused, problem-oriented, and measurable. This facilitates ongoing evaluation and changes in therapeutic direction. It also allows for continuous quality control and improvement, and ultimately contributes positively to the final outcome.

From the vantage point of placement, two long-term goals are predominant, offer the necessary context for clinical goals and objectives, and are closely related to integrity of family of origin and to age. The first goal is family reunification, provided that the severity of family distress or psychopathology does not preclude a good prognosis. When reunification is the goal, length of stay tends to be shorter. In a systems model, both child and family of origin must receive all possible therapeutic interventions in support of family preservation. However, often this is not possible. In this case separation—through continued foster care, adoption, or eventual independent living—becomes the ultimate goal. (Obviously, the child's age is an important factor.) The therapeutic interventions depend on the goals.

In some instances long-term therapeutic foster care is a goal in itself because some children are difficult to adopt or because of chronological or developmental reasons. These children have a long road ahead toward independent living. Characteristically, many therapeutic foster parents are willing to make this difficult commitment.

Interaction with Other Interventions

Therapeutic foster care is actively used with all other forms of therapy. Referrals usually come from local and state child welfare agencies, hospitals, residential treatment centers, and the courts. During placement children often require any form of intervention—from hospitalization to an array of biological treatments, from special behavioral treatments to family therapy or individual psychotherapy. Prevention, assessment, early identification, emergency services, crisis intervention, outpatient treatment, day treatment, vocational and rehabilitation therapies, special education, and focused time-limited interventions are all part of the armamentarium for an individualized treatment. Children may also need therapeutic group homes, therapeutic camp, residential treatment centers or facilities, inpatient services, or independent living. They may also need many specialized services, including mental retardation or developmental disabilities follow-up, probationary and court hearings, psychiatric evaluations, special education, etc. Foster care agencies obtain these through a wide range of networking arrangements or contracts with other agencies or professionals. In fact, the essence of therapeutic foster care is the integration of services in the least restrictive fashion possible, considering quality of services and cost-effectiveness. Throughout, family conservation remains a clear priority.

Qualifications of the Clinician

Therapeutic foster care is essentially a team effort. Its success requires that the clinician empower, through education, the most logical agent to provide therapeutic interventions directly. Representatives of the traditional disciplines come into the team with various areas of expertise, but the points of convergence are the therapeutic foster parents and their immediate supervisor, the caseworker or social worker. The child psychiatrist must not only be well versed in diagnosis and psychopharmacology, but also in systems theory, family therapy, psychodynamics, and developmental and behavior modification theories. An in-depth knowledge of the child welfare and foster care fields is necessary. Cultural sensitivity and competence are a must for all clinicians and some degree of familiarity with postmodern epistemology is desirable because it can guide the negotiation of seemingly disparate cultural values (Murphy & Callaghan, 1989).

Indications

Children in therapeutic foster care bring with them a wide range of diagnoses in the categories of cognitive, emotional, and behavioral problems. It is perhaps severity rather than diagnosis that is the common denominator. Prereferral problems may be incorrigibility, problems with peers, dependency, poor self-esteem, depression, withdrawal, destruction of property, medical problems, use of drugs, enuresis, encopresis, hallucinations, delusions, mood swings, hyperactivity, autism, running away, truancy, school problems, suicide attempts, self-destructiveness, gender and sexual problems, tantrums, aggressiveness, dishonest behavior, and mental retardation (Meadocroft & Trout, 1990). In one study the presenting problems were conduct problems in 79 percent of cases, with a history of abuse and neglect in 70 percent and of incest in 15 percent. In the same study all except two of seventy-one children had one or more *DSM-III* Axis I disorders and one third had two or more psychiatric disorders. Conduct disorder was the diagnosis in 46 percent of the cases, anxiety disorder in 20 percent (particularly in children under age 5). Other diagnoses were adjustment disorder, attention deficit disorder, oppositional disorder, major depressive disorder, pervasive developmental disorder, and organic personality disorder. Eighteen percent had severe to borderline mental retardation; 14 percent suffered from enuresis or encopresis. Specific developmental disorders in this sample were

present in twenty-five of the seventy-one children. A range of associated medical conditions was present. In a subsample considered representative of the whole group and studied in depth, all children had had psychosocial stressors during the year prior to admission (Fine, 1993). Conduct disorder and dual diagnosis were the most frequent problems in the group studied by Chamberlain (1994). Other disorders represented in Chamberlain's group were borderline personality, posttraumatic stress disorder, alcohol dependency, schizophrenia, and dysthymic disorders.

The ability to serve children is related to agency philosophy and the professional quality of foster parents as well as to the specific diagnosis and severity of the children's problems. Since one of the main purposes of this modality is to avoid institutionalization, children who used to be considered in need of such treatment are candidates for therapeutic foster care. Many of these children were in the past placed out of state. In the foster care lingo, these children have been often grouped as exceptional, classified, or handicapped. Many of the children that have been placed in therapeutic foster care have a history of previous psychiatric or residential institutionalization or of regular foster care, and some have been rejected by more restrictive programs as unmanageable. A high proportion carried dual diagnoses. Many children have a history of physical and/or sexual abuse. Children with mental retardation, conduct or emotional disorders, psychosis, or histories of deliquency are candidates for this approach when their family may be thought to be absent, noxious, or in need of a therapeutic respite period.

Regarding families of origin, parents' problems may include marital discord; alcohol and substance abuse; psychiatric history; criminal history; unemployment; child abuse, neglect, or abandonment; or death (Meadocroft & Trout, 1990). Children with complicated health care needs, those with multiple disabling conditions, and teenage mothers or those with severe conduct disorders are candidates for therapeutic foster care. The major advantage of therapeutic foster care is its potential for providing service that is tailored to the specific needs of the particular child, family, and foster family. Therapeutic parents' attitudes, knowledge, and skills vary widely in regard to children's and families' sociocultural and developmental characteristics or psychopathology.

Contraindications and Risks

There are no contraindications to therapeutic foster care, except when a less restrictive environment may be applicable. Actively psychotic children who may be a danger to self or others; the severely retarded; and those with a chronic, recurrent, or present history of serious firesetting, sexual abuse, drug abuse, running away, and violence may represent a high risk. A more restrictive environment may be necessary in these cases.

Measures of Clinical Progress

As in any other therapeutic modality, baseline assessment of severity is important in order to measure progress. Measurement is problem specific. It follows the same guidelines as other approaches and is dictated by the diagnosis or type of problem. However, additional measurements of general adjustment are necessary and often provided by behavior modification levels, accrual of privileges, or number and severity of unwarranted incidents during specific periods of time. These measurements are inclusive of different spheres, such as school, family visits, etc. When working with the family of origin toward the goal of reunification, measurement of family progress is also an important factor.

Duration and Termination

Length of stay is variable and contingent on type of problem, diagnosis, agency philosophy, and whether the placement is deemed permanent. Since the guiding principle is minimal restriction, planners must determine the capacity for return to family of origin or, alternately, for transition to regular foster care, a group home, or independent living. Even within these outcomes, many programs foster continuity of a relationship that may have become like the relationship a child has with an extended family. Here the guide is optimal distance as defined primarily by the needs of the child. A commitment to stay with the child for as long as necessary, thus providing continuity, is a feature of many therapeutic foster family programs.

Preparation for discharge may be a lengthy process and must be carefully planned to ensure a positive outcome. This is particularly true when independent living is the desired aftermath. Equally important is adequate follow-up contact to ensure a smooth transition. Unfortunately, not all agencies provide enough support for this kind of activity; often the foster parents must soon start with a new placement.

Economic, Ethical, and Social Issues

Therapeutic efficacy and cost-effectiveness are among the most compelling arguments in favor of therapeutic foster care, especially when foster care is compared with institutionalization. Although cost varies widely among agencies, the modality compares quite favorably across the board to hospitalization and residential treatment. Costs vary according to the scope of interventions included in the individualized treatment of the child and family. Networking and contracting avoid costly duplication. Compared to traditional foster care, the modality is expensive because of the added individualized therapeutic component. The significant difference of a custodial versus a therapeutic approach offsets any degree of concern about additional costs. The important aspect of behavioral generalization and its intended contribution to family restoration and reproduction makes therapeutic foster care highly useful from a social policy point of view. The emphasis on teamwork, networking, and utilization of available resources is a paradigm for service delivery. The abolition of the often-adversarial tone so typical of the relationship between natural and foster parents in the past is a qualitative change that seems to be becoming permanent. The conceptualization of the natural family not as a failure but as a group in an impasse and in need of respite is also positive for families. The incredible dedication, motivation, and generosity of some of the therapeutic families can only be described in terms of inspiration and hope.

Outcome Studies

Because of the wide range of characteristics of therapeutic foster homes, evaluating therapeutic foster care is difficult. The evaluator encounters problems similar to those present in evaluating the psychotherapies, except that difficulty is magnified by the great number of actors and overlapping systems. One way agencies have measured the success of their programs is through the very ambiguous concept of outcome (i.e., successful completion of treatment goals, particularly transition to a less restrictive setting). Stroul (1989) presents data from a dozen programs whose success rates range from 62 to 89 percent when measured in this fashion. This is indeed impressive, but it is a limited measure and offers no control or comparison. In their evaluation of three programs, Meadocroft and Trout (1990) found that different methodologies precluded generalization. However, in one of the programs they describe, the rate of discharge to less restrictive settings went from 50 to 86 percent in 7 years; the success rates of the other two programs were 79 percent and 89 percent, respectively. Another important measure was placement success, or the ability to sustain a child in a program to successful discharge. Here the findings were similarly impressive: 88 percent and 98 percent, respectively, for the two programs that provided data. Another index of effectiveness was target behavior improvement. In spite of the acknowledged subjective nature of these evaluations, an average of better than 75 percent of the behaviors were rated as significantly improved in the program that conducted this measurement. Fifty percent of cases of noncompliance were rated significantly improved, as were 100 percent of the cases of enuresis, hyperactivity, and poor self-help skills. Similarly, fine (1993) reported 74 percent behavioral improvement with 25 percent unchanged and only 1 percent worse after at least 1 year of treatment. Unfortunately, in a follow-up of a subsample after discharge, most children reported serious adjustment problems, although the social adjustment was considered remarkably positive and almost two thirds had a good relationship with their biological family. Chamberlain (1994) compared 16 children referred for delinquency, all of whom had been committed to an Oregon training school. She matched the group by age, sex, and date of commitment with youths court-referred to other treatment settings (group homes, secure residential center, intensive parole supervision at home, and another therapeutic foster care program). The groups were highly comparable in terms of 18 of 19 family risk factors, child risk factors, child dangerousness, and school adjustment. Of the experimental group, 75 percent completed the program, compared to 31 percent in the control group. Nineteen percent of the experimental group, compared to 25 percent of the control group, failed to complete the program because of incarceration, and 6 percent and 44 percent of the children in the experimental and control groups, respectively, ran away. The rate of success favored the experimental group (chi-square = 6.15; $p <$ 0.03). Similarly, during the first 2 years posttreatment, the number of incarcerated children in the experimental group was 50 percent and the number in the control group was 94 percent (chi-square = 5.56; $p = 0.018$). The success of the experimental group alone, there was a dosage effect, or indirect relationship between length of treatment and time in jail during follow-up. Although the author considered the study weak, she saw promising possibilities. Methodologically the Chamberlain study was a significant improvement over previous studies.

The same author reported results in a sample of twenty 9- to 18-year-old psychiatric cases randomly assigned to therapeutic foster care or treatment as usual from the Oregon State Hospital Child and Adolescent Treatment Program. The groups had been hospitalized an average of 245 and 236 days, respectively, during the year prior to the beginning of the program. On the average, all cases fell into the category of "major impairment in functioning in several areas" in the Child Global Assessment Scale. After 3 months of treatment, the experimental group showed a more than 50 percent reduction in problems reported per day (over twenty at baseline for both groups). There was no change for the control group. Both groups showed decline in 7 months.

Within-subject time-series evaluation of target behaviors at placement point, during placement, and after discharge has been conducted, on a very limited scale (Hampson, 1988). The results are encouraging—that is, the study showed gains in IQ or adaptive behaviors. Although the results may be inconclusive, therapeutic foster care shows a conclusive advantage in regard to cost-effectiveness (Hampson, 1988). Satisfaction with services is another area that has been evaluated, particularly professional parent satisfaction (Stroul, 1989). Some program planners are attempting to develop longer-term individual follow-up measurements to determine personalized effects. Better-designed studies and the use of controls are necessary to come to more definite conclusions (Friedman, 1989). One important area that needs further study is the implementation of outcome studies utilizing *DSM-IV* nomenclature. Such nomenclature would allow researchers to link effectiveness to diagnosis.

Clinical Standards

Clearly, therapeutic foster care is a treatment approach that has not only been widely accepted and developed progressively into a discrete therapeutic approach throughout half a century, but it has proven to be an effective treatment for children with a wide variety of diagnoses.

Conclusion: Future Directions

Throughout this century foster care has evolved dramatically and so have the institutions of the family and diagnostic nosology. Of all children in substitute care, over two thirds may be in foster family care. More and more children (about one third, according to studies) have fallen into the categories handicapped or exceptional. Many of these children have been institutionalized in hospitals, residential treatment centers, or training schools, and they are considered to be in need of specialized services. In fact, most children in foster care probably experience a wide variety of psychiatric problems: adjustment reactions; developmental, behavioral, and emotional disorders; and family and social problems of lesser severity. This has led some to postulate that all children in foster care should be considered as having exceptional needs; therefore, all foster care should be planned as therapeutic (Hampson, 1988). If the present trend continues and given favorable government support, it is possible that, like institutional care, traditional foster care will be replaced. It may be replaced by the different shades of therapeutic foster care.

REFERENCES

Chamberlain, P. (1994). *Family connections. A treatment foster care model for adolescents with deliquency.* Eugene, OR: Castalia Publishing.

Bryant, B., Snodgrass, R., Houff, J., Kidd, J., & Campbell, P. (1986). *The parental skills training.* Staunton, VA: People Places Inc. (Available from People Places Inc., Research and Training Dept, 1215 North Augusta Street, Staunton VA 24401; (703) 885–8841; fax (703) 886–6379.)

Fine, P. (1993). *A developmental network approach to therapeutic foster care.* Washington, DC: Child Welfare League of America.

Friedman, R. (1989). The role of therapeutic foster care in an overall system of care: Issues in service delivery and program evaluation. In R. P. Hawkins, & J. Breiling (Eds.), *Therapeutic foster care: Critical issues.* Washington, DC: Child Welfare League of America.

Gurdin, P., & Anderson, G. R. (1987). Quality care for ill children: AIDS-specialized foster family homes. *Child Welfare, 66,* 291–302.

Hampson, R. B. (1988). Special foster care for exceptional children. A review of programs and policies. *Children and Youth Services Review, 10,* 19–41.

Knitzer, J. (1982). *Unclaimed children: The failure of public responsibility to children and adolescents in need of mental health services.* Washington, DC: Children's Defense Fund.

Meadocroft, P., & Trout, B. A. (1990). *Troubled youth in treatment homes: A handbook of therapeutic foster care.* Washington, DC: Child Welfare League of America.

Minuchin, P. (1995). Foster and natural families: Forming a cooperative network. In L. Combrinck-Graham (Ed.), *Children in families at risk.* New York: Guilford Press.

Minuchin, P., Brooks, A., Colapinto, J., Genijovich, E., Minuchin, D., & Minuchin, S. (1990). *Training man-*

ual for foster parents based on an ecological perspective on foster care. New York: Family Studies Inc.

Murphy, J. W., & Callaghan, K. A. (1989). Therapeutic versus traditional foster care: Theoretical and practical distinctions. *Adolescence, 24,* 891–900.

National Resource Center on Family Based Services. (1995). Catalog and order form. (Available from The University of Iowa School of Social Work, 112 North Hall., Iowa City, IA 52242–1223; (319) 335–2200; fax (319) 335–2204.)

Rendon, M., Gurdin, P., Bassi, J., & Weston, M. (1989). Foster care for children with AIDS—a psychosocial perspective. *Child Psychiatry and Human Development, 19,* 256–269.

Stroul, B. A. (1989). *Therapeutic foster care* (Vol. 3). Series on Community-Based Services for Children and Adolescents Who Are Severely Emotionally Disturbed Washington, DC: CASSP Technical Assistance Center. Georgetown University Child Development Center.

---

42 / Therapeutic Adoption

Virginia McDermott

Over a span of approximately 35 years, major changes have occurred in the institution of adoption, the children to be adopted, and the parents who adopt them. Until the 1960s both professionals and parents identified adoption with the placement of healthy infants. In these traditional adoptive placements, the emphasis was on providing infertile couples a child to raise "as their own." There was little disclosure of information about the child's birth parents, genetic and social history, or potential risk factors. The match of parents with the infant might occur along ethnic, cultural, or physical similarities. "Less than perfect" infants or children freed for adoption at an older age often languished in foster care or grew up in orphanages.

Since the late' 60s, however, a subtle shift in the focus of adoption has resulted in broadening the definition of *adoptable*. Based on the premise that full family membership can be an important contributing factor in the healing of early trauma, separation, and loss, therapeutic adoption moves along the continuum finding families for children who traditionally have been viewed as difficult, hard to place, or even unadoptable. From "crack babies" to teens with serious emotional disturbances, children with special needs are finding family membership. These adoptions are characterized by changes in how children are identified; the process of recruiting and preparing families; the amount of information about the child's history and potential risks, which are disclosed; and

the kind of support available to the family in the years following the adoption.

The roots of most social movements are usually not found in one person or group, but if there is a birthplace of adoption reform, it is the Spaulding for Children agency established in Michigan in 1968. With strong support from parent advocates Peter and Joyce Forsythe, who saw the need and marshaled the resources to form and fund the agency, Kathryn S. Donley pioneered a new model of adoptive placement by recruiting families to parent children who were considered handicapped by reason of age; sibling membership; educational, physical, or emotional problems; or race. The commitment was not just to find families who were willing to take the children but to support the placement for as long after placement as was needed to ensure the child had an adequate opportunity to find family membership. The failure of children to find family membership in a first adoptive placement did not necessarily mean they were unadoptable but rather that further information about their needs and the type of family needed to parent them was now available and could be used both in terms of preparing children for placement and recruiting the family who could meet their needs. What set the agency apart was not just the adoption model that emerged but the ongoing commitment to articulating, both nationally and internationally, the principles of adoption practice through training.

Goals of Therapeutic Adoption

Why adoption? Why full family membership for children who are badly damaged and deeply distressed and who will likely cause considerable grief to the families who adopt them? Family membership is a critical component in helping youngsters grow into productive adulthood. It is within the family that values are formed and within the family that lifetime patterns of relating to others are developed. For children who have been placed, the worst fear of childhood has been realized. That is, they have lost a parent and, devoid of emotional support, they must endure and survive their loss. Caught in a cycle of separation and loss that affects the way they view themselves, their family relationships, and their futures, they most often have unmet dependency needs, critical gaps between their chronological age and emotional and academic functioning, and unclear expectations about what family membership can provide.

These are children who are damaged. They feel defective. And, often, they are convinced that they have an unlovable core. The commitment of continuous family membership offers them a different reality, providing a continuity of caring that has been too long absent from their lives. Full family membership helps repair the damage of loss.

Although we can't predict the way early trauma will be played out in later childhood and adolescence, we do know that most of these children will experience distress, be difficult to parent, and respond to the giving and receiving of affection in convoluted ways. These are children whose attachments have been made and broken, and they often spend significant portions of their lives repeating the pattern—making and breaking attachments. Adoption, offers the opportunity, is there to reattach and, it is hoped, lessen the effects of the early disruption.

As more is understood about the nature of trauma, the powerful impact of early breaks in the attachment process, and the significance of multiple losses on all phases of childhood development, professionals increasingly recognize that adoption can be an essential component in the process of healing. Families will need ongoing support and services: parenting programs, therapeutic intervention, respite care. The children may require residential treatment and/or hospitalization. Yet the experiences of the past 35 years suggest that many of these children have the capacity to ameliorate the impact of their early life experiences and even of their genetic loading when they are helped to heal by adoption.

The Children

IDENTIFYING THE CHILDREN

The promise of adoption is the promise of continuous family membership. Adoption is a public act that makes the psychological parent the legal parent as well. The question to be asked when assessing whether children should be considered for adoptive placement is straightforward: Does the parent who feeds, shelters, disciplines, and encourages the child have legal responsibility for him or her? If not, and if this condition has persisted for 18 months or longer, then the child is without continuous family membership and adoption should be seriously explored as one of several alternatives for providing that membership.

PREPARING THE CHILDREN

Adoption will succeed most of the time if the children are helped to understand who they are and what has happened to them. This section will briefly sketch major themes and issues that deserve attention in the preparation of children for adoptive placement. Even very young children require effort by adults to help them make sense of their experience. Donley (in Unger, Dwarshuis, & Johnson, 1977) states that toddlers are among the most difficult children to place in an adoptive family because of their low level of verbal development and the difficulty in knowing what they have comprehended.

Who Am I? It is a safe assumption that a child with a history of placement outside his or her family lacks an *organized* sense of his or her identity. Separated from "historians," old memories get reworked in isolation and without the dialog and interaction that normally characterizes this phase of development. In addition, with frequent moves, a child experiences additional losses: the loss of caregivers, neighborhoods, school mementos, etc. A young adult who had grown up in foster care recalled that the "youngest" picture he had of himself was from seventh grade. The absence of pictures from infancy and toddler stages always haunted him; he described feeling like he hadn't been born they way other children were. In addition, he recalled strong positive feelings that were evoked whenever he ate buttered noodles—and the pain of not recalling at whose table he ate them.

The work to prepare children for adoption should begin by locating and reviewing with the child's birth certificate and hospital newborn record. For children who never knew their birthweight, length at birth and Apgar score and never saw their infant footprint, these are exciting discoveries that help to establish a sense of continuity with the who they are today. While gathering these documents is a small thing to do, it helps the children begin the process of internalizing early family connections, and the records display concrete evidence that they entered the world like everybody else.

How Did I Get Separated from My Birth Family? Birth records help to begin the process of sorting early family connections; a group process simultaneously available can help children begin to accept what has happened to them. To be with other children who have experienced a similar loss—that is, separation from birth family—can help them let their guard down and access the feelings they have about what they have experienced. In the group they can sort out their expectations about family life and discover how other children, faced with similar circumstances, coped.

But these children must also address how they got separated from their birth family and allowed to remember other losses too. I remember well a 10-year-old girl who was obsessed with getting back a tutu that had been packed in an attic when she was barely 7 and left behind when she moved again. Slowly and over time she came to grips with the fact that the tutu, now lost, would not have fit her even if she could locate it. She cried bitter tears over many days for the lost tutu—and the lost childhood. Then she moved forward once again.

In some ways the most significant work with these children focuses on their losses. Helping a child with a placement history develop an account of his or her past, which is both psychologically and chronologically a reconstruction of their child's experience, is a difficult task. In addition to routine information about the family, shelter, or the child's home, the names of pets, schools attended, and other historical data should be offered. Where possible, visits to the places lived and other favorite neighborhood haunts are recommended. If adults who work with the child can comfortably handle the child's pain, the child can too, and working it through is an essential part of healing. This phase of work can help integrate the experience of separation and loss. There can be relief and healing in coming to understand that the feelings that have been experienced are normal reactions to grief and loss; so, too, in coming to understand that difficulty concentrating in school, not being able to keep friends, and other behavioral problems may have roots in early childhood losses. Children often experience relief that an explanation exists for what seemed inexplicable.

What Will Become of Me? For children in care this question is central. Many of them have fantasies of being reunited with birth family; others hope for a commitment from their foster family. Very few consider adoption as an option until they are helped to understand what continuous family membership can provide and can receive straight messages from the adults in their lives about the level of commitment that is available to them. These children need time to absorb distinctions between different types of parents—birth, legal, and psychological—parents and a forum for exploring the multiplicity of relationships available to them.

Perhaps, most importantly, they need help resolving issues of divided loyalties. This may be a lifelong task. Children have fantasies about their families of origin, of how they got separated from them, and of how they will be reunited with them. All children have fantasies of "all-good" parents who are different from the everyday parents who establish rules, bedtimes, chores, and limits. Confronted repeatedly with the reality of only one set of parents, who are both "good," and "bad," an integration occurs that is significant for its impact on later development. For children in care, no such reality check operates; there *are* two sets of parents. Fantasies that are unmodulated by reality (and that may be exacerbated by the abandonment the child feels) often become very powerful and organizing forces in a person's life. Therapeutic work that explores these fantasies and gently helps children to improve reality testing about idealized family relationships prior to placement will help the placement to hold. Additional work may be needed at developmental nodal points.

Adolescence: Added Risk and Added Promise

At adolescence the task of separating, begun when the child took the first halting steps away from the parent, is renewed and brought to completion. Sorting out their dependencies and establishing themselves as distinct personalities with their own styles and values actually escalates adolescents' need for family membership. Teenagers need someone with enduring values to react to; they need a wall to bounce off, over and over again, as they test the limits and define who they are.

While adolescents "try on" many identities to see how their families and friends will respond (and what will be tolerated), the task of separating and individuating is not directed to severing family ties but rather to re-creating those ties in new ways. Adolescence is not complete until enduring ways of relating are established and "character" is formed.

Teens need adults who can endure the testing and retesting they are put through—adults who set limits, yes, but also allow youngsters to remain connected in whatever way they can. They still need tethering; and they need adults who understand how early childhood experiences have left them vulnerable to fears of abandonment, have made them abandon rather than be abandoned.

In many respects, adolescence provides an opportunity to rework earlier developmental issues. It is, if you will, a second chance, a second individuation. This is one reason why adoption even at adolescence can be a crucial life event. It is, of course, just the opportunities inherent in adolescence that are also the most conflictual for adolescents with histories of placement. It is when a child reaches adolescence that the commitment of adoption often receives its severest testing and

parents feel most like failures,—especially if their success is measured only by their ability to contain the youngster within the home. But keeping the youngster within the home is not the same as keeping the youngster within the family.

Finding Families

CHILD-SPECIFIC RECRUITMENT

There has been great resistance to involving children who are in need of families in the marketing strategies to recruit prospective families. Yet, the experience of Spaulding, in Michigan, demonstrated convincingly that making the children visible, no matter the depth or degree of their problems, results almost always in families coming forward who are able to parent them. Recruitment techniques include photo listings of children, which are posted on state, regional, and national exchanges; television and newspaper features that provide thumbnail sketches of real children in need of families; and, with developing technologies, descriptions and photos on the internet.

The marketing strategy may appear exploitative. The assumption behind it is that adoption is about the creation and maintenance of a relationship. Families who have not even considered adoption in general often respond to the needs and/or personality of a particular child. That is, providing a snapshot description of a real child in need, and providing photo listings, or bringing children in need of family together with families considering adoption may stimulate a family to consider how a particular child may fit into their home. Something in the picture, description, or being of the child creates a connection. Likewise, making information about families available to children often lowers their resistance to considering adoption. They discover that there are real families out there looking to adopt youngsters like them.

PREPARING THE FAMILIES

The successful integration of children who are difficult to place into families of adoption requires time and effort before placement. The family and child must get to know each other and process their concerns. All parties must learn about the availability of multiple forms of support in the years following placement. For the family, preparing to adopt means learning about what children with histories of trauma need from family membership, the risks involved, and the potential range of behaviors the family may face. But, more importantly, once a specific child has been identified, the family must spend significant time learning about the child's history, needs, risks, and behavior.

Just as the faces and features of the children needing adoption have changed, the faces and features of the adults who adopt have changed. Adoptive parents are adults who are single, couples with children, biracial families, lesbian or gay adults, foster parents, and adults whose own family of origin may not be much different from that of the children presented for adoption.

The process of preparing families for therapeutic adoption is highly collaborative, with social workers and families working together to gather enough information so that the decision by a family to move forward or to stop the adoption process can be made with reasonable confidence. From the parents' perspective the prevailing question is What do we need to know about this child and about ourselves to make an intelligent decision about our capacities to integrate this child into our family?

In order to provide prospective parents with this information, adoption must be viewed as a partnership by those professionals who have access to information about the child's social history, genetics, and behavior. It requires tenacity, empathy, and restraint as well as integrity to help a family explore the likely risks and potential of adding a child to their family. Information about the child's psychological, academic, and birth history; early childhood development; and medical, dental, and neurological background should be provided and examined to provide the prospective family with realistic information. Follow-up studies on placement suggest that, when families are provided with realistic information about the child in a format they can understand and assimilate, placements are more stable.

Preparing families for adoption using a group setting permits the adoption process itself to func-tion as a recruitment tool, allowing the broadest possible range of individuals and families to explore the backgrounds of the children available for adoption and the strengths and resources they will need to parent them. It also provides the beginnings of a support group for these families, modeling directly and indirectly the benefits of sharing what is going on within their families, the potential for learning new ways to assess problems and issues, and the possibilities of new ideas for addressing them.

From the first meeting families need to hear from the folks in the trenches—parents who have adopted children who have added risks and foster parents who have cared for them. With the help of these parents and experienced social workers they can begin to understand the daily demands and to assess their capacities to meet the children's needs.

In addition, the parents must begin to explore how their own histories give them both strengths and vulnerabilities—and how knowing these will help them to identify the kinds of children they will most likely be able to parent. In essence, the more they know about themselves and the children, the better able they will be to determine how to proceed. In helping families to make informed decisions, social workers must help them to feel in their bones the tremendous power that abused and neglected children have to invite adults into reenactments of their early life, again and again and yet again. To help parents to understand what might happen, social workers themselves must understand the significance of the children's life events and the developmental line along which the trauma occurred. For instance when trauma occurs preverbally, it is carried as a body memory and the child is likely to act out repetitions of the traumatic event when similar feelings are stirred. Furthermore, since the event and the feelings were never linked verbally, the child's feelings are split off from the experience. The child doesn't recognize the links between the feelings and the acting-out behavior.

Just as children need to know what they are getting into before choosing adoption as an option, adults need to know as much as is possible about the risks inherent in adoption, the psychological and genetic risks of the children, the range of difficulties they might encounter, and the intensity and level of support available to them when their children are presenting with difficulties and their families are in distress.

In the past, secrecy surrounded adoption. Even now, workers are sometimes reluctant to share the details of history with prospective parents; yet, the very key to survival as a family may be knowing what has occurred, because knowledge may offer some preparation for what may occur. And no parent should be allowed to adopt until he or she accepts that the worst can occur. Although it is not possible to configure the specific ways that early damage will impact a particular child, there are some generalizations that will apply to all adoptions of children past infancy.

1. The earlier the damage and/or the more times attachment has been broken, the greater the risks.
2. Traditional ways of parenting will not be effective and new strategies are necessary.
3. In myriad ways the limits of adult caring and commitment will be tested.
4. The children will likely provoke adults beyond limits in an effort to receive emotional and physical blows that repeat patterns in their histories, and they will not respond as expected when they are motivated by rewards or threats of punishment.
5. They will find every adult vulnerability and push the appropriate button.

MAKING THE MATCH

At some point in the process, a match is made—that is, a specific child is identified for a particular family and a plan about how to proceed is developed. Ideally, at the time of initiating the process of adoption, a family has a specific child in mind. More often, that decision evolves over the course of the adoption study. However, the adoption study of the family should not be written "generically" but only in terms of a specific child. By utilizing this approach, the worker preparing the study can focus on the specific strengths and weaknesses of the family in regard to a child who has a specific constellation of needs.

For parents to have the information they need about the child they wish to adopt, important work in three areas must be done. Essential information about the child's history must be obtained and missing information located so that the fullest possible picture of the child's circumstances is available to the adopting family. Then the information must be shared and interpreted so the family can understand the implications of the information for their family (or for them). To ensure that a prospective family has weighed the implications of a child's history and functioning, ask the family to predict behaviors, developments, concerns, or issues that will likely occur if the child joins the family. What can they anticipate will happen to the family? To other children in the family? What might the adopted child do at school? In the neighborhood? Who might be offended? Who might be supportive? By taking extensive notes of this discussion and sending a copy to the family, a valuable tool is created. The notes will help the family integrate the information about the child and think about how the child will fit within their family. At every stage of the placement process and in the contacts that occur after placement, these predictions can be reviewed and revised if necessary.

When parents reach an understanding of their capacities and limitations, professionals must resist the urge to "stretch" a family beyond its comfort zone. (If the stretch occurs, it should be parent-initiated and very likely it may occur at an adoption party or similar event that brings children and families together.) At this point in the process, families should be encouraged to bring other relatives and/or close friends to the group meetings so they too can hear about the children, their issues, likely behaviors, and the commitment to parenting that is demanded. Often members of the extended family don't understand much about adoption and add to the difficulties the family is experiencing as they work to of integrating the adopted child into the family system. Extended families and close friends need information about the kinds of behaviors children with histories of placement bring with them and the reparative nature of family membership. Such information helps the prospective adopting families develop a support system, and a support system increases the likelihood that the families will receive compassion when the going gets tough. Extended family members and close friends should learn about the recurring defensive strategies that the child develops to ward off the anticipated pain of rejection and fear of abandonment. Such preparation helps those close to adopting families to understand that, although the behaviors appear designed to break connections, they may actually represent a desperate search for connection.

There is another important reason for helping adopting families communicate well with extended family and friends about their children: Adopting families need to know who will parent their children if something happens to them. When death, illness, or disability disrupts family functioning, many families are able to turn to kin for continuity of care for their birth children. Blood and history incorporate these children into the family system. Children exhibit patterns of behavior and/or recognizable features that allow them to be maintained within the extended family. For children of adoption—especially children who bring high-risk factors with them—the same permeability of boundaries may not exist. These children are at risk for not being viewed as kin. Consequently, adopting families and their extended families must be helped to address these issues directly and concretely as part of the placement process and in ongoing ways during the years following placement.

Bringing Children and Families Together

PREPARATION FOR MEETING

The family feels ready to move forward. The preparation work with the child has been done. Now it is time to think about introducing the family and child to each other. This is an important step in the adoption process, and it benefits from the same care, time, and commitment that has gone into the previous stages. Altogether too often children and families are brought together without a specific plan in mind, and the placement is endangered.

The presentation should occur before the first meeting. Exchanging pictures, letters, and/or videos will help everyone to develop an increased comfort level before they meet each other.

THE FIRST MEETING

The actual meeting should be simple, on the child's turf, and short. In addition to the prospec-

tive adoptive family, the current foster family and the social worker should be there. That first meeting will be stressful for everyone and there should be an opportunity for both the child and the family to process the experience with their workers before proceeding to further visits.

ADDITIONAL CHILD-FAMILY CONTACTS

Frequent visits of increasing length should occur over a period of several weeks—in public places, at home, on weeknights, over weekends—all timed to the pace of the child. In between times, the social worker should be talking to the adopting family, the child's caregivers, the child, and other adults who understand how the child functions and can help make sense of what the child is experiencing. Hesitation, a wish to slow down the process, a desire to speed it up—all are signals that should be treated respectfully and understood. The child will signal a readiness to move, perhaps by leaving clothes behind or beginning to pack boxes for the move.

At the same time the child is being helped to form a new attachment, help should be forthcoming to end the current placement without breaking the relationship. Mixed feelings and outright sadness are to be expected. The child may be disappointed that the family he or she now lives with did not come forward to adopt. That will feel like another rejection and another loss. It is and deserves to be recognized as such.

MOVING IN

Eventually, the child and the family will decide on moving forward, and a date for the child to move in will be set. As with every step in the process, care must be taken to plan for this day. It is a significant event and deserves to be treated as such. For the child and the family, it marks a new way of relating to each other, an ending and a beginning. A ceremony that celebrates the incorporation of the child into the family—and acknowledges the importance of the child's history to this moment—helps highlight this passage.

SUPPORTING THE PLACEMENT

Successfully parenting these children through therapeutic adoption will require a commitment to working with other professionals to maintain the semblance of family living. Parent support groups can be extremely helpful, but they are not enough. Respite care can allow time for regrouping. But it is a Band-Aid, not a cure. Therapeutic intervention (outpatient therapy, residential treatment, day treatment programs, or inpatient hospitalization) will be helpful, but only if the parents have been able to identify mental health professionals who understand the dynamics behind the behaviors and who remain committed to working with the family through the crises that arise. In addition, built into the adoption plan at placement, there has to be a team available to provide ongoing postplacement services through the legal adoption and beyond. The success of the endeavor is just about directly proportional to the degree of involvement the family has maintained with the agency since placement. Red flags should go up when families withdraw following placement or after the adoption is final. No high-risk adoption can afford the luxury of disengaging from its support group and social worker contact.

In addition, there has to be access to funds for treatment if it is necessary. Otherwise, when children act out, and the costs of treatment exceed family resources and insurance, parents discover a significant disparity between foster care and adoption: too often funds are available for the acting-out child or adolescent in foster care, but not for the child, with similar life experiences and history, who has been adopted.

Contraindications for Adoption

Are there children who can't be adopted? Yes, although probably fewer than commonly believed. The need for treatment is not a contraindication to placement. Neither is the statement by the current foster parents that they won't adopt but will raise the child to age 18. Traumatizing life events and/or the failure of previous placements are not in themselves contraindications to placement.

In most cases, knowing the child well enough to identify the family who can meet the child's needs will significantly increase the likelihood of a placement succeeding. Adequate preparation of the child and of the family, coupled with ongoing support and the availability of necessary re-

sources, are the sine qua non of a child achieving full family membership.

When a family is not found for a child or the placement of a child within a family doesn't hold, it may be that the available information about the child was inaccurate or incomplete or not fully understood. Or the preparation of the child for adoptive placement was inadequate to meet the child's needs. Being unsuccessful may be disappointing, but it can also be informative, providing useful feedback in the planning for the child.

However, if the steps in the process have been carefully followed—with adequate support offered, and outside resources accessed, and feedback from failures utilized, and still the child cannot find full family membership, then for this child, at this time, adoption may not be the best choice. But when the child reaches a different developmental stage, the issue should be revisited.

Reaching the Goal

Frequently, therapeutic adoptions are troubled. Yet, despite the very real pain, most families make it. In fact, 85 percent of the matches result in stable adoptions. With slight variations this figure has held constant over several studies on special needs adoptions. And, when first matches do not result in stable adoptive placements, the second adoptive placement has a chance for success of about 55 percent. Some families adopt again. In addition, many children who exhibited significant behavior problems during latency and adolescence achieve a measure of stability and integration that allows them to pursue worthwhile lives as adults. In many cases they break the cycle of abuse and neglect that first propelled them into the system.

The research of Barth and Berry (1988) provides a framework for adoption placement policy. Their analysis of adoption placements offers important insights about the range of services that result in positive outcomes for children and families at highest risk of adoption disruption. Furthermore, their research broadens the criteria for successful adoption beyond placement stability and proposes that the broadened criteria are useful when comparing adoption with other placement alternatives: foster care, guardianship, or residential care.

Even when early trauma has compromised physical, emotional, and intellectual development, children of therapeutic adoption often grow up to live rewarding and productive lives. In the course of their progress, they falter. Those who attempt to parent them may falter too. But, for most who have made the choice, the pain is balanced, in the end, by the pleasure of having touched one life and having made a difference. In the words of Goldstein, Freud, and Solnit (1973), "Each time the cycle of grossly inadequate parent-child relationships is broken, society stands to gain a person capable of becoming an adequate parent for children of the future."

REFERENCES

Barth, R., & Berry, M. (1988). *Adoption and disruption: Rates, risks and responses.* New York: Aldine de Grutyer.

Brinich, P. M. (1989). Adoption from the inside out: A psychoanalytic perspective. In D. M. Brodzinsky & M. D. Schechter (Eds.), *The psychology of adoption* (pp. 42–61). New York: Oxford University Press.

Brodzinsky, D. M., Schechter, M. D., & Henig, R. M. (1992). *Being adopted.* New York: Doubleday.

Cole, E. S., & Donley, K. S. (1989). History, values and placement policy issues in adoption. In D. M. Brodzinsky & M. D. Schechter (Eds.), *The psychology of adoption* (pp. 273–294). New York: Oxford University Press.

DeWoody, M. (1993, May/June). Adoption and disclosure. *Child Welfare, 72,* no. 3, 195–218.

Donley, K. S. (1975). *Opening new doors.* Monograph. London: Association of British Adoption Agencies. (Available through, National Resource Center for Special Needs Adoption, 16250 Northland Drive, Suite 120, Southfield, MI 48075.

Donley, K. S. (1978). The dynamics of disruption. *Adoption and Fostering, 92,* 34–39.

Fahlberg, V. (1996). *A child's journey through placement.*

Geiser, R. L. (1973). *The illusion of caring.* Boston: Beacon Press.

Goldstein, J., Freud, A., & Solnit, A. (1973). *Beyond the best interests of the child.* London: Free Press.

Jewett, C. (1982). *Helping children cope with separation and loss.* Harvard, MA: Harvard Common Press.

Karen, R. (1994). *Becoming attached.* New York: Warner Books.

Kirk, H. D. (1984). *Shared fate.* New York: Free Press.

Littner, N. (1956a). *The child's need to repeat his past: Some implications for placement.* New York: Child Welfare League of America.

Littner, N. (1956b). *Some traumatic effects of separation and placement.* New York: Child Welfare League of America.

Littner, N. (1974). *Treatment for the adopted adolescent.* Unpublished manuscript.

McDermott, V. (1987). Life planning services: Helping older placed children with their identity. *Child and Adolescent Social Work, 4,* 97–115.

McDermott, V. (1996). Therapeutic adoptions. *The adoption support and preservation curriculum.* Southfield, MI: Spaulding for Children's Training and Leadership Center.

Nickman, S. L. (1985). Losses in adoption: The need for dialogue. *Psychoanalytic Study of the Child, 40,* 365–398.

Sroufe, A., & Waters, E. (1977). Attachment as an organizational construct. *Child Development, 48,* 1184–1199.

Stern, D. N. (1985). *The interpersonal world of the infant.* New York: Basic Books.

Triseliotis, J., & Hill, M. (1989). Contrasting adoption, foster care, and residential rearing. In D. M. Brodzinsky & M. D. Schechter (Eds.), *The psychology of adoption* (pp. 107–120). New York: Oxford University Press.

Unger, C., Dwarshuis, G., & Johnson, E. (1977). *Chaos, madness and unpredictability . . . placing the child with ears like Uncle Harry's.* Chelsea, MI: Spaulding for Children.

Warren, S., Huston, L., Egeland, B., & Sroufe, A. (1997). Child and adolescent anxiety disorders and early attachment. *Journal of the American Academy of Child and Adolescent Psychiatry, 36,* no. 5, 637–645.

Weisman, M. (1994). When parents are not in the best interests of the child. *The Atlantic Manthly,* July, 43–63.

43 / Art Interventions

Helen B. Landgarten

Introduction

Art psychotherapy intertwines the theories of art and psychology and is synergistic with all other psychotherapeutic approaches. Although its goals are similar to those of other interventions, the means (an art task orientation) is unique to this modality.

In a therapeutic session, I focus on the psychological needs of each child or adolescent and immediately translate them into a metaphoric art task. Strategic directives are given to meet the objectives of the session. For example, tasks may be formulated with attention to the following: (1) emotional experiencing, (2) gaining awareness, (3) revealing unconscious material, (4) problem solving, (5) catharsis, (6) socialization, (7) reality testing, (8) concretizing and working through conflicts, (9) uncovering covert messages, (10) surfacing repressed material, (11) sublimation, (12) understanding cause and effect, (13–14) dealing with separation and loss, and (15) individuation. Participants are purposely given simple art materials to facilitate their involvement. These include oil pastels, crayons, felt markers, magazine photos, construction paper, plastilina (a plastic clay-like substance), scissors, and glue. The youngsters' familiarity with these supplies makes the techniques of art psychotherapy a less threatening mode of intervention.

Persons in the process of art psychotherapy may make a conscious choice of what to convey through their art or may start out in a random fashion. With art as a new means of communication—a means that the client has probably not used in a therapeutic way before—the usual "editing" defenses are less available; therefore, his or her artwork may contain underlying meanings of which the youngster is totally unaware. In spite of resistance to exposure, hidden emotions, thoughts, and modes of functioning are regularly depicted.

Since art involves the primary process, (Bemporad, 1980) repressed material often surfaces. In such cases careful consideration must be given whether to avoid, delay, or deal with the symbolic material that has unconsciously been revealed.

While viewing the art, I make interpretive guesses that are not shared with the client at that time. It is of paramount importance to hear the child's explanation, for it is a disservice to place a fixed meaning onto any specific symbol. To illustrate this point, the image of an "octopus" has had many different meanings for different children.

To a 5-year-old boy, it represented his nightmarish fears that a "creature from space will come and hurt me." In contrast, a 9-year-old girl said it reminded her of "one of my favorite soft and funny stuffed animals that I like to sleep with." An adolescent once explained that her drawing of an octopus represented "my parent's grabbing hands that are always pulling at me with their constant demands."

An essential feature of the art psychotherapy process is the therapeutic value of the medium itself (Landgarten, 1987). Art materials are given that match the objectives, since they have the power to evoke emotional responses; this is especially true with adolescents, who have weak ego strength and may be particularly venerable.

Art techniques are employed to control boundaries or to give greater freedom to the participants (Linesch, 1988). In one-to-one sessions and group work, the limitation or expansiveness of the physical space is also a factor. Reactions to supplies or to the task itself can offer clues to the child's or adolescent's personality. For example, low frustration tolerance is likely to be displayed by youngsters who have difficulty manipulating the material, staying focused, and/or problem solving. They may exhibit anger by acting out, degrading themselves verbally, expressing their despair, and/or withdrawing altogether. Later, as a follow-up, these same supplies and tasks are given to compare any changes in reactions.

An advantage to the creative process is that it

distances the participants from talking about their problems. As a result, the artwork comes as a relief and frequently helps to hasten the therapeutic alliance (Wood, 1984).

Elementary school–age children have the option of recording their comments by themselves or dictating the information to the therapist. Young children are impressed that their words and thoughts are valued enough to be recorded, also that their artwork is saved in locked cabinets. Hence, they view the art therapist as a person who values them as worthy individuals.

In art psychotherapy the products become a permanent self-record of the individual's therapeutic process. The documents, with their visually telling statements, make disownership of feelings and thoughts impossible.

During the "termination" phase, the art portfolio is invaluable as tangible evidence and a means for recapitulating all the work that has taken place (Landgarten, 1991). It is particularly reassuring to adolescents to see the actual proof of what they have accomplished. It is an opportunity for them to assess their gains and receive further validation of and reinforcement for their achievements; they end their therapeutic intervention with pride and self-confidence.

This chapter contains case histories of children and adolescents. It presents a developmental model with a focus on presenting difficulties. The illustrations include examples of assessment plus individual and group interventions.

Assessment

The assessment procedure requires explicit art tasks (Landgarten, 1983). As the child or adolescent is engaged, observations are made in regard to their attitude toward the task, response to the medium, procedural approach, content of the art, and free associations to the imagery.

The task orientation begins in the initial session. If the individual is resistant, the therapist uses himself or herself as a role model to demonstrate how a few simple lines can be expressive. For instance, a blue wavy line can mean feeling peaceful or a red jagged line may stand for anger, and a scribble may represent frustration. Another

effective medium is the magazine photo collage (Landgarten, 1993), where pictures are self-selected and the youngster makes associations to them. The metaphoric images give additional clues to the assessment process.

Three examples of assessment follow.

CASE EXAMPLES

Seven Years Old: Revealing Secrets: Felice, age 7, was referred to therapy because of her depression and anxiety. During the assessment phase she created two pictures of her own choice titled *Mommy and Little Girl Ghosts.* The first showed a "little girl ghost who gets home from school and finds her mommy ghost in bed." The child explained that the mommy· ghost was saying, "Honey, I'm sick and I gotta stay in bed." When questioned about the little ghost's thoughts, Felice haltingly replied, "I better take care of my mommy."

The second picture contained a "smiling mommy ghost," who said to her little girl, "Hi, honey. Let's have fun." In response the little ghost (who she unconsciously labeled "me") was thinking, "My mother's acting funny again . . . I'm scared."

Younger children frequently slip into first person when the story is analogous to their own circumstances. These ghost stories and similar ones led to the suspicion of mother's alcohol abuse and child neglect. The case was reported and the investigator found it necessary to remove Felice from her mother's care.

Twelve Years Old, Fantasies Exposed: Thirteen-year-old Sally was causing trouble at home because she played one parent against the other. To find out what precipitated this maneuver she was told, "Draw how you feel when you are with your mother and draw another picture that shows how you feel when you are with your father."

Sally created a picture of herself and her mother. Both figures looked like young girls who stood under a small rainbow composed of three different colors. She claimed it meant there were "nice feelings" between them.

In the painting about her father, she created herself as a sexy adult woman dressed up as a queen. The figure was standing in the middle of a road surrounded by rolling hills and a blue sky with billowy clouds. A rainbow composed of many colors stood over her head. Sally explained, "My father makes me feel like a queen. I feel really special. He tells everyone how wonderful I am."

The imagery identified the adolescent's fantasies of competing with her mother to gain the adult and prime position in the eyes of her father.

Sixteen Years Old, Suicidal Ideation: Sixteen-year-old Earl was suffering from the loss of his girlfriend, who had moved to a different state. The young couple stayed in touch with each other almost daily for several months. In spite of their mutual love, the girlfriend's parents insisted that the contact be stopped. They believed that their daughter was not adjusting to her new environment because of her yearnings for Earl. The lack of connection put the boy into a state of depression. His parents insisted that he receive some psychotherapy in hopes that it would help him cope with his predicament.

During the initial assessment session, the therapist asked Earl to make a magazine photo collage (Landgarten, 1993). The adolescent was supplied with a large selection of photographic images and was instructed, to "Select pictures and paste them down on the blank page." Afterward Earl was told, to "Free-associate to them." Several images were of sad people. He identified them with persons who had lost their loved ones or were lonely. When asked what these people were thinking, he referred to their sense of hopelessness. Other photos of concern showed a "noose" and "a hand holding out pills."

Considering the boy's state of mind, these symbols indicated the possibility of a suicidal ideation. Earl was questioned about suicide. Although reticent he admitted giving serious thought to such a gesture. When asked if he had a specific plan, Earl confessed that he was considering taking pain pills from the family's medicine chest. Although unaware that the medication would not kill him, the intent was taken very seriously and the matter dealt with clinically.

Individual Art Psychotherapy Intervention

This section presents examples of individual art psychotherapy interventions.

Children who are preparing for surgery are given the opportunity to work on the trauma through art psychotherapy. They are relieved by the opportunity to express their rage over the violation of their persons. It is therapeutic for the young child to have a chance to feel in control. An effective technique is to shift the child from being the passive patient to playing out the active physician. The following is a typical example of a child's responses to upcoming surgery.

CASE EXAMPLE

Five Years Old, Crisis Intervention: Rae was about to have minor surgery on an outpatient basis. Since play is a natural process, she was pleased when she was told that she and the therapist would use the plastilina to form figures of a little girl, a nurse, and a doctor. Although leery at first, she was quickly involved when the therapist placed a toy hypodermic needle, stethoscope, and tongue depressors onto the tray before her. When she was invited to play out a hospital scene, her attention went immediately to the hypodermic needle. Rae used it on the plastelina child figure. Giving it a voice, she loudly yelled, "Ouch! Ouch! Ouch!" Rae smiled as she picked up the doctor figure to twist and squeeze his nose out of place. The child giggled with delight when she gave the doctor sculpture shots in his arms and buttocks, all the while shouting "There. There. You mean man! See how it hurts!" Extraordinarily pleased with herself she continued on, delivering him a number of kicks. Rae did not mind the fact that the doctor figure got all bent out of shape. Finally, with disgust, she threw it into the pile of unformed plastilena. Feeling satisfied, she finished off by slapping her hands together as she said, "Well, that's that."

Toward the end of the session the therapist picked up the plastilena nurse, placed it in front of the girl sculpture, and gave it a voice by stating, "Everything is going to be just fine now. In a week or so you'll be able to go out and play or you might even be able to go back to school." Rae turned to the therapist with a furtive look when she realized that this message was more than a part of the play.

In contrast to her appearance when the meeting began, the cathartic experience relaxed the child. Rae requested a box of crayons to keep. As she skipped out of the room she assured the therapist, "I'll draw you a picture when I get home."

CASE EXAMPLES

Eight Years Old Mastery Through Metaphoric Art: Elementary school–age children use metaphoric art as a part of their mastery process. The comic strip format, in which drawings are done in sequence and words written in balloon configurations, is best suited for their pictorial story. The tales are steered toward animals who are undergoing parallel situations. With this type of distancing, children are, as a rule, easily engaged in the task. At times it is necessary for the therapist to offer a therapeutic ending (Gardener, 1971). The following is an example of this procedure.

Kay's parents wished to provide her with their personal care. Consequently, the mother worked a day shift, from 11:00 A.M. to 7:00 P.M., and the father worked at night, from 11:00 P.M. to 7:00 A.M. Kay's mother took her child to school and her father brought her home. Against the father's wishes his employer changed his work schedule so that he could no longer pick his child up from school. A babysitter was hired to care for Kay from 3:00 P.M. to 7:00 P.M.

With the new arrangements, the child seldom saw her father, to whom she was very attached. Kay became enuretic and often awoke at night, screaming. Early in the intervention phase, Kay was instructed, "Draw a story about a little kitty whose father cat had to work a lot and did not have much time to spend at home."

Stimulated by the theme she created a tale titled *The Sad Little Kitty*. As Kay drew, she dictated the following story:

One upon a time there was a little kitty who loved her father very much. The little kitty and her father played a lot. They had fun. When the father got kitty home from school, she was happy. He'd give his little girl milk and a sandwich. The father always asked the little kitty What did she do in school? Kitty was happy. Kitty went out to play with friends. One day the father said he wouldn't be home anymore to take her home from school. The kitty cried and cried. The kitty was sad. The little kitten worried. Father wasn't home to give the little kitty a sandwich and milk when she got home from school. She didn't want to go out and play anymore. The kitty worried because her father would forget to come home from work. The little girl would not get any food. The kitty had a nice babysitter, but she did not make her sandwiches. She didn't know how to cook. The babysitter did not even ask her about school. The kitty was very sad. She worried about her father. The end.

The therapist made *therapeutic art interventions* by adding comforting images onto the child's pictures. This technique was used whenever necessary, on an ongoing basis. For instance, when Kay drew a worried or frightened kitty, the therapist added a babysitter cat who learned how to make special sandwiches and cookies. In other stories, the therapist made a kitty who said to the catsitter, "Would you like to hear about what I did in school today? I used to tell my daddy cat what I did in school when I came home." Kay would look at the therapist quizzically when such statements were made. After several sessions the child reported that she had told her babysitter what the kitty in the story said.

Aside from ventilating her feelings, Kay was able to incorporate ideas that had come from the pictorial storytelling techniques. As the child became assured that she would be well taken care of by the babysitter, her fears were alleviated and the enuresis ceased.

Conjoint Session, Expression of Emotions: Mrs. Jones wanted her 9-year-old son to discontinue art therapy because his encopresis had ceased. Although the child had made great gains, the therapist believed they were not fully integrated.

During a conjoint meeting the boy drew while his mother talked. As the session began he sketched his positive transference through hearts and flowers. However, when the mother approached the subject of termination, Don drew a tree that was on fire with a little boy standing underneath it. As Mrs. Jones spoke of her child's therapy benefits, he reached for a blue oil pastel and covered up the fire to transform it into a sky.

The child interrupted his mother to show her his picture. She barely acknowledged it and continued, setting a date for the last session. In response, Don made a picture of a boy and a tree, with red streaks of lightning headed toward each one. Immediately afterward, he regressed to his pretherapy behavior. The boy became belligerent and purposely dropped the pastels and markers onto the floor, then proceeded to squeeze out large amounts of glue and sloppily dripped it all over his picture.

At first the mother was unaware of the reason for her son's performance. An interpretation was withheld in hopes that Mrs. Jones herself would understand her child's actions. When the enraged boy crushed up the picture and dumped it into the wastebasket, she got his nonverbal message. It was obvious that he believed his work in art psychotherapy had been for nothing and the gains he received were being trashed.

Even though Mrs. Jones did not want to take the recommendation for continued work, her son's feelings of annihilation were poignantly displayed. Both the art and his regressive behavior helped the mother to realize that ending treatment was premature. When she expressed her willingness to continue, he created a large smiling sun and a boy standing beneath it.

Ten Years Old, Recognizing and Displaying Emotions: Brent was recommended for treatment by a school psychologist who was concerned about the boy's blunted affect and selective mutism. Although Brent responded to his teachers, he seldom spoke to peers. His parents did not understand why he needed any mental health intervention because, they claimed, "He was no trouble at home."

During the initial session the boy drew a dog yelping "Help, help!" The next week he made a plastilena sculpture of a "boy with the face of a dog." He jokingly titled it *Dog-Faced*.

Again, in the following session, he drew a dog calling for help. This time Brent was told that it seemed that he, like the dog, wanted some help and that the therapist was there for that purpose. Instead of responding verbally he drew two connected hearts. The art was acknowledged as his way of communicating that he was pleased.

In subsequent meetings his positive transference was creatively displayed many times. This therapeutic alliance motivated Brent to reveal his inner thoughts. Released from the pressure to speak, he gathered courage to take both nonverbal and verbal risks.

Because art tasks were designed to help him get in touch with emotions, he was instructed to make a "'feeling faces chart' that shows different types of expressions. It could be done through drawings or magazine pictures." The finished chart included a variety of facial expressions representing anger, envy, hate, happy, sadness, excitement, love, boredom, and disgust.

In another session Brent's instructions were "Create a series of different situations." Afterward, he was told, "Look over the chart and pick out the feelings that match each situation." Several meetings later Brent was told, "Create a situation that you have experienced," followed by the instructions "Match feelings from the chart that fit that particular situation."

In the succeeding sessions, whenever the boy drew real-life circumstances, he had to include a "feeling self-portrait." There were also meetings when the boy had to imitate those images in front of a mirror. In this way he could experience and rehearse his affect.

It was necessary to deal with Brent's need to be "nice" all the time. He confessed that his restricted speech came from his belief that it was "better to say nothing than the wrong thing." The art enabled him to gain awareness about the messages that his parents had sent out. He drew his mother and father along with quotations of what they had often said: "Always be nice to people"; "Be quiet, I'm busy now"; "Keep your feelings to yourself"; "Don't be a crybaby"; and "Be brave." With time, Brent realized that he conformed to his parents messages out of fear of their disapproval and fantasies of their abandonment.

In summary, through art psychotherapy Brent was given permission to experience himself and, through metaphor, to gain insight. The feeling charts and the practice of matching his affect to each emotion were primary elements in the therapeutic intervention.

Twelve Years Old, Grief and Mourning: Jim was being considered for placement by his biological father and stepmother. The child was incredibly dirty, seldom washed, and emphatically refused to bathe. The family considered his actions as stubborn, oppositional, and hostile. In school the boy's unkempt demeanor became the brunt of the students' jokes. His belligerent attitude triggered a great deal of discord among his stepmother, father, and himself. The stepmother threatened to leave her husband if his son remained in the home.

In one of Jim's art therapy sessions he was told, "Draw about your birthday that is coming up." Somehow this led him into drawing a series of his past birthdays. As he did so he became unusually engrossed in detailing two particular pictures. The first showed a person in the bathroom talking to a boy in the shower, and the second picture depicted pallbearers carrying a coffin.

When Jim began to explain the art he burst into tears. He wept as he remembered, "My mother went to the hospital on my birthday, and she died a couple of weeks later. I was in the shower when they told me she was dead!"

An interpretation tied his fear of water to the connection of hearing about his mother's death while he was washing. In the following months he did a great deal of work regarding–abandonment, loss, grief, and mourning. This took place as he created various scenes of his mother, her illness, and her death.

His fury over her abandonment was shown many times. It was only through the art that he could eventually say good-bye to a mother that he could no longer see but could now remember without anger and with love.

Acting-out behavior in adolescence is sometimes a means by which young people divert their underlying depression. This phenomenon may be poignantly demonstrated by the adolescent's artwork. Unconsciously, teenagers may simultaneously draw both their behavior and their dichotomous depression. Their pictures make plain how their conduct serves as a means of fending off the emotions that lie beneath the surface. Images such as these are useful subjects for interpretations. They are effective in gaining insight and maintaining a focus on feelings instead of behavior. Adolescents begin to realize that the conflicting themes in their art actually show the different parts of themselves. The following is an example of such a case.

CASE EXAMPLES

Fifteen Years Old, Diverting Depression. Without being aware of it, John expressed the two parts of himself in a drawing. On half a page he created a "loose design with a variety of colored markers." He said it represented all of his activities that kept him busy. On the other half, instead of continuing with the markers, he replaced them with a lead pencil and made a "minuscule stick figure." When asked to talk about it, he brushed it off by saying the tiny figure was just a "lost person." John did not connect the picture to himself.

On one occasion John drew his usual colorful picture on one side of the page. On the other side, he created a "garbage can with a little stick figure next to it." He stated, "It is a person who feels rotten. Empty and sad."

At this juncture an interpretation was made. Though John denied it at the time, he gave it some thought. A month later John decided to start dealing with his inner feelings and face his depression rather than push it away.

Seventeen Years Old Evidence of Induced Psychosis: Jan, an adolescent from an intact family, suddenly began to exhibit acting-out behavior. This was manifested in her negative attitude at home, a drop in academic grades, and the theft of clothes from a department store. Her parents suspected their daughter of taking drugs. The store brought charges against Jan, and the court placed her on probation and ordered mental health intervention.

Since the intervention was not the girl's choice, she resented therapy sessions. When questioned about drugs Jan emphatically denied ever taking any. She was hostile and balked at tasks that seemed too revealing. In one session she appeared "off mark." When asked if she had recently taken drugs, she became enraged, vehemently denied such activity, and angrily accused the therapist of being inappropriately suspicious. The issue was about to be dropped when Jan began to draw a bizarre picture of a person with red eyes, purple lips, and a cross on one cheek. The therapist wondered if this was "punk art" and if Jan was testing the therapist's reactions to it. Still, nothing was said.

To gather more information, instructions to draw a tree (Buck, 1966) were given. Again the picture had a strange flavor. The tree had twisted roots that grasped at the ground yet did not make any connections. The bark was heavily defined and the leafless branches were tangled. Subsequent drawings became less and less defined until the pictures contained only a few disconnected lines. These drawings exposed the dissolution of Jan's defenses and her disintegration. This type of art is generally made by someone who is prepsychotic or in the midst of a psychotic episode. It appeared that drug abuse was probably the cause of an induced psychosis. A consultation was requested and Jan was hospitalized.

Art psychotherapy was continued on the inpatient unit. When she finally admitted her use of drugs she defended it, convinced that it heightened her awareness and made her more creative. She insisted that it enabled her to do everything "better." Draw better, dance better, and make love better.

Since Jan's prehospitalization pictures were proof that her perceptions were distorted, she was shown those images. Only this evidence enabled her to see that drugs did not heighten her capabilities, but in fact unrealistically distorted them. The art made an impact on Jan and, for the first time, she began to look at her self-destructive behavior.

Group Intervention

Group art psychotherapy is often the intervention of choice for elementary school–age children and adolescents. The techniques inherent in this modality facilitate involvement, help children focus, lengthen their attention span, and improve their social skills.

Groups are often composed of boys and girls with behavioral difficulties. The participants frequently lack impulse control, are self-destructive in relationships, and have trouble staying focused in a purely "talk therapy" group. A number of youngsters are diagnosed with attention deficit disorders.

To hold the attention of such a group, psychological and spacial containment are imperative. Initially this is accomplished through (1) restrictive art materials, (2) avoidance of physical closeness, (3) art tasks that give symbolic structure, and (4) the use of tolerable themes.

In contrast to the overly active members, there are those who are withdrawn, shy, fearful, lack social skills, and suffer from poor peer relations. The immediate and spontaneous aspects of creating art actively catalyze group process. In this environment the reticent child need not be pushed aside by the stronger, verbal members. Here all persons have an equal chance to express themselves when rounds are made. At that time each person shares his or her artwork and talks about its meaning. The encounter is corrective for the timid child who manages to practice a new role in which thoughts and feelings are voiced.

Cooperative art projects are ideal for addressing the interpersonal aspects of group therapy. Interaction is stimulated when all members become involved in the decision-making and problem-solving issues. The combined efforts establish a means for appraising the actions of self and others. As a "here and now" happening, all excuses are bypassed and self-destructive behavior examined. Thus *cause and effect* are sighted and explored, with insight as the goal.

Several group case examples follow. on: The Unifying Function of Space and Theme, Establishing a Therapeutic Alliance, Revealing Family Dynamics, A Bonding Process, and Displaying the Internal Self.

CASE EXAMPLES

Elementary School–Age Children, Unifying Function of Space and Theme: A group of elementary school–age children had difficulty working together as a unit. When they were near each other, the interaction provoked stimulation and chaos.

To set boundaries and to help the children tolerate physical closeness, everyone was placed as far apart as possible. And were asked to produce their own pieces of art. The next step was working in dyads, then triads. Group size was gradually increased until the children could handle working in a small cluster. The cluster was then enlarged, until they were ready for a total-group cooperative effort, where they could create a single piece of art.

Besides building up spatial tolerance, themes were pivotal for maintaining the group's attention. Since some participants had been labeled "bad," the therapist instructions were to, "create a mural about the feelings or imagined feelings of being called bad." This subject became a catalyst for serious involvement as everyone drew their metaphoric reactions.

During the sharing portion, children who were burdened with a "bad" tag vented their rage and their suffering. Those participants who pretended to have such an experience caught glimpses into their peers' pain. This incident and others like it were invaluable for establishing an atmosphere of honesty and trust.

Elementary School–Age Children Establishing a Therapeutic Alliance: When, a group begins it is profitable to deal directly with the childrens reasons for being present. Elementary school–age children are relieved when they realize that they are not alone in having problems. Therefore, in the first session the instructions were "Show your troubles through your art."

Jane promptly made a picture that represented her mother. Without being asked she volunteered to show her art. When she explained the metaphor, she complained about this parent's lack of communication. In her next drawing, which was undirected, Jane scribbled over an entire page. She said it stood for her frustration and resentment toward this parent.

This topic motivated other participants to share their own feelings about their families' type of communication. Since some members did not respond to this theme they were told, "Draw any situation where you were disappointed for not being heard."

One girl drew her "teacher" because she felt neglected by her. Another made a "store salesperson" who made her feel demeaned because she ignored children and attended to adults only. A boy who came from a different cultural background drew himself as an "outsider" in school.

The commonality of the subject of not being heard gave the group an impetus to further their interaction. The children developed the courage to deal openly with their problems, both with and through other members.

Preadolescent: Revealing Family Dynamics: In a preadolescent group the participants were instructed, "Paint pictures of your own choice." Twelve-year-old Jonas made a watercolor painting that caught the attention of everyone. The image showed "two persons with smeared and blurred faces." The title was *The Perfect Couple.* As a caption he wrote, "Jurgle gurgle" and other nonsense words. Members were puzzled over the meaning of this picture. Though they pressed Jonas for an explanation, he insisted, "It's just a funny picture."

When the therapist asked the group members what they thought the painting meant, they projected their own meanings onto it. The boy denied all their interpretations, stating that they did not apply to him. After much urging to explain what the words on the art meant, Jonas finally acquiesced. He admitted that the couple's smeared faces represented their disguised feelings. The group questioned him about the personal significance of the image. In the face of this pressure, he confessed that his art stood for his "parents' doubletalk." He complained that their double messages drove him "crazy," because it put him in a double-bind; no matter what he did, he could never win.

Jonas agreed with the therapist suggestion to take his picture to a family session. He hoped that it would open his parent's eyes so they could work on the issue of miscommunication.

During the family meeting Jonas' mother and father were surprised by their son's symbolic picture. The image jarred them into paying attention to his complaint. From then on *jurgle gurgle* was used as a buzzword for unclear messages. When Jonas reported this to the group, they too, used *jurgle gurgle* as a way to stop any of the members' doubletalk.

Early Adolescents: A Bonding Process: A small art therapy group was formed for youngsters in early adolescence. The members had similar presenting problems, social ineptness along with school peformances that did not reflect their intelligence. Due to the social problems, it was difficult to develop a group spirit. Their art was benign and did not divulge the difficulties that troubled them. They tended to express information that was outside themselves. They circumvented revealing themselves by creating art about sports, movies, news items, and complaints about teachers.

On one occasion, quite by chance, a participant named Paul poignantly drew himself trying to stop the walls from closing in on him. He labeled it *Pressures.* He went on to explain that one wall stood for school and the other represented his mother and father. Paul's picture, more powerful than words, depicted the suffocating and frightening feelings that were evoked through his parents' pressures about education. Many of the members were empathic; they, too, found themselves in this predicament. Through collages the participants worked on their reactions to pressure. Some displayed the ways they "got even." For the most part they did so through passivity, although some acted out through drugs, taking their parents cars without permission, and stealing from stores.

The art often portrayed self-images as helpless victims. To assist them in looking at alternatives, they were instructed, "Create a collage that shows how pressure might be alleviated."

An array of pictorial answers were produced. For instance, Joe selected a magazine photo of a "boy doing his homework" and onto it he drew a "clock set at 4:00." He said, "If I do my homework when I get home instead of playing Nintendo, I could stop being nagged by my dad and maybe get better grades." The group agreed with the reality of this solution.

The members laughed when they saw Patty's magazine picture of a refrigerator that she transformed into a female figure." The metaphor meant, "If I stopped eating so much my mother would stop being so mad at me all the time. I guess life would be more peaceful then."

Bill, the shy boy, shared his collage that it represented "Me talking to other guys and learning to play tennis." He claimed that such activities would satisfy his parent's complaints about him being too isolated. Bill became aware that, if he could manage to be more social, then he would have little time to get lost in his daydreams. He added that under these circumstances his grades might even improve.

Because of the mutually shared problems, a support system was established. To reinforce it the author directed the group, "Make a symbolic gift for each member." When this task was given in the past, the art response showed: candy, tickets to ballgames, money, a radio, a VCR, and other material items. However, this time, as proof of their sensitivity for each other, they created different kinds of thoughtful gifts. For instance,

the shy member received pictures that showed him participating in events with his peers, doing homework with another group member, and having fun skateboarding with friends.

The boy who called himself stupid received a handshake, a book titled *Good Friends,* and a "baseball bat" that was labeled "You are the best." The girl who acted out got a "stop sign" and a poem called "Getting It Together." Because of the presents they received, the participants were touched emotionally and, for the first time, expressed their appreciation for one another. The thought and understanding that the gifts evoked helped them to form a close bond.

Adolescence: Revealing Internal Selves. During an adolescent group a particular task made a profound impression on members. The directions were "Draw or make a collage that represents two portraits of yourself, one that displays the face you show to the world and the other that symbolizes what you hide inside."

There were only a few images where the outside and inside were congruent; for the most part, the pictures revealed disparities. For example, participants were shocked when they saw the drawing that the very attractive Vera made. Although her self-portrait was a great likeness, the picture of her buried secret self exhibited a "dried-up old woman."

Phil also made two images that were diametrically opposed. For the outside image he used a magazine picture of a "male hulk." He knew that was how people perceived him. For the inside image he selected the photo of "a little boy just learning to walk."

Sara, a bulimic girl, drew her external image as a "fat girl," but her internal vision was an "empty circle." Other members presented "happy" facades while their buried parts were "frightened or worried."

The participants declared their feelings of "being privileged" for witnessing what was beneath the skins of their peers. Their own bravery amazed them as they realized that they had achieved trust suffered to allow them to expose so much of themselves.

All the participants agreed that the encounter made a profound impact upon them. From that time on all barriers for revealing themselves were removed and a support system firmly established. This phenomenon enabled the group members to deal with troubling issues that were frequently shared by their peers.

REFERENCES

Bemporad, J. R. (1980). Theories of development. In J. R. Bemporad (Ed.), Child development in normality and psychopathology. New York: Brunner/Mazel.

Buck, J. N. (1966). *House-Tree-Person Technique.* Los Angeles Western Psychological Services.

Gardner, R. A. (1971). *Therapeutic communication with children.* New York: Science House.

Landgarten, H. B. (1981). *Clinical art therapy: A comprehensive guide.* New York: Brunner/Mazel.

Landgarten, H. B. (1987). *Family art psychotherapy: A clinical guide and casebook.* New York: Brunner/Mazel.

Landgarten, H. B. (1991). Termination: Theory and practice. In H. B. Landgarten & D. Lubbers (Eds.), *Adult art psychotherapy: Issues and applications* (pp. 174–200). New York: Brunner/Mazel.

Landgarten, H. B. (1993). *Magazine photo collage: A multicultural assessment and treatment technique.* New York: Brunner/Mazel.

Linesch, D. G. (1988). Adolescent art therapy. New York: Brunner/Mazel.

Warren, L. A. (1995). An Interview. American Journal of Art Therapy. Vol 34, No 2. Nov. 1995.

Wood, M. (1984). The child and art therapy: A psychodynamic viewpoint. In T. Dalley (Ed.) Art as therapy. New York, London: Tavistock Publications.

44 / Dance and Movement Interventions

Nana Koch and Barbara Melson

Throughout history, movement has been a primary means of communication, forming the basis of interaction among people. Movement precedes formal language, both historically and developmentally, and is expressive of how we feel about ourselves and the world around us. The body is the channel for emotional experience, which is felt and then reflected through posture, muscular tension, facial expression, gestural language, and breathing patterns.

Movement behavior can either replace or augment the spoken word. As we move through our daily lives, we often rely on the language of our bodies for self-expression and communication. A person may express joy through physically exuberant, expansive movement or may sink into the chest when feeling sorrowful. We share a rhythm with people with whom we feel comfortable and stand far away from someone who is angry. We breathe evenly when relaxed and irregularly when tense. Regardless of the unique ways in which body movement is consciously or unconsciously used for self-expression, it is clear that psyche and soma are connected and that movement plays a significant role in expressing the inner worlds of thought and feeling.

Historically and cross-culturally dance which can be viewed as an extension of movement behavior, has long been utilized as an outlet for emotional expression and as a way to define the identity of individuals and groups. In both ancient and indigenous cultures, dance is an activity that functions as an integral part of life (Serlin, 1993). In these cultures dance marks individual milestones and significant societal events, such as birth, coming of age, marriage, death, and war. In Western society various forms of social dance provide people with relaxation, socialization, and a means of self-expression. In dance/movement therapy, to dance with others is to form a bond that enhances self-esteem and self-image. It enables individuals to experience unity and to feel less isolated physically and psychologically.

Dance/movement therapy, as defined by the American Dance Therapy Association is the psychotherapeutic use of movement which furthers the emotional, cognitive and physical integration of the individual. At the foundation of this holistic approach is the belief in the inherent therapeutic and healing value of dance.

The field of dance/movement therapy developed out of postwar America in the 1940s. It has its roots in the part of dance history that emphasizes creative self-expression; communal experience; and spontaneous, unstylized movement. The dance/movement therapy pioneers came from a dance tradition that embraced these specific aspects of modern and ethnic dance. Recognizing the psychotherapeutic power of dance, they adapted teaching methods used in their dance classes to therapeutic work with psychiatric patients and neurotic clients.

Today, dance/movement therapy is practiced by registered dance/movement therapists, trained on the graduate level and credentialed by the American Dance Therapy Association. Dance/movement therapists work with a wide range of individuals and groups (i.e., infants, children, adolescents, adults, geriatrics, and families). Methods of group or individual treatment vary, depending upon the setting, type of client, and the particular needs and problems presented. Although dance/movement therapists serve the needs of people with a wide variety of dysfunctions, the focus in this paper is on how group dance/movement therapy serves the needs of children and adolescents.

Dance/movement therapists typically treat children and adolescents who have unsuccessfully negotiated the social world. Clients from these populations often experience developmental delays as a result of neurological and cognitive dysfunctions, affective disorders, and emotional disturbances. These problems are frequently combined with environmental stressors. In many instances clients have low self-esteem, a poor body image, disorganized thinking, an inability to adapt to new situations, poor communication and social skills, a lack of understanding about what they feel, and an overall inability to establish and maintain relationships. Their ability to identify and discuss personal difficulties and connect them to present-day functioning may also be limited.

Clients with the kinds of problems described are particularly amenable to dance/movement therapy treatment. Research conducted by and clinical reports of dance/movement therapists, have shown that this modality is effective for accomplishing the following goals: raising self-esteem and self-awareness; improving body image; developing greater situational adaptability; improving social and communication skills; enhancing relationships; and increasing an awareness of the relationship between thought and action, emotions, and behavior (Erfer, 1995; Kalish, 1974; Loughlin, 1993; Naess, 1982; Downes, 1980; Leventhal, 1980; Duggan, 1978).

Dance/Movement Therapy Groups

Group work provides children and adolescents with many opportunities for growth. Within the group they can work interactively and cooperatively, gain awareness and confidence with self and others, experience psychological and physical integration, feel the success of being in control of their impulses, and improve self-esteem.

In dance/movement therapy groups, content and method vary for children and adolescents. Session structure, however, is similar for both populations. Structure is marked by stages of group development and spatial formations.

Stages in dance/movement therapy were identified by Marion Chace as warm-up, development and closure (Chaiklin, 1975). In the warm-up, group members activate and mobilize their bodies and become acquainted with each other, the modality, and the tasks to be accomplished (Schmais, 1981). The material that emerges in the warm-up is explored in the development stage of the session. Members move with others; share the range of their feelings (literally or symbolically); try out new behaviors; and, when possible, individuate (Schmais, 1981). During the closure stage the task is to process the group and its accomplishments; to identify how the group has dealt with its tasks; and to acknowledge, verbally or in movement, the end of the session. Separation issues often emerge here and are dealt with in the closing discussion or group movement. Closure provides a sense of completion, readying members for what awaits them after the session.

Spatial formations occur within each stage and generate particular interactions and relationships (Schmais, 1981). All formations reflect the developmental level of a given group. Additionally, the group process and dynamic informs the choice of formation. For example, circles have traditionally been used to unify group members, symbolizing community, where everyone belongs and has equal status. Members can readily become aware of one another and the leader. Other formations include line, clump, cluster, and scatter (Schmais, 1981).

The movement that clients do in the warm-up and subsequent stages are often everyday, unstylized movements that express their feelings and help them connect with others. Movement is valued as self-expression regardless of whether positive or negative feelings and thoughts are shared. The belief is that feelings expressed within the group can be safely contained and symbolically worked through with a sense of control.

Clinical descriptions provided in the following sections are meant to serve primarily as examples of how the dance/movement therapist specifically addresses the needs of children and adolescents. Exercises included in these sections are most often used during the development stage of a session, when they relate to issues that emerge in the warm-up. They are not prescriptions for use by professionals who are not trained in the discipline.

Treatment of Children

THEORETICAL BASIS

The modality of dance/movement therapy is one that most children respond to readily because children live in and through their bodies. Developmental life begins with mobility and throughout childhood aliveness is evidenced in the activities of exploring, discovering, and growing. The child copes with the world largely on a bodily level and is involved in a continuous dance of feeling and expression.

It is through the body that the ego develops and both body image and self-concept are formed. Freud (1927) suggested that the ego is first a bodily concept. Greenacre (1958) speculates that "... the infant's inner sensations form the core of the self. They seem to remain central, the crystallization point of the 'feeling of self', around which a sense of identity will become established" (p. 613).

Changes in the body image are influenced by movement and lead to an alteration in the psychic attitude (Schilder, 1950). The development of the body image evolves from early sensations and movement behaviors. According to Schilder (1950), it is in and through movement that we come to know our bodies and understand our relationship to the outside world. Body image is conceptualized as the expression of personality and emotional life.

Since body ego concepts are central to development, it follows that treatment dealing directly with the body is particularly meaningful for children who experience disturbances in development and functioning. For such children dance/movement therapy makes dynamic use of the interrelationship of the body, emotions, and movement.

Disturbances in development and functioning vary greatly among children. When a developmental or behavioral disturbance occurs, there is a concurrent bodily disturbance. For example, the child may appear listless, withdrawn, rigid, fragmented, hyperactive, or agitated. Leave in treatment dance/movement therapists observe these movement behaviors. The child's body presentation is seen as a totality, an expression of the whole person, including thoughts, feelings, attitudes, and behaviors. Additionally, the children are viewed in the context of their environment, considering school, religious affiliations, culture and community.

A basic tenet of dance/movement therapy is to begin to work with the health and/or strength of each child (Evan, 1949). That is, what is unique to each child, regardless of the dysfunction or disturbance. Clinically the dance/movement therapist first identifies 'where' the child is, in the moment, and what the child 'can do'. Behavior is assessed, relative to the norm for the age. The therapist recognizes a child's need and functional level and begins the process of therapy at that point.

The success of dance/movement therapy depends largely on the relationship between the therapist and the children. The dance/movement therapist establishes rapport, creates a holding environment and develops a trusting relationship in which a child can feel safe and supported. Within this therapeutic framework children have a chance to be themselves and to gradually experience a degree of self-respect and self-worth. The dance/movement therapist functions on many levels within any one children's group: leader, playmate, good caregiver and teacher.

GROUPS WITH CHILDREN

In group work with children, the dance/movement therapist must be particularly aware of and sensitive to the balance between structure and freedom (Erfer, 1995). Structure is needed to provide the support that allows freedom. In a typical session the choices that provide structure are many and varied. They include: definition of the space as in forming a circle or line; the use of music, sound accompaniment, or silence; the type of movement experience as in basic body mobilization, creative movement exploration, improvisation, enactment and skill building; the use of props, i.e. balls, elastic bands, scarves, hoops; and the verbal guidance and direction given by the therapist.

Groups often begin with children sitting or standing in a circle formation. In many cases, each child has a special place on a mat or chair. This provides the child with a sense of security and helps to contain the group in the space. Although the circle is often used during the warm-up stage (and frequently again for closure), the child's need to move freely outside such a structure is respected and encouraged in the development phase. Spatially, it is not uncommon for members to form line or scatter formations, dyads, or small groups. Children might be encourage to find their own spot in the room; create a silly walk with a partner to move close together without bumping.

The typical warm-up begins with group members making sounds and using rhythm. This may occur through hitting a small hand drum, singing, tapping different parts of the body, or clapping. These are ways to encourage listening and responding to others which are basic communication (Polk, 1974). Rhythm is also an important tool to use with children because it helps to establish an internal connection to the heartbeat and breath. These are then related to the external rhythms of other people and the environment.

It is possible for children who have difficulties relating to others to relate to rhythm. When a group of children are in unison in rhythmic synchrony, the feeling is profound. Moving simultaneously with others in rhythm provides a rare experience of group unity and harmony (Erfer, 1995).

Usually basic mobilization follows this beginning, to enliven their bodies and to release tensions. Children might be directed to stretch, bend, shake, twist and/or swing the whole body, as well as specific body areas. These types of movements may be accompanied by verbally naming and identifying body parts. This helps children gain or relearn body boundaries while increasing body awareness. In this way children can gain a sense of where they begin and end. On a body level they start to answer the question 'Who am I?' The increased awareness of self and the development of comfort with ones own body and movement is a bridge to improved self-esteem and the ability to relate to others. The movement experiences are encouraged and facilitated by the leader's verbal and nonverbal directives, which are simple, clear, and supportive.

Throughout the session the leader mirrors or reflects the children's movements. This technique allows the therapist to join the children, thus giving them the message that who they are and how they move is valued (Erfer, 1995). In the further development of the session, the therapist continues to observe and reflect the specific movements, qualities of movement, and feelings that spontaneously emerge from the members.

In the development stage many things occur. There may be sadness or anger, which can be danced. There may be energy that needs to be expended. These dances may be created individually or as a group, where, for example, the children symbolically embody the form of a stalking lion or a racing car. A child's inherent sense of play is encouraged within this stage. Goals include having fun and experiencing the pleasure that can be derived from moving with others. For example, when children explore and play with props—such as bubbles, balloons, and scarves—they often experience pleasure. Playful aspects of a group are developed so that children can experience enthusiasm, fun, and joy in an accepting, safe environment. During the group development children are given opportunities to run, skip, jump, balance, or throw and catch a ball. They have the chance to practice these activities repeatedly, to improve basic motor skills and to develop a sense of competence.

Simultaneously, on emotional and psychological levels, children experience feelings, such as fear or excitement, that are generated when they do basic locomotor movements. At the same time they learn to tolerate their feelings and experience physical and emotional mastery. In addition, children are socially challenged and encouraged, in such tasks as taking turns, leading the group, moving with others, and creating and relating through movement.

While a session develops in the moment, it also involves predictability and repetition, however. Children who regularly have dance/movement therapy come to know and expect the following: They are likely to begin in a circle, they will move their bodies, there may be sound and/or music, there will be time to move alone, there is the likelihood of using a prop, and at the end of there time to gather together and share their experiences.

CLINICAL EXAMPLE

Working with opposites is a common movement framework to use with children. They relate to opposites cognitively, physically, and psychologically. Some examples of frequently used opposites include big and small, fast and slow, strong and soft. A movement exercise that children respond to and enjoy is Freeze, which uses the opposites of stop and go.

This exercise is effective for children with diverse diagnoses, from ages 3 to 12. The therapist stands on the periphery of the group, which is in a scatter formation. The therapist's function is to regulate the music or sound accompaniment. When the music plays, the children are directed to move in response to the music. When it stops, they must freeze. The specific selection of music is critical. The therapist must know the group well enough to understand the kind of music the children will respond to spontaneously, without losing control.

Freeze can continue for a long period, with stop and go directives given close together or with more time for moving while the music plays. When the freeze position is held for a long period the children have opportunities to experience feelings or conflicts that may not have been conscious or expressed before the exercise began. With older children, this can develop into intensifying the freeze positions, remembering them and then creating a movement phrase with several of the positions.

In group of approximately eight children, 8- to 10-year-olds, the theme of stopping and starting emerged early in the session. Before the group the children felt that limits had been placed on them when they became loud and exuberant in their classroom. They were shouting and were told to stop. In the dance/movement therapy session, they described this event to the therapist who directed them to do strong, outwardly directed actions and to abruptly stop them. Loud sounds were added to the strong actions. The interaction developed into the Freeze exercise described previously.

The children spent several minutes moving to percussive music, making very strong, and expansive actions. Their freeze positions expressed an equal amount of feeling. The quality of the children's movement changed once they had the opportunity to fully vent their feelings. Softer music was introduced, and the children continued the exercise with lighter, smaller and more contained movements.

This exercise helped the children to feel that big, expansive actions were acceptable within the time and place of the dance/movement therapy session. The session also enabled them to experience opposite or contrasting responses while exploring the meaning and appropriateness of their behaviors in specific contexts. In discussion, they focused on the consequences of their earlier behavior.

Treatment of Adolescents

THEORETICAL BASIS

Working with adolescents poses special challenges for the dance/movement therapist. Of all the creative arts therapies, dance/movement therapy may be one of the most difficult for adolescents to embrace. There is little opportunity for emotional concealment when the object of expression and outlet is ones own body. This focus can threaten the defensive structure and facade that adolescents construct in the struggle to redefine their identity and integrate their changing body image and sexual and aggressive impulses. The irony is that the very therapy that can help the adolescent cope with the new feelings brought on by bodily change, is a therapy with which the adolescent may have difficulties. Therefore, for this therapy to be effective as a treatment modality, the dance/movement therapist must pay special attention to the developmental changes that upset the equilibrium of the adolescent. To understand why particular clinical interventions are made by the dance/movement therapist, it is necessary to first look at the breadth of change and the issues raised during the adolescent years.

In adolescence, upset is marked by developmental changes that cause alterations and disturbances simultaneously in physical, cognitive, psychological, and social growth. While change occurs in all realms, the most outstanding are physical and hormonal in nature (Blos, 1962). The adolescent body looks, feels, and moves differently than the child and prepubescent body. Sexual maturity, a prominent aspect of this time period, occurs simultaneously with growth spurts; increases in the drives of the id, which often translate into sexual and aggressive impulses; and increases in physical activity, as the need grows for tension outlets. Although the growth pattern for each individual varies, the changes can be extreme, uneven and dramatic, regardless of their period of onset, duration and termination. Overall, these changes, in the extreme, may be accompanied by a decrease in self-esteem, a distortion in the body image, and feelings of being powerless and out–to–control.

Cognitively, adolescents have the capacity to think logically and abstractly, because they have reached the level of formal operational thought. However, they may not always be able to reason adequately and problem-solve while they are learning how to cope with their changing bodies and sexual and aggressive impulses. Intense feelings may be coupled with a lack of introspection, leading to explosive and antisocial behavior. A false sense of mastery of tasks and emotions may also produce grandiosity and narcissism. At this time logical and methodical verbal processing may be too demanding for adolescents to master. Therefore, the integration of unconscious thoughts and feelings are facilitated best in activities and therapies that encourage adolescents to act out their often aggressive impulses in symbolic actions.

Psychosocially adolescents are forming a more complete identity as they make the shift out of childhood and into the adult world. There is a struggle between integrating the "physiological revolution" within, and assimilating the roles and tasks of childhood with those of the adult (Erikson, 1963). Childish behaviors are rejected for fear of appearing regressive and being identified with the childhood they are leaving. Feelings of infantalization often contribute to the adolescent's rejection of working on the body level.

In response to the struggle for identity, autonomy, and individuation, adolescents may seek affirmation outside of the family. In this process they may also devalue authority figures and seek recognition from peer groups that serve the social function that families once had.

GROUPS WITH ADOLESCENTS

Adolescents who pass through these years with more than normal upheaval are those referred to dance/movement therapy. They are often seen in groups, in as close to homogeneous groupings (age and functioning level) as possible, regardless of whether they are in out-patient or inpatient facilities.

Dance/movement therapy group work provides an environment in which adolescents can try out new behaviors, in the safety of a peer group going through similar upheavals. Through the use of dance/movement activities (which may include play and drama), adolescents can familiarize themselves with their bodily sensations and verbalize the associative meaning of these sensations (Johnson & Eicher, 1990).

Dance/movement therapists must assume various roles when working with adolescents. These include:

- Initiator of movement for the most regressed patients, who have limited focus and movement repertoires and need someone to help them begin to move and participate (i.e., schizophrenic and psychotic patients).
- Director and facilitator. providing encouragement and direction for those patients who need specific structures created for them so they can feel safe and trusting in the environment (i.e., character-disordered and borderline patients).
- Guide and supportive observer. providing guidance, organization, and support, the therapist can help patients conduct-disordered patients.

What is clear from defining the types of roles assumed by dance movement therapists is that they take on supportive, rather than policing roles. The roles are meant to foster trust rather than creating power struggles.

Although the methodology used with adolescent groups may vary from that used with children, the spatial formations and the stages of group development are the same as those described previously. What is important to remember is that how the structure of the group evolves emanates from the developmental needs and interests of the members (Duggan, 1995).

For adolescents the circle formation can be confining and too reminiscent of formations used in childhood games. The need for autonomy is strong, and the implied focus on unity in a circle may not provide enough room to explore issues of separation and individuation (Duggan, 1995). Clump and cluster formations give adolescents opportunities to move in small groups rather than in required interaction with many members. Either formation requires adaptability to others. The scatter formation requires little interaction, and adolescents who need to work on issues fostering autonomy and self-determination do best when activities incorporate this formation. Single-line formations can provide opportunities to take a leader or follower role; parallel-line formations provide a structure for confrontation.

Sessions with adolescents begin in a myriad of ways, depending upon the tenor of the group. An adolescent girls group might begin with exercises taken from gymnastics. This helps them activate their bodies, focus their energy, and gain confidence doing physical tasks they can master. A boys' group might focus on a martial arts warm-up that would accomplish similar goals. A mixed group of females and males might begin with aerobic exercises. In each group, members can take turns leading the warm-up to try out their ability to take responsibility for themselves and others.

Warm-up exercises might bring up feelings of confidence or inadequacy, depending upon the ability of the members to adapt their bodies to new movements and/or positions of leadership. In the development stage, members are encouraged to verbalize their feelings and reexperience uncomfortable movements; learn new behaviors; and take risks, emotionally and physically. Group members who are more proficient physically often help those who are not. Thus, issues are addressed that relate to self-esteem, self-awareness, and relating to others.

Directly verbalizing feelings is often an onerous task for adolescents. Therefore, it may be more acceptable to use a range of bodily positions and gestures to externalize feelings symbolically. After initial body warm-ups, enactment and improvisa-tions offer adolescents ways to use the body to "say" what might be unspeakable.

CLINICAL EXAMPLE

A Yes-No exercise provides group members with structure and a forum for venting feelings and individual choice. Group members are paired and instructed to stand and face each other at arm's length. They may not touch and can only use the words *yes* and *no*. However, they can use their bodies and voices in any way they choose. In subsequent stages of the exercise, pairs join other pairs, form parallel lines, and face each other. The exercise is timed to last from 5 to 20 minutes *to allow* for emotional regrouping and verbal processing. The exercise can be extended or repeated, depending upon the needs of the group.

The session discussed herein was held with a group of conduct-disordered, inpatient adolescents.

Group members chose their own partners. They worked in dyads spaced around the room. A male and female pair distinguished themselves by initially speaking softly and politely. Their movements were light, fluid, and indirect. As they progressed, the male become stronger and more direct with his movements and voice. The female become progressively more tense, losing strength and directness in her movements and voice. The discussion that followed focused on the experiences the girl had with a domineering older brother. What would begin as a playful interaction with him often ended with her submitting to his will. Her submission was reinforced by the actions of a verbally abusive father, who dominated the entire family. On the other hand, the boy in this exercise revealed that he felt powerless in his family as well and enjoyed yelling and physically dominating his partner. The therapist suggested that this particular dyad do the exercise a second time, assuming personalities that contrasted with the ones they revealed in the last sequence. Group members observed the interactions of the working pair. When necessary, the members coached the pair to move and verbalize in ways that would help them express their feelings of inadequacy. Peer interaction made interventions more acceptable and also provided opportunities for experiencing empathy with others. Eventually, the girl assumed a more confident stance, the boy a less threatening one. During the closure stage, the entire group shared feelings about being in abusive relationships and feeling powerless to change established roles and interactive patterns. The exercise helped the members feel more in control of themselves, establish boundaries, and try out new behaviors.

Conclusion

This discussion has focused on significant theoretical and clinical aspects of dance/movement therapy when applied to treatment with children and adolescents. It describes ways in which the needs of these two populations can be served by a modality that gives special attention to the body as a basic means of communication and expression. When used as a primary therapy or in conjunction with other therapies, dance/movement therapy provides a unique and powerful tool for healing.

REFERENCES

Blos, P. (1962). *On adolescence*. New York: Free Press.

Chaiklin, S. (1975). Dance therapy. In S. Arieti (Ed.), *American handbook of psychiatry*. New York: Basic Books. pp 701–715.

Downes, J. (1980). Movement therapy for the special child: Construct for the emerging self. In M. B. Leventhal (Ed.), *Movement and growth: Dance therapy for the special child* (pp. 13–17). New York: New York University Press. The Graduate Dance Therapy Program, Department of Dance and Dance Education with the cooperation of the center for Educational Research.

Duggan, D. (1978). Goals and methods in dance therapy with severely multiply handicapped children. *American Journal of Dance Therapy, 2* (1), 31–34.

Duggan, D. (1995). The "4's": A dance therapy program for learning-disabled adolescents. In F. J. Levy (Ed.), *Dance and other expressive arts therapies* (pp. 225–240). New York: Routledge.

Erfer, T. (1995). Treating children with autism in a public school system. In F. J. Levy (Ed.), *Dance and other expressive arts therapies* (pp. 191–211). New York: Routledge.

Erikson, E. (1963). *Childhood and society*. New York: W. W. Norton.

Evan, B. (1949). The child's world: Its relation to dance pedagogy. 1949–1951. In originally in *Dance Magazine*, now in *Collected works by and about Blanche Evan*. Blanche Evan Dance Foundation. Edited by Ruth G. Benov.

Freud, S. (1927). *The ego and the id*. London: Hogarth Press.

Greenacre, P. (1958). "Early Physical Determinants in the development of the sense of identity." In Journal of the American Psychoanalytic Association, 6, 612–627.

Johnson, D. R., & Eicher, V. (1990). The use of drama activities to facilitate dance therapy with adolescents. *The Arts in Psychotherapy, 17*, 157–164.

Kalish, B. (1974). Working with an autistic child. In K. Mason (Ed.), *Focus on dance VII: Dance therapy* (pp. 38–40). Reston, VA: American Alliance for Health, Physical Education, and Recreation.

Leventhal, M. B. (Ed.). (1980). *Movement and growth: Dance therapy for the special child*. New York: New York University Press. The Graduate Dance Therapy Program, Department of Dance and Dance Education with the cooperation of the Center for Educational Research.

Levy, F. (1988). *Dance movement therapy: A healing art*. Reston, VA: American Alliance for Health, Physical Education, and Recreation.

Loughlin, E. (1993). "Why was I born among mirrors?" Therapeutic dance for teenage girls and women with Turner syndrome. *American Journal of Dance Therapy, 15* (2), 107–124.

Mason, K. (1974). *Focus on dance VII: Dance therapy*. Washington, DC: American Association for Health, Physical Education, and Recreation.

Naess, J. A. (1982). A developmental approach to the interactive process in dance/movement therapy. *American Journal of Dance Therapy, 5*, 43–55.

Polk, E. (1974). Dance therapy with special children. In K. Mason (Ed.), *Focus on dance VII: Dance therapy* (pp. 56–58). Washington, DC: American Association for Health, Physical Education, and Recreation.

Schilder, P. (1950). *The image and appearance of the human body*. New York: International Universities Press.

Schmais, C. (1981). Group development and group formation in dance therapy. *The Arts in Psychotherapy, 8*, 103–107.

Serlin, L. (1993). Root images of healing in dance therapy. *American Journal of Dance Therapy, 15* (2), 65–76.

Stanton-Jones, K. (1992). *Dance/movement therapy in psychiatry*. New York: Routledge.

45 / Drama and Poetry Interventions

Steve Harvey

Introduction and Nature of the Modality

Poetry and drama are used in the psychotherapy of children, adolescents, and their families. In typical examples, patients in individual, group, or family sessions are encouraged to improvise role-playing scenes, write song lyrics or poems, keep journals, and/or develop dramatic performances that have personal relevance. This activity, which is designed to lead to behavioral and emotional change, has as its central feature the development of the patient's capacity to create metaphor. Metaphor making occurs as patients are assisted to give external form to their inner experiences along with the associated emotion and thoughts. By focusing on specially adapted aspects of the dramatic and poetic forms, children and adolescents can become engaged in expressing, organizing, understanding, and ultimately changing their personal conflicts in creative ways.

As disciplines, poetry and drama therapy draw on their respective artistic traditions. Many, if not all, therapists who use the creative, expressive arts have experienced the connections between a young patient's personal experience and his dramatic or poetic expressions. The actual practice of these therapies is thus quite different from the general making of drama and/or poetry. In both drama and poetry therapy, the entire process of making metaphors, as well as the resultant dramas or poems, offer ways for the therapist to intervene. The therapist can thus help child patients and their families observe themselves and become active in making behavioral and emotional changes. For example, an angry teenager in a drama therapy session might be encouraged to enact a fantasized role of a rebellious figure; he can then be helped to generate several endings to the dramatic scenes involving this character. Through a therapist's questioning, this adolescent could presently be led to gain an understanding of various methods of solving problems related to his own anger and its consequences. In a poetry therapy session, this same adolescent might be encouraged to choose rock-song lyrics related to his personal situation and then either add lines to these lyrics or even generate original songs along the same theme. In both these situations, the therapist's efforts would be directed toward helping this patient connect the various verbal and dramatic expressions with his own personal situation.

Throughout this personal expressive process, the therapist can take on several roles and functions. These include exposing patients to various forms of poetic and/or dramatic expression; helping patients develop needed skills to observe and/or produce such expression; providing feedback about how these expressions might be related to real-life concerns; questioning patients about how their own process of metaphor making relates to their current situation or past history; and, occasionally, playing minor roles or directing drama or song production. This would assist a patient in playing or replaying expressions more fully in quasi-public or group performances. The main thrust of drama and poetry therapy is to help unite the process and content aspects of written and dramatic expression with a patient's life.

Background and Conceptual Framework

The use of poetry and drama in psychotherapy have developed from the efforts of multitalented individuals who had interest and experience within the expressive arts and mental health and understood the relationship between these fields. Early in this century, Jacob Moreno, became extremely interested in how the dramatic expression involved in role-playing influenced the emotional life of individuals and groups. He observed how individuals became more spontaneous in their social presentation following dramatic enactments related to current real-life situations. Reflecting on this, Moreno developed psychodrama, a powerful therapeutic form in which individuals enact personal dramatic events, and sociodrama, a form in which group members develop and improvise dramas based on common themes, conflicts, and concerns. Johnson (1982), Landy (1986), and Emunah (1993), among others, incorporated methods from dramatic improvisation involving nonverbal communication as well as role-playing. In addition they utilized public performance of dramas developed from personal and group real-life experiences to expand the range of possibilities in drama therapy. Similarly, Leedy (1969) and other psychiatrists began integrating into psychotherapy the reading, writing, and speaking of poetry and personal journals.

In the current practice of developmental drama and poetry therapy, a conceptual framework has emerged. Generic elements of the experience of making dramatic and poetic metaphors have been identified as being particularly helpful in guiding young patients to engagement in behavioral change. To facilitate more productive work, these parts of a patient's expressive experience are emphasized in psychotherapy sessions. These elements of the expressive experience include (1) encouragement of creative abilities; (2) encouragement of a sense of challenge and intrinsic motivation to become active in poetic and dramatic metaphor making; and (3) the development of therapeutic, artistic expression as a type of lab in which experimentation and active exploration of behavioral change can occur. In this lab, mistakes are expected and employed, thus (4) increasing the experiences of the self as a creator of expression to help counter feelings of helplessness and (5) encouraging group and family cohesion, inclusiveness, and intimacy as patients and their families generate and share spontaneous imagery. In psychotherapy with children and adolescents, each of these parts of the creative process can be developed and nurtured through concrete writing and dramatic activity. Ultimately, drama and poetry therapy with these younger populations involve a very active approach with an accent on doing.

Poetry Therapy

Poetry therapy employs a wide range of poetic and literary expressive techniques. These techniques include (1) use of existing poems, stories, and song lyrics; (2) various expressive methods, such as writing and reading original poetry and/or stories; children to contribute additional word lists to describe these emotions. Using the word collage, groups can then develop collaborative poems to which each child adds a line.

Poetry can be a particularly important activity for adolescents. Many teenagers write to express themselves and poetry is their chosen form. Moreover, when one considers adolescent interest in popular music, it is clear that teenagers have great interest in verbal expression. By encouraging teenagers to develop and then share their private writing, the therapist can gain access to these patients' internal thoughts, which are too painful to be expressed in other ways. Such writing can reveal self-destructive thoughts through themes that emphasize death or plots that leave protagonists in very bad situations. In such cases, patients can be encouraged to use their writing to address their unhappiness.

Poetry groups with adolescents can start with existing poems that highlight certain issues. These poems can stimulate discussion effectively. Discussion can be directed to the collaborative development of poetry, with each member contributing lines or images.

When using existing poems, it is wise to use works related to the mood of the individual patient or group. Poems should be chosen not only to demonstrate difficulties, but also to suggest the ability to surmount obstacles. An effort should be made to anticipate children's reactions and turn to particular poems to serve specific purposes. In using existing poems, the problems to be addressed can be introduced at the beginning of the session by presenting specifically chosen poems. The next poem should introduce a complementary mood or idea. Poems should be short, not too abstract, likely to elicit strong feelings, and related to the therapeutic goals in the group. Usually poems written in the first person are the most effective for the purpose of therapy.

Before using such poems, therapists should do a careful preliminary reading, in which they endeavor to identify all possible meanings. A through understanding will, help facilitate group discussion. In general, therapists should anticipate the reactions and explore the child's understanding of the poem. This precaution is necessary because children may reach silent conclusions that are counterproductive. For example, a poem may cause a child to experience guilt or anxiety that he or she the does not verbalize. Again, when using existing poems, children can become more personally involved if they are given the chance to develop different endings or change specific images or lines.

Various forms of creative writing, including oral creations, are utilized in poetry therapy. This use of verbal metaphor making can provide a safe distance for children and adolescents to express their feelings when all of their other channels of communication are closed. Poetry and other forms of writing can foster self-reflection and establish a sense of competence in using disciplined self-disclosure. Such creative writing can be used with children as young as 6 years of age. Interventions with first- and second-grade children may take the form of providing certain key "feeling" words and asking experience was very helpful to them. According to the therapist, this girl was unable to engage in any other more traditional therapeutic intervention; the poetic metaphors were offered spontaneously within the therapeutic relationship.

To illustrate several of these ideas, Weisberger, in a personal communication in 1993, describe a case in which a 7-year-old girl spontaneously provided imagery to described her emotional experience of watching her grandmother slowly die of cancer.

In a conversation with her therapist, the girl kept saying that inside her she had an "oval" that had burst. In further sessions, the girl used this image to describe how she had been holding all of her feelings inside (the oval) until she needed to express them (the bursting). The therapist wrote these images down for the girl in the form of a poem. When the grandmother did die, the girl and her mother placed a typed version of the poem in the coffin. This act helped the girl actively participate in the funeral rite and express her grief and was very emotionally cathartic for her. The girl's mother reported how important the poem was in understanding and empathizing with her daughter's feelings. Both mother and daughter reported that this experience was very helpful to them. According to the therapist, this girl was unable to engage in any other more traditional

therapeutic intervention; the poetic metaphors were offered spontaneously within the therapist's relationship.

This case illustrates the effectiveness of metaphor making in helping children express what they cannot do in any other way.

Drama Therapy

Drama therapy involves the intentional use of dramatic expression to address emotional and behavioral conflict and to attain symptom relief. The primary techniques include role-playing and patient enactment of real events, fantasized or make-believe stories, or therapist-prescribed themes. This role-playing can employ many media, including puppet play, use of dolls, and various game enactments (e.g., follow the leader, hide-and-seek, or specifically created games). In more typical dramatic play, the most commonly used form of enactment involves children actually assuming roles and generating improvised action. Action can take the form of nonverbal gestures, facial expressions, and interactive movement. In individual therapy, the therapist often takes on the smaller and complementary roles; in group or family intervention, the therapist functions as an observer or director while other group or family members provide the interactive enactment and role-playing of the dramas. Some techniques also involve the use of specially trained therapists, actors, and dancers who perform improvisations of children's and families' real-life stories or expressed feeling states (Salas, 1993). Finally, groups of children or teenagers have been helped to produce and generate their own plays about their common experiences.

Typical drama therapy sessions include some kind of role-playing and dramatic expression in combination with some verbal expression and consideration of how these improvised dramas can apply to life conflicts. As sessions progress, the therapist must decide how much emphasis to place on using the drama to help children and adolescents talk about their conflicts in order to gain understanding and control of their conflicting feelings. The therapist must also decide how much attention given to helping patients elaborate their ongoing improvisations in order to search experientially for more action-oriented solutions. These questions—(1) how and when to stop and reflect on personal meaning and (2) when to continue with dramatic experience in search of problem resolution—are central therapeutic considerations in drama therapy. Typically, patients with less control of expression need more verbal reflection. Conversely, withdrawn and less motivated patients need to continue and extend their dramatic action creatively.

To accomplish these goals, drama therapists have developed various techniques. To facilitate interpretation, the therapist can reflect on the process of the drama, noticing how conflicts arise in various enactments and stories and how the process of role-playing furthers, hinders, or disguises essential core difficulties. Such observations are then used to discuss current or past difficulties. These are various interventions designed to help patients extend their enactments more productively. In one intervention the therapist freezes the drama and directs the development of alternative endings and/or new lines within a conflict situation. A therapist can also help patients develop fantasy scenes to replace conflict-laden enactments with creatively engendered positive feelings, such as hope. Patients can extend important dramatic moments by using movement expression to fill out their statements more fully. This is particularly useful for patients who are less verbally able. In group or family situations, other members or the therapist can play out a particular patient's inner thoughts and feelings and/or develop alternative solutions for the central characters within an enactment. Incorporating resistance (especially with teenagers) by allowing development of dramas that include rebellious characters and angry, strong emotional expression can also be helpful.

Audience performance and video recording of improvised enactments can highlight organizational and communicative abilities that performances call for. In general, performance is used with targeted groups of preteen and adolescent children to help improve social skills, including the development of trust, interpersonal problem solving, and positive peer relations. When using performances, these children and adolescents become involved in writing, improvising, organizing, directing, and participating in a final performance. Performance can also be a very important vehicle through which adolescents can satisfy their need to express strong feelings to their com-

munities in a positive fashion. The enactments can be done in school and community situations and involve themes including substance abuse, AIDS, date rape, family problems, homophobia, and gender roles.

Drama therapy can be applied very effectively in family therapy situations. One intervention with young children and their families involves using specifically designed dramatic and interactive game playing to address difficulties with trust and disorganized attachment styles. Such dramatic interaction can help children build an understanding of intimate relationships. This work has important implications when working with children who have, as a result of severe abuse and separation from caregivers, developed significant insecurities and disturbed attachment styles.

In family drama therapy structured games help repair a child's social development by facilitating the emergence of a new quality of intrafamilial relationship. The games involve sensitive, moment-to-moment turn taking and the abilities to imitate; find cause and effect in nonverbal, intimate communication; and of parents and children create dramatic images collaboratively.

Interactive game playing with children and their families usually begins with a simple starting activity, such as a parent and child making faces at one another while rolling a ball back and forth. As such interaction continues, children showing major difficulties with trust often introduce major deviations and impasses, causing the game playing to stop or break down. The therapeutic strategy at this point is to incorporate these deviations into the action and help the family make a new, improvised game. These play breaks include things like small injuries, the child changing the rules of the game, the child introducing rapid emotional state changes, and refusal to play. In general, these occurrences function to stop play interaction between parents and children. Such breaks from the simple initial game are seen as enactments of the disorganization of the attachment relationship within the family. As the family is helped to improvise using such recurring interactive patterns, through interactive play they can develop alternative metaphors that are healing.

An example of this style of parent-child play occurred when treating an adopted 7-year-old boy who during his infancy had a history of failure to thrive in several foster home placements.

The therapist asked the boy to play face games with his adoptive mother of 5 years. As mutual face making progressed, the mother made more than adequate efforts to provide a fun, playful atmosphere. Despite her efforts the boy repeatedly looked away, remained dazed, and had difficulty to producing faces. The therapist asked the boy to look around the room and find the point that most interested him. His gaze led to a pile of pillows, and he was asked to go there. The boy then crawled under the pillows, became more animated, and stated he was a squirrel in a treehouse. He and his mother began to develop face games where he could look out of "windows" at her and continue in the role of his chosen animal. Eventually, as the boy began to enjoy the face game at a distance from his mother, he invented a new part of the game in which he left his house to join her for a meal. By including the boy's looking away as part of the game, the child was able to continue his improvisation in a new and creative way. Presently, his basic fears and strong emotional conflict related to trust and becoming close to his adoptive mother underwent a change. In this illustration, the game had clear emotional significance, which was later discussed. In the course of this conversation, the adoptive mother was able to recognize the dazed look as relating to her son's difficult infancy. Though the boy could not report any verbal insight into how the game was connected to his past, he and his mother began to play "squirrel," which included more interactive play, in his home. It was this active parent-child creation, in combination with some reflection by the parent, that helped bring about a change in the climate of intimacy in this relationship.

Developmental Considerations

Drama and poetry therapy in some form can be successfully applied to children of many ages. Interactive dramatic play can be used to facilitate the development of attachment relationships with families with infants, toddlers, and preschoolers. Along this line, group drama therapy can serve children with significant developmental delays. Here the positive sensory experiences help such children express themselves in dramatic play. Such approaches usually need to utilize adult modeling of dramatic play and humor, this leads to more independent performances of dramas that have a symbolic meaning. Throughout the preschool and elementary years, dramatic expression can be developed using puppetry and dramatic storytelling in group, family, and individual therapy. As children become developmentally able to conceptualize expression, they are increasingly able to use poetry and other verbal means in their metaphor making.

Drama therapy can be particularly useful in working with the resistance and acting out common in adolescence. At this age, patients typically need to express high intensity and complex emotions, and they evidence a wish to explore real-life possibilities with safety and distance. Drama therapy can be adapted to help groups of teenagers express such intensity and then use more neutral acting out to explore the possibilities of their actions. The therapist can also help teenagers develop a sense of mastery over their emotions by using the skill building and decision making involved in making dramatic and theatric metaphors.

Qualifications of the Clinician

Clearly, in addition to a background in mental health, clinicians who use poetry and drama therapy should have some direct experience with these creative art forms. Typically, programs that train graduate-level poetry and drama therapists include academic coursework in clinical and abnormal psychology, professional issues related to ethics and research, as well as coursework dealing with the theory and skills of drama or poetry therapy. Such programs usually require supervised clinical practicum and internship experiences as preparation for being an independent poetry or drama therapist. Some psychotherapists with training in psychiatry, social work, or psychology incorporate poetry and drama therapy into their work with children, adolescents, and their families. Such practitioners have usually taken additional training in creative arts therapies and have experience in the creative arts.

Equipment and Technological Considerations

The materials involved in poetry therapy range from pen and paper to collections of poems and literature that can be read and presented in different group activities. Haynes and Haynes-Berry (1986) have compiled a collection of literature, poems, and writing activities that can be used in bibliotherapy, especially with groups of young abused children.

When necessary, drama therapists working with young children use a variety of props, costume pieces, puppets, and video equipment to stimulate dramatic enactment and facilitate performance. When engaging children in puppet play, it is wise to use a wide range of puppets, ranging from the realistic to the supernatural. This range is helpful in allowing children to project a variety of interactive scenarios and emotional states into their play. In regard to costume pieces and props, provide neutral pieces such as colored scarves, pieces of cloth, and different kinds of hats. Unlike specific costumes, neutral pieces tend to encourage and develop the use of creative fantasy rather than restrict imagination. Some drama therapists use of makeup and facepaint. To encourage dramatic family enactment with young children, other therapists use stuffed animals of different sizes and props that are as large as the participants. Large pillows can be used to make houses and walls and define different spots of the room. Videotaping dramatic enactment can help patients observe themselves and organize their expressions.

Indications, Contraindications, and Risks

Many children and teenagers engage in writing and dramatic play quite naturally. Where verbal methods have proven difficult, drama and poetry therapy have been shown to be an excellent way to engage children in activities that can be therapeutic. As with several of the other creative arts therapies, drama and poetry therapies are especially helpful in dealing with children who have experienced abusive trauma. Initially, it is often easier for child victims to express their feelings about what has happened to them and their emotional experience by using poetry or dramatic enactions than by to communications verbally. Quite

often, the experience of abuse is so traumatic that children are unable to use everyday words, and the imagery of the various expressive arts provides the only avenue of expression available.

Poetry and drama therapy are, of course, not without risks. Some disturbed children and teenagers may not be ready for engagement in expression, and caution should be exercised. Usually, the drama and poetry therapist has the skill and training to determine whether a child is appropriate for involvement in expressive arts activities, and how much expression an individual child can tolerate. Appropriate follow-up after expressive activities is recommended; follow-up helps children integrate their expressive experiences. During follow-up interviews the therapist can look for signs—such as disintegration, disconnected thinking, or emotional withdrawal—that suggest that further use of poetry or drama therapy may not be beneficial.

The mental health field has recently been the arena for controversy about practitioners influencing children's accounts of abuse. Clinicians must not lead children to develop false "memories" or make false statements concerning past experiences with trauma. This is particularly relevant when the therapist participates in a dramatic enactment or in the development of a metaphor. In such cases, the therapist must be particularly sensitive and use only the child's cues in an appropriate fashion, without adding pieces to suggest that a given person may have committed assaulted the child or that a particular event occurred. Generally, it is recommended that the process of evaluation of abuse on the one hand, be kept completely separate from drama or poetry therapy on the other, to help guard against undue influence.

Measures of Clinical Progress

Because the creative arts therapies involve the process of developing metaphors, a child, group, or family's involvement in intrinsic, independent metaphor making serves as an excellent indicator of clinical progress. A therapist may use various structures to help begin a therapeutic activity; as progress is being made, participants become more able to engage in expressive activity independently. To the extent that various group and/or family clients are able to sustain creative activities for a longer time, progress is occurring. Also, an examination of the content of the metaphors yields some indications of change. As clients are able not only to develop metaphors, but also to create strategies that lead to positive endings and to depict their self-images in a more positive light, therapy can be assumed to be beneficial.

Duration and Termination

The activities of creative arts therapies are very adaptable. Consequently, when appropriate clinical goals are set, these interventions can be used on a short- or long-term basis. If a child is to be seen on a short-term basis, such as in a crisis intervention, the primary goal is to help the him or her use the distance provided by the expressive media. Initially and concretely, distance can help the youngster define the problem situation along with its emotional components. In long-term cases, the therapeutic goal is for the clients to experience more of the expressive process and then, at his or her own pace, connect the process with life.

Termination is determined when the individual, group, or family can realistically engage in creative metaphor making in a way that addresses the presenting problem. Because poetry and drama therapy emphasize the externalizing of internal experience, the clinician can engage the clients themselves in judging when the metaphor making adequately resolves their initial conflict. In the course of the termination process, the therapist can review the client's, group's, or family's progression of themes and imagery. Final sessions can include some sort of good-bye ritual, including positive enactments or poem making to summarize the treatment and the client's involvement with the therapist.

Ethical and Social Issues

Generally, all information exchanged between a therapist and client or client group is confidential and cannot be shared outside the therapeutic context without expressed, written consent. This is important when considering that clients often produce poems, videotapes, or other lasting expressive pieces as part of the therapy. When performance is part of the therapeutic process, even if expressed consent is given, the drama or poetry therapist must carefully consider the client's reaction. In this case, therapists must both prepare and include the clients involved in the performance as part of the therapeutic process.

Although it is very important to maintain a client's confidentiality, the expressive aspect of performance provides an extremely important avenue for communication within a community. When appropriate therapeutic attention is given to performance and/or publication, drama and poetry can be powerful tools in helping patients present very real human issues in an organized and understandable form, and educating communities about the inner emotional experience of different client groups.

Conclusion: Outcome Studies, Future Directions, and Unanswered Questions

Very few outcome studies involving appropriate control groups exist. Despite this lack of research, anecdotal and observational evidence suggest that both poetry and drama therapy can be highly effective. Therefore, these forms should be considered as clinically useful, though as yet unproven.

The use of poetry and drama is relatively uneven across the country. This is due more to logistical than professional reasons. In areas close to creative arts therapy training centers and universities and where creative arts therapists have been able to obtain licensure as mental health counselors, these intervention styles have become accepted and a part of mainstream delivery. In areas of the country where poetry and drama therapists do not have the same visibility, these interventions are not being utilized. Hopefully, with the growth of university training programs and as interested psychotherapists and researchers from other disciplines become involved in drama and poetry therapy, these gaps will disappear.

Perhaps the most interesting facet of successful engagement of children and teenagers in drama and poetry therapy interventions is the way creativity affects day-to-day human behavior in schools, families, and social interaction. As many therapeutic experiences show, the process of making metaphors that are relevant to the lived experiential moment can have benefit.

REFERENCES

Emunah, R. (1993). Acting for real: Drama therapy process, technique, and performance. New York: Brunner/Mazel.

Haynes, A. N., & Haynes-Berry, M. (1982). Bibliopoetry therapy: A resource bibliography. St. Joseph, NM: Bibliotherapy Roundtable.

Haynes, A. N., & Haynes-Berry, M. (1986). Bibliotherapy—The interactive process: A handbook. Boulder, CO: Westview Press.

Johnson, D. (1982). Developmental approaches in drama therapy. The Arts in Psychotherapy, 9, 183–190.

Johnson, D. (1991). The theory and technique of transformations in drama therapy. The Arts in Psychotherapy, 18, 285–300.

Landy, R. J. (1986). Drama therapy: Concepts and practices. Springfield, IL: Charles C Thomas.

Landy, R. J. (1993). Persona and performance: The meaning of role in drama therapy in everyday life. New York: Guilford Press.

Leedy, J. (1969). Poetry therapy. Philadelphia: J. B. Lippincott.

Leedy, J. (1993). Poetry the healer. Philadelphia: J. B. Lippincott.

Salas, J. (1993). Improvising real life. Dubuque, IA: Kendall-Hunt.

46 / Music Interventions

Amy Hammel

History of Music as a Therapy

Music has been used therapeutically in the treatment of emotional, physical, and mental illnesses for many centuries. In ancient times it was claimed that music could heal the soul, body, and mind through the rhythms and sounds of songs and incantations. The histories of the Egyptians, Persians, Greeks, and Hebrews contain many instances of music as therapy for mental problems, such as David's use of the harp to help alleviate King Saul's depression (In I Sam., 16:23).

Definition

Music therapy is the use of music in treatment by a trained and accredited person within a clinical relationship that is established to instill, alleviate, modify, or enhance desired changes in thoughts, feelings, or behaviors. The emphasis in music therapy is on the process of music in the therapeutic relationship, not on the actual product of a musical creation or event. The therapeutic relationship is established over time, and music is an integral element of this relationship. The music therapist must be adept on a variety of instruments, because communicating musically is inherent to music therapy. In addition, the music therapist needs to be well-trained as a psychotherapist in order to respond effectively to the nonmusical issues that arise during the therapeutic process.

Settings and Goals

Music therapy is used in a wide variety of environments. Some of these include

- psychiatric hospitals, outpatient clinics, and centers
- general hospitals (delivery rooms, burn units, surgical areas)
- specialty hospitals (for the treatment of physical impairments, terminal illnesses, neurological traumas)
- nursing homes and residential centers
- developmental centers and institutes (for treatment of the visually impaired or hearing impaired, mentally retarded, cerebral palsy-afflicted patients)
- special community and private programs (for persons with substance abuse problems, AIDS, posttraumatic stress disorder)
- educational systems (for children who are gifted or who have multiple handicaps, or youngsters with communicative, learning, or emotional disorders)
- correctional systems (prisons, jails, and forensic units)
- private practice (for those seeking pain relief, stress reduction or self-growth)

The music therapy goals for children and adolescents with psychiatric diagnoses might be increased self-esteem; reduced anxiety, depression or unwanted feelings and/or thoughts; increased self-expression and communication skills; increased range and flexibility of behaviors; improved peer and family relations and social interactions; and heightened insight and resolution of internal conflicts.

In research investigating children's and adolescents' psychological responses to music, benefits include increased verbalization, increased self-esteem, heightened cooperation and trust, greater facility with task performance, and increased peer acceptance.

Elements of Music Therapy Treatment

A therapeutic relationship between a patient or client and the music therapist is based upon the powerful elements that music can provide. This music therapy relationship can be created through music listening, music creation, and music discussions. This can be done in individual, dyad, or group sessions. The client's needs determine how the music is used. For example, some children with psychiatric disorders may need to participate in small groups using instruments, whereas certain adolescents may be able to participate in larger groups where the focus is on listening to and exploring the meanings of particular songs that are important to them.

The musical equipment used is also contingent upon the patient population. The instrumentation and music must be not only age appropriate, but culturally congruent. For example, the inner city child will probably relate more quickly and genuinely to the drum machine than to the violin. Generally, instruments that produce authentic sounds and that are not toy-sized will aid the client in creating a fulfilling sound production. Prerecorded music (often popular songs) needs to come from the patient's own listening repertoire to be most useful in the therapeutic context.

Music therapy may be effective for any person who can experience and enjoy music. It is contraindicated for anyone who finds music unpleasant. Most people use music as a part of their everyday lives. Listening to music frequently takes place throughout the day and is often a primary leisure activity for children, adolescents, and adults. A risk of using music as a therapy is the recalling of fears or negative thoughts that stem from previous associations. These fears might be manifested by an unwillingness to sing or play an instrument because of negative experiences of feeling unmusical in prior music education or performance settings (i.e., piano lessons). This type of risk would need to be worked through with sensitivity in the context of the music therapy relationship in order for the negative, performance-oriented associations to diminish.

Creating Music

Sometimes psychiatric patients are thought to be unavailable for participation in a group process because of the level of their disturbances. Often music can provide several ingredients that make participation in a group a successful experience. It may contain a structure that can feel safe and secure. Music can be expressive without evoking feelings of fear of rejection from others. It can offer simultaneously both individuation and group cohesion, especially when instruments are being played. A group can play together as a unit while individuals have simultaneous opportunities for self-expression within the group's music making. Music is generally found by most people to be enjoyable; therefore when music is created successfully and sounds good to the creator(s), it can raise self-esteem.

"We Sound Great!": A group of children, ages 9 to 11, in a day treatment program were deemed unsuitable for any group therapy because of their levels of aggressiveness, psychosis, and hyperactivity. The children recognized this exclusion and spoke of feeling like "failures" for being left out. Therefore, a less verbal group therapy, music therapy, was selected by the staff as a possible accommodation for these children.

The children formed their own rules for their group and with the music therapist wrote these rules in the form of a rap song with which they began each group session. Singing these rules seemed to establish an important ritual, which in turn appeared to create an environment of safety within the group while offering an element of control to each of the contributing composers.

The group would then sing a song to each member inquiring how each individual was feeling on that day. To this each would respond by playing on an instrument of choice (from a variety of percussion instruments). It was then the music therapist's duty to verbalize her interpretation of the feelings. The member corrected or approved each interpretation. Hearing verbal descriptions of feelings that they first expressed musically, afforded the children a feeling-oriented vocabulary.

Often the children would then choose follow-the-leader types of musical events. For example, each would take a turn being the leader on the largest of the drums, and the group would have to listen and watch to know when and how to play their smaller drums. As the group became more and more adept at playing music

together, they demanded more and more from each other musically. They needed to listen intently and for prolonged periods in order to replicate intricate rhythmic patterns. The concentrated, silent attention of the group would give the leader a feeling of power and validation as he heard his musical ideas echoed in responses from the others.

At other times the group wanted to play together, and the music therapist would set up a rhythmic, harmonic background on the guitar while the members improvised with their own individual rhythms on various percussive instruments. This group of children, who previously felt like failures and were thought incapable of remaining seated with others in a group, proclaimed that their group's music "sounded great" and congratulated each other.

As the group became more adventurous, the children decided to draw on cardboard circles faces depicting various feelings. They put these faces into a bag and took turns picking a face, but not showing it to peers. Each child selected an instrument to portray the emotions through musical improvisations and physical postures. He or she positioned the body in a fashion congruent with the feeling to be portrayed musically. The music often seemed to increase the capacities to role-play emotions, perhaps by making the feeling seem more real. The other patients guessed which feeling was being portrayed. This technique afforded the group the opportunity to learn and expand musical, physical, and verbal vocabularies, thus giving the members increased modes of self-expression in positive ways.

Musical Identification

A song can serve not only as a vehicle for self description, but as a way to speak the unspeakable, particularly for a child. The music can express the mood of the child and the lyrics can help label or describe the specific events creating the feelings.

"My Name is Luka": Sue, a shy and nervous 8-year-old girl, was a newcomer to a music therapy group and had come to the inpatient unit with an admitting diagnosis of dysthymia. Her condition had no known precipitating cause, according to the parents. On the unit she generally was polite and superficial and made little contact with her peers or the staff. During one of her first music therapy groups, she listened to another group member talk about her favorite song, Suzanne Vega's "Luka." This song portrays a young girl who is abused

in her home but tells the neighbors not to ask her what is wrong. After the song ended, Sue spoke very quietly to a peer; "That's like my house." The peer knew what Sue was talking about and replied, "It's mine too." Together they began to sing the lyrics and speak about the similarities between their lives and the life of the girl depicted in the song. The group, which was often loud and rambunctious on the unit, sat attentively as the girls spoke. The music therapist played and sang the song on the piano, leaving spaces for the two girls to fill in their own names and experiences into the song. Soon the entire group was singing this personalized song together. When the session ended, many of the members offered Sue signs of support, such as kind words and hugs. During Sue's hospitalization she was especially friendly with the particular peer who shared the song, and Sue continued to brighten up and speak about abuse in her home during sessions.

The mood of the music therapy group was powerfully set by the initial song which helped the group speak about a sensitive issue, parental abusiveness. Although some members of the group did not share these experiences, they were able to empathize with the two girls because of the emotional content of the song. Music can create a supportive atmosphere, enabling members of a group to feel more comfortable and communicative. This cohesive environment helps the members share experiences on a deep emotional level, thereby fostering empathy.

Songwriting

Sometimes people experience fears they cannot express verbally. This is often more pronounced in children with psychotic disturbances. Through the vehicle of songwriting, anxiety can be allayed and information about dangers that cause fears can be shared. A Music Therapy group of children first wrote a song, then repeated their song in different ways in order to control the effect their fear had on them. In this way they were able to experience and to express their freedom from their original anxiety.

"FIRE" A music therapy outpatient group contained five 4 to 7-year-old boys with varying diagnoses from psychosis to oppositional defiant disorder. They met in a session immediately prior to Halloween. One member brought up the possibility of his being "burned to death" if someone came near him with a cigarette while he was wearing his Halloween costume. This fear ignited the group's anxiety about fire, especially relevant since some of them had histories of firesetting. Their actions became more and more disruptive and aggressive, and their words became more loosely associated. They were then presented with the idea of writing a song about what they were feeling.

After they voted to write their first song, the music therapist drew a series of lines on a posterboard, to simplify the idea of writing a song and to concretize the rhythm of the song to ensure its success or appeal.

The group was asked to pick a title and place it in the first and last lines of the song. Their title was "Fire" and each member contributed words to the song. They experimented with ways to sing their song to the therapist's guitar accompaniment, sometimes singing loudly and quickly, like "football players" softly and slowly, like "little babies," or with accents, like "cowboys." Later they added verses and requested firehats to wear as they sang. They decorated their song poster with tissue paper resembling flames and hung the poster in the music therapy room.

During the following year the group often asked to sing this particular song because they claimed it "felt good" to sing it. It offered the boys a chance to control their fears instead of being controlled by their fears.

"FIRE"
by the Boy's Music Therapy Group

Fire
Frightening Scary
Call The Fireman
Don't Play With Matches
Fire

Fires are dangerous
Don't mess with gasoline
They burn down houses
You'll have no home

Communicating Through Music

Adolescents often expend huge amounts of energy listening to music and expressing their musical tastes. Music is part of their daily lives and is very often an important emblem of identification within a particular subculture. It is something adolescents take with them wherever they go—even into psychiatric hospitalization. They may bring their music with them physically (e.g. in the form of cassette tapes or lyrics on clothing) or emotionally (by remembering music). Generally, the music they listen to is quite purposeful and meaningful. It expresses their beliefs, hopes, fears, and feelings. The music therapist who speaks the youngster's language with regard to music (knows the adolescent's favorite songs) has a powerful tool in opening up lines of communication. The beginning of a trusting relationship is often created by the mere fact that an adult is not only familiar with the names of the adolescent's favorite groups or songs, but recalls specific lyrics or plays musical patterns from these songs.

"Fade to Black": Dave, an angry and isolative 16-year-old inpatient, claimed to have no psychological, social, or emotional concerns (despite his diagnosis of depression), just anger at his parents for their censorship attempts on his music and his "life." The staff had been concerned that Dave rarely spoke, responding only with monosyllabic grunts, if at all, to their questions. He refused to see any doctors and sat silently when his parents visited. In response to the music therapist's initial questions about the type of music he liked, he said that his favorite group was a heavy-metal band named Metallica. The music therapist verbally recalled names of a few of the group's records, and she asked him which of the group's songs was his favorite. His surprise at the therapist's ability to speak his language sparked him to complete his first spontaneous, lengthy utterance of his hospitalization. Dave told the music therapist, "My song is "Fade to Black". That's my insides. Only my friends knew it, and it scared them so they quit hanging out with me. My parents would freak if they knew what my song said, but all they ever told me was to turn it down or turn it off."

Dave and the music therapist then listened to a recording of the song together, and he stopped the tape several times to point out the key lyrics with which he identified. Most of these lyrics had to do with death and the feeling that life was not worth living. As Dave spoke about the lyrics, he shared specific aspects of his life that troubled him and he recognized that he needed help understanding his troubles. Often by obtaining a "musical history", the music therapist is allowed access to far more personal and pertinent information than is revealed through the psychosocial history taken upon admission.

The sharing of Dave's song not only created a close therapeutic alliance, but it provided the treatment team with valuable information about his level of suicidality.

This information probably would not have been revealed on such an immediate and profound level without the medium of music and the ability of the music therapist to access it through the common language they shared.

A person selects music that matches his or her thoughts and/or feelings. Songs can serve as an outward reflection of an inner thought process. If "inappropriate" behaviors appear to surface when a youngster listens to certain music, a closer analysis of the music and its meanings for the youngster is warranted. That will give the youngster an opportunity to develop insight into his or her reactions.

Conclusion

Music therapy can have simultaneous diagnostic and therapeutic implications. Music can be pleasurable and is therefore desirable to patients as a form of therapy. Because music can be nonthreatening, barriers of defense are often lowered within the music therapy relationship. Creating music is a collaborative process that instills a sense of trust in the participants, since it involves mutual musical risk-taking. Moreover, when structured successfully by the music therapist, the creation of music is intrinsically reinforcing and can thus raise the self-esteem of the participants.

The case example, "We Sound Great!", illustrated how the acquisition of musical vocabulary can instill a verbal and physical vocabulary. Youngsters with psychiatric disorders often have enormous difficulties identifying and then communicating their feelings successfully. Through the creation of music, specifically musical role-playing of emotions, these youngsters gained the opportunity to learn and practice effective communication skills.

"My Name Is Luka," the second case described, is a case of how songs can provide a safe distance from which to disclose painful experiences without revealing too much. Songs can confirm feelings and offer a sense of validation, a sense that someone else has had similar perceptions. The inherent structure of a song—with a beginning, middle and end—offers the listener a feeling of security, the sense that his or her conflicts or problems will also have a resolution.

"Fire" demonstrated how, through the process of songwriting, a group can conquer fears. The participants were able to change their own moods by selecting different musical elements—such as rhythm, key, tempo, and timbre—thereby gaining control of their fears which otherwise controlled them. In addition, music is based in time, which provides the necessary structure for treatment of psychoses by giving feedback on a moment-to-moment basis both auditorily and visually.

"Fade To Black," the final case example, was an example of how music can be used as a metaphor to express feelings. Music, specifically songs, can evoke paired associations. The listener can be transported back to where he was and how he felt when he originally heard the song. This musical association can include many differing aspects simultaneously: For example, the lyrics can convey a sad feeling while the music evokes an angry mood, thus reflecting conflictual or complex feelings.

Music therapy focuses on the process of music in the patient's life as well as in the therapeutic relationship. Very often music is already present in a patient's life and already used intentionally or unintentionally, to gain insight or confirmation regarding perceptions or to reflect, enhance, or alter mood. Music can serve as a form of self-expression and communication, facilitate the therapeutic relationship, and aid group cohesion. The music therapist incorporates these various properties into the therapeutic process as a primary or a parallel therapy.

REFERENCES

Alvin, J. (1966). *Music therapy*. London: Baker.

Chomet, H. (1875). *The Influence of music on health and life*. New York: G. P. Putnam's Sons.

Gaston, E. T. (1968). *Music therapy*. New York: Macmillan.

Nordoff, P., & Robbins, C. (1971). *Therapy in music for handicapped children*. New York: St. Martin's Press.

Priestley, M. (1994). *Essays on analytical music therapy*. Phoenixville, Pa: Barcelona.

Tyson, F. (1981). *Psychiatric music therapy: Origins and development*. New York: Fred Weidner & Son.

Wigram, T., Saperston, B., and West, R. (Eds.) (1995). *The art and science of music therapy: A handbook*. Switzerland: Harwood.

47 / **Recreational Therapy**

CeEtta Medlock Crayton

During the course of history many organizations have called upon recreation professions to intervene in social disorders throughout the world. The recreation profession has responded by presenting programs of social development that have interacted well with many forms of social problems in the United States and other countries. Recreation programming is a vital aspect of the intervention process for growth of individuals, especially in the areas of social development and physical well being.

It is important to stress the thrust of social interactions in recreation intervention. The interactions of intervention include physiological and psychological benefits: a five phase process of 1) assessment, 2) development (planning), 3) implementation, 4) evaluation, and 5) modification (carpenter and Howe, 1985). The main thrust of this chapter is to define and analyze the process involved in recreation intervention.

Recreation Defined

Recreation is often seen as an activity that is engaged in during one's free time, is pleasurable, and which has socially redeeming qualities (Kraus 1990). Recreation participation however, usually must result in constructive, positive, socially accepted behavior in order to be seen as rewarding. Whatever the activity, recreation can be used as an intervention strategy to promote wellness and physical well-being, and to combat negative aspects of behavior, such as loneliness, shyness, shutting off the outside world and a break-down in family life.

Play Defined

Play is universal, it has shaped the values, norms and customs of all cultures. (Edington 1995) Play may be considered the "business" of childhood. Children often engage in play spontaneously, with no inhibitions, joyfully and with a sense of freedom. Thus, play can be used as an intervention tool for children to promote socially accepted behavior and encourage normal growth patterns.

Games Defined

Games are leisure experiences with formal rules that define the interaction content, attempt to equalize the players, and define the role that skills and chance will play in determining the outcome (Rossman, 1995). In every culture we see people playing games. Whether it be the young Asian boy learning martial arts, or the young American girl learning to play the game of Monopoly, both are preparation for roles that will be assumed in adulthood. Gender and other roles are seen in games and are often acted out in the play environ-

ment where according to Edington, "our earlier notion of who we are is formed."

Recreation Activities

Recreation activities encourage normal growth and educational opportunities for children. It should be noted that play for children and adolescents can be used to help them learn to communicate and share feelings, release stress and help channel surplus energy, and to provide choices which promote problem solving and decision making, and simulate competitive experiences similar to adult life situations. It is also important to have activities that temporarily release aggressive urges, and to practice social interaction with peers which will hopefully lead to lasting friendships.

Physiological Benefits

It has been researched in recreation activities that persons that socially interact together secrete higher levels of immunoglobin "A" and an increase in positive thinking chemicals such as norephinephrine. Additional benefits from recreation intervention activities include social activities which develop close, warm friendships and highly visible action activities that will increase physiological benefits in those who participate.

Psychological Benefits

The positive psychological benefits of recreation intervention are: enhanced self-esteem, closeness to others, and positive moods. Recreation activities promote social development and the formation of warm and close friendships. Negative aspects of life, such as, loneliness, shyness, health, weight problems, shutting off from the outside world, and a break-down in family life can be dealt with in supportive, carefully planned recreation activity programs.

The Recreation Intervention Process

The recreation intervention process involves 5 phases: Phase 1) assessment, Phase 2) development (planning), Phase 3) implementation, Phase 4) evaluation and Phase 5) modification (Carpenter and Howe 1985).

PHASE 1 — ASSESSMENT

In order to understand the patient's physical limitations; abilities; socialization needs; and levels of confidence, self-esteem, and cognitive skills, an assessment must be the first step in recreation intervention.

An assessment will assist in developing an awareness of a patient's strengths and weaknesses at the beginning of the intervention process.

For example: Susan (age 11), while playing Monopoly, can be involved in a situation where a recreation professional can observe her social interactions with her peers. Her abilities to follow rule and regulations, to play fairly, to concentrate and stay on task are very important in her social development.

We can also observe her problem-solving and decision-making abilities within the rules of this game. Her ability to grasp small pieces, count spaces, and move directionally will help her spatial and cognitive awareness and development.

Recreation assessment occurs at three levels: physical, cognitive, and social interaction (Peters 1985). One of the best recreation assessment programs for children is the "Recreation Behavior Inventory" developed by D. Berryman and C. La-Fevvre. It utilizes a variety of games and activities to assess the three levels of functioning and includes leadership tips and measurements for recreation intervention based on the clinician's observations.

PHASE 2 — DEVELOPMENT (PLANNING)

In the second phase, the development or planning phase, the recreation intervener uses data produced by the assessment phase to plan intervening activities for patients. It is during this phase that the recreation intervention professional matches patients with the assessed goals and program objectives. The development and planning phase should introduce structured and unstructured play activities to meet assessed needs.

For example, the clinician might strongly suggest that Bob, age 16, go to social dance classes in order to work on social interaction skills, dating behaviors, developing new dance skills. This therapy may also aid him in the use of appropriate grooming skills and help him to have a normalized teenage experience.

Unstructured play is a time that is set aside for play, where the child is escorted to the play area and allowed to freely select activities of choice. Unstructured play allows the clinician to observe choice of play items, selection of playmates, level of concentration and interaction skills with peers and staff without professional intervention.

PHASE 3 — IMPLEMENTATION

The third phase of the intervention process is the implementation period, the actual provision of the recreation experience to the participants (Carpenter and Howe, 1985). This is where activities are conducted that compliment the program and individual patient goals. During this stage games are played, crafts are created, team sports are played, and fitness programs are conducted. Patients are either referred to or voluntarily select activities. During this stage the clinician should observe patient reaction to the activities, and their level of skill, involvement, and participation in the activities. Their social interaction skills, their physical abilities, and their cognitive levels and skills also should be recorded. These observations are recorded at regular intervals and later used in progress notes as a record of patient intervention and treatment.

PHASE 4 — EVALUATION

The discipline of recreation intervention must define this phase in its most basic form: Evaluation is the process of judging the merit, worth, and value of something. It is a systematic inquiry within which some judgment of merit or worth is made based on certain criteria (Carpenter and Howe, 1985). Evaluation is a two-way communication tool. It can be used between recreation intervention personnel and the clientele to assess continued treatment needs.

Based on the observation and written reports of the patient's participation in recreation activities, an evaluation of the patient's progress is conducted. The clinician should consider all phases of the program goals, and make changes and corrections as warranted.

Example, Bob, age 16, is now participating cooperatively in the social dance group. He shares feelings in the debriefing group and contributes to the discussion appropriately. He appears friendly and seems to anticipate participating in social group activities. Based on these observations he is advanced to a higher-level activity, "community Re-integration," one day a week to begin to bridge the gap between the hospital and the community. The evaluation process allows the clinician to monitor Bob's progress and to continuously intervene in a planned positive therapeutic manner.

PHASE 5 — MODIFICATION

The modification phase is necessary when data from the evaluations prompt a change to satisfy the patient's needs. The recreation intervening professional must carefully review the outcomes or findings of an evaluation. The key point is that program revision results in action-modification of the program based upon the results of the evaluation. Thus revision occurs in response to evaluation (Carpenter and Howe 1985).

Modifying programs is an essential part of program management (Rossman 1995). Certain modification may run into resistance from patients. A recreation intervention team must undertake methods to overcome such resistance. The professional must have the skills to analyze programs, to note their deficiencies, and be able to recommend and gain the patient's acceptance of the modifications that will keep the programs viable (Rossman 1995).

Conclusion

Recreation programming is a vital aspect of the intervention process for children and adolescents. It allows youngsters to participate in normal growth activities while hospitalized and provides opportunities for planned and casual observation of social and physical skill building that can be addressed within the recreation environment.

REFERENCES

Austin, D. R. (1991). *Therapeutic Recreation Processes and Techniques* second edition, Champaign, IL Sagamore Pub.

Berryman, D. L. and LaFervre, C. B. (1991). *Recreation Behavior Inventory* Denton, TX: Leisure Learning System.

Carpenter, G. M. and Howe, C. Z., (1995). *Programming Leisure Experiences*, NJ: Prentice Hall.

Edington, C, Jordan, D, DeGraff D, Edington C.

(1995). *Leisure and Life Satisfaction,* Boston: Brown and Benchmark Pub.

Kraus, R. (1989). *Therapeutic Recreation Service,* Boston: Wm Brown Pub.

Peterson, C. A., Gunn, S. L. (1984). *Therapeutic Recreation Program Design,* Second Ed. Englewood Cliffs, N. J.: Prentice Hall.

Rossman, J. R., (1995). *Recreation Programming* second edition, Sagamore Publishing: Champaign, IL.

48 / Occupational Therapy

Susan Haiman and Sandra Greene

Occupational therapy is based on the process of doing, or being engaged in occupations as both the means of intervention and the desired end. Activities or occupations are introduced to match a child's or adolescent's abilities and to provide opportunity to experience success, thereby enabling a "stretch" for even better performance at a higher level of demand. Interventions are planned to meet individual goals, but the service may be provided either individually or in groups. It is important that there is a rightness of fit between the performance components or skills needed to succeed and the demands of the environment. If either is too complex or, alternatively, not appealing enough, engaging the young patient in the process is doomed to failure. When supplies are limited, rooms too barren or overstimulating, parents unavailable or too demanding, or the neighborhood too violent, even normal children must struggle to function adequately. An environment that facilitates and enhances functioning is what is needed for any interventions to be effective.

This chapter presents examples of individual and group strategies used with both children and adolescents. In each section readers will find interventions that emerge from understanding the patient and the artful adaptation of occupations.

Interventions with Children

INDIVIDUAL INTERVENTION

The initial assessment process identifies the child's strengths and problem areas. A child's problems are the basis for establishing goals of intervention; the strengths are used to facilitate goal achievement. Problems are prioritized based on the severity of their impact on performance. For example, if a child has the problems of short attention span, inability to tolerate peers at the same table during group activities, and decreased interest in activities, then intervention priorities might be to gradually attempt to engage the child on a one-to-one basis in simple games and crafts. Once activities the child enjoys are identified, the next priority is to introduce a peer to share the environment for short periods of time. An attempt to lengthen the child's attention span, through highly structured short-term activities, follows.

In general, interventions are carried out in an environment with access to social interaction with peers and the availability of a variety of play materials, including toys, crafts, and games. These are meant to develop social interactions, perceptual-motor skills, play exploration, mastery, and trust in the social and physical environment. During intervention sessions there are two primary principles of attention. One is to provide activities for the child at an appropriate skill level in a safe environment. The second is to be provided activities as a part of the child's daily routine, using normal community play and social activities. For example, a group designed to encourage exploration in play can take place at a community park. Practitioners can help each child reach goals in a normal, nonclinical setting.

Many children with psychiatric illness experience repeated failures in play and social interactions over time. These failures can exacerbate some of the symptoms associated with that illness. For example, a child may have advanced academic abilities yet be unable to get along with peers on the playground during recess. While providing a successful experience, interventions are designed to provide activities that enable skills needed to cooperate with peers, follow simple game rules, or structure free time. For example, to help this child develop skills at playing board games, he or she might be enlisted as a helper for younger peers. During that session, a simple board game is played. The older child does not lose face by participating in and learning the skills of a younger child's game, and he or she may also gain self-esteem by taking on the assistant role.

To assist children in structuring free time, short periods of unstructured time are programmed into the therapy sessions. The practitioner limits free-time choices by limiting available supplies. He or she provides support while the child engages in any of the choices. As the child demonstrates increased ability to structure time, the structure the practitioner provides can be reduced. The goal is for the child to choose and carry out independently an activity with a peer, with no intervention needed. Progress can be monitored during recess and outside school by child, practitioner, teachers, and parents.

A GROUP INTERVENTION WITH CHILDREN

This section describes a group program design that incorporates occupational therapy intervention within the context of a normal childhood occupation, scouting. One program, through a psychiatric service, offers scout meetings, held twice per week for 1 hour. This is a combined Girl and Boy Scout troop, with charters from both the Girl and Boy Scouts of America. Uniforms are provided for the children to wear while they attend the meeting. The objectives of the group are to gain skills and pride in being a group member; develop leadership skills; and, by accomplishing the skills required for scout badges and patches, develop craft, social, community, and physical abilities.

Among the observable outcomes of the program is the pride the children express in being part of the troop. Many of these children were unable to participate in scouting programs at their own schools because of their odd or disruptive behavior. In general they are delighted to be part of something in the mainstream of childhood experience. Behavior usually improves on scout meeting days, as the children know what the behavioral expectations are for attendance. And—without drawing attention to sensory, motor, cognitive, neuromuscular, and psychological performance deficits—interventions become part and parcel of the scouting activities.

Leadership of the group meeting rotates among the scouts. Being the leader entails calling the roll, asking for old and new business, explaining what the day's activity will be, and organizing cleanup at the end of the meeting. For children who are depressed and isolated, this is a structured, supported opportunity to be more assertive and experience a leadership role. For children who have difficulty with appropriate social skills, the scout meeting gives opportunity to cope with interpersonal situations while receiving assistance and support. Although one scout leads the group, all the scouts are reminded that they are leaders and are expected to behave as leaders toward their peers and adults in the group. This expectation often results in performance of social and play skills similar to those in the average daily setting.

Parents, used to receiving negative feedback, are relieved and pleased when hearing that their children are doing well in the scout program. In regard to ensuring their child's success in community scouting, they can gain pointers from practitioners and pass these on to new troop leaders. And everyone can receive positive feedback from the child's ability to engage in a developmentally consonant experience, despite the disruption of a psychiatric illness.

Interventions with Adolescents

INDIVIDUAL INTERVENTIONS

For the adolescent with psychiatric illness, the demands of adolescent development can overwhelm the capacity for successful occupational role performance in one or multiple roles. Especially at risk are social relationships with peers, which are so critical to negotiation of this phase. Thus, much intervention occurs in settings where peers are present, but group interaction is minimized. This allows patients to grapple with issues they have in common while promoting peer group identification and independence from the watchful eyes of parents, teachers, tutors, or therapists. The task for the practitioner is to create a context in which the adolescents' strengths are maximized, without overwhelming an already tenuous self-concept, while addressing functional problems in a variety of spheres. For example, for the young patient who is always late to session, thus disrupting others, an individual goal might be "At the end of 3 months, the patient will be awake, showered, and dressed by 8:00 A.M., without parental prodding." To this end, the patient and the practitioner might design one step toward the goal: "Patient will purchase the alarm or clock radio of his choice by the end of the first 2 weeks."

Other examples of "individualized" interventions in a group setting include making English muffin pizzas with patients as yet unable to cooperate to make a single large pizza. Or, in the case of the patient who constantly interrupts the group but has excellent arithmetic and computer skills, asking the patient to create a price list for a group bake sale. Not only does this intervention play to the patient's strengths, it uses the computer as a modality to diminish distractibility in a socially acceptable fashion. Or consider the 14-year-old who cannot manage a woodworking project without hammering his own finger. For him an individualized intervention might involve giving him a choice among projects that have limited options for self-injury and expansiveness but do contain options for creative color, design, and shape. Individualizing the activity ensures success, increases the ability to perform with minimal supervision, and eliminates the conflict between child and practitioner.

A GROUP INTERVENTION WITH ADOLESCENTS

When planning groups, attention should be paid to both present and expected contexts in which the adolescent will be functioning. Scheduling should replicate normal activity, with events occurring after school, in the evening, or on weekends. Groups should serve as "laboratories for living," in which social values and norms can be explored.

Adolescents in the Arts and Through the Ages is a group that meets weekly for 2 hours. Promoted as an extracurricular "course," the group is based in beliefs that adolescents can expand their limited horizons through plays, films, and music. The visual images and characters help young patients to examine adolescent issues—such as peer relationships, family relationships, and sexuality—from an emotional distance that makes the material manageable.

Group leaders identify several plays, movies, and pieces of music that were popular in the past, have been updated to have popular appeal, and represent common concerns of adolescents. A successful sequence of group meetings began by focusing on Shakespeare's Romeo and Juliet. During the first session, the balcony and feud scenes were read aloud by members of the group. The adolescents discussed the unfamiliar language and identified relevant themes. The themes of fear and membership in neighborhood gangs were quickly mentioned. The second week, patients watched a videotaped version of the Romeo and Juliet ballet, which provided a visual and musical experience. Again, only the balcony and feud scenes were shown. By the end of this session, patients began to discuss their own attitudes toward sexuality. By the third week, longer segments of the film by Franco Zefferelli were shown. Patients had gained comfort in discussing sexuality; independence from parents; and suicide, a topic they avoided when they began to emerge in group psychotherapy.

The next phase began in the fourth week. A modernized, culturally relevant version of this tragedy was introduced through the script and music of West Side Story. Again, group members read segments of the script. Then the group listened to the music and watched scenes from the film. Again, the feud scene and balcony scenes were featured initially. More was offered when patients reported being ready to see or hear more. During final group sessions the patients wanted to watch Romeo and Juliet and West Side Story in their entirety. A 14-year-old—a Hispanic girl who was impulsive, disruptive, and attention seeking—asked "Where can I buy that movie? And who did you say was the director?" Her enthusiasm was a clear indication that important growth had occurred.

Conclusion

The intervention strategies presented in this chapter have occupational performance or functional independence as both the essence of program design and the desired outcome. Practitioners intend to help their young patients use their strengths to develop skills to better accomplish the tasks and routines of daily living. They provide real experiences and the opportunity to practice skills in normal or normalized environments. Sometimes the child or adolescent needs to learn new skills, sometimes the activity must be graded to ensure mastery, and at times the environment needs to be adapted. In any and all of these instances, it is through culturally relevant, goal-directed occupations that patients, therapist, and parents all receive direct and objective feedback about progress toward adult roles—despite psychiatric illness, developmental delays, and identified behavioral problems.

REFERENCES

Allen, C. K. (1985). *Occupational therapy for psychiatric diseases: Measurement and management of cognitive disabilities.* Boston: Little, Brown.

Baum, C., & Christiansen, C. (Eds.). (1991). *Occupational therapy: Overcoming human performance deficits.* Thoroghfare, NJ: Slack Inc.

Bonder, B. (1995). *Psychopathology and function.* Thoroghfare, NJ: Slack Inc.

Breines, E. B. (Ed.). (1994). *Occupational therapy activities: From clay to computers.* Philadelphia: F. A. Davis.

Cotrell, R. (Ed.). (1993). *Psychosocial occupational therapy: Proactive approaches.* Bethesda, MD: American Occupational Therapy Association.

Cynkin, S., & Robinson, A. (1990). *Occupational therapy and activities health: Toward health through activities.* Boston: Little, Brown.

Reilly, M. (1974). *Play as exploratory learning: Studies of curiosity behavior.* Beverly Hills, CA: Sage Press.

---

49 / Vocational Therapy

Elissa Lang and Barbara Milone

Vocational interventions for children and adolescents require a coordinated effort to facilitate development in areas of delay; approximate or include real play, real school, real work, and real social behaviors; and acknowledge normal expectations while creatively remediating disabling conditions that may interfere. As with modern adult psychiatric rehabilitation intervention, it is critical for the child or adolescent to receive vocational treatment based upon developmental need and role or function demands rather than inpatient or outpatient residency.

To quote Kirkland (1985): "Occupational choice is a developmental process that begins with the imaginative play of the child. This period is followed by a stage of tentative choices and finally a period of realistic choices, corresponding to adolescence and young adulthood respectively" (p. 1). *Vocational therapy* can be defined as the process of assessing and treating deficits in performance components that interfere with the individual's ability to participate in productive occupations through the life span. *Independent living skills* refers to the abilities needed to perform physical, psychological, and emotional self-care, work, and leisure to a level of independence appropriate to age, life space, cultural background, and disability (Knitzer, 1982).

For children, "play is their work." Children use play to interact with their environment and with each other and to increase their understanding of human roles and situations. In early childhood play is the primary activity. Imaginary play fosters the ability and willingness to tolerate the structure and rules needed for satisfying social interactions. The play of toddlers imitates the activities and roles they observe in their world. Play can be viewed as a continuum leading to both work and leisure.

As children mature, time is divided between school and free time, later work and non-work. Play experiences lay the foundation for work and leisure through exploration; manipulation and investigation; learning; social interaction; competition, cooperation, learning of rules; and the development of competence, self-determination and personality.

Shannon and Reilly (1974) noted that certain crucial work skills—such as attention span and cognitive, physical, and interpersonal skills—are learned through play. They examined the ways in which play contributes to occupational choice skills and prevocational readiness:

In play the child learns to cope with his environment and with himself. It is in play that the child's habits and attitudes are molded into an orientation toward life, congruent with his value orientation. Play provides for the development of the child's physical and intellectual capacities and is thereby a major force in shaping self-concept. Play is the arena in which the child discovers his creative potential and has opportunities to learn and practice organizational and leadership skills. Play teaches discipline, responsibility and citizenship. Cooperation, competition, loyalty and a respect for others are learned in the play environment. Play encourages risk-taking, trial and error and commitment, all essential to the development of problem-solving or decision-making skills. Play also provides for identification with the worker role through the simulated experiences of role-playing and daydreaming. Most important, the repetitive nature of play lends itself well to the child's expressive needs and to the development of self-confidence and competence; it is in the exploratory experimental play milieu that the child's human achievement endeavors are tried and rehearsed in the interest of task mastery.

Adolescence is considered one of life's most difficult and turbulent transitions. The struggle for independence, the search for identity, and the interest in becoming self-sufficient are ever present. Shannon (1983) considered employment preparation an important part of an adolescent's work.

The central feature in the transition from adolescence to adulthood is preparation for employment. The major components of a successful transition are identified as: education; opportunities to acquire a degree of personal autonomy; preparation for a social lifestyle, including personal and recreational pursuits; experiences to acquire the skills for optimal independent living; and training and services to enhance the ability to earn one's own living.

Under the best of circumstances, the nondisabled adolescent receives guidance and support from family and school counselors. This help is based on individual potential, intellectual capacity, social maturity, personality, interests, academic achievement, and opportunities. Ideally these teens have vocational exposure through volunteer work or a part-time job, and through this experience they develop some work skills.

Shannon and Reilly (1974) maintained that innovative and quality programming is essential to meet the needs of psychiatrically disabled youth.

Formal Individualized Student Plans focusing on the coordinated vocational transition of the disabled student must be developed, initially as part of the students *Individual Education Plan* (IEP) and adjusted post-school as a component of the client's *Individual Written Rehabilitation Plan* (IWRP). The plan should first be developed at least 4 years prior to an individual's graduation and then modified at least once per year until the individual has successfully adjusted to a postschool vocational placement.

Educating parents and involving them in vocational planning and training help to focus parents on how to help their children cope with the practical tasks of everyday life and increase the likelihood of future vocational success (Wehman, 1991). Nelson and Condrin (1987) emphasized the need for early programming.

Because occupational choice is a dynamic process, programming must begin at an early age with the introduction of activities to foster career awareness and exploration of vocational capabilities and interests. Although such awareness and exploration must be re-inforced with normal children, it is particularly critical for programming to be presented developmentally and initiated at an early age for special needs children. The reasons for this are their limited exposure (or lack of exposure) to the world of work, and limited career expectations for them on the part of parents and society.

The growth-promoting interventions for psychiatrically disabled children include *activity dyads* and *therapeutic play*, which foster the development of *"play-to-work"* (*play-to-work* is defined later in this chapter) skills and help with community reintegration. Such interventions combine traditional age-appropriate play activities with adapted creative play techniques to meet the disabled child's needs. Most strategies that promote successful play experiences for this population are developmental in nature. Children are initially introduced to familiar play and varied task experiences that build on existing skills. Structured dyadic activity provides opportunities for satisfying play with a peer, promotes relaxation, and encourages motivation and confidence to develop new skills. As new and needed coping skills develop, the child has a better repertoire of strategies with which to manage interaction and task performance. Experiences in a larger group, with reciprocal activity, help each youngster learn and elaborate on dyadic play and play-to-work and socialization skills. Much like the ideal home environment, the overall goal of developmental dyadic and play interventions is to provide a safe environment within which a child can take the risks needed to experience both success and failure. Ultimately, this fosters self-discovery and serves as preparation for interacting successfully in home, school, and natural community. That play therapy so obviously mirrors good parenting as a preventive "intervention" strategy has done little to legitimize its prescriptive use in early childhood educational, clinical, and vocational remediation. Virtually every investigation of early vocational interventions substantiates the significance of "parent or caretaker involvement, normalization of activity (play) experiences, and coordinated service efforts" as ingredients for positive outcome (Wehman, 1991).

Play-to-work and vocational therapy groups represent several levels of prevocational development for psychiatrically disabled children and adolescents from 6 to 12 years old.

Work groups foster an acceptance of routine, an increased sense of responsibility for others, basic work skills, and basic money management. Tasks assigned must benefit the therapeutic or academic community. These might include feeding fish, setting the table, making signs, making to sell, putting toys away, and potting plants. Specific tasks are assigned and performed independently, after initial training. They are then checked by an adult who gives the positive feedback first and then reteaches whatever skill is deficient. Completed jobs can be charted and the children paid play money which can be spent at a group store or for a special treat. A weekly worker's meeting should allow youngsters to discuss work tasks, difficulties faced, and new assignments. Children

must be helped to decide whether to save or spend their money, and the group's leader should be available to assist *every day*.

Community projects groups plan activities and complete that contribute to the well-being of other children in the milieu. Activities could include making holiday decorations, trick-or-treat bags, or birthday cakes. Group members must be ready to work cooperatively and negotiate with peers, build on basic social and interactional skills, help others, and experience delayed gratification for their work.

Play-to-work groups model real work closely in that the demand group decision making, problem solving, and implementation to produce a product or event open to the "public." An example of a play-to-work task is the organization of a summer carnival by the children and adolescents in the milieu. Members design carnival games by problem solving and experimentation. All game equipment is constructed by members, and tickets, points, prize values, and distribution are within their control. Professional staff act as consultants and intervene only to facilitate group process.

Big kid–little kid groups assign adolescents and children to big brother or big sister roles in relation to others in the group. Such groups encourage both youngsters in a pair to increase their ability to play, learn flexibility, problem-solve, cooperate, and compromise with others while working together in a positive way.

Newspaper and literary groups encourage members to demonstrate their ability to exceed prework skills and function in a larger peer group. In addition to writing responsibilities, each child can be assigned, on a rotating basis, to positions such as editor-in-chief, art editor, or collating editor. Participants gain skills in the areas of time management, communication, giving and following instructions, computer skills, grammar, and overall collaboration in a worklike setting. *Parent-child groups* can provide parents with concrete experience and practice in pleasurable interaction with their child through structured play and activities. Parents should be assisted to structure, engage in, and adapt mutual activities to the child's capacities. The goal is to encourage and increase the ability of families to spend productive, growth-promoting, and pleasurable time together.

Parent-adolescent groups provide an opportunity for parents and adolescents to develop appropriate and positive mutual relationships through joint pleasurable activities. Activities such as cooking, art, games, construction tasks, or homework can be introduced to families each week. The choice of the activity must be based on the known interests, values, and skills of the adolescent. As families gain comfort in the group, they can plan their own weekly activity with leader assistance. In this setting families have an opportunity to witness their child's new skills and assets or be reintroduced to skills they have developed over the years. The constant stress experienced by families with a psychiatrically disabled child often overshadows the child's positive attributes. Enhancement and acknowledgment of these positive skills is crucial to vocational development, planning, and success.

Specific programs are notable for their work with special-needs adolescent. One such program, *World of Work,* is a prevocational discussion and fieldtrip group. It helps adolescents determine long-range career goals and college choices by increasing their knowledge about themselves and actual work sites. It teaches skills needed to obtain entry-level jobs and apply to college. The group participates in peer discussions, uses written materials, vocational testing, computer programs, and community trips to prepare the involved teens for work and school. Ideally, these adolescents should also participate in some kind of volunteer experience appropriate to their entry-level stage. Such an encounter provides real-life exposure to the demands and rewards of work and results in an increased sense of responsibility, productivity, and self-esteem. Fostering an adolescent's self-concept as a worker is the ultimate goal of this type of intervention.

Vocational rehabilitation programs can offer psychiatrically disabled adolescents needed career experiences and occupational exploration. The transitional school-to-work phase is an especially critical time for disabled adolescents, since it highlights special problems for both the adolescent and the surrounding family group.

The traditional educational system provides a two-tiered program for high school students: college preparatory and vocational technical tracks. Susan Knox (1993) interviewed high school graduates with disabilities to explore their view of services most helpful in making the transition from school to work. "Included in their suggestions were the need for a planned transition process, a job-related school curriculum, and structured procedures to facilitate community integration." The disabled adolescent requires a complete vocational rehabilitation assessment, external clinical and natural supports within and outside the school setting, and an experience-based education. External supports include career education, testing, supported education, supported employment, individual vocational counseling, and parent-adolescent activities.

As a developmentally determined and dynamically informed behavior and skill development treatment modality, the psychiatric rehabilitation of child and adolescent social and vocational disabilities requires exquisite knowledge, attitude, and skills on the part of practitioners. A capacity to provide palatable remediation within the context of developmentally relevant normal activity is of primary importance.

CASE EXAMPLES

Child: R. is a 10-year-old black male who was admitted to an inpatient children's unit for aggression, toward peers and adults, apparently unrelated to actual events. During his 5 and one-half-month hospitalization, R. hoarded supplies and materials at home and school, though he did not use them in any purposeful manner. He ate anything, including frozen food and feces. R. displayed many specific cognitive deficits, receptive and expressive language difficulties, memory problems, poor gross and fine motor coordination, a limited attention span, and extreme impulsivity. He generally played by himself, and interactions with peers usually ended in verbal or physical arguments.

R.'s biological mother is mildly retarded and emotionally disturbed. R. was removed from her home at 6 months because she left him alone for up to 9 hours at a time without food or a change of diaper. R. is presently living with his sixth foster family.

R. attended individual activity therapy twice each week. The goals of the work were to increase attention span and repertoire of play activities decrease distractibility and impulsive behavior, improve social relationships, and enhance visual motor and cognitive abilities. R. participated in the parent-child activity group with his foster mother as well as the unit community meal.

With great difficulty R. was able to remain on task for up to 20 minutes, albeit with moderate redirection and encouragement. He showed improved frustration tolerance and an increased ability to speak rather than act out his feelings. R. continued to have difficulty accepting offers of assistance with challenging tasks. R. was placed in a dyadic construction group with a younger peer, S., whose task skills were comparable to, if not exceeding, R.'s skills. R. was very excited to be placed in this dyad, which was presented as a big kid–little kid group in which R. would have to help this younger peer. Initially, R. was brusque, physically intimidating, and tried to restrict S's behavior. As the group progressed, opportunities arose for R. to have to deal with such issues as being liked by S., having S. want to imitate him, and having increased responsibilities. R. also began to appreciate the need to give and request help, and slowly became more willing to take on the roles of being both a helper with S. and accepting staff help for himself. R. progressed far enough in his play, task, and social skills to join the community projects group with two male peers. Though highly motivated to participate, R. continued to be impulsive and exhibit poor boundaries, but he could respond to verbal limits set on his behavior. R. had difficulty waiting to get paid in play money, and only toward the end of hospitalization was he able to make the connection between the length of a project and his earnings. R. was quite proud of the projects the group made and of his continuing efforts in the group. He often announced to the unit that the group was "making a surprise" and talked about how good this made him feel.

R.'s mother spoke frequently about the positive progress she saw in R.'s behavior and marked changes in her relationship with him during their work in parent-child activity group and on home visits. R.'s foster mother consulted with the practitioner to implement similar work situations so she could continue the rehabilitation process through positive experiences after discharge.

Adolescent: J. was a 17-year-old Caucasian female admitted to an adolescent inpatient unit following a suicide attempt. J. was in outpatient care with a psychiatrist for her depression prior to admission. J. experienced problems with peers, poor concentration in school, lack of appetite, and increased arguments with her parents and boyfriend. The suicide attempt followed an argument with the boyfriend and J.'s fear of a possible breakup.

J. was an average student with many peer relationships and held an after-school and weekend job at a chain ice cream store. J.'s peer relationships decreased; she became more isolated, spending time with her boyfriend only. J.'s school performance and relationship with her boyfriend were a major source of stress for her parents.

J. consistently reported that "her job was the part of her life where she felt best." She continued to have a good relationship with co-workers, and her job performance remained the same. J. stated she enjoyed the feeling of independence her job gave her, but felt her boss and co-workers really did not know her.

During J.'s hospitalization she participated in social skills group, World of Work group, parent-adolescent group, and anger management, and she worked in the Adolescent Canteen [the patient-run restaurant] as well as on the unit newspaper.

Initially J. was quite withdrawn and depressed and refused to participate in any unit or therapeutic activities. About 2 weeks into her 4-month stay, J. was able to identify skills and goals she needed to work on. J. identified a need to resolve conflicts with parents and boyfriend without taking it out on herself. She acknowledged that her difficulty with expressing disagreement, expressing her opinion, requesting help, responding to feedback, and managing her time affected all areas of her life.

In the social skills group, J. quickly became comfortable participating in role-playing, in which she focused on difficult social interactions she had experienced in the past and explored current conflicts that arose with peers and family in the hospital.

In parent-adolescent group, J. and her parents used joint activity to change their perceptions and communication styles with each other. J.'s parents were able to accept her need for more independence, be reintroduced to their daughter's many assets, and negotiate mutually agreeable conditions for spending enjoyable time together. J.'s parents were able to be more supportive of her work interests and goals, and they reached a compromise about peer relationships and ground rules at home.

The newsletter group was an area where J. received a great deal of recognition and praise for her writing and ability to express many feelings. She became an editor and, although at times she had to struggle with maintaining a leadership role, was able to work on issues with support.

J.'s participation in world of work and the restaurant was the "highlight of her week." She felt these experiences were the most normalizing and similar to home. She was able to explore and work out difficulties similar to those she experienced at her job and found these groups to be helpful in her transition out of the hospital and back to school and work. Subsequently, J. was re-hospitalized for a brief 2-week period but has reportedly finished high school and is working while taking courses at a local community college.

REFERENCES

Black, B. (1988). *Work and mental illness*. Baltimore, MD: Johns Hopkins University Press.

Crowell, S. (1989). A new way of thinking: The challenge of the future. *Educational Leadership, 47* (1), 60–63.

Gorski, G., & Mujake, S. (1985). The adolescent life/work planning group: A prevention model. *Occupational Therapy in Health Care, 2* (3), 139–150.

Kirkland, M., & Robertson, S. (1985). *Planning and implementing vocational readiness in occupational therapy (PIVOT)*. Rockville MD: American Occupational Therapy Association.

Knitzer J., & Olson, L. (1982). *Unclaimed children*. Washington, DC: Children's Defense Fund.

Knox, S. H. (1993). Play and leisure. In H. L. Hopkins & H. D. Smith (Eds.), *Willard & Spackman's occupational therapy*. (8th ed.). Philadelphia: J. B. Lippincott.

Nelson, R., & Condrin, J. (1987). A vocational readiness and independent living skills program for psychiatrically impaired adolescents. *Occupational Therapy in Mental Health,* Summer.

Shannon, P. (1983). The adolescent experience. *Occupational Therapy in Mental Health, 3* (2), 73–87.

Shannon, P., & Reilly, H. (Ed.). (1974). Occupational choice: Decision-making play. In H. Reilly (Ed.), *Play as exploratory learning: Studies in curiosity behavior*. Beverly Hills, CA: Sage Publishing.

Wehman, P. (1991). Transition from school to work. *Journal of Vocational Rehabilitation, 1* (4). MA: Andover Medical Publishers, Inc.

50 / Educational Interventions

Gail B. Werbach

Educational therapy is the clinical arm of special education. It is the process of evaluation, intervention, and remediation of learning problems. (Directory of Occupational Titles 1977) The educational therapist serves a population of young children, adolescents, and adults that includes those who demonstrate dyslexia, test anxiety, reading/writing/language/math problems, attention deficit hyperactivity disorder, and other school problems affecting school performance.

The therapist works in the educational domain (private practice, schools, hospitals, or public agencies) and is skilled in:

1. Administering and/or interpreting formal and informal educational assessment
2. Synthesizing information from other specialists and from parents as a case manager
3. Developing and implementing appropriate remedial programs for school-related learning and behavior problems within the school setting.
4. Forming supportive relationships with the student and with those involved in their educational development and rehabilitation
5. Applying strategies for addressing social and emotional aspects of learning disabilities outside of school
6. Facilitating communication among the individual, the family, the school, and involved professionals.

While the main emphasis is on individual therapy, the approach is not limited to therapists who work with individual students, but includes those who work with groups, such as resource specialists (special education teachers who work temporarily with a small group of children outside the regular classroom) and special education teachers in the school system. Unique to the field is the emphasis on psychoeducational intervention, defined as: "Any intervention or coming between that fosters and enables the acting, thinking, and feeling necessary for learning to take place" (Ungerleider, 1991).

Individuals who enter into educational therapy often are being seen concurrently by other specialists. Often the primary physician has made the original referral to a neurologist, psychiatrist, or clinical psychologist. Subsequent intervention by a speech and language therapist, educational psychologist, or guidance counselor is common. The educational therapist prioritizes and coordinates the interventions and clarifies the needs of the client.

Situations in Which Psychoeducational Intervention Is Indicated

Psychoeducational intervention is indicated in a number of situations.

CHILDREN WITH LEARNING DISABILITIES

Children with developmental lags in language/auditory/visual processing and/or memory deficits that interfere with academic achievement can profit from psychoeducational interventions. (Auditory perceptual problems are difficulties in understanding what is heard despite normal hearing. Visual perceptual problems are difficulties in interpreting what is seen. Processing disorders are difficulties in extracting meaningful information from sensory impressions.) Most learning disabilities are not diagnosed until about third grade. However, some high risk children can benefit from early intervention. Some examples of children at risk for learning disabilities are those whose parents are substance abusers, children with many ear infections during ages 2–5; very distractible children; children with markedly poor fine or gross motor skills, or speech and language development; and children whose parents have a history of learning problems.

Barry was a 9-year-old boy functioning at least 2 years behind his fourth grade class in reading and math. He had an above-average IQ but significant visual and auditory processing deficits as well as poor fine motor coordination. He always forgot to bring home his assignments and had difficulty with long-term assignments, such as book reports.

Barry was seen twice weekly for 2 years. Sessions consisted of specific reading exercises, identifying the main idea and oral reading. Barry was asked to begin reading a book at home, and a home reading log was designed to follow up his work. Mother was instructed to check the log daily and reward Barry with a star for appropriate reading. A weekly reward was issued for completion of this task. In the sessions, the therapist followed up the reading with contextual clues and summary work. The therapist presented Barry with a monthly calendar with which to organize long-term assignments. This way he could plan for his work to be completed on time. Since the family already owned a computer, the therapist encouraged Barry to do as much work as possible on the computer while also working on his handwriting. As a result Barry began to turn in neat, legible papers and was praised by his teacher.

The treatment plan included parent counseling and coordination between parents and teachers. On a weekly basis the therapist would speak to the teacher and then give feedback to the parents. Communication facilitated the accomplishment of common goals. The parents began to see the teacher as an ally, not an enemy.

Barry improved his reading and math skills and learned both compensatory strategies for his deficits and how to structure his time so that his assignments were completed and handed in on time.

CHILDREN WITH ATTENTION DEFICIT HYPERACTIVITY DISORDER

The inability to focus makes some children with attention deficit hyperactivity disorder unable to achieve age-appropriate academic performance. While many distractible young children do not cause alarm in their households, school success necessitates the ability to sustain attention. Academic success is often measured by the amount of work completed by a student. For those students who are constantly distracted from the task at hand, it is difficult to be successful. In addition, these children often prevent other students from completing their work.

Bobby made his first-grade teacher throw up her hands in despair. He was obviously bright but was constantly asking questions and volunteering information without raising his hand. During reading he was easily distracted by noise, movement, or other children. He played with his pencil, looked around, spoke to others, and generally missed the lesson being presented.

Bobby was seen twice weekly during the summer and weekly during the school year. In addition, Bobby was referred to a pediatric neurologist for an evaluation for attention deficit hyperactivity disorder; treatment with Ritalin was begun. The referral was preceded by 2 sessions with the parents to help them overcome their fears of "drugging" their son. They refused a referral until the therapist gave them appropriate articles to read about the efficacy of the medication and Bobby's prognosis with its use. There was a 4-month interval between these 2 sessions, as they were convinced he would improve without this intervention. The therapist coordinated their visit with the medical doctor to whom they sent relevant observations on the child before their visit.

The educational therapist held monthly school meetings with the teacher and counselor to ameliorate any problem areas. A home visit was conducted to teach the parents how to deal with homework problems. At the house, the therapist explained to the family the necessity of a large clean desk, proper lighting, a quiet study area, and a regular study time. This helped the student complete his assignments in a timely fashion.

At the end of the second grade, Bobby was on grade level and able to complete his work without any special help. His self-image had improved and he had developed a positive attitude toward school. In addition, his parents were pleased with the changes made by medication and less anxious about this treatment.

CHILDREN ATTENDING A SCHOOL THAT IS INAPPROPRIATE FOR THEIR NEEDS AND TALENTS

Some children could function well in many school settings but are currently in a school that is inappropriate. There is a wide variety of types of schools, public and private, in the United States. Schools differ in size and philosophy. While some follow strict guidelines, others allow children to choose the activity they want at a particular time. There is no consensus at the current time on the best way to teach the basic subjects of reading and math. In addition, parents are not always capable of choosing the correct type of school for their child.

John's parents had enrolled him in the same private school his siblings attended. "This is our school. We have contributed financially and emotionally and expect him to succeed," said his physician father. At the outset, John did not fit into the very structured fast-paced academic atmosphere. He was struggling, even at the bottom of his first-grade class.

Informal evaluation of John's skills, weekly educational therapy sessions from September to November, and consultation with school personnel yielded data indicating some changes had to be made. From the school's point of view, John was taking too much teacher time and could not keep up with the work. When asked, John readily admitted to disliking school because "the work is hard, the teacher yells, and I am bored." John's parents met with the educational therapist who advised a school change and promised to help them select the most appropriate school. The parents were encouraged to deal with their disappointment in John's inability to fit in and to focus on his very many good qualities. The therapist visited and evaluated several appropriate alternative schools and made recommendations.

John made a good adjustment to the second grade in a less structured, more humanistic neighborhood school that stressed the visual arts, had little or no homework, and placed little emphasis on grades.

SLOW LEARNERS

Some schools cannot provide extra help with academic subjects. Classrooms frequently have 28 or more children. It is very difficult for a teacher to individualize in the core areas of reading and math. Thus a child who needs extra time or instruction to grasp a subject is often unable to get this help.

Billy had a low-average IQ and a severe auditory processing deficit. He was a pleasant, quiet boy from a high-achieving family. In the fifth grade, he was reading and writing at about the second-grade level. His parents were very concerned about his future vocational opportunities.

During a 2-year period Billy was tutored in academic subjects and word processing skills. Goals were set that would enable Billy to function independently once he left school. With the use of the computer Billy learned to compose letters, use a spell checker, and touch-type. The therapist met with his parents to outline realistic job situations and the needed skills he had to have at this point in his academic career. For example, he was taught to use a calculator and a hand-held spell checker so that he could be more independent and correct in his math computations and spelling.

Billy continued to need supportive intervention throughout his high school career. He was in a program at school where he met in a separate room with a resource specialist for 1 hour per day. Upon graduation, he enrolled in a program at a local community college for people with learning disabilities. Throughout this process, the therapist facilitated communication between Billy and his support personnel and his family.

CHILDREN WITH POOR ORGANIZATIONAL SKILLS OR POOR STUDY HABITS

Some children fail to achieve their academic potential because of poor organizational skills or poor study habits. Teachers give multi-part homework assignments during the school day. Many children either do not copy the assignment, copy it incorrectly, forget to bring home the necessary books, or miss some verbal instruction given by the teacher. In addition, some parents are unaware that younger children especially need help in developing good study habits.

Josh was a bright boy in the 10th grade whose backpack, notebooks, and room were in disarray. He complained that his parents were forever planning dinners or family events that interfered with his studies or when he had work due at school. He never read a book in the scheduled time and usually turned in assignments late. His room contained a radio, a television, a videocassette recorder, a telephone, and a guitar—all of which were used at times while he was studying.

Josh was seen weekly for a year with emphasis on organizational skills. He was taught to keep a weekly calendar, plan out study in advance of tests, and keep a record of time spent daily doing work. He learned to take responsibility for his own work. A home visit and consultation with his parents resulted in the removal of the TV and telephone from his room. (The home visit was necessary because students are expected to do a good deal of work at home; the therapist needs to see what the work environment is like and suggest changes if needed.) A behavior modification chart with reward system was set up on a weekly basis with the family, the student, and the school. This provided clear, consistent feedback of his work. The parents learned not to be manipulated by him to approve unacceptable behavior, and were able to motivate him to get his work in on time.

Josh finished the school year with excellent grades and much improved study organizational skills.

CHILDREN FROM DYSFUNCTIONAL FAMILIES

Often dysfunctional families are unable to provide the support and guidance children need for learning. In order to be successful students, children need to know their parents' goals for them, family finances (as they near college age), and receive general appropriate feedback to motivate academic success. This seems to be missing in many modern families.

Janice was a 15-year-old high school student with a history of average school grades. Her parents were concerned about her college plans. Janice's father was an alcoholic who worked long hours and then isolated himself in his study. Her mother was depressed and contemplated separation from her husband. Neither parent was available on a regular basis to monitor study habits or to help her set goals.

Janice was seen weekly for 9 months and encouraged to become more responsible for her own actions. The first few sessions were centered on her identifying appropriate colleges, sending for information, and analyzing her own preferences for type of school. She identified 3 schools in the immediate area that she could visit to compare their size and facilities. A joint session was held with her parents and the therapist so that Janice could discuss the financial aspect of college with them. The therapist also conducted individual sessions with each parent, recommending marital counseling to them both as well as an Alcoholics Anonymous program for the father and an Alanon program for the mother. Throughout the therapy Janice's grades and college testing needs were monitored by the therapist.

Upon graduation from high school, Janice enrolled in college and eagerly looked forward to living in a dorm. The therapist remained an ally during her parents' subsequent divorce and helped Janice make a good college adjustment.

CHILDREN WHO ARE INADEQUATELY MOTIVATED TO ACHIEVE ACADEMICALLY

Cultural and familial expectations regarding the importance of education vary among the many families whose children attend school in the United States. Many children need motivation, structure, and good limit setting from their family to perform well in school. Reading is not usually considered as much fun as is watching television or playing a video game.

Bill was a fifth-grade student referred by his private school because of poor performance. His family was extremely wealthy and his parents were not well educated.

Bill was seen weekly for 9 months. His parents were seen additionally in counseling sessions regarding their role in motivating Bill. They had been giving him the message that upon graduation he would take over their successful air-conditioning business. It was pointed out to them that if, in fact, he did take over the business, he would need adequate math and reading/writing skills to run it. They were resistant at the beginning but after several months began to see Bill's needs. Once their message to Bill began to change, he became more accessible to remedial work. The therapist taught him more efficient ways to do calculations and helped him memorize his times tables. In the area of writing, he was taught how to write a power paragraph of main idea, supporting details, and conclusion and how to proofread his work. He began to work on his computer and found that this facilitated his ability to edit his work. By involving him with reading athletes' biographies and the newspaper's sports page, he began to get more comfortable with reading. The next step was to limit his free-choice reading to every other book, with the therapist or teacher supplying the alternate books, so that he read a variety of material. In addition, the therapist worked with the classroom teacher to make Bill a peer tutor to a first-grade student. This improved his self-esteem.

After 9 months of therapy, Bill was eagerly looking forward to a summer park program where he would be helping other children with their reading. His basic skills were much improved.

CHILDREN NOT GIVEN THE STRUCTURE AND SUPPORT NEEDED FOR ACADEMIC ACHIEVEMENT

Many parents are too busy, uneducated themselves, or make poor choices regarding discipline. This often fosters lowered academic achievement in students who need support and motivation to be successful.

Allan was a bright boy in the second grade at a liberal, fairly unstructured private day school. His mother had attended parochial schools, which she thought were too rigid. She wanted her son's education to be more individualized. The school was concerned that his moderate visual perceptual problems might interfere with his learning. Assignments were rarely completed at home, and Allan was frequently absent from school.

Allan was seen twice weekly to strengthen his visual perceptual skills. Materials such as letter identification, figure ground work, and mazes were used to help him with visual discrimination. Allan was encouraged to keep a copy book, where he did daily copying exercises to help his writing become more automatic. In addition, Mother and Father were instructed to read to Allan on a daily basis. In order to stimulate his interest in reading, they were to use material that was interesting but too difficult for Allan to read himself. Weekly consultations were held with his mother to help her understand limit setting and structure with relation to the educational process. It was explained to her that students behave in school generally as they do at home so that if he were to succeed at school, he needed a consistent approach.

Through parent education, appropriate student behavior, and teacher/therapist/parent coordination, Allan made great gains in internalizing structure and organization and began to function better in school.

CHILDREN WITH OVERPROTECTIVE PARENTS

Some children have not learned to be independent learners due to overprotective parents. As children mature they need to become independent learners. This means that parents need to separate from their children's school work gradually. In some cases, a student has to fail an assignment to learn that he is responsible for his own work.

Susan was in the sixth grade and experiencing moderate school problems. Her mother sat next to her at home while she did all her assignments. In addition, Susan was not allowed to participate in after-school activities. Initially, in reporting on Susan's work to the therapist, the mother would state, for example, "We didn't finish our book report this week."

After several consultations with the mother, a home visit was conducted by the therapist to model behavior for Mother while Susan was doing her work. At first, Mother would go over work plans with her and be available to help. After several weeks, she was able to let Susan plan her own work schedule and ask for help if needed. The teacher was made aware of this change so that the work in this transition period could be monitored. Mother became less anxious as Susan proved her ability. The family was encouraged to allow Susan one after-school activity as long as her homework was completed. The therapist shifted the focus to remediating specific reading and math areas of weakness. In reading, work was done on answering inferential questions and identifying the main idea. In math, Susan was given extra help with word problems, starting with easy one-step problems to give her confidence before she attached more difficult problems.

Susan gradually improved her school performance. However, the therapist felt that the parents were continuing to have difficulty letting their only child become independent. They refused, however, the recommendation for conjoint psychotherapy. The parents' terminated Susan's therapy with the issue of separation only partly resolved.

Professionals Interested in the Field Should be Aware of the Following Factors

In educational therapy, the goals and objectives of the therapist must reflect the client's long-term needs. These needs must be realistic in terms of the client's cognitive/social/emotional potential. At times such needs are in conflict with those of the parents. Following evaluation of the learning problems and current concerns, the therapist formulates goals with the client, parents, or other involved family members. There are usually both short-term and long-term goals, which need to be reevaluated on a regular basis. It is not uncommon for goals to be changed because new information originally withheld by the family is revealed. Changes also take place in current school situations as a result of medical evaluations or psychoeducational testing.

As a professional, the educational therapist has unique training and expertise in the treatment of individuals with learning disabilities and learning difficulties. Frequently, there are consultations and cross-referrals with professionals in related fields. Not uncommonly, clients are seen concurrently by both an educational therapist and another professional, most often a speech and language therapist, educational psychologist, guidance counselor, clinical psychologist, or psychiatrist.

In general, educational therapists see clients in an office or in a school setting. Their equipment consists of assessment materials; reading/math/language/writing books and workbooks; games—educational, therapeutic, and social; electronics—calculators, computers, and tactile/kinesthetic/art supplies.

There are no absolute contraindications to educational therapy. Candidates first need to be evaluated adequately so that the appropriateness of this treatment can be ascertained. Because these children often have multiple and complex problems, treatments need to be prioritized to determine whether educational therapy is indicated.

It is most important that the therapist be aware of when and how to refer to other professionals. A thorough intake with both parents, if possible, and an initial few sessions with the child provide the data that allow the therapist to begin a course of treatment or immediately refer to another professional. For example, such a study would rule out any eye, ear, neurological, or speech problems that might be interfering with learning. In addition, the therapist must confer with the teacher and other professionals working on the case. It is very helpful for the therapist to have a referral network in place so that recommendations can be made appropriately. In addition, as the case progresses, issues come up and goals sometimes need to be changed. After having worked for some time with the child, it is not uncommon to refer to psychotherapists, psychiatrists, neurologists, speech and language therapists, and educational psychologists. Risks to the client are minimal in this type of noninvasive therapy.

The following are examples of timely referrals which facilitated the educational therapy treatment.

Sue was a 14-year-old girl who had a history of learning problems. She had been in educational therapy for 3 years, making good gains in her basic skills. Her performance plateaued and further progress seemed difficult. Sue was referred to it by her to a psychotherapist. During a course of psychotherapy, the girl revealed that her mother was suicidal and using Sue as a sounding board for her unhappiness. The girl could not concentrate on her schoolwork until she was able to separate from her mother's anxieties. Consequently, the mother, not Sue, became the psychotherapy patient, and Sue began to make continued progress in educational therapy.

Bill was in the sixth grade and very resistant to educational therapy and general schoolwork. He was cognitively able and had no other apparent deficits. His teachers reported that he did not put any effort into daily assignments. Parents were cooperative but had no ideas as to how to change his attitude. The therapist used materials related to sports and rock stars that he liked, played games such as Scrabble, and used the computer to write stories. None of these was effective. As his behavior at home became more belligerent, the family was referred to a psychologist. During the course of therapy, the parents revealed their feelings of inadequacy regarding schoolwork. Neither had gone to college and both were afraid their son would be ashamed of them if he were a college graduate. They had been giving him an unconscious message not to succeed in schoolwork. Only after working through their own feelings of inadequacy were they able to be effective parents and motivate their son toward learning.

Measures of clinical progress are not standardized and often tend to be anecdotal. Some educational therapists do pre- and posttests of basic school subjects on an annual basis. Usually a combination of tests, school reports (formal and informal), student feedback and parent reports serves as the basis of ascertaining clinical progress.

Sessions are generally 50 to 60 minutes in duration, once or twice a week. There is no standard duration of therapy. In general, clients remain in treatment 1 to 2 years. In some cases, brief intervention is satisfactory; in others, prolonged support during the school years is necessary. Termination, ideally, takes place with the consent of the client, family, and therapist. There are, of course, premature terminations due to financial limitations, family relocations, family pathology, or when the therapist's style or personality does not fit the client or the family.

For the most part, educational therapy is currently available primarily to those clients who can pay private practice fees. Insurance reimbursement is sometimes available, especially for cases that have been medically diagnosed as attention deficit hyperactivity disorder. There are limited one-to-one services available for the poor through volunteer programs and school special education programs.

Ethically, educational therapists operate under guidelines similar to those established by other helping professions. A detailed Code of Ethics guides therapists (CODE OF ETHICS, 1985). These include integrity and competence, commitment to clients, validation of ethical practice, and collaboration with other professionals.

There have been no scientific studies measuring the outcome of this treatment modality, due in part to the newness of the field and to the multiplicity of intervention techniques. There have been, however, studies of the efficacy of various individual treatment techniques, such as behavioral intervention, sensory integration techniques, biofeedback, metacognitive strategies, the effects of colored filters on reading, and memory tools.

The future of educational therapy depends on improved training programs, research validating the efficacy of the techniques employed, (Johnson 1984) and the growing acceptance of this treatment model by the professional community and the public. With advances in science and technology, more precise knowledge of brain functioning should provide the educational therapist with increasingly effective diagnostic and remedial tools. While the field continues to grow, the widespread availability of this therapy is hampered by the lack of insurance reimbursement and the failure of most health maintenance organizations to offer it to their subscribers.

As we approach the end of the twentieth century, the need for educational therapy is great. Jails are crowded with criminals who have failed in school. A federal study has shown that learning disabled youths are more than twice as likely to be judged delinquent by the courts than non-LD youths (The GRAM, 1995a). 31% of adolescents with learning disabilities will be arrested 3–4 years out of high school. (The GRAM, 1995b). Inside jails and juvenile facilities, prioritization of testing for learning disabilities needs to be established. (Franklin, 1995). Programs such as the ones in Maryland which educate reading disabled and special education students exist in every major correctional institution are a model for the future. (Steurer, 1995).

Currently more babies are being born with psychological and learning disabilities due to their mothers' abuse of drugs and alcohol. The research on ecocultural context, those complex cultural-environmental conditions that influence families and their children's development underscores the relationship between substance abuse and risk of becoming learning disabled (Spekman et al., 1993). Public funding for school programs in special education constantly is being reduced which means that students will receive less remedial work in school and need more work with therapists outside of the classroom.

It is hoped that the growing ranks of educational therapists will be able to fill the void and provide the needed remediation field. Educational therapy training programs are beginning to set up clinics for the indigent students, libraries continue to provide free tutoring and private practitioners are participating in community programs which provide remediation on a sliding scale. An expanded collaborative role with other therapists and continued multidisciplinary training should assure educational therapists a unique role in helping the professionals committed to the remediation of individuals with learning disabilities.

REFERENCES

Code of Ethics. (1985). (Available from Association of Educational Therapists, 1804 W. Burbank Blvd., Burbank, California 91506.)

Directory of Occupational Titles. (1977). Washington, DC, U.S. Department of Labor.

Franklin, P. (1995). GED testing accommodations for poor and incarcerated special needs students. The GRAM, 29(3), 18. Available from Learning Disabilities Association of California, 655 Lewelling Blvd. #355 San Leandro, California 94579.

Johnston, C. L. (1984). Educational therapy: Past perspectives, current practices and a proposal for change. Journal of Learning Disabilities, 17(4); 200–204.

Spekman et al. (1993). An exploration of risk and resilience in the lives of individuals with learning disabilities. Learning Disabilities Research and Practice, 8(1), 11–18.

Steurer, S. (1995). Educating the reading and learning disabled behind bars. The GRAM, 29, 3; 10.

The GRAM (1995a), 29(3); 4.

The GRAM (1995b), 29(3); 3.

Ungerleider, D. (1991). Psychoeducational perspectives. p. 19 (Available from Association of Educational Therapists, 1804 W. Burbank Blvd., Burbank, California 91506)

51 / Physical Therapy

Elisabeth B. Guthrie

Introduction

Physical therapy, or PT, is the rehabilitation of neuromuscular function, particularly gross motor movement and mobility. The terms *rehabilitation* and *habilitation* are often used to distinguish between interventions for acquired or congenital deficits, respectively. Rehabilitation deals with the restoration of lost function; habilitation addresses the compensation for a lifelong functional deficit. In this chapter the term *rehabilitation* will be used to include both concepts.

Pediatric physical therapy involves the functional rehabilitation of congenital and acquired childhood disabilities. It differs from adult rehabilitation in two significant ways. First, in children, all function and functional deficits must be viewed in a developmental context. Second, the child is relatively immature and dependent, and usually must be seen as a member of a family unit.

The long-range goal of therapeutic intervention is to maximize physical capability in the least restrictive environment. Short-term goals vary according to musculoskeletal, neurological, and psychological development. Orthotics, assistive devices, and wheelchairs are important components of therapy programs; their implementation is greatly determined by neuromuscular and cognitive maturity.

A wide variety of pediatric diagnoses require physical therapy. Congenital lesions—such as myelomeningoceole, cerebral palsy, and limb deformities—are nonprogressive deficits; however, the secondary complications change over the course of development. Progressive diseases include neuromuscular dystrophies, rheumatoid disorders, malignancy, and infectious illnesses. Trauma injury, which is usually preventable, accounts for a significant amount of inpatient pediatric rehabilitation. Motor vehicle accidents remain the most common cause of mortality and major morbidity. Gunshot injuries have been seen with increasing frequency in the teenage and pediatric population. Burns, near drownings, internal injuries, and musculoskeletal trauma from falls and sporting accidents are also major causes of the need for pediatric rehabilitation.

Development-Specific Issues

INFANCY

Ideally, an infant with suspected or known neuromuscular abnormalities should be assessed for physical therapy within the first 6 months of life. Interventions attempt to reproduce motor functions along normal developmental milestones. Thus, the infant should gain increasing muscle control in a cephalo-caudal progression, starting with neck control, truncal equilibrium, upper extremity stabilization, weight bearing, and ambulation. With each of these gross motor milestones, crucial developmental consequences occur. Eye contact is facilitated, hands join together midline and become involved in complex manipulations, and truncal stability followed by mobility allows for greater exploration and independence.

Parents may be instructed in exercises and handling techniques that they may then integrate into the child's daily activities. Manipulation of posture promotes the regression of tonic neck reflexes and/or steadies head control, which in turn fosters improved mutual gaze, communication, and midline activities. Stabilization of the trunk facilitates sitting and use of upper extremities. Tone-reducing, or "inhibitive," splints and braces may be applied to the lower extremities to maximize stretch and maintain good joint alignment, both in preparation for weight bearing. These splints and braces are lightweight, molded plastic shells that infants generally tolerate with ease. Infants with limb deficiencies have been shown to learn to manipulate a prosthesis as early as 6 months of age, provided that prosthesis is light and comfortable.

The infant and his or her family require routine follow-up at intervals dictated by each individual circumstance. This can vary from several times weekly to 4 times per year. Active handling and manipulation of premature infants is often prohibited by multiple medical problems and regulatory instability. When feasible, passive range-of-motion manipulation; positioning; and exposure to tactile, auditory, and visual stimuli are indicated. Even in the intensive care unit, a clear explanation of therapy goals can facilitate the parent's role and incorporate the parent into aspects of caregiving.

The development of attachment is paramount for the emotional health and well-being of the infant and future parent-child relationship. Helping to maximize parental caregiving and foster the confidence of parents' in their role as adjunct physical therapists is critical in these early months of life.

PRESCHOOL

The preschool period contains numerous major milestones in motor and social functioning. The physically challenged child needs special skills to achieve these milestones on a schedule that is as close to "normal" as possible. Emphasis is placed on establishing a therapy routine, with particular attention paid to maintenance of "good habits" and prevention of secondary complications. Therapeutic exercise should become a more interactive process, and play is introduced to foster cooperation and pleasure. Parents need to be educated so that they can carry out the PT regimen once or twice daily. The rationale behind the exercises should be explained clearly to parent and child in developmentally appropriate terms. Parents are often apprehensive and uncertain about their competency in carrying out therapy routines, and they require support and reassurance. Passive range-of-motion manipulation may be an uncomfortable process but should not be a painful one. At the end of a slow stretch, apprehension may distress a child, but this distress should resolve upon discontinuation of the movement. Persistent discomfort suggests excessive manipulation. Posturing and splinting provide added support and counter asymmetric torque on joints and skeletal muscles. The motivation to ambulate and explore should be exploited to maximize active range of motion. If ambulation is deemed inadvisable or impossible, most children should begin training in wheelchair mobility after the first birthday. Repetitions and aerobic exercise, such as bike riding with foot or hand pedals, build strength and endurance and provide the fun of speed and motion to an otherwise slow-moving child.

Speech therapy focuses on the facilitation of communication. Communication can be verbal, through the use of communication boards, and/or signing. Toilet training is a significant milestone usually achieved during the third year. Disabled children need to begin toilet training along with their peers, provided they are cognitively capable of doing so.

Peer interactions must also be sought out for this age group. It is preferable to have toddlers with special needs enrolled in an early-childhood program that will meet their physical, occupational, and speech therapy needs, in the context of a stimulating social environment.

By the end of the preschool period, a toddler should have mastered some degree of mobility and feel capable and proud of his or her newfound autonomy and sociability.

SCHOOL AGE

Overall, the goals of the school-age child are to maintain the gains achieved during the preschool period, integrate PT needs into as unrestricted a lifestyle as possible, proceed with surgical interventions when necessary, and optimize learning skills and success. Therapy continues to focus on establishing daily routines that maximize mobility, strength, and endurance. These routines need to fit into the child's day as unobtrusively as possible, minimizing interruption of academic and social life.

The center of a child's world generally shifts from home to school and the child's relationship with peers. This transition may be delayed for the disabled child. The disabled child may come to rely on his or her parents for PT and occupational therapy (OT) functions, some of which may well lie within the child's own capability. Parents may feel competent in their caregiving role and become anxious at the thought of giving it up. It is the role of the therapist to encourage self-care and provide assistive devices—such as a dressing stick, Velcro closures, or easy-to-handle utensils—to further this goal. Physical activities that promote PT goals can be incorporated into recreational pursuits, taking some of the pressure to motivate the child away from the parent. For example, many disabled children battle the challenges of gravity; swimming negates gravity and is a great source of exercise and fun. Horseback riding provides mobility, a locus of control, and mastery. Children with disabilities can expend large amounts of energy during exercise. A conscious effort must be made to ensure that rest and calorie consumption are commensurate with the demands of increased activity.

Problems with visuoperceptual, graphomotor, and other higher integrative functions commonly arise during these years. Previously diagnosed learning disabilities can become more problematic in school. For the child with speech delays, communication augmentation may become more sophisticated as he or she learns to use computer-based programs designed to meet multiple needs. Mainstreaming may be a more difficult and less positive experience, requiring reassessment by educators, psychologist, or PT and OT therapists.

Musculoskeletal asymmetry that is not reversed by intensive physical therapy may require surgery during the schoolage period. Causes for such a condition include scoliosis, dislocated hips secondary to chronic contractures or malalignment, disturbances of gait, and persistent postural maladjustments. Hospitalization and immobilization disrupt the child's schooling, social life, and short-range rehabilitation. Relative stiffness and loss of function is common after surgery. In addition, postoperative pain increases the child's anticipatory anxiety upon resuming physical therapy.

Thus, the goals of the schoolage child include further separation from the home, greater participation in peer group activities, and academic success. Physical therapy may complicate the task of separation. Compliance with therapy may be forfeited in lieu of social acceptance and the need to fit in. Learning disabilities as well as school absenteeism may interfere with academic performance.

ADOLESCENCE

The goals of social acceptance, identity formation, and functional independence pertain to disabled and nondisabled teenagers alike. Unfortunately, social difficulties and dependency may interfere with successful resolution of the disabled adolescent's identity crisis. Poor self-esteem and identity diffusion weaken motivation and pervasively undermine physical therapy goals. Splints, braces, exercise routines, and assistive devices must be aesthetically pleasing to the adolescent and meet with acceptance by the peer group, or they will not be well tolerated. For the chronically disabled teenager, PT routines should be well established and remain the same as in earlier years. The adolescent who was well until illness or injury resulted in disability usually undergoes a period of intense denial and resistance to therapy. Children who oppose therapeutic interventions place themselves at risk for developing complications and further loss of function.

Issues regarding self-care and personal hygiene are a priority. Patients with spinal cord deficits must learn a skin care regimen to avoid the complications of decubiti. The problems of incontinence and its complications must be addressed. A scheduled program of bowel emptying and frequent self-catheterization hopefully provides a socially acceptable lifestyle while minimizing risks of intestinal obstruction, urinary tract infection, and autonomic dysreflexia. Because physical therapy involves bodily contact, respect and appreciation of how touching may impact the developing sexual identity of an adolescent are necessary. Undressing and physical manipulations must be handled in a discreet and sensitive manner at all ages, but this is even more true for the teenager who is undergoing pubertal changes.

Adolescence is a time of concern in physical therapy because of the rapid rate of growth that occurs. This growth spurt can have detrimental effects on therapeutic goals. Increases in height result in a changing center of gravity, compromising previously established balance. Musculoskeletal deformities also grow with rapidity during these years, creating new therapeutic challenges. Although the majority of surgery is performed prior to adolescence, scoliosis repair, leg lengthening, and surgical joint stabilization may be necessary following a growth spurt. Ambulation takes greater effort; it is not uncommon to see changes in mobility due to high energy costs and slow progress. For example, a teenager who had been ambulatory at school may become a home ambulator, relying on the use a wheelchair outside the home. Understandably, the child and family experience this change as a set back; PT practitioners must help them view the change as the most efficient way to maximize mobility in the long run. Weight gain often occurs because of limited mobility, overeating, and endocrine changes. Obesity further compromises physical activity, resulting in the regression of function. Efforts to intervene include greater aerobic movement as well as behavioral and psychological treatment.

Adolescence is a time when physical therapy must promote an individual's independence by helping him or her understand and accept limitations while maintaining a positive self-concept. Attention to the concerns and priorities of the teenager, however trivial they may appear in the eyes of the therapist, is crucial for a successful outcome.

REFERENCES

Alexander, M., Nelson, M. R., Shah, A. (1992). Orthotics, adapted seating and assistive devices. In G. E. Molnar (Ed.), *Pediatric rehabilitation* (2nd ed., pp. 181–201). Baltimore, MD: Williams & Wilkins.

Annest, J. L., Mercy, J. A., Gibson, D. R., & Ryan, G. W. (1995). National estimates of nonfatal firearm-related injuries. *Journal of the American Medical Association, 173* (22), 1749–1753.

Asher, M., & Olson, J. (1983). Factors affecting the ambulator status of patients with spina bifida cystica. *Journal of Bone and Joint Surgery Ann, 65,* 350–357.

Challenor, Y. (1992). Limb deficiencies in children. In G. E. Molnar (Ed.), *Pediatric rehabilitation* (2nd ed., pp. 400–424). Baltimore, MD: Williams & Wilkins.

Cromer, B. A., Enrile, B., McCoy, K., et al. (1990). Knowledge, attitudes and behavior related to sexuality in adolescents with chronic disability. *Developmental Medicine and Child Neurology, 32,* 602–616.

Deluca, P. A. (1996). The musculoskeletal management of children with cerebral palsy. *Pediatric Clinics of North America, 43* (5), 1135–1150.

Dormans, J. P. (1993). Orthopedic management of children with cerebral palsy. *Pediatric Clinics of North America, 40* (3), 645–658.

Emery, H. M., Bowyer, S. L., & Sisung, C. E. (1995). Rehabilitation of the child with a rheumatic disease. *Pediatric Clinics of North America, 42* (5), 1263–1283.

Greenspan, A. I., & Mackenzie, E. J. (1994). Functional outcome after pediatric head injury. *Pediatrics, 94* (4), 425–432.

Jaffe, K. M., Polissar, N. L., Fay, G., & Liao, S. (1995). Recovery trends over three years following pediatric traumatic brain injury. *Archives of Physical Medicine and Rehabilitation, 76,* 17–26.

Kurtz, L. A., & Scull, S. A. (1993). Rehabilitation for developmental disabilities. *Pediatric Clinics of North America, 40* (3), 629–643.

Michaud, L. J., Duchaime, A. C., & Batshaw, M. L. (1993). Traumatic brain injury in children. *Pediatric Clinics of North America, 40* (3), 553–565.

Molnar, G. E. (1988). A developmental perspective for the rehabilitation of children with physical disabilities. *Pediatric Annals, 17,* 766–777.

Molnar, G. E., & Kaminer, R. (1992). Growth and development. In G. E. Molnar, (Ed.), *Pediatric rehabilitation* (2nd ed., pp. 21–47). Baltimore, MD: Williams & Wilkins.

Ponsford, J. (1995). Traumatic brain injury in children. In J. Ponsford (Ed.), *Traumatic brain injury: Rehabilitation for everyday adaptive living* (pp. 295–326). Hillsdale, NJ: Lawrence Erlbaum.

Sarwark, J. F. (1996). Spina bifida. *Pediatric Clinics of North America, 43* (5), 1151–1159.

Shapiro, B. K., & Gallico, R. P. (1993). *Learning disabilities. Pediatric Clinics of North America, 40* (3), 491–506.

Soifer, L. H. (1992). Development and disorders of communication. In G. E. Molnar (Ed.), *Pediatric rehabilitation* (2nd ed., pp. 88–118). Baltimore, MD: Williams & Wilkins.

Taggart, P. J., & Matthews, D. J. (1992). Developmental intervention and therapeutic exercise. In G. E. Molnar (Ed.), *Pediatric rehabilitation* (2nd ed., pp. 166–180). Baltimore, MD: Williams & Wilkins.

Vaughn, C. L., Berman, B., & Peacock, W. J. (1991). Cerebral palsy and rhizotomy: A 3-year follow-up evaluation with gait analysis. *Journal of Neurosurgery, 74*, 178–184.

Watt, J., Sims, D., Harckham, F., et al. (1986). A prospective study of inhibitive casting as an adjunct to physiotherapy for cerebral palsied children. *Developmental Medicine and Child Neurology, 28*, 480–488.

Zavouski, R. W., Lapidus, G. D., Lever, T. J., & Banco, L. I. (1995). A population-based study of severe firearm injury among children and youth. *Pediatrics, 96* (2).

52 / Clinical Pastoral Care

Linda Mans Wagener

It would be rare for a child to reach school age without having constructed some image of God (Fowler, 1981; Rizzuto, 1979). Though children's religious conceptualizations are subject to developmental limitations, they nevertheless hold fairly complex beliefs about the nature of God; God's role as a creator; and the far-reaching extent of God's influence in regard to suffering, death, spirit, and afterlife. Many children have formed these beliefs as early as 3 to 4 years of age (Fowler, 1981). Due to the pervasive presence of religious symbols and language in culture, this is true for children whether or not they have been raised in religious homes or been subject to religious instruction (Rizzuto, 1979).

Despite this, clinicians have been slow to address spiritual issues with youths in crisis. Likewise, spiritual leaders, who have long considered pastoral care for suffering adults to fall within their domain, have not routinely offered the same services to their young parishioners. There are various reasons for this neglect, including (most significantly) a lack of appropriate education (Lester, 1985).

CASE EXAMPLE

Ten-year-old Ellen, raised in a devout Christian home, witnessed the shooting death of her grandmother during a mugging. Prior to being shot by the perpetrator, the grandmother fell to her knees, begging God to spare her life. Following this event, Ellen suffered from post-traumatic stress disorder, evident in her recurrent and distressing recollections of the murder, nightmares, and fears that she would not live to adulthood. In addition to the psychological problems engendered by this experience, Ellen also underwent a spiritual crisis that could be observed in her obsessive questioning of how God could have allowed this evil act to occur. Underlying her questioning were complex theological issues, including fear that God had abandoned her and her family; anger that God did not protect her grandmother; and desire to be in a loving, caring relationship with a benevolent and protective God. A negative resolution of Ellen's crisis of faith could lead to her conviction that she and her grandmother were being punished by God. This could result in her turning away from God and her faith community. A positive resolution could lead ultimately to an increased understanding of pain, suffering, and evil—an understanding that would sustain Ellen throughout her life and result in her turning toward God and her faith community in times of need.

Most clinicians, with the tools to understand Ellen's developmental status, could use verbal communication and other modalities, such as play, to help her with her loss; however, they probably would lack a theology of suffering that would guide her spiritual needs. On the other hand, clergy would have the requisite theology but may lack the necessary clinical tools to engage Ellen in a psychological healing process. Ellen presents an especially challenging case for clinician and clergy because she has not yet achieved the ability to think in terms of formal philosophical systems.

Clinical pastoral care integrates the tools of clinicians and clergy to help children and adolescents make theological sense out of their circumstances. What distinguishes clinical pastoral care from other approaches is a framework which that links life experiences to the understanding of meaning and purpose in a system of faith and strengthens connections between people in a religious community. Clinical pastoral intervention can facilitate the interpretation of both the crisis and its resolution in spiritual terms and thus contribute to healthy spiritual and religious development. When young people in crisis do not receive adequate clinical pastoral care, they may reach maladaptive conclusions about the nature of God and God's way of relating to people.

Stages of Faith

To address spiritual issues with children and adolescents, the practitioner should understand the various stages of religious development. James Fowler (1981) has articulated a developmental progression of stages of faith, in Western monotheistic culture, that spans from infancy through adulthood. The stages of faith parallel the cognitive developmental stages described by Jean Piaget (1958) and the stages of moral development articulated by Lawrence Kohlberg (1969). Understanding these stages is necessary to ascertain the ability of youngsters to understand and make use of theological principles.

In infancy, the foundations for trust and love or their opposites are laid through the infant's experience of the caregiving environment. The infant's initial awareness of self as separate from but dependent upon an infinitely more powerful other sets the foundation for the child's image of God. In a loving, secure, and sensitive environment, the child will associate feelings of trust and being cared for with an image of God. In an environment that is unpredictable, frightening, intrusive, or insensitive, children will associate fear and anxiety with an image of God.

The preschool child is able to use language and symbols in speech and play. Fantasy and imagination as well as imitation dominate his or her thinking and behavior. Children's concepts of God, death, creation, the afterlife, and other religious matters are marked by egocentrism, fluidity, and a lack of logic during this time. Four-year-old Teddy, for example, had no problem with the infinite nature of God, simply explaining "God is everywhere at one time, inside my heart and all through everything, sky, trees, and everybody." In addition, preschool children tend to focus on issues such as reward and punishment, size and power, authority and dependence. Teddy also commented that God would "know for sure if you did something bad, like tell a lie, 'cause he knows everything."

In contrast to younger children, school-age children have a religious understanding that is logical, orderly, and literal. School-age children can become familiar with and accurately retell the stories, beliefs, and rituals of their communities. Through the drama of narrative, children assimilate and conform to the standards and values of their immediate culture. Rigidly held beliefs about right and wrong, without regard to individual circumstances, would be a hallmark of this stage. God would typically be experienced in anthropomorphic forms offered by the child's culture; for example, a child might conceptualize God as a good parent. Nine-year-old Elizabeth described God as "a kind old man with a beard, sitting on a throne in heaven with angels and saints all around him. God knows what's best for us and does it even if we don't like it."

In adolescence the emergence of formal operational thinking and the subsequent abilities for complex perspective taking and reflection allow for the transition into a personal faith that is deeply interwoven with individual identity. God assumes qualities of companionship, support, guidance, and personal love that reflect the intensely interpersonal nature of faith at this stage. Sixteen-year-old Abe said, "God is my best friend. . . . God is always there for me when I need someone to listen."

Rarely seen in children, but common in adulthood, is an understanding of faith issues that moves beyond the conventional premises of the faith community of one's origin. Recognition of the unavoidable tensions between individual responsibility and group membership, subjectivity and objectivity, and service to others versus self-fulfillment leads to a transition to faith that may be characterized as individuative-reflective, conjunctive, or universalizing (Fowler, 1981).

Gender differences may also be reflected in children's conceptions of God. Girls tend to describe an aesthetic, relational creator; boys tend to describe God as rational and active (Hellner, 1986).

Understanding children's perceptions of spiritual leaders is also relevant to effective service delivery. Benjamin Griffin (1975) found in his interviews with children between the ages of 3 and 12 that they linked the clergy with God and the faith community. For children, spiritual leaders are a physical representation of God, religious tradition, and a community of faith. This unique symbolic function can be used to communicate to children the trustworthiness, forgiveness, and love of God. However, it is also possible that a child may fear such an individual or attribute magical powers either to the clergy or to symbols and rituals of the religion.

Method and Procedures of Pastoral Care

ASSESSING THE YOUNG PERSON

Pastoral care of individuals typically begins with contract for the interaction. Decisions must be made as to the focus of the intervention; the unit of care, whether it be the child, the family, or some variation thereof; and whether it is an appro-

priate contract. Structuring also includes gaining the permission of parents and determining where meetings will occur; frequency of meetings; and fee structure, if appropriate. An evaluation of the child's clinical status must be included and consultation with other professionals arranged if necessary.

Guidelines for pastoral evaluation focus on theological rather than medical aspects of the child's functioning (Pruyser, 1976). Either through conversation or play, the practitioner may want to observe the youngster's spiritual status in terms of awareness of the holy, providence, grace, repentance, communion, and vocation. These concepts may require some adaptation to the developmental level of the child (Ludwick & Peake, 1982).

Awareness of the Holy What, if anything, is sacred and approached with reverence in the experience of the young person? In the earlier story of Ellen, the girl had observed her grandmother's piety and reverence for God, yet God seemed not to respond. This set the stage for Ellen's conflicted between her own feelings and her reverence for God.

Providence What does the youngster believe about how God is working in the world? Questions such as Couldn't God have done anything about this? and Does God care? reflect issues of providence. Ellen had more struggles with this aspect of her faith than any other as she wondered if God was really in charge and paying attention to what was happening in the world.

Grace Does the child believe that he or she can be forgiven and loved despite personal imperfections? The need for grace is closely associated with feelings of guilt, sinfulness, atonement, and forgiveness. As Ellen worked through her spiritual crisis, it became apparent that she was unsure whether God would accept her, given the intensity of her anger toward God. Within her faith tradition, Christianity, were many examples from the Bible of individuals pouring out their feelings of anger toward God and yet remaining loved and accepted by God. No special grace from God is needed in the case of anger, even when it is directed toward God. A deeper understanding of this issue helped Ellen toward resolution of her faith crisis.

Repentance Does the youngster take responsibility for the troubled situation? Either a lack of responsibility or excessive self-blame or guilt can indicate a spiritual problem.

Communion Does the young person experience a feeling of connectedness to creation or, conversely, does the child experience alienation or feelings of separation?

Vocation Does the child or adolescent feel a sense of purposefulness and involvement in creation? As Ellen's spiritual crisis resolved, her fears that she would not live to adulthood dissipated and she was again able to engage in the normal developmental tasks of play, relating to friends and family, and school accomplishments.

CASE EXAMPLE

Four-year-old Matt, dying of cancer, prayed each night, "Now I lay me down to sleep, I pray the Lord my soul to keep. If I die before I wake, I pray the Lord my soul to take." He told his night nurse, who sat with him while he prayed, "I'm going to be with God. I won't hurt anymore and all the owees will be gone." In this moment he demonstrated his faith in God's providence. In other conversations Matt expressed a sense of purpose and meaning for his life by saying, "I'm glad I was born even though I had to get sick. I know God wanted me to love my mom and my dad and for them to love me too."

ASSESSING THE FAMILY

Assessment that places the youngster in the context of family functioning can also give important information to the practitioner. A systems perspective can be helpful in understanding the relationship between the child's behavior and the child's role in the family. Asking the questions that follow can help the practitioner to understand the young person in crisis (Treadway & Florell, 1987). What is the overall functioning of this family? How effectively can this family communicate? What is the life-cycle stage of this family? What are the influences from the past that are affecting this family? How does this family interacts?

CASE EXAMPLE

Terry, an active, outgoing eight-year-old, had a serious skateboarding accident in which he sustained a head injury. The injury affected his ability to concentrate. The boy was certain that the accident was a punishment from God, since Terry had been told not to ride his skateboard before finishing his homework and Terry

had disobeyed. His beliefs became understandable when the practitioner found that the family frequently tried to control their children's behavior by telling stories of God inflicting punishment on the wicked. Furthermore, Terry's father stated that "Terry is just like my brother who ended up in jail" and elaborated his fears that Terry would end up in a similar situation. Understanding these aspects about family functioning helped the practitioner work with Terry.

EXPERIENCING RELATIONSHIP

Following an appropriate structuring and assessment, the relationship between the practitioner and the young person becomes the vehicle through which the work will occur. The pastoral relationship is particularly significant because it is a direct and personal relationship to a member of God's community of faith. The attention paid to the young person immediately communicates that he or she is a valued member of this community. Including the child as an active participant during a crisis increases the young person's sense of competence and belonging. In cases where children are ignored, overly protected, or physically separated during a crisis, their sense of community is disrupted. The relationship with the pastoral care professional sets the stage for the child's experience of what God is like, how God works, and how God feels about him or her.

Techniques of Pastoral Care

The traditional metaphor for pastoral care is shepherding. The pastoral practitioner is the shepherd of the faith community (Hiltner, 1958). Guiding, protecting, nurturing, seeking, and consoling are primary functions of the shepherd. At a glance these functions can be seen to be relevant to the needs of youths in crisis (Lester, 1985). Oates (1969) defined the dimensions of pastoral care as *healing*, characterized as movement toward wholeness following brokeness stemming from a crisis; *reconciling*, referring to the repairing of fractured relationships; *sustaining*, in which support is offered and a means of sharing burdens is suggested; *confronting*, wherein the laws and standards of the faith tradition are applied to individual behavior; *guiding*, or assisted decision making; and *informing*, the clarification of alternatives by providing new information.

The tools clinical pastoral practitioners use in their work with young people include play and art therapy, storytelling, sentence completion, journal writing, behavior modification, and conversation. What sets the pastoral method apart in these cases is the inclusion of content that is specifically faith-oriented. Pastoral care might include retelling stories from sacred texts; frank discussion of concepts such as grace, blessing, sin, and forgiveness; or drawing the face of God. Interpretation is used as a technique in pastoral conversation. However—unlike forms of interpretation used in exploratory psychotherapy, which seek to clarify unconscious psychological processes—pastoral interpretation seeks to reveal the spiritual significance of internal processes and life events. Experiences are told, understood, and then interpreted in the light of the religious community's beliefs about life's meaning and the person's relationship to God. In this regard it is essential to take into consideration the developmental level of the child or adolescent and the particular beliefs of his or her religious community.

Unlike most clinical interventions, pastoral care may also include prayer or meditation, blessing, worship, and adjunct services. As in all professional contact with minors, it is important to gain permission of both the youngster and the parents before engaging in these activities.

PRAYER

Pastoral prayer is the process of assisting people to communicate with God in their time of need. If coupled with the telling or reading of religious texts and scriptures, it can become a form of conversation with God that includes both speaking and listening. Prayer can be used when the young person in question can be helped by articulating their concerns to God. In addition, prayer can provide a source of comfort in the remembering of God's presence and interest and can serve to awaken faith and hope.

The style of prayer varies within various traditions of faith. It can differ in structure from the silence of contemplative meditation to a repetition of a well-known and familiar prayer such as the Lord's Prayer, the Song of Moses, the Vedas, or the Serenity Prayer from the Twelve-Step movement, to a spontaneous production based on the needs of the moment as revealed in pastoral conversation. Prayer, appropriate to the developmental level of the child, may be offered by the practitioner, by the youngster, or in some cases by a group of concerned others from the faith community. Prayer frequently results in overwhelming emotions, and it is best to be prepared for this possibility.

In deciding when to pray with young people, it is important to determine their comfort level and desire in this regard. It is common for children to have the impression that prayer is a magical method of getting one's way or to controlling God. Such misinterpretation need to be addressed without giving the child the impression that he or she is wrong for desiring such an outcome.

BLESSING

A blessing typically gives God's gift of grace to the young person and communicates that he or she is special in the sight of God (Smalley & Trent, 1986). It may include meaningful touch, which can take the form of the practitioner laying a hand on the head, shoulder, or back; holding a hand; giving a hug; or holding a child on his or her lap. This must of course be done with sensitivity to the individual's sense of personal territory and comfort level in regard to being touched. The practitioner must also ensure that the family is comfortable about the practitioner touching the child. An important aspect of the blessing is a spoken message that confers special significance upon the youngster, giving him or her value and a special place and future in God's plan. A blessing is normally offered in the context of a spiritual community that supports the individual.

WORSHIP

Worship can take many forms but most often is a form of symbolic ritual that conveys the deep meanings of a faith. During worship a child may experience at an unconscious level the faith elements that contribute to the healing of spiritual wounds. Participating in the Christian communion ritual, a Hebrew blessing, or lighting a lamp before a representation of God may allow a child to feel the power and mystery of religious experience when an intellectual understanding of the event is well beyond his or her capabilities. In addition, community worship strengthens the ties among participants and contributes to identity.

ADJUNCT SERVICES

The pastoral practitioner can frequently act as a conduit to a variety of services provided by organized faith communities. These may include but are not limited to religious education, youth groups, community agencies, retreats, care groups, wilderness therapy experiences, seminars, home and hospital visits, child care, opportunities for social service, and financial aid.

Common Crises

Faith issues associated with problems such as divorce, abuse, or bereavement may have common features. Children who are in the midst of these crises may frequently engage in "magical prayers" that ask God to intervene to bring about a desired outcome. Many children whose parents are divorcing have prayed to God to "make Mommy and Daddy love each other again." Failure of the parents as well as God to relieve the youngster's distress may lead to problem of trust. The child may have difficulty trusting those with power to do what is right and good for the child. Also, children in preschool and early school years often feel guilty and responsible for their experience and can benefit from an understanding of forgiveness, both of self and of other. Children who experience bereavement, chronic illness, or disability will commonly ask Why me? and wonder about the nature of a God who allows suffering. In addition to these common themes, the practitioner who listens and carefully observes will discern the individual nature of the spiritual concerns of the child or adolescent in crisis.

In *Amazing Grace: The Lives of Children and the Conscience of a Nation,* author Jonathan Kozol (1995) tells the story of how one child, Anabelle, described heaven to him.

"'People who are good go to heaven, 'she begins in a singsong voice, as if this part is obvious. 'People who are bad go down to where the devil lives. They have to wear red suits, which look like red pajamas. People who go to heaven wear a nightgown, white, because they're angels. All little children who die when they are young will go to heaven.'" (pg 129)

Kozol describes Anabelle as "one of the most joyful children I have ever met. There is seldom any hint of sorrow in her voice." Yet, she lived among many children who had lost family members to AIDS. When asked how the children thus orphaned handled that pain, Anabelle became solemn and replied, "They cry. They suffer. People die. They pray."

In addition to the delight that listening to children's descriptions of spiritual matters can bring, it also serves as a window to the wounds and coping strategies that mark their faith journey.

REFERENCES

Erickson, E. H. (Ed.). (1963). *Childhood and society.* New York: Norton.

Fowler, J. W. (1981). *Stages of faith: The psychology of human development and the quest for meaning.* San Francisco: Harper.

Griffin, B. T. (1975). *Pastoral care of children in crisis.* Unpublished manuscript, Lancaster Theological Seminary.

Hellner, D. (1986). *The children's god.* Chicago: University of Chicago Press.

Hiltner, S. (1958). *Preface to pastoral theology.* Nashville: Abingdon Press.

Kohlberg, L. (1969). Stage & sequence: The cognitive developmental approach to socialization. In D. A. Goslin (Ed.), *Handbook of socialization theory and research* (pp. 347–480). Chicago: Rand McNally.

Kozol, J. (1995). Amazing Grace: The Lives of Children and the Conscience of a Nation. New York: Harper Perennial.

Lester, A. D. (1985). *Pastoral care with children in crisis.* Philadelphia: Westminster Press.

Lester, A. D. (Ed) (1987). *When children suffer.* Philadelphia: Westminster Press.

Ludwick, C. & Peake T. H. (1982). Adapting a clinical

religious history format for pastoral intervention with adolescents in psychiatric treatment. *J of Psychology and Christianity* 1:2, (pp. 9–15).

Oates, W. (1969). *On becoming children of God*. Philadelphia: Westminster Press.

Piaget, J. (1958). *The growth of logical thinking from childhood to adolescence*. New York: Basic Books.

Pruyser, P. W. (1976). *The minister as diagnostician: personal problems in pastoral perspective*. Philadelphia: Westminster Press.

Rizzuto, A. (1979). *The birth of the living God*. Chicago: University of Chicago Press.

Rowatt, G. W. (1989). *Pastoral care with children in crisis*. Louisville: Westmister/John Knox Press.

Smalley, G. & Trent, J. (1975). *The blessing*. Nashville: Thomas Nelson.

Treadway, C. W. & Florell, J. L. (1987). Pastoral assessment of the child and the family. In A. D. Lester (Ed.), *When Children Suffer* (pp. 184–192). Philadelphia: Westminster Press.

53 / Therapeutic Camping

Elizabeth Doone

The out-of-doors provides a wealth of opportunities to facilitate the therapeutic process, and the outdoors heightens the senses. Utilizing the out-of-doors in camping-and adventure-based programs has evolved into a field in which such programs have become alternative or supplemental to traditional mental health, juvenile court, school, health, and enrichment programs. These diverse camping and adventure programs serve a range of clientele from adjudicated youths, to women with cancer, substance abusers, children labeled by the school system, to anyone seeking adventure. Camping programs are part of the continuum of services available to troubled youths, including those diagnosed as severely emotionally disturbed, behavior-disordered, or emotionally handicapped. Week-long or summer-long programs are considered short-term and may be supplemental to school services or hospital treatment programs. Such programs, such as Outward Bound, may provide adventure, intensity, and challenge, but not the added components of consistency and duration typical of year-round camping programs.

Residential camping programs are often long-term, with campers remaining for 12 to 18 months or more. Total immersion with caring adults in a humane environment is a fundamental aspect of milieu therapy. The first aspect of therapeutic camping involves removing the child from an environment in which he or she has not experienced success. The second is placing the child in a supportive, caring environment in the great outdoors, where significant adult role models provide opportunities for success and create an atmosphere that facilitates the building of positive self-esteem and the therapeutic process.

According to Remar and Lowry (1974), whose experiences include camp therapy in the Massachusetts mental hospital system, the camp milieu proves beneficial for three types of patients: disturbed adolescents, chronic patients, and less disturbed patients in outpatient treatment or rehabilitation. Disturbed adolescents benefit from camp therapy because the camp environment meets their need for close supervision and muscle activity. Chronic patients, who need arousal from their torpor, benefit from the stimulation and adventure of camp therapy. Less disturbed patients in rehabilitation programs, who need a retreat from their daily living conditions, benefit from short camp programs.

History of Camping

Camping as a formal institution began to proliferate during the latter part of the 19th century. Summer camps for wealthy boys were instituted to keep them from idling away their time, poor boys were sent to camp for fresh-air outings, and churches sent youths to be converted during the summer. The YMCA, Boy and Girl Scouts of America, and other youth and recreational organizations established a stronghold in camping, with the goals of promoting strong values in a out-of-doors atmosphere.

An early form of milieu therapy, tent treatment, was developed out of necessity and refined out of existence before its basic benefits were isolated. In 1901, the fear of a tuberculosis epidemic in the overcrowded wards at a New York hospital prompted the medical director to order the erection of isolation tents on the hospital grounds. The marked physical and mental improvements of the patients astonished the staff, and more tents were erected. Again the gains were incredible; formerly hopeless patients improved. The prominence of tent treatment faded as fresh air and sunshine became the sole focus. The esprit de corps patients developed in small groups vanished. The overcrowded wards had moved outside (Caplan, 1974).

Developed in 1921, the Michigan Fresh Air Camp was probably one of the first therapeutic camps specifically for maladjusted boys. Morse (1957) states that the philosophy of the camp was that, through proper socialization, boys with inadequate backgrounds can develop into better citizens. The campers were boys from metropolitan Detroit who were burdened with severe emotional problems and/or delinquency. By incorporating a mental hygiene philosophy and changing the complete milieu of the child, the camp evolved to deal effectively with this special population.

By the 1930s growth in the fields of psychology, education, and sociology was making its mark on camping programs. The objectives of psychological self-reliance and survival were influential in the development of the Outward Bound programs of the early '40s. British officers were intrigued that young, fit soldiers died at sea while older soldiers survived. Although originally a form of training for British seamen, Outward Bound has expanded into an outdoor adventure program that tests self-imposed limits and builds self-esteem through challenge and adventure in the great mountains, deserts, rivers, oceans, and jungles around the world.

Advantages of a Camp Milieu

Therapeutic camping can provide an alternative to incarceration, traditional institutionalization, psychiatric placement, and other especially designed programs for children who cannot function in a normal school, family, or community setting. Camping programs also provide families with the least traumatic choice of separation and the least stigma for the child. The recent increase in the number of adjudicated youths being sentenced to therapeutic camps is attributed to the value of such programs and the lack of rehabilitation in incarceration. Camping and adventure programs offer at-risk youths the stimulation and excitement that they often seek in street-gang or other delinquent activities, but in a positive, child-centered, esteem-building environment.

Historically, there has been a progression from punitive to custodial to rehabilitative programs for juvenile delinquents and troubled youths. Therapeutic camping is an innovative treatment program that combines the advantages of peer group treatment, recreation therapy, reality therapy, and experiental education in a wilderness setting. Such a setting is a unique and atypical place for the juvenile delinquent. The tasks at hand reinforce the basic reality of living: survival. Campers are responsible for all aspects of daily living as well as planning and carrying out daily and weekly goals. Campers are given respect and the responsibility of making their own life decisions. Then they have the opportunity to experience the consequences of those decisions (Bailey et al., 1978).

Elements of Successful Programs

The diversity of camp programs is extensive due to the variety of populations served, the length and depth of the various programs, program sponsorship guidelines, facilities, philosophy, and intervention methods. Despite program variety, experts agree that the best programs have much in common. Lingle (1980) summarizes the factors about whose essential for successful camping experiences. First and foremost is the quality of leadership and staff. Common goals for campers include the reestablishment of respect and trust in adults, as well as each camper's belief in his or her own potential, a belief that improves self-esteem. This is accomplished by emphasizing accomplishments rather than failures. Basic rules of conduct are stressed at camp as is a respect for the capabilities, strengths, weaknesses, and rights of others. Campers are also taught to think objectively and make rational decisions through a natural-consequences approach (Lingle, 1980; Loughmiller, 1965). The use of small groups, usually peer groups, for support and as influential entities is a very effective therapeutic tool that as such most camping programs use.

The Loughmiller Model

Camp Woodland Springs was founded in the 1920s. By 1946 it had evolved from a summer recreation program for children into a year-round camping program for emotionally disturbed boys. Campbell Loughmiller directed Camp Woodland Springs for 20 years and served as a consultant to his camp and many others for more than a decade. The extension of the camp into a year-round facility is one of the primary distinctions of the Loughmiller model. Because of Loughmiller's pioneering efforts in the field and the broad use of his constructs in year-round residential camping programs serving disturbed and delinquent youths, the main components of his model are outlined in this section.

SETTING

An open, out-of-doors setting, sufficiently removed from civilization and with few permanent structures, is the backdrop for camp. Tent construction is part of the therapeutic process; therefore, campers are responsible for building and maintaining their own shelters, latrines, cook tents, chuck tent, tool racks, wash area, and garbage facilities. Permanent structures include a centrally located office, warehouse, kitchen–dining room, and a bathhouse. The five campsites are sufficiently isolated from each other to afford each group its independence.

GROUP PROCESS

Laughmiller (1979) writes "A group has common goals, mutual respect and concern for each other, and a plan of procedure. Without these there can be chaos" (p. 64). The task is getting an aggregation of ten boys to function like a group. Part of the process involves the ownership of the plans and the goals of the group. The counselor has the responsibility of facilitating the group democratic process. Learning and utilizing problem-solving skills are goals of camp; therefore, daily problems are dealt with by the group. This process reinforces the respect and responsibility afforded each member. The problem must be resolved to the group's satisfaction in order to continue with daily plans. The constant focus on resolving problems, which places the boys' needs above the agenda, reinforces the camper-centered philosophy. At the end of each day, the group evaluates the day's activities in a sacred nightly ritual that provides an opportunity for reflection and ends the day on a positive note. Campers leave the program with an acquired skill that becomes an important part of their coping repertoire. These skills and the campers' increased ability to verbalize their feelings are positive outcomes of the camping experience.

PARENTS

Unless extreme circumstances dictate otherwise, successful integration of the camper back into the family is a goal of camp. Parental involvement is vital for this to happen. Camp social workers keep parents informed about their child's progress in camp, and the social workers conduct monthly meetings. Parents are invited to camp for group meetings where better parent-child relationships are often promoted. Once every 6 weeks a camper goes home for 4 days. This home visit is a time for practicing the skills learned at camp, not a retreat from camp. Campers write goals before going home and evaluate and discuss the experience when they return.

COUNSELORS

Loughmiller (1979, 1965) describes the camp counselors as the single most important element in the camp program. Counselors provide the main interactions with the camper; group work supervisors, director, and family workers provide support to both counselors and campers. The home lives of many campers do not include nurturing parents, so the young, energetic, committed camp counselor becomes a significant adult in the campers life, modeling positive values and taking on the role of friend, parent, and teacher or tutor.

Counselors are taught basic camping skills to ensure that equipment is correctly handled and manipulated. The counselors teach the boys the same skills. Because the physical skills of camp life can be easily taught, the counselors' attitude and faith in people is of utmost importance. A counselor must be intact enough to experience group failure without feeling inadequate and then learn from the experience. A counselor must recognize the inherent danger of a situation and understand when to call for reinforcement. The continuity of group functioning is maintained by the counselor's rigorous schedule. The campers' relationship with their counselors, not fences and gates, is the bond that keeps campers at camp. Therefore, the counselor must be able to relate to the camper on his level, use good judgment, communicate a true interest in each camper, and utilize the democratic process. The goal is to build a strong group in order to deal effectively with the individual and build each boy's sense of self-worth (Loughmiller, 1979).

EDUCATION

Campers experience real-life education in their daily camp activities. Their immersion in nature piques interest; the environment becomes the classroom. Students formerly not interested in wildlife become able to identify the variety of birds, snakes, and other animals that share their surroundings. Construction of campsites does more for the camper's self-esteem than learning the mathematical formulas that he now grasps because of their new-found relevance. The building process teaches a myriad of skills including planning (the campers must design a tent according to its function), ecology, (the campers learn the value of reforestation after cutting down pine trees for

the new structure), teamwork and cooperation, (without which a project could not completed), and satisfaction, (which is gained by carrying through a project from start to finish). The tent serves as a constant reminder of how capable the campers are and what they are able to accomplish. Tent construction is one experiential aspect of the camping program. Writing skills are developed in a variety of daily activities: by composing short- and long-term goals, menu plans, trip itineraries, requisitions, and so forth. Each of them develops an array of other skills.

The Loughmiller model does not include a formal classroom component, but because of changes in state guidelines many derivative programs now do. Such a classroom in the woods offers a campers the opportunity to move from his role as camper back into a student role in a tested, safe, and secure environment. The boy moves into a campsite in which the structures are of a more permanent nature. The classroom is reminiscent of a one-room schoolhouse, although it is fully equipped with kitchen and computers. The students range in age and level of functioning; therefore, individual and thematic approaches are utilized. The teacher is a state-certified special education major. The group process is still utilized, but the behavior of the campers in the transitional group has also evolved. The problems are now related to the anxiety of going home, adjustment to school, and reimmersion in an environment that formerly provided failure. For most campers this 3- to 4-month period is used for dealing with these anxieties as well as remediating basic academic skills.

OUTINGS

Trips are a result of careful planning and are often tied into a thematic goal or group interest. Most trips of any duration take at least a month to plan because the experiences are real and careful attention to details is necessary. The planning process is a wonderful opportunity for learning. Groups become familiar with a region as they study maps, plot courses, and plan for provisions. Trips provide adventure and challenge for groups and often include backpacking, canoeing, and rafting.

Contraindications and Risks

Camping programs are not recommended for people who are nonambulatory, diabetic, in delirium tremens, or in active withdrawal from addiction. The stresses of camp life can not handle the added complexities of these four groups of patients without special and expensive facilities (Remar & Lowry, 1974).

Fritz Redl (1974), a proponent of therapeutic camping, asserts, " . . . because I am so firmly convinced of the tremendous value of camping, educationally and as a means of therapy, I can afford to discuss [psychopathologic risks] without fear of being misunderstood" (p. 76). He believes that adjusting to nature for some children can be an anxiety-laden process. "Fantasy fears and real discomfort are mixed into a frightening blend" (p. 78). The handling of these anxieties is difficult because the child's experiences and protective understandings have not developed adequately for the management of these fears. Most of the anxieties are displaced into complaints about camp life in general or into an "unreasonable bravado" that may result in the total disregard of health and safety regulations. Adjusting to the separation from parents, home, and family life—no matter how dysfunctional the family—takes time and proper guidance from camp counselors. Home life is familiar; even in confused and unhappy homes children have developed coping mechanisms to survive. The camper must deal with these anxieties before the camping experience can be effective.

Another contraindication to long-term camping programs is the development of dependence on the program and staff. Such dependence makes adjustment to home life difficult. Redl (1974) suggests that the best safeguard against pathological risks in therapeutic camping programs is remembering that the program is a process—it is neither good nor bad. Therefore, the best that camp staff can strive for is the constant monitoring and questioning of programming and policies, on the one hand, and human relations and the child on the other.

Conclusion: Evaluation

Although most sources agree that camp provides positive experiences for camper and results in increased self-esteem, the dearth of process and outcome evaluation for such programs limits the reliability of the claims about therapeutic camping.

Camping programs that are unable to affect the life decisions of their clientele, even for the short term, should be critically viewed. The positive human aspects of the program should be considered over the political utilization of power.

Many programs have developed and changed to meet accreditation as hospitals or secure facilities. As therapeutic camping moves in this direction, it may be moving backward. The acquisition of state moneys becomes a moot point if the programs are no longer effective. Loughmiller (1979, 1965) asserts that those who make the decisions regarding the child should be those with the most contact with the child. Therefore, broad-based changes involving campers should be made at the camp. Instead of becoming models for experiential education and positive experiences, camps may be returning to the holding facilities of the past. To exclude an essential component of the program is to lose focus. Self-reflection; physical improvements; and constant monitoring of progress, utilizing qualitative and quantitative methodologies, are appropriate. Losing sight of the physical goals and philosophies that have come to make therapeutic camping effective is not.

REFERENCES

Bailey, B. E., Selman, G. L., Faherty J. K., Dromnes D., & Ray, P. E. (1978). *Wilderness therapeutic camping: An alternative treatment approach for the juvenile offender.* Paper presented at the annual meeting of the Texas Psychological Association, Dallas, TX.

Caplan, R. B. (1974). Early forms of camping in American mental hospitals. In T. P. Lowry (Ed.) *Camping therapy* (pp. 8–12). Springfield, IL: Charles C Thomas.

Griffin, W. H., & Carter, J. T. (1979). *An evaluation program for the Eckerd Foundation therapeutic wilderness camping program: An evaluation of an atypical alternative education program.* Paper presented at the fifth evaluation network annual conference, Cincinnati, OH.

Lingle, K. I. (1980). Alternative for youth at-risk: Outdoor experiences for a special population. (Occasional paper issued by the Fund for Advancement of Camping). *Camping Magazine,* 15–25.

Loughmiller, C. (1965). *Wilderness road.* Austin, TX: Hogg Foundation for Mental Health, University of Texas.

Loughmiller, C. (1979). *Kids in trouble.* Tyler: TX: Wildwood Books.

Lowry, T. P. (Ed). (1974). *Camping therapy: Its uses in psychiatry and rehabilitation.* Springfield, IL: Charles C Thomas.

Morse, W. C. (1957). The background of therapeutic camping. *Journal of Social Issues, 13* (1), 15–22.

Redl, F. (1974). Psychopathologic risks of camp life. In T. P. Lowry (Ed.). *Camping therapy* (pp. 76–88). Springfield, IL: Charles C Thomas.

Remar, E. M., & Lowry, T. P. (1974). Camping therapy in the commonwealth of Massachusetts. In T. P. Lowry (Ed.), *Camping therapy* (pp. 13–15). Springfield, IL: Charles C Thomas.

Name Index

Subject Index

Subject Index

Subject Index